Applied Economics

Visit the Applied Economics Companion Website at
www.booksites.net/griffithswall
to find valuable teaching and learning material

For Students:

• Study material designed to help you improve your results
• Learning objectives for each chapter
• Multiple choice questions to help test your learning
• Up-to-date facts in the field of Economics
• Links to relevant sites on the web

Also: This site has a syllabus manager, search functions, and email
results functions.

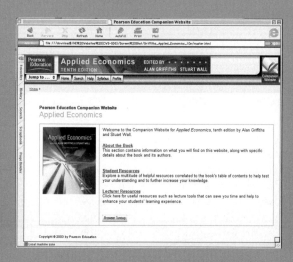

TENTH EDITION

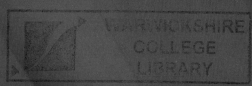
Applied Economics

Edited by **ALAN GRIFFITHS & STUART WALL**

FT Prentice Hall
FINANCIAL TIMES

An imprint of **Pearson Education**

Harlow, England • London • New York • Boston • San Francisco • Toronto • Sydney • Singapore • Hong Kong
Tokyo • Seoul • Taipei • New Delhi • Cape Town • Madrid • Mexico City • Amsterdam • Munich • Paris • Milan

Pearson Education Limited
Edinburgh Gate
Harlow
Esssex CM20 2JE
England

and Associated Companies throughout the world

Visit us on the World Wide Web at:
www.pearsoned.co.uk

First published 1984
Second edition 1986
Third edition 1989
Fourth edition 1991
Fifth edition 1993
Sixth edition 1995
Seventh edition 1997
Eighth edition 1999
Ninth edition 2001
Tenth edition 2004

ISBN 0273 68432 9

British Library Cataloguing-in-Publication Data
A catalogue record for this book is available from the British Library

10 9 8 7 6 5 4 3 2 1
08 07 06 05 04

Set in 9/11½pt Sabon
Typeset by 25
Printed and bound by Ashford Colour Press, Gosport

The publisher's policy is to use paper manufactured from sustainable forests

Brief contents

Contents

Part II: Environmental, regional and social economics

Part III: Macroeconomics

Contents of Companion Website – www.booksites.net/griffithswall

For students

Study material
Learning objectives
Multiple choice questions
Up-to-date facts in the field of Economics
Links to relevant sites on the web

For lecturers

Teaching material
Instructor's manual
Topical events and case study material
Outline answers to all discursive questions
Full solutions to all calculation-type questions
Extra case material

This site has a syllabus manager, search functions, and email results functions

Guided tour

A synopsis at the beginning of each chapter explains what students will learn on reading the chapter

Regular revision of data ensures book is up-to-date

Thorough examination of policy issues in the UK, Europe and the global economy

Key points at the end of each chapter reinforce students' learning

The booksites logo directs students to further on-line study material

Chapter 25   Globalization

'Globalization' is a widely used but often loosely defined term. In this chapter we take forward many of the ideas touched on in Chapter 7 (The multinational corporation). We review the major characteristics of globalization, including new markets, new actors, new rules and norms and new methods of communication.

Some indicators of these characteristics are identified and measured over recent decades to establish some of the quantitative and qualitative patterns and trends underpinning globalization. After assessing some of the strategic implications for firms operating in a global environment, attention turns to the multi-dimensional aspects of such an environment. In addition to the economic dimension, political, legal and sociocultural dimensions are briefly reviewed, including terrorism (with a review of the impacts of 9/11) and health-related issues within a globalized environment. The perspectives behind the raft of contemporary anti-globalization protests are reviewed and evaluated. The chapter concludes by reviewing the move towards global engagement by the economy most directly associated with globalization, namely the USA.

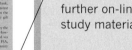

References and further reading at the end of each chapter encourage students to research topics in depth

A guide to sources highlights useful sources for statistical data on the economy

Weblinks refer students to useful data and information

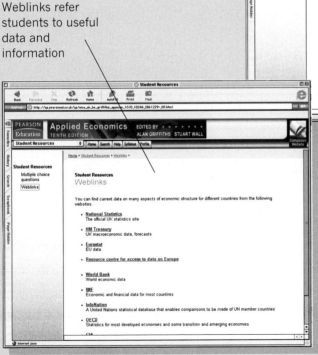

Multiple choice questions help test students' learning

As any teacher or student of economics well knows, the vitality of the subject depends largely upon a continual synthesis of theory with observation, and observation with theory. Unfortunately this exercise is costly in terms of the time and the effort involved in finding sources, in assembling and interpreting data, and in searching journals and periodicals for informed comment on contemporary events. That the exercise is, however, ultimately worth while, is eloquently expressed by the late Professor James Meade in the following quotation taken, with his permission, from a letter to the authors:

> The great tradition of Political Economy in this country is the application of basic economic analysis to the central economic problems of the time. For this purpose students must have a knowledge of institutions and quantitative relationships over a very wide range of sectors of the economy; and this instruction about the facts must be accompanied with guidance about methods of applying economic theory to the problems which arise over a very wide range of topics. Guidebooks to the UK economy which combine information and analysis in this way are all too rare; and the authors are to be highly commended for undertaking a comprehensive survey of this kind.

Our hope is that *Applied Economics* will take the reader some distance along this route, by combining information with analysis over thirty separate topic areas. The book also examines in detail the major economic issues arising within each topic area. Although the focus of *Applied Economics* is the UK, extensive reference is made throughout to the experience of the other advanced industrialized countries, helping the reader place any observations on the UK in a broader international context.

Each chapter concentrates on a particular topic area and begins with a synopsis, setting out the issues to be investigated, and ends with a conclusion, reviewing the major findings. The largely self-contained nature of each chapter gives the book a useful degree of flexibility. For instance chapters can be read selectively, in any order appropriate to the reader's interest or to the stage reached in a programme of study. This may be helpful to the reader as courses rarely follow the same sequence of topics. On the other hand the topics have been arranged with an element of progression, so that the reader may begin at Chapter 1 and read the following chapters, arranged in four separate 'parts', consecutively. The book then takes the form of a 'course' in applied economics.

Applied Economics is designed for undergraduate students taking degree courses in economics, the social sciences, business studies and management, and for those taking professional and postgraduate courses with an economic content. The material will also be useful to many involved in Foundation Degrees and in Higher and National Diplomas and Certificates, and to the serious A level student. Much of the content begins at an introductory level and is suitable for those with little or no previous exposure to economics, although the diverse nature of the various topic areas inevitably means some variation in the level of analysis, and indeed in the balance between information and analysis. Overall, the book is best read in conjunction with a good introductory text on economic theory.

We are indebted to many individuals for help during the course of this project, not least the help of so many library staff at APU, crucial to our exploring the wide range of journal and on-line sources of data and information captured by this book. The major debt is, however, clearly owed to those who contributed the various chapters, and this is acknowledged more fully at the end of the book. Finally, for patience and forbearance during many months of absence from normal family activities, our thanks go to Sylvia and Eleanor. Of course any errors and omissions are entirely our responsibility.

We were delighted that the first nine editions of *Applied Economics* were so well received by teachers and students across a wide range of courses. Our intention is to keep the book at the forefront of economic debate and events. Accordingly, in this tenth edition we have thoroughly updated all the data and empirical material and added new economic analysis where appropriate.

You can find a variety of self-check questions on each chapter and further up-to-date information and data on the Companion Website to this book at www.booksites.net/griffithswall.

Alan Griffiths, Stuart Wall.
Cambridge 2004

Editors' acknowledgements

The Editors would like to thank Gavin Peebles for his helpful comments.

Publisher's acknowledgements

We are grateful to the following people for permission to reproduce copyright material:

Tables 1.7, 1.8, 1.10, 1.11, 1.12 and 1.13 from O'Mahoney, M. & de Boer, W., 2002a, Britain's relative productivity performance: Update to 1999: Final Report to DTI/Treasury/ONS. *National Institute of Economic & Social Research*; Figures 2.1, 2.2, 2.3, 2.4, 2.5, 2.6, 2.7, 2.8 and 2.11 from Tesco plc reproduced with permission; Table 3.3 from Bureau van Dijk: FAME, July 2000; Table 3.4 Reprinted from *European Management Journal*, Vol. 19, No. 6, Canals, J. How to Think about Corporate Growth. © (2001), with permission from Elsevier; Figure 7.2 from US Dept of Labor (2002), Bureau of Statistics; Tables 7.1, 7.2, 7.3, 7.4, 7.6, 7.7, Figure 7.8, Table 7.9 from UNCTAD Division on Investment, Technology & Enterprise Development. Reprinted with permission; Tables 11.4, 12.1, 12.2, 12.3, 12.5 and 12.7 from DETR 2002, Annual Report, Crown copyright reproduced with permission of HMSO; Table 12.4 Family Spending 2003 (National Statistics), Crown copyright reproduced with permission of HMSO; Table 12.6 from *The Capital at Risk*, the Transport of London Task Force Report, reprinted by permission of the Confederation of British Industry; Table 14.1 Goodman, A., & Shephard, A. 2002, *Inequality & Living Standards in Great Britain*, from Institute of Fiscal Studies, Briefing Note No. 19; Table 16.2 Reprinted by permission of Sage Publications Ltd, from © *National Institute Economic Review*, 2003; Table 17.2 from *Economic Outlook*, OECD © 2002; Figure 19.7 from *Poverty* (1998) reproduced with permission of the Child Poverty Action Group; Tables 20.2, 21.5, 21.6 & 22.3, Figures 21.4, 22.1 and 24.4 from the Bank of England, reproduced with permission; Table 21.2, Figures 21.6, 21.7 and 21.8 from the British Banking Association Annual Abstract of Banking Statistics, Vol. 19, Tab. 4.04, Vols. 12 7 19. Tables 5.01, 5.02 & 5.03, Vol. 19, Tab. 3.09 & Vol. 19, Tab. 3.09, reprinted with permission; Figures 22.2, 22.3, 22.9, 23.2, 23.3 from ONS, Crown copyright reproduced with permission of HMSO; Tables 22.1, 22.2, 23.1, 23.2 and 27.9 from ONS, Crown copyright reproduced with permission of HMSO; Table 24.2 Cabinet Office 2001, Crown copyright reproduced with permission of HMSO; Table 25.1, 25.2, and 25.3 from *World Investment Reports 1999 and 2002*, reprinted with permission of the Director, UNCTAD, Division on Investment, Technology and Enterprise; from Insurance Information Institute, New York & Geneva, reprinted with permission; Table 25.7 from Comptroller of New York, reproduced with permission; Table 28.3 WTO International Statistics 2002, reprinted with permission HM Treasury 2002, Crown copyright reproduced with permission of HMSO; Table 29.5 from ONS 2002, HM Treasury 2002 European Community Finances and Table 29.7 from ONS 2002, United Kingdom Balance of Payments, Crown copyright reproduced with permission of HMSO.

We are grateful to the Financial Times Limited for permission to reprint the following material:

Figure 11.5 Job changes by urban-rural categories (000s), © *Financial Times*, 30 November 1999.

Whilst every effort has been made to trace the owners of copyright material, in a few cases this has proved impossible and we take this opportunity to offer our apologies to any copyright holders whose rights we may have infringed.

Chapter 1 Changes in the UK
economic structure

In this chapter we review the changing economic structure of the UK,
particularly the declining significance of industrial output and employment
as compared with the service sector. Some comparisons are made with
international experience. Alternative explanations of industrial decline are
examined, such as economic 'maturity', low-wage competition, the advent of
North Sea oil, 'crowding out' by the non-market public sector, and low UK
productivity *vis-à-vis* its competitors. We consider whether the changes
observed in the UK are a cause for concern, or merely a reflection of
changes experienced in other advanced industrialized countries.

The popular view of the UK as an industrial economy, a manufacturing
nation, is now inaccurate. Over the past 30 years the structure of the
economy has been transformed. Manufacturing now contributes only around
18% of total output and employs over 5 million fewer people than in 1964.
One of the most prominent of today's industries, North Sea oil and gas, did
not even exist 28 years ago, and service activities now dominate the
economy in terms of both output and employment. There are even
suggestions that the UK is becoming a 'post-industrial' economy, i.e. one in
which information-handling activities are predominant. We shall consider
the causes and consequences of these changes, and in so doing point out
that structural change has implications for other important economic issues.

Structure defined

An economy may be analysed in terms of its component parts, often called 'sectors'. Sectors may be widely drawn to include groups of industries (e.g. the engineering industries) or narrowly drawn to identify parts of industries (e.g. fuel-injection equipment), depending on our purpose. Structural change is often discussed in terms of the even more widely drawn 'primary', 'secondary' and 'tertiary' (service) sectors. It will be useful at the outset to define these, and other conventional sector headings:

1 The *primary sector* – includes activities directly related to natural resources, e.g. farming, mining and oil extraction.

2 The *secondary sector* – covers all the other goods production in the economy, including the processing of materials produced by the primary sector. Manufacturing is the main element in this sector which also includes construction and the public utility industries of gas, water and electricity.

3 The *tertiary sector* – includes all the private sector services, e.g. distribution, insurance, banking and finance, and all the public sector services, such as health and defence.

4 The *goods sector* – the primary and secondary sectors combined.

5 The *production industries* – includes the entire secondary sector except construction, together with the coal and coke industries and the extraction of mineral oil and natural gas. There is an index of industrial production on this basis, and the term 'industry' usually refers to this sector heading.

Structural change means change in the relative size of the sectors, however defined. We may judge size by output (contribution to Gross Domestic Product (GDP)),[1] or by inputs used, either capital or labour. Usually more attention is paid to labour because of the interest in employment and also because it is more easily measured than capital.

Through time we should *expect* the structure of an economy to change. The pattern of demand for a country's products will change with variations in income or taste, affecting in turn both output and employment. If economic growth occurs and real incomes rise, then the demand for goods and services with high and positive income elasticities will tend to increase relative to those with low or even negative income elasticities.[2] For example, between 1983 and 2001 real household expenditure grew by 74.6% whilst expenditure on financial services rose by as much as 165%, and on 'durable goods, transport and communication' by 97.2%. On the other hand, food consumption grew by only 21.2% whilst the consumption of 'alcohol, drink and tobacco' actually fell by 12.3%. Such changes have clear implications for the pattern of output and employment.

The pattern of demand is also responsive to changes in the age structure of the population. The UK, like other developed countries, is experiencing important demographic changes which mean that by 2001 there were 1.8 million fewer people in the 15–24-year-old age group than in 1981. So, for example, the 'recreation, entertainment and education' sector may find this a constraint on its growth, unless it can adapt to the changing characteristics of the market. This smaller age cohort will form fewer new households than previous cohorts, so reducing demand for housing, furniture and consumer durables below what it would otherwise have been. In the longer term, a further demographic factor will be the continuing rise in the numbers of people aged over 75, who will place increasingly heavy demands on the medical and care services.

It is not only the demand side which initiates structural change. The reduced supply of young people in the labour market in the early 1990s increased their earnings relative to other workers, which encouraged firms such as supermarkets to recruit older workers. Employers may also respond by substituting capital for labour and so changing employment patterns, or by raising product prices which would reduce the growth of output and in turn influence employment.

Also on the supply side, technical progress makes possible entirely new goods and services, as well as new processes for producing existing goods and services. In Chapter 23 we note that microelectronics not only gives us new products, such as word processors and video games, but also reduces costs of production, whether through the introduction of robotics in manufacturing, or of computerized accounting methods in banking services. Where such 'process innovation' raises total factor productivity, unit costs fall. The supply side is therefore itself initiating new patterns of demand, output and employment, by creating new products or by reducing the prices of existing products and raising quality.

Changes in resource availability may also initiate structural change, as happened so dramatically with oil in 1973 and again in 1979. When the oil-producing and exporting countries (OPEC) restricted world output, oil-based products rose sharply in price, with *direct* consequences for substitutes (e.g. coal and gas) and complements (e.g. cars). In response to higher oil prices not only did the demand for substitutes rise, and for complements fall, but decisions had also to be taken throughout the economy, by both producers and consumers, to use less energy. As a result there was a decline in output and employment in energy-intensive industries, a prime example being steel.

Oil has had further *indirect* effects on the structure of the UK economy by means of the exchange rate. The development of North Sea oil production enabled the UK to be self-sufficient in oil by 1980, but also bestowed 'petro-currency' status on the pound. This meant that the sterling exchange rate was now responsive to changes in oil prices, which between 1979 and 1983 tended to keep the pound higher than would otherwise have been the case. The result was to make UK exports dearer and imports cheaper in the early 1980s, with adverse consequences for output and employment in sectors facing international competition, both abroad and at home. During 1986 this was partially reversed. The oil price halved and sterling fell 9.2% (on average), providing a stimulus to industrial output during 1987. Although by 1990 the UK was not much more than self-sufficient in oil, the pound still behaved as a petro-currency during the first Gulf war. Following the invasion of Kuwait by Iraq, and the consequent rise in the oil price, the pound appreciated by just over 6% during July and August 1990. The trade surplus in oil peaked at £8.1bn in 1985 and fell to a low of £1.2bn by 1991. Since then it has been rising with the rapid growth in oil production and reached £5.4bn in 2001.

International competition is a potent force for change in the economic structure of the UK. Changing consumer tastes, the creation of new products and changing comparative costs result in the redistribution of economic activity around the world. The demise of the UK motorcycle industry in the face of Japanese competition, for example, was the result of UK manufacturers failing to meet consumer demand for lighter, more reliable, motorcycles which Japan could produce more cheaply. As we see in Chapter 27, for most products the major impact on UK output and employment has come not from

Japanese producers, but from those EU countries which, unlike Japan, have unrestricted access to the UK market. Membership of the EU inevitably meant accepting some restructuring of the UK economy, in accordance with European comparative advantages. This is certainly true for industrial production, with the EU a protected free trade area, though less true for agriculture (see Chapter 29).

Decisions on the location of industrial production are increasingly taken by *multinational enterprises*. In the UK motor industry, decisions taken by Ford and General Motors during the 1970s and early 1980s to supply more of the European market from other EU plants contributed to the fall in UK car output from 1.3 million in 1977 to 1.1 million in 1987, despite real consumer spending on cars and vehicles more than doubling in that period. By 2001 inward investment by Nissan, Toyota, Honda, BMW and Peugeot-Citroën had contributed to an increase in car production to over 1.8 million.

Structural change in the UK

Changes in output

Table 1.1 presents index numbers of output at constant factor cost,[3] recording changes in the volume of output for the various sectors. Data for GDP at factor cost are also given so that comparisons can be made between the individual sectors and the economy as a whole.

In the **primary sector**, *agriculture, hunting, forestry and fishing* grew slower than GDP between 1964 and 1979. After 1979 this sector's output was more influenced by the agricultural policy of the European Union than by the UK business cycle. So agricultural output grew strongly through the recession of the early 1980s and, just as perversely, fell during the upswing of 1994 and 1995. Within *mining and quarrying* there are two very contrasting industries: coal, which is the only industry where output has fallen throughout the period, and the oil and gas extraction industry which grew very rapidly in the late 1970s and early 1980s. *Coal* output fell by just over half between 1964 and 1979. High real energy prices after the 1973 and 1979 oil price 'shocks' improved the prospects of the coal industry, but at the

Table 1.1 Index numbers of output at constant basic prices (1990 = 100).

	1964	1969	1973	1979	1981	1990	2001
Primary							
Agriculture, hunting, forestry and fishing	55.0	59.0	69.5	71.3	81.2	100	88.8
Mining and quarrying	187.0	136.1	104.3	109.2	115.7	100	138.6
Coal and nuclear fuel	295.0	213.2	166.1	144.4	143.8	100	29.6
Oil and gas extraction	–	–	–	88.8	99.2	100	175.9
Secondary							
Manufacturing	72.6	85.4	94.6	90.6	77.7	100	105.2
Construction	65.9	74.4	77.4	69.4	60.5	100	92.3
Electricity, gas and water supply	45.3	55.1	69.6	80.4	81.9	100	131.9
Tertiary							
Distribution, hotels and catering, repairs	61.0	65.5	76.0	76.6	69.9	100	114.2
Transport and storage	60.2	66.7	79.3	81.5	77.9	100	133.2
Post and telecommunication	30.6	40.2	50.2	59.7	62.7	100	248.3
Financial, intermediation, real estate, renting and business activities	27.6	34.5	42.3	49.6	54.3	100	154.1
Public administration, national defence and social security	85.1	89.1	98.0	98.0	102.2	100	96.4
Education, health and social work	57.9	67.2	76.5	92.4	94.2	100	121.4
Other services	51.8	54.7	59.0	68.3	70.5	100	146.7
GDP	58.7	66.4	74.9	80.0	76.5	100	127.4
Production industries	62.6	73.3	81.4	87.6	78.9	100	110.2

Source: ONS (2002) *United Kingdom National Accounts*, and previous issues.

same time made feasible the rapid exploitation of high-cost North Sea oil, which was increasingly to act as a substitute for coal. Coal output fell by around 30% between 1979 and 1990 and then by a further 70% between 1990 and 2001 as the privatized electricity generating companies made their 'dash for gas'. *Oil and gas extraction* had peaked at an index number of 137 in 1987 before falling to the 100 in 1990 shown in the table (the halving of the oil price in 1986 may have been a factor in this decline). Since 1990 the offshore oil and gas extraction industry has enjoyed a remarkable revival in which output increased by nearly 76% over the 11 years to 2001 to register an all-time high. Earlier forecasts of declining output proved to be wrong as new techniques enabled more oil and gas to be profitably produced both from existing fields and also from new smaller fields which might previously have been uneconomic.

In the **secondary sector**, 1973 is again a significant date. Output from both manufacturing and construction rose steadily between 1964 and 1973 (at annual rates of 2.9% and 1.8% respectively), but between 1973 and 1979 output from both these subsectors actually fell, and fell still more sharply in the recession between 1979 and 1981. *Manufacturing* output fell by as much as 12.9 points or 14.2% in this recession. The recovery after 1981 took manufacturing output to a new peak by 1990 which was just 5.4 points above the previous peak 17 years earlier in 1973. All of that gain in output was then lost in the recessionary years of 1991 and 1992, before the upturn from 1993 which left manufacturing output in 2001 only 5.2% above that of 1990 and just 10.6 points (or 11.2%) above the level of 1973. Over a period of 28 years this rate of growth represents virtual stagnation.

Output in the *construction* industry follows a similar path to that in manufacturing up to 1981. The industry was then a leading sector in the boom of the eighties, far outstripping manufacturing, with growth of almost 40 points or 66% between 1981 and 1990 (i.e. 5.7% per annum). Output of the industry then fell by 7.7% between 1990 and 2001. *Electricity, gas and water supply* shows none of the volatility of construction. The long-run growth of output in this sector tends to exceed that of GDP and does not become negative during recessions.

The index of output for the *production industries* (see earlier definition) is presented in the last row of Table 1.1. We see that industrial production grew between 1964 and 1973 by 18.8 points, an annual rate of 2.9%, but then grew more slowly between 1973 and 1979, and fell sharply between 1979 and 1981. This definition includes the contribution of North Sea oil and gas, which helped to compensate for the sharp decline of output in manufacturing since 1973. Exploitation of a non-renewable natural resource is, however, more akin to the consumption of capital than it is to the production of goods and services. The North Sea is providing the UK with a once-and-for-all 'windfall' gain in output over other less fortunate countries. To some extent this masked the full extent of the decline in *non-oil industrial output* which fell by 14.6% between 1973 and 1981, resulting in *non-oil GDP* being 2.5% lower in 1981 than in 1973.

After 1981, growth of UK industrial output resumed, led by the recovery of manufacturing output, and averaged 2.9% per year through to 1988. Industrial output in the 1980s was again growing at the rates of the 1960s, and changing oil output did not significantly affect the index. Industrial production then fell back under the impact of recession, falling 4.1 points between 1990 and 1992 before recovering after 1993.

International comparisons highlight the failure of British industry during the 1960s and 1970s. Industrial production in the industrial market economies (OECD) grew at a weighted average of 6.2% per annum between 1960 and 1970, slowing to what in the UK would still have been regarded as a healthy 2.3% per annum between 1970 and 1983. So British industrial output in the 1960s grew at less than half the average rate of the industrial market economies as a whole, and during the late 1970s contracted as industrial production in these countries continued to grow. However, during the 1980s the growth of UK industry relative to the rest of the OECD clearly improved. The OECD index of industrial production shows growth in the UK of 42% for the period 1981–2001, against an average growth for the whole OECD of 44%. We can conclude that although the UK's rate of relative decline as an industrial producer has been greatly reduced since the 1970s, it has not yet been halted.

In the **tertiary or service sector**, Table 1.1 shows that output grew in every subsector throughout the whole 1964–79 time period. Even during the recession of 1979–81 output fell in only two of the eight subsectors. The pace-setters have been the communications, financial services and real estate sectors. The thrust of government policy since 1979 has ensured that public sector services have grown more slowly than the rest of the sector. Indeed, since 1990, public administration along with defence and social security as a group has seen a fall in measured output.

The contrast in growth experience between the service sector and the industrial sector has changed the share of total output attributable to each (see Table 1.2). However, even in the service sector, growth of output in the UK at 2.9% per annum between 1964 and 1981 lagged behind the average for the industrial market economies which was 3.9%. Between 1981 and 2001 UK service sector growth was, at 3.4% per annum, a relative improvement as the average for the industrial market economies had fallen to a similar figure. The poor UK industrial performance outlined above may also have contributed to this relatively poor service sector performance, since many services are marketed to industry or to people whose incomes are earned in industry. A growing industrial sector generates an induced demand for the output of the service sector.

The GDP can be obtained by aggregating the various sectors outlined above. It grew from 58.7 in 1964 to 80.0 in 1979, i.e. by around 36%. This represents an average annual growth rate of about 2.2% between 1964 and 1979, slowing to 1.1% between 1973 and 1979. The GDP actually declined between 1979 and 1981 by 4.4% whilst the OECD average GDP continued to rise slowly. By international standards the UK growth performance was poor between 1964 and 1981. For instance, the weighted average annual growth rate for industrial market economies, our key trading partners, was 5.1% between 1960 and 1970 and 3.2% between

Table 1.2 Percentage shares of GDP at factor cost.*

	1964	1969	1973	1979	1990	2001
Primary	5.8	4.3	4.2	6.7	3.9	3.9
Agriculture, forestry and fishing	1.9	1.8	2.9	2.2	1.8	1.0
Mining and quarrying including oil and gas extraction	3.9	2.5	1.1	4.5	2.1	2.9
Secondary	40.8	42.0	40.9	36.7	31.5	24.8
Mineral oil processing	0.5	0.5	0.4	0.6	} 22.5	} 17.6
Manufacturing	29.5	30.7	30.0	27.3		
Construction	8.4	8.4	7.3	6.2	6.9	5.4
Electricity, gas and water supply	2.4	2.4	2.8	2.6	2.1	1.8
Tertiary	53.8	53.0	54.9	56.5	64.4	71.3
Distribution, hotels, catering, repairs	14.0	13.3	13.1	12.7	13.5	15.6
Transport and storage	4.4	4.4	4.7	4.8	} 7.6	} 8.0
Post and telecommunication	1.6	1.9	2.3	2.5		
Financial intermediation, real estate, renting and business activities	8.3	8.6	10.7	11.0	} 22.6	} 24.7
Ownership of dwellings	5.4	5.5	5.1	5.8		
Public administration, national defence and social security	7.6	7.0	6.1	6.1	6.3	4.8
Education, health and social work	6.9	7.1	7.7	8.1	8.9	13.0
Other services	5.6	5.2	5.1	5.7	5.5	5.2

Calculated from GDP at factor cost, at current prices and unadjusted for financial services and residual error.
* Totals may not sum to 100 due to rounding.
Source: ONS (2002) *United Kingdom National Accounts*, and previous issues.

1970 and 1979. In the eight years following the recession of 1981, UK real GDP grew at an average of 3.3% per annum, well above the UK rates of the 1960s, and above the OECD average of 3.1%. During the 1980s, therefore, the UK's relative economic decline was halted, but even at these higher rates its reversal was likely to be a slow process. Events since 1988 have confirmed this view, with UK real GDP growing at 2.4% per annum between 1988 and 2001 compared to the OECD average of 2.5%.

Changes in shares of output

Table 1.2 uses percentage shares of total output (GDP at factor cost) to show changes in the relative importance of the sectors presented in Table 1.1.

The **primary sector** was in relative decline between 1964 and 1973 because of the contraction of output in coal-mining. From a low point of 4.2% of GDP in

1973, the primary sector sharply increased its share to 6.7% in 1979 and 9.5% in 1984 (not shown), an unusual trend in a developed economy and almost entirely attributable to the growth of North Sea oil and gas production. By 1990 the primary sector's share had slumped to 3.9%. This dramatic change was caused, in part, by the collapse of oil prices during 1986. Self-sufficiency in oil has meant that the UK's national interest in energy prices is no longer necessarily the same as that of the other (non-oil-producing) industrial nations.

The **secondary sector's** share of output fell from a peak of 42.0% in 1969 to only 31.5% in 1990; the recession then further reduced this to 24.8% by 2001. This long-term decline in the secondary sector is inevitable as the share of manufacturing in GDP falls. By 1990 manufacturing produced only 22.5% of UK output, which fell further to 17.6% by 2001.

The **tertiary sector's** share of output has grown throughout the period since 1969, necessarily so as the shares of the primary and secondary sectors have fallen. The financial sector trebled its share of output between 1964 and 2001 to become the largest sector in output share.

With the exception of the growth of the North Sea sector, these changes in economic structure have occurred throughout the advanced industrial countries (see Table 1.3). The fall in the share of manufacturing in GDP in the UK is typical of the other industrial market economies, and the growth in the share of the service sector has been similar to the average for such economies. This has led some to interpret the changes in UK economic structure as inevitable, giving more recently industrialized countries a glimpse of the future. However, to be complacent because the *relative* position of the sectors in the UK has changed in line with that in other advanced industrialized countries is to ignore the UK's dramatic and unrivalled fall in the *volume* of non-oil industrial production between 1973 and 1981, outlined above in the section on changes in output. Of especial concern has been the negligible growth rate of manufacturing output in the UK between 1973 and 2001; indeed the volume figure for UK manufacturing in 2001 is only 11.2% above that for 1973 (see Table 1.1 above).

Changes in employment

Employment has obviously been influenced by the changes in output already described. It has also been influenced by changes in technology, which have affected the labour required per unit of output. Table 1.4 gives numbers employed in each sector, together with percentage shares of total employment.

Table 1.3 Industrial market economies, distribution of GDP: percentages.

	1960	**1980**	**1985**	**2001**
Agriculture	6.0	3.1	2.6	1.7
Industry	41.0	36.5	34.2	28.6
(manufacturing)	(30.4)	(24.7)	(23.2)	(20.1)
Services	53.0	60.4	63.2	69.7

Sources: OECD (2002) *OECD in Figures*, and previous issues; OECD (2002) *Country Surveys* (various).

The table shows that in the **goods sector** (primary and secondary) there were fewer jobs in 1979 than in 1964, with a still more rapid decline in jobs between 1979 and 2001.

In the **primary sector**, employment was reduced by 60% between 1964 and 1990. The contraction in coal output inevitably sent employment in *mining and quarrying* into severe decline. After 1990 this accelerated as the coal industry lost some of its electricity generation market to gas and was itself made ready for privatization. By 2001 coal industry employment stood at only 14,000, having been over 300,000 in the early 1970s. Such was the growth of output per worker in *agriculture, forestry and fishing* that employment was reduced by 2001 to 50% of its 1964 level, despite an increase in output of 61%. The rise of the North Sea sector had directly created only 24,000 jobs in *oil and natural gas* by 1981. Renewed interest in gas helped raise this to 36,000 by 1990 but although output soared after 1990, employment again fell. The outcome was that between 1964 and 2001 the primary sector's share of total employment fell from 5.1% to 1.4%.

In the **secondary sector**, employment fell by 2.07 million between 1964 and 1979, and again by 3.8 million between 1979 and 2001. Manufacturing, as the largest part of this sector, suffered most of these job losses, with manufacturing employment falling by over 5 million in the period 1964–2001. The *share* of manufacturing in total employment fell from 38.1% in 1964 to as little as 14.9% in 2001.

As employment fell in the goods sector between 1964 and 1979, employment in the **tertiary sector** expanded by 2,378,000, enabling total employment to be held at around 23 million. This expansion was concentrated in the financial sector, and in various professional and scientific services.

The rough balance between employment losses in the goods sector and gains in the service sector broke down after 1979. Between 1979 and 1981 service sector employment actually fell slightly. Not until 1984 did the growth of service sector employment again compensate for the loss of goods sector employment. However, over the whole period 1979–2001 service sector employment grew by 6.7 million whilst employment in the goods sector fell by 3.8 million. As a result total employment rose by 2.9 million.

Similar changes in the pattern of employment have, however, taken place throughout the industrial world (see Table 1.5). By comparison with other

Table 1.4 Employees in employment, UK at mid-June.

	1964 (000s)	1964 (% of total employment)	1973 (000s)	1973 (% of total employment)	1979 (000s)	1979 (% of total employment)	1981 (000s)	1981 (% of total employment)	1990 (000s)	1990 (% of total employment)	2001 (000s)	2001 (% of total employment)
Agriculture forestry and fishing	540	2.3	432	1.9	368	1.6	363	1.6	314	1.4	271	1.1
Mining and quarrying			336	1.5	304	1.3	285	1.3	126	0.5	44	0.2
Extraction of mineral oil and natural gas			5	–	20	0.1	24	0.1	36	0.2	30	0.1
Total primary	**1,201**	**5.1**	**773**	**3.4**	**692**	**3.0**	**672**	**3.0**	**476**	**2.1**	**345**	**1.4**
Manufacturing	8,909	38.1	7,861	34.7	7,259	31.3	6,221	28.4	4,709	20.5	3,837	14.9
Construction	1,659	7.1	1,320	5.8	1,253	5.4	1,130	5.2	1,143	5.0	1,201	4.7
Other energy and water supply			364	1.6	366	1.6	366	1.7	241	1.1	105	0.4
Total secondary	**10,978**	**46.9**	**9,573**	**42.4**	**8,911**	**38.5**	**7,748**	**35.4**	**6,093**	**26.6**	**5,143**	**20.0**
Distribution, hotels and catering, repairs	1,665	7.1	3,950	17.4	4,252	18.4	4,172	19.1	4,912	21.4	6,117	24.0
Transport			1,062	4.7	1,051	4.5	987	4.5	921	4.0	1,023	4.0
Communication			445	2.0	422	1.8	438	2.0	471	2.0	534	2.1
Banking, finance, insurance, business services and leasing			1,442	6.4	1,663	7.2	1,738	7.9	3,480	15.2	4,994	19.1
Public administration, defence and social security	9,513	40.7	1,664	7.3	1,721	7.4	1,623	7.4	1,442	6.3	1,411	5.4
Education and health			2,781	12.3	2,876	12.4	2,908	13.3	5,125	22.4	6,168	24.0
Other services			976	4.3	1,571	6.8	1,600	7.3				
Total tertiary	**11,178**	**47.8**	**12,320**	**54.4**	**13,556**	**58.5**	**13,465**	**61.4**	**16,351**	**71.3**	**20,247**	**78.6**
Total employment	**23,357**		**22,664**		**23,158**		**21,891**		**22,920**		**25,735**	

Sources: ONS (2002) *UK National Accounts*, and previous issues; *Labour Market Trends* (2002), December.

Table 1.5 Industrial market economies, distribution of the labour force: percentages.

	1960	1980	2000
Agriculture	17.3	6.5	2.5
Industry	36.7	34.5	24.6
(manufacturing)	(27.2)	(25.0)	(17.4)
Services	46.0	59.0	72.9

Sources: OECD (2002) *OECD in Figures,* and previous issues; OECD (2002) *Country Surveys* (various).

Table 1.6 Changes in industrial employment (%).

	1964–79	1979–83	1983–2001
UK	−14.8	−18.9	−10.4
Canada	+35.7	−8.7	+21.1
USA	+27.2	−6.4	+6.7
Japan	+28.3	+4.1	−1.9
Austria	−3.2	+8.3	−8.1
Belgium	−18.6	−15.2	−13.4
France	+2.3	−7.4	−19.6
Germany	−10.3	−8.5	+11.4
Italy	+2.2	−3.8	−6.9
The Netherlands	−14.0	−12.4	+20.3
Norway	+9.1	−2.7	−5.9
Sweden	−10.9	−7.1	−20.2
Switzerland	−21.1	−3.3	−11.4

Source: Calculated from data in OECD (2002) *Labour Force Statistics 1981–2001.*

advanced economies the UK now has relatively small agricultural and industrial sectors, leaving services with a larger than average share of total employment.

Causes of structural change

Stage of maturity

As the world's oldest industrial nation the UK might reasonably lay claim to being its most developed or 'mature' economy. Several variants of the maturity argument provide explanations of industrial decline which appear rather reassuring.

A first variant suggests that the changing pattern of UK employment since 1964 may be seen as analogous to the transfer of workers from agriculture to industry during the nineteenth century, a transfer necessary to create the new industrial workforce. In a similar way, the argument here is that those previously employed in industrial activities were required for the expansion of the service sector in the 1960s and 1970s. However, this line of argument looks rather weak from the mid- to late 1970s onwards, with rising unemployment surely providing the opportunity for service sector expansion without any marked decline in industrial sector employment.

The hypothesis that economic maturity is always associated with falling industrial employment may be crudely tested by reference to Table 1.6. In the period 1964–79 the experience of the UK, Austria, Belgium, West Germany, the Netherlands, Sweden and Switzerland lends support to the hypothesis, whilst the experience of Canada, the USA, France and Norway contradicts it. Italy and Japan also experienced rising

industrial employment, but it might be contentious to call these economies 'mature' in this period. Between 1964 and 1979, the evidence does therefore suggest that decline in industrial employment in the UK was not necessarily an inevitable result of economic development. The data between 1979 and 1983 are more difficult to interpret as they cover a period of recession, but only Japan and Austria experienced a rise in industrial employment in these years. However, data for the years 1983–2001 do seem to refute any simple hypothesis that economic maturity must inevitably bring with it a fall in industrial employment. Canada, the USA, Germany and the Netherlands all experienced increases in industrial employment. In fact, if we take the period 1994–2001 for the OECD countries, total industrial employment actually increased by 0.7%. In the UK the decline in industrial employment accelerated during the early 1990s, resulting in an overall fall of over 10% for the 1983–2001 period as a whole.

A second variant of the 'maturity' argument is that our changing economic structure simply reflects the changing pattern of demand that follows from economic development. It has been argued that consumer demand in a mature economy shifts away from goods and towards services (higher income elasticities) and that this, together with increased government provision of public sector services, adds impetus to the growth of the tertiary sector. This may be a sound explanation for some of the UK's structural change, but not all. The pattern of UK demand simply does not fit such a stylized picture; for instance, UK trade data clearly show UK demand for manufactured imports growing faster than UK manufactured exports (see Chapter 27). This growth in manufactured imports is hardly consistent with a major switch of UK demand away from industries producing goods.

In a third variant of the 'maturity' argument, Rowthorn and Wells (1987) have pointed out that the demand for manufactured goods is at least as income elastic as the demand for services, when valued at constant prices, that is, in terms of volume. A successful industrial sector would therefore achieve increases in the volume of output at least matching the growth of GDP. Faster growth of productivity in the industrial sector could then cause prices to fall relative to those in the service sector, thereby reducing the industrial sector's *share* of both output at current prices and employment. The 'maturity' argument should, in the view of Rowthorn and Wells, be based on *productivity* changes and not on demand changes. In the case of the UK, the relatively slow growth in the *volume* of industrial output hardly supports this variant of the 'maturity' argument.

A fourth variant of the argument is that the UK has always been a reluctant manufacturing nation, and that we are now specializing in services, a sector in which we enjoy a comparative advantage and a protected domestic market. However, since the mid-1970s, any need to exploit comparative advantages in services could again have been met from unused resources rather than by reducing industrial output and employment.

Low-wage competition

Foreigners, especially from the Third World, make a convenient scapegoat for UK problems and are particularly blamed for providing 'unfair', low-wage competition. Wages in the Third World are extremely low but are often accompanied by low productivity, a lack of key categories of skilled labour, and a shortage of supporting industrial services and infrastructure. The UK is not unique in facing this competition and is itself a low-wage economy by developed country standards. In some sectors (e.g. textiles and cheap electrical goods) Third

World competition has been important but, as yet, the scale of Third World involvement in the export of world manufactures is too small (around 16% of OECD-manufactured exports in 2001) to be regarded as a major cause of UK structural change. As we see in Chapter 27, the main competition comes from other industrial market economies, not from low-wage developing countries. We should also remember that countries like the previously high growth Asian 'Tiger' economies provide important export markets for manufactured goods, and so have contributed to world economic growth, with the recent slump in the late 1990s in these economies creating problems for the export sectors of many industrialized economies, such as the UK.

The North Sea

Free-market economists often argue that the contribution of North Sea oil to the UK balance of payments has meant inevitable decline for some sectors of the economy. The mechanism of decline is usually attributed to the exchange rate, with the improvement in the UK visible balance (via removal of the oil deficit) bringing upward pressure on sterling. In terms of the foreign exchange market, higher exports of oil increase the demand for sterling, and lower imports of oil decrease the supply of sterling. The net effect has been a higher sterling exchange rate than would otherwise have been the case, particularly in the late 1970s and early 1980s. The status of sterling as a petro-currency may also attract an increased capital inflow, further raising the demand for sterling, and with it the sterling exchange rate. The higher price of sterling then makes UK exports more expensive abroad, and imports cheaper in the UK. United Kingdom producers of industrial exports, and import substitutes, are the most seriously disadvantaged by a high pound, since the major part of UK trade is in industrial products (around two-thirds of both exports and imports). In this way a higher pound produces a decline in industrial output and employment.

The argument that North Sea oil, through its effect on the exchange rate, inevitably resulted in the decline in UK manufacturing output and employment observed in the late 1970s and early 1980s is rather simplistic. The government could have directed surplus foreign exchange created by oil revenues towards imported capital equipment. This increase in imports of capital equipment would have eased the upward pressure on the pound,[4] whilst providing a basis for increased future competitiveness and economic recovery. Equally, the upward pressure on sterling could have been alleviated by macroeconomic policies aimed at raising aggregate demand, and with it spending on imports, or by lower interest rates aimed at reducing capital inflow.

North Sea oil cannot be wholly to blame for the observed decline in UK industrial output and employment. These structural changes began in the mid-1960s, yet North Sea oil only became a significant factor in the UK balance of payments in 1978. The periods of high exchange rate between 1978 and 1981, whilst certainly contributing to industrial decline, were by no means an inevitable consequence of North Sea oil. Different macroeconomic policies could, as we have seen, have produced a lower exchange rate, as happened after withdrawal from the Exchange Rate Mechanism in September 1992.

'Crowding out'

Bacon and Eltis (1976) argued that the decline of British industry was due to its being displaced ('crowded out') by the growth of the non-market public sector. Some of the (then) public sector, such as steel, is itself industrial and markets its output in the same way as any private sector company. However, some of the public sector, such as health and education, provides services which are not marketed, being free at the point of use. This non-market public sector uses resources and generates income, but does not supply any output to the market. It requires investment goods for input, and consumes goods and services, all of which must be provided by the market sector.

We might usefully illustrate the 'crowding out' argument by first taking a closed economy with no government sector. Here the income generated in the market would equal the value of output. The income-receivers could enjoy all the goods and services they produced. However, they could no longer do so if a non-market (government) sector is now added, since the non-market sector will also require a proportion of the goods and services produced by the market sector. The market sector must therefore forgo some of its claims on its own output. It is one of the functions of taxes to channel resources from the market sector to support non-market (government) activity. The rapid growth of the public sector after 1945, it is argued, led to too rapid an increase in the tax burden (see Chapter 19), which adversely affected investment and attitudes to work, to the detriment of economic growth. Also, in the face of rising tax demands, workers in both market and non-market sectors sought to maintain or improve their real disposable income, thereby creating inflationary pressures.

If the market sector does not accommodate the demands of a growing non-market sector by forgoing claims on its own output, then in an open economy adjustment must be made externally. The higher overall demand *of both sectors combined* can then only be met either by reducing the exports of the market sector, or by increasing imports. A rising non-market public sector in this way contributes to balance of payments problems.

Bacon and Eltis saw the rapid growth of the non-market public sector as the cause of higher taxes, higher interest rates (to finance public spending), low investment, inflationary pressures and balance of payments problems. The growth of the non-market public sector has in these ways allegedly 'crowded out' the market sector, creating an economic environment which has been conducive to UK decline.

These ideas provided intellectual backing to the Conservative Party's approach to public spending and tax policies after 1979. The irony is that attempts to cut public spending and taxation after 1979 simply accelerated industrial decline, eroded the tax base and prevented the desired reduction of the tax burden (see Chapter 19). Bacon and Eltis's ideas provide a coherent theory of industrial decline, helping us to appreciate some of the complex linkages in the process. However, experience since 1979 calls into question their basic propositions. High unemployment during the 1980s made it impossible to argue that industry was denied labour, although it did lack capital investment. It may be that low investment had more to do with low expected returns than with the high interest rates said to be necessary to finance the growth of public expenditure. There are, of course, several other determinants of UK interest rates in addition to public expenditure. The 'crowding out' argument also neglects the importance of public sector services as *inputs* to the private sector. Of the non-marketed services, education is especially important in increasing the skills of the workforce.

Productivity

The total output of any economy is determined partly by the quantity of factor input (labour, capital, etc.), and partly by the use to which factors are put. Different economies may achieve different volumes of total output using similar quantities of factor input, because of variations in productivity. Productivity is the concept relating output to a given input, or inputs.

Productivity is usually expressed in terms of labour as input, i.e. labour productivity, or of capital as input, i.e. capital productivity. However, a productivity measure which relates output to *both* labour and capital inputs is called *total factor productivity* (TFP). We now seek to investigate the UK's productivity performance relative to other countries with the aid of these measures.

The most widely used measure of a country's economic efficiency is *labour productivity* and this is often defined as output (or value added) per person employed. However, since there may be changes in the structure of jobs between full- and part-time or in the length of the working week or number of holidays, then a more useful measure of labour productivity is arguably output (value added) *per person hour*.

A major issue in recent years has been whether the UK has been able to catch up with its major competitors in terms of productivity. In this context, the most comprehensive study of the UK's relative productivity performance over the last few years was that by Mary O'Mahoney and Willem de Boer in 2002 (O'Mahoney and de Boer 2002a). Some of the results of their detailed study form the basis for many of the tables shown below.

Table 1.7 shows the growth rate of labour productivity, defined in terms of value added per hour worked, for the UK and its main competitors between 1979 and 1999. These growth rates are expressed as an average across all sectors of the economy and include agricultural, industrial and service sectors. We see that the UK's growth rate of labour productivity averaged 2.16% per annum over the whole 1979–99 period, a figure significantly higher than the 1.21% per annum recorded for the USA and similar to those of France and Germany but below that for Japan. When we break this 20-year time period down into sub-periods, we can see that the US's productivity growth performance was relatively poor during the 1980s, though recovering somewhat

Table 1.7 Growth in output per hour worked, 1979–99.

Period	USA	UK	France	Germany	Japan
1979–99	1.21	2.16	2.13	2.29	2.79
1979–89	0.97	2.41	2.94	1.92*	3.37
1989–99	1.46	1.91	1.32	2.67	2.14
1989–95	1.15	2.28	1.42	3.13	2.57
1995–99	1.92	1.37	1.16	1.98	1.28

*West Germany.
Source: Adapted from O'Mahoney and de Boer (2002a).

during the 1990s, especially in the latter part of that decade. On the other hand, the UK's labour productivity performance deteriorated in the 1990s, being somewhat better than that for France but worse than those for Germany and Japan. Of particular concern is the apparent *deceleration* in the UK's productivity performance in the second half of the 1990s, matching that of recession-hit Japan.

What matters, of course, is not only the growth rate of labour productivity but also the *base level* from which that growth takes place. Table 1.8 compares absolute levels of labour productivity in the UK with those in three of its main competitors, namely the US, France and Germany. It provides a sectoral breakdown of absolute labour productivities (column L) using index numbers based on UK = 100. We can see that in the 'market economy' in 1999, labour productivity in the US was 39% above that of the UK, with labour productivity in France (+22%) and Germany (+19%) also significantly above UK levels. Table 1.8 also provides some useful comparisons of absolute levels of total factor productivity (column T). In this case we see that in the 'market economy' in 1999, total factor productivity (TFP) in the US was 29% above that of the UK, but with the relative advantage in terms of this productivity measure rather small for Germany (+9%) and France (+4%). Before we investigate these aspects in more detail it might be interesting to note that over the decade 1989–99, the UK's relative labour productivity and TFP ratios did not change significantly in relation to the US, but improved slightly in relation to France and deteriorated slightly in relation to Germany (O'Mahoney 2002).

Table 1.8 Labour productivity and total factor productivity by sector, 1999 (UK = 100).

Sector	USA		France		Germany	
	L	**T**	**L**	**T**	**L**	**T**
Agriculture, forestry and fishing	189	136	104	84	51	50
Mining	78	99	43	128	20	31
Gas, electricity and water	157	145	114	115	65	80
Manufacturing	155	143	132	110	129	121
Construction	114	102	108	98	101	85
Transport and communications	113	94	101	89	88	72
Distributive trades	161	139	150	112	112	103
Financial and business services	153	124	126	99	161	122
Personal services	97	139	93	106	147	151
Non-market services	84	80	107	101	87	83
Market economy	139	129	122	104	119	109

L = Labour productivity, T = Total factor productivity.
Source: Adapted from O'Mahoney and de Boer (2002a).

Table 1.8 also provides information on the levels of labour productivity and TFP in the most important *sectors* of the respective economies. In general, the UK appears to have a general advantage over the other economies in mining, but this is largely due to the fact that in Britain this sector is weighted towards the relatively efficient oil and gas extraction business. Its relative performance on transport and communications and on construction was also sound. However, if we concentrate on manufacturing, distributive trades and financial and business services (which account for some 60% of GDP in these countries), we find that the UK still faces a significant disadvantage in terms of both labour productivity and TFP in many of these sectors as compared to the US, France and Germany.

- First, taking *labour productivity*, the UK's relative disadvantages in 1999 compared to the US in the manufacturing, distributive trades and financial/business services sectors were 55%, 61% and 53% respectively. For France the figures were 32%, 50% and 26% respectively, and for Germany, 29%, 12% and 61% respectively.

- Second, taking *total factor productivity*, the UK's relative disadvantages in 1999 compared to the US in the manufacturing, distributive trades and financial/business services were 43%, 39% and 24% respectively. For France the figures were 10% and 12% for the first two of these sectors, but the French performance was virtually equal to the UK's in financial and business services. For Germany the relative disadvantages were 21%, 3% and 22% respectively.

These figures suggest that the UK's overall productivity performance continues to lag behind those of the other three main economies and that the UK cannot necessarily depend on higher productivity in services to compensate for any relative productivity deficiencies in manufacturing. At this point it will be useful to consider productivity in UK manufacturing in rather more detail.

Manufacturing productivity

The UK's productivity in manufacturing has always been in the forefront of discussion because the sector is so open to global competitive forces. Table 1.9 gives a brief summary of trends in labour productivity for the whole economy and for manufacturing, together with trends in manufacturing output in the UK between 1964 and 2002. We see that output per person employed in manufacturing has risen by 90.3

Table 1.9 United Kingdom productivity and manufacturing output (1990 = 100).

Year	UK output per person employed		Manufacturing output
	Whole economy	Manufacturing	
1964	58.1	45.3	72.6
1969	67.0	53.8	85.4
1973	76.2	63.4	94.6
1979	81.7	65.8	90.6
1990	100.0	100.0	100.0
2002	123.1	135.6	103.2

Source: ONS (2003) *Economic Trends,* March, and previous issues.

Table 1.10 Labour productivity growth rates in manufacturing, 1989–99.

	1989–99	1989–95	1995–99
USA	3.38	2.85	4.18
Germany	3.52	4.46	2.10
France	2.74	2.76	2.72
UK	2.32	3.31	0.83

Source: Adapted from O'Mahoney and de Boer (2002a).

points on 1964, much more than the 65 points recorded for the whole economy. This is certainly supportive of the view that manufacturing is a vital 'engine for growth'. However, we can also see that manufacturing *output* has increased by only 30.6 points since 1964. Indeed, since 1990 UK manufacturing output has been essentially static, growing by only 3.2 points. It is hardly surprising, then, that we noted significant job losses in the manufacturing sector in Table 1.4, since a relatively rapid labour productivity growth and a static output are invariably associated with a reduction in employment.

The problems experienced in UK manufacturing can also be seen in Table 1.10 where UK labour productivity growth rates in this sector are compared to those for three of its main rivals. Here we see that the UK's growth rate for labour productivity in manufacturing was below those of its three rivals over the decade 1989–99. Despite a relatively improved performance in the early 1990s, there was a significant reversal of growth in the years leading to the new millennium.

Although much discussion of the UK's performance in terms of productivity has centred on the manufacturing sector, it should be noted that this sector is not a cohesive entity; rather it is made up of many subsectors with divergent records over time. A major study of UK manufacturing productivity (Cameron and Proudman 1998) showed that although the overall growth of manufacturing output

may have been stagnant, there were significant differences between subsectors of manufacturing. The study investigated output growth and labour productivity in 19 subsectors of manufacturing over the period 1970–92. Their results suggest that there has been an important shift in the contribution of the various subsectors to manufacturing output, with nine sectors experiencing positive rates of output growth (led by computing, pharmaceuticals, aerospace, electronics and precision instruments), whilst the other 10 sectors experienced negative rates of growth of output (led by iron and steel, basic metals, minerals and machinery). Interestingly, the sectors experiencing positive rates of growth of output also tended to be those which experienced higher rates of growth of labour productivity.

Two further conclusions of the study might also be noted. First, the authors investigated whether changes in overall manufacturing productivity were due to the relocation of resources *between* sectors (i.e. from low to high productivity sectors) or due to productivity growth *within* the sectors over time. They concluded that over 90% of the increase in labour productivity was due to *within*-sector productivity growth. This suggests that explanations of changes in productivity should concentrate on factors which affect productivity *within* industries and even plants. Second, the study looked at whether productivities across the various sectors of manufacturing have tended to converge. They concluded that whilst productivity in a number of sectors appeared to settle at levels just below the manufacturing mean, the productivities of a few sectors (such as computing, pharmaceuticals and aerospace) remained consistently above the mean and tended to move further above the mean over time.

Despite these differential performances between sectors within UK manufacturing, the UK falls behind the US, Germany and France in absolute labour productivities in most of the subsectors of manufacturing. For example, the O'Mahoney and de Boer study (2002a) points out that in the basic metals sector, the absolute productivity levels in the US, France and Germany in 1999 (UK = 100) were 198, 148 and 166 respectively. For the electrical and electronic equipment sector the figures were 173, 145 and 135 respectively, whilst in textiles, clothing and footwear the absolute productivity figures were 159, 196 and 129 respectively. Such divergent productivity performances between different UK manufacturing sectors, and also between the UK and other countries' manufacturing sectors, raises interesting questions. For example, are these differences due to the nature of technologies used in these sectors, or are they the result of other factors involving capital intensity, labour skills or openness to trade? We will return to some of these questions later in the chapter.

Productivity and capital investment

The contribution of *capital investment* to variations in the rate of output growth between nations has been an important topic of research for many years, the argument being that the greater the investment in plant and equipment, the greater the capacity of the economy to grow (see Chapter 17). Recent research has looked at the role of investment in tangible assets (plant, machinery and equipment) and in human capital (training, etc.) in influencing the growth of nations (Dougherty and Jorgenson 1997). Dougherty and Jorgenson found that for the period 1960–89, the two main factors explaining the recorded differences in levels of output per head between countries were identified as the *level* of capital input and the *quality* of labour input. They concluded that one of the most serious deficiencies in the UK *vis-à-vis* other countries was the low recorded level of capital per head.

A later study by O'Mahoney and de Boer (2002a) provides further evidence on this issue of capital intensity, i.e. different levels of capital per unit of labour across nations and sectors. Table 1.11 shows capital per hour worked in the US, France and Germany in 1999 as compared with the UK (base of 100). As far as the whole 'market economy' is concerned, the US had a capital intensity advantage of 25%, France 60% and Germany 32% in terms of capital per hour worked. More specifically in terms of ICT capital per hour worked (i.e. in computers, software and communication equipment), the US had a capital intensity advantage of 162% over the UK as compared to 15% for France.

Table 1.11 also gives a sectoral breakdown of the relative capital intensity per hour worked, and here we see that the UK has a disadvantage *vis-à-vis* the US, France and Germany in all sectors other than mining and personal services. When we look at the three major sectors of manufacturing, distributive trades and financial/business services, we can see some important patterns.

Table 1.11 Relative capital per hour worked by sector, 1999 (UK = 100).

Sector	USA	France	Germany
Agriculture, forestry and fishing	198 (167)	221 (34)	109
Mining	73 (434)	27 (352)	20
Gas, electricity and water	112 (175)	99 (156)	72
Manufacturing	130 (228)	180 (70)	130
Construction	170 (432)	188 (90)	212
Transport and communications	174 (251)	150 (59)	183
Distributive trades	166 (369)	236 (151)	136
Financial and business services	190 (314)	209 (159)	199
Personal services	25 (340)	71 (355)	93
Non-market services	182 (316)	196 (131)	178
Market economy	125 (262)	160 (115)	132

Figures in brackets are for ICT capital per hour worked.
Source: Adapted from O'Mahoney and de Boer (2002a).

- In the *manufacturing* sector, all three countries have a capital intensity advantage over the UK. In 1999, the US had 30% more capital per hour worked in manufacturing than the UK, with corresponding figures of 80% for France and 30% for Germany. In terms of ICT capital intensity the US had a still greater advantage of 128% over the UK, although the UK was ahead of France in this respect.

- In the *distributive trades* sector, again all three countries have a capital intensity advantage over the UK. In 1999, the US had 66% more capital per hour worked in the distributive trades than the UK, with the corresponding figures of 136% for France and 36% for Germany. ICT capital investment per hour worked was 269% higher in the US and 51% higher in France than in the UK.

- In the *financial/business services* sector the capital intensity figures again show the UK at a major disadvantage. The US was 90% more capital intensive than the UK, and the figures for France and Germany were 109% and 99% higher respectively. ICT capital per hour worked was also 214% higher in the US and 59% higher in France.

In general, these figures show the UK's generally inadequate performance in terms of capital intensity per hour worked in 1999. Additional research over the period 1989–99 shows that the overall gap between the UK's relative levels of capital per hour worked compared to the US, France and Germany did narrow a little over the decade but that the convergence began to falter in the late 1990s (O'Mahoney 2002).

A relatively low level of capital intensity for the UK is of some concern in the context of studies such as that of Oulton (1997). In a more general survey of growth in 53 countries over the period 1965–90, Oulton found that the most important way of raising growth rates was by increasing the growth rate of capital stock, i.e. raising capital per worker. Of course, the relatively low levels of investment in the UK may be a rational response to low returns, so that whilst low investment may contribute to low productivity, low productivity may in turn discourage investment. For example, Oulton noted that the pre-tax rate of return for investment in UK companies (excluding North Sea oil) averaged only 8.7% per annum between 1988 and 1997, with the private rate of return on human capital around the same figure.

Since the cost of capital averaged around 5–7% per annum over the same period, the payoff for investing in either physical or human capital in the UK was hardly attractive!

Productivity and labour skills

The above account points to the importance of capital intensity in enhancing productivity. Of course the productivity of a nation also depends on the skills of its management and workforce in making the best use of whatever resources are available. Management is responsible for selecting projects, organizing the flow of work and the utilization of resources, so that effective management is a 'necessary' condition for good productivity performance. It is not, however, 'sufficient' since a labour force which possesses inappropriate skills, or which refuses to adapt its work practices and manning levels to new technology, will prevent advances in productivity, whatever the merits of management. A major issue in many industries is workers' lack of flexibility between tasks, resulting in overmanning and also acting as a disincentive to innovation. Lack of flexibility can result from union restrictive practices, but is also caused by badly trained workers and managers who are unable to cope with change. There is evidence of low standards in UK education which mean that many school leavers are ill-equipped for the growing complexity of work.

Throughout British industry there is less emphasis on training than in other countries. Only around 52% of 18-year-olds in the UK were in full-time or part-time education or training in 1999, much less than the 80% figure for Germany, France, the Netherlands and Belgium, suggesting that young people as a group in the UK are among the least educated and trained in Europe. When considering the whole labour force, that is the stock of human capital rather than the flow, the situation is probably even worse. Davies and Caves (1987) had pointed out that British managers were only marginally better qualified than the population at large: for example, very few production managers were graduate engineers. Amongst production workers only a quarter in Britain had completed an apprenticeship compared with about half in Germany. Very few British foremen had formal qualifications for their job, but in Germany foremen were trained as craftsmen and then took the further

and hence investment plans. Investment is also required in many industries to raise productivity, and thereby profits, and so we come full circle. Profits depend on productivity, which is affected by investment, which depends on profits! The process is self-reinforcing; low productivity gives low profits, low investment and therefore little productivity improvement. In contrast, once productivity is raised, profits and investment increase, which further raises productivity. This cumulative upward spiral is still further reinforced in that market share and factor incomes rise, so that demand is created for still higher output. New technology is also more easily accepted in situations of rising output, perhaps leading to still higher profits, stimulating further investment, and so driving the process on. The UK's problem is to further improve on its productivity performance, given the substantial gaps which still persist relative to its main competitors across a number of industrial and service sectors.

The consequences of low productivity and poor competitiveness have been felt mainly in the manufacturing sector of the economy, largely because its exposure to international competition is greater than that of the service sector. Structural change, in the form of a *reduced share* of output and employment for the manufacturing sector, is then almost inevitable. Indeed, Hadjimatheou and Sarantis (1998) present simulations for the UK economy over the period 1994–2010, and show that even in the 'most optimistic scenario' the share of manufacturing in total UK employment falls to 14.5%, whilst the 'most pessimistic scenario' suggests that the share falls as low as 11.4%. In the UK this has also become a decline in the *absolute level* of employment in manufacturing and, since 1973, virtual stagnation of the absolute level of output of the manufacturing sector.

Consequences of structural change

Deindustrialization

There is little agreement as to what 'deindustrialization' actually means. For some time politicians on the left have used the term to mean loss of industrial employment. Others extend the term to include situations of declining industrial output, and still others to include declining *shares* of employment or output.

We have shown that the UK has undergone deindustrialization on each and every one of these criteria. Declining industrial employment is not unusual in other advanced economies (see Table 1.6), and neither is a decline in the industrial sector's share of employment (Table 1.5) or of GDP (Table 1.3). Where the UK is unusual is in the insignificant growth of non-oil industrial production in the 28 years since 1973.

Declining industrial employment need not be a problem; there is every indication that many British people would not freely choose industrial employment. There will, however, be the problem of rising unemployment if declining industrial employment is not compensated by increasing non-industrial employment. Until 1979 this problem did not arise; as we saw in Table 1.4, employment levels were broadly maintained until 1979, but since then the growth of service sector employment has *not* compensated for falling industrial employment. The costs of deindustrialization have been particularly felt in those regions where declining industries were concentrated. The Midlands, the North, Yorkshire and Humberside, the North West, Wales and Scotland all experienced a prolonged period with unemployment rates well above 10% during the 1980s, as the industrial base contracted. However, there has been a considerable narrowing of the unemployment differential between regions as the recession of the early 1990s bit deep into the previously expanding service sector activities throughout the UK (see Chapter 23).

Some writers view these changes as part of a move towards a post-industrial society, where the main activities involve the creation and handling of information. However, a decline in the *share* of industrial activity within the economy would be less worrying if *absolute* industrial output had grown since 1973 at the same rate as in other advanced economies.

A decline in manufacturing activity may cause a still more serious employment impact than that given by the official statistics. This is because manufacturing is characterized by many more *backward-linkages* than is the service sector (Greenhalgh 1994). For example, in order to make cars the vehicle manufacturer will buy in some engine components, metal products and textiles from other manufacturers and will also purchase the services of vehicle transporters, accountants, bankers, designers, etc. Manufacturing and services display very different patterns of inter-industry purchases, which can be examined using statistical input–output tables. In particular, the rate of purchase of service output by manufacturing firms is a much larger proportion per unit of gross output than is the purchase of manufactured goods for use as inputs by services. Whereas Greenhalgh found that each £1 spent on manufacturing gross output created £1.61 of employment income in *all* sectors, that same £1 spent on service gross output created only £0.56 of employment income in *all* sectors. Clearly manufacturing sustains a far higher proportion of jobs (*directly and indirectly*) than it might appear to us from data on sectoral shares, such as Table 1.4 above.

Deindustrialization may put not only these back-ward-linkages at risk but also a variety of *forward-linkages*. The suggestion here is that innovations, whether measured by patents or survey records, are heavily concentrated in the manufacturing sector. Again Greenhalgh (1994) found that 87% of innovations were developed in the manufacturing (and primary) sector, and 80% of all first commercial adoptions of innovations took place in this sector. Deindustrialization clearly puts at risk the 'seed-corn' of domestic technology, which in turn has balance of payments implications (see below) as UK trade becomes progressively geared to high-technology products.

Growth prospects

As we saw in Table 1.9, it is manufacturing which has led the way in productivity growth. Manufacturing lends itself to rapid growth of labour productivity because of the scope for capital investment and technical progress. Growth of manufacturing output, of GDP and of productivity are closely related, and manufacturing has in the past been the engine for growth. As workers found new jobs in manufacturing during the nineteenth century they left agriculture and other relatively low-productivity sectors. Those in the new jobs raised their productivity, and the average productivity of those remaining in agriculture was raised by the removal of marginal workers. At the same time rising incomes in manufacturing generated new demand for goods and services, the multiplier process encouraging still further growth of output, and with it productivity. Indeed Greenhalgh (1994)

points out that in the eight-year period 1985–93, manufacturing contributed about 70% of the average rise in output per worker in the whole economy.

In parts of the service sector there is little scope for improved productivity; even the concept itself is often inappropriate. First, there is often no clear output – how do you measure the output of doctors, or nurses? Second, even where a crude output measure is devised, it often fails to take into account the quality of service – are larger class sizes an increase or a decrease in educational productivity? The national accounts often resort to measuring output by input (e.g. the wages of health workers), so that productivity is by definition equal to 1. There are, however, some services where productivity can be meaningfully measured and in these there is scope for productivity growth, especially where the new information technologies can be applied. But many workers who lose manufacturing jobs move into service sector jobs, where their productivity may be lower, into unemployment or out of the labour market altogether. There is no mechanism for growth in this process, but quite the reverse.

Nevertheless, as the process of deindustrialization progresses, the overall growth of productivity will depend on productivity gains in the service sector. This is in line with the theory of 'asymptotic stagnancy' which indicates that if there are two activities, one of which is 'technologically progressive' whilst the other is 'technologically stagnant', then it can be shown mathematically that in the long run the average rate of growth of an economy will be determined by the sector in which productivity growth is the slowest (Baumol, Blackman and Wolff 1989). In this context manufacturing can be regarded as the 'technologically progressive' sector with services 'technologically stagnant' in comparison, suggesting that the growth rate of the economy as a whole will depend on the growth of productivity in the service sector. Future developments in information technology will be a key element in further raising productivity in a broad range of service sector activities. The process of deindustrialization is clearly making productivity in the service industry a major determinant of the prospects for future economic growth and increases in welfare in the UK. In this context the modest comparative performance of the UK in service sector productivity, noted in Tables 1.8 and 1.11 above, may be seen as of particular concern and a focus for remedial policy action.

Balance of payments

An alternative definition of deindustrialization is offered by Singh, based on the traditional role of manufacturing in UK trade flows. Historically the UK was a net exporter of manufactures, so that surplus foreign exchange was earned which enabled the country to run a deficit on its trade in food and raw materials. Singh (1977) defines an 'efficient' manufacturing sector as one which 'not only satisfies the demands of consumers at home but is also able to sell enough of its products abroad to pay for the nation's import requirements'. Singh also states that this is subject to the restriction that 'an efficient manufacturing sector must be able to achieve these objectives at socially acceptable levels of output, employment and exchange rate'. A country such as the UK would then be 'deindustrialized' if its manufacturing sector did not meet these criteria, leaving an economic structure inappropriate to the needs of the country. It can be argued that this is indeed the position in the UK. The current account can only be kept in balance by surpluses in the oil and service sectors and by earnings from overseas assets. Any reflation of aggregate demand stimulates an even faster growth in imports of manufactured goods which pushes the current account towards deficit. By the end of the 1980s boom the UK again had a worryingly large current account deficit (see Chapter 27). The decline of UK manufacturing has recreated the balance of payments constraint on macroeconomic policy which many had hoped North Sea oil would remove. This, allied to the fact that UK output and employment are hardly at *socially acceptable* levels, suggests that the UK could be regarded as 'deindustrialized' on Singh's definition.

It might be argued that the service sector can take over the traditional role of manufacturing in the balance of payments accounts. A difficulty here is that unlike manufactures many services cannot, by their nature, be traded internationally (e.g. public sector services), with the result that trade in manufactures is on a vastly bigger scale than trade in services (see Chapter 27). The House of Commons Trade and Industry Committee (1994) pointed out that a 2.5% rise in service exports is required merely to offset a 1% fall in manufacturing exports. In some services which can be traded, the UK is already highly successful (e.g. financial services), and if even bigger surpluses are to be earned then the UK would have to move towards a monopoly position in those services.

In fact, international competition is increasing in traded services and the UK may find it difficult to hold its current share of the market.

Other economists have pointed out that Singh's definition would leave most of the non-oil-producing industrial countries categorized as 'deindustrialized' because, despite growing industrial output, their macroeconomic policies were constrained by their balance of payments positions after the 1973 and 1979 oil price rises. This observation does not invalidate the conclusion that deindustrialization in the UK has had serious balance of payments consequences.

Inflation

If deindustrialization in the UK is so advanced that the economy is not capable of producing goods to match the pattern of market demand, then there may be implications not only for imports but also for prices. Any increase in overall demand will meet a shortage of domestic suppliers in many industrial sectors. This will both encourage import substitution and provide opportunities for domestic suppliers to raise prices. As a result, despite continuing high unemployment, there may be little effective spare capacity in the UK in sectors where deindustrialization has been excessive. Supply-side constraints created by structural change may then have increased the likelihood of the UK experiencing demand-led inflation in the event of a sustained increase in aggregate demand, such as that of the late 1980s. In response to such constraints government policy has moved towards strengthening the supply side, as with the Conservative government's labour market reforms and Labour government measures such as the New Deal.

Industrial relations

Deindustrialization is having important implications for the nature of industrial relations. Trade unions originally gained their strength from the industrial sector, in which it was easier to organize and to engage in centralized bargaining because of the broadly similar work undertaken by large groups of workers. Although centralized bargaining has helped to narrow the wage differentials within manufacturing (see Chapter 15), as the UK economy continues to shift towards services this form of bargaining will become more difficult to achieve as the nature of work in the service sector varies considerably across different activities. For example, the levels of skill and security of employment vary significantly between financial services and retailing. The wage differentials will be needed to compensate for these skill differences, and centralized union bargaining designed to narrow wage differentials will clearly be perceived by employers as having adverse effects on the growth of service sector productivity. The roles of trade unions will clearly have to adapt, with the diversity of the service sector making the retention of union membership more difficult and weakening the traditional systems of wage bargaining.

Conclusion

There have been profound structural changes in the UK economy since 1964, resulting in relative stagnation of industrial output and declining industrial employment, and these have transformed the sectoral balance of the economy. The causes of these changes are not agreed. We reviewed various suggestions, such as economic 'maturity', low-wage competition, the advent of North Sea oil, 'crowding out', and low productivity. Our view has been that low productivity, resulting in a substantial loss of competitiveness, has been central to the structural changes observed. Certainly no other major industrial country has experienced the fall in volume of non-oil industrial output recorded in the UK after 1973. The consequences of industrial decline are widespread, contributing to unemployment and balance of payments problems, increasing inflationary pressures and hampering growth. Judged by the growth of output and productivity there was an improvement in the performance of the UK economy during the 1980s. The UK has reduced the productivity gap with other OECD countries and has increased industrial output at a rate close to the OECD average. Nevertheless, UK manufacturing output in 2002 was only 12.6% more in volume terms than it had been in 1973.

Key points

- Whereas the secondary sector contributed some 41% of GDP in 1964, by 2001 this had fallen to 25%.

- Manufacturing (within the secondary sector) saw its share of GDP fall from around 30% in 1964 to just under 18% by 2001.

- Nearly 6 million jobs have been lost from the secondary sector since 1964, around 5 million having been lost from manufacturing.

- The service (tertiary) sector has provided almost 9 million extra jobs since 1964, and has managed to match the loss of manufacturing employment.

- Not all advanced industrialized countries have seen a decline in industrial employment.

- Suggested causes of 'deindustrialization' have included maturity of the economy, low-wage competition, North Sea oil, 'crowding out' and low productivity.

- UK productivity *growth rates* in manufacturing and in the whole economy fell behind those of its main competitors during the 1960s and 1970s but kept pace in the 1980s and early 1990s before falling behind again since the mid-1990s. However, the *absolute levels* of UK productivity and capital intensity remain well below those of its competitors.

- UK productivity per employed worker in manufacturing has grown by some 4.5% per annum since 1979. Unfortunately total UK output has grown at a much slower rate, resulting in fewer workers being employed.

- True competitiveness depends not only upon relative productivity but also upon relative labour costs and the sterling effective exchange rate. This is best measured by relative unit labour costs (RULC).

- The UK is still, on average, some 40% less competitive overall (in terms of RULC) in 2002 than it was in 1976.

Now try the self-check questions for this chapter on the Companion Website. You will also find up-to-date facts and case materials.

Notes

1. The GDP is the total value of output produced by factors of production located in a given country.

2. Income elasticity of demand is given by:

$$\frac{\text{\% change in quantity demanded}}{\text{\% change in income}}$$

3. 'Factor cost' means that 'market price' valuations of output have been adjusted to take account of the distortions caused by taxes and subsidies. Taxes raise market prices above the true cost of factor input and so are subtracted. Subsidies reduce market prices below factor cost and so are added. 'Constant factor cost' means that the valuations have been made in the prices of a given base year. This eliminates the effects of inflation, so that the time series shows 'real' output.

4. Buying the foreign currency to pay for the extra imports would increase the supply of sterling on the foreign exchange market, reducing the price of sterling.

References and further reading

Bacon, R. and Eltis, W. (1976) *Britain's Economic Problem – Too Few Producers*, Macmillan.

Baumol, W. J., Blackman, S. and Wolff, E. N. (1989) *Productivity and American Leadership: The Long View*, MIT Press.

Bosworth, D., Davies, R. and Wilson, R. (2002) Management qualifications and organisational performance: An analysis of the Employers Skill Survey 1999, *Labour Market Trends*, August.

Cameron, G. and Proudman, J. (1998) Growth in UK manufacturing between 1970–92, *Bank of England Quarterly Bulletin*, May.

Carr, C. (1992) Productivity and skills in vehicle component manufacturers in Britain, Germany, the USA and Japan, *National Institute Economic Review*, February.

Crafts, N. and O'Mahoney, M. (2001) A perspective on UK productivity performance, *Fiscal Studies*, 22(3).

Davies, S. and Caves, R. E. (1987) *Britain's Productivity Gap*, CUP, Cambridge.

Dougherty, C. and Jorgenson, D. W. (1997) There is no silver bullet: investment and growth in the G7, *National Institute Economic Review*, 4.

Eltis, W. and Higham, D. (1995) Closing the UK competitiveness gap, *National Institute Economic Review*, November.

Feinstein, C. and Mathews, R. (1990) The growth of output and productivity in the UK, *National Institute Economic Review*, August.

Grant, S. (1994) Challenges to UK competitiveness, *British Economy Survey*, Spring.

Greenhalgh, C. (1994) Why manufacturing still matters, *Economic Review*, September.

Hadjimatheou, G. and Sarantis, N. (1998) Is UK deindustrialisation inevitable?, in Buxton, T., Chapman, P. and Temple, P., *Britain's Economic Performance* (2nd edn), Routledge.

HMSO (1996) *Competitiveness – Forging Ahead*, Cm 2867.

House of Commons Trade and Industry Committee (1994) *Competitiveness of UK Manufacturing Industry*, Second Report and Vol. II Memoranda of Evidence, HMSO, April.

Kaletsky, A. (1998) Where Britain can learn to improve productivity, *Times*, 3 November.

Kitson, W. and Mitchie, J. (1996) Britain's industrial performance since 1960, *Economic Journal*, January.

Mason, G. and Finegold, D. (1997) Productivity, machinery and skills in the United States and Western Europe, *National Institute Economic Review*, 4.

McKinsey Co. (2002) *Reviving UK manufacturing*, October.

McKinsey Report (1998) *Driving Productivity and Growth in the UK Economy*, McKinsey Global Institute.

O'Mahoney, M. (2002) Productivity and convergence in the EU, *National Institute Economic Review*, 180, April.

O'Mahoney, M. and de Boer, W. (2002a) Britain's relative productivity performance: Updates to 1999. Final Report to DTI/Treasury/ONS, *National Institute of Economic and Social Research*, March.

O'Mahoney, M. and de Boer, W. (2002b) Britain's relative productivity performance: Has anything changed?, *National Institute Economic Review*, 179, January.

O'Mahoney, M. (1998) Britain's relative productivity performance 1950–1996: estimates by sector, *National Institute of Economic and Social Research*, September.

Oulton, N. (1994) Labour productivity and unit labour costs in manufacturing: the UK and its competitors, *National Institute Economic Review*, May.

Oulton, N. (1997) Total factor productivity growth and the role of externalities, *National Institute Economic Review*, 4.

Proudfoot Consulting (2002) *Untapped potential: the barriers to optimum corporate productivity*, October.

Rowthorn, R. E. and Wells, J. R. (1987) *Deindustrialization and Foreign Trade*, CUP, Cambridge.

Singh, A. (1977) UK industry and the world economy: a case of deindustrialization? *Cambridge Journal of Economics*, 1(2), June.

Steedman, H., Mason, G. and Wagner, K. (1991) Intermediate skills in the workplace, *National Institute Economic Review*, May.

Part I # Theory of the firm

Chapter 2   Company accounts as a source of financial information

Companies in the UK are required by Act of Parliament to publish financial information on an annual basis.

This chapter examines the content and presentation of annual reports, and identifies a number of useful accounting ratios which can be calculated. The 2002 accounts of Tesco p.l.c. have been used for illustration. Tesco is one of Britain's leading food retailers, with 979 stores throughout the United Kingdom. It also operates stores in the Republic of Ireland, France, Central Europe and Asia. The chapter concludes with a detailed analysis of the Financial Times Share Information Service, and the indices and ratios it contains.

Company accounts and the assessment of company performance

The separation of control and ownership in the majority of public companies[1] creates an atmosphere in which management might wish to present to shareholders as favourable a picture as possible of the company's activities. Fear of the effects of competition and of adverse investor reaction may also mean that companies seek to give away as little as possible – usually by disclosing the legal minimum of information. Most p.l.c.'s, however, regard the presentation of their annual report as a matter of corporate pride, and pay great attention to the quality and relevance of the documents.

Published financial statements should provide sufficient information to enable shareholders and potential shareholders to make economic decisions about whether to buy, hold or sell shares in a company.

An examination of the typical elements that make up a company report reveals a mixture of statutory items, requirements of the accounting profession, additional Stock Exchange requirements and voluntary disclosures. The most important items within annual reports are the following:

(a) Operating and financial review
(b) Directors' report
(c) Balance sheet
(d) Profit and loss account
(e) Statement of total recognized gains and losses
(f) Note of historical cost profits and losses
(g) Notes to the accounts (including statement of accounting policies)
(h) Cashflow statement
(i) Auditors' report
(j) Historical summary.

Each of these is summarized below.

Operating and financial review (OFR)

At present, there is no statutory requirement for an OFR, but the Accounting Standards Board (see below) recommends its inclusion in the annual reports of large companies. Areas covered by the OFR include:

- commentary on the operating results;
- review of the group's financial needs and resources;
- commentary on shareholder returns and risks.

Tesco's OFR stated that:

> Total shareholder return, which is measured as the percentage change in the share price plus the dividend, has been 20.2% over the last five years, compared to the FTSE average of 6.2%. Over the last three years it has been 15.0%, compared to the FTSE average of –2.7%. In the last year, total shareholder return in Tesco was –2.7%, compared to the FTSE average of –14.3%.

In addition, there may be a Chairman's report, which is a reflective, personal appraisal of company performance.

Directors' report

This includes a statement of the principal activities of the company and of any significant changes that have taken place in the holding of fixed assets (e.g. property sales or the acquisition of subsidiaries). Details of the directors and their shareholdings in the company are also mentioned, as any significant change in their holdings may reflect their view of the company's future prospects.

Balance sheet

This shows the position of the company at its financial year end, usually 31 December, but for a retailer like Tesco, the relatively 'quiet' date of the last Saturday in February 2002 (23rd) was used. It details the assets of the business and balances them against its liabilities; in other words, what the company *owns* (assets) is exactly matched by what it *owes* (liabilities) in terms of funds required to finance those assets.

Assets are divided between *fixed* and *current*. Fixed assets are those expected to be retained by the business for at least a year from the balance sheet date and are of significant value, e.g. land, machinery and vehicles. Current assets constantly change value during the course of a business's activities, e.g. stock, debtors and bank balances.

Some fixed assets might be *intangible* (i.e. not 'physical') such as the price paid for the reputation (goodwill) of a business which has been taken over. Most fixed assets are *depreciated*, which ensures that a reasonable amount is included in the company's total expenses to recognize any loss in value due to wear and tear, obsolescence, etc.

Accounting ratios

The construction of several simple ratios from the information contained within the balance sheet can give a clear assessment of the company's performance by making the following comparisons:

■ with its *own* performance in previous time periods,

■ with that of *other companies* in the same sector, and/or

■ with *accepted standards* of performance, i.e. with particular values ('norms') for each ratio.

Figure 2.1 shows the 2002 balance sheet for Tesco p.l.c. Several accounting ratios have been calculated

Group Balance Sheet

23 February 2002

	2002 £m	2001 £m
Fixed assets		
Intangible assets	154	154
Tangible assets	11,032	9,580
Investments	317	304
	11,503	10,038
Current assets		
Stocks	929	838
Debtors	454	322
Investments	225	255
Cash at bank and in hand	445	279
	2,053	1,694
Creditors: falling due within one year [1]	(4,809)	(4,389)
Net current liabilities	(2,756)	(2,695)
Total assets less current liabilities	8,747	7,343
Creditors: falling due after more than one year [2]	(2,741)	(1,927)
Provisions for liabilities and charges	(440)	(402)
Total net assets	5,566	5,014
Capital and reserves		
Called up share capital	350	347
Share premium account	2,004	1,870
Other reserves	40	40
Profit and loss account	3,136	2,721
Equity shareholders' funds	5,530	4,978
Minority interests	36	36
Total capital employed	5,566	5,014

1. Includes £1,474m bank loans and overdrafts (2001: £1,389m) and trade creditors £1,830m (2001: £1,538m).
2. Assume that this is all loan stock.

Fig. 2.1 Balance sheet.
Source: Adapted from Tesco p.l.c., 2002.

by extracting the 2002 figures from the table and comparing them with the corresponding (net of VAT) annual sales turnover (£25,654m for Group sales to outside customers – see the profit and loss account of Fig. 2.2). For comparative purposes the same ratios have been calculated for Kingfisher p.l.c., also in the

Group Profit and Loss Account

52 weeks ended 23 February 2002

	2002 £m	2001 £m
Sales at net selling prices	25,654	22,773
Turnover including share of joint ventures	23,804	21,096
Less: share of joint ventures' turnover	(151)	(108)
Group turnover excluding value added tax	23,653	20,988
Operating expenses		
– Normal operating expenses	(22,273)	(19,770)
– Employee profit sharing	(48)	(44)
– Goodwill amortization	(10)	(8)
Operating profit	1,322	1,166
Share of operating profit of joint ventures and associates	42	21
Net loss on disposal of fixed assets	(10)	(8)
Profit on ordinary activities before interest and taxation	1,354	1,179
Net interest payable	(153)	(125)
Profit on ordinary activities before taxation	1,201	1,054
Profit before net loss on disposal of fixed assets and goodwill amortization	1,221	1,070
Net loss on disposal of fixed assets	(10)	(8)
Goodwill amortization	(10)	(8)
Tax on profit on ordinary activities	(371)	(333)
Profit on ordinary activities after taxation	830	721
Minority interests	–	1
Profit for the financial year	830	722
Dividends	(390)	(340)
Retained profit for the financial year	440	382
	Pence	Pence
Earnings per share	12.05	10.63
Adjustment for net loss on disposal of fixed assets after taxation	0.14	0.12
Adjusted for goodwill amortization	0.14	0.12
Adjusted earnings per share	12.33	10.87
Diluted earnings per share	11.86	10.42
Adjusted for net loss on disposal of fixed assets after taxation	0.14	0.12
Adjusted for goodwill amortization	0.14	0.12
Adjusted diluted earnings per share	12.14	10.66
Dividend per share	5.60	4.98
Dividend cover (times)	2.17	2.14

Fig. 2.2 Profit and loss account.
Source: Tesco p.l.c., 2002.

retailing sector (Woolworths, Superdrug, Comet, etc.), and, as a contrast, for RMC Group p.l.c. in the manufacturing (building materials) sector.

Gearing ratio

This reflects the financial risk to which the company is subject, by measuring the capital structure of the company and the degree to which it relies on external borrowings. Gearing can be calculated in various ways, including:

$$\text{Gearing ratio} = \frac{\text{external borrowing}}{\text{total capital employed}}$$

$$= \frac{\text{loan capital} + \text{bank overdraft}}{\text{loan capital} + \text{bank overdraft} + \text{ordinary shares and reserves}}$$

The total capital employed is made up of external borrowings (debentures,[2] other loans and bank borrowing) and internally generated funds (ordinary shares and reserves). The *cost* of external borrowing is loan interest payments, whilst that for internal funds is the dividend that must be paid to shareholders.

The gearing ratio shows the proportion of total capital that is provided externally and gives an indication of the burden of interest payments to which the company is committed irrespective of its profitability. A gearing ratio of about 33.3% is usually regarded as acceptable for a company, suggesting that it is not over-reliant on external borrowing. A figure in excess of this indicates a relatively highly geared company. High gearing ratios are most suitable to those companies with steady and reliable profits, whose earnings are sufficient to cover interest payments and where total dividends are low. Wide fluctuations in profitability make the highly geared company extremely vulnerable to a downturn in market conditions – profits may be so low that interest payments cannot be covered, leading to receivership. The 2002 accounts reveal a gearing ratio of 43.1% for Tesco, $(1,474 + 2,741)/(1,474 + 2,741 + 5,566)$, a value higher than the 15% of RMC and Kingfisher's 33%. Tesco had £670m investments and cash at bank and in hand at the balance sheet date, which, when offset against loans and overdrafts, effectively reduces its gearing level to 36.2%.

A drawback of the ratio is that it is concerned only with borrowings on which interest charges are incurred. It ignores completely liabilities which constitute interest-free loans. One such major item is that of 'trade creditors' – money which is owed by the company to its suppliers. The ratio tends to understate the dependence of companies on external borrowings, so it is useful to extend the 'loan' item to 'all liabilities'. The numerator would then become 'short- and long-term liabilities' and produce a ratio which is a more realistic basis for comparison when linked with 'shareholders' funds'. The ratios for the three companies are: Tesco 77%; RMC 110%; Kingfisher 86%.

Operating ratios

These can be used to gauge the efficiency with which various aspects of the company's trading are managed.

Stock turnover ratio

The holding of stock, in the form of unsold finished and partly finished goods, is an expensive activity for companies, so that considerable attention is paid to the stock turnover ratio:

$$\text{Stock turnover ratio} = \frac{\text{average stocks}}{\text{sales turnover}}$$

This ratio reflects the level of stockholding used to support sales (see Fig. 2.2). We would expect companies to carry the minimum level of stock (inventories) consistent with the efficient running of the business. The figure will vary widely according to the industrial sector involved. Tesco's ratio is only 3.74%, $((838 + 929)/2)/23,653$, a figure which reflects the extremely fast throughput of their stock, on average being sold every 14 days. Kingfisher's ratio was 16.3% (60 days) whilst RMC had a ratio of 6.5% (24 days).

Debtors' turnover ratio

This ratio can be used to monitor a company's credit control procedures, by comparing the amount it is owed by consumers, to whom credit facilities have been extended, with its total sales.

$$\text{Debtors' turnover ratio} = \frac{\text{debtors}}{\text{sales turnover}}$$

$$= \frac{\text{average amount owed to the group by customers}}{\text{sales turnover}}$$

Businesses like retail supermarkets are run almost exclusively on a cash-and-carry basis so have virtually zero debtors. However, the tendency for retail supermarkets to introduce their own charge card for credit trading (e.g. Marks and Spencer, 1985, Tesco, 1996) increases the debtors' figure. Even so, it may generate sufficient additional sales actually to reduce the debtors' turnover ratio. For other businesses an average credit period might be nine weeks, equivalent to a debtors' turnover figure of around 17%. Retailers Tesco and Kingfisher showed figures of 1.64% (i.e. ((322 + 454)/2)/23,653) (6 days' sales) and 8.71% (32 days' sales) respectively, though RMC's ratio was 16% (57 days).

Creditors' turnover ratio

This ratio indicates the size and period of credit a company receives from its suppliers, by comparing its sales with the total amount the company owes to its creditors.

$$\text{Creditors' turnover ratio} = \frac{\text{creditors}}{\text{sales turnover}}$$

$$= \frac{\begin{array}{c}\text{average amount owed by}\\ \text{the group to its suppliers}\end{array}}{\text{sales turnover}}$$

It may (after evaluating the possibility of prepayment discounts) be very much in the company's interests to exploit its suppliers by extending the credit period. However, Tesco shows a figure of 7.12% (i.e. ((1,538 + 1,830)/2)/23,653) (26 days), reflecting its close links with its suppliers. Kingfisher (10% or 36 days) and RMC (9.6% or 35 days) show these companies taking an extra 10 days to pay creditors.

It is important to avoid confusion between the term 'creditors' when meaning 'trade creditors' (i.e. money owed to suppliers) as against meaning 'total creditors' (i.e. liabilities of all varieties). All further references in this chapter will equate 'creditors' with 'trade creditors'.

Liquidity ratios

These give an indication of the company's short-term financial position, in other words, the availability of cash or marketable assets with which to meet current liabilities.

Current ratio

The current ratio measures the extent to which currently available assets cover current liabilities, i.e. those requiring repayment within one year.

$$\text{Current ratio} = \frac{\text{current assets}}{\text{current liabilities}}$$

$$= \frac{\text{stocks} + \text{debtors} + \text{cash}}{\text{overdraft} + \text{creditors} + \text{taxation} + \text{dividends}}$$

A figure of 1.5 may be taken as prudent, showing that current liabilities are more than covered by current assets. A ratio of more than 1.5 is not necessarily a sign of strength, since it may mean excessive stocks or debtors, or an uneconomic use of liquid funds.

Food retailers are unusual in that their rapid turnovers, together with the cash-and-carry nature of their business, will give relatively low 'stock' and 'debtor' items respectively. In this way 'current assets' will be small, and so a very low current ratio is to be expected. Tesco's 2002 figure of 0.43 (2,053/4,809) must be viewed in this context. By comparison, RMC's 1.1 reflects the high level of stocks which manufacturers carry. Kingfisher's ratio of 0.98 is typical of a predominantly 'non-food' retailer.

Quick assets ratio (acid test)

This ratio provides a better indication of short-term liquidity by ignoring stockholdings and concentrating on those assets which are more easily convertible into cash.

$$\text{Quick assets ratio} = \frac{\text{current assets} - \text{stocks}}{\text{current liabilities}}$$

A yardstick of 1.0 is usually sought, indicating that sufficient liquid assets are available to cover current liabilities. RMC is just below the manufacturing sector average with a ratio of 0.8.

Traders with a rapid turnover of cash sales will have a lower level of current assets, and often a very low ratio. This is the case with Tesco's quick assets ratio of only 0.23 ((2,053 – 929)/4,809) for 2002. Kingfisher's ratio is 0.49.

The current and quick assets ratios are probably the best-known and most widely used financial ratios. It is no surprise that some companies might resort to 'window-dressing' of the accounts in order to create an impression that these ratios are a little better than they actually are, particularly by delaying fixed asset purchases until after the balance sheet date.

The calculation of the above six ratios from balance sheet information, i.e. (a) *gearing* ratio, (b) *operating* ratios (stock turnover, debtors' turnover, creditors' turnover) and (c) *liquidity* ratios (current, quick assets), permit an assessment of a company's performance with regard to accepted standards across a given sector. This assessment is further improved by considering the information provided by the profit and loss account (see Fig. 2.2).

Profit and loss account

This is a summary of transactions for a stated period, usually a year, and sets revenues against costs in order to show the company's profit or loss. The statement discloses summarized figures for the expenses of the business (e.g. the cost of goods sold), but makes no evaluation of the risks incurred in order to earn the given profit levels. Neither is there any indication of the degree to which the given profit level conforms with the company's objectives.

Figure 2.2 shows the profit and loss account of Tesco for 2002 and indicates the various deductions that take place from sales revenue to derive profit or loss. Part of the profit is distributed to shareholders in the form of dividends, with the balance being retained by the company to boost reserves. Dividends may still be paid to shareholders even when losses have been incurred, if profits from previous years are available.

The profit figure remains the single most important figure in the company accounts and various profitability measures can be employed to assess relative performance.

Profit margin

$$\text{Profit margin} = \frac{\text{profit before interest and tax}}{\text{sales turnover}}$$

The profit margin is a ratio of profit, after the deduction of trading expenses but before the payment of interest on borrowings (financing charges) and corporation tax, to sales turnover. A figure of 6–8% would be typical for manufacturing industry. Activities such as food retailing, with high volumes and competitive prices, might expect a ratio around 4%, which might still yield high absolute levels of profit. In fact, Tesco exhibits an encouraging result with a ratio of 5.7% (1,354/23,653) for its profit margin. Kingfisher earned only 0.8% in a difficult year, whilst RMC produced 6.1%.

Return on assets

$$\text{Return on assets} = \frac{\text{profit before interest and tax}}{\text{total assets}}$$

Measurement of the rate of return on total assets offers a popular alternative assessment of profitability, despite the fact that it compares a 'dynamic' item (profits) with a 'static' item (total assets). On this basis the Tesco figure is 10% (1,354)/(11,503 + 2,053), whereas RMC yields 5.6%, and Kingfisher only 1.3%.

Calculations of the return on assets will clearly vary, sometimes substantially, with the basis used for measurement. This is a strong argument for using a standard approach and accountants are expected, under their *Financial Reporting Standard (FRS) 15*, to reassess the value of assets at regular intervals to avoid outdated valuations being used.

A consideration of these profitability ratios, together with earlier information on gearing, operating and liquidity ratios, can give an overall impression of Tesco's financial position in 2002. The company has maintained a relatively high profit margin and return on assets, whilst having a low gearing ratio. Its working capital situation would cause alarm in a different type of business, but the very fast throughput of stock ensures that the cashflow is more than adequate to meet liabilities as they fall due.

Statement of total recognized gains and losses

This is a primary financial statement (i.e. of equal standing to the profit and loss account, balance sheet and cashflow statement), which was introduced by *Financial Reporting Standard (FRS) 3* in 1992. It enables users of accounts to consider *all* gains and losses (not just 'trading' profits) in assessing the company's overall performance. Figure 2.3 shows Tesco p.l.c.'s statement which, for 2002, showed that the company, whilst making an after-tax profit of £830m (as shown in the profit and loss account), gained £12m on foreign exchange adjustments, bringing the total 'recognized' gains up to £842m, before an adjustment of £45m caused by a change in an accounting standard implemented in the previous year. The statement was introduced to prevent companies from misleading shareholders by 'hiding' non-trading losses (e.g. on revaluation of properties and foreign currency transactions) in *notes* to the accounts, rather than giving them the prominence they warranted. The classification of the statement of

Statement of Total Recognized Gains and Losses

52 weeks ended 23 February 2002

	2002 £m	2001 £m
Profit for the financial year	830	722
Gain/(loss) on foreign currency net investments	12	(2)
Total recognized gains and losses relating to the financial year	842	720
Prior year adjustment	(45)	
Total recognized gains and losses since last annual report and financial statements	797	

Fig. 2.3 Statement of total recognized gains and losses.
Source: Adapted from Tesco p.l.c., 2002.

total recognized gains and losses as a *primary* statement ensured that such vital information can no longer be concealed.

Note of historical cost profits and losses

This is a memorandum statement, also introduced by FRS 3, designed to present the profits or losses of companies which have *revalued* their assets on a more comparable basis with those that have not. Neither Tesco nor RMC revalued their assets, but Fig. 2.4 is the statement of Kingfisher p.l.c. showing that if assets had not been revalued, reported profits would have been £198.6m higher in the year.

Notes to the accounts (including statement of accounting policies)

There is far more information contained in notes to the accounts than within the balance sheet and profit and loss account. The regulatory framework of accounting has broadened since the early 1970s to include not only the Companies Acts but also *Statements of Standard Accounting Practice and Financial Reporting Standards*, which are issued by the accountancy profession to standardize procedures and suggest 'best practice'.

The notes always commence with a statement of the accounting policies adopted by the company (an extract is shown in Fig. 2.5), and there follow many pages of detailed information needed to comply either

Note of Historical Cost Profits and Losses

year ended 2 February 2002

	2002 £m	2001 £m
Profit on ordinary activities before tax	28.0	691.2
Prior year property revaluation surplus now realized	196.9	14.2
Difference between historical cost depreciation charge and the actual depreciation charge calculated on the revalued amount	1.7	1.9
Historical cost profit on ordinary activities before tax	226.6	707.3
Historical cost profit (loss) for the year retained after tax, minority interests and dividends	(657.7)	211.4

Fig. 2.4 Note of historical cost profits and losses.
Source: Adapted from Kingfisher p.l.c., 2002.

TESCO PLC

Accounting Policies

BASIS OF PREPARATION OF FINANCIAL STATEMENTS

These financial statements have been prepared under the historical cost convention, in accordance with applicable accounting standards and the Companies Act 1985.

In November and December 2000, the Accounting Standards Board issued FRS 17, 'Retirement Benefits' and FRS 19, 'Deferred Tax' respectively.

FRS 17 will be adopted by the Group over the next two years. The FRS has an extended transitional period during which certain disclosures will be required in the notes to the financial statements. The Group is required to make these phased disclosures in the current year, which are shown in note 27(b).

FRS 19 has been adopted with effect from 25 February 2001. This standard addresses the recognition, on a full provision basis, of deferred tax assets and liabilities arising from timing differences between the recognition of gains and losses in the financial statements and their recognition in a tax computation. Prior to 25 February 2001, the Group's accounting policy was to provide for the deferred tax which was likely to be payable or recoverable.

BASIS OF CONSOLIDATION

The Group financial statements consist of the financial statements of the parent company, its subsidiary under-takings and the Group's share of interests in joint ventures and associates. The accounts of the parent company's subsidiary undertakings are prepared to dates around 23 February 2002 apart from Global T.H., Tesco Polska Sp. z o.o., Tesco Stores ČR a.s., Tesco Stores SR a.s., Samsung Tesco Co. Limited, Tesco Taiwan Co. Limited and Ek-Chai Distribution System Co. Ltd which prepared accounts to 31 December 2001. In the opinion of the Directors it is necessary for the above named subsidiaries to prepare accounts to a date earlier than the rest of the Group to enable the timely publication of the Group financial statements.

The Group's interests in joint ventures are accounted for using the gross equity method. The Group's interests in associates are accounted for using the equity method.

TURNOVER

Turnover consists of sales through retail outlets and sales of development properties excluding value added tax.

STOCKS

Stocks comprise goods held for resale and properties held for, or in the course of, development and are valued at the lower of cost and net realisable value. Stocks in stores are calculated at retail prices and reduced by appropriate margins to the lower of cost and net realisable value.

MONEY MARKET DEPOSITS

Money market deposits are stated at cost. All income from these investments is included in the profit and loss account as interest receivable and similar income.

FIXED ASSETS AND DEPRECIATION

Fixed assets are carried at cost and include amounts in respect of interest paid on funds specifically related to the financing of assets in the course of construction.

Depreciation is provided on a straight-line basis over the anticipated useful economic lives of the assets.

The following rates applied for the year ended 23 February 2002:

- Land premia paid in excess of the alternative use value – at 2.5% of cost.
- Freehold and leasehold buildings with greater than 40 years unexpired – at 2.5% of cost.
- Leasehold properties with less than 40 years unexpired are amortised by equal annual instalments over the unexpired period of the lease.
- Plant, equipment, fixtures and fittings and motor vehicles – at rates varying from 10% to 33%.

GOODWILL

Goodwill arising from transactions entered into after 1 March 1998 is capitalised and amortised on a straight-line basis over its useful economic life, up to a maximum of 20 years.

All goodwill arising from transactions entered into prior to 1 March 1998 has been written off to reserves.

Fig. 2.5 (Extract from) accounting policies.
Source: Adapted from Tesco p.l.c., 2002.

Group Cashflow Statement

52 weeks ended 23 February 2002

	2002 £m	2001 £m
Net cash inflow from operating activities	2,038	1,937
Dividends from joint ventures and associates		
Income received from joint ventures and associates	15	–
Returns on investments and servicing of finance		
Interest received	44	49
Interest paid	(232)	(206)
Interest element of finance lease rental payments	(4)	(4)
Net cash outflow from returns on investments and servicing of finance	(192)	(161)
Taxation		
Corporation tax paid	(378)	(272)
Capital expenditure and financial investment		
Payments to acquire tangible fixed assets	(1,877)	(1,953)
Receipts from sale of tangible fixed assets	42	43
Purchase of own shares	(85)	(58)
Net cash outflow for capital expenditure and financial investment	(1,920)	(1,968)
Acquisitions and disposals		
Purchase of subsidiary undertakings	(31)	(41)
Invested in joint ventures	(46)	(35)
Invested in associates and other investments	(19)	–
Net cash outflow from acquisitions and disposals	(96)	(76)
Equity dividends paid	(297)	(254)
Cash outflow before use of liquid resources and financing	(830)	(794)
Management of liquid resources		
Decrease in short-term deposits	27	–
Financing		
Ordinary shares issued for cash	82	88
Increase in other loans	916	928
New finance leases	–	13
Capital element of finance leases repaid	(24)	(46)
Net cash inflow from financing	974	983
Increase in cash	171	189

Fig. 2.6 Cashflow statement.
Source: Adapted from Tesco p.l.c., 2002.

with the Acts or with the relevant accounting standards required by the profession. It is unusual for companies to give more than the minimum requirements, but the auditors' report (see Fig. 2.7 below) will confirm whether or not such requirements have been met.

Cashflow statement

The usual accounting convention followed when preparing a profit and loss account is that *all* relevant income and expenditure must be included, whether or not it resulted in a cash inflow or outflow in that period. Hence turnover will include sales invoiced but not yet paid for (debtors) and cost of sales and overheads include goods and services received from suppliers which are owing at the end of the financial year (creditors). Some expenses, notably *depreciation*, do not result in a cashflow. A company might have major cashflows which are not reflected in the profit and loss account – for example, loans might be issued or repaid in the period, share capital might be issued and fixed assets bought or sold. Profitability alone is not sufficient to ensure the survival of a company – its cash resources must be adequate to ensure that it can meet its liabilities when they fall due. Aggressive expanding companies such as Tesco often show a cash inflow considerably less than their profit, as fixed asset acquisitions soak up the net cash generated from trading.

Figure 2.6 shows Tesco's cashflow statement for 2002. It shows an overall increase in cash of £171m, considerably less than the retained profit for the same period of £440m as shown in its profit and loss account. Trading activities generated over £2bn of cash, but interest payments (£232m), taxation (£378m), purchase of fixed assets (£1,877m) and the payment of dividends (£297m) reduced the overall cashflow significantly.

Auditors' report

The auditors are required to report to shareholders ('the members') on whether the company accounts have been properly prepared, in accordance with the Companies Act and accounting standards, and whether they give a true and fair view of the activities of the company. Figure 2.7 provides a typical example. The auditors may qualify their approval of the accounts if they feel that the records have not been well kept or if all the information they require is not available. Such qualifications usually fall into two categories: (1) those relating to accounting policy, and (2) those relating to unsatisfactory levels of information.

Historical summary

Companies subject to the requirements of the Stock Exchange Listing Agreement usually provide some

sort of historical summary, usually over a five- or ten-year period, but with no uniform approach to content (Fig. 2.8). It gives a simple overall picture of the company's progress, along with difficulties encountered, such as problems of coping with inflation over the period or with changing accounting standards.

International accounting standards

In addition to the accounting standards produced by the UK profession, many other countries have their own 'national' standards. In 1973, an organization called the International Accounting Standards Committee (IASC) was established with the object of harmonizing standards on a worldwide basis and of encouraging compliance between national standards and those agreed by the IASC. In 2001, the IASC was reorganized and from 1 April in that year, a new body, the International Accounting Standards Board (IASB), assumed accounting standard setting responsibilities. There is a growing move towards the adoption of international standards to avoid a repetition of major accounting scandals such as those seen in the US in 2001 and 2002, including the collapse of Enron and Worldcom. In Europe, all companies listed on stock markets will be required from January 2005 to follow international accounting standards when producing their annual reports.

External sources of financial information

Of the various elements in the company accounts, the operating and financial review is probably the most widely read. None of the other elements, despite the importance of the information contained, receives more than the passing attention of the average, non-specialist, reader. Users of financial information still often prefer to use secondary sources of information, including those provided by the financial press and other external agencies. Two specific features are considered in detail on page 42: the FTSE All-Share Index, and data on individual share price movements.

Auditors' Report

To the Members of Tesco p.l.c.

We have audited the financial statements which comprise the profit and loss account, the balance sheets, the cash-flow statement, the statement of total recognised gains and losses and the related notes, including the information on Directors' emoluments and share details included within tables one to five, in the report of the Directors on remuneration, which have been prepared under the historical cost convention and the accounting policies set out in the statement of accounting policies.

RESPECTIVE RESPONSIBILITIES OF DIRECTORS AND AUDITORS

The Directors' responsibilities for preparing the annual report and financial statements, in accordance with applicable United Kingdom law and accounting standards, are set out in the statement of Directors' responsibilities.

Our responsibility is to audit the financial statements in accordance with relevant legal and regulatory requirements, United Kingdom Auditing Standards issued by the Auditing Practices Board and the Listing Rules of the Financial Services Authority.

We report to you our opinion as to whether the financial statements give a true and fair view and are properly prepared in accordance with the Companies Act 1985. We also report to you if, in our opinion, the Directors' report is not consistent with the financial statements, if the company has not kept proper accounting records, if we have not received all the information and explanations we require for our audit, or if information specified by law or the Listing Rules regarding Directors' remuneration and transactions is not disclosed.

We read the other information contained in the annual report and consider the implications for our report if we become aware of any apparent misstatements or material inconsistencies with the financial statements. The other information comprises only the Directors' report, the Chairman's statement, the financial highlights, the operating and financial review, the corporate governance statement and the report of the Directors on remuneration.

We review whether the corporate governance statement reflects the company's compliance with the seven provisions of the Combined Code specified for our review by the Listing Rules, and we report if it does not. We are not required to consider whether the Board's statements on internal control cover all risks and controls, or to form an opinion on the effectiveness of the company's or Group's corporate governance procedures or its risk and control procedures.

BASIS OF AUDIT OPINION

We conducted our audit in accordance with auditing standards issued by the Auditing Practices Board. An audit includes examination, on a test basis, of evidence relevant to the amounts and disclosures in the financial statements. It also includes an assessment of the significant estimates and judgements made by the Directors in the preparation of the financial statements, and of whether the accounting policies are appropriate to the company's and the Group's circumstances, consistently applied and adequately disclosed.

We planned and performed our audit so as to obtain all the information and explanations which we considered necessary in order to provide us with sufficient evidence to give reasonable assurance that the financial statements are free from material misstatement, whether caused by fraud or other irregularity or error. In forming our opinion we also evaluated the overall adequacy of the presentation of information in the financial statements.

OPINION

In our opinion the financial statements give a true and fair view of the state of affairs of the company and the Group at 23 February 2002 and of the profit and cashflows of the Group for the year then ended and have been properly prepared in accordance with the Companies Act 1985.

PriceWaterhouseCoopers

Chartered Accountants and Registered Auditors
London 9 April 2002

Fig. 2.7 Auditors' Report.
Source: Adapted from Tesco p.l.c., 2002.

Five Year Record

Year ended February

Financial statistics	1998 £m	1999 £m	2000 £m	2001 £m	2002 £m
Turnover excluding VAT					
UK	14,971	15,835	16,958	18,372	20,052
Rest of Europe	1,481	1,167	1,374	1,756	2,203
Asia	–	156	464	860	1,398
	16,452	17,158	18,796	20,988	23,653
Operating profit					
UK	875	919	993	1,100	1,213
Rest of Europe	37	48	51	70	90
Asia	–	(2)	(1)	4	29
	912	965	1,043	1,174	1,332
Operating margin					
UK	5.8%	5.8%	5.9%	6.0%	6.0%
Rest of Europe	2.5%	4.1%	3.7%	4.0%	4.1%
Asia	–	(1.3)%	(0.2)%	0.5%	2.1%
Total group	5.5%	5.6%	5.5%	5.6%	5.6%
Share of profit/(loss) from joint ventures	(6)	6	11	21	42
Net interest payable	(74)	(90)	(99)	(125)	(153)
Underlying profit	832	881	955	1,070	1,221
Ireland integration costs	(63)	(26)	(6)	–	–
Goodwill amortisation	–	(5)	(7)	(8)	(10)
Net loss on disposal of discontinued operations	(8)	–	–	–	–
Net loss on disposal of fixed assets	(1)	(8)	(9)	(8)	(10)
Profit before taxation	760	842	933	1,054	1,201
Taxation	(228)	(237)	(259)	(333)	(371)
Minority interest	–	1	–	1	–
Profit for the financial year	532	606	674	722	830
Adjusted diluted earnings per share	8.84p	9.37p	10.18p	10.66p	12.14p
Adjusted earnings per share	9.05p	9.59p	10.36p	10.87p	12.33p
Dividend per share	3.87p	4.12p	4.48p	4.98p	5.60p
Return on shareholders' funds	21.3%	21.3%	20.9%	22.7%	23.2%
Return on capital employed	18.7%	17.2%	16.1%	16.6%	16.1%
UK retail productivity £					
Turnover per employee	149,799	151,138	156,427	161,161	165,348
Profit per employee	8,755	8,771	9,160	9,649	10,002
Wages per employee	15,079	15,271	15,600	16,087	16,821
Weekly sales per sq. ft.	20.48	21.05	21.43	22.01	22.33
UK retail statistics					
Number of stores	618	639	659	692	729
Total sales area – 000 sq. ft.	15,215	15,975	16,895	17,965	18,822
Average store size (sales area – sq. ft.)	25,490	25,627	26,641	27,636	28,576
Full-time equivalent employees	99,941	104,772	108,409	113,998	121,272
Group statistics					
Number of stores	781	821	845	907	979
Total sales area – 000 sq. ft.	18,254	21,353	24,039	28,362	32,491
Full-time equivalent employees	119,127	126,914	134,896	152,210	171,794

Fig. 2.8 Five year record.
Source: Adapted from Tesco p.l.c., 2002.

FTSE All-Share Index: sector share movements

The All-Share Index[3] integrates the movements of some 800 constituent shares, covering 10 sector groups, and 39 individual sectors, based on April 1962 = 100. Figure 2.9 shows a small extract of the information provided. Various indices (see below) and trends are published separately for each sector group, as well as for selected sectors within those groups.

A comparison of *sector* index numbers with that for the All-Share Index allows the buoyant and depressed sectors to be quickly and clearly identified. For instance, of the sectors shown in the extract, the utility companies (electricity, gas and water) have done comparatively well (3270.86) when compared with the depressed information technology sector, still suffering from the 'dotcom' collapse, at only 268.94.

FT data on individual share movements

The *individual company* Share Information Service – of which Fig. 2.10 is an abstract – can usefully be

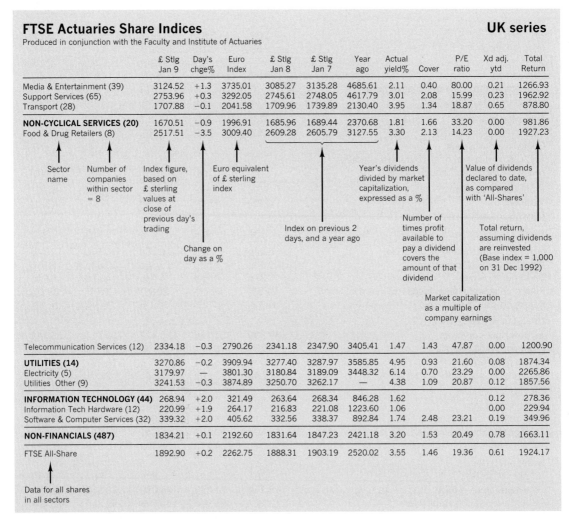

FTSE Actuaries Share Indices   **UK series**
Produced in conjunction with the Faculty and Institute of Actuaries

	£ Stlg Jan 9	Day's chge%	Euro Index	£ Stlg Jan 8	£ Stlg Jan 7	Year ago	Actual yield%	Cover	P/E ratio	Xd adj. ytd	Total Return
Media & Entertainment (39)	3124.52	+1.3	3735.01	3085.27	3135.28	4685.61	2.11	0.40	80.00	0.21	1266.93
Support Services (65)	2753.96	+0.3	3292.05	2745.61	2748.05	4617.79	3.01	2.08	15.99	0.23	1962.92
Transport (28)	1707.88	−0.1	2041.58	1709.96	1739.89	2130.40	3.95	1.34	18.87	0.65	878.80
NON-CYCLICAL SERVICES (20)	1670.51	−0.9	1996.91	1685.96	1689.44	2370.68	1.81	1.66	33.20	0.00	981.86
Food & Drug Retailers (8)	2517.51	−3.5	3009.40	2609.28	2605.79	3127.55	3.30	2.13	14.23	0.00	1927.23

Sector name

Number of companies within sector = 8

Index figure, based on £ sterling values at close of previous day's trading

Euro equivalent of £ sterling index

Year's dividends divided by market capitalization, expressed as a %

Value of dividends declared to date, as compared with 'All-Shares'

Index on previous 2 days, and a year ago

Number of times profit available to pay a dividend covers the amount of that dividend

Total return, assuming dividends are reinvested (Base index = 1,000 on 31 Dec 1992)

Change on day as a %

Market capitalization as a multiple of company earnings

	£ Stlg Jan 9	Day's chge%	Euro Index	£ Stlg Jan 8	£ Stlg Jan 7	Year ago	Actual yield%	Cover	P/E ratio	Xd adj. ytd	Total Return
Telecommunication Services (12)	2334.18	−0.3	2790.26	2341.18	2347.90	3405.41	1.47	1.43	47.87	0.00	1200.90
UTILITIES (14)	3270.86	−0.2	3909.94	3277.40	3287.97	3585.85	4.95	0.93	21.60	0.08	1874.34
Electricity (5)	3179.97	—	3801.30	3180.84	3189.09	3448.32	6.14	0.70	23.29	0.00	2265.86
Utilities Other (9)	3241.53	−0.3	3874.89	3250.70	3262.17	—	4.38	1.09	20.87	0.12	1857.56
INFORMATION TECHNOLOGY (44)	268.94	+2.0	321.49	263.64	268.34	846.28	1.62			0.12	278.36
Information Tech Hardware (12)	220.99	+1.9	264.17	216.83	221.08	1223.60	1.06			0.00	229.94
Software & Computer Services (32)	339.32	+2.0	405.62	332.56	338.37	892.84	1.74	2.48	23.21	0.19	349.96
NON-FINANCIALS (487)	1834.21	+0.1	2192.60	1831.64	1847.23	2421.18	3.20	1.53	20.49	0.78	1663.11
FTSE All-Share	1892.90	+0.2	2262.75	1888.31	1903.19	2520.02	3.55	1.46	19.36	0.61	1924.17

Data for all shares in all sectors

Fig. 2.9 (Extract from) FTSE actuaries share indices.
Source: Adapted from *Financial Times* 10 January 2003.

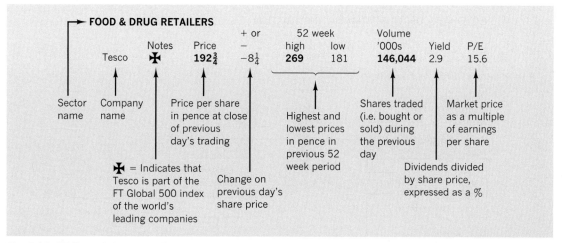

Fig. 2.10 FT Share Information Service.
Source: Adapted from *Financial Times* 10 January 2003.

viewed in conjunction with the All-Share Index. The performance of an individual company can then be assessed in the context of the performance of the industrial sector in which it operates.

Share (equity) price movements are published daily, with shares ordered alphabetically within particular industrial sectors. The price quoted is the middle price, i.e. midway between the buy and sell prices on the stock market. Figure 2.10 shows the specific information provided for Tesco p.l.c. in the food and drug retailers sector.

The FT of Friday 10 January 2003 (see Fig. 2.10) revealed that at the close of the day's trading the Tesco share price stood at $192\frac{3}{4}$p, down $8\frac{1}{4}$p from the previous day's closing price. We can make a more thorough assessment of Tesco's current position if we examine some of the technical headings of Figs 2.9 and 2.10, in conjunction with Tesco's own annual report. Figure 2.11 shows the derivation of Tesco's key data.

Price/earnings ratio: Tesco 15.6, Sector 14.23, All-Share 19.36

$$\text{P/E ratio} = \frac{\text{share price}}{\text{earnings per share}}$$

where earnings per share is profit after tax divided by the number of ordinary shares.

The price/earnings (P/E) ratio is the most important single measure of how the market views the company, and is the most common means of comparing the market values of different shares. The P/E ratio tells us the number of times the market price exceeds the last reported earnings. The more highly regarded the company, the higher its P/E ratio, with the market anticipating a sustained earnings performance over a lengthy period. The P/E ratio will depend in part upon the company's past record, but also upon that of the industrial sector of which it is a part, and upon the overall level of the stock market. A P/E ratio of 17–20 was regarded as typical in January 2003.

The sector figure of 14.23 for food retailers (see Fig. 2.9) is itself much lower than average (19.36), whilst Tesco's own P/E ratio of 15.6 probably indicates market sentiment regarding Tesco's dominant place within the sector whilst recognizing the intense competition from other retailers such as J. Sainsbury and Asda. Changes in future expectations will affect both share price and the P/E ratio, of which the share price is the numerator.

Cover: Tesco 2.1, Sector 2.13, All-Share 1.46

This indicates the level of safety regarding the payment of dividends compared with profit levels. The average number of times that the profit *available* for dividend 'covers' the dividend itself is 2.13 in the food retailers sector; i.e. for every £1 paid in

EXTERNAL SOURCES OF FINANCIAL INFORMATION

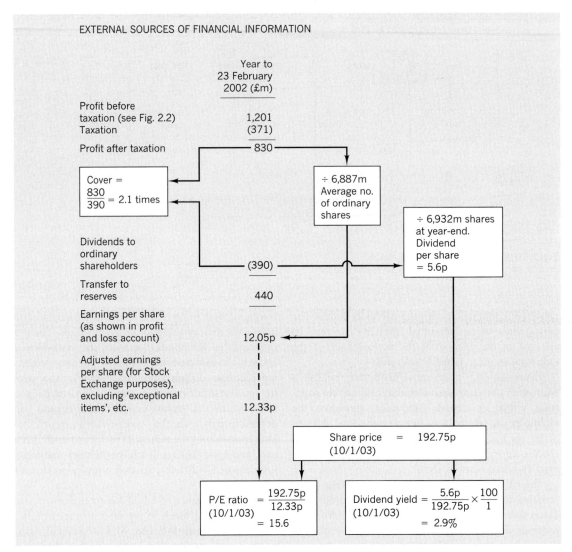

Fig. 2.11 FT ratios: Tesco p.l.c. (2002).

dividends, there was £2.13 of profits available. This is significantly safer than the overall 'All Share' average of only 1.46.

Dividend yield: Tesco 2.9%, Sector 3.3%, All-Share 3.2%

This shows the return on the investment as a percentage of the share price.

Gross dividend yield

$$= \frac{\text{gross dividend per share}}{\text{share price}} \times 100$$

The sector and all-share yields are similar, but Tesco's lower yield reflects the fact that its share price has kept strong relative to the market as a whole. Therefore dividends as a percentage of the price to be paid for shares in that company are lower than in a comparable company whose share price has fallen.

These technical figures, particularly the P/E ratio and the dividend yield, provide an excellent indication of current company performance and prospects. If this FT information is used alongside balance sheet information, company reports and press statements about recent company activities, then the shareholder will be better able to assess the management of his or her investment.

Conclusion

Various accounting ratios, properly understood, give useful insights into specific aspects of company performance. Taken together they can also provide a more general guide to overall company prospects. The content of the published accounts, together with external sources, notably the FT Share Information Service, provide an excellent basis for the assessment of company performance and the evaluation of investments.

Key points

■ All limited companies in the UK have to publish financial information.

■ All p.l.c.s have to appoint an independent auditor to report to the shareholders on the truth and fairness of the financial statements.

■ The majority of the financial information contained within the annual report is required by either legislation (the Companies Acts), Stock Exchange regulations or accounting standards.

■ There are four primary financial statements: the balance sheet, the profit and loss account, the cashflow statement and the statement of total recognized gains and losses.

■ The cashflow statement was introduced to show whether the company had a net cash inflow or outflow during the year. Even though a company may be profitable, it may go out of business through its inability to pay its creditors or repay a loan (or loan interest) which falls due.

■ The FTSE All-Share Index shows key information for nearly 40 sectors. Individual share information is found each day (except Sunday) in the Share Information Service pages of the *Financial Times*.

Now try the self-check questions for this chapter on the Companion Website. You will also find up-to-date facts and case materials.

Notes

1. Evidence suggests that in the majority of public companies, the controlling management has little or no stake in the ownership of the company. The directors of Tesco p.l.c., for example, had beneficial ownership of only 0.13% of the company's issued equity capital (9.1m shares out of a total issued share capital of over 6.9 billion).

2. Fixed-interest stocks issued by companies, usually redeemable at a set date, and backed by an agreement similar to a mortgage. Also known as 'bonds'.

3. The All-Share Index is an arithmetic average of price relatives weighted to reflect the market valuation of the shares included.

All-Share Index
$$= \frac{w_1(P_1/S_1) + w_2(P_2/S_2) + \cdots + w_{800}(P_{800}/S_{800})}{w_1 + w_2 + \cdots + w_{800}}$$

where

w_{1-800} = market valuations (i.e. current share price × number of ordinary shares) for each share included;

P_{1-800} = current share price of each share;

S_{1-800} = base year share prices for April 1962.

References and further reading

Financial Reporting Standard 1 (1991)
Accounting Standards Board.
Financial Reporting Standard 3 (1992)
Accounting Standards Board.
Financial Reporting Standard 15 (1999)
Accounting Standards Board.

The following websites are relevant to this chapter:

http://www.tesco.co.uk
http://www.kingfisher.co.uk
http://www.rmc-group.com

http://www.ftse.com
http://www.asb.org.uk
http://www.iasb.co.uk

Further general reading on accounting and accounting standards:

Black, G. (2000) *Introduction to Accounting*, Financial Times Prentice Hall.
Black, G. (2003) *Student's Guide to Accounting and Financial Reporting Standards*, Financial Times Prentice Hall.

Chapter 3   Firm objectives and firm behaviour

Economists have put forward various theories as to how firms behave in order to predict their reaction to events. At the heart of such theories is an assumption about firm objectives, the most usual being that the firm seeks to maximize profits. The first part of the chapter examines a number of alternative objectives open to the firm. It begins with those of a maximizing type, namely profit, sales revenue and growth maximization, predicting firm price and output in each case. A number of non-maximizing or behavioural objectives are then considered. The second part of the chapter reviews recent research into actual firm performance, and attempts to establish which objectives are most consistent with how firms actually operate. We see that although profit is important, careful consideration must be given to a number of other objectives if we are accurately to predict firm performance. The need for a perspective broader than profit is reinforced when we consider current management practice in devising the corporate plan.

Firm objectives

The objectives of a firm can be grouped under two main headings: maximizing goals and non-maximizing goals. We shall see that marginal analysis is particularly important for maximizing goals. This is often confusing to the student who, rightly, assumes that few firms can have any detailed knowledge of marginal revenue or marginal cost. However, it should be remembered that marginal analysis does not pretend to describe *how* firms maximize profits or revenue. It simply tells us *what* the output and price must be if they do succeed in maximizing these items, whether by luck or by judgement.

Maximizing goals

Profit maximization

The profit-maximizing assumption is based on two premisses: first, that owners are in control of the day-to-day management of the firm; second, that the main desire of owners is for higher profit. The case for profit maximization as 'self-evident' is, as we shall see, undermined if either of these premisses fails to hold.

Profit is maximized where marginal revenue (*MR*) equals marginal cost (*MC*), i.e. where the revenue raised from selling an extra unit is equal to the cost of producing that extra unit. In Fig. 3.1 total profit (*TP*) is a maximum at output Q_p, where the vertical distance between total revenue (*TR*) and total cost (*TC*) is the greatest ($TP = TR - TC$). Had the marginal revenue and marginal cost curves been presented in Fig. 3.1, they would have intersected at output Q_p.

To assume that it is the owners who control the firm neglects the fact that the dominant form of industrial organization is the public limited company (p.l.c.), which is usually run by managers rather than by owners. This may lead to conflict between the owners (shareholders) and the managers whenever the managers pursue goals which differ from those of the owners. This conflict is referred to as a type of

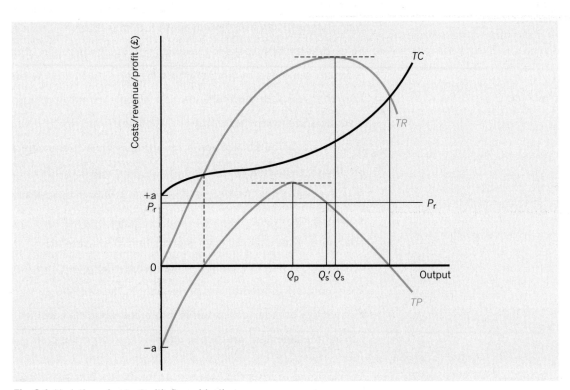

Fig. 3.1 Variation of output with firm objective.

principal–agent problem and emerges when the shareholders (principals) contract a second party, the managers (agents), to perform some tasks on their behalf. In return, the principals offer their agents some compensation (wage payments). However, because the principals are divorced from the day-to-day running of the business, the agents may be able to act as they themselves see fit. This independence of action may be due to their superior knowledge of the company as well as their ability to disguise their actions from the principals. Agents, therefore, may not always act in the manner desired by the principals. Indeed, it may be the agents' goals which predominate. This has led to a number of managerial theories of firm behaviour, such as sales revenue maximization and growth maximization.

Sales revenue maximization

Baumol (1959) has suggested that the manager-controlled firm is likely to have sales revenue maximization as its main goal rather than the profit maximization favoured by shareholders. His argument is that the salaries of top managers, and other perks, are more closely correlated with sales revenue than with profits.

Williamson's (1963) managerial theory of the firm is similar to Baumol's in stressing the growth of sales revenue as a major firm objective. However, it is broader based, with the manager seeking to increase satisfaction through the greater expenditure on both staff levels and projects made possible by higher sales revenue. Funds for greater expenditure can come from profits, external finance and *sales revenue*. In Williamson's view, however, increased sales revenue is the easiest means of providing additional funds, since higher profits have in part to be distributed to shareholders, and new finance requires greater accountability. Baumol and Williamson are describing the same phenomenon, though in rather different terms.

If management seeks to maximize sales revenue without any thought to profit at all (pure sales revenue maximization) then this would lead to output Q_s in Fig. 3.1. This last (Q_sth) unit is neither raising nor lowering total revenue, i.e. its marginal revenue is zero.

Constrained sales revenue maximization

Both Baumol and Williamson recognize that some constraint on managers can be exercised by share-

holders. Maximum sales revenue is usually considered to occur well above the level of output which generates maximum profits. The shareholders may demand at least a certain level of distributed profit, so that sales revenue can only be maximized subject to this constraint.

The difference a profit constraint makes to firm output is shown in Fig. 3.1. If P_r is the minimum profit required by shareholders, then Q_s' is the output which permits the highest total revenue whilst still meeting the profit constraint. Any output beyond Q_s' up to Q_s would raise total revenue TR – the major objective – but reduce total profit TP below the minimum required (P_r). Therefore Q_s' represents the constrained sales revenue maximizing output.

So far we have assumed that the goals of owners (profits) have been in conflict with the goals of management (sales revenue). Marris (1964), however, believes that owners and managers have a *common* goal, namely maximum growth of the firm.

Growth maximization

Marris (1964) argues that the overriding goal which *both* managers and owners have in common is growth. Managers seek a growth in demand for the firm's products or services, to raise power or status. Owners seek a growth in the capital value of the firm to increase personal wealth.

It is important to note, therefore, that it is through the *growth* of the firm that the goals of both managers and owners can be achieved. Also central to the analysis of Marris is the ratio of retained to distributed profits, i.e. the 'retention ratio'. If managers distribute most of the profits (low retention ratio), shareholders will be content and the share price will be sufficiently high to deter takeover. However, if managers distribute less profit (high retention ratio), then the retained profit can be used for investment, stimulating the growth of the firm. In this case shareholders may be less content, and the share price lower, thereby increasing the risk of a takeover bid.

The major objective of the firm, with which both managers and shareholders are in accord, is then seen by Marris as maximizing the rate of growth of the firm's demand *and* the firm's capital ('balanced growth'), subject to an acceptable retention ratio. Figure 3.2 shows the trade-off between higher balanced growth and the average profit rate.[1]

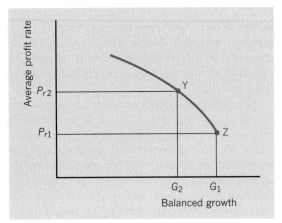

Fig. 3.2 Trade-off between average profit and balanced growth.

For 'balanced growth' to increase, more and more investment in capital projects must be undertaken. Since the most profitable projects are undertaken first, any extra investment must be reducing the average profit rate. Point Z is where the balanced growth rate is at a maximum (G_1), with an implied retention ratio so high that all profitable investment projects have been pursued, giving an average profit rate P_{r1}. Risk avoidance by managers may, however, enforce a lower retention ratio with more profits distributed. Point Y is such a constrained growth-maximizing position (G_2), with a lower retention ratio, lower investment and higher average profit (P_{r2}) than at point Z. How close the firm gets to its major objective, Z, will depend on how constrained management feels by the risk of disgruntled shareholders, or a takeover bid, should the retention ratio be kept at the high rates consistent with points near to Z.

Non-maximizing goals

The traditional (owner control) and managerial (non-owner control) theories of the firm assume that a single goal will be pursued. The firm then attempts to achieve the highest value for that goal, whether profits, sales revenue or growth. The *behaviouralist* viewpoint is rather different, and sees the firm as an organization with various groups, workers, managers, shareholders, customers, etc., each of which has its own goal, or set of goals. The group which

achieves prominence at any point of time may be able to guide the firm into promoting its goal set over time. This dominant group may then be replaced by another giving greater emphasis to a totally different goal set. The traditional and managerial theories which propose the maximization of a single goal are seen by behaviouralists as being remote from the organizational complexity of modern firms.

Satisficing

One of the earliest behavioural theories was that of Simon (1959) who suggested that in practice managers are unable to ascertain when a marginal point has been reached, such as maximum profit with marginal cost equal to marginal revenue. Consequently, managers set themselves *minimum* acceptable levels of achievement. Firms which are satisfied in achieving such limited objectives are said to 'satisfice' rather than 'maximize'. This is not to say that satisficing leads to some long-term performance which is less than would otherwise be achieved. The achievement of objectives has long been recognized as an incentive to improving performance and is the basis of the management technique known as management by objectives (MBO). Figure 3.3 illustrates how the attainment of initially limited objectives might lead to an improved long-term performance.

At the starting point 1, the manager sets the objective and attempts to achieve it. If, after evaluation, it is found that the objective has been achieved, then this will lead to an increase in aspirational level (3B). A new and higher objective (4B) will then emerge. Thus, by setting achievable objectives, what might be an initial minimum target turns out to be a prelude to a series of higher targets, perhaps culminating in the achievement of some maximum target, or objective. If, on the other hand, the initial objective is not achieved, then aspirational levels are lowered (3A) until achievable objectives are set. Simon's theory is one in which no single objective can be presumed to be the inevitable outcome of this organizational process. In fact, the final objective may, as we have seen, be far removed from the initial one.

Coalitions and goal formation

If a firm is 'satisficing', then who is being satisfied – and how? Cyert and March (1963) were rather more specific than Simon in identifying various groups or coalitions within an organization. A *coalition* is any

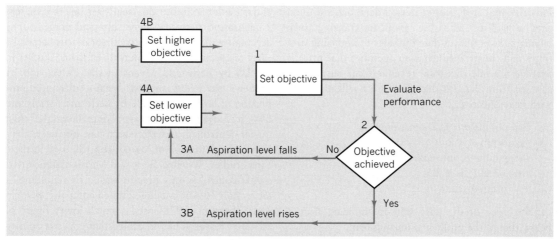

Fig. 3.3 Development of aspiration levels through goal achievement.

group which, at a given moment, shares a consensus on the goals to be pursued.

Workers may form one coalition wanting good wages and work conditions and some job security; managers want power and prestige as well as high salaries; shareholders want high profits. These differing goals may well result in group conflict, e.g. higher wages for workers may mean lower profits for shareholders. The behavioural theory of Cyert and March, along with Simon, does not then view the firm as having one outstanding objective (e.g. profit maximization), but rather many, often conflicting, objectives.

It is not just internal groups which need to be satisfied. There is an increasing focus by leading organizations on *stakeholders*, i.e. the range of both internal and external groups which relate to that organization. Freeman (1984) defined stakeholders as 'Any group or individual who can affect or is affected by the achievement of the organization's objectives'. Cyert and March suggest that the aim of top management is to set goals which resolve conflict between opposing groups. This approach has been reinforced by the *Tomorrow's Company Inquiry* Report (RSA 1994) which noted that sustainability of the *company* can only occur where it meets the expectations of its stakeholders.

Contingency theory

The contingency theory of company behaviour suggests that the optimal solutions to organizational problems are derived from matching the internal structure and processes of the firm with its external environment. However, the external environment is constantly changing as industrial markets become more complex, so that the optimum strategy for a firm will change as the prevailing environmental influences change. The result of this is that firms may not have a single goal such as the maximization of profits or sales, but will have to vary their goals and strategies as the environment changes around them. Contingency theory helps us to understand why firms will not always be able to follow a single optimizing course through time.

To summarize, the various behavioural theories look at the *process* of decision-making. They recognize that the 'organization' is not synonymous with the owner, nor with any other single influence, but rather that the firm has many objectives which relate to the many different groups acting within the organization. These objectives may be in conflict and so management will use a number of techniques in order to reduce that conflict. The behavioural approach has been criticized for its inability to yield precise predictions of firm activity in particular settings. However, where management processes are recognized, such as in strategic planning (see p. 56), then specific short-term predictions can be made.

Does firm objective matter?

The economist is continually seeking to predict the output and price behaviour of the firm. Figure 3.1

indicates that firm *output* does indeed depend upon firm objective, with the profit-maximizing firm having a lower output than the sales-maximizing firm (pure and constrained). If we remember that price is average revenue (i.e. total revenue/total output) we can see from Fig. 3.4 that firm *price* will also vary with firm objective.

Price in the *pure sales-maximizing*
firm = $\tan \theta_s = R_1/Q_s$
Price in the *profit-maximizing*
firm = $\tan \theta_p = R_2/Q_p$
$\tan \theta_s < \tan \theta_p$

i.e. the price of the pure sales-maximizing firm is below that of the profit-maximizing firm.

It is clear that it really *does* matter what objective we assume for the firm, since both output and price depend on that objective. We turn now to firm performance to assess which of the objectives, if any, can be supported by how firms actually behave.

Firm behaviour

Ownership and control in practice

Profit maximization is usually based on the assumption that firms are owner-controlled, whereas sales and growth maximization usually assume that there is a separation between ownership and control. The acceptance of these alternative theories was helped by early research into the ownership of firms. Studies in the US by Berle and Means in the 1930s, and by Larner in the 1960s, suggested that a substantial proportion of large firms (44% by Berle and Means and 85% by Larner) were manager-controlled rather than owner-controlled. Later research has, however, challenged the definition of 'owner-control' used in these early studies. Whereas Berle and Means assumed that owner-control is only present with a shareholding of more than 20% in a public limited company, Nyman and Silberston (1978) used a much lower figure of 5% after research had indicated that effective control could be exercised by owners with this level of shareholding. This would suggest that owner-control is far more extensive than previously thought. Leech and Leahy (1991) found that 91% of British public limited companies are owner-controlled using the 5% threshold figure, but only 34% are owner-controlled using a 20% threshold figure. Clearly the degree of ownership control is somewhat subjective, depending crucially on the threshold figure assigned to shareholding by owners in order to exercise effective control.

A further aspect of owner-control involves the role of financial institutions and pension funds. Between them they now own over 76% of the shares of public

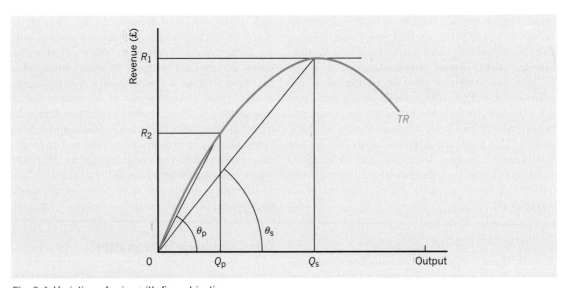

Fig. 3.4 Variation of price with firm objective.

companies in the UK, compared to only 36% in 1963, while individual share ownership has declined from 54% to around 20% over the same period. Financial institutions are more likely than individuals to bring influence to bear on chief executives, being experienced in the channels of communication and sensitive to indices of firm performance. The effect of this influence is seen by many as moving the firm towards the profit-maximizing (owner-controlled) type of objective.

Profit

Profit maximization

In a major study, Shipley (1981) concluded that only 15.9% of his sample of 728 UK firms could be regarded as 'true' profit-maximizers. This conclusion was reached by cross-tabulating replies to two questions shown in Table 3.1.

Because answers to questionnaires can often be given loosely, Shipley considered as 'true' maximizers only those who claimed both to maximize profit (answered (a) to Question 1) and to regard profit as being of overriding importance (answered (d) to Question 2). Only 15.9% of all the firms replied with both 1(a) and 2(d), and were considered by Shipley as true profit-maximizers.

A similar study by Jobber and Hooley (1987) found that 40% of their sample of nearly 1,800 firms

had profit maximization as their prime objective. In a more recent study of 77 Scottish companies by Hornby (1994), 25% responded as 'profit maximizers' to the 'Shipley test'. The percentage of satisficers was very similar in both studies (Shipley 52.3%, Hornby 51.9%).

Given the significance of the profit-maximizing assumption in economic analysis, these results may seem surprising. However, some consideration of the decision-making process may serve to explain these low figures for profit maximization. Firms in practice often rely on preset 'hurdle' rates of return for projects, with managers given some minimum rate of return as a criterion for project appraisal. As a result they may not consciously see themselves as profit-maximizers, since this phrase suggests marginal analysis. Yet in setting the hurdle rates, top management will be keenly aware of the marginal cost of funding, so that this approach may in some cases relate closely to profit maximization. In other words, the response of management to questionnaires may understate the true significance of the pursuit of profit.

Profit as part of a 'goal set'

Although few firms appear to set out specifically to maximize profit, profit is still seen (even in response to questionnaires) as an important factor in decision-making. In the Shipley study the firms were asked to list their principal goal in setting price. Target profit

Table 3.1 Sample of 728 firms.

	All respondents (%)
(1) Does your firm try to achieve:	
(a) maximum profits?	47.7
(b) 'satisfactory' profits?	52.3
(2) Compared to your firm's other leading objectives, is the achievement of a target profit ... regarded as being:	
(a) of little importance?	2.1
(b) fairly important?	12.9
(c) very important?	58.9
(d) of overriding importance?	26.1
Those responding with both 1(a) and 2(d)	15.9

Source: Adapted from Shipley (1981).

was easily the most frequently cited, with 73% of all firms regarding it as their principal goal. Even more firms (88%) included profit as at least part of their 'goal set'.

Profit – long term versus short term

Long-term profit may be even more important than short-term profit in firm objectives. Senior managers are well aware that poor profitability in the long term may lead to their dismissal or the takeover of their firm, quite apart from an increased risk of insolvency. Indeed Shipley found that 59.7% of his sample gave priority to long-term profits, compared to only 20.6% giving priority to short-term profits. Shipley found long-term profit to be a significant influence in all sizes of company, though particularly in those of medium/large size. More recently, a survey by the *Financial Times* (1998) of 77 Finance Directors of FTSE 100 companies found that 98% considered the priority of investors to be long-term performance of the company rather than its performance in the short term.

Studies of the behaviour of firms in technology-based markets has provided further support for the emphasis on longer-term profit perspectives (Arthur 1996). Arthur suggests that when a technology reaches a certain critical mass of usage, then the market is 'locked in' and the only rational choice for new users is then to adopt the established technology. He cites Microsoft Windows as being a typical example of this, with the continued increase in use of Windows providing an example of a market system operating positive feedback. Arthur suggests that average (and marginal) revenues might even rise in technology-based markets as volume exceeds the 'critical mass' for that established technology, rather than decline as in standard theory. This phenomenon has often led to a strategy of giving away products reflecting new technologies at their introduction stage in order to create lock-in. The objective of this strategy for technology-based markets might arguably still be profit maximization, but only in the longer term.

Profit and reward structures

There was a great deal of concern throughout the 1990s that managers in large firms have paid too little regard to the interests of shareholders, especially as regards profit performance of the company. Indeed a number of celebrated cases in the press have focused on the apparent lack of any link between substantial rises in the pay and bonuses of chief executives and any improvements in company performance.

The majority of empirical studies have indeed found little relationship between the remuneration of top managers and the profit performance of their companies. In the UK, Storey *et al.* (1995) found no evidence of a link between the pay of top managers and the ratio of average pre-tax profits to total assets, with similar results for studies by Jensen and Murphy (1990) and Barkema and Gomez-Meija (1998) in the US. Table 3.2 confirms this picture, with only one of the 20 firms appearing in the 10 highest sales revenue and 10 highest profit rankings being in the list of the 10 highest paid CEOs. This apparent lack of a clear relationship between executive pay and company performance became an important issue during 2002–03 as the chief executive officers of companies such as Royal & Sun Alliance, Lloyds TSB, Kingfisher, Shell and ICI received large pay rises and special cash deals at the same time as company profits and share prices fell.

However, the absence of any proven link between the profitability of a firm and the reward structures it offers to its CEO and other top managers does not necessarily mean that profit-related goals are unimportant. Firms increasingly offer top managers a total remuneration 'package' involving bonus payments and share options as well as salary. In this case higher firm profitability, and therefore dividend earnings per share, may help raise the share price and with it the value of the total remuneration package. Indeed Ezzamel and Watson (1998) have suggested that the total remuneration package offered to CEOs is directly related to the 'going rate' for corporate profitability. It may therefore be that top management have more incentives for seeking profit-related goals than might at first be apparent.

To summarize, therefore, although there may be no open admission to profit maximization, the strong influence of owners on managed firms, the use of preset hurdle rates and the presence of profit-related reward structures may in the end lead to an objective, or set of objectives, closely akin to profit maximization.

Sales revenue

Sales revenue maximization

Baumol's suggestion that management-controlled firms will wish to maximize sales revenue was based

Table 3.2 The 10 highest-ranked US corporations by sales revenue growth, profit growth and CEO remuneration.

Rank	Sales revenue maximizers[1]	Profit maximizers[2]	Highest paid CEOs[3]
1	AdvancePCS	Nvidia	Oracle
2	Murphy Oil	Dynacq International	Dell Computer
3	Ebay	P.F. Chang's China Bistro	JDS Uniphase
4	Nvidia	Frontier Oil	Forest Labs
5	Frontier Oil	XTO Energy	Capital One Financial
6	Evergreen Resources	Patina Oil & Gas	Nabors Industries
7	Micromuse	Quicksilver Resources	Lehman Bros Holdings
8	Quanta Services	Cytyc	Qwest Communications
9	Siebel Systems	St Mary Land & Exploration	Stilwell Financial
10	MGM Mirage	Hot Topic	Siebel Systems

[1] % change in revenue from 2001 to 2002.
[2] % growth in earnings per share from 2001 to 2002.
[3] Using 2002 remuneration data.
Sources: Sales Revenue and Profit Maximization (Fortune 2001); CEO Pay (Forbes 2002).

on the belief that the earnings of executives are more closely related to firm revenue than to firm profit. A number of studies have sought to test this belief. For example, in a study of 177 firms between 1985 and 1990, Conyon and Gregg (1994) found that the pay of top executives in large companies in the UK was most strongly related to *relative sales growth* (i.e. relative to competitors). They also found that it was only weakly related to a long-term performance measure (total shareholder returns) and not at all to current accounting profit. Furthermore, growth in sales resulting from takeovers was more highly rewarded than internal growth, despite the fact that such takeovers produced on average a lower return for shareholders and an increased liquidity risk. These findings are in line with other recent UK research (Gregg *et al.* 1993; Conyon and Leech 1994) and with a study of small UK companies by Conyon and Nicolitsas (1998) which also found sales growth to be closely correlated with the pay of top executives.

As well as a linkage between the growth of sales revenue and executive income, there is also general support for the contention that *firm size* is directly related to executive income. Studies by Gregg *et al.* (1993) and Rosen (1990) concur with much earlier studies, such as that of Meeks and Whittington (1975), who found that the larger the asset value of the company, the larger the executive salary.

What does seem clear from these various findings is that top management appears to be able to revise the rules for their own remuneration according to circumstance. Principals (shareholders) would appear to have little effective control over the remuneration of agents (management) in major public corporations where ownership and control are separated.

Sales revenue as part of a 'goal set'

The results of Shipley's analysis tell us little about sales revenue *maximization*. Nevertheless, Shipley found that target sales revenue was the fourth-ranked principal pricing objective, and that nearly half the firms included sales revenue as at least part of their set of objectives. Larger companies cited sales revenue as an objective most frequently; one-seventh of companies with over 3,000 employees gave sales revenue as a principal goal compared to only one-fourteenth of all the firms. Since larger companies have greater separation between ownership and management control, this does lend some support to Baumol's assertion. The importance of sales revenue as part of a set of policy objectives was reinforced by the study of 193 UK industrial distributors by Shipley and Bourdon (1990), which found that 88% of these companies included sales revenue as one of a number of objectives. However, we see below that the nature of planning in large organizations must also be considered and that this may temper our support for sales revenue being itself the major objective, at least in the long term.

Strategic planning and sales revenue

Current thinking on strategic planning would support the idea of short-term sales maximization, but only as a means to other ends (e.g. profitability or growth). Research in the mid-1970s by the US Strategic Planning Institute linked market share – seen here as a proxy for sales revenue – to profitability. These studies found that high market share had a significant and beneficial effect on both return on investment and cashflow, at least in the long term. However, in the short term the high investment and marketing expenditure needed to attain high market share reduces profitability and drains cashflow. Profit has to be sacrificed in the short term if high market share, and hence future high profits, are to be achieved in the long term.

Constrained sales revenue maximization

The fact that 88% of all companies in Shipley's original study included profit in their goal set indicates the relevance of the profit constraint to other objectives, including sales revenue. The later study by Shipley and Bourdon (1990) reached a similar conclusion, finding that 93% of the UK industrial distributors surveyed included profit in their goal set.

Growth

There are a number of reasons why firms should wish to grow, although in the 1990s the term 'growth' would appear to apply to asset value and market share rather than workforce. Marris (1964) suggests that managers seek to increase their status by increasing the 'empire' in which they work. Others would argue that although growth is an important company objective it is a means to an end, e.g. higher profit, rather than an end in itself as Marris would suggest.

When we examine the facts, however, there is little to indicate that faster growth really does mean higher profits. To illustrate this, consider Table 3.3. This shows the top 10 highest-growth firms (percentage change in total assets) amongst the leading 100 UK p.l.c.'s. To the right-hand side of the table, however,

Table 3.3 The 10 fastest-growing UK p.l.c.'s in 1998 (% change in total assets over 1997–98) and their position in the profitability ranking (% profit margin 1997–98) of the top 100 UK p.l.c.'s.

Rank in growth	Firm	Rank in profitability
1	Pearson	6
2	Invensys	78
3	Scottish and Southern Energy	35
4	Somerfield	91
5	Powergen UK	98
6	Marconi	10
7	Kingfisher	42
8	United News & Media	18
9	BP Amoco	54
10	Gallaher	51

Source: Financial Analysis Made Easy (FAME) (DVD), July 2000.

we can see that, ranked in terms of profitability (percentage profit margin), only Pearson and Marconi can be ranked as fast growing *and* highly profitable. Indeed, the other nine high-growth p.l.c.'s are low in the profitability rankings, with Scottish and Southern Energy third in growth but only 35th in profitability. Table 3.3 is in line with the results of a study by Whittington (1980) who found that profit levels did *not* increase as the firm grew in size. This lends some support to those, like Marris, who see growth as a separate objective to profit.

In fast-moving markets, such as high-technology electronics and pharmaceuticals, companies need flexibility to move rapidly to fill market niches. To achieve this, some firms are moving in quite the opposite direction to growth, i.e. they are 'de-merging'. De-merging occurs when the firm splits into smaller units, each separately quoted on the Stock Exchange. For example, since 1996 Hanson plc, the US–UK conglomerate, has de-merged its coal, power, tobacco and chemical interests to concentrate on building materials, rather similar to the situation of ICI which, in 1992, had de-merged its pharmaceutical interests, giving 'birth' to the new company Zeneca. Such de-merging is a clear sign that professional investors do not merely equate larger size to greater profit.

In a similar vein, Tom Peters, co-author of *In Search of Excellence*, says that 'quality and flexibility will be the hallmarks of the successful economy for the foreseeable future'. This premiss leads to a view that size, with its inherent inflexibility and distance from the end-customer, is a *disadvantage*. Indeed, analysis by the Strategic Planning Institute (Buzzel and Gale 1987) shows an *inverse* relationship between market size and the rate of return on investment in the US. In market segments of less than $100m (£61m), the return on investment averaged 27% in their study; however, where firms operated in market segments of over $1bn (£610m), the return averaged only 11%. They found that organizations sought to reduce the disadvantages of size by restructuring, either by de-merging or by the creation of smaller, more dynamic Strategic Business Units (SBUs), which are able to meet the demands of the market more rapidly. This is well illustrated by the decision of DuPont, in its 1994 restructuring programme, to split its six Chemicals and Specialities sectors into 23 SBUs, for precisely this reason.

Despite the comments made above, a company which fails to grow over a period of time, even though its profits are relatively healthy, is in danger of becoming an ineffective innovator. Growth is important because it attracts good, young entrepreneurial talent, as dynamic firms such as Nokia, Goldman Sachs and L'Oréal have found. It also helps companies to attract new capital and to be innovative as regards new products and processes. The dynamics of the growth process depend on the interaction between a firm's external environment (industry, markets and customers) and the internal environment of the company (resources and abilities). Table 3.4 shows four corporate growth paths with examples of companies which seem to have taken these paths (Canals 2001).

Basically speaking, *corporate renewal* is a determinant of growth when companies use their current resources and abilities to expand their customer base. For example, Swatch succeeded in becoming dynamic once more as a result of greater attention to costs, product design and differentiation. *Innovation* is an important determinant of growth, as companies like Nokia can attest. The company moved from one which operated across different industries to one which increasingly concentrated on communication systems. It focused more clearly on cellular phones by increasing investment in R&D and increasing its manufacturing capabilities. Some companies grow by *expanding their capabilities* through merger, as was the case with Glaxo and Wellcome. The synergy of two pharmaceutical companies (which had strong R&D capabilities and complementary areas of expertise) meant that the new company, Glaxo Wellcome, could produce an array of new products. Finally, *exploiting external opportunities* involves companies utilizing the benefits of growth in order to exploit external opportunities, such as new markets. For example, in the 1990s, Merck, the giant US pharmaceutical company, acquired Medco, a firm that ran a network of 48,000 pharmacies in the US. Through Medco's direct sales links, Merck was able to control distribution and sell its goods direct to patients.

As we can see from the above examples, growth is still an important strategic variable because it acts as a catalyst to firms that want to become leaders in their respective fields. Firms that stand still often die, so that corporate growth provides the way for firms to ensure their long-term survival.

Non-maximizing behaviour

We have seen that the non-maximizing or behavioural theories concentrate on how firms actually operate within the constraints imposed by organizational structure and firm environment. Recent evidence on management practice broadly supports the behavioural contention, namely that it is unhelpful to seek a single firm objective as a guide to actual firm behaviour. This support, however, comes from a rather different type of analysis, that of portfolio planning.

Work in the US by the Boston Consulting Group on the relationship between market share and industry growth gave rise to an approach to corporate planning known as 'portfolio planning'. Firms, especially the

Table 3.4 Patterns of corporate growth.

Corporate renewal	Innovation	Expanding capabilities	Exploiting external opportunities
Swatch	Nokia	Glaxo	Merck
L'Oréal	Hewlett-Packard	Volkswagen	Bertelsmann
Disney	Canon	BP	Merrill Lynch
Lloyds	Goldman Sachs	Compaq	Wal-Mart

Source: Canals (2001), Table 3 (modified).

larger ones, can be viewed as having a collection or 'portfolio' of different products at different stages in the product life cycle. If a product is at an early stage in its life cycle, it will require a large investment in marketing and product development in order to achieve future levels of high profitability. At the same time another product may have 'matured' and, already possessing a good share of the market, be providing high profits and substantial cashflow.

The usual strategy in portfolio planning is to attempt to balance the portfolio so that existing profitable products are providing the funds necessary to raise new products to maturity. This approach has become a classic part of strategic decision-making.

If a firm is using the portfolio approach in its planning then it may be impossible to predict the firm's behaviour for individual products or market sections on the basis of a single firm objective. This is because the goals of the firm will change for a given product or market sector *depending on the relative position of that product or market sector within the overall portfolio*. Portfolio planning, along with other behavioural theories, suggests that no single objective is likely to be useful in explaining actual firm behaviour, at least in specific cases.

The non-maximizing behaviour of large companies can be seen clearly in the approach taken by some large companies (Griffiths 2000). For example, between 1997 and 2000 Cadbury Schweppes, the chocolate and confectionery multinational, explained its objectives in terms of 'Managing for Value' (MFV). To meet the MFV criterion the company stressed the importance of:

- increasing earnings per share by at least 10% every year;
- generating £150 million of free cashflow every year;
- doubling the value of shareholders' investment in the four years to 2000;
- competing in the world's growth markets by effective internal investment and by value-enhancing acquisitions;
- developing market share by introducing innovations in product development, packaging and routes to market;
- increasing commitment to value creation in managers and employees through incentive schemes and share ownership;

- investing in key areas of air emissions, water, energy and solid waste.

From the above list it is clear that the first three preoccupations are related to the profit objectives while the third and fourth relate to company growth and market share. In addition the final two objectives encompass both human resource and environmental issues. In this context, it can be seen that maximizing a single corporate goal seems unrealistic in the dynamic world of multinationals.

Conclusion

The traditional theory of the firm assumes that its sole objective is to maximize profit. The managerial theories assume that where ownership and control of the organization are separated, the objective which guides the firm will be that which the management sets. This is usually thought to be maximization of either sales revenue or growth. It is important to know which, if any, of the maximizing objectives are being pursued, since firm output and price will be different for each objective. Behavioural theory tends to oppose the idea of the firm seeking to maximize any objective. For instance, top management may seek to hold the various stakeholder groups in balance by adopting a set of minimum targets. Even where a single group with a clear objective does become dominant within the firm, others with alternative objectives may soon replace it.

In practice, profit maximization *in the long term* still appears to be important. Sales revenue seems quite important as a short-term goal, though even here a profit target may still be part of the goal set. The prominence of the profit target may be an indication that ownership is not as divorced from the control of large firms as may once have been thought. One reason why sales revenue may be pursued in the short term is found in an analysis of current strategic planning techniques, which link short-term sales revenue to long-term profit. Sales revenue may therefore be useful for explaining short-term firm behaviour, but with profit crucial for long-term behaviour. Those who, like Marris, argue that growth is a separate objective from profit find some support in the lack of any clear relationship between growth and profitability. Growth may also be a means of securing greater stability for the firm. It may reduce internal conflict, by being an objective around which both owner–shareholders and managers can agree, and possibly reduces the risk of takeover. Also large firms experience, if not higher profits, then less variable profits (Whittington 1980; Schmalensee 1989). A widely used technique in the management of larger firms, portfolio planning, would seem to support the behaviouralist view, that no single objective will usefully help predict firm behaviour in a given market.

Key points

- Separation between ownership by share-holders (principals) and control by managers (agents) makes profit maximization less likely.
- Maximization of sales revenue or asset growth (as well as profit) must be considered in manager-led firms.
- The objectives pursued by the firm will influence the firm's price and output decisions.
- Different groupings (coalitions) may be dominant within a firm at different points of time. Firm objectives may therefore change as the coalitions in effective control change.
- Organizational structure may result in non-maximizing behaviour; e.g. the presence of diverse stakeholders may induce the firm to set minimum targets for a range of variables as a means of reducing conflict.
- Shipley's seminal work (supported by later studies) found less than 16% of the firms studied to be 'true' profit maximizers.
- However, Shipley found that 88% of firms included profit as part of their 'goal set'.

- Separation between ownership and control receives empirical support, though small 'threshold' levels of share-holdings may still secure effective control in modern p.l.c.'s.
- Profit remains a useful predictor of long-term firm behaviour, though sales revenue may be better in predicting short-term firm behaviour.
- Profit maximization may not be acknowledged as a goal by many firms, yet in setting 'hurdle rates' senior managers may implicitly be following such an objective.
- Profitability and executive pay appear to be largely unrelated, suggesting that other managerial objectives might be given priority (sales revenue, growth, etc.). However, total remuneration 'packages' for top executives may be linked to profitability, helping to align the interests of managers more closely to the interests of shareholders.
- Portfolio planning points to a variety of ever-changing objectives guiding firm activity rather than any single objective.

Now try the self-check questions for this chapter on the Companion Website. You will also find up-to-date facts and case materials.

Note

1. Average profit rate is total profit divided by total capital employed.

References and further reading

Arthur, W. B. (1996) Increasing returns and the new world of business, *Harvard Business Review*, July–August, 100–9.

Barkema, H. G. and Gomez-Meija, L. R. (1998) Managerial compensation and firm performance, *Academy of Management Journal*, **41**(2).

Baumol, W. J. (1959) *Business Behaviour, Value and Growth*, Macmillan.

Berle, A. A. and Means, G. C. (1934) *The Modern Corporation and Private Property*, Macmillan, New York.

Buzzel, R. and Gale, B. (1987) *The PIMS Principles*, Strategic Planning Institute.

Canals, J. (2001) How to think about corporate growth, *European Management Journal*, **19**(6).

Conyon, M. and Gregg, P. (1994) Pay at the top: a study of the sensitivity of top director remuneration to company specific shocks, *National Institute Economic Review*, August.

Conyon, M. and Leech, D. (1994) Executive compensation, corporate performance and ownership structure, *Oxford Bulletin of Economics and Statistics*, **56**, 229–47.

Conyon, M. J. and Nicolitsas, D. (1998) Does the market for top executives work? CEO pay and turnover in small UK companies, *Small Business Economics*, **11**(2).

Cyert, R. M. and March, J. G. (1963) *A Behavioural Theory of the Firm*, Prentice-Hall, New York.

Ezzamel, M. and Watson, R. (1998) Market compensation earnings and the bidding-up of executive cash compensation: evidence from the United Kingdom, *Academy of Management Journal*, **41**(2).

Financial Times (1998) Shares in the action, 27 April.

Forbes (2002) http://forbes.com/tool/toolbox/ceo/asp/CEORankIndex.asp?year=2000

Fortune (2002) http://www.fortune.com/fortune/fortune500/perform.html

Freeman, R. E. (1984) *Strategic Management: a stakeholder approach*, Pitman, Boston.

Gregg, P., Machin, S. and Szymanski, S. (1993) The disappearing relationship between directors' pay and corporate performance, *British Journal of Industrial Relations*, **31**, 1–9.

Griffiths, A. (2000) Corporate objectives, risk taking and the market: the case of Cadbury Schweppes, *British Economy Survey*, **29**(2), Spring.

Henderson, B. (1970) Intuitive strategy, *Perspectives*, **96**, The Boston Consulting Group, Boston.

Hornby, W. (1994) *The Theory of the Firm Revisited: a Scottish perspective*, Aberdeen Business School.

Jensen, M. C. and Murphy, K. J. (1990) Performance pay and top management incentives, *Journal of Political Economy*, **98**.

Jobber, D. and Hooley, G. (1987) Pricing behaviour in UK manufacturing and service industries, *Managerial and Decision Economics*, **8**, 167–77.

Leech, D. and Leahy, J. (1991) Ownership structure, control type classifications and the performance of large British companies, *Economic Journal*, **101**.

Main, B. G. M. (1991) Top executive pay and performance, *Management and Decision Economics*, **12**, 219–29.

Marris, R. (1964) *The Economic Theory of Managerial Italism*, Macmillan.

Meeks, G. and Whittington, G. (1975) Directors' pay, growth and profitability, *Journal of Industrial Economics*, **24**(1), September.

Nyman, S. and Silberston, A. (1978) The ownership and control of industry, *Oxford Economic Papers*, **30**(1), March.

Rosen, S. (1990) Contracts and the market for executives, *NBFR Working Paper*, 3542.

RSA (1994) *Tomorrow's Company Inquiry*.

Schmalensee, R. (1989) Intra-industry profitability in the US, *Journal of Industrial Economics*, **36**(4).

Shipley, D. D. (1981) Primary objectives in British manufacturing industry, *Journal of Industrial Economics*, **29**(4), June.

Shipley, D. and Bourdon, E. (1990) Distributor pricing in very competitive markets, *Industrial Marketing Management*, **19**.

Simon, H. A. (1959) Theories of decision making in economics, *American Economic Review*, **69**(3), June.

Storey, D., Watson, R. and Wynarczyk, P. (1995) The remuneration of non-owner managers in UK unquoted and unlisted securities market enterprises, *Small Business Economics*, **7**.

Whittington, G. (1980) The profitability and size of United Kingdom companies, *Journal of Industrial Economics*, **28**(4).

Williamson, O. E. (1963) Managerial discretion and business behaviour, *American Economic Review*, **53**, December.

Chapter 4

The small firm

The small firm is the subject matter of this chapter. It begins by outlining the difficulties of finding an adequate definition, along with problems of measurement. Fragmentary statistical evidence is reviewed, to see whether the small firm really is becoming more important in UK employment and net output, and to compare the small firm in the UK with its position in other countries. We consider the historical reasons for the neglect of the small firm, and why, in more recent times, there has been a resurgence of interest in them. Measures to help the small firm are outlined, from both government and private sources. The chapter concludes with a cautionary note against placing too heavy a reliance on the small firm for economic regeneration.

Definition of the small firm

There is no single comprehensive definition of the small firm sector. This is largely because most advanced economies have a wide diversity of business enterprises across both industry and service sectors. An early attempt at identifying the key characteristics of a small firm in the UK was the Bolton Committee Report of 1971, which concluded that three main characteristics had to be taken into account:

1 A small firm is one that has a relatively small share of its market.

2 It is managed by its owners or part-owners in a personalized way, and not through the medium of a formalized management structure.

3 It is independent, in the sense that it does not form part of a large enterprise, so that its owner-managers are free from outside control when taking their principal decisions.

The Report also recognized that the precise definition of a 'small firm' might also depend on the sector in which the firm operated: for example, a firm of 200 employees or less might be regarded as small in the manufacturing sector but a firm having 25 employees or less might be regarded as small in the construction sector.

Since the 1970s, there have been attempts to standardize definitions of small and medium-sized enterprises (SMEs) using variables such as the number of employees, turnover, balance sheet totals and ownership. In the UK two broad approaches have been followed:

■ The Department of Trade and Industry (DTI) uses the employee criterion and defines firm size as follows: *micro firm* (0–9 employees); *small firm* (0–49 employees); *medium firm* (50–249 employees); and *large firm* (over 250 employees).

■ However, the Companies Act of 1985 (Section 248) states that a company is 'small' if it satisfies at least two of the following criteria:

	Small company	Medium company
Turnover	Not more than £2.8m	Not more than £11.2m
Balance sheet total	Not more than £1.4m	Not more than £5.6m
Employees	Not more than 50	Not more than 250

These are the main statistical definitions used in the UK, although specific schemes often adopt a range of practical definitions depending on their particular objectives. For example, the British Bankers Association defines small businesses as those having an annual account turnover of less than £1m.

In the European Union the definition of an SME involves four criteria, as listed below.

	Micro firm	Small firm	Medium firm
Turnover	–	Not exceeding €7m	Not exceeding €40m
Balance sheet total	–	Not exceeding €5m	Not exceeding €27m
Employees	Less than 10	Less than 50	Less than 250
Independence criteria	–	25% or less	25% or less

To qualify as an SME both the employees and independence criteria must be satisfied together with *either* the turnover *or* the balance sheet criteria. An SME is defined as an 'independent enterprise' when the amount of capital or voting rights in that firm held by one or more non-SME firms does not exceed 25%. The values shown in the above table for turnover and balance are liable to be changed over time as the absolute monetary values require adjustment because of inflation.

The importance of the small firm

Since 1995, information on the size distribution of all UK firms has been improved with the introduction of the new Inter-Departmental Business Register (IDBR). This register keeps statistics of all businesses registered for VAT and also those businesses which operate a PAYE scheme. This means that the IDBR includes small businesses below the VAT threshold but with a PAYE system, together with those businesses trading in goods exempt from VAT but operating a PAYE system, e.g. small firms in finance, insurance and education. Of course, the IDBR does not collect information on unregistered businesses, i.e. those which do not register for VAT or operate

PAYE systems. Thus, figures for activities such as sole proprietors and partnerships have to be estimated from the Labour Force Survey (LFS) and added to the IDBR figures.

Table 4.1 shows that there were some 3,746,000 businesses in the UK in 2001. The new category 'class size zero' includes enterprises which consist of one or more self-employed people with *no employees*. This category reflects the growth of self-employment in the UK, but while it accounts for 69.3% of the total number of businesses it accounts for only some 12.8% of total employment and 7.2% of total turnover. Small businesses with fewer than 50 employees can be seen from the table to account for over 43% of total employment and around 38% of total turnover. If we include small and medium-sized enterprises (SMEs), i.e. businesses employing fewer than 250 employees, then such businesses account for around 55% of employment and 51% of turnover. The total number of businesses in the UK rose from 2.4m in 1979 to over 3.7m in 2001 and, since most of the *new* businesses are small, this reflects a significant growth in the small firm sector.

As we see later in the chapter, the 1980s saw a renewed interest in the role of the small firm in the UK, with a variety of policy measures directed towards its support. As a result the relative size of the small firms sector in the UK is now much closer to that in other countries than it was at the beginning of the 1980s. As Table 4.2 indicates, in 2000 the small (micro) firm in the UK employing fewer than 10 persons made up 95% of all enterprises and provided some 30.3% of all employment and 22.8% of total turnover.

While the figures for the contribution for micro enterprises were similar in the UK and the EU, it is interesting to note that small and medium-sized enterprises tended to contribute rather less to employment and turnover in the UK than in the EU. The mirror image of this can be seen in the greater contribution that large firms make to employment and turnover in the UK as compared to the EU.

The neglect of small firms

Early economic theory was broadly favourable to the small firm. The theory of perfect competition had shown that in markets where many small firms produced identical products, the eventual equilibrium would be at the 'technical optimum', i.e. the level of output with lowest average cost. Monopoly, on the other hand, was regarded with suspicion, the exploitation of market power giving the opportunity for restricting output and raising prices (see Chapter 9, Fig. 9.1).

Table 4.1 Number of businesses, employment and turnover share by size band (2001).

Employment size band	Number of businesses (thousands)	Share of total (%)		
		Businesses	Employment	Turnover
0	2,596	69.3	12.8	7.2
1–4	748	20.0	9.9	8.2
5–9	200	5.3	6.3	5.8
10–19	113	3.0	6.9	9.0
20–49	55	1.5	7.5	8.0
50–99	18	0.5	5.5	6.7
100–199	8	0.2	4.9	5.4
200–249	2	–	1.6	2.0
250–499	3	0.1	5.0	7.4
500+	3	0.1	39.6	41.2
Total	3,746	100.0	100.0	100.0

Note: figures rounded.
Source: Adapted from Small Business Service (2002a).

Table 4.2 Shares of enterprises, employment and turnover: UK and EU (2000).

%	Micro (0–9)	Small (10–49)	Medium (50–249)	Large (250+)
Enterprises:				
UK	95.0	4.2	0.6	0.2
EU	93.1	5.9	0.8	0.2
Employment:				
UK	30.3	13.4	11.4	44.9
EU	34.0	19.0	13.0	34.0
Turnover:				
UK	22.8	14.5	13.9	48.8
EU	18.0	17.4	19.3	45.3

Sources: European Commission (2002); Small Business Service (2002b).

The rise of limited liability and the development of the capital market had, by the end of the nineteenth century, made it easier for firms to raise finance for growth. There was also a greater awareness that increased size could secure substantial economies of scale. These developments shifted the focus of attention away from small firms and towards large firms. During the inter-war period, economic theory gave further grounds for viewing large-scale production in a more favourable light. The theory of imperfect competition developed during the 1930s showed that many small firms producing differentiated products could, as with monopoly, produce output below the technical optimum, with prices above the competitive level.

Bannock (1981) argues that after the Second World War attitudes towards large firms became still more positive, with attention being focused on the innovatory role of large firms. Particularly influential was the American economist Schumpeter, who wrote in 1943 that 'the large-scale establishment ... has come to be the most powerful engine in [economic] progress and in particular of the long-run expansion of total output' (Bannock 1981). Price competition in traditional competitive theory was, to Schumpeter, less important than the 'gales of creative destruction' which replaced old products, processes and organizations with new ones. Technical progress to bring about these innovative changes would, in Schumpeter's view, require substantial monopoly profits to fund research and development (R & D). The large sums needed to research and develop products in the aerospace, nuclear and computer industries lent weight to this argument. The fact that in the two decades after the Second World War, increasing industrial concentration coincided with the most rapid and sustained period of economic growth in the twentieth century was seen by many as supporting Schumpeter's view.

British government policy reflected this growing preoccupation with larger size as a means of reaping economies of scale and reducing unit costs of production, so that UK products would become more competitive on world markets. For example, in 1966 the government announced the formation of the Industrial Reorganization Corporation (IRC). The White Paper inaugurating the IRC had emphasized the need for increased concentration in British industry, so that firms could benefit from economies of scale in production and increase expenditure on R & D. The IRC was set up to encourage the reorganization of UK industry, which in practice led to it promoting mergers through financial and other assistance. Although the IRC was wound up in 1971, the Industry Acts of 1972 and 1975 continued to offer financial help to industry on a selective basis in order to encourage modernization, efficiency and expansion, in particular through the activities of the National Enterprise Board (NEB). However, emphasis on increasing size as a means of achieving greater efficiency began to wane by the early 1970s, with a reawakening of interest in small firms.

The renewed interest in small firms

Empirical and other evidence began to accumulate in the late 1960s which challenged the views of Schumpeter that large firms must be the engine of economic progress.

First, it began to be felt that large firms might not always be the most innovative. Instead of large firms growing still larger by capturing new markets as a result of product and process innovation, they often grew by taking over existing firms with established products and processes. A study by Hannah and Kay (1977) had shown that virtually all the increase in concentration that occurred in the UK between 1957 and 1973 resulted from mergers between existing companies and not from internal growth.

Second, evidence began to be published which indicated that small firms were themselves beginning to play an important role in innovation. The Bolton Committee had found in its survey of important innovations between 1945 and 1970 that small firms accounted for only some 10% of these innovations, but that this was twice as high as their share of total R & D. It has been argued, therefore, that small firms use skilled manpower and research equipment more efficiently than larger firms. Similarly, in a nationwide study of 800 firms covering 1,200 innovations, Oakey *et al.* 1980) had found that 23% of these innovations came from single-site independent companies. In the fast-growing instrument engineering and electronic sectors, the small firms' share of innovations was even higher. The fact that small firms had been prominent in the most dynamic, high-technology sectors suggested that they still had an important role to play as innovators. The role of small firms as innovators continued into the 1990s, as illustrated in an important report by the Cambridge University Centre for Business Research which compared the innovative nature of SMEs over the 1990–95 period. The report showed that over 20% of SMEs in their sample produced 'original' product innovation, i.e. innovations which were not only new to the specific firm but also new to the industry in which the firm operated (Cosh and Hughes 1996).

Third, Prais (1976) produced evidence that the growth in size of firms (business units) was not, in the main, due to the growth in size of plants (production units). According to his calculations, the share of the 100 largest manufacturing plants remained at about 11% between 1930 and 1968, whilst the share of the 100 largest *firms* rose from about 22% to 41% in the same period. Concentration had increased because firms had built or acquired more plants, not because they had built larger ones. Put another way, Prais showed that increasing concentration was not explained by increased technical economies of scale at plant level. The small firm may therefore be able to compete with the large firm even though it produced in relatively small plants.

Fourth, evidence began to accumulate that acquisitions do not always have particularly beneficial effects on financial performance. A number of studies (Singh 1971; Meeks 1977) showed that the profitability of the combined enterprise usually fell after merger. In fact Newbold (1970) found that only 18% of all the mergers investigated could be linked in any way to technical or financial economies of scale.

Again, such evidence gave grounds for optimism that the small firm may be at less of a disadvantage in terms of profitability than had earlier been thought.

Fifth, there was evidence that small firms had contributed a major part of the recorded gains in employment whilst larger firms had been shedding labour. Birch (1979), in his study of changes in employment in the USA, concluded that small firms (those with 20 or fewer employees) generated 66% of all new jobs in the USA in the period 1969–76. More recent studies have tended to confirm these earlier findings. For example, the European network for research on SMEs found that small and medium-sized companies accounted for no less than 94% of the UK *net* employment growth over the 1987–91 period. Keeble (1997) found that between 1990 and 1995 the number of people employed by small firms in the UK rose by 19%. However, it is also important to note that net employment creation in the UK's SME sector has been mostly generated by new, innovative, technology-based companies (TUC 2000).

Sixth, the role of small firms in foreign trade had been shown to be more significant than had previously been thought. Hannah and Kay (1977) quoted unpublished figures from a survey undertaken in 1973 by the Department of Trade. These showed that firms with a turnover of less than £10m exported 14.5% of turnover, whilst firms with a turnover of over £250m exported only 10%. By the mid-1990s, figures for exports show that the small-firm sector as a whole exported an average of 12% of their turnover, whilst small firms in manufacturing exported as much as 14% of their turnover (Keeble 1997). Such an export performance may also have been underestimated because small firms also provide 'indirect exports' since they supply intermediate goods for large export firms (European Commission 2002).

For all these reasons there has been a renewed interest in the small firm, which has been reflected in recent government policy.

Measures to help small firms

Small firms and government

Since the early 1980s the then Conservative government and the current Labour government have sought to stimulate the supply side of the economy, with special attention being paid to the small-firms sector. Specifically, action has been taken in three directions.

Equity and loan capital

The flow of equity and loan capital has been augmented to enable an individual who wishes to exploit an idea or to expand his business to do so. The Department of Trade and Industry introduced a new Enterprise Fund in 1998 designed to provide flexible support for those SMEs with growth potential. The fund had £100m to spend in 2002/03 on the first three items listed below.

Small Firms Loan Guarantee Scheme

This was introduced in June 1981 as a pilot scheme for three years. It was intended to cover situations where potential borrowers were unable to provide sufficient collateral, or where the banks considered the risk went beyond their normal criteria for lending. From April 2003 the scheme was made available to UK companies with an annual turnover of more than £3m (non-manufacturing) and £5m (manufacturing). The government encourages 'authorized' financial institutions such as the main UK banks to lend to small firms by guaranteeing 75% of each loan up to £100,000 for new companies and £250,000 for established businesses, with the loans being guaranteed for between two and 10 years. In return for the guarantee, the borrower pays the Department an extra interest premium of 2% per year on the outstanding balance of all new loans. Some £204m was spent on the scheme in 2002/03 and since its inception in 1981 a total of £3bn has been spent on guaranteeing some 80,000 individual loans.

Regional Venture Capital Funds

These are public–private partnerships, receiving government financial help from the DTI's Enterprise Fund. These partnerships are aimed at encouraging equity venture capital investment by the private sector in small firms across the English regions. The government intends to invest up to £80m in the nine Regional Venture Capital Funds (RVCFs) during the 2000–03 period and this will, it is hoped, encourage up to £187m from private sector investors.

High Technology Fund

During 1999–2000 the Enterprise Fund began working in partnership with a private firm, Westport

Private Equity Ltd, to raise finance for the creation of a further fund of up to £125m to invest in existing UK high technology venture capital funds. The aim of this 'fund of funds' is to stimulate companies in the early stages of high technology development which, by definition, are likely to be SMEs. By 2003, almost £35m of the fund had been invested in 69 companies working in areas such as pharmaceuticals, communications, internet technologies and bio-sciences.

Phoenix Fund

The DTI established a Phoenix Fund in 2000 to help tackle social exclusion by encouraging entrepreneurship in disadvantaged areas of the UK and supporting those groups under-represented in business ownership. For example, the Phoenix Fund includes a Development Fund which is designed to help support business projects in ethnic minority communities, providing grants and loan guarantees to Community Development Finance Institutions (CDFIs) which in turn use such resources to help promote enterprise amongst disadvantaged groups not able to obtain finance from conventional sources. The Development Fund also supports a national network of volunteer mentors to help pre- and early stage business start-ups. Between 2000 and 2003 the Development Fund had supported 96 projects at a total cost of £30m, while the Community Development Finance Institutions initiative had allocated £26m to 42 individual projects.

The Enterprise Investment Scheme

The Enterprise Investment Scheme (EIS) was introduced in January 1994 and is the successor to the former Business Expansion Scheme (BES) which had been operating since 1983. The BES had become expensive to run and only a fraction of the funds had actually found their way to small manufacturing companies. Much of the equity investment had been placed in private rented properties which gave 'safe' returns, rather than being invested in the more dynamic but risky manufacturing sector.

The EIS was introduced to encourage equity investment in small (and therefore 'high risk') unquoted companies. It also sought to encourage 'business angels' (outside investors with some business background who might contribute both capital and management expertise) to invest in such companies. The scheme was modified in 1998 and offers income tax relief at 20% on annual investments of up to £150,000 a year in the ordinary shares (equity) of companies which qualify. A person who was previously unconnected with the company can also become a paid director and qualify for tax relief.

Gains made on the sale of equities held for the full three years are exempt from capital gains tax. Also, any losses experienced when selling the shares after this period can be set off against income tax. To qualify for the EIS, companies must have carried on an approved trade wholly or mainly in the UK for a period of three years after the date of issue of shares, but they need not be resident or incorporated in the UK.

Venture Capital Trusts

The Venture Capital Trust (VCT) was introduced by the Finance Act 1995 to encourage individuals to invest in smaller, unlisted trading companies. By January 2003 a total of 50 VCTs had invested over £1bn in small companies since the inception of the scheme. Basically the VCT invests in a range of trading companies whose assets must not exceed £10m, i.e. it invests in relatively small companies. VCTs are exempt from corporation tax on any capital gains arising on the disposal of their investments. Individuals who invest, i.e. buy shares, in a VCT are exempt from income tax on their dividends from ordinary shares and are also exempt from capital gains tax when they dispose of their shares.

Alternative Investment Market (AIM)

The Unlisted Securities Market (USM) was introduced in November 1981 to enable small and medium-sized firms to acquire venture capital on the London Stock Exchange. Its attractiveness declined in the early 1990s partly because the Stock Exchange rules regarding a full listing had been relaxed in response to changes in European Union directives. This meant that the advantages to companies of being on the USM rather than on the Official Stock Exchange List had been eroded. The USM ceased trading in December 1996.

The demand for a replacement market to the USM was evident in the early 1990s with the growth of trading under Rule 4.2 of the London Stock Exchange. This rule permitted member firms to deal in specific securities which were neither listed nor quoted on the USM. It had been formulated to provide an occasional dealing facility in unquoted companies for members of the Stock Exchange. The main benefit of trading under Rule 4.2 was that trading rules were less stringent than under the full listing or the USM.

In June 1995 the *Alternative Investment Market* was opened to meet the demand for a low-cost and accessible investment market for small and growing companies. Its trading rules are less demanding than those for the full listing and the old USM but are on a more formal basis than trading under Rule 4.2. For example, the cost of a full listing is often high because companies need to appoint mandatory 'sponsors' who check whether the listing rules have been followed. In the new market, the responsibility for the accuracy of the documents rests on the company directors alone. The new market would, in addition, be accessible to companies raising small amounts of capital and those with few shareholders. Investors in AIM companies benefit from the same tax breaks as apply to unquoted companies, including inheritance tax relief, capital gains tax relief and relief under the Enterprise Investments Scheme and Venture Capital Trusts. Further, there would be no minimum or maximum limits set on the size of the company joining the market, nor on the size of the issue. In brief, the Alternative Investment Market operates under rules which depend more on companies themselves disclosing the basic information rather than on their having to fulfil the strict suitability criteria for a full listing. The hope is that the market will be attractive to small companies, providing the finance and flexibility they need.

By November 2003, there were 693 companies trading on the AIM with a total of £5bn having been raised since 1995. Companies on the AIM include Peel Hotels, Majestic Wine and Ask Central (restaurants) and Aberdeen Football Club. By the late 1990s some observers began to point out that the cost of an AIM float could be as high as £250,000, not too far short of the cost of a full listing. The result has been that many very small firms are beginning to use the Ofex market, leaving AIM for those companies looking to raise £2m or more.

Tax allowances and grants

In order to help small businesses, tax allowances have been modified, and grants offered.

Corporation tax

Corporation tax has been made more generous for small firms over the last few years. For example, the corporation tax for 'very small companies' with less than £10,000 taxable profits was brought down from 10% in 1996 to zero in 2003, while the corporation tax rate fell from 24% to 19% for 'small' companies and from 33% to 30% for 'large' companies over the same period. SMEs were also entitled to an additional deduction from taxable income of 50% of their current spending on certain research and development activities while also receiving a first-year tax relief of 40% on investment in plant and machinery.

Enterprise Grants (EG)

This is a scheme for firms employing fewer than 250 people in the new Enterprise Grant areas of England (pp. 201–2) introduced in November 1999 with some £52m committed to the EG scheme over the period 2000–03. Under this scheme, companies investing up to £500,000 may apply for a once-and-for-all grant of 15% of the fixed costs up to a maximum of £75,000. The Small Business Service (SBS) administers the scheme, with advice from the Regional Development Agencies.

The Small Firms Merit Award for Research and Technology (SMART)

Under the SMART scheme individuals and independent small companies with fewer than 50 employees can submit proposals for funding 75% of the total cost (up to £45,000) of feasibility studies into innovative technology. Larger independent businesses with fewer than 250 employees can apply for funding up to 30% of the total development cost of new products and processes. In 1999 there was a major expansion of the scheme to cover R & D and consultancy costs for smaller projects undertaken by individuals or 'micro-enterprises' with fewer than 10 employees. Such grants are available to those who want to develop simple low-cost prototypes of new products which involve technological advance and/or novelty. The expenditure on such grants was £28m in 2002/03.

Other sources of advice and training for small firms

By 2003 there were a number of providers of advice, information and training for small firms.

Training and Enterprise Councils (TECs)

The network of 79 TECs in England and Wales were charged with the responsibility of taking forward the government's strategy for training in the 1990s. These independent companies are run by boards of directors led by private-sector business leaders and are contracted by the government both to provide the whole country with a skilled workforce and to support and coordinate local economic development. The TECs provide advice, counselling, training and consultancy facilities for small firms.

Chambers of Commerce

These also provide information and support services for small firms, while the *Local Enterprise Agencies* (LEAs) offer advice and counselling to new and expanding businesses and often work under contract to the local TEC. There are now over 150 LEAs throughout the UK.

Business Links

These were established in 1993 and form the final major source for the provision of core services which local small businesses may need. These are partnerships between the TECs, Chambers of Commerce, LEAs and local authorities, and bring together the most important business development services in a single, accessible location. Business Link services are provided by Business Link Operators in 45 areas of England with a total of £162m spent on these services in 2002/03. Each Business Link Operator provides small and medium-sized firms with access to the most appropriate public, private or voluntary sector support in areas such as export, consultancy, innovation, design and business skills.

Small Business Service (SBS)

Established in April 2000, the SBS is designed to act as an effective voice for small firms in government. In this context, the SBS will influence the direction of government policy in three ways: first, by acting as a centre of expertise, by bringing knowledge about SMEs together, analysing it and disseminating it to those who can use such information; second, by acting as an innovator in order to develop new ideas and new approaches which better meet the needs of SMEs; and third, by acting as an engine of change by working with partners both within and outside government to help the small firm sector. In 2003/04 some £380m was allocated to the SBS with most of the expenditure being used for various business support and training initiatives.

All these training initiatives are absolutely essential, since surveys in the early 1990s showed that between 80% and 90% of small companies had no business training and received no formal preparation for company board responsibility. The continued need for such support was highlighted in a major study of 1,300 SMEs by the Centre for Business Research of Cambridge University (Cosh and Hughes 2000). This study found that less than half of all the firms investigated had formal structures for their management organization and less than half provided formal training within their companies.

Another useful survey of the problems facing UK SMEs involved a sample of around 1,000 small firms compiled by NatWest/SBRT in their *Quarterly Survey of Small Business* (2000). Figure 4.1 shows that the three most important problems faced by UK SMEs over the last 16 years have involved low turnover, government regulations and cashflow/payments. Low turnover was identified by almost 45% of firms as the most important problem in the immediate aftermath of the economic slowdown of the early 1990s and is still cited as such by around 25% of SMEs. Cashflow payments problems are seen as the main source of concern by around 10% of UK SMEs with government regulations and paperwork cited as a problem by nearly 15% of respondents. Sometimes the source of this problem may be high interest rates on loans or the lack of demand in times of recession. However, a persistent element would seem to involve late payments. For example, a recent survey by Grant Thornton (Bank of England 2002) found that the UK was as low as seventh in the EU league as regards average payment periods. It had an average payment delay of 41 days, longer than countries such as Denmark (33 days), Norway (30 days) and Germany (31 days), but shorter than France (58 days) and Italy (78 days). It is interesting to note that the NatWest/SBRT survey found a lack of skilled employees to be in fourth place as regards the most important problem faced by UK SMEs.

Small firms and the banks

Sources of finance for UK industry vary with the size of company. Smaller firms rely on personal savings at the start-up stage but then obtain some 60% of external finance from banks, although very small firms also use hire purchase and leasing arrangements. The relationship between smaller firms and banks is therefore of vital importance for this sector of UK industry. As has been noted in many surveys, the central problem of financial support for small firms is not necessarily the *availability* of finance but its *cost*. The rate of interest for the smallest firms employing fewer than 30 employees is between 3% and 5% above base rates and this is often doubled if the overdraft is exceeded, even if only briefly.

Another issue for UK small firms relates to the *structure* of their debt. The UK dependence on overdraft finance for external funding is above the EU average, as can be seen from Table 4.3. This often restricts the ability of smaller firms to take a long-term

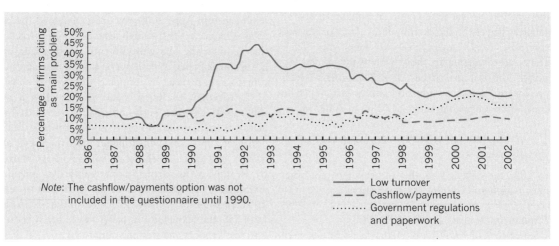

Note: The cashflow/payments option was not included in the questionnaire until 1990.

——— Low turnover
– – – Cashflow/payments
·········· Government regulations and paperwork

Fig. 4.1 Problems facing small firms.
Source: Bank of England (2002) and previous issues.

Table 4.3 Sources of external funding (%) and lengths of loans.

Country	Sources of external funding (%)			Length of loans (%)		
	Overdraft	Lease & hire-purchase	Loans	Up to 3 years	3–5 years	Over 5 years
UK	59	42	34	24	29	47
EU average	50	39	46	25	37	37

Source: Adapted from Bank of England (2002).

view because overdrafts are payable on demand. As far as the length of loans is concerned, some 24% of UK companies have loans of up to three years, which is similar to the EU average. On the other hand, a smaller proportion of UK firms have loans of three to five years, and a larger proportion of UK firms have loans of over five years, as compared to the EU average.

A final problem is that UK banks have been criticized for not providing small firms with sufficient *liquidity* to avert bankruptcy, unlike the German banking system which is more flexible in such situations. This seems to indicate that there may be failures of understanding among UK banks of how to help small businesses in both growth and recession periods. In contrast with Germany and Japan, the UK has no regional banks which are likely to have greater knowledge of local industry and can develop mutual trust with small local firms. Also the big UK commercial banks often lack a strong local or regional career structure, so that managers are often shifted across country and find it difficult to get to know their locality before they are moved on.

European Union policy for small firms

Within the European Commission, policies relating to small and medium-sized firms are now the responsibility of the Enterprise DG which was created in January 2000 and comprises three previous Directorate-Generals (DGs), namely Industry, SME and Information Society. Help for SMEs in the EU is provided by many agencies and it might be useful here to mention a few initiatives in this area. For example, a framework plan entitled 'The Multinational Programme for Enterprise and Entrepreneurship

2001–05' was designed to enhance European business in general but with special reference to SMEs. The objectives of the framework plan are pursued through a series of activities that fall under three headings. The first is to provide adequate *advice, information and assistance* to SMEs through 259 Euro Info Centres located in most European countries. These centres can also refer SMEs to other specialized networks or organizations when specific assistance is required. The second is to improve the *financial environment* for SMEs with many schemes managed by the European Investment Fund (EIF). For example, Seed Capital Action is designed to stimulate the supply of capital for the creation of innovative new businesses by partially funding the recruitment of more investment managers, whilst the European Technology Facility (ETF) start-up scheme invests in funds which provide risk capital to smaller businesses, and the SME Guarantee Facility, also managed by the EIF, provides guarantees to those financial institutions which lend to qualifying SMEs. The third objective is to identify *best practice* amongst SMEs by introducing benchmarking activities across the EU. The information gathered from the most efficient SMEs as a result of benchmarking is then disseminated to other SMEs.

Other funds for SMEs are available through the *European Regional Development Fund* (ERDF), which spends 10% of its budget on SMEs. The *European Social Fund* (ESF) spends 14% of its funds on promoting a systematic approach to training by SMEs in the poorer regions of the EU. Finally, Enterprise DG has supported the development of European stock markets specifically designed to help SMEs. For example, the Nouveau Marche in Paris and the EASDAQ in Brussels specialize in helping young, relatively small companies gain access to equity funds more easily and cheaply.

Conclusion

Renewed interest in small firms derives from changes in economic thought and has been given impetus by the particular policies pursued by the government, partly for ideological reasons, partly as a means of producing new jobs, and partly as a corollary of 'supply side' monetarist policies. However, there is a danger in placing too heavy an emphasis on the role of small firms in rebuilding the UK's industrial base. Figures from the DTI in 2002 showed that 45% of VAT registered businesses failed to survive the first three years. Storey (1982) had already shown that most small firms stay static or die. In his study of all the new manufacturing firms started in Cleveland, County Durham, and Tyne and Wear from 1965 to 1978, he found that only 774 survived out of 1,200. Of the survivors, more than half still had fewer than 10 employees in 1982, and nearly three-quarters had fewer than 25. In fact, the probability of a new business employing more than 100 people after a decade was less than 0.75%. For every new job created by a small firm in these three counties over the 13-year period, four jobs were lost from large companies employing over 1,000 persons. Storey *et al.* (1987) found that in their survey of single-plant independent manufacturing companies in northern England, one-third of the new jobs were found in less than 4% of the new starters. Further research (Storey 1994) also showed that it is incorrect to assume that countries which have experienced the most rapid increase in new firm formation (measured in terms of increase in self-employment) are those which have experienced the fastest growth of employment creation. The same survey also pointed out that investment in government training schemes for small-company entrepreneurs at the start-up or at later stages is not necessarily related to the future success of small companies. The evidence shows that success is more closely related to the original educational attainment of the business owner. In other words, it may be more important to improve the level of the UK's general education as a whole, if small firms are to thrive.

For all these reasons, the net advantages of small firms may be less than is commonly supposed. Nevertheless, small firms are able to find market niches, especially where economies of scale are not easily obtained, as in providing specialized items for small markets, and in developing products used as components by large firms. Also the movement towards a higher proportion of employment being in the service sector, where traditionally smaller firms have been dominant, suggests an increasingly important role for smaller firms in the UK economy. For example, a recent report has shown that UK-based SMEs performed relatively well over the period 1988–2001 as compared to large companies when measured in terms of growth in real value added, employment and profitability (European Commission 2002). However, in *absolute* terms there are still major gaps between small and large firms. For example, in the UK at the beginning of the new millennium, the value added per occupied person (labour productivity) in small firms was still only 87% of the UK average as compared to 120% for large firms (TUC 2000).

Key points

- Definitions of the small firm vary within and between countries.

- Across all industrial sectors in the UK, firms with fewer than five employees account for around 90% of the total number of firms. However, such firms account for only around 23% of total employment and 15% of total turnover.

- The small firm is increasingly seen by governments as a focus of new growth and employment opportunities.

- Small-firm support has focused on three main areas: easier access to equity and loan capital, increased tax allowances and grants, and less government interference.

- Banks provide the main source (59%) of external finance for small firms (via overdraft) in the UK, increasingly in the form of medium- to longer-term loans, though high exposure to such overdraft finance remains a problem in the UK.

- Small firms in the UK see interest rate policy, general macroeconomic policy and taxation policy as the governmental policies with most impact on themselves.

■ Low turnover is by far the most important single problem identified by small firms in the UK.

■ European policy towards SMEs is becoming increasingly influential with large-scale funds available to support a broad range of initiatives.

Now try the self-check questions for this chapter on the Companion Website. You will also find up-to-date facts and case materials.

References and further reading

Bank of England (2002) *Quarterly Report on Small Business Statistics*, Business Finance Division, October.

Bannock, G. (1981) *The Economics of Small Firms*, Blackwell, Oxford.

Bannock, G. and Daly, M. (eds) (1994) *Small Business Statistics*, Paul Chapman.

Birch, D. L. (1979) *The Job Generation Process*, Massachusetts Institute of Technology (mimeo).

Cosh, A. and Hughes, A. (eds) (1996) *The Changing State of British Enterprise: Growth, Innovation and Competitive Advantage in Small and Medium Sized Firms 1986–95*, ESRC Centre for Business Research, University of Cambridge.

Cosh, A. and Hughes, A. (2000) *British Enterprise in Transition: Growth, Innovation and Public Policy in the Small and Medium Sized Enterprise Sector 1994–99*, ESRC Centre for Business Research, University of Cambridge.

Department of Trade and Industry (1996) *Small Firms in Britain Report 1996*.

Department of Trade and Industry (1999) *Small and Medium-sized Enterprises (SME) Statistics for the United Kingdom 1998*, Small Firms Statistical Unit, July.

European Commission (2002) *Observatory of European SMEs 2002/No. 2*.

Hannah, L. and Kay, J. A. (1977) *Concentration in Modern Industry*, Macmillan.

Keeble, D. (1997) Small firms, innovation and regional development in Britain in the 1990s, *Regional Studies*, 31(3), May.

Meeks, G. (1977) *Disappointing Marriage: a study of the gains from merger*. University of Cambridge, Department of Applied Economics, Occasional Paper 51, CUP, Cambridge.

Newbold, A. (1970) *Management and Merger Activity*, Guthstead, Liverpool.

Oakey, R. P., Thwaites, A. T. and Nash, P. A. (1980) The regional distribution of innovative manufacturing establishments in Britain, *Regional Studies*, 14(3).

Prais, S. J. (1976) *The Evolution of Giant Firms in Britain*, CUP, Cambridge.

Singh, A. (1971) *Takeovers*, CUP, Cambridge.

Small Business Service (2002a) *SME – Statistics for the UK 2001*.

Small Business Service (2002b) *SME – Statistics for the UK 2000*.

Storey, D. (1982) *Entrepreneurship and the New Firm*, Croom Helm.

Storey, D. (1994) *Understanding the Small Business Sector*, Routledge, London.

Storey, D., Keasey, K., Watson, R. and Wynarczyk, P. (1987) *The Performance of Small Firms*, Croom Helm.

TUC (2000) *Small Business – Myths and Reality*, March.

Chapter 5

Mergers and acquisitions in the growth of the firm

A well-established maxim suggests that a company must grow if it is to survive. Mergers and acquisitions have become two of the more widely used methods of achieving growth in recent years, accounting for about 50% of the increase in assets and 60% of the increase in industrial concentration. The years 1984–89 and 1994–2000 provided a sustained merger boom greater than that experienced in either 1968 or 1972, in that the *expenditure* on mergers was extremely high compared to the number of mergers involved. This chapter examines the types of merger activity, such as horizontal, vertical, conglomerate and lateral mergers, and the motives for such activity. These include financial motives which may be related to valuations placed on a firm's assets, the desire to increase 'market power' or to secure economies of scale and managerial motives related more to firm growth than to profitability. Trends in merger activity and legislation affecting merger activity are considered in both the UK and the EU. The UK approach to mergers is then contrasted with that of the USA. The chapter concludes with a brief review of recent tendencies to de-merge.

One of the most significant changes in the UK's industrial structure during this century has been the growth of the large-scale firm. For example, the share of the 100 largest private enterprises in manufacturing net output has risen from 22% in 1949 to a maximum of 42% in 1975, before falling back to around 30% by 2000. Most of the growth in size was achieved by acquisition or merger rather than by internal growth.

A *merger* takes place with the mutual agreement of the management of both companies, usually through an exchange of shares of the merging firms with shares of the new legal entity. Additional funds are not usually required for the act of merging, and the new venture often reflects the name of both the companies concerned.

A *takeover* (or acquisition) occurs when the management of Firm A makes a direct offer to the shareholders of Firm B and acquires a controlling interest. Usually the price offered to Firm B shareholders is substantially higher than the current share price on the stock market. In other words, a takeover involves a direct transaction between the management of the acquiring firm and the stockholders of the acquired firm. Takeovers usually require additional funds to be raised by the acquiring firm (Firm A) for the acquisition of the other firm (Firm B), and the identity of the acquired company is often subsumed within that of the purchaser.

Sometimes the distinction between merger and takeover is clear, as when an acquired company has put up a fight to prevent acquisition. However, in the majority of cases the distinction between merger and takeover is difficult to make. Occasionally the situation is complicated by the use of the words 'takeover' and 'merger'. For example, in 1989 the press announced that SmithKline Beckman, the US pharmaceutical company, had 'taken over' the UK company Beecham for £4,509m. However, technically speaking it was a 'merger' because a new company SmithKline Beecham was created which acquired the shares of the two constituent companies to form a new entity.

Four major forms of merger activity can be identified: horizontal integration, vertical integration, the formation of conglomerate mergers, and lateral integration.

Horizontal integration

This occurs when firms combine at the same stage of production, involving similar products or services. During the 1960s over 80% of UK mergers were of the horizontal type, and despite a subsequent fall in this percentage, some 80% of mergers in the late 1990s were still of this type. The British Airways takeover of British Caledonian in 1988, the merger of Royal Insurance and Sun Alliance to form Royal & Sun Alliance in 1996, and Imperial Tobacco's acquisition of the German tobacco firm Reemtsma Cigarettenfabriken in 2002, were all examples of horizontal mergers. Horizontal integration may provide a number of economies at the level of both the plant (productive unit) and the firm (business unit). *Plant economies* may follow from the rationalization made possible by horizontal integration. For instance, production may be concentrated at a smaller number of enlarged plants, permitting the familiar technical economies of greater specialization, the dovetailing of separate processes at higher output,[1] and the application of the 'engineers' rule' whereby material costs increase as the square but capacity as the cube. All these lead to a reduction in cost per unit as the size of plant output increases. *Firm economies* result from the growth in size of the whole enterprise, permitting economies via bulk purchase, the spread of similar administrative costs over greater output, and the cheaper cost of finance, etc.

Vertical integration

This occurs when the firms combine at different stages of production of a common good or service. Only about 5% of UK mergers are of this type. Firms might benefit by being able to exert closer control over quality and delivery of supplies if the vertical integration is 'backward', i.e. towards the source of supply. Factor inputs might also be cheaper, obtained at cost instead of cost + profit. The takeover of Texas Eastern, an oil exploration company, by Enterprise Oil in 1989, serves as an example of backward vertical integration. Of course, vertical integration could be 'forward' – towards the retail outlet. This may give the firm merging 'forward' more control of wholesale or retail pricing policy, and more direct customer contact. An example of forward vertical integration towards the market was the acquisition by the UK publishing company Pearson PLC of National Computer Systems (NCS) in 2000 for £1.6bn. NCS was a US global information service company providing Internet links and curriculum and assessment testing facilities for schools. The takeover allowed Pearson to design integrated educational programmes for schools by providing students with customized learning and assessment testing facilities. It could also use the NCS network to reach both teachers and parents. In this way, Pearson was able to use its NCS subsidiary to sell its existing publishing products while also developing new on-line materials for the educational marketplace.

Vertical integration can often lead to increased control of the market, infringing monopoly legislation. This is undoubtedly one reason why they are so infrequent. Another is the fact that, as Marks and Spencer have shown, it is not necessary to have a controlling interest in suppliers in order to exert effective control over them. Textile suppliers of Marks and Spencer send over 75% of their total output to Marks and Spencer. Marks and Spencer have been able to use this reliance to their own advantage. In return for placing long production runs with these suppliers, Marks and Spencer have been able to restrict supplier profit margins whilst maintaining their viability. Apart from low costs of purchase, Marks and Spencer are also able to insist on frequent batch delivery, cutting stock-holding costs to a minimum.

Conglomerate merger

This refers to the adding of different products to each firm's operations. Diversification into products and areas with which the acquiring firm was not previously directly involved accounted for only 13% of all mergers in the UK in the 1960s. However, by the late 1980s the figure had risen to 34%. The major benefit is the spreading of risk for the firms and shareholders involved. Giant conglomerates like Unilever (with interests in food, detergents, toilet preparations, chemicals, paper, plastics, packaging, animal feeds, transport and tropical plantations – in 75 separate countries) are largely cushioned against any damaging movements which are restricted to particular product

groups or particular countries. The various *firm economies* outlined above may also result from a conglomerate merger. The ability to buy companies relatively cheaply on the stock exchange, and to sell parts of them off at a profit later, became an important reason for conglomerate mergers in the 1980s. The takeovers by Hanson p.l.c. of the Imperial Group, Consolidated Goldfields and the Eastern Group in 1986, 1989 and 1995 respectively provide good examples of the growth of a large conglomerate organization.

Despite these benefits of diversification, the recession of the early 1990s led many firms to revert to more familiar 'core' businesses. As a result, only some 10% of new UK mergers in the 1990s could be classified as conglomerate mergers. For example, the de-merger of Hanson p.l.c. in 1996 produced four businesses with recognizable 'core' activities, namely tobacco, chemicals, building and energy.

Lateral integration

This is sometimes given separate treatment, though in practice it is difficult to distinguish from a conglomerate merger. The term 'lateral integration' is often used when the firms which combine are involved in different products, but in products which have *some element of commonality*. This might be in terms of factor input, such as requiring similar labour skills, capital equipment or raw materials; or it might be in terms of product outlet. The Swiss company TetraLaval's offer for the French company Sidel in 2001 (which was finally cleared by the EU competition authorities in 2002) provides an example of the difficulty of distinguishing the concepts of conglomerate and lateral integration. TetraLaval designs, manufactures and sells packaging for liquid food products as well as manufacturing and marketing equipment for milk and farm products. Sidel designs and sells machines used in the manufacture of plastic bottles and packaging. The European Commission regarded the merger as conglomerate in that the companies operated in different sectors of the market and were to be organized, post merger, into three distinct entities within the TetraLaval Group. However, it was still the case that the merger would resemble a case of lateral integration in that the companies had a commonality of experience in the packaging and container sector.

Economic theory and merger activity

A number of theories have been put forward to explain the underlying motives behind merger activity. However, when these various theories are tested empirically the results have often been inconsistent and contradictory. An interesting survey article on merger activity in 1989 noted that as many as *fourteen* separate motives were frequently cited in support of merger activity (Mueller 1989). Despite these obvious complications, it may be useful at this stage to explain some of the main factors which seem to motivate mergers, if only to understand the complexity of the process.

The value discrepancy hypothesis

This theory is based on a belief that two of the most common characteristics of the industrial world are imperfect information and uncertainty. Together, these help explain why different investors have different expectations of the prospects for a given firm.

The value discrepancy hypothesis suggests that one firm will bid for another only if it places a greater value on the firm than that placed on the firm by its current owners. If Firm B is valued at V_A by Firm A and V_B by Firm B then a takeover of Firm B will only take place if $V_A > V_B +$ costs of acquisition. The difference in valuation arises through Firm A's higher expectations of future profitability, often because A takes account of the improved efficiency with which it believes the future operations of B can be run.

It has been argued that it is in periods when technology, market conditions and share prices are changing most rapidly that past information and experience are of least assistance in estimating future earnings. As a result differences in valuation are likely to occur more often, leading to increased merger activity. The value discrepancy hypothesis would therefore predict high merger activity when technological change is most rapid, and when market and share price conditions are most volatile.

Evidence

Gort's (1969) test of the value discrepancy hypothesis in the USA gives some support, finding a statistically significant relationship between merger rate and the parameters noted above. Interestingly, recent work on mergers and acquisitions has tended to concentrate on the relationship between industry-level shocks (and associated expectational changes) and merger activity, so reminiscent of the Gort hypothesis. For example, one such study (Andrade *et al.* 2001) indicates that mergers which occurred between the 1970s and the 1990s were often the result of industrial shocks triggered by technological innovations (which can create excess capacity and the need for industry rationalization), supply-side shocks (e.g. oil price changes) or industrial deregulation (greater competition). Arguably the UK merger booms of the late nineteenth century, the 1920s, the 1960s, the mid-1980s and the 1990s often occurred during periods characterized by industry-level shocks. However, although the industrial shock theory with its effects on expectations does give some indication of the forces at work in merger activity, it does not always give sufficient insight into the particular reasons behind such merger activity.

The valuation ratio

One factor which may affect the likelihood of takeover is the valuation ratio, as defined below:

$$\text{Valuation ratio} = \frac{\text{market value}}{\text{asset value}}$$
$$= \frac{\text{no. of shares} \times \text{share price}}{\text{book value of assets}}$$

If a company is 'undervalued' because its share price is low compared to the value of its assets, then it becomes a prime target for the 'asset stripper'. If a company attempts to grow rapidly it will tend to retain a high proportion of profits for reinvestment, with less profit therefore available for distribution to shareholders. The consequence may be a low share price, reducing the market value of the firm in relation to the book value of its assets, i.e. reducing the valuation ratio. It has been argued that a high valuation ratio will deter takeovers, whilst a low valuation ratio will increase the vulnerability of the firm to takeover. In the early 1980s, for example, the property company British Land purchased Dorothy Perkins, the womenswear chain, because its market value was seen as being low in relation to the value of its assets (prime high street sites). After stripping out all the freehold properties for resale, the remainder of the chain was sold to the Burton Group.

In recent years the asset value of some companies has been seriously underestimated for other reasons. For example, many companies have taken years to build up brand names which are therefore worth a great amount of money; but it is often the case that these are *not* given a money value and are thus not included in the asset value of the company. As a result, if the market value of a company is already low in relation to the book value of its assets, then the acquirer gets a double bonus. One reason why Nestlé was prepared to bid £2.5bn (regarded as a 'high' bid, in relation to its book value) for Rowntree Mackintosh in 1988 was to acquire the 'value' of its consumer brands cheaply, because they were not shown on the balance sheet. Finally, it is interesting to note that when the valuation ratio is low and a company would appear to be a 'bargain', a takeover may originate from *within* the company; in this case it is referred to as a management buyout (MBO).

Evidence

Kuehn (1975), in his study of over 3,500 companies in the UK (88% of companies quoted on the Stock Exchange) between 1957 and 1969, found that those firms which maintained a high valuation ratio were much less susceptible to takeover. Figure 5.1 indicates

this inverse relation between valuation ratio and the probability of acquisition. The suggestion is that potential raiders are deterred by the high price to be paid, reflecting a more realistic market valuation of the potential victims' assets. However, the valuation ratio may not be as important as Kuehn's study implies. For example Singh (1971), in a study of takeovers in five UK industries (which included food, drink and electrical engineering industries) between 1955 and 1960, found that a relatively high valuation ratio may not always guarantee protection against takeover. An even stronger conclusion against the valuation ratio hypothesis was drawn by Newbold (1970), when he compared the valuation ratios of 'victim' firms with those of the 'bidding' firms during the merger period of 1967 and 1968. His conclusion was that the valuation ratio of actual 'victim' firms exceeded the average for the industry in 38 cases but was below the average in only 26 cases. In other words, a high valuation ratio did not seem to deter takeover activity. Levine and Aaronovitch (1981) came to a similar conclusion in their study of 109 mergers in manufacturing and services, noting that as many as 14% of the successful 'bidding' firms had a valuation ratio below 1, which one might have expected to result in their becoming 'victim' firms.

Some confirmation of the view that a high valuation ratio may not deter takeover activity has come from a survey of merger activity in the US manufacturing and mining sectors, between 1940 and 1985. This survey related merger activity to a measure called the Tobin q. This measure is similar to the valuation ratio explained above, except that the market value of a company is measured against the 'replacement value' of the company's assets. The study found a *positive* relationship between mergers and the Tobin q, i.e. a high Tobin q or valuation ratio was associated with a high level of merger activity – the reverse of the more usually accepted hypothesis (Golbe and White 1988).

The market power theory

The main motive behind merger activity may often be to increase monopoly control of the environment in which the firm operates. Increased market power may help the firm to withstand adverse economic conditions, and increase long-term profitability.

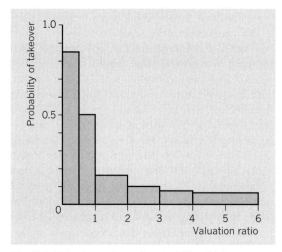

Fig. 5.1 Valuation ratio and probability of takeover.

Three situations are particularly likely to induce merger activity aimed at increasing market power:

1 Where a fall in demand results in excess capacity and the danger of price-cutting competition. In this situation firms may merge in order to secure a better vantage point from which to rationalize the industry.

2 Where international competition threatens increased penetration of the domestic market by foreign firms. Mergers in electronics, computers and engineering have in the past produced combines large enough to fight off such foreign competition.

3 Where a tightening of legislation makes many types of linkages between companies illegal. Firms have in the past adopted many practices which involved collusion in order to control markets. Since restrictive practices legislation has made many of these practices illegal between companies, merger, by 'internalizing' the practices, has allowed them to continue.

For these reasons merger activity may take place to increase a firm's market power. However, the very act of merging usually increases company size, both in absolute terms and in relation to other firms. It is clear, therefore, that increased size will be both a by-product of the quest for increased market power, and itself a cause of increased market power.

Evidence

Newbold (1970), in his study of 38 mergers between 1967 and 1968, found that the most frequent reason cited by managers for merger activity was risk reduction (48% of all mergers), as firms sought to control markets along the lines of market power theory. These conclusions were substantiated in a study by Cowling *et al.* (1980) of nine major UK mergers, which concluded that the mergers did generate elements of market power, often to the detriment of consumers. Further support for this view has come from a study of UK merger trends across 200 industry sectors, ranging from pharmaceuticals to road haulage, which showed that merger activity over the period 1991–95 was closely related to industry concentration. Industries with lower concentration ratios tended to be the industries with the highest rates of merger activity as incumbent firms tried to grow larger in order to increase their market power (Schoenberg and Reeves 1999). Similarly, a global

research report covering merger deals involving 107 companies worldwide by the accountancy firm KPMG found that as many as 54% of the executives concerned stated that mergers and acquisitions were aimed at gaining new market share, or protecting existing market share (KPMG 1999).

There is also fragmentary evidence that the termination of restrictive agreements encouraged some firms to combine formally. Elliot and Gribbin (1977) found that the five-firm concentration ratio increased faster in industries in which restrictive practices had been terminated than in those in which no such practices existed.

Empirical work does suggest that an increase in the size of a firm raises its market power. For example, Whittington (1980) found that large firms often experience less variability in their profits than small firms, indicating that large firms may be less susceptible to changing economic circumstances as a result of their greater market power. Studies by Aaronovitch and Sawyer (1975) also show that large firms are less likely to be taken over than small or medium-sized ones, and that a given percentage increase in size for an already large firm reduces the probability of takeover much more than the same percentage increase for a small to medium-size firm. It would appear that size, stability and market power are closely interrelated.

It may also be that profitability and market power are closely related. This would seem to be the implication of the results of a survey into 146 out of the top 500 UK firms. A questionnaire was sent to these companies asking for the responses of their respective Chief Executive Officers to a number of questions relating to merger activity (Ingham *et al.* 1992). From the responses to questions relating to the motives for mergers, the survey found that the single most important reason for mergers and acquisitions was the expectation of increased profitability. This was closely followed by the second most important reason – the pursuit of market power. It is therefore possible that the desire for market power and the profit motive are highly interrelated, or at least are thought to be so by significant 'players' in the market.

Nevertheless the *actual results* of merger activity provide little evidence that any increase in market power is effective in raising firm profitability. For example, Ravenscraft and Scherer (1987) conducted a detailed analysis of 6,000 acquisitions in the US between 1950 and 1976 and revealed that post-merger profitability was generally disappointing, with the profitability of around two-thirds of the merged companies *below* the average achieved prior to merger. Interestingly, the report by KPMG noted above (KPMG 1999) also found that only 17% of the mergers studied had resulted in an increase in shareholder value, with as many as 53% of the deals actually destroying shareholder value.

Economies of scale

It is often argued that the achievement of lower average costs (and thereby higher profits) through an increase in the scale of operation is the main motive for merger activity. As we noted in the earlier part of this chapter, such economies can be at two levels: first, at the level of the plant, the production unit, including the familiar technical economies of specialization, dovetailing of processes, engineers' rule, etc.; and second, at the level of the firm, the business unit, including research, marketing, administrative, managerial and financial economies. To these plant- and firm-level economies we might add the 'synergy' effect of merger, the so-called '2 + 2 > 4' effect, whereby merger increases the efficiency of the combined firm by more than the sum of its parts. Synergy could result from combining complementary activities as, for example, when one firm has a strong R & D team whilst another firm has more effective production control personnel.

Evidence

Economies of scale seem less important in merger activity than is traditionally supposed. Prais (1976) points out that technical economies, through increased plant size, have played only a small part in the growth of large firms. For instance, the growth of the 100 largest plants (production units) in net output has been much slower than the growth of the 100 largest firms (business units) in net output. Firms seem to grow not so much by expanding plant size to reap technical economies, but by acquiring more plants. Of course, evidence that firms seek to grow as an enterprise or business unit, through adding extra plants, could still be linked to securing 'firm level' economies of scale.

Newbold (1970), however, found that only 18% of firms surveyed admitted to any motive that could be linked to plant- or firm-level economies of scale.

Cowling *et al.* (1980) concluded in similar vein that the 'efficiency gains' (economies of scale) from mergers were difficult to identify in the firms examined. Finally, Whittington (1980) found profitability to be independent of firm size, and we have already noted that the study by Ravenscraft and Scherer (1987) noted a decline in the profitability of two-thirds of the now larger combined firms in the period following the mergers. This might also seem to argue against any significant economies of scale, otherwise larger firms, with much lower costs, might be expected to secure higher profits. Similarly, research carried out on the performance of 11 major media companies which had been actively involved in mergers during the period up to 2000 found no significant correlation between firm size (and thus the benefits of economies of scale and scope) and company performance (Peltier 2002).

Although we cannot test the synergy effect directly, there is case evidence that it plays a part in encouraging merger activity. Nevertheless, the hopes of substantial benefits through this effect are not always realized. Unsuccessful attempts at pursuing synergy are widespread, notably by companies who mistakenly believe that they have the management and marketing expertise to turn around loss-making companies into efficient, profitable ventures. Indeed the survey by Ingham *et al.* (1992), mentioned earlier, placed the 'pursuit of marketing economies of scale' as the third most important reason for mergers. However, this reason was given rather infrequently, i.e. it was ranked well behind 'profitability' and 'market power'. Again, although recent EU annual reports on competition policy seem to indicate that the synergies to be derived from 'combining complementary activities' are an important motive for merger activity, this reason was also ranked well behind 'strengthening of market share' and 'expansion'.

Managerial theories

In all the theories considered so far, the underlying principle in merger activity is, in one way or another, the pursuit of profit. For example, market power theory suggests that through control of the firm's environment, the prospects of profit, at least in the long run, are improved. Economies of scale theory concentrates on raising profit through the reduction of cost. Managerial theories, on the other hand (see also Chapter 3), lay greater stress on non-profit motives.

With the rise of the public limited company there has been a progressive divorce between ownership by shareholders and control by management. This has given managers greater discretion in control of the company, and therefore in merger policy. The suggestion by Marris, Williamson and others is that a prime objective of managers is growth of the firm, rather than absolute size. In these theories the growth of the firm raises managerial utility by bringing higher salaries, power, status, and job security to managers. Managers may therefore be more interested in the rate of growth of the firm than in its profit performance.

Managerial theories would suggest that fast-growing firms, having already adopted a growth-maximization approach, are the ones most likely to be involved in merger activity. These theories would also suggest that fast-growing firms will give higher remuneration to managers, and will raise job security by being less prone to takeover.

Evidence

It does appear that it is the fast-growing firms that are mainly involved in merger activity. For example, Singh (1971, 1975) noted that the acquiring firms had a significantly higher growth rate than the acquired firms, and possessed many of the other attributes of a growth maximizer, such as a higher retention ratio (see Chapter 3), higher gearing and less liquidity (Chapter 2). Similarly Aaronovitch and Sawyer (1975) reported that in the period before an acquisition, the acquiring firm generally grew much faster than the acquired firm. Ravenscraft and Scherer (1987) in their major study of 6,000 US acquisitions concluded that the pursuit of growth rather than profit was a key factor in explaining merger activity.

As regards higher managerial remuneration through growth, Firth (1980) found a significant increase in the salaries of directors of the acquiring company after merger. The chairman's salary increased by an average of 33% in the two years following merger, compared to only 20% for the control group of companies not engaged in merger activity. More recent research carried out between 1985 and 1990 on a sample of 170 UK firms (Conyon and Gregg 1994) showed that the remuneration of the top director was closely related to sales growth. The research also showed that company sales growth through acquisition raised the top

directors' remuneration significantly above that which could have been achieved by internal or organic growth. The research by Schoenberg and Reeves (1999) into UK merger activity in some 200 industrial sectors, referred to above, also found that the frequency of industry-wide mergers was closely related to the growth of sales revenue. This is in line with the growth and managerial utility motives for mergers suggested by Marris and Williamson, respectively.

Managerial theories place less stress on profit performance, and more on growth of the firm. The fact that, at least in the short run, the profit level often deteriorates for the acquiring firms is taken by some as further evidence in support of the managerial approach. A number of studies have showed that firms involved in mergers tended to have lower profitability levels than non-merging firms; in studies by Meeks (1977), Kumar (1985), Cosh *et al.* (1985) and Ravenscraft and Scherer (1987), mergers were found to have negative effects on profitability.

We have already noted that large firms, whilst not necessarily the most profitable (Meeks and Whittington 1975), were less likely to be taken over than small to medium-sized firms. In fact, any given percentage increase in size was much more significant in reducing the probability of takeover for the large firm than it was for the small to medium-sized firm (Aaronovitch and Sawyer 1975; Singh 1975). The small to medium-sized firm has therefore an incentive to become large, and the large firm still larger, if takeovers are to be resisted. Further evidence in support of the suggestion that small to medium-sized firms are active in acquisitions came from a survey of some 2,000 firms in UK manufacturing industry between 1960 and 1976 (Kumar 1985). The study concluded that there was indeed a tendency for firm growth through acquisitions to be *negatively* related to firm size. Once firms become large they appear to be more 'stable' and less prone to takeover. Such evidence is consistent with managerial theories which stress the importance of growth as a means of enhancing job security for managers. However, it should be noted that the merger boom of the late 1980s showed that even large firms were no longer safe from takeovers; this was in part due to firms now having easier access to the finance required for takeover activity.

The evidence clearly points away from traditional economies of scale, whether at the level of 'plant' or 'firm', as the motive for merger. Survival of the firm, and control of its environment, seems to be at the heart of most merger activity. This often implies the sacrifice of profit, at least in the short run. Such an observation is consistent with market power and managerial theories, both of which concentrate on objectives other than short-run profit (see also Chapter 3).

Mergers and the public interest

Although there is clearly much debate about the motivation behind merger activity, there is a broad consensus that the resulting growth in firm size will have implications for the 'public interest'. Before a more detailed investigation into the legislation and institutions involved in regulating merger activity in the UK, EU and US, it may be helpful to consider the potential impacts of a merger on economic efficiency and economic welfare, which are two key elements in any definition of the 'public interest'.

Economic efficiency

The idea of economic efficiency may usefully be broken down into two separate elements.

■ *Productive efficiency*. This involves using the most efficient combination of resources to produce a *given level* of output. Only when the firm is producing a given level of output with the *least-cost* methods of production available do we regard it as having achieved 'productive efficiency'.

■ *Allocative efficiency*. This is often taken to mean setting a price which corresponds to the marginal cost of production. The idea here is that consumers pay firms exactly what it costs them to produce the last (marginal) unit of output; such a pricing strategy can be shown to be a key condition in achieving a so-called 'Pareto optimum' resource allocation, where it is no longer possible to make someone better off without making someone else worse off. Any deviation of price *away from* marginal cost is then seen as resulting in 'allocative inefficiency'.

What may pose problems for policy makers is that the impacts of proposed mergers may move these two

aspects of economic efficiency in *opposite directions*. For example, economies of scale may result from the merger having increased firm size, with a lower cost of producing any given output thereby improving productive efficiency. However, the greater market power associated with increased size may give the enlarged firm new opportunities to raise price above (or still further above) its costs of production, including marginal costs, thereby reducing allocative efficiency.

We may need to balance the gain in productive efficiency against the loss in allocative efficiency to get a better idea of the overall impact of the merger on the 'public interest'.

Economic welfare

Economic welfare is a branch of economics which often involves ideas of consumer surplus and producer surplus.

■ *Consumer surplus*. This is the benefit to consumers of being willing to pay *more* for a product than they actually have to pay in terms of the going market price. It is usually measured by the area underneath the demand (willingness to pay) curve and above the ruling market price. So in Fig. 5.2, if the ruling market price is P and quantity sold Q, then area afd corresponds to the 'consumer surplus', in the sense that consumers are willing to pay $OafQ$ for Q units, but only have to pay $OdfQ$ (price × quantity), giving a consumer surplus of afd.

■ *Producer surplus*. This is the benefit to producers of receiving a price *higher* than the price they actually needed to get them to supply the product. In Fig. 5.2 we shall assume for simplicity that the MC curve is the firm's supply curve (you should know that this actually *is* the case in a perfectly competitive industry!). So in Fig. 5.2, if the ruling market price is P and the quantity sold Q, then area $dfig$ corresponds to the 'producer surplus', in the sense that producers are willing to supply Q units at a price of g but actually receive a price of P, giving them a producer surplus of dg per unit, and a total producer's surplus of $dfig$ on all Q units sold.

Figure 5.2 is useful in illustrating the fact that a proposed merger might move productive and allocative

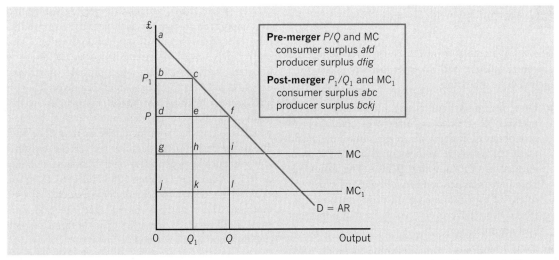

Fig. 5.2 Mergers, economic efficiency and economic welfare. Welfare gain (*ghkj*) and welfare loss (*cflk*) from merger.

efficiencies in opposite directions. For simplicity we assume the curves displayed to be linear, and the firm to be at an initial price/quantity equilibrium of P/Q with marginal cost MC (for a profit-maximizing firm MR would have intersected MC at point i). Now suppose that the merger/takeover results in the (enlarged) firm[2] using its market power to raise price from P to P_1, cutting output from Q to Q_1, *but* that at the same time the newly available scale economies cut costs so that MC shifts downwards to MC_1.

Clearly we have to balance a loss of allocative efficiency against a gain in productive efficiency in order to assess the overall impact on the 'public interest'. To do this we can usefully return to the idea of economic welfare, and the associated consumer and producer surpluses.

If we regard the total welfare resulting from a resource allocation as being the sum of the consumer surplus and the producer surplus, we have:

- Pre-merger   *afd* + *dfig*

- Post-merger   *abc* + *bckj*

In terms of total welfare (consumer surplus + producer surplus) we can note the following impacts of the merger:

- Gain of welfare   *ghkj*

- Loss of welfare   *cflk*

The 'gain of welfare' (*ghkj*) represents the improvement in productive efficiency from the merger, as the Q_1 units still produced require fewer resources than before, now that the scale economies have reduced costs (shifting MC down to MC_1).

The 'loss of welfare' (*cflk*) represents the deterioration in allocative efficiency from the merger; price has risen (P to P_1) and marginal costs have fallen (MC to MC_1), further increasing the gap between price and marginal cost. As a result of the price rise from P to P_1, output has fallen from Q to Q_1. This loss of output has reduced economic welfare, since society's willingness to pay for these lost $Q - Q_1$ units (the area under the demand curve from $Q - Q_1$, i.e. *cfQQ₁*) exceeds the cost of producing them (the sum of all the marginal costs from $Q - Q_1$, i.e. *klQQ₁*) by *cflk*.

Clearly the overall welfare effect ('public interest') could be positive or negative, depending on whether the welfare gains exceed the welfare losses, or vice versa (in Fig. 5.2 the losses outweigh the gains). No pre-judgement can therefore be made that a merger will, or will not be, in the public interest. As Stewart (1996) notes, everything depends on the extent of any price rise and on the demand and cost curve configurations for any proposed merger. It is in this context that a Competition Commission investigation and other methods of enquiry into *particular* proposals might be regarded as important in deciding whether any merger should proceed or be abandoned.

Merger booms

The most notable features which have tended to galvanize merger and takeover activity have often included the following.

- First, the growth of national and international markets has created circumstances favourable to economies of scale, while at the same time world tariff barriers have been reduced under the guidance of GATT (now the WTO). The result has been fierce competition between nations which has often led to a rationalization of production since larger firms have been seen as having important cost advantages.

- Second, improved communication methods, often involving information/telecommunication technologies, have made it easier for large companies to grow, while the adoption by many companies of a multi-divisional structure has encouraged horizontal mergers.

- Third, there has been a rapid growth in the number and type of financial intermediaries, such as insurance companies and investment trusts. They have begun investing heavily in company equity, thereby providing a ready source of finance for companies who want to issue more shares and then to use the money received to support a takeover bid. At the same time, there has been a dilution of managerial control (see Chapter 3). This 'divorce of ownership from control' has made takeover activity easier because directors now have a less close relationship with the company, and are therefore less committed to its continuing in an unchanged form.

- Fourth, many of the periods of intense merger activity have seen an increase in the 'gearing ratio' of companies, i.e. an increase in the ratio of debt (debenture and bank borrowing) to shares (equity). Loan finance has proven attractive because the interest paid on debentures and loans has been deducted from company profits *before* it is taxed. Therefore companies have had a tax incentive to issue loan stock, the money from which they have then been able to use to mount a takeover bid.

The motives for such intense takeover activity have been varied. For example, many of the 1985–87 mergers were of the *horizontal* type, suggesting that one important motive for such activity was production economies arising from rationalization. This motive may have been strengthened by the desire to integrate technology and to improve marketing expertise in order to increase market power. There is also some evidence that *target* companies in this period tended to be less dependent on debt finance, which suggests that some acquisitions may have been due to the desire of the *acquirer* to increase cashflow and to reduce its dependency on debt finance. A study of 38 UK takeovers between 1985 and 1987 (Manson *et al.* 1994) seemed to provide some evidence of such motives. These authors found that the takeovers studied did produce operating gains in terms of both cashflow and market values.

During this period, mergers were largely financed by share issues. The value of the more dynamic bidder's share would often tend to be higher than the value of the target company's share, giving the bidder the opportunity to exchange the minimum number of its shares for every one of the target company's. This meant that the takeover deal was relatively 'cheap' for the bidder so that its earnings per share (EPS – total earnings/total number of shares) would not fall too much to worry its existing shareholders and the stock market in general. After the stock market crash in late 1987, however, the decrease in share prices and the rise in interest rates meant that takeovers increasingly involved cash deals rather than share issues.

Merger and acquisition activity during 1992–2002 has been triggered by many factors, including merger opportunities in utilities such as electricity and water, and attempts to secure greater market share in the pharmaceutical, telecommunications and finance industries in order to gain scale economies and provide a base for global expansion. Examples of such mergers in the UK utilities sector include the acquisition of the Lattice Group by the National Grid Group for £5.1bn in 2002 to form National Grid Transco plc, a major supplier of electricity and gas. In the telecommunication industry, the takeover of the German company Mannesmann AG by the UK's Vodafone Air Touch plc in 2000 created Europe's largest telecommunication company. In the same year the £120bn merger of UK companies Glaxo Wellcome and SmithKline Beecham to form GlaxoSmithKline resulted in one of the largest pharmaceutical companies in the world.

The control of mergers and acquisitions

We have seen that mergers may be a means of extending market power. We now consider how the UK, the EU and the USA have sought to exercise control over merger activity in order to prevent the abuse of such power.

The UK experience

United Kingdom legislation has been tentative in its approach to merger activity, recognizing the desirable qualities of some monopoly situations created through merger; it therefore seeks to examine each case on its individual merits. The first UK legislation, the Monopolies and Restrictive Practices (Inquiry and Control) Act, dates from 1948 and set up the Monopolies Commission. The power of the 1948 Act was extended to mergers by the Monopolies and Mergers Act of 1965 under which the newly established Monopolies and Mergers Commission (MMC) could now report on situations where a merger resulted in a combined market share of 25% or more of a particular good or service, or involved combined assets of over £30m.

The next major Act having implications for merger activity was the Fair Trading Act 1973, under which the Office of Fair Trading (OFT) was formed with a Director-General of Fair Trading (DGFT) as its head. Over the next quarter of a century, the DGFT advised the Secretary of State for Trade and Industry as to which mergers should be referred to the MMC for investigation. However, the Secretary of State could overrule both the DGFT and the MMC if he or she felt that the merger was in the 'public interest', which was nowhere clearly defined. This vague 'public interest' test often led to complaints by business of undue and arbitrary government involvement in the decision-making process as regards permitting or prohibiting merger activity.

Problems with UK merger policy

As already noted, by the 1990s the effectiveness of the MMC and the role of the Secretary of State in merger investigations were increasingly being called into question. For example, the MMC was criticized for lacking both resources and a professional attitude. It had one full-time chairman, three part-time deputy chairmen, 31 part-time commissioners and only 100 full-time staff. Many argued that the MMC was often 'outgunned' by lawyers representing firms under investigation and, with its scarce resources, was unable to properly scrutinize many potentially important merger proposals. For example, between 1950 and 1995 the MMC had investigated only 171 merger cases.

The traditional UK approach to mergers was based on the principle that they can be forbidden by the Secretary of State if they operate against the public interest. The vagueness of the term 'public interest', together with the differing approaches to mergers of individual Secretaries of State, led to what many saw as inconsistent decision-making in merger policy over time. For example, the Labour government had recommended in 1978 that the MMC should recognize the benefits as well as the costs of merger activity in their deliberations. However, the following Conservative government issued guidelines in 1984 suggesting that the MMC should concentrate on 'loss of competition' as the most important aspect when assessing mergers. By 1992, the Conservative government's approach to mergers seems to have shifted ground yet again, with the DTI placing greater emphasis on creating 'national champions' capable of competing in international markets – thereby supporting larger mergers even when some 'loss of competition' was inevitable. Yet by 1996, Ian Laing, the new Conservative Secretary of State for Trade and Industry, announced that 'fostering competition' rather than the creation of national champions should be the guideline for assessing merger policy. This followed the refusal of the minister to allow either National Power's £2.8bn bid for Southern Electric or PowerGen's £1.9bn bid for Midland Electricity to proceed. These ever-shifting approaches to merger activity indicate some degree of strategic confusion in the implementation of merger policy.

In addition to the problems noted above, there were also increasing complications as regards the power of the Secretary of State during merger references. For example, the Secretary of State had the power to overrule recommendations from both the DGFT and the MMC if he or she was so minded. For example, in 1993 the then Secretary of State at the DTI, Michael Heseltine, rejected the recommendation of the DGFT to refer both GEC's acquisition of Philips' infra-red components business and the hostile bid by Airtours for Owners Abroad, to the MMC. The Secretary of State argued that the mergers might help rationalize the industry and create strong competitive companies so that, despite the competition-based concerns of the DGFT, he declined to refer these proposed mergers to the MMC for further scrutiny. Again, in August 1998 Margaret Beckett, the Secretary of State for Trade and Industry, overruled the recommendation of the MMC in the case of First Group, a transport company which had made a £96m acquisition of Glasgow-based SB Holdings. The MMC believed that First Group should be allowed to acquire SB Holdings only if it agreed to sell a division of its Scottish operations to decrease the company's market power. However, the Secretary of State allowed the merger to proceed without any such restriction on the grounds that a rival company, Stagecoach, had entered the Glasgow bus market, thus creating sufficient competitive conditions.

These inconsistencies in merger policy continued even after the replacement of the MMC by the Competition Commission (CC) under the provisions of the 1998 Competition Act. Again there was criticism of inadequate resources in the CC, which had a relatively small staff of 78 persons and a grant income of only £5.9m, the concern being that it might become a 'toothless tiger', used only for appeals against merger decisions rather than itself being a key decision taker. A series of consultation documents were published between 1999 and 2001 culminating in the Enterprise Act of 2002, which received the Royal Assent on November 2002 and was brought into force, in stages, from the spring of 2003 onwards.

Current merger legislation: Enterprise Act 2002

The Enterprise Act 2002 overhauled UK competition law and, amongst other things, restated the UK merger control framework by introducing significant amendments to previous legislation in this area. The main aspects of current merger legislation now include the following.

1 **Relevant merger situation**. Under the Act, a 'relevant merger situation' to which the new procedures potentially apply is one in which *three* criteria are met:

   ■ First, that the two or more enterprises involved in the merger cease to be distinct as a result of the merger.

   ■ Second, that the merger must not have taken place, or have taken place not more than four months before the reference is made to the OFT.

   ■ Third, *either* that the enterprise being taken over has a UK turnover exceeding £70m (the 'turnover test') *or* that the merged enterprises together supply, or acquire, at least 25% of all those particular goods or services supplied in the UK or a substantial part of the UK (the 'share of supply' test). It is implicit in this criterion that at least one enterprise must trade within the UK.

2 **Competition authorities evaluation test**. Under the Act, for a 'relevant merger situation', the test which the OFT will apply when evaluating whether a merger should be referred to the CC is whether the merger or proposed merger has resulted, or may be expected to result, in a substantial 'lessening of competition' within the relevant market or markets in the UK. 'Lessening of competition' would generally mean a situation where product choice would be reduced, prices raised, or product quality or innovation reduced as the result of merger activity. However, the OFT might decide *not* to make a reference to the CC if it believes that customer benefits (e.g. higher choice, lower prices, higher quality or innovation) resulting from the merger outweigh the substantial lessening of competition noted above. Similarly, the CC when considering a merger in more depth will also weigh the 'lessening of competition' effect against the 'public benefits effect' before making its final decision.

3 **Competition authorities**. Under the Act, the OFT was established as an independent statutory body and the post of DGFT was abolished.

   ■ As a result of its new statutory power the OFT can require the provision of information and documents, enter premises under warrant, and seize material. It has explicit duties to keep markets under review and to promote competition. It publishes an annual report on its activities and performance which is laid before Parliament. It also has the functions of advising the Secretary of State on mergers which might fall under the scope of the 'public interest'.

   ■ The CC, which was already an independent statutory body, continues its in-depth investigation of any merger cases referred to it by the OFT or less frequently by the Secretary of State.

The CC determines the outcome of such cases and reports its decision to the Secretary of State.

■ The Secretary of State for Trade and Industry has retained power to make decisions for mergers involving newspaper transfers and in certain public interest cases such as those that deal with national security. Apart from these specified types of merger situations, the main decisions relating to mergers are now dealt with by the OFT and CC without resort to the Secretary of State.

■ There is also a new appeals mechanism giving a right to those parties involved in the merger to apply to the Competition Appeal Tribunal (CAT) for a statutory judicial review of a decision of the OFT, CC or the Secretary of State. There is also a further right of appeal (on a point of law only) to the Court of Appeal.

Putting merger policy into practice

To understand the main procedures for merger investigation, a brief account will be given here of the process. When the OFT is made aware of the 'relevant merger situation', it may choose to undertake a 'first stage' investigation. It might seek to assess the potential effect of the merger on market structure. For example, if it is a horizontal-type merger then market shares, concentration ratios or the Herfindahl–Hirschman Index (see below, page 92) might be used as initial indicators of potential competition concerns. This market structure assessment could be followed by an examination of whether the entry of new firms into the market is easy or difficult and whether any 'lessening of competition' is likely to occur. The OFT will then make its own decision on the case without reference to the Secretary of State. The OFT will give one of three possible decisions:

■ First, the merger is given an unconditional clearance.

■ Second, the merger is given a clearance only if the parties agree to modify their uncompetitive behaviour or decrease their market power.

■ Third, the merger may turn out to be serious enough to refer it directly to the CC for a 'second-stage' investigation. At this point the Secretary of State can intervene in the proceedings, but under the new regime this intervention can be done only in *very specific* circumstances involving mergers with media, national security or other narrowly specified implications.

If the OFT refers the merger to the CC, the Commission will consider the evidence of the OFT but will also make its own in-depth report on the merger. After consideration of the evidence and basing its views on both the 'lessening of competition' and 'customer benefits criteria', the CC will recommend that one of three possible actions be taken: (i) an unconditional clearance, or (ii) a clearance subject to conditions proposed by the CC, or (iii) an outright prohibition. If the CC recommends conditional clearance then the companies involved may be asked to divest some of their assets or to ensure in some specified way that competition is maintained (e.g. giving licences to their competitors). Again, the Secretary of State may intervene only in very limited circumstances as in the media, national security or other specified issues (e.g. if one of the parties to the merger is a government contractor). If the decision of the CC is to prohibit the merger, the parties can appeal to the CAT.

In essence, the Enterprise Act has *depersonalized* competition authority by abolishing the post of DGFT. It has also improved the overall *predictability* of the mergers investigation procedure by de-politicizing the process of merger control. It has done this by severely curtailing the involvement of the Secretary of State and by giving expert independent bodies (the OFT and CC) more power. Basically, the OFT and CC have been transformed from essentially advisory bodies to the Secretary of State to independent bodies with their own decision-making powers. The Act has also *clarified* merger control policy by introducing the 'lessening of competition' test in place of the old 'public interest' test and by allowing potential benefits (including public benefits) to be considered. In addition, the Act made the mergers regime more *transparent* by obliging both the OFT and the CC to consult fully with companies involved in mergers and provide the parties involved with their provisional findings. Finally, the new mergers regime seeks to introduce a *fairness* criterion in that companies now have the right of appeal to the CAT.

Self-regulatory controls

As well as the legal controls noted above, there are also self-regulatory controls on UK merger activity which are imposed by the Stock Exchange and the Panel on Takeovers and Mergers, both of which are responsible to the *Council for the Securities Industry*. The London Stock Exchange imposes self-regulatory controls on all companies which are listed on the Stock Exchange or on the Alternative Investment Market (AIM). These rules were developed mainly in order to keep all shareholders adequately informed of certain important changes in share ownership. For example, the quotations department of the Stock Exchange must be given certain information about listed companies which acquire more than 5% of the assets of another company or which divest more than 5% of their own assets. If the figure is between 5% and 15%, only the Stock Exchange and the press need be notified; but if the figure rises to 15% or more, the Department of Trade and Industry, the shareholders and the press should be notified. The Council for the Securities Industry also issues a 'City Code on Takeovers and Mergers'. This is administered by the Panel on Takeovers and Mergers and relates to both listed and unlisted companies but not to private companies. One function of the Code is to make sure that each shareholder is treated equally during takeover bids. For example, an offer given to some shareholders early in a bid, and which they have accepted, must also be left open to all other shareholders. Another function of the Code is to set out 'rules' for the conduct of companies during a takeover, covering items such as 'insider dealing' and other complicated aspects of such bids. If companies fail to follow these rules, the Council can refuse them the facilities of the securities market.

Insider dealing

On a wider issue, the whole question of 'insider dealing' came to the fore during this period. This type of dealing occurs when company shares are bought by those who have special privileged information about the future of the company, e.g. the possibility of an imminent takeover. By buying shares *before* a takeover announcement, for example, they can make huge gains as share prices rise when the excitement of the takeover begins. Basically, the UK has some of the most advanced insider-dealing regulations in the world.

The latest UK legislation regulating insider dealing came into force in 1994 and extended the scope of the main Companies Securities (Insider Dealing) Act of 1985. The new provisions were contained in the 1993 Criminal Justice Act and followed a requirement to implement an EU Directive on the subject. Under the new law it is a criminal offence for an individual who has inside information to deal in price affected securities (such as shares, debt securities, gilts and derivatives whose price movements could be sensitive to certain information), or to encourage another person

to deal. It is also a criminal offence for such an individual to disclose the information to another person, other than as part of his or her professional work. The dealing in question must be either on a regulated market (basically all EU primary and secondary markets) or off-market but involving professional intermediaries who deal in securities.

The new legislation expands the scope of the 1985 Act by widening the definition of who can be considered an 'insider' and by extending, for the first time, the definition of the securities covered to derivative products. The definition of dealing has been widened to include subscribing for shares (as well as the buying and selling of shares), thus making the legislation applicable to underwriting transactions. Also the territorial scope of the legislation was extended to most EU markets rather than only UK markets and the burden of proof was shifted from the prosecution to the defence. Whether the legislation achieves its main aim of making convictions for insider dealing easier remains to be seen, especially since insider dealing is a criminal offence, so that the amount of proof needed for conviction is substantial, leading to few being convicted. For example, in 1995 the Stock Exchange investigated 1,500 unusual share trading operations but only 43 were referred to the prosecuting authority. A city 'think tank' report in 1996 recommended that to increase the number of convictions, insider dealing should be made a *civil* offence. This would mean that a lower burden of proof would then be required for conviction and those harmed by insider dealing would be able to recover damages.

The EU experience

Many European countries have long histories of state intervention in markets so it is hardly surprising that the European Commission accepts the case for intervention by member governments. Apart from agriculture, competition is the only area in which the EU has been able to implement effectively a common policy across member countries. The Commission can intervene to control the behaviour of monopolists, and to increase the degree of competition, through authority derived directly from the Treaty of Rome:

1 Article 81 prohibits agreements between enterprises which result in the restriction of competition (notably relating to price-fixing, market-sharing,

production limitations and other restrictive practices). This article refers to any agreement affecting trade between member states and therefore applies to a large number of British industries.

2   Article 82 prohibits a dominant firm, or group of firms, from using their market power to exploit consumers.

3   Articles 87 and 88 prohibit government subsidies to industries or individual firms which will distort, or threaten to distort, competition.

Mergers and EU industry

A good indicator of the nature and intensity of merger and acquisition activity in the EU can be gauged by a brief analysis of mergers and acquisitions which were notified to the European Commission between 1990 and 2002 and were deemed by the European Commission as having the potential to exercise 'unacceptable power' within the EU. Although they do not represent the total number of mergers and acquisitions actually occurring in the EU, they do reflect merger activity involving the most important companies operating in the EU. From Table 5.1 we can see that 2,169 mergers were notified to the EU between 1990 and 2002 for preliminary investigation as to whether their likely impacts came under the scope of EU rules on merger activity. Some 834 or 38% of the total involved companies located in different member states, while 622 or 29% involved merger activity between EU and non-EU companies. Finally, some 490 or 23% involved mergers between companies

Table 5.1 Merger and acquisition activity: notifications to the EU Commission 1990–2002.

Total number of notified cases	2,169
Borders of operations	
Cross-border: inside EU	834
Cross-border: EU–non EU	622
Cross-border: non-EU–non-EU	73
No cross-border: inside EU	490
No cross-border: outside EU	150
Type of concentration (% of total)	
Joint ventures	45
Acquisition of majority of assets	41
Agreed bid	6
Merger	4
Others	4
Main countries involved in merger activity (% of total)	
Germany	20
UK	14
USA	12
France	11
Netherlands	7
Others	36
Top five sectors involved in merger activity (% of total)	
Chemical and chemical products	9
Telecommunications	8
Financial intermediation	5
Insurance and pension funding	5
Manufacture of motor vehicles	5

Source: Adapted from European Commission (2003) Statistics: European Merger Control 1990 2002, Competition Directorate General.

from the same country in the EU, i.e. 'home' mergers.

The word 'merger' is often used to cover a wider range of different types of concentrative activity. In Table 5.1 we can see that joint ventures and acquisition of the majority of assets account for 86% of notifications, while 'agreed bids' account for only 6% of total activity. We can also see that five countries account for 64% of all merger notifications within the EU, with US companies being the main non-EU country involved. Finally, the top five sectors most active in merger notifications account for a third of all cases. It is interesting to note that they are in the most technologically advanced sectors and in the increasingly competitive service sectors such as finance and insurance.

An interesting strategic view of the merger process has been indicated by surveys of top executives across six of Europe's most actively acquisitive countries (Angwin and Savill 1997). The results showed that the top four reasons for expanding into other countries through acquisitions were, in order:

- the growing similarity between both national and EU markets;

- the ability to find a good strategic fit;

- establishing a market presence overseas ahead of others; and

- obtaining greater growth potential at a lower cost abroad than at home.

The most appropriate *target company* for acquisition was quoted as being a company which has a good strategic fit with the acquirer, is financially healthy, and has a relatively strong market (or market niche) position. Over the last decade corporate mergers have tended to involve the core activities of the merging companies, resulting in more horizontal-type mergers. For example, the purchase by Volkswagen of Rolls-Royce for £430m in 1998 was aimed at strengthening its core activities, with higher volumes permitting the scale economies which might allow more effective competition in world markets, while at the same time improving the strategic fit, since Volkswagen wanted to compete more actively in the luxury car market in which Rolls-Royce had a greater presence.

A number of advantages were cited by the top executives surveyed for using acquisitions rather than joint ventures or other methods of entry into other EU markets, with an important one being that acquisitions were seen as a faster and less risky method of building up a critical mass in another country.

European competition policy has been criticized for its lack of comprehensiveness, but in December 1989 the Council of Ministers agreed for the first time on specific cross-border merger regulations. The criteria for judging whether a merger should be referred to the European Commission covered three aspects. First, the companies concerned must have a combined world turnover of more than €5bn (though for insurance companies the figure was based on total assets rather than turnover). Second, at least two of the companies concerned in the merger must have a Community-wide turnover of at least €250m each. Third, if both parties to the merger have two-thirds of their business in one and the same member state, the merger was to be subject to national and not Community controls.

The Commission must be notified of merger proposals which meet the criteria noted above within one week of the announcement of the bid and it will vet each proposed merger against a concept of 'a dominant position'. Any creation or strengthening of a dominant position will be seen as incompatible with the aims of the Community if it significantly impedes 'effective competition'. The Commission has one month after notification to decide whether to start proceedings and then four months to make a final decision. If a case is being investigated by the Commission it will not also be investigated by national bodies such as the British Monopolies and Mergers Commission, for example. Member states may prevent a merger which has already been permitted by the Community only if it involves public security or some aspects of the media or if competition in the local markets is threatened.

Review of EU merger regulation

A number of reservations were expressed about the 1990 legislation. First, a main aim of the legislation was to introduce the 'one stop shop' which meant that merging companies would be liable to either European *or* national merger control and not both. However, as can be seen above, there were situations where national merger control could override EU control in certain instances so that there may be a 'two stop shop'! Second, it was not clear how the rules would apply to non-EU companies. For example, it was quite possible that two US or Japanese companies each with the required amount of *sales* in the Community, but with no actual Community *presence*, could merge. While such a case would certainly fall within the EU merger rules, it was not clear how seriously the Commission would pursue its powers in such cases. Third, guidelines were also needed on joint ventures.

In March 1998 a number of amendments were made to the scope of EU cross-border merger regulations, in effect increasing the number of mergers which can be referred to the EU Commission. The threshold (turnover) figures noted earlier had been criticized for being set at too high a level, so that only large mergers could be referred *exclusively* to the Commission, thereby meeting the 'one stop shop' principle. Of course, such an approach suited many individual member countries of the EU which did not want to cede to the Commission their own national authority to investigate mergers. However, by 1996 the EU Commission had suggested a 'middle road' whereby the old higher thresholds could remain but in which other thresholds would be introduced to allow more mergers to be dealt with exclusively by the Commission.

The result of these amendments is that the three original criteria for exclusive reference to the Commission remain, but other criteria have been added to cover some mergers which would not be large enough to qualify under the €5bn and €250m rules described earlier. For example, the Commission can now assume exclusive jurisdiction for any merger if the following three new, and rather complicated, conditions *all* hold true: first, if the combined aggregate worldwide turnover of the undertakings concerned exceeds €2.5bn; *and* second, if in each of at least three Member States, the combined aggregate turnover of the undertakings concerned is more than €100m; *and* third, if in each of the same three Member States, the aggregate turnover of each of at least two of the undertakings concerned exceeds €25m. The Commission believes that the new thresholds may result in more companies having the choice of making only one filing to the Commission instead of multiple national filings (i.e. there will now be more 'one stop shop' opportunities). Of course, the difficulty of calculating more turnover figures than before will add to the complexity of the whole process. To date the Commission has handled around 80 merger cases per year since 1991, and the new legislation will perhaps increase this by another eight mergers per year.

As regards joint ventures, the new regulations make a distinction between 'concentrative' joint ventures and 'cooperative' joint ventures, with the new Commission rules applying to the first type (which was seen to concentrate power) but not to the second (which was merely seen as a method to coordinate competitive behaviour). The second type was to be covered by Articles 81 and 82 (formerly Articles 85 and 86) of the Treaty of Rome, as before.

In 2000, a review of the merger approval system was instigated by the EU. By November 2002 it was announced that a package of reforms would be introduced that would take effect from May 2004. One aspect of the reforms includes the retention of the rule that a merger is unlawful if it 'creates or strengthens a dominant position' but also adds an amendment to the merger regulation to include situations where a merger may be deemed unlawful if it creates 'collective dominance' in a market. This situation might occur when a merger results in the formation or strengthening of an oligopolistic market structure within which a few large firms can coordinate their activities to the detriment of consumers. Another aspect of the changes will be the publication of guidelines on mergers dealing with issues such as ease of market entry and efficiency. Finally, a number of other reforms are designed to improve the decision-making process, to base judgements on solid economic analysis and to enhance the opportunities for the views of merging firms to be taken more fully into account.

The US experience

American legislation reflects a much more vigilant attitude towards mergers, dating from the Sherman Anti-Trust Act of 1890. Monopolies were considered illegal from the outset, resulting in a much less flexible approach to the control of monopoly power. Present merger legislation in the US is covered under the Clayton Act (1914), the Celler/Kaufman Act (1950) and the Hart–Scott–Rodino Act (1976), with the laws being enforced by the Federal Department of Justice and the Federal Trade Commission.

Since 1968 US merger guidelines have directed attention to the market power exerted by the four largest companies in any market. The rigidity of using merely the four largest companies (see Fig. 5.3 and the discussion below) for evaluating merger proposals has been extensively criticized, and in June 1982 the US Justice Department issued new proposals. These included establishing a new 'screening' index to alert the Justice Department as to which merger proposals were worthy of closer scrutiny and which should be immediately prohibited or 'nodded through'. That index was to reflect the whole market and not just the four largest firms.

The so-called 'Herfindahl–Hirschman Index' of market concentration was devised for this screening purpose, together with a number of guidelines for policy action. This index is constructed simply as:

$$\sum_{i=1}^{n} (\% \text{ market share})^2$$

for all n companies in the market. Using a squaring procedure places greater emphasis on the large firms in the market. We can illustrate this by first considering an index which adopts an additive procedure. If a simple additive procedure had been used over all n companies:

Market A: Index = $1(70) + 30(1) = 100$
Market B: Index = $4(20) + 20(1) = 100$

Here the markets would be evaluated as equally competitive, yet a strong case could be made for Market B being the more competitive. Using the Herfindahl–Hirschman Index we have:

Market A: Index = $1(70)^2 + 30(1)^2 = 4,930$
Market B: Index = $4(20)^2 + 20(1)^2 = 1,620$

The lower the index, the more competitive the market, so that Market B is deemed more competitive. The index could, in fact, vary in value from 10,000 (i.e. 100^2) for a pure monopoly, to almost zero for a perfectly competitive industry. For example, an industry consisting of 1,000 companies each with a tiny 0.1% share of the market would produce an index value of only 10 (i.e. $1,000 (0.1)^2$).

Once constructed, the interpretation of the index is still, however, subjective. Figure 5.4 illustrates the range of the index and the three zones of index value identified by the US Justice Department for policy purposes. The chosen dividing lines appear somewhat arbitrary, though it is clear from the guidelines that the two extreme zones are viewed in radically different lights. The central zone (1,000–1,800) represents a policy 'grey' area, requiring more detailed scrutiny of the proposed merger. In practice, mergers in this zone will receive approval only if there is evidence of easy entry into the market, freely available substitutes and no collusive arrangements between existing members. The intention in this central zone is to prevent further acquisitions in the market by a market leader, whilst allowing smaller companies to combine more freely. The 'highly concentrated' zone (>1,800)

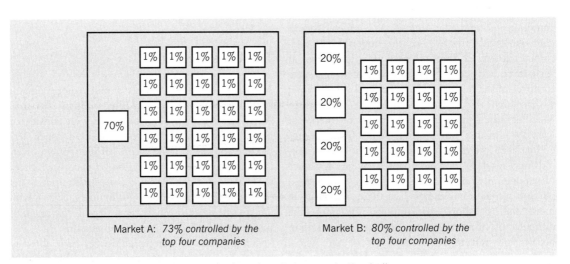

Market A: *73% controlled by the top four companies*

Market B: *80% controlled by the top four companies*

Fig. 5.3 Hypothetical markets in the construction of market concentration indices.

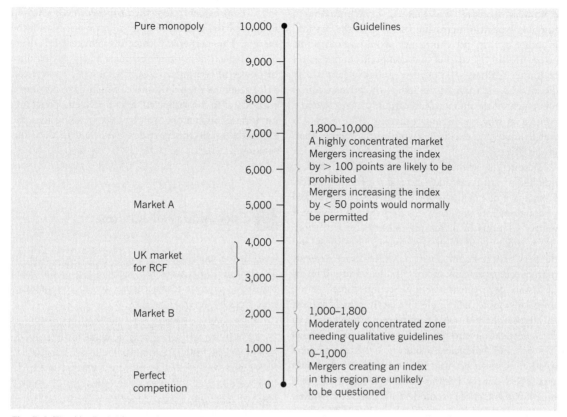

Fig. 5.4 The Herfindahl–Hirschman Index as an instrument of merger policy.

of the index would, for instance, include any market in which two companies have shares of over 30%, so that their potential for growth of market share by further acquisition is slim – even the addition to one of these firms of a further 2% of acquisition would trigger the 100-point condition. Yet in the same market, two smaller companies with market shares of less than 5% each could combine without infringing anti-trust policies. The purchase of just one of the competing companies in hypothetical Market A of Fig. 5.3 by the dominant firm would increase the index to 5,070 (i.e. $1(71)^2 + 29(1)^2$), triggering the 100-point condition in the process and attracting the attentions of the Justice Department.

To see how such guidelines would operate within the UK context, it might be interesting to take the Monopolies and Mergers Commission report on the UK insulation market, published in May 1991. The merger which was investigated was between Morgan Crucible Plc, an international group based in the UK,

and Manville Corporation, a US company. Both companies produced RCF (Refractory Ceramic Fibre) which is used in the steel, petrochemical and aluminium industries as a high temperature heat insulator. The market for RCF in the UK was supplied by the following companies; Carborundum (50%), Morgan Crucible (27%), Kerlane (12%), Manville (9%) and others (2%).

Under the Herfindahl–Hirschman index the industry would already have been regarded as concentrated, with a value of 3,458 (i.e. $1(50)^2 + 1(27)^2 + 1(12)^2 + 1(9)^2 + 1(2)^2$). However, the merger would have increased the market share of the combined group to 36%, so that the index would have risen to 3,944 (i.e. $1(50)^2 + 1(36)^2 + 1(12)^2 + 1(2)^2$). The increase of 486 would have been much higher than the 100-point criterion for attracting the attention of the US Justice Department. Interestingly, this merger was allowed to go ahead in the UK on the basis that Carborundum, the BP-owned company, was continuing to grow, and that the French company, Kerlane, was also increasing its share of the market. In other words, all companies would retain some power in the UK market and competition could still continue. Although US merger policy is not *solely* dictated by the value of the index, the adverse initial movement of the index would certainly have created a context in which subsequent investigation in the US was less likely to decide in favour of the merger than in the UK.

Despite the attractive simplicity of this index, a number of criticisms have been directed towards it. First, the index cannot cope adequately with vertical or conglomerate mergers since they cannot be viewed merely in terms of increasing market concentration. As a result, even with this index, non-horizontal mergers between companies in different industries or market sectors remain an area of uncertainty in terms of Justice Department reaction. Second, there is often no clear way to determine in exactly which market the market share should be measured. For example, in the investigation into the proposed alliance of British Airways and American Airlines in 1998, the carriers themselves asserted that the relevant market was travel between the US and Europe (where their combined market share is modest), while EU officials focused on travel between the US and the UK (where their combined market share is substantial). Third, even where the definition of the market is clear, the relation between changes in the index and changes in market power may be rather obscure. For example, although two firms, Coca-Cola and Pepsi-Cola, control 75% of sales of the US soft drinks industry, such market concentration has in no way diminished the aggressive price competition between these rivals.

Officials have increasingly resorted to a range of indicators in addition to the Herfindahl–Hirschman index in order to evaluate proposed mergers. For example, a key issue may be whether mergers are likely to drive prices higher. In 1997, the proposed merger of Staples and Office Depot, the two superstore office chains, seemed to provide no problem in terms of market concentration as thousands of other US retailers also sell office supplies. However, when the Federal Trade Commission (FTC) used electronic scanners to scrutinize data on sales price and quantities for every item sold, they found a distinctive pattern. Staples' prices were found to be lower in cities where Office Depot had a store compared to cities where Office Depot had none. This was seen by

the FTC as evidence that the proposed merger would in all probability allow Staples to raise prices after the merger. The merger was therefore blocked. It is often technological developments, such as the availability of powerful computer resources and electronic retail price scanners in this example, which have permitted such data to be collected and analysed, providing additional indicators to be used alongside the Herfindahl–Hirschman index as an aid to decision-making.

Corporate restructuring

Two of the most important developments during the 1980s and 1990s were the acceleration in the trend towards corporate restructuring, and the financing of takeovers by 'leveraged debt'.

While larger mergers continued, other forms of restructuring seemed to go against this trend. Restructuring took two directions: the taking apart of diversified conglomerates, and the putting together of focused global companies. There are obvious advantages in creating diversified conglomerates, such as less risk of financial distress and a decreased threat of being taken over. However, in recent years many larger conglomerates have found that they need to concentrate on operating a more limited range of companies or divisions, especially those which can generate cash. For example, Pearson p.l.c., which owns the *Financial Times* and a large number of publishing companies (e.g. Penguin, Pitman, Addison Wesley Longman, Prentice-Hall), sold many of its non-media-related companies during 1997/98, such as those involved with leisure interests (e.g. Madame Tussaud's, Warwick Castle) and financial services, in order to focus on its core, media-related activities. During 2001–02, Kingfisher, the home improvements and electrical/furniture retailer giant, was involved in a large restructuring programme designed to focus on its core activities (B&Q stores) in order to strengthen its market power and financial position in the home improvements sector. For example, in 2001 it de-merged from Woolworth and sold off its Superdrug and Time Retail Finance businesses and went on to acquire the French home improvement company, Castorama, in 2002. Finally, a major phase in Kingfisher's strategy of focusing on the home improvements sector occurred when it de-merged its electrical division (including its Comet stores) in 2003. For similar reasons, Hays, the large UK conglomerate operating in such diverse areas as personnel, commercial, mail and logistics, announced in early 2003 the decision to break up a £1.5bn empire in order to focus on its personnel/recruitment services division.

The restructuring of companies into a relatively more focused area of operation during the 1980s and 1990s was made more possible by the emergence in the UK and abroad of the 'leveraged buyout'. This means that companies obtain a high percentage of the finance they need in order to take over another company by issuing high interest unsecured bonds (Junk Bonds) or by borrowing through high interest unsecured loans (mezzanine finance). The former was a method favoured in the US while the latter form of borrowing is the favoured UK method. This development has had two important repercussions for corporate strategy. First, it has meant that even managers of very large companies can be subject to a takeover bid from a smaller company which has managed to borrow large amounts of debt finance. Being large *per se* is, therefore, no guarantee of safety from being taken over. Second, it has become easier, through leveraged buyouts, to take over a large diversified conglomerate, to sell off parts of it, and then to refocus the company on its 'core' activity. There has been a tendency in recent years for such 'deconglomeration' to be used in order to increase the cashflow of an acquiring company, thereby helping to service the larger debt created by the takeover, while also increasing the competitiveness of the company in its core activities, to the benefit of shareholders.

However, one should also remember that financial factors alone cannot account for all the restructuring and subsequent merger activity in the UK over the last decade. For example, one of the most powerful forces influencing recent restructuring has been the shift towards privatization and deregulation (see Chapter 8). Schoenberg and Reeves (1999) found that the most important single determinant of merger activity in the UK between 1991 and 1995 was the deregulation of industry. Industrial restructuring (in the form of privatization programmes, Single Market developments, etc.) can clearly play an important role in stimulating merger activity.

Conclusion

Corporate restructuring through mergers and acquisitions became increasingly important in the late 1980s and again in the mid- to late 1990s, as had previously been the case during certain periods of the 1950s and 1970s. The 1980s saw the build-up of conglomerate types of mergers, while the 1990s saw a shift towards mergers between companies within the same sector, as companies moved closer to their 'core' activities. Economic theory and statistical analysis do little to suggest that there are substantial benefits from merger activity, although such activity does appear consistent with managerial motives, such as higher status and remuneration.

UK legislation on mergers and takeovers has required some modification in order to tighten controls on anti-competitive arrangements and to bring UK and EU policy into closer alignment. On a more global scale, the chapter has looked at merger regulation in the US and in the EU.

Key points

- Types of merger activity include horizontal, vertical, conglomerate and lateral.

- Suggested reasons for merger include at least one company believing it can add value beyond the costs of merger (value discrepancy hypothesis), a low valuation of share price relative to assets (valuation ratio) and the desire for greater market power.

- Other reasons include the securing of substantial economies of scale at plant and/or enterprise level. The former would be mainly technical economies by rationalization of production into larger plants.

- There is little evidence to suggest that merger activity increases shareholder value but considerable evidence to suggest that merger activity may diminish profitability and shareholder value.

- Mergers which result in 25% or more of the industry's UK supply being in the hands of the merged enterprise may be referred to the Competition Commission (formerly Monopolies and Mergers Commission, MMC). So too may mergers where an enterprise being taken over has a UK turnover exceeding £70m.
- Few mergers were actually referred to the Competition Commission (and previously the MMC) – only 219 between 1950 and 2000. Less than 3% have been disallowed.

- 'Competition factors' seem to be the most important reason for referral to the OFT, Competition Commission (and the previous MMC).
- UK regulations of mergers have moved closer to the EU model, with prohibition and legal redress (e.g. fines) more available as remedies to injured parties.

Now try the self-check questions for this chapter on the Companion Website. You will also find up-to-date facts and case materials.

Note

1. This refers to the fact that a higher level of output may be required before the separate processes involved in producing the good 'dovetail' so that there is no idle capacity. Suppose two processes are required to produce good X. Process A needs a specialized machine which can produce 20 units per hour and Process B needs a machine able to produce 30 units per hour. Only when output has risen to 60 units per hour will there be no idle capacity. For smaller output than 60 at least one machine cannot be fully used.

2. There is an element of 'contrivance' in this analysis. Strictly speaking, the demand curve for the (now) enlarged firm is likely to be further to the right than D(=AR) in Fig. 5.2. We also assume that the now enlarged firm is seeking a non-profit maximizing solution since, if demand *were* unchanged at D(=AR), the existing MR curve would intersect the new (lower) MC↑ curve to the right of Q, implying a lower price and higher quantity.

References and further reading

Aaronovitch, S. and Sawyer, M. (1975) Mergers, growth and concentration, *Oxford Economic Papers*, 27(1), March.
Andrade, G., Mitchell, M. and Stafford, E. (2001) New evidence and perspectives on mergers, *Journal of Economic Perspectives*, 15(2), Spring.

Angwin, D. and Savill, B. (1997) Strategic perspectives on European cross-border acquisitions: a view from top European executives, *European Management Journal*, 15(4), August.
Conyon, M. J. and Gregg, P. (1994) Pay at the

top: a study of the sensitivity of top director remuneration to company specific shocks, *National Institute Economic Review*, **149**, August.

Cosh, A. D., Hughes, A. and Singh, M. S. (1980) The causes and effects of takeovers in the UK: an empirical investigation for the late 1940s at the microeconomic level, in Mueller, D. C. (ed.), *The Determinants and Effects of Mergers*, Gelschlager, Gunn and Hain.

Cosh, A. D., Hughes, A. and Singh, M. S. (1985) *Institutional investment, company performance and mergers: empirical evidence for the UK*. A report to the Office of Fair Trading, mimeo, Cambridge.

Cowling, K., Cubbin, J. and Hall, S. (1980) *Mergers and Economic Performance*, CUP, Cambridge, Ch. 5.

Elliot, D. and Gribbin, J. D. (1977) The abolition of cartels and structural change in the United Kingdom, in Jacquemin, A. P. and de Jong, H. W. (eds), *Welfare Aspects of Industrial Markets*, Leidin Nijhoff, The Hague.

Firth, M. (1979) The profitability of takeovers and mergers, *Economic Journal*, **89**.

Firth, M. (1980) Takeovers, shareholders' return and the theory of the firm, *Economic Journal*, **82**.

Golbe, D. L. and White, L. (1988) A time-saving analysis of mergers and acquisitions in the US economy, in Auerbach, A. J. (ed.), *Corporate Takeovers: Causes and Consequences*, University of Chicago Press.

Gort, M. (1969) An economic disturbance theory of mergers, *Quarterly Journal of Economics*, **82**.

Griffiths, A. (1992) Competition policy and EC industry, in Griffiths, A. (ed.), *European Community Survey*, Longman.

Ingham, H., Kran, I. and Lovestam, A. (1992) Mergers and profitability, *Journal of Management Studies*, **2**, March.

KPMG (1999) Unlocking shareholder values: the keys to success, in *Merger and Acquisition: a Global Research Report*.

Kuehn, D. A. (1975) *Takeovers and the Theory of the Firm*, Macmillan.

Kumar, M. S. (1985) Growth, acquisition and firm size: evidence from the United Kingdom, *Journal of Industrial Economics*, **33**, March.

Levine, P. and Aaronovitch, S. (1981) The financial characteristics of firms and theories of merger activity, *Journal of Industrial Economics*, **30**.

Manson, S., Stark, A. and Thomas, H. (1994) *A cashflow analysis of the operational gains from takeovers*, The Chartered Association of Certified Accountants, Research Report No. 35.

Meeks, G. (1977) *Disappointing Marriage: a study of the gains from merger*. University of Cambridge, Department of Applied Economics, Occasional Paper 51, CUP, Cambridge.

Meeks, G. and Whittington, G. (1975) Director's pay, growth and profitability, *Journal of Industrial Economics*, **24**(1), September.

Mueller, D. C. (1989) Mergers, *International Journal of Industrial Organization*, **7**.

Newbold, A. (1970) *Management and Merger Activity*, Guthstead, Liverpool.

Peltier, S. (2002) Mergers and acquisitions in the media industries: a preliminary study of the impact on performance, ACEI Conference, Rotterdam.

Prais, S. J. (1976) *The Evolution of Giant Firms in Britain*, CUP, Cambridge.

Ravenscraft, D. J. and Scherer, F. M. (1987) *Mergers, Sell-offs and Economic Efficiency*, Brookings Institution, Washington, DC.

Schoenberg, R. and Reeves, R. (1999) What determines acquisition activity within an industry?, *European Management Journal*, **17**(1).

Singh, A. (1971) *Takeovers*, CUP, Cambridge.

Singh, A. (1975) Takeovers, economic natural selection and the theory of the firm: evidence from the post-war United Kingdom experience, *Economic Journal*, **85**, September.

Stewart, G. (1996) Takeovers, *Economic Review*, **14**(1, 2).

Whittington, G. (1980) The profitability and size of UK companies, *Journal of Industrial Economics*, **28**(4), June.

Chapter 6   Oligopoly

In this chapter we first record the growth of market domination by the few, using the most recent statistics on the size distribution of firms, on concentration ratios, and on advertising expenditures. We then consider attempts to explain and predict behaviour in oligopoly markets, closely relating theory to actual practice. Attempts to explain firm behaviour when there is no collusion have involved various reaction curve models (including kinked demand), and more recently game theory. However, collusion can and does take place, sometimes formally, as in cartels, or more often tacitly, under various types of price leadership.

The definition and measurement of oligopoly

Oligopoly may be defined as an industry in which there are few firms and many buyers. However, this definition begs two important questions. First, how many is 'few'? Broadly speaking, the number of firms should be sufficiently small for there to be 'conscious interdependence', with each firm aware that its future prospects depend not only on its own policies, but also on those of its rivals. Second, what is an industry? In theory, an industry is defined as a group of firms whose products are close substitutes for one another (i.e. the products have high and positive cross-elasticities of demand).[1] In practice, precise calculations of cross-elasticities of demand are impossible to make, and an industry is defined either by approximate similarity of output (such as the confectionery industry) or by similarity of the major input (such as the rubber industry, which makes a wide variety of goods from shoe soles to tyres).

Bearing in mind these problems of precise definition, the rise of oligopoly can be charted in a variety of ways.

Concentration ratios

Perhaps the most usual method of measuring the degree of oligopoly is through concentration ratios. These show the proportion of output or employment in a given industry or product group which is accounted for by the dominant firms operating in those areas. The oldest concentration ratio used in the UK within manufacturing is the 100-firm ratio which measures the share of the 100 largest private firms in total manufacturing net output. This ratio increased from 16.0% in 1909 to 41.7% in 1975, before falling back to 32% by 2001, indicating the progressive concentration of economic power within UK manufacturing over the first three-quarters of the twentieth century, followed by a fall in such domination over the last quarter century.

The more normal way of measuring concentration ratios is to calculate the proportion of output or employment contributed by the three, four or five largest firms in that industry or product group. By the 1990s, industrial sectors in the UK such as Tobacco, Motor Vehicles and Cement already had five-firm

concentration ratios of above 80%, which meant that the top five firms in these sectors accounted for more than 80% of the UK's total net output or employment. On the other hand, the printing and leather goods industries, for example, were more fragmented, with less than 20% of the net output or employment being accounted for by the five largest firms.

Evidence of market domination by the few is also present in manufacturing at the European level. Table 6.1 shows the 10 *most concentrated* industries and the 10 *least concentrated* industries in the EU, using the five-firm concentration ratios for the respective industries. It can be seen that the most concentrated EU industries are in either the advertising intensive industries (A), the research intensive industries (R), or industries which are *both* advertising and research intensive (AR). On the other hand, the least concentrated EU industries are all in the so-called conventional industries (C) producing fairly homogeneous products for which competition is based mainly on price.

The advertising and/or research intensive industries are characterized by product differentiation rather than product homogeneity, and by non-price competition rather than price competition. High advertising and/or research and development expenditure in relation to turnover can create competitive advantages which allow a small number of large enterprises to dominate these industrial sectors. These competitive advantages may relate to successful branding created and reinforced by advertising and/or technological innovations resulting from substantial R&D investment. Non-technical scale economies tend to be more important for these industries than the plant-based technical scale economies, with the opposite the case for the 'conventional' industries.

The concentration figures given in Table 6.1 and in the text above, for both the UK and the EU, help show the dominance of a few firms in relatively large sectors. However, these figures sometimes hide the intense competition which actually occurs between the few large firms within that specific product group. Table 6.2 provides an insight into competition between a few large firms in 10 selected product groups in that it shows the percentage share of the UK market in those products accounted for by the three and five largest firms. For example, the plastic card market is dominated by Visa, Switch and Mastercard International respectively, whilst the cigarette market

Table 6.1 Five-firm concentration ratios (C5EU) at the EU level by industry and type.

Ten most concentrated	%	Ten least concentrated	%
Optical instruments (AR)	73.1	Metal structures (C)	5.7
Computers/office equipment (R)	71.2	Meat products (C)	5.7
Electric lamps/lighting (R)	64.7	Plastics (C)	5.6
Motor vehicles (AR)	62.9	Wooden structures (C)	5.5
Domestic/office chemicals (R)	62.9	Silk (C)	5.3
Artificial fibres (R)	62.6	Clothing (C)	4.3
Aerospace (R)	57.0	Wooden containers (C)	4.1
Tobacco (A)	56.1	Metal treatment (C)	3.8
Rubber (A)	48.7	Other wood products (C)	3.2
Domestic electrical appliances (AR)	46.4	Wooden furniture (C)	3.1

Notes: The % figures represent the combined production of the five largest EU firms as a percentage of total EU production, for each industry. The industry 'types' are in brackets, where:
   A = advertising intensive
   AR = advertising and research intensive
   R = research intensive
   C = conventional.
Source: Adapted from Davies and Lyons (1996).

Table 6.2 Company shares of the UK market by sector/product group, 2001.

	Percentage share of UK market by volume	
Sector/product group	Three largest companies	Five largest companies
Plastic cards	83.5	99.6
Cigarettes	80.6	91.6
Chocolate confectionery	77.5	81.9
Refrigeration appliances	56.0	68.2
Household cleaning products	55.2	62.1
Beer	54.1	68.6
Cars	38.8	53.1
Wrist watches	34.5	45.0
Stationery products	33.0	37.4
Bottled water	31.9	39.9

Sources: *Euromonitor* (2002), *Market Research GB* (various).

is essentially a duopoly with Imperial Tobacco and Gallaher alone accounting for around 75% of the market in 2001.

The chocolate confectionery market is dominated by Cadbury, Mars and Nestlé and the refrigeration appliances group by well-known names such as General Domestic Appliances Ltd (which produce Hotpoint), Electrolux UK Ltd and Lec Refrigeration plc. Some of the product groups which show less concentrated control include stationery, bottled water ((Evian Volvic (UK and Ireland) Ltd, Perrier Vittel (UK) Ltd and Highland Spring Ltd)) and wrist watches (Seiko Ltd, Time Products (UK) and the Inter-City Watch Company). The main reasons for the lower concentration ratios in some product groups such as stationery products is the presence of own/private labels (such as the WHS own brand) or, as in the case of bottled water, the fact that the product group provides market space for small, specialized (niche) producers.

Often consumers are not aware that a few firms dominate certain markets because each company produces a variety of models or brands that appear on the surface to be unrelated to each other, as for example with Diageo plc which produces brands such as Smirnoff vodka, Bell's whisky and Gordon's gin, and controls 20% of the UK spirit market. It is often useful to examine *product groups* if we wish to see the true extent of market domination by a few firms.

Advertising expenditure

Data on advertising provide a useful, if indirect, method for gauging both the rise of oligopoly markets and the tendency towards product differentiation. Advertising is essentially aimed at binding consumers to particular brands for reasons other than price. Estimates in the USA of branded, processed foods put their prices almost 9% higher than 'private label' equivalents – similar products packaged under the retailer's own name – due solely to more extensive media advertising.[2]

One way of understanding the impact of advertising on oligopolistic markets is to study the total advertising expenditure of the top 10 *companies*, as listed in Table 6.3. For example, the two companies which dominated UK advertising in 2001 were Unilever and Procter & Gamble. The figures shown here include the advertising expenditure of all the major subsidiaries of the two groups operating in a wide range of sectors from food and household goods to health, beauty and cosmetics. If we take the clothes washing market, Procter & Gamble's products (such as Ariel Future and Daz Automatic) are in competition with Lever Brothers' products (such as Persil Automatic and Persil New Generation). In 2000, for example, one of the major competitive battles between the two companies occurred in the deodorant sector with Procter & Gamble's deodorant product, *Secret*, competing aggressively against Unilever's deodorant, *Dove*. In the *automobile industry*, companies such as Ford, Vauxhall, Peugeot and Renault are all included in the top 10 advertisers. Finally, it is also worth noting the presence of three very large *confectionery* groups in the top advertisers.

Table 6.3 Top 10 advertising companies in the UK, 2001.

Rank	Company	Advertising (£m)
1	Unilever	142.63
2	Procter & Gamble	114.23
3	BT	91.79
4	Ford Motor Company	82.14
5	Renault	64.29
6	Vauxhall Motors	55.49
7	DFS Northern Upholstery	50.65
8	L'Oréal Golden	49.12
9	Sainsbury's	46.00
10	Peugeot Motor Company	45.62

Note: Advertising by the Central Office of Information is omitted and the Unilever figure is the total for its four divisions.
Source: Modified from *Marketing* (2002a).

Mars Confectionery was the eleventh largest advertiser in 2001, with Nestlé Rowntree (22) and Trebor Basset (72) also intensive advertisers. Thus the UK confectionery market is in the hands of a few firms which sell extensive ranges of branded goods and compete vigorously with each other.

The companies noted above all advertise their branded products intensively in order to 'bind' the consumer to the product for reasons other than price. Where successful, such advertising may help *shift* the demand curve outwards, raising market share, while simultaneously causing the demand curve to pivot and become steeper. Demand then becomes less price elastic, creating new opportunities for raising both price and revenue. Table 6.4 shows the advertising expenditure on the top 10 branded products in the grocery, drink and personal care sectors and also gives figures for brand penetration. Brand penetration is defined as the percentage of UK households that purchased these brands during the year 2000. These figures provide an interesting insight into the intensity of the demand for each brand product. For example, Walkers Crisps achieved the highest penetration rate as a result of its intensive advertising to larger households in the C2 and D social classes and capitalized on this in its May 2002 launch of its upmarket brand 'posh crisps' with adverts by Victoria Beckham and Gary Lineker. Some other classical examples of the role of branding in creating new market opportunities

Table 6.4 Top 10 brands in the grocery, drink and personal care sectors by advertising spend, 2002.

Rank	Brand	Company	Penetration (%)	Advertising (£m)
1	Coca-Cola	Coca-Cola	59	23.37
2	Persil	Lever Brothers	47	19.62
3	Walkers Crisps	PepsiCo	78	16.48
4	Wrigley's	Wrigley's	35	16.34
5	Ariel	Procter & Gamble	42	15.72
6	Budweiser	Anheuser Busch	9	13.81
7	Nescafé	Nestlé	55	13.77
8	Müller	Müller	71	13.55
9	KitKat	Nestlé Rowntree	66	12.83
10	Bold	Procter & Gamble	24	8.45

Source: Adapted from *Marketing* (2002b).

to 'bind' consumers to a new product include Wrigley's launch of its new X.Cite mini-mint chewing gum in April 2002 with an £8m advertising campaign. Such spending can also be undertaken to help relaunch products, as in the case of Procter & Gamble's £12m advertising spend in 2002 on relaunching its Sunny Delight drink. Branding activity is, of course, also rife in other sectors such as automobiles where the top five companies (Ford, Vauxhall, Renault, VW and Fiat) account for 53% of the UK market and brands such as the Ford Focus, Vauxhall Vectra, Renault Megane and Fiat Stilo are all extensively advertised.

Oligopoly in theory and practice

The central task of market theory is to predict how firms will set prices and output. In perfect competition and pure monopoly we can make definite predictions. In perfect competition it can be shown that in the long run price will be equal to the lowest possible average costs of the firm – what Adam Smith called 'the natural price'. In pure monopoly the firm seeking to maximize profits will restrict output and raise prices until marginal revenue exactly equals marginal cost.

In oligopoly, where there are few firms in the market, and where there is product differentiation, there can be no such precision. Where the number of firms is sufficiently small for each firm to be aware of the pricing policy of its rivals, it will have to try to anticipate its rivals' reactions to its own pricing decision. Further, where products are differentiated, the firm will have to estimate the degree of brand loyalty customers have for its products – the greater that loyalty, the smaller the effect of price changes on consumer demand. This constant need to anticipate the reaction of both rivals and consumers creates a high degree of uncertainty in oligopoly markets.

Despite this uncertainty, the importance of the oligopoly-type of market structure in modern economies has encouraged the quest for theories to explain and predict firm behaviour. Although little progress seems to have been made in devising a general theory of oligopoly behaviour, some progress has been made in understanding the behaviour of *particular* firms in *particular* oligopoly situations. We might usefully review a number of such theories, keeping a close eye on firm practice.

Non-collusive oligopoly

First, we consider situations in which each firm decides upon its strategy without any formal or even tacit collusion between rivals. There are essentially three approaches the firm can adopt to handle interdependence when oligopoly is non-collusive:

1   The firm could assume that whatever it decides to do, its rivals *will not* react, i.e. they will ignore its

strategies. This assumption may reasonably be valid for day-to-day, routine decisions, but is hardly realistic for major initiatives. The Cournot duopoly model is, however, of this type. Each firm simply observes what the other does, and then adopts a strategy that maximizes its own profits. It makes no attempt to evaluate potential reactions by the rival firm to its own profit-maximizing strategy.

2 The firm could assume that rivals *will* react to its own strategies, and use past experience to assess the form that reaction might take. This 'learning' process underlies the reaction-curve model of Stackleberg. It also underlies the kinked-demand model (see below), with firms learning that rivals do not match price increases, but certainly do match any price reductions.

3 Instead of using past experience to assess future reactions by rivals, the firm itself could try to identify the *best possible* move the opposition could make to each of its own strategies. The firm could then plan counter-measures if the rival reacts in this (for the rival) optimal way. As we see below, this is the essence of game theory.

Approaches (2) and (3) might lead us to expect a considerable amount of price movement, as rivals incessantly formulate strategy and counter-strategy. In practice, however, the oligopolistic industries experience *short bursts* of price-changing activity (often linked to price warfare), together with longer periods of relatively stable or rigid prices. We briefly review these two types of situation, noting the relevance of kinked-demand theory to stable prices, and conclude our discussion of non-collusive behaviour with an outline of game theory.

Price warfare

Price-cutting is a well-attested strategy for oligopoly firms, for both raising and defending market share. This can, of course, lead to a competitive downward spiral in firm prices, resembling a 'price war'. Examples of this abound. We will see, in Chapter 9, how price warfare developed amongst petrol retailers. In 1996, for example, stagnant demand for petrol due to increasing taxes, and more fuel-efficient cars coupled with competition from supermarkets, led the UK's largest petrol retailer, Esso, to announce aggressive price cuts to maintain its dominant position.

Shell, BP and Conoco (Jet) responded by matching or undercutting Esso's price cuts. The catalyst for the new strategy was that Esso's share of the petrol market had fallen to around 17% as compared to the supermarkets' share of 25%.

In 1996, the cross-channel transport business saw a fierce outbreak of price warfare. Of the 35m passengers using the cross-channel route, 35% went by Eurotunnel, 32% by P&O European Ferries and 20% by Stena Line. Between 1993 and 1996, peak season cross-channel fares fell by 60% as the ferries tried to resist the challenge of the Channel Tunnel. For example, the standard brochure fares for a crossing in the summer of 1996 involving a car and four passengers were heavily discounted on the shorter Dover/Calais (ferries) and the Folkestone/Calais (Le Shuttle) routes. Actual ferry prices were cut to around 40% of the standard return price while Le Shuttle prices were cut to 80% of their normal fares. Most of the operators were charging around £100 for a return fare involving a car and four passengers. In order to use its ships to capacity, P&O's policy was to match any rival company's discount. The presence of price warfare is also endemic in the financial sector as illustrated by the price competition between Visa and Europay, the two payments card groupings, over the fees they charge to their member banks in Europe for using their product. After a four-year cost-cutting programme prior to 1998, Europay (which runs the Eurocard debit card scheme and Mastercard) decided to undercut Visa's fees by 20% in early 2000. Visa's response was to announce a programme aimed at undercutting Europay by 25% between 2000 and 2001.

One of the most dynamic areas for oligopolistic price warfare activity in more recent times occurred in the games console market during the period 2001–02 when Sony (Playstation 2), Microsoft (Microsoft XBox) and Nintendo (GameCube) fought for market share. In November 2001 Sony decreased the price of its Playstation 2, a move which led Microsoft to decrease the price of its new Microsoft XBox from £300 to £199 in April 2002. Nintendo followed in May 2002 with a discounted price of £129 for its new GameCube console. By October 2002, the most aggressive aspect of the console price war seemed to be over as the protagonists concentrated on the next generation of consoles due in 2005. The main logic behind such price wars was the desire for market share. Microsoft was able to lift its UK market share to 20%, ahead of Nintendo (10%) but still behind the leader Sony (70%). Price decreases were made possible not only by the economies of scale achieved in the production of consoles, but also by companies cross-subsidizing their consoles in order to drive up software sales (e.g. in 2003 Microsoft was known to be losing £60 on each XBox sold). Such examples of product line pricing are considered in more detail in Chapter 9.

Clearly in oligopolistic markets, where only a few firms dominate, a price-cutting strategy by one is likely to be followed by others. After short bursts of price warfare, the market may settle down into prolonged periods of price stability, although the fact that firms no longer compete in price may not mean an absence of competition. In periods of price stability, non-price competition often becomes more intense, with advertising, packaging and other promotional activities now used to raise or defend market share. For example, in the food retailing business, advertising is a well-known form of non-price competition. In 2001, Sainsbury spent £46m on advertising, Tesco £24m and Asda £24.7m. Coupled with this overall advertising strategy, there have been other efforts at product differentiation, such as the 'green grocer' campaigns to promote environmentally friendly products. Similarly, the loyalty cards introduced by Tesco (Clubcard), Safeway (Added Bonus Card) and Sainsbury (Reward card) were designed to reinforce brand loyalty and make customers less price sensitive. In economic terms, this was designed to make demand curves less elastic, giving the supermarkets more opportunity to raise prices at a later date if necessary.

Non-price competition may take forms other than advertising and quality considerations. In the mid-1990s when price competition was intense in the travel industry, there were still signs that companies were using other non-price methods to increase market share. For example, Thomson's industrial strategy of *vertical integration* towards the market (owning Lunn Poly and Britannia Airways) was strengthened further in 1994 by its purchase of the Country Holidays Group which gave it a major interest in the UK holiday lettings industry. Vertical integration was also involved in the acquisition by Thomas Cook in 1998 of the US Carlson group (owner of Caledonian Airways and the tour operator 'Inspirations'). Between 2001 and 2002 both Thomson and Thomas Cook experienced further integration when each was taken over by a German-

owned leisure group in a period of fierce competition in the European holidays industry. Such takeover strategies are an important 'non-price' method by which firms in oligopolistic industries continue to compete with one another.

Price stability

That price in oligopoly will tend to have periods of stability is, in fact, predicted by economic theory.

Kinked demand

In 1939 Hall and Hitch in the UK and Sweezy in the USA proposed a theory to explain why prices often remain stable in oligopoly markets, even when costs rise. A central feature of that theory was the existence of a kinked-demand curve.

To illustrate this we take an oligopolistic market which sells similar but not identical products, i.e. there is some measure of product differentiation. If one firm raises its price, it will then lose some, though not all, of its custom to rivals. Similarly, if the firm reduces its price it will attract some, though not all, of its rivals' custom. How much custom is lost or gained will depend partly on whether the rivals follow the initial price change.

Extensive interviews with managers of firms in oligopoly markets led Hall and Hitch to conclude that most firms have learned a common lesson from past experience of how rivals react. Namely, that if the firm were to raise its price above the current level (P in Fig. 6.1), its rivals *would not* follow, content to let the firm lose sales to them. The firm will then expect its demand curve to be relatively elastic (dK) for price rises. However, if the firm were to reduce its price, rivals *would* follow to protect their market share, so that the firm gains few extra sales. The firm will then expect its demand curve to be relatively inelastic (KD') for price reductions. Overall the firm will believe that its demand curve is kinked at the current price P, as in Fig. 6.1.

One can intuitively see why this belief will lead to price stickiness, since the firm will rapidly lose market share if it raises price, and gain little from reducing price. A kinked-demand (average revenue) curve of the form dKD', will have a discontinuity (L–M) in its associated marginal revenue curve below the kink point K.[3] The marginal cost curve could then vary between MC_1 and MC_2 without causing the firm to alter its profit-maximizing price P (or its output Q).

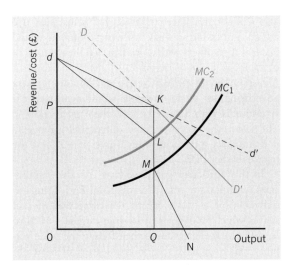

Fig. 6.1 Kinked demand curve and price stability.
Notes: d–d′ = Demand curve when rivals *do not* follow price changes.
D–D′ = Demand curve when rivals *do* follow price changes.
dKD′ = Kinked demand curve.
dLMN = Associated marginal revenue curve.

A number of industries have exhibited price stability, despite rising costs. The UK confectionery industry, presently dominated by Mars, Nestlé Rowntree (which absorbed Rowntree Mackintosh in 1988) and Cadbury Schweppes, is a good example of this tendency. During some periods in the 1980s, price wars were often avoided, though competition between these companies still continued in other forms. For example, in the mid-1980s non-price competition took the form of product weight. In one such period, Mars raised the weight of Mars bars by 10%, Cadbury raised the weight of its Fruit and Nut by 14% and Rowntree Mackintosh raised the weight of Cabana by 15% and increased the chocolate content of KitKat by 5%. In all of these cases the firms accepted rises in their costs, i.e. more ingredients per bar, *without changing price*.

Similarly in 1990, competition in the UK snacks market increased as the three major companies, KP Foods, Smiths and Walkers (owned by the US company, PepsiCo), and Golden Wonder (the Dalgety subsidiary), looked for new ways of competing. KP foods introduced its new crisp-like snack called 'Frisp' and spent £4.4m on marketing it in the first three months alone. To prevent being squeezed out by its two big rivals, Golden Wonder planned to launch

a few new products in the middle of 1990 and in the meantime increased the packet size of all its crisps and snacks from 28 grams to 30 grams *without raising prices*. In terms of our kinked oligopoly model, the companies noted above preferred to accept the higher costs of non-price competition (which can be illustrated by the upward shift in the MC curve), rather than engage in price warfare, in order to gain market share. The reason for this is that companies sometimes believe they have a better idea of the costs and benefits involved in *non-price competition* as compared to the unknown risks of getting involved in price competition. When a company becomes involved in price competition, gains and losses are more difficult to assess because they depend on the *reactions* of competitors to the initial company's pricing strategy.

Despite the usefulness of the kinked oligopoly model as a descriptive tool in the understanding of oligopoly behaviour, it still faces a number of problems:

1   The theory does not explain how oligopolists actually *set* an initial price, but merely why a price, once set, might be stable. Kinked demand is *not* a theory of price determination.

2   The observed stickiness of prices may have little to do with the rival-firm reaction patterns of kinked-demand theory. It is, for instance, administratively expensive to change prices too often.

3   The assertion, implicit in kinked-demand theory, that prices are more 'sticky' under oligopoly than under other market forms, has not received strong support from empirical studies (Wagner 1981). For instance, Stigler, in a sample of 100 firms across 21 industries in the USA, had concluded as early as the 1940s that oligopoly prices hardly merited the description 'sticky'. Domberger, in a survey of 21 UK industries, found that the *more* oligopolistic the market, the more variable was price (Domberger 1980).

4   The precise nature of any kink in the demand curve may depend on the economic conditions prevailing at the time. For example, a study of 73 small owner-managed firms in Scotland found that price increases were more likely to be followed during booms, whilst falls were more likely to be followed during times of recession (Bhaskar *et al.* 1991).

Game theory

One of the more recent attempts to assess non-collusive behaviour by oligopolists has involved game theory. The intention is to go beyond the rather general reaction patterns of earlier theory, to more explicit assessments of strategy and counter-strategy. We might usefully illustrate the principles involved by a simple two-firm (duopoly) game, involving market share. By its very nature, a market share game must be 'zero sum', in that any gain by one 'player' must be offset exactly by the loss of the other(s).

Suppose Firm A is considering two possible strategies to raise its market share, a 20% price cut or a 10% increase in advertising expenditure. Whatever initial strategy A adopts, it anticipates that its rival, Firm B, will react by using either a price cut or extra advertising to defend its market share. Firm A now evaluates the market share it can expect for each initial strategy and each possible counter-strategy by B. The outcomes expected by A are summarized in the payoff matrix of Table 6.5.

If A cuts price, and B responds with a price cut, A receives 60% of the market. However, if B responds with extra advertising, A receives 70% of the market. The 'worst' outcome for A (60% of the market) will occur if B responds with a price cut. If A adopts the strategy of extra advertising, then the 'worst' outcome for A (50% of the market) will again occur if B responds with a price cut. If A expects B to play the game astutely, i.e. choose the counter-strategy best for itself (worst for A), then A will choose the price-cut strategy as this gives it 60% of the market rather than 50%. If A plays the game in this way, selecting the best of the 'worst possible' outcomes for each initial strategy, it is said to be adopting a 'maxi–min approach' to the game.

If B adopts the same maxi–min approach as A, *and* has made the same evaluation of outcomes as A, it also will adopt a price-cut strategy. For instance, if B adopts a price-cut strategy, its 'worst' outcome would occur if A responds with a price cut – B then gets 40% of the market (100% minus 60%), rather than 50% if A responds with extra advertising. If B adopts extra advertising, its 'worst' outcome would again occur if A responds with a price cut – B then receives 30%. The best of the 'worst possible' outcomes for B occurs if B adopts a price cut, which gives it 40% of the market rather than 30%.

In this particular game we have a stable equilibrium, without any resort to collusion. Both firms initially cut price, then accept the respective market shares which fulfil their maxi–min targets – 60% to A, 40% to B. There could then follow the price stability which we have seen to be a feature of some oligopoly situations. In some games the optimal strategy for each firm may not even have been an initial price cut, but rather non-price competition (such as advertising). Game theory can predict both price stability and extensive non-price competition.

The problem with game theory is that it can equally predict unstable solutions, with extensive price as well as non-price competition. An unstable solution might follow if each firm, faced with the payoff matrix of Table 6.5, adopts entirely different strategies. Firm B might not use the maxi–min approach of A, but take more risk.[4] Instead of the price cut it might adopt the 'extra advertising' strategy, hoping to induce an advertising response from Firm A and gain 45% of the market, but risk getting only 30% if A responds with a price cut. Suppose this is what happens. Firm A now receives 70% of the market, but B only receives 30%, which is below its initial expectation of 45%. This may provoke B into alternative strategy formulation, setting off a further chain reaction. The game may then fail to settle down quickly, if at all, to a stable solution, i.e. one in which

Table 6.5 Firm A's payoff matrix.

		Firm B's strategies	
		Price cut	**Extra advertising**
Firm A's strategies	Price cut	60*†	70†
	Extra advertising	50*	55

* 'Worst' outcome for A of each A strategy.
† 'Worst' outcome for B of each B strategy.

each firm receives a market share which meets its overall expectation. An unstable solution might also follow if each firm evaluates the payoff matrix differently from the other. Even if they then adopt the same approach to the game, one firm at least will be 'disappointed', possibly provoking action and counteraction.

If we could tell *before the event* which oligopoly situations would be stable, and which unstable, then the many possible outcomes of game theory would be considerably narrowed. At present this is beyond the state of the art. However, game theory has been useful in making more explicit the *interdependence* of oligopoly situations. Here we have used game theory in a situation in which the firms did not collude. Game theory can also show (in games which are *not* zero sum) that collusion between firms may sometimes improve the position of all. It is to such collusive behaviour that we now turn.

Collusive oligopoly

When oligopoly is non-collusive, the firm uses guesswork and calculation to handle the uncertainty of its rivals' reactions. Another way of handling that uncertainty in markets which are interdependent is by some form of central coordination; in other words, collusion. At least two features of collusive oligopoly are worth emphasizing: first, the objectives that are sought through collusion; and second, the methods that are used to promote collusion – these may be formal, as in a cartel, or informal, via tacit agreement.

Objectives of collusion

Joint profit maximization

The firms may seek to coordinate their price, output and other policies to achieve maximum profits for the industry as a whole. In the extreme case the firms may act together as a monopoly, aggregating their marginal costs and equating these with marginal revenue for the whole market. If achieved, the result would be to maximize joint profits, with a unique industry price and output (P_1Q_1), as in Fig. 6.2.

A major problem is, of course, how to achieve the close coordination required. We consider this further below, but we might note from Fig. 6.2 that coordination is required both to *establish* the profit-maximizing solution for the industry P_1Q_1, and to *enforce* it once established. For instance, some agreement must be reached on sharing the output Q_1 between the colluding firms. One solution is to equate marginal revenue for whole output with marginal cost in each separate market,[5] with Firm A producing Q_A and Firm B producing Q_B. Whatever the agreement, it must remain in force – since if any firm produces above its quota, this will raise industry output, depress price and move the industry away from the joint profit-maximizing solution.

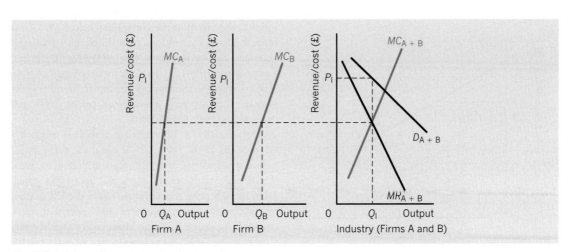

Fig. 6.2 Joint profit maximization in duopoly.

Deterrence of new entrants – limit-pricing

Firms may seek to coordinate policies, to maximize not so much short-run profit but rather some longer-run notion of profit (see Chapter 3). A major threat to long-run profit is the potential entrance of new firms into the industry. Economists such as Andrews and Bain have therefore suggested that oligopolistic firms may collude with the objectives of setting price below the level which maximizes joint profits, in order to deter new entrants. The 'limit price' can be defined as the highest price which the established firms believe they can charge without inducing entry. Its precise value will depend upon the nature and extent of the 'barriers to entry' for any particular industry. The greater the barriers to entry, the higher the 'limit price' will be.

Substantial economies of scale are a 'barrier to entry', in that a new firm will usually be smaller than established firms, and will therefore be at a cost disadvantage. Product differentiation itself, reinforced by extensive advertising, is also a barrier – since product loyalty, once captured, is difficult and expensive for new entrants to dislodge. Other barriers might include legally enforced patents to new technologies in the hands of established firms, and even inelastic market demands. This latter is a barrier in that the less elastic the market demand for the product, the greater will be the price fall from any extra supply contributed by new entrants.

The principle of 'limit-pricing' can be illustrated from Fig. 6.3. Let us make the analysis easier by supposing that each established firm has an identical average cost (AC) curve, and sells an identical output,

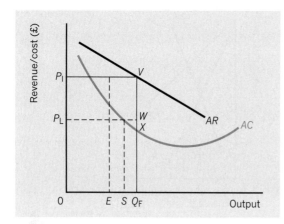

Fig. 6.3 Limit-pricing as a barrier to entry.

Q_F, at the joint profit-maximizing price P_I set for the industry. Suppose a new firm, with an identical cost profile, is considering entering the industry, and is capable of selling E units in the first instance. Despite the initial cost disadvantage the new firm believes it can survive. One way of preventing the survival of the new firm, perhaps even deterring its entry, would be for the colluding established firms to reduce the industry price to P_L. Although this would reduce their own excess profits in the short run (by VW per unit) the new entrant would make a loss selling E at price P_L, since price would be less than average cost at that output. It would have needed to produce as much as output S *immediately* at the price P_L, even to have just covered its average costs.

The greater the barriers to the entry of new firms, the higher the 'limit price', P_L, can be, i.e. the closer P_L can be to P_I. The most favourable situation for established firms would be if barriers were so great that P_L were at, or above, P_I. In other words, established firms could set the joint profit-maximizing price without inducing entry.

An example of the occurrence of high barriers to entry and relatively high limit prices could be seen in the French market for natural spring water during the early 1990s. In 1992 the French market for such bottled water was dominated by three companies, Nestlé, Perrier and BSN, and the barriers to entry into the industry were high. For example, the transport costs of bringing non-French water to the market were substantial and persuading French retailers to stock new brands was difficult. Advertising costs were also heavy, helping create strong brand loyalties in France for the products of the three companies. Finally, the fact that the companies held 82% of the market share by volume constituted an additional problem for prospective new entrants (European Commission 1994). As a result, these companies were able to increase their prices substantially during the period, thus keeping their limit prices high and maximizing their joint profits.

Occasionally a limit-pricing policy is explicitly adopted, as in the early 1960s when the three major petrol wholesalers, Shell/BP, Esso and Regent, were threatened with new entrants. In 1963 Shell announced a price reduction 'to make the UK market less attractive to newcomers and potential newcomers'. Again, in 1973 the Monopolies and Mergers Commission (MMC) found evidence of limit-pricing by Kellogg, concluding that 'when fixing its prices, therefore, Kellogg has as an objective the preservation of its share of the market against potential competitors'.

An obvious constraint to limit-pricing is that prices cannot be set below X in Fig. 6.3, the level at which the established firms begin to make excess profits (normal profit included in average cost), at least not for any length of time. The established firms may therefore resort to non-price competition to reinforce barriers against new entrants. For instance, the petrol companies sought extensive 'solus' agreements, giving discounts to retailers dealing exclusively with them, and sought to buy up retail outlets directly. In the detergent industry, Lever Brothers, by introducing new brands, have increased product differentiation and raised barriers to entry. As much as 58% of their turnover comes from new brands introduced in the past 16 years. Extensive advertising (as shown by Tables 6.3 and 6.4) is yet another way of increasing barriers to entry into a market or industry. Advertising can be used to increase brand loyalty, thus making it difficult for new firms with a new product to enter a market. Increased advertising can be used by firms already in the industry not only to keep other firms out, but also to drive out existing firms which have newly entered the industry.

To investigate this latter proposition, a study was undertaken into the behaviour of 42 companies operating in various consumer goods markets, such as electric shavers, deodorants, washing-up liquids and kettles, over the period 1975 to 1981. The study investigated the advertising strategy of companies *already in* these oligopolistic markets after new firms with new products had managed to enter those markets (Cubbin and Domberger 1988). The results of the study showed that increased advertising was used as a weapon in an attempt to drive out new entrants in 38% of markets studied, and that the response of the firms already in the market to the new entrants depended on the *structure of the oligopoly* and the *nature of the market*. For example, in a tightly competitive oligopoly situation, where a dominant firm controlled more than 30% of the market, it was more likely that the new entrant would be exposed to increased advertising competition than in a looser oligopoly where there was no clear dominance by one firm. Similarly, increased advertising competition was more likely to face new entrants in static markets, i.e. those in which demand is not growing. This is partly because growing markets tend

to be dominated by new consumers with less attachment to the products of existing firms. Advertising in this situation is therefore a less certain weapon for driving out a new entrant, as compared to a market in which demand is static.

We now turn briefly to the methods which firms have actually used to promote collusion in oligopolistic markets.

Methods of collusion

Formal collusion – cartels

Formal collusion often takes the form of a cartel – in other words, the establishment of some central body with responsibility for setting the industry price and output which most nearly meets some agreed objective. Usually it also has the responsibility for sharing that total output between the members. Cartels are against the law in most countries, including the UK. However, in the UK the Cement Makers' Federation was an exception. Up to 1987 it still held monthly meetings in which deliveries, prices and market shares were discussed. The three main companies sharing the market were Blue Circle (60%), Rio Tinto Zinc (22%) and Rugby Portland (18%), with their common price calculated on a formula which averaged the costs of different producers. The Restrictive Practices Court permitted the cartel to continue on the basis that a common price agreement enables cement capacity to be controlled in an orderly way. Nevertheless, increased concentration of the cement industry in the last few years raised the possibility of intervention by the MMC (now the Competition Commission) and this, together with international competition from cheap European imports (especially from Greece), caused the cartel to be abandoned in 1987. However, cartel-type collusion still persists in the UK cement industry. In 2000, the three largest UK producers of ordinary Portland cement (OPC), i.e. Blue Circle plc, Castle Cement Ltd and the Rugby Group, refused to supply bulk OPC to customers such as ready-mix concrete producers who had intended to resell it in bags to builders' merchants. This was because they themselves sold OPC in bag form to customers. In September 2000 the Office of Fair Trading (OFT) found that such a policy was anti-competitive and told the companies to desist from such supply-fixing cartel behaviour.

An example of a price-fixing cartel operating in the UK was discovered and prohibited by the OFT in

1999. Vitafoam Ltd of Rochdale, Carpenter plc of Glossop, and Recticel Ltd of Alfreton had met to agree on price rises of 8% for foam rubber and 4% for reconstituted foam which they supplied to the upholstery business. Cartel members agreed that the price rises announced by Vitafoam, the market leader, would be matched immediately by similar announcements from Carpenter and Recticel.

Various cartels operate internationally. The most famous is OPEC, in which many but not all (the UK is not a member) oil-exporting countries meet regularly to agree on prices and set production quotas. Whilst OPEC worked successfully in the mid-1970s in raising oil prices, in the worldwide economic slump of the early 1980s coordination proved increasingly difficult. As demand for oil fell, exporters were faced with the necessity of cutting production quotas to maintain prices; and some, such as Iran and Nigeria with major internal economic problems, were unwilling to do this, preferring to cut prices and seek higher market share. Of course the Iraqi pressure on OPEC countries to curtail production and raise prices, and the subsequent Kuwait invasion, contributed to higher oil prices in the early 1990s. However, by 1992/93, the continued fall in demand for oil under worldwide recessionary conditions, allied to some additional oil supplies (e.g. from the Gulf States), revived the disagreements between those cartel members in favour of price cuts and those in favour of tighter quotas. In more recent times, OPEC's ability to enforce the cartel led to a cut in the supply of oil available to industrial countries in March 1999. This resulted in a trebling of the price of a barrel of crude oil from $10 to $34 by March 2000.

The International Air Transport Association (IATA) is the cartel of international airlines, and has sought to set prices for each route. During the 1970s it was seriously weakened by price-cutting competition from non-member airlines, such as Laker Airways. It was further weakened by worldwide recession in the late 1980s and early 1990s, with lower incomes causing demand for air travel, with its high-income elasticity, to fall dramatically. To fill seats, the member airlines began to compete amongst themselves in terms of price, often via a complex system of discounts. The experiences of OPEC and IATA suggest that cartels are vulnerable both to price-cutting amongst members when demand for the product declines, and to competition from non-members.

Another example of an international cartel was brought to light by investigations during 1990 into the activity of the International Telegraph and Telephone Consultative Committee (CCITT), a Geneva-based 'club' consisting of the main international telephone companies of the major industrial countries (*Financial Times* 1990). Major international telephone companies such as AT&T (USA), British Telecom (UK), Deutsche Bundespost (Germany), France Télécom (France), Telecom Canada (Canada) and KDD (Japan) belong to the group. The CCITT had a book of 'recommendations' for its member companies which included two important features. First, it suggested a complicated method of sharing the revenues received from international telephone calls. When international phone calls are made from the UK to Japan, for example, BT receives the money for the call but it has to pay KDD in Japan for delivering the call to its final destination in that country. The particular method used to calculate the distribution of the revenue received for the call between the various international telephone companies tended to penalize any company that attempted to cut its telephone prices. This in turn made it difficult for both existing and new companies to decrease prices because their profits would also fall. Second, it suggested that members of the group should not lease too much of their international telephone circuits to other private companies, since this could increase potential competition.

The effect of the first 'rule' was to provide high profit margins for telephone companies because prices were kept artificially high by the peculiar revenue-sharing scheme. Meanwhile, new technological advances had decreased the *real* costs per minute of using a transatlantic cable from $2.53 in 1956 to $0.04 in 1988. While costs had fallen drastically, the price charged for a peak call from the US to the UK and Italy remained at $2 and $4 per minute respectively! As a result, profit margins on international calls (i.e. profits divided by revenue) of some of the top earners were as follows: Japan 75%, Canada 68%, USA 63%, Britain 58%, West Germany 48%, and France 43%. British Telecom earned a profit of between £600m and £800m on its international business during the 1988/89 financial year, depending on the accounting definitions used. The second 'rule' made it difficult for new companies to enter this market because most of the international cables were built by members of the CCITT and new operators had to get permission from these companies in order to lease cable space from them. If they were not allowed more space on international cables, then new companies had to use satellite links which were more expensive and of lower quality than cable links.

Tacit collusion – price leadership

Although cartels are illegal in most countries, various forms of tacit collusion undoubtedly occur. In 1776, Adam Smith wrote in his *Wealth of Nations* that entrepreneurs rarely meet together without conspiring to raise prices at the expense of the consumer. Today the most usual method of tacit collusion is price leadership, where one firm sets a price which the others follow.

1. Dominant-firm leadership. Frequently the price leader is the dominant firm. In the late 1960s Brooke Bond controlled 43% of the market for tea, well ahead of the second largest firm Typhoo with only 18% of the market. Brooke Bond's price rises were soon matched by those of other firms, bringing the industry to the attention of the Prices and Incomes Board in 1970. Sealink, with 34% of the cross-channel ferry market, seems to have been the price leader in ferry travel to the Continent in the 1980s. In the car industry, Ford has frequently acted as the dominant market leader by being first with its price increases. In 1990, companies that bought fleet cars from Ford, Rover, Vauxhall and Peugeot Talbot, accused the big car manufacturers of operating a price cartel led by Ford. By initiating two separate price rises (amounting to a total of 8.5% by the middle of 1990), Ford was seen as the dominant leader of a 'cartel' by the fleet car buyers. We have already noted that Vitafoam acted as a dominant price leader for reconstituted foam in the upholstery business in the UK in 1999.

2. Barometric-firm leadership. In some cases the price leader is a small firm, recognized by others to have a close knowledge of prevailing market conditions. The firm acts as a 'barometer' to others of changing market conditions, and its prices are closely followed. In the mid-1970s Williams and Glyn's, a relatively small commercial bank, took the lead in reducing bank charges in response to rising interest rates. Maunder also found this sort of price leadership in the glass bottle and sanitary ware markets of the 1960s and early 1970s (Maunder 1972). Since the mid-1970s there have been signs that the 'minor'

petrol wholesalers have had an increasing influence on petrol prices (see Chapter 9). Again the barometric form of price leadership can be seen in the North American newsprint industry where some 30 firms produce most of the newsprint. In a major study, Booth *et al.* (1991) found a tendency for a leader to emerge which then acts as an 'anchor' for the calculations of other firms in the industry and as a 'trigger' for any price adjustment within the group when cost or demand conditions change.

3. Collusive-price leadership. This is a more complicated form of price leadership; essentially it is an informal cartel in which prices change almost simultaneously. The parallel pricing which occurred in the wholesale petrol market (noted in Chapter 9) until the mid-1970s suggested this sort of tacit group collusion. In practice it is often difficult to distinguish collusive-price leadership from types in which firms follow price leaders very quickly. The French market for spring water, referred to earlier in the chapter, is one where both the setting of parallel prices and price leadership were present. Between 1987 and 1992 the prices of bottled water sold by Nestlé, Perrier and BSN rose in almost a simultaneous or parallel way, with Perrier being the price leader. Although the three companies did not have a collusive price arrangement, their behaviour was reminiscent of a close 'tacit' form of oligopolistic interdependence.

Conclusion

That oligopoly has become a progressively more important form of market structure in the UK is clear from the data, particularly from concentration ratios. Interdependence is a key feature of such markets, which makes the outcome of any strategy by a firm uncertain, depending to a large extent on how the rivals react. Price competition may be a particularly hazardous strategy, perhaps leading to a 'price war'. In any case, to the extent that kinked-demand theory is valid, the profit-maximizing price may not change even for wide variations in cost. For both these reasons there may be extensive periods of price stability. Even so, there may still be close competition between firms for market share, though this will be mainly of the non-price variety – advertising, packaging, new brands, etc. Non-price competition, by increasing product differentiation, real or imagined, may benefit firms not only by raising market share, but by providing greater future control over price – extra brand loyalty making demand curves less price-elastic.

The uncertainty of rival reactions, whether price or non-price, can be mitigated by guesswork, based on past experience (reaction curves), or by trying to evaluate the rivals' optimal counter-strategy (game theory). Collusion between firms may be a still more secure way of reducing uncertainty and avoiding mutual damage. This could be arranged formally, as in cartels, or informally by some form of tacit collusion (information agreements, price leadership, etc.). Although we may be no nearer a general model of oligopoly behaviour, we have made some progress in predicting how firms react under particular circumstances at particular times.

Key points

- Concentration ratios for both product and industry groups have risen over time, implying a more oligopolistic market structure.

- 'Recognized interdependence between the few' is a key feature of oligopoly markets.

- Where firms develop their own strategies independently we speak of 'non-collusive behaviour'.

- Even in this case firms will seek to anticipate how their rivals might react to any strategy they might adopt.

- Past experience might be a guide to rival reactions, as in the 'kinked demand' model. Firms learn that rivals match price cuts but not price rises. The model predicts price stability.

- Even where there is little price competition, there may be extensive non-price competition.

- 'Game' simulations may be used to predict the outcomes of different combinations of action/reaction. Games may or may not have stable equilibria depending on the strategies each firm adopts.

- To avoid uncertainty, collusion may occur, whether formal (cartels) or informal (tacit).

- Informal collusion may include various types of price leadership models as well as agreements of various kinds.

- To be successful firms must abide by the rules of collusive agreements, e.g. producing no more than their allocated quotas.

Now try the self-check questions for this chapter on the Companion Website. You will also find up-to-date facts and case materials.

Notes

1. Cross-elasticity of demand is defined as the percentage change in the quantity demanded of X, divided by the percentage change in the price of Y. If X and Y are close substitutes, then a small fall in the price of Y will lead to a substantial decrease in demand for X. This gives a high positive value for the quotient.

2. See, for instance, Jump (1982), which suggested that brand loyalty permitted prices to be 9% higher for branded processed foods in the USA than for supermarket own-brand equivalents.

3. This is because each demand curve, *dd'* and *DD'* respectively, will have its own separate marginal revenue curve, bisecting the horizontal between the vertical axis and the demand curve in question.

4. The maxi–min approach is a rather conservative strategy in that it assumes that the rival reacts to your strategy in the worst possible way for you.

5. A distribution of the joint profit-maximizing output such that aggregate $MR = MC$ in each separate market is often called the 'ideal' distribution. From Fig. 6.2 we can see that there is no other distribution which will raise total profits for the industry. For instance, one extra unit produced by Firm B will add more to cost than is saved by one fewer unit produced by Firm A (i.e. $MC_B > MC_A$). Whether the firms will acquiesce in such a share-out is quite another matter.

References and further reading

Bhaskar, V., Machin, S. and Reid, G. (1991) Testing a model of the kinked demand curve, *Journal of Industrial Economics*, 39(3), March.

Booth, D. I., Kanetkar, V., Vertinsky, I. and Whistler, D. (1991) An empirical model of capacity expansion and pricing in an oligopoly with barometric price leadership: a case study of the newsprint industry of North America, *Journal of Industrial Economics*, 39(3), March.

Cubbin, J. and Domberger, S. (1988) Advertising and post-entry oligopoly behaviour, *Journal of Industrial Economics*, 37, December.

Davies, S. and Lyons, D. (1996) *Industrial Organisation in the EU*, Clarendon Press, Oxford.

Domberger, S. (1980) Mergers, market structure and the rate of price adjustment, in Cowling, K. *et al.*, *Mergers and Economic Performance*, CUP, Cambridge, Ch. 13.

European Commission (1994) *European Economy*, No. 57, Part C.

Financial Times (1990) Reconnecting charges with costs, 3 April.

Jump, N. (1982) Corporate strategy in mature markets, *Barclays Bank Review*, 57(4), November.

Marketing (2002a) The UK's top 100 advertisers, 21 February.

Marketing (2002b) Britain's biggest brands, 15 August.

Maunder, P. (1972) Price leadership: an appraisal of its character in some British industries, *Business Economist*, 4.

Wagner, L. (ed.) (1981) *Readings in Applied Micro-economics*, 2nd edn, OUP, Oxford.

Chapter 7 The multinational corporation

This chapter focuses on the 'globalization' of business and the growing importance of the multinational corporation. Aided by a host of 'enabling technologies', notably inexpensive air travel and microchip-based communications systems, the world's largest companies have become truly global in scope. From Beijing to London to Tierra del Fuego, today's teenagers universally drink Coca-Cola, eat McDonald's hamburgers and wear Levi jeans. Their parents drive cars produced by a handful of global auto makers, filling them up with petrol refined by an even smaller number of worldwide oil companies. This chapter reviews the changing pattern of production by multinational corporations, going on to consider the reasons for the increasing globalization of business. It then considers the implications of this phenomenon for the UK economy.

What is a multinational corporation?

The terms 'multinational', 'transnational' and 'international' corporation (or enterprise) are often used interchangeably. A multinational may be defined as a company which owns or controls production or service facilities in more than one country. In other words, a multinational is *not* simply a company which trades internationally by exporting its products (or by licensing overseas producers); it actually *owns* (via a wholly or partly owned subsidiary) or *controls* (via a branch plant, joint venture or minority shareholding) productive facilities in countries outside its home country. Such overseas productive facilities may be acquired by taking over existing locally-owned capacity (e.g. Coca-Cola's acquisition of parts of Cadbury Schweppes in 1999) or by investing directly in new (or 'greenfield site') plant and equipment (e.g. Nissan's plant in Washington or Toyota's car factory in Derby).

From a statistical point of view, there are two main methods of ranking the world's top multinationals: first, according to the amount of foreign assets they control, and second, in terms of a 'transnationality index'. Table 7.1 ranks the top 10 multinationals according to the value of foreign assets they control. We can see that three of the top 10 companies are from the US, three from the UK, and one each from France, Japan, Spain and Italy. They are primarily based in the telecommunications, petroleum and motor vehicle sectors. However, Table 7.1 also provides each company's transnationality index and its transnationality ranking. The *transnationality index* takes a more comprehensive view of a company's global activity and is calculated as the average of the following ratios: foreign assets/total assets; foreign sales/total sales; and foreign employment/total employment. For example, we can see that the second largest multinational company is General Electric in terms of the foreign assets it owns. However, its transnationality index of 40% means that it is ranked only 73rd in terms of this criterion. The reason for this is that even though it has large investments overseas in absolute value, in *percentage* terms most of its assets, sales and employment are still located in the US. This is in contrast with Exxon Corporation where over 68% of its overall activity is based abroad.

If we wanted to find the companies which operate mostly outside their home country, then we would have to look at the top 10 multinationals in terms of the *transnationality index*. These are shown in Table 7.2 and here we see the dominance of EU companies in sectors such as food/beverages, pharmaceuticals/chemicals and electrical/electronics. The companies with the highest transnationality index are often from the smaller countries, as a more restricted domestic

Table 7.1 World's top 10 non-financial multinationals ranked by foreign assets, 2000.

| Rankings | | | | | Transnationality |
Foreign assets	Transnationality index	Company	Country	Industry	index (%)
1	15	Vodafone	UK	Telecommunications	81
2	73	General Electric	USA	Electrical/electronics	40
3	30	Exxon/Mobil	USA	Petroleum	68
4	42	Vivendi Universal	France	Diversified	60
5	84	General Motors	USA	Motor vehicles	31
6	46	Royal Dutch/Shell	UK	Petroleum	57
7	24	BP	UK	Petroleum	77
8	80	Toyota Motor	Japan	Motor vehicles	35
9	55	Telefonica	Spain	Telecommunications	54
10	47	Fiat	Italy	Motor vehicles	57

Source: Modified from UNCTAD (2002), Table 2, p. 2.

Table 7.2 World's top 10 non-financial multinationals ranked by transnationality index, 2000.

Rankings					
Transnationality index	Foreign assets	Company	Country	Industry	Transnationality index (%)
1	39	Rio Tinto Zinc	UK	Mining	98.2
2	49	Thomson	Canada	Media	95.3
3	24	ABB	Switzerland	Machinery/equipment	94.9
4	18	Nestlé	Switzerland	Food & beverages	94.7
5	31	BAT	UK	Tobacco	94.7
6	91	Electrolux	Sweden	Electrical/electronics	93.2
7	86	Interbrew	Belgium	Food & beverages	90.2
8	26	Anglo American	UK	Mining/quarrying	88.4
9	52	AstraZeneca	UK	Pharmaceuticals	86.9
10	25	Philips Electronics	Netherlands	Electrical/electronics	85.7

Source: Modified from UNCTAD (2002), Table IV.8, p. 97.

market induces them to operate abroad if they are to maximize their growth in terms of revenue or profits.

Technical definitions of multinationals, however, fail to convey the true scope and diversity of global business, which covers everything from the thousands of medium-sized firms which have overseas operations to the truly gigantic multinationals like IBM, General Motors and Ford. Some multinationals are vertically integrated, with different stages of the same productive process taking place in different countries (e.g. British Petroleum). Others are horizontally integrated, performing the same basic production operations in each of the countries in which they operate (e.g. Marks and Spencer). Many multinationals are household names, marketing global brands (e.g. Rothmans International, IBM, British Airways). Others are holding companies for a portfolio of international companies (e.g. Diageo) or specialize in capital goods that have little name-recognition in the high street (e.g. BTR).

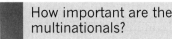

How important are the multinationals?

In 2002 the United Nations Division on Transnational Corporations and Investment estimated that there were 65,000 multinationals at that time,

collectively controlling a total of 850,000 foreign affiliates. Table 7.3 provides an overview of multinational activity. It shows that in 2001 the sales of multinationals' foreign affiliates exceeded global exports and amounted to 58% of world Gross Domestic Product (GDP). It also shows that foreign direct investment (FDI) has grown at approximately twice the rate of growth of exports for much of the period since 1986. Multinationals' affiliates also accounted for 33% of world exports. Ranked by either turnover or GDP, half of the world's largest economic 'units' are multinationals, rather than countries. Only 14 nation states have a GDP which exceeds the turnover of Exxon, Ford or General Motors.

Historically, the bulk of multinational activity was concentrated in the *developed* world. Indeed, as recently as the mid-1980s, half of all multinational production took place in only five countries – the United States, Canada, the UK, Germany and the Netherlands. This pattern is now changing rapidly. The rapid industrialization and economic growth in the newly industrializing nations of the world has led to a sharp increase in multinational investment in Asia and (to a lesser extent) Latin America. Some of these countries, notably the 'four tigers' (Taiwan, South Korea, Hong Kong and Singapore), now have per capita GDP levels which exceed those of most European nations and their indigenous companies are

Table 7.3 Multinational activity in a global context.

	2001 ($bn)	Average annual growth rates (%)			
		1986–1990	1991–1995	1996–2000	2001
FDI outflows	621	24.3	15.8	36.7	−55.0
FDI outward stock	6,582	19.8	10.4	17.8	7.6
Sales of foreign affiliates	18,517	16.9	10.5	14.5	9.2
World GDP at factor cost	31,900*	11.5	6.5	1.2	2.0
World gross fixed capital formation	6,680	13.9	5.0	1.3	–
Exports of goods and non-factor services	7,430†	15.8	8.7	4.2	−5.4

*2000 figure.
†Estimate.
Source: UNCTAD (2002), Table 1.1.

now beginning to establish production facilities in the 'old world', although the 1997 'Asian crisis' may temporarily slow or even reverse this process. Figure 7.1 shows that the old bipolar world (dominated by North America and Europe) is now giving way to a tripolar economy, comprising the 'triad' of North America, the European Union, and East and South-East Asia. These three regions account for approximately 75% of the world's exports and 60% of manufacturing output and almost all multinational activity.

It is estimated that in the next 10 years, world GDP will nearly double from its present level of $30,000bn to $55,000bn, with the share of the devel-

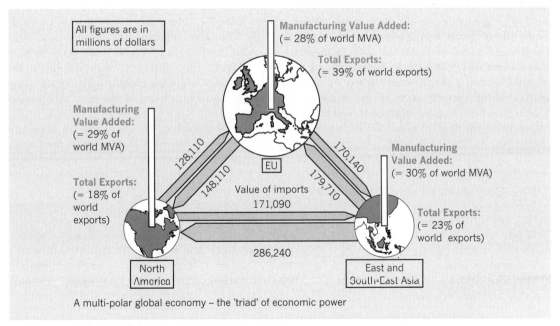

A multi-polar global economy – the 'triad' of economic power

Fig. 7.1 The changing global map of production and trade.
Source: Adapted from Dicken (2003).

oping world rising from one-third to one-half over the same period. Table 7.4 shows the changing pattern of foreign direct investment by which domestic companies acquire control over productive facilities overseas. While a strong cyclical pattern is evident, with FDI in the rich industrial countries higher during the world boom than in the recessionary years of the early 1990s, investment in the developing countries shows a strong secular increase over the period 1989–2001.

Table 7.4 also reflects the reintegration of the former centrally planned economies of central and eastern Europe into the world economy. These former centrally planned economies are included in the category 'developing countries'. Although the total volume of inward foreign investment is still relatively low (central and eastern Europe attracted only 2.4% of total global inflows in the period 2000–01), inflows have increased strongly since the transition process began in 1989. In this region, 60% of the inflows are associated with the privatization of former state-owned enterprises (compared with 8% in the other developing countries). Unsurprisingly, countries that have pushed ahead with market reform, and privatization in particular, have attracted the bulk of the foreign investment, both by creating international confidence in their future economic and political stability and by providing the opportunities for foreign companies to buy local production and distribution facilities. Poland and the Czech Republic, for example, have been highly successful in attracting multinationals such as Ford, Volkswagen and Philip Morris. Countries which have resisted or delayed market reform, notably many of the states of the former Soviet Union, have, in contrast, found foreign companies unwilling to risk large-scale inward investment.

Multinationals and the UK economy

Multinationals play a central role in the UK economy. Table 7.5 gives one indication of their importance. It lists the top 20 non-financial UK corporations ranked by market value, most of them being well-known multinational companies. Royal Dutch/Shell and BP boast production and distribution facilities in over 100 countries, while Vodafone and BT in the telecommunications sector have increased their international scope in recent years. The giant pharmaceutical companies GlaxoSmithKline and AstraZeneca also illustrate well the growth of UK transnationals in the competitive environment of the pharmaceuticals industry.

The UK still ranks as a major home to multinationals, reflecting its colonial past and the vast assets accumulated 1914. Although Table 7.6 suggests that the *number* of home-based multinationals is smaller than in the other countries represented, the *value* of their contribution to multinational activity is substantially greater, as can be seen in Table 7.7. Outward foreign investment from Britain has remained high ever since the Second World War, with UK home-based multinationals responsible for over 17% of all FDI outflows from the developed economies between 1996 and 2001, whilst representing only around 6% of all home-based multinationals (see Table 7.7). Moreover, despite the UK's increasingly close economic and political ties with other member states of the European Union (EU), the bulk of *outward* foreign direct investment still goes to the United States where UK multinationals retain a pre-eminent position in terms of the value of US assets controlled.

As a host country, the UK is also an important destination for *inward* direct investment by foreign

Table 7.4 Inflows of foreign direct investment ($bn).

Region	1990–95 (annual average)	1996	1997	1998	1999	2000	2001
Developed countries	145.0	219.9	267.9	484.2	837.7	1,227.5	503.1
Developing countries	74.3	152.7	191.0	187.6	225.1	237.9	204.8
Central and Eastern Europe	6.0	13.5	19.1	22.6	25.4	26.6	27.2

Note: Figures are rounded.
Source: Modified from UNCTAD (2002), Annex Table B.1.

Table 7.5 The UK's top 20 non-financial companies by market value (£m).

Rank	Company	Sector	Market value (£m)
1	Royal Dutch/Shell*	Oil and gas	93,125
2	BP	Oil and gas	90,238
3	Vodafone	Telecommunications services	76,831
4	GlaxoSmithKline	Pharmaceuticals/biotechnology	66,932
5	Unilever*	Food products and processors	38,516
6	AstraZeneca	Pharmaceuticals/biotechnology	36,948
7	Diageo	Beverages	20,399
8	BT Group	Telecommunications services	14,104
9	Anglo American	Mining	13,209
10	Tesco	Food/drug retailers	12,987
11	BAT	Tobacco	12,656
12	British Sky Broadcasting	Media and entertainment	12,300
13	National Grid Transco	Utilities	11,892
14	BG Group	Oil and gas	8,586
15	Reckitt Benckiser	Personal care/household products	7,740
16	Imperial Tobacco	Tobacco	7,288
17	Scottish Power	Electricity	7,026
18	Cadbury Schweppes	Food producers/processors	6,963
19	Marks & Spencer	General retailers	6,863
20	Centrica	Utilities	6,230

*Anglo/Dutch companies. Market value converted from dollars at the rate £1 = $1.60.
Source: Modified from *Financial Times* (2003).

Table 7.6 Home and host to multinationals.

	Parent corporation based in country: home	Foreign affiliates based in country: host
France	1,922	9,473
Germany	8,522	13,267
United Kingdom	3,208	8,609
Japan	3,786	3,359
United States	3,263	15,699
Total (five countries)	20,701	50,407
Developed countries	50,250	100,825

Source: Modified from UNCTAD (2002), Annex table A.1.3.

Table 7.7 FDI outflows from five main home economies for multinationals ($bn).

	1990–95 annual average	1996	1997	1998	1999	2000	2001
France	23.7	30.4	35.6	48.6	120.6	175.5	82.8
Germany	23.4	50.8	41.8	88.8	109.5	49.8	43.3
United Kingdom	25.6	34.0	61.6	122.8	201.4	253.9	39.5
Japan	25.0	23.4	26.0	24.2	22.7	31.6	38.1
USA	58.1	84.4	95.8	131.0	174.6	165.0	114.0
Total	155.8	223.0	260.8	415.4	628.8	675.8	317.7
Developed countries	221.0	332.4	395.0	631.3	966.0	1,271.2	580.6

Source: Modified from UNCTAD (2002), Annex table B.2.

multinationals (see Table 7.6). Of the *Financial Times* top 500 companies operating in the UK, 313 are foreign-owned, with Germany (87), France (77), Switzerland (28) and the Netherlands (17) being the most important European nations. Just as UK multinationals dominate foreign direct investment in the United States, however, so US multinationals account for the lion's share of foreign direct investment in the UK; and led by Nissan, Sony, Toyota and Honda, Japanese and Korean multinationals are also increasing their stake in the UK economy. In recent years, 120 major Japanese companies have set up in the UK. Over 30% of all Japanese foreign direct investment in the EU to date has been in the UK, and the Confederation of British Industry (CBI) estimates that, by 2010, subsidiaries of Japanese multinationals alone could produce as much as 20% of the UK's industrial output.

The UK economy is thus particularly affected by the globalization of business, being simultaneously home of, *and* host to, a large number of multinationals producing a rapidly growing proportion of its output. Multinational companies (both UK companies and foreign companies in the UK) account for an estimated 30% of GDP in the UK and almost half of all manufacturing employment. Most activity is concentrated in capital-intensive, high technology sectors – computers, automobiles, electronics, pharmaceuticals and chemicals. One-third of UK exports and imports by value are estimated to be *intra-firm* (within firm) transactions, as multinationals import and export the intermediate products which tie together production processes which are vertically integrated across national frontiers.

Why do companies become multinational?

Multinationals are very heterogeneous in nature. Most large companies are multinational, but there are many medium-sized companies which also have overseas operations. This heterogeneity makes it difficult to generalize about the reasons why firms become multinational. Nevertheless, there is broad agreement amongst economists that the primary motivation for multinational activity is to seek higher or more

secure profits in the long term – for example, by strengthening the company's market position.

Ultimately, any such consideration of the motives for establishing overseas operations must focus on one or other side of the profit and loss account; that is, becoming multinational is driven either by a desire to cut costs or, alternatively, by the prospect of greater revenues. One way of categorizing these two motives is to distinguish between multinationals which are *cost-oriented* and those which are *market-oriented*.

- **Cost-oriented multinationals** are those which internationalize their operations by *vertical integration*; e.g. integrating backwards in search of cheaper or more secure inputs into the productive process. Oil companies such as Exxon, Shell and BP were early examples of this approach. In order to secure control of strategic raw materials in oil fields around the world, they established overseas extraction operations in the early years of the twentieth century with the aim of shipping crude oil back to their home markets for refining and sale. More recently, many US and European companies have integrated forwards by establishing assembly facilities in South East Asia in order to take account of the relative abundance of cheap, high quality labour (see Fig. 7.2). Companies such as America's ITT ship semi-manufactured components to the region, where they are assembled by local labour into finished products which are then re-exported back to the home market. Such home countries are sometimes termed 'production platforms', which underscores their role as providers of a low-cost input into a global, vertically integrated production process.

- **Market-oriented multinationals** are those whose internationalization is motivated by the promise of new markets and greater sales; i.e. the internationalization process takes the form of *horizontal* (rather than vertical) *integration* into new geographic markets, with companies gradually switching from exporting (or licensing) to establishing first a sales outlet and finally full production facilities overseas (see Fig. 7.3).

Figure 7.4 shows the spectacular divergence in economic performance between the world's major economies which is expected over the next 15 years. It shows that currently, in terms of market size, the

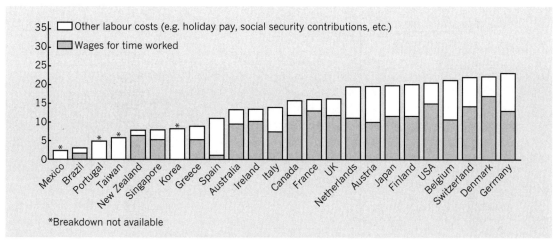

Fig. 7.2 Manufacturing labour costs ($ per hour, 2002).
Source: US Department of Labor (2002), Bureau of Statistics, September.

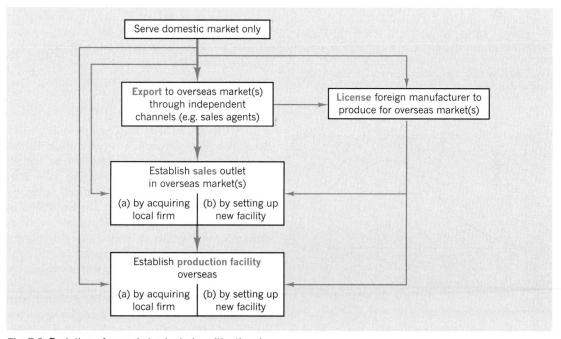

Fig. 7.3 Evolution of a market-oriented multinational.

global economy is dominated by rich industrial countries like the United States, Japan, Germany, France, Italy and the UK. However, by the year 2020, China will be the world's largest market, with India, Indonesia, South Korea, Thailand and Taiwan all moving into the 'top 10'. Therefore it is increasingly likely that market-oriented companies will be drawn to these areas.

Extending the product life cycle

A more subtle variation on this theme is that firms may internationalize in order to extend the 'product life cycle' of their products. The underlying thesis is that products have a finite economic life, going through four stages or phases (see Fig. 7.5). In the *introduction phase*, the product is slow to win over

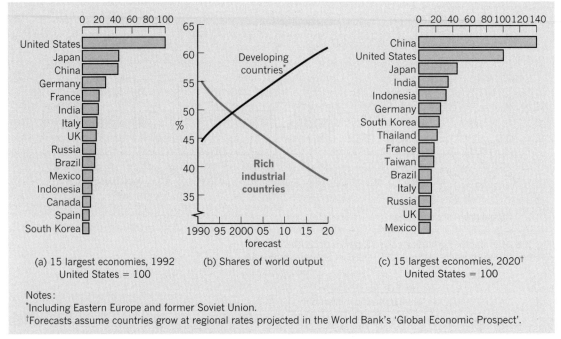

(a) 15 largest economies, 1992
United States = 100

(b) Shares of world output

(c) 15 largest economies, 2020†
United States = 100

Notes:
*Including Eastern Europe and former Soviet Union.
†Forecasts assume countries grow at regional rates projected in the World Bank's 'Global Economic Prospect'.

Fig. 7.4 Growth of the global economy, 1992–2020.
Source: World Bank.

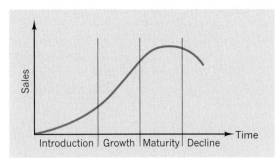

Fig. 7.5 Product life cycle.

consumers, who are unfamiliar with the innovation; many products fail at this stage. But for those which are successful, sales gradually build up in the following *growth phase*, as the product becomes established. At some point, the product reaches *maturity* – there are few new users to win over and most sales are on a replacement basis; the product becomes standardized and competition becomes cut-throat. Finally, either because a new substitute challenges the product or because consumer tastes simply move on, the product moves into a period of *decline*, with sales

steadily falling. The Sony Walkman provides a useful illustration of this cycle. It was first introduced to a sceptical Japanese market, where it was initially derided as a 'portable cassette player with no speakers and no facility to record tapes'. Gradually, it became established, stimulating a raft of 'me-too' copies by other companies until the market became saturated. Currently, the market is under attack from new formats, including portable CD players and the mini-disc system which allows material to be recorded onto small CD-like diskettes.

The link between the product life cycle and internationalization stems from the fact that a product may be at *different stages of its life cycle* in *different geographic markets*, giving rise to changing configurations of supply and demand which variously favour local production, and/or exporting, and/or importing from cheaper overseas suppliers.

Consider Fig. 7.6, which illustrates one possible scenario for a US manufacturer. In *Phase I* (introduction), production is concentrated in the United States, with the innovating companies exporting to other countries. As the US market matures and production techniques become standardized, production starts up

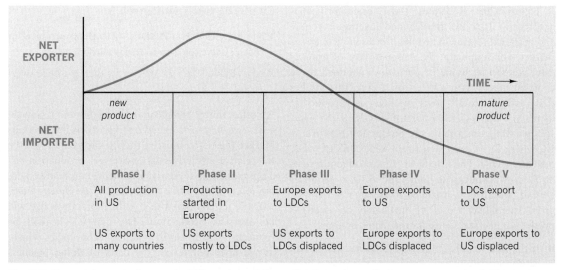

Fig. 7.6 Stages/phases in the product life cycle and the switch from domestic to overseas production.

in the expanding, lower-cost European market; these new lower-cost producers are able to initially displace imports into Europe from the United States (in *Phase II*) and then increasingly challenge US competitors for a share of developing country markets (in *Phase III*) and finally the US market itself (in *Phase IV*). In due course, however, the technology spreads to the developing world, whose producers are gradually able to take on and out-compete the now higher-cost European companies, first in their own markets (*Phase IV*) and ultimately in the US market as well (*Phase V*). In this way, the product life cycle drives production *out* of the innovating country to lower-cost producers overseas.

Advances in enabling technologies

While cost orientation and market orientation clearly provide important *motives* for investing and producing overseas, the acceleration in the pace of globalization is also intimately tied up with advances in *enabling technologies* which have reduced the costs of doing business across national frontiers. These include:

1 *improved communications*, including cheap air travel, satellite telephone and fax facilities, computers and IT-based communications systems such as the Internet;

2 *the globalization of consumer markets*, through television, video and popular music which make it

cheaper for established producers to penetrate new markets in developing countries; and

3 *new organizational technologies*, e.g. the rise of the divisional corporate structure based on product or geographic divisions or matrices. This makes managing complex global companies more feasible.

Benefits of producing overseas compared to exporting

One way of exploring the decision by a domestic company to internationalize its production is to consider the advantages of producing at home *vis-à-vis* overseas.

Consider a **market-oriented** company first. By exporting, the company can concentrate production in a single plant at home, reaping the advantages of lower production costs which flow from economies of scale and avoiding the costs of managing an overseas facility. By producing overseas, however, the company can avoid the costs of transporting its products and incurring tariffs. All other things being equal, the greater the scope for economies of scale and the higher the costs of managing offshore facilities, the more likely a firm will be to forego internationalization in favour of a large domestic plant; conversely, the smaller the scope for economies of scale and the higher the transports costs and tariffs faced when exporting, the greater the incentive to invest directly in overseas capacity.

Figure 7.7(a) illustrates these basic principles graphically. It shows the demand (average revenue) and marginal revenue schedules it faces in its *overseas* market. For simplicity, the *marginal cost of production*, whether at home or abroad, is assumed to be constant at C_1 (with a given fixed cost, this implies that average total costs decline as production increases). The *marginal cost of supplying the overseas market* from a domestic production platform is C_2, where $C_2 - C_1$ is equal to the unit costs of *transport* and *tariffs*. The firm faces *fixed* production costs of F_1 if it produces at home and F_2 if it produces abroad, where F_2 is assumed to be greater than F_1, given the higher costs of managing an overseas production facility. Consider the firm's options.

- If the firm *exports to the overseas market*, it will set C_2 equal to marginal revenue, charging a price P_2 and earning profit equal to $P_2 A C C_2 - F_1$.

- If the firm *establishes an overseas production facility*, then it will set C_1 equal to marginal revenue, charging a price P_1 and earning profit equal to $P_1 B D C_1 - F_2$.

Clearly, the firm's decision rule is:

1 if $P_2 A C C_2 - F_1 > P_1 B D C_1 - F_2$, then produce at home and export to overseas market;

2 if $P_1 B D C_1 - F_2 > P_2 A C C_2 - F_1$, then produce overseas.

All other things being equal, the *higher the transport costs and/or tariffs levied on exports* to the overseas market (i.e. C_2 compared to C_1), the greater will be the relative attractiveness of overseas production *vis-à-vis* exporting; similarly, all other things being equal, the *lower the relative fixed costs of producing overseas* (i.e. F_2 compared to F_1), the more attractive will be overseas production. The gap $F_2 - F_1$ will be reduced by advances in enabling technologies which, as we have noted, cut the costs of doing business across national frontiers.

Hence, the decision for a market-oriented firm to locate overseas rather than export hinges critically on the transport and tariff costs of serving overseas markets and the relative fixed costs of production. The greater the former, and the smaller any gap as

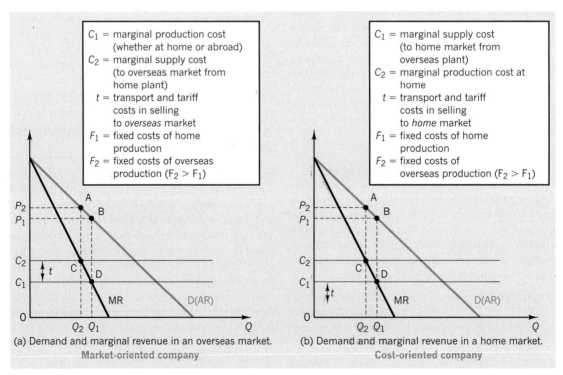

(a) Demand and marginal revenue in an overseas market. Market-oriented company

(b) Demand and marginal revenue in a home market. Cost-oriented company

Fig. 7.7 Demand and marginal revenue depending on company and market.

regards the latter $(F_2 > F_1)$, the more favourable the situation is to multinational activity.

The same diagram can also be reinterpreted to illustrate the decision facing a **cost-oriented** multinational. In this case (Fig. 7.7(b)), the demand and marginal revenue schedules are drawn for the *home market*. C_2 is now the company's marginal cost of producing at home for its domestic market, while C_1 represents the marginal cost of supplying the home market from an overseas production platform and shipping back to the home market. Despite the costs of transport and tariffs, it is assumed here that overseas production is subject to lower supply costs, for example because of lower labour costs.

- If the firm *produces at home*, it sets marginal production cost C_2 equal to marginal revenue, charging a price P_2 and earning profit $P_2 ACC_2 - F_1$.
- If the firm *produces abroad*, it sets marginal supply cost C_1 equal to marginal revenue, charging a price P_1 and earning profit $P_1 BDC_1 - F_2$.

Its decision rules are now:

1. if $P_2 ACC_2 - F_1 > P_1 BDC_1 - F_2$, then produce at home;
2. if $P_1 BDC_1 - F_2 > P_2 ACC_2 - F_1$, then produce overseas and export to the home market.

All other things being equal, the *lower the relative marginal costs of supplying from overseas* (i.e. C_1 compared to C_2), the greater will be the relative attractiveness of overseas production *vis-à-vis* domestic production; similarly, all other things being equal, the *lower the relative fixed costs of producing overseas* (i.e. F_2 compared to F_1) the more attractive will be overseas production.

Hence, the decision for a cost-oriented firm to serve its home market from an offshore production facility rather than producing at home hinges on the relative variable costs of overseas production and relative fixed costs. The greater the (variable) cost discrepancy in favour of overseas supply, and the smaller any gap as regards overseas fixed costs compared to domestic fixed costs (i.e. F_2 compared to F_1), the more favourable the situation is to multinational activity.

It should be remembered that labour cost (an important variable cost) can be an important determinant of production location even within major industrialized countries. For example in 2002, the US Department of Labor calculated that the hourly compensation costs of production workers in the UK were \$16.1 as compared to the US (\$20.3), France (\$15.9), Japan (\$19.6) and Germany (\$22.9). The 1,500 German subsidiaries operating in the UK see the relatively low labour costs in the UK as giving them an attractive production advantage which they can exploit by exporting their UK-produced goods back to Germany and to other European countries.

Location and internalization

The above explanations of internationalization are, however, only partial. They fail to explain why cost-oriented companies do not simply import the inputs they need from independent producers in low-cost countries rather than integrating backwards; similarly, they do not explain why market-oriented companies should operate their own production facilities in foreign markets rather than licensing local manufacturers to produce their products. A full explanation needs to account for both 'location' (i.e. why a good is produced in *two or more* countries rather than simply one) and 'internalization' (i.e. why production in different locations is done by the *same* firm rather than different firms).

Dunning (1993) attempted to synthesize different theoretical perspectives on multinationals with the evidence provided by case studies. He concluded that companies will only become involved in overseas investment and production when the following conditions are all satisfied:

1. companies possess an 'ownership-specific' advantage over firms in the host country (e.g. assets which are internal to the firm, including organization structure, human capital, financial resources, size and market power);
2. these advantages are best exploited by the firm itself, rather than selling them to foreign firms. In other words, due to market imperfections (e.g. uncertainty), multinationals choose to bypass the market and 'internalize' the use of ownership-specific advantages via vertical and horizontal integration (such internalization reduces transactions costs in the presence of market imperfections); and
3. it must be more profitable for the multinational to exploit its ownership-specific advantages in an

Table 7.8 Types of international production: some determining factors.

Types of international production	(O) Ownership advantages (the 'why' of MNE activity)	(L) Location advantages (the 'where' of production)	(I) Internalization (the 'how' of involvement)	Strategic goals of MNEs	Illustration of types of activity that favour MNEs
Natural resource seeking	Capital, technology, access to markets; complementary assets; size and negotiating strengths	Possession of natural resources and related transport and communications infrastructure; tax and other incentives	To ensure stability of supplies at right price; control markets	To gain privileged access to resources vis-à-vis competitors	(a) Oil, copper, bauxite, bananas, pineapples, cocoa, hotels (b) Export processing, labour intensive products or processes
Market seeking	Capital, technology, information, management and organizational skills; surplus R&D and other capacity; economies of scale; ability to generate brand loyalty	Material and labour costs; market size and characteristics; government policy (e.g. with respect to regulations and to import controls, investment incentives, etc.)	Wish to reduce transaction or information costs, buyer ignorance, or uncertainty, etc; to protect property rights	To protect existing markets, counteract behaviour of competitors; to preclude rivals or potential rivals from gaining new markets	Computers, pharmaceuticals, motor vehicles, cigarettes, processed foods, airline services
Efficiency seeking (a) of products (b) of processes	As above, but also access to markets; economies of scope, geographical diversification, and international sourcing of inputs	(a) Economies of product specialization and concentration (b) Low labour costs; incentives to local production by host governments	(a) As for second category plus gains from economies of common governance (b) The economies of vertical integration	As part of regional or global product rationalization and/or to gain advantages of process specialization	(a) Motor vehicles, electrical appliances, business services, some R&D (b) Consumer electronics, textiles and clothing, cameras, pharmaceuticals
Strategic asset seeking	Any of first three that offer opportunities for synergy with existing assets	Any of first three that offer technology, markets and other assets in which firm is deficient	Economies of common governance; improved competitive or strategic advantage; to reduce or spread risks	To strengthen global innovatory or production competitiveness; to gain new product lines or markets	Industries that record a high ratio of fixed to overhead costs and which offer substantial economies of scale or synergy
Textile and distribution (import and export)	Market access; products to distribute	Source of inputs and local markets; need to be near customers; after-sales servicing, etc.	Need to protect quality of inputs; need to ensure sales outlets and to avoid under-performance or misrepresentation by foreign agents	Either as entry to new markets or as part of regional or global marketing strategy	A variety of goods, particularly those requiring contact with subcontractors and final consumers
Support services	Experience of clients in home countries	Availability of markets, particularly those of 'lead' clients	Various (see above categories)	As part of regional or global product or geographical diversification	(a) Accounting, advertising, banking, producer goods (b) Where spatial linkages are essential (e.g. airlines and shipping)

Source: Adapted from Dunning (1993).

overseas market than in its domestic market, i.e. there must additionally exist 'location specific' factors which favour overseas production (e.g. special economic or political factors, attractive markets in terms of size, growth or structure, low 'psychic' or 'cultural' distance, etc.).

The decisions of multinationals to produce abroad are, therefore, determined by a mixture of motives – ownership-specific, internalization and location-specific factors – as noted above. These are also summarized in a more effective way in Table 7.8.

Honda case study

However, to understand the complexity of motives which underlie multinational activity it may be helpful to consider an actual example, namely Honda Europe. Figure 7.8 shows the Honda motorcycle network in Europe together with its outside supply links. Honda is very much a multinational company with a *transnationality index* of over 50%. It began by exporting motorcycles to Europe, but this was quickly followed by its first European overseas affiliate in 1962. This affiliate, Honda Benelux NV (Belgium), was set up in order to establish strong bonds with

European customers as well as to provide a 'learning' opportunity before Honda brought its automobile production to Europe. Figure 7.8 shows that, by the late 1990s, Honda's operations had widened significantly, with its affiliates in Germany acting as its main European regional headquarters. Honda Deutschland GmbH coordinates the production and marketing side, while Honda R & D Europe is engaged in research, engineering and designing for all the affiliates in Europe.

Honda's key *assembly* affiliates are Honda Industriale SpA (Italy) which is wholly owned, and Montessa Honda SA (Spain) which is majority owned (88%). These companies were originally designed to concentrate on the assembly of specific types of motorcycle model appropriate to the different European locations in order to benefit from various economies of scale. At the same time, each assembler exported its own model to the other Honda locations in Europe in order to gain economies in joint production and marketing; in other words any given model is produced in one location, but a full range of models is offered for sale in all locations. Finally, in the international context, Honda's European models are also exported to its subsidiaries in the US, Brazil

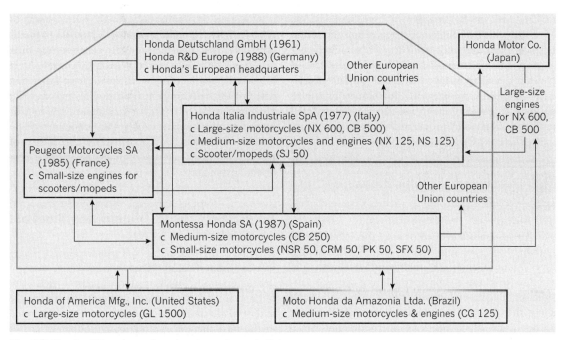

Fig. 7.8 Honda: EU motorcycle networks and supply links.
Source: UNCTAD (1996), p. 102.

and Japan, while its European network imports large and medium-sized motorcycles from its US and Brazil affiliates.

As far as motorcycle parts are concerned, engines and key parts were initially supplied from Japan. However, in 1985 Honda acquired a 25% stake in Peugeot Motorcycles SA and began producing small engines in France for scooters and mopeds. These engines were then supplied to its Italian and Spanish assemblers of scooters and mopeds. Following this, medium-sized engines began to be produced in Honda Italia Industriale, both for its own models and for Montessa Honda, while the latter began producing frames and other parts locally. Large-sized engines were still, however, supplied from Japan.

This study of Honda illustrates the complex set of motives underlying multinational activity which were discussed earlier. The traditional technical economies of scale were exploited to reduce average costs as were the more market-based advantages from producing within the EU with its 370 million consumers. In addition, the improved communications within the EU and the rise of more sophisticated corporate structures enabled Honda to integrate operations both horizontally, through affiliate specialization in particular models, and vertically, through specialization of affiliates in the production of parts. Honda was able to capitalize on its well-known ownership-specific advantages of excellent quality engineering and sound business skills, and to combine this with an intelligent strategy for locating production within the largest consumer market in the world. The Honda experience also helps to illustrate the nature of multinational *inter-firm* activity within a sophisticated market dominated by product differentiation.

 ## The impact of multinationals on the UK economy

The UK is unusually exposed to the influence of multinationals. As noted above, the UK is an important *home* country of multinationals, with the majority of its top companies operating overseas subsidiaries. By the end of the 1990s, official records show that the UK was the home for 1,059 parent corporations which operated internationally. Since the register does not give a complete picture of the involvement of smaller companies, we can take this to

be an underestimate of the total number, although it provides a useful guideline as to the number of medium to large UK multinational companies. However, we can supplement this data by using the flows of foreign direct investment from the UK as a measure of the UK's multinational involvement in the world's economy. Here we find that during the 2000–01 period the UK accounted for 22% of total EU outflows of FDI, ahead of Germany and France.

The UK is also a major *host* country for foreign multinationals. For example, in 2000, although foreign-owned businesses in agriculture, manufacturing and distribution accounted for only 0.5% of total UK enterprises, they accounted for as much as 12% of total UK employment and 25% of total UK turnover. Three countries, namely the US, Germany and Japan, had a particularly strong presence in the UK, accounting for over 60% of all foreign multinational employment and turnover in the UK. The US had, by far, the most dominating presence in the UK, accounting for some 42% of all foreign multinational employment in the UK and 37% of all foreign multinational turnover in the UK. In manufacturing, the presence of foreign multinationals is even more dominant, accounting for 19% of UK manufacturing employment and 26% of manufacturing net output (Duffus and Gooding 1997).

What are the implications for the UK economy of such openness to multinationals? Advocates of multinationals argue that the economy benefits from their activities, with outward and inward foreign direct investment accelerating industrial restructuring and ensuring the most efficient allocation of resources. On the other hand, critics argue that outward FDI by UK-owned multinationals denies the economy sorely-needed investment and jobs, while the influx of foreign multinationals undermines the nation's economic sovereignty.

An economic cost–benefit appraisal of multinational activity

It is clear that there are strongly contrasting views of multinationals. However, such divergent views are often coloured by implicit assumptions about the nature of the multinationals involved and, as noted in the introduction, international companies are so heterogeneous in their nature that generalizations are both difficult and potentially dangerous. For example, the precise balance of economic costs and benefits that a foreign multinational imposes on the UK economy depends upon:

1 how the multinational establishes itself in the UK (e.g. via a greenfield site investment or the takeover of locally owned productive assets, etc.);

2 whether funds used for the investment are raised locally or 'imported';

3 the function of the multinational (e.g. whether it is cost- or market-oriented); and

4 characteristics of host and parent economies (e.g. the extent to which there is 'culture dissonance').

These costs and benefits can be explored in more detail under six main headings. Consider each in turn.

Foreign direct investment and economic welfare

Direct investment by a foreign multinational is widely regarded as an unambiguous improvement in economic welfare. Figures 7.9(a) and (b) illustrate the potential economic gains from cross-border investment by multinationals in search of the highest marginal rate of return on capital. These figures show the marginal product of capital in both the home country (MPK_H) and overseas (MPK_F) respectively. Initially, in the absence of multinational activity, capital is relatively less abundant in the home country

and with a capital stock, K_1, the marginal product of capital is B. GDP is given by the area under the curve, $0ACK_1$, of which $0BCK_1$ is the reward to capital and BAC is the reward to labour. Similarly, in the overseas sector, the capital stock is K_4, giving rise to a marginal product of capital equal to J and a GDP of $0GLK_4$, of which $0JLK_4$ is the reward to capital and JGL the reward to labour.

Given this disparity between the marginal productivity of capital in different countries, profit-maximizing multinationals will reallocate capital from overseas to the home country, increasing the capital stock from K_1 to K_2, while reducing it overseas from K_4 to K_3. GDP in the home country will rise to $0AFK_2$, an increase of K_1CFK_2. GDP overseas will fall to $0GIK_3$, a reduction of K_3ILK_4. However, remember that a proportion of GDP is a reward to capital and, in the case of multinational investment in the home country, this profit will be repatriated overseas. Hence, for the home country, the net gain from the inward investment is only EFC (the reward to labour), with K_1EFK_2 being repatriated by the foreign multinationals. Conversely, overseas, the loss of GDP (K_3ILK_4) is offset by the repatriated profit K_1EFK_2. Since K_1K_2 (the increase in the capital stock in the home country) is equal to K_3K_4 (the decrease in the capital stock overseas), and D (new marginal product of capital at home) is equal to H (new marginal product of capital overseas), then area K_1EFK_2 must exceed area K_3ILK_4. Thus, the home country benefits as a result of the multinational activity (by the

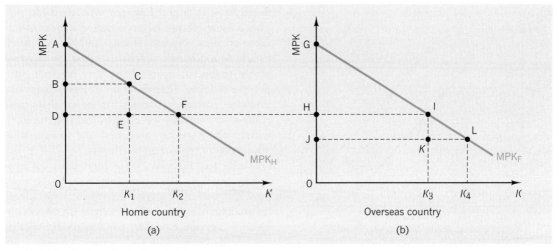

Fig. 7.9 Marginal product of capital, home and overseas.

amount of the value-added by its domestic labour force) and overseas producers gain (because the reward from the extra production generated by the use of their capital exceeds its opportunity cost in the overseas market).

This conventional analysis of the impact of multinational investment implicitly assumes, however, that the investment constitutes a reallocation of productive capital from overseas to the host country. In practice, this assumption may be violated in two ways.

First, multinationals frequently finance overseas investment either from the retained profits earned by their existing productive or sales operations in the target country or by raising the capital on the local capital market. In both cases, the multinational's investment may simply displace domestic investment that would otherwise have taken place. Figure 7.10 illustrates this dilemma.

An investment financed by a capital inflow from the parent multinational overseas bypasses the domestic market for loanable funds, leaving the balance of domestic savings and investment unchanged at I_2, with rate of interest r_0. However, raising funds locally to finance the investment increases the demand for loanable funds (from D to D'), leading to a rise in interest rates (from r_0 to r_1) and the crowding out of domestic investment (which falls from I_2 to I_1).

Secondly, multinational investment more frequently involves the takeover of existing assets, rather than

greenfield site investment in new plant and equipment. Table 7.9 gives details of the largest foreign acquisitions of UK companies that took place in 2001. In this case, the total capital stock of the host country is unaffected by the foreign direct investment, with the ownership of existing assets simply being transferred from local investors to the foreign multinational. Figure 7.11 gives an impression of the scale of such takeover activity, in both the UK and overseas markets. Note here that UK *domestic* refers to acquisitions by UK companies in the UK; UK *outward* refers to UK companies acquiring overseas companies; UK *inward* refers to overseas companies acquiring UK companies.

Technology transfer

It is widely held that multinational activity by more efficient foreign multinationals promotes technology transfer to the benefit of domestic companies. For example, when Nissan established a car plant in north-east England, it demanded much higher standards of UK component suppliers than the incumbent national producers such as Ford and Rover. Nissan's engineers assisted these supplying companies to upgrade their production processes in order to meet their requirements. The result was the creation of a strong positive externality: the international competitiveness of the UK car supply industry was strengthened and, as a direct consequence, the quality of the inputs to domestic auto makers improved.

This so-called 'technology transfer' is clearly maximized by such 'direct linkages' with domestic suppliers, which occurs when incoming multinationals such as Sony, Nissan, Honda and Toyota work closely with domestic suppliers to raise the standard of UK-produced inputs. There are, however, also positive indirect 'demonstration effects' which may promote technology transfer. At its simplest, these relate to attempts by less efficient local producers to imitate the superior processes and organization advantages of the foreign interlopers.

There are, however, clear limitations to technology transfer. Most obviously, one of the most powerful drivers for foreign investment is the advantage to a multinational of internalizing an ownership-specific advantage. Such considerations militate against the notion that a foreign multinational will willingly share the technologically based sources of its

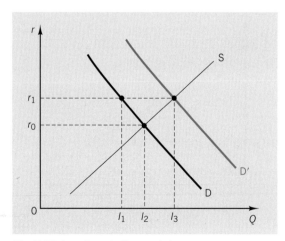

Fig. 7.10 Investment financed from overseas versus investment financed locally.

Table 7.9 The 10 largest foreign takeovers of UK companies completed in 2001 valued at over $1bn.

Acquired company	Sector	Acquiring company	Sector	Acquirer's nationality
Billiton Plc	Metal ores	BHP Ltd	Steelworks/rolling mills	Australian
GKN Plc suport services	Industrial supplies	Brambles Industries Ltd	Equipment rental/leasing	Australian
LASMO Ltd	Oil drilling/gas wells	ENI SpA	Petroleum refining	Italy
Blue Circle Industries Plc	Cement, hydraulic	Lafarge SA	Cement, hydraulic	France
AMS-Missiles Systems Division	Guided missiles and space vehicles	Matra BAe Dynamics	Guided missiles and space vehicles	France
Freesave Plc (Dixon's group)	Information retrieval services	Wanadoo (France Télécom SA)	Information retrieval services	France
Laporte Plc	Industrial organic chemicals	Degussa SKW Co.	Investors	Germany
IPC Group (Cinven)	Periodicals/publishing	AOL Time-Warner Inc.	Television broadcasting stations	US
Glynwed International pipe systems	Plastic pipes	Etex Group SA (Fineter SA)	Plastic pipes	Belgium
Marconi Plc medical operations	Surgical/medical instruments	Koninklijke Philips Electronics	Household audio/ video equipment	Netherlands

Source: Modified from UNCTAD (2002), Annex Table A.1.2.

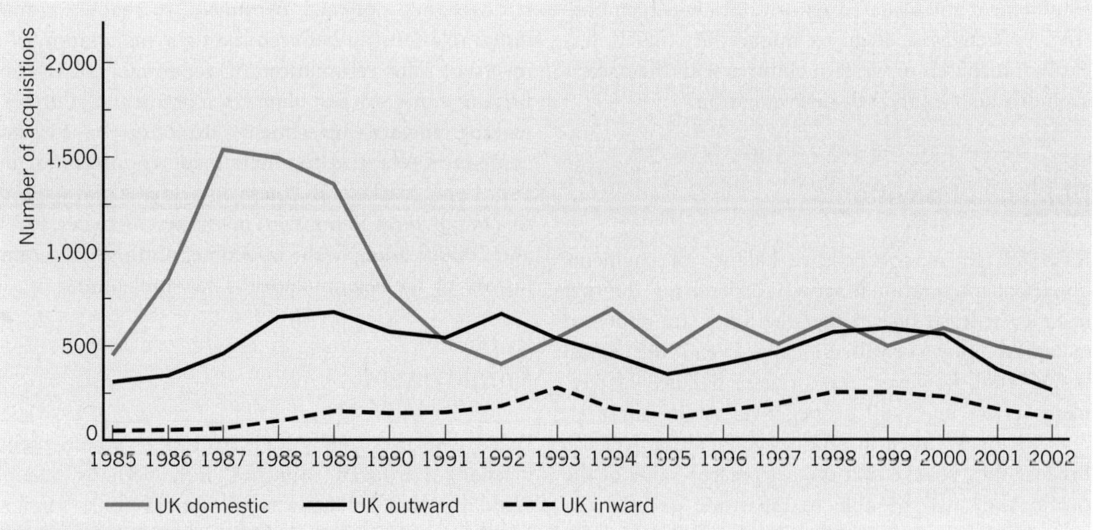

Fig. 7.11 Acquisition activity.
Sources: Amdata; ONS: Mergers and Acquisitions data 1969–2003.

competitive advantage over local rivals. Moreover, in the case of Japanese multinationals, their historical advantage was built upon close relationships with Japanese suppliers. For example, the big four Japanese motorcycle companies (Honda, Yamaha, Suzuki and Kawasaki) rely heavily on a very limited number of domestic suppliers (e.g. Bridgestone for tyres, Nippon Denso for electronic components, etc.). Early dissatisfaction with UK suppliers with regard to quality and reliability of deliveries has led to a number of these Japanese suppliers following their major customers into the European market, thereby reducing the potential scope for technology transfer via linkages with local suppliers.

A final problem relates to the issue of cultural dissonance. The psychic distance between US and UK companies is relatively small. Both share a broadly common culture, a common language and a reasonably high level of mutual understanding. The success of multinationals from, say, Japan or other parts of East and South-East Asia is built on a very different set of social and cultural values, which are not easily transferable to the UK setting. Companies such as Sony, Nissan and Honda have all reported difficulties in establishing Japanese-style work practices, which many economists regard as an integral part of that country's corporate success. The operation of 'just-in-time' (or 'kanban') production processes and 'quality circles' relies on employee loyalty to his or her company, which in Japan is reinforced by lifetime employment and a shared set of values which emphasizes collectivism. Such techniques are much less easily transposed to western cultures with their stress on individualism and self-determination.

Balance of payments

As noted above, the positive balance of payments impact of multinational activity depends, in the first instance at least, on whether the funds are imported (a capital inflow) or raised locally. Even if the capital is imported, however, the ultimate balance of payments effect may still be negative. At its simplest, multinationals invest in productive facilities overseas because they believe that the net present value of the profits they will be able to repatriate exceeds the capital investment they will make. It follows that, if a multinational invests rationally, the initial capital inflow must be at least matched by the net present value of future outflows on current account (i.e. net payments of interest, profit and dividend abroad). In crude money terms, the total value of the repatriated returns to capital will dwarf the original investment made.

Moreover, the speed with which an initial capital inflow is reversed by outflows on the current account depends critically on the function of the multinational. In the case of a market-oriented company intent on 'jumping tariffs', the multinational may attempt to import part-finished products, using cheap local labour to assemble the final product. Volkswagen was accused of this technique during the 1970s in Brazil, when it established a manufacturing plant in which workers assembled 'complete knock-down kits' into finished cars which were sold, tariff-free, in the Brazilian market. The impact on the current account was strongly negative, with visible imports being inflated by the cost of the kits and invisible imports being increased by the repatriated profits. Most countries (including Brazil) now have extensive 'rules of origin' to prevent such 'screw-driving operations' being used by multinationals as a device for evading tariffs.

In Britain's case, however, inward foreign direct investment has historically been generally outweighed by higher outward capital flows. Table 7.10 shows that both inward and outward investment fell during the 1990–92 recession. During the subsequent recovery, inward investment picked up much more strongly than outward investment, so that the traditional relationship between the two was temporarily reversed. The resumption of economic growth in Britain came earlier than in continental Europe, making inward investment attractive to foreign companies strapped for investment opportunities in their home markets. Recovery in overseas markets led to a major surge in outward investment between 1997 and 2000, leading to the largest net outflows in recent history by the beginning of the new millenium.

Employment

Faced with persistently high levels of unemployment in many European countries, it is perhaps understandable that so many states should court foreign multinationals in the belief that their investments will create local employment. Recent investments by major Japanese and US multinationals have, for example,

Table 7.10 The impact of multinationals on the UK's balance of payments.

	Direct inward investment (£m)	Direct outward investment (£m)	Net direct investment (£m)
1980	4,365	4,876	−511
1981	2,939	6,018	−3,079
1982	3,034	4,099	−1,065
1983	3,393	5,428	−2,035
1984	−181	6,055	−6,236
1985	4,514	8,448	−3,934
1986	5,850	11,674	−5,824
1987	9,469	19,188	−9,719
1988	12,034	20,893	−8,859
1989	18,581	21,472	−2,891
1990	18,566	10,588	−7,978
1991	9,086	9,059	27
1992	9,213	11,061	−1,848
1993	10,326	17,895	−7,569
1994	6,103	22,208	−16,105
1995	12,936	28,165	−15,229
1996	16,554	22,508	−5,954
1997	20,296	37,619	−17,323
1998	44,877	74,159	−29,282
1999	54,376	124,508	−70,132
2000	78,495	154,242	−75,747
2001	41,972	45,929	−3,957

Source: ONS, Business Monitor MA4 (Various).

been accompanied by strong competition on the part of national and regional governments in the EU to attract the investment in the hope of generating work. The relationship between government regional assistance and the presence of foreign multinational activity is dealt with more specifically in Chapter 11 on Regional and Urban Policy. The ultimate employment effect of multinational activity is, however, rather more complex. The net employment effect is a function of three factors:

1 direct job creation, which depends on the size of the foreign-owned subsidiary and the labour (or capital) intensity of its production processes;

2 indirect job creation, which depends on linkages with local suppliers and the value-added by domestic factors of production; and

3 the 'Trojan horse' effect, namely the displacement of domestic incumbents by the more efficient

multinational company, which depends upon the latter's market power.

In practice, it is difficult to gauge the net employment effect of multinational activity in the UK. There is no question that direct job creation has been significant, as witnessed by the eagerness of local authorities in areas of high unemployment to woo potential investors to their region. The UK government estimated that nearly 500,000 jobs were created by overseas businesses in the country between 1979 and 1998. However, indirect job creation (like technology transfer) is clearly limited by the extent to which foreign multinationals rely on imported intermediate products (e.g. inputs shipped from the parent company for local assembly). Under pressure from the EU, Japanese multinationals in the UK, for example, are attempting to raise the percentage of 'local' (i.e. EU) content in finished products to 80%, but the recent average is only 67%. Finally, to the extent that (by definition) foreign multinationals enjoy owner-ship-specific advantages over domestic rivals, their success is likely to be at the expense of the declining market share enjoyed by the existing incumbents – direct (and indirect) jobs gains may thus be offset by induced job losses in the adversely affected companies. The difficulty of estimating this Trojan horse effect in the UK is that the foreign multinational's output may compete with (and displace) exports from other countries, rather than with domestic production; by the same token, part or all of the multinational's output may be exported (e.g. to other states in the EU). Hence, the UK may enjoy the direct job gains, while the Trojan horse losses (which could well be larger) may fall on third countries, inside or outside the EU. In recent years, certain EU governments, notably France, have expressed precisely this fear, suspecting that the Japanese-led renaissance of the UK's consumer electronics and car industries will be at the expense of French, German and Italian workers.

In the UK, the Trojan horse effect is seen when foreign multinationals, often with UK government subsidies, create employment in the UK but at a high cost per worker and by displacing indigenous companies. For example, it has been calculated in the late 1990s that the subsidy given to the Korean Lucky Goldstar (LG) electronics company to locate production in South Wales amounted to £40,000 per job created – while indigenous investment could generate more high quality jobs for a much lower subsidy of between £2,000 and £3,000 per job (*Financial Times* 1998b). The problems of such investment became even clearer in May 2003 when economic difficulties at home in Korea, coupled with adverse market trends, led LG to announce the closure of its computer screen plant in South Wales with the loss of 900 jobs. The semiconductor plant built by LG on the same site in Newport did not even open for business.

Industrial structure

The ownership-specific advantage often enjoyed by foreign multinationals is their market size and power. One consequence of this is, inevitably, the displacement of less efficient domestic producers. Under certain circumstances, it is sometimes argued that foreign direct investment may result in the truncation of the host economy (i.e. the gradual loss of those economic sectors critical to self-sustained growth) and its subsequent dependence on overseas multinationals for continued growth and employment. *In extremis*, it is sometimes claimed that the widespread presence of foreign multinationals may lead to a loss of economic sovereignty on the part of the host country's government. The counter argument is that, at least in the case of the UK, foreign direct investment has positively benefited the UK's economic structure, channelling funds into those sectors (e.g. high technology manufacturing, car production, etc.) in which the economy enjoys a comparative advantage and thereby accelerating economic restructuring.

Taxation

Multinationals are widely accused by governments of arranging intra-company transactions in order to minimize their tax liabilities, effectively forcing countries to compete to provide the lowest tax regime. Consider a simplified example in which a multinational's production is vertically integrated, with operations in two countries. Basic manufacture takes place in country A and final assembly and sale in country B (see Table 7.11). In country A, the corporate tax rate is 25%, while in country B it is 50%. Suppose the company's costs (inputs, labour, etc.) in country A are $40m and it produces intermediate products with a market value of $50m; if it were to sell these intermediate products in the *open market*, it would declare a profit of $10m in country A, incurring a tax liability of $2.5m in that country.

However, suppose the products are actually intended for the parent company's subsidiary in country B. In Scenario 1, the 'transfer price' (i.e. internal price used by the company to calculate profits in different countries) is set at the market price of $50m in country A for the intermediate products which are now to be 'shipped' to country B for incorporation into the final product. The operation in country B incurs additional costs of $40m, after which the final product is sold in country B for $100m; thus the subsidiary will declare a profit of $10m and incur a tax liability of $5m. The company as a whole will face a total tax liability of $7.5m in countries A and B taken together.

Consider an alternative scenario (Scenario 2), in which the company sets a transfer price *above* the market price for the intermediate products manufactured in the low-tax country, A. With a transfer price

Table 7.11 Multinational tax avoidance.

$m	Scenario 1		Scenario 2	
	Country A	Country B	Country A	Country B
Costs	40	90	40	100
Sales	50	100	60	100
Profit	10	10	20	0
Tax liability	2.5	5	5	0
Total tax	7.5		5	

of $60m rather than $50m and the same costs of $40m, the subsidiary in country A incurs a higher tax liability (25% of $20m), but this is more than offset by the lower (in fact, zero) tax liability incurred by the subsidiary in country B. Because the latter is now recording its total costs (including the cost of the intermediate products 'bought' from the subsidiary in country A) as being $100m rather than $90m, its profits and tax liability fall to zero. As a result, the total tax liability faced by the company on its international operations is only $5m, rather than $7.5m.

The basic issue is that the multinational has earned a total profit of $20m on its vertically integrated operation, i.e. $100m actual sales revenue in B minus $80m costs in A + B. However, by setting transfer prices on intra-company sales and purchases of intermediate products appropriately, the company can 'move' this profit to the lowest-tax country, thereby denying the higher tax country (in this case, country B) the tax revenue to which it is entitled. Such transfer pricing can, of course, only succeed when there is no active market for the intermediate products being traded. If the tax authorities in country B can refer to an open market price for the intermediate product, the inflated transfer price being paid can be identified. However, to the extent that many multinationals internalize cross-border operations because they have ownership-specific advantages (e.g. control of a specific raw material or technology), it may be that comparable intermediate products are not available on the open market. For this reason, high-tax countries may find they lose tax revenues to lower tax centres as business becomes increasingly globalized. This creates, in turn, an incentive for countries to 'compete' for multinational tax revenues by offering low tax rates; the result of such competition is a transfer of income from national governments to the shareholders of multinational companies.

Conclusion

Multinationals play a more influential role in the UK economy than in any other major, developed country in the world. Most of the household-name companies in Britain – BP, Unilever, Ford, Kellogg, Heinz, Cadbury Schweppes – are multinationals. In the past, companies became multinational to secure resources and markets or to overcome the transport costs associated with exporting. Increasingly, multinationals are becoming genuinely global, performing different stages of an integrated productive process in different countries to exploit natural and government-induced differences in factor costs as we saw in the case of Honda. There is a fierce debate about the benefits and costs of multinational activity for individual economies such as that of the UK. What is clear, however, is that the growth of multinationals will continue into the next century and that an increasing proportion of UK companies will do the majority of their business overseas, while an ever-higher share of UK production will be controlled by foreign companies.

Indeed, it is already becoming increasingly meaningless to think of companies as 'British' or 'foreign'. Is Ford, an 'American' company which designs and builds cars in the UK, 'foreign'? Is Attock Oil, a 'British' oil exploration and production company which operates only in North America and SE Asia, 'British'? As companies become increasingly global in nature, the convention of labelling a company's nationality by reference to the nationality of its controlling shareholders will become redundant. Imagine the Ford Motor Company, owned by Japanese shareholders, run by an American chief executive, producing components across the EU and assembling them in Turkey for sale in Russia. In what sense is such a multinational 'American', 'Japanese' or even 'European'? The multinational of the future is likely to be genuinely 'stateless'. Already the trend towards statelessness is well underway and the implications of this phenomenon are liable to be profound.

Key points

- A 'multinational' is a company which owns or controls production or service facilities in more than one country.

- There are some 65,000 multinational companies, the sales revenue of which amounts to around 58% of world GDP. Only 14 nation states have a GDP greater than the annual turnover of Exxon, Ford or General Motors.

- Multinationals account for around 30% of GDP in the UK and almost half of manufacturing employment.

- Foreign multinationals account for 11% of UK employment and 23% of UK turnover. The US dominates the scene, accounting for 42% of all foreign multinational employment in the UK and 37% of all foreign multinational turnover.

- Successful multinational activity from the home base usually depends on the possession of 'ownership-specific' advantages over firms in the host country, together with 'location-specific' advantages which favour overseas production.

- Cost-oriented multinationals focus mainly on reducing costs of production via overseas production (often via vertical integration); market-oriented multinationals focus mainly on easier sales access to overseas markets via overseas production (often via horizontal integration).

- Being both a 'home' country to (UK) multinationals as well as a 'host' to foreign multinationals results in substantial flows of outward and inward foreign direct investment (FDI).

- The costs and benefits of multinational activity for the UK (or indeed any country) can usefully be assessed under six main headings:
  (i)   FDI and economic welfare
  (ii)   technology transfer
  (iii) balance of payments
  (iv)   employment
  (v)   industrial structure
  (vi)   taxation.

Now try the self-check questions for this chapter on the Companion Website. You will also find up-to-date facts and case materials.

References and further reading

Buckley, P. J. (1992) *New Dimensions in International Business*, Edward Elgar.

Cleeve, E. (1994) Transnational corporations and internationalisation: a critical review, *British Review of Economic Issues*, 16(40).

Crum, R. and Davies, S. (1991) *Multinationals*, Heinemann Educational.

Dicken, P. (2003) *Global Shift: Transforming the World Economy*, 4th edn, Paul Chapman.

Duffus, G. and Gooding, P. (1997) Globalisation: scope, issues and statistics, *Economic Trends*, No. 528, November.

Dunning, J. (1996) Globalisation, foreign direct investment and economic development, *Economics and Business Education*, 4(3).

Dunning, J. H. (1993) *Multinational Enterprises and the Global Economy*, Addison-Wesley.

Economist (1996) *Economic Indicators*, 27 April.

Financial Times (1998a) West-Midlands popular as manufacturing base, *Reporting Britain*, 16 July.

Financial Times (1998b) Regions take an inward look at a growing problem, 21 May.

Financial Times (2003) *FT Global 500*.

Greenaway, D. (1993) Trade and foreign direct investment, *European Economy*, No. 52.

Kene, P. B. (1994) *The International Economy*, Cambridge University Press.

Kobrun, S. J. (1991) An empirical analysis of the determinants of global integration, *Strategic Management Journal*, **12**.

Norman, G. (1995) Japanese foreign direct investment: the impact on the European Union, in N. Healey (ed.), *The Economics of the New Europe: from Community to Union*, Routledge.

Thomsen, S. (1992) Integration through globalisation, *National Westminster Bank Quarterly Review*, August.

UNCTAD (1996) *World Investment Report: Investment, Trade and International Policy Arrangements*, Geneva.

UNCTAD (2002) *World Investment Report 2002*, Geneva.

Winters, L. (1991) GATT: the Uruguay Round, *Economic Review*, **9**(2), November.

Young, S., Hood, N. and Hamill, J. (1988) *Foreign Multinationals and the British Economy*, Croom Helm.

Chapter 8 | Privatization and deregulation

Public ownership of industries is now in retreat throughout the world as governments privatize. Since the early 1980s the UK has provided a model of privatization which has been influential in policy making, both in other industrial countries and in developing countries. The collapse of the Soviet Union and the Eastern European Communist regimes has led to privatization programmes which totally dwarf those of the UK. This chapter summarizes the original case for nationalization and considers the arguments for and against privatization. There is also a discussion of the case for regulating the activities of the privatized companies as well as the contrary view in favour of less regulation (i.e. deregulation).

Nature and importance

Public (or state) ownership of industry in the UK has mainly been through *public corporations*, which are trading bodies whose chairpersons and board members are appointed by the Secretary of State concerned. These *nationalized industries*, as they are often called, are quite separate from government itself. They run their businesses without close supervision but within the constraints imposed by government policy. These constraints include limits to the amounts they can borrow and therefore invest and may also include limits to the wages and salaries they can offer. Not all public corporations are, however, nationalized industries. There are some public corporations, such as the BBC, which are not classed as nationalized industries.

Public ownership can also take the form of direct share ownership in private sector companies. So, for example, after the collapse of the DAF motor vehicle group in 1993, the Netherlands government provided 50% of the equity and loan capital for DAF Trucks NV which took over some of the failed group's activities. In a similar way the UK government held a majority holding in British Petroleum for many years prior to its complete privatization in 1987.

Privatization in the UK has reduced the number of nationalized industries to a mere handful of enterprises accounting for less than 2% of UK GDP, around 3% of investment and under 1.5% of employment. By contrast, in 1979 the then nationalized industries were a very significant part of the economy, producing 9% of GDP, being responsible for 11.5% of investment and employing 7.3% of all UK employees. The scale of the transfer of public sector businesses since 1979 to private ownership is further indicated in Table 8.1 below, which lists the businesses privatized by sector.

Reasons for nationalization

Looking back from the perspective of the new millennium, the reader may well ask why the state ever became so heavily involved in the production of goods and services. Yet between the 1940s and the 1980s this was one of the most contentious issues in British politics, both between the major parties and within the Labour Party. The first post-war Labour government (1945–51) achieved a major programme of nationalization which was opposed by the Conservative Party at the time but broadly left in place by subsequent Conservative governments. The apparent consensus on the scale of the nationalized industries was, however, broken after 1979 as Conservative governments under Mrs Thatcher developed the policy of privatization. We now consider a range of arguments used in favour of nationalization.

Political

The political case for nationalization centred on the suggestion that private ownership of productive assets creates a concentration of power over resources which is intolerable in a democracy. Until 1995 the Labour Party appeared to embrace this idea in Clause 4 of its constitution which promised public ownership of the means of production, distribution and exchange. The founders of the Labour Party saw public ownership as a necessary step towards full-scale socialism and one which would aid economic planning. This developed into a policy of nationalizing the 'commanding heights' of the economy which the 1945 Labour government identified as the transport industries, the power industries and the iron and steel industries; the Post Office had always been state owned and at that time also included telephones. There were always many in the Labour Party who were opposed to a literal interpretation of Clause 4 and saw that there were other means of regulating economic activity besides outright public ownership. By the 1990s, after the collapse of the Eastern European socialist economies, there were few remaining advocates of economic planning and the Labour Party abandoned the old Clause 4 by a large majority at a special conference in 1995.

Post-war reconstruction

After the Second World War some industries, e.g. the railways, were extremely run-down, requiring large-scale investment and repair. For these, the provision of state finance through nationalization seemed a sensible solution. In other industries, e.g. steel, nationalization was a means of achieving reorganization so that economies of scale could be fully exploited. In still other industries, e.g. gas and electricity, reorganization was required to change the industry base from the local to the national.[1] A different government might, of course, have used policy measures other than nationalization, such as grants and tax reliefs, to achieve these objectives.

The public interest

There are many situations where commercial criteria, with their focus on profitability, are at odds with a broader view of the public interest, and in such cases nationalization is one solution. For instance, the Post Office aims to make a profit overall, but in doing so makes losses on rural services which are subsidized by profits made elsewhere – a 'cross-subsidy' from one group of consumers to another. Some object to cross-subsidization, arguing that it interferes with the price mechanism in its role of resource allocation when some consumers pay less than the true cost of the services they buy, whilst others pay more than the true cost. However, in the case of the Post Office cross-subsidization seems reasonable, if only because we may all want to send letters to outlying areas from time to time, and all derive benefit from the existence of a full national postal service. A private sector profit-orientated firm might not be prepared to undertake the loss-making Post Office services.

State ownership may also be a means of promoting the public interest when entire businesses are about to collapse. The state has sometimes intervened to prevent liquidation, as in 1970 when the Conservative government decided to rescue Rolls-Royce rather than see the company liquidated. Prestige, strategic considerations, effects on employment and on the balance of payments all played a part in the argument, as the judgement of the market was rejected in favour of a broader view of the public interest. In the long run the markets were proved wrong and the decision to intervene commercially correct, as the company is now a world leader in aero-engine technology and has been successfully returned to the private sector.

State monopoly

The 'natural monopoly' argument is often advanced in favour of nationalization of certain industries. Economies of scale in railways, water, electricity and gas industries are perhaps so great that the tendency towards monopoly can be termed 'natural'. Competing provision of these services, with duplication of invest-

ment, would clearly be wasteful of resources. The theory of the firm suggests that monopolies may enjoy supernormal profits, charging higher prices and producing lower output than would a competitive industry with the same cost conditions. However, where there are sufficient economies of scale, the monopoly price could be lower and output higher than under competition (see Chapter 9, Fig. 9.1). Monopoly might then be the preferred market form, especially if it can be regulated. Nationalization is one means of achieving such regulation.

Presence of externalities

Externalities occur when economic decisions create costs or benefits for people other than the decision-taker; these are called social costs or social benefits. For example, a firm producing textiles may emit industrial effluent, polluting nearby rivers and causing loss of amenity. In other words, society is forced to bear part of the cost of private industrial activity. Sometimes those who impose external or social costs in this way can be controlled by legislation (pollution controls, Clean Air Acts), or penalized through taxation. The parties affected might be compensated, using the revenue raised from taxing those firms creating social costs. On the other hand, firms creating external or social benefits may be rewarded by the receipt of subsidies. In other cases nationalization is a possible solution. If the industry is run in the public interest, it might be expected that full account will be taken of any externalities. For instance, it can be argued that railways reduce road usage, creating social benefits by relieving urban congestion, pollution and traffic accidents. This was one aspect of the case for subsidizing British Rail through the passenger service obligation grant which, in the mid-1990s, amounted to around £1bn. The grant enabled British Rail to continue operating some loss-making services. Nationalization is therefore one means of exercising public control over the use of subsidies when these are thought to be in the public interest.

Improved industrial climate

There was hope after 1945 that the removal of private capital would improve labour relations in the industries concerned, promoting the feeling of co-ownership. The coal industry in particular had a bitter legacy of industrial relations. From nationalization until the strike of 1973, industrial relations in the coal industry, judged by days lost in disputes, seemed to have dramatically improved over pre-war days. Nevertheless, for the nationalized industries as a whole, it is fair to say that the hopes of the 1940s were not fulfilled, perhaps because the form of nationalization adopted in the UK did little to involve workers in the running of their industries. Participation in management, worker directors, genuine consultation and even an adequate flow of information to workers are no more common in the UK public sector than they are in the private sector.

Redistribution of wealth

Nationalization of private sector assets without compensation is a well-tried revolutionary means of changing the distribution of wealth in an inegalitarian society. Nationalization in the UK has not, unlike the Soviet Union in 1917, been used in this way; in the UK there has almost always been 'fair' compensation. Indeed, the compensation paid between 1945 and 1951 was criticized as over-generous, enabling shareholders to get their wealth out of industries which, in the main, had poor prospects (e.g. railways, coal) in order to buy new shareholdings in growth industries (e.g. chemicals, consumer durables). Once 'fair' compensation is accepted in principle in state acquisitions of private capital, then nationalization ceases to be a mechanism for redistribution of wealth.

An alternative to 'fair' compensation is confiscation. However, this would have serious consequences for UK capital markets. Ownership of assets in the UK would, in future, carry the additional risk of total loss by state confiscation, which could influence decisions to invest in new UK-based plant and equipment, and to buy UK shares. The ability of UK companies to invest and to raise finance might therefore be undermined. The transfer of assets might also prove inequitable, since shares are held by pension funds and insurance companies on behalf of millions of small savers who would then be penalized by confiscation.

Privatization

Privatization means the transfer of assets or economic activity from the public sector to the private sector. As we noted earlier, privatization in the UK has reduced the number of nationalized industries in 2003 to a mere handful of enterprises accounting for less than 2% of UK GDP, around 3% of investment and under 1.5% of employment. Indeed the public ownership of industries is now in retreat throughout the world as governments privatize. However, privatization can often mean much more than denationalization. Sometimes the government has kept a substantial shareholding in privatized public corporations (initially 49.8% in BT), whereas in other cases a public corporation has been sold in its entirety (e.g. National Freight Corporation). Where public sector corporations and companies are not attractive propositions for *complete* privatization, profitable assets have been sold (e.g. Jaguar Cars from the then British Leyland and also British Rail Hotels). Yet again, many public sector activities have been opened up to market forces by inviting tenders, the cleaning of public buildings and local authority refuse collection being examples of former 'in-house' services which are now put out to tender. Private sector finance and operation of facilities and services is also now established in a vast array of public/private finance initiatives (PFI). In other words, the many aspects of privatization also involve aspects of *deregulation*, e.g. in allowing private companies to provide goods and services which could previously only (by law) be provided in the public sector.

Early privatizations, for example BT in 1984, were usually simple transfers of existing businesses to the private sector. Increasingly privatizations have become much more complex, often being used to restructure industries by breaking up monopolies and establishing market-based relationships between the new companies. For example, the privatization of British Rail involved separating ownership of the track (Railtrack) from the train operating companies and also the train leasing companies. The train operating companies are in this case franchisees who have successfully tendered for contracts to operate trains for a specified period.

Market forces have also been introduced into the unlikely areas of social services, the health services and education – especially higher education. In health and social services this has involved the purchaser/provider model in which, for example, doctors and 'primary care groups' have used their limited budgets to buy hospital services needed by their patients. Funds, and hence the use of resources, are then controlled by *purchasers* rather than by the *providers*. As a result, these purchasers have an incentive to use hospitals offering, in their judgement, the 'best' service as described by some combination of quality and value for money. (However, as we note in Chapter 13, the Labour government has sought to modify some of these market arrangements.) In higher education, the funding of universities has been closely linked to the numbers of students enrolling. It follows that any failure to enrol students, perhaps through offering unpopular courses, would drive a university into deficit and possible bankruptcy. Resources in this sector were previously allocated by administrators; now a market test is applied.

Table 8.1 shows the extent of privatization in the UK to 2003, in terms of both the number of businesses and their spread across major sectors of the economy. The total value of privatization receipts to the Treasury has been estimated at over £70bn.

Table 8.1 Major privatizations: a sectoral breakdown.

Mining, Oil, Agriculture and Forestry
British Coal, British Petroleum, Britoil, Enterprise Oil
Land Settlement, Forestry Commission, Plant Breeding Institute

Electricity, Gas and Water
British Gas
National Power, PowerGen
Nuclear Electric
Northern Ireland Electric, Northern Ireland Generation (4 companies)
Scottish Hydro-Electric, Scottish Power
National Grid
Regional Electricity Distribution (12 Companies)
Regional Water Holding Companies (10 Companies)

Manufacturing, Science and Engineering
AEA Technology
British Aerospace, Short Bros, Rolls-Royce
British Shipbuilders, Harland and Wolff
British Rail Engineering
British Steel
British Sugar Corporation
Royal Ordnance
Jaguar, Rover Group
Amersham International
British Technology Group Holdings (ICL, Fairey, Ferranti, Inmos)

Distribution, Hotels, Catering
British Rail Hotels

Transport and Communication
British Railways
National Freight, National and Local Bus Companies
Motorway Service Area Leases
Associated British Ports, Trust Ports, Sealink
British Airways, British Airports Authority (and other airports)
British Telecommunications, Cable and Wireless

Banking, Finance, etc.
Girobank

Clearly the scope for further privatization among the remaining nationalized industries is now limited as there are so few left, but there are many possibilities in the activities currently run by the Civil Service and Local Authorities.

The case for privatization

A commitment to privatize wherever possible became established in the Conservative Party during Mrs Thatcher's first term. By 1982 the late Mr Nicholas Ridley, then Financial Secretary to the Treasury, expressed this commitment as follows:

> It must be right to press ahead with the transfer of ownership from state to private ownership of as many public sector businesses as possible. ... The introduction of competition must be linked to a transfer of ownership to private citizens and away from the State. Real public ownership – that is ownership by people – must be and is our ultimate goal.

Mr Ridley made a case for privatization which focused on the traditional Conservative antipathy to the state. On this view the transfer of economic activity from the public to the private sector is, in itself, a desirable objective. By the early 1980s privatization was also supported by adherents of 'supply side' economics with its emphasis on free markets. Privatization would expose industries to market forces which would benefit consumers by giving them choice, and also lower prices as a result of efficiency gains within the privatized companies.

Supply-side benefits

The breaking of a state monopoly would, in this view, enable consumers to choose whichever company produced the service they preferred. That company would then generate more profit and expand in response to consumer demand, whilst competitive pressure would be put on the company losing business to improve its service or go into liquidation. BT's progressive reductions in telephone charges and Internet access charges in recent years have clearly been at least partly in response to competition. The pressure to meet consumer requirements should also improve internal efficiency (X efficiency) as changes can be justified to workers and managers by the need

to respond to the market. The old public corporations had increasingly been seen as producer led, serving the interests of management and workers rather than those of consumers and shareholders (in this case taxpayers). Privatization introduces market pressures which help to stimulate a change of organizational culture.

Trade unions can be expected to discover that previous customs and work practices agreed when in the public sector are now challenged by privatization, as the stance taken by management changes from when the industry was nationalized, and thereby raises corporate efficiency. Similarly competition in the product market will force moderation in wage demands and increased attention to manning levels, again raising efficiency. Privatization contributes in these various ways to the creation of 'flexibility' in labour markets, higher productivity and reduced unit labour costs.

The stock market provides a further market test for privatized companies. Poor performance in meeting consumer preferences or in utilizing assets should result in a share price which underperforms the rest of the market and undervalues the company's assets, ultimately leaving it vulnerable to takeover by a company able to make better use of the assets. Supporters of privatization place more faith in these market forces than in the monitoring activities of Departments of State and Parliamentary Committees.

Wider share ownership

The Conservative Party in its drive towards privatization also emphasized wider share ownership. By 2003, share ownership in the UK had spread to 22% of the adult population, having been only 7% as recently as 1981. The total number of UK shareholders is about the same as the number of trade unionists. This increase in shareholding is largely due to privatization. A new group of shareholders has been attracted and become participants in the 'enterprise culture'. Additionally 90% of the employees in the privatized companies have become shareholders in the companies they work for, at least initially. Worker share ownership is advocated as a means of involving workers more closely with their companies and achieving improved industrial relations. This has been taken further by selling companies to their managers (e.g. Leyland Bus in 1987) or to consortiums of managers and workers (e.g. National Freight in 1982). The latter is regarded as a highly successful example, profits having grown more than tenfold since privatization.

Reductions in PSBR

Privatization has also been seen as a way in which the PSBR can be cut, at a stroke! The finance of external borrowing by the nationalized industries is regarded in accounting terms as being part of public expenditure, which then ceases when these industries become privately owned. Sale of assets or shares also increases government revenue, again reducing the PSBR in the year of the sale. Over the period 1979–2002 the Treasury gained £70bn from asset sales. Privatization made a very significant contribution to the budget surpluses of the late 1980s and to curbing the size of the budget deficits of the 1990s. Privatization proceeds reduced the PSBR as a proportion of GDP by more than 1.5% during the late 1980s, and by a still significant, if smaller, percentage in other years.

Managerial freedom

The activities of state-owned organizations are constrained by their relationship with the government. They lack financial freedom to raise investment capital externally because the government is concerned about restraining the growth of public expenditure (see Chapter 18). Privatization is then seen as increasing the prospects for raising investment capital, thereby increasing efficiency and lowering prices.

A further limitation on nationalized industries is the political near-impossibility of diversification. In many cases this would be the sensible corporate response to poor market prospects but it is not an option likely to be open to a nationalized concern. Since privatization, however, companies have been able to freely exploit market opportunities. So, for example, most of the regional electricity companies have become suppliers of gas as well as electricity.

The 'globalization' of economic activity also, in this view, leaves nationalized industries at a distinct disadvantage. For example, no private oil company would have followed the nationalized British Coal in confining its activities to one country where it happened to have reserves. This international perspective is an important reason why the Post Office management saw privatization as 'the only (option) which offers us the freedom to fight off foreign competition'.

In the postal services, increased competition has arisen from the Dutch Post Office, which has been privatized, and is expected from further liberalization of other national postal services expected within the European Single Market. The difficulties of an international strategy for nationalized industries are shown by the failure of the attempted Renault–Volvo merger in 1993. The then nationalized status of Renault contributed substantially to Swedish (Volvo) shareholder opposition to the merger.

Privatization, then, is seen by its supporters as a means of greatly improving economic performance.

The case against privatization

Privatization may be opposed for all the reasons that nationalization was originally undertaken (see above). Additionally both the rationale of the policy and its implementation may be criticized.

Absence of competition

An essential aspect to the case *for* privatization is the creation of competitive market conditions. However, some state-owned industries have always faced stiff competition in their markets (for example, Post Office Parcelforce from DHL), so that privatization of these industries might be considered irrelevant on the basis of this 'competitive market conditions' argument.

The government also faces a dilemma as regards creating competitive market conditions when privatizing public utilities which are monopolies, namely that it has another, and potentially conflicting, objective which is to raise money for the Treasury. Breaking up state monopolies in order to increase competition reduces the market value of the share offer; monopolies are likely to be worth more as share offers because they reduce uncertainty for investors. Critics would say that the government has allowed the creation of competition to be secondary to creating attractive share issues which sell easily. The result has been the transfer of public utility monopolies intact to the private sector, creating instead private sector monopolies.

Nevertheless, competitive pressures are being applied to some of the previously public utility monopolies in their newly privatized form. For example, at the time of privatization, British Gas appeared to be a classic natural monopoly. Since then consistent pressure from the regulatory authorities has created competitive market conditions in the supply of gas to industry, to such an extent that by 2003 the British Gas share of the industrial market was below 30% and competitive supply had been extended to the domestic market for gas across the whole country. As regards BT, opportunities for new entrants created by rapid technological change have been even more significant in eroding the market dominance of BT. Cable TV companies can now provide highly competitive phone services using their fibre optic cable systems; additionally many large organizations have created their own phone networks and the Internet and digital TV are creating still further opportunities for communication.

The technical and regulatory changes in the telecommunication and gas industries have benefited consumers but should not be confused with the issue of the desirability of privatization. Consumers might well feel that these desirable outcomes could have been achieved under public ownership. If so, critics might then argue that consumers could have experienced still greater benefit from technical innovation because, under privatization, lax regulatory regimes have allowed excessive levels of profit, to the benefit of shareholders and executives rather than consumers.

Presence of externalities

The rationale for privatization is at its weakest when externalities exist. Indeed the former nationalized industries contained many examples of such externalities, which was one of the reasons for their original public ownership. The now privatized rail companies are *not* able to charge road users for any benefits (e.g. less congestion) created by the lower levels of road traffic which rail services create. In the water industry there is a vested interest in encouraging consumption to increase turnover, even if this means the need to build new reservoirs with a consequent loss of land, disruption to everyday life and dramatically changed landscapes. In the case of the electricity industry, the competitive market among the generators has had nearly terminal implications for the coal industry. New contracts for coal supplies to the electricity generating companies have only been secured by British Coal at world prices, well below the prices previously agreed. As employment in mining has plummeted, the cost has been borne by society. Miners' families and local communities have become

much poorer, whilst public expenditure on unemployment and social security benefits has risen and tax revenues have been reduced by the rising unemployment. At a time of high unemployment, organizations which lower their *private* costs by making more workers redundant invariably create *social* costs (externalities). There is also the issue of the long-term *strategic* role of the coal industry. The German government has long recognized these wider aspects of industrial policy and has arranged a levy on electricity users to compensate the electricity generators for offering coal prices which are over three times the world price. German electricity prices in the early years of the millennium were some 30–40% higher than those in the rest of Europe. The UK government has taken a contrary view and decided that the nuclear industry rather than the coal industry should be subsidized. In doing so it has, of course, departed from its free market philosophy and further endangered the coal industry by subsidizing a competitor.

Undervaluation of State assets

The extension of share ownership does not in itself attract much criticism. The issues which have provoked criticism include the pricing and the marketing of the shares. It is argued that valuable national assets have been sold at give-away prices. This criticism is made of both privately negotiated deals and the public share offers. An example of the former is the offer for Austin Rover made by British Aerospace in March 1988 which valued a company which has received a total of £2.9bn of public funds at only £150m and this on condition that the government wrote off £1.1bn of accumulated losses and injected a further £800m. The deal could be presented as giving away £650m and a company with net assets of more than £1.1bn. The generosity of the government's approach was confirmed when the European Commission ruled that the £800 million government injection of capital must be reduced to £572 million, in the interests of fair competition in the EU motor market. The Commission also insisted that British Aerospace repay £44.4 million which it received from the government as 'sweeteners' during the deal. The government's prime objective was to return Rover to the private sector as quickly as possible in the belief that the benefits would soon outweigh any losses on the deal. There were also the provisos that the company remain under British ownership (see below) and that employment be maintained. These provisos severely restricted the number of potential buyers.

In most cases public share offers have been heavily over-subscribed and large percentage profits have been made by successful applicants. Rolls-Royce shares, for example, were issued part paid at 85p on 20 May 1987 and moved to 147p by the close of business that day, a profit of 73% before dealing costs. British Telecom shares reached a premium of 86% on the first day. The electricity privatization has, to date, raised some £6.5 billion, but the assets involved have a value of £28 billion. Hardly surprisingly, the regional electricity company shares had a first-day premium of almost 60%, and those of the electricity generating companies a premium of almost 40%.

Underpriced issues have cost the Treasury substantial revenues and have also conditioned a new class of small shareholders to expect quick, risk-free capital gains. These expectations were encouraged by barrages of skilful advertising. Not surprisingly many of the new shareholders cashed in their windfall gains by selling their shares. As a result share ownership in the new companies quickly became more concentrated. For example, the 1.1 million BA shareholders at the flotation in February 1987 had reduced to 0.4 million by early October. Despite this, there is no doubt that there has been a considerable extension of share ownership, although the majority of shareholders have shares in only one company. In fact 54% of investors hold shares in only one company and only 17% have shares in more than four companies. Parker (1991) concludes that privatization has *widened* share ownership but not *deepened* it. Indeed, the institutional investors raised their proportion of shareholdings during the 1980s at the expense of the private investor, whose proportion of total shareholdings fell from 30% to 20% during this period.

Short-termism

The discipline of the capital markets may prove a very mixed blessing for some of the privatized companies if they become subject to the City's alleged 'short-termism'. The large investment fund managers are often criticized for taking a short-term view of prospects. This would be particularly inappropriate for the public utilities where both the gestation period for investment and the pay-back period tend to be lengthy. The freedom with which ownership of assets

changes hands on the stock market is not always in the public interest. The acquisition of B Cal in 1987 by the newly privatized BA, for example, was investigated by the Monopolies and Mergers Commission (MMC) and approved on condition that BA gave up some of the routes acquired. There was also concern at the 22% holding in BP which the Kuwait Investment Office acquired very cheaply in the aftermath of the 1987 stock market crash. The MMC ruled that the Kuwait holding be reduced to 11%. The limitations of privatization and excessive reliance on the markets was illustrated in 1994 by BMW's takeover of the Rover Group from British Aerospace. The government had originally set a period of five years in which Rover could not be sold to a foreign buyer but, within a few months of the expiry of the limitation, the last British-controlled volume car producer was sold to the German company. Of course it is by no means clear that retaining national control of companies is a desirable objective. The takeover could arguably be welcomed as a benefit of European integration which will strengthen the European car industry. However, if national control *is* desired, as it was when British Aerospace bought Rover, then this is an example of the weakness of privatization as a substitute for industrial policy. The French government's plans to retain a controlling majority interest in Renault after privatization illustrates an alternative approach, although the UK government would tend not to view such a compromise as a 'privatization'.

Opportunity costs

The flow of funds into privatization offers has been diverted from other uses. It is reasonable to suppose that applicants for shares are using their savings rather than reducing their consumption. Large sums of money leave the building societies during privatizations, and other financial institutions are also deprived of funds. This raises the possibility that what is merely a restructuring and change of ownership of state industry may be reducing the availability of funds for other organizations which would use them for real capital investment. The effects of privatization issues on the financial markets are much the same as the effects of government borrowing, raising the same possibilities of 'crowding out'.

The contribution of privatization to reducing the PSBR has been widely criticized as 'selling the family silver'. The sales involve profitable assets and, after privatization, the Exchequer loses the flow of returns from them. Schwartz and Lopes (1993) have pointed out that the sale price of assets should equal the net present value of expected future returns on them. If this were the case, then the 'family silver' argument would lose some of its power and rest on the use to which the proceeds were put – that is consumption or investment. However, most privatization issues in the UK *have* been underpriced in the view of the markets (see above).

Burden on taxpayers

A final criticism of privatization is a moral one, that the public are being sold shares which, as taxpayers, they already collectively own. The purchasers of the shares benefit from the dividends paid by the new profit-seeking enterprises, at the expense of taxpayers as a group. Those taxpayers who do not buy the shares, perhaps because they have no spare cash, are effectively dispossessed.

Regulation of privatized companies

The privatization of public utility companies with 'natural' monopolies creates the possibility that the companies might abuse their monopoly power. In these cases UK privatizations have offered reassurance to the public in the form of regulatory offices for each privatized utility, for example OFTEL for telecommunications and OFWAT for the water industry. Where privatized companies such as Rover and British Airways are returned to competitive markets, arguably there is no need for specific regulation beyond the normal activities of the Office of Fair Trading (OFT) and the Competition Commission (CC). If a privatized company finds its regulator's stipulations unacceptable, then it may appeal to the Competition Commission.

Objectives of regulators

Regulators have two fundamental objectives. Firstly, they attempt to create the constraints and stimuli which companies would experience in a competitive market environment. For example, companies in competitive markets must bear in mind what their competitors are doing when setting their prices and are under competitive pressure to improve their service to consumers in order to gain market share.

Regulation can *simulate* the effects of a competitive market by setting price caps and performance standards. Secondly, regulators have the longer-term objective of encouraging *actual* competition by easing the entry of new producers and by preventing privatized monopoly power maintaining barriers to entry. An ideal is the creation of markets sufficiently competitive to make regulation unnecessary. The market for gas has moved substantially in this direction. British Gas, when first privatized, had an apparent classic natural monopoly in the supply of gas to industry, but by the end of 2002 the British Gas market share was below 30% for industrial users and since 1998 the company has faced nationwide competition in the supply of gas to domestic consumers. Similarly, the Regulator insisted on the introduction of competition into the supply of electricity to domestic consumers by 1998.

Problems facing regulators

Regulators have an unenviable role as they try to create the constraints and stimuli of a competitive market. Essentially they are arbitrating between the interests of consumers and producers. *Other things being equal*, attempts by regulators to achieve improvements in service levels will cause increases in costs and so lower profits, whilst price caps on services with price inelastic demand will also reduce profits by *preventing* the regulated industries raising prices and therefore revenue. Lower profits, and the expectation of lower profits, have immediate implications for dividend distributions to shareholders and so for share prices. At this point other things are unlikely to remain equal. The privatized company subject to a price cap may well look for ways of lowering costs to allow profits to be at least maintained, or perhaps raised. In most organizations there are economies to be gained by reducing staffing levels, and the utility companies have dramatically reduced their numbers of employees. Investment in new technology may also enable unit costs to be lowered so that profits are greater than they otherwise would have been.

Establishing a price cap

In deciding on a price cap the regulator has in mind some 'satisfactory' rate of profit on the value of assets employed. A key issue is then the valuation of the assets. If the basis of valuation is *historical*, using the market value at privatization plus an estimate of investment since that date, then the company will face a stricter price cap than if *current* market valuations are used for assets. This is because historical valuations will usually be much smaller than the current valuations and so will justify much smaller total profits and therefore lower prices to achieve that profit.

Price caps are often associated with job losses. In an economy with less than full employment it may then be argued that such cost savings in the privatized companies are only achieved at the expense of extra public expenditure on welfare benefit. However, a counter-argument is that lower public utility prices benefit all consumers, with lower costs of production across the economy stimulating output and creating employment.

It may be over-simplistic to assume that privatized companies will invariably respond to a price cap by cutting costs as much as possible in order to maximize profits over the medium-term period of the price cap. The planning period in public utilities is likely to be much longer than the four or five years of a regulator's price review period. If a company meets its price cap and service requirements by making excessively large efficiency savings so that its profits and share price grow quicker than the average for large companies, then there will be great public pressure on the regulator to be much tougher next time. The goals of regulated companies probably include avoiding the long-term regulatory regime becoming too 'tight'. At the same time the regulator may depend on the company for a great deal of the information needed for the task of regulation. So there is the possibility of the regulator's independence being compromised, which has been called 'capture' of the regulator. Clearly the relationship between regulator and regulated company is complex, so that simple predictions of action and reaction are difficult to make.

Costs of regulation

Whilst regulation should produce clear benefits for the consumers of each privatized company, there are inevitable costs involved in running regulatory offices and also costs for the regulated company which has to supply information and present its case to the regulator. It is likely that companies will go further than this and try to *anticipate* the regulator's activities, so incurring further costs. It is not at all clear that having separate regulatory offices for each industry is a cost-

effective arrangement. Concentration of *all* regulation in one agency might be more efficient and lead to more consistency in the treatment of different industries. It would also enable a consideration of the implications of decisions in one industry on competitive conditions in other industries. OFTEL, for example, has sought to increase competition in the rapidly changing telecommunications market by forcing BT to allow cable TV companies favourable access to its transmission networks. Yet these cable companies themselves have monopoly power in their own markets!

Differences in the regulatory regimes have certainly contributed to the astonishing difference between the weak share performance of the gas and telecommunications industries and the strong share performance of the water and electricity industries which have outperformed the FTSE 100 index by 60% and 101% respectively. High returns in the stock market are usually associated with risk. However, neither the water industry nor electricity can be viewed as risky; indeed they would normally be seen as unspectacular but steady income generators rather than as growth stocks.

Regulation and deregulation

Regulation

Regulation may be defined as the various *rules* set by governments or their agencies which seek to control the operations of firms. We have already discussed the role of the regulators for the privatized industries who themselves are part of this broad regulatory process.

Regulation is one of the mechanisms available to governments when dealing with the problem of 'market failure'. Of course market failure can take many forms although, as Stewart (1997) points out, four broad categories can usefully be identified.

■ *Asymmetric information*. Here the providers may have information not available to the purchasers. For example, in recent cases involving the mis-selling of pensions the companies involved were found to have withheld information from purchasers. Stricter regulation of the sector has been the government's response to this situation.

■ *Externalities*. In the case of negative externalities, regulations may be used to bring private costs more closely into line with social costs (as with environmental taxes) or to restrict social costs to a given level (as with environmental standards).

■ *Public goods*. Regulation may be required if such goods are to be provided at all. The idea of a public 'good' (which may, of course, be a service) is that it has the characteristics of being non-excludable and non-exhaustible, at least in the 'pure' case. Non-excludable refers to the difficulty of excluding those who do not wish to pay for the 'good' (e.g. police or defence); non-exhaustible refers to the fact that the marginal cost of providing an extra unit of the 'good' is effectively zero (e.g. an extra person covered by the police or defence forces). The non-excludable condition prevents a private market developing, since it is difficult to make 'free riders' actually pay for the public good. The non-exhaustible condition implies that any price that is charged should, for allocative efficiency (see Chapter 5, p. 82), equal marginal cost and therefore be zero. Private markets guided by the profit motive are hardly in the business of charging zero prices! Both conditions imply that the 'good' is best supplied by the public sector at zero price, using general tax revenue to fund provision (in the 'pure' public good case).

■ *Monopoly*. Regulation may be required to prevent the abuse of monopoly power. In Chapter 5 we considered a variety of regulations implemented by the Office of Fair Trading. Figure 5.2 (p. 83) was used to show that regulations involving the Competition Commission may be used to prevent or modify certain proposed mergers which are arguably against the public interest (e.g. where gains in 'productive efficiency' are more than offset by losses in 'allocative efficiency').

The *forms* of regulation are too innumerable to capture in a few headings. The various rules can involve the application of maximum or minimum prices, the imposition of various types of standards, taxes, quotas, procedures, directives, etc., whether issued by national bodies (e.g. the UK government or its agencies) or international bodies (e.g. the EU Commission, the World Trade Organization, etc.).

Although a strict classification of the numerous types of regulation would seem improbable, McKenzie (1998) makes a useful distinction:

■ regulations aimed at *protecting* the consumer from the consequences of market failure;

■ regulations aimed at *preventing* the market failure from happening in the first place.

In terms of the Financial Sector, the Deposit Guarantee Directive of the EU is of the former type. This *protects* customers of accredited EU banks by restoring at least 90% of any losses up to £12,000 which might result from the failure of a particular bank. In part this is a response to asymmetric information, since customers do not have the information to evaluate the credit-worthiness of a particular bank, and might not be able to interpret that information even if it were available.

The Capital Adequacy Directive of the EU is of the latter type. This seeks to *prevent* market failure (such as a bank collapse) by directly relating the value of the capital a bank must hold to the riskiness of its business. The idea here is that the greater the value of capital available to a bank, the larger the buffer stock which it can use to absorb any losses. Various elements of the Capital Adequacy Directive force the banks to increase their capital base if the riskiness of their portfolio (indicated by various statistical measures) is deemed to have increased. In part this is in response to the potential for negative externalities in this sector. One bank failure can invariably lead to a 'domino effect' and risk system collapse with incalculable consequences for the sector as a whole.

In these ways the regulatory system for EU financial markets is seeking to provide a framework within which greater competition between banks can occur, while at the same time addressing the fact that greater competition can increase the risks of bank failure. It is seeking both to protect consumers should any mishap occur and at the same time to prevent such a mishap actually occurring.

Overall we can say that those who support any or all of these forms of regulation, in whatever sector of the economy, usually do so in the belief that they improve the allocation of resources in situations characterized by one or more types of market failure.

Deregulation

Deregulation may be defined as efforts to *remove* the various rules set by governments or their agencies which seek to control the operation of firms.

One of the major arguments in favour of deregulation involves 'public interest theory'. The suggestion here is that regulations should be removed whenever it can be shown that this will remove or reduce the 'deadweight loss' typically shown to result from various types of market interference.

Figure 8.1 can be used to show how a particular market regulation, here a quota scheme, can result in a 'deadweight loss'. In this analysis *economic welfare* is defined as consumer surplus plus producer surplus. The *consumer surplus* is the amount consumers are willing to pay over and above the amount they need to pay; the *producer surplus* is the amount producers receive over and above the amount they need for them to supply the product.

In Fig. 8.1 we start with an initial demand curve *DD* and supply curve *SS* giving market equilibrium price P_1 and quantity Q_1. However, the *regulation* here is that should the market price fall below a particular level P_2, then the government is directed to intervene. It is required to use a *quota* arrangement to prevent market price from falling below P_2; in other words P_2 is a minimum price which is set by regulation at a level which is above the free market price P_1. In terms of Fig. 8.1, if the quota is set at Q_2, then the effective supply curve becomes SvS', since no more than Q_2 can be supplied whatever the price. The result is to raise the 'equilibrium' price to P_2 and reduce the 'equilibrium' quantity to Q_2. However, the quota regulation has resulted in a *loss of economic welfare* equivalent to the area B plus area C. The reduction in output from Q_1 to Q_2 means a loss of area B in consumer surplus and loss of area C in producer surplus. However, the higher price results in a gain of area A in producer surplus which exactly offsets the loss of area A in consumer surplus. This means that the *net* welfare change is negative, i.e. there is a 'deadweight loss' of area B + area C.

'Public interest theory' is therefore suggesting that deregulation should occur whenever the net welfare change of *removing regulations* is deemed to be positive. In terms of Fig. 8.1 it might be argued that removing the regulation whereby the government (or its agent) seeks to keep price artificially high at P_2 will give a *net* welfare change which is positive, namely a net gain of area B + area C. In other words, allowing the free market equilibrium price P_1 and quantity Q_1 to prevail restores the previous deadweight loss via regulation. Put another way, public interest theory is suggesting that deregulation should occur whenever the outcome is a net welfare gain, so that those who gain can, at least potentially, more than compensate those who lose.

Of course a similar analysis can be carried out in terms of other types of regulation incurring a deadweight loss *vis-à-vis* the free market equilibrium. In Chapter 29 we show how the operation of price support schemes using *central purchasing* arrangements by the Common Agricultural Policy of the EU can incur deadweight loss, when intervention prices are set above the world market price for certain agricultural products.

The empirical difficulties of placing a money value on changes in consumer surplus and producer surplus should not, of course, be underestimated. In terms of Fig. 8.1 it involves accurate estimates of both the demand and supply (or cost) curves facing the firm or industry. Issues of 'weighting' must also be considered, for example whether a £1 gain of producer surplus is the same in welfare terms as a £1 loss of

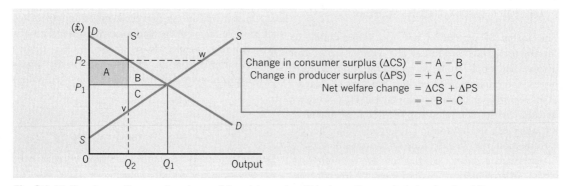

Fig. 8.1 Welfare loss with a quota scheme $0Q_2$ raising price (P_2) above the market clearing level P_1.

consumer surplus. Certainly such a 'one for one' weighting was used in Fig. 8.1, with +A gain of producer surplus under the quota regarded as exactly offsetting the −A loss of consumer surplus previously earned under the initial free market situation. Some might argue that a given monetary value to consumers should be given a greater 'weight' in terms of economic welfare than a similar monetary value received by producers!

Whether deregulation will yield a net welfare gain or loss (i.e. be in, or against, the public interest) clearly involves both theoretical and empirical aspects, and may need to be considered on a case-by-case basis. Certainly deregulation is gathering momentum in the major industrialized economies. For example, it has been estimated that in 1977 some 17% of US GNP was derived from the output of fully regulated industries, whereas that figure has declined to around 5% of GNP in current times. Winston (1993), in a wide-ranging study of the impacts of deregulation across the US industrial and service sectors, found substantial net gains to have resulted from deregulatory activity. For instance, in the US airlines sector he estimated the net benefit of the elimination of all regulations on air fares in 1983 to have been in the range of $4.3bn to $6.5bn over a 10-year period.

Interestingly, empirical estimates of the impact of deregulation have had the greatest difficulty in placing monetary values on predicted or actual changes in the *quality* of goods or services. For example, predictions as to the likely impact of deregulation on the mean and variance of travel times for passengers and freight in the transport sector have been noticeable by their absence from empirical studies or their inaccuracy when compared with eventual outcomes.

Our earlier discussion in Chapter 5 (pp. 82–3) reinforced this point about the difficulty of evaluating the net welfare change from deregulation. It showed how 'public interest theory' may often have to weigh the gains in terms of 'productive efficiency' against the losses in terms of 'allocative efficiency' when trying to evaluate whether a regulation (e.g. restricting a proposed merger) is, or is not, operating in the overall public interest.

Conclusion

Despite the advance of privatization, there remains a strong case for some form of government intervention in selected industries, for example to protect the public interest, prevent abuse of monopoly power and compensate for externalities. It does not, however, follow that nationalization is the best form of government intervention. The extent of privatization since 1979 has radically changed the role of the state in the UK economy and makes it very unlikely that there will ever again be the range of state industries which existed at that date. Indeed, there is now a worldwide shift of policy in favour of privatizing state-owned assets. The performance of both state-owned and privatized industry is difficult to evaluate. It has not been convincingly demonstrated that the form of ownership of an organization is the most important influence on its performance. Of much greater importance would seem to be the degree of competition and the effectiveness of regulatory bodies. Certainly greater powers are being given to many of the regulators of the previously nationalized industries in an attempt to prevent the abuse of monopoly power by the now privatized utilities. Regulators may impose price-caps and use other devices to prevent consumers being 'exploited' in monopoly-type situations. They may also seek to open markets to additional competition by encouraging new entrants. Nevertheless there is also a counter-movement which seeks to *remove* regulations where these are thought to operate against the public interest. Such attempts at deregulation are widespread, though it should not be forgotten that the reason many regulations exist is to protect consumers from the adverse consequences of various types of 'market failure'.

Key points

- In 1979 the nationalized industries produced some 9% of GDP, 12% of investment and 7% of total employment.

However, by 2003 their contribution was much smaller, only around 2% of GDP, 3% of investment and 2% of total employment.

- Privatization is the transfer of assets or economic activity from the public sector to the private sector.

- The term 'privatization' is often used to cover many situations: the outright sale of state-owned assets, part-sale, joint public/private ventures, market testing, contracting out of central/local government services, etc.

- The case *for* privatization includes allegedly greater productive efficiency (lower costs) via the introduction of market pressures. These are seen as creating more flexibility in labour markets, higher productivity and reduced unit labour costs. More widespread share ownership, a lower PSBR, easier access to investment capital, greater scope for diversification, and the absence of civil service oversight, are often quoted as 'advantages' of privatization.

- The case *against* privatization includes suggestions that state monopolies have often merely been replaced by private monopolies, with little benefit to consumers, especially in the case of the public utilities. The loss of scale economies (e.g. 'natural monopolies'), the inability to deal effectively with externalities, undervaluation of state assets, the subsequent concentration of share ownership, and 'short-termism' of the city, are often quoted as disadvantages of privatization.

- Regulators have been appointed for a number of public utilities in an attempt to *simulate* the effects of competition (e.g. limits to price increases and to profits), when there is little competition in reality.

- Other regulations are widely used in all economic sectors in order to protect consumers from 'market failure' and to prevent such failures actually occurring.

- There is considerable momentum behind removing regulations (i.e. deregulation) where this can be shown to be in the 'public interest'. However, evaluating the welfare change from deregulation is a complex exercise.

Now try the self-check questions for this chapter on the Companion Website. You will also find up-to-date facts and case materials.

Note

1. For example, the transition from private to public ownership meant the takeover of some 550 separate local concerns in the electricity industry and over 1,000 local concerns in the gas industry.

References and further reading

Bishop, M., Kay, J. and Mayer, C. (1994) *Privatization and Economic Performance*, Oxford University Press.

Helm, D. (1994) British utility regulation theory, practice and reform, *Oxford Review of Economic Policy*, **10**(3).

Humphreys, I. and Francis, G. (2002) Airport privatisation, *British Economy Survey*, Spring.

Ingham, A. (2003) Rail privatisation revisited, *Economic Review*, February.

McKenzie, G. (1998) Financial regulation and the European Union, *Economic Review*, April.

McWilliams, D. and Pragnell, M. (1996) Who will miss the PSBR? *Financial Times*, 30 September.

Myers, D. (1998) The Private Finance Initiative – a progress report, *Economic Review*, April.

Oxford Review of Economic Policy (1997) *Competition in Regulated Industries*, **13**(1), Spring.

Parker, D. (1991) Privatization ten years on: a critical analysis of its rationale and results, *Economics*, Winter.

Schwartz, G. and Lopes, P. S. (1993) Privatization: expectations, trade-offs and results, *Finance and Development*, June.

Stewart, G. (1997) Why regulate?, *Economic Review*, September.

Wilson, J. (1994) Competitive tendering and UK public services, *Economic Review*, April.

Winston, C. (1993) Economic deregulation, *Journal of Economic Literature*, **31**, September.

Chapter 9 Pricing in practice

The first part of this chapter briefly illustrates how economic *theory* can predict a variety of prices for a product, depending on the structure of the market and the objectives of the firm. The second and major part looks at pricing in *practice*, using recent research findings to illustrate how firms actually price their products. Costs clearly play a role in price-setting, although a variety of other factors must also be considered, including market-share strategies, the phase of the product life cycle, the degree of product differentiation, product line and prestige pricing strategies, and the role of distributors. Chapter 3, 'Firm objectives and firm behaviour', could usefully be read before beginning this chapter.

Pricing in theory

Price and market structure

For simplicity we shall initially assume that the firm's objective is to maximize profits. Given this objective the price charged may still vary depending on the type of market structure within which the firm operates. This is well illustrated by a comparison between the extreme market forms of perfect competition and pure monopoly.

Perfect competition versus pure monopoly

Under perfect competition, price is determined for the industry (and for the firm) by the intersection of demand and supply, at P_C in Fig. 9.1. As the reader familiar with the theory of the firm will know, the supply curve, S, of the perfectly competitive industry is also the marginal cost (MC) curve of the industry. Suppose now that the industry is taken over by a single firm ('pure monopoly'), and that costs are initially unchanged. It follows that the marginal cost curve remains in the same position; also that the demand curve for the perfectly competitive industry becomes the demand (and average revenue (AR))

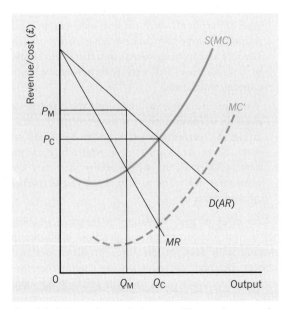

Fig. 9.1 Price under perfect competition and monopoly.

curve for the monopolist. The marginal revenue (MR) curve must then lie inside the negatively sloped AR curve. The profit-maximizing price for the monopolist is P_M, corresponding to output Q_M where $MC = MR$. Price is higher under monopoly than under perfect competition (and quantity, Q_M, is lower). This is the so-called 'classical' case against monopoly.

Our intention here is merely to point out that price will tend to *differ* for firms depending on the type of market within which they operate. In our comparison of extreme market forms, the final outcome for price may or may not be higher under monopoly than under competition. It is in part an empirical question. If economies of scale were sufficient to lower the MC curve below MC' in Fig. 9.1, then the monopoly price would be below that of perfect competition. Price will, however, except by coincidence, *be different* under these two market forms, as it would under other market forms, such as monopolistic competition or oligopoly.

Price and firm objective

So far we have assumed that the firm has a single objective, i.e. profit maximization. If there are other objectives then there will tend to be a still wider range of possibilities for price. We saw in Fig. 3.4 (p. 52) that a sales-maximizing objective would usually lead to a lower price than would a profit-maximizing objective. The situation becomes even more complicated when we examine behavioural or non-maximizing objectives, as these yield not a unique price, but a range of price outcomes for any given market structure. Clearly firm price depends also on firm objective.

Price, market structure and firm objective

Price thus depends on both market structure and firm objective. Since there are many possible combinations of these, any given product or service can experience a wide array of possible prices.

From Fig. 9.2 we see that the four market structures can lead to at least four different price outcomes (P_1-P_4) for objective 1. A further four prices (P_5-P_8) might result from objective 2, and so on, giving at least 16 prices[1] for the four market structures and the

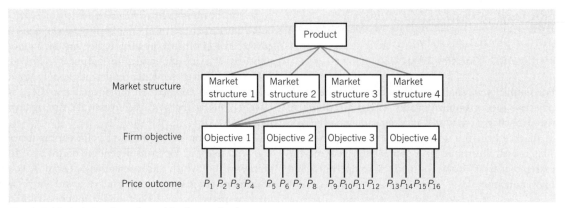

Fig. 9.2 Market structure, firm objective and price.

four firm objectives. To derive guidelines for price-setting from theory, which will have general validity, is clearly a daunting if not impossible task.

<h2>Pricing in practice</h2>

We now turn to practice to see whether observation will give us more help than theory in determining price.

Cost-plus pricing

We first examine the influence of cost on price. The suggestion here is that it is not so much the demand side of the market that affects price, but rather the supply side, via costs of production.

Cost-plus pricing is a description given to a number of practices whereby price is closely related to costs of production. Most cost-plus pricing strategies add a certain percentage profit mark-up to the firm's costs, in order to arrive at a final price. The precise outcome for price will vary from firm to firm for three main reasons:

1 There is the problem of selecting which costs to include in the pricing decision. Some firms may include only variable costs in the base for the mark-up. Interestingly this is called 'marginal costing' by accountants even when the base is average variable cost. Other firms may include both variable and fixed costs in the base (full-cost

pricing). When the firm is producing more than one product, full-cost pricing faces the problem of apportioning total fixed costs between the various products. For instance, if a factory was already producing Product A, and a new Product B was introduced using the same machinery, what part, if any, of the unchanged capital costs should be allocated to B? Product B may be asked to 'absorb' some proportion of the fixed costs already included in the price of A. Different firms will make different decisions on how to absorb fixed costs across their various products.

2 Whatever the costs to be included in the base, there is the problem of estimating the 'normal' level of output at which the firm will operate. This estimate is important since *average cost* (both the variable and fixed elements), and therefore the size of the cost base, will vary with output, i.e. with capacity utilization.

3 Whatever the costs included, and the estimate of capacity utilization, there is the problem of calculating the percentage mark-up to be added to costs. Some firms may set a relatively constant percentage mark-up, whilst others may vary the percentage according to firm objective and market circumstance.

An array of price outcomes is therefore possible for a firm, depending on the practices it adopts in dealing with each of the three problems outlined above. Although cost-plus pricing cannot therefore yield precise predictions for firm price, it does put price-setting in a particular perspective. The emphasis is upon *costs* influencing price, and then producers selling what they can at that price. Demand has little influence on price-setting in cost-plus theory, except perhaps in affecting the size of the mark-up to be added to costs. Any extra demand is met from stocks, or by lengthening the order book, rather than by the immediate price rise predicted by market theory.

Empirical evidence

The empirical evidence for cost-plus pricing, in one firm or another, is rather impressive. Hall and Hitch (1939), in their survey of entrepreneurs in the 1930s, found that most adopted a full-cost pricing approach. Hague (1948) came to a similar conclusion in his study of 20 firms in the Midlands, finding that price was set by adding a largely conventional profit margin to average total cost. An intensive study by Coutts et al. (1978) of seven UK industries also lent support to cost-plus pricing. Their study set out to test the relative importance of costs, demand, taxes, government intervention, and international trade, on the price of manufactured goods in the UK over the period 1957–73. The results suggested that firms had very limited and specific rules about the process of price determination and that costs of production were the most important single influence on price. More recently, Shipley and Bourdon (1990) found that in their sample of 193 industrial distributors almost 52% used a cost-plus pricing approach, whilst Blinder (1992) found cost-plus pricing to be ranked third highest in his study of 72 US companies. Hall et al. (1996), in a major survey of the pricing policy of 654 UK companies, found that cost-based pricing was recognized as 'important' by over 47% of these companies. It was ranked overall as the second most important pricing strategy which those companies actually pursue.

In practice, there are a number of reasons for the popularity of cost-based pricing methods. One reason is that many firms do not change their prices very often, in part because of the substantial costs involved in searching for the information necessary to *identify* the profit-maximizing price. Moreover, even having identified some 'optimal' price, firms also face the cost of *implementing* the adjustments to current pricing and policy strategies. Given such costs, Blinder (1992) found that firms in his US study usually changed their prices only annually. Similarly Dahlby (1992) showed that the average length of the pricing period for Canadian insurance premiums was

as high as 15 months, whilst the Small Business Research Trust (1995) found that 42% of a sample of 350 small UK firms changed their prices at most only once a year and often even less frequently. Hall et al. (1996) also found that the firms studied tended to let at least six months elapse before changing prices. Of course, the frequency of price change tends to vary from sector to sector, with retailers much more likely to change their prices more frequently than construction or manufacturing firms. Nevertheless, the general sense is that prices appear to be 'sticky', i.e. relatively unresponsive to the frequent changes affecting the general demand conditions, and more closely associated with cost than demand.

Reinforcing this view is the evidence that firms often tend to rely upon changes in material costs as a reason for changing prices. For instance Hall et al. (1996) found that firms were approximately four times more likely to *raise* their price due to increases in costs as opposed to increases in demand. Similarly, they found that firms were much more likely to *reduce* their prices due to decreases in costs as opposed to decreases in demand.

A more recent major study of the pricing behaviour of UK firms (Batini et al. 2002) appears to substantiate the importance of costs in the determination of prices. The study investigated the factors determining prices at the sectoral level in both UK industry and services between 1969 and 1998. The study came to three strong conclusions. First, price determination across various UK sectors was strongly dependent on marginal cost levels in those sectors. Second, prices in various sectors of the UK were also significantly related to cost levels, expressed in domestic currency, of *foreign* firms competing with the UK in those sectors. In other words, the prices charged by UK firms across various sectors were strongly determined both by their own domestic marginal costs, and also by the cost structure of foreign rival firms. Third, the study showed that the more open the sector was to international trade (e.g. aerospace, electronics, motor vehicles, etc.) the greater was the effect of foreign competitors' costs on the prices charged by UK firms. The study illustrated the continued relevance of costs, both domestic and international, in determining prices charged by UK companies.

Nevertheless, although it is clear that the prices of both domestic and internationally traded products are related to cost, market factors can still play a part. For example, when demand is relatively price inelastic, Eichner (1987) found that the mark-up on costs is likely to be higher. He found a higher mark-up to be particularly likely in market situations where there are fewer substitutes available, when new entrants face substantial barriers and when there was little chance of government retaliatory action (e.g. anti-trust referrals to the Monopolies and Mergers Commission, etc.). These are obviously situations in which higher profits can more easily be made. Some therefore see cost-plus pricing as being less divorced from market factors than might at first appear. Shipley and Bourdon (1990) support this view, finding that 27% of the industrial distribution firms they studied raised the mark-up when demand increased and 41% reduced the mark-up when demand decreased.

Much of this analysis, whilst finding empirical support for cost-plus pricing strategies, suggests that firms do respond to major shifts in market situations by varying the percentage mark-up according to the ease or difficulty of making profit. This has led some commentators to argue that cost-plus pricing is actually a rule of thumb for setting the profit-maximizing price in situations when firms rarely have detailed knowledge of marginal revenue and cost, and even if they had would find it administratively too difficult and expensive to change the profit-maximizing price (MC = MR) with every market fluctuation.

We now turn to price-setting practices that are more broadly based than cost.

Market-share strategies

Although the importance of costs in the determination of prices cannot be doubted, it is nevertheless true that prices are also changed for strategic reasons. For example, prices may be reduced in order to raise market share, or to defend an existing market share in the face of competition. Jobber and Hooley (1987) found that market share pricing objectives were more often practised by larger firms. In this context, the experience of the UK's retail petrol market is instructive. As we can see from Table 9.1, the five major oil companies accounted for 59.5% of the volume of petrol sold in the UK in 2003 and also controlled 58.2% of the total number of forecourt sites which sold petrol.

There is evidence that these 'majors' have often followed a pattern of *parallel pricing* at certain times,

i.e. a situation where prices charged by the various oil companies follow each other with only a very brief lag. In some cases, such patterns of pricing have followed changes in the world oil market such as when price fell across the board for a few months after the Iraq war of 2003. However, such pricing periods have sometimes been followed by more aggressive pricing policies designed to defend or increase market shares. The growth in the shares of petrol sold by the hypermarkets from 9% in 1990 to 28% by 2003 has often acted as a catalyst for price wars designed to maintain or increase market shares. Such competitive pricing strategies were also stimulated by a fall in the number of UK petrol forecourt sites over the same period. For example, Esso launched its 'PriceWatch' campaign in January 1996. This saw prices cut to the extent that its margin on the price per litre fell to 1p (OFT 1998). Since petrol is a relatively homogeneous product with little attendant brand loyalty, the other oil majors and the supermarkets also had to cut their prices to support their *relative* market share. When prices are dictated in this way by market-share strategies they may bear little relationship to the costs of production, at least in the short run. For example, between 1992 and 1996 the net profit margins of all the majors fell as they became involved in price wars designed to defend their relative market share (OFT 1998).

From this analysis we can see that short-term pricing policy can be dictated by market-share strategies. Parallel pricing has been used by the majors to avoid mutually damaging encroachment on their respective market shares. However, when times get difficult, price wars can still break out. When prices *are* dictated by market-share strategies they may bear little relationship to costs of production, at least in the short run. This view was confirmed by Hall *et al.* (1996) in a survey of 654 UK companies. Over 65% of companies stated that their most important pricing strategy was 'market-led pricing', with prices set either at the highest level the market could bear or at a level which has taken full account of their competitors' pricing strategies.

The strategy of pricing a product in order to gain market share can sometimes be taken to the extreme as when a firm is engaged in *predatory pricing* designed not only to create or maintain market dominance, but often to eliminate rivals. For example, in the period up to 2001, Napp Pharmaceuticals was found to be selling its slow release morphine drug

Table 9.1 Shares of the UK petrol retail market, first quarter of 2003.

Brand	Number of sites	Market share (sites %)	Market share (volume %)
BP	1,431	12.5	15.2
Esso	1,245	10.9	13.8
Shell	1,142	10.0	11.9
Total*	1,406	12.3	9.6
Texaco	1,444	12.6	8.9
Branded majors	**6,668**	**58.2**	**59.5**
Other brands	2,606	22.8	10.7
Hypermarkets	1,107	9.7	27.8
Unbranded	1,067	9.3	2.0
Total	**11,448**	**100.0**	**100.0**

* TotalFinaElf was formed from mergers between Total and Petrofina in June 1999 followed by a merger with Elf Aquitaine in autumn 1999. The name was changed from TotalFinaElf to Total SA in May 2003.
Source: Catalist Ltd (2003).

MST at below its direct costs of production. The aim was to eliminate its three rival firms, BIL, Link and Sanofi-Winthrop, from the market (Griffiths and Ison 2001).

Life-cycle strategies

The pricing strategy of the firm will be affected not only by considerations of market share. The position of the product in its life cycle will also influence price. It has long been recognized that products frequently have a finite market life, and that within that life they change their strategic role (see also Chapter 3 on portfolio planning). The three broad phases of the life cycle which products go through after their successful introduction (most products fail!) are often described as the growth phase, the maturity phase and the decline phase.

Growth phase

In the growth phase the product's market share, and possibly the total market size, is increasing. It is normal for those first into a market to support growth by high marketing expenditure. Market leaders may be forced in this phase to make a choice between two types of strategy. They can adopt a 'skimming' strategy, charging a *high* price which creams off a small but lucrative part of the market. Producers of fashion products, which have a short life and high innovative value as long as only a few people own them, often adopt a skimming strategy. Companies such as IBM, Polaroid and Bosch have operated such price skimming systems over time. Bosch used a successful skimming policy, supported by patents, in its launch of fuel injection and antilock braking systems. Similarly, in 2001 both Unilever and Procter & Gamble launched liquid soap capsules, i.e. capsules of pre-measured doses of liquid detergent which could be placed into washing machines, to save people the bother of working out how much soap to use per wash. As 'premium priced' products, the capsules seemed to offer good profit skimming opportunities.

Alternatively, market leaders can adopt a 'penetration' strategy, charging a *low* price and raising marketing expenditure in order to establish a much larger market presence. The penetration strategy is more likely to deter early competition and may ultimately prove more profitable if the firm can afford to wait for a return on its initial outlay. The firm can then delay raising the price of its product until *after* it has secured a substantial market presence. Redmond (1989) concluded that penetration pricing by pioneer firms in a range of industries had a measurable influence in raising the eventual concentration of those industries in maturity.

How much of a role cost plays in the determination of price during the growth phase will depend on the individual firm. It is not unknown for companies which market aggressively to set prices *below* average cost in order to gain high market share, in the expectation that costs will fall as output and experience increase. This is particularly so in high-technology industries. In similar vein a strategy of giving away products based on the ownership of high-technology processes and products has been adopted by firms offering global products. The rationale is to lock the market into that technology, thereby making any change to alternative technologies and their associated products too expensive. The battle between AOL Time Warner, Microsoft and Yahoo! to provide Internet services is an example of this.

Maturity phase

As time passes the product reaches maturity. Both the firm and the market are then in a situation which can be expected to continue for some time. The strategic pricing decisions will in this phase depend largely on the market share that has already been established and on the quality of the product compared to that of its competitors.

For a company with a high market share and a high-quality product, the policy is often to charge relatively high prices, supported by high marketing and product development expenditure in order to maintain the position of leadership. Prices may, however, still be well in excess of average total cost, since technical costs in the maturity phase are often low as a result of scale economies. Again, prices may diverge from cost during the maturity phase of the product life cycle.

Take, for example, the disposable nappy. This is a relatively mature product, yet producers are constantly seeking ways of updating the design of disposable nappies, with higher prices often associated with the updated version of this (mature) product. The point here is that the 'update' gives some latitude for price variation (increase). Vishwanath and Mark (1997) have shown that Procter & Gamble, the makers of Pampers Baby-Dry and Pampers Premium disposable nappies, have continuously invested in strategic products such as these in order to maintain the 'mature phase' for as long as possible, i.e. to use updating-investment as a means of delaying the onset of the 'decline phase'.

Decline phase

Over time many products fall into 'decline', perhaps through changing social habits or because of technological innovation. Even so, manufacturers will usually try to maintain their high price in the decline phase by relying upon the brand loyalty of those customers who remain. When products become 'obsolete', such as video games like 'Doom' and 'Quake', manufacturers may attempt to repackage such products as 'classics'. Where successful this strategy will allow them to continue to profit from earlier investment in such products, even during the decline phase.

Pricing policy may in these various ways be shaped by factors other than cost; here the phase of the product life cycle has played an important role.

Market segmentation strategies

There is a trend in advanced economies towards wider variety in consumer choice and greater specialization in industrial products. In other words, the markets are far less homogeneous than had been thought, being constructed of *segments* which can be distinguished from each other. For example, shampoo was once considered one market, but new product development, branding and packaging have segmented this in many ways. Shampoo products may be seen to be segmented into medicated hair products (Head & Shoulders™), two-in-ones (Wash & Go™), children's shampoos (L'Oréal Kids™), 'balanced' shampoos (Organics™, Fructis™) and environmentally sensitive shampoos (The Body Shop™ range). Such strategies permit manufacturers such as Unilever and Procter & Gamble to place a higher premium on many of their shampoo products. These forms of *lifestyle segmentation* are now used by many firms in preference to the social class distinctions of the previous four decades.

The price of goods and services may increasingly be related to the demand characteristics of the market segment, rather than to the actual costs of production. For example, the changing lifestyles of consumers are giving rise to changes in demand elasticity and buying habits. A number of studies have confirmed the idea that, by assembling goods in one place, a shop saves its customers 'search' costs. The *one-stop shop* customers are prepared to *pay more* for the convenience of being able to buy all the household groceries in one shopping visit.

The beer market provides a further example of how market segmentation can form the basis of pricing strategies, rather than the costs of producing the various products. For example, the Office of Fair Trading, in its latest report on the supply of beer in 2000 (OFT 2000), concluded that the production costs of ale and lager were relatively similar, but that lager prices continued to be higher than those of ale. It reported that this was probably due to the relatively inelastic demand for lager as a result of the drinking preferences of young 18–25-year-olds. This demand shift towards lager was clearly evidenced by the fact that between 1989 and 2000, lager's share of the market increased from 51% to 61%, while the shares of ale and stout fell from 49% to 39% of the market. The demand for lager therefore displays a lower price elasticity, and, in consequence, a higher mark-up on costs can be charged.

Price discrimination strategies

Price discrimination may also result in prices bearing little or no relation to cost. Conventional economic theory tells us that two conditions are necessary for price discrimination, i.e. the charging of *different prices for the same product in different markets*. First, for price discrimination to be *possible*, there must be barriers (e.g. distance, time, etc.) preventing consumers switching from the dearer to the cheaper market. Second, for price discrimination to be *profitable*, there must be differences in price elasticity of demand between the markets. The profit-maximizing condition would then be that marginal cost for the whole output be equal to marginal revenue *in each separate market*. In this way economic theory would predict higher prices in markets for which demand was less elastic, irrespective of cost conditions.

In 2000 the market for motor vehicles provided a clear example of price discrimination. The European Commission found that a Land Rover Discovery was 55.5% more expensive in the UK than in Italy. Smaller cars such as the Nissan Micra were also found to be 37.1% more expensive in the UK than in Finland (European Commission 2000). Another example is the differential prices charged for accessing the Internet. A further example of price discrimination strategies was brought to light in 2001 when

Napp Pharmaceuticals were selling their slow release morphine drug MST at a very much higher price to the general practitioner (GP) market (who were reluctant to experiment with new products, i.e. relatively inelastic demand) than to the hospital market (who were more likely to 'shop around' for cheaper substitute drugs, i.e. relatively elastic demand) (Griffiths and Ison 2001).

Product differentiation strategies

Product differentiation refers to attempts by the firm to make its product different from other products. This may be achieved by changing the characteristics of the product through R & D expenditure, or by changing consumer perceptions of the product through additional marketing expenditure. Product differentiation enables the firm to lessen the prospect of facing direct competition and to move towards a more monopolistic position, with greater control over price.

In some cases product differentiation is becoming more difficult. Petrol companies, for instance, found product differentiation virtually impossible after the star/octane ratings were made public. Similarly, packaged food manufacturers with well-known brands such as Birds Eye and Heinz are being put under increasing pressure from retailers' own brands, some of which are now perceived as being of higher quality. Despite these difficulties many manufacturers are successful in differentiating their products and in gaining premium prices because of it.

An example of this was the introduction of 'Pepsi Max' by PepsiCo Inc. As a result of market research, PepsiCo established that the majority of consumers of Diet Pepsi were female. Further research concluded that the reason for this was that men objected to purchasing goods that were labelled 'diet'. In order to allow full exploitation of the low-calorie cola market, PepsiCo launched Pepsi Max, a sugar-free cola drink, with no connotations with diet whatsoever. So, through the use of extensive market research, PepsiCo were able to identify an under-exploited niche in the cola market and create a unique product to exploit this (Sellars 1994).

It is in the firm's interest to establish the *extent* to which product differentiation gives it control over price, i.e. what the customer is prepared to pay. Kraushar (1982) describes how market research helps solve the problem of discovering exactly what the market will bear. Two techniques are frequently used: buy–response questions and multi-brand choice.

Buy–response and multi-brand choice

The buy–response test is where a large sample of respondents are shown the product and asked 'If you saw this product in your local store, would you pay £x, £y, £z ... etc. for it?'. The list will typically contain 10 prices. A large number of responses makes it possible to construct a buy–response curve, giving the percentage of buyers at different price levels. In the example shown in Fig. 9.3, 90% of those willing to buy would pay up to 40p for the product, and 35% would pay up to 56p. The flatter the buy–response curve the more control the firm has over price.

The multi-brand choice test is where respondents are asked to rate the products in question against similar products. The question may take the form 'If we add this feature to our product, making it different from those of our competitors, would you pay an extra £x, £y, £z ... etc. for it?'. The aim is to establish a *relative* price for the product.

Kraushar (1982) cites a number of examples where these two approaches to price determination

have been used successfully. Using buy–response curves, a manufacturer's undercoat paint was found to be more price-sensitive than his gloss paint. The manufacturer decided therefore to keep the price of his undercoat paint at the same level as that of cheaper competitors' 'own brands'. However, with gloss paint being less sensitive to price, the manufacturer was able to raise the price of this product relative to those of his competitors.

Product line pricing

Where a firm produces a set of related products in a *product line*, the pricing of one item may be influenced by factors other than the cost of producing that item. Suppose, for example, that a firm manufactures a product line consisting mainly of *complementary products*, as with a particular type of camera and its various accessories. The manufacturer may seek to maximize return on the *whole product line*, setting a price for the 'core' or central product (car or camera) low enough to attract customers to the components or accessories which can then be priced with a higher mark-up on cost. For example, in 2002 computer

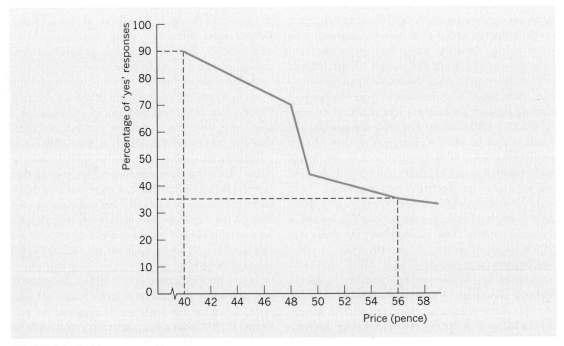

Fig. 9.3 A typical buy–response curve.

printer manufacturers such as Hewlett Packard were said to be selling their printers at below manufacturing costs, and then recouping profits by charging high prices for ink cartridges. The assumption made by such manufacturers was that consumers would buy cartridges at any prices once they had been 'captured', i.e. bought the printer. 'Clever chips' placed in printer cartridges tended to prohibit non-company brands from being used in such printers, thus often allowing prices of cartridges to remain high (geek.com news 2002).

In a similar way, companies such as Microsoft (XBox) or Sony (Playstation 2) sold their consoles at around £60–£80 below cost during 2000–2003 period but then made their extra profit on the software. This was done not always by the company producing the actual software themselves, but by gaining exclusive rights to games such as Gran Tourismo, Final Fantasy or Tomb Raider, and also by limiting the type of games the consoles could play. This meant that once consumers had been 'captured' by the loss leading consoles, the companies could control the software market and kept these prices high (Games Investor 2002).

On the other hand, the product line may consist mainly of *substitute products*, e.g. the manufacture of standard and de-luxe models of car or camera. Where two or more products in the line are substitutes, the price of the bottom-of-the-line product may be set artificially below that which a conventional mark-up on cost might suggest. If consumers are satisfied with the inexpensive first-time purchase, then the next time they make a repeat purchase they may buy a product in the higher quality range which earns the manufacturer a larger mark-up. The sale of automobiles tends to follow such considerations.

We can therefore see that the determination of prices in a *product line* is dependent on many factors other than costs. For example Sony, which produces the Walkman personal stereo, had a range of prices in 2002 from about £18 for the basic WM-EX190 personal stereo, to £80 for a top-of-the-range WM-GX400 personal stereo, with each successive model in the range offering additional features. The prices of the various different models in the product range are determined not only by cost differences but also by competitors' prices, consumers' perceptions of the additional features offered, and the producers' objective (in many cases) to maximize the return to the *whole* product line rather than any single item contained within it. Psychology also plays a part in product line pricing, since if the increments in price

between two successive models in a range are too small, consumers, in the main, will opt for the more advanced model.

Prestige pricing strategies

This type of pricing practice occurs when manufacturers price their products at a deliberately high level in the belief that consumers equate high prices with high quality. In this way an *increase in price* may even lead to an *increase in demand*, as in the case of Gillette's razors. Indeed, through the introduction in 1999 of a new super-premium product, Mach3™, the company was able to convince consumers that this was a true prestige product. Despite being priced 40% higher than Gillette's Sensor Excel™, the Mach3™ razor was able to command a 15% share of the US market. *Prestige pricing strategies* can also occur in markets where consumers may have no other means of judging the product's exact quality so that they take the price as the best indicator of quality. For example, people often feel that branded drugs are more effective than the chemically equivalent generic drugs because they have been priced at a higher level.

If manufacturers can create an association in consumers' minds that premium prices mean higher quality and exclusiveness, then they can engage in prestige pricing. For example, *designer* jeans and sports apparel sold in stores are often four times the price of mass market jeans and shirts, but the quality is rarely four times as high!

Influence of retailers on price

Whatever lengths manufacturers go to in establishing the retail price for a product, they have to take account of the profit margins of the intermediaries – the distributors, both wholesalers and retailers. The power to control prices would in some markets appear to be moving out of the hands of producers and into the hands of distributors.

Brewers distribute their beers to a number of different types of trade channels. A Monopolies and Mergers Commission report in 1989 stated that the price, and the amount of contribution to profits, varied according to the channel used. In *managed houses* where brewers have most control, the wholesale price of draught lager averaged £128.23 per bbl (a beer barrel (bbl) is 36 gallons or 288 pints). In *free houses* the price averaged £116.49 per bbl. However, in free houses where a low-interest loan had been provided by the brewery (giving the brewery more control), the price was £126.11 per bbl.

However, as retailers become more powerful, they may be able to wrest control of prices from the producer, as was shown by a Competition Commission report in 2000 into the operation of UK supermarkets (Competition Commission 2000). The study investigated the influence which supermarkets such as Tesco, Sainsbury's, Aldi, Marks & Spencer, and Safeway had on their supplier prices. It was found that the big retailers often asked for discounts from suppliers for bulk orders and that between 40% and 50% of any decrease in price offered by the retailer as a promotional strategy was borne by the supplier. Often suppliers of branded goods would contribute financially to any promotions which the supplier was undertaking in order to get their goods placed in advantageous positions in the store. In these ways, supermarkets were able to force prices below what many suppliers could bear. Some 25% of suppliers of non-branded foods complained that they were just about breaking even as a result of the power the supermarkets possessed over their prices.

The power of large retailers has been further enhanced in recent years as they set out to dominate the distribution of goods to their stores instead of depending on suppliers such as manufacturers (and/or independent wholesalers) to do that work. This means that the large retailer has much more control over total delivery costs, and therefore over final prices. The extreme case is the *factory gate* pricing system where the supplier is required to sell its products on the basis of their being made available for collection at the factory gate, with the large retailer arranging onward transportation through its own distribution centres from that point (Ginns 2002). Large retailers such as Tesco can then introduce computerized stock control to distribute their goods to various stores, enabling costs to be decreased even further. A summary of the development of the system in relation to large retailers can be seen in Fig. 9.4.

The 'original system' gave those who supplied to retail stores (i.e. either manufacturers directly or through wholesalers) more power in the value chain, in that they processed/delivered the goods direct to the store. Over time, this has shifted towards the 'current system' whereby suppliers merely transport their goods to Regional Distribution Centres (RDC) to be collected from there by large retailers who own the RDCs. The third stage is the so-called 'factory gate pricing' system, where the large retailer has now

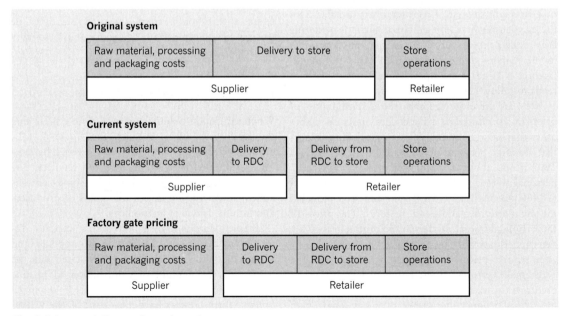

Fig. 9.4 Large retailers and supply costs.

taken over all the distribution network between the supplier (manufacturer or wholesaler) and the retail store.

This section has shown that large retailers have power to control suppler price through discounts and promotional demand. Coupled with their increasing dominance of the distribution system, this means that they have plenty of scope to vary retail prices. An example of the amounts involved can be seen in the case of Tesco. In 2002, the breakdown of Tesco's supply costs was as follows.

Supplier delivery to the Tesco distribution centre	18%
Tesco distribution centre operations and delivery to store	28%
Store replenishment	46%
Replenishment systems	8%
Total	100%

Store replenishment involves refilling the shelves, storage within the store, disposal of packaging, etc., and takes up 46% of total supply costs. An equally large proportion of 46% (18% + 28%) of total costs is accounted for by costs of transport from supplier to the Tesco distribution centre and then to the store. A similar example of Douwe Egbert, the coffee company, found that total distribution costs from supplier to store accounted for 47% of supply costs. The drive by large retailers to control more and more of the supply chain means that they will then be able to control goods availability times, stocking requirements and distribution costs. Greater control of their total supply costs gives large retailers much more flexibility when deciding the final price they will charge for their product.

 ## Conclusion

Pricing decisions depend both on the structure of the market in which the firm operates and on the objectives it pursues. There are, in fact, a variety of market structures and a variety of firm objectives, so that theory predicts a wide range of price outcomes. Can observation of firm practice lead us to more definite conclusions? Costs certainly determine the price floor, since in the long term price cannot fall below average total cost if the firm is to stay in business. However, those who support cost-plus theories would argue that everyday prices are closely related to cost. There is a considerable body of empirical support for cost-plus price-setting, though there is also evidence that the percentage mark-up on cost varies with both market circumstance and firm strategy. The phase of the product life cycle may also influence price, as may the firm's degree of 'success' in setting prices which discriminate between markets, or in establishing product differentiation. Finally, the nature of the retail outlets used by the firm will affect the price, with the producer having less freedom to dictate price where retail outlets themselves begin to control more and more of the supply chain.

Key points

- Estimates of the level of output and decisions as to the costs to be included are vital elements in cost-plus pricing.

- The percentage mark-up on cost seems to rise as market conditions improve, suggesting that demand factors as well as costs play a part here.

- In a major survey of 654 UK companies, over 47% regarded cost-based pricing as 'important' (Hall *et al.* 1996). Another important survey found that prices charged by UK firms were strongly determined by both their domestic costs and the cost structures of their foreign rivals (Batini *et al.* 2002).

- Other influences on price include firm objective, market structure, stage reached in the product life cycle, pursuit of market segmentation or price discrimination strategies, etc.

- Product differention, product-line pricing and prestige pricing strategies may also influence price.

- The major survey of 654 UK companies reported above also found 'market led' pricing to be the most important pricing strategy for over 65% of companies (Hall *et al.* 1996).
- Although often neglected by economists, the market power of distributors may influence price at least as much as producers. As a result, large retailers have begun to take over control of more of the supply chain in order to control costs, and therefore final prices.

Now try the self-check questions for this chapter on the Companion Website. You will also find up-to-date facts and case materials.

Note

1. For instance, it is assumed in Fig. 9.2 that the four firm objectives are of the maximizing type, with only a single price outcome for each objective. Equally, Fig. 9.2 assumes that for each objective and market structure there is a single price outcome covering both short- and long-run time periods. If either of these assumptions is relaxed, there might be more than 16 different price outcomes from our figure.

References and further reading

Batini, N., Jackson, B. and Nickell, S. (2002) The pricing behaviour of UK firms, Bank of England Discussion Paper No. 9, April.

Blinder, A. (1992) Why are prices sticky? *American Economic Review*, May.

Competition Commission (2000) *Supermarkets: A report on the supply of goods from multiple stores in the United Kingdom*, cm. 4842, 10 October.

Coutts, K., Godley, G. and Nordhaus, W. (1978) *Industrial Pricing in the UK*, Cambridge University Press.

Dahlby, B. (1992) Price adjustment in an automobile insurance market, *Canadian Journal of Economics*, 25.

Eichner, A. S. (1987) Prices and pricing, *Journal of Economic Issues*, December.

European Commission (2000) http://europa.eu.int/comm/competition/car_sector

Games Investor (2002) Console strategies for 2001–2005, *Think Pieces*, January.

geek.com news (2002) EU bans 'clever chips', 23 December.

Ginns, S. (2002) Driving improvement: cost reduction in the supply chain, *British Economy Survey*, 32(1), Autumn.

Griffiths, A. and Ison, S. (2001) *Business Economics*, Heinemann.

Hague, D. C. (1948) Economic theory and business behaviour, *Review of Economic Studies*, 16.

Hall, R. L. and Hitch, C. J. (1939) Price theory and business behaviour, *Oxford Economic Papers*, 2, May.

Hall, S., Walsh, M. and Yates, T. (1996) How do UK companies set prices?, *Bank of England Quarterly Bulletin*, May.

Jobber, D. and Hooley, G. (1987) Pricing behaviour in UK manufacturing and service industries, *Managerial and Decision Economics*, 8, 167–77.

Kraushar, P. (1982) How to research prices, *Management Today*, January.

MMC (1981) *Discounts to Retailers*, House of Commons Papers, 311, HMSO.

Office of Fair Trading (1998) *Competition in the Supply of Petrol*, OFT229.

Office of Fair Trading (2000) The supply of beer, OFT 317, December.

Redmond, W. H. (1989) Effects of new product pricing on the evolution of market structure, *Journal of Product Innovation Management*, 6(2), June.

Sellars, P. (1994) Pepsi opens a second front, *Fortune*, 8, August.

Shipley, D. and Bourdon, E. (1990) Distributor pricing in very competitive markets, *Industrial Marketing Management*, **19**.

Small Business Research Trust (1995) *Pricing Policies*, 3(4).

Vishwanath, V. and Mark, J. (1997) Your brand's best strategy, *Harvard Business Review*, May–June.

Chapter 10   The economics of the environment

In recent years there has been considerable interest in the impact of economic decisions on the environment. In this chapter we start by reviewing the position of the environment in models of national income determination. We then look at a number of important contemporary issues involving the environment, such as the debates on sustainable growth and global environmental change. The application of cost–benefit principles to environmental issues is also considered, together with problems of valuation. The use of market-based incentives in dealing with environmental problems, such as taxation and tradeable permits, is reviewed, as is the use of 'command and control' type regulations. We conclude by examining a number of case studies which show how environmental considerations can be brought into practical policy making, paying particular attention to global warming and transport-related pollution.

The role of the environment

The familiar circular flow analysis represents the flow of income (and output) between domestic firms and households. Withdrawals (leakages) from the circular flow are identified as savings, imports and taxes, and injections into the circular flow as investment, exports and government expenditure. When withdrawals exactly match injections, then the circular flow is regarded as being in 'equilibrium', with no further tendency to rise or fall in value.

All this should be familiar from any introductory course in macroeconomics. This circular flow analysis is often considered to be 'open' since it incorporates external flows of income (and output) between domestic and overseas residents via exports and imports. However, many economists would still regard this system as 'closed' in one vital respect, namely that it takes no account of the constraints imposed upon the economic system by environmental factors. Such a 'traditional' circular flow model assumes that natural resources are abundant and limitless, and generally ignores any waste disposal implications for the economic system.

Figure 10.1 provides a simplified model in which linkages between the conventional economy (circular flow system) and the environment *are* now introduced. The natural environment is seen as being involved with the economy in at least three specific ways.

1. *Amenity Services (A).*   The natural environment provides consumer services to domestic households in the form of living and recreational space, natural beauty, and so on. We call these 'Amenity Services'.

2. *Natural Resources (R).*   The natural environment is also the source of various inputs into the production process such as mineral deposits, forests, water resources, animal populations and so on. These natural resources are in turn the basis of both the renewable and non-renewable energy supplies used in production.

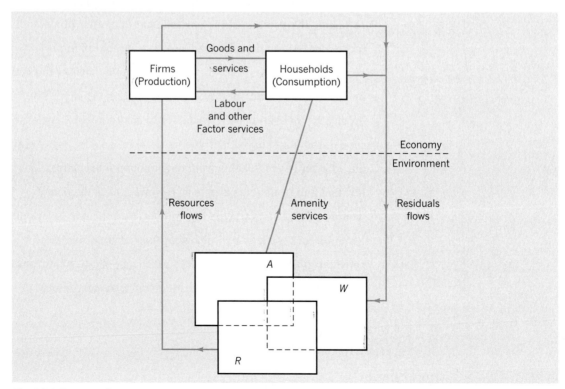

Fig. 10.1 Economy/environment linkages.

3. *Waste Products* (W). Both production and consumption are activities which generate waste products or residuals. For example, many productive activities generate harmful by-products which are discharged into the atmosphere or watercourses. Similarly, sewage, litter and other waste products result from many consumption activities. The key point here is that the natural environment is the ultimate dumping place or 'sink' for all these waste products or residuals.

We have now identified three *economic* functions of the environment: namely, it functions as a direct source of consumer utility (A), as a resource supplier (R) and as a waste receptor and assimilator (W). Moreover, these functions interact with other parts of the economic system and also with each other. This latter point is the reason for showing the three boxes A, R and W as overlapping each other in Fig. 10.1. For example, a waterway may provide amenity services (A) to anglers and sailors, as well as aesthetic beauty to onlookers. At the same time it may also provide water resources (R) to firms situated alongside which can be used for power, for cleaning, as a coolant or as a direct input into production. Both consumers and producers may then discharge effluent and other waste products (W) into the waterway as a consequence of using this natural resource. All three functions may readily coexist at certain levels of interaction. However, excessive levels of effluent and waste discharge could overextend the ability of the waterway to assimilate waste, thereby destroying the amenity and resource functions of the waterway. In other words the three economic functions of the natural environment constantly interact with each other, as well as with the economic (circular flow) system as a whole. Later in the chapter we shall look at ways of providing economic incentives or regulations which might bring about *optimum* levels of interaction between each function and within the economic system as a whole.

By bringing the environment into our modelling of the economy we are essentially challenging the traditional view that the environment and the economy can be treated as separate entities. Everything that happens in the economy has a potential environmental impact. For example, excessive price support for agricultural products under the Common Agricultural Policy (CAP – see Chapter 29) will encourage overproduction of agricultural produce. Land which

might otherwise be left in its natural state may then be brought into agricultural use, and increased yields may be sought by additional applications of fertilizers and pesticides. Hedgerows may be cut back to provide larger and more economical units of cultivation, and so on. In other words, most types of economic policy intervention will impact upon the environment directly or indirectly. Equally, policies which seek to influence the environment will themselves impact upon the economic system. As we shall see, attempts to reduce CO_2 (carbon dioxide) emissions may influence the relative attractiveness of different types of energy, causing consumers to switch between coal, gas, electricity, nuclear power and other energy forms. There will be direct effects on output, employment and prices in these substitute industries and, via the multiplier, elsewhere in the economy. We must treat the traditional economic system and the environment as being dynamically interrelated.

Sustainable economic welfare

Rather more sophisticated attempts to capture environmental costs within a national accounting framework have been made by economists such as Jackson and Marks (1994 and, with Ralls and Stymne 1997). An Index of Sustainable Economic Welfare (ISEW) has been calculated for the USA and UK. Essentially, any increase in the GNP figure is *adjusted* to reflect the following impacts which are often associated with rising GNP:

1 monies spent correcting environmental damage (i.e. 'defensive' expenditures);

2 decline in the stock of natural resources (i.e. environmental depreciation);

3 pollution damage (i.e. monetary value of any environmental damage not corrected).

By failing to take these environmental impacts into account, the conventional GNP figure arguably does *not* give an accurate indication of *sustainable economic welfare*, i.e. the flow of goods and services that an economy can generate without reducing its future production capacity. Suppose we consider the expenditure method of calculating GNP. It could be argued that some of the growth in GNP is due to expenditures undertaken to mitigate (offset) the impact of environmental damage. For example, some double-glazing may be undertaken to reduce noise levels from increased traffic flow, and does not therefore reflect an increase in economic well-being, merely an attempt to retain the status quo. Such 'defensive expenditures' should be subtracted from the GNP figure (item 1 above). So too should be expenditures associated with a decline in the stock of natural resources. For example, the monetary value of minerals extracted from rock is included in GNP but nothing is subtracted to reflect the loss of unique mineral deposits. 'Environmental depreciation' of this kind should arguably be subtracted from the conventional GNP figure (item 2 above). Finally, some expenditures are incurred to overcome pollution damage which has not been corrected; e.g. extra cost of bottled water when purchased because tap water is of poor quality. Additional expenditures of this kind should also be subtracted from the GNP figure, as should the monetary valuation of any environmental damage which has *not* been corrected (item 3 above).

We are then left with an *Index of Sustainable*

Economic Welfare (ISEW) which subtracts rather more from GNP than the usual depreciation of physical capital.

ISEW = GNP *minus* depreciation of physical capital
minus defensive expenditures
minus depreciation of environmental capital
minus monetary value of residual pollution

As we can see from Fig. 10.2 the effect of such adjustments is quite startling. The UK GNP per capita (unadjusted) was 2.5 times greater in real terms in 1996 than it was in 1950 (Jackson *et al.* 1997). This corresponds to a 2.0% average annual growth in real GNP over the period 1950–96. However, the adjustment outlined above for each year over the period gives an ISEW per head for the UK which is just 1.25 times higher in real terms than it was in 1950. This corresponds to a mere 0.5% average annual growth in real ISEW over the period 1950–96. Such 'environmental accounting' is suggesting an entirely different perspective on recorded changes in national economic welfare.

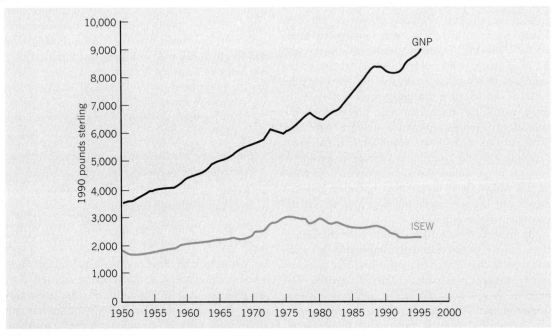

Fig. 10.2 Real GNP and ISEW per capita, UK, 1950–96.
Note: ISEW = Index of Sustainable Economic Welfare.
Source: Adapted from Jackson *et al.* (1997).

Valuing the environment

A number of approaches may be used in seeking to place a 'value' on environmental changes, whether 'favourable' (benefits) or 'unfavourable' (costs). Sometimes the market mechanism may help in terms of monetary valuations by yielding prices for products derived from environmental assets. However, these market prices may be distorted by various types of 'failure' in the market mechanism (e.g. monopolies or externalities), so that some adjustment may be needed to these prices. For example 'shadow prices' may be used, i.e. market prices which are adjusted in order to reflect the valuation to *society* of a particular activity.

On other occasions there may be no market prices to adjust, in which case we may need to use questionnaires to derive *hypothetical* valuations of 'willingness to pay' for an environmental amenity or 'willingness to accept' compensation for an environmental loss. These 'expressed preference' methods of valuation differ from 'revealed preference' methods which seek to observe how consumers *actually* behave in the marketplace for products which are substitutes or complements to the activities for which no market prices exist.

The issue of *time* is particularly important for monetary valuation of environmental impacts which may take many years to materialize. It is therefore important to pay close attention to the process of calculating the *present value* of a stream of future revenues or costs, using the technique of discounting (see Chapter 17, p. 323).

We return to these valuation techniques below, but first it will be useful to consider why valuing environmental costs and benefits is so important to policy makers.

Finding the socially optimum output

Figure 10.3 presents a simplified model in which the marginal pollution costs (MPC) attributable to production are seen as rising with output beyond a certain output level, Q_A. Up to Q_A the amount of pollution generated within the economy is assumed to be assimilated by the environment with zero pollution costs. In this model we assume that pollution is a

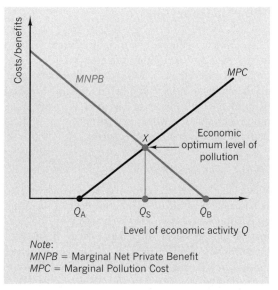

Note:
MNPB = Marginal Net Private Benefit
MPC = Marginal Pollution Cost

Fig. 10.3 Finding an optimum level of pollution.

'negative externality', in that firms which pollute are imposing costs on society that are not paid for by those firms.

At the same time the marginal *net* private benefit (MNPB) of each unit of output is assumed to decline as the level of economic activity rises. MNPB is the addition to private benefit received by firms from selling the last unit of output minus the addition to private costs incurred by producing that last unit of output.

If the pollution externality was *not* taken into account, then firms would produce up to output Q_B at which MNPB = 0. Only here would total net private benefit (i.e. total profit) be a maximum. However, the *socially optimum* level of output is Q_S, where MNPB = MPC. Each unit of output *beyond* Q_S adds more in pollution costs to society than it does to net private benefit, and is therefore socially inefficient to produce. Equally it would be socially inefficient to forsake producing any units *up to* Q_S, since each of these units adds more to net private benefit than to pollution costs for society.

Note that in this analysis the social optimum does *not* imply zero pollution. Rather it suggests that the benefits to society are greatest at output Q_S, with pollution costs being positive at $Q_S X$. We return to this idea of seeking 'acceptable' levels of pollution below.

The valuation issue

A key element in finding any socially efficient solution to the negative environmental effects of increased production clearly involves placing a *monetary value* on the marginal private and social costs (or benefits) of production. In terms of Fig. 10.3 we need some monetary valuation which will permit us to estimate both the MNPB and the MPC curves.

Using 'shadow prices'

Where market prices exist, it is at least feasible to obtain monetary valuations of future net revenues from an environmental asset. However, where one or more market failures occur, these prices may be deemed 'inappropriate' and in need of adjustment to reflect more accurately the true benefits and costs to society. Such adjustments give rise to '*shadow prices*', i.e. prices which do not actually exist in the marketplace but which are assumed to exist for purposes of valuation.

Demand curve methods

'Expressed preference' and 'revealed preference' methods are widely used here.

Expressed preference methods

Where no market price exists, individuals are often asked, using surveys or questionnaires, to express how much they would be *willing to pay* for some specified environmental improvement, such as improved water quality or the preservation of a threatened local amenity. In other words an 'expressed preference' approach is taken to valuation. An example of the use of this approach was used in Ukunda, Kenya, where residents were faced with a choice between three sources of water – door-to-door vendors, kiosks and wells – each requiring residents to pay different costs in money and time. Water from door-to-door vendors cost the most but required the least collection time. A study found that the villagers were willing to pay a substantial share of their incomes – about 8% – in exchange for this greater convenience and for time saved. Such valuations can be helpful in seeking to make the case for extending reliable public water supply even to poorer communities. Questionnaires and surveys of willingness to pay have been widely used in the UK to evaluate the recreational benefits of environmental amenities. They can help capture 'use value' (see p. 178) where market prices are inappro-

priate or do not even exist, as well as 'option' and 'existence' values.

These 'expressed preference' methods are sometimes referred to as 'contingent valuation' methods, since the user's 'willingness to pay' (WTP) is often sought for different situations 'contingent upon' some improvement in the (environmental) quality of provision. The same approach may involve asking individuals how much they are 'willing to accept' (WTA) to avoid some specific environmental degradation.

Revealed preference methods

This approach seeks to avoid relying on the use of questionnaires or surveys to gain an impression of the *hypothetical* valuations placed by consumers on various environmental costs and benefits. Instead it seeks to use direct observation of the consumers' *actual* responses to various substitute or complementary goods and services to gain an estimate of value in a particular environmental situation. The focus here is on the 'revealed preferences' of the consumers as expressed in the marketplace, even if this expression is indirect in that it involves surrogate goods and services rather than the environmental amenity itself.

1. Travel Cost Method (TCM). Where no price is charged for entry to recreational sites, economists have searched for private market goods or services whose consumption is *complementary* to the consumption of the recreational good in question. One such private complementary good is the travel costs incurred by individuals to gain access to recreational sites. The 'price' paid to visit any site is uniquely determined for each visitor by calculating the travel costs from his or her location of origin. By observing people's willingness to pay for the private complementary good it is then possible to infer a price for the non-price environmental amenity.

In Fig. 10.4, the demand curve D_{VISITS} shows the overall trend relationship between travel costs and visit rates for all the visitors interviewed. Using this information we can estimate the average visitor's (V_1) total recreational value ($V_1 \times P_1$) for the site. Multiplying this by the total number of visitors per annum allows us to estimate the total annual recreational value of the site.

2. Hedonic Price Method (HPM). A further technique often used in deriving valuations where no prices exist, is the so-called 'hedonic price' method.

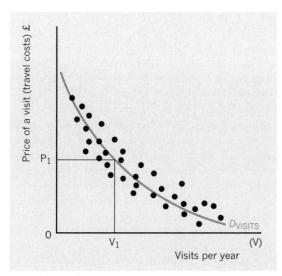

Fig. 10.4 The relationship between the number of visits to a site and the price of the visit.

This estimates the extent to which people are, for example, willing to pay a house price premium for the benefit of living within easy access of an environmental amenity. It could equally be used to estimate the house price discount resulting from living within easy access of a source of environmental concern.

House and other property prices are clearly determined by a number of independent variables. Some of these will involve variables related to the following:

- *Characteristics of the property*: number of rooms, whether detached, semi-detached or terraced, garage facilities available, etc.

- *Characteristics of the location*: number (and reputation) of schools, availability of shopping and recreational facilities, transport infrastructure, etc.

- *Characteristics of the environment*: proximity to favourable or unfavourable environmental factors.

Statistical techniques (such as multiple regression analysis) can be used to estimate the influence of these possible 'explanatory' (independent) variables on house and property prices. For example, a 'classic' statistical study of the impact of traffic noise in Washington, DC, established an inverse relationship between house prices and the environmental factor 'noise pollution' with each extra decibel of noise found to be statistically correlated with a 0.88% fall in average house prices.

Non-demand curve valuations

Essentially both the expressed preference and revealed preference methods are making use of demand curve analysis in placing monetary values on aspects of environmental quality. However, a number of valuation methods may be used which depart from this approach.

Replacement cost method. The focus here is on the cost of replacing or restoring a damaged asset. This cost estimate is then used as a measure of the 'benefit' from such replacement or restoration. For example, if it costs £1 million to restore the façade of buildings damaged by air pollution, then this £1 million cost is used as an estimate of the benefit of environmental improvement.

Preventative expenditure method. The focus here is on using the costs incurred in an attempt to prevent some potential environmental damage as a measure of 'benefit'. For example, the expenditure incurred by residents on double-glazing to avoid 'noise pollution' from a new trunk road might be used as a proxy variable of the value placed by residents on noise abatement.

Delphi method. The focus here is on valuations derived from consulting a group of recognized experts. Each member of the group responds independently to questions as to the valuations that might be placed on various (environmental) contingencies in their area of expertise. The initial responses of the group are then summarized in graphical or tabular form, with each member given the opportunity to re-evaluate their individual responses. The idea here is that through successive rounds of re-evaluation, a consensus valuation of the expert group may eventually emerge.

Cost–benefit analysis (CBA)

Under cost–benefit analysis, the techniques already discussed and others are used to assign monetary values to the gains and losses to different individuals and groups, often weighted according to some perception of the contribution of these individuals or groups to social utility (social welfare). It is for this reason that this approach is sometimes referred to as 'social' cost–benefit analysis. Some of the 'market failures' previously identified are taken into account, with some existing market prices adjusted (e.g. via weighting) and values attributed to some situations where no market prices currently exist. If the proposed reallocation of resources via new investment in some (environmental) project is evaluated as creating benefits that are greater, in present value terms, to those who gain than the costs imposed on those who lose, then the project is potentially viable from society's perspective. In other words, if the net present value to society of a project is positive, then the project is at least worthy of consideration. Whether or not it will be undertaken may depend upon what restrictions, if any, apply to the level of resources (finance) available. If such resources are limited and must be rationed, then of course only those projects with the highest (positive) net present values to society may be selected.

Total economic value

In recent years there has been considerable discussion as to how to find the 'total economic value' (TEV) of an environmental asset. The following identity has been suggested:

Total economic value ≡ use value
+ option value + existence value

The idea here is that 'use value' reflects the practical uses to which an environmental asset is currently being put. For example, the tropical rainforests are used to provide arable land for crop cultivation or to rear cattle in various ranching activities. The forests are also a source of various products, such as timber, rubber, medicines, nuts, etc. In addition, the forests act as the 'lungs' of the world, absorbing stores of carbon dioxide and releasing oxygen, as well as helping to prevent soil erosion and playing an important part in flood control.

There are clear difficulties in placing reliable monetary estimates on all these aspects of the 'use value' of the rainforest. However, it is even more difficult to estimate 'option value', which refers to the value we place on the asset *now* as regards functions which might be exploited some time in the *future*. For example, how much are we willing to pay to preserve the rainforest in case it becomes a still more important source of herbal and other medicines? This is a type of insurance value, seeking to measure the willingness to

pay for an environmental asset now, given some probability function of the individual (or group) wishing to use that asset in various ways in the future.

Finally, 'existence value' refers to the value we place on an environmental asset as it is today, independently of any current or future use we might make of that asset. This is an attempt to measure our willingness to pay for an environmental asset simply because we wish it to continue to exist in its present form. Many people subscribe to charities to preserve the rainforests, other natural habitats or wildlife even though they may never themselves see those habitats or species. Existence value may involve inter-generational motives, such as wishing to give one's children or grandchildren the opportunity to observe certain species or ecosystems.

Although much remains to be done in estimating TEV, a number of empirical studies have been undertaken. For instance, the Flood Hazard Research Centre in the UK estimated that in 1987/88 people were willing to pay £14 to £18 per annum in taxes in order that recreational beaches (use value) be protected from erosion (Turner 1991). The researchers also surveyed a sample of people who did *not* use beaches for recreational use. They estimated that these people were willing to pay £21 to £25 per annum in taxes in order to preserve these same beaches (existence value).

Overall, many estimates are finding that the 'option' and 'existence' values of environmental assets often far exceed their 'use' value. For example, existence values for the Grand Canyon were found to outweigh use values by the startling ratio of 60 to 1 (Pearce 1991a). In similar vein, *non-users* of Prince William Sound, Alaska, devastated by the Exxon Valdez oil spill in 1989, placed an extremely high value on its existence value (O'Doherty 1994). The amounts non-users were estimated (via interviews) as willing to pay to *avoid* the damage actually incurred came to $2.8 billion, i.e. $31 per US household. This approach, whereby interviewees are asked about the value of a resource 'contingent' on its not being damaged, is often termed 'contingent valuation'.

We now turn to the important policy issue of how we can provide market incentives or regulations which will result in a socially optimum level of environmental damage (output Q_S in Fig. 10.3), rather than the higher levels of environmental damage which would result from an unfettered free market in which externalities were ignored (output Q_B in Fig. 10.3).

Market-based and non-market-based incentives

In free-market or mixed economies the market is often seen as an efficient means of allocating scarce resources. Here we look at ways in which the *market* could be used to provide incentives to either firms or consumers in order to bring about a more socially optimum use of environmental assets.

Market-based incentives

Environmental taxes

An environmental tax is a tax on a product or service which is detrimental to the environment, or a tax on a factor input used to produce that product or service. An environmental tax will increase the *private* costs of producing goods or services which impose negative 'externalities' on society. In terms of Fig. 10.3 (p. 175) an appropriate tax could convert the marginal *pollution* cost curve (MPC) into the firm's own marginal cost curve (MC). This is because the firm itself now has to pay a 'price' (the tax) for the pollution it imposes on society. The firm itself would then have a profit-based incentive to produce the socially optimum level of output Q_S, since its own profits would now be maximized at MNPB = MPC, instead of producing the socially inefficient output Q_B. Using environmental taxes in this way is often said to be a policy of 'internalizing' the externality. In other words the firm itself now has the incentive to take the externality into account in its own decision making.

Of course, in practice, there are many problems in devising a tax rate which will exactly equate marginal pollution cost (MPC) with marginal cost (MC) for the firm. Such a (Pigouvian) tax would need to impose private costs which vary with output in a way which exactly mirrors the amount of marginal pollution cost related to each additional unit of output.

A move towards environmental taxes is in line with the 'polluter pays' principle adopted by the OECD in 1972. This principle states that 'the polluter should bear the cost of measures to reduce pollution decided upon by public authorities to ensure that the environment is in an "acceptable state" '. The idea behind adopting this principle across member states was to avoid the distortions in comparative advantages and trade flows which could arise if countries tackled environmental problems in widely different ways. Slightly less than 2% of UK total tax revenue is currently yielded by explicitly environmental taxes, although if general taxes on energy are also included in a looser definition of 'environmentally related' taxes, then this figure rises to some 8.5% of UK total tax revenue.

Tradeable permits

Another market-based solution to environmental problems could involve tradeable permits. Here the polluter receives a permit to emit a specified amount of waste, whether carbon dioxide, sulphur dioxide or whatever. The *total* amount of permits issued for any pollutant must, of course, be within currently accepted guidelines of 'safe' levels of emission for that pollutant. Within the overall limit of the permits issued, individual polluters can then buy and sell the permits between each other. The distribution of pollution is then market directed even though the overall total is regulated, the expectation being that those firms which are already able to meet 'clean' standards will benefit by selling permits to those firms which currently find it too difficult or expensive to meet those standards.

Put another way, the case for tradeable permits rests on some firms being more efficient than other firms in 'abating' (avoiding) pollution. The *marginal abatement cost* (MAC) curves in Fig. 10.5 show the extra cost incurred by abating (avoiding) the last unit of pollution. Suppose two firms, A and B, both emit carbon dioxide but with different MACs, as illustrated in Figs 10.5(a) and (b). It can be seen that the MACs for firm A rise more quickly than for firm B as abatement increases and emissions are reduced.

With no controls on emission levels so that no abatement takes place, total emissions of carbon dioxide are 240 million tonnes per annum. Suppose, however, the authorities desire a reduction in emission levels of 50%, so that 120 million tonnes (*m*) is the maximum emission level from the two firms. This can be achieved by the issue of 120 (*m*) tradeable permits. Suppose these permits are issued on the basis of past levels of emissions (grandfathering). In this case firm A would receive 50 (*m*) tradeable permits and firm B 70 (*m*) tradeable permits. This being the case, A would have to reduce emissions to 50 and B to 70 million tonnes per annum respectively.

If A were to reduce its emissions to 50 million tonnes, its MAC would then be £5,000 per tonne. If A

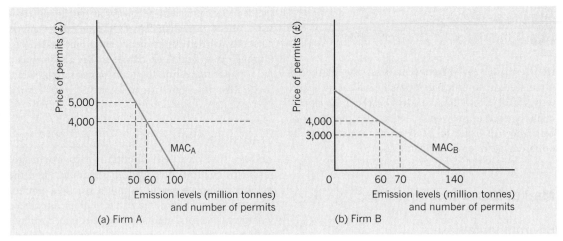

Fig. 10.5 Differences in MACs as a basis for trading permits.

can *buy* permits for less than £5,000 it will do so, since it would then be cheaper for A to buy a permit and pollute, than to abate (avoid) the last unit of pollution. If firm B were to reduce its emissions to 70 million tonnes, its MAC would be £3,000 per tonne. If B can *sell* its permits for a price greater than £3,000 per tonne it will do so, since the revenue earned from the sale would be greater than the extra cost of abatement incurred by reducing emissions, A will be willing to buy permits at prices between £3,000 and £5,000 per tonne. There is thus the basis for trade between the two firms. The two firms will continue to trade whilst their MACs are different. As can be seen in Figs 10.5(a) and (b), such trade can continue until their respective MACs are equalized at a price of £4,000, with 60 million tonnes emitted by both firm A and firm B, with B selling 10 permits to A. The overall total of emissions, however, remains constant at 120 million tonnes.

The Kyoto agreement in December 1997 has, for the first time, accepted the principle of carbon trading between nations. Countries are to be allocated quotas for maximum annual emissions of carbon dioxide. Should any country produce *less than* its quota, it will be able to sell its 'right to pollute' to other countries. We return to the issue of the Kyoto Protocol and tradeable permits in the discussion of global warming below (p. 184).

Bargains

The idea here is that if we assign 'property rights' to the polluters giving them the 'right to pollute', or to the sufferers giving them the 'right not to be polluted', then bargains may be struck whereby pollution is curbed. For instance, if we assign these property rights to the polluters, then those who suffer may find it advantageous to compensate the polluter for agreeing *not* to pollute, the suggestion being that compensation will be offered by the sufferers as long as this is less than the value of the damage which would otherwise be inflicted upon them. Alternatively, if the property rights are assigned to the sufferers, who then have the 'right' not to be polluted, then the polluters may find it advantageous to offer the sufferers sums of money which would allow the polluters to continue polluting, the suggestion being that the polluters will offer compensation to the sufferers as long as this is less than the private benefits obtained by expanding output and thereby increasing pollution. Under either situation, economists such as R. Coase have shown that clearly assigned property rights can lead to 'bargains' which bring about output solutions closer to the social optimum than would otherwise occur.

From Fig. 10.6 we can see that, with no regulation, the polluter will seek to maximize *total* net private benefits (profits) producing at Q_B, whereas Q_S is the social optimum.

The introduction of property rights can, however, change this situation. If the *polluter* is given the property rights, then the sufferer will (provided polluter and sufferer have the same information!) find it advantageous to *compensate/bribe* the polluter to cease output at Q_S. For any *extra* output beyond Q_S the losses to the sufferer exceed the benefits to the

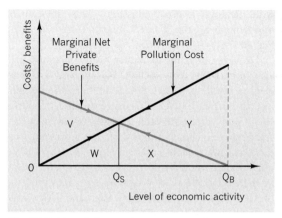

Fig. 10.6 Negotiation under property rights.

polluter (e.g. $X + Y > X$ at output Q_B). There is clearly scope for a negotiated solution at output level Q_S.

A similar negotiated outcome can be expected under the Coase theorem if the *sufferer* is given the property rights. This time the polluter will (given symmetry of information) find it advantageous to *choose* the socially optimum output Q_S and offer compensation equivalent to W to sufferers. For any *extra* output beyond Q_S the gains to the polluter are more than offset by the (actionable) losses to the sufferers (e.g. $X > X + Y$ at output Q_B). There is, again, clearly scope for a negotiated solution at output level Q_S.

The principle of 'sufferer pays' is already in evidence. For example, Sweden assists Poland with reducing acid rain because the acid rain from Poland damages Swedish lakes and forests. Similarly, the Montreal Protocol of 1987 sought to protect the ozone layer by including provisions by which China, India and other developing countries were to be compensated by richer countries for agreeing to limit their use of chlorofluorocarbons (CFCs). On this basis, Brazil has argued that it is up to the developed countries to compensate it for desisting from exploiting its tropical rainforests, given that it is primarily other countries which will suffer if deforestation continues apace.

Non-market-based incentives: regulations

Many current environmental policies make use of regulations. Standards are set for air or water quality

and the polluter is then left free to decide on how best to achieve these minimum standards. The regulator then monitors the environmental situation and takes action against any producers found to be in violation of the standards set.

In the UK, the Environmental Protection Act (1989) laid down minimum environmental standards for emissions from over 3,500 factories involved in chemical processes, waste incineration and oil refining. The factories have to meet these standards for all emissions, whether into air or water or onto land. Factory performance is monitored by a strengthened HM Inspectorate of Pollution, the costs of which are paid for by the factory owners themselves. The Act also provided for public access to information on the pollution created by firms. Regulations were also established on restricting the release of genetically engineered bacteria and viruses and a ban was imposed on most forms of straw and stubble burning from 1992 onwards. Stricter regulations were also imposed on waste disposal operations, with local authorities given a duty to keep public land clean. On-the-spot fines of up to £1,000 were instituted for persons dropping litter.

Regulations have also played an important part in the five 'Environmental Action Programmes' of the EU, which first began in 1973. For example, specific standards have been set for minimum acceptable levels of water quality for drinking and for bathing. As regards the latter, regular monitoring of coastal waters must take place, with as many as 19 separate tests undertaken throughout the tourist season.

Of course regulations may be part of an integrated environmental policy which also involves market-based incentives. A tradeable permits system for sulphur dioxide emissions has been long established in the US and works in tandem with the standards imposed by the US Clean Air Act.

We now review two key environmental issues to examine the relative merits of market-based and non-market-based incentives for dealing with environmental problems, namely global warming and transport-related pollution.

Global warming

This refers to the trapping of heat between the earth's surface and gases in the atmosphere, especially carbon dioxide (CO_2). Currently some six billion tonnes of carbon dioxide are released into the atmosphere each year, largely as a result of burning fossil fuels. In fact carbon dioxide constitutes some 56% of these 'greenhouse gases', with chlorofluorocarbons (CFCs), used mainly in refrigerators, aerosols and air-conditioning systems, accounting for a further 23% of such gases, the rest being methane (14%) and nitrous oxide (7%). By trapping the sun's heat these gases are in turn raising global temperature (global warming). On present estimates, temperatures are expected to increase by a further 1 °C in the next two decades, when an increase of merely half a degree in world temperature over the past century is believed to have contributed to a rise of 10 cm in sea levels. Higher sea levels (resulting from melting ice caps), flooding, and various climatic changes causing increased desertification and drought, have all been widely linked to global warming.

The whole debate on curbing emissions of CO_2 and other 'greenhouse gases' in an attempt to combat global warming usefully highlights a number of issues:

■ a non-zero level of pollution as socially efficient;

■ the respective advantages and disadvantages of market-based and non-market-based incentives in achieving socially efficient solutions.

We have already addressed some of the environmental implications of global warming. There are clearly significant social damage costs associated with emissions of CO_2, which rise at an increasing rate

with the total level of emissions. This situation is represented by the *Total Damage Costs* curve in Fig. 10.7(a).

However, seeking to reduce CO_2 emissions will also impose costs on society. For instance we may need to install expensive flue-desulphurization plants in coal-burning power stations, or to use (less efficient) sources of renewable energy (e.g. wind, wave, solar power). These various costs are represented by the *Total Abatement Costs* curve in Fig. 10.7(a). We might expect these Total Abatement Costs to rise at an increasing rate as we progressively *reduce* the level of CO_2 emissions, since the easier and less costly means of cutting back on CO_2 emissions are likely to have been adopted first.

In Fig. 10.7(a), we can see that the consequence of taking *no action* to reduce CO_2 emissions would leave us at Q_p, with zero abatement costs but high total damage costs.

What must be stressed here is the importance of seeking to identify *both* types of cost. On occasions environmentalists focus exclusively on the damages caused by global warming, whereas producers concern themselves solely with the higher (abatement) costs of adopting less CO_2 intensive methods of production.

The analysis is simplified (Fig. 10.7(b)) by using *marginal* changes in the damage costs or abatement costs related to each extra tonne of CO_2 emitted or abated. The socially optimum level of CO_2 emissions is where marginal damage costs exactly equal marginal abatement costs, i.e. output Q_s in Fig. 10.7(b). To emit more CO_2 than Q_s would imply marginal

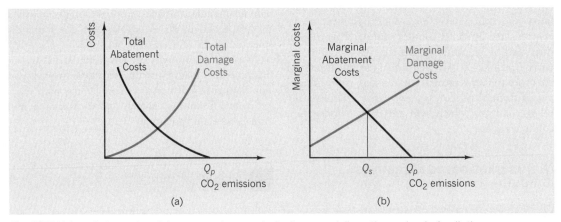

Fig. 10.7 Using abatement and damage cost curves in finding a socially optimum level of pollution.

damage costs to society *greater than* the marginal cost to society of abating that damage. Society is clearly disadvantaged by any emissions in excess of Q_s. Equally, to emit less CO_2 than Q_s would imply marginal damage costs to society *less than* the marginal cost to society of abating that damage. In this case society is disadvantaged by seeking to cut CO_2 emissions below Q_s.

Setting the targets

If we are to apply our analysis in practical ways we must seek to *value* both the marginal damage and the marginal abatement cost curves. Again we are faced with the conceptual problem of placing a valuation on variables to which monetary values are at present only rarely attached, if at all. In addition, in a full cost–benefit analysis we must select a rate of discount (see Chapter 12) to enable a comparison to be made between effects in the distant future and the costs of policies introduced today.

Uncertainty will therefore clearly be involved in any attempt to evaluate the costs and benefits of policy action or inaction. The target for *reducing* CO_2 emissions ($Q_p - Q_s$ in Fig. 10.7(b)) to the socially optimum level will clearly be affected by such uncertainty. Analysts often use 'scenarios' of high, medium and low estimates for marginal damage and marginal abatement cost curves. For instance, Nordhaus (1991) estimated each of these marginal cost curves for both CO_2 emissions and for the broader category

of greenhouse gases, based on US data. His *high* estimate of marginal damage costs was calculated at $66.00 per tonne of CO_2, his *low* estimate at only $1.83 per tonne of CO_2. We can use Fig. 10.7(b), above, to illustrate this analysis. In the high estimate case, the marginal damage cost curve shifts vertically upwards, Q_s falls, and the 'target' reduction in CO_2 emissions (i.e. $Q_s - Q_p$) increases. On this basis Nordhaus advocates reducing CO_2 emissions by 20%. It is hardly surprising (in view of the valuation discrepancy noted above) that in his low estimate case, the marginal damage cost curve shifts vertically downwards in Fig. 10.7(b), Q_s rises, and the target reduction in CO_2 emissions (i.e. $Q_s - Q_p$) falls. On this basis Nordhaus advocates reducing CO_2 emissions by only about 3%.

Cooperative solutions and regulations

The arguments in favour of cooperative solutions to problems such as global warming have led many to support some type of regulatory framework such as that embedded in the Kyoto Protocol (see below). We can review some of these arguments using Fig. 10.8, which represents a situation in which the benefits to a country, A, from pollution reduction accrue only partly to itself, the remaining (and more substantial) benefits from A's pollution reduction being the rest of the region (here the world) of which A is but a part. However, A is faced with having itself to pay the costs of any pollution reduction (abatement) it undertakes.

In Fig. 10.8 A_{MB} and A_{MC} are country A's marginal benefits and marginal costs of pollution reduction (note that the horizontal axis is pollution reduction, so more pollution reduction in Fig. 10.8 – moving left to right – is the same as less pollution emission – moving right to left – in Fig. 10.7(b) above), whilst R_{MB} is the whole region's (rest of the world's) marginal benefit from country A's pollution reduction.

Note that the maximum net benefit for the *whole region* ($MW0$) occurs with pollution reduction by country A of P_R. But the maximum net benefit for *country A* ($LV0$) occurs with pollution reduction by country A of only P_A. To induce A to undertake pollution reduction beyond P_A is in the best interest of the whole region (world) but any further reduction in pollution by A beyond P_A brings extra benefit to itself only up to X (area VXP_A) and this is insufficient to

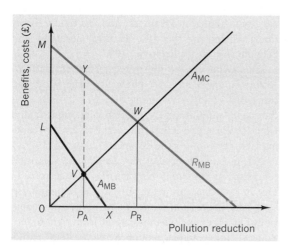

Fig. 10.8 Regional reciprocal pollution and the need for negotiation.

cover its additional costs. In other words A will require extensive compensation to induce it to reduce pollution to P_R or at least a regulatory framework in which A can recognize benefits to itself from other countries also acting with a regional or global perspective in mind, rather than merely their own self-interest. It was in an attempt to provide such a global perspective for pollution reduction that the Kyoto Protocol was signed in 1997.

Kyoto Protocol

Provisionally agreed in December 1997 via the UN Framework Convention on Climate Change, the main features of the Kyoto Protocol are as follows.

- Developed countries to collectively reduce 1990 emission levels of six greenhouse gases by 5% by 2012.
- Individual country targets to be set within this average.
- Penalties for non-compliance.
- Emissions trading to be allowed (via permits).
- 'Clean Development Mechanisms' to be applied by which greenhouse gas reductions in developing countries resulting from investments by developed countries can be credited to those developed countries, thereby reducing the pollution reduction targets set for them in the Kyoto agreement.

To ratify the Kyoto Protocol needs the signatures of countries responsible for at least 55% of 1990 emissions of greenhouse gases. An initial problem was the unwillingness of the US to ratify the protocol, given that it alone represented some 35% of 1990 greenhouse gas emissions. Only in 2003 was the Kyoto Protocol provisionally ratified with the initial reluctance to ratify of Russia (18% of 1990 emissions), Canada and some other countries finally being overcome. Having a major source of greenhouse gas emissions such as the US outside the Kyoto Protocol is clearly a weakness for this cooperative approach to tackling global warming.

Achieving the targets

Whatever the targets set for reduced emissions, which policy instruments will be most effective in achieving those targets? The discussion by Ingham and Ulph (1991) is helpful in comparing market and non-market policy instruments. Many different methods are available for bringing about any given total reduction in CO_2 emissions. Users of fossil fuels might be induced to switch towards fuels that emit less CO_2 within a given total energy requirement. For instance oil and gas emit, respectively, about 80% and 60% as much CO_2 per unit of energy as coal. Alternatively, the total amount of energy used might be reduced in an attempt to cut CO_2 emissions.

Another issue is whether we seek to impose our target rate of reduction for CO_2 emissions on *all* sectors of the UK economy. For example, some 40% of CO_2 emissions come from electricity generation, 20% from the industrial sector and around 20% from the transport sector. Should we then ask for a *uniform* reduction of, say, 25% across all sectors? This is unlikely to be appropriate, since *marginal abatement* cost curves are likely to differ across sectors and, indeed, across countries. For instance, it has been estimated that to abate 14% of the air pollution emitted by the textiles sector in the USA will cost $136m per annum. However, to abate 14% of the air pollution emitted by each of the machinery, electrical equipment and fabricated metals sectors will cost $572m, $729m and $896m respectively (World Bank 1992). As well as differing between industrial sectors *within* a country, abatement costs will also differ between countries. For example, it has been estimated that a 10% reduction in CO_2 emissions by 2010 (as compared to 1988 emission levels) will cost €400 per tonne of CO_2 abated in Italy, but only €200 per tonne abated in Denmark, and less than €20 per tonne abated in the UK, France, Germany and Belgium (*European Economy* 1992).

This point can be illustrated by taking just two sectors in the UK – say electricity generation and transport – and by assuming that they initially emit the same amount of CO_2. Following Ingham and Ulph (1991) suppose that the overall target for reducing CO_2 emissions is the distance $O'O$ in Fig. 10.9.

We must now decide how to allocate this total reduction in emissions between the two sectors. In Fig. 10.9 we measure reductions in CO_2 emissions in electricity generation from left to right, and reductions in CO_2 emissions in transport from right to left. Point A, for example, would divide the total reduction in emissions into OA in electricity generation and $O'A$ in transport. A *marginal abatement cost* (MAC)

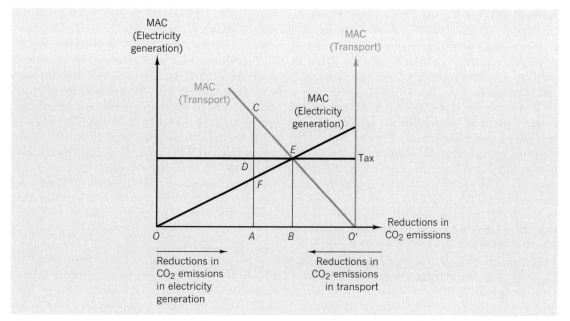

Fig. 10.9 Finding the 'efficient' or 'least-cost' solution for reducing CO_2 emissions in a two-sector model.

curve is now calculated for each sector. In Fig. 10.9 we draw the MAC curve for electricity generation as being lower and flatter than that for transport. This reflects the greater fuel-switching possibilities in electricity generation as compared to transport, both within fossil fuels and between fossil and non-fossil (solar, wave, wind) fuels. In other words, any marginal reduction in CO_2 emissions in electricity generation is likely to raise overall costs by *less* in electricity generation than in transport. In transport there are far fewer fuel-substitution possibilities, the major means of curbing CO_2 emissions in transport being improved techniques for energy efficiency or a switch from private to public transport.

Given these *different* marginal abatement cost curves for each sector in Fig. 10.9, how then should we allocate our reduction between the two sectors? Clearly we should seek a solution by which the given total reduction in emissions is achieved at the least total cost to society: we shall call this the *efficient* or *least-cost* solution. In Fig. 10.9, this will be where marginal abatement costs are the same in both sectors, i.e. at point *B* in the diagram. We can explain this by supposing we were initially *not* at *B*, but at *A* in Fig. 10.9, with equal reductions in the two sectors. At point *A*, marginal abatement costs in transport are

AC but marginal abatement costs in electricity generation are only *AF*. So by abating CO_2 by *one more* tonne in electricity generation and *one less* tonne in transport, we would have the same total reduction in CO_2 emissions, but would have saved *CF* in costs. By moving from point *A* to the 'efficient' point *B*, we would save the area *CFE* in abatement costs.

It follows, therefore, that for any given target for total reduction in CO_2 emissions, 'efficiency' will occur only if the marginal cost of abatement is the same across all sectors of the economy (and indeed across all methods of abatement). Pollution control policies which seek to treat all sectors equally, even where marginal abatement costs differ widely between sectors, may clearly fail to reach an 'efficient' solution.

Policy implications

We have previously seen that environmental policy instruments can be broadly classified into two types: market-based and non-market-based. *Market-based* policy instruments would include setting a tax on emissions of CO_2 or issuing a limited number of permits to emit CO_2 and then allowing a market to be set up in which those permits are traded. *Non-*

market-based policy instruments would include regulations and directives. For example, in the UK, the Non-Fossil Fuel Obligation currently imposed on privatized electricity companies requires them to purchase a specified amount of electricity from non-fossil fuel sources.

We can use Fig. 10.9 to examine the case for using a tax instrument (market-based) as compared to regulation (non-market-based). A tax of *BE* on CO_2 emissions would lead to the 'efficient' solution *B*. This is because polluters have a choice of paying the tax on their emissions of CO_2 or of taking steps to abate their emissions. They will have an incentive to abate as long as the marginal cost of abatement is lower than the tax. So electricity generating companies will have incentives to abate to *OB*, and transport companies to *O'B*, in Fig. 10.9 above. Since every polluter faces the same tax, then they will end up with the same marginal abatement cost. Here 'prices', amended by tax, are conveying signals to producers in a way which helps coordinate their (profit maximizing) decisions in order to bring about an 'efficient' (least cost) solution.

The alternative policy of government regulations and directives (non-market-based instruments) in achieving the 'efficient' solution at *B* in Fig. 10.9 would be much more complicated. The government would have to estimate the marginal abatement cost curve for *each sector*, given that such curves differ between sectors. It would then have to estimate the different percentage reductions required in each sector in order to equalize marginal abatement costs (the 'efficient' solution). It is hardly reasonable to suppose that the government could achieve such fine tuning in order to reach 'efficient' solutions.

The market-based solution of tax has no administrative overhead. Producers are simply assumed to react to the signals of market prices (amended by taxes) in a way which maximizes their own profits. Regulations, on the other hand, imply monitoring, supervision and other 'bureaucratic' procedures. Ingham and Ulph (1991) found that using a tax policy, as compared with seeking an *equal proportionate reduction* in CO_2 emissions by regulations, resulted in total abatement costs being 20% lower than they would have been under the alternative regulatory policy.

In a simulation by Cambridge Econometrics (Cowe 1998), a 'package' of seven green taxes, including a carbon tax based on industrial and commercial energy use, was estimated as cutting CO_2 emissions by 13% on 1990 levels by 2010. Rather encouragingly, this package of green taxes was estimated as raising a further £27 bn in tax revenues by 2010, which could be used to cut employers' national insurance by 3%, leading to almost 400,000 extra jobs. Only a small (−0.2%) deterioration was predicted for the balance of payments and for inflation (prices rising by 0.5%) by 2010 and GDP was even predicted to have received a small boost (+0.2%) by this package of green taxes. Such simulation studies are useful in that they 'model' impacts of tax measures throughout the economy, although one must carefully check the assumptions which underlie the equations used in computer models.

The Climate Change Levy

In the 1999 UK Budget, the Chancellor, Gordon Brown, announced that a *Climate Change Levy* (CCL) would be imposed on business use of energy from April 2001. The CCL is a tax applying to fossil fuel used by non-domestic (mainly commercial and industrial) users, applying at different rates to different fossil fuels. The rates are 0.42p per kWh for electricity, 0.15p per kWh for gas and 1.17p per kilogram for coal. Fuel oils are not liable for CCL as they are already liable for separate duty. The CCL is a revenue-neutral tax, meaning that the revenue produced by the tax will be recycled to companies so that for industry as a whole there will be no net increase in taxation. The revenues are recycled through a reduction of 0.3% in employers' national insurance contributions, an increase in tax allowances for certain energy-saving investments by a company, and payments from an energy-efficient fund for small and medium-sized companies. Certain large polluters are able to enter into negotiated voluntary agreement with the government to reduce energy consumption in exchange for a reduction (up to 80%) of CCL. Note that the tax does not apply to domestic energy use, although households will bear some of the burden of this tax in so far as firms pass the tax forward.

Critics have suggested that a carbon tax which was based solely on CO_2 content would be preferable, since the energy content of fuel does not necessarily reflect its carbon content. However, an energy tax is believed to be simpler to administer, being applied at a uniform rate per kilowatt-hour for all 'primary' fuels (coal, gas, oil), rather than a more complex differential rate depending on their carbon content.

Transport and the environment

Many of the detailed issues involving transport are considered in Chapter 12. Here we focus on the environmental implications of various scenarios envisaged for the growth of transport, and the various policy instruments which might be applied to influence transport outcomes.

That transport has moved to centre-stage as regards environmental concern is amply illustrated by the plethora of major reports on transport and the environment (e.g. Royal Commission on Environmental Pollution 1994, 1997; House of Commons 1994). This is hardly surprising, given facts such as the following and our earlier discussions on global warming and climatic change:

- Total UK carbon dioxide emissions fell by 10% between 1970 and 1990, but emissions from transport increased by 65%.

- Transport accounts for the whole of the net increase projected in UK carbon dioxide emissions between 1970 and 2020 (an increase of 39 million tonnes of carbon a year).

- Two-thirds of that projected increase in carbon dioxide emissions is accounted for by private cars.

Nor is there any longer much doubt as to the serious impact of the negative externalities associated with road transport, as Table 10.1 usefully indicates. This table excludes congestion costs (see Chapter 12) and a number of other environmental costs, yet still

calculates the environmental costs of road transport at between £8.3bn and £32.3bn per annum, depending on which of the three studies is used and on whether the lower or upper estimates are selected in any given study. This is equivalent to between 1% and 4% of UK GDP per annum. Even allowing for the uncertainty indicated by the differing estimates of each study and by the lower and upper ranges of the calculations, negative externalities of such magnitude have forced transport to the forefront of environmental debate.

The Royal Commission on Environmental Pollution (1994) set a range of *targets* for transport-related pollutants at specific future dates, for example to limit emissions of carbon dioxide from surface transport in 2000 to the 1990 level, and in 2020 to no more than 80% of the 1990 level. To achieve such targets it proposed a range of *policy instruments* which included a blend of market-based and non-market-based instruments.

Market-based instruments

There is a clear preference to use such instruments wherever feasible, yet a recognition that other approaches may sometimes be needed:

> Although economic instruments utilising the price mechanism are not a complete alternative to direct regulation, they tend to be more efficient.
> (Royal Commission 1994, p. 106)

The commission reviews a number of possible road charges which relate the amount paid to the

Table 10.1 Transport and environmental costs (£bn per annum in 1994 prices).

	Eighteenth Report	Newbery	Maddison *et al.*
Air pollution	2.0–5.2	2.8–7.4	19.7
Climate change	1.5–3.1	0.4	0.1
Noise and vibration	1.0–4.6	0.6	2.6–3.1
Total environmental costs	4.6–12.9	3.8–8.4	22.4–22.9
Road accidents	5.4	4.5–7.5	2.9–9.4
Quantified social and environmental costs other than congestion costs	10.0–18.3	8.3–15.9	25.3–32.3

Note: 'Eighteenth Report' refers to the Royal Commission on Environmental Pollution (1994). Details of the studies by Newbery (1995) and Maddison *et al.* (1996) can be found at the end of the chapter.
Source: Adapted from Royal Commission on Environmental Pollution (1997).

environmental costs imposed by journeys or movements. These included charges related to distance travelled, to use of road space (road pricing), to pollutants emitted, to parking space, and to fuel used. The 'pollutant emitted' charge was attractive to the commission as it would correspond to the Pigouvian environmental tax previously discussed (p. 179). A German proposal is for data on the use of the vehicle during the year to be stored in an electronic management system, displayed during an annual test on emissions and passed on to the tax authorities. The technology and necessary EU legislation for such a tax is not immediately available, although the London congestion charge of £5 per day introduced in February 2003 indicates a renewed interest in at least moving in this direction. Nevertheless, the focus of attention has mainly been on the charge on fuel used.

Fuel duty was regarded as having a number of advantages as an economic instrument for influencing decisions about additional journeys:

- *The amount of tax paid varies with the environmental costs.* The amount of fuel used and duty paid is in the main proportional to the amount of carbon dioxide emitted, and (for any given vehicle) is closely reflected in the quantities of other substances emitted. Fuel consumption is substantially higher in congested urban traffic, and is therefore correlated to some degree with situations in which a vehicle is contributing to higher concentrations of pollutants, and where there is a higher exposure to the noise and vibration it is producing.

- *It is simple to administer.* It costs little to collect, is difficult to avoid or evade, and can easily be modified.

- *Road users have discretion about how to respond.* Road users may respond either by reducing the number or length of their journeys or by reducing their use of fuel in other ways, such as switching to a smaller or more fuel-efficient vehicle or driving in a more fuel-efficient way.

- *It is possible to vary the rate of fuel duty to provide an incentive to use environmentally less damaging forms of fuel,* as in the case of the existing small differentials in favour of diesel and unleaded petrol.

- *A fuel duty already exists.*

Empirical studies have indicated that variations in fuel duty do indeed have an effect on road transport use. The Department of Transport has estimated that a 10% increase in the price of fuel in real terms would lead to a fall in fuel use of up to 3%, of which half would be the result of reduced vehicle use. The Royal

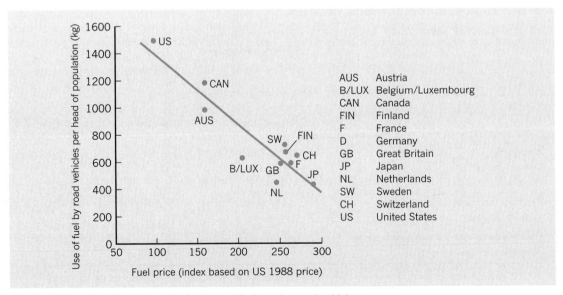

Fig. 10.10 Relationship between fuel price and fuel use by road vehicles.
Source: Adapted from Royal Commission on Environmental Pollution (1994).

Commission concluded that in order to meet the target of limiting carbon dioxide emissions from road transport to 1990 levels by this means alone, the price of fuel would need to double, relative to the price of other goods, by 2005. This would require an increase in fuel duty of some 9% a year (in real terms) for 10 years (a further 4% above the government's already stated intention of 5% a year). Certainly there is international evidence to indicate the effectiveness of higher fuel prices deterring fuel use by road vehicles, as can be seen in Fig. 10.2.

Non-market based instruments

The Royal Commission's recommended measures for achieving its CO_2 targets for 2000 and 2020 are set out in Table 10.2. These clearly involve a mix of market- and non-market-based instruments. For example, emissions of various pollutants (including CO_2) increase fairly rapidly at vehicle speeds over 55 mph, as do car accidents. There is therefore a recommendation for stricter enforcement by the regulatory authorities of the speed limits on various roads. Note that *all* the measures in Table 10.2 are needed to meet the target of carbon dioxide at 80% of 1990 levels by 2020.

Many other subsidiary *regulations* also underly these recommendations, for example 'that more stringent standards be applied in the emissions element of the annual MOT test, and that this element become obligatory for all cars a year after registration' (instead of three years as at present). This recognizes the fact that there is a tendency for pollution emissions to increase with age of vehicle, for any given distance travelled.

As the Royal Commission concludes:

> Government must use an appropriate combination of direct regulation and economic instruments to force the pace of technological development and foster markets for new products. In the case of noise levels and the emission of pollutants, direct regulation in the form of EU legislation should continue to be the primary method used to reduce the environmental impact of vehicles. Direct regulation should extend beyond compliance with limits for new vehicles to include much more effective enforcement of environmental standards applying to the existing fleet. (Royal Commission 1994: 144)

Conclusion

The World Bank has concluded that 'regulatory policies, which are used extensively in both industrial and developing countries, are best suited to situations

Table 10.2 Combined effect of recommended measures on CO_2 emissions from surface transport (million tonnes carbon per year).

		Cars 19.7	Road 30.5	Total 32.3	% of 1990 100
	1990				
Baseline	2000	22.4	34.7	36.4	113
Doubling of fuel prices by 2005		20.2	31.3	33.2	103
Enforcement of 60 mph and 70 mph speed limits		19.1	30.1	32.0	99
40% improvement in fuel efficiency of new cars by 2005		18.4	29.1	31.1	97
Halving of growth of car traffic in urban areas		18.2	28.9	30.9	96
Baseline	2020	26.9	42.9	44.7	138
Doubling of fuel prices by 2005		18.2	29.5	32.0	99
Enforcement of 60 mph and 70 mph speed limits		17.1	28.4	30.9	96
40% improvement in fuel efficiency of new cars by 2005		13.1	23.8	26.3	82
Halving of growth of car traffic in urban areas		12.6	23.2	25.7	80

Source: Adapted from Royal Commission on Environmental Pollution (1994), Appendix D.

that involve a few public enterprises and non-competitive private firms' (World Bank 1992). It also concludes that economic incentives, such as charges, will often be less costly than regulatory alternatives. For instance, to achieve the *least-cost* or *efficient* solution of point *B* in Fig. 10.9 is estimated as costing some 22 times more in the US if particulate matter is abated by regulations, rather than by using market-based instruments. Similarly, achieving this least-cost solution by regulating sulphur dioxide emissions in the UK is estimated as costing between 1.4 and 2.5 times as much as achieving it by using market-based instruments.

However, regulatory policies are particularly appropriate when it is important not to exceed certain thresholds, e.g. emissions of radioactive and toxic wastes. In these cases it is clearly of greater concern that substantial environmental damage be avoided than that pollution control be implemented by policies which might prove to be more expensive than expected. However, where the social costs of environmental damage do not increase dramatically if standards are breached by small margins, then it is worth seeking the least-cost policy via market incentives rather than spending excessive amounts on regulation to avoid any breach at all.

With market-based policies, all resource users or polluters face the same price and must respond accordingly. Each *user* decides on the basis of their own utility/profit preferences whether to use fewer environmental resources or to pay extra for using more. On the other hand, with regulations it is the regulators who take such decisions on the behalf of the users, e.g. *all* users might be given the same limited access to a scarce environmental resource. Regulators are, of course, unlikely to be well informed about the relative costs and benefits faced by users or the valuations placed on these by such users.

Market-based policies have another advantage, namely that they price environmental damage in a way which affects all *polluters*, providing uniform 'prices' to which all polluters can respond (see Fig. 10.9), thereby yielding 'efficient' or 'least cost' solutions. By contrast, regulations usually affect only those who fail to comply and who therefore face penalties. Further, regulations which set minimizing standards give polluters no incentives to do better than that minimum.

Our review of environmental concerns and possible remedial policies has, of necessity, been selective. We have considered the competing claims of market- and non-market-based incentives towards achieving socially efficient solutions. Market-based incentives often help avoid the necessity of external bodies seeking to evaluate marginal abatement cost and marginal damage cost curves. This is certainly an advantage in an area where such valuations are notoriously difficult. Nevertheless there are situations where regulations, or a judicious mix of markets and regulations, may be the most appropriate way forward. In any case all the interdependences of any proposed solution must be fully taken into account before any final decisions are made. What is beyond dispute is that the environment and the economic system are highly interrelated, and neither can be considered in isolation from the other.

Key points

- The environment interacts with the circular flow, providing amenity services, natural resources and the assimilation of waste products.

- An 'Index of Sustainable Economic Welfare' (ISEW) adjusts the conventional GNP figure for environmental impacts. On this basis the growth of ISEW per head for the UK in the period 1950–96 is a mere 0.5% per annum, much less than the growth in real GNP per head of 2.0% per annum over the same period.

- The optimum level of pollution for society is unlikely to be zero. Rather it will occur at the (positive) level at which marginal damage costs exactly equal marginal abatement costs.

- Assessing such an optimum involves finding solutions to problems of *valuation* of environmental impacts, especially where no market prices exist.

- Policy instruments which might be used to achieve a social optimum include both market-based incentives (taxes, tradeable permits and negotiation) and

- non-market-based incentives (various standards and regulations).
- There is evidence to suggest that in most cases a given objective can be achieved at least cost by a combination of market-based policy instruments.
- Where the benefits of pollution reduction measures extend beyond the country concerned, there is a case for cooperative and international agreements along the lines of the Kyoto Protocol if socially optimum outcomes are to be achieved.

Now try the self-check questions for this chapter on the Companion Website. You will also find up-to-date facts and case materials.

References and further reading

Cowe, R. (1998) Green taxes come up against pain barrier, *Guardian*, 2 February.

European Economy (1992) The climate challenge, economic aspects of the Community's strategy for limiting CO_2 emissions, *European Economy*, **51**, May.

House of Commons (1994) *Transport-Related Air Pollution in London*, Vol. 1, Report, Minutes of Proceedings and Appendices.

Ingham, A. and Ulph, A. (1991) Economics of global warming, *Economic Review*, **9**(2).

Ison, S., Peake, S. and Wall, S. (2002) *Environmental Issues and Policies*, FT/Prentice Hall.

Jackson, T. and Marks, N. (1994) *Measuring Sustainable Economic Welfare – A Pilot Index: 1950–1990*, Stockholm Environment Institute.

Jackson, T., Marks, N., Ralls, J. and Stymne, S. (1997) *Sustainable Economic Welfare in the UK 1950–1996*, New Economics Foundation, London.

Kerry Turner, R., Pearce, D. and Bateman, I. (1994) *Environmental Economics*, Harvester Wheatsheaf, Hemel Hempstead.

Lawrence, P. (2002) Can the World Bank rescue Africa's economies?, *Economic Review*, **19**(4), April.

Maddison, D., Pearce, D. *et al.* (1996) *Blueprint 5: The True Costs of Road Transport*, Earthscan Publications Ltd.

Markandya, A. and Mason, P. (1999) Air pollution and health, *Economic Review*, **17**(2).

Newbery, D. M. (1995) Economic effects of (18th Report) recommendations, *Economic Journal*, **105**, September.

Nordhaus, W. (1991) To slow or not to slow: the economics of the greenhouse effect, *Economic Journal*, **101**.

O'Doherty, R. (1994) Pricing environmental disasters, *Economic Review*, **12**(1).

Palmer, A. (2001) Organic food, *Economic Review*, **19**(1), September.

Pearce, D. (1991a) Towards the sustainable economy: environment and economics, *Royal Bank of Scotland Review*, **172**, December.

Pearce, D. (1991b) Economics and the environment, *Economics, Journal of the Economics Association*, **27**(1), 113.

Pearce, D. (1998) Sustainable development: taking stock for the future, *Economic Review*, **16**(1).

Royal Commission on Environmental Pollution (1994) *Transport and the Environment*, Eighteenth Report.

Royal Commission on Environmental Pollution (1997) *Transport and the Environment – Developments since 1994*, Twentieth Report.

Sheppard, P. and Walter, M. (2002) The Dibden Bay project: a matter of choice, *Economic Review*, **19**(4), April.

Turner, K. (1991) Environmental economics, *Developments in Economics: an Annual Review*, 7.

UK Environmental Accounts (2003) HMSO.

Willis, K. (1991) The priceless countryside: the recreational benefits of environmental goods, *Royal Bank of Scotland Review*, **172**, December.

World Bank (1992, 1994) World Development Reports.

Chapter 11   Regional and urban policy

This chapter surveys the regional and urban problems experienced by the UK over the last 30–40 years. The difficulties of defining a region are examined, together with 'convergent' and 'divergent' theories of regional development. The policies used by successive governments to alleviate the 'regional problem' are noted, and their effectiveness is assessed. The urban dimension to the regional problem is then discussed and government policy outlined. The chapter ends with a brief assessment of the effectiveness of urban policy.

The regions and their characteristics

Simply defined, a region is a portion of the earth's surface that possesses certain characteristics (physical, economic, political, etc.) which give it a measure of unity and differentiate it from surrounding areas, enabling us to draw boundaries around it. The commonly perceived regions of the UK, mainly counties, were formalized into 'economic planning regions' in 1964. Although certain economic criteria were used in the groupings of counties, the regions were largely established on the basis of administrative convenience.

There is nothing absolute about these planning regions. The Local Government Act of 1972 dramatically altered the county boundaries, and this led to the redrawing of the economic planning regions. These were then called Standard Planning Regions but in 1994 the system changed once more with the establishment of the Government Offices for the Regions (GORs).

The GORs act as regional arms for three government departments, namely the Department of the Environment, Transport and the Regions, the Department for Education and Employment, and the Department of Trade and Industry. Their role is to work in partnership with local communities, including local government, in order to promote economic prosperity in the region as a whole. With the introduction of the GORs in April 1994, the boundaries of the UK regions were redrawn, and as from 1998, statistics for the regions have been based on the GOR boundaries.

In a further change, local government reorganization between 1995 and 1998 has introduced Unitary Authorities (UA) to replace the County and Local District Authorities in some areas of England and Wales, whilst Unitary Councils were established in Scotland and Unitary Boards/Districts in Northern Ireland. The new GOR regions and their sub-regions are shown in Figs 11.1 and 11.2.

Economic planning in the regions is now based on the Government Offices for the Regions (GORs), which act as the regional arms of three government departments, namely the Department of the Environment, Transport and the Regions, the Department for Education and Employment and the Department for Trade and Industry. Their role is to work in partnership with local communities, including local government, in order to promote economic prosperity in the regions as a whole.

The new GORs also became the basic geographic location for the eight new Regional Development Agencies (RDAs) set up in April 1999, followed by a further new RDA for London created in 2000 with the establishment of the Greater London Authority. They resemble the RDAs already in existence in Wales and Scotland and have the task of producing an economic strategy for each region while at the same time administering many of the government's regional and urban programmes.

The regional problem

Traditionally a 'regional problem' is said to exist when a region departs from the 'national average' in a number of important respects:

1   High and persistent unemployment.

2   Low level and growth of GDP per head.

3   Heavy dependence upon a narrow industrial base.

4   Rapid decline in manufacturing.

5   Inadequate levels of infrastructure.

6   Net migration out of the region.

Table 11.1 gives some indication of the regional disparities with reference to the first two criteria.

A number of attempts have been made to group regions in terms of common economic characteristics. For instance, the terms 'core' and 'periphery' are often used. The 'core area' of the UK includes those regions which have experienced the most rapid economic advance in the past three decades. The South East, East Midlands and the Eastern region are usually placed in this category. In 2001, for example, unemployment in the South East was 63% of the national average, but in 2000 the standard of living, as indicated by GDP per head, was 19.9% above the national average. The 'periphery' can be subdivided into an 'inner periphery', which contains the West Midlands, the South West, and Yorkshire and the Humber, and an 'outer periphery', which contains the North West, the North East, Wales, Scotland and Northern Ireland. Regions in the 'outer periphery' are characterized by relatively slow growth, stagnation or decline, and contain most of the old industrial areas of the UK. In 2001, unemployment in the North East was 54% above the national average whilst in 2000

Fig. 11.1 The boundaries of the Government Offices for the Regions (GORs).

GDP per head was 23.9% below that average. Regions in the 'inner periphery' are somewhat in between these two extremes, showing rather more signs of 'economic health' than regions in the 'outer periphery'. In 2001, for example, these areas were 7% below the national average as regards unemploy- ment, and in 2000 they were 11.5% below as regards GDP per head.

Attempts to group regions on these broad economic grounds are, however, becoming less meaningful. The rise of microelectronic technology, the growing impor- tance of multinational activity (see Chapter 7), and the

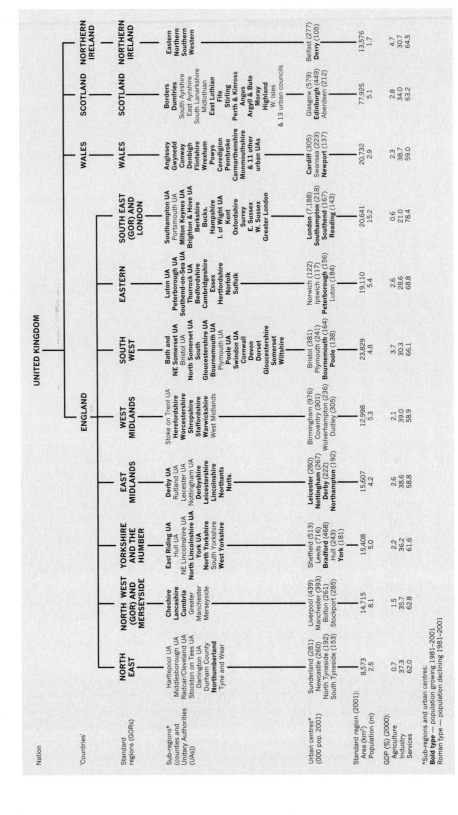

Fig. 11.2 The UK: regional, sub-regional and urban organization.
Sources: ONS (2002), adapted from *Regional Trends* and other ONS updates.

Table 11.1 Index of regional variation in GDP per head and unemployment (UK = 100).

		GDP per head			Unemployment		
		1971	1981	2000	1971	1981	2001
Core	South East	113.8	114.5	119.9	59	71	63
	East Midlands	96.5	100.0	91.7	85	90	102
	Eastern	93.8	97.3	109.9	91	81	75
Inner periphery	West Midlands	102.7	90.6	90.3	85	120	104
	South West	94.7	95.9	89.0	95	87	73
	Yorks/Humber	93.2	93.0	86.2	112	104	102
Outer periphery	North West	96.1	94.3	89.9	113	122	106
	North East	87.1	94.3	76.1	163	130	154
	Wales	88.4	86.8	78.8	128	128	119
	Scotland	93.0	98.7	94.4	170	120	121
	Northern Ireland	74.3	72.2	78.2	221	159	129

Sources: ONS (2002) *Annual Abstract of Statistics,* and previous issues.
　　　ONS (2003) *Regional Gross Value Added,* 20 Aug.

effects of the Single European Act (see Chapter 29) have all contributed to a more 'footloose', and therefore geographically mobile, pattern of industrial location. In today's complex and rapidly changing industrial environment, any spatial grouping of 'standard' regions into 'core' or 'periphery' may be less appropriate than hitherto. Indeed there is evidence to suggest the emergence in the 1990s of 'areas of prosperity' centred on urban regions, which are likely to grow much faster than other parts of their GOR region.

However, the three core areas defined in Table 11.1 still contributed 49.4% of total UK GDP in 2000 and have an important weight in the economy. A similar concern still remains about the continuing influence of the North/South 'divide', which involves a broader definition of Britain's regions than that given in Table 11.1 The recession of the early 1990s tended to hit the UK's service-orientated industries more than manufacturing, so that the North appeared to have been relatively less affected by the recession than the South. However, in 2000 the South (defined as East Midlands, Eastern, South East and South West) still contributed 56.9% of UK GDP as compared to 52.6% in 1979. As a result, the core and periphery and similar concepts still remain useful tools of reference during the early years of the new millennium.

Free market or government intervention?

From Table 11.1 it is clear that regional disparities do exist in the UK in terms of both unemployment and income per head. Whether or not these disparities constitute a 'problem', requiring government intervention, depends on one's view of the economic system. Certainly changes in demand and supply in any economy will have different effects on individual regions, since each has its own particular industrial structure. A change in the pattern of demand can cause some regions to increase production, employment and income, when they contain the industries which produce the goods and services now demanded. Similarly, regions which produce commodities for which demand has decreased will find themselves with declining production, employment and income. As a result, growing regions will diverge positively from the national norm, while declining regions will diverge negatively.

It has been argued that in a dynamic economy regional disparities will be short-run, as in time market forces will tend to equalize the situation across regions (convergence). This could occur through a movement into the high-unemployment/low-income regions of firms attracted by lower wage costs. At the same time there will be an outward migration of labour from these 'disadvantaged' regions to the relatively prosperous regions where demand, employment and wages are higher. It follows that if labour and capital are perfectly mobile, with no impediment to firms moving into and out of regions, regional differences should disappear. For example, in the disadvantaged regions unemployment would fall and wages would rise as firms relocate themselves in these areas. Similarly, in the more prosperous regions unemployment would rise and wages fall as firms move out to low-wage/low-cost areas. Given sufficient time, and no imperfections, this view suggests that there would be no need for government intervention to solve the 'regional problem', since market forces will eventually cause regions to 'converge'.

The case for intervention

In practice, imperfections exist and even those who believe in the market mechanism may still advocate some form of regional policy. First, neither labour nor capital is perfectly mobile. There may be a lack of knowledge on the part of employees or employers of opportunities in other regions; or there may be high 'costs' of movement as with the need for rehousing, the breaking of social ties and the expensive relocation of plant and machinery. Second, there may be restrictions on the price of labour or capital, such as maximum or minimum wages, or limits on the dividends which firms issue. These imperfections may reduce the incentives for both labour and capital to flow out of 'disadvantaged' and into 'advantaged' regions and vice versa. Under these circumstances even the free-market adherent might admit the need for government intervention to offset these market imperfections. This may take the form of policies to promote labour mobility or to coax firms to move into more disadvantaged regions. Government intervention is then seen as necessary to *enhance* the workings of the market mechanism.

Another view of the regional problem sees a still more urgent need for government intervention. Market forces are regarded as acting in a way which will aggravate rather than ameliorate regional disparities. Intervention is no longer a *supplement* to market forces but must be strong enough to *offset* them. Any fall in output and employment in a region will reduce the size of the regional market and erode economies of scale. Also labour migration from declining regions may consist of the younger, better educated, more adaptable component of the regional labour force, leaving behind a less productive labour force. New firms may no longer wish to locate production in such regions even if wages are lower. As regional output declines and unemployment rises, local authority rates may become inadequate to sustain basic infrastructure and services, further disadvantaging a region already in decline. In this view, government policy has to be strong enough to prevent regions constantly 'diverging', with poor regions getting poorer and rich regions getting richer. Such a policy might seek to inhibit the movement of labour out of disadvantaged regions by giving firms incentives to locate in these regions.

To sum up, if, as in the first view, the regions are seen as 'converging' over time, then government intervention need only strengthen the 'natural' market forces making for equality. However, if, as in the second view, the regions are seen as 'diverging' over time, then a greater degree of government intervention may be needed. Otherwise market forces will cause regions to become 'polarized' into areas of very low output, employment and income on the one hand, and very high output, employment and income on the other.

Regional policy in the UK

In the UK the need for government intervention in the regions was accepted as far back as 1934, with the passing of the first of three Special Areas Acts. These aimed to help the depressed areas by setting up government trading estates, subsidizing rents and providing low-interest loans. Since then legislation affecting the regions has been embodied in a variety of Industry and Finance Acts.

The Assisted Areas (AAs)

During the 1990s three types of area were designated for regional assistance, namely Development Areas (DAs), Intermediate Areas (IAs) and 'split' areas which were a mixture of Development and Intermediate Areas. These areas were designated according to the degree of economic deprivation in those regions as measured by indices such as structural unemployment, long-term unemployment, economic activity rates, and so on. The degree of assistance given to these areas varied from those which needed most help (DAs) to those which needed less help (IAs), and in-between areas with pockets of localized problems ('split' areas). Once the assisted regions had been defined, then UK policy was designed to offer incentives to firms to move into those areas while controlling the expansion of firms outside those areas.

The latest decision to modify the coverage of the areas to be offered regional assistance began in 1999 when the government announced a review of the Assisted Areas of the UK in response to the new European Commission guidelines on regional aid introduced in 1997. This was part of the EU's drive to reduce the overall level of aid in the Community and to prepare for the possible accession of new member states in the near future. It was hoped that the new areas will help to make the regional aid system both transparent and comparable across all EU member states. The new Assisted Areas map became operational in July 2000 and is shown in Fig. 11.3. Here the *Tier 1* areas are those in which GDP per capita measured in purchasing power parity (PPP) is below 75% of the EU average. These areas are automatically granted Assisted Area status by the EU Commission. The *Tier 2* areas are more discretionary, being areas designated by the UK government using indictors which are acceptable to the EU, such as unemployment rates, labour participation rates, local dependency on manufacturing, etc., which suggest significant disparities in economic conditions.

Although the UK can propose the boundaries for Tier 2 areas, the EU can veto the national proposals. The new Tier 1 and Tier 2 areas cover about 29% of the UK as compared to 34% under the previous assisted areas regime. Firms in the Tier 1 areas will be eligible for grants of up to 40% of the net project costs whereas firms in Tier 2 areas will be eligible for grants of up to 20% of such costs. In addition Fig. 11.3 shows those areas covered by the new Enterprise Grant.

The policy instruments

Financial incentives

In 1988, the then Conservative government recommended an overhaul of the Department of Trade and Industry (DTI) in order to improve Britain's competitiveness, innovativeness and the skills of individuals, especially in AAs and inner cities. Regional financial assistance was seen by the government as a subsidy that was damaging industry's efficiency and therefore its ability to compete, especially in view of the 'open market' of the EU after 1992. These revisions to regional policy were undertaken in the belief that payment of continuous subsidies to industries in AAs was an inappropriate way for central government to encourage an attitude of self-help and a spirit of enterprise and competitiveness. Hence, it was argued that if the regions were ever to experience *convergence*, much of the impetus would have to come from within the regions themselves, and government could only really facilitate this process – it could not legislate it, nor could it make certain areas or industries forever dependent upon the public purse.

A major consequence of the DTI's reorganization was to shift the focus of regional aid away from support for traditional industries and more towards encouragement of new company formation. This meant changing the balance of regional financial assistance – Regional Development Grants (RDGs), long the mainstay of regional policy aid, were terminated in 1988, and the emphasis shifted to Regional Selective Assistance and to a new scheme of other grants and incentives for smaller firms in both AAs and under various government Urban initiatives.

Regional Selective Assistance (RSA)

This is the main instrument of UK regional industrial policy. It is a discretionary grant towards projects of any size in both the manufacturing and service sectors, is open to both domestic and international investors and is available to help with the investment costs of projects with capital expenditures above £500,000. It has three overlapping objectives: first, to create and safeguard jobs; second, to attract and retain internationally mobile investment; and third, to contribute to improving the competitiveness of disadvantaged regions. The RSA is usually administered as either a capital-related or a job-related grant. Capital-related project grants are normally used to help cover the costs of land purchase and site preparation or the acquisition of plant and machinery; job-related project grants are normally used to help

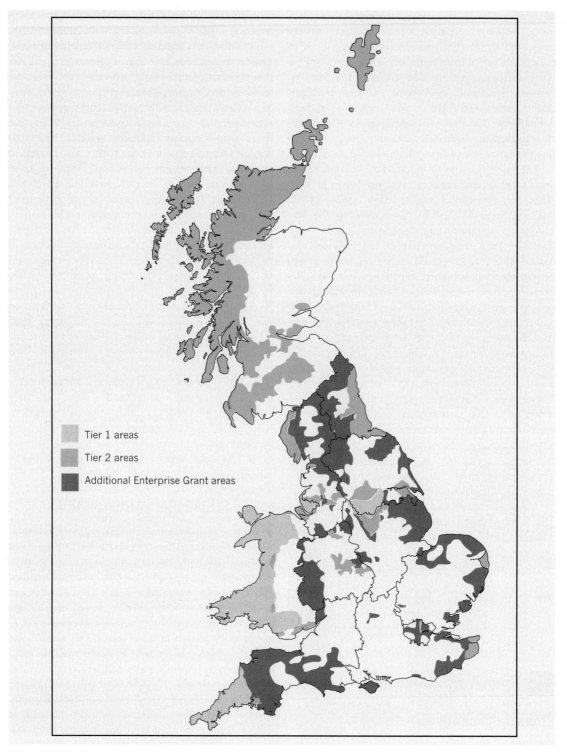

Fig. 11.3 The Assisted Areas from July 2000.
Source: Department of Trade and Industry website (www.dti.gov.uk).

cover the costs of hiring and training staff. The DTI administers the scheme and spent £110m on RSA grants in 1999/2000, with around 850 grants being offered and 36,000 jobs created or safeguarded in that year alone. The cost per job was estimated at around £4,000 during this period with the scheme helping stimulate around £1.3bn of total investment. Between 2000 and 2004 a further £450m was spent on RSA grants. An example of such efforts to safeguard jobs in the regions was the £45m grant to Nissan in 2001/02 in order to secure production of the Primera and Micra cars at its Sunderland car plant.

Regional Enterprise Grants (REG), the Enterprise Grant (EG) and other assistance

One of the main aspects of the government changes to regional incentives in 1988 was its emphasis on schemes designed to support the wealth-creating process among small and medium-sized firms. As a result companies in Assisted Areas employing fewer than 25 people were able to apply for two Regional Enterprise Grants. The first was an *investment* grant of 15% towards the costs of fixed assets, subject to a maximum grant of £15,000. The second was an *innovation* grant of 50% designed to support product and process development in small companies with a maximum grant limit of £25,000. However, both REGs were discontinued in 1996/97 after evaluations of the schemes concluded that they were less effective than alternatives available through the RSA. To replace the REG, a new simplified *Enterprise Grant* (EG) was introduced in 2000 to stimulate the growth of small and medium-sized firms in the newly created Enterprise Grant Areas of England (see Fig. 11.3). Companies investing up to £500,000 in capital expenditure can apply for a once-and-for-all grant of up to 15% of the fixed capital costs of a project, up to a maximum of £75,000. The scheme is administered by the Small Business Service (SBS) and £52m has been committed to the scheme for the period 2000–04. In addition a new Regional Innovation Fund (RIF) was introduced in the Budget of 2000 to support business clusters and 'incubators' in the regions. The aim of the RIF is to support collaborations and joint innovation projects among participating companies (e.g. universities and private

companies). Over the period 2001–04, £154m was provided for such funding.

European Regional Development Fund

Since 1973 the UK has had access to a further potential source of regional assistance, the EU. It was only in 1975, however, with the establishment of the European Regional Development Fund (ERDF), that EU funds became available for regional support on a systematic basis. The ERDF is financed out of the general budget of the EU and allocates most of its funds to member countries on a quota basis rather than for specific regional projects. The funds are given directly to member governments, and are intended to be *additional to* regional aid already given by those governments. Between 1975 and 2004 the UK received over £10.8bn from the fund. Unfortunately there have been criticisms that these funds were used to replace rather than supplement regional expenditure by member governments. In an attempt to counter this, 5% of all ERDF funds have been allocated on a non-quota basis, linked to specific projects proposed by member governments. Some 80% of the cost of the regional/social fund is now allocated to the four poorest members of the EU and the fund is encouraging designated Assisted Areas in all EU countries to construct *coherent* development programmes rather than submit large numbers of individual projects.

The ERDF is part of the wider *European Structural Funds* initiative which designated six objectives for European areas suffering from structural decline. Of those six, three objectives have been identified for regional enterprise initiatives. Objective 1 covers the most problematic regions lagging behind the rest of the EU, i.e. where GDP per capita is 75% or less of the EU average. From 2000 onwards, the Objective 1 areas were Merseyside, South Yorkshire, West Wales and the Valleys, Cornwall and the Isles of Scilly. The areas previously included under this category (i.e. Northern Ireland and the Highlands and Islands) will receive transitional help until 2005. Objective 2 covers regions in industrial decline, such as the North East, North West, Yorkshire and Humberside, West Midlands and South Wales, as well as certain rural areas of the South West, Wales, the North of England and Scotland. Some 2.8% of the UK's population is covered under Objective 1, and 40% under Objective 2, thus covering some 43% of the UK population in total. ERDF grants normally pay up to 50% of the eligible cost of a project, although it can be more in Objective 1 areas. The rest, i.e. 'matching funds', must be found by the prospective ERDF recipient from its own funds or from funds it can raise from other grant-awarding bodies. Objective 3 areas have also been designated as needing support for education, training and employment. Over the period 2000–06 the total allocated from the EU Structural Funds for all these areas will be £10.7bn, with £3.9bn for Objective 1 areas.

Expansion control

Industrial Development Certificate

The principal method used by successive British governments between 1947 and 1981 to try to control the regional distribution of manufacturing industry was the Industrial Development Certificate (IDC). This was first introduced in the Town and Country Planning Act of 1947. Under the Act, any proposed new industrial development in excess of 5,000 square feet (465 square metres) had to obtain an Industrial Development Certificate (IDC) from the Board of Trade before planning permission for development could be granted. The certificate could be withheld at the discretion of the Board of Trade if

| The effectiveness of regional policy |

the development would create industrial congestion or if it was not consistent with the 'proper' distribution of industry.

It is difficult to assess the effectiveness of regional policy, for a number of reasons. First, detailed statistics on the regions have been readily available only since the mid-1970s. Second, the areas qualifying for assistance have themselves been frequently redefined. For example, since 1979 the Development Areas have been 'reduced' in size to such an extent that they now include only 16% of the employed population in Britain, in contrast to 40% in previous years. Third, any assessment of the impact of regional policy involves a comparison of the actual situation with an *estimate* of what would have happened had there

been no such regional policy.

Despite these problems attempts have been made to assess the effects of regional policy over the last 40–50 years. These attempts fall into two broad categories: first, those which measure the total impact of policy on employment creation and factory/office building in AAs; and second, those which assess the effectiveness of particular instruments of regional policy, such as grants, tax incentives and IDCs.

Effects of policy on employment and firms

The 1960–79 period

A detailed study of the impact of regional policy on job gains and firm relocations in Assisted Areas (AAs) by Moore *et al.* (1986) came to the conclusion that over two decades of 'active' regional policy covering 1960–81, about 945,000 jobs were created or safeguarded in AAs as a result of government programmes. Some 90% of these jobs were still in place in 1981. As far as firm relocations are concerned, policy-induced movements of factories from more prosperous areas to AAs yielded a net gain of 2,085 firms between 1945 and 1978, with 58% of the moves occurring during the more active policy period of 1966–78. However, in general, some 8,000 firms moved from one county to another between 1945 and 1980, of which only about 12% appear to have been 'persuaded' to move by government policy.

As well as trying to determine the total impact of regional policy on the economies of AAs by aggregating gross and net gains in numbers of jobs and of factory moves, regional economists have also sought to demonstrate relationships between the *actual numbers involved*, and *variations in the intensity of government intervention policy* over given time periods. Figure 11.4 shows the relationship between the growth of manufacturing employment in selected regions and changes in regional policy.

In Fig. 11.4 an attempt is made to define periods when regional policy was 'active' or strong, and periods when regional policy was 'passive' or weak. Periods of 'active' as distinct from 'passive' regional policy were defined as those periods in which the amount spent on regional incentives increased significantly and in which IDCs were issued far more sparingly in the non-assisted areas.

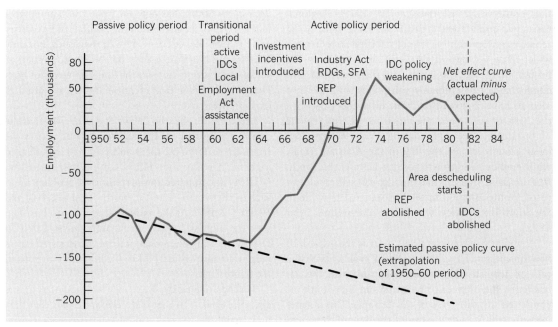

Fig. 11.4 The growth of manufacturing employment in Scotland, Wales, the Northern region and Northern Ireland relative to the UK.
Sources: Adapted from Gudgin *et al.* (1982) and Moore *et al.* (1986).

The amount of employment in any region will depend in part on the balance of industries in that region (i.e. industrial structure), and in part on the growth of output from such industries. Given the industrial structure of an Assisted Area, the maximum employment which that region could be 'expected' to create would occur if each of its industries grew at the national average rate. This 'expected' level of employment was calculated for the four named Assisted Areas as a whole, for each year since 1950, and compared with the actual level of employment in those areas in each year. If actual employment in the Assisted Areas had reached the 'expected' level, then the 'net effect' curve (actual *minus* expected) would have recorded zero on the vertical axis. The fact that in the first few years 'actual' employment was around 100,000 below that 'expected', suggests that the Assisted Areas really do have more serious employment problems than elsewhere.

During the 'passive' period from 1950 to 1959, with little or no regional assistance, actual unemployment fell progressively further behind the 'expected' level. This provides some support for the 'divergent' view of the regional problem (see earlier), i.e. that

without intervention the position of the assisted regions will progressively deteriorate. The dashed line in Fig. 11.4 projects this trend during the 'passive' period through to 1981. In other words, it provides an indication of what might have happened if regional policy had not become more 'active'. However, from 1963 a variety of incentives were introduced (see above) in the Assisted Areas, together with a more stringent application of IDCs preventing expansion in the advantaged regions. We can see from Fig. 11.4 that actual employment gets closer and closer to the 'expected' level up to 1970, and after 1970 even exceeds it. 'Active' policy began to slacken in the mid-1970s, with a number of incentives abolished (e.g. Regional Employment Premium (REP) in 1976 – see below), and a less stringent application of IDCs. As a result actual employment had begun to fall towards the 'expected' level in the late 1970s and early 1980s.

The 1980–2002 period

As noted previously, the importance attached to regional policy initiatives decreased after the return of the Conservative government in 1979. Regional assistance became less general and more selective in scope, as government philosophy shifted away from a wider view of the regional problem towards the promotion of new enterprises and the growth of self-employment. Unfortunately, this policy shift does not seem to have narrowed the basic differences between the Assisted Areas and the more prosperous regions of Britain. For example, during 1979–90, employment growth fell by 100,000 in the Assisted Areas, while employment growth rose by 1.3m in the South. Within these figures, the number of self-employed rose by only 200,000 in the Assisted Areas while in the South the increase was 1.3m (Martin and Tyler 1992).

A similar picture emerges as regards the growth of new businesses. Here it is useful to look at both the rate of *new* business registrations and also the *net change* in the number of businesses in the 'South' as compared to the 'North' of Britain. The former measure will provide an idea of the dynamic changes in new business *formation*, while the latter (since it takes into consideration both the births and deaths of firms) gives a picture of the overall *net effect* on the total stock of businesses. Between 1981 and 1989, new business registrations per 1,000 employees were

94.5 in the South, but only 66.5 per 1,000 employees in the North. Net changes in the number of businesses per 1,000 employees were 17.5 in the South, but only 11.4 in the North. Clearly, the North continued to suffer more problems than the South in terms of both lower rates of new firm creation and the retention of existing firms.

However, in the mid-1990s it was argued that the tide had now turned. It was pointed out that in the recession of 1990–92 the South East had experienced a greater than average fall in net business formation (−3.1%) as compared to the traditional problem areas such as the North (−2.4%), North West (−2.4%) and Wales (−2.5%). At the same time the South East had seen the highest growth in unemployment. Partly in response to this phenomenon, the UK Assisted Areas map was redrawn in 1993 to include more regions in the South East.

Perhaps one of the ways in which regional grants are still relevant to regional development is that they may make the regions somewhat more attractive to foreign multinationals. Table 11.2 provides some information which may be relevant to this debate. It includes figures for each region in terms of GDP, shares of manufacturing output contributed by UK and by foreign firms, and the number of UK and

Table 11.2 GDP, regional assistance, and the location of foreign manufacturing output.

	GDP[1]	Manufacturing[2]		RSA assistance[3]	
		UK	Foreign	UK	Foreign
Scotland	99	65	35	411	365
Wales	83	70	30	342	356
North East	84	70	30	181	184
West Midlands	94	74	26	133	134
North West	91	78	22	127	63
Yorks/Humber	90	83	17	126	37
Merseyside	–	73	27	63	32
South West	95	84	16	40	40
East Midlands	94	84	16	26	5
South East	115	70	30	17	6
London	123	74	26	10	3
Eastern	109	72	28	7	3
UK	**100**	**75**	**25**	**1,482**	**1,416**

[1] GDP (1996) based on UK = 100.
[2] Percentage of gross value added in each region, 1995.
[3] Number of companies receiving RSA, 1987–97.
Sources: *Financial Times* (1998) *Reporting Britain*, 11 June, and Table 11.1.

foreign firms in receipt of government assistance via the RSA. We can see from Table 11.2 that the share of foreign firms in regional manufacturing output is greater in Scotland, Wales and the North East. These three regions also account for 77% of the total number of foreign firms receiving government assistance under the RSA. The government estimates that some 500,000 jobs have been created in the UK by such overseas business since 1979. However, the situation is not without its critics. For example, it has been argued that regions of the UK such as Wales still have below-average GDP even though they have high ratios of foreign inward investment. It has also been argued that the concentration of foreign manufacturing production in Wales has given that regional economy a bias towards middle- to low-quality jobs in export-orientated manufacturing companies which are highly vulnerable to changes in world market conditions; further, the relatively small contribution of the service sector in Wales, which tends to include activities of a higher value-added nature than manufacturing, has arguably only compounded the situation. Such critics argue that the role of government assistance as a means of promoting inward investment and jobs cannot be divorced from the need to create a balanced view of development in each region.

However, improved job prospects and the growth of new companies depend not only on the prospects of government grants but also on how macroeconomic forces (such as relatively lower wages in the UK) and microeconomic policies (such as urban policies) affect the *regions*. Nevertheless, whichever way we look at the problem, a regional perspective is still critical if we wish to enjoy a healthy and prosperous national economy.

Effectiveness of policy instruments

Criticism of regional policy instruments has become part of a 'performance evaluation' procedure since the mid-1970s, particularly when it has been able to identify their 'cost-effectiveness' on a job creation basis. Research into the gross Exchequer *cost per job* in British Development Areas during 1960–81 demonstrated that the most cost-effective instrument was IDC policy with its minor administrative cost. The next least expensive instrument was RSA, with a cost per job (at 1981 prices) of £17,000, followed by investment incentives at £25,000 per job and by REP,

the most expensive instrument, at £73,000 per job (Moore *et al.* 1986). Not surprisingly, with governments determined to reduce spending from the late 1970s onwards, RSA emerged as the favoured policy instrument.

Investment incentives have formed a central part of regional policy since its inception in 1934. Investment grants and tax incentives were designed to encourage firms to set up in the disadvantaged regions. Surveys in the 1960s and 1970s seemed to show that capital grants may have had a significant effect on the movement of industry to Assisted Areas. However, financial incentives have been criticized for being capital-biased, thus encouraging the movement of capital- rather than labour-intensive firms into the Assisted Areas. Another criticism was that these incentives, whether grants or tax allowances, were often 'automatic', being given to *all* firms in the Assisted Areas irrespective of whether they were creating new employment or not. It was this persistent criticism and the suspicion that grants were going mostly to companies that would have invested in the Assisted Areas even *without* government assistance which led to the termination of RDG schemes in 1988 and the creation of the discretionary RSA assistance, which was much more selective in the projects chosen for help.

There has been much debate about the effectiveness of the RSA grant (Armstrong 2001). On the positive side, the grant's consistent focus on using criteria such as 'competitiveness' and 'employment creation' when allocating resources has been a positive step, as has its focus on providing financial help to the manufacturing sector, thereby slowing down the UK's manufacturing decline. Its assistance in attracting inward investment to the UK has also been important for the UK regions. However, there have been various concerns about the grant. First, despite targeting RSA grants to selective projects, only around 45% of the total number of jobs created by RSA spending in the 1980s and 1990s were *additional* ones – in the sense that the RSA grants were *critical* in helping companies bring employment to the regions. In other words, 55% of the total jobs created by RSA-assisted companies would have been created *in any case*, i.e. such companies would have come to the region even without the RSA grant. Second, certain parts of the UK (in particular Scotland and Wales) have tended to obtain higher per capita shares of the RSA budget than elsewhere partly because the grant is 'demand determined'. Third, there has been criticism that the RSA grant has been too small – a mere 0.2% of GDP, and that it has only had a marginal effect on the industrial structure of the assisted regions (Wren and Taylor 1999). Finally, the effectiveness of the RSA has been constrained by EU policy guidelines which led to a decrease in the areas eligible for help after the new assisted areas map was drawn in 2000.

The *Regional Employment Premium* (REP) was used as a policy weapon in the UK from 1967 to 1976 and was, in effect, a direct-labour subsidy paid to all employers in the Assisted Areas to encourage the retention of existing employment and the creation of new employment. However, the benefits of a flat-rate subsidy such as the REP were eroded by inflation during the early 1970s, reducing its attractiveness to employers. Also, as with financial incentives, the REP was criticized for being available to all manufacturing establishments in the Development Areas 'whether new or old, expanding or contracting, progressive or asleep' (Moore and Rhodes 1976, p. 218). Another criticism was that the REP may well have encouraged firms to retain a higher labour/capital ratio than might have been dictated by economic efficiency alone. The REP was abolished in early 1976.

Industrial Development Certificates (IDCs) were simple to operate and were of only minor administrative cost to the Exchequer. However, there was no guarantee that a firm refused an IDC in, say, the South East, would actually build the factory in an Assisted Area. Projects for expansion could be shelved or moved abroad, particularly if the company refused permission to develop was a multinational. Industrial Development Certificate-type controls were more effective in redistributing employment when the economy was relatively buoyant than they were in recession when every region became desperate for jobs. In such circumstances all regions, including the relatively prosperous ones, were reluctant to accept restrictions on the expansion of firms through IDC control. It was partly as a result of this inadequacy that the use of IDCs was suspended in December 1981.

The urban problem

Urban–rural shift

One of the most striking features of the post-war period has been the shift in employment and population from London and the large conurbations towards towns and cities in more rural areas. This shift is clearly seen in Fig. 11.5 which summarizes some research by the TCPA (Town and Country Planning Association 1999). It shows that London,

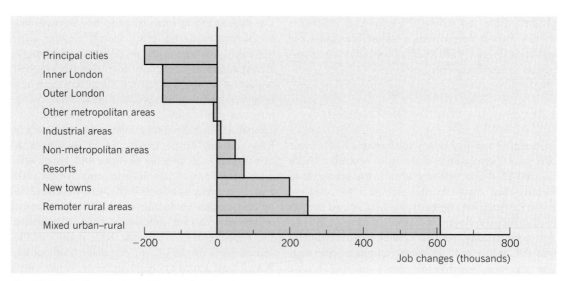

Fig. 11.5 Job changes by urban–rural categories.
Source: *Financial Times* (1999), 30 November.

the principal cities and other metropolitan areas lost a total of 500,000 jobs between 1981 and 1996, with most of the jobs lost being in manufacturing. At the same time, small towns and rural areas gained nearly 1.7m jobs. The report stated that cities tended to underperform in sectors where they might have been predicted to do well, such as in financial services, hotels and catering, and cultural industries.

Such shifts in employment and population away from the large urban areas have been due to a number of reasons. First, it became increasingly obvious that urban areas could not provide adequate factory floorspace for industries to expand. Automation and the adoption of new techniques led to a demand for greater floorspace per employee, causing firms to seek suitable sites outside major conurbations. Second, the cost of acquiring land in urban areas to establish new factories or to extend old ones was high compared to that in other regions. Third, some surveys have shown that over 60% of UK manufacturing industry is now 'footloose', being less affected by specific locational factors. Reinforcing this tendency is the fact that the growth of information technology has also freed both manufacturing and service companies from having to be located in city centres. Finally, the growth in the number of professional workers has tended to increase job mobility, making commuting more 'acceptable'.

Finally, the urban–rural shift has been explained in terms of an 'enterprise theory' (Keeble and Tyler 1995). The suggestion here is that rural settlements (as distinct from urban locations) are more able to attract a relatively high proportion of actual or potential entrepreneurs because of the more desirable residential environment. This in turn creates a pool of specialized and complex skills which results in the growth of niche markets, producing new and innovatory products. The improved accessibility of many rural settlements to modern telecommunications, transport and financial services make the rural locations increasingly more attractive than their urban counterparts.

All these factors have encouraged the movement of employment and population away from large urban areas, presenting a major problem for the inner core of many large cities.

The urban and inner-city problem

Since the Second World War employment and population have declined in the major conurbations, with the greatest decline occurring in the inner-city areas of such conurbations. For instance, between the early 1950s and the mid-1970s employment declined by 20% in the conurbations as a whole, but by 33% in the inner-city areas. However, in the suburban areas employment remained steady, whilst in small towns and rural areas employment rose.

The movement of manufacturing employment away from the inner-urban areas was encouraged by the government's *New Towns* policies in the 1950s and 1960s. This was later followed by increased availability of grants and incentives for firms locating in the Assisted Areas. Inner-urban areas also suffered from the more active use of IDC policy, which made it more difficult for firms to locate within inner-urban areas. The general improvement in communications and rising real incomes were further factors in encouraging more people to live outside inner-urban areas, in suburbs, smaller towns and rural communities. By the early 1990s research had found that small firms in rural areas were likely to take on more labour than similar firms in urban areas, especially when the expansion of the rural firms was due to higher wage and other costs in the urban areas (North and Smallbone 1993).

The severity of the urban and inner-city problem can be clearly seen in Table 11.3 which provides unemployment and deprivation figures for various urban and inner-city districts. The districts vary in size, but provide useful insights into the nature of unemployment and poverty in both small and large districts and conurbations. Each district is made up of a number of smaller wards (over 8,400 in England) so that the district level unemployment and deprivation figures given here are derived from these smaller ward figures. The *unemployment index* compares unemployment in each district with the UK average level of unemployment, while the *deprivation index* is a composite index made up of six different measures of deprivation, namely income, employment, health, education, housing, and access to services.

The 'extent score' figures show the proportion of the district's population who live in wards which are included in a list of the most deprived 10% of wards in England. For example, *all* the people in the London borough of Hackney live in wards that are included in the list of the 10% most deprived wards in England. Similarly, some 57.62% of the people in South Tyneside live in wards that are included in the list of the 10% most deprived wards in England. What is interesting from Table 11.3 is that whilst data and studies suggest that the 'North/South divide' still exists in England (e.g. see Table 11.5 below), there are clearly serious pockets of inner-city poverty in London as well as in Manchester, Liverpool and the North East (South Tyneside and Middlesborough). In fact, London boroughs account for four out of the ten most deprived districts of England, suggesting that urban and inner-city problems have a country-wide dimension. These inner-urban areas also tend to suffer from having a higher proportion of unskilled and semi-skilled workers, making it difficult for them to move outside the inner-urban areas to obtain work.

 ## Urban policy in the UK

Since the Second World War government policy towards the plight of urban and inner-city areas can be divided into four phases: 1945–65, 1965–77, 1977–88 and 1988–2002.

1945–65

During this phase the government's policy was to limit the growth of major conurbations in an attempt to solve some of the pressing problems of urban congestion. *Green Belts* were established around major conurbations to prevent their expansion, and *New Towns* were built outside the major conurbations to take up any urban overspill. After 1947 the use of IDCs further restricted the growth of industries in the urban areas, whilst the Location of Offices Bureau sought to redistribute office work away from the conurbations, especially London.

1965–77

From the middle of the 1960s the government's attitude towards the inner-city problem began to change. Attention began to be drawn to the fact that the UK non-white population had grown to some half a million and was largely concentrated in cities. Fears were expressed that race riots similar to those of the US in 1967–68 might occur in the UK and this helped focus government attention on the urban problem. This emphasis was strengthened by the findings of the Plowden Report on children's education in 1967. This report identified deprived areas in inner cities which needed special help and led to the setting-up of *Educational Priority Areas* (EPAs) in 1969. In 1968 an *Urban Programme* was also established which, under the Local Government Grants (Social Needs)

Table 11.3 Unemployment and deprivation in urban and inner-city areas of England, 2000–02.

Region	District	Unemployment (2002) UK = 100[1]	Multiple Deprivation Index (2000) Extent score (%)[2]	Multiple Deprivation Index (2000) Extent ranking
London	Hackney	230	100.00	1
London	Tower Hamlets	230	96.99	2
London	Newham	221	95.38	3
North West	Manchester	174	79.29	4
Merseyside	Knowsley	160	79.13	5
North East	Easington	190	78.49	6
Merseyside	Liverpool	194	72.29	7
North East	Middlesborough	215	59.86	8
London	Islington	171	57.98	9
North East	South Tyneside	236	57.62	10

[1] Unemployment is ILO-based.
[2] Percentage of district population living in wards which rank with the most deprived 10% of wards in the country.
Sources: Adapted from DETR (2000) *Indices of Deprivation 2000: Regeneration Research Summary No. 31*; ONS (2001/02) *Annual Local Labour Force Survey*.

Act of 1969, was provided with a fund of £20–25m over four years. The aim of the Urban Programme was to provide resources for capital projects and educational schemes, such as pre-school playgroups, in order to raise the level of social services in areas of acute social need. In 1969 the *Community Development Project* was established to research into new ways of solving social deprivation in large urban communities.

1977–88

During this period the focus of attention began to shift to the economic problems of inner cities. The seeds of change began with the Labour government's White Paper *Policy for the Inner Cities* in 1977. This sought to strengthen the economies of inner-city areas, to improve the physical fabric of such areas to alleviate social problems, and to secure a new balance between inner-city areas and the rest of the region in terms of population and jobs. The White Paper also proposed the extension of local authority power to assist industry, and this was introduced through the Inner Urban Areas Act of 1978 which empowered local authorities to declare industrial and commercial improvement areas and to give financial assistance to companies which located in such areas.

With the election of the Conservative government in 1979 new initiatives were introduced to add to, and modify, existing legislation. Under the Local Government Planning and Land Act of 1980, Enterprise Zones and Urban Development Corporations (UDCs) were set up. In 1984 the first Free Zones (originally called Freeports) were designated, and in 1988 Simplified Planning Zones (SPZs) were created, having fewer financial advantages than Enterprise Zones but retaining the benefits of fewer planning regulations.

Enterprise Zones reflected the government's desire to release the private sector from restrictive financial and administrative controls, encouraging firms to set up in the more derelict parts of inner-city areas. Initially, 11 zones were designated in 1981, with the number rising to a maximum of 27 by the end of 1989. These Enterprise Zones enjoy a number of privileges for 10 years from their date of inception, the most important being exemption from the Business Rate, and 100% tax allowances for capital expenditure on commercial or industrial buildings. Companies setting

up in Enterprise Zones are also exempt from development land tax, and face fewer local authority planning regulations and controls than they would in other areas. However, in 1988 the then Conservative government announced that no more zones would be created in England, as it was becoming particularly worried about the consequences of the cost of the zones to the Exchequer.

Urban Development Corporations (UDCs)

The role of the local authorities in allocating resources has been eroded by such legislation as Enterprise Zones. Their powers were further reduced under the 1980 Act by the creation of new agencies for urban renewal with special powers and resources, the Urban Development Corporations (UDCs). The UDCs were designed to undertake substantial programmes of land acquisition and reclamation in an attempt to secure the greatest possible involvement of the private sector companies in their areas. Similarly, the UDCs are involved in environmental improvement and infrastructure provision in these areas. The first generation of Urban Development Corporations were formed in the London Docklands and in Merseyside in 1980 and were given special powers to promote urban renewal in those areas. The second generation, formed in 1987, included Trafford Park, the Black Country, Teesside and Tyne and Wear. By the late 1980s these had been joined by a third generation covering Central Manchester, Leeds, Sheffield and Bristol. The fourth, and most recent, generation of UDCs included the Birmingham Heartlands and Plymouth, designated in 1992/93. These corporations are financed mainly by Exchequer grants and employ around 500 permanent staff in total. The UDCs are limited-life bodies and are now preparing their completion and succession strategies. Leeds and Bristol UDCs were wound up in 1995 and all the UDCs had been wound up by March 1998.

Free Zones

Six areas were designated for Free Zone status in 1984, including Birmingham, Belfast, Cardiff, Liverpool, Prestwick and Southampton. However, by 1994, Belfast and Cardiff had left the list but Hull, Tilbury and Humberside had been added. Within the Freeports, goods are to be exempt from customs duties and (possibly) VAT, unless the goods are subsequently transported from the Freeport to the rest of the UK. The intention of the Freeports is to attract business and investment into the areas, particularly since goods *not destined for import into the UK* can be handled *without* tariff charges. This should help the UK gain a greater share of the rapidly growing intermediate processing and servicing activities via global specialization (see Chapter 7).

In addition to the measures noted above, this period saw the growth of a 'package' of measures to combat inner-city problems. These included the Urban Programme, the Urban Development Grant and the Derelict Land Programme.

Urban Programme

Up to the early 1990s the Urban Programme was the major mechanism for allocating funds to the inner cities. The programme continued to operate, despite changes in emphasis, up to the late 1990s when other schemes took over. The Urban Programme was designed to provide support for a wide range of projects submitted by 57 local authorities, called Urban Programme areas (UPs). In particular it provided funding to enable local authorities to make assistance available in their locality for *specific projects* which involved the private sector organizations and which encouraged enterprise and the development of new businesses. Broadly speaking the main aims of the Urban Programme were:

1 To promote the regeneration of local economies. This involved supporting projects which built new, or converted old, factory units and which created training opportunities and jobs for the labour force in those areas.

2 To improve the physical environment of local economies. This involved modernizing shops and other buildings while also improving parks, waterways, footpaths, etc.

3 To meet social and housing needs directly. Social needs included the provision of community centres, sports facilities and health projects while housing needs encompassed improvements in refuge accommodation and helping to improve conditions on housing estates which had environmental problems.

Up to 1988, the key instrument for funding parts of the Urban Programme was the *Urban Development Grant* (UDG) but this was abolished in May 1988 and was replaced by the *City Grant* explained

below. However, since 1994/95 the funding of the Urban Programmes came directly from the Single Regeneration Budget (see below) and most of the remaining Urban Programme projects were completed by 1997.

Another component of the urban package, although not strictly defined as being within the Urban Programme, was the *Derelict Land Programme*. Under the Derelict Land Act of 1982, the Secretary of State for the Environment was empowered to pay grants to public bodies, voluntary organizations, private firms and individuals to enable derelict land to be reclaimed, improved or brought into use again. The grant varied between 50% and 100%, depending on the location of the site and the institutions or persons applying.

1988–2002

As noted earlier in the chapter, in March 1988 the Conservative government launched a series of new initiatives to help promote enterprise investment and employment in the inner-city areas and also published a new government booklet entitled *Action for Cities*. The booklet defined a range of inner-city initiatives which were to be the foundation of government urban policy during the 1990s. Some of the initiatives included in the booklet, such as the Urban Programme and the Urban Development Corporations, were not in fact new, but were now collected together under the Action for Cities 'umbrella'. However, other initiatives were new, including the following elements.

First, a new, simplified *City Grant* noted above was introduced to replace the Urban Development Grant (UDG), the Urban Regeneration Grant (URG) and the private-sector part of the Derelict Land Grant (DLG). It was designed to support capital investments undertaken by the private sector in property and business development, especially in the priority areas. The total project value must be above £200,000 and the private sector must convince the Department of the Environment that the project will provide jobs, private housing or other benefits. Also, to receive the grant the Department must be satisfied that the project is unable to proceed because the costs incurred in the development (including allowance for a reasonable profit) exceed the market value of the project. If the application is successful then the grant would cover this deficit and would therefore allow projects which benefit the community to continue despite the apparent problems of covering all essential costs. The *City Grant* applications are made directly to the local offices of the DOE (instead of through the local authorities as with the UDG) and appraisals of the projects are to be made within ten weeks. These procedures simplified and streamlined the grant system.

Second, measures were introduced to make more unused and under-utilized land in urban areas available for development by requiring publication of information about land held in public ownership.

Third, the government factory builder, the English Industrial Estates, provided grants for the conversion of suitable buildings for use as managed workshops.

Fourth, the Manpower Services Commission (the forerunner of the Training Agency) was allowed to increase its staff in inner-city areas in order to advise unemployed people and also to give financial support to inner-city areas (Compacts). Here groups of employers work with schools to guarantee a job with training for all young people aged 16–18 leaving school and who have met an agreed standard while at school. Many of these initiatives were then taken over in modified form by the 104 *Training and Enterprise Councils* (TECs) which were responsible for delivering a range of training programmes on behalf of the Department for Education and Employment. A new body, the *Learning and Skills Council*, has replaced the TECs in implementing a wide range of such schemes.

To add to the plethora of different measures which were introduced, it is worth noting two additional schemes and one major reorganization.

First, from 1985 onwards the Department of Trade and Industry created eight City Action Teams (CATs). These teams consist of senior officials and other representatives who attempt to coordinate the work of their different government departments within inner-city areas. They also encourage partnerships between business, local and central government and the voluntary sector in inner-city areas and act as the primary focal point with local authorities for the City Challenge (see below). The work of these teams was subsumed within the Government Offices for the Regions in 1994. In 1986, under the same initiative, 16 Inner-City Task Forces, composed of smaller teams of civil servants and people on secondment from the private sector, were formed to work directly with local businesses or local councils in an attempt to stimulate economic development, employment and training in inner-city areas. In 1997/98 the Task

Forces assisted around 2,000 businesses and provided up to 6,000 jobs and 19,000 training places, before being wound up in 1998.

Second, in order to improve the targeting of government resources as part of the Action for Cities programme, the *City Challenge* was introduced in 1991. Under this scheme local authorities, in conjunction with the private sector, compete for government resources (i.e. funds diverted from various existing inner-city schemes) by submitting *action plans* for scrutiny. These plans must be environmentally imaginative whilst also helping to sustain economic activity in key inner-city localities. By 1998 a total of 31 City Challenge action plans were each receiving £7.5m a year, ongoing for five years. All these action plans were completed by 1999.

Third, a major reorganization occurred in 1994 when the *Single Regeneration Budget* (SRB) was introduced. The SRB provided regeneration funds for schemes developed and implemented by local partnerships and aimed to improve urban areas in terms of employment, education, business start-ups and housing. During 1999–2002, 80% of the funds were spent on schemes in the most deprived areas, whilst 20% were spent on schemes to tackle pockets of need in rural coalfields and some coastal areas. In April 2002, the government announced that there would be no more national rounds of the SRB, since these resources would be included in a new single programme budget allocated to each *Regional Development Agency* (RDA) from central government funds.

Table 11.4 provides a summary of regional and urban expenditure between 1998 and 2004 and shows clearly the shift of funding towards the RDAs. As can be seen, the SRB has been phased out and the responsibility for regeneration shifted to the RDAs.

EU funding for the regions remained at a relatively steady rate over the period. The voluntary *Regional Chambers* are composed of local authorities and other social partners which provide a voice for the regions and can scrutinize the work of the RDAs. The *English Partnerships* (EP) are designed to bring sustainable economic regeneration and development in England and work closely with government and the RDAs. In 2001 the *English Cities Fund* (a joint venture between EP, Legal & General, and AMEC plc) was launched and £250m allocated to encourage greater private investment to help regenerate under-performing city centres and city centre fringes in the assisted areas of England. The final item in

Table 11.4 Regional and urban expenditure, 1998–2004 (£m).

	1999–2000	2001–02 (outturn)	2003–04 (plans)
Regional Development Agencies (RDAs)	12.8	1,120.2	1,425.7
Regional Chambers	–	3.6	–
European Regional Development Fund	231.1	166.2	254.0
Single Regeneration Budget	558.9	–	–
English Partnerships			
Urban Regeneration Agency	156.3	100.0	106.4
Commission for New Towns	32.9	–44.3	–42.7
Coalfields	26.4	34.3	28.7
Total	**1,018.5**	**1,380.0**	**1,772.2**

Source: Adapted from Department of Transport, Local Government and the Regions (2002), *Annual Report*.

Table 11.4 relates to the regeneration of the former English coalfields in order to bring about the government's long-term programme of bringing better physical, social and economic regeneration to these areas.

In addition to the expenditure shown in Table 11.4, it should be noted that in April 2002 central government set up the *Neighbourhood Renewal Unit* (NRU). This unit is designed to concentrate resources on the 88 local authority districts which account for 82% of the total number of 'deprived' wards in England. Through the *Neighbourhood Renewal Fund* (NRF), £900m was allocated between 2001 and 2002 to local authorities to tackle deprivation. In addition, the central government organization called *New Deal for the Communities* (NDC) funded 39 local partnerships (e.g. local authorities and the private sector) worth £50m per partnership over the period 1998–2008 in order to help improve community services.

 The effectiveness of urban policy

Although greater emphasis has been placed on urban policy over the last few years, it has not been without its critics.

First, it has been argued that resources directed to urban policies have been insufficient, accounting for only 4% of the Department of the Environment, Transport and the Regions' planned spending in 1998/99. In the same period, for example, the total amount to be spent on the English Partnerships (£298m) and the Challenge Fund (£567m) combined

was less than central government spending on arts and libraries.

Second, it is claimed that urban policies have failed to ensure that new jobs created in the inner cities were filled by unemployed inner-city residents. Evidence suggests that higher-skilled commuters from outside the inner-city areas often 'crowd out' inner-city residents in the competition for employment. To redress the balance it has been suggested that marginal subsidies be provided for firms which recruit unemployed inner-city residents. Such schemes could also be designed to favour employers making the greatest contribution to improving the skill and job experience of inner-city residents.

Third, the UDG and similar support schemes have been criticized for being more helpful in attracting renewal schemes to areas which *already* have a reasonable degree of economic activity. In a study of 41 UDG-sponsored projects in operation during the mid-1980s it was found that many of the schemes would have gone ahead even without UDG grants. In fact 64% of the total employment generated by the UDG-sponsored projects would have been created even without the government subsidy. In other words, companies were likely to have come to those areas even if they had not been offered subsidies (Martin 1998).

A report by Price Waterhouse on the impact of the City Grant and its predecessors (the UDG and the Urban Regeneration Grant) covering 36 projects was completed in 1993. It indicated that the grants had been important in creating confidence in the local economies but that the actual job creation had been 19% below the figure initially predicted for the schemes. Further, some 46% of the jobs created were jobs displaced from other premises in the area. Hence, the *net* additional jobs were only half the numbers initially predicted. Hotels were the most efficient at generating net additional jobs and they also employed the highest proportion of employees from within the inner-city areas. However, they were also the most 'expensive' in that they absorbed £1 of government grants for every £2.8 of private investment (i.e. 35%) as compared to retail (14%), offices (15%) and industrial (25%). In general, the cost per job at £14,280 for the City Grants compared relatively favourably with other public-sector job creation initiatives.

Fourth, there is a danger that programmes such as the Urban Development Corporations may not solve the unemployment problem because many of the jobs created in these areas often go to people who live outside the area. For example, a report by the House of Commons Employment Committee in 1988 found that although overall employment in the London Dockland Corporation area had risen from 27,213 in 1981 to 36,000 in 1987, the majority of this increase represented a relocation of jobs from outside Docklands. It also pointed out that the skills demanded by the new companies entering the London Dockland Development Corporation scheme did not match the skills of the local population. Finally, the committee found that most of the new jobs created in this area tended to be in office or service work and that manufacturing employment had actually declined. As a result the unemployment level in this area was higher in 1988 than at the launch of the scheme in 1981. The problems of unemployment and deprivation continue in the urban areas despite the myriad of schemes shown in Table 11.4.

A survey assessing the impact of urban policy on the Urban Programme Areas (UPAs) found that the *unemployment* gaps between UPA and non-UPA areas had narrowed over the last part of the 1980s but that there was no discernible narrowing of the difference between the two types of areas in terms of *job creation* or *new firm foundation*. In fact, the benefits accruing to the deprived inner-city areas were less than those accruing to the areas on the periphery of these deprived inner-city areas (Department of the Environment 1994).

A report on 13 Enterprise Zones which had completed their 10-year life cycle in 1993/94 serves to illustrate some of these problems (Department of the Environment 1995). Out of 51,100 permanent jobs created in the 13 zones over the 10-year period, 33,424 would have been there even without the zone designation and some 26,269 of the jobs had merely been diverted to the zones from nearby areas. Taking other multiplier effects into consideration, the net additional permanent jobs created by the zones was estimated as 23,150, at a total cost of between £1,450 and £1,850 per job, per year.

Fifth, the effectiveness of urban policy depends on a rational and clear strategic view of how to tackle urban problems. The City Challenge initiative could be usefully assessed in this light. Unfortunately, the City Challenge promoted centralization rather than a free market, in that the government (through the competitive bidding process) was given more control over how Urban Programme authorities spend their resources. Also, cooperation between authorities was hindered by the fact that authorities were made to bid against each other for funds. On top of this, the City Challenge did not provide a net addition to the general Urban Programme fund, since the resources were taken from other urban initiatives. Lastly, local authorities that were successful in obtaining City Challenge funds often had to bring more of their own funds into the scheme, sometimes at the cost of reducing spending on other deprived areas within the local authority (Atkinson and Moon 1994).

Finally, the trend over the last 20 years has been for people to leave the inner cities for the suburbs and smaller towns, further weakening the inner-city economies. Between 1990 and 1997 much reliance was placed on property-led regeneration (London Docklands, Cardiff Bay, etc.) in the hope that there would be 'trickle-down effects' which would benefit disadvantaged residents in nearby areas. In this context, evaluations of the early rounds of the SRB showed that resources had been spread too thinly across too many projects and across too many regions (Robson *et al.* 2000). A key element often missing from such initiatives is the need to develop *sound economies* in problem-ridden urban and inner-city locations (Gripaios 2002).

The Regional Development Agencies (RDAs)

Over the last few years, the concept of 'new regionalism', with its stress on the creation of regional systems of economic governance, has become official policy in both the UK and the EU. The publication by the Treasury of a consultative document entitled 'A Modern Regional Policy for the United Kingdom' in 2003 clarified the government's aims of creating economic dynamism through devolution and decentralization in both the UK and the EU. Under such plans, UK regions are seen as vital platforms for increasing the country's competitiveness within the global marketplace. In this context, the incoming Labour government of 1997, as well as devolving power to Scotland and Wales, also established nine English *Regional Development Agencies* (RDAs). They resembled those already in existence in Wales and Scotland, i.e. the Welsh Development Agency (WDA) and Scottish Development Agency (SDA) respectively. The boundaries of the RDAs are the same as those already existing under the Government Offices of the Regions (GORs). Each RDA is, in effect, a non-departmental public body with the Secretary of State appointing each RDA Board member (between eight and 15). Those appointed to Board membership in each region reflect a mix of interests such as business, education, the voluntary sector, etc.

The functions of the RDAs are defined to include taking a leadership role in developing and implementing regional economic strategies designed to improve the competitiveness of the region. Each RDA is provided with a single budget each year from central government funds and is allowed to spend this money wherever it can have the greatest impact. The RDAs are monitored by government and are given challenging targets to achieve – for example, the RDAs have been set a target of reducing deprivation in the 20% most deprived wards in their region. In addition, the government sets 'milestones' for measuring the activities of the RDAs. For example, during 2002–03 and 2003–04 the RDAs collectively were asked to support or safeguard some 193,147 jobs, recycle 2,841 hectares of brownfield sites, support the creation of learning opportunities for 208,598 individuals, and support the creation and/or attraction of 8,713 new businesses (DTLR 2002). If we take as an example one of the RDAs, e.g. the Office for the North East (ONE), we find that in 2001/02 it spent over 65% of its income on urban and rural regeneration projects with one of its targets being to create 12,753 new jobs. Its actual performance was an extra 12,878 jobs, i.e. 101% of this specified target over the period.

The introduction of the RDA model for regional regeneration and competitiveness has not been without critics. First, it has been argued that the RDAs are inevitably involved in wasteful competition as regions use their scarce resources to compete against each other to attract inward investment. Second, there is the argument that RDA plans place too much emphasis on economic development, with the result that environmental or sustainable development objectives are often hardly mentioned. Third, the RDAs can find themselves involved in inter-organizational disputes in the regions, because central government departments have also set up institutions which sometimes act as an alternative focus to the RDA. For example, both the Local Learning and Skills Councils (LSCs) established by the Department for Education and Skills (DfES), and the Small Business Service (SBS) established by the DTI, operate at the regional/local level, making the role of the RDAs more complicated (Fuller *et al.* 2002). Finally, many argue that there is little reason to believe that the RDAs can make a major difference to the economic performance of the problem regions, given that the average spending on *all* RDAs between 2001 and 2004 was only £1.2bn per year, a total of only 60% of the value paid by Cadbury Schweppes in 2003 for Adams, a chewing gum company!

Given these constraints, the RDAs clearly have a number of problems on their hands in trying to redress these UK regional inequalities often described as the 'North/South divide'. The nature of the continuing problem can be seen in Table 11.5, which provides an overall index of *regional competitiveness*, a composite measure that incorporates regional data on unemployment, number of businesses per head, number of knowledge-based businesses, etc. Other indices shown in Table 11.5 include average gross weekly household income, pass rates at GCSE, and households receiving income or family benefits. The table suggests the continued existence of the so-called 'North/South divide'. However, it also shows the anomalous situation in London which has a very high average gross weekly household income figure, but also has pockets of inner-city poverty, as indicated by the income/family support figures and the below-average educational achievement (see also Table 11.3 earlier). The data in Table 11.5 certainly point to a continuing regional problem.

Other studies confirm this picture. A more detailed study by Huggins of the regional 'competitive index'

Table 11.5 English regions and the North/South divide, 2001/02 (UK average = 100).

	Regional competitiveness	Average gross weekly household income	Pass rate for GCSE[1]	Households receiving income/family support
London	119.2	128.1	95.3	100.0
South East	107.2	122.1	108.8	62.5
Eastern	104.8	106.3	105.9	68.8
South West	97.0	93.5	107.1	87.5
East Midlands	95.6	93.5	96.3	93.8
West Midlands	95.4	96.3	93.0	112.6
North West	93.8	89.6	94.1	118.8
Yorks and Humber	92.6	90.0	87.1	118.8
North East	86.5	79.2	86.1	131.3
UK	**100.0**	**100.0**	**100.0**	**100.0**

[1] The percentage of pupils receiving five or more grades A–C at GCSE or equivalent.
Sources: Adapted from Huggins (2003); ONS (2002) *Regional Trends*.

shown in Table 11.5 concluded that the gap between the top three regions and the worst three regions in the table widened by as much as 30% during 1997–2001 (Huggins 2001). In addition, it has been pointed out that although traditional indices of the North/South divide using claimant count unemployment data appear to have converged over time, such patterns may be misleading (Fothergill 2001). If labour market indices are broadened to include inactivity such as premature retirement and long-term limiting illness, then the numbers of workers in the 25–64 age group who are 'economically inactive' are as much as 30% greater in the North than in the South. The 'Southern-centric' bias in economic development also means that any overheating and inflationary pressures in the South may be tackled by tight economic policy, when in the disadvantaged North the reverse policy may be required. The new regional policy, as exemplified by the RDAs, is designed to raise the economic potential of *all* regions rather than improving the North *relative* to the South, which may arguably be a more appropriate policy focus.

Conclusion

Despite the problems of definition, it has long been recognized that some areas of the UK suffer a greater degree of economic difficulty than do others. Government policies have attempted to alleviate such problems and have experienced some measure of success, creating up to 800,000 extra jobs in the Assisted Areas since the 1960s. However, critics have commented that the 'costs' have been high, at £40,000 per job created, with much of the benefit going to companies such as ICI, Shell and BP, which often would have located plants in the Assisted Areas without financial help.

In the 1970s the regional problem was aggravated by economic and social difficulties experienced in the large conurbations, especially within the inner cities. Policies to counteract these problems were slow to develop, though in the 1980s and 1990s government policy has been much more active with the development of Enterprise Zones, UDCs and inner-city initiatives such as *Action for Cities*, and with the new organizational changes brought about by the Single Regeneration Budget in 1994. However, an integrated policy may be required, incorporating both government and industry views, and taking account of both the regional and urban dimension, if the UK is successfully to combat the difficulties noted above. To promote such integration, from April 1999 the new Regional Development Agencies have been given the task of coordinating the various policy initiatives at the regional level. The long-run 'costs' of *not* developing an effective, integrated policy may far outweigh any short-term monetary 'benefits' from reduced government spending.

Key points

- A *regional problem* exists where a region departs from the 'national average' in terms of various characteristics: e.g. levels of unemployment, GDP per head, outward migration, etc.

- 'Core' regions are those which have experienced the most rapid economic advance in the past three decades or so: e.g. South East, East Midlands, East Anglia.

- 'Periphery' regions have experienced less favourable conditions: 'inner' and 'outer' peripheries are often identified.

- Intervention in terms of regional policy is usually advocated by those who feel that market forces alone will not eliminate regional disparities.

- Various types of *Assisted Area* (AA) are now identified in the UK. *Tier 1* receive most help and *Tier 2* rather less, with Enterprise Grants being more widely available over the UK.

- Most policy instruments now involve a range of financial incentives rather than direct controls.

- The *Urban Problem* involves aspects such as the urban–rural shift of population and economic activity, often reflected in particular inner-city problems.

- Policies have included Enterprise Zones, Urban Development Corporations and Grants and various inner-city initiatives.

- The Regional Development Agencies (RDAs) are playing an increasingly important role in regional and urban policy in England.

Now try the self-check questions for this chapter on the Companion Website. You will also find up-to-date facts and case materials.

References and further reading

Armstrong, H. W. (2001) Regional Selective Assistance: is the speed enough and is it targeting the right places?, *Regional Studies*, 35(3), May.

Atkinson, R. and Moon, G. (1994) The city challenge initiative: an overview and preliminary assessment, *Regional Studies*, 28(1).

Blake, N. (1995) The regional implications of macroeconomic policy, *Oxford Review of Economic Policy*, 11(2), Summer.

Department of the Environment (1994) *Assessing the Impact of Urban Policy*, Inner City Research Programme.

Department of the Environment (1995) *Final Evaluation of Enterprise Zones*, PA Cambridge Economic Consultants.

DTLR (2002) *Annual Report*, Department of Transport, Local Government and the Regions.

Financial Times (1998) Regions take an inward look at the growing problem, May, p. 11.

Financial Times (1999) Warning on flight of jobs from cities, 30 November.

Fothergill, S. (2001) The true scale of the regional problem in the UK, *Regional Studies*, 35(3), May.

Fothergill, S. and Gudgin, G. (1982) *Unequal Growth: urban and regional employment change in the UK*, Heinemann.

Fuller, C., Bennett, R. J. and Ramsden, M. (2002) The economic development role of English RDAs: the need for greater discretionary power, *Regional Studies*, 36(4), June.

Gripaios, P. (2002) The failure of regeneration policy in Britain, *Regional Studies*, 36(5), July.

Gudgin, G. (1996) Regional problems and policy in the UK, *Oxford Review of Economic Policy*, 11(2).

Gudgin, G., Moore, B. and Rhodes, J. (1982) Employment problems in the cities and regions of the UK: prospects for the 1980s, *Cambridge Economic Policy Review*, 8(2), University of Cambridge, Department of Economics, Gower.

Huggins, R. (2001) *UK Competitiveness Index: Regional and Local Benchmarking*, Huggins Associates, Cardiff.

Huggins, R. (2003) Creating a UK Competitiveness Index: regional and local benchmarking, *Regional Studies*, 37(1), February.

Keeble, D. and Tyler, P. (1995) Enterprising behaviour and the urban–rural shift, *Urban Studies*, 32(6).

Martin, R. (1998) Regional incentive spending for European regions, *Regional Studies*, 32(6).

Martin R. and Tyler, P. (1992) The regional legacy, in J. Michie (ed.) *The Economic Legacy 1979–1992*, Academic Press.

Martin, S. (1989) New jobs in the inner city: the employment impacts of projects assisted under urban development Grant Programme, *Urban Studies*, 26(6), December.

Moore, B. C. and Rhodes, J. (1976) A quantitative analysis of the effects of the regional employment premium and other regional policy instruments, in A. Whiting, (ed.) *The Economics of Industrial Subsidies*, HMSO.

Moore, B. C. and Rhodes, J. (1977) *Methods of Evaluating the Effects of Regional Policy*, OECD, Paris.

Moore, B., Rhodes, J. and Tyler, P. (1986) *The Effect of Government Regional Economic Policy*, DTI, HMSO.

North, D. and Smallbone, D. (1993) Employment generation and small business growth in different geographical environments, Small Firms Conference, Nottingham.

Robson, B. (1997) Urban renewal and regional development, *Developments in Economics*, 13, Causeway Press.

Robson, B., Parkinson, M., Boddy, M. and Maclinnon, D. (2000) *The State of English Cities*, DETR.

Town and Country Planning Association (1999) *The people: where will they work?* TCPA report.

Tyler, J., Moore, B. and Rhodes, J. (1979) Regional policy and growth in development areas, paper presented to the Social Science Research Council Urban and Regional Economic Seminar Group, Newcastle.

Wren, C. and Taylor, J. (1999) Industrial restructuring and regional policy, *Oxford Economic Papers*, 51.

Chapter 12   Transport

Transport is an important sector of the UK economy and has been the subject of increasing debate in recent years. This chapter will deal with certain aspects of that debate, notably the problems of road transport congestion and the move to a deregulated transport sector. The last 50 years have seen a dramatic change in the patterns of demand for transport. For example, in 1952 only 27% of passenger kilometres travelled were by car, van and taxi, while public transport (both road and rail) accounted for 60%. Today, however, the share has changed, with 85% of passenger kilometres now being by car, van and taxi and with public transport accounting for only 12%. Such a substantial change has significant implications for road congestion and the environment. In this chapter we therefore concentrate mainly on the *road transport sector*, and on the car in particular.

The characteristics of transport

Firstly, transport is a service which is seldom demanded for its own sake and can be viewed as a 'derived demand'. In other words, the demand for the private car, public transport and freight haulage is 'derived' from the need to transfer passengers and goods from one destination to another. Each journey undertaken can be seen as 'unique' in terms of both time and space, and cannot therefore be stored or transferred.

Secondly, the transport sector (both passenger and freight operators) is affected by the peak and off-peak nature of demand. There will be periods of maximum or peak demand, e.g. on a *daily* basis when commuters travel into a major conurbation to work, or on a *seasonal* basis when holidaymakers use road, rail or airline transport during summer periods. Peak periods are present in the transport sector because of

the derived nature of demand and because transport is consumed immediately and is therefore non-storable. Spare capacity at one time of the day or season *cannot* be used at another time of the day or season. Also the indivisibility of supply means that public transport may be running at full capacity into the urban area in the peak period, but operating empty on the return journey. As a result there are often problems of over-supply during off-peak periods.

Thirdly, the transport sector has, over the years, been subject to varying degrees of state intervention. In the 1970s, the transport sector was characterized by public ownership and substantial government intervention, particularly in the provision of public transport. The 1980s and 1990s saw a period of rapid change, with a substantial scaling-down of state intervention in the sector. For example, the *1980 Transport Act* deregulated the long-distance express coach market, allowing increased competition. The National Freight Corporation was privatized in 1982

Table 12.1 Passenger transport by mode, 1990–2001.

	Billion passenger kilometres/percentage														
	Road														
	Buses and coaches		Cars and vans[1]		Motor cycles		Pedal cycles		All road		Rail		Air		All models[2]	
		%		%		%		%		%		%		%		%
1990	46	7	588	85	6	1	5	1	645	94	39	6	5	1	689	100
1991	44	6	582	86	6	1	5	1	637	94	38	6	5	1	681	100
1992	43	6	583	86	5	1	5	1	636	94	38	6	5	1	679	100
1993	44	6	584	86	4	1	4	1	637	94	36	5	5	1	678	100
1994	44	6	591	86	4	1	5	1	643	94	35	5	5	1	684	100
1995	44	6	596	86	4	1	4	1	648	94	36	5	6	1	690	100
1996	44	6	606	86	4	1	4	1	658	94	38	5	6	1	703	100
1997	44	6	614	86	4	1	4	1	666	93	42	6	6.8	0.9	714	100
1998	45	6	618	86	4	1	4	1	671	93	44	6	7.0	1	722	100
1999[3]	45	6	616	85	5	1	4	1	671	93	46	6	7.3	1	724	100
1999	45	6	613	85	5	1	4	1	667	93	46	6	7.3	1	721	100
2000	45	6	618	85	5	1	4	1	672	93	47	6	7.6	1	726	100
2001	46	6	624	85	5	1	4	1	679	92	47	6	7.7	1	734	100

[1] Includes taxis.
[2] Excluding travel by water within the UK (including Channel Islands), estimated at 0.7 billion passenger kilometres in 2000.
[3] Figures for 1999 onwards have been produced on a new basis and are not strictly comparable with earlier figures.
Source: Department for Transport (2002).

and subsequent years saw the deregulation of local bus provision as a result of the *1985 Transport Act*. Other transport companies were privatized, such as British Airways in 1987 and NBC in 1988. In addition there was the franchising of rail services from 1995 onwards.

Fourthly, 'externality' effects are a characteristic of transport. These include effects such as pollution through emissions from car exhausts, noise from aircraft and motorways, and traffic congestion. At present 69% of carbon monoxide and 43% of nitrogen oxide emissions are associated with road transport in the UK. These impose costs on the community and are generally not taken into account by the transport provider (company or individual) who is usually only concerned with the *private costs* (such as fuel, wear and tear, etc.) of the journey undertaken. Intervention by the state has therefore been required to deal with these external effects, especially where companies or individuals have failed to take full account of the *social* implications of their actions.

This has led, for example, to the introduction of emission tests for carbon monoxide as part of the MoT test for cars and light vehicles and an increase in roadside enforcement programmes in order to remove the worst offenders from the road.

Fifthly, other characteristics of transport may be gauged from the changing nature of travel over the last 15 years. Table 12.1 gives a summary of passenger travel in Great Britain over the period 1990–2001. It shows that, even with revised figures (see table notes), there was an increase in passenger transport by 4% over the period, with travel by cars and vans increasing by 6%. *Cars* and *vans* dominate passenger transport, accounting for 85% of all passengers kilometres travelled in 2001, with *bus* and *coach* travel accounting for 6% of all passenger kilometres in 2001. Domestic air travel, although it has grown, still accounts for only 1.0% of overall travel.

Table 12.2 compares Great Britain with a number of other countries in terms of passenger kilometres travelled between 1990 and 2000. In all of these

Table 12.2 Passenger transport by national vehicles on national territory, 1990 and 2000.

	Billion passenger kilometres							
	Cars and taxis		Buses and coaches		Rail excluding metro systems		Total of these modes	
	1990	2000	1990	2000	1990	2000	1990	2000
Great Britain	588.0	613.0	46.0	45.0	33.2	39.2	667.2	697.2
Belgium	89.2	105.9	10.9	12.4	6.5	7.8	106.6	126.1
Denmark	47.8	66.6	9.3	11.3	4.9	5.3	62.0	83.2
France	585.6	699.6	41.3	45.3	63.8	69.6	690.7	814.5
Germany	683.1	723.4	73.1	69.0	64.5	74.0	820.7	866.4
Greece	48.8	77.1	17.7	21.7	2.0	1.9	68.5	100.7
Irish Republic	18.1	33.3	3.9	6.1	1.2	1.4	23.2	40.8
Italy	522.6	665.2	84.0	94.0	44.7	43.8	651.3	803.0
Netherlands	139.3	151.5	13.0	12.6	11.1	14.8	163.4	178.9
Spain	220.0	331.6	33.4	50.6	16.7	20.1	270.1	402.3
Sweden	85.7	92.9	9.0	11.1	6.0	8.3	100.7	112.3
European Union[1]	3,186.3	3,776.6	370.0	412.6	272.5	301.7	3,828.8	4,490.9
Japan	530.0	–	110.0	–	390.0	–	1,030.0	–
USA	5,280.0	–	196.0	–	21.0	–	5,497.0	–

[1] Not including Northern Ireland.
Source: Adapted from Department for Transport (2002).

countries the major mode of transport is the private road vehicle. In Great Britain some 88% of total passenger travel in 2000 was by cars and taxis, compared with 84% in the EU as a whole and as much as 96% in the USA for the latest period available. The figure for Japan for passenger travel by cars and taxis is much lower (51%), with rail travel being much more significant (38%) than elsewhere.

Finally, another characteristic of transport is the changing nature of the *freight* market. In terms of freight transport, Table 12.3 gives figures in billion tonne kilometres and percentage, by mode, over the period 1991–2001. It shows that there has been a 21% increase in freight transported by road over the 10-year period and, as with passenger transport, roads can be seen as the major form of transport, with 64% of the share in the most recent time period.

The demand for transport

The quantity of a good or service demanded is dependent upon a number of factors, such as its own price, the price of other goods or services (particularly close substitutes and complements), and income. For example, private car ownership is a function not only of the price of motor vehicles, but also of fuel prices, the price of alternative forms of transport, and income levels. Income is an important factor in determining both the demand for transport in general, and the *particular mode* of transport a passenger uses.

Table 12.4 gives figures for motoring expenditure, fares and other travel costs for households with different levels of income in the UK over the 2001–02 period. As one would expect, it clearly shows that travel expenditure increases with income, with those households in the lowest 10% income group having an average weekly expenditure on *transport* of £10.30 whilst the highest 10% spend £132.70. For *all* households the average is £57.70. For *bus and coach* fares the figures reveal that expenditure declines at higher income levels. As illustrated in Table 12.4, the ninth income decile group spent £2.00 on average per week whilst the top decile group spent £1.20 per week, leading one to suggest that bus and coach travel can be viewed in economic terms as an *inferior good*.

For *rail transport, Family Spending 2001–02* (National Statistics 2003) reveals a different trend, with higher income groups spending more on that mode of travel. As illustrated in Table 12.4 the

Table 12.3 Domestic freight transport by mode (in billion tonne kilometres and percentages), 1991–2001.

	1991	1993	1995	1997	1999	2001
All traffic						
Road[1]	130.0	134.5	149.6	157.1	156.7	156.9
Rail	15.3	13.8	13.3	16.9	18.2	19.7
Water[2]	57.7	51.2	53.1	48.1	58.7	–
Pipeline	11.1	11.6	11.1	11.2	11.6	11.5
All modes	214.1	211.1	227.1	233.3	245.2	–
Percentage of all traffic						
Road[1]	61	64	66	67	64	–
Rail	7	7	6	7	7	–
Water[2]	27	24	23	21	24	–
Pipeline	5	5	5	5	5	–
All modes	100	100	100	100	100	–

[1] All goods vehicles, including those under 3.5 tonnes gross vehicle weight.
[2] Figures for water are for UK traffic.
Source: Adapted from Department for Transport (2002).

Table 12.4 Detailed household expenditure by gross income decile group.

Commodity or service	Lowest 10%	Second decile group	Third decile group	Fourth decile group	Fifth decile group	Sixth decile group	Seventh decile group	Eighth decile group	Ninth decile group	Highest 10%	All households
					Average weekly household expenditure (£)						
Transport	10.30	16.30	28.00	34.90	44.10	57.60	70.10	82.00	101.10	132.70	57.70
Purchase of vehicles	3.00	6.20	11.00	13.40	15.90	26.20	31.90	37.10	49.80	62.10	25.70
New cars and vans	1.30	1.40	3.30	7.00	5.80	10.10		[14.00]	20.10	31.70	10.60
Second-hand cars or vans	1.70	4.60	7.60	6.30	9.50	15.10	19.50	21.80	28.60	29.10	14.40
Motorcycles					[0.40]	[0.80]	[0.70]		[0.90]		0.40
Other vehicles											0.20
Operation of personal transport	4.80	6.90	12.00	16.60	22.10	24.20	30.00	34.60	36.00	48.60	23.60
Spares and accessories		0.40	0.90	0.90	2.00	2.50	2.60	3.30	2.50	4.50	2.00
Petrol, diesel, other motor oils	3.20	4.30	7.40	10.30	13.30	14.80	18.80	22.60	23.60	29.30	14.70
Repairs and servicing	1.10	1.80	2.90	4.30	5.00	5.00	6.60	6.30	7.20	10.50	5.10
Other motoring costs	0.40	0.40	0.80	1.20	1.70	1.90	2.00	2.50	2.80	4.40	1.80
Transport services	2.50	3.20	5.00	4.80	6.10	7.20	8.20	10.20	15.40	21.90	8.40
Rail and tube fares	0.40	0.20	0.60	0.70	1.00	1.20	1.60	2.10	3.80	7.00	1.90
Bus and coach fares	0.90	1.10	1.20	1.40	1.40	1.90	1.80	1.70	2.00	1.20	1.50
Air travel							[2.00]		[3.10]	[1.60]	1.20
Combined fares	[0.30]	[0.40]	[0.20]	[0.30]	0.40	[0.50]	0.60	1.40	2.10	4.10	1.00
Other travel and transport	0.70	1.10	1.80	1.70	2.50	2.40	2.20	4.50	4.30	7.90	2.90

Source: Adapted from National Statistics (2003) *Family Spending*.

highest 10% of income earners spent on average £7.00 per week on rail and tube fares compared to an average for *all households* of £1.90.

Predicting the demand for transport in the future is a difficult process, since it depends on how the variables affecting demand change over time. For example, forecasts in terms of car ownership and, in particular, cars per head of population are predicted to increase by 41% between 1996 and 2031. In terms of vehicle kilometres the forecast for cars is an increase of between 30% and 75% over the same period, whereas goods vehicles are forecast to increase by between 96% and 165%. In 2001 there were approximately 23.9m private cars licensed in Great Britain. As Table 12.5 reveals, however, we have not yet reached saturation level in terms of car ownership, for there are still 26% of households who do not own a car.

With regards to forecasting car ownership, the Department of Transport used the *National Road Traffic Forecasts* 1988 (Goodwin 1990) to make the following observation:

> Many factors are likely to influence the growth of car ownership and use. They include income, the cost of buying and running cars, journey requirements (work and non-work), quality of public transport services and the way people's expectations and preferences about car ownership change over time. … It seems likely that car ownership will eventually reach a limit – or

'saturation level' – as a larger proportion of the population acquires cars. Since no country appears to have reached this limit yet, the level of saturation must be assumed. For these forecasts, saturation has been assumed to occur when 90% of the driving age group of 17–74-year-olds owns a car (100% car ownership is unlikely because some people will be prevented or deterred by disabilities or other factors). On this basis, saturation would correspond to 650 cars per thousand people. The forecasts of growth in national car ownership are essentially about the rate and path with which the saturation level is approached.

Forecasts of future traffic, particularly the private car, are essential for a central government which has to decide on the allocation of funds for future road development. For, as stated by the Department of Transport in 1989:

> Traffic forecasts are important in assessing whether the benefits from a road improvement, over its life-time, justify the initial cost and in determining the standard of provision. They enable a balance to be struck between providing extra capacity before it is needed and the cost of adding to capacity at a later stage. Traffic forecasts also play a part in predicting the environmental impacts of traffic, such as noise and air pollution.

Table 12.5 Households with regular use of cars, 1992–2001.

| | Percentage of households | | | | |
	No car	One car	Two cars	Three or more cars	Great Britain (millions)
1992	32	45	20	4	22.6
1993	31	45	20	4	22.9
1994	32	45	20	4	23.1
1995	30	45	21	4	23.3
1996	30	45	21	4	23.5
1997	30	45	21	4	23.7
1998	28	44	23	5	23.9
1999	28	44	22	5	24.1
2000	27	45	23	5	24.4
2001	26	46	22	5	–

Source: Department for Transport (2002).

Such forecasts are difficult to determine owing to the high degree of uncertainty about the future and for this reason the basis of the forecasts involves two differing assumptions, namely that of low economic growth and that of high economic growth. The forecasts therefore provide a range of values ('scenarios') to cover the uncertainties involved. It is possible, however, for the outcome to fall outside the forecast range, with the Department of Transport being unable to forecast traffic levels accurately. A good example of this was seen with the M25, for which forecasts were undertaken in the 1970s when oil prices were high and economic growth low. This led the Department of Transport to underestimate the likely demand for transport along the route. For example, between 1982 and 1987 they forecast an increase in road traffic of between 9% and 16%, but the actual increase was 22%. The main reason for this was that the forecast assumed a growth of GDP of between 8% and 15% over the five-year period, but GDP actually grew by 18%. Also the price of fuel was forecast to rise in real terms, whereas it actually fell.

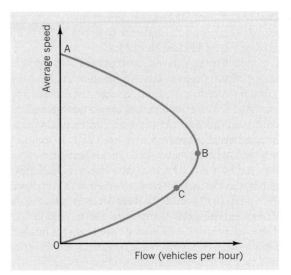

Fig. 12.1 Speed–flow curve.

Road transport congestion

Congestion costs arise because the addition of more vehicles onto a road network reduces the speed of other vehicles and so increases the average time it takes to complete any particular journey.

It is possible to gain some understanding of congestion by studying the relationship between speed and flow along a particular route. Figure 12.1 shows a *speed–flow curve* for the movement of vehicles along a particular road. It shows how motorists interact and impose delays and costs on each other. In a free-flow situation (around point A) there is little or no interaction between vehicles, and therefore speeds (subject to the legal speed limit) are relatively high. However, as extra vehicles join the road, average speed is reduced; nevertheless an increased flow will still occur until point B is reached. The flow of vehicles depends upon the number of vehicles joining the road and the speed of the traffic. For the *individual user*, maximum efficiency is where the speed is at its highest, i.e. point A. In terms of the *system as a whole*, however, the maximum efficiency is at point B, before the speed–flow curve turns back on itself

(i.e. where the maximum flow of vehicles is achieved). Once at point B, the road is said to have reached its capacity at the maximum flow level. Motorists may continue to enter the road after B because they may lack perfect information, thus slowing down the whole flow. Point C may therefore be used to represent the speed–flow situation during a peak period. At this point the traffic is in a stop–start situation, perhaps where the traffic flow is subject to a bottleneck. This gives rise to high *external* costs which the motorist is not taking into account. These costs will tend to increase the closer the road is to full capacity.

The costs of congestion

It is clear that a major strategy is needed to tackle the congestion problem, not only in urban areas but also on inter-urban routes. Congestion undermines competitiveness and hinders certain conurbations, particularly London, from attracting people and business. It also imposes a financial cost on the business community in terms of increased commuter times and delays in the delivery of goods. The British Road Federation has estimated that congestion costs are over £3bn per year in London and the six major English conurbations alone, and has suggested that the total national congestion bill could be in the region of £10bn per year.

The Confederation of British Industry estimates that delays on the M25 cost £1bn per year, and that London's inadequate transport system costs the nation around £15bn per annum, almost two-thirds of which relates to London and the South East. In the CBI report 'The Capital at Risk', published in 1989, the following figures were given for the average additional costs incurred in London and the South East. This information was compiled from data provided by those national companies which could compare their distribution costs in London and the South East with other areas. The results are shown in Table 12.6 and reveal that the £15bn per annum consists of, amongst other things, increased staff and vehicle requirements and additional fuel costs. This figure should, however, be treated with extreme caution.

Specific businesses such as British Telecom and the Royal Mail put the cost of congestion to themselves at £7.25m and £10.4m per annum, respectively. These costs were measured in terms of fleet inefficiency, lost driver's time, and extra vehicle costs. According to the CBI, every British household has to spend at least £5 per week *more than it needs to* on goods and services

Table 12.6 Average additional costs due to congestion incurred in London and the South East.

Productivity lost due to lateness of staff	1%
Delivery time and cost penalties within M25	30%
Additional staff/drivers needed to beat congestion	20%
Additional vehicles needed	20%
Additional vehicle service/repair costs	20%
Additional fuel costs	10%
Estimated total additional transportation costs in the London area	20%

Statistics were compiled from information provided by national organizations that could compare distribution costs in London and the South East with other areas.
Source: Confederation of British Industry (1989).

in order to meet the costs to business of road and rail congestion. This is equal to 2p on the basic rate of income tax. The CBI estimate that if traffic delays could be reduced, thereby raising average speeds by 1.5 mph, then London's economy would be better off

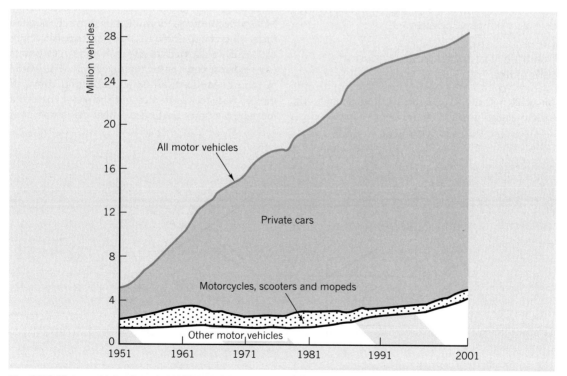

Fig. 12.2 Motor vehicles licensed, 1951–2001.
Source: Adapted from National Statistics (2002).

by £1m per day. In 1997 the National Economic Research Associates (NERA) estimated the total cost of road congestion to road users to be £7bn. This can be split into the cost to business (£2.5bn) and the cost to private motorists, private van drivers and bus passengers (£4.5bn). More recent estimates of congestion costs are even more substantial; for example the RAC (2000) has estimated that congestion costs the motorist around £23bn in time losses alone each year. This is approximately £800 per annum for every motorist in Britain irrespective of the extra fuel and wear and tear costs associated with congestion. Whilst estimates of the cost of congestion have been made, the government has admitted that 'an ideal measure [of congestion] has yet to be identified' (House of Commons Transport Committee 2003).

In terms of traffic speeds, the situation has worsened over the last 30 years. In Central London, the morning and evening peak period travel speeds were 12.7 and 11.8 mph respectively in 1968–70, whereas by 2003 they had fallen to 9.9 and 10.2 mph respectively (National Statistics 2003). Figure 12.2 gives some indication of the causes of congestion. There has been a dramatic rise in the number of licensed vehicles over the period 1951–2001, made up almost entirely of private cars.

The theory of urban road transport congestion

An economic model can be used to simplify the various issues involved in transport congestion, as shown in Fig. 12.3. The horizontal axis measures the flow of vehicles per hour along a particular route. The vertical axis measures the cost per trip, including time costs. Two demand curves are shown, both of which have a negative slope because it is assumed that motorists will reduce their driving if the cost of driving increases. The demand curve D_1 refers to the *off-peak* demand for the route. It is the aggregate demand of all motorists who wish to use the route. If the cost per trip is C_0, and demand is D_1, then this will produce a flow of F_0 along the route. When making a journey, a motorist is not likely to take account of the congestion cost of that journey and may in fact consider only his or her own *marginal private cost* (MPC). MPC includes costs such as the price of petrol used and the opportunity cost of the time the motorist spends travelling. There can, however, be costs incurred on *other* road users which the individual motorist will not take into account. These are 'external costs' and include such things as the pollution and noise borne by society as a whole and the congestion borne by other road users. These are shown by the *marginal social cost* curve (MSC) in Fig. 12.3. For simplicity Fig. 12.3 assumes that congestion is the *only* externality; hence MPC is shown as equal to MSC for some range of traffic flow up to F_1 because there is no congestion until that flow is reached. (Of course, if we allowed for the pollution which occurs from exhaust gases at low mileage, then MSC would be above MPC at all levels of traffic flow.) If motorists *did* take into account the social costs of a journey, then they might decide that the journey was

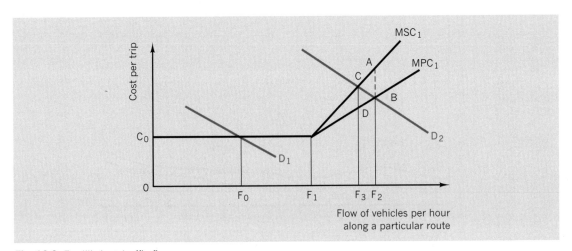

Fig. 12.3 Equilibrium traffic flow.

not worth making, at least not at that time of day or by that particular route.

In the figure it can be seen that the flow of traffic can increase up to F_1 without congestion, because it is possible for the additional cars to enter the road without slowing down any other driver. It can be seen, therefore, that there is no divergence between marginal private cost and marginal social cost. However, at flows above F_1, congestion is apparent because additional drivers slow down the overall traffic flow and the individual motorist's MPC per trip increases. Each motorist is now beginning to interfere with other road users, affecting their costs but ignoring those costs when deciding whether or not to make a particular trip. As the flow of traffic increases beyond F_1 there is also a *divergence* between the MPC and the MSC, as shown in the figure by lines MPC_1 and MSC_1 (MSC is equal to MPC plus the social cost of congestion). This is brought about mainly through increased travel times, as each additional driver entering the road imposes an extra delay (perhaps only small) on every other driver. If the demand for the route at the peak period is of the normal shape D_2, then the traffic flow will be F_2. Here F_2B will be the (private) cost per trip *to the motorist*, and the external costs which the motorist has *not* taken into account will be equal to AB. At a flow of F_2 there is therefore *allocative inefficiency*, as the 'real' or social cost of congestion has not been accounted for by the private motorist.

Policy options for urban road congestion – demand policies

There are various policies which have been designed to improve the use of existing road capacity. These include policies which can be introduced to influence the *demand* for road space; there are also policies designed to expand road capacity, which can be viewed as *supply* side policies. These various policies will be covered in this section. However, at this stage it is also worth mentioning that there is a '*laissez-faire*' approach which is an alternative solution for permitting an equilibrium level of road transport congestion to emerge. For instance, if congestion gets 'too bad' in a particular region, then it may persuade companies and individuals to move to less prosperous regions which do not have the same level of congestion. The problem with this '*laissez-faire*'

approach is that the transport network may be operating at, or near, full capacity at certain times, and therefore even small fluctuations in demand can cause long delays and create problems for safety.

Road user charging

When undertaking a journey, each driver is comparing the private benefit of each trip with the private cost of each trip. Drivers will add their vehicles to the flow whenever their marginal private benefit exceeds their marginal private cost. New roads could be built to meet the demand during the peak period, or demand could be restrained, or a mixture of the two policies could be undertaken. In Fig. 12.3 above, the flow of F_3 could be achieved by placing a charge of CD on the road user, so raising marginal private costs from MPC_1 to equal those of MSC_1; this would thereby reduce the traffic flow from F_2 to F_3. This road user charging option would bring about a 'more efficient allocation' of a scarce resource, because the marginal private benefit (as measured by the demand curve) is now equal to the marginal social cost curve. Road user charging is an option which is gaining in popularity. D. Newbery has commented that 'As road space is a valuable and scarce resource, it is natural that economists should argue that it should be rationed by price – road-users should pay the marginal social cost of using the road network if they are to make the right decisions about whether (and by which means) to take a particular journey, and, more generally, to ensure that they make the correct allocative decisions between transport and other activities' (Newbery 1990).

Road user charging was suggested as a possible solution to the urban congestion problem as long ago as 1964, when the Ministry of Transport produced the Smeed Report. Road user charging could be introduced by using meters attached to cars in the form of an electronic numberplate. As a car entered a congested area or stretch of road, the meter would be activated by sensors in the road. A charge would then be registered. As well as dissuading the marginal car user from using the road, it would also provide the authorities with revenue which could be used to construct more roads or to improve the public transport system. The government has recognized this and in their White Paper on the Future of Transport (1998) stated that 'We will introduce legislation to allow local authorities to charge road users so as to reduce congestion, as part of a package of measures in a *local transport plan* that would include improving public transport. The use of revenues to benefit transport serving the area where charges apply ... will be critical to the success of such schemes.' The government agreed that the revenue should be *ring-fenced*, with local authorities able to retain all the revenue generated for a period of 10 years from the implementation of a scheme, provided there are worthwhile transport-related projects to be funded. The Transport Bill (2000) included powers to enable local authorities outside London, if they wanted to, to introduce road user charging and/or a workplace parking levy (see below) as part of their local transport plan. Such powers had already been given to London's mayor and the Boroughs through the Greater London Authority Act 1999.

On 17 February 2003 in London the Mayor, Ken Livingstone, launched the first major congestion charging scheme in Britain, a scheme to charge motorists for the use of the road network within a specified area of Central London between certain times. The aim of the scheme is to reduce congestion and it forms one of only a small number of charging schemes worldwide, the Singapore Electronic Road Pricing scheme being the other main example.

Britain is one of the most congested countries in Europe and London one of the most congested cities. As shown in Table 12.7, average vehicle speeds in London have declined over time since 1974. This reduction in average speeds has been experienced in both the morning and evening peak periods with, perhaps surprisingly, the daytime off-peak period in Central London being most congested of all (in terms of lowest vehicle speeds). Clearly this is something the London authorities, namely Transport for London, have been keen to address. According to the *Financial Times* (17 February 2003), 3.3m London residents work and of these 36% use a car to travel to work compared with 19% and 11% using the tube and bus respectively. Some 2% cycle and 1% use a motorbike or scooter.

Congestion charging covers 21 square km of Central London. Motorists entering the zone between the hours of 7.00 am and 6.30 pm, Monday to Friday (excluding public holidays), are charged £5. It is predicted that congestion charging will raise around £130m per annum which can be used to invest in the improvement of London's transport infrastructure.

Table 12.7 Average vehicle speeds in London for selected time periods, dates and locations.

Morning peak period	Central area	Inner area
1974–76	14.2	15.9
1980–82	12.1	14.2
1986–90	11.5	11.8
1994–97	10.9	13.4
2000–03	9.9	–
Daytime off-peak		
1974–76	12.9	18.6
1980–82	11.6	17.2
1986–90	11.0	14.6
1994–97	10.9	15.0
2000–03	9.0	–
Evening peak period		
1974–76	13.2	15.5
1980–82	12.2	14.1
1986–90	11.0	11.6
1994–97	10.8	12.8
2000–03	9.6	–

Source: Adapted from National Statistics (2002).

Enforcement

Enforcement of the scheme is via 700 video cameras, which are able to scan the rear numberplate of the 250,000 vehicles that on average enter the area during a working week. It is predicted that every vehicle in the charging zone will pass an average of five cameras over the $11\frac{1}{2}$ hours that the charge is in operation each day. Each evening the information obtained is matched against a database of motorists who have paid the charge. Payment can be made by phone, using the Internet, at shops or at petrol stations. In fact there are 100 machines in car parks, 112 BT Internet kiosks within the zone and more than 1,500 retail locations with paypoints. If the motorist has failed to pay the charge before midnight, a fine of £80 is imposed. If the offender pays within 14 days, then the fine falls to £40.

Exemptions

A number of exemptions have been built into the scheme.

- Certain listed vehicles receive a 100% discount – this includes all alternative fuel vehicles, namely gas, electric and fuel cell vehicles, which are exempt on environmental grounds. Blue and orange badge holders are also exempt; that is, vehicles driven by disabled people. In addition, certain NHS staff, patients and emergency vehicles (fire engines, police vehicles and ambulances) have been brought within this category. Certain other vehicles are also exempt, such as those with more than nine seats and military vehicles used by the armed forces.

■ Residents within the charging zone are eligible for a 90% discount.

■ Motorbikes and mopeds, black cabs and London-licensed mini-cabs are also exempt.

Early estimates suggest that there were 25% fewer vehicles in the charging zone on the first day of the scheme, i.e. some 190,000 vehicles as compared with the 250,000 vehicles on a typical working day. Of these 100,000 vehicles paid the charge and approximately 45,000 vehicles were exempt from paying either because they involved a particular type of vehicle (e.g. bus or emergency vehicle) or they were registered for 100% exemption (e.g. either a blue badge holder or using alternative fuels).

If the scheme is perceived to work then other cities in the UK such as Bristol and Edinburgh may follow suit and the London scheme will most likely be extended, but any decision on this will not be taken until after the mayoral elections in May 2004. Pressure for inclusion within the zone is coming from those living in adjoining boroughs such as Kensington, Westminster and Tower Hamlets. Additional money raised from widening the scheme is likely to be limited, however, since many drivers now paying the £5 charge to enter the zone would then be entitled to the 90% discount for residents.

The scheme utilizes a rather simplistic technology, namely cameras on all the roads into the central area. It also incorporates a fixed price of £5, the charge not changing in line with the level of congestion experienced. As we noted in Chapter 10, the 'pure' environmental tax (Pigouvian tax) would equal the marginal external damage and would therefore rise as the marginal external damage increases (e.g. at peak time). The current fixed charge may, however, be changed to a variable charge as the scheme evolves. For example, the scheme might use global positioning satellites (GPS) and cars fitted with satellite receivers in order to allow the charge to vary with distance, time and location.

One of the criticisms levelled at road user charging is its effect on increasing the inflation rate. However, if it succeeded in reducing the total costs of commercial activities, then this is a false worry. Road user charging should not be viewed as a revenue maximizing charge, but as an efficiency maximizing charge. It could then be the key to medium-term relief from congestion and could provide the funds for the long-term upgrading of roads and public transport.

In addition, there are a number of problems to be addressed when considering the implementation of a road pricing policy. First, there need to be accurate estimates of elasticities of demand and of marginal external costs. Second, the issue of equity and the problem of practically implementing the scheme both need to be considered. For example, what charge should be made for congestion and how would it vary depending on the level of traffic and the time of day? Third, road user charging could be seen as an invasion of privacy, which was one of the reasons for it not being continued in Hong Kong after the initial experiment in 1983–85.

Subsidizing public transport

Another approach designed to shift the demand to the left in Fig. 12.3 is *subsidizing public transport*. This method was used in the 1970s by a number of UK metropolitan councils. For example in Sheffield, bus fares were reduced by 55% in real terms over the period 1975–81. In addition to financial implications, the problem faced by this method is in persuading car users to *transfer* from private to public transport, since they often perceive themselves as being the *victims* of congestion rather than the *cause* of it. To be successful this policy requires a long-term improvement in public transport and a cross-elasticity of demand between public and private transport substantially greater than zero. An added problem is that increased income levels lead to increased car ownership, thus lowering the demand for public transport, as stated above in the section 'The demand for transport'. The public transport sector therefore becomes more reliant on certain groups of travellers, namely the young, the elderly and those on low incomes, i.e. on a market which is getting smaller (Goodwin 1990). The Department of Transport commented that 'The level of traffic on roads in London is a reflection largely of individual choice, not the non-availability of other modes of travel'. However, it could be the case that individuals are not paying the true cost of motoring, i.e. there are 'hidden subsidies' which have the effect of making single car occupancy an attractive proposition, particularly in the peak period. This results in an inefficient use of road capacity.

Parking restrictions

One policy which has been extensively used in urban areas since the 1960s is *parking restraints*. The aim has been, through parking meters and restrictions on on-street parking, to limit the supply of parking spaces, so reducing the demand for urban routes. This policy, too, has limitations in that removing parking facilities from a road essentially increases the size of the road and may therefore encourage extra traffic flows. At the same time, parking restraints encourage illegal parking which may add to congestion. This is one of the main reasons for the introduction of wheel clamps in Central London in 1986 and policies such as the tow-away scheme introduced in Cambridge in 1991, subsequently abandoned in 1996 given its unprofitability.

City Councils have sought to use pricing policies at their car parks to encourage shopping and other short-stay motorists, while at the same time discouraging long-stay commuters. However, the success of this policy has been hindered to some extent by their lack of control over privately operated car parks and by high volumes of through traffic in most congested areas. Parking charges are also unable to discriminate between length of journey or route taken. Pricing policies could be used to encourage motorists to park at peripheral, out of town, car parks that are part of park-and-ride schemes, which are now operating in many British cities.

The lack of control over private parking was addressed by the Transport Bill (2000) which gave local authorities the power not only to introduce road user charging but also to levy a mandatory charge on workplace parking across all or part of their area. The levy would act as a *licence fee* with the owners or occupiers of premises applying to the traffic authority for a licence stating the maximum number of vehicles that would be parked on their premises at any one time. A workplace parking charge per vehicle would then be multiplied by that maximum number. The aim is 'to reduce the amount of free workplace car parking available as a means of reducing car journeys and promoting greater use of alternative modes' (DETR 1998b). It is intended that the levy will act as

an incentive for occupiers of property to reduce the total number of parking spaces, restricting the maximum number of vehicles for which a licence is sought. As with road user charging there are a number of issues which need to be addressed. These include the need for *complementary policies* to be adopted, such as the introduction or strengthening of existing on-street parking restrictions and the adjustment of tariffs for both on- and off-street parking outside the workplace to levels consistent with those applied to workplace parking. There is also the problem of which premises or vehicles should be exempt, if any, and what the exact parking levy per vehicle should be in order to achieve the desired objective. To date only Nottingham City Council is seriously considering the introduction of a workplace parking levy as a means of reducing congestion.

Limiting car ownership and use

Further ways of influencing the demand for road space include:

- *Limit on car ownership* This could be achieved by imposing either import restrictions, a registration tax, or a system of rationing on cars. As yet, this is not something which has been advocated in the UK but it does occur in certain parts of the world, not only to deal with traffic congestion but also to save energy. For example, in Singapore a quota system is in operation where vehicle owners tender for a 'certificate of entitlement' without which they cannot own a vehicle.

- *System of car sharing* If successful this would also shift demand to the left in Fig. 12.3.

- *Increase in road fuel duty* This was introduced by the Chancellor of the Exchequer in the March 1993 Budget. The road fuel duty was increased by 10% and it was announced that in future Budgets the duty would be increased, in real terms, by at least 3%, though this was subsequently abandoned after the fuel price protests of 2000. Although the stated reason for this policy was environmental, directed towards reducing carbon dioxide emissions, it would also act as a disincentive to car ownership and use. This policy, whilst being welcomed by the Royal Commission on Environmental Pollution (1994), was perceived to be insufficient to achieve its environmental objectives. The Commission recommended that the duty on fuel should be doubled in price, relative to the prices of other goods, by 2005, if emission targets are to be achieved. The increase in fuel duty met with a certain amount of resistance, not least among road hauliers.

Policy options for urban road congestion – supply policies

As well as demand policies to deal with the urban road congestion problem, *supply-side policies* (such as new road building) can be implemented. An urban road building strategy can be examined by the use of Fig. 12.4.

Increasing the number of lanes, or building new roads, will shift the marginal private cost and marginal social cost curves from MPC_1 and MSC_1 respectively, to MPC_2 and MSC_2. The diagram implies that before the road capacity was expanded, congestion occurred beyond a traffic flow of F_1, but now occurs at a point beyond F_4. The reason for this is that road construction increases road capacity, so that an increased flow is now possible before the costs of congestion appear. If demand is taken to be D_2, then a flow of F_5 will now use the road, and although there will be some congestion (note that MSC_2 is greater than MPC_2 at F_5 by the distance GH) this will be somewhat less than the congestion *before* the new road expansion, which was AB in Fig. 12.4.

There is, however, a limitation with this strategy. If the road network is expanded and improved, then individuals who previously used public transport may now begin to use their own car. New traffic will therefore be *generated*, as those who did not make a particular trip previously are now encouraged to do so, and motorists who travelled via a different route may now be persuaded to use the route(s) in question. Also peak and off-peak travel can, to some extent, be viewed as substitutes, so that off-peak travel may fall. It could therefore be argued that increasing a road's capacity will result in more vehicles using the route, i.e. a case of supply generating its own demand. This means that the level of demand may well be underestimated. In fact demand could become almost perfectly elastic, as with demand curve D_3 in Fig. 12.4. If this were to be the case, then the flow of traffic along the particular route would be F_6 and not F_5, and the social cost which had not been taken into account would be EF and not GH. The final situation may not, then, be significantly different from the initial external cost of AB in Fig. 12.4. In other words, a similar congestion problem would still persist.

■ Government transport policy

In July 1998 the government published a White Paper on the Future of Transport entitled 'A New Deal for Transport: Better for Everyone' in which it was

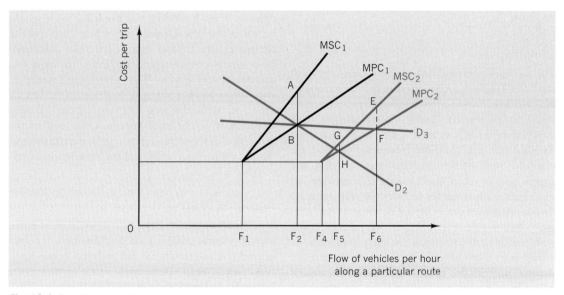

Fig. 12.4 Equilibrium traffic flow: supply-side policies.

recognized that there was a need to improve public transport and reduce car dependency. As such, a commitment was made to create an improved integrated transport system more able to tackle congestion and its associated pollution. The main aim of the White Paper was perceived to 'increase personal choice by improving the alternatives and to secure mobility that is sustainable in the long term'. There is a recognition that road building ('predict and provide') is not the answer to the growth in traffic. Integration is central to the government's thinking as stated in the White Paper (DETR 1998a).

By an *integrated* transport policy the government means:

- integration *within and between different types of transport* – so that each contributes its full potential and people can move easily between them;

- integration *with the environment* – so that our transport choices support a better environment;

- integration *with land use planning* – at national, regional and local level, so that transport and planning work together to support more sustainable travel choices and reduce the need to travel;

- integration *with our policies for education, health and wealth creation* – so that transport helps to make a fairer, more inclusive society.

Over the years, the state has attempted to influence transport in a number of ways, concerning quality, quantity, ownership, resource allocation and construction.

Quality

This has been concerned mainly with safety. In 1930 the Road Traffic Act was introduced, which required both bus operators and freight hauliers to license their vehicles with regional Traffic Commissioners. This policy was viewed, essentially, as one of protecting the public interest. This follows from the fact that, for both the road haulier and the bus operator, the capital costs of vehicle purchase are relatively low, so that there is a low barrier to entry into the industry. As a result profits can be driven down, which in turn could lead to operators trying to reduce their costs, with possibly adverse effects on safety standards. In recent years there have been a number of transport disasters and this has clearly made the whole area of transport safety a major political issue. An important

question is whether increased competition will lead to reduced safety standards!

Quantity

The licensing system has also been used as a form of regulatory control. Successive governments have been of the opinion that quantitative controls on transport were necessary in order to make sure that existing capacity was fully utilized. Such controls have applied to the road haulage and bus industries. One of the implications of licensing has been the cross-subsidization of bus services. Until 1986, the provision of unprofitable services was closely linked to the granting of licences for route monopolies by the traffic commissioners. Although certain services, such as late evenings, weekends and certain rural routes, were unprofitable, they were viewed as being 'socially' worthwhile. The financial losses on such routes were supported from the profits which the operators earned on the more profitable routes, so that cross-subsidization clearly took place. However, cross-subsidization was possible only as long as operators had monopolies; with a deregulated bus sector this was less likely.

Ownership

In the past railways and parts of the road haulage and bus passenger transport sector have been under public ownership. The main reasons put forward for such ownership include the suggestion that if the subsidization of such services was needed, then it would be easier for the government rather than private companies to control that particular operation. Government control would also allow for improved coordination of services. The government's stance on state ownership has changed, however, in the last 25 years, as with the sale of the National Freight Corporation to its employees in 1982, and of the National Bus Company following the deregulation of the bus industry in 1986 and the franchising of rail services.

Resource allocation

A major area of direct government involvement in the transport sector concerns the large amounts of public expenditure invested in the rail and road network.

In July 2000 the Department of the Environment, Transport and the Regions published *Transport 2010:*

The 10 Year Plan (DETR 2000). The Plan outlined a spending package designed to achieve the government's priorities of reduced congestion, better integration and a wider choice of quicker, safer, more reliable travel on road, rail and other public transport.

In 'Opportunity and security for all: investing in an enterprising, fairer Britain' (Treasury 2002), the government reaffirmed its commitment to providing the resources needed to deliver the improvements spelt out in the DETR's 10 Year Plan. These include:

- spending on UK transport rising at an average rate of 8.4% a year after inflation;

- the Department for Transport's own budget rising at over 12% a year on average in real terms, so that spending will be over £4 billion higher in 2005/06 than in 2002/03;

- increased purchasing power for Railtrack's successors to spend on track and infrastructure renewals and maintenance;

- delivery of new strategic road schemes through the Targeted Programme of Improvements;

- continuing increases in funding for local authority transport;

- reforms to create a more integrated system of transport planning and implementation, providing better value for money and more cost-effective delivery of this huge investment programme;

- some £370 million from unallocated capital within the 10 Year Plan being brought forward into the Spending Review to accelerate delivery;

- new funding of around £1bn per year being added to the 10 Year Plan to support the delivery of the improvements to the London Underground to be provided through the Public–Private Partnership.

Government intervention in the transport sector, characterized by state monopolies, public ownership and investment based on state priorities, can be contrasted with a '*laissez-faire*' approach. The latter involves leaving the sector to the workings of the free market, with quality, quantity and resource allocation being determined by consumer preferences. In a 'pure' *laissez-faire* situation, transport services are provided by privately owned firms and the finance of those services is based on customer fares. In this free market there would be no statutory control on entry into the sector and no financial support for those operators facing difficulties. However, the transport sector has not been left to the free market, for many of the reasons mentioned above, although there has been a move in recent years to allow certain parts of the transport sector to operate in a 'freer' market. This has been the case with the private financing and construction of the Channel Tunnel, the deregulation of the bus industry and the private financing of road construction. There is now a general consensus that road supply cannot realistically be expanded sufficiently to meet demand. The need for demand management policies has therefore become more widely accepted and these will become an increasingly important part of any government's transport policy in the foreseeable future.

Private road construction

In May 1989 the government published a Green Consultation Paper entitled 'New Roads by New Means' which set out proposals for the private funding of roads. Private-sector companies would now be invited to bid for contracts to design, build, finance and operate (DBFO) privately financed road schemes. As well as building new motorways, improvement to existing roads was also envisaged.

The rationale for private-sector roads is based on the premise that it allows (in theory at least) more roads to be built than would be the case if government-funded road schemes were the only ones undertaken. Also, because private road builders would be using their own finance plus that of their shareholders, they would have to bear the risk of financial failure. This being so, greater care would be taken to ensure that projects were completed on time and within the financial constraints laid down. Essentially, it would mean that the risk would be transferred from the public sector to the private sector.

Roads would, of course, be built only if the construction company believed that demand was sufficient to generate an adequate return on the capital investment. The private road builders would charge for the use of such roads, which would ensure that the users paid directly for the resources they consumed. In return for being charged for the use of the road, the user would receive a higher-quality road service. However, there are a number of issues which need to be considered as regards private-sector road projects. If a system of tolls were used they could create problems in being collected, which could in itself create congestion. They may also create problems of road design, because the number of toll exits has to be limited. However, the problem of toll collection could, to some extent, be dealt with by having vehicles fitted with an electronic identity plate. This would allow cars to pass through a toll point with a pre-paid bank account being directly debited. Tolls would be based on what motorists were prepared to pay, although in monopoly situations (such as river crossings) the government would have to fix a maximum charge in line with the 'public interest'. It is likely, however, that private-sector finance would be attracted only to those parts of the country which were experiencing relatively high levels of economic growth, and that the public sector would have to provide for the less economically attractive regions.

In saying this, a number of roads have been constructed, such as the A1(M) improvement near Peterborough which is based on the DBFO contractual arrangements. The contract involves the private sector in providing or improving a particular road and with its management over a 30-year period. The private sector raises the funds and is remunerated by the government based on the usage of the road. Essentially a 'shadow toll' system is used. A 'shadow toll' is one where the private construction company makes an agreement to build or improve a road and is then reimbursed by the government, depending on the number of vehicles which use the road. One benefit of using such a 'shadow toll' is that it avoids the disruption of the traffic flow caused by the collection of actual tolls. The Birmingham northern relief road, in order to relieve congestion, has been financed privately. It opened in January 2004 and is intended to take pressure off the M6, which carries up to 180,000 vehicles a day through the suburbs of Birmingham. A differential pricing system of £3 per trip for cars but £11 for lorries has been criticized as too expensive for the latter.

Deregulation of the bus industry

Prior to 1930, the local urban and rural bus industry operated in a competitive market structure with no government regulation. There was fierce competition between rival bus companies (using surplus war vehicles) and this period was associated with a high number of accidents, unscheduled and irregular intervention by 'pirate' operators at peak times, and other types of wasteful duplication.

It was for these reasons that, in 1930, the *Road Traffic Act* was introduced, which was to form the basis of bus industry regulation for 50 years. Under the Act, Traffic Commissioners were responsible for the issue of road service licences (a licence being required for each route operated), the quality of vehicles and the level of fares.

The period 1930 to 1980 was therefore a restrictive one for the local bus service industry. A comprehensive public transport network was provided under a protectionist system, with a licence acting as a barrier to entry, since a licence gave the operator a monopoly on a particular route for the duration of the licence. In 1930 the industry was dominated by private bus operators but, as it developed, the state took a progressively larger role, as with the formation in 1968 of the National Bus Company (NBC) and the Scottish Bus Group (SBG). This meant that by 1986 the industry consisted of state-owned operators, the local authority sector and independent companies which mainly operated in the contract hire sector (including school bus provision).

Changes were regarded as necessary by the mid-1980s. There had been a steady decline in patronage, with bus and coach passenger travel falling from 42% of total travel in 1953 to 8% in 1983. The growth in the use of the private car, fare increases in excess of the inflation rate, increased operating costs and the decline in services were seen as the chief reasons for the decline in bus/coach travel.

The Conservative government started on the changes with the *1980 Transport Act*, which abolished road service licences for long-distance express coach travel, and with the decision to establish the 'trial areas' of Devon, Hereford and Worcester, and Norfolk, for local bus service deregulation. For long-distance coach travel, the Act allowed companies which met certain safety standards to enter the market and to offer whatever service they chose. By 1989, passenger prices on the main trunk roads were 15% lower in real terms, and coach frequency 70% higher, as compared to the position prior to deregulation (Thompson and Whitfield 1990).

The 1984 White Paper on Buses stated:

> The total travel market is expanding. New measures are needed urgently to break out of the cycle of rising costs, rising fares, reducing services, so that public transport can win a bigger share of this market. We must get away from the idea that

the only future for bus services is to contract painfully at large cost to taxpayers and ratepayers as well as travellers. Competition provides the opportunity for lower fares, new services, more passengers. For these great gains, half measures will not be enough. Within the essential framework of safety regulation and provision for social needs, the obstacles to enterprise, initiative and efficiency must be removed.

The White Paper led to the *1985 Transport Act*, through which (by October 1986) road service licensing requirements were abolished outside London. Provision was also made in the Act for the privatization of the National Bus Company. The Passenger Transport Executives operating in metropolitan areas were to be converted into independent companies, still owned by the local authorities, but those authorities now had the option to privatize them. Local bus operators had to register their routes and times and to give sufficient notice of withdrawal of services. There was also the introduction of competitive tendering for the unprofitable bus routes.

So the main objective of the 1985 Act was to introduce competition into the bus sector, providing the opportunity for independent bus operators which did not offer licensed services before 1986, now to do so. It was envisaged that there would be a number of benefits from deregulation:

- firstly, increased competition, allowing greater choice for the consumer and providing a service which is more responsive to the preferences of the consumer;

- secondly, a closer relationship between bus operating costs and the fares charged, the reason being the ending of cross-subsidization, whereby certain routes were overcharged in order to subsidize non-profitable routes. This was helped, of course, by the freedom of entry for new operators after 1986, which in principle should compete away any 'monopoly profits' from charging excessive fares on routes, unrelated to costs;

- thirdly, providing a greater potential for innovation in bus travel under deregulation, which was less likely in the absence of competition. One such innovation following deregulation has been the introduction of minibus services;

- fourthly, a reduction in the subsidies obtained by bus operators to undertake unprofitable services.

The revenue support from government had increased from £10m in 1972 to £529m in 1982. It could be argued that such subsidies created a protective wall behind which bus operators could operate inefficient services.

There were, however, reservations as to the likely success of bus deregulation, most notably the view that it could lead to a wasteful duplication of services on the profitable routes, especially at peak periods, with a resulting increase in the level of congestion in a number of urban areas. Further, it was feared that the intended reduction in the level of subsidy to the bus sector after deregulation might lead to a rise in the level of fares, thereby diminishing bus use.

Bus services since deregulation

In terms of local bus services in England (outside London), there has in fact been an increase in annual bus kilometres travelled. In 1985/86, the year before deregulation, 1,423m bus kilometres were undertaken, whereas by 2000/01 around 1,774m bus kilometres were recorded, an increase of 25%.

Although there has been an *increase in bus kilometres travelled* since deregulation, there has also been a *decrease in passenger journeys* in England from 4,808m in 1985/86 to 3,798m in 2001/02, a decline of 21%. There is little doubt that deregulation has been a contributing factor to the decline in bus use by passengers. One reason, at least immediately after deregulation, is the confusion which passengers experienced due to the changes in service times, routes and operators resulting from deregulation. Higher fares may also have played a part in the reduction in passenger journeys. In Great Britain between 1995 and 2001/02, local bus fares increased by 30.6%, whereas the RPI increased over the same period by only 16.6%. A factor in these price increases has been the reduction in Local Authority subsidies for bus services, which fell by over £520m in real terms between 1985/86 and 1996/97. Another factor in the recorded price increases was the ending of the 'cheap fares policies' by the Public Transport Executives (PTEs) in metropolitan areas over the period 1985–87. Of course the reduction in passenger use of buses has been a trend over a long period of time, closely related to the increase in car ownership and use.

Deregulation of buses can also be assessed in terms of its impact on operating costs. Over the period

1990–91 to 2000–01 bus operating costs fell from 124p per vehicle kilometre (excluding depreciation at 2000/01 prices) to 99p in 2000/01.

According to the government's White Paper on the Future of Transport 1998 bus deregulations outside London caused substantial upheaval because of 'bus wars' and confusion over changing service patterns. There have been some good examples of innovation, but frequent changes to bus services, poor connections and the reluctance of some bus operators to participate in information schemes or through-ticketing has undermined bus services. In this climate, it was not easy for buses to match the levels of comfort, reliability and access offered by the private car.

In response to this, 'Quality Partnerships' made statutory by the Transport Bill (2000) have been developed. These already exist in a number of towns and cities but the view is that they need to be more widespread. These partnerships are between local authorities and the bus operators, with local authorities providing traffic management schemes such as bus priority at traffic lights, bus lanes and park-and-ride sites, and operators providing an improved quality of service. The partnerships have seen substantial investment by bus operators in recent years, resulting in fleets of new buses, improved services and passenger growth.

British Rail privatization

In July 1992 the government published a White Paper entitled *New Opportunities for the Railways* (Cm 2012) in which it put forward plans for the privatization of BR, the objective being to 'improve the quality of railway services by creating many new opportunities for private sector involvement'. The ensuing Railways Act 1993 provided for the privatization of British Rail and incorporated a number of major changes.

A track authority was established, namely *Railtrack*, which owned and managed the railway infrastructure, in particular the track, signalling and stations. Railtrack was also responsible for coordinating the timetable of services, for making sure that safety standards were adhered to (although ultimately the safety of the network is the responsibility of the Health and Safety Executive) and for investing in new, and modernizing existing, infrastructure.

Railtrack has now been replaced by a national railway infrastructure provider, namely *Network Rail Infrastructure Limited*. The majority of the infrastructure provider's revenue comes from charging the users of the track and from income obtained through the leasing of stations. Stations, given their prime site location in many towns and cities and thus their potential for new office and shopping development, are in fact likely to prove important sources of revenue.

The *Office of the Rail Regulator* (ORR) has specific objectives:

- to promote the interests of passengers;
- to promote the development of rail freight;
- to ensure that Network Rail Infrastructure Limited acts as a responsible and efficient steward of the national rail network by operating, maintaining, renewing and developing the network to provide the improvements expected by passengers, freight users and funders;
- to ensure that where workable competitive structures can be achieved and can benefit users, these are promoted and that monopoly is controlled to protect and benefit users; and
- to ensure that regulated contracts and licences operate, develop and improve in a way that promotes the interests of passengers and freight users, making clear where ORR shall intervene.

ORR works closely with other key stakeholders within the sector, including the Strategic Rail Authority (SRA) and the Health and Safety Executive (HSE). The SRA sets down railway strategies and represents the interests of passengers and freight via the provision and management of passenger train operating franchises, the provision of rail freight grants and the enforcement of consumer protection conditions which are contained within the operating licence.

The goods for the SRA are:

- growth over the period of the government's 10 Year Plan of 50% in passenger traffic (measured in passenger kilometres) and 80% in freight traffic (measured in freight tonne kilometres);
- reducing overcrowding on services within the London area to meet standards set by the SRA; and
- improved performance in the form of train service punctuality and reliability.

The implications

The privatization of British Rail has offered a number of opportunities, although difficulties have been experienced. In terms of the opportunities, the Department of Transport, in a paper entitled 'Britain's Railways: A New Era' (March 1994), stated that privatization would:

■ allow competition to be introduced into the provision of rail services, improving efficiency and the quality of service;

■ mean that additional investment could be provided by the private sector; and

■ allow subsidies to continue, but their allocation would be such that it would be clearer to see where they were being spent.

It is certainly the case that a privatized sector has allowed companies such as bus operators to run rail services. This has created a number of attractive opportunities in that they have similar skills, bus companies being experienced public transport operators with considerable market knowledge in terms of service design, passenger requirements, publicity and marketing.

A view has been expressed that British Rail was too bureaucratic in the past, which meant it was slow to change and take advantage of new ideas. It has also been stated that British Rail had a management structure which was engineering dominated and weaker in terms of customer relations. Proponents of privatization argue, therefore, that it allowed managers the opportunity to become more customer oriented.

There have, however, been a number of difficulties associated with rail privatization. Potential franchisees have been deterred from entering the rail sector by the fear that they would have insufficient control over their operation. The provision of a train service is the total sum of many factors. The franchisee, however, has only a limited influence over certain aspects of its operation. This has certainly been the case in terms of the track, the signalling, and the quality and availability of the rolling stock.

It has been argued that rather than reducing the level of bureaucracy there has been an increase, with hundreds of contracts and a fragmentation of responsibility. Since the franchising of services began there appears to have been a deterioration in the punctuality and reliability of rail services. In the first quarter of 1998, for example, passenger complaints almost doubled compared with the same period in 1997. In October 2000, after a number of high-profile rail accidents, Railtrack was placed into administration, emerging as *Network Rail*.

Conclusion

This chapter has attempted to identify, and analyse, a number of the current issues facing the transport sector, notably road congestion and the role of the state in transport provision. Transport, as a derived demand, is an important sector of the UK economy, accounting for some 15% of household expenditure. The period 1990–2001 saw a 4% increase in the demand for passenger transport and this is expected to continue, with the car dominating. Income has been viewed as a major factor in determining that demand and its future growth. Forecasting the future patterns of demand is seen as essential for governments when deciding on the allocation of funds to possible new road developments. The increased reliance on the car has created a major problem of congestion, particularly in urban areas, and in recent years this has become more of a political issue. A number of possible solutions have been examined, originating from both the supply and demand sides. On the supply side, it is clear that it is not possible to provide sufficient road capacity to meet the likely growth in demand. Demand needs therefore to be 'managed', and demand-side policies have been extensively used. Road user charging is viewed by many to be the best method of dealing with the congestion problem, albeit part of a package of measures.

The public sector plays an important role in the transport sector, as regards both its expenditure on such aspects as the national roads system and its ownership of parts of the sector. The last 30 years have, however, seen a move towards a transport sector operating in a 'freer' market. Major parts of the sector have been privatized, the bus industry has been deregulated and there has been increased private-sector involvement in the provision of the transport infrastructure. This chapter has sought to examine the possible reasons for this move towards a free-market sector, together with the likely advantages and disadvantages.

Key points

- In the 1950s only 25% of passenger journeys were by car; today the figure has risen to over 80%.

- Transport is a service which is a *derived* demand, with important peak and off-peak characteristics.

- Transport, particularly road transport, is a major source of pollution and of other externalities, e.g. congestion.

- A *speed–flow curve* is a useful means of analysing congestion.

- The CBI estimates that every British household must spend at least an *extra* £5 per week in order to meet the costs to business of road and rail congestion.

- Policy options to deal with congestion are various. Those involving *demand* include road user charging, subsidies to public transport, parking restrictions and limits to car ownership. Those involving *supply* include more extensive and better integrated transport networks.

Now try the self-check questions for this chapter on the Companion Website. You will also find up-to-date facts and case materials.

References and further reading

Confederation of British Industry (1989) *The Capital at Risk: Transport in London Task Force Report*.

Department for Transport (2002) *Transport Statistics Great Britain 2002*, London, The Stationery Office.

Department of the Environment, Transport and the Regions (DETR) (1998a) *A New Deal for Transport: Better for Everyone*, Government's White Paper on the Future of Transport (Cm. 3950).

Department of the Environment, Transport and the Regions (DETR) (1998b) *Breaking the Log Jam; The Government's consultation paper on fighting traffic congestion and pollution through road user and workplace parking charges*, London, The Stationery Office.

Department of the Environment, Transport and the Regions (DETR) (2000) *Transport 2010: The 10 Year Plan*, London, The Stationery Office.

Department of Transport (1984) *Buses*, HMSO (Cmnd 9300).

Department of Transport (1989) *New Roads by New Means – Bringing in Private Finance*, HMSO (Cmnd 698).

Department of Transport (1992) *New Opportunities for the Railways*, HMSO (Cmnd 2012).

Goodwin, P. B. (1990) Demographic impacts, social consequences, and the transport debate, *Oxford Review of Economic Policy*, 6(2), Summer.

House of Commons Transport Committee (1993) Fourth Report, The Government's Proposals for the Deregulation of Buses in London, HMSO.

House of Commons Transport Committee (2003) First Report of Session 2002–03 Urban Charging Schemes, London, The Stationery Office, HC390-I.

National Economic Research Associates (NERA) (1997) The Costs of Road Congestion in Great Britain, NERA Briefing Paper.

National Statistics (2002) *Transport Statistics, Great Britain*, London, The Stationery Office.

National Statistics (2003) *Family Spending, a Report on the 2001–02 Expenditure and Food Survey*, London, The Stationery Office.

Newbery, D. M. (1990) Pricing and congestion: economic principles relevant to pricing roads, *Oxford Review of Economic Policy*, **6**(2), Summer.

Royal Commission on Environmental Pollution (1994) Eighteenth Report, Transport and the Environment, HMSO (Cm2674).

Thompson, D. J. and Whitfield, A. (1990) Express Coaching: Privatization, Incumbent Advantage and the Competitive Process, Centre for Business Strategy Working Paper, London Business School.

Treasury (2002) Opportunity and security for all: Investing in an enterprising, fairer Britain, *New Public Spending Plans 2003–2006*, London, The Stationery Office, Cm5570.

Chapter 13 Social policy

This chapter will focus on the various methods by which resources might be allocated within the social policy area. In this sense it might be more accurately titled 'The economics of social problems' or even 'Welfare State economics'. After briefly reviewing the nature of the Welfare State, we look at a number of market and quasi-market means of resource allocation. The context for our analysis will be three key areas of welfare provision, namely health care, education and housing. Of course relevant materials can also be found in other chapters, especially those involving the distribution of income and wealth (Chapter 14), public expenditure (Chapter 18), taxation (Chapter 19), and unemployment (Chapter 23).

The Welfare State

The term 'Welfare State' is broadly applied to those social welfare services in an economy which are organized and provided by the government. Indeed some two-thirds of public spending is represented by welfare services such as health, education, housing and social security (see Chapter 18).

It may be useful at the outset to identify what the Welfare State seeks to achieve. The popular view is that it seeks to relieve poverty – but far broader aims have been advanced in favour of the Welfare State. At least four key (if overlapping) aims can be identified in support of the public provision or finance of welfare services:

1 Relief of poverty and redistribution of income towards the long-term poor.

2 Smoothing out the level of income over the life cycle, i.e. acting as a kind of 'savings bank' between periods of high and low earning and during periods of non-employment, e.g. while undertaking education or in retirement.

3 Insurance for everyone against life's risks, e.g. long-term illness, unemployment, early retirement, family breakdown and so on.

4 Redistribution towards particular groups with greater needs, e.g. the sick, the disabled, the unemployed or those with pressing family circumstances (e.g. single parents).

Given these broad aims of welfare policy it would be unrealistic to expect only the poor to receive welfare services. Nevertheless there is much debate as to whether the 'wrong' people are benefiting from welfare spending, such as middle-class households receiving child benefit or high-income households receiving state pensions. The period of economic recession in the early 1990s helped to heighten such concern, since all welfare services either are direct transfer payments from tax revenue or involve government provision at (subsidized) prices considerably below cost, and sometimes even at zero prices.

Demographic patterns are placing considerable strain on the operation of the Welfare State in its present form. For example, the current system relies on those generations *in work* paying more into the system than they receive in benefits to cover the needs of those generations currently in retirement. In other words the system works on a 'pay as you go' principle, rather than banking the contributions of each generation for the future use of that generation once it has retired. Those who are currently aged 59 years have, on average, paid £40,000 more into the system than they have as yet received; the implied inter-generational contract is that they will receive most, if not all, of this back over the rest of their lives during retirement. However, if the share of GDP allocated to the welfare state is reduced, with greater emphasis on private insurance to cover future welfare needs, then this inter-generational contract will be breached. Those in work will then have to pay much more over their working lives (to cover both their own future needs and those currently retired or about to retire) than they can expect to receive back over their entire life cycle. In some sense they will be 'paying twice' – once for previous generations who, now being too old, lack the opportunity of private insurance provisions, and once for themselves.

Demographic pressures are also putting the welfare state under great strain. By 2030 the proportion of the population over 65 years is expected to be 18.4%, almost 4% higher than in 2003. Such an ageing population is expected to increase the UK *dependency ratio* – the non-working population divided by the working population – from 0.52 in 2003 to 0.62 by 2030, implying that those in work will need to support a greater number of retired persons. This is, of course, a key reason why some policy-makers regard it as inevitable that the implied inter-generational contract will be breached, as already discussed. If the present system were to continue, each worker would be required to contribute some 18% *more* in real income to sustain the current level of welfare provision into 2030. To improve the quality of welfare provision in the future would require still greater real income contributions from those in work.

Quasi-markets in welfare provision

The provision of many welfare services is increasingly being undertaken by what might be called *quasi-markets* or *internal markets* instead of being directly controlled by a government department, as previously. In many cases the state ceases to provide the services in question, relying instead on independent institutions to compete against each other to win contracts to supply such services. As well as competition on the supply side there is usually a purchasing aspect on the demand side of the quasi-market, often state funded. Since outcomes (in terms of allocation of resources) are determined by the interaction of supply and demand, typical of any market, we can reasonably use the term 'market' to describe these emerging mechanisms of welfare provision. However, there are a number of aspects on both the supply and demand sides which are untypical of any market – hence the term 'quasi':

- On the supply side there is a wider variety of *types of service provider* than is usual in a market – for example, private 'for profit' organizations, private 'not for profit' organizations (e.g. voluntary bodies and charities), various public organizations, etc. There is therefore a greater than usual diversity of ownership structures and organizational objectives than is typical of more conventional markets.

- On the demand side, consumer purchasing power is often expressed in terms of *vouchers*, or *budgets* allocated for specific purposes, rather than in terms of cash changing hands.

- On the demand side, instead of market preferences being expressed by the consumer directly, as in normal markets, the consumer's preferences are often expressed indirectly by an *agent* or *intermediary* (e.g. a GP, health authority, care manager, etc.).

Many advocates of these emerging quasi-markets argue that they promote greater efficiency in supply, respond more rapidly to consumer preferences and are more accountable to those who fund their operation. Critics argue that the market conditions necessary for such favourable outcomes do not exist in most welfare sectors. As a consequence, movements towards quasi-market provision will increase administrative and other transaction costs and lead to greater inequalities amongst recipients of such services. Before considering the operation of these quasi-markets in the particular sectors of health care, education and housing, it may be useful to consider the contribution of conventional economic theory to an understanding of their operation. Indeed, economic theory suggests a number of conditions which must be met if the more favourable outcomes claimed for quasi-markets are to occur.

1 *The market structure must be competitive in both supply and demand, with many providers and many purchasers.* If markets are to operate 'efficiently', in terms of price, output and quality, dissatisfied purchasers must be able to seek alternative sources of supply (i.e. there must be an absence of monopoly in supply). Similarly suppliers must not be dependent on a few, powerful purchasers, otherwise price can be kept artificially low and many potentially efficient suppliers can be driven out of business (i.e. there must be an absence of monopsony in demand).

2 *Accurate, easily accessible information as to the cost and quality of provision must be available to both suppliers and purchasers.* Otherwise suppliers will be unable to cost and price their activities appropriately, and purchasers will be unable to monitor the price and quality of the services they receive. 'Market failure' in respect of this condition could, for example, lead to suppliers reducing costs by lowering the quality of services without purchasers being aware of the fact.

3 *Profit must be a significant factor in motivating suppliers.* Price is a key 'signal' in markets and if suppliers do not respond to the signal of higher prices and profits by increasing supply, because profit is not a motivating factor, then resource allocation will be impaired. It follows that an over-representation of voluntary and charitable bodies in provision, pursuing various 'praiseworthy' aims, may lead to unpredictable and arguably 'inefficient' responses by suppliers to market signals.

4 *There must be few opportunities in the market for 'adverse selection' or its opposite, 'cream skimming'.* Both are the consequence of a lack of symmetry in the information available to sellers and buyers and may inhibit the existence of a market. In the case of 'adverse selection', purchasers who know themselves to be 'bad risks' but who are not known to be so by providers, may be over-represented in the market. This will reduce profitability for providers and may even cause the welfare provision to cease as suppliers make excessive losses. On the other hand, 'cream skimming' can impair market efficiency by permitting providers to use information available only to themselves to select purchasers who are 'good risks', thereby raising profits. In this case welfare services may fail to reach those who most require them.

We shall refer back to some of the aspects of quasi-markets considered in this section as we look in more detail at the provision of particular welfare services.

Health care

Since the National Health Service (NHS) was instituted in 1948 following the earlier Beveridge Report (1942), the majority of health care services have been provided via a relatively centralized administrative structure. A single organization funded by the state, namely the Department of Health, both purchased and provided health care services along two main routes:

■ via the Family Practitioner Committees (FPCs) to the general practitioners (GPs), dentists and pharmacists, who had contracts with the NHS to provide 'front-line' medical care; and

■ via the Regional Health Authorities (RHAs) and the District Health Authorities (DHAs), which operated the hospitals and the community units, e.g. midwives and district nurses.

Those in the front-line services would either treat patients themselves or refer them to the hospital sector. Costs would be incurred at the point of treatment and would be covered by a budgetary allocation at each point in the system.

The mandate of the NHS is to provide health care services according to need, free at the point of delivery. It was, and continues to be, financed from central government tax revenues via the Consolidated Fund. Some 80% of funding is via these tax revenues with another 14% via a proportion of the National Insurance contributions of employers and employees, with only around 4% of NHS receipts currently funded via charges for prescriptions, dental services, etc. The consequence for resource allocation of providing health care services essentially free at the point of delivery can be discussed using Fig. 13.1.

We assume demand for health care services to be downward sloping with respect to price, i.e. people demand fewer treatments per time period if price rises. If a market were established with demand D_1 and a short-run supply S_1 (here perfectly inelastic supply), then a price P_1 would be established with an equilibrium number of treatments demanded and

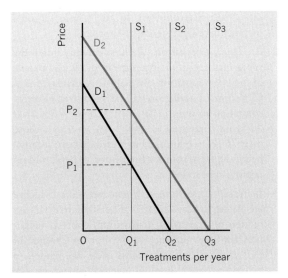

Fig. 13.1 Demand and supply of health care.

supplied per year of Q_1. If demand now increases to D_2, then *price adjusts* in the market, rising to P_2 to allocate the unchanged Q_1.

However, as we have seen, the NHS does not operate by price adjustment but by *quantity adjustment* (since service is free at the point of treatment); with the initial demand D_1, at zero price $0Q_2$ treatments are demanded. This requires the supply curve of treatments to shift rightwards to S_2 if the NHS is to satisfy this demand. If demand now rises to D_2, supply must further increase to S_3, since no price adjustment is permitted, otherwise $Q_3 - Q_2$ patients would be untreated, leading to a rise in waiting lists. It is clear that by relying mainly on quantity adjustment, the NHS must either allocate more resources to health care in the face of increased demand or accept a rise in waiting lists.

Factors behind the demand for health care services

A commonly observed trend in the UK, as in other advanced industrialized countries, has been that of a substantial and persistent increase in demand for health care services. A number of well-attested factors underlie this increase:

1 *A high income elasticity of demand for health care services.* The rise in NHS spending has grown

more than in proportion to any rise in national income (here GNP at constant prices).

2 *An ageing population.* We have already noted the rapid increase in the proportion of elderly people in the UK population. By 2011 it is estimated that 17% of the population will be aged over 65 years compared to only 11% in 1951, with 4.5% over 80 years compared to only 1.4% in 1951, those over 75 years old (together with newborn infants) being the main source of increased expenditure on health care services.

3 *Increased deprivation/economic recession.* Evidence has begun to accumulate that health care needs are related to aspects of deprivation, such as unemployment, low income, etc. We note in Chapter 23 that each successive business cycle has tended to exhibit a higher level of unemployment at any given stage than have previous business cycles. Evidence has been collected which indicates that those Regional Health Authorities with the highest unemployment rates are those which issue the most prescriptions per year, suggesting that rising unemployment is associated with increasing ill health.

4 *Advances in medical technology.* New methods and procedures are available today to treat conditions which previously would have been left untreated.

5 *Higher expectations.* With greater awareness by patients of rights and opportunities (e.g. Patients' Charter), there is a progressively higher expectation of treatment than in earlier times.

Of course the list could readily be extended; what has become abundantly clear is that demand has outstripped supply in many health care specialities, with waiting lists frequently growing as a means of rationing by quantity adjustment rather than price adjustment.

Supply and cost factors

In addition to the problem of ever-increasing demand, the NHS faces substantial *cost increases* in real terms with *health care price inflation* in the UK estimated to be rising twice as fast as general price inflation (Chalkley 2001). With the NHS costing over £68bn per year (second only to Social Security among the spending departments), accounting for some 20% of UK government total spending, employing over one million persons, dispensing 435m drug prescriptions per year, and treating 8m in-patients and 20m out-patients per year, the scope for governmental concern at rising costs and expenditures is obvious.

In 2003, total health care spending in the UK was only some 7% of GDP, much less than the 'average' of 8.6% of GDP for the EU countries and the 13.6% of GDP for the US. In an attempt to close this 'health care gap', the Chancellor has committed the UK government to a 7.3% annual real-term growth in expenditure on the NHS over the period 2002–05.

Creating an internal (quasi-)market

In April 1991 the then Conservative government introduced major changes into the UK health care market. The responsibility for *purchasing* health care was to be separated from the responsibility for *providing* it.

According to the White Paper preceding the 1991 reforms, the health service reforms were intended to achieve two objectives, namely:

> To give patients, wherever they live in the UK, better health care and greater choice of the services available [and to produce] greater satisfaction and rewards for those working in the NHS who successfully respond to local needs and preferences.

These objectives were to be accomplished by the implementation of a number of key measures.

- First, increased delegation of responsibilities from central to local levels, for example the delegation of functions from Regions to Districts, and from Districts to individual hospitals.

- Second, certain of the larger hospitals were invited to apply to become NHS Hospital Trusts. Trust status would permit the hospital increased freedom of action in terms of local pay settlements, easier access to borrowing, more choice in deciding upon output mix (e.g. types of speciality) and new opportunities to retain profit. There would then be hospitals managed directly by the District Health Authority (DHA) and hospitals with NHS Trust status.

■ Third, all hospitals in the future were to be free to offer their services, at agreed prices, to any DHA in the UK, and to the private sector. Previously hospitals within a given area normally treated only patients originating from within that area.

■ Fourth, a facility was to be provided for the larger general practices to hold and operate their own budgets, for the purchase of services directly from hospitals and to cover drug prescribing costs. This meant the creation of a new category of General Practitioner Fund Holders (GPFH). For smaller practices the GPs could *combine* to form various types of commissioning groups, purchasing on behalf of individual GPs within such groups.

The new NHS structure introduced in 1991 was to be as shown in Fig. 13.2(a). The Department of Health (through the NHS Executive) allocates funds to Regional Health Authorities (RHAs) according to demographic 'needs'. These are in turn allocated to District Health Authorities (DHAs), NHS Trusts and GP Fund Holders. Notice the beginnings of extensive contractual relationships between the various 'players' (dashed lines).

Note that the internal market established in 1991 was *not* a private market in the normal sense. It was not the patients who were to make the purchasing decisions, as they do in the case of US health care, for example; rather it was the DHAs and the GPs who were to have the spending power, allocated to them from the RHA or, as in the case of the GP Commissioning Groups, allocated to them from the DHA. On the basis of this budget allocation, the purchaser can then effect a health treatment on behalf of the patient in any one of three ways. Treatment may be purchased first, from a (managed) hospital administered by a DHA; second, from a hospital with Trust status; or third, from a private sector hospital, i.e. one totally outside the NHS.

Table 13.1 shows the main purchasers and providers of health care services. Note that we have included the private sector. The 'purchasers' include private patients paying directly for treatment or, more usually, through health insurance schemes (e.g. BUPA).

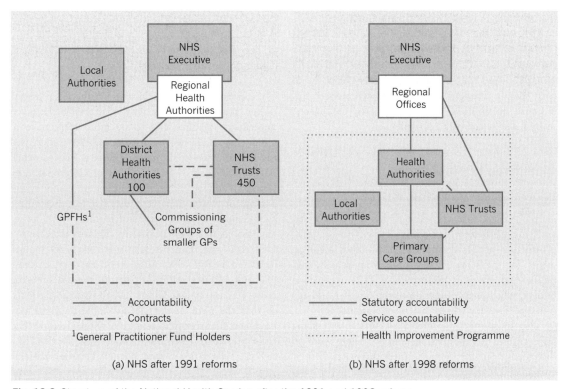

Fig. 13.2 Structure of the National Health Service after the 1991 and 1998 reforms.

Table 13.1 Purchasers and providers of health care.

Purchasers	Providers
District Health Authority (DHA)	NHS Trust hospitals
GP Fund Holders (GPFH)	District managed hospitals
GP Commissioning Groups	
Private patients	Private hospitals

The 'providers' include private hospitals which may offer services to NHS patients. Equivalently, NHS hospitals may offer services to private patients. Some exchange between the public and private sector has occurred previously but its extent was expected to increase under the new reforms.

The Conservative government argued in 1991 that the introduction of competition on the supply side would encourage efficiency. Providers competing for contracts with purchasers would have to be efficient or face a possible loss of business. Purchasers, because they had finite budgets, would have incentives to seek out efficient providers. The government also argued that this system would increase patient choice.

However, the efficiency benefits claimed for this internal (quasi-)market in health care depend upon the 'signals' or incentives given to both providers and purchasers and the nature of their likely response to such signals (Propper 1993). We now consider this in more detail: first, the incentives to purchasers; second, the incentives to providers.

Incentives to purchasers

District Health Authority (DHA)

As purchasers, districts were to be responsible for assessing the health care needs of their populations, prioritizing needs, developing contracting arrangements for the services they wish to purchase, and monitoring provider performance. They received a budget, which was a function of the number and age of the persons for whom they were responsible.

The incentives for increased efficiency facing DHAs were, however, rather limited. There were no direct sanctions for failing to meet the needs of their consumers. Managers were not rewarded on the basis of health care outcomes and so were not directly rewarded for doing what the new system intended them to do. It was relatively costly for districts to gather information about the *outcomes* of care from different providers since they had no direct contact with patients. This high cost of acquiring information meant that at the margin, districts probably under-collected such information.

General Practitioner Fund Holders (GPFH)

Alongside districts, the 1991 reforms gave larger general practices (providers of primary care) the opportunity to become fund holders and to assume a purchasing role. The financing for this role came from top-slicing part of the budget of the DHA in which the fund holding practice was located. Fund holders were free to place contracts with whichever hospitals they wished, and in some cases to substitute their own services for existing ones, e.g. they could now offer minor surgical procedures directly.

GP fund holders had more discretion than non-fund-holding GPs about how and when their patients were treated. They had better access than the DHAs to information about the outcomes of care from different providers, since they saw patients both *before* and *after* treatment. The costs of gathering information were therefore lower and, in this respect, fund holders were likely to be more efficient than DHAs in acting as consumers' agents.

Competition on the purchasing side between agents rather than individuals may arguably have given purchasers the incentive to be more responsive to patient needs. However, it may also have increased the risk of 'cream skimming'. This is because each purchasing agent – DHA, GPFH or Commissioning Group of smaller GPs – receives a sum of money per person for whom they were responsible, adjusted for age. General Practitioner Fund Holders were, as we have noted, in a good position to identify directly any 'bad risks', i.e. patients who were likely to require recurrent health care. They could then reject these 'bad risks' from their list of patients, thereby reducing costs. In contrast the DHAs had to treat *all* patients, so that the pool of patients available to them may have become over-represented by those deemed 'bad risks' (i.e. adverse selection). Many saw the risks of a two-tier system developing in which healthier patients would receive priority treatment from GP fund holders.

Incentives to providers

The *providers* were to be the NHS managed hospitals, NHS trust hospitals and private hospitals. The difference between the first two, the directly managed hospitals under DHA control and the trust hospitals responsible to the Department of Health, was mainly in terms of the greater contractual freedom of the latter. Trust hospitals could set their own pay scales, and decide themselves on the quantity and mix of factor inputs and types of specialism they offered (output mix).

Neither managed nor trust hospitals could make a profit on their services. Prices had to be based on *average cost*, with no cross-subsidies or price discrimination. However, this average cost pricing policy could itself lead to inefficiencies. In Fig. 13.3 we assume, for simplicity, that two hospitals, A and B, have *identical* average and marginal cost curves. We can see that although each hospital treats a different number of patients, they each have the same average cost $\overline{C}$ in a situation where Q_A treatments take place in hospital A and Q_B treatments take place in hospital B, and therefore both hospitals charge the same price according to the earlier directive on average cost pricing. However, an efficient allocation of resources (patients) would be one which allowed hospital A to charge a *lower price* than B, since scale economies are still potentially available to A which would reduce average costs with extra treatments (unlike hospital B where average costs would increase with extra treat-

ments). This lower price would then attract patients to hospital A which can provide treatment at a lower (average) cost than hospital B. Therefore the regulation insisting on average cost pricing did not permit the (quasi-) market for health care to send appropriate signals to patients. Resource allocation would then be inefficient where patients (or their agents) chose the identically priced hospital B rather than A. (Note that a marginal cost pricing principle would be more appropriate here – since MC_A at $Q_A < MC_B$ at Q_B.)

Put another way, the internal market was not structured in such a way as to allow profit signals on particular activities to guide resource allocation. Even if such profit signals had existed, the fact that all three types of provider (including even the private hospitals) may not have followed a clear profit-maximizing objective might have deflected them from reacting 'appropriately' to the profit signals. It is sometimes argued that the publicly owned managed and trust hospitals are dominated by senior managers or medical staff who seek 'break even' targets, rather than maximum profits. Such non-profit maximizing objectives may even extend to private hospitals, some of which have charitable status. It can hardly be surprising if non-profit maximizing hospitals fail to respond to profit-related signals in ways predicted by economic theory, even when such profit signals *are* transmitted in the market!

Another criticism of the operation of the internal market was that funds did not always follow the patient immediately, the result being that the efficient providers have sometimes been unable to treat more patients even when the demand has been there, since they have run out of funds. As a result treatments have had to cease in some 'efficient' hospitals once their initial targets have been met.

Characteristics of an internal market and health care provision

It may be that certain aspects of the 1991 reforms establishing an internal market were unlikely to succeed because of *intrinsic characteristics* of the market for health care provision. For example, competition is likely to yield efficiency gains only where excess capacity exists in a market. This is hardly the case in health care provision where almost all indicators point to under-supply (i.e. excess demand). In a

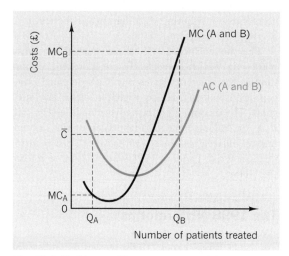

Fig. 13.3 Problems with average cost pricing.

case of under-supply in a pure market, *price* will allocate the restricted supply amongst the competing consumers (see Fig. 13.1 above). In a quasi-market, where regulations of various kinds are imposed which prevent a 'pure' price adjustment, an element of *rationing* may be inevitable. Arguably it may then be better to use certain 'objective' means of rationing rather than consumer purchasing power or the arbitrary judgements of the service providers.

A number of other problems were seen, by critics, as likely to prevent the internal market from making a significant contribution to the improvement of health care.

Asymmetry of information

When the provider and purchaser were one and the same, as with the DHAs before 1991, the quality of health care provision could be monitored through internal channels. However, they became separated after the creation of the internal market in 1991, the problem then being that while the providers may be aware of any diminution in quality of service, the purchasers may not. This *asymmetry of information* between seller and buyer is a classic instance of 'market failure' which may lead to an inefficient allocation of resources, with purchasers paying more than the competitive price for any given quality of service.

High transaction costs

The main means by which purchasers seek to gain assurances as to the price and quality of provision is by the issuing of contracts, which may of necessity be rather detailed. Drawing up such contracts takes time and money, as does the whole tendering process between rival providers and the eventual requirements for issuing and processing invoices and other documents between contracting parties. These *transaction costs* may absorb some or all of any efficiency gains via the internal market. Before the creation of the internal market some 5% of total health care spending in the UK involved administrative costs; there were fears that the internal market might raise this figure nearer to the 20% of total health care spending involving the various transaction costs commonly experienced in the US.

Non-contestable markets

To avoid excessive transaction costs, there may be the incentive for individual providers and purchasers to develop *long-term relationships* in response to the creation of an internal market. The billing and invoicing system of the respective parties might then be simplified and made compatible, as might other aspects of provision. Familiarity and convenience may then serve to make it difficult for *potential new entrants* to secure existing contracts when these are due for renewal. This lack of opportunity for new entrants may permit existing providers in the internal market to be less efficient than is technically feasible, as a result of the long-term relationships established between providers and purchasers. In other words these long-term relationships may make the internal health care market less contestable (by new entrants) than hitherto.

Monopoly provision

Some districts and regions within the internal market may be too small, in themselves, to support more than one (or perhaps even one) 'efficient' service provider. This may be the case where significant economies of scale are available in respect of various types of treatment, giving large hospitals a cost advantage. Significant travel costs (transport, time and convenience) may then deter patients (or their agents) from undermining the higher cost provision in these local monopoly cases by seeking treatment in other regions and districts.

Table 13.2 would suggest that in the case of processing blood samples, for example, very significant economies of scale do exist. A tenfold increase in throughput spreads the fixed equipment costs over much larger output, thereby reducing average fixed costs and contributing to a significant reduction in average total costs.

The move since 1991 to an internal or quasi-market in health care clearly created some opportunities for efficiency gains but it also created other conditions which may in principle offset any such gains. The incoming Labour government in 1997 felt that, on balance, the disadvantages of the internal market outweighed the advantages. It therefore introduced a White Paper in 1998 which sought to reform the NHS.

The 1998 NHS reforms

The NHS White Paper (1998) set out to replace the internal market by a system of integrated care,

Table 13.2 Average total costs for blood samples at different scales of operation.

Item	Cost per test in pence Throughput: thousands of samples				
	50	100	200	400	500
Labour	2.5	2.5	2.5	2.5	2.5
Consumables	2.5	2.5	2.5	2.5	2.5
Equipment	10	5	2.5	1.25	1
Overheads and phlebotomy costs	25	25	25	25	25
Average total cost	40	35	32.5	31.25	31

Source: Adapted from Bowers (1994).

outlined in Fig. 13.2(b) (p. 245). The focus of the reforms can be seen as providing a greater emphasis on *national planning* of health provision, with delivery a matter of *local responsibility* and involving *partnership* between the various providers.

The White Paper set out a 10-year programme for reform. The Health Authorities (HAs) were reconstituted and given stronger powers to improve the health of residents in their region and district. Over time they are to lose their responsibility for direct commissioning. Instead their main objective is to work with local authorities, NHS trusts and Primary Care Groups (PCGs) to draw up three-year Health Improvement Programmes within which all local NHS bodies operate.

HAs allocate funds to PCGs which then take the responsibility for commissioning services, working closely with local authority social services. The PCGs serve about 100,000 patients, and non-fund-holding GPs are able to influence purchasing priorities by these Groups. The independent contractor status of existing GP fund holders was allowed to continue, though no new GP fund holders would be created and the commissioning role of existing GP fund holders would progressively be undertaken by the PCGs. By these reorganizations the government claimed that the total number of commissioning bodies was drastically cut from the 3,600 or so under the internal market to around 480 PCGs and 100 HAs.

The NHS trust hospitals retain much of their operational independence but are now required to integrate their activities with local Health Improvement Programmes and to enter into long-term service agreements with the PCGs.

No matter what the nature of the reforms of health provision, in the foreseeable future there will remain a situation of under-supply (i.e. excess demand) for many types of service. This inevitably raises the issue of allocating scarce resources amongst competing possible uses. If the price mechanism is to play little, if any, role in such resource allocation (see p. 243), then alternative mechanisms must be devised. It is in this context that a number of, allegedly, more 'objective' mechanisms for resource allocation have been proposed.

Foundation hospitals and public-interest companies

Public-interest companies (PICs) are a hybrid between privatization and public ownership. They are private sector but are not driven by the profit motive, since any money they do make must be reinvested in the service. The idea is that PICs will free parts of the public sector from central control and bureaucratic structures, thereby becoming more responsive to the needs of local communities. PICs would be technically independent of the state but would have governors drawn from the local community and other stakeholders.

The *Foundation Hospitals* broadly fall into the PIC category, with potential governors including representatives of medical staff, patients and other members of the local communities. The suggestion is that all NHS hospitals should achieve Foundation Hospital status by 2008. However, the Treasury has concerns that while the debts of Foundation Hospitals would not, as private sector entities, appear on the public sector balance sheet, in practice it would be the public sector that would pick up the bill of 'rescuing' any Foundation Hospital facing financial difficulties. A Foundation Hospital might, in the Treasury's view, be free to borrow funds on capital markets without sufficient financial discipline, since it would know that the government would ultimately intervene to prevent it facing bankruptcy or administration.

Quality Adjusted Life Year (QALY) indicators

The idea here is that for individuals of specific ages a certain quality of life can be expected, as an average for such individuals. A *Quality Adjusted Life Year* (QALY) index score of 1 is then assigned to this expected life profile. Any deterioration in the expected quality of life from a given illness will reduce the QALY index below 1 and towards zero. This approach is being used to develop models for each type of treatment, and is illustrated in Fig. 13.4.

Here a patient with a particular illness has a 0.5 QALY score; in other words the particular illness has halved the expected quality of life for a patient of that age. The patient, if untreated (line A), can expect to live for three more years with a progressive deterioration in his or her condition and therefore in the QALY index. On the other hand, if treated (line B), the patient can expect to recover to a 0.9 QALY within one year (i.e. 90% of the expected quality of life), sustain that quality over a further eight years, then progressively deteriorate in the tenth year before dying.

The area between the axes and line B gives the number of Quality Adjusted Life Years from treatment. These QALYs from treatment can be compared with the number of QALYs from non-treatment (area between axes and line A), the *difference* between the areas being the QALY gained from providing appropriate treatment for that person with that illness.

Clearly a vast array of statistics are available to identify the likely prognosis and life-pattern for those with certain types and severity of illness, which should help to identify both line B (treatment) and line A (no treatment). One can then compare the QALY *gains* from treatment (B – A) with the *costs* of such treatment and can then calculate the 'cost per 1 QALY gained' for the different types of treatment. Such 'objective' data can help in making more informed decisions as to how scarce resources might be allocated.

In the UK, data has suggested a cost of £750 per QALY gained via hip replacements compared to £70,000 per QALY gained via brain surgery. An extra £1m could then yield either 1,333 QALYs if spent on hip replacement surgery, or 14 QALYs if spent on brain surgery. Table 13.3 indicates some further examples of costs per QALY. It is data such as this which is being used by bodies such as the National Institute of Clinical Excellence (NICE) which advises the government whether particular drugs and therapies are, or are not, cost-effective.

Of course there are many value judgements underlying such 'objective' measures, not least in assessing the comparative degrees of discomfort of particular illnesses and therefore the estimated pattern of decline in QALY. Further, a 'civilized' society may arguably

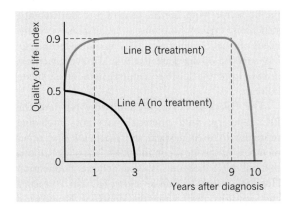

Fig. 13.4 The QALY gains from treatment.

Table 13.3 Examples of cost per QALY in the UK.

Cost of one year of quality-adjusted life arising after treatment	
Orlistat, new anti-obesity drug	£46,000
NHS smoking cessation clinic	£209
Breast cancer screening	£5,780
Kidney transplant	£4,710
Viagra	£3,639
EPO for kidney failure	£3,000–£9,000

Source: Walker (2002).

be expected to cater for *all* treatable illnesses, regardless of cost. Nevertheless the use of QALYs may at least serve as additional information to guide policy-makers in situations of under-supply where some means of rationing health care services is sought other than by pure market price.

Education and training

Clearly this is an area of wide scope and considerable complexity which merits an in-depth analysis. Here we consider only those aspects of education and training particularly relevant to the debate on market versus non-market means of resource allocation.

Benefits of education and training

Additional education or training can clearly be regarded, in part, as yielding *consumption benefits*, e.g. positive utility or pleasure to those directly involved in the process of gaining knowledge or acquiring skills. However, the main motivation to both suppliers and purchasers of education and training is likely to take the form of securing *investment benefits*, in other words, the use of scarce resources by suppliers (labour, capital) and purchasers (time, energy, money, income expended, income foregone, etc.) to yield higher future returns.

At the *micro level* this return on 'human capital investment' may originate from a rightward shift in the Marginal Revenue Product Curve (see Chapter 15). This rightward shift raises the value of labour input to both the firm and (via higher wages) the individual undertaking the education or training. At the *macro level* such investment is seen as shifting the production possibilities frontier for the economy to the right, i.e. raising what is often referred to as 'sustainable growth'. This is growth which can be attained *without* running into capacity constraints, causing inflationary or balance of payments pressures. The term 'endogenous growth' is also sometimes given to investment in education or training, 'endogenous' meaning here 'growth which develops from within'. Research by Robert Barro, for example, suggests that a 10% increase in educational attainment increases growth by 0.2% per year.

To what extent is the market capable of providing an appropriate level of education or training? What role might there be for an internal or quasi-market in this area? Before seeking to address these issues it may be useful to review the circumstances under which the purchaser or provider, respectively, might be induced to invest in a given amount of education or training.

In Fig. 13.5, suppose the individual can leave school without training at 16 years and progress along the income pathway S_1S_1'. Alternatively the individual can 'invest' in 0A years of training, paying directly the sum 0ACD as costs for this training. On completion, the higher marginal revenue product of the employee raises his or her earning potential to S_2S_2'. In addition the (full time) training period has meant an opportunity cost of $0AXS_1$ income foregone during the training period. Only if lifetime benefits exceed the lifetime costs of training is it likely that the 'investment' in training will be regarded as worthwhile. In other words the extra benefits $XS_1'S_2'S_2$ must be greater than the extra costs $0ACD + 0AXS_1$. All sums must, since they occur at different times, be discounted to a present value equivalent.

Perhaps the most comprehensive survey of this issue (IFS 1998) involved the life profiles of 2,500 individuals born in a particular week in March 1958. The study concluded that male graduates in their early 30s earned 15–20% more than men of similar age who completed A levels but did not undertake higher education. For women the average gain due to a degree was even higher, around 35%. The OECD has estimated an annualized *private* rate of return for an individual's human capital investment in a degree of around 18.5% per annum for the UK, with the *social* rate of return even higher (OECD 2001). Similarly attractive returns have been reported in other studies, with the UK government justifying its

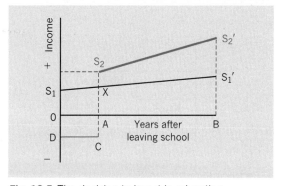

Fig. 13.5 The decision to invest in education.

recent move towards top-up fees in higher education by quoting figures suggesting that the average graduate in the UK can expect to earn about £400,000 more than a non-graduate over a lifetime (Bunting 2002).

Problems for a pure market

It is unlikely that a pure market will lead to an 'efficient' level of provision for education or training. This can be illustrated in Fig. 13.6. Suppose untrained labour has a Marginal Revenue Product of MRP_0 to the firm, and is paid the wage ($= MRP_0$) of W_0. Suppose also that the firm which provides the training does so at a cost of ($V - W_0$) per week. The total cost to the firm of providing training during the training period is therefore given by area A. However, at the end of the training period, suppose the Marginal Revenue Product of trained labour rises to MRP_1 ($> MRP_0$). To recoup the training costs the firm will now need to pay a wage *below* MRP_1 (say W_1). The minimum condition necessary to make it worthwhile for the firm to support training is that:

$$\underset{\begin{pmatrix} \text{cost of training} \\ \text{during training period} \end{pmatrix}}{\text{Area A}} = \underset{\begin{pmatrix} \text{excess of MRP after} \\ \text{training over wage paid} \end{pmatrix}}{\text{Area B}}$$

Again, of course, this equation must be expressed in present value terms, with all future sums involved discounted to their present value equivalents.

A problem for a *pure market* to be established in training would be the risks of 'poaching'. For example, a rival firm could offer to pay the trained worker at the end of the training period between W_1 and MRP_1 and still find this transaction profitable since it has not itself incurred the training costs A. If the worker leaves the company which has funded the training *before* sufficient time has elapsed for area B (in present value terms) to at least equal area A, then the company has lost at the expense of its rival. Such 'poaching', if extensive, would negate any incentives for individual firms themselves to offer an appropriate level of training opportunities.

Quasi-markets in education and training

Many of the reforms proposed for enhancing access to education and training involve aspects of the quasi-markets discussed earlier.

On the *provider* side a centralized state agency (Department for Employment and Education, or Department of Trade and Industry) is being progressively replaced by market-type mechanisms for resource allocation. In the schools, inducements have been provided for schools to 'opt out' of local authority control and to receive direct grants from central government. Budgets are increasingly allocated to schools according to their individual characteristics (formula funding) – if more pupils are attracted, more income is received. Schools have also been given greater opportunities for managing their own budgets (Local Management of Schools – LMS), becoming in effect semi-independent providers, a trend further boosted by the creation of specialist schools with additional sources of funding.

On the *purchaser side*, under open enrolment parents have greater choice, within limits, as to the school to which they send their child. The Learning and Skills Council or equivalent organizations can act as agents for consumers, selecting the educational institutions or training bodies they will fund to provide particular vocational or training courses, or even providing such courses themselves. Greater awareness of the results of different educational institutions (e.g. National League Tables) are aimed at giving 'purchasers' better information as to the quality of service provision. In total, many of these reforms have similarities with a *voucher system*, whereby parents, students or government agencies choose a particular provider, and a budget allocation directly follows that choice. Indeed, pilot projects have been run whereby education and training vouchers have been allocated to students directly to a given value which can then be spent on courses of their choice.

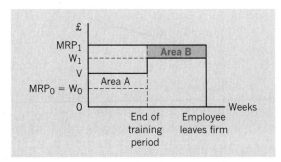

Fig. 13.6 The firm's decision to train labour.

As in the case of health care, the view of recent governments has been that increased competition among providers for the vouchers/expenditure of purchasers would raise both the efficiency of supply and the choice of consumers. We now consider a number of broad issues raised by the development of such quasi-markets in education and training.

Problems for quasi-market provision

Cream skimming and adverse selection

As with health care, the extent of efficiency gains from quasi-markets depends upon providers being unable to 'cream skim' by taking only those most likely to succeed. If certain schools *are* able to do this, other (non-specialist, non-opted-out) schools will have a progressively adverse pool from which to draw their pupils, and disparities between schools will widen rather than narrow. There is evidence to suggest that a quasi-market in which only a minority of schools become specialist or opt out is indeed likely to result in elements of selection. For example, detailed studies such as Mortimore *et al.* (1988) found that over 64% of the variance in pupil achievements could be explained by initial attainment and social background. With such a large part of the likely outcomes for pupils outside the direct influence of the schools, Glennerster (1993) concluded that 'any school entrepreneur acting rationally would seek to exclude pupils who would drag down the overall performance of the school, its major selling point to parents', a prediction even more likely to be fulfilled given the emphasis placed on testing and school 'league tables' over the past decade.

Poor information and externalities

Following on from the previous point, a selective system might (say critics) create rather misleading information and a variety of negative externalities as compared to an initially non-selective system. This is in line with the earlier point that in quasi-markets there needs to be *symmetry of information between providers and purchasers*. In a competitive and selective system, educational providers may have incentives *not to reveal* relevant factors, and parents (purchasers) may be unable to extract that information. Of course such 'secrecy' may also be the case in non-selective schools as a defence mechanism for

teachers. In any case Parents' Charters and National League Tables may help remedy information deficiencies by ensuring that schools reveal specific aspects of information about themselves. 'Value added' league tables may give still more relevant information to parents (prospective purchasers).

Selectivity may also lead to certain *negative externalities*, for example, the loss of local community ties fostered by non-selective local schools, and the loss of the improved educational outcomes attributed to average and below-average children mixing together in non-selective schooling. Opponents of this view would cite the *positive externalities* selection might give to brighter children able to progress more rapidly in a cohort of children with similar ability.

Sunk costs

A quasi-market will lead to 'winners' and 'losers', with some schools expanding and others contracting. The corollary of this is that there will be more frequent entry to, and exit from, individual schools by children. *Sunk costs* are costs which cannot be recovered on exit from a market, and arguably these will be high in an educational context where schools have become part of a community. Any closure of the less successful schools will then incur substantial sunk costs. Similarly the disruption costs to children from frequent upheaval will be considerable. Critics of this view would argue that the decline and even closure of inadequate schools is a 'price worth paying' for higher standards.

As in the case of health care, there can be no presumption that quasi-markets in education and training must of necessity create greater efficiency and choice. The issues are complex and require thorough analysis and empirical investigation. Certainly the momentum is towards extending such quasi-markets with reports such as Social Justice (1994) recommending the creation of individual learning accounts (i.e. transferable vouchers) for both pupils and employees, a scheme eventually introduced but suspended in 2001 after widespread allegations of fraud. However, the Social Justice Report recognized that pure market solutions will not work in the case of training, so it also proposed that *minimum standards* be set for all employers. For instance all employers, whether providing training or not, might be required to set aside up to 2% of payroll, reclaimable in part or full depending on the amount of training they themselves actually provide. Employers unable or unwilling to provide that level of training themselves would be required to put the *difference* into their employees' individual learning accounts or to pay the Learning and Skills Council to reimburse companies who do provide such training. Again the aim was to use quasi-markets rather than 'pure' markets to redress a situation in which nearly two-thirds of UK employers invest less than 2% of payroll costs in training, whereas three-quarters of French employers invest more than 2% and in Germany an average of 3.5% of payroll is given towards training-related programmes.

Housing

As in the case of health care and education, resources in the *housing sector* are increasingly allocated via quasi-markets. The housing associations have largely replaced the local authorities as the main providers of social housing in the UK. Government policy has largely switched from subsidizing bricks and mortar to subsidizing individual 'purchasers', via means-tested housing benefit. These 'purchasers' can then exercise some choice, subject to certain restrictions, as to the sector (whether local authority, housing association or private landlord) and type of property which will receive their 'voucher-type' payment.

Before examining some of the quasi-market issues involving housing, it may be useful to review briefly some of the main developments in so vital a sector.

Housing market developments

Growth of owner occupation

Owner-occupied housing is both an *asset* (wealth) and a *consumption good* (providing housing services which must otherwise be paid for). A rise in house prices is therefore significant in terms of a wealth effect (leading to extra consumer spending) and in changing in favour of owner occupation in preference to the now more expensive renting of property. The fact that wealth in housing has been seen over the past few decades as being more easily *transformed* into purchasing power than wealth in other assets such as insurance policies or pensions, further increased the attractiveness of owner occupation. As we can see

Table 13.4 Trends in housing data in the UK.

	Owner occupation %	Stock of dwellings (millions)	UK population: stock of dwellings	Index of real house prices (1971 = 100)
1901	10.0	8.01	4.78	–
1911	–	8.94	4.71	–
1921	–	7.98	5.52	–
1931	–	9.40	4.90	–
1939	33.0	11.50	4.20	51
1945	–	11.10	4.32	61
1951	34.5	12.39	4.05	87
1961	44.4	16.42	3.21	71
1971	52.1	18.20	3.05	100
1981	58.6	21.18	2.64	140
1991	68.0	23.00	2.52	182
1994	67.8	23.70	2.49	174
1998	69.4	24.60	2.48	207
2001	70.0	25.00	2.44	274

Sources: *Annual Abstract of Statistics* (various); *Social Trends* (2002); Miles (1992).

from Table 13.4, owner occupation rose dramatically over the twentieth century, from 10% in 1901 to 70% in 2001, with particularly rapid growth in the 1981–91 period, partly due to attractive terms for the purchase of council houses by tenants (an average of 40% discount for existing tenants wishing to purchase). Of the 25m dwellings in the UK, some 17.4m are owner occupied and around 150,000 new houses are built each year. As the supply of houses is relatively inelastic, at least in the short run, the main influence on the price of houses comes from the demand side.

Decline in rented sector

In parallel with the growth of owner occupation there has been a significant decline in the rented sector, from 90% in 1914 to around 30% in 2001. The switch towards owner occupation has come mainly from the local authority (public rented) sector which declined from 31.4% of the housing stock in 1979 to only 21% in 2001.

Increase in availability and real price of housing

Other interesting trends shown in Table 13.4 include the data on the rise in the stock of dwellings from some 8m units in 1901 to 25m units in 2001. This increase in the stock of dwellings has occurred at almost twice the rate at which the population has increased, so that the *number of persons per dwelling* has roughly halved from 4.78 to 2.44 over the period. We can also see that since shortly before the Second World War the index of *real house prices* increased more than fivefold, with real house prices rising by over 15% per annum in recent years.

Increase in housing contribution to net wealth

The rises in the stock of dwellings, in the rate of owner occupation and in real house prices have all contributed to a significant increase in *housing net wealth* held by the personal sector. Whereas housing was only 20% of the total net wealth of the personal sector in 1968, by 2001 that figure had more than doubled to around 46%. This is hardly surprising, since between 1939 and 2001 the total number of houses more than doubled and the real price increased fivefold, giving a tenfold increase in the

value of the real stock of housing. Clearly a strong housing market has played a key part in consumer confidence via a positive wealth effect, especially during the 'boom' years of the 1980s, mid- to late 1990s and early years of the millennium. Indeed there is ample evidence to support the view that the housing market led to significant 'equity withdrawal', supporting consumer spending during those years. *Equity withdrawal* is where net new lending on housing *exceeds* the amounts recorded as having actually been spent on housing!

Negative equity

The corollary of the above is that in periods characterized by the onset of recession, the housing market has played a key part in eroding consumer wealth and confidence via the mechanism of a significant rise in *negative equity*. This is the situation whereby the value of the mortgage debt outstanding on a house *exceeds* the current market value of the house. The decline in house prices between 1988 and 1995 led to a situation where over one million houses were estimated as having negative equity in 1995. The effect of this decline in house prices on consumer confidence was particularly important in the UK which has a higher ratio of net equity in housing to GDP (at 1.68) than has any other industrialized country except Japan.

Housing market and bequests

The housing market is a key factor in the transmission of wealth from one generation to another. Hamnett *et al.* (1991) found that in a random sample, 60% of all persons inheriting over £1,000 did so via the houses of their parents. The substantial rise in owner occupation noted above and the continued rise in life expectancy will make bequests of housing wealth still more important in the future. It is expected that the number of housing bequests will exceed 200,000 per year by 2010, and will double in the following 25 years.

Quasi-markets in housing

Although an extremely diverse sector, many of the current developments and proposed reforms involving housing incorporate aspects of *quasi-markets* (p. 241). In particular, moves in the rented sector towards subsidizing people (rather than bricks and mortar) with portable housing benefits are, in effect, voucher-type purchasing power characteristic of quasi-markets on the demand side. On the supply side quasi-market characteristics are also developing in the housing sector. For example, Housing Associations with an approximately 55 : 45 public–private mix are increasingly replacing local authorities as providers of new social housing. The *Social Justice* report (1994) had called for Local Housing Companies, with a mix of private and public capital, to play a leading role in providing new social housing. Although beyond our brief to investigate the relative merits of these various quasi-market solutions, we can clearly state a number of principles as to why *some form* of 'quasi' as opposed to 'pure' market solution will be needed in a housing context.

Externalities

The widespread presence of *externalities*, both positive and negative, in the housing market makes it unlikely that 'pure' market solutions will be efficient. For example, if one person renovates his house, he and his neighbours may benefit from a rise in house value. Yet only if the marginal *private* benefit exceeds the marginal private cost to the renovator will he go ahead with the housing investment. Such calculations will usually be made without taking into account any marginal *social* benefits, here the rise in house values of neighbours. In this case underprovision of housing investment would occur in a 'pure' market because of 'market failure' in the context of unaccounted positive externalities.

Complementary markets

A related argument for intervention involves cases where a market operates efficiently only for a *combination of products* rather than for a single product in isolation. There are many situations in the housing sector where an appropriate 'price' can be assigned only if *all* the aspects of housing redevelopment are brought together in a single package, hence the need for public or quasi-public bodies to be involved in major housing schemes, such as the London Dockland Development Corporation.

Institutional conventions

Certain *conventions* by the lending institutions may

preclude a market being established, even where benefits exceed costs. For example, building societies have sometimes 'red-lined' *entire geographical areas as high risk* and precluded all mortgage applications from such areas, independently of their individual merits. Similarly, 'statistical screening' practices by lenders may disadvantage entire groups of potential borrowers (e.g. the self-employed are ascribed a 'high risk' score). For these and other reasons there may need to be public provision or at least a public guarantee of loan finance advanced by private sector lenders.

Imperfect information

Efficient markets depend on full knowledge of the prices and qualities of the products traded in the market. Clearly building societies, banks and estate agents go some way to resolving this informational problem in the housing market, especially where they have branches throughout the country and can therefore advise on regional price variations. However, the fact that long and complex selling chains are still frequent (often breaking down and preventing purchase), and that building surveys are often the source of dispute or have to be repeated, suggests that the market is some way from entirely resolving this problem of imperfect information. Arguably the state has a role to play in at least guaranteeing minimum standards of professional competence for those involved in the market, though others would advocate that it should play a much more extensive informational role.

Absence of market makers

An alleged 'flaw' in the market for housing is the absence of a market maker. The function of a market maker is to both buy and sell the commodity in question, thereby establishing a market for it. Unlike, say, dealers in second-hand cars, none of the professional agencies in the housing sectors appear willing to act as market makers. The mortgage providers (building societies, banks, etc.) see their role as merely funding a contract for property; the estate agents see their role as merely introducing prospective sellers to prospective buyers. No one (except the occasional housing developer) sees their role as being that of taking the prospective buyer's *existing* property onto their books at an agreed price, thereby enabling the buyer to complete the purchase. Of course such market making would be expensive for those acting as 'principal agent' in this way, and wide margins would be required between the purchase and sale price. Nevertheless this may be a 'price' traders would be willing to pay to reduce the delay, uncertainty and frequent breakdown of selling chains. The state may again have a role to play in facilitating the operation of such 'market makers' in one way or another.

In all these ways, 'quasi' as opposed to 'pure' markets are arguably more appropriate for the housing sector. Whether in any particular situation a quasi-market is more efficient than a centralized administrative system of resource allocation must be decided on a case-by-case basis.

 ## Conclusion

The chapter has reviewed some of the four key aims, outcomes and prospects for social policy in the context of the welfare state. Three particular areas of policy have been examined: health care, education and training, and housing. It has been noted that many of the emerging means of provision in these areas involved 'quasi' rather than 'pure' market provision, as an alternative to the previously centralized and administrative means of resource allocation. Some of the conditions under which quasi-markets are likely, or unlikely, to yield 'efficient' allocative solutions have been noted, both in general and in each particular area or sector.

Key points

- Welfare services such as health, education, housing and social security make up around two-thirds of all public spending.

- The Welfare State has several objectives, including relief of poverty, life-cycle redistribution and help for particular disadvantaged groups, such as the sick, disabled and unemployed.

- The provision of welfare services is making increasing use of *quasi* or *internal* markets.

- Quasi-markets have particular characteristics: many types of service provider, use of vouchers rather than cash, use of intermediaries (agents) in purchasing.

- An excess demand at zero price in the market for health care can only be closed by increased supply or some form of 'rationing'.

- Such 'rationing' might be made more explicit and objective by the use of indicators such as QALYs (Quality Adjusted Life Years) and estimates of the cost per QALY gained.

- The UK internal market in health care has sought to separate *purchasers* from *providers* and to introduce more accountability and competition. Since 1998 various reforms have started to move the NHS away from an internal market.

- Problems such as *cream skimming*, *adverse selection*, *asymmetry of information*, presence of *negative externalities*, etc., are present in most types of welfare provision, whether health, education and training, or housing.

Now try the self-check questions for this chapter on the Companion Website. You will also find up-to-date facts and case materials.

References and further reading

Bowers, P. (1994) *Managerial Economics for the Service Industries*, Chapman and Hall.

Bunting, C. (2002) Money back guaranteed?, *Times Educational Supplement*, 8 November.

Chalkley, M. (2001) Is the NHS affordable?, *Economic Review*, **19**(2), November.

Frayne, C. (2001) Encouraging education, *Economic Review*, **19**(2), November.

Glennerster, H. (1993) The economics of education, in N. Barr, and, D. Whynes, *The Economics of the Welfare State*, Weidenfeld and Nicolson.

Hamnett, C. *et al.* (1991) *Safe as Houses*, Paul Chapman.

IFS (1998) *Higher Education, Employment and Earnings in Britain*, Institute of Fiscal Studies.

Maclennan, D. and Gibb, K. (1993) Political economy, applied welfare economics and housing in the UK, in N. Barr, and D.Whynes, *The Economics of the Welfare State*, Weidenfeld and Nicolson.

Mason, T. (2003) The housing market and the economy, *Economic Review*, **20**(3), February.

Miles, D. (1992) Housing and the wider economy in the short and long run, *National Institute Economic Review*, February.

Mooney, G. (1994) *Key Issues in Health Economics*, Harvester Wheatsheaf.

Mortimore, P. *et al.* (1988) *The Junior School Project: Understanding School Effectiveness*, ILEA Statistics Section.

OECD (2001) Investment in human capital through post-compulsory education and training, *OECD Economic Outlook*, **70**, December.

Propper, C. (1993) Incentives in the new UK health care market, *Economic Review*, February.

Smith, P. (2002a) Education and poverty, *Economic Review*, **19**(3), February.

Smith, P. (2002b) The market for higher education, *Economic Review*, **20**(2), November.

Social Justice (1994) Strategies for National Renewal.

Social Trends (2002) National Statistics.

Swift, S. (2002a) Financing health care, *British Economy Survey*, **31**(2), Spring.

Swift, S. (2002b) The Budget and the NHS, *British Economy Survey*, **32**(1), Autumn.

Walker, D. (2002) Far too nice, *Guardian*, 16 October.

Chapter 14

Distribution of income and wealth

In this chapter we review the changes that have taken place in the distribution of income and wealth in the UK. We see that there has been a significant increase in inequality of incomes in the UK since the late 1970s, though not at every income level. We assess the usefulness of the Gini coefficient as an index of inequality, and use it to compare the income distribution of the UK with that of other countries. Income from employment is examined in some detail as this provides over 65% of all income received. Factors resulting in income inequality are considered together with policies which might correct the inequalities observed. Although wealth is difficult to measure, we note a progressive tendency towards a more equal distribution in the 1970s, but then a widening of the gap once more in the 1980s, 1990s and early years of the millennium. In fact there is also clear evidence of greater inequality after 1979 at the top and bottom ends of the income distribution. This chapter concludes with a brief review of poverty in the UK.

Distribution and justice

Throughout the history of economics, the distribution of income and wealth has been a major concern. There has been not only a desire to explain the observed pattern of distribution, but also a belief that basic issues of justice and morality were involved. Positive and normative economics are therefore difficult to separate in this area.

Commutative justice

There are two main views of justice in distribution. The first may be called 'commutative justice', where it is held that each person should receive income in proportion to the value of labour and capital they have contributed to the productive process. This view underlies the ideology of the free market economy, with some economists seeking to show that commutative justice will automatically be achieved under free competition, since each factor will receive the value of its marginal product. Disparities in the distribution of income and wealth are then seen as being quite consistent with 'commutative justice'.

Distributive justice

The second view may be called 'distributive justice', where it is believed that people should receive income according to need. Given that people's needs are much the same, 'distributive justice' implies approximate equality in income distribution. This view underlies the ideology of socialism. The socialist sees the free market as a kind of power struggle, through which certain groups are exploited; hence their advocacy of various forms of social control of the economy to achieve 'distributive justice'.

Issues in distribution

In the debate about distribution, there are five specific areas of concern:

1 The distribution of income between persons, irrespective of the source of that income. Included here is income from labour (wages and salaries), and from the ownership of capital (dividend and interest) and land (rent).

2 The distribution of income between factors of production, in particular between labour and capital. Advocates of the free market believe that income accrues to labour and capital according to their relative productivity, whilst critics explain their relative shares as the outcome of a continuous conflict in which capital seeks to exploit labour, and labour to resist.

3 The distribution of earnings between different types of labour. Again, believers in the free market see differences in earnings between occupational groups as being caused by differences in relative productivity. Critics explain such differentials through the relative bargaining power of the labour groups in question.

4 The distribution of wealth. In the nineteenth century virtually all wealth was held by a small elite, who lived off the profits from it, whilst the majority lived by the 'sweat of their brows'. The injustice of this was a major spur to socialism. More recently, defenders of capitalism have argued that wealth has become progressively more evenly distributed, so that the majority benefit from profits – 'We are all capitalists now'!

5 Poverty. Free market ideologists have always acknowledged that a small minority will be unable to compete in the labour market, and will therefore be poor; so from Adam Smith onwards most economists accepted the need for some protection of the poor. Critics, however, have argued that poverty was, and remains, widespread.

In this chapter, we shall attempt to assess the facts in each of these five areas of concern, and to look more closely at the conflicting explanations. We shall start by looking at the overall distribution of income between people.

Income distribution between people

The overall picture

The most vivid illustration of income distribution is Pen's 'Parade of Dwarfs' (Pen 1971). In the course of *an hour* the entire population passes by, each person's height in relation to average height signifying their income in relation to average income. In the first minute we see only matchstick people such as women doing casual work. After 10–15 minutes dustmen and ticket collectors pass by, though only three feet high. After 30 minutes, when half the population has passed, skilled manual workers and senior office clerks appear, though these are still well under five feet tall. In fact we only reach the average height 12 minutes before the hour ends, when teachers, executive class civil servants, social workers and sales representatives pass by. After this, height increases rapidly. Six minutes before the end come farmers, headmasters and departmental heads of offices, standing about six feet six inches. Then come the giants: the fairly ordinary lawyer at eight feet tall, the family doctor at 21 feet, the chairman of a typical public company at over 60 feet, and various film stars and tycoons resembling tower blocks.

This illustration demonstrates two little-understood features of personal income distribution. First, the mean or average income is way above median income, the median-income receiver being the person who arrives after 30 minutes, with half the population poorer and half richer. Roughly three-quarters of the population have less than the mean or average income. Put another way, the median income is only about 85% of average income. Broadly speaking, this is because at the top end there are considerable numbers of very rich people who pull the average up. Second, amongst the top quarter of income receivers are people in fairly ordinary professions, such as teachers and sales representatives, who would perhaps be surprised to learn that the great majority of the population were significantly less well off than themselves.

Definition of income

When we come to collect precise data about income we find various problems of definition. Should we deduct taxes and add transfer payments? Should we count capital gains as income? This latter question raises the problem of distinguishing between income which is a flow, and wealth which is a stock. Income is defined in theory as *the amount a person could have spent whilst maintaining the value of his wealth intact*. By this definition capital gains should count as income, but for simplicity of data collection they are excluded from official tables. A further question is whether an imputed rent should be credited as income to those who own their dwelling. Again, strictly it should, as a dwelling is a potential source of income which could be spent without diminishing wealth, but for simplicity it is usually excluded. Finally, what should count as the income receiver, the individual or the household? In practice we normally use the 'tax unit' – the individual or family which is defined as one unit for tax purposes.

The Lorenz curve and the Gini coefficient

The conventional means of illustrating income distribution is the Lorenz curve, shown in Fig. 14.1. The horizontal axis shows the cumulative percentage of population; the vertical axis the cumulative percentage of total income they receive. The diagonal is the 'line of perfect equality' where, say, 20% of all people receive 20% of all income.

Table 14.1 presents figures for the distribution of income in the UK at selected dates since 1961. The data for 2001 are plotted in Fig. 14.1 as a continuous line, and are known as the Lorenz curve. The degree of inequality can be judged by the extent to which the Lorenz curve deviates from the diagonal. For instance, the bottom 20% received only 7.5% of total

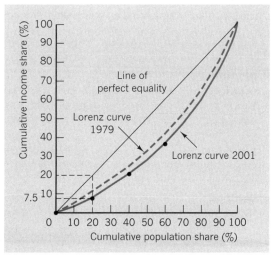

Fig. 14.1 Lorenz curve and Gini coefficient.

income in 2001, so that the vertical difference between the Lorenz curve and the diagonal represents inequality. To assess inequality over the whole range of the income distribution, the Gini coefficient is calculated. It is the ratio of the area enclosed between the Lorenz curve and the diagonal, to the total area underneath the diagonal. If there was no inequality (i.e. perfect equality), the Lorenz curve would coincide with the diagonal, and the above ratio would be zero. If there was perfect inequality (all the income going to the last person) then the Lorenz curve would coincide with the horizontal axis until that last person, and the above ratio would be 1. The Gini coefficient therefore ranges from zero to 1 with a rise in the Gini coefficient suggesting less equality. The value of the Gini coefficient is, in fact, calculated for each year in Table 14.1.

The figures from Table 14.1, as well as confirming the conclusions we drew from Pen's 'Parade of Dwarfs', show that during the 1960s and early 1970s the Gini coefficient remained relatively constant, suggesting no significant change in the distribution of income. The period from 1971 to 1979 saw a sustained fall in the coefficient, suggesting that the income distribution became progressively more equal. However, the trend has been broken since 1979, with the Gini coefficient rising, i.e. less equality.

The Gini coefficient can, however, only give an overall impression. More detailed inspection shows that the bottom 20% of income receivers were worse off in 2001 with only 7.5% of income, compared to 9.9% in 1979. What has happened is that the relative position of the lower-income groups has worsened, and that of some of the higher-income groups improved. The top 10% received 27.7% of income in 2001 but only 20.4% in 1979. When one Lorenz curve lies below another *at every point* we can confidently say that a rise in the Gini coefficient must mean less equality. This appears to be the case for *all* deciles of income in 2001 as compared to 1979. If the Lorenz curves intersect we have to balance less equality at one part of the income distribution with greater equality at another part.

If we had compared the 1961 and 1971 Lorenz curves, we would have found just such an intersection. For instance, there was *less equality* for the bottom 50% of income earners in 1971 (32.2% of income) than in 1961 (32.7% of income). However, there was *greater equality* for the bottom 20% of income earners in 1971 (9.5% of income) than in 1961 (9.4% of income). So the rise in the overall Gini coefficient, from 0.260 in 1961 to 0.262 in 1971, must be treated with some care as it does not, in this case, mean less equality throughout the income distribution.

In more recent times the Gini coefficient has continued to rise, despite attempts by successive Labour governments since 1997 to reverse this trend through the introduction of new tax and benefit systems designed to be redistributive in nature (i.e. benefit the lower-income groups much more than higher-income groups). In fact the average incomes of the

Table 14.1 Percentage shares of income after tax in the UK (before housing costs).

Income receivers	1961	1971	1979	1981	1985	1991	2000–01
Bottom 10%	3.7	4.0	4.2	4.1	4.0	3.0	2.8
Bottom 20%	9.4	9.5	9.9	9.8	9.4	7.4	7.5
Bottom 30%	16.3	16.1	16.7	16.3	15.7	12.9	13.1
Bottom 40%	24.1	23.2	24.3	23.8	22.8	19.5	19.6
Bottom 50%	32.7	32.2	32.9	32.2	30.9	27.2	27.2
Bottom 60%	42.2	41.7	42.5	41.6	40.2	36.2	35.8
Bottom 70%	52.9	52.3	53.2	52.3	50.8	46.6	45.9
Bottom 80%	64.8	64.2	65.5	64.5	63.0	58.9	52.8
Bottom 90%	78.8	78.3	79.6	79.0	77.4	74.0	72.3
Bottom 100%	100.0	100.0	100.0	100.0	100.0	100.0	100.0
Gini coefficient	0.260	0.262	0.248	0.259	0.279	0.337	0.347

Source: Goodman and Shephard (2002).

higher-income groups have grown at least as fast as those of the lower-income groups during 1997–2001 (Griffiths 2003). We discuss possible reasons behind such an outcome later in the chapter.

International comparisons

International comparisons of income distributions and their associated Gini coefficients have been difficult to undertake because various countries have different definitions of income and different methods of collecting data. However, work by A. B. Atkinson has provided an important insight into income distribution in both Europe and the US (Atkinson 1996). Table 14.2 presents the income distribution for various countries in the late 1980s, using cumulative decile shares. This table contains the same information as Table 14.1. For example, the income distribution for Finland shows that the bottom 10% of income earners (S_{10}) earn 4.5% of all income, whereas the bottom 20% of income earners (S_{20}) earn 10.8% of all income, and so on. The Gini coefficient for the entire distribution is given in the last column on the right (G_0).

If these figures were drawn for each country then we would have a series of Lorenz curves of the kind shown in Fig. 14.1 with each Lorenz curve representing a country's income distribution. The countries in Table 14.1 are ranked from low to high inequality, using the share of the *bottom decile* income group as the initial indicator; i.e. the greater the share of income accounted for by the bottom 10% of income earners, the less inequality we initially assume to occur in that country's distribution of income. Of course we know that the Lorenz curves can intersect each other, making generalizations about the bottom decile less useful.

The Gini coefficients based on the *whole distribution* are given on the right of Table 14.2 and yield a similar ranking (from low to high) of inequality to that implied by the bottom decile of income earners, although the ordering is not exactly the same. Despite these problems, useful conclusions can be drawn from such tables. For example, if all the Lorenz curves were mapped, there would be a clear group of mainland Northern European countries at the top (Finland, Belgium, Luxembourg, Norway and Sweden), i.e. with the lowest income inequalities. In the middle

Table 14.2 Income distribution in European countries and the US in the 1980s: cumulative decile shares of total income (%).

	S_{10}	S_{20}	S_{30}	S_{40}	S_{50}	S_{60}	S_{70}	S_{80}	S_{90}	G_0
Finland	4.5	10.8	18.1	26.4	35.6	45.6	56.6	68.6	82.2	0.207
Luxembourg	4.3	10.2	17.1	24.8	33.5	43.1	53.9	66.0	80.4	0.238
Belgium	4.2	10.2	17.1	25.0	33.8	43.5	54.3	66.4	80.3	0.235
Netherlands	4.1	10.1	16.9	24.5	33.0	42.5	53.2	65.3	79.4	0.268
Germany	4.0	9.8	16.6	24.2	32.9	42.5	53.2	65.3	79.4	0.250
Norway	3.9	9.8	16.9	24.9	33.9	43.7	54.6	66.7	80.6	0.234
Portugal	3.4	8.0	13.9	20.9	28.9	38.1	48.5	60.8	75.8	0.310
Sweden	3.3	9.5	16.9	25.3	34.6	44.8	55.9	68.2	81.9	0.220
Italy	3.1	8.0	13.9	20.7	28.7	38.0	48.7	61.2	76.2	0.310
France	3.0	8.3	14.6	21.8	29.9	39.1	49.5	61.6	76.3	0.296
Switzerland	2.8	8.0	14.1	21.0	29.0	37.8	47.7	58.9	72.5	0.323
Spain	2.8	7.4	13.2	20.1	28.2	37.5	47.9	60.2	75.5	0.320
UK	2.5	7.5	13.5	20.5	28.7	38.2	49.1	61.8	77.1	0.304
Ireland	2.5	7.1	12.6	19.3	27.1	36.3	47.0	59.6	75.1	0.330
US	1.9	5.7	11.2	18.0	26.2	35.7	46.9	60.2	76.3	0.341

Note: The results are for the distribution among persons of household disposable income adjusted by an equivalence scale equal to (household size)$^{0.5}$.
Source: Modified from Atkinson (1996).

would be countries such as France, Italy and Portugal, and at the bottom, i.e. with highest income inequalities, would be a grouping containing Switzerland, Spain, the UK and Ireland, together with the US. The Gini coefficient for the US suggests the least equal distribution of income of all the countries considered. The weighted average Gini coefficient for Europe was 0.288 as compared to that for the US of 0.341, indicating that inequality of income in Europe as a whole is still less than such income inequality in the US. Interestingly, this 5% (0.053) *difference* in Gini coefficient between Europe and the US is less than the difference between some European countries. For example, when comparing Finland with Switzerland or Sweden with Ireland, we find the differences in Gini coefficients are closer to 10%. The UK has more inequality in terms of the overall Gini coefficient (0.304) than has Europe as a whole (0.288), though some six countries (see Table 14.2) have still greater inequality than the UK. However, in terms of the bottom 10% of income earners, the UK's ranking is lower still, with only Ireland equivalent to it and the US below it, suggesting that this group of income earners is particularly vulnerable in the UK.

These trends were substantiated by another major cross-country comparison of income inequality (Gottshalk and Smeeding 1997). Gottshalk and Smeeding calculated an inequality measure which they called the '90/10 ratio'. The 90 refers to the ratio of the income of a person at the 90th percentile to the median income for the whole country, whereas the 10 refers to the ratio of the income of a person at the 10th percentile to the median income. By *dividing* these two ratios we derive the 90/10 ratio for the UK in the mid-1990s as 206/44 or 4.67, suggesting that a person at the 90th percentile enjoys nearly five times the income of a person at the 10th percentile. Only the ratio for the US at 5.78 was found to be higher than the UK's, while the ratio for most European countries varied within the range from Finland (2.74) to Ireland (4.30).

The next question which might be asked in the international context is what has happened to the distribution of income *over time*? Has it become more or less unequal? Atkinson (1996) presented data pertaining to *changes* in the Gini coefficient of different countries over time. A rise in the index suggests that overall inequality has risen, and a fall in the index suggests that overall inequality has fallen. Income inequality appeared to have remained relatively

steady or actually fallen in the US, Germany, France, Italy and Finland, whilst in the UK there had been a significant increase in inequality, indicated by a rise of over 40% (0.40) in the Gini coefficient between 1977 and 1991. This trend is substantiated by the rise of 36% (0.36) in the Gini coefficient between 1979 and 1991 shown in Table 14.1 earlier. No other country experienced this rate of increase, Sweden since 1988 being the only other major country experiencing a clear increase in inequality. This trend was further confirmed by Gottshalk and Smeeding (1997), who concluded from their data that the UK Gini coefficient had risen at twice the rate of the US between 1978 and 1991.

Income distribution between factors of production

Definition of factors

In analysing the share of income between labour, capital and land there are initial problems of definition. First, under labour do we include workers and managers, thereby combining wages and salaries, since both are paid in return for work? Some argue that salaries for managers include a profit element, since managers exert direct control over capital and they carry entrepreneurial risks. In practice it is impossible to separate any profit element in salaries, and payments to workers and managers are counted together. More difficult is the income of the self-employed, since this undoubtedly includes payment for both labour and capital services; a separate category is, in fact, usually made for the self-employed.

Measurement of factor shares

Table 14.3 shows the income to various factors as a percentage of gross value added at factor cost (national income before adjustment for taxes/subsidies) and provides an insight into the distribution of national income by factor shares. The table is in the new format introduced in 1998 by the government to conform to European national income practices. The 'compensation of employees' corresponds to incomes which employees earn from employment, while 'gross operating surplus' covers mainly the profits to various corporate bodies, both private and public. The 'other income' includes what is called 'mixed income' (largely income from unincorporated businesses owned by householders) and the operating surpluses of other unincorporated bodies such as partnerships. Although not precise, the 'other income group' can be thought of as a proxy for 'self-employed income'.

Labour's share of total income has increased from approximately 50% in 1900 to 65.1% in 2001. Table 14.3 shows that over the last 30 years, the percentage shares going to various factors have been relatively steady, although the share of total income going to labour fell and to profits rose significantly between 1981 and 1989 as the relatively slow rise in real wages and the economic recovery helped shift income away from employment and towards corporate profits.

One may question the importance of factor shares in overall income distribution. Whether the changes in factor shares shown in Table 14.3 reflect greater inequality in household incomes depends on how unequally distributed these earnings from different factor sources are across the various income groups. For example, the table suggests that the distribution of factor shares has shifted away from employment and towards self-employment and profits ('gross operating surplus' and 'other income') since 1981. If we knew that income from these two sources is more unevenly distributed across income groups than income from employment, then this shift in factor shares towards self-employment and profits could result in an increase in the overall inequality of income between different groups of people. Studies have, in fact, shown that income from self-employment and from investments (rent, dividends and interest) are more important sources of income for the lowest and highest income groups than for the middle income groups. For example in 1992/93, income from self-employment accounted for 18% of total income for the *bottom 10% income group* while investment income accounted for 13%. For the *top 10% income group* the figures were only 17% and 10% respectively (Ryan 1996).

There are two main types of theoretical explanation of factor shares. The first emphasizes the role of market forces and starts with a microeconomic analysis of factor markets. If there is perfect competition in goods and factor markets, each factor will receive precisely its marginal revenue product; in other words, it will receive income in proportion to its productive value. The rising share to the factor labour would be viewed from this standpoint as reward for a greater contribution to production.

An alternative approach has been to explain factor shares in terms of power. Marx saw capitalists as exploiting labour, receiving 'surplus value' from the fact that the efforts of workers yield returns over and above their wages. Marx believed that this exploitation would increase as production became more

Table 14.3 Factor shares as a percentage of gross value added at factor cost.

	1973	1977	1981	1989	2001
Compensation of employees	66.4	66.6	67.9	63.8	65.1
Gross operating surplus	24.5	24.9	23.4	27.1	24.6
Non-financial companies					
Private corporations	17.8	17.5	17.4	23.1	21.9
Public corporations	3.2	3.8	3.7	1.5	1.1
Financial corporations	3.5	3.6	2.3	2.5	1.6
Other income*	9.1	8.5	8.7	9.1	10.3
Total	100.0	100.0	100.0	100.0	100.0

* Includes mixed income and the operating surplus of the non-corporate sector (proxy variable for self-employment income).
Source: ONS (2002) *Economic Trends*, Annual Supplement, and previous issues.

capital-intensive and labour was displaced, creating a pool of unemployment which would depress wages, and therefore the share of labour in National Income. Eventually, the decline in people's ability to purchase the output of the capitalist factories, combined with the workers' resentment at their poverty, would cause crisis and revolution.

Neither theory is wholly adequate. Assumptions, such as perfect competition in labour markets, required by orthodox theory are clearly unrealistic (see Chapter 15). Similarly, Marx's prediction of a declining wage and factor share for labour has not been fulfilled.

The earnings distribution

Since over 65% of total income accrues to the factor labour (Table 14.3), it follows that differing returns to the various factors (labour, capital or land) are unlikely to be the main explanation of income inequality. Rather, we must turn our attention to variations in income between different groups *within* the factor labour, i.e. the earnings distribution.

Earnings by occupation

Table 14.4 shows the relative earnings of the main occupational groups according to the Standard Occupational Classification (SOC) introduced for the first time in 1991. Each figure represents the average earnings of the members of that group as a percentage of overall average male earnings. We can see that the first three categories of non-manual workers earn significantly more than the average. These categories include managers in industry and in local/central government; professionals, such as engineers, teachers, scientists and solicitors; and associate professional and technical employees such as technicians, surveyors and computer programmers. However, it is also true that non-manual workers in occupations such as clerical and secretarial earn, on average, less than workers in manual occupations such as craft workers and machine operators. Indeed a more detailed analysis also reveals that certain manual occupations, such as plant drivers and scaffolders, earn as much as teachers and certain classes of management. Although the overall picture is

Table 14.4 Earnings of occupational groups: average (gross weekly) earnings of full-time male employees in selected occupations, as a percentage of average (gross weekly) earnings of all full-time male employees (April 2002).

Non-manual	
Managers and administrators	152
Professional occupations	132
Associate professional and technical	113
Sales	76
Personal and protection services	76
Clerical and secretarial	63
Manual	
Craft and related occupations	78
Plant and machine operators	71
Other occupations	60

Source: Adapted from ONS (2002) *New Earnings Survey, Part D.*

complicated, it can be seen that inequalities of earnings are clearly present in UK society.

A hidden source of inequality between occupations is the difference in value of fringe benefits and pension entitlement. As early as 1979 the Diamond Commission found that this typically adds 36% to the pre-tax salary of a senior manager, and 18% to that of a foreman, whilst unskilled workers enjoy few or no such benefits.

Earnings by sex

Table 14.5 shows female earnings in relation to male earnings. The position of women improved significantly during the 1970s – a period which saw the introduction of equal pay legislation – though women continued to earn substantially less than men. The momentum towards equal pay seemed to slow down during the 1980s and 1990s, with the earnings of both manual and non-manual females making little further progress as compared to males.

Earnings trends

Figure 14.2 shows that there have been significant changes *over time* in the real earnings gap between

Table 14.5 Average gross weekly female earnings as a percentage of average male earnings.

	1970	1976	2002
Manual	50	62	67
Non-manual	51	61	67

Source: ONS (2002) *New Earnings Survey, Part A*, and previous issues.

high and low wage earners. The figure traces the growth in real hourly (male) earnings between 1966 and 2002 of people positioned at three different points on the income distribution scale. The 50th percentile line traces the increases in the real hourly earnings of workers receiving the median ('average') wage over the period. Similarly, the 90th percentile represents the growth of real hourly earnings of workers who are 90% of the way up the income distribution, while the 10th percentile shows the growth of real hourly earnings for those whose income is only 10% of the way up the income distribution. Of course the 90th percentile is likely to include some of the people in the non-manual 'managers and admini-

strators' category in Table 14.4, while the 10th percentile will include some of those in the manual 'other occupations' category.

Between 1966 and 1978 the three categories moved roughly in line with each other. However, major differences have emerged since then between those on low and high pay. For example, the real pay for average earners (50th percentile) increased by 50% between 1978 and 2002, whilst the real pay for those near the top of the income scale (90th percentile) increased by as much as 65% over the same time period. On the other hand, those with earnings near the bottom of the income scale (10th percentile) hardly benefited at all over this period. The *relative position* of workers near the bottom of the income scale was in fact the lowest since records began in 1886.

The study by Gottshalk and Smeeding (1997) on the '90/10 ratio' confirms this pattern for the UK and considers the same ratio in other countries. For example, in terms of the '90/10' ratio they found that the US had the highest *increase* in earnings inequality (rise in the ratio) between 1979 and the early 1990s for males as compared to other industrial countries. Their results show that the UK's increase in earnings inequality over the period was just over 80% of that

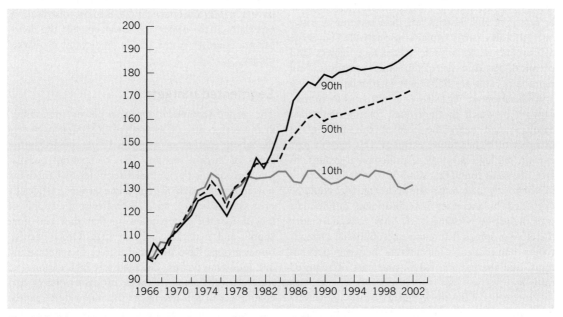

Fig. 14.2 Real hourly male earnings by percentile (Index 1966 = 100).
Sources: *Financial Times* (1994); *New Earnings Survey* (2002).

of the US, followed by Canada and Australia (in the range 50–80% of the US figure) and France, Japan, the Netherlands, Sweden and Finland (in the range 10–50% of the US figure). Finally, Italy and Germany experienced no measurable increase in earnings inequality. From these figures we note that the growth of male earnings inequality in the UK has been second only to the US over the recent past.

Explanation of earnings differentials

In seeking to explain the earnings distribution there are two main theoretical approaches, similar to those we considered above for factor shares.

Market theory

The first, the 'market theory', starts from an assumption of equality in *net advantages* for all jobs, i.e. that money earnings *and* the money value placed on working conditions are equal for all jobs. It also assumes that labour has a high degree of occupational and geographical mobility, so that if there is any inequality in net advantages, labour will move to the more advantageous jobs until equality is restored. Thus, differences in *actual* earnings must be caused by compensating differences in other advantages. Job satisfaction is one compensating advantage: enjoyable or safe jobs will be paid less than irksome or risky ones; this may partly explain the relatively high wage of manual workers such as coalface miners and chemical, gas and petroleum plant operators. Still more important are differences in training. Training and education are regarded as investments in 'human capital', in which the individual forfeits immediate earnings, and bears the cost of training, in the prospect of higher future earnings; this may in part explain the high earnings of professional groups. In fact, one study found that some 30% of the disparities in real hourly male wages shown in Fig. 14.2 could be explained by increases in educational differentials over the period (Gosling *et al.* 2000). Market theory therefore proposes that relative occupational earnings reflect non-monetary advantages between occupations, and the varying length and cost of required training.

Proponents of this theory agree that it is not wholly adequate, and would recognize differences in natural ability as also affecting earnings. However, others, whilst still broadly advocating market theory, have suggested a more fundamental objection, namely that labour is in fact highly immobile. The most recent study of income immobility among the rich and poor found that groups of people at the extreme ends of the income distribution tend to be subject to intergenerational immobility (Johnson and Reed 1996). This research attempted to assess whether the income level and unemployment experiences of fathers were related to the subsequent experiences of their sons. The results were interesting in that the sons of those fathers who were unemployed were also more likely to end up being unemployed. Indeed, the sons of fathers whose income was in the bottom 20% of income earners were three times more likely to remain in the same income group than those sons whose fathers' incomes were above average. Similarly, the sons of fathers whose income was in the top 20% of earners were three times as likely to end up in the same income group as their father than those sons whose fathers' incomes were in the bottom 20% of income earners. However, the survey also showed that the more able children of poor parents do have a better chance of moving into higher income bands than less able children, making it very important to make sure that good quality education is available to all. From what we have noted above, a combination of social, occupational and geographic immobility can have a significant effect on the earnings distribution, especially at the upper and lower ends of the distribution, contrary to the simple predictions of market theory.

Segmented markets

The second theoretical approach places 'immobility' at the very centre of its analysis. This approach sees the labour market as 'segmented', i.e. divided into a series of largely separate (non-competing) occupational groups, with earnings determined by bargaining power *within* each group. Some groups, especially professional bodies, have control over the supply of labour to their occupations, so that they can limit supply and maintain high earnings. Other occupational groups have differing degrees of unionization and industrial power. The relatively high earnings of the relatively small number of printworkers and coalminers in the UK up to the mid-1980s may be explained in part by their history of effective and forceful collective bargaining, whilst the fragmented nature of agricultural and catering work may have contributed to their low pay. In this approach bargaining power is held to outweigh the effects of free market forces. A UK study on the relationship between wage inequality and union density during the 1980s largely substantiated these conclusions (Gosling 1995). It found that wage inequality increased as trade union influence weakened. The significant weakening of trade union power in the UK in the 1980s may therefore have played a part in the observed increase in the inequality of income. In particular, various groups of labour which do not have strong market power will suffer more than proportionately as a result of any decline in trade union bargaining positions. In similar vein, recent research by the IMF (Prasad 2002) identified inequalities in circumstances as between occupations as the major factor in accounting for the observed growth in UK wage disparities.

These two theoretical approaches to the distribution of earnings need not be regarded as mutually exclusive. Market theory can itself be used to analyse bargaining power, with professional bodies and trade unions affecting the supply of labour, and the elasticity of labour demand determining the employment effects of their activities. More fundamentally, it may be suggested that labour, whilst fairly immobile in the short run, is highly mobile in the long run. Thus, whilst the exertion of bargaining power may affect differentials in the short run, in the long run labour will move in response to market forces, and thereby erode such differentials.

However, it is obvious from Fig. 14.2 that the wage differential between those on low and those on high wages has *not* been eroded; in fact it actually *widened* between 1978 and 2002. Although the reasons for such a trend are complex, they seem to lie in both inter-industry and intra-industry shifts which have occurred in the UK labour market (Gregg and Machin 1994). For example, the *inter-industry* employment shift from manufacturing to services has tended to increase the number of lower-paid jobs. However, there also seem to have been *intra-industry* employment shifts, namely a shift in demand *within* industries in favour of non-manual, better educated, workers. Even when the proportion of workers with degrees rose from 8% to 11% during the 1980s, their wages continued to rise as demand for such workers rose even faster than their supply. At the other end of the scale, although the percentage of workers with no

qualifications fell from 46% to 32%, the unemployment rate among this group actually rose from 6.5% to 16.4% over the 1980s. In other words the demand for such workers fell even faster than the fall in their supply. The drive towards international cost competitiveness and the introduction of new technology have increased the demands for a more skilled and flexible workforce (OECD 1996), leaving workers with low skills, poor family backgrounds and inflexible work attitudes to occupy the low-paid jobs. These trends are also linked to age. For example, young people who are poorly qualified and have low earnings are less likely to experience increasing real earnings with age than are their predecessors (Gosling *et al*. 1994).

Another interesting theory linked to the segmented market hypothesis has been suggested by Daniel Cohen (Cohen 1998). He suggests that there is no longer a single market even for a particular kind of skill or occupation, i.e. there is an *intra-skill* dimension to earnings differentials. For example, top law firms may require secretaries whose pay will reflect their value to the company, while secretaries of similar capabilities working for less profitable law firms will earn considerably less. In other words, an individual's earnings prospects may depend on the nature and profitability of the company which employs them, so that even modest differences in skill may be magnified into significant earnings differentials. In this sense earnings differentials may substantially exceed any skill differentials, even within a given occupation.

The above attempts to explain the presence of wage differentials did not explicitly seek to clarify the reasons for earnings differentials by *sex*, so clearly shown in Table 14.5. Such differentials could be due, for example, to some element of *discrimination* which might exist in the labour market between men and women, even though they were identical workers. For instance, until December 1975, when it was made illegal, collective agreements between employers and employees often included clauses which prescribed that female wage rates should not exceed a certain proportion of the male wage. The examples of wage differentials noted above were made possible because of the preponderance of males in most unions. The state has also been active in allowing this wage differential to exist. For example, up to 1970 when the Equal Pay Act was passed, the police pay structure provided for a differential wage structure for men and women up to the rank of ordinary sergeant, while the pay structure for more senior sergeant ranks included only male rates. Obviously, female policewomen were felt to be able to achieve only the lower grades and even here were not seen as of equal value to males (Tzannatos 1990).

On the other hand, the observed differentials could be regarded as being due to *genuine differences* which exist (or are perceived to exist) between male and female labour. For instance, it is often observed that employers make certain assumptions about the 'average' female worker, i.e. as being one who will not be working for long before leaving to have a child. As a result, employers may be more reluctant to train female workers, who are then placed at a disadvantage as compared to their male counterparts. By acquiring fewer skills, the female worker inevitably receives less pay. Again, female workers are often constrained in competing with male workers by the need to seek employment in the catchment area of their husbands' employment. Such restrictions can again result in a lower wage as compared to that received by the more mobile male counterpart.

Whatever the causes of wage differentials between males and females, there is no doubt that they still exist, even after the initial improvements in the early 1970s following the Equal Pay Act of 1970 and the Sex Discrimination Act of 1975.

 The distribution of wealth

Definition of data collection

Wealth is notoriously difficult to define. The most obvious forms of wealth are land, housing, stocks and shares and other financial assets. In addition, many households hold several thousands of pounds-worth of durable goods: cars, carpets and furnishings, electrical goods and so on. All these together are known as 'marketable wealth'. But many ordinary families, whilst owning little land and few shares, may have substantial pension rights. In the case of private schemes these usually derive from contributions into a fund, which in turn is used to buy assets; whilst in the state scheme it derives from contributions which entitle people to future income from government revenues. It is the ownership of marketable wealth plus occupational and state pension rights which is often presented in the data (e.g. Table 14.6).

There are also considerable problems in obtaining information about wealth. Britain has no wealth tax, and so no regular wealth valuations are made. Attempts have been made to do this via sample surveys, but people are often reluctant to reveal their economic circumstances in sufficient detail to draw reliable conclusions. The only time that wealth *is* publicly evaluated is when substantial amounts are transferred from one person to another, usually at death, when wealth is assessed for capital transfer tax. By analysing these figures in terms of age and sex, it is possible to take the dead as a sample of the living, and so estimate the overall wealth distribution. Of course, there is an obvious likelihood of sampling error, especially in estimating the wealth of the young. The procedure also ignores certain bequests, such as those to surviving spouses, which are not liable to tax. Nevertheless, it is the best method available.

Concentration of wealth

Table 14.6 shows the Inland Revenue's estimate of the overall wealth distribution, excluding occupational

Table 14.6 Ownership of marketable wealth.

Percentage of wealth owned by:	1971	1976	1986	2000
Most wealthy 1% of population	31	24	18	22
Most wealthy 5% of population	52	46	36	42
Most wealthy 10% of population	65	61	50	54
Most wealthy 25% of population	87	84	73	74
Most wealthy 50% of population	97	95	90	94

Source: Inland Revenue Statistics (2002) and previous issues.

and state pension rights. As we might expect, wealth is much more unequally distributed than income. For example, the most wealthy 1% of the population own 22% of the wealth, whilst the top 10% own as much as 54% of wealth and the top 50% own 94% of wealth (i.e. the bottom half own only 6% of wealth).

But perhaps more significant than the absolute figures is the astonishingly rapid reduction in inequality, especially in the early 1970s. The wealth of the richest 1% fell in five years from 31 to 24% of the total, whilst for the richest 10% it fell from 65 to 61% (Table 14.6). This reflects the high rate of inflation in those years, which rapidly eroded the value of financial assets, and also the steep decline in the prices of stocks and shares and commercial land. Over a much longer period we observe a steady reduction in wealth inequality. In 1924 the wealthiest 1% owned 60% of *marketable* wealth (i.e. excluding occupational and state pension rights); this had fallen to 42% in 1951, and is now 22%. A major reason for this has been death duties, and more recently capital transfer tax (inheritance tax). This is a progressive tax, and helps break up the largest wealth holdings as they pass from one generation to another.

Despite the continuing influences of these factors, changes in the distribution of wealth were much more modest in the 1980s and 1990s, as can be observed from Table 14.6. Recently, however, it has been argued that 'new wealth' is being created in the UK as the rapid spread of home ownership and the rise in house prices means that inheriting such properties may allow both middle- and working-class people to benefit in the future. The percentage of UK households owning their own homes rose from 56% in 1980 to 76% in 2002. Although this may improve the wealth situation of many middle- and working-class income earners, it will create even more problems for the children of the 25% or more parents who may never own their own homes. It may also further increase the regional disparity of wealth as a result of regional house price differentials.

Though it is an emotive issue, one may doubt that the wealth distribution is a primary source of income inequality. We have already seen that the main source of income inequality is not between capital and labour, but between different groups of labour.

Poverty

Definition

There has been much debate as to the definition of poverty. Some have tried to define it in *absolute* terms. For example, Rowntree (1901), who made a major study of poverty just over a century ago, concluded that poverty was having insufficient income to obtain the minimum means necessary for survival, namely basic food, housing and clothing. Others have sought to define it in *relative* terms: Townsend (1973), in his survey of poverty, saw it as the inability to participate in the customary activities of society, which then might have included taking an annual holiday away from home, owning a refrigerator, having sole use of an indoor WC, and so on.

In some ways, the grinding poverty experienced in pre-Second World War Britain is no longer present. For example, studies by the Department of Social Security on 'Households below average income' have shown that amongst the poorest 10% of UK income earners, the percentage who have access to some basic consumer benefits were as follows: fridge/fridge freezer (99%), washing machine (88%), central heating (77%), telephone (76%), video (72%) and car or van (53%). Although these figures suffer from measurement problems, the improvement over the last 20 years in these percentages has been significant. However, such data do not always capture the more complicated aspects of poverty and the *relative* positions of different groups in UK society.

On a more practical level the 'official' poverty level (defined as the minimum acceptable income level) used by many researchers in the UK is given by the level of Income Support. On the other hand, the Child Poverty Action Group (CPAG) has defined the 'margins of poverty' as those people whose incomes are below Income Support plus 40%. Income Support is set by governments, and may be affected not only by the needs of the poor, but also by general political policy. It also ignores other aspects of economic deprivation not directly related to money income, such as inadequate housing, schools, health care and suchlike.

Another important source of statistics on poverty is derived from the *Households Below Average Income* published by the government's Department for Work and Pensions. Using these statistics, the poverty line is most often defined as those households whose income is *either* below 50% of the mean household income *or* below 60% of the median household income. In recent years the government has tended to use the latter definition because it is in line with EU practice, and because it is arguably a better measure for capturing the gap between the standard of living enjoyed by the poorest families and the 'typical' (median) family. Even so, there is sometimes inconsistency, as when using a poverty measure of below 50% (not 60%) of the median household income (as in Table 14.7). The CPAG, on the other hand, continues to use the former definition.

These various measures, together with information on the distribution of income which is supplied by the Institute for Fiscal Studies (Table 14.1), provide useful insights into the incidence of low income and poverty. However, they fail to account for other forms of poverty such as those frequently shown in statistics of homelessness or of ill-health.

Incidence of poverty

When we look at some of these suggested measures of poverty we find some disturbing results. Data show that the number of people *receiving* Income Support (including income-based Jobseeker's Allowance) has risen from 3.0m in 1978 to 4.6m in 2002. If we add to these figures the people who *depend upon* these benefits, e.g. children, then the total number dependent on these benefits in 2002 was 11.1m people, or 19.5% of the total population.

To help clarify the growth of poverty in the UK it may be helpful to study the results of the *Households*

Below Average Income report, published in 2002 (Table 14.7). Using the definition of 'poverty' as those households who earn less than 50% of the average income after housing costs, we can see that between 1979 and 2001 the total number of people in poverty has increased from 5m to 13.7m, suggesting that the percentage of the total population in poverty has nearly trebled over the period. The number of children who live in poverty has increased from 1.4m to 4.1m over the same period, suggesting that the percentage of children in poverty has more than trebled between 1979 and 2001. By 2001, therefore, some 24% of the total UK population and 32% of UK children were living in households earning less than half the average income.

Of course different family types face different risks of falling into poverty. Table 14.8 shows that there has been a significant increase in the numbers of people in poverty over all the groups, with the exception of married pensioners. In terms of the proportion of the total UK population in poverty, we find that couples with children and single-parent families together comprise over half (52%) of all those defined as being in poverty in the UK in 2001. When we focus on *each group separately*, we find that by 2001, 57% of all lone parents, 33% of all single pensioners and 22% of all couples with children can be regarded as in poverty. Table 14.8 also indicates the rapid rise in the proportion of these (and other) groups defined as in poverty since 1979.

Research has also suggested a close relationship between poverty and illness. For example, poor people are one and a half times as likely to have a long-standing illness and twice as likely to have a disability than those who are better off. The problem of

Table 14.7 The growth of poverty (defined as earnings less than 50% of average income), 1979–2001.

	Total population (m)			Child population (m)		
	Total population	Number in poverty	Percentage of population	Child population	Number in poverty	Percentage in poverty
1979	54.0	5.0	9.2	13.8	1.4	10.1
1994/95	55.8	13.3	23.8	12.7	4.0	31.5
2000/01	56.9	13.7	24.1	12.3	4.1	32.0

Source: National Statistics (2002) *Households Below Average Income 1994/5–2000/1*, and previous issues.

Table 14.8 The growth of poverty (defined as earnings less than 50% of average income) by status, 1979–2001.

Group	Total numbers in poverty (000s)			Percentage of total population[1] 2000/01	Percentage of group in poverty[2]		
	1979	1994/95	2000/01	2000/01	1979	1994/95	2000/01
Single without children	530	2,231	2,329	17	7	23	22
Single with children	460	2,310	2,740	20	10	55	57
Couples without children	490	1,380	1,507	11	5	12	13
Couples with children	2,220	4,784	4,384	32	8	23	22
Single pensioners	520	1,376	1,370	10	12	32	33
Married pensioners	1,020	1,219	1,233	9	21	23	23

[1] Indicates the group as a proportion of the total population in poverty.
[2] Indicates the proportion of each group in poverty.
Source: As for Table 14.7.

poverty would also seem to have an effect on the incidence of crime – for example, the incidences of assault and theft in the most deprived neighbourhoods of the Merseyside region are, respectively, more than five and ten times higher than those for the least deprived neighbourhoods (Hirschfield *et al*. 1996).

It may be useful to compare the UK with other EU countries as regards 'poverty' using one of the EU definitions for low income, generally the percentage of people with incomes below 60% of the median. On this measure some 20% of the UK population could be defined as 'in poverty' during the 1990s, this figure being the fourth highest out of 13 major European countries. Again the UK fares rather poorly using comparative figures for *child poverty* in 25 major countries published by UNICEF in the late 1990s. This data showed that the UK had the third highest level of child poverty (after Russia and the USA) with 21% of its children living in households in which the income level was below 50% of the median income (compared to 26% of children in Russia and the USA). This figure was found to be considerably more than in other EU countries with the exception of Italy (Bradbury and Jantti 1999).

The prospects for government policy being able to reverse this situation rapidly would appear rather slim. For example, it was calculated that if all families with children who were below the poverty line in 2001 (defined here as below 60% of median household income) were given an extra £46 per week, then half of those families would reach the median income

level and child poverty could be halved (Brewer *et al*. 2002). To provide help for those in poverty, the government introduced the Child Tax Credit (CTC) and the Working Tax Credit (WTC) in 2003, aimed at providing new income-related support to families and low-income households. Calculations of the possible effects of the new Child Tax Credit (£27.75 per child, per week) introduced in 2003 indicate that it should decrease child poverty by between 3 and 4 percentage points, i.e. a fall of some 400,000 children in poverty, at a cost of around 0.2% of GDP. The more ambitious target set by the government to reduce child poverty by half was estimated as requiring a much higher CTC of £46.45 per child, at a cost of around 1% of the UK's GDP.

Recent research has confirmed that government policies *do* have a role to play in alleviating poverty. For example, the Labour government's policies to combat child poverty between 1997 and 2001 were found to lead to a fall in the number of children in poverty (defined by below the 60% median income level) by around 400,000. If the '50% of mean income' definition is taken as the poverty level, then the decrease in the number of children in poverty fell by around 300,000 over the period (Brewer *et al*. 2002).

Whatever our definition, there are clearly large numbers of adults and children in 'poverty', suggesting that it is most effectively tackled by a wide range of initiatives over a prolonged period of time. For example, the National Minimum Wage (NMW) introduced in 1998 has, as one of its objectives, the reduction of income inequalities at work. However, in this respect its impacts have been rather modest, perhaps because the NMW has not been uprated in line with average earnings (Dickens and Manning 2002).

Conclusion

After some move towards greater equality of income distribution between 1961 and 1979, the process has been significantly reversed since the end of the 1970s. Income from employment provides over 65% of all income received, and must be a focus for any attempt to explain the inequality that does exist. Variations in income by occupation, by sex and by skill levels clearly contribute to such inequality. Together with the rise of inequality of income from employment, the growth of self-employment in recent years has also contributed to greater inequality in overall income. Wealth is more unequally distributed than income, and although there has been a progressive tendency towards a more equal distribution since the early 1970s, this process slowed down markedly in the 1980s and actually went into reverse in the 1990s with growing wealth inequality. Poverty is a serious and growing phenomenon in the UK, no matter how we define it. The large numbers and varied characteristics of those in poverty suggest that government policy must be wide-ranging and sustained if poverty levels are to be reduced substantially.

Key points

- The Gini coefficient (G) is the ratio of the area between the Lorenz curve and the diagonal to the total area beneath the diagonal.

- Where $G = 0$, we have perfect equality; where $G = 1$, we have perfect inequality.

- Where Lorenz curves intersect, we must be particularly careful in using the Gini coefficient.

- Since 1979, the Gini coefficient has tended to rise in the UK.

- Inequality as measured by the Gini coefficient is higher in the UK than for the *average* of EU countries, but is lower than for the US.

- Since employment accounts for around 65% of all factor income, the labour market must be a major source of any income inequalities observed.

- Significant differences in earnings can be observed by type of occupation and by gender, though the latter gap has narrowed in recent years.

- Household characteristics such as age, unemployment, single parenthood, etc., also play a key role in income inequality.

- The distribution of wealth is even more unequal than the distribution of income.

- Poverty can be expressed in both absolute and relative terms. Using a variety of indicators, the incidence of poverty has clearly increased in the UK since 1979, although some progress has been made in combatting poverty in recent times.

Now try the self-check questions for this chapter on the Companion Website. You will also find up-to-date facts and case materials.

References and further reading

Adam, S. and Brewer, M. (2003) Children, well-being, taxes and benefits, *Economic Review*, 20(3), February; 20(4), April.

Atkinson, A. B. (1996) Income distribution in Europe and the United States, *Oxford Review of Economic Policy*, 12(1).

Atkinson, A. B. (1999) The distribution of income in the UK and OECD countries in the twentieth century, *Oxford Review of Economic Policy*, 15(4).

Bradbury, B. and Jantti, M. (1999) Child poverty across industrialized countries, *Innocenti: Occasional Papers, Economic and Social Policy Series*, No. 17, Florence: UNICEF International Child Development Centre.

Brewer, M., Clark, T. and Goodman, A. (2002) The government's child poverty target: how much progress has been made?, *Institute for Fiscal Studies, Commentary No. 87*.

Cohen, D. (1998) *The Wealth of the World and the Poverty of Nations*, MIT Press.

Department of Employment (1999) *New Earnings Survey*, Part D.

Dickens, R. and Manning, A. (2002) Has the national minimum wage reduced UK wage inequality?, *Centre for Economic Performance, LSE, Discussion Paper No. 533*.

Goodman, A. and Shephard, A. (2002) Inequality and living standards in Great Britain: some facts, *Institute for Fiscal Studies, Briefing Note no. 19*.

Gosling, A. (1995) Wages and unions in the British labour markets, Working Paper, University College, London.

Gosling, A., Machin, S. and Meghir, C. (1994) What has happened to wages?, *Institute for Fiscal Studies, Commentary No. 43*.

Gosling, A., Machin, S. and Meghir, C. (2000) The changing distribution of male wages in the UK, *Review of Economic Studies*, 67.

Gottshalk, P. and Smeeding, M. (1997) Cross-national comparisons of earnings and income inequality, *Journal of Economic Literature*, 35(2), June.

Gregg, H. and Machin, S. (1994) Is the UK rise in inequality different?, in R. Barrell (ed.) *The UK Labour Market: Comparative Aspects and Institutional Developments*, Cambridge University Press.

Griffiths, A. (2003) Taxes, transfers and the distribution of income: UK experience 1997–2001, *British Economy Survey*, 32(2), Spring.

Hirschfield, A. *et al.* (1996) *Crime and Spacial Concentration of Disadvantage*, ESRC Programme.

Jenkins, S. P. (1996) Recent trends in the UK income distribution: What has happened and why?, *Oxford Review of Economic Policy*, 12(1).

Johnson P. and Reed, H. (1996) Intergenerational mobility among the rich and poor: results from the National Child Development Survey, *Oxford Review of Economic Policy*, 12(1).

Machin, S. (1996) Wage inequality in the UK, *Oxford Review of Economic Policy*, 12(1).

OECD (1996) *Technology, Productivity, and Job Creation*, April.

Pen, J. (1971) *Income Distribution*, Pelican.

Prasad, E. S. (2002) Wage inequality in the UK 1975–1999, *IMF Staff Papers*, 49(3).

Rowntree, S. (1901) *Poverty – A Study of Town Life*, Macmillan.

Ryan, P. (1996) Factor shares and inequality in the UK, *Oxford Review of Economic Policy*, 12(1).

Sutherland, H. and Piachaud, D. (2002) *Reducing Child Poverty in Britain: an Assessment of Government Policy 1997–2001*.

Townsend, P. (1973) *The Social Minority*, Allen Lane.

Tzannatos, Z. (1990) Sex differences in the labour market, *Economic Review*, May.

Chapter 15   Trade unions, wages
and collective
bargaining

This chapter first identifies the main institutions involved in the
process of collective bargaining in the UK. The structure and growth
of trade unions are then traced, and the role of employers and
government examined. A simple 'marginal productivity' model of
wage determination is presented, before assessing the degree to
which unions can use their 'bargaining power' to modify the
predictions of this model. Other factors affecting the wage bargain,
such as comparability, work conditions, cost of living and
productivity agreements, are considered. The role of government in
setting a minimum wage is assessed, as are the impacts of the
minimum wage. The chapter concludes by examining the impact of
collective bargaining on pay differentials, restrictive practices and
strike activity.

Types of trade union

A trade union has been described as 'a continuous association of wage-earners for the purpose of maintaining or improving the conditions of their working lives' (Webb and Webb 1896, p. 1). Although useful, this definition does not reflect the whole range of trade union objectives. The Trades Union Congress (TUC) outlines 10 general objectives of unions, with improved wages and terms of employment at the top of the list. Other aims, such as 'full employment', 'industrial democracy' and a 'voice in government', are included, but the emphasis is on the unions' 'capacity to win higher wages through collective bargaining as one of their most effective methods of attracting membership'.[1]

Despite having some objectives in common there is still a considerable amount of diversity between unions in the UK (Table 15.1). Most unions are relatively small. In 2002 some 50% of unions had fewer than 1,000 members each, but together they accounted for only 0.36% of total union membership. There has been a progressive reduction in the number of unions, from the peak of 1,384 unions in

1920, to 226 in 2002. The reduction has been particularly marked for small unions. The number of unions with fewer than 1,000 members has more than halved since 1979. In 2002 the 10 largest unions (Table 15.2) accounted for 71% of total membership. The trend towards fewer and larger unions, largely as a result of mergers, is well established, but the 226 British unions provide a contrast with the 17 industrial unions in the former West Germany.

Four broad headings have been traditionally used to classify trades unions in the UK, namely craft, general, industrial and 'white-collar' unions.

Craft unions

These were the earliest type of union, and are mainly composed of workers regarded as 'qualified' in a particular craft. Most craft unions now include workers with the same skill across the industry or industries in which they are employed, such as the Associated Society of Locomotive Engineers and Firemen (ASLEF). Another contemporary example is the Graphical, Paper and Media Union.

Table 15.1 Unions and union membership, 1979 and 2002.

| Members | Number of unions | | All membership (000s) | | Percentage of | | | |
| | | | | | No. of unions | | Membership of all unions | |
	1979	2002	1979	2002	1979	2002	1979	2002
Under 100	73	50	4	2	16.0	22.1	0.0	0.0
100–499	124	41	30	12	27.3	18.1	0.2	0.2
500–999	47	21	33	14	10.4	9.3	0.3	0.2
1,000–2,499	58	28	92	47	12.8	12.4	0.7	0.6
2,500–4,999	43	21	152	74	9.5	9.3	1.1	1.0
5,000–9,999	24	12	155	86	5.3	5.3	1.2	1.1
10,000–14,999	7	4	83	48	1.6	1.8	0.6	0.6
15,000–24,999	19	12	358	223	4.2	5.3	2.7	2.9
25,000–49,999	17	15	623	515	3.7	6.6	4.7	6.6
50,000–99,999	15	6	919	361	3.3	2.7	6.9	4.6
100,000–249,999	16	5	2,350	765	3.5	2.2	17.7	9.8
250,000 and more	11	11	8,490	5,633	2.4	4.9	63.9	72.4
All members	454	226	13,289	7,780	100.0	100.0	100.0	100.0

Source: Adapted from *Annual Report of the Certification Officer, 2001–2002*.

Table 15.2 The top 10 largest TUC unions, 2002.

Rank	Name	Membership
1.	UNISON[1]	1,272,700
2.	Amicus[2]	1,080,046
3.	Transport and General Workers' Union (T & G)	848,809
4.	GMB[3]	689,276
5.	Royal College of Nursing of the UK	334,414
6.	Union of Shop, Distributive and Allied Workers (USDAW)	310,337
7.	Public and Commercial Services Union	281,923
8.	Communication Workers Union[4] (CWU)	279,679
9.	National Union of Teachers (NUT)	217,224
10.	National Association of School Masters and Union of Women Teachers (NASUWT)	200,257

[1] UNISON was formed in July 1993 and is composed of the three main public sector unions, NALGO, NUPE and COHSE.
[2] Amicus was established in 2002 as a result of a merger between the Amalgamated Engineering and Electrical Union (AEEU) and the Manufacturing, Science and Finance Union (MSF).
[3] GMB is the formal designation of the Boilermaker and Allied Trades Union (composed of seven sections which cover both blue- and white-collar workers).
[4] This union was formed in 1995 as a result of a merger between the National Communications Union and the Union of Communications Workers.
Source: Adapted from TUC (2003) Britain's Unions, *Annual Report of the Certification Officer 2001–2002*.

General unions

These unions originated in the 1880s in the attempt to organize semi-skilled and unskilled workers not covered by the craft unions. General unions do not restrict their membership to workers with specific skills, nor to particular industries or occupations. Examples include the Transport and General Workers' Union (T&G) with around 849,000 members, and the GMB with some 690,000 members.

The distinction between craft and general unions is not always clear. Over the last decade or so, this problem has been complicated by the growth of merger activity in the trade union movement. For example, in May 1992 the Amalgamated Engineering Union (AEU) merged with the Electrical, Electronic, Telecommunications and Plumbing Union (EETPU) to form the Amalgamated Engineering and Electrical Union (AEEU). The new union included occupations within the engineering and electrical sectors, which can be classified as 'craft' type occupations, as well as a variety of semi-skilled and unskilled machine operators who could legitimately be placed in the 'general union' category.

Industrial unions

These attempt to place under one union all the workers in an industry, whatever their status of occupation. The National Union of Mineworkers (NUM) comes closest to this in the UK, covering most of the occupations engaged in mining operations, though now very much reduced in size. Other examples of industrial unions include the Iron and Steel Trades Confederation (ISTC) and the Communication Workers Union. Most industrial unions in the UK are 'a matter of degree rather than kind'. In other words, they usually cover a large number of those engaged in the industry, but by no means all.

'White-collar' unions

These restrict their membership to professional, administrative and clerical employees. 'White-collar' unions have expanded faster than any other type of union in the post-war period. Large numbers of professions are now organized as unions, such as the Royal College of Nursing of the UK with over 334,000 members and the National Union of Teachers (NUT) with over 217,000 members.

As in the case of general and craft trade unions, the distinction between white-collar and manual unions is also becoming clouded by merger. This was exemplified in July 1993 by the formation of UNISON as a result of an amalgamation of the white-collar National and Local Government Officers' Association (NALGO) with the two primarily manual workers' unions, the National Union of Public Employees (NUPE) and the Confederation of Health Service Employees (COHSE). Similarly, in January 2002, the Amalgamated Engineering and Electrical Union (AEEU) and the Manufacturing, Science and Finance Union (MSF) merged to form Amicus which brought together skilled and semi-skilled workers in the electrical and engineering sectors with supervisory and managerial grades in the manufacturing, science and finance sectors. In fact, the overwhelming majority of unions now have features taken from more than one category of union, suggesting the need for new and alternative classifications. For example, some unions may now be more usefully classified as either 'closed' or 'open'. They may be said to be 'closed', in that they restrict membership to a clearly definable trade or profession such as the British Airline Pilots' Association (BALPA), or to a particular industry as with the National Union of Mineworkers (NUM). In contrast, 'open' unions seek to recruit a diverse membership, such as the large general unions, thereby making them less susceptible to decline as particular industries ebb and flow.

It is difficult to provide an accurate pattern of trade union membership by *industry*, as over 4 million members belong to unions recruiting over several industries. The fact that the UK does not have just a few industrial unions as in West Germany, or enterprise unions as in Japan, poses problems not only for classification but also for collective bargaining. The 'multi-union' structure of the UK means that many unions are involved in negotiations at both plant and enterprise levels. This can cause problems for both management and unions. Management may experience difficulties in coordinating negotiations with several different unions, often in the same plant. Unions may have to compromise individual aims and policies when part of a 'team' negotiating with employers. Multi-union plants or enterprises may also lead to inter-union rivalry and conflict. For instance, the Rail and Maritime Transport union (RMT) and ASLEF compete for membership among London Underground employees. There is also rivalry among the teaching unions in both schools and university sectors for membership.

The Trades Union Congress

The TUC was founded in 1868 with the aim of improving the economic and social conditions of working people, and of promoting the interests of its affiliated organizations. In 2002 there were 69 affiliated trade unions representing 88% of trade unionists in the UK. The TUC is mainly concerned with general questions which affect trade unions both nationally and internationally, and has participated in discussions relating to the national economy through its membership of the National Economic Development Office (NEDO), although the government's abolition of NEDO in 1992 removed a major residual channel of communication. The General Council of the TUC represents the organization in the period between one annual Congress and another and is responsible for putting Congress decisions into effect. The General Council has no authority to call strikes, or to stop strikes called by its members, but can offer advice on disputes. Under Rule 11 the General Council can intervene in unofficial strikes and make recommendations to the unions and employers concerned.

The TUC has also been successful through its Organising Academy in training union recruiters and improving the professionalism of unions' recruitment strategies. Although the influence of the TUC on the UK government has waned considerably since the 1970s, it has an influence on European legislation as a member of the European Trade Union Confederation (ETUC). The ETUC represents the interests of some 57 million trade unionists in Europe, both within and outside the EU, and is one of the 'social partners' in the EU along with the employers' organizations UNICE and CEEP (see below). The partners have negotiated 'frameworks agreements' that have been adopted as EU Directives and which are binding in UK law. These Directives are considered more fully in the section on the Social Chapter (p. 288).

Trade unions and change

Until 1980 the fall in employment, and therefore the number unionized, in the primary and secondary industries was more than compensated for by the rise in employment, and so the number unionized, in the service industries. Since 1980 this trend has been broken (see Table 15.3) and with it the sustained growth in trade union membership over the post-war period. In fact, membership fell substantially by 41.5% between 1979 and 2001, with union density declining from a peak of 54.5% in 1979 to 28.5% in 2001. A breakdown of membership by sex reveals that of the 8 million or so union members in 2001, 47% were women, giving a density of around 28% compared to a density of 30% for men.

Factors affecting union growth and decline

Explanations of the factors which affect union membership (and in particular the decline in the density figure since its peak in 1979) can be grouped under three broad headings.

Labour force composition

This set of explanations highlights the role of changes in the *compositions of the workforce* as a factor

affecting the decline in union density, the argument being that the composition of employment has moved away from the industries, occupations and regions where union density was relatively high, and towards those industries, occupations and regions where union density tends to be relatively low.

For example, union membership differs *by sector*. In the public sector, national government (65%) and local government (72%) tend to have high union densities. These figures remain above the average for manufacturing (27%). As far as *occupations* are concerned, union density is high for employees such as teachers (82%) and for the skilled engineering trades (57%), but low for secretarial (24%) and various sales occupations (11%). In terms of *employment status* (i.e. whether a person is full-time or part-time, self-employed or a trainee), the statistics show that union density is much higher for full-time workers (32%) than for part-time workers (20%) or for full-time self-employed (10%). It also seems that the *size of workplace* is an important factor. For example, the average union density in workplaces employing 25 or more employees is 36%, while that for workplaces employing fewer than 25 employees is only 15%. *Gender* is also a factor, with union density higher for males (30%) than for females (28%) and

Table 15.3 Trade union membership and density in the UK, 1979–2001 (000s and %).

Year	Civilian employees in employment	Unemployed	Potential trade union membership	Trade union membership	Density[1] (%)
1979	23,173	1,295	24,368	13,289	54.5
1981	21,892	2,520	24,412	12,106	49.6
1983	21,067	3,104	24,171	11,236	46.5
1985	21,423	3,271	24,694	10,821	43.8
1987	21,584	2,953	24,537	10,475	42.7
1989	23,661	1,799	25,460	10,238	40.2
1990	22,918	1,665	24,583	9,947	40.5
1992	23,198	2,779	25,977	9,048	34.8
1994	22,937	2,796	25,733	8,278	32.2
1996	23,624	2,388	26,012	7,935	30.5
1998	24,569	1,822	26,397	7,851	29.7
2001	25,844	1,472	27,316	7,779	28.5

[1] Union density defined as: $\dfrac{\text{actual union membership}}{\text{potential union membership}} \times 100$

Sources: *Labour Market Trends* (2003) March, and previous issues.

increasing with age and length of service for both males and females. Finally, union density is affected by *region*, being highest in Wales, the North and Northern Ireland (40%) and lowest in the South East (outside London) (22%). Given these figures, it is obvious that the recent changes in the structure of the working population (see Chapter 1, Table 1.4) have had an adverse effect on union density.

The privatization of much of the public sector, the loss of engineering and related jobs via de-industrialization, the sharp increase in the number of self-employed and part-time workers, the growth in the number of small companies, and the growth of female participation in the labour force, are just some of the changes which have tended to decrease union density.

Another key factor behind falling trade union membership is the widespread failure of unions to organize workers in businesses that were set up after 1980. The proportion of British establishments which recognize manual and non-manual trade unions for collective bargaining over pay and conditions is 30 percentage points lower in post-1980 establishments than in the rest of the business community (Machin 2000). Although the largest decreases in recognition occurred in private sector manufacturing companies, there were also sharp falls in private-sector services companies. Such organizations were often faced with particularly severe competitive conditions during 1980–2000 which tended to restrict their capacity to sustain the potential 'costs' of union recognition. In fact, unions were recognized for collective bargaining in only a fifth of such 'new' enterprises. However, Charlwood (2002) reports that four out of 10 non-union employees would join unions if one existed in their workplace. This tends to indicate that a combination of employer resistance and relatively weak trade union organizational power might account for the trends indicated above.

Macroeconomic factors

Macroeconomic factors such as economic growth and unemployment, as well as movements in prices and wages, also have an effect on union membership and density.

Unemployment has obviously had a significant negative impact on union growth. Historically the major upswings in trade union membership have occurred in periods when unemployment has been relatively low or falling – for instance, 1901–20 and

1934–47. A study by Bain and Elsheikh (1982) found that in 15 of the 19 industries studied during the inter-war and post-war years, slow growth of unionization was correlated with periods of high unemployment, and vice versa. The Bain–Elsheikh model suggests that relatively high unemployment will reduce union bargaining power, and therefore discourage union membership. This conclusion is also supported by a survey which investigated the effects of the 1990–93 recession on TU membership (Geroski *et al.* 1995). That recession was shown to cause a still more rapid decline in trade union membership than might otherwise have been predicted.

However, some have suggested that the *threat* of unemployment may even act as a *stimulus* to union growth. Hawkins (1981) sees this as one factor in raising union density amongst white-collar workers threatened by technological and organizational change during the 1970s. Technology is something of a two-edged sword for unions; on the one hand it may create unemployment, whilst on the other it often confers substantial industrial 'muscle' on the key workers operating the new computer-based systems.

Price and Bain (1976) suggest that the *rate of change of prices* and *the rate of change of wages* may also influence union growth. Rising prices have a 'threat' effect so that workers unionize to defend real wages, particularly in the early years of an inflationary period. Wage rises have a 'credit' effect for unions, in that they are attributed to their bargaining power, and this promotes membership. Bain and Elsheikh (1982) found that the real wage variable, in one form or another, had a significant and positive impact on union growth in 15 of the 19 industries they studied. Also the desire to protect established *pay relativities* may affect union growth. For example, in advanced stages of incomes policies, when pay differentials have been substantially eroded, there is evidence that union membership increases. The suggestion here is that a series of injustices leads workers to seek greater bargaining power by joining unions in the hope of restoring differentials.

The rapid decline of both union membership and density in the 1980s and early 1990s suggests that macroeconomic factors may have a negative influence on union growth. Some of the macroeconomic factors also appear to have different effects on union density than those shown by some of the earlier studies quoted above. For example, Carruth and Disney

(1987) tried to capture the effects of the main macro-economic factors on union density by separating out the changes in union membership into two components: a 'trend' component influenced by changes in total employment, and a 'cycle' component which varies with macroeconomic variables such as wages, prices and unemployment. They note that when unemployment and real wage growth are high relative to the trend, membership growth is depressed. The 'threat' and 'credit effect' noted in earlier studies seem to have become much less effective. Interestingly, a more recent study of the 1988–90 period (Metcalf 1994) noticed that the reverse relationship did not seem to hold; i.e. falling unemployment and slower real wages did not seem to halt the fall in union density. This may suggest that union density may be experiencing a long-term, secular decline rather than being affected only by short-run cyclical changes in macroeconomic variables.

Industrial relations environment

This set of reasons relates to the influence on union membership and density of such factors as government and employer policies, and the trade unions' own responses to such policies.

Carruth and Disney (1987) found that, in a historical context, *Conservative governments* have tended to exercise a negative impact on membership rates. Freeman and Pelletier (1990) and Minford and Riley (1994) also accord a strong negative impact on membership rates of the post-1979 legislative programme of the UK Conservative governments. Although it is difficult to be precise, there is little doubt that the post-1979 legislative reforms significantly weakened the position of trade unions. To these legislative reforms should be added the effects of government supply-side policies, with their emphasis on privatization and cost savings. For example, the total number of public sector employees decreased from just over 7m in 1979 to 5m in 1995 – a fall of 29%. Central government employment fell by 29%, local government employment fell by 9% and employment in the public corporations fell by 21%, over the same period. Given that the density of unionization is higher in the public sector than in the private sector, it is hardly surprising that the Conservative governments' economic policies have been directly associated with a decline in union density.

Changes in the *attitudes of employers* have also affected union membership over the last 20 years. For example, the incidence of companies refusing to recognize unions has increased. 'De-recognition' refers to the complete withdrawal of a trade union's rights to negotiate pay on behalf of its members, although they may be represented for consultation purposes or during grievance and disciplinary hearings. De-recognition was a feature of several heavily publicized disputes in the 1980s, notably News International's de-recognition of the print unions, P&O's of the seafarers' union and the government's decision that union membership was incompatible with national security at Government Communications Headquarters (GCHQ). Although these were far from being typical instances, they did serve to indicate a change in management power and the declining attractiveness of union membership in such circumstances.

The 1998 Workplace Employee Relations Survey (Cully *et al.* 1999) found that the proportion of workplaces with over 25 employees that recognized trade unions had fallen from 66% in 1984 to 45% by 1998. However, the Labour government's Employee Relations Act 1999 (Schedule 1) introduced a statutory right to union recognition when certain qualifications are fulfilled. Since this came into force in June 2000, the number of new recognition agreements has continued to rise (IDS 2002). As a result of such measures the unions have recruited members in businesses with anti-union reputations, including, for example, the re-recognition of the National Union of Journalists in national and provincial newspapers. Unions have also made inroads into areas in which it has traditionally been difficult to recruit, such as hotels and catering and retailing. Such successes have, however, been offset by membership losses in manufacturing and finance, leaving total union membership relatively stable.

The employers

Employers' associations

Many employers in the UK are members of employers' associations which seek to regulate relations between employers and trade unions. These associations are usually organized on an industry basis rather than a product basis, as with the Engineering Employers' Federation with over 5,000 members. Their role includes negotiating with unions at industry level, the operation of procedures for the resolution of disputes, and the provision of advice to members on employment law, manpower planning and other personnel matters. In some industries there are local or regional employers' associations, combined into national federations, as with the Building Employers' Confederation. Altogether there are about 150 national employers' associations which negotiate the national collective agreements for their industry with the trade unions concerned, and most of these belong to the Confederation of British Industry (CBI).

Membership of employers' associations has tended to fall over the past 20 years as the trend towards company bargaining has gained ground. Large companies, such as the car manufacturers, BP, ICI and Shell, prefer to bargain on a company basis with unions rather than be part of a multi-employer bargaining team.

The Confederation of British Industry

This is the largest central employers' organization in the UK, representing over 12,000 companies which employ around 10 million people. Membership includes all sizes and types of company, both private and nationalized, and covers the primary, secondary and tertiary sectors of industry, although manufacturing predominates. Policy is determined by a council of 330 members, and there are 360 permanent staff members, including representatives with the EU in Brussels. The CBI seeks to represent the broad interests of businessmen in discussions with the government, with national and international institutions, and with the public at large. It nominates the employers' representatives for such bodies as the Advisory, Conciliation and Arbitration Service (ACAS). Like the TUC, the CBI is affiliated to a Europe-wide representative organization, the Union of Industrial and Employers' Confederations of Europe (UNICE), which represents central employers' confederations from 25 European countries. It also works in tandem with the European Centre of Enterprises with Public Participation (CEEP) that represents public sector employers.

Individual employers

Over the last 15 years the influence of management has increased as the pressures of unemployment and international competition shifted power away from unions and towards management. Recent management initiatives to increase employee flexibility, to improve quality, and to introduce more performance-related pay, have begun to create a 'cultural change' within individual workplaces. One such change has been the issue of trade union recognition within the company.

The most difficult aspect of collective bargaining in the UK is the fact that workers of a given company often belong to different unions, i.e. multi-union companies. As a result, management often have to negotiate with each union separately. The changing competitive environment mentioned above has caused a shift in the locus of power away from employers' association bargaining with unions and towards individual company bargaining. This shift in power has often resulted in company management attempting to limit bargaining rights to a single trade union within the workplace, i.e. 'single unionism'. The advantage to management of such arrangements is that it simplifies the bargaining process and prevents conflict over demarcations between different skill groups represented by different trade unions within the same enterprise. Although only around 200 firms concluded single-union agreements prior to the advent of statutory recognition (e.g. BICC cables, Ikeda, Hoover and Bosch), the new procedure has substantially increased the number of such arrangements.

Another approach to collective bargaining has been the rise of 'single-table bargaining' which means that, unlike 'single unionism', more than one union is allowed to exist within the company but they have to bargain jointly as a single unit with management rather than separately. These arrangements are supported by the TUC and by individual unions as preferable to single-union deals. Examples are to be found in engineering, the privatized water companies and in car manufacturing, e.g. Rover. Both single-union and single-table bargaining have tended to reflect a shift in power within the workplace, namely towards management and away from unions.

In addition to the issues of union representation, management have been involved in trying to increase employee flexibility by 'multi-skilling', i.e. by widening the skills of each worker (functional flexibility) and by varying the hours worked or employing more part-time or sub-contracted workers rather than full-time workers (numerical flexibility). This trend has threatened union bargaining power, since part-time or sub-contracted workers have a lower union density, as noted earlier in this chapter. Multi-skilling also tends to restrict the ability of shop stewards to negotiate such subjects as staffing levels, job demarcations and the pace of work. Similarly the growth of performance-related pay (PRP), by linking reward to actual performance, may weaken the trade unions because part or all of the individual's annual pay award is no longer subject to collective bargaining.

Finally it is worth noting that the growth of quality consciousness in UK industry has enhanced the importance of *teamwork*. The introduction of such devices as quality circles, where groups of around 10 workers meet to discuss their work and suggest improvements, has increased employee involvement in the firm. The large-scale survey of workplace practices by the DTI in 1998 showed that many 'new' management practices had been introduced to create more employee commitment. Such practices included teamwork activity, team briefings and also performance appraisal meetings in which staff were invited to participate in setting targets and goals. The net effect of these increased attempts by management to involve employees has been to circumvent or marginalize unions while retaining union recognition, leaving the future of 'collective' (i.e. union) representation of the workforce rather unclear.

The emergence of 'partnership agreements' between management and trade unions in recent years suggests an attempt to prevent the marginalization of unions noted above. A formal partnership agreement between unions and management usually involves reciprocal agreements whereby employers receive union commitment to flexible work practices whilst union members receive greater work security and greater participation in the affairs of the company. Such partnerships have occurred in a variety of organizations such as Natwest Retail Banking and Tesco, and are encouraged by a 'Partnership Fund' established by the Labour government.

The government

The government's role in industrial relations is threefold: as an employer, as a legislator and as an economic and social policy-maker.

The government is a major direct *employer of labour*, with central government employing 1.1 million persons, or 4% of the workforce in 1997. It influences not only these pay settlements but also those of the local authorities and the remaining nationalized industries, in total an extra 4.1 million persons. The government can, through its position as a primary source of finance, and by using cash limits (see Chapter 8), affect wage bargaining and employment levels in the local authorities and the nationalized industries.

As a *legislator*, the previous Conservative administration was particularly active, and made extensive use of the law in an effort to reduce what it perceived as excessive union bargaining power, resulting in high UK wage cost and low labour productivity. An examination of the major legal changes introduced since 1979, mainly in the 1980, 1982, 1988, 1989 and 1990 Employment Acts, and in the 1984 Trade Union Act, reveals important changes in the context of collective bargaining. The previous Conservative government consolidated its 'step by step' reforms with the passing of the Trade Union and Labour Relations (Consolidation) Act 1992 (TULR(C)A) as amended by the Trade Union Reform and Employment Rights Act 1993. The former Act was a measure designed to rationalize all previous relevant statutory provisions into a *single act* rather than to change the substance of the law. The latter Act aimed to modify some sections of the 1992 Act by enhancing the rights of individual employees and union members while also imposing certain regulations relating to industrial action. The Labour government has retained most of these legal reforms, and introduced important new statutes (e.g. setting a national minimum wage), as will be discussed later in this chapter.

The closed shop

This is a situation where employees obtain or retain a job only if they become a member of a specified trade union. Its advantages to unions *and* management are discussed below. This practice was progressively weakened by legislation in the 1980s and 1990s making unions liable to legal action from both employees and management if they tried to enforce the closed shop. The relevant legislation which deals with this aspect is contained in Part III of TULR(C)A. A sample study of 529 firms in the mid-1990s found that only 9% of firms still had formal closed-shop arrangements (Geroski *et al.* 1995). However, two important studies (Wright 1996; Addison and Siebert 1998) have shown that while formal union arrangements such as the closed shop may have collapsed among white-collar workers, manual workers and other groups have still retained informal methods of maintaining a closed shop, as in the case of closed-shop arrangements *agreed* between managers and labour.

Strikes and other industrial action

Since the end of the nineteenth century it has been impossible for a trade union to organize a strike without committing a *tort*, that is the civil wrong of interfering with the contract of employment between employer and employed. The committing of a tort enables the employer to obtain an injunction against, or claim damages from, the union. However, since 1906 Parliament has protected unions from this liability by providing them with immunity from civil action, and a major aim of the post-1979 legislation has been to narrow the scope of this immunity by rendering certain types of dispute 'unlawful'.

Industrial action is unlawful when the union is no longer covered by immunity from civil actions brought by employers or other affected parties in the courts. If successful, the employer will obtain a court injunction prohibiting the dispute, and the union will face fines or the sequestration of its assets for failure to comply. An employer can also subsequently claim damages arising from losses sustained during the action.

An important provision in the 1982 Employment Act restricted 'lawful trade disputes' to those between workers and their own employer, making 'political' strikes and inter-union disputes unlawful (s. 219). Also rendered unlawful by the 1980 Employment Act was secondary action, i.e. action against an employer not party to a dispute (s. 224). Picketing is now almost wholly restricted in law to the union members' 'place of work', often even excluding another plant of the same employer. Restrictions on illegal picketing are effected by making unions liable to pay damages in civil actions brought against them by employers. The 1984 Act also meant loss of legal immunity in certain circumstances. Official industrial action, i.e. that approved by the union leadership, must be sanctioned by a secret ballot of the membership. The ballot must be held no more than four weeks before the event, and a majority of union members must be

in favour of the action. If the action takes place without majority consent, then the union loses any legal immunity for organizing industrial action that it may have enjoyed in the past. These provisions were strengthened by the 1988 Employment Act which gave the individual union member the right not to be called out on strike without a properly held secret ballot and, most controversially, in view of the stated opposition of both the CBI and the Chartered Institute of Personnel and Development, the right not to be disciplined by his or her union for refusing to strike or for crossing a picket line. The Act also established a Commissioner for the Rights of Trade Union Members to provide funds and advice to individuals wishing to take legal action to exercise these rights (s. 62). However, this office was abolished by the Employment Act of 1999, which also gave the Certification Officer the power to hear the complaints of trade union members against their unions.

The Employment Act 1999 also strengthened the rights of those employees engaged in 'official' industrial action, i.e. action which has been officially authorized by the unions involved. Previously employees could, in certain circumstances, deem to have been fairly dismissed for such union activity. However under the new Act the dismissal of such employees is deemed automatically unfair for the first eight weeks of the action, a period which may be extended if the employer fails to take 'reasonable steps' to resolve the dispute. Such changes follow the expressed desire of the Labour government to create a workplace environment of greater trust and cooperation.

The 1990 Employment Act took the control of union behaviour even further by requiring that the union leadership must take positive steps to repudiate 'unofficial action', i.e. actions undertaken by union members without union consent (that is of the executive committee or president or general secretary). For instance, the union must do its best to give written notice to all members participating in the action that it does *not* receive the union's support. Failure by the union to take such steps could mean loss of immunity for the union, even though the action is unofficial. In addition, the Act allowed employers to dismiss unofficial strikers selectively at the place of work (e.g. the strike leaders) and deny those dismissed the right to claim unfair dismissal. Any industrial action because of such dismissal would now be deprived of immunity (s. 223).

The Trade Union Reform and Employment Rights Act 1993 passed two main provisions relating to the organization of industrial action. First, ballots held in support of action should be fully postal and subject to independent scrutiny, effectively restricting the initiation of action at 'rank-and-file' level. Second, unions are to be required to give seven days' written notice before industrial action can be taken. This affords a longer waiting period to help settle any dispute. The unions argue, however, that it also gives employers rather longer to prepare for any dispute. The Act also provided government assistance for members of the public to seek damages from trade unions for the effects of unlawful industrial action, but this was abolished by the Employment Relations Act 1999 (ERA). ERA also amended the rules on ballots, enabling employers and trade unions to continue negotiations beyond the four-week deadline for the commencement of industrial action after the date of the ballot. In addition, ERA issued a code of practice on how ballots should be conducted that can be used by courts to determine breaches of the law. It also made it clear that an overtime ban constituted industrial action short of a strike, and not full strike action.

Legal regulation of wages and conditions of work

Many legal regulations which had originally been designed to place a 'floor' on both wages and conditions of work were dismantled after 1979 by successive Conservative governments in order to remove alleged disincentives to employment and to help increase labour flexibility. For example, the abolition of the Wages Councils in 1993 took away minimum-wage guarantees for low-paid workers in the industries for which these Wages Councils existed. In addition, the UK also initially 'opted out' of the 'Agreement on Social Policy' contained in the Social Protocol of the Maastricht Treaty – commonly known as the Social Chapter. This absolved the UK government from the need to implement certain EU Directives regulating employer/employee relations, a policy reversed in 1997 by the incoming Labour government.

Although also committed to workforce flexibility, the Labour government has tended to reverse some of this earlier legislation. It established the Low Pay Commission to make recommendations for a *National Minimum Wage* (NMW), which is considered further

below (p. 293). It also legislated against the blacklisting of union members and sought to improve the rights of workers on 'zero hours' contracts (i.e. where workers have no guaranteed paid hours). ERA 1999 also gave employees the statutory right to be represented in formal disciplinary and grievance proceedings, which unions have seen as a possible route to recognition and new members as it implies union access to previously non-union workplaces (McKay 2001).

The Employment Act 2002 introduced further individual rights for employees, the most significant of which address certain 'family-friendly' practices to promote 'work/life balance'. From April 2003, maternity leave was increased and working fathers have been given the right to two weeks' paternity leave. Employees are also able to request flexible working from their employers, such as job sharing, flexi-time, home-working and part-time work. Employers have the right to refuse such requests, but must explain their reasons for this to the employee in writing.

Trade union democracy

The Trade Union Act 1984 and Employment Act 1988 embodied a number of provisions for internal union democracy in addition to those pertaining to strike action. Members of the main executive committee of a trade union must have been elected in a secret ballot of the union's members within the previous five years. The Employment Act of 1990 contained the right of members to a postal vote in elections for all members of union governing bodies and for key national leaders. In addition, the 1984 Act required trade unions with political funds to ballot their members at least every 10 years. Only if this is done, and majority assent for the fund achieved, can the union continue to spend money on 'political' matters, such as a campaign against new legislation or in support of a political party. To date, of all ballots which have been held on this matter, a substantial majority have been in favour of retaining the fund.

The Trade Union Reform and Employment Rights Act 1993 modified some sections of the TULR(C)A by taking the issue of democracy further. Firstly, it strengthened the rights of *individuals* by giving them greater freedom to belong to the union of their choice. For example, an individual could belong to more than one union and unions could not dismiss a member for failing to support a strike. This had obvious implications for relationships between unions and their members. Secondly, it also gave *trade union members* the right not to have union subscriptions deducted from their pay except with their written consent. The latter 'check off' arrangements were seen as threatening union membership levels and were repealed in 1998 by the Labour government.

Statutory recognition of trade unions

An important legislative change relating to trade union recognition was introduced in June 2000 under Schedule 1 of the Employment Relations Act 1999, which amended the Trades Union and Labour Relations (Consolidation Act) 1992. This schedule covers workers in organizations with at least 21 employees where a trade union has made a request to be recognized as the representative of employees for bargaining purposes. If an employer rejects the request, the union can apply to the Central Arbitration Committee (CAC) which has to decide whether the union has the support of the majority of the workforce that comprises the proposed 'bargaining unit', i.e. the group of employees to be covered by collective bargaining. If 50% or more of the bargaining unit are members of the union applying for recognition, then the CAC may award automatic recognition. If this criterion is not met, then a ballot can be held. In this case recognition will depend on the union receiving a majority of the votes in a ballot *and* at least 40% of the workers entitled to vote having done so. The recognition agreement lasts for three years.

The impact of this legislation on union membership was considered earlier in the chapter, and its use has proved less problematic for trade unions than they envisaged, given the formidable qualifications for recognition that the procedure imposed. From June 2000 to the end of March 2002, 175 applications for recognition were received by the CAC, of which 86 were ultimately withdrawn, 12 were rejected by the CAC, 34 were pending and in 14 cases recognition was decided by the Committee without a ballot. Only 29 cases proceeded to a ballot and 20 of these led to union recognition. The relative success of the unions involved in the procedure reflects their avoidance of making applications where they were not very confident about membership levels and support for recognition in the bargaining unit.

Probably the most difficult part of the recognition procedure is the decision about the appropriateness of the bargaining unit, which must be 'compatible with effective management'. Not only has this been a source of conflict between unions seeking recognition and management, but it can also cause friction between unions competing for membership. For example, the TGWU was recognized by Eurotunnel to represent its train drivers in the teeth of opposition by ASLEF, the train drivers' union (Walsh 2000). Whilst the Labour government has extended the rights of employees to collective representation, UK law places more restrictions on industrial action than anywhere else in the EU, with the Labour government remaining committed to the outlawing of strikes called in sympathy with other unions, or union actions that can broadly be deemed as political.

In its legislative capacity, therefore, the government can alter the balance of power between employer and employee. However, it is difficult to assess how far any legislation can be effectively used by employers, as this depends upon a complex array of factors, such as management style, the firm's size and position within both product and labour markets, the availability of alternative tactics and the anticipated repercussions of recourse to law on a firm's industrial relations.

The European Union and UK industrial relations

The European Union is discussed more fully in Chapter 29, but the current proposals of the European Commission are of potentially great significance to the UK. The most important measures are contained in the *European Social Charter* and the accompanying 'Action Programme' for its implementation. The Charter contains provisions relating to both the individual and collective rights of workers, but it is important to recognize that it is a statement of *principles* or intent and that by itself it creates no legally enforceable rights. However, the Commission plans to give legal form to the Charter's contents over the next few years, which at present enjoy majority support in the Council of Ministers.

Only a brief outline of the Charter can be given here, but measures pertaining to individual employee rights include greater freedom of movement within the Community, the right to training, protection regarding health and safety and against discrimination, provisions to safeguard the employment conditions of the young, disabled and elderly, and employees at large, and minimum rules on work duration, rest periods and holidays, shift work and systematic overtime. Broadly similar rights are to be extended to part-time, casual and temporary workers. The Charter excludes a commitment to minimum wage legislation. Measures relating to collective labour law are more limited, and the Charter does not propose any legally enforceable right to bargain for trade unions where this is not already part of a member state's law. However, the Charter does include important prospective rights to information and consultation plus the 'participation' of employees before companies make decisions on redundancies and closures.

Implementing the Social Chapter

The Labour government's reversal of the 'opt-out' from the Social Chapter has led to the adoption of EU Directives which have had important implications for industrial relations. Under the Social Chapter, the European Commission must consult with the social partners (ETUC, UNICE and CEEP) about the content of its proposals, with much of the ensuing legislation arising out of 'framework agreements' negotiated at European level by the partners. Successful agreements which have been adopted by the Commission include the *Parental Leave Directive* (which gave parents the right to leave work after the birth or adoption of a child), the *Part-time Workers' Directive* (which extended equal rights and pro-rata benefits to part-time staff) and the *Fixed-Term Contracts Directive* (which strengthened the rights of workers under such contracts, as well as discouraging their use). This last Directive is unique in that it is the first to be initiated by UNICE in the employment field (Gennard and Judge 2002). However, the Labour government has restricted the impact of the part-time workers' regulations by limiting the scope for comparison between such employees and full-time staff to those working under the same type of contract and at the same location (McKay 2001).

The *Working Time Directive* was implemented in the UK in 1998 and contained provisions for a legal right to four weeks' paid holidays and an upper limit to the working week of 48 hours (averaged over 14 weeks), together with various other entitlements, such

as the right to rest periods. The impact so far has been marginal, with the government allowing both individual and collective 'opt-outs' by employees from the legislation. British employee relations have also been affected by the *European Works Council Directive* of 1994 (extended to the UK in 1998). The European Works Council (EWC) is a term used for a pan-European forum of employee representatives set up for the purpose of information and consultation. Multinationals with at least 1,000 employees working in the EU and with at least 150 employees working in two or more of its member states, are required to establish an EWC, which consists of managers and elected representatives from the workforce across its European operations. It must meet at least once a year to discuss the progress and prospects of the company, as well as any decisions likely to affect more than one EU member state, e.g. closures or mergers.

A significant new measure that extends the principle of consultation is the *Information and Consultation Directive* (2002), which is opposed by the Labour government. This gives employees in establishments with at least 50 employees rights to information and consultation on the performance of the business and on decisions relevant to employment, including substantial changes to work organization, particularly where jobs are threatened. Whilst the Directive is not due for full implementation in the UK until early 2008, it can be expected to increase substantially the incidence of formal, joint consultation beyond its current level of 53% (Cully *et al.* 1999).

As a complement to EU statutes, the *Human Rights Act* 1998 (HRA) came into force in 2000, with important implications for British employee relations. For example, it includes the requirement that internal disciplinary procedures in the public sector organizations must conform to standards of proof and procedures expected of courts and tribunals. The HRA's effects on the private sector are less clear, but employment practices are likely to be subjected to more rigorous examination under the Act which, like the EU Charter, also enshrines a right to freedom of association.

The structure of collective bargaining

Collective bargaining has been defined by Clegg as referring to 'the whole range of dealings between employers and managers on the one hand, and trade unions, shop stewards and members on the other, over the making, interpretation and administration of employment rules'. These rules are both *substantive*, determining pay, hours, overtime, manning levels, holidays, etc., and *procedural*, governing the way in which substantive issues are settled. One of the most significant changes which has taken place in UK industrial relations over the last 20 years has been the decrease in the percentage of employees covered by collective bargaining agreements. For example, between 1984 and 2001, the percentage of total employees covered by collective bargaining arrangements fell from 71% to 36%. The effects of decreased union density, the legal changes introduced by government, the privatization movement, and the increased power of management, all contributed towards this downward trend. Despite this radical change, collective bargaining between unions and employers is still of major importance in most of the UK's key sectors, and occurs at a number of levels.

bargaining has already disappeared from a number of sectors, including the clearing banks, the cable industry, provincial newspapers and independent TV companies. Nevertheless, a potentially important development in multi-employer bargaining is the growth of 'coordinated bargaining' across Europe, defined as 'an attempt to achieve the same or related outcomes in separate negotiations' (Sisson and Marginson 2002). At EU-sector level, ETUC and its constituent industry federations, such as the European Metalworkers' Federation, have initiated procedures to combat 'social dumping' by multinational companies (MNCs). In MNCs, many of which operate across Europe, there is pressure from top management to implement 'best practice' policies (such as team-working and annualized hours) across their European subsidiaries as, for example, in the case of General Motors. This type of coordinated bargaining is at an early stage but nevertheless could have an impact on UK industrial relations, although significant decentralization is likely to remain.

National or multi-employer bargaining

This level of negotiation predominates in the public sector in which centralized bargaining gives rise to relatively formal, fixed-term and comprehensive agreements, leaving little scope for localized or workplace bargaining. However, there is now a clear trend towards more decentralized bargaining in the public sector. The 'local management of schools' initiative, together with the creation of semi-autonomous NHS Trusts, necessarily imply further moves towards local bargaining. Moreover, both the privatized water companies and electricity generators have withdrawn from industry-level agreements, and decentralization is becoming the norm for the privatized elements of British Rail. Finally, the 'contracting out' to private tender of many services previously supplied by local authorities clearly reduces the coverage of national bargaining in this sector.

In the private sector national bargaining occurs on an industry level, between employers' associations and trade unions, or federations of unions. This was once the main type of collective bargaining, but has declined in importance in many industries so that by the late 1990s it covered only about 15% of employees in the private sector (e.g. electrical contracting). In fact, industry-wide and multi-employer

Single-employer bargaining

This occurs at two levels: (a) *corporate*, i.e. at the level of the company or whole organization; and (b) *establishment*, i.e. at the level of the workplace, such as the factory, plant or office.

The widespread practice of informal bargaining at workplaces in the 1960s, generally in the manufacturing sector, was criticized by the Donovan Commission in 1968. The Commission recommended that tacit, unwritten deals between local managers and shop stewards should be replaced by written formal agreements of specified duration and on clearly delineated issues. This encouraged the rise of corporate or company-level bargaining and the greater involvement of senior management.

However, this shift to company agreements, largely initiated by US-owned multinationals to exert greater control over collective bargaining, has not been universal. In fact, establishment or plant-level bargaining remains important in many industries, such as clothing, and the footwear, brick and timber industries. More significantly, recent changes in managerial practice, which have devolved more responsibility to middle management for running individual establishments as separate budget or profit centres, have enhanced formal plant bargaining at the expense of company-wide negotiation. The growth of multi-product or multi-divisional firms such as Unilever, Philips, Coates Viyella and Lucas, for example, is evidence of such trends towards division and establishment level bargaining. However, this development has been accompanied by a decline in the range of substantive issues which many managements are prepared to negotiate with unions. Moreover, and of perhaps greater future importance for workplace bargaining, there has been a marked increase in systems of individual assessment and reward, some linked to the profit performance of the company, which could further undermine collective representation. Studies have shown that 14% of non-managerial employees in the private sector have their pay negotiated at corporate level and 9% at workplace level. This compares with 16% and 35% respectively in the public sector (Cully *et al.* 1999). Bargaining has become more decentralized over time, moving from the multi-employer to the corporate level, and on the other hand from the corporate level to the establishment or plant level. The main reasons cited for the growth of establishment- or plant-level bargaining include better control of profitability levels by taking into consideration local labour market conditions and more ability to reward individual employees according to performance.

Advisory, Conciliation and Arbitration Service (ACAS)

ACAS was established as an independent statutory body on 1 January 1976 and is formally independent of direct ministerial intervention. The agency stemmed from the Department of Employment's Conciliation and Arbitration Service which had often been criticized as not being independent since it was directly under the control of a government minister. Its role is to provide impartial information (advisory) and to help prevent or resolve problems between employers and their workforces (conciliation and arbitration). The service is controlled by a council consisting of 12 members, including an independent chairman and 11 other members with experience of industrial relations (e.g. trade unionists, academics and others), all of whom are appointed by the Secretary of State for Industry. For example, in 2001/02 it acted in its advisory capacity on 506 projects, completed 1,270 conciliation events and arbitrated or mediated in 68 disputes. *Conciliation* is

the process of bringing parties together in a dispute in order to move forward towards a settlement, whilst *arbitration* involves an independent arbitrator or board of arbitrators,[2] who decide on the outcome of a dispute and whose decision may have legal force. Of the 68 arbitration cases dealt with by ACAS in 2001/02, pay and conditions of employment accounted for 56% of the cases undertaken, followed by dismissal and discipline matters (32%), issues of employee grading (7%) and redundancy and demarcation issues 5% (ACAS 2002).

Wage determination and collective bargaining

The neo-classical view of wage determination is embodied in 'marginal productivity' theory. With many small buyers of labour (firms) and many small suppliers (i.e. non-unionized individuals), the wage rate would be determined by the intersection of demand and supply curves for labour.

The demand curve for any factor, including labour, is seen as being derived from the demand for the product or service it produces. Additional labour will always be required if the revenue gained from selling the output produced by the last person, the marginal revenue product of labour (MRP_L),[3] is greater than the extra cost of employing that person, the marginal cost of labour (MC_L). In a competitive labour market (see Fig. 15.1), the supply of labour

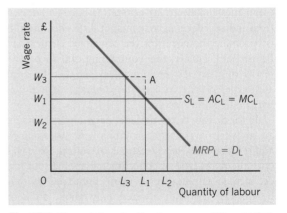

Fig. 15.1 Wage determination in a competitive market.

(S_L) to each firm would be perfectly elastic at the going wage rate (W_1), so that the wage rate is itself the marginal cost of labour.[4] The profit-maximizing firm would then hire people until MRP_L equalled MC_L, i.e. L_1 persons in Fig. 15.1. If more than L_1 persons were hired, then the extra revenue from their hire would fail to match the extra cost incurred.

Under these conditions the MRP_L curve becomes the demand curve for labour (D_L), since at any given wage rate the profit-maximizing firm will employ labour until MRP_L equals that wage rate. For example, if the wage rate falls to W_2 in Fig. 15.1, then demand for labour rises to L_2.

Wages and unions

If the labour force is now unionized, then the supply of labour to the firm (or industry) may be regulated. However, even though unions bring an element of monopoly into labour supply, theory suggests that they can influence only price *or* quantity, but not both. For example, in Fig. 15.1 the union may seek wage rate W_3, but must accept in return lower employment at L_3. Alternatively, unions may seek a level of employment L_2, but must then accept a lower wage rate at W_2. Except (see below) where unions are able to force employers off their demand curve for labour (MRP_L), then unions can raise wages only at the 'cost' of reduced employment. However, a *given rise* in wages will reduce employment by less, under the following circumstances:

1 The less elastic is final demand for the product.

2 The less easy it is to substitute other factors for the workers in question.

3 The lower the proportion of labour costs to total costs of production.

All of these circumstances will make the demand curve for labour, MRP_L, less elastic.

Unions and bargaining power

Unions may seek to force the employer off his demand curve for labour so that he makes less than maximum profits. It may then be possible for wages to rise from W_1 to W_3 with no loss of employment, i.e. at point A in Fig. 15.1. How effective unions will be in such strategies will depend upon the extent of their 'bargaining power'.

Chamberlain defines union bargaining power as:

$$\frac{\text{Management costs of disagreeing (to union terms)}}{\text{Management costs of agreeing (to union terms)}}$$

Although this ratio cannot be measured, as it relies on subjective assessments, it is a useful analytical tool. If unions are to exert effective influence on management the ratio must exceed unity. That is to say, it must be more costly for management to disagree (e.g. loss of profits, or market share as a result of strike action) than to agree (e.g. higher labour costs and manning levels). The higher the ratio, the more inclined management may then be to agree to the union's terms.

The level of the wage demand will affect union bargaining power. The more modest the wage claim, the lower the management cost of agreement, and the higher Chamberlain's ratio, i.e. the greater is union bargaining power. This will increase the prospects for securing higher wages with stable employment.

Union density will also affect bargaining power. The greater the proportion of the industry unionized, the less easy it will be to substitute non-union labour. The management costs of disagreeing to union terms will tend to be higher, so that the ratio, i.e. union bargaining power, rises. Equally, the higher is union density in the industry as a whole, the easier it is for any particular company to pass on higher wage demands as price increases to consumers without losing market share. This is because competing firms in the industry will also be facing similar wage-cost conditions. High union density therefore reduces the management costs of agreeing to union terms, and again raises the ratio, i.e. union bargaining power. High union density will therefore also increase the prospects for securing higher wages with stable employment.

Even macroeconomic factors can be brought into this analysis. The higher the level of real income in the economy, the higher will be demand for 'normal' goods. Management will then be able to pass on cost increases as higher prices with relatively less effect on demand. This will reduce management costs of agreeing to union terms, raise the ratio, and with it union bargaining power.

Another main factor which affects the bargaining power of trade unions is the degree of competition in the *product market*. For example, Gregg and Machin (1991) found that those unionized firms facing increased competition in the market for their product, experienced slower wage growth than those unionized firms that did not. In other words, increasing competition in the product market tends to *reduce* the bargaining power of unions to raise wages. This seems to indicate that unions are becoming more aware of the potential 'costs' to them in terms of unemployment if they bargain for higher wages when their firm is experiencing intense competition.

However, one must recognize the existence of many other dimensions to union bargaining power, such as the degree of unanimity or conflict within unions over bargaining goals and methods. Unions will also vary in the militancy of their members and the bargaining abilities of their leaders. All this makes the assessment of bargaining power extremely difficult. It is also important to note that the 'resource' theory of the impact of trade unionism on the firm does not accept that the exercise of this power will necessarily raise production costs. Instead, the theory argues that unions can significantly increase productivity by providing an efficient means for the management and settlement of disputes. Thus, collective bargaining reduces the costs of individual expressions of grievances, which may raise the 'quit' rate of key employees and the incidence of absenteeism or poor-quality work. Further, the 'shock' effect of unions' negotiation of pay rises may force managements to increase efficiency in order to absorb higher costs.

Wages and employers' associations

Wages are determined by a variety of factors, of which union bargaining power is but one, admittedly important, element.

Employers' associations are themselves able to create an element of monopoly on the *demand* side of the labour market (i.e. 'monopsony'). These associations bring together the employers of labour in order to exert greater influence in collective bargaining. Standard theory suggests that monopsony in the labour market will, by itself, reduce both wages and employment in the labour market.

In Fig. 15.2, under competitive labour market conditions the equilibrium would occur where the supply of labour ($S_L = AC_L$) equalled the demand for labour (MRP_L), giving wage W_C and employment L_C. If monopsony occurs, so that employers bid the wage rate up against themselves, then it can be shown that

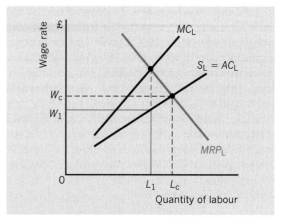

Fig. 15.2 Wage determination with monopsony in the labour market.

the MC_L curve will lie above the $S_L = AC_L$ curve. For example, if by hiring the fourth worker, the wage ($= AC_L$) of all workers is bid up from £5 to £6, then the AC_L for the fourth worker is £6 *but* the MC_L for the fourth worker is higher at £9 (£24 − £15). The profit-maximizing employer will want to equate the extra revenue contributed by the last worker employed (MRP_L) to the extra cost of employing the last worker (MC_L). In Fig. 15.2 this occurs with L_1 workers employed. Note, however, that the employer only has to offer a wage of W_1 in order to get L_1 workers to supply themselves to the labour market. The wage W_1 is *below* the competitive wage W_C and the level of employment L_1 is *below* the competitive level of employment L_C. This is the standard case against monopsony in a labour market, namely lower wages and lower employment as compared to a competitive labour market.

When monopoly on the demand side (employers' associations) is combined with monopoly on the supply side (trade unions), the wage and employment outcome becomes indeterminate. This is often called 'bilateral monopoly'.

The existence of employers' associations will clearly affect the strength of union bargaining power. The greater the density of their coverage within an industry, the smaller might be the management costs of disagreement, e.g. in the case of a strike there is less likelihood of other domestic firms capturing their markets. By reducing the numerator of the ratio, union bargaining power is reduced.

Wages and government: the National Minimum Wage

The National Minimum Wage (NMW) was introduced in April 1999 in the UK at a rate of £3.60 per hour for workers aged 22 years and over, with a lower 'development rate' of £3.00 per hour for workers aged between 18 and 21 years. The rates have been adjusted upwards at roughly yearly intervals since then, so that by October 2003 the adult rate had reached a level of £4.50 per hour and the development rate stood at £3.80 per hour.

Figure 15.3 illustrates the problem of setting too high a minimum wage. If the NMW is set above the competitive wage (W_C) for any labour market, then there will be an excess supply of labour of $L' - L^*$, with more people supplying themselves to work in this labour market than there are jobs available. In Fig. 15.3 the actual level of employment falls from L_C to L^*.

However, there have been a number of studies suggesting that in the US, a higher minimum wage has actually increased wages *and* employment (Atkinson 1996). But it has been noted that many of the US studies have involved labour markets (e.g. fast food) which are dominated by a few large employers of labour, i.e. *monopsonistic* labour markets.

In fact our earlier analysis of monopsony might have led us to expect this. For example, if in Fig. 15.4 the initial monopsony equilibrium was wage W_1 and employment L_1, then setting a minimum wage of W^* would result in a rise in both wages (W_1 to W^*) and

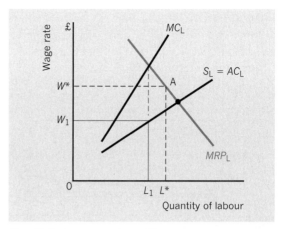

Fig. 15.4 Minimum wage (W^*) raising both wages and employment with monopsony in the labour market.

employment (L_1 to L^*). Since no labour is supplied below the minimum wage W^* this is the *effective labour supply curve* at W^* ($W^* = AC_L = MC_L$). The profit-maximizing situation is at point A on the MRP_L curve, where the marginal cost of hiring the last person (MC_L) exactly equals the extra revenue resulting from employing that last person (MRP_L). So imposing a minimum wage on a labour market that is already imperfect (here monopsony) can increase both wages and levels of employment.

The impact of the minimum wage legislation on low pay since 2000 can be seen in Fig. 15.5 which gives the number of people aged 22 and over who were paid *below* a range of hourly wage rates. The figures are given in the form of four lines, each representing a different period in time and indicating the number of people earning below the specified hourly wage rate at the date shown. The NMW levels at the different dates are also provided.

First, it can be seen that there is a tendency for a significant increase in the number earning just above the minimum wage shortly after the introduction of the NMW, suggesting that employers are responsive to raising pay just above the minimum wage around the time the NMW was introduced or subsequently changed. Second, over the period 1999 to 2002, each successive time line is below the one representing the previous time period, indicating that a change in the NMW threshold has impacts that continue into future time periods, with progressively fewer people paid below that 'new' benchmark as time moves on. Overall it would seem that the numbers of jobs

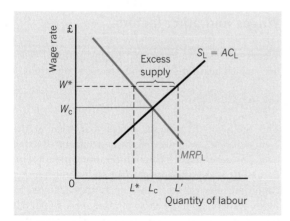

Fig. 15.3 Minimum wage (W^*) set above the competitive market wage (W_C).

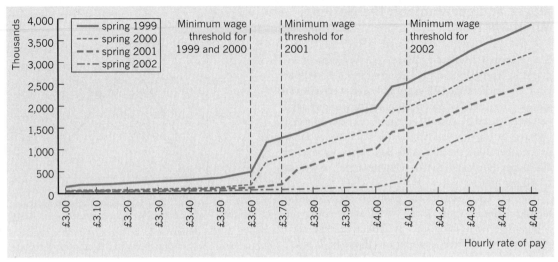

Fig. 15.5 Numbers of jobs paid below different hourly rates of pay for people aged 22 and over, UK, 1999–2002. Source: Heasman (2003).

paying wage levels below the NMW threshold appear to be very responsive to the threshold changes but with something of a time lag (Heasman 2003).

Despite the decreases in numbers of workers earning low wage rates (as shown in Fig. 15.5 by the downward shift in the lines over time), there are still a significant number of low-paid workers in some sectors of economic activity. For example, the percentage of workers paid less than £5 per hour is higher in sectors such as Hotels and Restaurants (44% below £5 per hour), Wholesale, Retail and Motor trades (29%), Agriculture, Hunting and Fishing (22%) and the Community, Social and Personal sector (21%). Similarly, part-time jobs are about five times as likely to be low paid as full-time jobs, whilst women's jobs are three times as likely to be low paid as men's jobs (Heasman 2003).

The effect of the successive increases in NMW on employment in such low-paid jobs has been a matter of intense study. Reports by the Low Pay Commission (LPC) and Income Data Services (IDS) between 2000 and 2003 have shown that the NMW has had no major negative effects on employment (IDS 2000). In fact, between 2001 and 2002 employment in low-paid sectors actually increased by 60,000, especially in low-wage sectors such as retail, hospitality, social care and hairdressing. Where employment has fallen, as in the cleaning, textile and clothing sectors, the reasons were to do with factors such as changes in

basic economic conditions, changes in product demand or in overseas competition (Low Pay Commission 2003). To offset higher wage costs as a result of the NMW, successive Low Pay Commissions have pointed out that firms have responded by changing their work organization, increasing their training and improving the quality of their service rather than by decreasing their employment. However, the period since the NMW has been introduced in the UK has been marked by rising real incomes and demand, and firmer conclusions must await the observation of firm responses in periods of declining economic activity.

Wages and other factors

Wages can also be influenced by institutional practices which bear little relation to market conditions.

'Spillover' and comparability

The 'spillover' hypothesis argues that wage settlements for one group of workers are transmitted ('spill over') to other groups through the principle of comparability, irrespective of product and labour market conditions. For example, the pay awards achieved by 'wage leaders' often give rise to a sequence of similar settlements in the same 'wage round' for other workers.

Non-pecuniary advantages or disadvantages

Not all jobs have the same conditions of work. Some are hazardous, dirty, boring, require the working of unsocial hours, or receive various perquisites ('perks'). These will inevitably form part of the collective bargain, and ultimately affect the wage outcome. In some circumstances wage demands may be modified as the union places greater emphasis on non-wage factors.

Cost of living

The cost of living is an important factor in determining the wage claim, and has even been a formal part of wage settlements. When inflation is accelerating, unions become still more preoccupied with securing cost-of-living increases. This can trigger a wage–price spiral when unions overestimate future rates of inflation.

Productivity agreements

Part of the wage bargain may include the abandonment of restrictive practices, and the raising of production in return for higher wages. During the 1960s a whole series of formalized productivity agreements were concluded. The first and most celebrated of these was negotiated between Esso and the unions at the oil refinery at Fawley. A whole range of restrictive practices, including demarcation rules, excessive overtime and time-wasting, were 'bought out' by management for higher wages.

The effects of collective bargaining

The process of collective bargaining has had a number of important effects on the UK labour market.

Pay differentials

A number of studies have suggested a significant pay differential between unionized and non-unionized workers. During the 1980s studies by economists such as Nickell and Andrews placed this differential as high as 20% in favour of unionized workers, though studies in the 1990s by Metcalf (1994)

suggested a lower figure of around 10%. The more recent research of Blanchflower (1996) also suggests a pay differential of around 10% between unionized and non-unionized workers. The evidence also suggests that such differentials have decreased over time and that they depend, in part, on the degree of union density across sectors; the greater the union density, the greater the pay differential (Addison and Siebert 1998).

However, the nature of the pay differential observed between union and non-union labour may be due to more than simply collective bargaining. First, union labour may be of higher quality than non-union labour, with some of the pay differential due to the higher marginal revenue product of union labour. Second, employers may raise the wages of non-union labour in an attempt to forestall unionization, thereby eroding the pay differential. Third, incomes policies imposed by governments may affect the union/non-union pay differential. Flat-rate norms which are often a part of incomes policy will compress the pay differential that union bargaining power might otherwise have secured.

In practice, the particular effect of trade unions on pay is very difficult to disentangle from those of other labour market conditions. It is interesting to note, however, that both union and non-union workers have on average been able to secure very large increases in real wages, even during periods of high unemployment. This may suggest a fall in the price elasticity of demand for labour as the capital/labour ratio has increased, thereby reducing labour costs as a proportion of total costs (see above), and may also indicate a low and negative unemployment elasticity of real wages.[5] In fact, unemployed workers have perhaps ceased to exert a *permanent* influence on wage determination.

Restrictive practices and labour utilization

It has been suggested that the process of collective bargaining reinforces the unions' perception that they have 'property rights'. These rights may include a variety of established practices which have been used to protect jobs or earnings. These practices have important consequences for labour utilization and may form part of the collective bargain. They include the closed shop, minimum staffing levels, demarcation rules, seniority principles, strikes, etc. We briefly review a number of the most important 'restrictive practices'.

The closed shop

Closed shops confer a number of advantages on trade unions. First, they permit monopoly control over labour supply. This increases the union's ability to disrupt production through industrial action, and therefore raises its 'bargaining power'. In terms of Chamberlain's ratio (p. 291), it raises the 'management cost of disagreeing', and therefore union bargaining power. Second, closed shops prevent the 'free rider' problem, whereby non-union labour benefits from union bargaining power. Third, closed shops make it easier to enforce agreements reached between unions and management. Indeed, despite restricting the freedom of employers to choose whom they will employ, the closed shop has the benefit of bringing more order and certainty to industrial relations.

As we have seen, legislation since 1979 has made the closed shop legally unenforceable, reflecting the government's desire to reduce union bargaining power and to protect the right of an individual not to join a trade union. The incidence of closed shops has decreased rapidly since 1979 with contemporary estimates suggesting that only some 9% of firms continue to have some form of closed shop agreement with unions.

Established practices

In industries such as printing, the railways and car production, unions often have, by tradition, some control over staffing levels, job speeds, the introduction of new technologies and demarcation issues, in other words, which type or grade of workers should undertake particular types of work. As a result, management decisions over the allocation of labour within an enterprise are subject to union influence.

The seniority principle

This is the principle whereby union members with the longest service in a firm are the first to be promoted and the last to be made redundant. This principle may conflict with the firm's desire to employ younger, more flexible and cheaper workers. However, companies may sometimes wish to retain senior workers, having already made a substantial investment in them through specific training.

These restrictive practices may enter into the collective bargain. Unions may seek to trade them for higher wages – as in the productivity agreements noted above. Through 'buying out' restrictive practices in this way, management seeks a more efficient utilization of labour, and thereby higher productivity.

The strike weapon

One of the most powerful 'property rights' perceived by the unions is their ability to affect the collective

Table 15.4 Strikes: international comparisons, 1989–2001 (working days lost per 1,000 employees – annual averages).

Country	1989–93	1994–2001	1989–2001
Spain	428	238	333
Canada	255	190	223
Italy	250	94	172
United Kingdom	72	20	46
France	34	95	65
United States	65	51	58
Germany[1]	19	3	11
Japan	3	2	3
EU average	105	60	83
OECD average	86	53	70

[1] From 1993 data covers entire Federal Republic of Germany.
Source: Adapted from *Labour Market Trends* (2003) April, and previous issues.

bargain by withdrawing their labour, i.e. going on strike. This is viewed by some as the ultimate form of restrictive practice. The use of the strike weapon by unions in the UK has been the subject of much research and debate.

Table 15.4 demonstrates that compared to its major economic competitors the UK was less strike-prone than the OECD and EU averages over the whole period shown. It is often in the context of strikes that governments and employers see union 'property rights' as detrimental to Britain's economic performance, while the unions themselves perceive the withdrawal of labour as a response to the failure of management. Disputes over pay are the most common cause of working days lost, accounting for 71% of the total in 1989–2001, followed by staffing and redundancy issues (9%) and work allocation issues (7%), although attributing strikes to a single cause often masks the existence of other contributory factors. The threat of industrial action by a trade union may alone be sufficient to achieve its aims, but one must be careful not to overestimate its role or that of actual strike incidence in the process of bargaining. The CBI has reported that both are only rarely given as a reason for employers conceding wage increases.

Although the improvement in Britain's strike record is clear and indisputable, there has been a dramatic rise in notified individual grievances. For example, the Advisory, Conciliation and Arbitration Service (ACAS) has reported a substantial rise in cases received for conciliation, i.e. prior to a hearing by an industrial tribunal. Perhaps the lack of actual strike activity may not be a good indicator of the actual stresses and strains experienced within the labour market!

Conclusion

We have seen that the trade unions play an important role in the wage-bargaining process, despite the recent decline in union density. The employers' associations and the government are also important role-players in the process of collective bargaining. In recent years there has been a shift in the private sector from national or industry-wide bargaining to single-employer and, increasingly, establishment bargaining of a largely 'formal' nature. Wage negotiation is, however, a complex procedure, and the outcome depends upon the relative 'bargaining power' of both management and unions. Wages are also affected by a variety of 'non-market' factors, such as comparability, work conditions, cost of living, and the 'trading' of restrictive practices. Government legislation in the form of the National Minimum Wage will also influence the wage outcome. Collective bargaining can have an important effect on pay differentials and may even help enshrine a variety of established (restrictive) practices which have been used to protect jobs or earnings. However, the use of the strike weapon appears to be limited to large plants in specific industrial sectors, though the fact that these are often the basic UK or export-orientated industries may still leave the UK at a disadvantage *vis-à-vis* her international competitors.

Key points

- Most trade unions are relatively small; around 50% have fewer than 1,000 members. However, these unions have less than 0.5% of total union membership. In fact very large unions with over 250,000 members have around 72% of total union membership.

- Trade unions in the UK can be one of four types: craft, general, industrial or white-collar. In Europe most unions are industrial.

- There has been a sharp fall in union membership: in 1979, 54.5% of all employees were unionized, but by 2001 this figure had fallen to only 28.5%.

- Unions can usually secure higher wages only at the 'cost' of less employment unless their bargaining power is strong. If this is the case, they may be able to force employers off their labour demand curves, securing higher wages with no loss of employment.

■ Chamberlain defined union 'bargaining power' as the ratio between the management costs of disagreeing and of agreeing to union terms. The larger the ratio, the greater the union bargaining power.

■ A *given rise* in wages will usually reduce employment by less: (a) the less elastic the demand for the final product, (b) the less easy it is to substitute labour by other factors of production, (c) the lower the proportion of labour costs in total production costs.

■ The government has legislated to reduce union power in various ways, e.g. removing the closed shop, imposing conditions on strikes and other union activities, deregulating the setting of wages and other working conditions, and promoting trade union democracy. It has also legislated to introduce a National Minimum Wage.

■ Other factors influencing the wage settlement include spillover and comparability, non-pecuniary advantages/disadvantages, the cost of living and any productivity agreements made between employers and employees.

■ Fewer strikes currently occur in the UK than is the average for the advanced industrialized countries; e.g. over the period 1989–2001, only 46 working days were lost per 1,000 employees in the UK compared to 68 for all advanced industrialized countries.

Now try the self-check questions for this chapter on the Companion Website. You will also find up-to-date facts and case materials.

Notes

1. Trades Union Congress evidence to the Royal Commission on Trade Unions and Employers' Associations (1968).

2. It may also refer to a Central Arbitration Committee. This is an independent national body which provides boards of arbitration for the settlement of trade disputes.

3. The marginal revenue product of labour (MRP_L) equals the marginal physical product of labour (MPP_L) times the price of output. Because of diminishing returns to labour, the MPP_L curve will eventually begin to slope downwards. This is the part of the curve reflected in Fig. 15.1, since, if MPP_L slopes downwards, so will MRP_L.

4. In Fig. 15.1 we assume the firm to be small, so that changes in its demand for labour are insignificant relative to total demand for that type of labour. As a result it can purchase all the labour it requires at the going wage rate. For this firm, the supply curve of labour can be regarded as perfectly elastic at the market wage rate. Therefore wage rate = average cost of labour = marginal cost of labour.

5. Unemployment elasticity of real wages =

$$\frac{\% \text{ change in real wages}}{\% \text{ change in unemployment}}$$

Oswald estimates a coefficient of about −0.10, i.e. 'we can expect a doubling of unemployment to lower wages by (*ceteris paribus*) a little under 10%.'

References and further reading

ACAS (2002) *Annual Report 2001/2*.

Addison, J. and Siebert, W. (1998) Union security in Britain, *Journal of Labour Research*, **19**(3), Summer.

Atkinson, B. (1996) National Minimum Wage, *Developments in Economics*, **13**.

Bain, G. S. and Elsheikh, F. (1980) Unionization in Britain: an inter-establishment analysis based on survey data, *British Journal of Industrial Relations*, **18**(2), July.

Bain, G. S. and Elsheikh, F. (1982) Union growth and the business cycle: a disaggregated study, *British Journal of Industrial Relations*, **20**(1), March.

Blanchflower, D. (1996) The role and influence of trade unions within the OECD, *Centre for Economic Performance, LSE Discussion Paper No. 310*.

Carruth, A. A. and Disney, R. (1987) Where have 2 million trade union members gone?, *Economica*, **55**.

Charlwood, A. (2002) Why do non-union employees want to unionize? Evidence from Britain, *British Journal of Industrial Relations*, **40**(3), September.

Cully, M., Woodland, S., O'Reilly, A. and Dix, G. (1999) *Britain at Work: as depicted by the 1998 Workplace Employee Relations Survey*, Routledge.

Daniel, W. W. and Millward, N. (1983) Workplace industrial relations in Britain: survey by the Department of Employment, Policy Studies Institute.

Disney, R. (1994) The decline of unions in Britain, *Economic Review*, November.

Freeman, R. R. and Pelletier, J. (1990) The impact of British union legislation on trade union density, *British Journal of Industrial Relations*, September.

Gennard, J. and Judge, G. (2002) *Employee Relations*, 3rd edn, Chartered Institute of Personnel and Development.

Geroski, P., Gregg P. and Desjonqueres, T. (1995) Did the retreat of UK trade unionism accelerate during the 1990–93 recession?, *British Journal of Industrial Relations*, **33**, March.

Gregg, P. and Machin, S. (1991) Changes in union status, increased competition and wage growth in the 1980s, *British Journal of Industrial Relations*, **29**(4), December.

Heasman, D. (2003) Patterns of low pay, *Labour Market Trends*, **111**(4), April.

IDS (2000) *Report 822*, Incomes Data Services, December.

IDS (2002) *Report 863*, Incomes Data Services, August.

Low Pay Commission (2003) The National Minimum Wage: building on success, *Fourth Report of the Low Pay Commission*, March.

Machin, S. (2000) Union decline in Britain, *British Journal of Industrial Relations*, **38**(2), December.

McKay, S. (2001) Between flexibility and regulation: rights, equality and protection at work, *British Journal of Industrial Relations*, **39**(2), June.

Metcalf, D. (1994) Transformation of British industrial relations? Institutions, conduct and outcomes 1980–1990, in R. Barrell, (ed.) *The UK Labour Market*, Cambridge University Press.

Millward, N. and Stevens, M. (1987) *British Workplace Industrial Relations, 1980–1984*, The DE/ESRC/PSI/ACAS Survey, Gower.

Minford, P. and Riley, J. (1994) The UK labour market micro rigidities and macro obstructions, in R. Barrell, (ed.) *The UK Labour Market*, Cambridge University Press.

Nickell, S., Wadhwani, S. and Wall, M. (1989) Unions and productivity growth in Britain, 1974–86, *CLE Discussion Paper No. 353*.

Price, R. and Bain, G. S. (1976) Union growth revisited, *British Journal of Industrial Relations*, **14**(3), November.

Price, R. and Bain, G. S. (1983) Union growth in Britain: retrospect and prospects, *British Journal of Industrial Relations*, **21**(1), March.

Sisson, K. and Marginson, P. (2002) Co-ordinating bargaining: a process for our times?, *British Journal of Industrial Relations*, **40**(2), June.

Smith, P. and Morton, G. (2001) New Labour's reform of Britain's employment law, *British Journal of Industrial Relations*, **39**(1), March.

Walsh, J. (2000) Eurotunnel single union battle provides an early test for CAC, *People Management*, 22 June.

Webb, S. and Webb, B. (1896) *The History of Trade Unionism*, Longman.

Wedderburn, L. (1990) *The Social Charter, European Company and Employment Rights*, Institute of European Rights.

Wright, M. (1996) The collapse of compulsory unionism? Collective organization in highly unionized British companies 1979–1991, *British Journal of Industrial Relations*, **34**, December.

Chapter 16   Consumption and
saving

Consumption is the most important single element in aggregate
demand, accounting for almost half of gross final expenditure (GFE),
so that its accurate estimation is essential to the management of the
economy. J. M. Keynes related consumption to current disposable
income, and for many years this was widely accepted. However, in
the 1950s evidence began to appear of a discrepancy between the
consumption function estimated from long-run time-series data, and
the much flatter consumption function estimated from short-run
time-series and cross-section data. The Keynesian consumption
function could not resolve this discrepancy, and it was this, together
with the need for more accurate forecasts of consumption, that led
to the development of the Permanent Income and Life-Cycle
Hypotheses. In this chapter the Keynesian and alternative theories
of consumption are considered in detail, their predictions are
compared with actual fact, and their different implications for policy
analysis are noted. We also look carefully at the mirror image of
consumption, namely the savings ratio.

Consumption

The consumption function – the relationship between consumer expenditure and income – is probably the most widely researched relationship in macro-economics. The impetus to this research was given by Keynes's initial conceptual breakthrough in *The General Theory of Employment, Interest and Money* (Keynes 1936). In the Keynesian view of the economic system, both output and employment are determined by the level of aggregate demand. Consumer spending is by far the largest element in aggregate demand. Typically it accounts for between half and two-thirds of total final expenditure, so it is essential that the factors influencing consumer spending be identified in order that it may be forecast accurately. This forecast for consumer spending can then be added to forecasts for the other elements of aggregate demand, namely investment, government spending, and net exports (exports minus imports), to derive an overall forecast for *total aggregate demand*. Policy-makers can then decide whether this projected level of demand is appropriate for the economy, and if not, what corrective fiscal or monetary action should be taken.

The central position of the consumption function in Keynesian economics has therefore led to many attempts to estimate an equation that would indeed predict consumer expenditure. Unfortunately, most of the early Keynesian types of equation failed to explain some of the more interesting features of aggregate consumer behaviour. Alternative theories were therefore developed in the 1950s and 1960s which, it was claimed, fitted the facts rather better than the simple Keynesian view of consumption.

The development of these new theories, and the relative economic stability of the 1950s and 1960s, led economists to believe (over-optimistically as it turned out) that consumer spending was probably one of the best-understood and best-forecast variables in economics. We see from Table 16.1, however, that there was a sharp fall in the proportion of personal disposable income consumed (the average propensity to consume, a.p.c.) in the early and late 1970s, early 1980s and early 1990s which was *not* predicted by the existing equations. This fall in the a.p.c. was reflected in the sharp rise in the savings ratio, and we return to this, along with the subsequent changes in the savings ratio in the 1980s and 1990s, later in the chapter.

The Keynesian consumption function

In the *General Theory*, Keynes argued that 'The fundamental psychological law ... is that men are disposed, as a rule and on the average, to increase their consumption as their income increases, but not by as much as the increase in their income' (Keynes 1936, p. 96). From this statement can be derived the Keynesian consumption function[1] which is usually expressed in the following way:

$$C = c_0 + bY$$

where C = consumer expenditure;
c_0 = a constant;
b = the marginal propensity to consume (m.p.c.), which is the amount consumed out of the last pound of income received; and
Y = National Income.

The Keynesian view is that when income rises, consumption rises, but by less than income, which implies that b, the m.p.c., is less than 1. Keynes also argued that 'it is also obvious that a higher absolute level of income will tend, as a rule, to widen the gap between income and consumption' (Keynes 1936, p. 97). This is usually taken to mean that he thought that the proportion of income consumed, C/Y (i.e. a.p.c.), will tend to fall as income increases. In fact the positive constant c_0 in the above equation ensures that this will happen, since

$$\text{a.p.c.} = \frac{C}{Y} = \frac{c_0}{Y} + b$$

and this will decrease as Y increases if, and only if, c_0 is positive. This also implies, of course, that the a.p.c. is greater than the m.p.c. by an amount c_0/Y.

Drawing the consumption function as a straight line, as in Fig. 16.1, means that we are assuming that the m.p.c., b, is a constant, as it is the slope of the consumption function. The a.p.c. is found, for any level of income, by measuring the slope of the radian from the origin to the appropriate point on the consumption function. For example, if income is Y_1, then consumption would be C_1, and the a.p.c. would be C_1/Y_1, which is the tangent of the angle α. It can be seen that as Y increases, the slope of the radian from the origin to the consumption function falls, which

Table 16.1 Household income, consumption and savings ratio (£m at 1995 prices), 1970–2002.

	1	2	3*	4	5	6*	7
	Disposable Income	Consumption	Average propensity to consume (a.p.c.)	Change in income	Change in consumption	Marginal propensity to consume (m.p.c.)	Households' savings ratio (%)
1970	252,132	237,369	0.94	–	–	–	6.6
1971	255,204	245,105	0.96	3,072	7,736	2.52	5.0
1972	276,571	260,881	0.94	21,367	15,776	0.74	7.3
1973	294,328	275,372	0.94	17,757	14,491	0.82	8.2
1974	291,330	270,832	0.93	–2,998	–4,540	1.51	8.4
1975	293,811	270,334	0.92	2,481	–498	–0.20	9.2
1976	292,642	271,446	0.93	–1,169	1,112	–0.95	8.8
1977	286,726	270,381	0.94	–5,916	–1,065	0.18	7.6
1978	307,896	284,793	0.92	21,170	14,412	0.68	9.4
1979	325,303	297,379	0.91	17,407	12,586	0.72	10.9
1980	330,463	297,031	0.90	5,160	–348	–0.07	12.4
1981	328,858	296,964	0.90	–1,605	–67	0.04	12.1
1982	328,157	299,573	0.91	–701	2,609	–3.72	10.9
1983	335,969	312,888	0.93	7,812	13,315	1.70	9.0
1984	348,235	319,296	0.92	12,266	6,408	0.52	10.3
1985	359,979	331,084	0.92	11,744	11,788	1.00	9.8
1986	374,866	352,689	0.94	14,887	21,605	1.45	8.2
1987	388,129	371,301	0.96	13,263	18,612	1.40	6.4
1988	408,762	398,851	0.98	20,633	27,550	1.34	4.9
1989	427,603	412,276	0.96	18,841	13,425	0.71	6.6
1990	442,420	415,557	0.94	14,817	3,281	0.22	8.0
1991	450,409	408,865	0.91	7,989	–6,692	–0.84	10.0
1992	464,011	411,204	0.89	13,602	2,339	0.17	11.4
1993	478,766	422,273	0.88	14,755	11,069	0.75	10.8
1994	486,458	435,350	0.89	7,692	13,077	1.70	9.3
1995	499,059	443,367	0.89	12,601	8,017	0.64	10.0
1996	510,926	460,760	0.90	11,867	17,393	1.47	9.1
1997	533,211	478,738	0.90	22,285	17,978	0.81	9.5
1998	532,300	496,231	0.93	–911	17,493	–19.20	6.0
1999	552,639	519,222	0.94	20,339	22,991	1.13	5.3
2000	578,408	545,751	0.94	25,769	26,529	1.03	4.3
2001	617,494	567,903	0.92	39,086	22,152	0.57	5.7
2002	631,591	589,862	0.93	14,097	21,959	1.56	5.1

* Column 3 = column 2 divided by column 1; column 6 = column 5 divided by column 4.
Source: Adapted from *Economic Trends* (various).

means that the proportion of income consumed (a.p.c.) falls. Indeed some early Keynesian economists were concerned that private sector investment would not grow as a proportion of income to fill the gap left by a declining average propensity to consume, in which case the economy would be subjected to 'secular stagnation'.

For Keynes, the main influence on consumption in the short run was current disposable income, i.e. income minus direct taxes. When this fluctuated, so

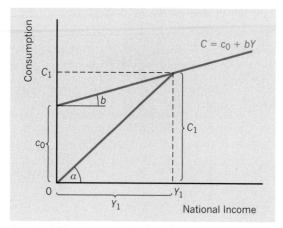

Fig. 16.1 The consumption function.

line, or line of 'best fit',[3] to the data in Table 16.1. Using linear regression we can derive the following equation:

$$C = 6{,}021 + 0.91Y_D$$

where Y_D is real disposable income (£m).

This consumption function (1970–2002) not only appears to fit the data well, as can be seen from Fig. 16.2, but also seems to support the Keynesian view that the m.p.c. is less than 1 (in our case 0.91). The equation also has a positive (if rather small) intercept of 6,021 (£m), implying that the a.p.c. does indeed fall as income rises. However, the intercept term is, statistically, not significantly different from zero and so we cannot be certain that the consumption function fails to go through the origin. If it did, this would mean that the a.p.c. does *not* fall as income rises.

As a first attempt, therefore, the above equation, which explains changes in consumption in terms of changes in current disposable income, seems to fit the facts and the Keynesian theory rather well. To take an example from Table 16.1, in 2001 real disposable income was £617,494m; fitting this into our equation gives predicted consumption of £567,160m. Actual consumption was £567,903m, an error of less than 1%. The equation also gives a predicted a.p.c. of 0.918 for 2001 whereas the actual a.p.c. was 0.920, again only a small error.

would consumption, but because the m.p.c. was less than 1, consumption would change by an amount less than the change in disposable income. If we look at the actual data for the UK and plot consumption against disposable income, both measured in real terms (using 1995 prices), we can see from Fig. 16.2 that over the period 1970–2002 there appears to be a close positive relationship between consumption and disposable income.[2]

In order to find numerical estimates for c_0 and b for our consumption function, we can fit a regression

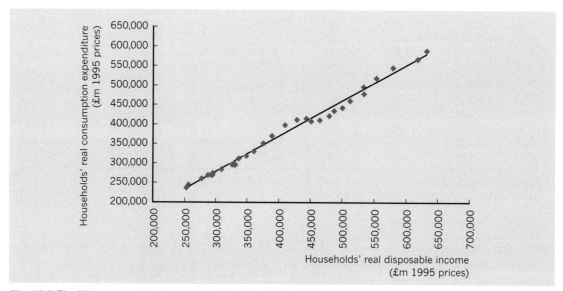

Fig. 16.2 The UK consumption–income relationship, 1970–2002.
Source: Table 16.1.

Closer examination of the data, however, indicates that using changes in current disposable income to explain changes in consumption may be less than satisfactory. It may help to look more carefully at the 'errors', i.e. the deviations of the *actual* observations for consumption from the *predicted* values on the regression line. At first sight, these 'errors' in our earlier Fig. 16.2 do not look very large. Nevertheless, policy-makers relying on the simple consumption function equation to forecast any future consumption would, in some years, still make substantial errors. A more striking picture of the errors can be seen in Fig. 16.3. Here the *differences* between actual and forecast consumption $(C - (6{,}021 + 0.91Y_D))$ are plotted.

Very large *negative* errors occurred, from 1975 to 1976 and again from 1978 to 1982. In these periods actual consumption was very much *less* than forecast, given the levels of real disposable income. It appears that consumers were acting very cautiously because they were pessimistic about their future incomes. In both periods, uncertainty was caused in part by oil-price shocks and rising unemployment. Similarly, in the early 1990s actual consumption was also lower than forecast by our equation, again in part because of uncertain future incomes as unemployment levels increased, but also because of falling asset prices (houses) and the desire of consumers to pay off accumulated debt.

At the other extreme, large *positive* errors were made in the late 1980s and in the period 1999–2002. Here people actually consumed more than would be forecast by our equation, given the levels of real disposable income. This period was one of falling unemployment, inflated house prices and rising incomes, all of which made consumers more optimistic about the future.

It appears from the above that consumers are a good deal more sophisticated than the simple Keynesian consumption function would imply. Consumers take into account not only their *current* income when deciding expenditure, but also their future *expected* income. Indeed one of the goals of the post-Keynesian theories of consumption considered in the next section is to attempt to include the influence of future income on consumer spending.

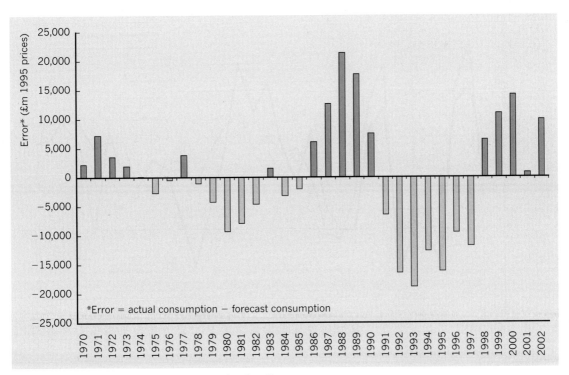

Fig. 16.3 Error analysis of simple consumption function.

One other feature of consumer behaviour ought to be noted at this stage. In general, consumers attempt to keep a relatively smooth consumption pattern over the business cycle. In periods when disposable income is rising rapidly, consumption will rise but not in proportion. In other words, during the recovery period consumers behave cautiously, at least at first. Similarly, in periods when disposable income is falling, consumers will on the whole attempt to maintain their consumption as best they can despite their reduced circumstances. Put simply, in the *short run*, consumption fluctuates less than disposable income (i.e. the short-run m.p.c. is smaller than the long-run m.p.c.). Figure 16.4 illustrates this point for the UK.

The major exception to this pattern occurred in the mid- to late 1980s and early 1990s. Financial deregulation and asset price inflation encouraged consumer borrowing in the mid- to late 1980s, which resulted in consumption increasing in those years by more than income. On the other hand the severe recession of the early 1990s, coupled with the

collapse of house prices and the hangover of indebtedness from the previous period, resulted in consumers cutting expenditure by more than income in an attempt to repay debt. It appears, therefore, that a Keynesian consumption function based only on *current disposable income* is insufficient to explain fully the short-run changes in consumer expenditure.

Post-Keynesian theories of the consumption function

The newer theories of the consumption function differed from that of Keynes in that they were more deeply rooted in the microeconomics of consumer behaviour. Two of the theories, Friedman's Permanent Income Hypothesis (PIH) and Modigliani's Life-Cycle Hypothesis (LCH), start from the position that consumers plan their consumption expenditure not on the basis of income received during the current

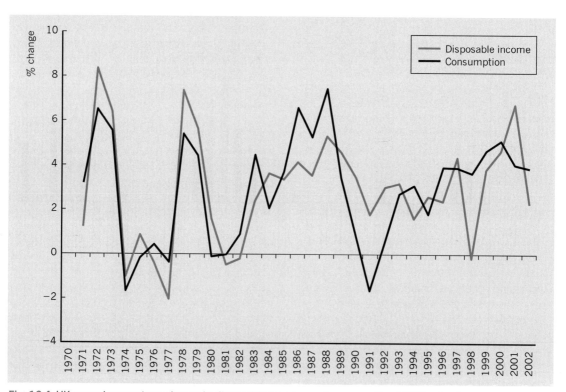

Fig. 16.4 UK annual percentage change in disposable income and consumption (1995 prices).
Source: Table 16.1.

period, but rather on the basis of their long-run, or lifetime, income expectations.

In both these theories, therefore, the link between current consumption and current income is broken. A consumer determines his or her consumption for a given period on the basis of a longer-run view of the resources available, taking into account not just current income but future expected income and any change in the value of their assets. Of course, if consumers cannot borrow on the strength of future income, i.e. if they are liquidity constrained, then they will have to adjust current spending to current income, as in the Keynesian theory.

The Permanent Income Hypothesis (PIH)

In Friedman's PIH an individual's consumption is based on that individual's permanent income (Y_p). Technically Y_p is defined as the return on the present value of an individual's wealth, and hence it is what can be consumed whilst leaving the individual's wealth intact. More generally Y_p could be thought of as some form of long-run average income, or 'normal income', which can be counted on in the future. An individual's actual or measured income (Y) in any time period will be made up of two parts – the 'permanent' part (Y_p), and the 'transitory' part (Y_t). Transitory income might be positive, if the individual is having an unexpectedly good year, or negative, if the individual is having a bad year. It follows that measured income is

$$Y = Y_p + Y_t$$

In the simplest form of the PIH, consumption is a constant proportion of permanent income, i.e.

$$C = kY_p$$

where

$$k = F(i, w, x)$$

The proportion k is determined by factors such as the interest rate (i), the ratio of non-human to human wealth (w), and a catch-all variable (x) which includes age and tastes as a major component. If i rises, then individuals are assumed to feel more secure as to the future returns from their asset holdings, so that k increases. Equally, k will increase if the ratio of non-human to human wealth (w) rises in total wealth holding. This is also thought to increase individual

security, since non-human wealth, such as money and shares, is assumed to be more reliable than human wealth, such as expected future labour income.

If the economy grows steadily, with no fluctuations, then Y_p would be approximately equal to Y (measured National Income), and not only would a constant proportion of permanent income be consumed, but also a constant proportion of measured National Income. A study by Simon Kuznets in the US showed that if *long-run* data were used (10-year averages of consumption and income) then the a.p.c. was roughly constant. Taking 10-year averages effectively eliminates short-run fluctuations in income, and so Kuznets's results are consistent with the constant proportion k in the PIH.

This long-run consumption function derived from time-series data averaged over the business cycle, with its constant a.p.c., seemed, however, at odds with the short-run consumption function derived either from time-series data on an annual basis or from cross-sectional data. The short-run consumption function was flatter than the long-run function (see Fig. 16.5), having therefore a lower m.p.c. and an a.p.c. that was not constant, falling when incomes rose (booms) and rising when incomes fell (slumps). The answer to this puzzle, according to Friedman, is that in booms more people will think that they are doing better than normal than will think they are doing worse than normal. For the economy as a whole, therefore, there will be positive transitory income (Y_t), so that measured National Income (Y) will be above permanent income (Y_p). The unexpectedly high measured income will, however, have little impact on consumer views of their permanent income unless it lasts for several years. Since consumer spending plans are based on permanent income, any boom that is not long-lived will have little effect on consumer spending. The unexpected increases in income are therefore largely saved, with the result that in a boom the average propensity to consume falls. This is seen in Fig. 16.5.

As the economy expands along its long-run trend, consumption should be a fixed proportion, k, of income. In reality, however, the economy fluctuates around this long-run trend. Suppose we start in situation Y_0, with measured and permanent income equal, consumption (kY_0) equal to C_0, and a.p.c. equal to k. The economy then experiences a boom with measured income rising to Y_1. Permanent income will, however, be less affected by the sudden increase in income, and in our figure rises only to Y_{p1}.

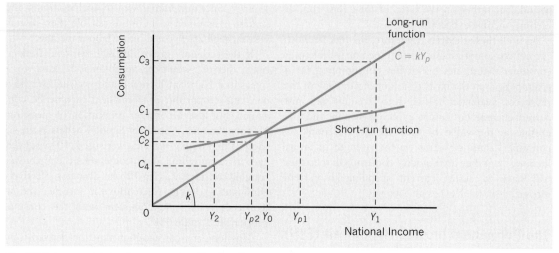

Fig. 16.5 Long- and short-run consumption functions.

Consumption, being based on permanent income, now rises to $C_1(kY_{p1})$. Only if measured income remained at Y_1 for *several years* would permanent income be revised upwards to Y_1, and consumption to $C_3(kY_1)$. If this is *not* the case, then the proportion of income consumed will be only C_1/Y_1, i.e. the a.p.c. will have fallen below the initial level k during the boom.

In a slump, income will fall, say from Y_0 to Y_2, and although permanent income may be revised downwards a little to Y_{p2}, it will fall proportionately less than measured income. Consumption will therefore be $C_2(kY_{p2})$, falling much less than if Y_2 had been regarded as permanent (when consumption would fall further to C_4). The a.p.c. will then be C_2/Y_2, which is *above* the initial level k.

It can be seen from this analysis that Friedman is able to explain why the short-run consumption function is flatter, with a variable a.p.c., whilst the long-run consumption function is steeper, with a constant a.p.c. Booms will, unless long-lived, cause a.p.c. to fall. There will be little upward revision of consumption plans, when higher income is largely regarded as transitory. Slumps will, unless long-lived, in a similar manner cause a.p.c. to rise.

The Life-Cycle Hypothesis (LCH)

The LCH, developed by Modigliani and his associates, is similar in many ways to the PIH. Consumption is again seen as being a constant proportion k of Y_p, with the same sort of variables affecting k as in Friedman's theory. Modigliani stresses, however, the age of the consumer, with the consumer trying to even out consumption over a lifetime in which income fluctuates widely. In youth and old age, when income is low, consumption is maintained by borrowing or drawing on past savings respectively, so that consumption is a high proportion of income; in middle life, when income is relatively high, a smaller proportion is consumed, with savings being built up to finance consumption after retirement.

One of the empirical facts that needed to be explained by any theory was why, from *cross-sectional* data, it was seen that low-income groups had a higher a.p.c. than high-income groups. The LCH argued that low-income groups contain a high proportion of very young and very old households, both of which have a high propensity to consume. On the other hand, the high-income groups contain a high proportion of middle-aged households, with a low propensity to consume.

The variations in a.p.c. observed using *time-series* data, when National Income rises or falls, can also be explained by the LCH. Any windfall or transitory income received in a boom is spread over the individual's remaining lifetime. For example, an unexpected increase in income of, say, £1,000 for someone with 20 more years to live would mean that they would revise their Y_p upwards by about £50 per annum, so that consumption in the year in which the windfall is received would increase by a relatively small amount (some proportion of £50). The a.p.c. would therefore fall with higher income because consumption (the numerator) will have risen by only a small amount, based on Y_p, but measured income (the denominator) has risen by the full £1,000. An unexpected reduction in income in a recession would likewise be spread over an individual's lifetime, with borrowing and/or the running down of past savings leading to only a small cut in that individual's current consumption, thereby causing a.p.c. to rise. The LCH has therefore been able, like the PIH, to reconcile the flatter short-run consumption function with the steeper long-run consumption function (with constant a.p.c.).

Both theories imply that the m.p.c., which is the slope of the consumption function, is lower in the short run than it is in the long run. In the PIH any unexpected increase in income is not consumed, but largely saved, whereas in the LCH it is spread over the consumer's lifetime. It follows that the multiplier[4] predicted by these theories will be small in the short run, because m.p.c. is low in the short run. Changes in government spending and taxation aimed at stabilizing the economy will therefore be relatively ineffective, especially if these changes are seen as being only temporary. A by-product of Friedman's work on the consumption function appears, therefore, to be an attack on the effectiveness of Keynesian short-run demand-management policies.

The PIH and LCH appear to have broken the link between current consumption and current disposable income by arguing that consumption depends not only on current disposable income but also on all future disposable income. It could be argued, however, that there are two reasons why the influence of current income may be more important than these theories imply. First, it is unreasonable to believe that all consumers will be able to borrow and lend in different periods to even out their consumption pattern. An unemployed worker is unlikely to be able to borrow money to maintain his consumption, even though he is convinced he will be able to repay the loan out of future earnings. In this case, once past savings are exhausted, the constraint on consumption will be current disposable income. Second, estimates of future disposable income, on which permanent income is based, are highly uncertain. It is reasonable to expect, therefore, that the consumer uses his or her recent experience, and current income, as an important basis for estimating long-run or permanent income, and hence wealth. For both these reasons, therefore, one could still argue that current disposable income is still a major influence on current consumption, even under the PIH and LCH.

Rational expectations and consumption

The theories of consumption developed by Friedman, Modigliani and others all involve some concept of permanent or (long-term) 'normal' income on which households plan their consumption decisions. In order to arrive at this concept, households need to come to some view of their *expected* future income. The early post-Keynesian theories made convenient, if rather naive, assumptions about this process. Friedman, for example, used *adaptive expectations*, which means that consumers adapt or change their view of their expected income in the light of any 'errors' made in previous time periods. In effect it can then be shown that 'permanent income' (which is supposed to capture future expected income) is simply a weighted average of past incomes.

Despite the empirical convenience of this method of modelling expectations (data on past incomes being readily available), economists have become increasingly dissatisfied with this approach to modelling the formation of expectations. This approach is too mechanistic, is backward looking and, apart from income, ignores all other relevant information that might affect future earnings. As an alternative many economists have adopted the hypothesis of *rational expectations*. Rational expectation theory argues that households form expectations not only on the basis of past experience but also on their predictions about the future. It is assumed that households possess some sort of 'model' of the economy which they then use to process relevant information and derive an expectation of future income. Of course most households do *not* possess any economic model of the economy. Nevertheless forecasts from actual models are freely available in the media and households can use these, together with any specific knowledge they might have of their particular industry and region, to make a rational forecast of anticipated future income. Although economists have had problems in applying this concept of rational expectations to empirical work, much of the current theoretical study of consumption is based upon it.

One application of rational expectations to the permanent income model has been developed by Robert Hall. Hall (1978) argued that under certain conditions a household's consumption should follow a '*random walk*'. If households have included all the available and relevant information in their forecast of future income then, assuming consumption smoothing, the only reason for a household to alter its consumption would be an unexpected change in income. Hence the best estimate of next year's consumption (C_{t+1}) will be this year's consumption (C_t), as this reflects all the available information on future incomes. That is to say, $C_{t+1} = C_t + e_{t+1}$ where e_{t+1} is a random amount that results from unexpected shocks. Hall found some evidence to support the view that next year's consumption is closely related to this year's consumption. However, he also found that other variables, including past income, influenced next year's consumption. One reason for this finding is, of course, the linkage between past income and current borrowing potential for householders as a means of financing future consumption.

The substantial variations in the savings ratio over the last economic cycle have, to a large extent, been explained by the impact of monetary policy. Monetary policy, operating through the house price channel, in an environment of financial liberalization, has been held responsible for the boom–bust cycle. Work by Catão and Ramaswamy (1996), however, suggests that although the monetary stance and wealth effects on consumption accounted for over half the contraction in economic activity, the role of 'true' shocks also played a significant role. True shocks are defined as those that cannot easily be explained by obvious economic factors. These could be caused by pessimism about the future or anxiety about the particular course of political or social developments. One policy conclusion that comes from their work is that although monetary policy is influential, it is difficult for monetary policy to fine-tune the economy in the face of expectational shocks.

Windfall gains and consumption

In 1996 consumers received around £3.5bn in special payments, sometimes called windfall gains. In 1997 the figure was around £35bn. These windfall gains were mainly the result of the merger of building societies and their demutualization, which converted building society assets into tradeable shares. There were also windfall gains via enforced (by the regulator) payouts to customers from the regional electricity companies and the sums received from maturing TESSA accounts.

Economic theory tells us that an increase in a consumer's wealth is unlikely to lead to a proportionate increase in consumption, with consumers maximizing utility by spreading the additional consumption over the rest of their lifetime. The increase in current consumption is likely, therefore, to be relatively small. The Bank of England Inflation Report in February 1997 adopted this viewpoint, arguing that previous windfall payouts by the Abbey National and TSB had resulted in only modest increases in current consumption. The Bank of England estimated that only around 5–10% of the £35bn of windfall gains expected in 1997 would be spent in the first year (i.e. up to £3.5bn). This view was further supported by a survey carried out by the Harris Research Centre, which found that only 36% of individuals who expected to receive a building society windfall in 1997 intended to spend all or most of it.

The *National Institute Economic Review* (1998) found that the effect of the windfalls on consumption had turned out to be larger than the Bank of England had anticipated a year earlier. It estimated that consumers' expenditure in 1997 had risen by a further £8bn because of the windfall gains received in that year. One explanation might be that more consumers had suffered from liquidity constraints in 1997 than the Bank of England had anticipated. If an individual is liquidity constrained then arguably they cannot achieve their optimum consumption pattern taking into account expected future income because they cannot, for various reasons, borrow on the strength of that expected future income. Any liquidity-constrained consumer who receives a windfall gain is then likely to spend more of it in the current period than they would have done had no such liquidity constraint been present.

A recent study by Banerjee and Batini (2003) suggests that about one-seventh of UK consumers consume an amount equal to their current income. This result is obviously at odds with the PIH and the LCH but is consistent with evidence on credit restrictions in the UK. The authors also argue that it ties in with the evidence that consumption in the UK is more responsive to changes in human wealth (labour income) than the PIH would suggest.

The savings ratio

Consumer spending has clearly been one of the most widely researched areas in macroeconomics. Despite this, there have been unexpectedly large movements in the proportion of income consumed, and hence saved, over the last 30 years. In the 1970s, household savings rose as a proportion of household disposable income, reaching a peak of 12.4% in 1980 (see the earlier Table 16.1). In the 1980s the savings ratio fell, reaching a low point of 4.9% in 1988, before rising again to 11.4% in 1992 as households sought to cushion themselves against uncertainty (and possible job loss) during a period of recession. In the latter part of the 1990s the savings ratio fell once more, and by 2002 it stood at 5.1%. These largely unanticipated swings in savings imply that the consumption function is less stable than Keynes had thought. The growth of consumer expenditure over the last 20

years has therefore proved very difficult to forecast. In the boom years of 1985–88, consumption was consistently *underestimated*; whereas in the recession years of 1989–92, it was consistently *overestimated*. The impact of these forecasting errors on economic policy, and the subsequent welfare losses resulting from policy failures, are a cause for serious concern. As we shall see later in this section, this concern has led to a re-examination of the determinants of consumption and especially of the role played by financial liberalization and the housing market.

Post-war behaviour of the savings ratio

The *household savings ratio* is defined as household savings as a percentage of total household resources, the latter itself being defined as the sum of gross household disposable income and the adjustment for the net equity of households in pension funds. Its value has fluctuated widely from around 2% just after the Second World War to over 12% in the early 1980s (Fig. 16.6). The period as a whole could be divided into five parts for further investigation.

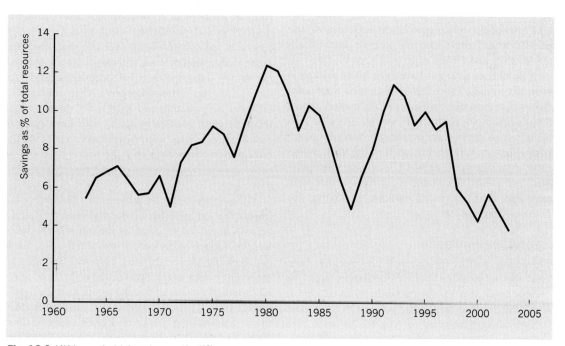

Fig. 16.6 UK households' savings ratio (%).
Source: *Economic Trends* (various).

Savings in the 1950s, 1960s and 1970s

The **first period**, from the end of the Second World War up to 1960, saw a rise in the savings ratio, from an exceptionally low level (0.1% in 1948) to what was considered at the time a more normal level (7.4% in 1960). The explanation for this appears to be that people in the early post-war years were catching up on consumption that had been postponed during the war years, so that the savings ratio in the early post-war period was uncharacteristically low. The rise in the savings ratio after these early years can therefore be seen as a return to normality.

The **second period**, from 1960 to 1971, revealed no marked upward trend, with the ratio fluctuating around an average of 8%. The fluctuations in the ratio coincided with variations in the rate of growth of National Income; the savings ratio fell when the economy slowed down, and rose when the economy accelerated. This period could therefore adequately be explained by any of the post-Keynesian theories of consumption.[5]

In the **third period**, from the early 1970s to around 1980, the upward trend in the savings ratio was re-established, reaching a peak of 12.4% in 1980. As we noted, this has been puzzling, being associated with high rates of inflation, negative real interest rates, and periods when real disposable income actually fell (1974, 1975 and 1977).

A number of attempts have been made to explain why the savings ratio has risen under these conditions. For example, the Bank of England has argued that increases in contractual savings (regular contributions to pension funds and life assurance companies) have at times contributed to the high savings ratio, especially in the early 1970s. Rising unemployment and related uncertainties, in times of recession, may also have led to an increase in savings for precautionary reasons.

Savings and inflation

The greater part of the research, however, has been into the relationship between inflation and the savings ratio. Most of the studies have found a positive connection between these two variables, but there is some disagreement as to why the inflation rate should affect the savings ratio.

One theory (Deaton 1977) explains the relationship in terms of consumers failing to perceive the actual rate of inflation. The suggestion is that consumers *underestimate* the average price level and are therefore unduly shocked at the apparently 'excessive' rise in the price of particular commodities. Until such time as consumers recognize the true (and higher) level of average prices, purchases of these commodities will have been cut back in response to the assumed sharp increase in individual prices. Savings will therefore rise as a result of this 'inflation surprise' effect. This theory suggests that it is unanticipated inflation that matters, so that the effect on consumption, and therefore savings, will be particularly strong in the early stages of inflation when the rate of inflation is accelerating.

A study by Bulkley (1981) has supplemented the above theory, showing that even if inflation is fully anticipated the savings ratio will still increase as long as anticipated inflation is itself increasing. Even if inflation is fully anticipated, workers' real wages will still have fluctuated throughout the year, since money wages are usually set on only one occasion in the year. Real wages will therefore be at a maximum when the money wage is first set, falling to a minimum a year later as prices progressively rise. In order to smooth out his or her real consumption pattern over the year, an individual will save more each week early in the contract period, and correspondingly less later in the contract period. If inflation is constant, and if wage contracts are spread evenly over the year, then the additional savings of some will cancel out the reduced savings of others, and there will be no aggregate effect on the savings ratio. However, when anticipated inflation is increasing and with it the money wage, then the extra savings by those who have recently received higher wage awards will more than offset the reduction in the savings of those nearing the end of their nominal wage contracts, and the savings ratio will rise.

Other explanations (Cuthbertson 1982) stress the impact that inflation has on the real value of an individual's liquid assets, affecting the individual's desire to save. Liquid assets include notes and coins, bank and building society deposits, National Savings and other short-term assets. Because the real rate of interest (nominal rate minus the rate of inflation) on liquid assets over this period has often been zero or negative, the real purchasing power of a given stock of these assets has fallen. If consumers wish to maintain the real value of their liquid assets, for reasons of security or flexibility, they must choose either to cash in less liquid assets, or to save more from current income. The real rate of return on some non-liquid assets such as housing and consumer durables has been positive over this period as a whole, and so rather than cash these in, one would expect the holdings of these to increase in inflationary times. Other non-liquid assets, such as life assurance and long-term contractual saving, are expensive to cash in, as are government bonds when the interest rate is high. Thus the desire to rebuild a given stock of real liquid assets could really only come from a reduction in non-durable consumption, i.e. saving. People have tended, therefore, during recent inflationary times to save a higher proportion of their disposable income in the attempt to maintain the real value of their liquid assets.

Savings since 1980

The **fourth period** embraces 1980 to 1988. During this period the household savings ratio fell from its peak of 12.4% in 1980 to a 30-year low of 4.9% in 1988. There appear to be a number of reasons for this.

First, in inflationary times some savings are needed just to maintain the *real* value of assets, the values of which are fixed in money terms. As the inflation rate falls, as it did from 1980 to 1983, the need for such saving declines. A second factor in the fall of the savings ratio seems to be the behaviour of pension funds. Conventionally, these funds are seen as the property of the personal sector and the income of these funds (including investment income and employers' contributions) is treated as part of personal income. However, movements in this element of personal income are unlikely to have much effect on consumption and for that reason are more likely to affect the savings ratio. As the earnings on the funds' assets rose from the low levels of the 1970s, the savings ratio increased. But in the 1980s it became apparent that the value of these pension funds had risen above the sum needed to meet pension liabilities; as a result employers' contributions to pension funds stopped rising from 1981. Indeed in 1986 and 1987 they actually fell in *nominal* as well as real terms. This 'contributions holiday' lowered personal income and so the *personal savings ratio* fell in favour of higher company saving.

A third factor influencing the savings ratio in this period has been the increased financial liberalization

of capital and money markets. Financial liberalization included the ending of quantitative controls on consumer credit in 1982 and the relaxation of the controls on mortgage lending. The average loan offered by building societies to first-time buyers rose from 76% of purchase price in 1980 to 86% by 1986. Deregulation at a time of rising house and other asset prices enabled consumers to gain easier access to credit markets at a time of growing consumer confidence. As a result, household borrowing rose rapidly in the 1980s with the ratio of debt to personal income rising from 57% in 1980 to 116% by 1990 (see Pain and Westaway 1994). Despite this increase in borrowing, the net wealth of the personal sector rose from 3.25 times income at the start of the decade to 5 times income by the end. This increase was mainly the result of the rise in home ownership and the buoyancy of share prices. Easier access to credit, and the confidence which came from rising incomes, falling unemployment and rising asset prices, all helped fuel the consumer boom and depress the savings ratio in the second half of the 1980s. Figure 16.7 illustrates the rise in consumer credit and mortgage equity withdrawal (that part of new mortgage lending used for consumption rather than investment in housing) at this time.

The fourth factor influencing the savings ratio in this period has been a demographic one. Recent research carried out by the London Business School suggests that the fall in the proportion of the population in the 45–64 year age group during this period

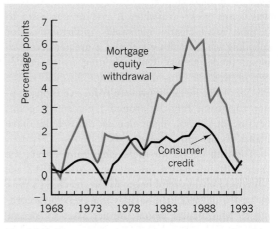

Fig. 16.7 Percentage changes in mortgage equity withdrawal and consumer credit.

has influenced savings. It is the people in this age group who are the principal savers in our society; younger people are borrowing to set up home and older retired people are living on past savings. A decline in the 45–64 year age group is therefore likely to reduce the savings ratio.

Finally, it has been claimed that the official figures actually underestimate the true savings ratio. Personal income, it is argued, is *underestimated* in official statistics, whereas consumption is *measured* reasonably accurately. This would lower the level of *measured* or recorded saving.

It is extremely difficult to quantify the role of the various influences on consumption and savings behaviour over the period 1980–88. However, econometric work by Muellbauer (1994) has attempted to identify the various factors that caused the unprecedented 10 percentage points rise in the consumption to income ratio (a.p.c.) between 1980 and 1988. In his view the contribution of *forecast income growth* was just over 2 percentage points (at the same time the rise in real interest rates reduced the ratio by 1 percentage point). *Reduced uncertainty* in the economy in the later part of the period was responsible for 3 percentage points upturn in the a.p.c.; of this some 2.5 points resulted from lower unemployment and 0.5 percentage points from reduced income volatility. By far the largest contribution, however, was a 5 percentage point rise in the ratio (i.e. half of the recorded total) caused by the rise in what Muellbauer calls 'spendability', more precisely the weighted net asset[6] to income ratio. Essentially not only was the net asset to income ratio increasing but, because of financial liberalization, asset-backed credit was more easily available. A rise in net asset to income ratio clearly increased opportunities for spending via a wealth effect and a greater access to liquid funds (credit). One offsetting factor in this period was the growth of income inequality; the impact of this inequality was to *reduce* the consumption to income ratio by around 1 percentage point, because in general higher income households have higher savings ratios (lower a.p.c.).

The **fifth period** for the savings ratio covers the years 1988 up to the present time. After 1988 the household savings ratio began to rise, reaching a peak of 11.4% in 1992. The savings rate peaked (according to Muellbauer) *before* the net asset to income ratio peaked. Several factors can account for this, including a sharp fall in expected income growth, a steep rise in the rate of increase of unemployment, an increase in income volatility, a rise in the real interest rate and the downturn in current income growth. Certainly the doubling of short-term interest rates over 1988–90 led, both directly and indirectly, to a fall in the net asset to income ratio. The impact of this sharp rise in real interest rates contributed to a lower real value of shares, a fall in real and nominal house prices and a high level of debt and debt repayments. All this led to a fall in the a.p.c. and an associated rise in the savings ratio. It is interesting to note that the Bank of England estimated that three-quarters of a million home owners in 1992 had properties valued at less than their outstanding mortgage. The value of this 'negative equity' was worth £5.9bn and obviously had a depressing effect on consumer spending as households saved harder to reduce this debt burden. These factors taken together clearly help explain the depths of the UK consumer recession in the period 1990–92 and the relatively sluggish recovery of consumption since the fourth quarter of 1992 despite lower interest rates. The savings ratio has fallen since economic recovery began in 1992.

Between 1995 and 2002 *household consumption* grew on average at 4.1% a year, the highest rate for any consecutive seven-year period in the past 100 years. The growth of *consumer durable* spending has in fact averaged 9.0% per year since 1995. The growth of consumption in excess of income growth (with the implied increase in debt) has further reduced the savings ratio, as can be seen from Fig. 16.6 above. Consumption and debt have increased not only because of the rise in disposable income associated with falling unemployment and improved terms of trade but also because of the rise in wealth associated with rising share prices until 2000 and, thereafter, rising house prices. Rising housing equity gives the consumer not only more confidence but also access to *secured borrowing* at extremely advantageous real rates of interest compared to those on unsecured loans. The Bank of England calculated that in the fourth quarter of 2002 the effective nominal interest rate on a secured loan was 5.3%, around one-half of the effective rate on an unsecured loan. The incentive for householders to borrow and spend can be seen from the estimate for the level of mortgage equity withdrawal for the fourth quarter of 2002 which at £13.3bn was 75% higher than for the same quarter of 2001.

National saving

National saving is the sum of saving by the public and private sectors. Table 16.2 illustrates the savings of the various sectors as a percentage of GDP. Overall, if the amount that is invested by a country exceeds the amount that is saved then the excess is represented by the financial account deficit on the balance of payments (see Chapter 24). In 2001 Britain's national savings rate of 15.1% was lower than that of any other OECD country except Turkey (12.4%) and Portugal (2.6%). It may be relevant to ask the question: is Britain's savings rate too low? Britain does not have the same requirement to save as, say, Germany (19.8%) or Italy (20.4%) with their rapidly ageing populations. However, as pointed out in the National Institute Economic Review (2003), over the last 15 years the low national savings ratio in the UK has constrained investment and hence wealth formation. Wealth has fallen as a percentage of income and the effects are visible in terms of low levels of public infrastructure and high house prices, both in part the consequence of not generating enough savings to be invested in these forms of capital.

Conclusion

The importance of having a clear idea of what factors determine consumption cannot be overestimated. Consumption expenditure is the largest element in total expenditure and so any fluctuations in consumption will have important implications for the overall level of demand in the economy. The failure to appreciate the strength of consumer demand in 1987 and 1988 was an important contributory factor to the subsequent deterioration in the inflation and balance of payments position that has posed such problems for the UK economy. Similarly the fall in consumer spending in the recession of the early 1990s was much sharper than in either of the previous two recessions of 1974–77 and 1979–82. Again this change in consumption expenditure was largely unforeseen by forecasters.

Post-Keynesian theories stress that, when deciding on consumption, consumers have a longer-term planning horizon than merely considering current income, the implication of post-Keynesian theories being that consumption is more stable than Keynesians thought. Evidence suggests, however, that in the face of uncertainty and liquidity constraints, current income may still be a key factor influencing consumption.

Table 16.2 National and sectoral savings and investment.

	As a percentage of GDP								
	Household sector		Company sector		Government sector		Whole economy		Finance from overseas
	Savings	Invest.	Savings	Invest.	Savings	Invest.	Savings	Invest.	
2000	2.9	4.0	9.4	12.3	2.9	1.0	15.3	17.3	2.0
2001	4.3	4.2	8.4	11.5	2.5	1.1	15.1	16.7	1.6
2002	3.8	4.3	10.1	10.1	0.4	1.4	14.5	15.7	1.2
2003	3.8	4.4	9.3	9.6	0.6	2.0	14.1	15.9	1.8

Source: *National Institute Economic Review* (2003), January.

Key points

- In the Keynesian view, current disposable income is the main determinant of consumer spending.

- The suggestion here is that the *average propensity to consume* (a.p.c.) will fall as disposable income increases.

- Further, the *marginal propensity to consume* (m.p.c.) will be less than 1.

- Using a line of 'best fit' to UK data over the period 1970–2002, the consumption function has been estimated as $C = 6,021 + 0.91Y_D$, where Y_D is real disposable income (£m).

- This suggests an m.p.c. of 0.91 and a low intercept term, suggesting a.p.c. will decline only slightly as disposable income increases.

- Evidence began to accumulate that the *short-run* consumption function was flatter than the *long-run* consumption function. In other words short-run m.p.c. is less than long-run m.p.c.

- Attempts to explain this discrepancy have resulted in independent variables *other than* current disposable income being proposed. The Permanent Income Hypothesis (Friedman) and Life-Cycle Income Hypothesis (Modigliani) have been suggested.

- Even models based on past experience and future expectations have been used (rational expectations).

- The policy consequences of errors in forecasting consumption (and therefore savings) are serious: *underestimates* of consumption cause economic policy to be overexpansionary (inflationary); *overestimates* of consumption cause economic policy to be overcautious (deflationary).

Now try the self-check questions for this chapter on the Companion Website. You will also find up-to-date facts and case materials.

Notes

1. This is a 'generalized' version of the Keynesian consumption function as it uses total income rather than disposable income as the independent variable.

2. However, this is not always the case, as can be seen on the rare occasions when m.p.c. is negative. A negative m.p.c. means that when disposable income falls, consumption actually rises. In 1982 consumption even rose by *more* than National Income fell, giving a value of –3.72 for m.p.c.

3. 'Best' in the sense that it minimizes the sum of squared deviations from the line.

4. The simple National Income multiplier is defined as 1/1 – m.p.c. for a closed economy with no government sector, and indicates the extent to which National Income changes following a given change in injections or withdrawals. If m.p.c. is low, the multiplier is low.

5. Remember that a fall in the savings ratio during 'recession' is the same as a rise in a.p.c.; and a rise in the savings ratio during 'boom' is the same as a fall in a.p.c.

6. 'Net asset' is essentially the market value of assets such as houses, stocks and shares, etc., *minus* any debt still outstanding on their acquisition.

References and further reading

Banerjee, R. and Batini, N. (2003) UK consumers' habits, *External MPC Unit Discussion Paper*, No. 13.

Bulkley, G. (1981) Personal savings and anticipated inflation, *Economic Journal*, **91**, March.

Catão, L. and Ramaswamy, R. (1996) Recession and recovery in the United Kingdom in the 1990s: identifying the shocks, *National Institute Economic Review*, **157**, July.

Chrystal, A. K. (1992) The fall and rise of saving, *National Westminster Bank Quarterly Review*, February.

Cuthbertson, K. (1982) The measurement and behaviour of the UK saving ratio in the 1970s, *National Institute Economic Review*, **99**, February.

Deaton, A. (1977) Involuntary saving through unanticipated inflation, *American Economic Review*, **67**(5), December.

Hall, R. (1978) Stochastic implications of the life cycle permanent income hypothesis, *Journal of Political Economy*, **86**, December.

Kennally, G. (1985) Committed and discretionary saving of households, *National Institute Economic Review*, **112**, May.

Keynes, J. M. (1936) *The General Theory of Employment, Interest and Money*, Macmillan.

Kuznets, S. (1946) *The National Product Since 1869*, The National Bureau of Economic Research.

Leighton Thomas, R. (1984) *The Consumption Function*, in D. Demery, *et al.*, *Macroeconomics, Surveys in Economics*, Longman.

Muellbauer, J. (1994) The assessment: consumer expenditure, *Oxford Review of Economic Policy*, **10**(2), Summer.

National Institute Economic Review (1998) **165**(3), July.

National Institute Economic Review (2003) **183**(1), January.

OECD (2000) *Economic Outlook*, No. 67, June.

Pain, N. and Westaway, P. (1994) Housing, consumption and borrowing: an assessment of recent personal sector behaviour in the UK, *National Institute Economic Review*, **149**, August.

Chapter 17　Investment

Although only around one-third as important as consumption in total aggregate demand, investment is arguably one of its most significant components. It is highly volatile, and through its impact on productivity affects both supply and demand sides of the economy. After briefly reviewing the definition and measurement of investment, this chapter considers the theory and evidence for a number of factors allegedly affecting fixed investment. The rate of interest, the Accelerator Theory, the Capital Stock Adjustment Model, profitability, 'crowding out', uncertainty, public policies, capital market imperfections and a poor skill set are all considered. The chapter concludes by assessing the role of investment in economic growth.

The nature of investment

Resources in an economy can be used to produce goods and services for immediate use (consumption), or to add to the stock of fixed capital (investment). This chapter concentrates on the latter.

In one sense consumption and investment are quite distinct. The act of investment usually involves abstaining from current consumption in order to acquire assets, which raise the productive potential of the economy, and therefore the possibilities for future consumption. Yet in another sense they are similar, both being components of aggregate demand, i.e. types of spending which create income for others in the economic system. We noted in Chapter 16 that consumption was around 49% of gross final expenditure (GFE) in 2002. Although smaller, fixed capital investment was 12% of GFE in 2002.

Stock and flow concepts

The total value of fixed capital at any time is a 'stock' concept. The rate of change of that 'stock' is a 'flow' concept. Investment in the National Accounts is entirely a 'flow' concept, as it is the addition to the stock of fixed capital in any given year. This helps explain why purchases of shares, paintings or antiques, although often termed 'investments' in everyday speech, are not regarded as such in the Accounts. Usually they merely represent a transfer of ownership from one person or institution to another, rather than an addition to the stock of assets. The difference between stock and flow valuations is often substantial.

Gross and net investment

'Gross' investment, though a flow concept, over-estimates the change in size of the stock of capital or inventories in the year. In the course of the year some fixed capital will have worn out or become obsolete, and some inventories will have become unusable. A part of 'gross' investment will therefore be needed simply to replace these assets used up in the course of production. If we subtract this 'replacement' investment from 'gross' investment, then we are left with 'net investment'. Net investment is then the estimate of the addition, in any year, to the stock of fixed capital and inventories, having allowed for depreciation of that stock during the year.

Of course, quantifying depreciation presents a number of problems. Estimating the loss in value of a machine in a year is difficult in itself, and may be guided less by the physical state of the asset than by the possibility of tax concessions. Also different accounting conventions will yield different measures of depreciation. For instance, historical cost accounting yields much lower figures for depreciation than does inflation accounting.

The majority of investment expenditure is on fixed capital formation rather than inventories and it is to this that we now turn.

Gross Fixed Capital Formation

Gross Fixed Capital Formation (GFCF) is defined in the National Accounts as 'expenditure on fixed assets (buildings, plant and machinery, vehicles, etc.), either for replacing or adding to the stock of existing fixed assets'. This apparently clear-cut definition turns out to be rather arbitrary in application. For instance, 'investment' in the National Accounts is restricted to the firm sector. If a household purchases a computer for personal use, it is classified in the National Accounts as 'consumption', yet the same purchase by a firm is classified as 'investment', even though in both cases the capital asset yields a stream of useful services throughout its life. This is because the National Accounts treat the household purchase as self-gratification, but the firm purchase as producing a flow of marketable goods and services.

The arbitrariness of this classification is well illustrated when an individual chooses, for tax purposes, to be regarded as self-employed. The purchase of a car by a teacher for travel to work as an employee is classed as 'consumption' expenditure. Should the teacher change his or her designation to self-employed and engage in privately contracted teaching, then the purchase of that same car could be classed as 'investment' expenditure.

Despite problems of classification, it is important to gauge changes in GFCF through time, both in total, and by sector and type of asset. Table 17.1 presents data for selected time periods since 1989 (the peak

Table 17.1 Gross Fixed Capital Formation by sector and by type of asset.

		Sector			
	Total	**Business investment**	**General government**	**NHS Trusts**	**Private dwellings**
1989	122,476	81,059	11,097	–	22,781
1992	108,556	71,189	14,233	644	17,311
2001	153,468	115,852	10,948	1,635	19,432
2002	148,592	106,619	12,635	1,335	22,091

		Asset			
	Transport & equipment	**Other machinery and equipment**	**Dwellings**	**Other new buildings**	**Intangible fixed assets**
1989	13,639	45,123	27,097	34,623	3,647
1992	9,279	38,429	20,041	36,572	3,917
2001	14,679	72,474	21,169	40,625	4,521
2002	14,689	64,800	23,716	40,628	4,759

Source: *Economic Trends* (various).

level of investment in the previous economic cycle). Given the problems we noted in measuring depreciation, the 'gross' concept is perhaps the most useful for purposes of comparison, whether through time or across countries. GFCF stood at around £149bn in 2002, which is some 20% higher than the figure recorded in 1989. Over this period the level of investment spending has, however, been quite volatile, falling sharply in the recession of the early 1990s before rebounding strongly in recent years.

For much of the past decade, the shift in the investment spend from the public to the private sector that was particularly pronounced during the 1980s has continued. However, over the last couple of years there have been some signs that the trend is finally being reversed. This is partly a result of a drop in private sector capital spending following the boom of the second half of the 1990s but is also a reflection of the government's decision to rebuild the infrastructure across much of the public sector. The private sector now accounts for some 88% of new capital spending compared with 91% in recent years. One reason why the public sector now contributes relatively little in the way of new investment is the privatization programme which has reduced the number of public corporations. However, it also reflects the desire of the previous government to keep spending under control. Because of difficulties involved in cutting back on current expenditure plans, capital projects have been sacrificed in a bid to fulfil this objective.

Investment by type of asset has changed since 1989. Investment in machinery and equipment has grown most rapidly, increasing by around 44%. It now accounts for around 43% of total GFCF. There has also been a healthy rise in the real level of investment in other new buildings and in transport equipment, which in 2002 together contributed some 37% of GFCF. The level of investment in dwellings has declined in real terms and now accounts for just 15% of GFCF. Within the housing investment component (dwellings) there has also been a transfer of resources from the public to the private sector. Investment in public sector housing fell from 16% of total dwelling investment in 1989 to only 7% in 2002.

Factors affecting fixed investment

Gross Fixed Capital Formation is so heterogeneous that any explanation must address itself to particular components. For instance, investment in dwellings is influenced by population trends, expected lifetime income, the availability and cost of mortgage finance, etc. Most attempts at theory and empirical work have, however, tended to concentrate on investment in plant and machinery, particularly in the manufacturing sector. Here we review the factors which allegedly affect this type of fixed investment.

The rate of interest

The earliest theories of investment placed considerable emphasis on the importance of the rate of interest, seen here as the compensation required for forgoing current consumption. Fisher used the rate of interest to derive the *present value* (PV) of an expected future stream of income. By calculating the PV of various alternative investment projects they could then be ranked against each other.

This approach was taken a stage further by Keynes who introduced the concept of the marginal efficiency of investment (MEI). The MEI was defined as that rate of discount which would equate the PV of a given stream of future income from a project, with the initial capital outlay (the supply price):

$$S = PV = \frac{R_1}{(1+i)} + \frac{R_2}{(1+i)^2} + \frac{R_3}{(1+i)^3} + \cdots + \frac{R_n}{(1+i)^n}$$

where S = the supply price;
     PV = the present value;
     R = the expected yearly return; and
     i = that rate of discount necessary to equate the present value of future income with the initial cost of the project.

The curve relating the marginal efficiency of investment (i) to the level of investment in Fig. 17.1 is negatively sloped, for two main reasons. First, the earliest investment projects undertaken are likely to be the most profitable, i.e. offering the highest expected yearly returns (R), and therefore having the highest marginal efficiencies of investment (i). As more projects are initiated, they are likely to be less and less profitable, with lower expected yearly returns, and therefore lower MEIs. Second, a rise in the level of investment undertaken is, at least in the short run, likely to raise the supply price (S), which in turn will reduce the MEI. This could follow if the industries producing capital goods faced capacity constraints in their attempt to raise output in the short run.

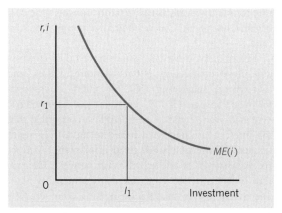

Fig. 17.1 The investment demand schedule.

The decision on whether to proceed with an investment project will depend on the relationship between the rate of interest (r) and the marginal efficiency of investment (i). If r is less than i, then the annual cost of borrowing funds for an additional project will be less than the expected annual return on the initial capital outlay, so that the project will be profitable to undertake. In Fig. 17.1, with interest rate r_1, it will be profitable to invest in all projects up to I_1, with I_1 itself breaking even. The MEI schedule is therefore the investment demand schedule, telling us the level of investment that will be undertaken at any given rate of interest. Expectations play an important role in this theory of investment. If, as is often the case, expectations are volatile, then the expected yearly returns (R) on any project will change, causing substantial shifts in the MEI schedule. At *any given rate of interest* investment demand will therefore be changing, which will reduce the closeness of any statistical fit between the interest rate and investment. In fact, it may be via expectations that interest rates exert their major influence on investment. A fall in rates is often a signal to investors of better times ahead, raising expected returns, shifting the MEI curve to the right, and raising investment (and conversely). Although this may dilute the statistical fit between r and I, there may still be an underlying linkage between the two variables.

Evidence

One problem in testing the influence of interest rates on investment is the selection of an appropriate interest rate. The average yield on debentures is a rate frequently used, as this broadly indicates the cost of new borrowing for a company at any point in time.

Historically, most UK studies have failed to show any close connection between interest rates and investment, suggesting that the latter is interest-inelastic. Savage (1978), in reviewing econometric evidence over a wide range of studies, concluded that the interest rate had been found to have little significance in influencing UK fixed investment. A more recent analysis of the relationship between the real rate of interest and gross fixed investment in plant and machinery in manufacturing was conducted by Turner (1989). He also found only a weak correlation between the two variables, as did Whitaker (1998) in his study of investment in the UK in the recovery period 1992–96. However, a study by Osler (1994), covering not only the UK but also Germany, France, Japan and Canada, found that the high level of real interest rates between 1990 and 1993 had substantially depressed private investment and consequently reduced output in the five countries by between $2\frac{1}{2}$ and $4\frac{1}{2}\%$ per year over the period.

Instead of focusing solely on the rate of interest, some research has looked for alternative measures of the cost of capital to firms. Cummins *et al.* (1996), for example, examined the role of the stock market in influencing investment trends. A rise in equity prices tends to make it cheaper to raise capital on the stock market while a fall can make it more expensive. They found that sudden share-price changes had a substantial impact on firms' investment plans in 12 of the 14 OECD countries examined, i.e. a rise in share prices leads to higher investment, and vice versa. A more recent study by Tevlin and Whelan (2000) which was based on US data suggested that over the previous decade the cost of capital had become significantly more important in determining the level of investment. They pointed out that much of the recent investment has been in the IT area and suggested that this is far more sensitive to the cost of capital than is investment in non-computing equipment. The Bank of England, in its model of investment spending, uses a variable described as the 'real cost of capital'. This is weighted to capture the proportion of corporate borrowing that is equity based and the proportion that is bond based. The numbers are then combined with equity and bond yields (long-term interest rates) before inflation expectations are deducted.

Accelerator Theory and Capital Stock Adjustment Model

The *Accelerator Theory* relates net investment to the rate of change of output. If the capital stock K is fully utilized, and the capital/output ratio v is a constant, then net investment (I) can be expressed in the following way:

$$K_t = vY_t$$
$$K_t - K_{t-1} = v(Y_t - Y_{t-1})$$
$$I_t = v(Y_t - Y_{t-1})$$
$$I_t = v\Delta Y_t$$

where Y is output and t and $t-1$ are time periods.

Net investment in year t is then a constant proportion of the change in output during that year. For example, if output rose by £2m for the economy ($\Delta Y_t = £2m$), and each extra £1 of output needed an average of £5 of capital equipment to produce it ($v = 5$), then $I_t = 5 \times 2m = £10m$. A number of criticisms have been levelled at the Accelerator Theory. First, the assumption that there is no excess capacity is particularly suspect. If there is spare capacity then a rise in output ΔY_t can be met from the existing capital stock, with no need for new investment. It has been estimated by the CBI that in the period 1979–2002, an average of just over 40% of firms were working at full capacity. Such a large amount of excess capacity must severely impair the effective functioning of the accelerator. Second, the assumption of a constant capital/output ratio, v, is becoming less and less plausible. The advent of new generations of micro-electronic technology is progressively reducing capital/output ratios. Third, it is also likely that prior to making an investment the firm would want to be sure that any upsurge in demand and in output is not a temporary phenomenon. *Expectations* of future demand, and therefore future changes in output, will then be important.

A more sophisticated version of this is the *Capital Stock Adjustment Model*. This was developed to overcome some of the problems of the simple Accelerator Theory. It states that investment is positively related to the expected level of output and negatively related to the existing capital stock. Any rise in investment will consequently depend not only on the expected level of output (demand) but also on the current size of the capital stock. Specifically,

$$I_t = bY_{t-1} - cK_{t-1}$$

where I_t = gross investment in the current year;

b and c = constant coefficients;

Y_{t-1} = last year's level of output;

K_{t-1} = the capital stock at the end of the preceding year.

If it is assumed that the expected volume of output is roughly equal to that experienced in the previous year, Y_{t-1}, then the higher is Y_{t-1} the greater will gross investment tend to be. However, the greater the inherited capital stock, K_{t-1}, the less need there will be for adding to the capital stock, or even replacing worn-out equipment.

Evidence

Even when varying lag structures are introduced into more refined versions of the Accelerator Theory, the evidence in its support is far from convincing. McCormick *et al.* (1983) found that changes in real GFCF by firms between 1962 and 1980 were not strongly related to the previous year's change in real consumer spending or demand. Kennedy (1997) noted that the Capital Stock Adjustment Principle was useful in explaining manufacturing investment in the UK between 1955 and 1970, though less so since then. Similar support for a modified accelerator theory as a determinant of investment has come from the studies of Catinat *et al.* (1987) and Ford and Poret (1990). A study by Oliner *et al.* (1995) in the US also found this approach helpful in explaining investment, albeit with the inclusion of other variables. However, Tevlin and Whelan (2000) suggested that the Capital Stock Adjustment Model actually broke down in the 1990s, with the actual level of investment in the US 7 percentage points higher in 1997 than could be explained by the model.

Profitability

There are at least three reasons why changes in profitability might be associated with changes in private sector investment:

1 Higher profits indicate a more favourable return on capital, which may encourage companies to reinvest any surplus rather than devote it to alternative uses.

2 Higher profits may improve business confidence and raise the expected future return on any project. An outward shift of the *MEI* schedule (see Fig. 17.1 above) might then raise investment at any given rate of interest.

3 Higher profits may raise investment by reducing its cost, as funds generated internally are cheaper than those obtained from the capital market, whether equity or debenture.

Evidence

In a major study of investment in the EU over the period 1961–90, the relation between net investment and the rate of profitability per unit of capital stock was found to be highly significant. Indeed variations in profitability were found to account for some three-quarters of the variations in capital stock during this period (European Economy 1991). In this study the profitability variable was lagged one period in order to take into account the unavoidable delays between changes in profit conditions and the effective realization of resulting investment decisions. More recent work by Carrauth *et al.* (2000) and Driver *et al.* (2001) has suggested that investment in the UK is significantly related to corporate profitability.

Given the more open product markets implied by a global economy, it is not only profitability in the *domestic economy* which now influences investment decisions but that in the *global economy*. A recent study has found that an increase in costs in the UK *relative to those in other countries* leads to a more than proportionate reduction in the UK investment, and of course vice versa (Young 1994). In other words, *relative* changes in UK factor prices and tax policies, and thereby in profitability, have a significant effect on UK investment. For example, Young found that a 1% rise in UK *relative factor prices* would lead to a 1.62% decline in UK investment, with an eight-quarter time lag.

Uncertainty

During periods of uncertainty (for example, after a shock rise in oil prices) it has been argued that firms will reduce the value they place on expected future returns on investment projects. In terms of the earlier Fig. 17.1, the *MEI* will shift leftwards and less investment will take place at any given rate of interest. Faced with such uncertainty, therefore, businessmen and women become more inclined to delay any planned capital spending.

Evidence

Until recently, there have been few attempts to model the relationship between investment and uncertainty. There is no general agreement as to how to account for uncertainty as a variable, although the majority of studies have used a variance measure to capture volatility in output, inflation or the exchange rate. Other options include the gold price, equity price volatility and information from the CBI survey. Work by Temple *et al.* (2001) and Bloom *et al.* (2001) amongst others confirms the relevance of uncertainty as an issue impacting upon capital spending decision-making.

Public policies

The post-war period until the late 1970s witnessed governments playing a positive role in stimulating demand through reflation of the economy. Booms were, however, generally interspersed with balance of payments crises. This prevented the application of reflationary policies over long time periods, since deflation of demand, to reduce spending on imports, was often used to correct balance of payments deficits. The uncertainty of such stop–go policies arguably reduced business confidence and discouraged investment.

Other public policies may also influence investment in the private sector. For example, changes in the rate of taxation of company profits, or in the capital allowances which can be set against tax, are believed by many to significantly affect levels of investment. The government introduced a tax credit for expenditure on Research and Development in 2002 to stimulate spending in an area seen as being of particular importance.

Evidence

Studies on the impacts of the reform of corporation tax and the phasing out of accelerated depreciation allowances on UK investment were undertaken by Sumner (1988) and Devereux (1989). The results suggested that such policies had relatively little impact on investment demand over the longer term. However, a more recent study by Bond *et al.* (1993) reopened the

debate. It suggested that recent corporation tax changes and the loss of capital allowances had created a strong fiscal bias against investment, equivalent to companies facing permanently higher interest rates of 1–2%. This conclusion is not dissimilar to the results produced by Cummins *et al.* (1994). They found that investment behaviour responded in a significant fashion to any changes in the tax regime which affected the cost of capital.

Capital market imperfections

It has been suggested that inefficiencies in the banking system and in the capital markets have prevented industry from obtaining the finance it requires for investment. Amongst the criticisms of UK financial institutions are the allegations that UK banks place too great an emphasis on lending to consumers, whereas overseas banks are primarily concerned with long-term industrial finance. Another criticism is that UK banks tend to concentrate on short-term lending, causing a shortage of long-term funds for investment. A further criticism is that financial institutions, which are major shareholders in many companies, place undue pressure on directors to distribute too high a proportion of total profit as dividend, the consequence then being that little profit is available to be 'ploughed back' as investment.

Evidence

Work carried out by Corbett and Jenkinson (1996) suggests that much of the criticism of the banking sector may be misplaced. Their study, which covers the period 1970 to 1994, suggests that banks provided a roughly similar share of funds for fixed investment in the UK as they did in Germany and the US. On average, bank finance in the UK accounted for 14.6% of investment spending. The corresponding figure for the US is 11.1% and that for Germany 10.8%. The economy where banks *have* played a more significant role is that of Japan. Over the period as a whole, Japanese banks provided 27% of the funds required for Japanese fixed investment.

Even though this research suggests that the UK is not markedly out of line with its main competitors, there remains considerable unease that 'short-termism' by the city discourages investment in another way, by inducing companies to pay too high a dividend in relation to profit. A related criticism is that dividend payments are too inflexible, not varying as profits rise and fall, with the result that funds available for investment are squeezed in times of recession. A House of Commons Trade and Industry Committee Report (1994) substantiated some of these concerns, showing a rising trend of dividend payments as a percentage of net earnings in UK companies, reaching levels in the UK above most other advanced industrialized countries, with the exception of the USA. The Report noted that: 'The Financial Secretary to the Treasury accepts that relatively high dividend pay-out ratios are a weakness in the UK economy' (p. 70). On the subject of corporate distributions, Whitaker (1998) concluded that relatively high dividend payouts during the UK economic recovery of 1992–96 may have diverted funds away from investment in fixed capital. Such concerns have resulted in changes to the tax treatment of dividends, making it relatively more attractive for firms to use profits for investment purposes rather than for dividend payments. Chapter 21 provides further background to this alleged cause of low levels of UK investment.

Skills and the labour market

A recent paper by the Department of Trade and Industry (2000) has argued that 'deficiencies in management and workforce skills' have contributed to the lack of investment in the UK. A major survey into UK competitiveness by Porter and Ketels (2003) reinforced this view, with American, French and German managers (especially the American managers) able to get more output from an equivalent amount of machinery and labour (i.e. they had demonstrably higher total factor productivities).

Evidence

There is only limited evidence of a relationship between investment and skill shortages. One study in this area was conducted by Nickell and Nicolitsas (2000). As a proxy for skill shortages they used the CBI industrial trends survey which contains a question as to the factors that are limiting output. The result of the study for UK manufacturing found that a 10 percentage point increase in the number of firms reporting skilled labour shortages reduced fixed capital investment by 10% and reduced R & D expenditure by 4%.

The rate of depreciation

Earlier in this chapter (p. 321) we noted that the difference between gross and net investment reflected the rate at which the existing capital stock is depreciated, which helped justify the focus on gross rather than net investment. However, Tevlin and Whelan (2000) concluded that a key reason for the recent pick-up in investment spending had been an increase in the rate at which businesses replace depreciated capital. While econometric models traditionally tend to assume a constant depreciation rate, Tevlin and Whelan argued that a structural shift of capital towards computers over the previous decade justified a faster rate of depreciation.

It is significant that the Office for National Statistics (ONS) in the UK has recently arrived at the same conclusion on the grounds that the lifespan of IT equipment tends to be shorter than for other types of capital. It follows that, although the (gross) investment to GDP ratio has climbed steeply in recent years, the ONS believes that the capital stock to GDP ratio has actually been falling.

The importance of investment

Investment has a dual role to play within any economy. In the short run, investment may be seen mainly as a component of aggregate demand which, if increased, will have the effect of stimulating the economy and, through the multiplier, substantially raising the level of National Income. Fixed investment made up some 12% of total final expenditure in 2002.

In the long run, investment will also affect the supply side of the economy, raising its productive potential and thereby pushing outwards the production frontier. Economic growth is sometimes strictly defined in this way, being that increase in GDP which results from raising productive potential. More usually it is loosely defined as any increase in GDP, even when that is within the existing production frontier.

There have been a number of studies into the importance of investment as a generator of growth, though the results have not been conclusive. For example, in 1961 Kuznets, using time-series data for a number of countries, found little relationship between the *share* of investment in GDP, and the growth in output over time. Similarly, a 1970 OECD survey based on cross-sectional data found no clear well-defined relationship between investment shares and growth in output.

Table 17.2 shows both the average annual growth in non-residential investment and the share of investment in GDP over the past 31 years for the seven major world economies. It suggests that it is difficult to identify too strong a relationship between either of these variables and the performance of the economy. While Japan and Canada achieved an identical growth rate in GDP over the period, their respective shares of investment in GDP were at either end of the spectrum, with Japan at the top and Canada near the bottom. However, in terms of the respective growth rates of non-residential investment, Canada was well ahead of Japan in this area. Interestingly, the UK experienced the lowest growth rate of GDP, with its share of investment in GDP near the bottom of the countries surveyed but its share of non-residential investment in the top half of the table.

Does the UK suffer from a lack of investment?

Some of the previous discussion suggests that the UK may be suffering from a relatively low level of invest-

ment. Certainly Porter and Ketels (2003) suggested that one key factor in the observed productivity gap between the UK and its main competitors was under-investment in the UK. Their survey showed that French workers have 60% more capital than in the UK, and those in Germany and the US between 25% and 30% more capital per worker. Recent work at the IMF (2003) casts some doubt on this judgement, particularly as it relates to the more productive forms of capital spending. In its analysis the IMF points out that the performance of the UK in *equipment investment* is broadly comparable to that of other OECD countries. The UK does, however, have significantly lower non-residential construction investment which may reflect historical factors or different public policies (since government spending tends to be more important in this area of investment).

Other studies such as that by Bloom *et al.* (2001) remain rather sceptical. They acknowledge that business investment as a percentage of GDP has risen in the UK since the mid-1990s but contend that it is still not relatively high when compared with the likes of the US and Germany. One point they make is that the use of 'consistent price investment' data distorts the picture (see Fig. 17.2). The authors of the report argue that over the period in question, the price of capital goods has fallen sharply while the overall price level has risen. In effect, there has been a significant decline in the *real price* of capital goods. Thus Bloom *et al.* point out that 'if firms had indeed bought the same capital goods they bought last year at the higher real prices prevailing in 1995, they would have had to spend substantially more money'.

Table 17.2 Investment and the growth of output, 1970–2001.

	GDP growth (%)	Non-residential investment (%)	Share of investment in GDP (%)
Japan	3.2	3.3	28.4
Canada	3.2	5.8	18.4
US	3.0	4.6	17.5
Germany	2.6	1.5	22.4
France	2.5	3.0	20.3
Italy	2.5	2.8	21.0
UK	2.3	3.7	18.4

Source: Adapted from OECD (2002) *Economic Outlook*, December.

Efficiency and investment

The level of investment is not the only factor contributing to growth. A number of economists see investment as a necessary, but by no means *sufficient*, condition for economic growth. Growth also depends on the efficiency with which any investment is utilized. One method of measuring the efficiency of investment is through the gross incremental capital/output ratio, i.e. the extra capital required to produce an additional unit of output.

Table 17.3 presents incremental capital/output ratios for five major economies. It demonstrates what appears to have been a major weakness of the UK economy in the past, namely that the UK has required

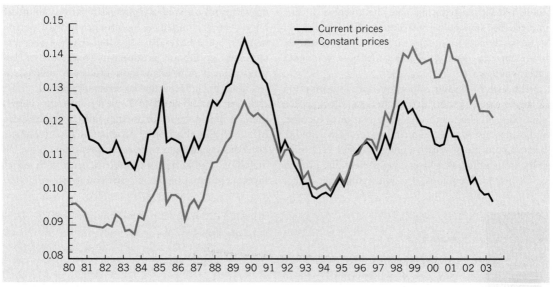

Fig. 17.2 Investment as a share of GDP.
Source: *Datastream.*

a higher rate of gross investment to produce a *given increase* in output, than have Germany, France, the USA or Japan. However, the data suggest a considerable improvement in the efficiency with which investment in the UK has been utilized during the 1990s. Some have suggested that the more flexible labour market in the UK following earlier reforms (see Chapter 15) has allowed capital to be used more productively in recent times.

Table 17.3 suggests that increased capital intensity within the UK has resulted in a *more than proportionate* increase in output during the 1990–2002 period, with only 0.7 units of capital required to yield a one-unit increase in output. It has been pointed out

in Chapter 1 that *total* factor productivity must rise in UK plants and enterprises if growth is to be sustained. It follows that increasing the efficiency of labour, and improving the organizational structure of UK firms, may be at least as important in generating economic growth as raising the absolute level of investment.

Studies such as Young (1994) suggest that in a global market with 'footloose' multinationals continually reappraising the location of investment decisions, it is *relative efficiency* which is becoming a crucial factor in investment decisions. Changes in total factor productivity (and thereby costs) in the UK relative to other countries may therefore have an increasingly significant influence on investment decisions in the UK.

Table 17.3 Incremental capital/output ratios.

	1970–79	1980–89	1990–2002
France	0.7	1.1	0.7
Germany	0.9	1.5	0.8
Japan	0.8	1.3	–0.4
UK	1.6	1.8	0.7
USA	1.3	0.9	1.7

Source: Adapted from OECD (2002), *Economic Outlook*, December.

Conclusion

Investment occurs in so wide a variety of assets and sectors that it must be disaggregated substantially if any close statistical fit is to be found. However, even when we concentrate on fixed investment in manufacturing, no single theory 'explains' much of the variation in investment. What evidence there is certainly suggests that UK investment is relatively interest-inelastic, reducing the effectiveness of the interest rate as a policy instrument. Nevertheless, in so far as changes in interest rates affect expectations, lower interest rates may still contribute to higher investment.

Although much less important than consumption in aggregate demand, investment has, through the multiplier, a significant effect on National Income, and is the most volatile element in aggregate demand. It also affects the productive potential of an economy. Even though the link between investment and growth is in some ways tenuous, it is interesting that higher growth rates of fixed investment in various countries have been accompanied by stronger growth performances. Some have also suggested that the observed increases in labour productivity suggest that UK investment is now being more efficiently utilized, as reflected by falls in the incremental capital/output ratio for the UK noted in Table 17.3, though clearly there is much scope for further falls in this respect. Increased globalization of production and investment decisions is placing a still greater premium on the UK matching, and surpassing, the efficiency with which investments are utilized in other countries.

Key points

- Investment is an important element of aggregate demand, contributing around 14% of total final expenditure (TFE).

- Investment also contributes to the 'supply side' of the economy, e.g. directly influencing real output per unit of factor input.

- Investment is a 'flow', as it involves a rate of change.

- Investment is volatile, having a significant impact on changes in National Income (via the multiplier).

- The share of investment undertaken by the public sector has edged up over the past few years but still remains a historically low 12%.

- Expectations as to future profitability are a key factor in influencing the level of investment.

- Other relevant factors include the rate of interest, the rate of change of output (accelerator theory), levels and rates of depreciation of capital stock, size of public sector, financial support available, etc.

- In a global economy, changes in UK costs *relative to other countries* have been identified as influencing UK levels of investment.

- As well as the levels of investment, the *efficiency* with which any investment is utilized is also important.

Now try the self-check questions for this chapter on the Companion Website. You will also find up-to-date facts and case materials.

References and further reading

Ashworth, P., Hubert, F., Pain, N. and Riley, R. (2001) UK fixed capital formation: determinants and constraints, *NIESR paper*, National Institute of Economic and Social Research.
Bank of England (2002) *Inflation Report*.

Bloom, N., Bond, S. and Van Reenen, J. (2001) The dynamics of investment under uncertainty, *IFS Working Paper*, No. 2001/05, Institute for Fiscal Studies.

Bond, S. and Jenkinson, T. (1996) The assessment: investment performance and policy, *Oxford Review of Economic Policy*, 12.2.

Bond, S. and Meghir, C. (1994) Financial constraints and company investment, *Fiscal Studies*, **15**.

Bond, S., Denny, K. and Devereux, M. (1993) Capital allowances and the impact of Corporation Tax on investment in the UK, *Fiscal Studies*, **14**.

Bond, S., Elston, J., Mairesse, J. and Mulkay, B. (1997) Financial factors and investment in Belgium, France, Germany and the UK, *NBER Working Paper*, No. 5900, National Bureau of Economic Research.

Carruth, A., Dickerson, A. and Henley, A. (2000) Econometric modelling of UK aggregate investment: the role of profits and uncertainty, *The Manchester School*, **68**(3).

Catinat, M. *et al.* (1987) The determinants of investment, *European Economy Annual Economic Report*, **31**, March.

Corbett, J. and Jenkinson, T. (1996) *The Financing of Industry: An International Comparison*, mimeo, University of Oxford.

Cummins, J. G., Hassett, K. A. and Hubbard, R. G. (1994) A reconsideration of investment behaviour using tax reforms as natural experiments, *Brookings Papers on Economic Activity*, **2**, 1–74.

Cummins, J. G., Hassett, K. A. and Hubbard, R. G. (1996) A cross-country comparison of investment expenditures, *Tax Reform Journal of Public Economies and Investment*.

Department of Trade and Industry (2000) *UK Competitiveness Indicators 1999*.

Devereux, M. (1989) Tax asymmetries, the cost of capital and investment: some evidence from the United Kingdom panel data, *Economic Journal*, **99**, pp. 103–12.

Driver, C., Temple, P. and Urga, G. (2001) The profit orientation of UK manufacturing investment: does Π beat Q?, *City University Business School, Department of Investment, Risk Management and Insurance, Working Paper*, No. 01/01.

European Economy (1991) The profitability of fixed capital and its relation with investment, *Annual Economic Report* 1991–92, 50, Dec.

Ford, R. and Poret, P. (1990) Business investment in the OECD economies: recent performance and some implications for policy, *OECD Working Paper* 88.

Gordon, R. J. and Veitch, J. M. (1987) Fixed investment in the American business cycle 1919–1983, in R. J. Gordon, *The American Business Cycle: Continuity and Change*.

House of Commons (1994) Trade and Industry Committee, *Competitiveness of UK Manufacturing Industry*, Second Report.

IMF (2003) *Selected Issues* Esolano, J., Koevaa, P. and Hollar, I. V., New York.

Kennedy, M. (1997) Economic activity and inflation, in M. J. Artis, (ed.) *The UK Economy*, 14th edn, Oxford.

Mullins, M. and Wadhwani, S. B. (1989) The effects of the stock market on investment, *European Economic Review*, **33**.

Nickell, S. and Nicolitsas, D. (2000) Human capital, investment and innovation: what are the connections?, in R. Barrell, G. Mason and M. O'Mahoney (eds), *Productivity, Innovation and Economic Performance*, Cambridge University Press.

Oliner, S. D., Rudebusch, G. D. and Sichel, D. E. (1995) New and old models of business investment; a comparison of forecasting performance, *Journal of Money, Credit and Banking*, **27**, August.

Osler, C. L. (1994) High foreign real interest rates and investment in the 1990s, *Federal Reserve Bank of New York Quarterly Review*, Spring 1994.

Porter, M. and Ketels, C. (2003) UK competitiveness: moving to the next stage, *DTI Economics paper*, Department of Trade and Industry.

Savage, D. (1978) The channels of manufacturing influence: a survey of the empirical evidence, *National Institute Economic Review*, **83**, February.

Sumner, M. (1998) Note on improving the effects of effective tax rates on business investment, *Journal of Public Economics*, **35**.

Temple, P., Urga, G. and Driver, C. (2001) The influence of uncertainty on investment in the

UK: a macro or micro phenomenon?, *Scottish Journal of Political Economy*, **48**(4).

Tevlin, S and Whelan, K. (2000) Explaining the investment boom of the 1990s, *Federal Reserve Board, Working Papers*.

Turner, P. (1989) Investment: theory and evidence, *Economic Review*, **6**(3).

Vittas, D. and Brown, R. (1982) *Bank Lending and Industrial Investment*, Banking Information Service.

Whitaker, S. (1998) Investment in this recovery: an assessment, *Bank of England Quarterly Bulletin*, February, **38**(1).

Young, G. (1994) International competitiveness, international taxation and domestic investment, *National Institute Economic Review*, May.

Chapter 18   Public expenditure

In this chapter we consider the growth of public expenditure and the difficulties
surrounding its control. The next chapter will examine the burden of taxation.

Here we look at public expenditure, its form, size and apparently inexorable growth.
Problems of definition and calculation are considered – for instance, current
estimates for the ratio of public spending to National Income vary from as little as
25% to over 50%. Resolving such ambiguities is extremely important since entire
economic and political platforms rest upon the outcome. Attempts to control public
expenditure are nothing new; they began long before Gladstone. Although the last
Conservative government was pledged to cut back public expenditure, the evidence
suggests that successive Conservative governments failed. Real public spending
between 1979 and 1997 showed an average growth rate of 1.4% per annum
compared with an annual rate of 1% under the previous Labour administration.
However, public expenditure has fallen as a *proportion* of GDP. In 1981/82 public
expenditure was 48.5% of GDP; in 2003/04 it was only around 41% of GDP. This
fall is largely because of the high growth rates of GDP in the mid- to late 1980s and
1990s. However, major increases in public expenditure over the period 2003–06
were announced in the Comprehensive Spending Review of November 2002,
raising the projected ratio of public expenditure to GDP to around 42% by 2005/06.

Although 'general government expenditure (GGE)' has been a widely used measure
of public spending, '*total managed expenditure* (TME)' has now been widely
adopted. Similarly any excess of public expenditure over revenue is no longer to be
called the public sector borrowing requirement (PSBR) but rather the *public sector
net cash requirement*.

Trends in UK public spending

As we can see from Fig. 18.1, the ratio of general government (now total managed) expenditure to GDP fell sharply during the growth years of the mid- to late 1980s. The Conservative government failed to sustain this objective during the early 1990s as the ratio rose, with social security and other demand-led expenditures placing upward pressure on public spending, and GDP falling relative to trend. Nevertheless the Conservative government reiterated its determination that, over time, public expenditure should continue to take a declining share of National Income and announced severe cuts in public expenditure in November 1993. The Conservative government believed that the result of such cuts would be lower borrowing which, combined with lower taxation, would mean that enterprise and efficiency would be encouraged and output and employment would grow.

Figure 18.1 indicates a sustained fall in general government (now total managed) expenditure as a percentage of GDP between 1993 and 2000, a fall initially continued under the incoming Labour government of 1997, before a series of boosts to public expenditure since 2000, especially in the Comprehensive Spending Review of November 2002. Table 18.1 identifies the major beneficiaries of that Review. As can be seen, in real terms, average annual spending is to grow by 4.3% per annum across all spending departments over

Table 18.1 Average annual spending growth, 2002/03 to 2005/06 (real terms).

Spending department	Average annual % (real terms)
Transport	+8.4
International Development	+8.1
Health	+7.3
Education	+5.7
Criminal Justice	+4.2
Housing	+3.5
Culture, Media and Sport	+2.8
Trade and Industry	+2.2
Social Security	+2.2
All other departments	+2.2
Total spending	+4.3

the period 2002/03 to 2005/06, with Transport, International Development, Health, Education and Criminal Justice the major beneficiaries.

Total Managed Expenditure (TME)

The *Economic and Fiscal Strategy Report* in June 1998 reformed the planning and control regime for public spending.

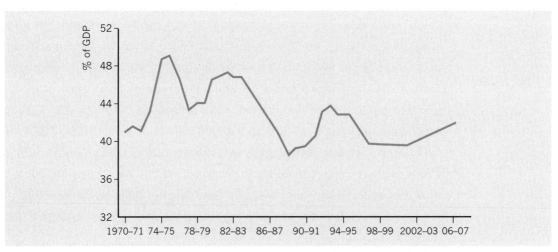

Fig. 18.1 General government expenditure as a percentage of GDP since 1970 (projections from 2003). Source: Adapted from Treasury (2002).

- Overall plans were to use a new distinction between current and capital spending.
- Firm three-year plans (*Departmental Expenditure Limits*, DELs) were to provide certainty and flexibility for long-term planning and management.
- Spending outside DELs, which could not reasonably be subjected to firm three-year spending commitments, was to be reviewed annually as part of the Budget process. This *annual managed expenditure* (AME) is also subject to constraints.
- Large public corporations, not dependent on government grants, were to be given more flexibility.
- *Total managed expenditure* (TME) was defined as consisting of DEL plus AME and was to be widely

Table 18.2 Historical series of government expenditure (% of GDP).

	Public sector current expenditure	Public sector net capital expenditure	General government expenditure (GGE)	Total managed expenditure (TME)
1970–71	32.1	6.4	41.0	42.2
1971–72	32.9	5.5	41.3	42.2
1972–73	32.7	5.0	40.8	41.4
1973–74	34.7	5.5	41.3	44.1
1974–75	38.4	5.8	47.6	48.5
1975–76	39.7	4.6	45.6	48.7
1976–77	39.7	4.6	45.6	48.7
1977–78	38.1	3.1	42.4	45.5
1978–79	38.0	2.7	43.0	45.0
1979–80	38.1	2.4	43.0	44.8
1980–81	40.8	2.0	46.0	47.3
1981–82	42.6	1.1	46.7	48.1
1982–83	42.6	1.6	46.6	48.5
1983–84	42.3	1.9	45.5	48.3
1984–85	42.5	1.6	45.5	48.0
1985–86	41.0	1.3	43.5	45.5
1986–87	40.0	0.8	41.6	43.9
1987–88	38.5	0.7	39.8	42.0
1988–89	36.0	0.4	37.2	39.2
1989–90	35.6	1.3	38.3	39.6
1990–91	35.8	1.5	38.5	39.7
1991–92	38.4	1.9	40.8	42.4
1992–93	40.3	2.1	42.8	44.3
1993–94	40.3	1.7	42.9	43.8
1994–95	40.0	1.5	42.2	43.3
1995–96	39.6	1.3	42.1	42.8
1996–97	38.8	0.7	40.3	41.2
1997–98	37.4	0.6	39.1	39.6
1998–99	36.5	0.6	38.3	38.7
1999–00	36.2	0.6	38.0	38.1
2000–01	36.5	0.6	–	38.4
2001–02	36.7	1.2	–	39.2
2002–03	37.1	1.4	–	39.8
2003–04	37.9	1.8	–	41.0

Source: Adapted from Treasury (2003).

used as the overall measure of government expenditure (replacing general government expenditure – GGE).

Making a clear distinction between public sector *current* expenditure and *capital* expenditure is a key element in the government's 'golden rule' (see below). A historical series for these various definitions is shown in Table 18.2.

The debate on the role of public expenditure continues. Nevertheless, both the previous Conservative government and the present Labour government have accepted that, as a cornerstone of the medium-term financial strategy, they should squeeze inflation progressively out of the economy, through a close control of the rate of growth of public expenditure. Continuing fiscal rectitude is seen as important for a government committed to the Maastricht criteria for fiscal convergence (see Chapter 29). These include a 3% target for the overall ratio of PSBR (now public sector net cash requirement) to GDP, and a 60% target for the ratio of public debt to GDP.

Fiscal 'rules'

In addition to its commitment to the Maastricht criteria for fiscal convergence, in 1998 the Labour government committed itself to the following two important 'fiscal rules'.

- The 'golden rule': over the economic cycle the government will only borrow to invest and will not borrow to fund current expenditure.

- The 'public debt rule': the ratio of public debt to National Income will be held over the economic cycle at a 'stable and prudent' level.

In effect the 'golden rule' implies that current expenditure will be covered by current revenue (see Chapter 19) over the economic cycle. Put another way, any PSBR (now public sector net cash requirement) must be used only for investment purposes, with 'investment' defined as in the National Accounts.

The 'public debt rule' is rather less clear in that the phrase 'stable and prudent' is somewhat ambiguous. However, taken together with the 'golden rule' it essentially means that, as an average over the economic cycle, the ratio of PSBR to National Income cannot exceed the ratio of investment to National Income. Given that, historically, government invest-

ment has been no more than 2–3% of National Income, then clearly the PSBR as a percentage of National Income must be kept within strict bounds.

This inevitably brings into focus the procedure for the planning, monitoring and control of public expenditure.

Planning, monitoring and control

Governments must seek to *plan* levels of public expenditure several years into the future, especially since any rise in public expenditure must be financed either by additional taxation or by increased borrowing. Governments must also develop and apply procedures to *monitor* and *control* public expenditure. All three elements are involved to some extent in the Public Expenditure Survey 'rounds', to which all the spending departments must submit on a regular and ongoing basis.

Public Expenditure Survey (PES)

Planning public expenditure for the next three years begins with the Public Expenditure Survey (PES). As part of this process the spending departments discuss their spending proposals with the Public Expenditure Division of the Treasury, with all proposals expressed in cash terms. This PES 'round' usually takes place between April and September of each year, with the results of the PES announced at the end of November when the Chancellor presents his Budget statement to Parliament. To avoid any planning 'surprises' the major spending departments, such as the Department of Social Security, actually undergo *two* PES rounds each year, the second lasting from October to April.

Control Total (CT)

We have already noted the importance attached to the 'golden rule', which has resulted in the government paying less attention to monitoring and controlling *cyclical* components of expenditure, such as unemployment benefit and various types of income support. This has led to the government establishing a new Control Total (CT) for public expenditure, which covers around 85% of the value of spending included in total managed expenditure (TME). An underlying objective of the CT is to help government focus on those items of expenditure which it can directly control and which are independent of cyclical fluctuations in the economy. As well as excluding unemployment benefit and income support, the CT also excludes central government gross debt interest (since borrowing and interest payments tend to rise during recession and fall during recovery).

Until 1992, the ministers in charge of the spending departments would seek to agree on spending limits for their departments in *bilateral* negotiations with the Chief Secretary to the Treasury. The agreed sums for each department would then be added together and announced in an 'Autumn Statement' on public spending plans.

Since 1993, however, the spending ministers have had to meet face-to-face in Cabinet in October or November to fight for a share of the already established overall value for the Control Total. Any extra given to one spending department must be funded at the expense of another spending department by reallocating the provisionally agreed CT. Clearly this procedure is intended to restrict the possibility of 'upward drift' in total public spending, which many critics claimed to have been a constant feature of the previous system of simply aggregating the outcomes of bilateral negotiations between spending departments and the Treasury.

Further, since 1993 we have had a unified Budget in March, in which both revenue raising and expenditure plans are discussed together. Prior to 1993, the spending totals were announced in the 'Autumn Statement' and the revenue-raising measures to finance them were announced some six months later in the March Budget. This separation of time between announcing planned expenditure and announcing methods for raising the tax revenue to fund that expenditure, was seen as encouraging public expenditure growth, since the public would be less likely to associate any need for higher taxes in the March Budget with announcements of higher public expenditure in the previous autumn. To remedy this, since 1993 we have had a 'unified' Budget, with planned expenditure and planned tax revenue announced together, reinforcing the linkage between the two.

Forecasts

Since the expenditure plans for each department must cover three years, *forecasts* are needed for the future expenditures required to implement the agreed policies over this time period. The expenditure forecasts for each department are based on the work of both *internal* departmental experts (e.g. statisticians and economists) and *external* experts (e.g. members of the independent Government Actuaries Department). Further, the basic assumptions on which these forecasts rest include estimates of future changes in variables such as retail prices, average earnings, unemployment rates, economic growth, etc. To ensure that the various departmental forecasts rest on *common* assumptions, the Treasury provides the spending departments with projections of the data on expected values for all these variables over the next three years.

Agreement by the government on the future spending plans of a department (departmental expenditure limits – DEL) implies agreement on the policy proposals produced by that department over the next three years. Such policy proposals are usually generated by the Policy Group which resides within each department. Members of the Policy Group will seek to reflect the political priorities of both the government and the departmental ministers, as well as taking into account the representation of various pressure groups and any current research findings in the field. These policy proposals, once agreed, are then costed by a specialist group within the department containing statisticians and economists, and these costings will in turn provide the basis for the department expenditure forecasts.

An outline of the various processes involved in a Public Expenditure Survey has been provided by Weir (1998), with the Department of Social Security (DSS) used to illustrate a system common to most spending departments (Fig. 18.2).

The DSS is the largest spending department and accounts for around 30% of planned public expenditure. Expenditure on Social Security benefits, such as the Retirement Pension, Housing Benefit and Child Benefit, account for 95% of the total DSS bill. Social Security expenditure is almost entirely demand led, so estimating future expenditure requires projections as to how that demand is likely to change in the future. Factors influencing Social Security expenditure can usefully be grouped into four key headings.

- *Demographic.* The size and the structure of the population are key variables here, for example an

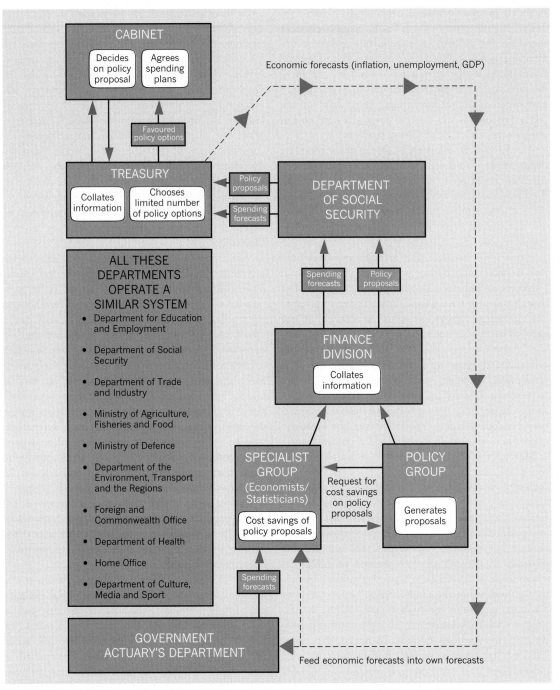

Fig. 18.2 The Public Expenditure Survey (PES) within the Department for Social Security (DSS).
Source: Adapted from Weir (1998).

ageing population will reduce spending on Child Benefit, but increase spending on retirement pensions.

- *Economic*. The projected levels of unemployment, earnings, prices and economic growth will affect the demand for various types of benefit and therefore the amount of benefit paid.
- *Social*. Changes in family structures, for example the frequency of divorce and of lone parenthood, will affect benefit expenditures.
- *Policy*. The introduction of new benefits, changes to entitlement, changes to benefit rates, etc. will all affect benefit expenditure.

The government is obliged to report the differences between *forecast* expenditure and *actual out-turn* for any given year; drawing attention to any discrepancies between what was planned to be spent and what was actually spent is seen as helping the process of monitoring and controlling public expenditure.

The planning, monitoring and control of public expenditure can therefore be seen to have undergone considerable change in recent years, with the underlying aim of curbing tendencies towards an upward drift in spending totals. The procedures involved in the PES, the introduction of a new Control Total, the unified budget, obligations to report any discrepancies between forecast expenditures and actual out-turn, are all parts of a more structured and accountable system for public expenditure.

A further element in such a system has been the so-called government drive for greater 'efficiency' in the public sector.

The drive for efficiency

Increasingly strident claims were made throughout the 1980s that, in the absence of competition, public services would always be produced inefficiently. One remedy might clearly be to increase such competition by privatizing the public services (see Chapter 8). Where this 'remedy' was not available then it was argued that efficiency could be improved by making sure that the delivery of public services conformed more closely to the needs of those who used them, rather than to the interests of those who provided them. This view led to a wave of reforms, including the introduction of contracting out and competitive tendering, the creation of Next Step Agencies, and the introduction of Value for Money Audits.

- *Contracting out and competitive tendering.* Putting services previously provided through the public sector out to tender has led to cost savings of varying magnitudes. For example, there have been estimates of savings of 20% in the case of NHS catering and laundry, and savings of 14% in the case of highway services. In a number of other cases savings of 7% have been realized (Griffiths 1998).
- *Next Step Agencies.* These have been introduced within government departments with the intention of improving the management of such departments. The idea here has been to separate the management of policy (the responsibility of central government) from operational management (the responsibility of the Agencies). For example the Department of Social Security (DSS) has five agencies – the Benefits Agency, the Contributions Agency, the Child Support Agency, the War Pensions Agency and the IT Services Agency. Such agencies have often been given the task of meeting a number of key performance indicators or targets, giving a yardstick against which their subsequent performance can be evaluated.
- *Value for money (VFM) audits.* These are part of the Financial Management Initiative (FMI) aimed at ensuring that public provision of goods and services is economic, efficient and effective. Under the FMI, central government departments have had to demonstrate to the Treasury that they have in place a VFM framework whereby audits are undertaken to check that managers are finding resource savings, while at the same time improving the quality of public services. Again, such procedures have often involved performance indicators.
- *Private Finance Initiative (PFI).* The intention here has been to identify projects which can attract private sector finance to be used alongside public sector finance (see Myers 1998).

The size of public expenditure

So far we have looked at changing *shares* within total public spending, but has the *absolute* level of public spending grown as fast as critics suggest? Such people usually point to a single statistic for evidence; for instance, that the public sector employs about 25% of the labour force or, as with Milton Friedman, that if public expenditure grows to around 60% of National Income then it will threaten to destroy freedom and democracy. Actually, estimates for the ratio of public spending to National Income vary widely, depending on the definitions used for each item. Figures for 2003/04 put total managed expenditure at around 41% of GDP at market prices (see Table 18.3). If, however, transfer payments are excluded from government expenditure, as they are from the measurement of National Income, then government expenditure falls dramatically to less than 30% of GDP at market prices. What, then, is the truth about the size of public expenditure?

An examination of data from the Office for National Statistics (ONS) suggests that as many as 10 measures could be used for estimating the size of public expenditure. The measure selected will depend on the question at issue. If the intention is to assess the *financial resources* passing through the hands of government, then a ratio involving total managed expenditure might be appropriate. However, the ONS's definition of National Income in the Blue Book excludes current grants and other transfers. Strictly, therefore, these same items should be excluded from government expenditure. They do not represent additional demand for resources; they are merely transfers of purchasing power from the taxpayer to other sectors of the community. Using this argument, a ratio of total managed expenditure on

goods and services of approximately 30% of National Income would appear to be the most appropriate measure.

No single measure of public expenditure has met with universal agreement, and even when one has been widely used for some time, it can be subject to change for a variety of reasons. In April 1977 the then widely used measure of general government expenditure was redefined to bring the UK into line with OECD accounting methods, and resulted in an apparent overnight reduction of some 6% in measured public expenditure. Again, what was previously tax relief may be reclassified as government expenditure, as with child tax allowances being replaced by Child Benefit in 1977. Public expenditure will also be affected by changes in the degree of 'privatization' (which is recorded as negative expenditure) or by changes in public sector pricing.

The National Income aggregate used for comparison will also influence our impression of the size of the public sector. Some ratios use domestic product, which measures resources produced *entirely within the domestic circular flow*. If, however, our interest was in the resources produced by UK nationals, *wherever they happen to be located*, then our ratio should use national product. Yet again, both domestic and national products could be valued 'gross' (including depreciation) or 'net' (excluding depreciation); at 'market prices', including the effects of taxes and subsidies, or at 'factor cost', excluding them.

For all these reasons, public spending ratios must be treated with caution when used in policy analysis.

Table 18.3 Government spending as a proportion of National Income.

(a) Government spending as a proportion of GNP at factor cost (%)

1790	1890	1910	1932	1951	1966	1970	1976	
12.0	8.0	12.0	29.0	40.2	40.2	42.2	48.7	

(b) Government spending as a proportion of GDP at market price (%)

1978/79	1982/83	1986/87	1988/89	1990/91	1992/93	1995/96	2000/01	2003/04
45.0	48.5	43.9	39.2	39.7	44.3	42.8	38.3	41.1

Note: From 1977 onwards, an approximately 6% upward revision should be made to any government spending/National Income ratio if comparison with pre-1977 figures is to be made.
Sources: Treasury (2003); Brown and Jackson (1982).

Explanations of the growth in public expenditure

No matter what the definition, statistics show that the government sector of the economy has expanded over the last 150 years (see Fig. 18.3), both in money and real terms, and as a percentage of National Income. In Table 18.3, Brown and Jackson (1982), quoting a variety of sources, showed a dramatically rising trend of government spending as a proportion of GNP at factor cost up to 1976. The trend (using a different statistical series) continued upwards for data after 1976, reaching a peak of 48.5% in 1982/83. Between then and 2000 there has been a sustained fall in government spending as a percentage of National Income, though for a few years during the recession of the early 1990s the percentage had risen before resuming its downward path. Since 2000, and especially since the Comprehensive Spending Review of November 2002, there has been a renewed upward drift in government spending as a percentage of National Income.

The 1979 government of Margaret Thatcher was returned with a mandate to cut public expenditure. Initially the results were very disappointing as public expenditure continued to grow. The explanation of the above trends and the difficulties involved in controlling public expenditure are based on two types of analysis: microeconomic and macroeconomic respectively.

Microeconomic analysis

Explanations based on microeconomic analysis suggest that additional public spending can be seen as the result of governments continually intervening to correct market failure. This would include the provision of 'public goods' such as collective defence, the police, and local amenities (Cottrell 2002). An extra unit of such goods can be enjoyed by one person, without anyone else's enjoyment being affected. In other words the marginal social cost of provision is zero, and it is often argued in welfare economics that the 'efficiency' price should, therefore, be zero. Private markets are unable to cope with providing goods at zero price, so that public provision is the only alternative should this welfare argument be accepted. Microeconomic analysis would also cover extra public spending due to a change in the composition of the 'market', such as an ageing population incurring greater expenditure on health care.

Macroeconomic analysis

There are also explanations of the growth of public spending based on long-run macroeconomic theories and models. The starting point in this field is the work of Wagner (see Bird 1971), who used empirical evidence to support his argument that government expenditure would inevitably increase at a rate faster than the rise in national production. Wagner suggested

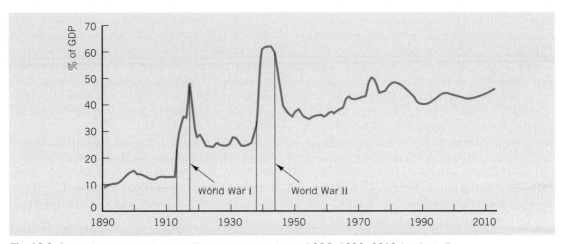

Fig. 18.3 General government expenditure as a percentage of GDP, 1890–2010 (projected).

that 'the pressures of social progress' would create tensions which could only be resolved by increased state activity in law and order, economic and social services, and participation in material production. Using the economists' terms, Wagner was in effect suggesting that public sector services and products are 'normal', with high income elasticities of demand. Early studies in the UK by Williamson during the 1960s tended to support Wagner, indicating overall income elasticities for public sector services of 1.7, and for public sector goods of 1.3, with similar results in other advanced industrialized countries. Further evidence in favour of Wagner's ideas came during the 1980s when studies by the OECD concluded that the proportion of GNP absorbed by public expenditure between 1954 and the early 1980s on 'merit goods' (education, health and housing) and 'income maintenance' (pensions, sickness, family and unemployment benefits) had doubled from 14% to 28%, as an average across all the advanced industrialized countries, with high income elasticities and low price elasticities playing a major part in this observed growth. Surveys of less developed economies were, however, more confusing, with econometric studies suggesting that little of the growth in public spending could be 'explained' by rising incomes (or low price elasticities).

Peacock and Wiseman's 'displacement theory', covering the period 1890–1953, suggested that public spending was not rising with the smooth, small changes predicted by Wagner, but that it was displaced (permanently) upwards by social upheavals associated, for instance, with depressions or wars leading to demands for new social expenditure (Fig. 18.3 above indicates the displacements of 1914–18 and 1939–45). Displacement theory has, however, been criticized for giving insufficient weight to political influences on the level of public expenditure. A further criticism of 'displacement' theory is the fact that for the UK there is little evidence that ratchet increases in public spending are long lasting. In fact, where the ratio of public expenditure to National Income continued to rise in the 1970s and 1980s, it was more easily explained by downward deviations of trend National Income in recession, with consequent increases in spending on unemployment benefits and social services, rather than through any upward revision of government expenditure plans.

The conclusion that must be drawn from reviewing such work is that there is no definite micro- or macro-explanation of the growth path for public expenditure. It then follows that there is no inevitable 'law' ensuring that public expenditure becomes a progressively rising proportion of National Income. However, in a recessionary period such as that of the early 1990s, increased spending on unemployment and social services may indeed cause a sharp increase in the share of public expenditure in National Income. The same result can be expected from explicit attempts by the UK government to raise the quality of public services and spending per head on those services to levels already reached within the EU economies (Griffiths 2002). Demographic changes may also conspire to raise the share of public expenditure. There has been considerable debate as to the mounting 'burden' on the working population likely to result from the growing number of pensioners in the next few decades. It has been estimated that the UK dependency ratio – the non-working population divided by the working population – will have risen from the current 0.52 to 0.62 by 2030. By 2030, therefore, each worker will be required to contribute 18% more real income to sustain the current level of welfare provision. It is scenarios such as this which have led to renewed scrutiny of the practicability of a welfare state along present lines.

International comparisons

Given that public expenditure has grown over time in the UK, how do we compare with other countries? Conclusions based on OECD surveys indicate that UK public expenditure patterns are similar to those in most other advanced industrialized countries, although inferences drawn from international surveys must be treated with caution. The OECD definitions are frequently different from national ones, public sector boundaries vary between countries, and fluctuating exchange rates compromise any attempt at a standard unit of value.

Table 18.4 indicates that the growing share of UK public expenditure in National Income has been paralleled in other countries. If anything, public expenditure has grown less quickly in the UK; in 1964 it was joint third highest, with Germany, of the 14 countries shown in Table 18.4; by 1989 it was only eleventh highest of those same 14 countries, and by 2003 it was still only tenth highest. Again, whereas

Table 18.4 Total outlays* of government as a percentage of GDP at market prices: some international comparisons.

	1964	1974	1979	1989	1999	2003†
Australia	22.1	31.6	31.4	33.1	32.4	32.1
Austria	32.1	41.9	48.9	50.0	49.9	47.8
Belgium	30.3	39.4	49.3	55.7	47.4	45.3
Canada	28.9	36.8	39.0	44.6	38.7	37.7
Denmark	24.8	45.9	53.2	59.4	52.5	49.3
France	34.6	39.3	45.0	49.4	49.6	48.5
Italy	30.1	37.9	45.5	51.5	46.7	45.4
Japan	N/A	24.5	31.6	31.5	36.1	37.6
The Netherlands	33.7	47.9	55.8	55.9	43.3	41.6
Norway	29.9	44.6	50.4	54.6	45.8	41.9
Sweden	31.1	48.1	60.7	59.9	55.0	51.8
UK	32.4	44.9	42.7	41.2	37.1	39.4
USA	27.5	32.2	31.7	36.1	30.2	30.5
Germany	32.4	44.6	47.6	45.5	46.2	45.4
Average EU countries	32.1	40.7	45.5	47.8	44.9	44.2
Average OECD countries	29.9	36.3	41.2	41.5	37.2	37.2

*Total government outlay = final consumption expenditure + interest on national debt + subsidies + social security transfers to households + gross capital formation.
† Projected
Source: Adapted from OECD (2003) *Economic Outlook*, June.

the government outlay ratio averaged 44.2% across all the EU countries in 2003, the UK at 39.4% was considerably below that average. In comparative terms it would appear that there is little cause for alarm at the growth path of UK public expenditure.

Should public expenditure be restricted?

Freedom and choice

Arguments for controlling or reducing the size of public expenditure are wide-ranging but not always convincing.

One argument is that excessive government expenditure adversely affects individual freedom and choice. First, it is feared that it 'spoonfeeds' individuals, taking away the incentive for personal provision, as with private insurance for sickness or old age. Second, it is feared that by impeding the market mechanism it may restrict consumer choice. For instance, the state may provide goods and services

that are in little demand, whilst discouraging others (via taxation) that might otherwise have been bought. Third, it has been suggested that government provision may encourage an unhelpful separation between payment and cost in the minds of consumers. With government provision, the good or service may be free or subsidized, so that the amount paid by the consumer will understate the true cost (higher taxes, etc.) of providing him or her with that good or service, thereby encouraging excessive consumption of the item.

Crowding out the private sector

The previous Conservative government had long believed that (excessive) public expenditure was at the heart of Britain's economic difficulties. It regarded the private sector as the source of wealth creation, part of which it saw as being used to subsidize the public sector. Sir Keith Joseph clarified this view during the 1970s by alleging that 'a wealth-creating sector which accounts for one-third of the national product carries on its back a State subsidized sector which accounts for two-thirds. The rider is twice as heavy as the horse.'

Bacon and Eltis (1978) attempted to give substance to this view. They suggested that public expenditure growth had led to a transfer of productive resources from the private sector to a public sector producing largely non-marketed output, and that this had been a major factor in the UK's poor performance in the post-war period. Bacon and Eltis noted that public sector employment had increased by some 26%, from 5.8 million workers to 7.3 million, between 1960 and 1978, a time when total employment was largely unchanged. They then alleged that the private (marketed) sector was being squeezed by higher taxes to finance this growth in the public sector – the result being deindustrialization, low labour productivity, low economic growth and balance of payments problems (see also Chapter 17).

Control of money

Another argument used by those who favour restricting public expenditure is that it must be cut in order to limit the growth of money supply and to curb inflation. The argument is that a high public sector borrowing requirement (PSBR) – now known as the public sector net cash requirement – following public expenditure growth, must be funded by the issue of Treasury bills and government stocks. Since there are inadequate 'real' savings to be found in the non-bank private sector, these bills and bonds inevitably find their way into the hands of the banks. As we will see in Chapter 20, they may then form the basis for a multiple expansion of bank deposits (money), with perhaps inflationary consequences.

A related argument is that public expenditure must be restricted, to limit not only the supply of money but also its 'price' – the rate of interest. The suggestion here is that to sell the extra bills and bonds to fund a high PSBR, interest rates must rise to attract investors. This then puts pressure on private sector borrowing, with the rise in interest rates inhibiting private sector investment and investment-led growth. A major policy aim of the government has, therefore, been to reduce public sector borrowing.

Incentives to work, save and take risks

There are also worries that increased public spending not only pushes up government borrowing to fund a high PSBR, but also leads to higher taxes, thereby reducing the incentives to work, save and take risks. The evidence linking taxes to incentives is reviewed in Chapter 19. Suffice it to say here that the evidence to support the general proposition that higher taxes undermine the work ethic is largely inconclusive.

Balance of payments stability

A further line of attack has been that the growth of public expenditure may have destabilized the economy. During the 1970s and early 1980s this view was implied by the Cambridge Economic Policy Group (CEPG), who used an accounting identity (see Chapter 24) to demonstrate that a higher PSBR must lead to a deterioration in the balance of payments. The common sense of their argument is that higher public spending raises interest rates and attracts capital inflows, which in turn raise the demand for sterling and therefore the exchange rate. A higher pound then makes exports dearer and imports cheaper, so that the balance of payments deteriorates.

These various lines of reasoning have been challenged by, amongst others, the New Cambridge School which suggested that the relationships between the public sector and economic management may by no means be so simple. In fact, one adherent of the New Cambridge School, Lord Kaldor, went so far as to say that there was no empirical support for a high PSBR leading either to substantial growth in money supply or to high rates of interest. Similarly, the claim that resources liberated by the public sector would automatically find their way into the private sector was hardly supported by the rising unemployment trend of the early 1980s and early 1990s. Another criticism has pointed to the fact that public expenditure cuts, rather than helping to control unemployment (by cutting inflation in a monetarist model), have either caused or exaggerated current unemployment (see Chapter 23).

Conclusion

The definition of public expenditure is by no means clear-cut and must depend upon the question at issue. Since National Income also has many variants, any public expenditure/National Income ratio must be treated with caution. The estimate for 2003/04 puts total managed expenditure at around 41% of GDP at market prices. If, however, we subtract grants and transfers from public expenditure, as we do from all the National Income measures, then the figure falls substantially to around 30%. Whatever the definition chosen, the proportion of government spending in National Income rose steadily throughout the twentieth century. The reduction in the growth of National Income played an important part in raising the ratio in the early 1980s and early 1990s, both directly, by restricting the denominator, and indirectly, by causing unplanned increases in expenditure on social security. Whether a growing public sector 'crowds out' or otherwise adversely affects the private sector is a matter of deep controversy. Certainly in comparative terms the UK is by no means exceptional, with the share of UK government spending in National Income well below the average for the EU countries. More 'rigour' has been imposed on procedures to plan, monitor and control public expenditure. This, together with renewed growth in National Income,

helped to progressively reduce the ratio of government spending to National Income to around 38% in 2000, though the renewed emphasis on increased government spending since then will see government spending at around 42% of National Income by 2005/06.

The move, in late 1992, towards a new 'control total' for public spending made it clear that the government would continue to seek a tight fiscal stance, especially on items of expenditure of a non-cyclical nature. The determination of the government to adhere to the Maastricht criteria of a ratio of PSBR to GDP below 3%, and of public debt to GDP below 60%, suggests that public expenditure will remain closely controlled despite substantial increases in the 2002 Spending Review based on the recent Budget surpluses (revenue greater than expenditure). This view is further strengthened by the announcement of fiscal 'rules' in 1998, especially the 'golden rule' whereby government borrowing will only be undertaken to support public investment and not current consumption.

Key points

- Although government spending rose in real terms by around 1% per annum between 1990 and 2000, this was less than the growth in real National Income.

- As a result the share of government spending in National Income fell from almost 45% in 1992/93 to around 38% in 2000/01.

- Successive government spending reviews since 2000 have resulted in substantial real-term increases in government spending, which is projected to take around 42% of National Income by 2005/06.

- Critics argue that too high a proportion of government spending goes on 'rescue' and 'welfare' and too little on 'renewal'. In this view more of the public purse should be used to support 'investment' type expenditures (on human or physical capital) directed towards raising future National Income.

- Total managed expenditure (TME) has now been widely adopted as a replacement for general government expenditure (GGE).

- International comparisons do *not* suggest that UK public expenditure is exceptionally high as a percentage of GDP. In 2003 it was only 10th highest out of 14 countries investigated, and some five percentage points below the EU average.

- Many of the reasons put forward for controlling public expenditure involve the desire to cut the PSBR (now the public sector net cash requirement). The government concern is that too high a PSBR will force higher taxes and interest rates, with adverse effects on incentives and investment in the private sector.

- Part of the 'convergence criteria' within the EU involves keeping the PSBR no higher than 3% of GDP, implying tight control of public expenditure.

- The government has also introduced two key 'fiscal rules', both of which imply a tight control of public expenditure.

- The procedures for planning, monitoring and controlling public expenditure have been modified. These include changes to the departmental PES, a new 'Control Total', a unified Budget, relating spending forecasts to out-turns, and various initiatives to increase efficiency in the public sector.

Now try the self-check questions for this chapter on the Companion Website. You will also find up-to-date facts and case materials.

References and further reading

Bacon, R. and Eltis, W. (1978) *Britain's Economic Problem: too few producers*, 2nd edn, Macmillan.

Beachill, R., Spoor, C. and Wetherly, P. (2002) Keeping the economy healthy, *Economic Review*, **20**(2), November.

Bird, R. M. (1971) Wagner's Law of Expanding State Activity, *Public Finance*, **26**(1).

Brown, C. V. and Jackson, P. M. (1982) *Public Sector Economics*, 2nd edn, Martin Robertson.

Cottrell, D. (2002) Public goods: an insoluble economic problem?, *Economic Review*, **20**(1), September.

Department of Trade and Industry (2002) *The Government's Expenditure Plans 2002–03 to 2003–04*.

Flemming, J. and Oppenheimer, P. (1996) Are government spending and taxes too high (or too low)?, *National Institute Economic Review*, July.

Griffiths, M. A. (1998) Government expenditure and efficiency, *Money Management Review*, **51**.

Griffiths, A. (2002) The Budget and the Comprehensive Spending Review 2002, *British Economy Survey*, **32**(1), Autumn.

Joseph, K. (1976) *Monetarism is not Enough*, Barry Rose.

Myers, D. (1998) The Private Finance Initiative – a progress report, *Economic Review*, **15**(4), April.

Papava, V. (1993) A new view of the economic ability of the government; egalitarian goods and GNP, *International Journal of Social Economics*, **20**(8).

Rowthorn, R. (1992) Government spending and taxation in the Thatcher era, in J. Michie, (ed.) *The Economic Legacy, 1979–1992*, Academic Press.

Treasury (2002) *Public Expenditure: Statistical Analyses 2002–03*.

Treasury (2003) *Public Expenditure: Statistical Analyses 2003–04*.

Weir, J. (1998) Government spending: a view from the inside, *Money Management Review*, **51**.

Chapter 19 Taxation

This chapter looks at the existing pattern of UK taxation and the changes that have taken place in recent years. We examine the degree of progressiveness of the UK tax system and the effects of the recent switches between direct and indirect taxation. The changing burden of taxation in the UK is charted, and international comparisons are presented. We then consider the effect of higher taxes on incentives to work, save and take risks, and on the rise of the 'black economy'. After a more general treatment of the direct versus indirect tax debate, we conclude with a brief look at recent reforms of local taxation and social security benefits.

The taxes that are collected: some taxation concepts

Taxes may be classified in a number of different ways:

- the method of collection
- the tax base
- the tax rate.

The method of collection

Taxes may be grouped by the administrative arrangement for their collection.

Direct or indirect

Income tax is paid *directly* to the Exchequer by the individual taxpayer (mainly through Pay As You Earn – PAYE), on the full amount of income from employment and investment in the fiscal year. The same is true of corporation tax, paid by firms on company profits. On the other hand, value added tax (VAT), though paid by consumers, reaches the Exchequer indirectly, largely through retailers acting as collecting agencies. Taxes may therefore be classified as either direct or indirect, according to the administrative arrangement for their collection. From Table 19.1 we see that direct taxes – in the form of income tax, capital taxes, corporation tax and petroleum revenue tax – were expected to produce 38.3% (152.2/397.1) of total government receipts in 2002/03. Income tax is by far the most important direct tax, alone contributing almost 29% of government receipts. Strictly speaking we should add the various National Insurance contributions to the total for direct taxation. These are a compulsory levy on employers, employees and the self-employed, expressed as a fixed percentage of total earnings, and paid directly to the Exchequer (shown under the 'Social Security receipts' heading). They total some £64.3bn in 2002/03 and provide around 16.2% of government receipts. They are not, however, included in the Consolidated Fund revenue tables.

Indirect taxes – VAT, a range of excise duties on oil, tobacco, alcohol and motor cars, and import duties – were expected to produce 27.4% of total government receipts in 2002/03. Of these VAT (16% of total 'receipts') was the most important. The indirect taxes are collected by Customs and Excise.

Table 19.1 How public spending is paid for: income of general government.

	General government receipts (£bn)		
	1998/99	2002/03	2002/03 %
Inland Revenue:			
Income tax	86.4	113.3	
Corporation tax[1]	30.0	26.2	
Petroleum tax	0.5	1.0	
Windfall tax	2.6	0.0	38.3
Capital Gains tax	1.8	1.7	
Inheritance tax	1.8	2.4	
Stamp duty	4.6	7.6	
Total Inland Revenue	**127.7**	**152.2**	
Customs & Excise:			
VAT	52.3	63.6	
Fuel duties	21.6	22.1	
Tobacco	8.2	8.1	
Betting	1.5	1.3	
Alcohol	5.9	7.3	27.4
Customs duties	2.1	1.9	
Air Passenger duty	0.5	0.8	
Insurance premium tax	1.2	2.1	
Others[2]	0.5	1.6	
Total Customs & Excise	**94.0**	**108.8**	
Vehicle excise duties	4.7	4.6	
Oil royalties	0.3	0.5	
Business rates	15.3	18.7	8.7
Others[3]	8.3	10.8	
Total taxes	**250.3**	**295.6**	**74.4**
Social security receipts	55.1	64.3	16.2
Council tax	12.1	16.6	4.2
Interest and dividends	4.3	4.1	1.0
Other receipts[3]	14.1	16.6	4.2
Total receipts	**335.9**	**397.1**	**100.0**

Note: Items may not add up to totals because of rounding.
[1] Includes company tax credits.
[2] Includes Landfill Tax (£0.5bn) and Climate Change Levy (£0.8bn).
[3] Net of own resource contributions to EU budget (£2.5bn).
Source: Modified from Treasury (2003) *Budget Report 2003.*

This Consolidated Fund revenue (£295.6bn), together with Social Security receipts (£64.3bn), business rates (some £18.7bn) and the Council Tax (£16.6bn) plus other miscellaneous receipts, are necessary to pay for the government's expenditure plans of around £395bn in 2002/03.

Details of the main items of government income and expenditure are shown in Table 19.2. The growing economy of the late 1980s helped contribute to increased tax revenue and the creation of *budget surpluses* from 1987/88 to 1990/91. However, these surpluses shrank rapidly after 1989 as government revenue fell and government expenditure rose in the wake of the most protracted period of recession since the inter-war years. The government's budget situation from the second half of the 1990s can be seen in Table 19.2. This format follows the new European system of accounts and shows the strong growth in public sector current receipts after 1996/97. For example, between 1998/99 and 2000/01 both the *public sector net borrowing* (formerly called the financial deficit) and the *net cash requirement* (formerly the public sector borrowing requirement) were negative, which meant that the government was in the healthy position of being able to repay debt. However, from 2001/02 onwards this trend was reversed as the government's borrowing increased once more. This reversal was mainly due to a slow-down in the rate of economic growth (slower growth in tax receipts) and the government's increasing commitment to public expenditure on education and health.

The tax base

The tax base is essentially the 'object' to which the tax rate is applied. Excluding National Insurance contributions, taxes are usually grouped under three headings as regards tax bases: taxes on income (income, corporation and petroleum revenue taxes); taxes on expenditure (VAT and customs and excise duties); and taxes on capital (capital gains and inheritance tax).

Figure 19.1 shows that for 2002/03, taxes on income were expected to yield 47.5% of the Total Tax Revenue of £295.6bn, taxes on expenditure 36.8% and taxes on capital 1.4%. In addition to these taxes (not in Fig. 19.1) there were compulsory levies in the form of Social Security receipts (National Insurance contributions) from individuals and companies of £64.3bn and council tax of £16.6bn, raising the burden further on income.

Classifying taxes in terms of tax base, rather than method of collection, is often of more interest to economists, especially when calculating tax incidence

Table 19.2 Public sector borrowing requirement, 1996–2003.

	£bn				
	1996/97	**1997/98**	**1999/2000**	**2001/02**	**2002/03**
Public sector current expenditure	299.4	306.3	326.6	366.6	395.0
Public sector current receipts	288.8	317.1	359.3	389.9	397.1
Depreciation	12.5	12.4	12.6	13.4	13.8
Surplus on current budget	**−23.1**	**−1.6**	**20.0**	**9.9**	**−11.7**
Net investment	5.3	4.9	4.4	9.6	12.2
Public sector net borrowing	**28.4**	**6.5**	**−15.7**	**−0.4**	**24.0**
(% GDP)	(3.6)	(0.8)	(−1.7)	(0.0)	(2.3)
Financial transactions	−5.7	−5.4	7.1	4.0	−1.5
Net cash requirement	**22.7**	**1.1**	**−8.5**	**3.6**	**22.5**
(% GDP)	(2.9)	(0.1)	(−0.9)	(0.4)	(2.1)

Note: Items may not add up to totals because of rounding.
Sources: Adapted from ONS (2003) *Financial Statistics*, No. 491, March; Treasury (2003) *Budget Report 2003*.

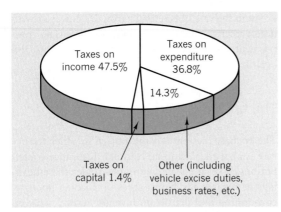

Fig. 19.1 Government revenue in 2002/03 and the tax base (as % of total tax revenue of £295.6bn).

(on whom the tax falls)! However, using the tax base does present problems of definition. For instance, Lord Wrenbury, in a legal judgment in 1925, defined income tax as being that which is 'within the Act, taxable under the Act'. National Insurance contributions, because they are based on calculations by actuaries, are not classified as a tax on income, yet they are levied as a percentage of income. Whatever the tax base, the taxes levied can be one of two types, either specific (lump sum) or *ad valorem*.

Specific and *ad valorem* taxes

A *specific tax* is expressed as an absolute sum of money per unit of the good. Excise duties are often of this kind, being so many pence per packet of cigarettes or per proof of spirit. An *ad valorem* tax is a percentage tax, levied not on volume but on value; e.g. in 2003/04 VAT was 17.5% of sales price, and corporation tax was 30% of assessable profits for larger companies and 19% for smaller companies.

Rate of taxation

Another useful classification is between progressive, proportional and regressive taxes. Tax is imposed as a rate or series of rates; e.g. income tax in 2002/03 was levied at 10%, 22% and 40% of taxable income whilst VAT items that are not exempted are zero-rated or pay 17.5%. These tax rates can be regarded as progressive, proportional or regressive, though such terms must be defined strictly as they are often

used loosely. For a tax to be regarded as progressive, its rate structure must be such that the tax takes a rising proportion of total income as income increases; a proportional tax takes a constant proportion, whilst a regressive tax takes a declining proportion.

The pattern of UK taxation

A broadly proportional tax system

Since a progressive tax means that the rich pay more, not only in an *absolute* sense, but *as a proportion of their total income*, we need to know more than that the *marginal* rate of tax rises with income.[1] If, for instance, tax allowances and exemptions are more easily acquired by higher-income groups (as with mortgage repayments, etc.) then, despite a rising marginal rate, the individual may pay a smaller proportion of a higher total income in tax. In fact, it is the *average* rate[2] that is the best guide to whether the tax or tax system is, or is not, progressive. If the average rate is rising with income, then the tax *is* taking a higher proportion of higher incomes, i.e. the tax *is* progressive.

As we know from any game, say cricket, only when an individual scores more on his last (marginal) innings than his average for all previous innings, will his overall average actually rise. In the same way, only when the *marginal rate of tax is higher than the average rate*, will the average rate rise as income rises, and the tax be progressive. If the marginal and average rates are equal, then the average rate will be unchanged as income rises, so that the tax is proportional. If the marginal rate is below the average rate, then the average rate falls as income rises, and the tax is regressive.

Figure 19.2 shows that, for the UK, direct taxes (the unshaded area in each bar) are progressive, taking a larger proportion of the total (gross) income of richer households. Indirect taxes are in contrast regressive, taking a declining proportion of such income. Overall, taking *both* direct and indirect taxes together, the UK tax system is broadly proportional to income.

Although indirect taxes as a whole are regressive, there is some variation between different types of indirect tax. As we observe from Table 19.3, VAT is a

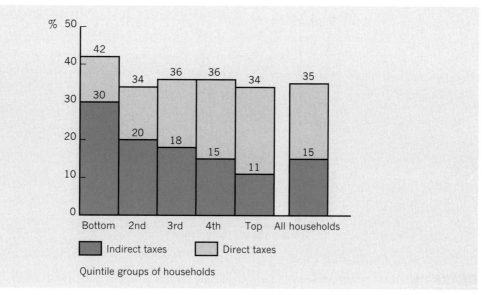

Fig. 19.2 Direct and indirect taxes as a percentage of gross household income (2001/02).
Source: Adapted from ONS (2003) *The Effects of Taxes and Benefits on Household Income, 2001/02,* April.

more mildly regressive tax, whereas other indirect taxes are strongly regressive.

A shift towards indirect taxation

We have seen that indirect taxes are more regressive than direct taxes. Here we chart the substantial changes that took place in the direct/indirect tax ratio during the 1970s and early 1980s.

As Fig. 19.3 indicates, throughout the 1950s and 1960s taxes on income (direct) and expenditure (indi-

rect) maintained a steady relationship, with taxes on income yielding around 10% more revenue. During the early and mid-1970s, however, the balance changed in favour of direct taxes on income as revenue providers for central government, due in part to inflation raising money incomes (and therefore direct tax receipts) and in part to fiscal drag. Fiscal drag is the extra tax yield which results from the fact that changes in both tax allowances and tax bands may not occur until *after* inflation has had its impact on money incomes. By 1975 direct taxes on income had peaked, providing some 60% more revenue than

Table 19.3 The regressiveness of indirect taxes (2001/02).

Quintile groups of households	Indirect taxes as percentage of *disposable* income per household		
	VAT	Other indirect taxes	Total indirect taxes
Bottom fifth	12.9	21.8	34.7
Next fifth	9.0	14.5	23.5
Middle fifth	8.5	12.9	21.4
Next fifth	7.5	10.7	18.2
Top fifth	5.9	7.2	13.1

Source: Adapted from ONS (2003) *The Effects of Taxes and Benefits on Household Income, 2001/02,* April.

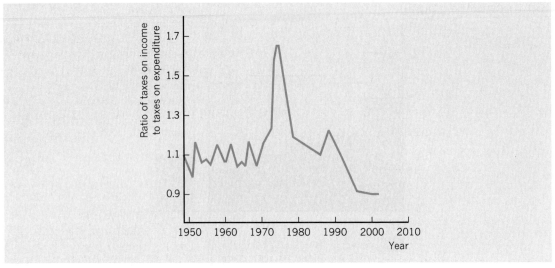

Fig. 19.3 The ratio of central government taxes on income to taxes on expenditure, 1949–2002.
Source: Treasury (2003) *Budget Report 2003*, and previous issues.

taxes on expenditure. The ratio fell substantially after that, and by 1986 direct taxes provided only some 10% more revenue than taxes on expenditure. After 1986 the ratio began to edge upwards again as incomes increased, with growing prosperity in the economy raising the yield from direct taxes. However, in 1988/89 the Chancellor once more reversed the trend by permitting a substantial over-indexation of tax allowances. This, together with the increase in VAT rates to 17.5% in the 1991 Budget, has caused the ratio to continue its downward path so that after 1994 it was below 1.

Income taxes are more 'visible' to individuals than expenditure taxes, which to some extent are hidden in product prices. This may well have contributed to the *feeling* that the UK was overtaxed, despite the fact that this is contradicted by the evidence (see Table 19.5 below). It may be helpful to look further into the factors helping to establish the pattern shown in Fig. 19.3.

With the slowing down of inflation in the mid- to late 1970s, the ratio of direct to indirect taxes in total revenue began to fall. The new Conservative government in 1979 then made a deliberate switch away from direct income taxation towards indirect taxation, cutting the standard rate of income tax from 33% to 30%, and raising VAT from 8% to 15%. We might have expected this switch to reinforce the downward trend in the ratio of direct to indirect tax receipts. In fact, higher inflation in the early years of that government prevented the ratio falling. Since the early 1980s, the receipts from direct taxes on income have fluctuated around an average figure some 10% above those from indirect taxes on expenditure; we have returned to the broad pattern of the 1950s and 1960s. The restored importance of indirect taxes, whatever its source, must, in the context of our earlier analysis, have made the UK tax system less progressive than it would otherwise have been.

A rise in the UK tax burden

We have seen that the *structure* of UK taxation has changed in recent years. What about the *level* of taxation? The ratio of total tax take to National Income is a frequently used measure of tax 'burden'. We can see from Table 19.4 that between 1964 and 1970 the total receipts from all taxes (including National Insurance) rose sharply as a proportion of GDP. Between 1970 and 1974 the tax ratio fell from 37.5% to 33.75% before rising to a peak in 1984/85. There was then a drift downwards in the figures until 1993/94 with substantial income tax reductions. However, the tax burden of 36.8% in 2001/02 was at a higher level than when the Conservatives came to power in 1979. The fear that the tax burden is likely to continue to rise during the first decade of the new

Table 19.4 The UK tax burden.

Fiscal year	Tax as a percentage of GDP*
1964–65	30.00
1969–70	37.50
1973–74	33.75
1978–79	33.30
1979–80	33.80
1980–81	35.80
1981–82	38.50
1982–83	38.70
1983–84	38.30
1984–85	38.90
1985–86	38.10
1986–87	37.80
1987–88	37.60
1988–89	36.90
1989–90	36.20
1990–91	35.90
1991–92	34.70
1992–93	33.70
1993–94	33.00
1994–95	34.40
1995–96	34.80
1996–97	34.90
1997–98	36.00
1998–99	36.50
1999–2000	36.60
2000–01	37.40
2001–02	36.80

* Net taxes and social security contributions as a
percentage of money GDP.
Source: Adapted from Treasury (2003) *Budget Report
2003* (March), and previous issues.

millennium has led to proposals for radical changes
in the Welfare State to curb growing government
expenditure in this area.

The UK tax burden: a comparative survey

Despite the rise in UK tax burden over the last few
years, and contrary to popular public opinion, the UK
is only a middle-ranked country in terms of tax
burden. From Table 19.5 we see that in 1981 the UK
was the eighth-ranked country out of 20 in terms of
tax burden, below the Scandinavian countries and
close to France. OECD data in 2001 gave the UK a
lower ranking of eleventh. Despite the high level of
tax revenue as a proportion of GDP over this 20-year
period, the UK tax burden in 2001 continued to lie
well below that in the Scandinavian countries, where
between 45% and 53% of GDP was taken in tax and
social security contributions in that year, and was
very similar to other major competitors such as
France and Germany.

Tax burden and economic growth

It can be concluded from the evidence of Table 19.5
that there is little relationship between low tax
burdens and faster economic growth. Finland, with
the fourth-highest tax burden in 2001, had an annual
average growth rate of 2.7% in the period
1981–2001, equal to the OECD average of 2.7% per
annum, and was also ranked as high as sixth in terms
of growth rate. On the other hand, Switzerland,
with one of the lowest tax burdens, had only the
thirteenth-fastest growth rate of 1.4% in that period,
well below the OECD average.

Tax schedules and tax rates

We should, however, bear one or two cautionary
points in mind before lapsing into complacency! A
study by Messere *et al.* (1982) suggests that published
tax schedules are a greater disincentive to effort than
the 'effective tax rates' (i.e. the tax actually paid after
all personal and other allowances have been calculated). The argument here is that it is tax schedules as
shown in Table 19.6, widely publicized in newspapers and annual tax returns, which form the basis for
the ordinary citizen's notion of tax burden.

In analysing tax schedules, the Messere study
found that a higher proportion of taxpayers (over
95%) paid the basic rate in the UK than elsewhere,
and that both the initial and top rates of tax on
earned income were higher in the UK than elsewhere.
Nevertheless, the taxpayer on average income in the
UK paid a marginal rate no higher than in other
OECD countries. Since 1987/88 the Conservative and
Labour governments have simplified the tax structure
and reduced the tax rates (as shown in Table 19.6 and
Fig. 19.4) in order to try to encourage incentives. By
the late 1990s the Treasury could safely claim that the
UK's top rate of income tax at 40% was below that of

Table 19.5 Comparative tax burdens and economic growth.

Tax* as a percentage of GNP	1981 Percentage	Rank	2001 Percentage	Rank	GDP growth (yearly average) 1981–2001 Percentage	Rank
Australia	33.5	14	31.5	15	3.4	3
Austria	49.6	4	45.7	3	2.4	=9
Belgium	49.6	4	45.3	5	2.0	=11
Canada	40.0	12	35.2	=13	2.8	=5
Denmark	55.6	3	49.0	2	2.1	10
Finland	39.6	13	45.4	4	2.7	6
France	47.6	7	36.4	=12	2.0	=11
Germany	42.3	9	36.4	=12	2.0	=11
Greece	31.6	16	40.8	9	1.9	=12
Ireland	41.6	10	29.2	17	5.5	1
Italy	33.4	15	41.8	8	1.9	=12
Japan	28.3	19	27.1	18	2.6	7
Luxembourg	40.0	11	42.4	7	5.2	2
Netherlands	49.4	6	39.9	10	2.4	=9
Norway	48.7	2	44.9	6	2.8	=5
Spain	27.2	20	35.2	=13	2.8	=5
Sweden	56.9	1	53.2	1	1.9	=12
Switzerland	30.8	18	34.5	14	1.4	13
United Kingdom	42.4	8	37.4	11	2.5	8
United States	31.1	17	29.6	16	3.1	4

* Including social security contributions.
Sources: OECD (2002) *Revenue Statistics 1965–2001*, and previous issues; OECD (2002) *Economic Outlook*, No. 71, June, and previous issues.

Table 19.6 UK income tax schedules, 1987/88 and 2003/04.

Rate of tax (%)	1987/88 Taxable income (£)	2003/04 Taxable income (£)
10	–	0–1,920
22	–	1,921–29,900
27	0–17,900	–
40	17,901–20,400	Over 29,900
45	20,401–25,400	–
50	25,401–33,300	–
55	33,301–41,200	–
60	Over 41,200	–

Note: Investment income surcharge on unearned income was abolished in March 1984.

its major competitors, as can be seen from Fig. 19.5.

A further reason for taxpayers believing that the burden of taxation is higher than it actually is may arise from a failure to understand the method of collection of income tax. Income tax is *not* collected on the total amount of income. Each individual is granted allowances or exemptions that reduce the total amount of income liable to tax. In 2003/04 each single person under 65 was, for example, given an allowance of £4,615. These allowances, plus a few others, are deducted from the total income to produce the *taxable income*. Tax rates of 10%, 22% and 40% (on taxable incomes over £29,900) are then applied to this *taxable income*. Thus the average burden of taxation for the average taxpayer is considerably below the main 22% and 40% seen in the tax schedules.

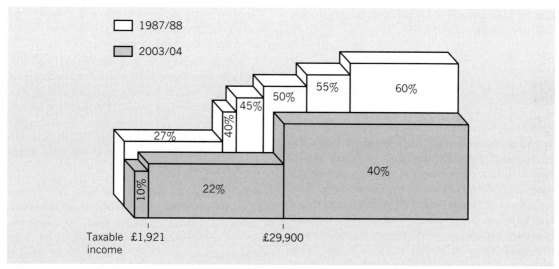

Fig. 19.4 Comparison of income tax between 1987/88 and 2003/04.

Overall there appears little evidence that the UK has an excessive burden of tax in comparison to other countries. Although the proportion of GNP taken in tax has tended to rise in the UK since the early 1970s, the UK is, in comparative terms, a lower-ranked country in terms of tax-take, with tax (including community charge) amounting to 36.8% of GDP in 2002. However, particular groups of UK taxpayers at the lowest and highest taxable income scales did suffer unusually high marginal rates during the 1970s and 1980s. This, together with the growing 'visibility' of the income tax and social security payments system in the UK, may have created the impression of a comparatively high tax burden, but this impression was, in fact, misleading for the *average* taxpayer. Unfortunately the post-1988/89 reduction in tax rates and simplifications of the system have done little to improve the tax burden on low-income earners, or to

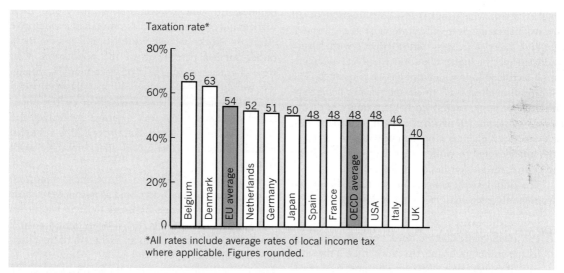

Fig. 19.5 Comparative maximum income tax rates, 2001.
Source: Adapted from OECD (2002) *Tax Database 2000–2002.*

alter the overall burden of the tax system over the last 15 years as seen in Table 19.4.

Does the level of taxation matter?

Clarke suggested in 1945, with the support of Keynes, that when taxation of all kinds was more than 25% of National Income, damaging pressures would follow. In fact, most industrial countries passed this figure over 30 years ago, with tax ratios of over 40% for some countries in the 1970s, yet they experienced low inflation and rapid growth of real incomes. However, perceptions of the benign nature of taxation have begun to change in more recent years, reverting back to those of Clarke and Keynes. Two of the major criticisms of a high tax burden relate to its (alleged) erosion of economic incentives and its encouragement of tax avoidance and evasion. We now consider these criticisms.

Impact of taxes on incentives to work, save and take risks

As the reader familiar with indifference curve analysis will know, a higher tax on income will have two effects, which pull in opposite directions. First, there is an 'income effect', with real income reduced via higher taxes, which means less consumption of all items, including leisure, i.e. more work is performed. Second, there is a 'substitution effect', with leisure now cheaper via higher taxes, since less real income is now sacrificed for each unit of leisure consumed. The substitution effect leads to cheaper leisure being substituted for work, i.e. less work. On grounds of theory alone we cannot tell which effect will be the stronger, i.e. whether higher taxes on income will raise or lower the time devoted to work rather than leisure (where, of course, the worker has some choice).

The only general conclusions that can be drawn from indifference analysis are the following:

1 Progressive taxes have higher substitution effects, and are therefore likely to cause a greater increase in leisure consumption (i.e. less work) than if the same sum of money were raised via a proportional tax.

2 Taxes on savings create a strong disincentive to future savings via their double-taxation effect.

Since saving takes place out of real disposable (net) income, to tax the returns on savings is to impose a further tax on net income.

3 Taxes on investment may discourage high-risk projects. Investment projects involve combinations of risk and yield, those with more risk usually providing more yield. If yields on investment income are more heavily taxed, then this may discourage high-risk investments, such as North Sea oil-prospecting, and encourage low-risk investments (including cash-holding).

Theory can take us little further than this general analysis. Beyond it we must look at actual behaviour to assess the impact of higher taxes on incentives. Empirical studies have taken three forms: (a) controlled experiments, usually observing how selected persons respond to higher benefits (negative taxes); (b) questionnaires based on random samples, and (c) econometric studies using data on how people have responded in the past to tax changes.

Studies up to 1970

Brown and Dawson (1969) conducted an exhaustive review of tax studies in the UK and USA from 1947 to 1968. They concluded that higher taxation had a disincentive effect on work (income < substitution effect) for between 5% and 15% of the population. These were mainly people who had the greatest freedom to vary their hours of employment – those without families, the middle-aged, the wealthy, and rural workers. In contrast, higher taxation had an incentive effect on work (income > substitution effect) for a rather smaller percentage of the population, who were characteristically part of large families, young, less well-off, urban dwellers. From a national viewpoint the small *net* disincentive effect on the population of higher taxes was regarded by Brown and Dawson as of little significance; over 70% appeared neutral (income = substitution effect) in their work response to higher taxes.

As regards the UK, two of the most important studies reviewed by Brown and Dawson were those based on questionnaires by Break in 1956 and Fields and Stanbury in 1968. In 1956, Break found a small *net* disincentive effect, with an extra 3% of the population claiming higher taxes to be a disincentive to further work than claimed it to be an incentive. In 1968 Fields and Stanbury updated Break's UK study and found the *net* disincentive effect to have grown to

8% of the population. In both studies the *net* disincentive effect was greater for higher-income groups, as one might expect with these paying higher marginal taxes (stronger substitution effects). This small growth in overall *net* disincentive effect between 1956 and 1968, and its being more pronounced at higher-income levels, was really all the empirical support there was in the UK for those suggesting that higher taxes discouraged work effort.

Studies after 1970

Controlled experiments and questionnaire results after 1970 gave no clearer a picture than those before 1970. If anything, they again pointed to a slight disincentive of higher taxes. For instance, Brown and Levin found that an increase in marginal tax rates for 2,000 Scottish workers in 1974 reduced hours worked, at least for higher-income groups. Fiegehen and Reddaway conducted a study on incentives amongst senior managers at board level in 94 companies in 1978, just before the large tax cuts introduced by the (then) newly elected Conservative government a year or so later. Similarly to Break, and Fields and Stanbury (see above), they showed that 12% of managers reported an incentive effect of high taxation on hours of work, while an equal percentage reported a disincentive effect. The most common response from 41% was 'no reply or don't know'. Fiegehen and Reddaway concluded: 'it is clear that, in total, any disincentive effects that operated on senior managers had a minimal impact on the activities of British industry'. Such studies were hardly a basis for advocating that tax *cuts* would lead to an upsurge in work effort! An important study by the Institute of Fiscal Studies (Dilnot and Kell 1988) tried to assess the effects of the 1979/80 reduction in the top rate of UK income tax from 83% to 60% on tax receipts. The argument used to support these top-rate tax cuts was that the lower income tax rates should provide extra incentives to work harder and thus boost tax revenue. The study found that the subsequent increase in tax revenue during the period to 1985/86 could be explained mostly by factors such as employment growth, growth of earnings and growth of self-employment rather than by any 'incentive' effects. Dilnot and Kell felt that any 'incentive' effect which may have been present could only account, at most, for £1.2bn or 3% of the total increase in tax revenues over the period studied.

Flemming and Oppenheimer (1996) also found little evidence to support the suggestion that reduced marginal tax rates at the upper end would unleash entrepreneurial talent and labour effort. They argued that if skilled or energetic workers supplied more effort (i.e. labour input/hours worked) as higher marginal tax rate fell, then one might expect that the *relative price* of their time/effort, i.e. wage per hour, would fall *vis-à-vis* other lower-skilled groups via an increase in relative supply resulting in a decrease in relative price (i.e. wage per hour). However, as noted in Chapter 14, pre-tax hourly earnings between different skill and occupational levels have widened considerably over the last 15 years, indicating that the higher-income earners have *increased* their relative wages. This rather suggests that the higher-income, higher-skilled segment of the workforce may not have increased the number of hours worked, i.e. the supply of effort, but may merely have benefited from *demand* changes which have moved in their favour, as discussed in Chapter 14. Interestingly, the disincentive to work resulting from high real marginal rates of tax is arguably more of a problem for those on below-average incomes, as the discussion of the poverty 'trap' indicates below.

The Laffer curve

Professor Laffer derived a relationship between tax revenue and tax rates of the form shown in Fig. 19.6. The curve was the result of econometric techniques, through which a 'least squares line'[3] was fitted to past US observations of tax revenue and tax rate. The dotted line indicates the extension of the fitted relationship (continuous line), as there will tend to be

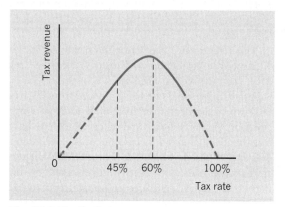

Fig. 19.6 The 'Laffer' curve.

zero tax revenue at both 0% and 100% tax rates. Tax revenue = tax rate × output (income), so that a 0% tax rate yields zero tax revenue, whatever the level of output. A 100% tax rate is assumed to discourage all output, except that for subsistence, again yielding zero tax revenue. Tax revenue must reach a maximum at some intermediate tax rate between these extremes.

The London Business School has estimated a Laffer curve for the UK using past data. Tax revenue was found to reach a peak at around a 60% 'composite tax rate', i.e. one which includes both direct and indirect taxes, as well as various social security payments, all expressed as a percentage of GDP. If the tax rate rises above 60% then the disincentive effect on output is so strong (i.e. output falls so much) that tax revenue (tax rate × output) actually falls, despite the higher tax rate. The Laffer curve in fact begins to flatten out at around a 45% composite tax rate. In other words, as tax rate rises above 45%, the disincentive effect on output is strong enough to mean that little extra tax revenue results. Econometric studies of this type have given support to those in favour of limiting overall rates of tax. It is interesting to note that shortly after this study, the top rate of tax on earned income in the UK was indeed reduced from 83% to 60%.[4]

The reduction in the top income tax rate to 40% in 1988/89 was inspired by the Laffer curve and supply-side economics. The Chancellor of the Exchequer believed that the tax cuts would increase revenue. He based his tax cuts on American research by Lindsey that concluded that reductions in the top tax rates to the American government in 1981/82 were costless as the top 170,000 taxpayers ended up paying $26.6bn under new legislation instead of $26bn under the old. Lindsey argued that the tax cuts not only created incentives but also increased the *cost of tax avoidance*.

This research has been criticized partly because it is American evidence and partly because the American rates were slashed by 23% over three years, with the top personal rate being reduced from 70% to 50% whilst the UK moved from 60% to 40% in just one year. Finally, Lindsey and other tax experts have consistently argued that as tax rates are cut, economic efficiency is raised by reducing tax breaks and shelters at the same time. However, fresh evidence on the impact of cuts in high rates of British taxation has been provided by Minford and Ashton (see Brown 1988). The latter study concluded that the cut in the

higher British tax rates to 40% would increase hours worked by 8%.

In summary, those who advocate 'supply-side economics', with tax reduction a key instrument for improving economic incentives, leading to an upsurge of productive activity, receive limited support from empirical studies. Only a small net disincentive effect has been found from studies using questionnaires, such as those by Break and by Fields and Stanbury. This conclusion was reinforced by the later study of Dilnot and Kell. On the other hand, the Laffer curve constructed for the UK by the London Business School, and work by Minford in the UK and Lindsey in the US, do indicate that *reductions* in the composite rate of tax below 60% and down as far as around 45%, have strong incentive effects on output – the converse of *rises* in tax rate between 45% and 60% having strong disincentive effects. However, we noted in Table 19.4 that the UK composite tax rate is currently less than 40%, and reductions below this level receive little support from econometric studies.

Poverty and unemployment traps

One area where the facts do strongly suggest that the current level and type of taxation may have eroded incentives, concerns the 'poverty' and 'unemployment' traps. The families in these traps are enmeshed in a web of overlapping tax schedules and benefit thresholds, developed and administered by two separate departments (Department of Social Security and the Treasury) with differing objectives in mind.

The 'poverty trap' describes a situation where a person on low income may gain very little, or even lose, from an increase in gross earnings. This is because as *gross* earnings rise, the amount of benefits paid out decreases while income tax deductions increase. In extreme circumstances, *net* income may actually fall when a person's gross earnings rise, i.e. an implicit marginal tax rate (or marginal net income deduction rate) of over 100%. After 1988, the government tried to resolve the gross disincentive effects of such high rates of deduction by relating benefits to net income after tax. However, the problems of the poverty trap dilemma still occur, if not to the same extent as before.

Table 19.7 shows the net income situation of a married man with two children in June 2002 when his gross income rises from £125 to £250 per week. We can see that net income rises little over this range. For example, an increase in income from £150 to £200,

Table 19.7 Married couple (one earner working more than 30 hours per week) with two children under 11 (rent £52.27, Council Tax £16.40 per week).

| | June 2002 | | | |
	(£ pw)	(£ pw)	(£ pw)	(£ pw)
Gross earnings*	125.00	150.00	200.00	250.00
*Plus:*Child benefit	26.30	26.30	26.30	26.30
Working family tax credit	112.26	99.88	80.56	61.86
Housing benefit	5.53	0.00	00.00	00.00
Council Tax Benefit	2.02	0.00	00.00	00.00
*Less:*Income tax	0.00	0.00	9.87	20.87
National Insurance	3.60	6.10	11.10	16.10
Net income	267.51	270.08	285.89	301.19

Notes: Calculations are for a married man with two children under 11, Local Authority rent of £52.27 a week and Council Tax of £16.40 a week.
* 30 hours per week at the minimum wage (June 2002) was £123.00.
Source: Adapted from DSS, Tax/Benefit Model Tables (June 2002).

i.e. £50 per week, gives only an extra £15.81 in income after deductions, i.e. £34.19 is lost. This results in an implicit marginal tax rate (or marginal deduction rate) of about 68% (34.19/50). In 1992, using a similar family situation and gross income change, the rate was as high as 124%. The improvements in the family credit arrangements since 1992 have eased such extreme situations but the rates are still high and often provide little encouragement for those in the area of the poverty trap to work harder. On a general level, the number of families where the head of the household faces a relatively high implicit marginal tax rate of 70% and over, nearly doubled after 1988 to 645,000 by 1999–2000 (HMSO 2000).

A high implicit marginal tax rate (marginal deduction rate) can therefore act as a major disincentive to low income earners. This point is further exemplified by Fig. 19.7 which simulates the net income of a family with two young children and only one income earner, under different income circumstances (*Poverty* 1998).

The vertical axis presents *net* pay after all benefits (here income support) and tax payments have been taken into consideration. The horizontal axis presents the hours worked per week. The income support level for such a family under the Jobseekers' Allowance would be around £125 per week and would correspond to the income that the family would receive if the only wage earner in the family was unemployed. The two other lines in Fig. 19.7 denote the change in net income which the family would receive if the person *was* in employment. The net income lines are plotted for wages of between £3.00 and £5.00 per hour and, as one would expect, net income tends to rise in line with increases in the number of hours worked. Notice, however, that when the wage per hour is only £3.00, net income barely rises between 10 and 20 hours' work per week, and for more than 30 hours' work per week. For example, if the worker increases the number of hours worked from 30 to 80 hours a week, the net pay rises by only about 3p for every pound earned. In fact the 'plateaux' broadly represent the impact of the poverty trap. If wages increase to £5.00 per hour then there is much less evidence of any such plateaux. This analysis would seem to suggest that the reason for the existence of a poverty plateau is a combination of the complexity of the benefit/tax structure (which creates very high implicit marginal tax rates at lower income levels), and the very low wages per hour paid to many workers. The extent of this problem can be gauged from the fact that there were still some 1.8m UK workers earning less than £3.40 per hour and some 3.75m earning less than £3.50 per hour prior to the introduction of the £3.60 hourly minimum wage in 1999.

As we have noted, the 'poverty trap' relates to people who are *in work* but find little incentive to improve their situation by extra work effort. On the other hand, some workers never even enter the labour

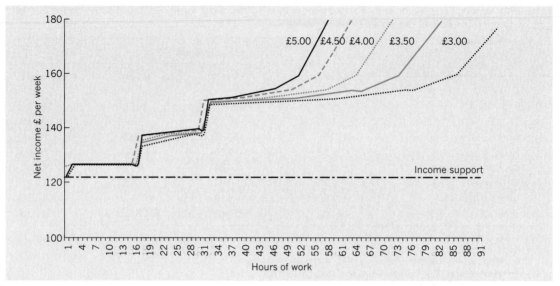

Fig. 19.7 Hours, wages and net family income: couple (one earner) with two children aged 4 and 6. Source: *Poverty* (1998).

market because of another problem, often called the 'unemployment trap'.

The 'unemployment trap' occurs when people find that their income when employed is no better than if they were unemployed. Taking figures for June 2002, Table 19.8 shows that when the gross wage of the married man in our example is £150 per week, the net income after various allowances and deductions is £270.08. If he was unemployed, his net income would be £253.82, i.e. the *replacement rate* is 94%. The replacement rate measures the proportion of a person's net income that will be 'replaced' by the benefit system if that person loses his or her job. The introduction of family credit in 1988 has helped to decrease the number of people with replacement rates of over 100%. The replacement rate for a person in the same situation as our present example in 1992 was 104%, so things have got marginally better. However, the fact that the income of a person when out of work is still 94% of his income when in work provides little incentive to work. There were still 590,000 people in the UK with replacement rates of 70% and over in 1999/2000 (HMSO 2000).

From these examples, we can see that both poverty and unemployment traps provide a disincentive to work because people caught in these problematic sit-

uations find it difficult, if not impossible, to improve their position through their own efforts.

Impact of taxes on avoidance and evasion

Tax avoidance is legal; tax evasion is illegal, involving concealment in one form or another, and therefore fraud.

The black economy

The Inland Revenue has estimated that tax evasion was equal to between 6% and 8% of GDP in the UK – often called the 'black economy'. However, other estimates have suggested that the black economy may even be as high as 10–12% of GDP. This would mean that the UK's black economy is the same size as Portugal's entire economy or is as much as the Treasury earns from income tax every year. One way in which the black economy can be estimated is through the difference between National Income when measured by the income method, and when measured by the expenditure method. Apart from errors and omissions, these are defined in the National Accounts in such a way that they come to the same value. If, however, people receive income and do not declare it in tax returns, it will not appear

Table 19.8 Unemployed married couple (one earner previously working more than 30 hours per week) with two children under 11 (rent £52.27, Council Tax £16.40 per week), June 2002.

In work	£ pw	Out of work	£ pw
Gross earnings	150.00	Jobseeker's Allowance	151.75
Child benefit	26.30	Child benefit	26.30
Working Family Tax Credit	99.88	Meals & welfare	7.10
Housing benefit	00.00	Housing benefit	52.27
Council Tax benefit	00.00	Council Tax benefit	16.40
Less Income tax	0.00		
Less National Insurance	6.10		
Net income	270.08	Net income	253.82
Replacement ratio	$\frac{253.82}{270.08} = 94\%$		

Notes:
Calculations are for a married man with two children under 11, Local Authority rent of £52.27 a week and Council Tax of £16.40 a week.
When employed he claims Working Family Tax Credit (WFTC) and is entitled to the £11.65 thirty-hour premium.
The figures when unemployed are illustrative for when the entitlement to WFTC has run out. The Jobseeker's Allowance is income-based and includes allowances for children.
Source: Adapted from DSS, Tax/Benefit Model Tables (June 2002).

on the income side, though expenditure will increase as the unrecorded income is spent on goods and services. In recent years the 'income' valuation – based on tax returns – has fallen short of the 'expenditure' valuation by progressively larger amounts.

Direct versus indirect taxes

In Fig. 19.3 above we observed a switch from direct to indirect taxation since the late 1970s. We noted that this switch entailed a move towards a more regressive system of taxation, i.e. one which takes a *smaller proportion* of higher incomes. This must follow since we move away from direct taxes which we saw to be progressive, towards indirect taxes, which at best are proportional (VAT), and more usually are regressive (the community charge – now the Council Tax, Uniform Business Rate, excise duties, import duties, etc.). It might be useful to consider in *more general terms* the advantages and disadvantages of direct and indirect systems of taxation. For convenience we shall compare the systems under four main headings, with indirect taxes considered first in each case.

Macroeconomic management

Indirect taxes can be varied more quickly and easily, taking more immediate effect, than can direct taxes. Since the Finance Act of 1961, the Chancellor of the Exchequer has had the power (via 'the regulator') to vary the rates of indirect taxation at any time between Budgets. Excise and import duties can be varied by up to 10%, and VAT by up to 25% (i.e. between 13.13% and 21.87% for a 17.5% rate of VAT). In contrast, direct taxes can be changed only at Budget time. In the case of income tax, any change involves time-consuming revisions to PAYE codings. For these reasons, indirect taxes are usually regarded as a more flexible instrument of macroeconomic policy.

Economic incentives

We have already seen how, in both theory and practice, direct taxes on income affect incentives to work. We found that neither in theory nor in practice need the *net* effect be one of disincentive. Nevertheless, it is often argued that if the *same sum* were derived from indirect taxation, then any net disincentive effect that did occur would be that much smaller. In particular, it is often said that indirect taxes are less visible (than direct), being to some extent hidden in the quoted price of the good. However, others suggest that consumers are well aware of the impact of indirect taxes on the price level. Let us look in more detail at the direct versus indirect argument, first in relation to incentives to work and second in relation to incentives to save and take risks.

Work effort

In terms of effects on the supply of work effort, a case against the current system of direct taxes and in favour of a switch towards indirect taxes might be made in the *specific* cases of poverty and unemployment traps. However, no *general* case can be made for such a switch. In fact, both income and substitution effects of a rise in indirect taxes are in the same direction as those for a rise in direct taxes. By raising the prices of goods, higher indirect taxes also reduce real income, and at the same time reduce the cost of leisure in terms of goods forgone. In other words, the income and substitution effects we considered above apply to higher indirect taxes as well as to higher direct taxes. Whether the *magnitude* of the income and substitution effects will be the same for indirect as for direct taxes is quite another matter. It will partly depend upon which items are taxed. If indirect taxes are levied on goods with highly inelastic demand curves, then the indirect taxes will be largely passed on to consumers as higher prices. Both income and substitution effects will then be substantial in magnitude. Of course the converse also applies – if the indirect taxes are levied on goods with elastic demand curves, both income and substitution effects will be small. We can make no general claim for 'superiority' of either type of tax with regard to work incentives.

Saving and risk-taking

With regard to incentives for saving, indirect taxes have the advantage of avoiding the 'double-taxation effect' imposed by direct income taxes. Saving takes place out of net income, i.e. income that has already been taxed. To tax the return on savings, via a tax on investment income (e.g. dividends), is to impose a type of double taxation on that income, an obvious disincentive to saving. This is, however, a weak argument in support of indirect taxes as it is quite possible to devise a system of direct taxation that avoids

double taxation (as currently with tax exemptions for returns on Post Office Savings and National Savings).

The argument that indirect taxes are to be preferred because they avoid the discrimination against risky investments of a direct tax system can also be rebutted. Risky investments do usually have higher yields, and do therefore pay more direct tax than less risky investments. However, such discrimination could be reduced, perhaps by raising the value of allowances (e.g. on exploration costs, etc.) that can be set against tax.

In terms of incentives, then, there is no general case to be made for or against one or other type of tax system. If we are to be more specific, we must compare one particular type of indirect tax system with one particular type of direct tax system.

Economic welfare

It is sometimes argued that indirect taxes are, in welfare terms, preferable to direct taxes, as they leave the taxpayer free to make a choice. The individual can, for instance, avoid the tax by choosing not to consume the taxed commodity. Although this 'voluntary' aspect of indirect taxes may apply to a particular individual and a particular tax, it cannot apply to all individuals and all taxes. In other words, indirect taxes cannot be 'voluntary' for the community as a whole. If a chancellor is to raise a given sum through a system of indirect taxes, individual choices not to consume taxed items must, if widespread, be countered either by raising rates of tax or by extending the range of goods and services taxed.

Another argument used to support indirect taxes on welfare grounds is that they can be used to combat 'externalities'. In Chapter 10 we noted that an externality occurs where private and social costs diverge. Where private costs of production are below social costs, an indirect tax could be imposed, or increased, so that price is raised to reflect the true social costs of production. Taxes on alcohol and tobacco could be justified on these grounds. By discriminating between different goods and services, indirect taxes can help reallocate resources in a way that raises economic welfare for society as a whole.

On the other hand, indirect taxes have also been criticized on welfare grounds for being regressive, the element of indirect tax embodied in commodity prices taking a higher proportion of the income from lower-paid groups. Nor is it easy to correct for this. It would be impossible administratively to place a higher tax on a given item for those with higher incomes, although one could impose indirect taxes mainly on the goods and services consumed by higher-income groups, and perhaps at higher rates.

In terms of economic welfare, as in terms of economic incentives, the picture is again unclear. A case can be made with some conviction both for and against each type of tax.

Administrative costs

Indirect taxes are often easy and cheap to administer. They are paid by manufacturers and traders, which are obviously fewer in number than the total of individuals paying income tax. This makes indirect taxes, such as excise and import duties, much cheaper to collect than direct taxes, though the difference is less marked for VAT, which requires the authorities to deal with a large number of mainly small traders.

Even if indirect taxes do impose smaller administrative costs than direct taxes for a given revenue yield, not too much should be made of this. It is, for instance, always possible to reform the system of PAYE and reduce administrative costs. The Inland Revenue is, in fact, considering a change from PAYE to an American system of income tax, with the obligation on taxpayers themselves to estimate and forward tax, subject to random checks. Also, the computerization of Inland Revenue operations may, in the long run, significantly reduce the administrative costs associated with the collection of direct taxes.

In summary, there is no clear case for one type of tax system compared to another. The macroeconomic management and administrative cost grounds may appear to favour indirect taxes, though the comparison is only with the *current* system of direct taxation. That system can, of course, be changed to accommodate criticisms along these lines. On perhaps the more important grounds of economic incentives and economic welfare the case is very mixed, with arguments for and against each type of tax finely balanced. To be more specific we must compare the particular and detailed systems proposed for each type of tax.

Tax and social security reform

The subject of tax reform is a topic in its own right and can only be touched upon here. Tax reform had been low on the political agenda before 1965, with the basic structure of taxes remaining unchanged for decades. Since then there have been more new taxes introduced than in any other equivalent peacetime period. Changes have included the introduction and repeal of selective employment tax; VAT replacing purchase tax; corporation tax replacing profits tax; the amalgamation of surtax and income tax; new taxes such as gambling and betting duties, and capital gains tax; and the replacement of estate duty first by capital transfer tax and subsequently by an inheritance tax.

Local taxation

In the late 1980s the Conservative government increased the pace of its tax reform. It introduced the Community Charge in England and Wales during 1990 (in Scotland during 1989), together with the Uniform Business Rate (UBR) in the same year. The unpopularity of the Community Charge or 'poll tax' led to its replacement in April 1993 by the Council Tax.

The 'rates' system

The Community Charge was introduced to replace what was seen as the 'unfairness' of the old local authority rates system. The rates were a property tax, paid by tenants and owner occupiers. The total amount paid per household in tax was based on two figures: first, on the 'rateable value' of the property, which was a value based on an assessment of what the property could earn if it were let out on the open market; and second, on a 'poundage' expressed as 'so many pence in the pound'. This was calculated by the local authority in accordance with the revenue it needed to raise to pay for local services. For example, if the local authority valued a house at £30,000 and the local poundage was 2p in the pound, then the total rates for that house would be £30,000 × 0.02 or £600 per year. There were persistent complaints that the rates system was complicated and inequitable, for instance because it was difficult to properly assess the rentable value of any property. It was also based on the household unit, irrespective of how many people were actually living in the household. Also the rates had a regressive effect on some members of the public, e.g. on elderly people who sometimes occupied large, highly rated properties but who could no longer afford to pay the rates demanded since their incomes were insufficient. Finally, the total rates collected by this method were often inadequate to meet the increasing cost of local government spending on education, etc. As a result, this system was abolished for domestic premises and replaced by the Community Charge in 1990. For business premises the rating principle was retained in a modified form known as the Uniform Business Rate (UBR).

Hypothecation

A recent approach favoured by many as a means of raising the tax take whilst retaining public support, involves the idea of *hypothecation*. This is the allocation of current or additional taxes to *specific* spending outcomes. An example is the suggestion in the 1992 election manifesto by the Liberal Democrats that an extra 1% should be added to the basic rate of income tax and the entire extra revenue raised be used for education spending.

The Uniform Business Rate (UBR)

The UBR payable on any commercial property is based on two factors – the rateable value of that property, and a UBR 'multiplier'. The rateable value represents the annual rental value of the property on the open market and is fixed by an independent valuation officer, with rateable values reviewed periodically throughout the UK. To determine the actual amount of UBR to be paid per year, the rateable value is then multiplied by a rating 'multiplier' or poundage. The UBR multiplier in England in 2003 was 44.4p in the pound.

One of the inevitable problems with this new tax was that business properties in the more dynamic or prosperous areas would find their valuations rising overnight to a much higher level than before, while other businesses in less prosperous areas would experience a fall in their valuations. The UBR also repre-

sented a change in that the 'poundage rate' under this scheme was now set by central government and not by the local authority. Although the local authorities actually collect the UBR, the receipts are paid into a central fund outside local authority control. The fund is then redistributed to local authorities at a fixed rate per adult, with extra finance made available to those local authorities with special problems. This is clearly a further curbing of local authority financial control.

The Community Charge

Unlike the UBR, the *Community Charge* sought to depart from the old rating system method of calculating local taxes. The Community Charge was to be based not on the household, but on the individual. In other words, the Community Charge (or poll tax) was a personal tax assessed on each adult and expressed in the form of a lump-sum payment per year.

The Community Charge was unpopular because it meant an increase in tax for many families, especially those with a number of adults living in one household. It was also accused of being a regressive tax, in that the fixed charge per head tended to affect low income earners more than high income earners despite the existence of rebates for poor families. Also, the cost of administering the tax was high, at some 4% of its yield, whereas other taxes cost less than half that amount to collect. Many of these costs were associated with the need to register individuals and with the problems of chasing non-payers. The tax also created tensions between central government and some local authorities who felt that their 'needs' were greater than was implied by their Standard Spending Assessment (see below). As a result, some local authorities (often in hard-pressed urban areas) put an extra levy on their Community Charge. This increase in the Community Charge in major urban areas resulted in a general dissatisfaction with this form of local taxation. The intense unpopularity of the Community Charge led to its replacement by the Council Tax on 1 April 1993.

Council Tax

The *Council Tax* is a hybrid tax, which is both part property or household tax and part personal tax. The Council Tax is based on the capital value of each

Table 19.9 Council Tax: bands and property values 2003/04 (England).

Band	Property value (£)	Property value (% of national average)	Council tax (% of average property)	Average bill* (£)
A	Under 40,000	up to 50	67	692
B	40,001–52,000	50–65	78	807
C	52,001–68,000	65–85	89	922
D	68,001–88,000	85–110	100	1,037
E	88,001–120,000	110–150	122	1,268
F	120,001–160,000	150–200	144	1,498
G	160,001–320,000	200–400	167	1,729
H	Over 320,000	400–500	200	2,075

*For a property in SE England (2 or more adults).
Source: Adapted from *Guide to 2003/4 Council Tax and Business Rate* (2003).

property, on the assumption that it contains two-adult members. If the property contains only one adult, then he or she will pay only 75% of the bill of a two-adult household. No additional tax is paid on a property where more than two adults reside. Also, personal discounts are given to certain classes of adults, e.g. those on very low incomes, handicapped people, those in full-time education, and so on. It has been calculated that about 25% of all households are entitled to some form of Council Tax rebate.

Properties are valued on a sample basis (e.g. one house may be taken as typical of that street or area) and assigned to specific property bands, as shown in Table 19.9. The average national property value is calculated and assigned to the appropriate band, i.e. band D in this case. From this base, the tax bills for properties in both higher and lower bands are calculated. For example, the average property value in England in 2003/04 was deemed to be £80,000, i.e. it is located in band D – between £68,000 and £88,000 (column one). This means that this band ranges from between 85% and 110% of the average property value (second column). Therefore the tax paid by property owners in band D is regarded as the 'average', i.e. 100 (third column). Properties which are valued at under £40,000 will pay 67% of the average bill, those valued at between £88,000 and £120,000 will pay 122% of the average bill, and so on.

The central government calculates a Standard Spending Assessment (SSA) for each authority based on its estimate of the amount of money the authority needs to provide a 'standard' level of service given the demographic and other characteristics of the local area. The government grant to each local authority is then equal to its SSA *minus* an estimate of how much the authority can raise from other sources, e.g. Community Charge and the UBR. If all authorities kept to their SSA, then the actual average household bill would be shown in column four of Table 19.9.

There are some points worth noting about this scheme. First, the Council Tax, as in the case of rates, is a regressive tax in that occupiers of properties of

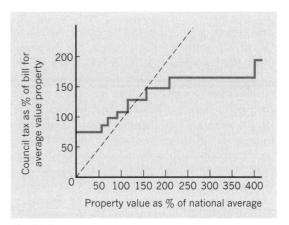

Fig. 19.8 Council Tax: property values and tax in each band.
Source: Adapted from *Guide to 2003/4 Council Tax and Business Rate* (2003).

below-average value pay proportionately more in tax, while occupiers of properties of above-average value pay proportionately less in tax. This can be seen from Fig. 19.8, in that the Council Tax line is flatter than the dotted 45% line, which would represent a proportionate tax. However, it may be said to be fairer than the Community Charge in that the tax does, at least, rise with the value of the house and it is reasonable to assume that those living in more expensive houses have higher incomes than those living in less expensive dwellings. Second, the administration of the scheme will be much easier because, unlike the Community Charge, collection is based on the household and not on the individual. Third, as with the Community Charge, the central government will still estimate the amount each local authority 'needs' to spend, i.e. the Standard Spending Assessment (SSA). If a local council exceeds this amount, then the local Council tax will be increased by a factor *greater than* the excess spending (i.e. the high-spending councils are penalized).

It has been calculated that some 37% of families were better off, and 37% worse off, as a result of the change from Community Charge to the Council Tax.

Tax, social welfare policies and work incentives

In addition to the significant changes which have taken place in local taxation, there have also been attempts by government to modify the tax structure in order to make it more equitable, while at the same time encouraging savings and increasing the base of UK share ownership. For example, the Approved Profit Sharing scheme (APS), the SAYE scheme and the Discretionary Share Option Scheme all provide tax incentives for employees to buy shares in their companies. Also the Personal Equity Plans (PEPs) introduced initially in 1986 encouraged small savers to invest in UK companies through unit and investment trusts. By making the income and capital gains from investing in such trusts free of tax, up to a maximum amount of £6,000 a year, it was hoped that savings would be encouraged, thereby helping to channel investment into UK industry. In April 1999, these were replaced by Individual Savings Accounts (ISAs). For example, during the 2003/04 tax year, savers can invest up to £7,000 tax free in an ISA with the advantage that they can have instant access to the

tax-free saving. ISAs will also be sold by a wider range of providers, e.g. by post offices and supermarkets, as well as by the financial institutions. It is difficult to measure the success of such share and savings schemes in stimulating UK industry, since any increase in share ownership by employees will not necessarily improve company performance *per se*.

On the personal taxation front, 1990 saw the introduction of a greater measure of equity, in that independent taxation for married couples was introduced. This gave married women independent status as taxpayers, i.e. they could control their own tax affairs. Since 1805 husbands had been legally responsible for the married couple's tax affairs and any married couple's allowance had been received by the husband. In the budget of 1992 it was announced that from 1993/94 onwards any extra married allowance can be claimed in its entirety by *either* husband or wife, or it can be shared equally between them, thus making the tax system fairer to married women. In 1999, the married couple's allowance was abolished, leaving a working husband and wife each receiving the single person's allowance.

As far as the social security system was concerned, the government introduced important measures in 1988 to modify the whole system. These covered unemployment benefits, pensions, income support, housing benefits, a family credit system and the social funds. The State Earnings Related Pensions Scheme (SERPS), which provided a pension based on National Insurance contributions, was cut back. Designated occupational pension schemes could now 'contract out' of SERPS. This meant that state pensions would be reduced, but the private scheme must then guarantee to at least make up the difference. Contracted-out workers pay a rate of National Insurance contribution reduced by 2%, as do their employers. At the same time the old supplementary benefit and heating allowances were abolished and a new system of income support was introduced.

The incoming Labour government of 1997 built on these reforms in order to tackle both the poverty and unemployment traps discussed earlier. A Jobseeker's Allowance (JSA) had already been introduced in 1996 to encourage more active job search during the first months of unemployment. Under the JSA the unemployed person and the Employment Service Adviser must draw up an agreement specifying what is expected of the unemployed person if they are to continue receiving the allowance. In April 1998 the government's 'New Deal' or 'Welfare to Work' initiative took such measures further by offering wage subsidies to employers to take on the unemployed and by offering new training and education opportunities. For example, young people between 18 and 24 who have been unemployed for more than six months can choose between various job options or study on a full-time approved course. If a New Deal place is refused, then benefits are reduced.

From April 2001 the government extended its New Deal programme to the long-term unemployed who are over 50 years old. They receive a £100 grant to ease the transition back to work, together with a minimum of £60 a week on top of their incomes for those earning up to £15,000 per annum. Lone parents are also encouraged to take up work by having to attend interviews with the employment service or risk losing their benefits. To help the transition to work, lone parents receive training fees and money to cover other back-to-work costs, including childcare allowances. The aim is to forge a new culture which puts work first.

Perhaps the biggest change in the 'welfare to work' system have been the introduction of tax credits as a means of alleviating poverty and improving incentives to work. Under this system, help is given to the needy through the tax system rather than as a 'handout' from the benefit agencies. The Working Family Tax Credit (WFTC) system operated from 1999 to 2003 but was replaced by the Child Tax Credit (CTC) and the Working Tax Credit (WTC) in April 2003. The Child Tax Credit is paid directly by the Inland Revenue to the main carer in the family, whilst the Working Tax Credit is paid through the wage packet to working people (those with or without children). For example, in 2003 the WTC guaranteed a minimum of £237 per week for a family with one child where the sole full-time worker earned the national minimum wage of £7,650 a year. It also guaranteed a minimum of £183 per week to couples without children, who were 25 years old or over and worked full-time (i.e. more than 35 hours a week). These amounts decreased gradually, depending on specific circumstances, as the yearly family income rose to £14,000 a year, at which point the WTC ceased.

For the poorest families whose earnings were less than £13,200 a year, the new CTC provided a maximum of £38.20 for the first child (making a total of £54.25 if the standard child benefit of £16.05 for the first child is added). This amount decreased to £10.45 per week (£26.50 including child benefit) for the first child of families whose income was less than £50,000 per year. The CTC also provides credits per additional child and allowances for childcare.

By guaranteeing minimum incomes and adjusting take-home pay through tax credits, the new system attempts to overcome the poverty and unemployment traps illustrated in Tables 19.8 and 19.9. The new system was designed to be more generous whilst at the same time providing an incentive to work by decreasing the implicit tax rates (marginal deduction rates) discussed previously. For example, it has been calculated that the number of families on implicit tax/marginal deduction rates of greater than 70% will fall from 740,000 in 1998 to 260,000 by 2004 as a result of the introduction of the new tax credit system (Treasury 2002). The hope is that the WTC and CTC will, over time, build on the old WFTC which had already begun to increase incentives to work for certain groups, i.e. unemployed households and single-parent families (Blundell 2000). A study carried out by the Institute for Fiscal Policy in 2001 attempted to analyse the potential effect of the new credits (WTC and CTC) and noted that the poorest 30% of families would probably gain an average of 2.7% in income as a result of the new changes. However, the report also indicated that the work incentive effect of the new credit system may not be very significant, because for people without children, entering work *already* increases income significantly above the welfare benefit level. In part this is because benefits currently available when such people are unemployed are relatively low (Clark and Myck 2001). It follows that the overall impact of the new system will become clearer only after the first few years of operation.

Conclusion

The UK tax system is broadly proportional. Direct taxes are, as a group, *progressive* in the UK, taking a larger proportion of the income of richer households. Indirect taxes are, as a group, *regressive*, though this is not the case for all indirect taxes. VAT is broadly proportional with the exception of the top fifth of income earners. The movement towards indirect taxation has therefore made the UK tax system less progressive than it would otherwise have been. The overall tax burden measured as a *percentage of GDP* has fluctuated since the late 1960s and rose during the 1990s to levels experienced in the early 1980s. However, the UK is not overtaxed compared to other countries. Neither does higher tax necessarily mean lower economic growth. Certainly the empirical case for higher taxes being a disincentive to effort and output is rather flimsy, whether from questionnaire or econometric study. There can be no general presumption in favour of either indirect or direct taxation, when we assess each system in terms of macro-management, economic incentives, economic welfare and administrative costs. The dilemma of how to construct an equitable and efficient form of local taxation remains, while the complicated relationships between tax changes and social security benefits still create difficulties for those families caught in the poverty or unemployment 'traps'. Various 'welfare to work' reforms are aiming to provide greater opportunities and incentives to those seeking employment.

Key points

- Taxes on *income* account for around 48% of all tax receipts, with taxes on *expenditure* around 37%.

- UK *direct* taxes are progressive while *indirect* taxes are regressive. Overall, the UK has a broadly proportional tax system.

- The UK tax burden as a percentage of GDP has averaged over 35% of GDP over the past decade.

- The UK is a middle-ranked country in terms of tax revenue as a percentage of GDP, i.e. in terms of 'tax burden'.

- There is no clear relationship between high income tax rates and disincentives to work. Detailed surveys show only a potentially small disincentive effect.

- The 'poverty trap' has improved since 1992 with implicit marginal tax rates for some households falling from 124% in 1992 to around 68% by 2002. Low hourly wages tend to worsen the poverty trap situation, though the minimum wage may help in this respect.

- The 'unemployment trap' has eased slightly, with replacement rates for an unemployed married couple with two children falling from 104% in 1992 to 94% by 2002.

- Labour market reforms, such as the Working Tax Credit (WTC) and the Child Tax Credit (CTC), and other 'Welfare to Work' initiatives should help further relieve the unemployment and poverty 'traps'.

Now try the self-check questions for this chapter on the Companion Website. You will also find up-to-date facts and case materials.

Notes

1. As it does in the UK, e.g. 10% on the first £1,920 of taxable income, 22% on taxable income up to £29,900 and 40% on higher income.

2. The average rate is total tax paid, divided by total income.

3. That is, that line which minimizes the sum of squared deviations from the line.

4. Note, however, that the Laffer curve strictly refers only to *overall* tax level, and not to that for any particular tax.

References and further reading

Blundell, R. (2000) Work incentives and 'in work' benefit reforms: a review, *Oxford Review of Economic Policy*, **16**(1), Spring.

Brown, C. (1988) Will the 1988 income tax cuts either increase work incentives or raise more revenue?, *Fiscal Studies*, **9**(4), November.

Brown, C. V. and Dawson, D. A. (1969) *Personal Taxation, Incentives and Tax Reforms*, Political and Economic Planning (PEP).

Clark, T. and Myck, M. (2001) Credit where it's due? An assessment of the new tax credits, *Institute for Fiscal Studies, Commentary No. 86*.

Crawford, M. and Dawson, D. (1982) Are rates the right tax for local government?, *Lloyds Bank Review*, 145, July.

CSO (1995) Taxes and Social Security contributions: an international comparison 1981–1993, *Economic Trends*, 505, November.

Dilnot, A. W. and Kell, M. (1988) Top-rate tax cuts and incentives: some empirical evidence, *Fiscal Studies*, **9**(4), November.

Flemming, J. and Oppenheimer, P. (1996) Are Government spending and taxes too high? *National Institute Economic Review*, 157, July.

HMSO (2000) The Government's expenditure plans 2000/01–2001/2: *Social Security Department Report*, Fig. 37, p. 81 (poverty trap) and Fig. 36, p. 81 (unemployment trap).

House of Commons (1990) *Low Income Statistics*, Social Services Committee, Fourth Report, House of Commons.

Kay, J. and King, M. (1990) *The British Tax System*, Oxford University Press.

Messere, K., Owen, J. and Teir, G. (1982) Tax trends and impact of taxes on different income groups, *The OECD Observer*, 25 January.

OECD (2000) *OECD in Figures*, Paris.

ONS (2000) 1998/99, The effects of taxes and benefits on household income, 537, April.

Poverty (1995) Fact and figures, *Journal of the Child Poverty Action Group*, 92, Winter, Fig. 1.

Poverty (1996) Fact and figures, *Journal of the Child Poverty Action Group*, 93, Spring, Table 1 (modified).

Poverty (1998) After the minimum wage: social security for working families with children, *Journal of the Child Poverty Action Group*, 99, Spring, Fig. 1.

Smith, D. (1996) Moonlighters cheat taxman out of £85bn, *Sunday Times*, 31 March.

Treasury (2000) *Budget Report 2000*.

Treasury (2002) *The Modernisation of Britain's Tax and Benefit System*, April.

Chapter 20 # Money and EMU

This chapter looks at the nature of money and the functions any money commodity must perform, before considering its importance from both monetarist and Keynesian perspectives. Before the money stock can be monitored and its effect on the economy considered, it must be measured. We therefore look at current definitions of the money stock, distinguishing between 'narrow' money and 'broad' money. We review the rules versus discretion debate and consider the importance of credibility and transparency. The development of monetary policy and the emergence of targets is considered with an emphasis on inflation targeting. A brief review of the euro is presented (see also Chapter 29), with particular emphasis on the advantages and disadvantages of the single currency.

The nature of money

We are all familiar with money. We use it almost every day of our lives, we recognize it when we see it, and most of us are all too aware that we don't have enough of it! Despite this, the effect of changes in the money supply on macroeconomic variables such as the rate of inflation, the rate of unemployment and the level of output are matters of deep controversy. One reason for this is that there is no completely watertight physical or legal definition of money. Instead, economists adopt a behavioural approach to the definition of money. This approach highlights the confidence element of money and emphasizes the importance of its *acceptability*. At the most basic level, money can be thought of as anything generally acceptable to others as a means of payment. History is littered with examples of commodities that have functioned as money at different times and in different places. The word 'pecuniary' is derived from the Latin for cattle and 'salary' is derived from the Latin for salt, indicating that both these commodities have functioned as money in the past. Other commodities such as stones, shells, beads and metals have also functioned as money.

In the UK, notes, coins, cheques and credit cards are used as means of payment to promote the exchange of goods and services and to settle debts, but cheques and credit cards are not strictly regarded as part of the money supply. Rather it is the underlying *bank deposit* of the cheque or credit card which is part of the money supply. Since cheques are simply an instruction to a bank to transfer ownership of a bank deposit, a cheque drawn against a non-existent bank deposit will be dishonoured by a bank and the debt will remain, as will also be the case if an attempt is made to settle a transaction by using an invalid credit card. Therefore a general definition of money in the UK today is notes, coins and bank and building society deposits.

In practice, for any asset to be considered as money it must perform certain functions and we turn now to a brief discussion of these.

Functions of money

Unit of account

One of the most important functions of money is to serve as a numeraire, or unit of account. Distance is measured in metres, weight in kilograms and so on. In the same way, when we measure the relative value in exchange of a house, a car or a haircut, our measuring rod is money. Money is therefore a common denominator against which value in exchange can be expressed. We then know that a litre of petrol is less

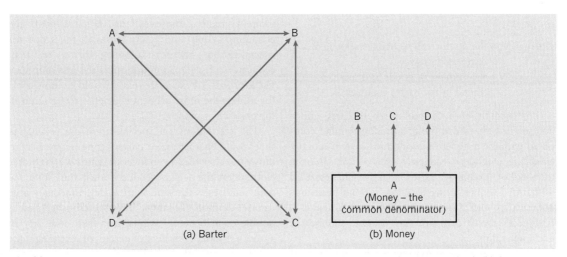

Fig. 20.1 (a) In a non-money economy producing four goods, six exchange ratios are required. (b) In a money economy producing four goods where one of the goods is money, only three exchange ratios are required.

valuable than a litre of whisky because we are able to express relative values in money terms. In the UK the basic unit of account is the pound sterling and all values in the UK are expressed in pounds sterling or fractions of a pound sterling.

The existence of a unit of account facilitates rational decision taking by consumers and producers. To understand the importance of this, consider a *barter economy*, i.e. an economy in which there is no unit of account. As an initial simplification, assume that only *four* consumer goods are offered for sale in this economy. To make decisions about how much of each good to acquire, consumers would need to consider the value of each good in relation to the value of all other goods. Figure 20.1(a) shows that consumers would need to express the value of good A in terms of goods B, C and D. Similarly, the value of good B would need to be expressed in terms of goods A, C and D, and so on. Without money, each good or service offered for sale would require an exchange value (or ratio) expressed in terms of *each* of the other goods and services offered for sale; *six* exchange ratios in all would be required. Figure 20.1(b) shows that when a unit of account does exist, the number of exchange ratios is reduced (here to only three) because the value of each good can be expressed in terms of the money commodity.

This is important because the number of exchange ratios increases rapidly as the number of goods and services offered for sale increases. In fact, we can calculate the number of exchange ratios that would exist in a *barter economy* if we substitute into the formula:

$$R_b = \tfrac{1}{2}N(N-1)$$

where R_b = the number of exchange ratios in a
           barter economy;
       N = the number of goods and services
           traded in the barter economy.

For example, in an economy where 1,000 goods and services are traded (quite a modest number compared with the number of goods and services actually traded in a modern economy such as the UK) the number of exchange ratios that would exist is 499,500! Imagine trying to make rational decisions about what and how much to produce when it is first necessary to compare such a large number of exchange ratios.

Contrast this situation with the number of exchange ratios that exist in a *money economy* and you immediately see one of the main advantages of money. In this case the number of exchange ratios is simply:

$$R_m = N - 1$$

where R_m = the number of exchange ratios in a
           money economy;
       N = the number of goods and services
           traded in the money economy.

Again, if 1,000 goods and services are traded, the number of exchange ratios is now only 999 for the money economy. Since each of these exchange ratios is expressed in the *same unit of account*, comparisons between relative goods and services as regards exchange value is very easy, taking the form of relative prices in a money economy. The fact that it is easy to compare relative prices makes it possible for consumers and producers to estimate the *opportunity cost* of any production or consumption decision. Economic theory tells us that in these circumstances resources are likely to be allocated much more efficiently than would otherwise be the case.

Medium of exchange

In this sense money is an interface between buyers and sellers which enables them to trade without the existence of a 'double coincidence of wants'. With a barter system those who trade must seek out others who have what they require and in turn require what they have. In functioning as a medium of exchange, money greatly improves the efficiency of the economic system and vastly increases the scope for specialization, thereby allowing firms to reap economies of scale. So important is the role of money in the process of exchange that it would be impossible for all but the most primitive societies to function in the absence of money.

The restrictions on specialization and exchange that would characterize a barter economy are easy to illustrate. Consider a producer of wheat who requires cloth. First the wheat producer must find someone who requires wheat and who is simultaneously able to offer cloth in exchange. Having established such a double coincidence of wants, it is then necessary to agree a mutually acceptable rate of exchange for wheat in terms of cloth. In such cases, the time and effort devoted to exchange might well exceed that devoted to production and there would be a tendency towards self-sufficiency.

Compare this with a money economy where the process of trade simply involves the exchange of money in return for the receipt of goods or services. Money clearly makes specialization and trade viable, but it also makes possible the vast economies of scale so characteristic of modern production. Remember, mass production is impossible without the existence of a mass market, and the existence of a common medium of exchange within an economy satisfies one of the conditions necessary for the existence of such a mass market. Without money it would be impossible for countries to support their current populations, far less for them to enjoy their current standard of living.

Store of value

The store of value function of money is closely bound up with its medium of exchange function. As a store of value, money permits a time-lag to exist between the sale of one thing and the purchase of something else. When goods and services are sold they are purchased with money which is then held by the sellers of goods and services until they themselves make purchases. In this sense money is an *asset* used for storing the value of sales until this value is required to make purchases. Most people receive payment for their labour at discrete intervals, usually a week or month, which do not coincide with the continuous flow of expenditures made over the same period. Money is therefore a convenient form in which to store purchasing power.

Money is not unique as a store of value and there are many forms in which wealth can be held, ranging from financial assets such as government bonds, to physical assets such as antiques. As a means of storing wealth these assets have advantages over money. For example, holders of government bonds receive interest income while holders of antiques usually experience a capital gain. Money, on the other hand, has the advantage of being immediately acceptable in exchange for goods and services. Economists use the term *liquidity* to describe assets which can easily and inexpensively be converted into money. Money is therefore the most liquid of all assets.

The liquidity which money possesses gives it a 'convenience value' over other assets, but whether it is an effective store of value depends on the behaviour of the price level. The nominal value of money is fixed by law but during periods of inflation, when prices rise, the real value of money falls. Clearly as inflation rises, money performs its store of value function less and less effectively. Indeed, inflation can be thought of as a tax on money holdings and the tax rate is equal to the rate of inflation. For example, between 1 January 2001 and 31 December 2002 the Retail Price Index in the UK increased from 173.3 to 176.2. This implied that the purchasing power of £1.00 on 1 January 2001 had a purchasing power of just over £0.98 on 31 December 2002, as the following calculation shows.

$$\text{£}1.00 \times \frac{\text{RPI on } 1.1.01}{\text{RPI on } 31.12.02} = \text{£}1.00 \times \frac{173.3}{176.2} = \text{£}0.98$$

Between 1 January 2001 and 31 December 2002, the real value of money had fallen by just over 2%.

The store of value function of money and the medium of exchange function are closely bound together. In periods of hyperinflation, money ceases to function both as an effective store of value and as an effective medium of exchange. Indeed those hyperinflations that have been documented are characterized by economic agents spending money balances as quickly as possible before they become worthless. A classic example of this occurred during the French Revolution of 1789 when assignants, the paper currency of the time, were issued in such quantity that their value declined so quickly that the peasants used them for the most ignominious purpose to which paper can ever be put. The German experience with hyperinflation in the inter-war period provides another classic example of money becoming ineffective as both a store of value and a medium of exchange. In extreme cases such as this, the value of money falls so quickly that it becomes increasingly difficult to make production and investment decisions. The result is that economic activity declines and economic agents resort to barter and exchange goods and services directly. The growth of the 'barter economy' during the hyperinflation in Russia in the late 1990s is a recently documented case in point.

A standard for deferred payments

Economists sometimes identify a fourth function of money: that it provides a standard for deferred payments. In this sense money provides a means of agreeing payments to be made at some future date, at the time when contracts are signed. Arguably, this is simply a particular aspect of its unit of account function.

Near money

Commodities which fulfil only some of the functions of money cannot be classed as money. Credit cards and luncheon vouchers, for instance, can sometimes be used as a medium of exchange for transactions, but they are not money because they cannot always be used, nor do they fulfil the other functions of money. Paper assets such as government securities serve as a store of value, but they cannot be used as a medium of exchange. However, liquid assets, i.e. those which can easily be converted into money without loss of value, form a potential addition to the money stock, and are often referred to as 'near money'. Assets normally classed as 'liquid' include time deposits, treasury and commercial bills, and certificates of deposit (Fig. 20.2). Other assets become more liquid the nearer is their maturity date. Many of the assets shown in Fig. 20.2 are considered in more detail later in this chapter and in Chapter 21.

Electronic money

The creation and use of electronic money, though still in its infancy, is likely to increase rapidly over the next few years. The possible implications of this are profound and far-reaching. So what is electronic money? Electronic money is a payment instrument whereby monetary value is stored electronically on

some device in the possession of the customer. The European Central Bank defines electronic money as 'an electronic store of monetary value on a technical device that may be widely used for making payments to undertakings other than the issuer without necessarily involving bank accounts in the transaction, but acting as a prepaid bearer instrument.'

The most obvious device for storing money is a computer chip embedded in a *smart card* and, for purposes of simplicity, our discussion here is restricted to this. The amount stored on the chip is increased or decreased every time it is used in some financial transaction or whenever funds are loaded onto, or unloaded from, the card. In this way, electronic money stored on a card can be thought of as being similar to cash stored in a wallet. The amount of money in the wallet goes up or down according to whether purchases or sales take place and additional balances can be loaded into the wallet or unloaded from it. This is entirely different from a credit card which simply gives its owner an immediate overdraft. E-money more closely resembles cash than credit card transactions and Fig. 20.3 shows the clearing and settlement of cash and E-money.

E-money is convenient and settlement is almost immediate. It is possible for E-money users to transfer balances onto their stored value cards from home and terminals that accept E-money transfer funds stored on a chip, into a bank account in settlement of transactions, almost invariably without delay. Another advantage of E-money is that it eliminates the necessity of carrying coins, which most people find inconvenient since they inevitably pile up in pockets and purses! The problems with E-money concern consumer resistance because of loss of anonymity when making transactions, security and the possibility of

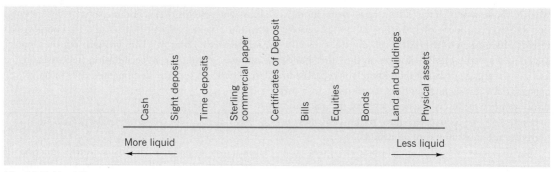

Fig. 20.2 Liquidity spectrum.

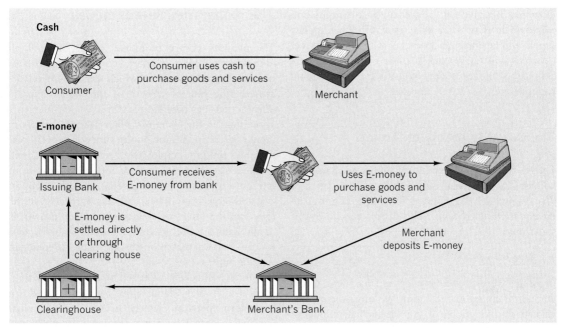

Fig. 20.3 Clearing and settlement of cash and E-money.
Source: Federal Reserve Bank of Dallas, *Southwest Economy*, March/April 1997, p. 6.

counterfeiting. These problems are technical and can probably be overcome relatively easily. For example, some institutions provide anonymity by offering E-money which, once it has been downloaded onto the card and balances are transferred from the individual's to the institution's account, cannot be 'matched' to the account from which it originated. Security and counterfeiting risks can probably be minimized by the development of sophisticated encryption techniques. When these are available and the public has trust in them, the use of E-money is likely to rise substantially.

The importance of money

Economists are in no doubt that 'money matters', but there is considerable disagreement as to how changes in the money stock influence macroeconomic variables (the so-called *transmission mechanism*) and as to the magnitude of its influence on these variables. Monetarists argue that although changes in the rate or growth of the money supply may influence 'real'

variables such as output and employment in the short run, in the long run they affect only nominal (or money) variables such as the rate of inflation, the rate of interest and the rate of exchange. The New Classical view is an extension of monetarist thinking and agrees that changes in the rate of growth of the money supply affect only nominal variables, but contends that this is the case in both the long run and the short run. Keynesians, on the other hand, argue that as well as affecting nominal variables, changes in the rate of growth of the money supply also affect real variables such as the level of output and employment in both the short run and the long run.

It is natural that we should focus on the differences between Keynesians and monetarists, but it would be a mistake to think that there are no similarities! Both groups agree that in the short run an increase in money supply will affect both real and nominal variables. They also agree that nominal variables will be affected in the long run, but they disagree over the nature of the transmission mechanism and over the influence of changes in money supply on the real economy in the long run. Keynes held the view that higher inflation was an acceptable price to pay for higher output and employment, whereas the monetarists argue that any changes in output and employment that occur as a result of higher money supply will be only transitory, i.e. in the long run real variables will revert back to their equilibrium rates and higher money supply will affect only nominal variables.

The quantity theory of money

The relationship between money on the one hand and nominal income (final output × the average price of that output) on the other, is formally recognized in the *equation of exchange*. The income version of this states that:

$$M \times V_Y = P \times Y$$

In other words, over any given time period, the amount of money in circulation (M) times the income velocity of circulation (V_Y) (i.e. the average number of times the money supply is spent on final output) must be identical to the average price of final output (P) times the volume of final output produced (Y).

Note that the income velocity of circulation (V_Y) is a measure of the speed at which money is spent on final output and is determined by several factors. One important factor is the frequency with which payments are made. For example, if wages are paid monthly and all other things are equal, money balances will, on average, be higher than if wages are paid weekly. This implies a lower income velocity of circulation.

There is nothing controversial in the equation of exchange. It is simply an identity and must be true by definition. It simply tells us that the value of spending on final output in one period (MV_Y) equals the value of output purchased in the same period (PY). However, if we assume that V_Y and Y are constant, then we have a relationship between M and P.

The *quantity theory of money* specifies the nature of this relationship and states that the relationship is *causal* from money to prices. In other words, an increase in the money supply will cause an increase in the average price level. Furthermore causation is one way, that is, the average price level cannot change unless there has been a prior change in the money supply. We shall see below that this strict interpretation of the *quantity theory of money* remains controversial.

The monetarist view of money

The quantity theory of money is the basis of all monetarist thinking. In short, monetarism is a set of beliefs about the ways in which changes in *money growth* (the rate of growth of the money supply) affect other macroeconomic variables. Monetarists argue that, in the *short run*, the effect of changes in money growth is ambiguous, affecting both real variables (output, employment, real wages, etc.) and nominal variables (the rate of inflation, the rate of interest, the rate of exchange, etc.), though in imprecise and largely unpredictable ways. However, in the *long run* the effect of changes in money growth is unambiguous, affecting only nominal variables. It is for this reason that monetarists focus on long-run relationships.

Monetarist beliefs are based on empirical relationships which they claim show a highly significant correlation between money growth and nominal national income. However, since they believe that real national income (output) is not affected by changes in money growth in the long run, the implication is that increased money growth leads to higher nominal income through inflation. In other words, increases in money growth lead, in the long run, to an increase in the rate of inflation.

The demand for money

All monetarists accept the quantity theory of money, but the emergence of monetarism as an economic doctrine focuses on the *demand for money*. Monetarists argue that the demand for money is determined by the same general factors which influence the demand for other goods and services and focus particularly on the *level of income*, the *price level*, and the *expected rate of inflation*. It is claimed that the relationship between these variables and the demand for money is stable over time. This is an extremely important claim because such stability could not exist unless the velocity of circulation was also constant. In other words, if it can be shown that the demand for money is stable, then the income velocity of circulation (V_Y) is also stable.[1]

For simplicity, the monetarist view implies that the demand for money is a stable function of nominal national income. The reasoning underlying this view is that in the long run the *actual* rate of inflation and the *expected* rate of inflation coincide. The main determinants of changes in the demand for money are therefore changes in the actual rate of inflation, that is, the rate of change of the price level, and changes in real income, that is, changes in nominal GNP divided by the price level. Monetarists therefore argue that when there is increased money growth, this will lead to changes in nominal GNP which will restore equilibrium between the demand for money and the supply of money.

To understand this more fully, the equation of exchange $(MV_Y = PY)$ can be written in the form $M = kPY$ where $k = 1/V_Y$. In equilibrium the demand for money equals the supply of money and so we can write:

$$M_s = M_d = kPY$$

Note that k is the proportion of nominal income (PY) that the population demand as money. Beginning with equilibrium between demand for money and supply of money, if the supply of money increases there will be disequilibrium between demand for money and supply of money. How is equilibrium restored? If, as the monetarists assume, V_Y is constant, then k must also be constant and equilibrium can only be restored by a rise in nominal income (PY). If V_Y is not stable, then k will not be stable. In this case, equilibrium following an increase in the money supply might be partially or totally restored by a change in the proportion of national income held as money. In other words, equilibrium is restored by a change in the demand for money that is not proportionately related to a change in nominal income.

Figure 20.4 is used as a basis for explanation. If the demand for money is constant at 25% of GNP, that is $k = \frac{1}{4}$, and the initial level of GNP is £1,000m then, assuming that demand for money and supply of money are in equilibrium, the quantity of money supplied and demanded is £250m. If the money supply now increases, nominal GNP will increase and, since k is assumed to be constant, demand for money will also increase. For example, if the money supply increases by £100m, equilibrium will be restored when demand for money increases by £100m and, with k constant at $\frac{1}{4}$, this implies that GNP increases to £1,400m.

The transmission mechanism

An important question to answer is *why* nominal GNP increases following an increase in money growth. In fact, the route by which the effect of a change in the money supply is transmitted to the economy is referred to as the *transmission mechanism*. The monetarists argue that an increase in the money supply will leave people holding excess money balances at the existing level of GNP. Consequently, spending on a whole range of goods and services will increase as economic agents (individuals and organizations) divest themselves of unwanted holdings of money. (This contrasts with liquidity preference theory which implies that it will be spent on *securities* – see the following section.) As aggregated demand increases, output and prices will rise until people are persuaded to hold an amount of money equivalent to

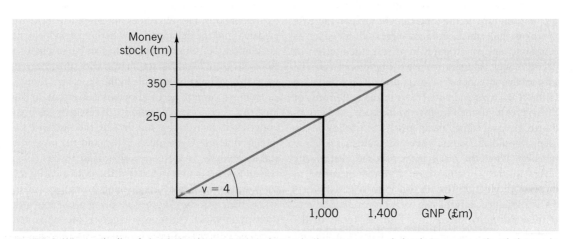

Fig. 20.4 When velocity of circulation is constant, a change in the money supply leads to a proportional change in nominal GNP.

the increased money supply in order to finance the increased value of their transactions. In other words, nominal GNP goes on rising until the increase in the supply of money is matched by an increase in the *transactions demand for money*, so that supply an demand for money are brought back into equilibrium.

However, this simple approach is ambiguous because an increase in nominal GNP can consist entirely of an increase in real income with prices unchanged, or entirely of an increase in prices with real income unchanged, or some combination of both. The monetarists claim that in the *short run*, the increase in nominal GNP will consist of an increase in both real income (output) and prices. However, in the *long run* they argue that there is an equilibrium 'natural rate of output' which is determined by institutional factors such as the capital stock, mobility of labour, the rate of social security payments, whether a minimum wage exists and so on (see Chapter 22). Such factors are not influenced by changes in money growth. Whilst it is possible that changes in money growth will bring about changes in real income in the short run, such changes will be only transitory since in the long run real income will return to the level that would have existed before the increase in money growth. Hence, an increase in money growth above the rate of growth of real income will, in the long run, simply lead to higher prices.

Short-run and long-run adjustment to a monetary shock

But why should output increase in the short run following an increase in money growth, and return to the 'natural rate' in the long run? In fact, an increase in money growth encourages increased spending as economic agents attempt to divest themselves of excess money balances at the existing price level. The inevitable consequence is rising prices. This implies a fall in real wages and an increase in the real profits of firms, providing the incentive to increase production. However, over time, rising prices are followed by rising nominal wages. The mechanism is now reversed. When the real wage is restored, real profits revert to their original level and the incentive to increase production (higher real profits) disappears. As a consequence, firms cut back on production and output reverts to the 'natural rate'. In terms of the quantity theory, the implication is that both velocity and output are constant in the long run and that an

increase in money growth merely causes an increase in prices.

Criticisms of the quantity theory

It is important to note that monetarism changes the relationship between M and P (given V_Y and Y) from that of an identity to that of a causal relationship. Although monetarism provides a theoretical rationale for doing this, a number of criticisms can be made of the view that a change in M will automatically lead, in the long run, to a proportionate change in P.

The first and perhaps most damaging criticism relates to assumptions about the behaviour of the velocity of circulation. The velocity has always fluctuated in the short run, sometimes in response to sudden changes in money growth. In the longer run, however, monetarists argue that velocity is relatively stable. Indeed Fig. 20.5 provides supportive evidence for the monetarist view. Broad money velocity (M4) – see the next section – fell dramatically in the 1980s in response to financial innovation and deregulation of the financial sector. This fall in the value of broad money velocity was widely anticipated and followed a broadly stable downward trend. In the 1990s broad money velocity again exhibited considerable stability, though minor short-run variations could be clearly identified. Narrow money velocity (M0) exhibits far less stability than broad money velocity (M4) – though the rise in narrow money velocity during the 1980s was also widely anticipated. Nevertheless most monetarists attach very little significance to the behaviour of narrow money and argue that the causal link is between broad money and prices.

Despite this, Fig. 20.5 does not provide conclusive evidence and the debate about whether the velocity of circulation (V_Y) can be regarded as stable in the long run is far from over. In fact there is widespread agreement that velocity is unstable in the short run, though economists cannot agree about its behaviour in the long run. A considerable amount of research has been undertaken to test the stability of the demand for money function (remember, if demand for money is stable, velocity is stable), with mixed results. One reason for this is that it is very difficult to identify the short-run influences on the demand for money and to assess their effects. Another involves problems with the way in which the money supply is measured and hence with the way in which velocity is calculated.[2] In this respect, some economists have argued that

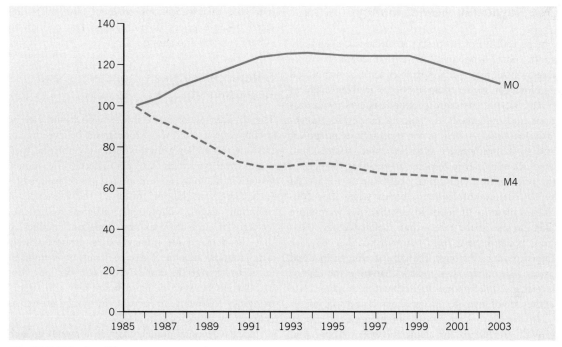

Fig. 20.5 Velocity of the money aggregates.
Source: *Financial Statistics*, ONS (various).

neither M0 nor M4 is a particularly useful measure of money and that *divisia* (see p. 383) is superior.

A further problem with the monetarist explanation of the effects of changes in M concerns the assumptions made about *goods market* behaviour. Monetarists assume that goods prices are demand determined rather than cost determined, and change as asset holdings, particularly money balances, change. Monetarists dismiss the possibility that goods prices are determined by costs. Their reasoning is simple. If money growth rises, then aggregate demand will rise. Since no business sells its products at a constant rate over time, businesses must hold stocks to meet changes in demand. A *general* rise in aggregate demand is not initially distinguishable from any other increase in demand, so the rise in aggregate demand will be met out of stocks and there will be no change in prices. However, if the higher level of demand persists, businesses will increase their purchases from suppliers to restore their stocks. The firms which supply the wholesalers and retailers will therefore experience higher than normal rates of sales and their stocks will be depleted more rapidly than expected. Suppliers of products will therefore increase production in order to restore their stocks to the desired level.

This process filters down the networks of markets until it reaches the markets for raw materials and labour (the primary inputs used to produce products). In the raw materials markets, the amount available is likely to be insufficient to meet the increased amount demanded at the old price, especially so when the increase in aggregate demand implies that all manufacturers want additional raw materials. The price of raw materials (and labour) will therefore be bid up until the market 'clears'. Because the higher price of raw materials (and labour) increases costs of production, manufacturers will charge wholesalers higher prices, citing increased raw material costs as the reason. Wholesalers will in turn charge retailers higher prices because of the higher prices they are compelled to pay. Retailers will then charge their customers higher prices and can, in truth, blame this on the higher costs they have incurred to supply customers with the product! However, rising costs are not the cause of the higher prices. The underlying cause is rising demand caused by increased money growth.

The Keynesian view of money

The perspective of Keynesian economics is essentially short run. Keynesians believe that changes in the money stock affect 'real' variables such as output and employment rather than money variables such as prices. Keynes envisaged economic agents (organizations and individuals) as holding money for *speculative motives* as well as for *transactions purposes*, and switching between financial assets (bonds) and holdings of money in response to expected changes in the price of financial assets. Economic agents would switch money holdings into bonds when they considered the price of bonds so low that they were more likely to rise in the future than to fall further. Now since bonds have a fixed coupon, i.e. they pay the same amount of money annually, a change in bond prices also implies an *opposite* change in the rate of interest.[3] A *fall* in bond prices therefore implies a rise in the rate of interest, raising demand and vice versa.

In the Keynesian model, an increase in money growth creates an imbalance between supply and demand for money which encourages economic agents to purchase bonds. In other words, an increase in money growth does not lead to a change in expenditures on goods and services and so has no immediate effect on the price of final output. Instead the price of bonds is driven upwards and interest rates fall, encouraging an increase in investment (see Chapter 17) and therefore in output, employment and incomes as the multiplier effect works through the economy. These changes in turn lead to an increase in the value of transactions and a consequent increase in the transactions demand for money to hold. The fall in interest rates also leads to a rise in the speculative demand for money to hold. These changes continue until there is an equilibrium between the supply of and demand for money.

An important issue is why the increase in money growth does not lead to an increase in prices in the Keynesian model. The answer is that, in the Keynesian view of the economy, different variables adjust at different rates. Market quantities, such as output or the number of jobs, adjust much more quickly than market prices. Prices may indeed rise as a result of an expansion in aggregate demand, but they will rise slowly, because it will take time for manufacturers to feel the effects of overall expansion on costs of production. Price rises will only accelerate when the economy nears full employment. The market is therefore in a permanent 'disequilibrium' state, because prices do not adjust fast enough to equate demand and supply.

Differences between monetarism and Keynesianism

The differences between the two positions can be summarized as follows. Monetarists believe that in the long run money growth affects only nominal variables. Real variables are not affected by money growth in the long run and instead are determined by such factors as labour mobility, the existence of minimum wages, technological progress and so on. Velocity of circulation exhibits long-run stability so that the demand for money varies proportionately with nominal income. Since real output is uninfluenced by changes in money growth in the long run, equilibrium between demand for money and supply of money following an increase in money growth is restored by an increase in prices.

In the Keynesian model, changes in money growth affect both nominal variables *and* real variables. However, a given increase in money growth has different effects because the velocity of circulation is unstable. In the Keynesian model an increase in money growth leads to a reduction in the velocity of circulation as more money is absorbed into idle balances and so is willingly held. This implies that part of any increase in money growth is willingly held at the existing price level.[4] This somewhat dissipates the effect of any increase in money growth. However, when there are unemployed resources in the economy, increased money growth will usually be associated with an increase in output and a fall in unemployment. This Keynesian implication that output is demand determined and that unemployment is due to insufficient aggregate demand is emphatically rejected by monetarist economists!

The debate between monetarists and Keynesians is not just about the role of money and the implications of this for monetary policy. It is also about ideology. Monetarists believe that the economy is inherently stable and tends towards a long-run equilibrium level of output. Because of this, they argue that resources are most efficiently allocated through the market and that government intervention destabilizes the economy and leads to a misallocation of resources by moving the economy away from its long-run equilibrium rate. They argue in favour of a 'monetary rule' whereby the money supply grows at a predetermined rate so that (by implication) markets have information about the expected long-run rate of inflation. The Keynesian view is exactly the opposite. They view the economy as inherently unstable and argue in favour of government intervention to stabilize the economy. They reject any kind of 'monetary rule' since this would restrict the scope for intervention and reduce the ability of government to respond to adverse shocks.

Debate between monetarists and Keynesians was fuelled in the 1970s and 1980s by the relatively high rates of inflation experienced then. More recently inflation targeting has provided the framework for successfully controlling inflation so that, although the debate between monetarists and Keynesians has not yet been resolved, it is certainly less important than it once was. Although economists still disagree on whether money growth is the only cause of inflation, they all agree that inflation must be financed by money growth. In other words, money growth, at the very least, plays a permissive role in the inflationary process (see also Chapter 22). It is to the measurement and control of the money stock that we now turn.

Issues in counting the money stock

Economists, governments and central bankers are interested in counting the money stock, not least because this is important if we are to test the propositions of monetary theory. Earlier we discussed the quantity theory of money in some detail, but how would we be able to test this theory without a clearly defined measure of the money supply? Another reason why we are interested in counting the money stock is that we wish to control its behaviour so as to achieve macroeconomic objectives, in particular controlling the rate of inflation. Without a measure of the money stock this would be impossible.

Narrow and broad money

Estimates of the money stock have been published in the UK since 1966 but there is no single measure of money that fully encapsulates monetary conditions.

Indeed it is usual to distinguish between narrow measures of money and broad measures of money. *Narrow* measures of money include the more liquid assets and are therefore concerned with the medium of exchange function of money, whereas *broad* measures of money also include a variety of less liquid assets and therefore also focus on the store of value function.

Definitions of money include notes, coins and assets such as bank deposits. The narrowest measure of money in the UK is M0 (pronounced M zero), which is sometimes referred to as 'base money' or 'high-powered money'. This consists of notes, coins and operational deposits of the banking sector. This is a very narrow measure of money and consists only of the most liquid assets.

No one would seriously argue that M0 provides a comprehensive definition of money. For example, other deposits such as sight deposits at banks and building societies also function as money and would certainly be included in any comprehensive definition of money. Indeed there are other assets, such as time deposits, which function as a store of value and which, after the required notice of withdrawal has elapsed, can be converted into assets which perform the medium of exchange function of money. The problem is not simply to distinguish between assets which function as money and assets which do not, but rather to identify that group of assets which provides a reliable and stable link between money growth and prices.

This is no easy task and measures of the money stock have changed frequently since they were first introduced. This is not only because of changing asset behaviour by the public, but also because of financial deregulation and innovation. The public holds deposits with the banking sector not only for *transactions* purposes but also as an *asset* on which they receive interest. Anything which changes the asset behaviour of the public, i.e. the volume of bank deposits held by the public, will be reflected in changes in the different money aggregates. This would weaken the link between money growth and prices. It is precisely for these reasons that the long-run behaviour of the velocity of circulation of money appears to have been less stable than it otherwise might have appeared.

In recent years financial innovation and deregulation have changed the nature of the assets which perform the functions of money and this in turn has changed the relationship between measures of the money stock and nominal income. Major changes occurred in the banking sector in the 1980s. For example, the Big Bang of 1986 removed the distinction between retail banks and wholesale banks, while the Building Societies Act of 1986 allowed building societies to offer transactions services (cheque books, cash cards and credit cards) and loans for purposes other than house purchase. This considerably blurred the distinction between banks and building societies and therefore rendered existing measures of the money supply, which excluded building society deposits, less reliable. In other words, measures of money supply growth failed to accurately predict changes in the rate of inflation, not necessarily because the demand for money was unstable, but possibly because existing measures of money no longer adequately measured the money stock. The increasing availability of new assets is sure to mean that measures of the money stock will continue to change for the foreseeable future.

In counting the money stock at least three issues are relevant.

Which deposits should be included?

Some measures of money include only sight deposits (chequing accounts where cash is available on demand) whereas others also include time deposits (requiring notice of withdrawal). In narrow measures of money we are particularly interested in counting transactions balances and therefore the question arises as to whether we should count only retail deposits up to a certain limit; if so, why should wholesale deposits up to the same limit be excluded (see Chapter 21 where we note that *retail deposits* are usually defined as individual deposits of £50,000 or less, and *wholesale deposits* as individual deposits in excess of £50,000)? There is a further problem about the ownership of deposits. In the UK only private sector deposits are counted as part of the money stock. Public sector deposits are therefore excluded, as are deposits of overseas residents. The same is not true in all countries.

Which liabilities should be included?

Traditionally only bank deposits have been counted as part of the money stock but, as the nature of the financial sector has changed, building society deposits are now included in some measures of the money stock. This simply reflects the fact that these institutions now provide banking services similar to those of the clearing banks. Some idea of the importance of this is illustrated by events in July 1989 when the Abbey National Building Society changed its status from a mutual society to that of a bank. To have included its very large deposits in measures of the money stock which did not already include building society deposits would have involved large breaks in the statistical series of those measures. Instead it was decided to discontinue publication of certain money aggregates and to introduce a new money aggregate (M4).

Which currencies should be included?

No money aggregate currently measured in the UK includes foreign currency deposits. However, these have been included in earlier measures of money and a dilemma certainly exists for the authorities. Capital controls have now largely been abandoned and the Single Market certainly allows the free flow of funds within the EU. One currency can readily be converted into other currencies and in particular euros can easily be converted into sterling. Foreign currency deposits might well become an even more significant component of the money supply in the future than they have been in the past. A strong case could therefore be made for their inclusion in a broad measure of the money stock.

Measures of money

Currently in the UK only two measures of money are published, M0 and M4.

M0

This is a *narrow* measure of money and consists of:

(a) notes and coin outside the Bank of England, plus

(b) bankers' operational (i.e. clearing) deposits with the Bank of England.

M0 is the cash base of the monetary system and is the only measure of the money stock which is unaffected by changes in the financial system. Indeed there are only two ways in which M0 can change:

1 the government issues more notes and coins, and/or

2 operational deposits change as a result of transactions between the private sector and the government. This might happen because of random factors, for example when a large company settles a tax demand, or it might happen because of government expenditure or as a result of open market operations. Any transactions between the private sector and the Bank of England will alter operational deposits at the Bank of England and will cause M0 to change.

M4

This is a *broad* measure of money first introduced in 1987, and now upgraded to the status of the sole broad measure of money in the UK. M4 consists of:

(a) notes and coin held by the M4 private sector (i.e. the private sector other than Monetary Financial Institutions (MFIs) such as the Bank of England and other banks and building societies), plus

(b) all M4 private sector retail and wholesale sterling deposits at MFIs in the UK (including certificates of deposit and other paper issued by MFIs of not more than five years' original maturity).

This money aggregate was introduced in 1987 because of the evolving role of the building societies which ceased to offer loans solely as mortgage finance for the purchase of property. Indeed building societies began to compete aggressively with banks as providers of loans for purchases other than property. The nature of the medium of exchange function of various financial intermediaries therefore evolved and to accommodate this it became necessary to widen the definition of money to include deposits with building societies. Table 20.1 shows the importance of these different components of M0 and M4 at January 2003. In particular, we can see the importance of interest-bearing retail deposits at banks ('other bank retail deposits') and the larger denominated wholesale deposits at banks ('bank wholesale deposits') which together account for over 77% of all bank deposits.

The Divisia Index

M4 items are simply summed to give a measure of the money supply. Each item in the aggregate has a weight of unity and so all assets are weighted equally. This approach takes no account of the 'moneyness' of the different assets. Thus notes and coin in circulation are treated in exactly the same way as interest-bearing time deposits and any substitution of one for the other has no effect on the measured magnitude of M4. However, notes and coin function as a 'pure' medium of exchange and are non-interest bearing, unlike interest-bearing deposits which function primarily as a store of value. The latter earn an explicit rate of return and, at different times, *switching* between assets is apparent. The implicit assumption of simple sum measures of the money supply, namely that all components are perfect substitutes, is therefore erroneous.

A different approach is to weight the different assets in the money stock according to their role in *transactions*, i.e. according to the extent to which they function as a medium of exchange. This is the reasoning behind the Divisia Index which is claimed to be more closely related to total expenditure in the

Table 20.1 Components of M0 and M4 (£m) as at January 2003.

M0		M4 private sector holdings of	
Notes and coin in circulation outside the Bank of England	37,163	Notes and coin	30,401
Bankers' operational deposits	73	Non-interest-bearing bank deposits	42,277
		Other bank retail deposits	494,898
		Building society retail shares and deposits	134,894
Total	**37,236**	**Total**	**702,470**

Source: Adapted from ONS (2003) *Financial Statistics*, April.

economy than conventional money aggregates. There are, of course, problems as to which variables to include in such a Divisia Index and the weight to be accorded to each variable. In practice the basic approach has been to weight each component according to the *difference* between its interest yield and the yield on a safe benchmark asset. In a Divisia Index, notes and coin therefore have a weight of 1, while high-interest-bearing savings accounts have a weight closer to zero, because the interest paid on them approaches the benchmark market rate and switching into and out of such accounts makes them less useful as a measure of the medium of exchange function.

The money supply process

The creation of deposits

The existence of a legal definition of money enables us to focus on an important question: how is money created? The answer is, not self-evident. Notes and coin are, of course, issued through the Bank of England and the Royal Mint, but they are not released without limit. If they were they would quickly lose value and would become unacceptable as a medium of exchange. However, before we focus on the importance of changes in base money (which includes notes and coin) in the money supply process, let us look at the creation of bank deposits. Even a cursory glance at the data for M4 in Table 20.1 shows that bank deposits are a significantly greater component of broad money such as M4 than of base (narrow) money such as M0.

In any discussion of the creation of bank deposits it is customary to begin by recognizing that not all of the funds deposited with a bank will be withdrawn at any one time. Indeed, under normal circumstances inflows and outflows of funds will be such that on any one day banks will require only a fraction of the total funds deposited with them to meet withdrawals by customers. This implies that the remainder can be lent to borrowers. But this is not the end of the story because funds lent by one bank will flow back into the banking system, again a fraction will be retained and the remainder will be available for lending to other borrowers. This process is known as the money supply multiplier.

The money supply multiplier

Models of the money supply multiplier link the money supply to the monetary base in a relationship of the following form:

$$M = mB$$

where M = the money supply;
m = the money supply multiplier;
B = the monetary base.

In models such as this, m tells us how many times the money supply will rise following an increase in the monetary base. But what determines the value of m? In fact, there are two factors: the decisions of depositors about their holdings of currency and deposits, and the level of reserves the banks hold to meet customer demands for currency. For simplicity let us assume that c is the desired ratio of currency (C) to total deposits (D) and that r is the desired ratio of reserves (R) to total deposits (D). Thus we have:

$$c = \frac{C}{D} \text{ and } r = \frac{R}{D}$$

Since $B = C + R$ and $M = C + D$, it follows that:

$$\frac{M}{B} = \frac{C+D}{C+R}$$

which, after dividing the right-hand side by D, can be written as:

$$\frac{M}{B} = \frac{\dfrac{C}{D}+1}{\dfrac{C}{D}+\dfrac{R}{D}}$$

Replacing C/D with c and R/D with r we have:

$$\frac{M}{B} = \frac{c+1}{c+r}$$

Since $m = \dfrac{M}{B}$ we can say that the money supply multiplier is determined by the public's desired ratio of cash to total deposits (c) and the bank's desired ratio of reserves to total deposits (r).

Whether the money supply multiplier is an adequate explanation of the money supply process depends partly on the stability of the ratios c and r. For the UK, the evidence suggests that c, the ratio of the public's demand for cash to deposits, can be unstable and unpredictable. Of course, there are bound to be seasonal variations and it might be expected that over the Christmas period and during the summer months when more holidays are taken, the c ratio will rise because of an increase in the public's demand for cash. However, empirical studies of the c ratio have concluded that the instability it exhibits arises for many reasons and changes do not always coincide with predictable changes in the seasons. One reason why the c ratio might be unstable is that changes in the rate of interest change the opportunity cost of holding cash. This is especially important because of the emergence of interest-bearing current account deposits. Whatever the reasons, for the UK it has been estimated that the c ratio varies between 0.16 and 0.21.

The empirical evidence on the stability of the r ratio is not so conclusive and some studies suggest that r is unstable while others suggest that it is relatively stable. Again, in the short run at least, changes in the rate of interest are likely to cause changes in the r ratio. For example, when interest rates are rising, banks have an incentive to reduce their holdings of reserves.

Certainly for the UK the general view is that the money supply multiplier is unstable in the short run, and that in the long run changes in the money supply depend more on changes in the monetary base.

The monetary base

In light of the above discussion an important issue presents itself: can the authorities control the *monetary base*? It can easily be shown that if public sector borrowing is not financed by sales of debt to the non-bank financial intermediaries or by sales of the foreign currency reserves, the banking sector will act as a source of residual finance and the monetary base will rise.

Let us begin with the following notation:

PSBR = public sector borrowing requirement
MAT = maturing government debt
MGD = marketable government debt
NMGD = non-marketable government debt
FE = sales of foreign exchange reserves
ΔB = change in the monetary base.

We can derive the following identity:

$$PSBR + MAT \equiv MGD + NMGD + FE + \Delta B$$

This simply tells us that total public sector borrowing requirement (plus redemption of maturing government debt) must be met by sales of debt and foreign currency or by an increase in the monetary base. Rearranging this identity tells us that changes in the monetary base represent the difference between public sector borrowing on the one hand, and sales of government debt and foreign exchange on the other. Thus:

$$\Delta B \equiv (PSBR + MAT) - (MGD + NMGD + FE)$$

The question naturally arises about the extent to which the authorities can control the determinants of the monetary base.

Controlling the PSBR

The PSBR is largely the central government's budget deficit and therefore controlling the PSBR implies that fiscal policy is geared to limiting the size of the budget deficit. In principle the authorities might very well be able to set targets for the budget deficit, but the problem is that expenditure and tax revenue are subject to short-term fluctuations which cannot easily be predicted. Indeed, during the *medium-term financial strategy* (see below) declining targets were announced for the PSBR, but these targets proved difficult to meet and were abandoned after only a few years. It is therefore not feasible to control the monetary base by controlling the PSBR.

Controlling MAT

The amount of government debt maturing at any given time depends on sales of debt in previous years. This is not under the immediate control of the authorities and indeed the size of the national debt is a particular problem for the authorities in the UK. Again, controlling the level of maturing government debt does not provide a feasible mechanism for controlling the monetary base.

Controlling MGD

Sales of marketable government debt have become the main means of financing the PSBR and maturing government debt. If the authorities were unconcerned with the monetary implications of their borrowing, this could be financed by sales of securities (debt) to the Bank of England. In this case the government's account at the Bank of England would be credited with an amount equivalent to the value of debt purchased by the Bank. However, once the government spent its newly acquired deposits they would flow into the banking system and the monetary base would rise. This is the modern equivalent of 'printing money'.

In practice the authorities are much more concerned to sell debt to the non-bank private sector such as insurance companies, pension funds, joint stock companies other than banks, private individuals and so on. Such sales result in a *fall* in banks' operational deposits at the Bank of England and the monetary base will tend to fall back towards its previous level. However, the extent to which the government can persuade the non-bank private sector to purchase debt depends on its willingness to accept higher and higher rates of interest. Given that changes in interest rates have become the main instrument for controlling the rate of inflation, it is inconceivable that sales of government debt to the non-bank private sector can be varied so as to control changes in the monetary base.

Controlling NMGD

Non-marketable government debt consists of such assets as national savings certificates, premium bonds and so on. Sales of the former depend again on rates of return but since these are unlikely to vary as freely as market rates on marketable government debt, it is not possible to rely on such sales as a means of controlling changes in the monetary base. The latter are sold on tap, that is, they are sold in response to public demand. The government makes no attempt to actively increase sales. Varying the sales of non-marketable government debt is not therefore an option open to the government in controlling the monetary base.

Changes in the foreign exchange reserves

When the authorities intervene to stabilize the exchange rate they buy or sell sterling in exchange for foreign currency. When imports exceed exports there will be downward pressure on sterling on the foreign exchanges. To preserve the exchange rate the authorities must sell foreign currency and purchase sterling on the foreign exchanges. The sterling deposits acquired by the Bank of England through intervention in the foreign exchange market imply an equivalent reduction in operational deposits of the

banking sector and the monetary base therefore tends to fall. In the event of upward pressure on sterling, intervention would tend to increase the monetary base since the Bank would be compelled to sell sterling on the foreign exchanges. It might be argued that the authorities could *sterilize* the effect of sterling inflows by open market sales of securities. However, as argued earlier, increased sales of securities imply an increase in the rate of interest which would tend to further increase upward pressure on the sterling exchange rate.

Two conclusions emerge from the above discussions: the monetary base is not exogenously determined by the authorities, and the money supply multiplier is an incomplete model of the money supply process. The first of these conclusions simply tells us that the monetary base is not under the direct control of the authorities unless they are prepared to allow interest rates and the exchange rate to be entirely determined by market forces. Given that the authorities clearly regard the interest rate and the exchange rate as instruments of economic policy, it is inconceivable that they would allow them to be entirely determined by the market. The second conclusion follows from the first and tells us that the monetary base is functionally related to changes in the rate of interest. Given that the two ratios which determine the money supply multiplier also depend on the rate of interest, it follows that the three determinants of the money supply in the multiplier model are interdependent. Any attempt by the authorities to offset changes in the c and r ratios by changes in the monetary base to achieve a particular money supply target are, therefore, likely to lead to further changes in c and r ratios!

The rules versus discretion debate

The rules versus discretion debate is one of the most enduring issues in monetary policy. It focuses on whether monetary policy should be conducted according to established rules, known in advance to all, or at the discretion of policy-makers. In the early years of the debate it was argued that the case for discretion in policy rested on the view that wages and prices adjust slowly in response to shocks such as a sharp increase in the price of oil. The slow adjustment of the economy results in lost output and unemployed resources. An activist policy allows freedom to vary policy to speed up adjustment and move the economy towards full employment or away from inflation. The counter-argument was that discretion succeeded only in raising the long-run rate of inflation and that a policy rule, such as a constant rate of growth for the money supply, facilitated a more effective adjustment and promoted a more stable economy.

The debate has now moved on and it is accepted that if economic outcomes (such as the rate of inflation) depend on expectations about future policies, then credible pre-commitment to a rule can have favourable effects on the economic outcomes that discretionary policies cannot have. In other words, a credible rule can influence expectations and in so doing can deliver more favourable outcomes than are possible when the authorities initiate discretionary changes in policy.

To understand how this can happen, imagine if the authorities announce a target for inflation for the 12-month period ahead which is below the existing rate of inflation. If the pre-commitment to deliver a lower rate of inflation is credible, that is, if it is widely believed that the authorities will adjust policy so as to deliver the target, this will influence wage and price setting to take account of the lower expected rate of inflation. As pressure on prices and wages falls, the authorities have an incentive to renege on their commitment to a lower rate of inflation, since an expansionary policy in these circumstances will boost output with little immediate impact on inflation. Economists refer to policy announcements that are subject to change as the *time inconsistency* problem.

The existence of time inconsistency raises a dilemma for the authorities. If their policy announcements are not deemed to be credible, they will have no effect on expectations and it will therefore be more difficult to deliver the target outcome without reducing output and increasing unemployment. Any policy that is not time consistent will therefore be unable to deliver favourable policy outcomes, that is, low inflation at a low cost in terms of output and unemployment. However, if the authorities pre-commit to a credible policy, favourable outcomes follow naturally because of the effect the pre-commitment has on inflation expectations. In other words, announcing a rule and sticking to it delivers favourable outcomes that cannot be achieved when the authorities exercise discretion.

This conclusion is now widely accepted, but several questions immediately present themselves: what should be the ultimate goal of policy, what variable should the authorities target to achieve their goal and how can they enhance the credibility of pre-commitments to the target? The first of these questions is easily answered. For most central banks, the overriding priority is to maintain low and stable inflation. It is well known that inflation imposes costs on the economy in terms of resource misallocation and so on, but it is also a widely held view that an environment of low and stable inflation is more likely to encourage investment and growth. The problem for central banks is therefore how best to achieve the aim, and this involves an analysis of the issues raised in the remaining two questions. We consider each in turn.

Monetary policy targets

Monetary targeting

One of the earliest proposals for a rule, particularly associated with Milton Friedman, was to establish a *monetary rule*. Such a rule involves setting a target rate of growth for the money supply. Monetary targeting can be analysed within the quantity theory framework. For example, if over some given period, V_Y is expected to fall by 1%, the target rate of inflation is 2% and Y is expected to grow by $2\frac{1}{2}$%, the quantity theory predicts that the inflation target will be achieved if the money growth target is fixed (and achieved) at roughly $5\frac{1}{2}$%.

In fact, it is no longer thought that inflation can be controlled directly by setting target rates of growth for the money supply. This does not necessarily imply that the quantity theory of money does not predict a causal link from money to prices. The predictions of the quantity theory are much more reliable in the *long run*, but over the *medium term* the relationship between money and prices is less precise. Because of this, as the following discussion shows, there are severe problems with monetary targeting and with interpreting the components of the quantity theory of money.

Problems with monetary targeting

Our simple example above assumes that variables in the quantity theory equation can be accurately measured. In reality the growth of output depends on the availability of factors of production and their productivity. These are very difficult to measure and forecast, especially if an economy is undergoing structural change. In the UK in the 1980s and 1990s structural changes occurred because of privatization and deregulation, trade union reform and so on. In the early years of the new millennium other structural changes are taking place, such as the rising number of school-leavers entering further and higher education rather than the labour market.

It is also unclear which definition of money most accurately captures the causal link from money to prices. Narrow definitions of money are more easily controlled, but they omit some liabilities of the banking system that have an important bearing on inflation. Divisia attempts to weight the various components of any definition of money according to their impact on prices. However, identifying appropriate weights has proved problematical and there is no agreement that divisia offers any advantages over more conventional measures of money.

Deregulation and development of the financial sector have also caused problems in predicting velocity of circulation. Financial deregulation usually results in a permanent reduction in velocity of circulation of broad money. To the extent that this happens, an increase in broad money growth might not imply an increase in the future rate of inflation. If there are frequent and unexpected changes in velocity, pursuing an inflexible money growth target can cause short-run swings in interest rates and real output as demand for money changes but supply of money does not respond.

Another problem with monetary targeting is that even if velocity is stable in the long run, short-run changes in velocity will cause unanticipated changes in interest rates. A change in velocity implies a change in demand for money and, with supply changing according to some fixed rule, interest rates will adjust in order to maintain equilibrium between demand for money and supply of money. Such unanticipated changes in interest rates will adversely affect investment and might have other adverse consequences on the economy through their effect on the exchange rate.

Exchange rate targeting

An exchange rate target simply involves fixing the external value of one currency against another, low-

inflation, currency. Over time this will result in the prices of tradeable goods and domestic inflation converging towards foreign levels. Maintaining the fixed exchange rate implies that domestic monetary policy must follow the monetary policy of the anchor currency, otherwise there will be pressure on the exchange rate.

A major advantage of exchange rate targeting over monetary targeting is that unanticipated changes in money demand have no effect on domestic interest rates because they will be matched by an equivalent and offsetting change in money supply through capital flows. Exchange rate targets are also transparent and easy for the general public to understand. To the extent that exchange rate targets are credible, they therefore provide information on which expectations can be based. The major problem with exchange rate targets is that they leave the authorities powerless to deal with adverse shocks to the economy, such as a deterioration in the terms of trade or a loss of export markets. Unless wages and prices are flexible, an adverse shock must be borne by the domestic economy and will result in declining output and rising unemployment. This will continue until the economy slows up sufficiently and wages and prices fall far enough to restore competitiveness.

Inflation rate targeting

When the authorities target the rate of inflation, the simplest case is when monetary policy is adjusted whenever the forecast rate of inflation rises above the announced target range. If inflation is above the target range, monetary policy is tightened and vice versa. However, central banks that target the rate of inflation have generally adopted a broader approach and, as well as monitoring forecast changes in the rate of inflation, also look at other factors: the overall state of the economy, rates of wage change and so on.

This is a much more flexible approach than a rigid monetary rule. It gives the central bank scope to respond to unanticipated shocks or cyclical changes in the economy which might require an easing or tightening of monetary policy to avoid some adverse effect on the economy. For example, if there is a downturn in economic activity which might develop into a recession, the central bank can cut interest rates to reduce the possibility of this eventuality. In adopting an inflation target which is to be interpreted flexibly, the central bank has some freedom to manoeuvre and is able to respond flexibly to changing circumstances without compromising its inflation target.

To see the advantage of this, consider the effect of a demand-side shock and a supply-side shock. When the economy is subject to a demand-side shock, output and inflation rise and fall together. For example, if there is a sharp fall in the demand for exports, inflation and output fall. In such cases, the optimal response of the central bank is clear and monetary policy should be loosened. Supply-side shocks, on the other hand, move the economy in opposite directions. For example, a sharp rise in the price of oil would push up input prices and would inject an inflationary impetus into the economy. Simultaneously the higher price of oil causes a reduction in aggregate demand and a consequent fall in output and employment. In this case the bank has to decide on the optimal response. Either it can bring inflation down rapidly by a sharp tightening of monetary policy so that the burden of adjustment falls entirely on output, or it can tighten monetary policy less severely so that the burden of adjustment is shared between prices and output. By changing the policy time horizon, the time by which inflation should be back within the target range, the central

bank spreads the output consequences of reducing inflation over a longer time period, thereby reducing the impact on employment, rather than compressing it into a shorter time horizon. Figures 20.6(a) and (b) illustrate the point.

In Figs 20.6(a) and (b), AD and AS are the original aggregate demand and aggregate supply curves. The price level is initially P and output is Y. In Fig. 20.6(a), an unanticipated fall in aggregate demand shifts the aggregate demand to AD_1. As a result prices fall to P_1 and output falls to Y_1. In this case the appropriate response of the authorities is to loosen monetary policy and so move aggregate demand back towards its original position. In Fig. 20.6(b), there is an unanticipated adverse supply shock which reduces aggregate supply to AS_1. In this case the bank has a range of policy responses depending on its priorities. It can tighten monetary policy severely enough so that aggregate demand, and through this, output, fall far enough to preserve price stability (Y_2). Alternatively, it can loosen monetary policy far enough so that output is unchanged but prices are given a further upward twist (P_2). Between these two extremes there exist an infinite number of policy choices which result in the burden of adjustment being shared between output and prices. The distribution of the burden depends on the preferences of the central bank.

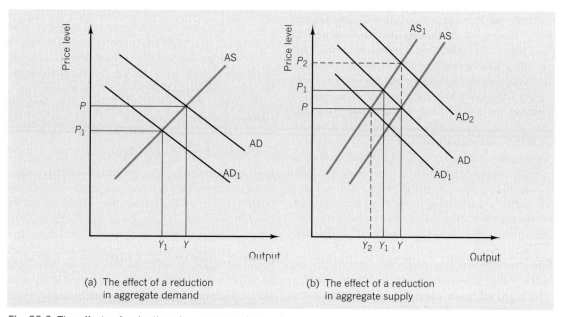

(a) The effect of a reduction in aggregate demand

(b) The effect of a reduction in aggregate supply

Fig. 20.6 The effects of reductions in aggregate demand and supply.

Central bank credibility

Central bank credibility refers to the degree of confidence the public has in the central bank's determination and ability to meet its announced targets. In reality, establishing credibility can sometimes be difficult because, as we have argued above, there are incentives for policy-makers to default on commitments that are widely believed. So how can credibility be improved and maintained?

In establishing and maintaining credibility, the overriding priority is that the authorities must be able to persuade the public that there is no inconsistency between their policy objectives. If policy objectives are inconsistent, any attempt to establish credibility will fail. Most central banks currently emphasize their commitment to price stability as their primary aim and promulgate the view that other aims, such as high and stable levels of employment, will be pursued only to the extent that they do not jeopardize price stability.

There would not seem to be any inconsistency in these objectives, but credibility will be more easily established and maintained in a stable economic environment in which the target rate of inflation is consistently delivered. If there is an economic downturn that monetary policy is unable to correct, it is possible that as unemployment rises the public might form the view that the government will reconsider its policy stance. To the extent that this creates the expectation of a higher rate of inflation, central bank credibility will be compromised. The old adage that 'nothing succeeds like success' is also true of central bank credibility. When the economy is performing well and the central bank is delivering its targets, credibility will be easier to establish than when the economy is not performing well.

As noted above, there are lags before changes in monetary policy take effect. In the meantime, inflation might be subject to change because of unforeseen events that make control in the short term difficult. Yet the central bank will be judged by outcomes, and where these differ from the central bank's announced targets, its credibility might be damaged. The central bank can minimize the damage by ensuring that the public is fully informed of events and why the measures it has taken are consistent with the announced policy objective.

Transparency in monetary policy

Central bank credibility is far easier to establish when policy is *transparent*. With respect to monetary policy, transparency is important whenever there is incomplete or imperfect information. Information might be incomplete or imperfect with respect to:

- the central bank's objectives;
- understanding the links between policy changes and the central bank's objectives; and/or
- the information the central bank has available on which to base policy changes.

We consider each in turn.

The central bank's objectives

As far as the objectives of the central bank are concerned, transparency involves more than the central bank simply stating its objectives. The public might be uncertain about the true nature of the objectives or the extent to which the central bank will trade off one objective (inflation) against another objective (unemployment). Transparency with respect to objectives requires the central bank to pursue clear objectives for aggregates which are familiar to the public. The public can then readily observe the behaviour of these target aggregates and judge for themselves the extent of transparency. Transparency is most likely to be achieved when the objectives of the central bank are either enshrined in its constitution or imposed on it by government. Currently many central banks pursue an inflation target (see p. 388). In some cases, such as the European Central Bank (ECB), the target value for inflation is set out in their constitution. In other cases, such as the Bank of England, the target rate of inflation is set by government.

The role of policy changes

Even if the central bank's objectives are clearly understood, transparency is not guaranteed, since the public might not understand the operation of the techniques used to achieve the target. For example, if the main policy instrument is interest rates, how big a change in interest rates is required each time the projected value of inflation deviates by $x\%$ from its target rate? Little can be said about this, since the relationship is imperfectly understood even by economists! What we can say is that transparency will be easier to achieve if interest rates move predictably in response to projected deviations in the rate of inflation from target.

The importance of information

The public might understand the central bank's objectives and the expected behaviour of interest rates in response to projected values for the rate of inflation, yet policy transparency might still not be achieved if the public do not have access to the same information as the central bank. For example, if the central bank has access to information that implies a slowdown in the economy and a significant reduction in the rate of inflation, the expected policy response would be a cut in interest rates. However, if the public do not have access to the same information they might misunderstand the motives behind the cut in interest rates. Ignorance of the expected recession might lead the public to form the erroneous view that policy was jeopardizing the inflation objective.

In reality, lack of information might not pose a serious problem if the public are informed of the reasons behind monetary policy decisions. It is for this reason that many central banks publish minutes of their monetary policy committee meetings. These minutes explain the information on which policy changes are based and the reasons for the particular extent of the policy change. Other information is often also made available to the public, such as the Inflation Report published by the Bank of England which details the bank's forecast of inflation for the period ahead.

Techniques of monetary policy

Over the years, a variety of techniques have been used to implement monetary policy. However, we can group the techniques of monetary policy into two broad approaches: those which impose direct controls on the banking sector, and market-based instruments which focus on interest rates. Both have been used by the Bank of England (as well as other central banks) to implement monetary policy.

Direct controls

Direct controls focus on the growth of bank deposits and often involve legal measures specifying that financial institutions are required to hold part of their assets in a defined form such as cash or other liquid assets, usually referred to as *reserve assets*. The central bank can then seek to control the growth of bank deposits by limiting the availability of reserve assets. There are various ways in which this can be done.

1 *Special deposits*. One technique used in the past was to impose *special deposits* on the banking sector. These deposits were 'frozen' at the central bank and the banking sector had no access to them (although they continued to earn interest at the treasury bill rate) until they were released by the central bank. A call for special deposits implied a reduction in the banks' operational deposits at the central bank and this again put pressure on the banking sector to reduce its lending. This technique was abandoned in 1971.

2 *Credit ceilings*. The central bank has also used credit ceilings, known as *supplementary special deposits*, to limit the growth of bank lending. These were imposed on the banking sector when their liabilities (bank deposits) rose above a specified level. In such cases, banks were required to make *non-interest bearing deposits* with the central bank in proportion to the growth of their liabilities. This technique was abandoned in 1980.

The principal advantage of direct controls is that they provide the central bank with a way of controlling the quantity or maximum price of credit. This might be particularly useful in a temporary crisis. They might also provide the only practicable way to implement monetary policy when financial markets are undeveloped. However, there are severe problems associated with these direct techniques of monetary control. Probably the major disadvantage is that they tend to be ineffective because they encourage *disintermediation*, that is, the diversion of business away from the regulated sector to unregulated sectors of the economy. This must be inefficient because if the unregulated sector was operating efficiently, it would already be providing a greater proportion of the business provided by the regulated sector! When direct controls are in place, savers and borrowers search for ways of circumventing the regulations. One obvious route through which regulations at home can be bypassed is by transferring business abroad. Regulations are also inefficient because they tend to stifle competition between banks and limit the benefits to borrowers and depositors.

Indirect controls

Indirect controls exert their influence through channels that leave the financial institutions free of direct controls (other than those necessary for prudential control of the banking system). Reserve asset ratios were abolished in 1981 and in more recent years the Bank of England has exercised control by measures which focus on the availability of *base money* (notes and coin held by the banking sector plus operational deposits at the Bank of England). Again these might take a variety of forms.

1　*Reserve requirements.* Reserve requirements impose restrictions on the form in which banks must hold their assets. They usually involve a requirement that total assets can be no greater than the maximum value of some defined group of assets (reserve assets). For example, if reserve assets are defined as the monetary base (see p. 385), then total assets can be no greater than some multiple of the monetary base.

2　*Funding.* During the 1980s, the Bank of England exerted its influence on the banking sector by *funding* the national debt. This technique involved the Bank in issuing fewer short-term securities and more long-term securities. Because treasury bills constituted part of the liquid assets ratio but long-term securities did not, the aim was to leave the banks short of liquid assets and compel them to cut their lending.

3　*Interest rates.* The Bank of England has considerable influence over short-term rates of interest because of the role it performs in the domestic money markets. As banker to the government and to the banks, it is able to forecast fairly accurately the daily flows of funds between the government's account and the accounts of the banks. When more money flows from the banks' accounts to the government's account the market will be short of funds; when funds flow in the opposite direction, the market will have a surplus of funds. The Bank of England operates on a daily basis to smooth these flows of funds but tends to conduct its open-market operations (see p. 420) in such a way as to leave the market short of funds. It then relieves this shortage by lending to the different institutions at a *repo* rate (official rate) of its own choosing. For example, if the Bank of England *sells* gilts (government bonds) in the open market there will be a transfer of deposits from the banks' operational balances at the Bank of England into the government's own account as cheques authorizing payment are cleared. As operational balances fall, banks are forced to borrow from the Bank of England.

Rather than dealing with every individual bank, the Bank of England uses the discount houses as an intermediary. The discount houses have borrowing facilities at the Bank of England and when the market is short of funds the discount houses are 'forced into the Bank'. The Bank of England provides them with cash either by re-discounting bills held by the discount houses or by lending direct. When the Bank changes the rate implied in the price at which it re-discounts bills or the repo rate at which it lends, all institutions quickly follow the Bank's lead and adjust their own rates of interest.

Central banks in developed economies rely almost entirely on indirect controls. Such controls are effective because they are non-selective and affect all institutions across the entire spectrum. For example, when interest rates are rising, this affects all institutions in exactly the same way. Indirect controls therefore avoid all of the problems associated with direct controls.

UK monetary policy since the 1950s

Monetary control in the 1950s and 1960s

In the 1950s and 1960s the Keynesian view of money was the consensus view. There was a widespread belief that money growth exerted its influence on the economy through changes in the rate of interest which stimulated changes in the rate of investment. However, monetary policy was viewed as having a weak effect, since the available empirical evidence strongly suggested that investment was interest-inelastic. The prevailing view was that investment by firms in fixed assets and stocks, if it was influenced at all by monetary factors, was influenced more by the *availability of credit* rather than by its *nominal cost*. Consequently monetary policy consisted primarily of ceilings on lending, although open-market operations and special deposits were also used during this period.

Competition and Credit Control (CCC), 1971

In 1971 the focus of monetary policy switched decisively. Interest rates were, ostensibly at least, to be market determined rather than imposed by the authorities. Furthermore, regulations were introduced compelling banks to observe a minimum 12.5% *reserve assets ratio* between eligible reserve assets and eligible liabilities. The former were defined as private sector non-bank deposits and building society deposits. The latter included balances at the Bank of England, money at call and short notice with the discount houses, British Government and Northern Ireland treasury bills, local authority bills and commercial bills eligible for rediscount at the Bank.

Whenever eligible reserve assets fell below the 12.5% minimum level, it followed that banks would be compelled to reduce their lending. Whenever it wanted to tighten monetary policy, the Bank of England could always engineer such an event, for example by calling for special deposits. In reality, although rates of interest were supposed to be market determined, the Bank of England frequently intervened to leave the banks short of funds, leaving it free to adjust interest rates.

Competition and Credit Control was in place for less than a decade. It failed to provide an effective framework for monetary policy for a variety of reasons. For example, it was unclear whether interest rates were market determined or whether the authorities were setting interest rates. (We have already argued that there are clear benefits arising from transparency.) Probably of more significance is that the regulations applied only to defined institutions and there was an explosion of growth in the unregulated sector. Rising inflation in the 1970s (see p. 445) also caused problems because it led to rising public sector borrowing and, rather than disrupt long-term interest rates through funding, the government borrowed short-term thus ensuring an adequate supply of liquidity to the banking sector. Despite these problems, it was the abolition of exchange controls in 1979 that finally brought the framework to an end. Capital flows between countries increased (see Chapter 26) to the extent that effective monetary control became impossible, since residents were enabled to open overseas bank accounts and to borrow abroad for current spending in the UK.

The medium-term financial strategy (MTFS), 1980

In March 1980 the government unveiled its new approach to monetary control, the *medium-term financial strategy* (MTFS). The MTFS was designed to provide a framework of control within which money growth could be targeted over a four-year period. The emphasis of control shifted in two ways:

1 from a short-term to a medium-term perspective; and

2 from controlling the availability of reserve assets to controlling the growth of bank assets, the so-called 'counterparts' to the money stock.

The rationale for shifting to a medium-term perspective is an admission that it is impossible to exercise control over money growth over a short time horizon. The rationale for controlling the counterparts to the money stock reflects the fact that, apart from the narrowest measures of money, definitions of the money stock focus on bank deposits. There is a famous banking maxim that 'every loan creates a deposit' because every loan granted by a bank is redeposited within the banking sector after being spent by the borrower. Controlling the counterparts of the money stock was therefore seen as a way of controlling money growth. In the UK, the authorities attempted to control growth of the (now defunct) broad measure of money known as sterling M3 (£M3). The MTFS set declining target rates of growth for £M3 annually so that as one year in the four-year cycle passed, another year began.

Bank deposits consist of lending to the *government*, the *private sector* and the *overseas sector*. The sum of lending to each of these forms the counterparts to the money stock, and the MTFS included specific measures to control each of these individually.

- Government expenditure was to be progressively reduced to rein back the PSBR. This was made easier because the proceeds from privatization were treated not, as might be expected, as a means of financing the PSBR, but as a means of reducing it!

- Debt sales to the non-bank private sector were encouraged by adjusting interest rates to the level required to persuade the non-bank private sector to take up offers of treasury bills.

■ Exchange rate policy was to be used to influence the external and foreign currency counterparts of the money stock.

Additional measures, designed to improve the effectiveness of monetary control by addressing some of the problems associated with Competition and Credit Control, were introduced in August 1981. Thenceforth banking regulations applied to all monetary institutions within the monetary sector. This is to avoid the emergence of disintermediation. The reserve assets ratio was abolished and a minimum figure (now abolished) was established for operational deposits.

The MTFS proved no more effective as a framework for monetary policy than did Competition and Credit Control. Monetary growth frequently exceeded the target growth rate and, in an attempt to improve control, target rates of growth for M0 were introduced in 1984. By 1987 targets for £M3 were abandoned, although the Bank of England continues to 'monitor' changes in M0. There are many reasons why it proved difficult to restrain £M3 within its target range. One reason is that private sector borrowing proved less sensitive to rising interest rates than anticipated. However, the main reason is that deregulation of the financial sector and product innovation distorted the money aggregates to the extent that they became unreliable as indicators of money growth.

Exchange rate and inflation rate targeting

As confidence in the efficacy of targeting money growth waned, the authorities turned to the exchange rate as an anchor for monetary policy. In the late 1980s sterling shadowed the Deutsche Mark before the official announcement in October 1990 that sterling was to join the ERM at a rate of £1 = DM2.95. It soon became clear that at this exchange rate sterling was hopelessly overvalued on the foreign exchanges, and in September 1992, with the UK deep in recession and interest rates at 15% to preserve the exchange rate, the Chancellor of the Exchequer bowed to the inevitable and withdrew sterling from the ERM. The following day interest rates were reduced to 10% and, free of exchange rate constraints, the focus of policy changed.

In October 1992, the Chancellor announced that monetary policy would henceforth target the rate of inflation. The first steps towards increasing transparency and credibility quickly followed when, later the same month, the Chancellor announced that the Governor of the Bank of England would produce a regular report on progress towards the inflation target. The *Inflation Report* is compiled by the Bank in the belief that it will be more credible than if it is produced by the government. In 1994, transparency was further increased when it was announced that minutes of meetings between the Chancellor and the Governor of the Bank of England to review the performance of monetary policy would be published. The Inflation Report and the Minutes of the MPC meetings (see below) remain an important mechanism through which the Bank communicates its views and actions to the general public.

The inflation target was initially set in the range 1–4% per annum, but in 1995 it was announced that a point target of 2.5% was to be introduced. It remains at this level.

Operational independence of the Bank of England

In furtherance of the aim of achieving credibility, on 6 May 1997, the Bank of England was given operational responsibility for setting short-term interest rates to achieve the inflation target, retained by the Labour government at 2.5%. However, the incoming Chancellor, Gordon Brown, made it clear that the government would retain a national interest in controlling inflation. This is effectively an escape clause allowing it to overrule the Bank's interest rates decisions in pursuit of the inflation target when it deems such action necessary. The government has not specified any formal process for implementing the escape clause, nor defined a set of conditions under which the Bank would be overruled. Nevertheless the point target now has a one percentage point threshold either side and if inflation breaches this, the Monetary Policy Committee (which decides on interest rate changes, see below) is required to publish an open letter outlining the reasons for the deviation and to explain the policy changes to be adopted so as to bring inflation back to target.

The Monetary Policy Committee (MPC), with a membership of nine and a quorum of six, meets monthly at the Bank of England to decide on the timing and extent of any change in the rate of interest for the month ahead. The broad aim is to keep the growth of demand in line with supply-side capacity as reflected by consistently low inflation. Subject to the primacy of hitting the inflation target, the MPC is required to support the government's economic policy, including its objectives for growth and employment. Monetary policy is therefore loosened or tightened in order to moderate the fluctuations that occur over the business cycle. It is anticipated that the target rate of inflation is consistent with delivering steadier growth, higher levels of employment and rising living standards into the medium and longer term.

The making of monetary policy in the UK

The making of monetary policy in the UK follows a clearly defined monthly cycle. Decisions are taken by a simple majority vote. The timetable for a typical monthly round of the MPC is set out in Table 20.2.

The euro

At midnight on 31 December 2001 the euro replaced 11 national currencies. For the first time in history, currencies which had not been debased through inflation had their legal tender states revoked. The adoption of the euro was the biggest event in the global financial system since the collapse of the Bretton Woods fixed exchange rate system in the early 1970s.

The euro changeover

It is widely agreed that the changeover from national currencies to the euro was a great success. The confusion and long queues outside retail outlets and railway stations, causing long delays which some had predicted, simply failed to materialize. Instead the euro was embraced with enthusiasm and appeared to cause few problems. No doubt this was partly due to

Table 20.2 Typical monthly round of the MPC.

Briefing	
Throughout the month	Circulation of briefing material and analysis of data releases and market developments by staff
Friday before policy meeting	Half-day pre-MPC meeting
Monday/Tuesday	Staff undertake follow-up work requested by the Committee
Policy meeting	
Wednesday	Policy meeting commences early afternoon. Committee identifies the key issues and debates their implications for inflation prospects
Thursday	Policy meeting concludes. Committee members provide their assessment of the appropriate policy stance and vote on the level of interest rates. Policy announcement at noon. Decision implemented immediately in a round of open-market operations at 12.15
Minutes	
Week following policy meeting	Draft of the Minutes circulated and comments from Committee Members incorporated
Monday (second week after policy meeting)	Committee meets and signs off the Minutes
Wednesday (two weeks after policy meeting)	Publication of the Minutes at 09.30

Source: Bean (2001).

the long gestation period before the introduction of euro notes and coin. The euro has been in existence as a unit of account since 1 January 1999, but did not exist as a physical currency until two years later. During that time, dual pricing existed and retailers displayed prices in local currency and simultaneously in euros. Settlement of all transactions prior to the changeover was, of course, in local currency.

A common criticism of the changeover was that businesses used the occasion to mark prices upwards. There is some possibility that this might have happened. Euro area inflation in January 2002 was 2.7%, up from the 2% recorded in the previous December. However, the issue is not so clear cut as these figures might imply. Some rounding upwards of prices was inevitable. For example, the conversion rate for Deutsche marks was €1 = DM1.95583 and for French francs €1 = FF6.55957. With such rates, a straight conversion from one price to another is a near impossibility. However, there is no reason to believe that all retailers would round prices upwards rather than being forced by competition to round them downwards! In fact, the increase in the euro inflation rate between December 2001 and January 2002 was in line with expected seasonal changes and increased fuel prices. A similar monthly increase was recorded in the UK for inflation in January 2002 and an even higher monthly increase was recorded in Sweden.

Advantages of a single currency

The creation of a single currency has several potential benefits which are briefly reviewed here.

Lower costs of exchange

When goods are imported the trader receiving the goods must obtain foreign currency to pay the exporter. Banks will happily supply foreign currency, but they will levy a service charge for the transaction. For the economy as a whole these charges are sizeable and, in general, they will be passed on to consumers through higher prices. For the EU as a whole the transactions costs associated with intra-community trade are estimated at 0.4% of EU GDP. These figures give an idea of the resource savings to those countries which adopted the euro and provide an encouraging argument about why these resource savings might be reflected in lower prices within the euro area.

Reduced exchange rate uncertainty

Inside the euro area, exchange rates are irrevocably fixed and there is no uncertainty over future rates of exchange. This is important because traders often negotiate contracts for delivery and payment stretching six months and longer into the future. Outside the euro area exchange rate risk exists for traders involved in international transactions. For example, if at the time a contract was agreed for $3m between a UK importer and a US exporter, the exchange rate for the US dollar against sterling was $1.60, and this fell to $1.55 by the time the contract became due for settlement, the importer would face an unanticipated increase in costs of more than £60,000.[5] It is, of course, possible for traders to hedge the foreign exchange risk in the forward market where rates of exchange can be agreed today for delivery of currency at some future point in time. However, such arrangements are costly and so raise the cost of a transaction. A different alternative might be for traders to find a domestic producer instead of trading internationally. The implication is that exchange rate risk might raise the cost of trading internationally or discourage international trade altogether. To the extent that this is the case, a single currency will reduce the cost of transacting business across frontiers (because of the costless elimination of exchange rate risk) and will increase international trade with all the associated benefits of comparative advantage. These advantages include the increased variety of products that become available, lower prices due to competition (because price differences between markets will no longer be masked by being quoted in different currencies) and greater economies of scale because of the larger market.

Eliminating competitive devaluations

Between the two world wars, several European countries engaged in what became known as 'competitive devaluations' when a devaluation in one country was matched by a devaluation in other countries. While such competitive devaluations have been avoided since that time, the possibility that they might recur still exists; in fact all devaluations adversely affect inflationary expectations in the devaluing country. Given the increasing scale of intra-European trade, any return to competitive devaluations (or any other form of protectionism) would have devastating effects on Europe's economies. The possibility of these disruptions disappears when a common currency exists.

Preventing speculative attacks

Where different currencies exist, there also exists the possibility of a speculative attack on one or more currencies. The problem is exacerbated when a fixed exchange rate exists because speculators have a one-way bet. If the currency they have bet against is not devalued, all they have lost is their transactions costs on the deal, whereas betting correctly can result in spectacular gains. Governments can defend currencies against such attacks, but this often involves raising interest rates which reduces business investment and hampers economic growth. The events leading up to sterling's withdrawal from the ERM provide a graphic example (see Chapter 29). To the extent that exchange rate disruption is avoided, trade, investment and economic growth will be encouraged. There will also be resource savings, since it will no longer be necessary for the authorities to hold reserves of foreign currency to defend the exchange rate and lower interest rates because higher rates will no longer be needed to defend the exchange rate. There is an opportunity cost associated with acquiring the former, and the latter will adversely impact on investment and growth. These problems are not completely avoided by adopting a single currency because not all trading partners will be included in the single currency. However, their impact is considerably diminished.

Disadvantages of a single currency

The advantages of adopting the euro seem encouraging, but these advantages do not come without costs. It is to a consideration of these that we now turn.

Loss of independent monetary policy

Countries participating in the euro relinquish the right to implement an independent domestic monetary policy. Instead they accept the monetary policy implemented by the ECB. However, this 'one size fits all' monetary policy might not suit all countries equally, for example when there is a recession in one country but not in others. If that country is outside the euro area then the country's central bank could reduce interest rates and stimulate economic activity. However, the ECB is unlikely to respond in this way if the recession is only country-specific because this will raise inflation throughout the Union. At present

unemployment is rising in several countries in the euro area, including France and Germany, but the ECB has not cut interest rates because of the impact this might have on the rate of inflation (see below).

The ECB has announced that monetary policy will target the rate of inflation. In other words, changes in monetary policy will be initiated whenever the forecast rate of inflation for the euro area as a whole rises above the ECB's target rate of 2%. Monetary policy actions for the ECB, as with the Bank of England, will involve changes in the rate of interest. However, changes in the rate of interest might not affect all countries equally. It has been suggested that at present in some countries (Germany, the UK, the Netherlands, Austria, Belgium and Finland) changes in interest rates might take up to three years before exerting their full impact on the economy, while in others (Denmark, France, Italy, Portugal, Spain and Sweden) the effect of changes in interest rates is felt much sooner – perhaps within 15–18 months. Furthermore, the effect of changes in the rate of interest is, at present, almost twice as strong in the first group as in the second. The implication is that in the euro area, a tightening of monetary policy would take more time to affect some countries and would exert a stronger impact in some countries than in others. Again a 'one size fits all' monetary policy might be less effective than the policy an independent country could pursue.

In part, the different effects of monetary policy in the UK compared with some other European countries stems from the fact that there are important differences in the size and role of the property market in the transmission mechanism. Typically UK mortgage finance is based on a variable interest rate so that changes in official interest rates are quickly reflected in mortgage rates. The effect on the economy is further reinforced because the UK has a relatively high rate of owner occupation and housing-related debt (outstanding mortgage debt is equivalent to about 90% of GDP). The effects of monetary policy in the UK might therefore be relatively long-lasting because of the effect of interest rate changes on property prices and through this on the wealth portfolio of property owners. There is ample evidence from the UK that these wealth effects exert a powerful influence on consumer expenditure. However, because of differences in the extent of home ownership and the types of mortgage finance, these effects are not uniform across member states. It is certainly not at all clear that a 'one size fits all' monetary policy will be appropriate for all countries within the euro area at all times; in particular it is unclear whether such a policy will be appropriate for the UK should it decide to adopt the single currency.

Loss of an independent exchange rate policy

Similarly, when a common currency exists, countries lose the ability to devalue the exchange rate to offset a loss of competitiveness. The exchange rate, like the rate of interest, is a powerful weapon for bringing about changes in demand and economic adjustment. In the event of a balance of payments deficit inside a common currency area, the burden of adjustment is thrown on to the domestic economy. For example, cutting aggregate demand to reduce imports and curb any price inflation will be reflected in lower domestic output and employment. This will continue until rising unemployment depresses real wages far enough to restore competitiveness. Adjustment is less painfully achieved when the rate of exchange can be devalued to restore competitiveness.

Loss of an independent fiscal policy

It might be argued that fiscal policy could fill the vacuum left by loss of monetary policy sovereignty and exchange rate policy sovereignty. However, since the maximum allowable budget deficit for any country in the euro area is 3% of that country's GDP,

scope for an active fiscal policy is clearly limited. It will be limited even further if current thinking on harmonizing taxation within the euro zone is adopted.

Lack of convergence

Loss of policy sovereignty might not be so important if economies are reasonably convergent, in which case country-specific shocks are less likely to occur. However, the convergence criteria agreed at Maastricht in 1992 focused entirely on 'nominal' variables. The problem for the UK is that the business cycle (a 'real' variable) is not entirely convergent with business cycles in Europe – even though on the nominal criteria agreed at Maastricht the degree of convergence in the UK compares favourably with convergence in many other European countries.

Figure 20.7 shows the *output gap* (the difference between actual and trend output) for Britain and the euro area countries between 1995 and 2004. On this indicator of convergence the UK is clearly out of step with the euro area. Therefore, a monetary policy which suits other European countries is unlikely at the present time to suit the UK. For example, if the output gap is negative and widening in the UK, because actual output is falling below trend output, the appropriate response would be a loosening of monetary policy in the UK. However, if, at the same time, the output gap for the rest of Europe were negligible, as in the period 2000–02, there would be no policy response from the ECB. Until there is clear evidence

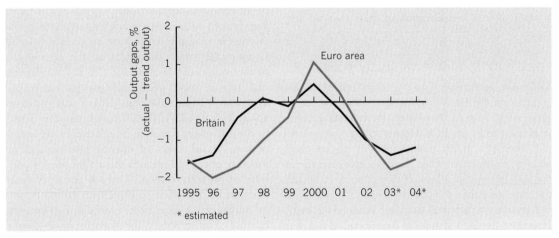

Fig. 20.7 Output gaps in Britain and the euro area.
Sources: Eurostat and OECD (various).

that business cycles are convergent, joining the euro area and accepting a Europe-wide monetary policy may well impose heavy economic costs on the UK.

Conclusion

A number of conclusions might be drawn from the UK experience of money growth and monetary control over the last three decades.

1 Financial innovation and deregulation make it impossible to define a set of assets which alone function as money. This is the major reason the broad money aggregates have been subjected to continuous redefinition.

2 Controversy remains about how useful the definitions of money are. In the UK one measure of narrow money (M0) and one measure of broad money (M4) are monitored. However, different measures of money are published in different countries and the accepted view is that when interpreting monetary conditions, definitions of money do not always include all of the relevant variables. There is also a view that weighted measures of the money stock (Divisia) might be more useful than 'simple sum' measures.

3 Doubt remains as to whether the direction of causation is from money to prices or from prices to money. However, growing evidence does support the view that the velocity of circulation of money follows a relatively stable trend, though there are short-run fluctuations about this trend.

4 Controlling a particular money aggregate is difficult because of financial innovation, deregulation and disintermediation. Monetary control is especially difficult because of disintermediation (see also Chapter 21).

5 The focus of monetary policy has switched from controlling intermediate variables such as the money stock or the exchange rate which were formally thought to be linked to the rate of inflation, to direct targeting of the rate of inflation.

6 Monetary policy actions focus on changes in the rate of interest which affect all institutions simultaneously and equally.

7 There are a number of clear advantages from adopting a single currency, though these do not come without costs and the latter may prove excessive unless business cycles become convergent.

Key points

- Money functions as a unit of account, a medium of exchange and a store of value.

- Money avoids the inefficiency of a barter system, permitting greater specialization and associated scale economies.

- M0 is the official definition of money which most closely corresponds to the idea of a 'cash base'.

- Deposits at financial institutions are the most important component of broad money.

- Definitions of money are constantly evolving because of financial deregulation and innovation.

- Monetary policy is most effective when it is both credible and transparent.

- Since 1992, the Bank of England has adopted an inflation target as the nominal anchor for monetary policy.

- The Bank of England was granted operational independence on 6 May 1997.

- In 11 Member States (now 12 with Greece), national currencies were replaced by the euro at midnight on 31 December 2001, and the UK must carefully assess the costs and benefits of possible entry.

Now try the self-check questions for this chapter on the Companion Website. You will also find up-to-date facts and case materials.

Notes

1. It is important to understand that in arguing that velocity is stable, the monetarists are not arguing that it is constant. Instead they have always claimed that velocity changes only slowly over time and in a predictable way. In this sense it can be regarded as stable from one time period to the next. We shall see later that this has important implications for policy purposes.

2. The quantity theory states that $MV_Y = PY$. If we multiply the average price of final output by the volume of final output we obtain GNP. The quantity theory can therefore be written as $MV_Y = GNP$ and hence $V_Y = GNP/M$. The problem is which measure of money do we use? If an inappropriate aggregate for M is substituted, the value obtained for V_Y will be inaccurate. Economists cannot agree on an appropriate definition of money and this has caused problems with attempts to test the stability of V_Y.

3. For example, a *consol* (an irredeemable bond) issued at 3% with a par value of £1m pays its owner £30,000 per annum. If the current market price of the consol is less than par, for example £0.9m, then the market rate of interest is $0.03/0.9 = 3.33\%$. Hence there is an *inverse relationship* between bond prices and the rate of interest.

4. It is sometimes argued that in the extreme a *liquidity trap* exists so that any change in the money supply leaves interest rates unchanged. Since the Keynesian transmission mechanism is through changes in interest rates, in this extreme situation an increase in money growth has no effect on the price level (P) or real output (Y). The increase in money growth has therefore been completely absorbed into idle balances, i.e. its effects have been offset by a reduction in the velocity of circulation. In other words, the increase in money supply is matched by an increase in the demand for money.

5. The current sterling value of the contract is $(\$3m/1.60)(£1) = £1,875,000$ and at the time of settlement the value of the contract is $(\$3m/1.55)(£1) = £1,935,484$.

References and further reading

Bank of England Inflation Reports (various) Supplements to *Bank of England Quarterly Bulletins*.

Bean, C. (2001) The formulation of monetary policy at the Bank of England, *Bank of England Quarterly Bulletin*, Winter.

Bean, C. (2002) The MPC and the UK economy: should we fear the D words? Speech delivered to the Emmanuel Society, *Bank of England Quarterly Bulletin*, Winter.

Chote, R. (1997) Treading the line between credibility and humility, *Financial Times*, 13 June.

European Central Bank (2000) Issues arising from the emergence of electronic money, *Monthly Bulletin*, November.

King, M. (2002) The inflation target ten years on, lecture delivered at the London School of Economics, *Bank of England Quarterly Bulletin*, Winter.

Pool, W. (1999) Monetary policy rules, *Federal Reserve Bank of St Louis*, *Economic Review*, March.

Rossell, M. (1997) Does electronic money mean the death of cash? *Federal Reserve Bank of Dallas, Southwest Economy*, No. 2, March/April.

Chapter 21 Financial institutions and markets

All modern, developed economies have a sophisticated financial system which incorporates both the financial institutions and financial markets. These institutions and markets exist to mediate between those who wish to save or lend and those who wish to borrow or invest. Mediation is necessary because lenders and borrowers have different needs in terms of maturity, liquidity and yield.

Lenders can be expected to prefer to lend for a short term before the loan matures, to get their money back quickly if their own need for liquidity changes, and to receive high returns on their loans. Borrowers can be expected to prefer to borrow over the long term and to offer low returns, though sharing the same desire for liquidity.

The whole process of matching the needs of lenders and borrowers is known as 'financial intermediation' and the institutions which play a part in this process are known as 'financial intermediaries'. Financial markets also play a key role in this system by allowing borrowers to issue IOUs such as bills or bonds which are acceptable to lenders and which can be traded on the secondary markets (i.e. markets dealing in securities which already exist).

Today, this whole financial system is undergoing rapid development and financial markets are becoming ever more complex, offering new types of financial instruments which reduce transactions costs, are more flexible and better targeted, whilst the traditional roles of the financial institutions are becoming increasingly blurred.

The role of the financial system

The basic rationale of a financial system is to bring together those who have accumulated an excess of money and who wish to save with those who have a requirement to borrow in order to finance investment. This process arguably helps to better utilize society's scarce resources, increase productive efficiency and ultimately raise the standard of living. Santomero and Babbel (2001) have usefully summarized this role of the financial system:

> Without a developed financial system, institutions, firms, and households would be forced to operate as self-contained economies. As a result, they could not save without deploying their resources somewhere, and they could not invest without saving from their own current

output. A financial system allows trade between individuals to accomplish both these ends. It allows savers to defer consumption and obtain a return for waiting. Likewise, it permits investors to deploy resources in excess of those that they have available from their own wealth in order to gain the productivity that such investment yields. The economy also gains from the financial system, as both households and firms advance the economy, total output, and economic growth.

Figure 21.1 provides an overview of the structure of the financial system in the UK. Essentially there are three kinds of operator in the UK financial system.

1 *Lenders and borrowers* – these include persons, companies and government.
2 *Financial intermediaries* – consisting of financial institutions which act as intermediaries between

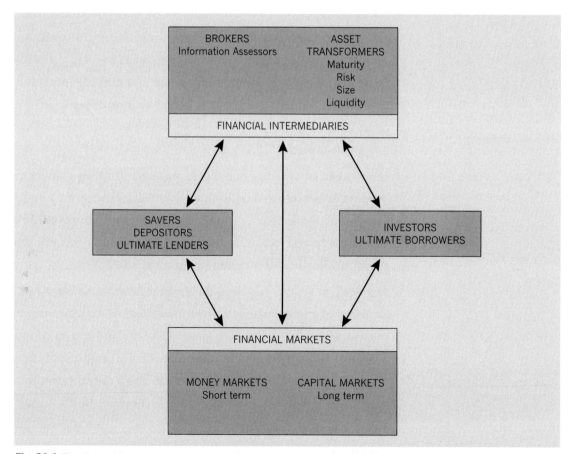

Fig. 21.1 The financial system.

lenders and borrowers. Financial intermediaries take one of two general forms: brokers (bringing together lenders and borrowers by evaluating market information) and asset transformers (transforming the financial assets of lenders by varying the maturity, risk, size and liquidity of the liabilities of borrowers).

3 *Financial markets* – where money is lent and borrowed through the sale and purchase of financial instruments. They play an essential role in reducing the cost of placing, pricing and trading such instruments. In the UK, the financial markets can be defined as short-term money markets and long-term capital markets.

The chapter will now consider in more detail the working of the financial system in the UK, beginning with the various financial instruments that are traded.

Financial claims

Operators within a financial system are essentially buying and selling paper IOUs in the form of financial claims. They are issued by those wishing to borrow and bought by those wishing to lend; lenders then hold a financial claim on the future income of the issuing company or person. Financial claims can be split into financial assets and financial liabilities. The purchaser of a claim holds it as a financial asset, whereas the issuer of the claim holds it as a financial liability.

An obvious example of a financial asset held by most people is a bank deposit account. The depositor holds a financial claim on the bank; and the bank, the borrower of the funds, holds a financial liability. Financial claims can take many forms, which are given the generic name financial instruments.

Characteristics of financial instruments

Financial instruments are classified according to various characteristics, the most important being the level of risk, liquidity and maturity. Other ways of classification may also be used, for example between those instruments that can be traded by third parties (e.g. Treasury bills) and those that cannot (bank deposits), or between those issued with a fixed or variable rate of interest.

Every financial instrument also provides the purchaser with a return or yield. The yield on any financial instrument is related to its characteristics and in general will be lower if the instrument is liquid, has a short time to maturity and has a lower level of risk. Thus, yields are usually higher for long-term investments because lenders require to be compensated for giving up their money for long periods of time and because the risk of default increases with time.

If financial instruments were perfect substitutes for one another, the yields on each would be identical. Any higher yield on one type of instrument would cause lenders to adjust their portfolios in favour of that instrument. The higher demand would then raise the market price of the instrument and thereby reduce the yield. Any variation in yields therefore represents a lack of perfect substitutability between different financial instruments. The various types of financial instruments traded in the UK are discussed in more detail when reviewing the functions of financial markets.

The role of financial intermediaries

Financial intermediaries come between these wishing to save (lend) and those wishing to invest (borrow). They provide a service that yields them a profit, via the *difference* which exists between the (lower) interest they pay to those who lend and the (higher) interest they receive from those who borrow. That they can earn such profits reflects the fact that they are offering a useful service to both lenders and borrowers, which can be disaggregated into at least four separate functions:

- Brokerage
- Maturity transformation
- Risk transformation
- Collection and parcelling – size transformation.

Brokerage

The brokerage function is rather different from the other three, which might all be regarded as including elements of 'asset transformation'. A broker is an intermediary who brings together lenders and borrowers who have complementary needs and does this by assessing and evaluating information. The *lender* may have neither the time nor the ability to undertake costly search activities in order to assess whether a potential borrower is trustworthy, is likely to use the funds for a project that is credible and profitable, and is able to pay the promised interest on the due date. By depositing funds with a financial intermediary the household avoids such information gathering, monitoring and evaluation costs, which are now undertaken by the specialized financial intermediary. The *borrower* needs to know that a promised loan will be received at the time and under the conditions specified in any agreement.

By bringing lenders and borrowers together in these ways, the various information and transactions costs are reduced, so that this brokerage function can command a 'fee'. The size of that fee will, of course, be greater the more difficult and expensive it is for the financial intermediary to develop procedures for evaluating and monitoring borrowers in order to minimize 'default risks'.

The next three functions involve elements of *asset transformation*, in which the liabilities (deposits) are transformed by the financial intermediaries into various types of asset with differing characteristics in terms of maturity, liquidity and risk.

Maturity transformation

Here the financial intermediaries bridge the gap between the desire of lenders to be able to get their money back quickly if needed, and the desire of borrowers to borrow for a long period. In fulfilling this function the financial intermediaries hold liabilities (e.g. deposits) that have a shorter term to maturity than their assets (e.g. loans), i.e. they borrow short and lend long. For example, a building society will typically hold around 70% of its liabilities in the form of deposits repayable 'on demand', i.e. which can be withdrawn at any time without penalty. In contrast, around 75% of its assets are repayable only after five years or more.

Financial intermediaries are able to perform this maturity transformation function in part because of the 'law of large numbers', which implies that while some depositors will be withdrawing funds others will be making new deposits. This means that, overall, withdrawals minus new deposits are likely to be small in relation to the value of total deposits (liabilities). As a result the 'funding risk', namely that depositors might wish to withdraw more funds than the banks have available in liquid form, is greatly reduced. This enables the financial intermediaries to hold a sizeable proportion of less liquid assets (e.g. long-term loans) in their portfolio.

Risk transformation

This involves the financial intermediaries in shifting the burden of risk from the lender to themselves. Their ability to do so depends largely on *economies of scale* in risk management. The large amounts of deposits (liabilities) the financial intermediaries collect allow them to diversify their assets across a wide variety of types and sectors. 'Pooling' risk and reward in this way means that no individual is exposed to a situation in which the default of one or more borrowers is likely to have a significant effect.

Collection and parcelling

Financial intermediaries also transform the nature of their assets through the *collection* of a large number of small amounts of funds from depositors and their *parcelling* into larger amounts required by borrowers. Often the financial intermediaries have relied on obtaining many small deposits from conveniently located branches of their operations. This process is known as 'size intermediation' and benefits borrowers because they obtain one large loan from one source, thus reducing transaction costs. Of course this loan is an asset to the financial intermediary and a liability to the borrower.

The common characteristics of all financial intermediaries are therefore as follows. First, they take money from those who seek to save, whether it be in exchange for a deposit account bearing interest or in exchange for a paper financial claim. Second, they lend the money provided by those savers to borrowers, who may issue a paper asset in return. Third, in exchange for such lending they acquire a portfolio of paper assets (claims on borrowers) which will pay an income to the intermediary, and which it may 'manage' by buying and selling the assets on financial markets in order to yield further profits for itself.

UK financial intermediaries

The UK financial system incorporates different types of financial intermediary, offering lenders and borrowers a variety of instruments which have different maturities, liquidities and risk profiles. A popular method of classification is to distinguish between the bank and non-bank financial intermediaries.

- *Bank sector.* All the UK financial institutions that have been issued with a *banking licence*, including the high street commercial banks, the corporate wholesale banks and the foreign banks, are regarded as being part of the bank sector. Currently there are 385 authorized banking institutions operating in the UK, a fall of over 150 from the 1990 figure of 548.

- *Non-bank sector.* The other financial intermediaries, including the building societies, insurance companies, pension funds, unit trust and investment trust companies, are classified as part of the non-bank sector. A further disaggregation of the non-bank sector brings together those institutions which are *deposit-taking institutions*, such as the building societies, and those which are *investing institutions*, namely all the non-bank sector except the building societies.

However, even this simple classification of bank and non-bank sector is becoming more difficult to sustain with the growth of competition between these sectors (*inter-sector competition*) and between the institutions within these sectors (*intra-sector competition*), so that the distinction between banking and non-banking institutions has become increasingly blurred. Nevertheless it may be helpful to consider the UK financial intermediaries under the following three headings: banking financial intermediaries, non-bank financial intermediaries, and the Bank of England.

The UK banking financial intermediaries

The UK bank sector includes a range of financial intermediaries.

The retail banks

These include banks which either participate in the UK clearing system or have extensive branch networks. The retail banks are sometimes known as the MBBGs (Major British Banking Groups) which includes all the UK's large retail banks. Listing these banks was once relatively simple but a spate of mergers and acquisitions has meant changes in ownership. However, the largest retail banks operating in the UK are Barclays plc (owner of Woolwich); the HBOS Group, which includes Halifax plc and Bank of Scotland; HSBC plc (formerly Midland); Lloyds TSB Group, which owns Cheltenham and Gloucester plc and Scottish Widows Bank plc; The Royal Bank of Scotland Group, owner of Direct Line Financial Services, Tesco Personal Finance, National Westminster Bank plc, Lombard Bank plc and Ulster Bank; Abbey National plc; Alliance and Leicester plc; Bradford and Bingley plc; and Northern Rock plc.

Retail banks, through their extensive branch networks, have historically been primarily engaged in gathering deposits and creating loans, usually at high margins given that they could obtain deposits at low interest rates and could offer loans to individuals and firms at high interest rates. Activities in this sector were highly regulated until the early 1970s and were often described as being 'supply led', since most arrangements appeared to be in the interests of the providers rather than the customers.

Today, the retail banks are highly competitive and more responsive to the needs of their customers. The retail banks offer a wide array of services to personal customers, including savings accounts, unsecured and secured loans, mortgages, overdrafts, automated cash machines, home banking, foreign currency transactions and general financial advice. They also offer a range of services to corporate customers, including leasing and hire purchase, export and import facilities, payroll services, and international financial transfers.

Total assets in the banking sector have increased substantially during the past 15 years, from around £1,233bn in 1990 to over £3,000bn in 2003, a figure boosted by the trend of mutually owned building societies converting to banks (see p. 407).

The wholesale banks

These include around 500 banks which typically engage only in large-scale lending and borrowing transactions, namely transactions in excess of £50,000.

The wholesale banks include the following.

- *merchant banks*, of which there are about 40 including the Accepting Houses;
- *other British banks*, a general category covering banks with UK majority ownership;
- *overseas banks*, which include American banks, Japanese banks and a variety of other overseas banks and consortium banks.

The wholesale banks actually include a large number of small providers. This, together with the fact that the majority of transactions are completed with knowledgeable corporate clients, usually results in margins being low. Nevertheless individual transactions are 'wholesale', that is of a high value (greater than £50,000 but, more typically, in excess of £1 million) so that sizeable absolute levels of profit can still be made. Wholesale banking takes place mainly in foreign currencies, which reflects the substantial presence of Japanese and American banks in this sector. However, the sector also includes the British merchant banks, whose major business includes the acceptance of bills, underwriting, consultancy, fund management and trading in the financial markets.

Historically, retail banks could be distinguished from wholesale banks by the nature of their business, in that they dealt in a high volume of small deposits, operated an extensive branch network, were actively involved in the cheque clearing system and relied heavily on the personal sector for their deposits (liabilities). However, these distinctions are becoming increasingly blurred due to the participation of all banks and other financial intermediaries in wholesale banking and to the growth of the inter-bank market.

Much of this convergence between the retail and wholesale banking sectors has been due to retail banks entering the wholesale arena, largely because of diminishing margins in the retail sector. We consider the response of the retail banks to a variety of competitive pressures later in this chapter (p. 421). Wholesale banking, however, has remained relatively unchanged in that the vast majority of transactions remain with the corporate sector and are undertaken in foreign currencies.

UK non-bank financial intermediaries

The institutions in this sector fulfil a number of specialist functions, such as providing mortgage finance, insurance and pension cover. They typically specialize in matching the needs of borrowers for long-term finance with the needs of lenders for paper assets denominated in small units which are readily saleable. The UK non-bank financial intermediaries include the building societies, insurance companies, pension funds, unit trusts and investment trusts.

The building societies

These are mutually owned financial institutions which have traditionally offered loans in the form of mortgages to facilitate house purchase. Mutuality means that they are owned by their 'members', namely those who have purchased shares in the form of deposits, and those who have borrowed from them. Until the early 1980s, building societies were the only institutions offering mortgages and competition was restricted by various agreements and regulations between the various building societies.

Competition in this sector has, however, intensified since the early 1980s when deregulation of the retail banking sector allowed banks to offer mortgage finance and thereby to threaten the position of the building societies. This led to demands for deregulation to be extended to the building society sector in order to allow the building societies to respond by competing with banks in financial and other markets, where previously they had been restricted. The Building Societies Act of 1986, the subsequent Orders in Council of 1988 and the Building Societies Act 1997 have permitted building societies to offer a whole range of new banking, investment and property-related housing services, in addition to their traditional savings and home loan business.

The Building Societies Act 1997 relaxed restrictions on *unsecured lending* and permitted building societies, subject to their own prudential controls, to lend out 25% of their assets on an unsecured basis. In addition, it allowed societies to have greater access to the wholesale money markets, permitting up to 50% of their funds (liabilities) to be in the form of borrowings on these markets. This meant that societies need not rely as heavily on costly retail deposits from savers to finance their lending, allowing them to compete more aggressively with the banking sector. In fact by the end of 2002 total wholesale liabilities in the building society sector were over £37 billion.

However, the 1997 Act, while granting societies more freedom, also ensured that the building societies' main function and basic purpose of attracting savings and making loans for house purchase remained. To this end, societies still have to raise at least 50% of their funds from individual investors (usually in the form of issuing a retail deposit) and remain restricted to having 75% of their commercial assets in the form of loans secured by a mortgage on housing.

The evidence indicates that building societies have remained true to their basic principles and remain predominantly mortgage finance providers. Table 21.1 shows that the building society sector provided around nine times more mortgage lending by value in 2002 than consumer credit lending. In fact the table shows that the building societies have made little impact on the consumer credit market, supplying less than 2% of gross lending for consumer credit in 2002. Rather more significantly, the share of the building societies in gross mortgage lending has declined substantially over the period, being only about one fifth the value of gross mortgage lending by banks during 2002. This reflects the trend in demutualization.

Table 21.2 shows that building societies are also losing their share of UK private sector deposits. In 1985, some 45.1% of UK private sector deposits were held in building society accounts, and 49.5% in UK banks. However, by 2001 the building societies' share had dropped to 13.5%, whilst the share of the banks had risen to nearly 80%. In fact such a trend had been

long established; for example, the building societies witnessed a fall in their share of UK private sector deposits of nearly 5% between 1985 and 1988. However, the trend accelerated as the larger building societies themselves began to convert to bank plcs (see Table 21.3).

Demutualization

As we have already noted, the building societies have been losing market share to the banks in the deposit, consumer credit and mortgage markets. Indeed in 1997 the banking sector for the first time had a greater share of gross mortgage lending than the building societies, a trend which is set to continue. However, this comparison is not entirely fair, as it does not represent a like-for-like comparison over time. In fact a major reason for these losses of market share involve the demutualization and conversion of the larger building societies into banks, which means that their business is now counted as part of the

Table 21.1 Bank and building society shares of gross lending for mortgages and consumer credit, 1997–2002 (£m).

	1997	1998	1999	2000	2001	2002
Gross mortgage lending						
Building societies	27,797	20,715	25,873	24,932	25,904	34,993
% of total	36.0	23.2	22.6	20.8	16.1	15.9
Banks	44,601	62,261	78,648	83,335	119,764	162,423
% of total	57.8	69.7	68.6	69.5	74.6	74.2
Other	4,828	6,390	10,103	11,599	14,768	21,423
% of total	6.2	7.1	8.8	9.6	9.2	9.8
Total	77,226	89,366	114,624	119,866	160,436	218,844
Gross lending of consumer credit						
Building societies	1,802	1,688	1,955	2,638	3,226	3,719
% of total	1.6	1.2	1.3	1.7	1.8	1.9
Banks	87,690	102,851	113,492	125,714	142,488	158,873
% of total	75.5	76.8	77.2	79.2	81.4	82.0
Other	26,644	29,348	31,566	30,361	29,389	31,139
% of total	22.9	22.0	21.5	19.1	16.8	16.1
Total	116,136	133,887	147,013	158,713	175,103	193,731

Source: Adapted from *Bank of England Monetary and Financial Statistics* (2003), Tables A5.3 and A5.6.

Table 21.2 UK private sector deposits with banks and building societies, 1985–2001.

	1985	1997	1998	1999	2000	2001
Total UK banks						
UK private sector deposits	114,905	573,976	611,912	625,346	696,707	743,627
% of total	49.5	77.8	77.8	77.7	79.9	79.7
Building societies						
UK private sector deposits	104,816	99,302	109,863	115,571	112,184	126,061
% of total	45.1	13.5	14.0	14.4	12.9	13.5
Other						
UK private sector deposits	12,486	65,343	65,046	63,394	63,207	63,140
% of total	5.4	8.8	8.3	7.9	7.3	6.8
Total	232,207	738,500	786,821	750,992	872,098	932,828

Source: Adapted from *British Bankers' Association Annual Abstract of Banking Statistics* (2003), Volume 19, Table 4.04.

Table 21.3 Building society conversions, total assets and market capitalization.

Building society	Date of conversion	Total assets (£m)*	Market capitalization (£m)*
Abbey National	July 1989	205,721	5,589
Cheltenham & Gloucester (merged into Lloyds Bank)	August 1995	n/a	n/a
National & Provincial (merged into Abbey National)	August 1996	n/a	n/a
Alliance & Leicester	April 1997	41,248	4,043
Halifax (now HBOS)	June 1997	355,080	26,061
Bristol & West (merged into Bank of Ireland)	July 1997	n/a	n/a
Woolwich (acquired by Barclays plc, August 2000)	July 1997	n/a	n/a
Northern Rock	October 1997	32,665	2,912
Birmingham Midshires (merged into Halifax)	January 1999	n/a	n/a
Bradford & Bingley	December 2000	25,386	2,001

*Total assets December 2002, market capitalization March 2003.
Sources: *Building Society Association Yearly Handbook* (2003), Annual Reports; *Financial Times.*

banking sector. Table 21.3 shows those building societies which have converted into banks, the date of conversion, the total assets and the market capitalization involved. A number of reasons have been suggested for this trend towards demutualization.

■ Banks are in a better position than building societies to compete in financial services and mortgage markets because they can issue shares. This will provide the funding to permit faster growth and enable speedier diversification into new areas.

■ Building societies which convert to banks cannot be taken over for five years, giving them time to establish themselves and compete with the larger banks.

- Building societies which convert can now compete under the same regulatory environment as banks, which means that they no longer have restrictions on access to the wholesale markets. This provides them with improved access to corporate clients and to cheaper funding, allowing them to compete more aggressively in the consumer credit market.

- Diversification into new and risky areas of business should, it is argued, be undertaken by using newly issued capital raised by newly constituted institutions rather than by using historical capital derived from relatively safe savings and mortgage business.

Such arguments were present in the conversion documents of both the Alliance & Leicester Building Society and the Halifax Building Society. The Alliance & Leicester document (1996) stated that the society intends to expand its commercial lending activities, extend its use of wholesale money markets, and increase its provision of 'personal financial services, such as unsecured lending, telephone banking, life assurance and unit trust products'. This will allow it to reduce its 'dependency on the mature residential mortgage market ... and to build new sources of revenue from cross-selling'.

Expansion and consolidation was also a central theme in the Halifax Building Society's transfer documentation (1996). Their strategy statement read:

> Halifax plc are seeking significant earnings growth in the areas of long term savings and protection products and personal lines insurance ... Halifax must continue to focus on its key competitive advantages of providing innovative and competitive products together with a high level of customer service.

Those who doubt the benefits of conversion have, however, expressed their concern. First, the costs of paying large dividends to shareholders will increase the interest rate to borrowers and decrease the rate for deposit holders (lenders). Second, capital markets have a tendency to be short term in their evaluation of strategy and performance, which may hinder long-term growth. Third, there is little evidence that banks are more accountable to their owners than are building societies. Fourth, takeover threats by other banks may still exist. At least one building society waived its right not to be taken over after conversion and in any case the protection from takeover for five years is removed if another building society initiates the takeover, as when Birmingham Midshires was acquired by the Halifax in 1999. Fifth, there are increased costs resulting from conversion, including the cost of compliance with a new regulatory code and the cost of retraining staff.

However, the comparison of building societies with banks and the debate as to the respective advantages and disadvantages of conversion have arguably become redundant issues, having been superseded by events. Those building societies that wish to remain specialist mortgage providers are likely to stay in the building societies sector and, by remaining as mutual institutions, may acquire a competitive edge in offering mortgages at lower interest rates. Much of the rationalization of this sector may already have occurred, there having been 481 building societies in 1970 but only 65 by the end of 2002.

On the other hand, most former building societies that have wished to expand their range of products and services, having found regulations in the sector somewhat restrictive, have already chosen to convert. Of the top 10 building societies in December 1996, only three exist today, namely Nationwide, Britannia and Yorkshire.

Insurance companies and pension funds

About half of all personal savings are channelled into these institutions via regular and single-premium life assurance and pension payments. These savings from the personal sector are used to acquire a portfolio of assets. The institutions then manage these assets with the objective that they yield a sufficient return to pay the eventual insurance and pension claims as well as providing a working rate of return for the financial institutions themselves. The insurance companies and pension funds are major investors in the financial markets and exert considerable influence in these markets. They hold large amounts of long-term debt and help absorb ('make markets in') large volumes and values of new issues of various equities, bills and bonds.

Although these insurance companies and pension funds compete strongly against each other in the personal savings market, their portfolio choices differ because the structures of their liabilities differ. For example, the life assurance companies hold a larger proportion of assets as fixed-interest securities, because many of their liabilities are expressed in nominal terms (e.g. money value of payments in the future on policies is known). Pension funds, however, hold a larger proportion of assets in the form of equities, which historically have yielded higher real rates of return, because many of their liabilities are expressed in real terms (e.g. pensions paid in the future are often index linked). However, both these institutions have been adversely affected by the recent downward trend in financial markets worldwide. At the beginning of 2000 they held quoted UK company shares to the value of £743bn, which made up 45% of their total financial assets of £1,657bn. As the UK share market dropped, the value of their investments in UK company shares halved and by the end of 2002 it was worth only £388bn. As a result, total financial assets held by insurance companies and pension funds also fell to 1998 levels of around £1,250bn. More seriously, it has affected both premiums and payouts in the sector.

Unit and investment trusts

Both unit and investment trusts offer lenders a chance to buy into a diversified portfolio of assets and thereby reduce risk while at the same time receiving attractive returns. These institutions can achieve this by pooling the funds received from a large number of small investors and then implementing various portfolio management techniques not available to such small investors.

There are over 1,400 *unit trusts*, provided by individual companies, banks and insurance companies. A lender looking to buy into a unit trust purchases the number of units they can afford at the current value and then pays a further 5% of the purchase price for the management of the fund. The price of each unit is given by the net value of the trust's assets divided by the number of units outstanding. The size of the unit trust fund varies with the amount of units currently in issue, which allows the fund to expand and contract depending on demand, thus unit trusts are termed 'open ended'.

There are over 300 *investment trusts* and they undertake a similar role, allowing individuals to benefit from a pooled investment fund. However, investment trusts are plcs and raise funds for investment by issuing equity and debt and by using retained profits. Unlike unit trusts they can also borrow money. If individuals or firms are to buy into an investment trust, they must purchase their shares, which are limited in supply, thus investment trusts are termed 'closed ended'.

Table 21.4 shows total investments by both unit and investment trusts. Two factors are worth noting. First, unit trusts hold nearly four times the value of assets held by the investment trusts. Second, both institutions invest heavily in foreign company shares, with unit trusts investing just under 40% and investment trusts about 37% in this type of investment.

An important issue is the extent to which insurance, pension fund, investment and unit trust companies are involved in *equity finance*. These institutions are responsible for holding around 50% of UK equity, which means that share prices will be significantly affected by the portfolio preferences of these institutions. That preference will be influenced by overall 'environmental' factors, such as the inflation rate, the exchange rate and the state of business expectations, as well as by the particular needs of the institutions themselves. A concern is that such institutions may tend to be affected in the same way by the same set of factors, so that share prices may be more volatile than would otherwise be the case. This could have significant repercussions on the individual companies concerned because share prices may then fluctuate in ways which do *not* reflect their true valuation in terms of yield. It follows from this that the ability of companies to raise funds on the Stock Exchange may be affected by the activities of these institutions, and possibly in ways unconnected to their underlying profit potential.

Table 21.4 Total investments of Investment and Unit Trusts, 2000 (market value, £m).

Investment	Unit Trust holdings	Investment Trust holdings
British Government securities	4,694	821
UK-listed company securities	131,441	34,129
Overseas company securities	82,813	22,323
Other	3,876	3,168
Total	222,824	60,449

Source: Adapted from National Statistics, *Financial Statistics*, Tables 5.2C and 5.2D.

The Bank of England

The Bank of England is at the head of the UK financial system, is owned by the government (having been nationalized in 1946), and has a monopoly on the note issue in England and Wales. As the central bank of the United Kingdom, the Bank is committed to maintaining a stable and efficient monetary and financial framework. In pursuing its goal, it has three core purposes:

1 *Maintaining the integrity and value of the currency.* Above all this involves maintaining price stability (as defined by the inflation target set by the government) as a precondition for achieving the wider economic goals of sustainable growth and high employment. The Bank pursues this core purpose through its decisions on interest rates taken at the monthly meetings of the Monetary Policy Committee, by participating in international discussions to promote the health of the world economy, by implementing monetary policy through its market operations and its dealings with the financial system, and by maintaining confidence in the note issue.

2 *Maintaining the stability of the financial system, both domestic and international.* The Bank seeks to achieve this through monitoring developments in the financial system both at home and abroad, including links between the individual institutions and the various financial markets; through analysing the health of the domestic and international economy; through close cooperation with the financial supervisors, both domestically and internationally; and through developing a sound financial infrastructure including efficient payment and settlement arrangements. In exceptional circumstances (in consultation with the Financial Services Authority and HM Treasury as appropriate) the Bank may also provide, or assist in arranging, last-resort financial support where this is needed to avoid systemic damage.

3 *Seeking to ensure the effectiveness of the UK's financial services.* The Bank wants a financial system that offers opportunities for firms of all sizes to have access to capital on terms that give adequate protection to investors, and which enhances the international competitive position of the City of London and other UK financial centres.

It aims to achieve these goals through its expertise in the marketplace, by acting as a catalyst to collective action where market forces alone are deficient, by supporting the development of a financial infrastructure that furthers these goals, by advising government, and by encouraging British interest through its contacts with financial authorities overseas (Bank of England Annual Report, 2000, p. 14).

In order for it to achieve its core purposes, the Bank is split into three main divisions, each of which has its own responsibilities to the UK financial system. These are the *Monetary Analysis and Statistics* division, the *Financial Market Operations* division and the *Financial Stability* division.

Monetary Analysis and Statistics division

This division is responsible for providing the Bank with economic analysis that helps the Monetary Policy Committee (see page 413) formulate its monetary policy to aid economic growth and control inflation. Within this division, economists at the Bank conduct research and analyse developments in international and UK economies and publish reports which are then made publicly available. These include the *Bank of England Quarterly Bulletin*, the *Inflation Report* and the monthly *Monetary and Financial Statistics*.

Financial Market Operations division

This division has three main areas of responsibility:

■ *Operations in the financial markets.* It is responsible for planning and conducting the Bank's operations in the core financial markets, especially the sterling wholesale money markets, where it aims to establish short-term interest rates at the level required by government in order to meet its monetary policy objectives (see page 419). This division also manages the UK's foreign exchange and gold reserves and contributes market analysis to aid the Monetary Policy Committee and the Financial Stability Committee in their operations.

■ *Banking and market services.* It undertakes the traditional role of providing banking services to the government, banks and other central banks and managing the note issue. In addition, the division also plays an important role in providing (and monitoring) a safe and efficient payment and settlement system for the UK financial markets and the wider economy.

■ *Risk analysis and monitoring.* It is responsible for analysing any risks that may arise from the Bank's operations in the financial markets and for assessing the effects that these may have on the Bank and the UK economy.

Financial Stability division

The Bank of England no longer has any supervisory or regulatory powers over the UK financial system, so the Financial Stability division undertakes to *maintain the stability* of the financial system as a whole. Its main areas of responsibility are domestic finance, financial intermediaries, international finance, financial market infrastructure and regulatory policy. This division works closely with the Financial Stability Committee which is chaired by the Governor of the Bank of England. In general, the work of the division covers the functioning of the international financial system as well as that of the UK. To this end it carries out research into developments in the structure of financial markets and institutions and makes proposals for changes to increase safety and effectiveness. The division is also responsible for publishing the *Financial Stability Review*.

In operational day-to-day terms the Bank of England has an important influence on three major markets: the sterling money market, the foreign exchange market, and the gilt-edged market.

1 *The Bank is a major player in the sterling money market* (see p. 419), buying and selling Treasury bills on a daily basis. The object is twofold: firstly the Bank buys or sells bills in order to ease cash shortages or to withdraw cash surpluses, which arise as a result of daily transactions between the government and the public. Such transactions by the Bank affect commercial bank clearing balances, alter the liquidity of these banks and hence their willingness to lend. Second, the 'Financial Market Operations' division of the Bank trades in bills with the government's interest rate policy specifically in mind. The buying and selling of bills by the Bank affects yields and therefore influences interest rates throughout the market (see p. 416). The Bank, in its daily dealings, attempts to reconcile these two separate objectives.

2 *The Bank has a major role in the foreign exchange market* as it is responsible for carrying out government policy with regard to the exchange rate. A strong pound has been seen by successive governments as essential if inflation is to be kept low. The combination in recent years of a floating pound and a weak balance of payments on current account has made it necessary to attract short-term funds on capital account by maintaining high interest rates. The Bank also uses the Exchange Equalization Account to intervene in the foreign exchange market by buying up surplus sterling should it need to support the external value of the pound.

3 *The Bank is also influential in the gilt-edged market* as it administers the issue of new bonds when the government wishes to borrow money. Various methods are used, depending on market circumstances. The 'tap' method is where bonds (gilts) are issued gradually in order not to flood the market and depress the price; the 'tender' method is where institutions are invited to tender for a given issue; and the 'auction' method is where bonds are sold to the highest bidders among the 20 or so gilt-edged market makers (GEMMAs). The Bank also manages the redemption of existing bonds in such a way as to smooth the demands on the government's financial resources. For instance, it buys up bonds which are nearing their redemption date, so as not to have to make large repayments over a short period of time.

The Bank faces a continual problem in that its actions in each of these markets have repercussions for the functioning of the other markets. For instance, intervention to purchase sterling in the foreign exchange market in order to support the sterling exchange rate is often ineffective because of the size of speculative outflows of short-term capital from the sterling money and gilt-edged markets. As a result interest rates may need to be raised in order to deter these short-term capital outflows. This often proves difficult, however, because of the way in which daily transactions between the government and the public affect the balances of the clearing banks with the Bank of England. For example, if the banks are short of liquidity the Bank of England may be purchasing bills on the Open Market in order to help replenish their cash balances. However, purchasing existing bills by the Bank of England will raise their market price and lower their yield, i.e. lower interest rates. This may then conflict with the need to keep interest rates high to prevent short-term capital outflows from depressing the sterling exchange rate.

Recent changes at the Bank of England

The three main purposes of the Bank of England were defined in May 1997, when the Chancellor of the Exchequer, Gordon Brown, proposed a number of institutional and operational changes to the Bank of England. First, it was given operational independence in setting interest rates which would now be the responsibility of a newly created Monetary Policy Committee (MPC) working within the Bank. Second, the regulation of the banking sector was taken away from the Bank and given to a newly established 'super' regulator called the Financial Services Authority (FSA). Third, although the government retained responsibility for determining the exchange rate regime, the Bank could now intervene at its discretion in support of the objectives of the MPC. Fourth, the management of the national debt was transferred from the Bank to the Treasury. These changes were set out in The Bank of England Act which came into force on 1 June 1998. The most important of these changes involved the creation of the MPC and the FSA.

The Monetary Policy Committee (MPC)

The Bank of England Act established that the responsibility for monetary policy and therefore for setting short-term interest rates was to reside with the MPC, a committee within the Bank of England. The MPC would be free from government intervention in all but extreme economic circumstances. The aim of short-term interest rate setting would be to restrict the growth of inflation to within a target range set by the government and announced in the annual Budget Statement. The present target has been set at 2.5% for annual retail price inflation, excluding mortgage interest payments (RPIX). Significantly, if inflation is more than 1% either side of this figure then the MPC is required to write an open letter of explanation to the Chancellor.

The MPC consists of the Governor of the Bank, two Deputy Governors, two members appointed by the Bank in consultation with the Chancellor, and four 'experts' appointed by the Chancellor. The MPC meets monthly, publishes its decisions within days of concluding any meeting and publishes minutes of the meeting within six weeks.

There has been much discussion as to the merits of these recent changes. In essence, they are an attempt by the Chancellor of the Exchequer to take the 'politics' out of setting interest rate policy. Hall (1997) makes the following points:

> As a device for enhancing the credibility of monetary policy the current regime, if allowed to work with optimal efficiency, is vastly superior to its predecessors, which had confirmed the worst fears of outside observers by allowing the Chancellor to attempt to extract the maximum political advantage from the interest rate setting process ... Moreover, if one believes in a high and positive correlation between the degree of independence enjoyed by a Central Bank and that country's success in fighting inflation, then the recent changes can only but serve to reinforce one's optimism about the UK's future inflation prospects.

It has been argued that as a result of such independence, the financial markets will gain additional confidence in the UK's ability to control future inflation. Some have pointed to the fact that long-term interest rates for UK government borrowing have reached a 30-year low since the Bank's independence was announced, as evidence of such confidence. Nevertheless, concerns over the new policy include fears that the Bank may set interest rates which are higher than necessary to control inflation, thereby stifling investment and raising the sterling exchange rate to levels which damage trading sectors of the economy, such as manufacturing. Others have argued that the MPC should have been given a target for economic growth as well as a target for inflation, to prevent an overemphasis on deflationary policies.

The Financial Services Authority (FSA)

Overall supervision of any banking system is essential to protect the interests of depositors, and although there was some degree of depositor protection in the 1960s it was not until the secondary banking crisis of the 1970s that formal supervisory structures were developed and embodied in the Banking Acts of 1979 and 1987.

Traditionally, the Board of Banking Supervision within the Bank concerned itself with three issues.

1 *Capital adequacy.* To what extent do banks have sufficient reserves of capital to cover the possibility of default by borrowers? This issue has become particularly important in recent years as the volume of Third World debt has grown to unmanageable proportions. The 1989 Solvency Ratio Directive established an EU-wide rule that a bank's capital reserves must be at least 8% of its risk-adjusted assets and off-balance-sheet transactions. Off-balance-sheet transactions include such things as an advance commitment to lend (rather than an actual loan) which may or may not ultimately lead to a future balance sheet entry.

2 *Liquidity.* There is currently no formal requirement as to adequate liquidity holdings by banks. However, the Bank of England required all banks under the Banking Act of 1987 to keep a ratio of 'primary liquid assets' to some definition of deposit liabilities. Such ratios may differ as between different types of banks, and deposits will be ranked according to their maturity. The shorter is the maturity structure of deposits, the higher will be the ratio of liquid assets required.

3 *Foreign currency exposure.* This issue relates particularly to banks which take deposits and lend in different currencies. Supervisors are concerned that banks should balance their assets and liabilities in each currency in such a way that their 'exposure' (to risk of loss on the foreign exchange market) should not exceed 10% of their capital base.

However, in May 1997 the Chancellor also reformed the regulatory structure of the financial system. As already noted, regulation and supervision of the *banking sector* was traditionally the responsibility of the Bank of England. In contrast, the regulation and supervision of the *non-bank sector* has historically been the responsibility of numerous different bodies, such as the Building Societies Commission and the Securities and Investment Board which itself headed three other self-regulating bodies. The Chancellor of the Exchequer highlighted problems with the then regulatory structure in a statement on 20 May 1997:

> It has long been apparent that the regulatory structure introduced by the Financial Services Act 1986 is not delivering the standard of supervision and investor protection that the industry and the public have a right to expect. The current two tier system splits responsibilities ... This division is inefficient, confusing for investors and lacks accountability and a clear allocation of

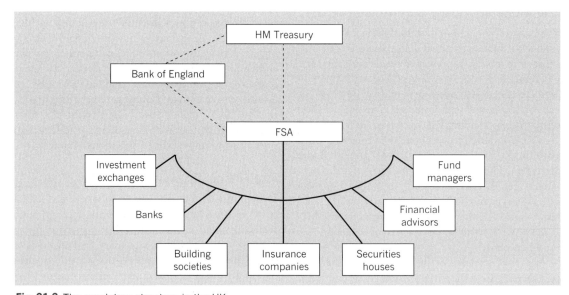

Fig. 21.2 The regulatory structure in the UK.

responsibilities. It is clear that the distinctions between different types of financial institutions – banks, securities firms and insurance companies – are becoming increasingly blurred ... [therefore] there is a strong case in principle for bringing the regulation of banking, securities and insurance together under one roof.

The Bank of England Act of 1998 transferred the regulatory functions of the Bank to a new regulatory authority called the Financial Services Authority (FSA), which was now to be responsible for regulating all financial institutions, whether bank or non-bank.

The Bank of England retains responsibility for monitoring the financial system, with the government establishing a structure whereby the Treasury, the Bank of England and the FSA work together to achieve stability. In a Memorandum of Understanding published in October 1997 the Chancellor set out the various roles of the Treasury, the Bank and the FSA, making it clear that these organizations should exchange information and consult regularly. A standing committee was established to provide the means for the three bodies to discuss any foreseeable problems.

The new regulatory structure was completed by the establishment of a new Financial Stability Committee whose functions were to oversee the stability of the system and detect any risk of system-wide failure. This Committee had the responsibility of liaising with the Standing Committee created by the Memorandum of Understanding. Figure 21.2 provides an overview of the new regulatory structure.

UK financial markets

The financial markets within the UK perform a variety of functions which make them attractive to both lenders and borrowers. Such functions include providing a place to trade financial instruments and a system by which to 'price' such instruments. The major UK financial markets are located in London, one of the three dominant financial centres together with New York and Tokyo. One reason for London's dominant position is the large number of overseas banks transacting in foreign currencies on the financial markets.

As with the financial intermediaries, there are a number of ways in which the financial markets might be classified. One of the most common is to separate the UK financial markets into the sterling wholesale money markets and capital markets.

The sterling wholesale money markets

Transactions undertaken in the UK 'money market' involve the borrowing and lending of short-term wholesale funds by financial institutions. 'Short-term' means for periods varying from one day to one year, and 'wholesale funds' means amounts in excess of £50,000. Money market activity in London has developed rapidly over the last 35 years, partly due to the growth of the financial sector in general, but also because of the increasing demand for sophisticated financial services by clients both in the UK and abroad.

In the UK, the money markets have been traditionally split into the *primary markets*, which issue new financial instruments, and the *secondary* (or *parallel*) *markets* which deal in previously issued financial instruments or securities (financial instruments which can be traded by third parties are known as *securities*). This distinction is no longer relevant today and it is best to think of the wholesale money market as one market issuing and trading short-term financial instruments. There are various money markets operating in the UK but it is useful to begin with the discount market.

The discount market

The discount market has always played an important role within the UK financial system. In this market, short-term (commonly 91 days) financial instruments known as 'bills' are bought and sold 'at a discount' to their redemption value on maturity (i.e. bought and sold at a price *below* their maturity value). The discount market has no physical location and only bills of the highest quality are traded. This is ensured by bills being accepted and underwritten (guaranteed) by creditable banking institutions (counterparties), with the Bank of England dealing only with 'eligible' bills that have been accepted by these registered counterparties.

During the nineteenth century the major function of the discount market was the discounting of commercial bills of exchange which financed the increasing volume of international trade. In general the functions of the discount market today are to allow commercial banks to adjust their cash positions, to provide short-term finance to the government and corporate sector, and to underwrite and 'make-a-market' in the weekly trade of government treasury bills.

Traditionally, the main players in the discount market were the discount houses that bought and sold discounted bills, thereby acting as a buffer between the Bank of England and the UK banking sector. This meant that if the banking sector needed more cash (liquidity), the Bank of England would provide this by purchasing bills from the discount houses. The discount houses would then make the cash from the sale of the bills available to the banking sector. However, over the past few years the Bank of England has started to provide direct support to the banking sector. The UK banks have also made growing use of the inter-bank market and other money markets to adjust their liquidity, which has somewhat nullified the role of the discount houses. Today many of the former discount houses have merged with larger financial institutions, so that the Bank of England now deals only with registered counterparties, which include banks, building societies, and securities firms. The Discount House Association, which was the overseer of the operations of the (now defunct) eight discount houses, has been replaced by the Finance House and Leasing Association.

The main functions of the counterparties are to:

■ underwrite the weekly tender issue of Treasury bills by bidding competitively for those bills not sold;

■ provide short-term finance for companies by discounting bills; and

■ maintain a secondary market in CDs and other short-term financial instruments.

The characteristics of bills

Bills are short-term financial instruments that are generally issued by large corporations (known as commercial bills) or by the Bank of England on behalf of the government (known as Treasury bills or Tbills) and traded on the discount market. The original purchaser (the lender) buys the bill at *below* its face or redemption value, i.e. at a discount, and earns a return by holding it until maturity. Alternatively, the original purchaser can sell the bill in the discount market before the bill matures. For example, the government might make an issue of £100,000, 91-day bills, at a discount of £2,000. This would mean that the purchaser would pay £98,000 for the bills and on maturity, in 91 days, would receive £100,000 back from the government. For the purchaser of the bill, it is important that they are aware of the annual percentage 'yield' or 'return' on the bill so that they can compare it with other financial instruments. The annualized 'discount yield' is calculated using the formula:

$$\text{Discount yield} = \left(\frac{\text{discount}}{\text{redemption value}}\right) \times \left(\frac{365}{n}\right) \times 100$$

In the above example the discount is £2,000, the redemption value of the bill is £100,000 and n equals the number of days to maturity, which is 91. Therefore the annual 'discount yield' on the above bill is given by

$$\text{Discount yield} = \left(\frac{2,000}{100,000}\right) \times \left(\frac{365}{91}\right) \times 100 = 8.02\%$$

The discount yield, however, is not the actual return that the investor enjoys, because in the above formula the redemption value of the bill has been used and not the *purchase price* of the bill. To convert the discount yield into the rate of interest enjoyed by the purchaser of the bill and one that is comparable with other financial instruments, it is necessary to change the denominator in the formula, thus:

$$\text{Interest rate} = \left(\frac{2,000}{98,000}\right) \times \left(\frac{365}{91}\right) \times 100 = 8.19\%$$

which is slightly higher than the discount yield.

Bills have a number of additional features:

■ They are issued in denominations of no less than £5,000 (but more typically £250,000).

■ They are *highly liquid* and *low-risk securities*. They gain their *liquidity* from being short-term and from being actively traded on the discount market. They are *low-risk* instruments because either they are issued by governments or, in the case of commercial bills, they have been underwritten by creditable banks – giving them eligible bill status, meaning that they are eligible for discount at the Bank of England.

■ They are *fixed income securities* because the purchaser of the security knows the amount they will receive from the bill at the time of purchase. However, their price fluctuates in line with any change in market or current interest rates.

The sterling inter-bank market

This market is now the largest and the most significant of the money markets. The inter-bank market allows financial institutions to borrow and lend wholesale funds amongst themselves (dealing through money brokers) for periods ranging from overnight to five years. By using such borrowings, banks have been able to make (profitable) lending decisions which are to some extent independent of the amount of personal deposits that they have been able to attract, because they could now obtain any extra funding they might acquire on the inter-bank market. The amounts involved are large, starting from £500,000, but £10–12 million is not untypical. Banks today borrow to finance lending, to balance out fluctuations in their books, and to speculate on future movements in interest rates. The London Inter-Bank Offer Rate (LIBOR) therefore represents the marginal or opportunity cost of funds to the banks and is the major influence on banks' base rates. The size of the market in 2002 was over £240 billion.

The sterling certificate of deposit market

Certificates of deposit (CDs) are paper assets issued by banks, building societies and finance houses to depositors who are willing to leave their money on deposit for a specified period of time. They are issued for periods ranging from 3 months to 5 years, but tend to be shorter rather than longer term and are issued at a rate of interest which can either be fixed or floating. Unlike Tbills and commercial bills, CDs are issued 'at par' (that is, its issue, nominal or face value) and the interest is added on to the face value at maturity, when the deposit is repaid. So, for example, the future (or *redemption*) value of a 91-day £100,000 CD that pays 5% interest can be found by the formula:

$$\text{Redemption value} = 100,000 \times \left[1 + \left(0.05 \times \frac{91}{365} \right) \right]$$
$$= £101,246.58$$

The purchaser of the CD can sell it on the market at any time if they have a requirement for liquidity.

This enables banks to lend for longer time periods because they can be certain of having access to liquidity. In addition, CDs are attractive to portfolio holders because the yield is competitive. By 2003, UK banks held over £200 billion in CDs and other short-term instruments as liabilities on their balance sheet.

The sterling commercial paper market

Since May 1986 companies have been permitted to issue short-term (7–364 days) unsecured promissory notes, which can then be traded at a discount. This provides a way of raising cheap short-term funds for businesses that require finance for general business purposes. The 1989 Budget extended the right to issue this form of sterling commercial paper to governments, overseas companies and certain overseas authorities, as well as to banks, building societies and insurance companies. In January 2003 the amount of commercial paper outstanding was £32.5 billion.

Large companies, or companies with high credit ratings, can borrow funds at more competitive rates than they can obtain from the banks. The creation and growth of this market has led to *disintermediation*, whereby companies circumvent the various financial institutions and deal directly with the wholesale markets themselves. This could be a concern for banks in that they may be left with borrowers who are of 'lower quality' and therefore riskier should a larger proportion of the 'higher quality' companies deal directly with the wholesale markets.

Euromarkets

Eurocurrency is currency held on deposit with a bank outside the country from which that currency originates. For example, loans made in dollars by banks in the UK are known as eurodollar loans. The eurocurrency market is a wholesale market and has its origins in the growing holdings of US dollars outside the US in the 1960s. Since that time, eurocurrency markets have grown rapidly to include dealing in all the major currencies, and have become particularly important when oil price rises create huge world surpluses and deficits, resulting in large shifts in demand for and supply of the major world currencies.

The major participants are banks, who use the euromarkets for a variety of reasons: for short-term inter-bank lending and borrowing, to match the currency composition of assets and liabilities and for global liquidity transformation between branches. However, the market is also extensively used by companies, and by governmental and international organizations. Lending which is longer-term is usually done on a variable-rate basis, where the interest is calculated periodically in line with changing market rates.

There are two important factors which make eurocurrency business attractive. The first is that the market is unregulated, so that banks which are subject to reserve requirements or interest rate restrictions in the home country, for instance, can do business more freely abroad. The other factor is that the margin between lending and borrowing rates is narrower on this market than on the home market, primarily because banks can operate at lower cost when all business is wholesale and when they are not subject to reserve requirements.

UK capital markets

In contrast to the short-term transactions undertaken in the UK wholesale money markets, the capital market provides an arena in which private and public sector companies can trade medium- and long-term financial claims. These financial claims can be either equity shares, interest-bearing debt instruments (bonds) or a mixture of the two types of instrument. Purchasers of *equity* have bought themselves a legal share in the ownership of the company, giving them the right to contribute in the determination of broad company strategy as well as a claim on the profits of the company. Purchasers of *debt*, in the form of *bonds*, in contrast, have purchased a long-term financial instrument which provides them with a flow of cash interest payments at specific times in the future. The purchasers of debt are classed as creditors or lenders and do not have ownership rights on the company.

The characteristics of equities

Equities (or shares) are non-redeemable financial instruments issued by companies. Any profits that are paid to shareholders are done so in the form of a *dividend*, which is usually paid annually. Shareholders usually have voting rights in the election of directors

and have a claim on any income left over if the company is liquidated. However, the major advantage of holding this kind of instrument lies in the possibility of capital appreciation if strong profit growth is anticipated some time in the future. In the case of *preference shares* the company pays a fixed annual sum to the shareholder and there is also the possibility of capital appreciation when the share is sold. *Ordinary shareholders* bear the largest risks since if the company goes out of business, the 'preferred' shareholders have first claim to a share of the money raised by selling assets (although only after the Inland Revenue, Customs and Excise and secured bank borrowers are paid). However, in good times, the ordinary shareholder will earn the greatest returns as dividend payments may be much greater than the fixed return received by the preference shareholders. As always in the financial markets, those who bear most risk have higher potential for returns.

The characteristics of bonds

Bonds are interest-bearing financial instruments issued by central and local governments, companies, banks and other financial institutions. The issuer of the bond (the borrower) undertakes to redeem the bond at 'par value' (£100) on a certain date and to pay the bondholder an annual fixed sum (the coupon rate) in interest each year. They are usually issued to mature in between five and 25 years' time with the year of maturity included in the bond's title, though some government bonds are undated and will never be redeemed. Bonds are also classified by their *residual maturity*, meaning the amount of time left until the bill will be redeemed by the issuer. Bonds with up to five years until maturity are known as 'shorts', those with between five and 15 years to maturity 'mediums', with those with over 15 years to run being known as 'longs'.

Bonds may be bought either as a new issue or second-hand on the secondary markets. The lender buying from the *secondary market* may have bought the bond at a price *below* par value and this makes the annual fixed interest payment more attractive, taking into account this lower price. For example, if 5% government bonds (gilts) of par value £100 are bought on the secondary market at £50, the buyer receives £5 a year from the government (that is, 5% of £100). However, the actual yield for the lender in this case is 10% (£5 from £50). In addition, the lender will gain a further £50 if they hold the bond until it matures when the government will redeem it for £100. Bonds normally bear a *fixed rate of interest* and this means that there will usually be an *inverse* relationship between the market price of an existing bond and movements in current interest rates. Therefore, in the above example, a *doubling* of the current interest rate from 10% to 20% would mean that the Treasury bond would *halve* in value (ignoring any later capital gain on maturity) to £25 because £5 return on £25 corresponds to an annual yield of 20% (£5/£25 × 100 = 20%). This would certainly be the market price for an existing Treasury bond with no future redemption date (known as consols) and therefore no future capital gain. If the price of such bonds did *not* fall by £25 when interest rates doubled, then investors would simply move their funds to financial instruments with similar characteristics where they could earn a return of 20%. Higher interest rates therefore reduce the market price of existing bonds and lower interest rates increase the market price or value of existing bonds.

UK capital markets can be split into primary and secondary markets.

■ *Primary capital markets.* New issues of debt and equity are originally placed on the primary capital market and then traded in the secondary market which includes the London Stock Exchange (LSE). The majority of primary markets are 'over-the-counter' markets which are a type of market with no location, reporting system or centralized market. In these markets information is dispersed using burgeoning computer networks.

■ *Secondary markets.* These are organized markets that enable the equity and debt of issuing companies to be traded. The ability to trade debt on a secondary market is an important part of any capital market, because it allows holders of long-term financial debt to liquidate their holding for cash at any time, for a known return. This means that new issues are more likely to be purchased. Also the holders of marketable financial claims can more readily maximize their utility by rearranging their consumption and risk profiles over time.

At the heart of the capital market in the UK is the London Stock Exchange (LSE). The LSE has a physical location where equity and debt instruments can be traded. However, the amount of business transacted on the floor of the LSE is minimal, with the majority of business taking place outside the physical location of the exchange using telephones and new technology. The market can be split into two: the *Main Market*, which is the largest and is where the majority of equity and debt prices are quoted; and *the Alternative Investment Market* (AIM) which opened in July 1995 to allow smaller companies access to the secondary market (see Chapter 4).

A major factor concerning capital markets today is the growing competition between financial centres, especially those within Europe. Traditionally, London has been the busiest European capital market: for example, the amount of international banking business undertaken from London at the beginning of the 1990s was three times that of the next busiest European country. Reasons advanced for this dominance have included London's geographical position between New York and Tokyo, the large amount of foreign banks operating in London, the availability of trained staff, and London's convenience in reaching the rest of Europe.

However, with the evolution of the Single Market, the increasing globalization of businesses and the advancement of technology, the competition from other financial centres has become intense. This has meant that European companies requiring long-term finance are increasingly looking throughout the European financial centres and not just at London.

The Bank of England and the sterling wholesale money markets

Having introduced both the Bank of England and the sterling wholesale money markets, it will be useful to consider the operations of the Bank of England in the money markets and the ways in which it seeks to influence the short-term interest rate.

We have already noted that setting interest rates is now the concern of the Monetary Policy Committee (MPC) which operates within the Bank of England. The aim of the Bank's operations on the money markets is to *guide* short-term interest rates to the level set by the MPC. The Bank does this by providing liquidity or cash to the banking system at the interest rate set by the MPC and by buying government securities at prices consistent with the interest rate set by the MPC. This exerts pressure on the short-term money market rate of interest to move to the 'official' rate set by the MPC.

To be able to do this, the Bank of England manages its accounts in ways which will ensure that the banking system as a whole is short of liquidity. The Bank of England can 'tighten' bank liquidity in the following ways.

- *Through taxation.* When people pay their taxes they do so from their bank accounts; the flow of these payments to the Bank of England (on behalf of the government) drains the banking sector of liquidity.

- *Through government borrowing.* Selling government securities (e.g. Treasury Bills) to individuals or institutions who pay for them from their bank accounts.

- *Through buying short-term claims on banks.* Such 'claims' are via the Bank of England lending to the banks for short periods. A number of these claims mature throughout the day and must be redeemed by the banks, draining them of liquidity.

- *Through regulations.* For example, regulations which require the clearing banks to maintain positive end-of-day balances with the Bank of England.

The Bank of England is aware that banks will always look to the money markets in general, and the Bank of England in particular, should they need to restore their liquidity. At this point the Bank will offer such liquidity at a 'price', namely one which will reinforce the interest rate level set by the MPC.

The Bank of England can, for example, raise short-term interest rates by first starving the banking sector of liquidity and then offering to restore that liquidity at its official rate of interest. This intervention often comes in the form of Open Market Operations (OMOs) on the money market. Figure 21.3 provides a simplified overview of such Open Market Operations. Where the Bank of England wants to *raise* interest rates it *sells* securities, and vice versa.

The Bank of England conducts its Open Market Operations by buying and selling high quality government securities such as Treasury bills and eligible bank bills, government foreign currency debt and gilt repos. By far the most significant of these securities are the gilt repos.

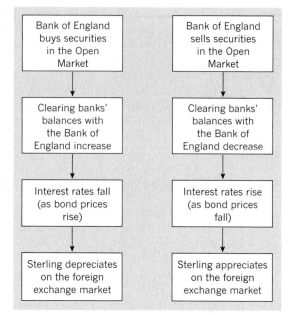

Fig. 21.3 Open Market Operations of the Bank of England.

The introduction of the gilt repo market

In March 1997 the Bank introduced reforms to its daily operations in the money markets. The aims of these reforms were threefold: first, to increase the efficiency of liquidity provision in the banking sector; second, to increase competition by raising the number of eligible institutions with which the Bank would trade (these institutions are known as 'counterparties' and now include banks, building societies and securities houses); and third, to introduce the gilt repo into its Open Market Operations, thereby providing the Bank with an additional instrument with which to influence short-term interest rates.

A *repo* is a transaction in which one party sells a financial asset to another party and agrees to repurchase an equivalent value of financial assets at some time in the future. The gilt repo market was introduced in January 1996 and quickly became a major tool with which the Bank of England could provide refinancing to the banking sector. Within three months of its introduction, over 50% of refinancing by the Bank was provided by the gilt repo and almost 50% of Open Market Operations by the Bank were

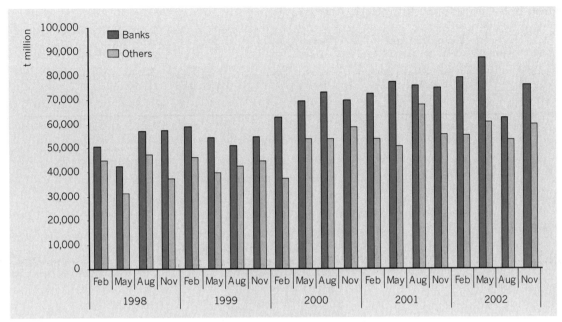

Fig. 21.4 Gilt repos outstanding at banks and other institutions, 1998–2002.
Source: Adapted from *Bank of England: Monetary and Financial Statistics,* March 2003, Table D3.1.

undertaken using the gilt repo. Figure 21.4 indicates that the value of gilt repos outstanding at banks and other financial institutions had expanded to over £135 billion by November 2002.

In addition the gilt repo market has made a considerable impact on the sterling money markets. As Table 21.5 shows, the gilt repo market is now of similar size to the CD market, with the CD market seeing £137bn worth of trade in 2002 compared with the gilt repo market's £136bn. The gilt repo market has witnessed a near doubling in value since 1997.

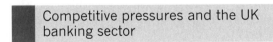

Competitive pressures and the UK banking sector

The UK financial system is undergoing a phase of major structural change brought about by changing economic conditions and increasing pressures in traditional markets. This change has impacted on all areas of banking business, including customer profile, delivery strategies and the type of business undertaken. This in turn has changed the structure of the various balance sheets and the sources from which their income is derived.

Figure 21.5 indicates some of the competitive pressures facing the retail banking sector. Response to these pressures within the retail banking sector has, however, been rather slow. Historically the retail banks in the UK herald from a stable, regulated and largely uncompetitive environment, which remained largely untouched in the decades preceding the 1970s. The absence of competition meant that by the 1970s retail banks had evolved into monoliths, with extensive branch networks employing managers who operated within a highly regulated market, typified by the cartel arrangements for fixing interest rates between the large retail banks. In such a regulated, uncompetitive environment it is hardly surprising that bank managers have been characterized as adopting conservative, risk-averse strategies towards lending decisions. However, the progressive build-up of competitive pressures on retail banks since the Competition and Credit Control Act of 1971 have brought about an entirely different landscape for the retail banks.

It will be useful at this stage to consider each of the factors identifed in Fig. 21.5 in rather more detail.

Table 21.5 The sizes of UK sterling money markets (£bn).

	Commercial paper	Treasury bills	CDs	Inter-bank	Gilt repo
1997	8	3	102	144	72
2000	18	3	130	151	128
2002	27	22	137	244	136

Source: Bank of England.

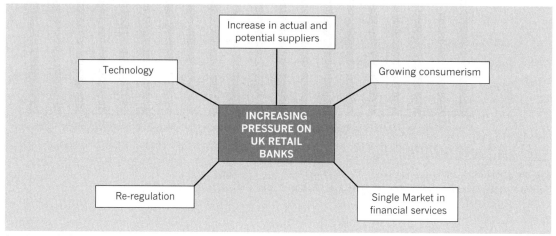

Fig. 21.5 Pressures on the UK banking sector.

Increase in suppliers

The increase in suppliers of services that were traditionally the preserve of the retail banks has come from three main sources: the financial markets, non-bank financial intermediaries and non-financial companies.

The financial markets

Traditionally, the retail banks have liaised between lenders and borrowers, using their deposits to benefit the economy by providing a variety of financial instruments with less risk and at a lower cost than would have been possible if the market had to rely on direct borrowing or lending. However, new financial instruments (e.g. repos) have been developed to enable borrowers and lenders to transact directly at lower cost. For example, companies faced with a funding gap may now find that it is cheaper to transact directly with the financial markets. This trend towards *disintermediation*, i.e. direct transactions between ultimate borrowers and lenders, reduces the need for financial intermediaries.

This increased use of the financial markets has been fuelled by the growing trend of *securitization*. Although technically the term securitization refers to the bundling up of mortgages into 'securities' which can be sold on the financial markets, it is more generally used to refer to the process of converting any existing (non-tradeable) loan into a *security* (tradeable). The seller of the asset (security) guarantees payment of interest in the new bundled security, which now becomes more liquid than the assets it replaces.

Although banks have lost business to the capital markets, securitization has enabled all financial institutions, including banks, to develop and market paper claims against what were previously non-marketable financial assets such as long-term loans, thereby reducing the risks and cost of holding them. Banks have also benefited by acting as advisor and broker to those companies wishing to finance future projects by issuing securities directly onto the markets.

Non-bank financial intermediaries

These financial intermediaries include the building societies, insurance companies and unit and investment trust companies. They have utilized changes in market regulations and technology to offer new, cheaper and more flexible products and services to lenders. In many cases these institutions are not exposed to the high operating costs of the banking sector. For example, the Halifax reported a cost/income ratio of 42.3% in 1996 covering its last year of trading as a mutual building society, whereas retail banks such as Lloyds and NatWest reported cost/income ratios of 57% and 68% respectively in the same year.

Non-financial companies

The threat of competition from non-financial companies to the retail banks has become real as the costs of entry into the banking sector have fallen. General retailers such as Marks & Spencer, and supermarkets such as Sainsbury's, Tesco, Asda, Safeway and Morrisons, all now offer many financial services, and even car manufacturers such as Vauxhall are developing their own financial products. These retailers can benefit from cheaper entry costs to many banking activities, due partly to advances in technology and also to their ability to utilize their extensive branch networks.

The term 'asymmetric competition' might be used to describe the competition pressures on the retail banking sector from these non-bank financial intermediaries and non-financial companies (Llewellyn 1997). It is asymmetric because changes in technology and regulation have made it easier for non-financial firms to diversify into banking business than for banks to diversify into non-financial business. This is mainly because of branding in that a strong reputation in general retailing gives a non-financial institution the possibility of using that reputation to sell financial products. However, the reverse is far less true, in that a bank with a strong reputation will find this of little help should it seek to diversify into general retailing. Further, whereas general retailers can put aside a small area within their current buildings to sell financial products, banks do not possess the spatial resources to sell tangible retail goods such as clothes, motor cars, etc. Generally speaking, these non-financial companies have entered the financial services sector for three main reasons: first, they have an established distribution network to provide such financial services; second, they have a strong brand image, especially as regards reputation; and third, in many cases (e.g. supermarkets) they can exploit information that they have gained from loyalty card and related schemes.

These new suppliers are clearly increasing the competitive pressures on the retail banking sector while at the same time restricting the ability of the banks themselves to diversify into new market segments. Further, the non-financial companies especially have the ability to cross-subsidize their financial services from other profitable activities and thereby out-compete the retail bank financial services.

Growing consumerism

At the same time there has been an increase in the awareness, expectations and demands of customers for newer, better and more targeted financial services. One possible reason for this growing 'consumerism' might include an increase in the number and quality of information flows available to consumers, for example via easier access to brokerage and other financial advice. Demographic changes might also have played a part; for example, an ageing population has increased its demand for savings and pension-related financial products, especially in the context of a more restricted Welfare State in the future, including even less generous provision for the state pension. A longer life expectancy and reduced job security might be other important factors in this increased desire for newer, better and more targeted financial services.

Table 21.6 shows the rapid growth in demand for savings products such as PEPs, TESSAs and ISAs. *PEPs* are Personal Equity Plans, introduced in 1987 to encourage savings by being exempt from income tax on any dividends or interest received. PEPs can involve investments in a variety of market-based financial instruments, such as UK and European company shares and corporate bonds. The growth in PEPs has been extremely rapid, growing by more than £76bn between 1991 and 2001, with the value of PEPs in the UK reaching more than £81bn in 2001. PEPs were closed to new subscriptions in April 1999. *TESSAs* are Tax Exempt Special Savings Accounts and are also exempt from income tax on savings up to £9,000 over five years. TESSAs grew to a value of over £30bn before the introduction of ISAs. *ISAs* are

Table 21.6 The demand for TESSAs[1], PEPs[2] and ISAs in the UK, 1991–2001 (£m).

Year	PEPs	TESSAs	ISAs
1991	4,520	7,326	–
1992	6,970	13,031	–
1993	11,890	18,455	–
1994	20,090	23,712	–
1995	23,800	28,047	–
1996	34,120	25,981	–
1997	49,530	27,257	–
1998	77,850	29,737	–
1999	91,920	30,040	–
2000	94,000	28,325	28,431
2001	81,120	13,284	29,778

[1] Tax exempt special savings accounts (TESSAs) could be opened between 1 January 1991 and 5 April 1999.
[2] Personal equity plans (PEPs) commenced on 1 January 1987 but were closed to new subscriptions from 6 April 1999.
Source: Inland Revenue Analytical Services Division: Inland Revenue Statistics 2002, Tables 9.1, 9.2, 9.3 and 9.4.

individual savings accounts and were introduced as a replacement for PEPs. Once again, they are tax free. Figures show the value of ISAs held in the UK to be nearly £30bn.

These identified trends suggest a shift in the balance of power from the *suppliers* to the *consumers* of financial services, and this shift is likely to continue as consumers demand more flexible, competitive and convenient financial products.

Single Market in financial services

The Ceccini report of 1988 had suggested that the Single Market Programme (SMP) for financial services would result in three main categories of benefit. First, financial institutions would benefit from economies of scale because they would be operating in a bigger market at higher volumes. Second, the increase in competitive pressure would reduce margins and financial institutions would be forced to reduce inefficiencies by reducing costs. Third, the increased competition would have non-price effects which would surface as higher product quality and more product innovation.

A major study has been published on the impacts of the SMP on credit institutions and banking since its initial implementation on 1 January 1993. The key findings of this study (Single Market Review 1997) are presented below.

■ Financial services firms have witnessed an increase in competition in the post-SMP period but the cost of loans to business has fallen only slightly in most markets.

■ The cost of loans to the personal sector, including mortgages, has fallen by even less than those to business.

■ The returns offered to depositors in both the personal and corporate sectors decreased slightly, but only 13% of financial institutions in the study believed this was due to the SMP.

■ Smaller banks have been pressurized into mergers and overall the number of banks in Europe has declined post-SMP.

■ There is little evidence that the SMP has increased productivity in European banking.

■ Significant price differences for identical products, for example chequing accounts, still remain across Europe.

■ The most common response by financial institutions to the SMP has been to diversify the range of products and services that they offer.

■ Trade in off-balance-sheet business in financial institutions of the Member States has increased but has not been mirrored by the retail financial sector.

Despite the comprehensive nature of the study, the trends identified have been difficult to disaggregate from changes which might in any case have occurred without SMP. What seems most likely is that the SMP has further intensified the competitive pressures that the European financial services industry was already experiencing.

Re-regulation

There are three broad categories of regulation, namely structural regulation, conduct (or prudential) regulation and investor protection. *Structural regulation* refers to rules about the actual separation of institutions. *Conduct regulation* refers to rules about the assets and liabilities of a bank, such as information disclosure, credit ceilings and capital adequacy requirements (CARs). *Investor protection* refers to rules which seek to prevent banks taking on excessive risk or undertaking fraudulent transactions.

Traditionally all three types of regulation were well represented in the UK banking sector, given its importance within the economy and the need to restrict excessive risk-taking which might lead to system-wide bank failures. In more recent times the trend towards more competitive markets has led to a near disappearance of structural regulation but an increase in conduct and investor protection legislation in the UK and other EU financial markets (see p. 413). This has typically been applied to all credit institutions, further blurring the demarcation applied between banks, non-banks and non-financial companies. With investors in these non-bank and non-financial companies now being equally well covered as those in banks as regards conduct and investor protection regulations, such re-regulation has further increased the competitive pressures on the banking sector.

Ultimately, this trend towards re-regulation will have two effects on the incumbent retail banks. First, profitability in the banking sector will be reduced as competition increases with other credit institutions and margins are reduced. Second, the increase in conduct and investor protection regulation will add to overall costs and reduce profits still further. This suggests that the UK retail banking sector is facing both increased competition from other credit institutions and increased costs in order to comply with new regulatory structures.

Technology

New technologies have tended to replace labour-intensive and costly processes with more capital-intensive and efficient processes. This is especially so as regards methods of storing and analysing information and assessing risk, thereby substantially increasing the volume of financial transactions that can be processed and reducing the cost per unit transaction. A simple illustration of the impact of new technology can be found in the growth of automated clearing. Although only introduced in 1985, by 1988 it had exceeded the annual value of the more costly paper-based clearing mechanism, and is now more than 10 times larger than paper-based alternatives, with an annual value of around £30,000 billion.

A significant impact of the new technologies has also been to reduce the costs of entry into the banking sector, thereby increasing competition. For example, new competititors no longer need an extensively staffed branch network, given the availability of telephone and Internet banking systems, which permit competitors to reach consumers in their homes.

It would seem that an increasing amount of future financial and non-financial business will be undertaken via the Internet. A recent report by Dougan (2003) states that by 2004 it is believed that 50% of all UK bank customers will have online accounts and by the end of 2004 there will be over 17 million users of online banking services. This can be contrasted with an estimated 6.5 million users of online banking services during 2002. Today, all the major UK banks now offer a comprehensive range of online facilities, and banks such as Cahoot, Intelligent Finance and Smile have been created as online-only subsidiaries of larger high street banks (Abbey National, HBOS and Co-Op). A number of reasons have been suggested as to why the rise in Internet banking has been, and will continue to be, so rapid. These include:

- the extremely low marginal cost of transactions;
- no requirement for a branch network;
- easy access to service and product information, which lowers search costs; customers can access information on all financial service providers quickly and cheaply and so price variation will fall, reducing margins in the sector;
- low costs of entry onto the Internet, further eroding margins;
- the consumer pays to connect to the service.

The increasing use of technology will therefore affect traditional banking business by increasing supplier access to customer information, reducing the costs of supplying various financial services and lowering entry barriers. Such impacts are forcing retail banks to reduce their cost structures in order to compete more effectively and maintain their profitability.

Responses of UK retail banks

Retail banks in the UK (and Europe) have made serious attempts to reduce their cost/income ratios in response to these various market pressures. The focus has been both to reduce cost and to increase income (revenue) in order to reduce this ratio.

Figure 21.6 suggests that retail banks have reduced fixed and variable costs by reducing the number of branches and staff. As can be seen, there has been a substantial fall in the number of staff employed by the 'big four' retail banks, from around 275,000 in 1990 to around 195,600 today, despite the figures having been inflated by the 'big four' takeover of mutual societies. These falls have been paralleled by a sustained increase in the number of Automatic Telling Machines (ATMs) from around 2,000 in 1979 to nearly 14,000 today.

Figure 21.7 suggests that the cost/income ratios of retail banks have indeed fallen to around 55%. Many believe further falls must occur if retail banks are to become competitive. A target of around 50% is widely accepted, given that other credit institutions such as building societies have cost/income ratios around 45%. It may be that more attention must be paid to generating extra *income* if further falls are to be achieved in this ratio.

Universal financial supermarkets

Although banks have reduced branch staff levels and closed some branches, this policy has met some resistance on both the political and economic (customer) fronts. An alternative approach which seeks to tackle *both* sides of the cost/income ratio has involved the retail banks developing into 'universal financial supermarkets'. This diversification into new markets has also helped to spread total costs over a wider product range. This allowed banks to spread their extensive assets into new areas using the same inputs and build on their solid reputation in the high street and access to customer financial data. Retail banks now offer a much broader array of products and services and increasingly receive income from other sources than interest payments, such as from foreign exchange and equity dealings and derivative-based income. This decline in importance of interest as a source of income is shown in Fig. 21.8. Whereas non-interest income was around 25% of all income in 1980, this figure had risen to over 40% by the turn of the new millennium.

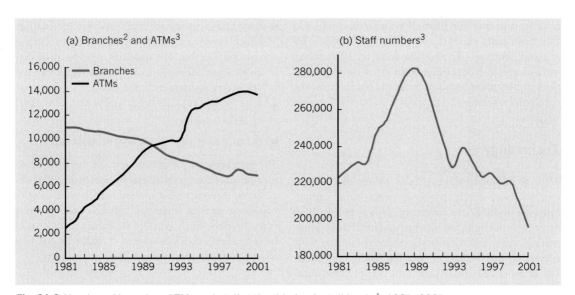

Fig. 21.6 Number of branches, ATMs and staff at the 'big four' retail banks[1], 1981–2001.
[1] Barclays, Nat West (now part of Royal Bank of Scotland (RBS branch level excluded for reasons of comparision)), HSBC (formerly Midland Bank) and Lloyds TSB (formerly Lloyds Bank)
[2] Figures prior to 1999 cover Lloyds Bank only
[3] Figures prior to 1994 cover Lloyds Bank only
Source: Adapted from *British Bankers' Association Annual Abstract of Banking Statistics* (2003), Volumes 12 and 19, Tables 5.01, 5.02 and 5.03.

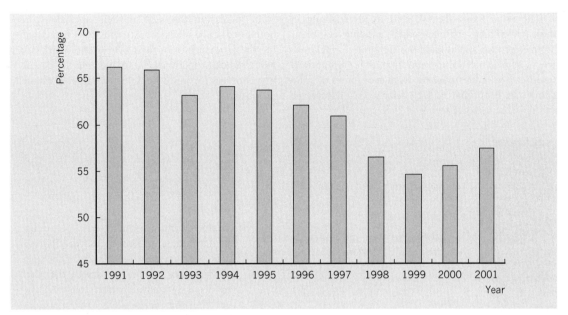

Fig. 21.7 Cost/income ratios for UK MBBGs[1], 1991–2001 (cost/income measured by operating expenses as a proportion of gross income).
[1] Major British Banking Groups, which consists of all the main retail banks in the UK
Source: Adapted from *British Bankers' Association Annual Abstract of Banking Statistics* (2003), Volume 19, Table 3.09.

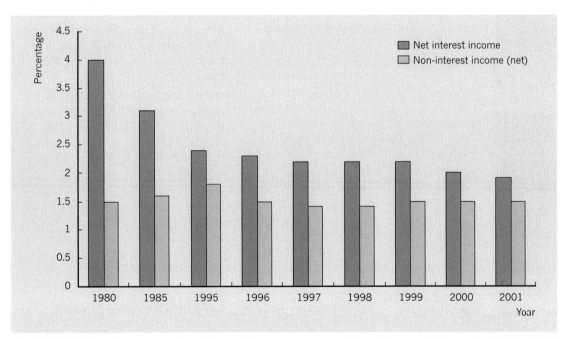

Fig. 21.8 Net-interest income and non-interest income as a proportion of average balance sheet total for UK MBBGs[1], 1980–2001.
[1] Major British Banking Groups, which consists of all the main retail banks in the UK
Source: Adapted from *British Bankers' Association Annual Abstract of Banking Statistics* (2003), Volume 19, Table 3.09.

The retail banks believe that by diversifying in these ways they are using their existing resources more effectively, including both tangible (branch networks and financial data) and intangible (reputation) resources, in order to benefit from economies of scale and scope. Economies of scale refer to cost reductions from increasing the size of their operations; economies of scope refer to cost reductions from changing the product mix of their operations. Further, the new financial supermarkets are meeting the demands of customers for more flexible and targeted financial products.

Key points

- Financial institutions exist to match the needs of borrowers and lenders, i.e. to *mediate* between them.

- Mediation may be necessary because borrowers and lenders have different requirements in terms of maturity, liquidity and yield.

- There are three main types of 'operator' in the UK financial system: lenders and borrowers, financial intermediaries and the various financial markets in which transactions take place.

- The Single European Act (1 January 1993) gave authorized financial institutions the right to do business anywhere in the EU.

- Financial intermediaries can take one of two main forms: brokerage intermediaries and asset-transforming intermediaries. *Brokerage intermediaries* assess information on lenders and borrowers but do not purchase or hold financial assets. *Asset-transforming intermediaries* acquire liabilities and transform them into assets with different characteristics in terms of maturity, liquidity and yield.

- UK financial intermediaries can also be categorized as *bank financial intermediaries*, which include the retail and wholesale banks, and *non-bank financial intermediaries*, which include building societies, pension funds, investment and unit trusts.

- Financial intermediation is becoming increasingly competitive and diversified. Not only are existing 'players' widening the range of activities in which they are involved but entirely new 'players' are entering the markets (e.g. supermarkets and banking services).

- The Bank of England has been granted independence in the setting of short-term interest rates and this is overseen by the Monetary Policy Committee (MPC) which is a committee within the Bank. The Bank manipulates short-term interest rates via open market operations in the money markets using predominantly gilt repos.

- Financial institutions are regulated by the Financial Services Authority (FSA). However, financial stability is maintained via frequent discussions between the FSA, the Bank of England and the Treasury department.

- Financial markets can be split into two main markets: the money markets which mainly deal in short-term financial assets, and the capital markets which mainly deal in long-term financial claims.

Now try the self-check questions for this chapter on the Companion Website. You will also find up-to-date facts and case materials.

References and further reading

Apps, R., Goacher, D. and Lipscombe, G. (1996) *The Monetary and Financial System*, Banker Books, London.

Bank of England (1997) The Bank of England's operations in the sterling money markets, *Bank of England Quarterly Bulletin*, May.

British Bankers' Association Statistical Unit (1998) Annual Abstract of Banking Statistics, *British Bankers' Association*, **15**.

Dougan, S. (2003) Branding financial services on the Internet, *Reuters Business Insight Finance Reports*, June.

Economist (1998) Capital of capital, *Economist*, 9 May.

Greenbaum, S. I. and Thakor, A. V. (1995) *Contemporary Financial Intermediation*, Dryden Press, Orlando.

Hall, M. J. B. (1997) All change at the bank, *Loughborough University Banking Centre Research Paper*, No. 110/97.

Howells, P. and Bain, K. (2003) *Monetary Economics: Policy and its Theoretical Basis*, Palgrave, Macmillan.

Llewellyn, D. (1997) Trends in the British financial system: the context for building societies, Loughborough University Banking Centre – Building Society Association Project Paper No. 5.

McKenzie, G. (1998) Financial regulation and the European Union, *Economic Review*, April.

Pilbeam, K. (1998) *Finance and Financial Markets*, Macmillan.

Rodgers, P. (1997) Changes at the Bank of England, *Bank of England Quarterly Bulletin*, August.

Rodgers, P. (1998) The Bank of England Act, *Bank of England Quarterly Bulletin*, May.

Santomero, A. M. and Babbel, D. F. (2001) *Financial Markets, Instruments, and Institutions*, 2nd edn, Irwin, Chicago.

Single Market Review (1997) Impact on services: credit institutions and banking, Subseries 2, Vol. 3, Kogan Page.

Webb, R. M. (1998) Operational efficiency of large UK retail banking groups, Middlesex University Business School, mimeo.

Relevant Internet sites

Bank of England: www.bankofengland.co.uk
British Bankers' Association: www.bba.org.uk
Building Societies' Association: www.bas.org.uk
Chartered Institute of Bankers: www.cib.org.uk
Financial Times: www.ft.com
London Stock Exchange: www.londonstockexchange.com

Chapter 22   Inflation

In this chapter we first examine a number of methods of measuring
inflation. We then consider the 'costs' of inflation, both when it is
fully anticipated, and when, as is usually the case, it is not. A basic
theoretical framework for understanding inflation is presented and is
used to explain recent UK experience. The issues of inflation
targeting and central bank independence are also considered.

The definition and measurement of inflation

Inflation is a persistent tendency for the general level of prices to rise. In effect the rate of inflation measures the change in the purchasing power of money, i.e. how much more money you would need to have this year when faced with this year's prices to be as well off as you were last year when faced with last year's prices. Until 1979 inflation in the UK was measured and reported almost exclusively by reference to the RPI; since then various additional measures have been introduced.

The Retail Price Index (RPI)

The RPI, which was formerly compiled by the Department of Employment, is now the responsibility of the Office for National Statistics. It measures the change from month to month in the cost of a representative 'basket' of goods and services of the type bought by a typical household.

A number of stages are involved in the calculation of the RPI. The first stage is to select the items to be included in the index and to weight these items according to their relative importance in the average family budget. Obviously items on which a family spends a large proportion of its income are given heavier weights than those items on which the family spends relatively little. For example, in 2003 the weight given to tea in the index was 1, whereas that for electricity was 14 (out of a total 'all items weight' of 1,000). The weights used are changed annually to reflect the changes in the composition of family expenditure. The new weights are derived from the Expenditure and Food Survey in which about 7,000 households, carefully chosen to represent all regions and types of household, take part each year. Each member of the household aged over 16 years records his or her day-to-day expenditure on items over a two-week period, together with any longer-term payments, such as telephone bills, season tickets, etc. It is from these records that the weights for the RPI are based. The new weights, which begin in January each year, are largely based on the pattern of expenditure shown in the survey over the year to the previous June. For some items, however, such as selected consumer durables (e.g. furniture and carpets) where sales fluctuate widely from year to year, expenditure is averaged over a three-year period.

The weights for this 'general RPI' are obtained by excluding those pensioner households who derive 75% or more of their income from state benefits and any households who are in the top 4% of income earners (these categories together accounting for 16% of all households). These two groups are excluded because the pattern of their expenditure differs markedly from that of the great majority of households.

The weights used for groups of items are shown in Table 22.1. It can be seen that food has been replaced as the largest item by housing (rent, mortgage interest rates and council tax, water charges, repairs and dwelling insurance). This is part of a longer-run trend associated with differing income elasticities of demand for the items in the 'basket'.

The second stage in deriving the RPI involves collecting the price data. For most items, prices are collected on a specific day each month, usually the Tuesday nearest the middle of the month. Prices are obtained from a sample of retail outlets in some 180 different areas. Care is taken to make sure a representative range of retail outlets, small retailers,

Table 22.1 General index of retail prices: group weights.

	1987	2003
Food	167	109
Catering	46	51
Alcoholic drink	76	68
Tobacco	38	30
Housing	157	203
Fuel and light	61	29
Household goods	73	72
Household services	44	61
Clothing and footwear	74	51
Personal goods and services	40	41
Motoring expenditure	127	146
Fares and other travel costs	22	20
Leisure goods	47	48
Leisure services	30	71
	1,000	1,000

Source: Office for National Statistics.

supermarkets, department stores, etc. are surveyed. In all, around 150,000 price quotations are collected each month. An average price is then calculated for each item in the index. For example, on 11 April 2000, 533 price quotations were taken for tomatoes; the prices ranged from 99p to 189p per kilo, with an average of 170p.

The final stage is to calculate the RPI from all these data. All index numbers must relate to some base period or reference date. In the case of the RPI the base period is January 1987 = 100. The index is calculated each month through a weighted price relative method.[1] Since the weights are revised each year to keep the index up to date, the index is calculated afresh each year with January counting as 100. Each yearly index is then linked back to the base year by means of a chain base method.[2] In February 2003 the RPI stood at 179.3, which means that average prices have risen by 79.3% between January 1987 and February 2003. As the index is an average, this figure conceals the fact that some prices have increased more rapidly (rent 153%, water 173% and cigarettes 205%), whilst other prices have fallen (audio-visual equipment by around 70%).

A separate index is calculated for one-pensioner and two-pensioner households. These have weights which differ from the general RPI because of the different pattern of expenditure of these households. For example, pensioners spend a higher proportion of their income on housing, fuel and food, and a smaller proportion on clothing, alcoholic drink, durable goods and transport. Despite this, 'pensioner' price indices have moved fairly closely in line with the general RPI for several years.

Once the RPI has been constructed, the rate of inflation can then be calculated, with the most usual measure being the twelve-monthly change in the RPI. For example, the RPI stood at 173.8 in February 2002. In February 2003 it stood at 179.3 and therefore the annual rate of inflation over that period is

$$\frac{179.3 - 173.8}{173.8} \times 100\% = 3.2\%$$

Inflation as measured by the RPI and the RPIX is shown in Fig. 22.1.

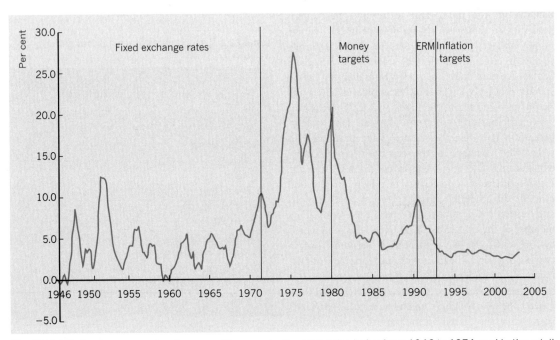

Fig. 22.1 Inflation is measured as the annual increase in the retail price index from 1946 to 1974, and in the retail price index excluding mortgage interest payments since 1974.
Sources: King (1997) and *Economic Trends* (various).

The RPIX and RPIY

The *RPI* is often referred to as the *headline* measure of inflation. For policy-makers, however, it has been superseded by the *RPIX* (the RPI excluding mortgage interest payments). The RPIX is referred to as measuring 'underlying' inflation and is the subject of the government's 2.5% inflation target.[3] Excluding mortgage interest rates from the RPI eliminates a rather perverse effect, namely that raising the interest rate to moderate inflationary pressure will actually increase the RPI measure of inflation!

However, both the RPI and the RPIX are influenced by increases in indirect taxes and the Council Tax. If these taxes increase, for example a rise in excise duty on cigarettes to discourage smoking, then the measure of inflation will increase without any increase in inflationary pressure in the economy. The Bank of England publishes the *RPIY* (RPIX minus VAT, local authority taxes and excise duty) to eliminate this effect.

Figure 22.2 shows the relationship between the RPI, RPIX and RPIY. The effect of the increase in interest rates in the second half of 1999 and the first half of 2000 can clearly be seen on the RPI, but the RPIX and RPIY were little affected.

Do the RPI and its related measures overestimate the cost of living?

The RPI (together with the various measures derived from it) is supposed to measure the movement in prices of goods and services that the average British family buys. In this respect the RPI has a pivotal role in the economy as a target for policy makers, for example in acting as a basis for indexing tax allowances and as a starting point for pay claims. The question might reasonably be asked as to how well the RPI reflects changes in the 'true' cost of living. In other words, if the RPI increases by 5% over the year, do households really need a 5% rise in disposable income to maintain their living standards? Some studies suggest that there is potential for systematic discrepancies between the RPI and a 'true' cost of living index. For example Cunningham (1996) notes four sources of 'bias' which might cause the RPI to overestimate the true increase

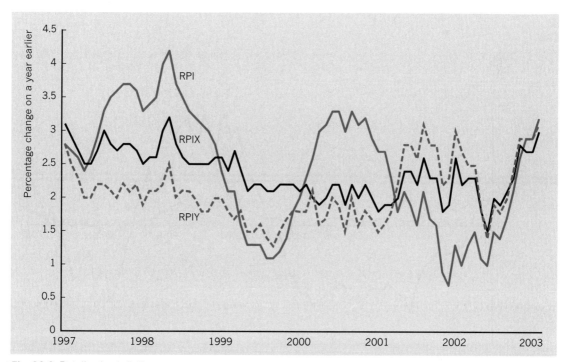

Fig. 22.2 Retail price inflation.
Source: Office for National Statistics.

in the cost of living. The first is a *substitution bias* which arises from consumers choosing relatively cheaper goods and services over time. However, the RPI has a fixed basket of goods and services for each year, preventing a switch to cheaper sources being reflected during that year. The second is a *new outlet bias*. Price quotes are taken from a wide range of outlets but are unlikely to fully reflect short-term changes in retailing patterns which might cause consumers to move to cheaper discount stores. The third is an *upward bias* which arises from new consumer durable goods not usually being included in the RPI index until the initial phase of rapidly falling prices (often associated with new entry) is over. The fourth is a *quality improvement bias*, with quality gains in durable goods and services not being fully captured in the RPI. Cunningham estimates that the RPI may actually *overestimate* the cost of living by at least 0.35 to 0.8% points per annum as a result of these biases.

Other measures of inflation

Although the RPI (with or without the mortgage interest adjustment) is the usual measure of inflation, there are others (see Fig. 22.3). The *Index of Producer Prices* (which has replaced the old Wholesale Price Index), for example, measures the rate of inflation before it is actually felt in the shops. This index has two parts, one giving the prices of raw materials and fuel as they enter the factory (input prices) and the other the rise in 'factory gate prices' as manufactured goods leave the factory (output prices). The main use of these two indices is to give an indication of the future trend of retail prices. The effect of the strong sterling exchange rate in 1996/97, together with the weakness in world commodity prices in the past few years, is clearly reflected in the *negative* input price inflation from mid-1996 to mid-1999. Oil price increases were mainly responsible for the upturn after 1999 and again in 2003.

In contrast to the RPI, which measures movements in the prices of a 'basket' of goods bought by a representative UK household, the *GDP deflator* seeks to measure movements in the prices of the *entire basket* of goods and services produced in the UK and can in this sense be regarded as the most comprehensive price index in the economy. It is, however, less up-to-date than the other indicators and is liable to greater revision. It is obtained by dividing the GDP at current

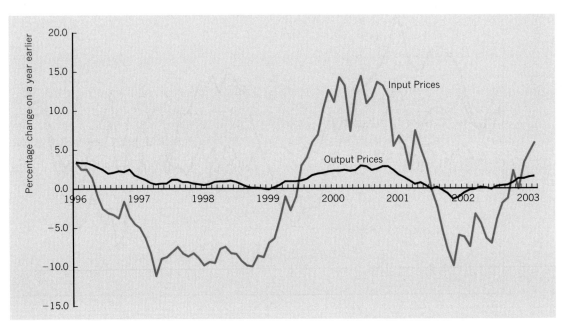

Fig. 22.3 UK manufacturers' input and output prices.
Source: Office for National Statistics.

factor cost by the GDP at constant factor cost, and is sometimes called the 'implicit' deflator because it is derived in this indirect way. Between the fourth quarter of 2001 and the fourth quarter of 2002, the GDP deflator rose by 3.1% compared to 2.5% for the RPI.

European comparisons of inflation: the HICP[3]

The *Harmonized Index of Consumer Prices* (HICP) is calculated in each EU country for purposes of comparison. The European Central Bank aims to keep EU inflation below 2% as measured by the HICP.

It is worth noting that the HICP and the RPI are different in a number of ways:

- The RPI is calculated using the arithmetic mean, whereas the HICP uses a geometric mean.

- The RPI excludes the richest 4% of households and the poorest pensioner households when calculating the weights.

- The HICP includes everyone, including foreign tourists and inhabitants of institutions.

- The basket of goods also differs mainly in its treatment of housing and related costs. A number of items included in the RPI are excluded from the HICP, such as Council Tax, mortgage interest payments, house depreciation and buildings insurance.

The HICP measure of inflation for the UK has systematically been below that of the RPIX. For example, over the first three months of 2003 HICP was 1.4% points less than the RPIX, mainly due to the exclusion of housing costs from the HICP. Table 22.2 shows EU inflation as measured by the HICP.[3]

 Low inflation as a policy objective

Much of the recent debate on inflation centres around how best to defeat it. Less is heard, at least in public debate, about the actual economic costs of inflation. It is important to identify these costs and to try and quantify them, so that they can then be compared with the costs of the policies aimed at reducing inflation. These latter costs are usually seen in terms of higher unemployment if restrictive monetary and fiscal policies are used to control inflation, or a mis-allocation of resources if prices and incomes policies are used. Traditionally the costs of inflation were seen in terms of its adverse effect on income distribution, as rising prices are particularly severe on those with fixed incomes, such as pensioners. However, Milton Friedman, in his Nobel lecture, shifted the focus of attention towards the adverse effects of inflation on output and employment.

In assessing the costs of inflation it is usual to distinguish two cases: that of perfectly anticipated inflation, where the rate of inflation is expected and has been taken into account in economic transactions, and that of imperfectly anticipated, or unexpected, inflation. We will consider perfectly anticipated inflation first, as it provides a useful benchmark against which to assess the more usual case of imperfectly anticipated inflation.

Perfectly anticipated inflation

Suppose we initially have an economy in which inflation is proceeding at a steady and perfectly foreseen rate, and in which all possible adjustments for the existence of inflation have been made. In this economy all contracts, interest rates and the tax system would take the correctly foreseen rate of

Table 22.2 EU harmonized indices of consumer prices (increase on year to January 2003).

EU	UK	France	Germany	Greece	Italy	Netherlands	Spain	Sweden
2.1	1.4	2.0	1.0	3.3	2.8	2.9	3.8	2.6

Source: Office for National Statistics, March 2003.

inflation into account. The exchange rate would also adjust to prevent inflation having any adverse effect on the balance of payments.

'Shoe-leather' costs

In such an economy the main cost of inflation would arise from the fact that interest is not normally paid on currency in circulation. The opportunity cost to the individual of holding currency would then be the interest the individual could have earned on other assets, such as deposits at the bank. Higher anticipated inflation will tend to raise interest rates and therefore the opportunity cost of holding currency, with the rational response to this being for the individual to economize on currency holdings by making more frequent trips to the bank. The costs of these extra trips to the bank are often called the 'shoe-leather' costs of inflation. Although these costs are small for low rates of inflation, they have been estimated as rising to about 0.3% of GDP for perfectly anticipated inflation rates rising to around 10% per annum.

'Menu' costs

A second cost, when inflation is fully anticipated, is that of having to change prices frequently. This is sometimes called the 'menu' cost of inflation. Presumably the more rapid the inflation, the more frequently things like price tags, cash tills, vending machines and price lists have to be changed, and this takes time, effort and money.

A study (Bakhshi *et al.* 1997) has attempted to estimate the benefits and costs of reducing perfectly anticipated inflation in the UK by 2% (which, given the overstatement of true inflation by the RPIX, would amount to achieving price stability). The annual welfare benefits of such a reduction in inflation were estimated at around 0.21% of GDP. Of course, the welfare benefits of lower inflation must be set against the lost output associated with the necessary deflation. Based on estimates of the UK 'sacrifice ratio' (the cost of cumulative lost output required for each percentage point reduction in inflation), Bakhshi *et al.* calculated the annual welfare loss of such a reduction in inflation to be around 0.18% of GDP. In other words, based on his estimates, there would be a net welfare gain of 0.03% of GDP per annum as a result of policies which reduce perfectly anticipated inflation in the UK by 2%.

Further costs arise from inflation when it is either not foreseen correctly, or not adjusted to fully. It is to these additional costs from imperfectly anticipated inflation that we now turn.

Imperfectly anticipated inflation

Redistribution effects

Unanticipated inflation leads to a redistribution of income and wealth. Debtors will gain at the expense of creditors if contracts do not take inflation fully into account and those on fixed incomes will suffer. In general there is likely to be a transfer from the private to the public sector. For example, inflation causes fiscal drag, taking individuals into higher tax brackets, thereby raising tax revenue for the public sector. Inflation also reduces the real value of the national debt, with government securities maturing at specified future dates for sums that are fixed in *money* terms, so that inflation reduces the real cost to the government of redeeming them. Inflation can, in effect, be regarded as an implicit tax on the holding of cash.

Costs of decision-taking

Uncertainty about future price levels is likely to lead to a misallocation of resources. For example, such uncertainty may discourage long-term contracts. This in turn is likely to inhibit investment which by its very nature tends to be long term. Savers and lenders may react to the uncertainty about future price levels by demanding a premium to cover the perceived extra risk. This premium will push up real interest rates and again discourage investment. Capital will also be misallocated if savers and investors form different expectations of inflation and hence different views as to expected real interest rates. There is evidence to suggest that the rate of inflation and the level of uncertainty are positively correlated (see Briault 1995).

Inflation and relative price movements

In market economies, changes in relative prices act as signals which serve to guide the allocation of resources. It is argued that economic agents find it difficult to discern *relative* price movements from *general* price level movements in times of inflation, especially when the rate of inflation is uncertain. In this case incorrect decisions will be made and resources will be misallocated.

The effects of inflation on economic growth

The previous analysis suggests that inflation (and especially uncertainty surrounding the future inflation rate) will lead to a misallocation of resources and a lower rate of economic growth. Testing this hypothesis empirically is extremely complex.

One approach is to use *time-series* data for single countries. Grimes (1991) found a significant *negative* relationship for 13 countries, which implied that a sustained increase in inflation from 0% to 9% would lead to a full percentage point reduction in annual growth rates. Others have found weaker but still negative relationships. The problem with simple regression equations used in such analyses is that it is difficult to get unbiased results. Difficulties arise in interpreting the overall negative relationship between inflation and growth. For example, in most countries, at least in the short run, inflation and economic growth are likely to be positively related, as in periods of boom. It might also be the case that the negative relationship might just be picking up the effects of policy measures; for example, a period of high inflation might precipitate a deflationary policy response which would slow the growth rate. The interested reader should consult Briault (1995) for further discussion of these issues.

An alternative approach is to use *cross-country* data. One example of this is the work done by Robert Barro (1995). He looked at data for 100 countries from 1960 to 1990. His regression results indicated that an increase in average inflation of 10% points per year reduces the growth or real per capita GDP by 0.2–0.3% points per year, and lowers the ratio of investment to GDP by 0.4–0.6% points. Although these effects may not appear particularly large, a reduction in growth rate of the above order of magnitude (brought about by a 10% rise in the average inflation rate) would mean that after 30 years real GDP would be 4–7% lower than otherwise. This would represent an estimated £30–50 billion shortfall in GDP at current UK values of output.

Another study by Sarel (1996) suggests that the effect of inflation on growth is non-linear. He found a *structural break* in the relationship at an inflation rate of around 8%, with inflation below 8% per annum having no significant negative effects on growth, but inflation above 8% per annum having significant negative effects on growth, the suggestion here being that policy makers should always keep inflation below the level (8%) consistent with this structural break. Another implication of Sarel's study is that there is nothing particularly 'optimal' about the UK inflation target of 2.5% per annum.

Economic theory and inflation

The causes of inflation can be illustrated using the standard aggregate supply/demand framework found in most economic texts, such as Lipsey and Chrystal (1995) and Parkin *et al.* (2003). Figure 22.4 illustrates this framework. The first point to make is that the distinction between the short-run and long-run aggregate supply curves is important.

The upward sloping *short-run aggregate supply* (SRAS) curve assumes that some input prices, particularly money wages, remain relatively fixed as the price level changes. It then follows that an increase in the price level, whilst input prices remain relatively fixed, increases the profitability of production and induces firms to expand output and employ more labour. An increase in the general price level will therefore lead, in the short run, to some increase in real GDP.

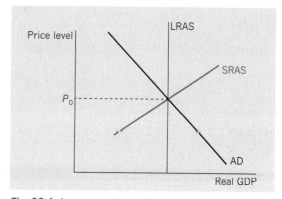

Fig. 22.4 Aggregate demand and supply.

There are two explanations as to why wages may remain constant even though prices have changed. First, many employees are hired under fixed-wage contracts. Once these contracts are agreed it is the firm that determines (within reason) the number of labour hours actually worked. If prices rise, the negotiated real wage will fall and firms will want to hire more labour time. Second, workers may not immediately be aware of price level changes, i.e. they may suffer from 'money illusion'. If workers' expectations lag behind actual price level changes, then workers will not be aware that their real wages have changed and will not adjust their wage demands appropriately. Both these reasons imply that as the price level rises, real wages will fall and the employment of extra labour hours will become more attractive to employers.

The long run is defined as the period in which all input prices (e.g. money wages) are fully responsive to changes in the price level. Workers in the long run can gather full information on price level changes and can renegotiate wage contracts in line with higher or lower prices. It follows that in the long run, a change in the price level is likely to be associated with an equal increase in money wages, leaving the real wage unchanged and by implication leaving employment and output unchanged. The *long-run aggregate supply* (LRAS) curve is independent of the price level; in other words, it is vertical.

Because, in the long run, all wages and prices can be renegotiated in line with supply and demand, the labour market will be in equilibrium (the real wage equating labour demand and supply) at the full employment level, with unemployment at the natural rate (see Chapter 23). The level of output associated with this level of employment is variously called the *full employment* level of output or the *natural* level of output. This level of output is obviously not constant but is determined by supply-side factors, such as the labour force, the capital stock and the state of technology. Through time this full employment or natural level of output can be expected to increase as the economy grows, i.e. the vertical LRAS curve can be expected to shift to the right.

Demand pull inflation

One-off demand inflation

Consider the case of a one-off increase in aggregate demand. The source of the increase could be an increase in the money stock, an increase in the budget deficit, or any autonomous change in consumption, investment or net exports. Whatever the cause, the aggregate demand curve AD_0 in Fig. 22.5 shifts to the right to AD_1 along the short-run aggregate supply curve $SRAS_0$. Excess demand now exists at the old price level P_0 and this pushes prices up to P_1. Such higher prices, with money wages lagging behind, increase the profitability of firms who then increase output beyond the full employment level Q_0, so that unemployment falls below the natural rate. However, the new short-run equilibrium (B) with the output Q_1

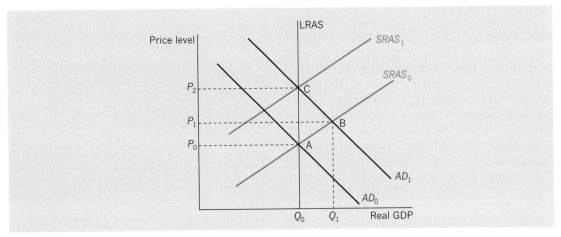

Fig. 22.5 A one-off increase in demand.

is not sustainable; labour is relatively scarce and workers will negotiate money wage increases to compensate for the increase in prices. The short-run aggregate supply curve now shifts up and to the left (i.e. from $SRAS_0$ to $SRAS_1$) in response to the increased costs of production, returning the economy to a new long-run equilibrium (C).

The economy experiences a period of 'stagflation' as output falls back to its *natural* level Q_0 and the price level continues to rise to P_2. The rise in price from P_1 to P_2 causing output to fall is usually explained in terms of rising prices reducing the real money supply, which in turn causes interest rates to rise and therefore interest-sensitive elements within aggregate demand to fall. Note that the inflation stops when the price level reaches P_2. A one-off increase in aggregate demand will not therefore generate a lasting inflation.

Continuous demand inflation

Inflation proper, by which we mean a *sustained* upward movement in the price level, can occur only if the growth in aggregate demand is maintained. In this case output does *not* fall back to its natural rate but remains above it. It seems unlikely that autonomous shifts in private aggregate demand will be repeated period after period, which leaves either fiscal or monetary policy as the most likely cause of persistent demand inflation. However, expansionary fiscal

policy, if funded by borrowing, is likely to lead to higher interest rates and therefore to the crowding-out of private spendings. This leaves monetary expansion as the most likely factor in turning a one-off inflation into a sustained inflation. The initial inflationary impulse could come from any demand-side factor, but an increase in the money supply is still necessary to prevent the price increases from reducing the real money supply, pushing up interest rates and eventually stopping the inflationary process. Figure 22.6 illustrates this case. As long as the money supply is allowed to expand in line with increasing prices, the aggregate demand curve continues to shift upward and the economy is kept above its natural level of output Q_0. The cost of this money supply strategy, however, is continuing inflation, with the price level rising in each time period.

Cost push inflation and supply shocks

Cost push or supply-side inflation results from an increase in costs of production which firms pass on in the form of higher prices. The source of the cost increases could be a rise in imported raw material costs, such as the two oil price shocks of 1973–75 and 1979–80. Alternatively, trade unions may use their market power to push wages up irrespective of the pressure of demand in the labour market. In both

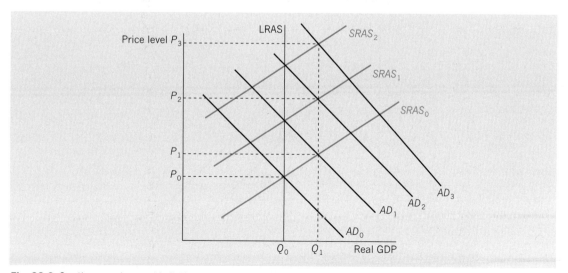

Fig. 22.6 Continuous demand inflation.

these cases one group, OPEC or unions, is using market power to try and secure a larger share of output; firms, in response, attempt to protect their profits by increasing prices. Figure 22.7 shows cost push/supply-side inflation.

Suppose the economy is initially in equilibrium (A) with output at the full employment or natural rate Q_0 and the price level at P_0 with zero inflation. An increase in oil prices then shifts $SRAS_0$, the short-run aggregate supply curve, to $SRAS_1$. The economy now faces a period of stagflation with falling output, increased unemployment and rising prices. The period of stagflation ends when the new short-run equilibrium B is reached. If aggregate demand remains unchanged at AD_0 then the excess supply in both goods and labour markets will eventually put downward pressure on costs and wages, causing the SRAS curve to return to its original position. This period of deflation returns the economy to its full employment equilibrium (A). However, this process is likely to be slow and painful, requiring a major adjustment in relative prices and a fall in real wages.

Expansionary monetary policy which shifts the aggregate demand curve to AD_1 would speed up the process of returning the economy to full employment, but at the cost of additional inflation (Q_0/P_2 at point C). Indeed if the government got the timing and strength of the demand expansion just right, the economy could move from one long-run equilibrium to another, with very little loss of output. It is highly unlikely, however, that the government has the appropriate information and macroeconomic tools to stabilize output precisely at the full employment level Q_0.

Continued cost push inflation is unlikely, unless accompanied by accommodating monetary policy. Union pressure for wage increases would be undermined by falling output and increased unemployment, and even oil producers would eventually find that the reduced activity of non-oil-producers would restrict their market power. Monetary accommodation would, however, alter the story and might lead to repeated supply shocks and continuing inflation. Unions, thwarted in their attempt to seek real wage increases because of the higher prices associated with the monetary expansion and without the deterrent of unemployment, might ask for wage increases in the next round, causing the short-run aggregate supply curve to shift to the left a second time. The choices for the government are, as before, either to allow unemployment to increase or to accommodate the new price increases by increasing the money supply and stimulating demand. The latter path could then lead to a continuous wage–price spiral.

There is no consensus as to the advisability of monetary accommodation of a supply-side shock. The policy decision depends to some extent on

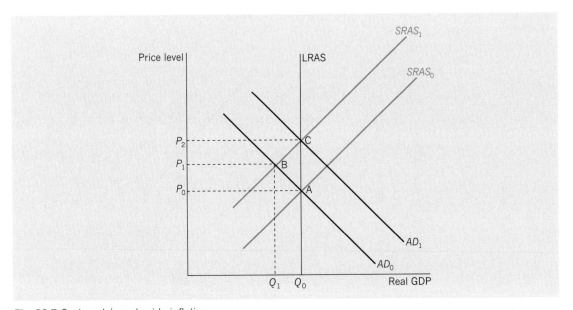

Fig. 22.7 Cost push/supply-side inflation.

judging the relative costs to the state of extra unemployment against those of extra inflation. The danger with accommodation is that once inflationary expectations become entrenched in the wage–price setting process, they might be eliminated only after a prolonged period of unemployment (see the section on the Phillips curve below).

In conclusion, the theoretical analysis of inflation indicates that the government can always stop inflation, whether the cause is demand or supply-side factors. All the government has to do is to halt the growth of the money supply. The bad news, however, is that the cost of halting inflation is likely to entail a reduction in output and a rise in unemployment.

The relationship between inflation and unemployment (the Phillips curve)

Very few articles in economics have generated as much subsequent interest as A. W. Phillips' study of UK wage inflation and unemployment over the period 1861–1957. In the article (Phillips 1958) he appeared to find a stable and inverse relationship between unemployment and inflation (strictly, changes in wage rates). If unemployment was low, inflation would be high, and vice versa. The so-called Phillips curve suggested that with unemployment of around 5.5% there would be zero *wage inflation* and that with unemployment of around 2.5% the wage inflation generated would be covered by productivity growth, resulting in zero *price inflation*. This is

depicted in Fig. 22.8. The relationship seemed to hold good over a long period of time and subsequent research found that it held good for many economies, and not just that of the UK.

The inverse relationship between inflation and unemployment was explained in terms of unemployment being an *indirect* measure of the level of excess demand in the economy. When unemployment is high and demand is low, the excess supply of labour holds wages and prices down; however, when unemployment is low and demand is high, the excess demand for labour will push wages and prices up more quickly. The Phillips curve appeared to offer the policy-maker a menu of choices from which could be chosen the preferred combination of unemployment and inflation, whilst at the same time highlighting the trade-off between the two policy objectives. If the economy was, say, at point A and the government wished to reduce unemployment by expanding aggregate demand, then it could do so but only at the cost of higher inflation, as at point B. Using the previous AD/AS framework, the expansionary fiscal or monetary policy would cause the AD curve to shift to the right, so that it now intersected further along the SRAS curve, thereby causing the price level to rise. The rise in prices will then push real wages down (because of either fixed contracts or workers' expectations lagging behind actual price increases), resulting in firms taking on more workers, unemployment falling and output rising. It is clear that some economists and policy-makers thought that point B could be maintained indefinitely if desired, but as we

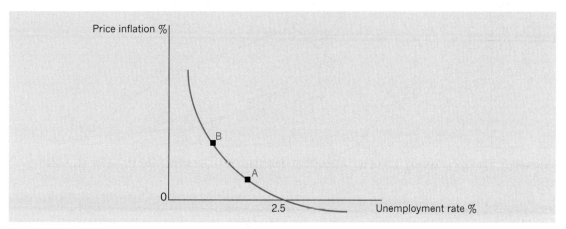

Fig. 22.8 The Phillips curve.

have seen and will confirm later, the existence of any such long-run trade-off (whereby a constant though higher rate of inflation can be achieved for a given fall in unemployment) is highly questionable.

Breakdown of the Phillips curve

Evidence of the breakdown of the Phillips curve came very soon after the 'discovery' of this relationship that had supposedly been stable for over 100 years. Figure 22.9 plots UK inflation against unemployment since 1966. Clearly the downward sloping Phillips curve is not always in evidence in the period 1966–2002.

Supply-side factors

One reason why the Phillips relationship might not be entirely stable is the existence of supply-side inflation. As we have seen, raw material prices or wage increases may push costs and prices up irrespective of the pressure of demand, at least in the short term. In this case, a given level of unemployment would be associated with higher levels of inflation than the original Phillips curve would predict. The two oil price shocks of 1973–75 and 1979–80 resulted in periods of increased inflation that were not associated

with falling unemployment, as the demand-side theory would have led us to predict.

Time-period factors

A more fundamental reason for the breakdown of the Phillips curve was proposed by Friedman (1968) and Phelps (1967). The new version of the Phillips curve makes the distinction between the short run and long run. It also assumes that markets are competitive enough in the long run to ensure that the real wage will be at the market clearing level. If this is the case, then labour supply will equal labour demand at the full employment level and unemployment will be at its natural rate. Note, however, that even when the market clears, not all workers who consider themselves to be part of the labour force will be either willing or able to accept a job at the going real wage. Some workers will be searching around for a better job offer (these are the *frictionally unemployed*), while other workers will not have the right skills or be in the right place (these are the *structurally unemployed*). The two groups together make up the *natural rate of unemployment* (NRU).

Figure 22.10 shows the market clearing or full employment real wage $(W/P)_F$ and the associated full employment level of employment (N_F); the natural

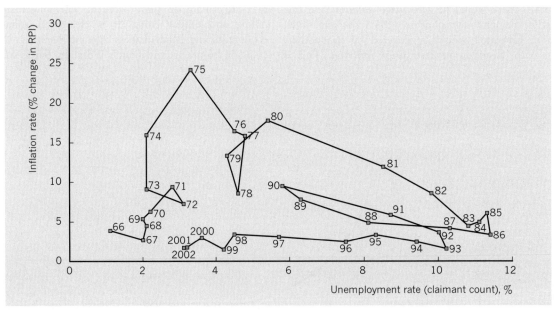

Fig. 22.9 The relationship between the unemployment and inflation rates in the UK, 1966–2002.
Source: Office for National Statistics.

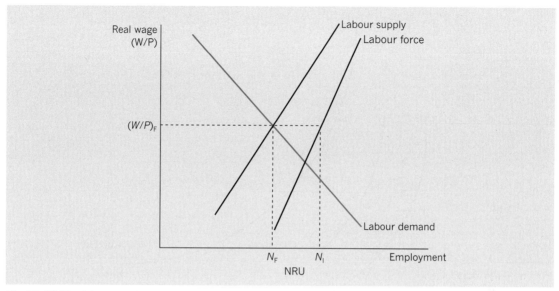

Fig. 22.10 The labour market.

rate of unemployment (NRU) is $N_1 - N_F$, the difference between the amount of labour demanded and the labour force.

Expectational factors

The final strand of the revised Phillips curve is to emphasize the role of *expectations* in the inflationary process. Friedman pointed out that what workers and firms are interested in is the *real* wages, not the *money* wage. Wage bargaining takes place in money terms but when considering a money wage offer the expected inflation rate will be taken into account. The implication is that for any given level of unemployment (labour market tightness) there will be any number of possible money wage claims (for a given target real wage), depending on the expected level of inflation. As these money wage deals are passed on in price increases, it means that a given level of unemployment can be associated with any level of inflation which in turn means the existence of not just one Phillips curve but a whole family of Phillips curves, one for each expected inflation rate.

In Friedman's view, once expectations are taken into account the unemployment/inflation trade-off is only a short-term possibility. Assume that the economy is currently at the natural rate of unemployment U_n and that zero inflation has been experienced for some time and hence is expected to continue (point A in Fig. 22.11).

The government attempts to increase output beyond the natural (full employment) rate by increasing the money supply. Aggregate demand shifts to the right and prices are forced up (as in Fig. 22.5 earlier). The increase in prices reduces real wages and so makes it profitable for firms to employ more labour. But why should previously unemployed labour take jobs they had previously rejected? As workers were expecting zero inflation, any money wage increase resulting from increased demand for labour will be interpreted as a *real* wage increase. As long as the money wage increase is less than the price increase, firms will be happy to employ the extra workers who have been 'fooled' into believing they have secured higher real wages by unexpectedly high inflation. Unemployment falls below the natural rate U_n to U_b, and inflation increases to b as the economy moves along the short-run Phillips curve (Ph_0) to B. (Note: this is equivalent to a movement up and to the right along the short-run aggregate supply curve in Fig. 22.5 earlier.)

If the inflation rate was to stay at b, workers would, sooner or later, adjust their inflationary expectations accordingly. Workers will then take the new and higher expected rate of inflation into account in their wage bargains. This is equivalent to the short-run aggregate supply curve shifting up and to the left, and the Phillips curve shifting up and to the right (Ph_1). The economy will now be at C, with

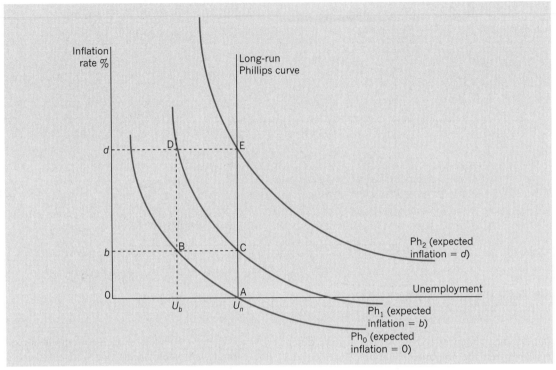

Fig. 22.11 The expectations-augmented Phillips curve.

unemployment and output falling back to their natural rates and with actual and expected inflation equal to b. In other words C is a long-run equilibrium possibility, with an inflation rate constant at b.

Suppose, however, that the government wishes to return unemployment to U_b. It must then increase the growth of the money supply more rapidly, so that actual inflation again exceeds expected inflation. If the government does do this the economy will move along the new short-run Phillips curve to point D. As before, this short-run equilibrium cannot be maintained because expectations will again catch up with actual inflation, and the economy will then move to E as the short-run Phillips curve again shifts upwards (Ph_2). At E the economy is once more in long-run equilibrium, with expected and actual inflation equal and the inflation rate constant at d.

Several interesting conclusions can be drawn from this modern view of the Phillips curve.

■ There is a short-run trade-off between unemployment and inflation but no long-run one.

■ Any rate of inflation is consistent with long-run equilibrium; all that is required is that *expected* inflation should equal *actual* inflation.

■ Attempts to push unemployment below the natural rate will result in increasing inflation. In fact the natural rate of unemployment is sometimes known as the non-accelerating inflation rate of unemployment (NAIRU).

■ Once inflationary expectations have become embedded in the system, a period of unemployment above the natural rate is required in order to lower the inflation rate. A movement down a given short-run Phillips curve to a level of unemployment above the natural rate will result in actual inflation being below expected inflation, leading to a downward revision of expectations, and hence falling inflation.

■ The natural rate of unemployment (and the NAIRU) are not constant over time. See Chapter 23 for a discussion of this issue.

UK inflationary experience 1970–92

During the 1970s and early 1980s the UK experienced its highest periods of inflation in recent history. Inflation peaked in 1975, reaching nearly 27% (% change over the 12 months to August); then after falling back it peaked again in the year to June 1982, reaching 21.9%. Another period of inflation occurred in the year to September 1990 when inflation reached 10.9%.

The first of these three periods to 1975 was preceded by very buoyant aggregate demand, stimulated by money supply growth (as a result of relaxation of the rules on bank lending), an expansionary budget and a booming world economy. All these led to the AD curve shifting to the right beyond the full employment level of output and increasing inflation. This period of rapid demand-led growth can be seen in Fig. 22.12. Our analysis tells us that even without the adverse supply shock given by oil and other commodity prices in 1973, prices would have been given a further boost (and output would fall) as *expectations*

of inflation were revised upwards in response to wage increases shifting the short-run AS curve up and to the left. The adverse supply shocks from oil and commodity price rises merely accelerated this process towards rising prices and falling output (note the fall in real GDP between 1973 and 1975 in Fig. 22.12).

The second inflationary episode occurred in the late 1970s and early 1980s. Again this period was marked by adverse supply shocks, including a doubling of oil prices, a near-doubling of VAT in 1979 (Q3) and an increase in wage costs, the last being the result of a catching-up process after a period of wage controls during 1974–79. The tightening of monetary and fiscal policy in late 1979 led to a further period of 'stagflation' in the following years (again note the fall in real GDP between 1979 and 1981 in Fig. 22.12).

It has been argued (Nelson and Nikolov 2002) that the reason why inflation was so troublesome in the late 1960s and the 1970s was partly due to policymakers *underestimating* the degree of excess demand in the economy and partly due to the neglect of monetary policy. Underestimating the rate of productivity slowdown in the 1970s meant policy-makers

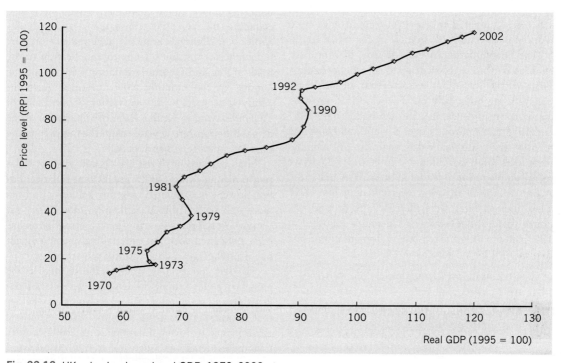

Fig. 22.12 UK price levels and real GDP, 1970–2002.
Source: ONS and author's calculations.

overestimated full employment output and hence *underestimated the level of demand pressure* (as measured by the output gap) in the economy. This was especially important over the 1972–74 period.

The reasons given for the neglect of monetary policy (meaning appropriate changes in interest rates) included:

- the view held by some that inflation was caused by factors other than excess demand;

- a feeling that incomes policy could be used as an alternative to demand management as a method of restraining inflation;

- an assumption that cost push inflation could continue indefinitely even in the absence of monetary accommodation (a view emanating from the Radcliffe Report of 1959 that argued that the velocity of circulation of money would adjust to offset any monetary policy); and

- a scepticism about the impact of interest rates on aggregated demand.

Nelson and Nikolov conclude that if appropriate interest rate changes had been made and if the output gap had not been mismeasured, then the 9.3% points actual increase in average inflation from 1970 Q1 to 1979 Q1 compared to the 1960s could have been reduced by around 7.2% points.

The third inflationary episode was, like the first, associated with excess demand in the economy. Financial liberalization, a relaxation of monetary policy, rising house and other asset prices, growing consumer confidence, tax-cutting budgets in 1987 and 1988 and buoyant world demand, all conspired to push aggregate demand beyond the full employment level. GDP was estimated to be over 4% above its full employment potential in both 1988 and 1989. Action to curtail inflation was taken in late 1988 when interest rates were increased by around 4% points to 12.8%. Further rate increases followed in 1989, but too little and too late to stop inflation rising to over 10% by the autumn of 1990.

Inflation targets and central bank independence: 1992–2003

In more recent years inflation policy has, in many countries, changed its emphasis. Instead of using *intermediate policy targets* such as the money supply or the exchange rate to achieve price stability, the emphasis has moved towards the use of *explicit inflation targets*. UK monetary policy has, since the departure from the ERM in 1992, been based on meeting an explicit target for inflation. Currently the target is to maintain inflation at 2.5% as measured by the RPIX (note that this is a *symmetrical target*, errors in either direction being regarded as equally bad). In addition to the inflation target, which is set by the Chancellor, a further significant change occurred in 1997 when the Chancellor delegated the power to decide interest rates to the nine-member Monetary Policy Committee (MPC) (see Chapter 20). The MPC is charged with setting short-term interest rates in order to meet the Chancellor's target. Put simply, if the MPC forecasts that the RPIX is going to be above the 2.5% target in approximately two years' time (given the time lag before interest rates have their maximum impact), then the MPC will raise the interest rates now, whereas if inflation is forecast to be less than the 2.5% target then interest rates will be lowered.

The new framework means that politics is taken out of interest rate decisions and this should give monetary policy added credibility. Credibility is also enhanced by increased transparency and accountability. Credibility is arguably achieved not only by the explicit target but also by the publication of the Bank of England Quarterly Inflation Report, and the minutes of the monthly MPC meetings. Accountability is secured by the Governor of the Bank of England having to write a letter of explanation if the actual inflation rate deviates from the target by more than 1% point in *either* direction.

In an assessment of the last decade or so of inflation targeting, King (2002) argues that inflation has been lower since inflation targeting and has also been more stable (see Table 22.3) than for most of the last century. At the same time low and stable inflation has been associated with not only falling unemployment but also relatively high and stable growth rates.

The key question is whether the change in the monetary policy framework has been the *cause* of low inflation and stability in the real economy or whether that causation runs from a more stable economic environment to lower inflation. King (2002) argues that the evidence, although not easy to assess, supports the former hypothesis and that crucially 'monetary policy is not adding to the volatility of the

Table 22.3 UK mean and standard deviation of inflation and GDP growth.

	Inflation			Real GDP Growth	
	Mean	St. Dev.		Mean	St. Dev.
1950–1959	4.14	1.06	1956–1959	2.42	1.22
1960–1969	3.65	0.72	1960–1969	3.15	0.92
1970–1979	13.07	1.81	1970–1979	2.12	1.42
1980–1992	6.40	1.14	1980–1992	1.86	0.84
1993–2002	2.49	0.24	1993–2002	2.76	0.36
1950–2002	5.93	1.41	1956–2002	2.42	0.98

Source: King (2002).

economy in a way that it did in earlier decades' (King, p. 461).

Conclusion

Inflation targeting and the MPC framework appear to have delivered low and stable inflation in the UK. However, some issues do still remain open to debate. One is the view that the MPC has held interest rates too high and has exhibited a deflationary bias. The evidence for this view comes from the fact that inflation has been below its target for most of the period in which the MPC has been in operation. The Treasury Select Committee End of Term Report on the workings of the MPC (2001) expressed its concern that in an attempt to establish credibility, the MPC might have biased its policy towards undershooting the target. Nickell (2002), on the other hand, examines the data and concludes that over the period 1999 Q2 to 2001 Q1 inflation would still have been below target even if interest rates had been 0.25% point lower during the relevant decision period 1997 Q2 to 1999 Q1. Nevertheless he concludes that the MPC was not guilty of a bias towards deflation because it

could not reasonably have been expected to predict the impacts that sterling appreciation and the new realism in the labour market were to have on keeping inflation down. During the period 2001 Q2 to 2002 Q3 inflation again undershot the target, but Nickell argues that if interest rates had been lower during the relevant decision period then inflation would have overshot the target.

A second area of concern is how, if at all, the MPC should respond to asset prices. If, for example, forecast inflation is below its target and yet there is a house price or shares price bubble, should the MPC refrain from lowering interest rates for fear of further stoking asset price inflation, or should interest rates be raised to prick the asset price bubble but with the danger of inflation undershooting its target? There is no consensus on this issue. Some argue that interest rates should be used to head off asset price bubbles to prevent the disruption to the real economy that occurs when they burst. Others argue that it is extremely difficult to identify asset price departures from 'fundamentals' and that if the interest rate were used in this further role, then the clear and predictable role it already has in controlling inflation would be lost along with the credibility and transparency of monetary policy.

Key points

- The RPI measures movement in the prices of a 'basket' of goods and services bought by a representative UK household.

- Items with higher income elasticities of demand (e.g. housing, leisure services, catering) are being given increasing weights in the calculation of the RPI.

- The RPI is linked back to January 1987 = 100 as base. With an RPI of 179.9 in March 2003, this indicates that average retail prices have risen by 79.9% since January 1987.

- RPIX is RPI *excluding* mortgage interest payments.

- RPIY is RPI *excluding* mortgage interest payments and indirect taxes.

- The GDP deflator seeks to measure changes in the prices of the *entire basket* of goods and services produced in the UK. It is found by dividing GDP at current factor cost by GDP at constant factor cost.

- The modern view of the Phillips curve is that there is a short-run trade-off between unemployment and inflation, but no long-run trade-off.

- Attempts to push unemployment below the *natural rate* will result in increasing inflation.

- This natural rate of unemployment is sometimes known as the Non-Accelerating Inflation Rate of Unemployment (NAIRU).

- The government sets the inflation target and the Monetary Policy Committee (MPC) changes interest rates in trying to meet that target.

- There is evidence that setting an inflation target may itself help to reduce inflation without inhibiting growth.

Now try the self-check questions for this chapter on the Companion Website. You will also find up-to-date facts and case materials.

Notes

1. If the price of an item in the index was 10p in January (P_0) and 12p in February (P_1) then the price relative would be 12/10 (P_1/P_0) and this would then be multiplied by the weight (W) for that item. The index for period 1 (where period 0 = 100) is given by $[\Sigma(P_1 \times W)/\Sigma(P_0 \times W)] \times 100$.

2. For example, if the index for January 2003 based on January 2000 was 120, and the index for July 2004 based on January 2003 was 110, then the July 2004 index, based on January 2000 = 100, would be calculated as follows: $120 \times 110/100 = 132$.

3. On 11 December 2003 the Chancellor of the Exchequer confirmed his intention to change the inflation target to one expressed in terms of the annual rate of inflation as measured by the *Harmonised Index of Consumer Prices* (HICP) – instead of the RPIX. The inflation target for HICP was set at 2% and was published for the first time in the February 2004 issue of the Bank of England's Inflation Report .

References and further reading

Bakhshi, H., Haldane, A. and Hatch, N. (1997) Some costs and benefits of price stability in the UK, *Bank of England Quarterly Bulletin*, 37(3), August.

Barclays Bank Economic Review (1992) February.

Barro, R. (1995) Inflation and economic growth, *Bank of England Quarterly Bulletin*, 35(2), May.

Briault, C. (1995) The costs of inflation, *Bank of England Quarterly Bulletin*, 35(1), February.

Cunningham, A. (1996) Measurement bias in price indices: an application to the UK's RPI, *Bank of England Working Paper*, No. 47.

Friedman, M. (1968) The role of monetary policy, *American Economic Review*, 58, March.

Friedman, M. (1977) Inflation and unemployment, *Journal of Political Economy*, 85(3).

Grimes, A. (1991) The effects of inflation on growth: some international evidence, *Weltwirtschaftliches Archive*, 127.

House of Commons Treasury Select Committee (2001), *The Monetary Policy Committee – an End of Term Report*, Ninth Report of the Treasury Select Committee (HC42).

King, M. (2002) The inflation target ten years on, *Bank of England Quarterly Bulletin*, 42(4), Winter.

Labour Market Trends (2000) June and July.

Lipsey, R. and Chrystal, K. (1995) *Positive Economics*, Oxford University Press.

National Institute Economic Review (2000) No. 172, April.

Nelson, E. and Nikolov, K. (2002) *Monetary Policy and Stagflation in the UK*, Bank of England Working Paper No. 155, May.

Nickell, S. (2002) Monetary policy issues: past, present, future. Speech delivered to Coventry and Warwickshire Chamber of Commerce, 19 June. Available on Bank of England website, www.bankofengland.co.uk

Parkin, M., Powell, M. and Matthews, K. (2003) *Economics*, Addison Wesley Longman, London.

Phelps, E. S. (1967) Phillips curves, expectations of inflation and optimal unemployment over time, *Economica*, 34, August.

Phillips, A. W. (1958) The relation between unemployment and the rate of change of money wage rates in the United Kingdom, *Economica*, 25, November.

Radcliffe Committee (1959) *Report on the Working of the Monetary System*, CMND. 827, HMSO.

Sarel, M. (1996) Nonlinear effects of inflation on economic growth, *IMF Staff Papers*, 43(1), March.

Soteri, S. and Westaway, P. (1993) Explaining price inflation in the UK: 1971–92, *National Institute Economic Review*, No. 144, May.

Wadhwani, M. L. (1984) Wage inflation in the United Kingdom, *Economica*, 52.

Chapter 23   Unemployment

In his conclusion to *The General Theory of Employment, Interest and Money*, Keynes wrote that 'it may be possible by a right analysis of the problem to cure the disease [of unemployment] whilst preserving efficiency and freedom' (Keynes 1936). The commitment to high and stable levels of unemployment of successive UK governments and the actual achievement of low rates of unemployment appeared to support Keynes' proposition, at least as far as unemployment was concerned. Indeed, in the 20 years after the Second World War the unemployment rate rarely exceeded 2%. This 'golden age', however, ended in the late 1960s and under the influence of two oil shocks during the 1970s and subsequent deflationary policy responses, unemployment in the UK rose to over 3 million by the mid-1980s, i.e. some 11% of the workforce. Although unemployment in the UK has fallen since then to its present level of around 4%, the 1990s average for the European Union has still exceeded 10% of the workforce. It appears that Keynes might have been over-optimistic in his prediction. In this chapter we look at the methods of counting the unemployed and at who the unemployed are. We then consider the contribution of economic theory to the issue of unemployment before concluding with an attempt to identify those policies that might lead the economy in the direction of higher employment.

Unemployment in the UK

It could be argued that the adoption, after the Second World War, of Keynesian demand-management policies secured nearly two decades of historically low unemployment (see Fig. 23.1). In recent years, however, although government commitment to full employment (first stated in the 1944 White Paper on employment policy) has never been revoked, we no longer appear to have the tools with which to do the job. The traditional reliance on macroeconomic policies as a means of reducing unemployment has largely been replaced by a greater emphasis on microeconomic supply-side measures that take into account the changing nature of the labour market, society and the global economy. Labour market reforms of this type during the 1980s and 1990s and measures such as the 'New Deal' of the incoming Labour government have, however, resulted in a UK unemployment rate that compares favourably with our EU partners. Nevertheless, the UK unemployment rate is still twice as high as it was in the 1950s and 1960s and there is an uneasy feeling that this period of very low unemployment may prove to have been the exception rather than the rule!

Before attempting to assess the causes of high unemployment, and to consider what, if anything, can be done, it is important to examine the unemployment statistics themselves to see what light they shed on the issue.

How unemployment is measured

Since January 2003 the UK government's only official and internationally comparable measure of unemployment has been provided by the *Labour Force Survey* (LFS). The LFS uses the internationally agreed definition of unemployment recommended by the International Labour Office (ILO). Unemployed people are 'those without a job who have actively sought work in the last four weeks and are available to start work within the next two weeks, or those who are out of work, but who have found a job but are waiting to start in the next two weeks'.

The LFS samples around 61,000 households in any three-month period and interviews are taken from approximately 120,000 people aged 16 and over. The LFS enables the publication of results for the latest available three months every month. Results for individual months are not published, however, as

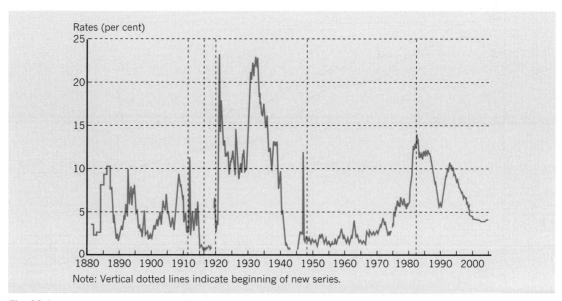

Note: Vertical dotted lines indicate beginning of new series.

Fig. 23.1 UK unemployment rate, 1881–2000 (excluding school-leavers).
Sources: *Labour Market Trends* (2000); London and Cambridge Economic Service (1967).

they are not thought to be statistically robust. Everyone surveyed is classified as either *economically active* (in employment or ILO unemployed) or *economically inactive* (either wanting a job but not meeting the ILO unemployment criteria, or not wanting a job).

In the three months from January to March 2003 unemployment in the UK stood at 1.5 million, a fall of 20,000 over the previous year. The figure of 1.5 million unemployed represents an *unemployment rate* of 5.1%. The unemployment rate is calculated by dividing the absolute number of unemployed by the total number of economically active (employed plus unemployed) and expressing this as a percentage.

Claimant Count data, which, in the past, has been used as an alternative measure, calculates unemployment in terms of those claiming unemployment-related benefits (Jobseeker's Allowance). Claimant Count data will continue to be published on a monthly basis and provides further information on the labour market, but it will no longer be presented as an alternative measure of UK unemployment. For the record the Claimant Count for March 2003 stood at 0.937 million, a rate of 3.1%.

Figure 23.2 shows both the Labour Force Survey (LFS) and Claimant Count measures of unemployment over the period 1992–2003.

Disaggregating unemployment statistics

Further insight can be gained by breaking down the total unemployment figures into a number of components as follows.

Regional unemployment

Some regions of the UK have experienced higher than average unemployment over the last 60 years. These high-unemployment regions have generally been the outer peripheral regions of the UK, namely Northern Ireland, Scotland, Wales, the North-East and the North-West. For example, in 1971 the Northern Ireland unemployment rate was double the UK average, whilst in Scotland the rate was 70% above the UK average. In comparison the rate for the South-East was only half the UK average (see also Chapter 11).

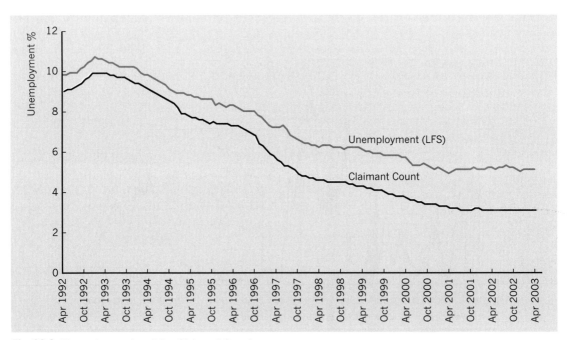

Fig. 23.2 Unemployment and the Claimant Count.
Source: Office for National Statistics.

Traditionally the explanation of such regional variation has been in terms of the depressed regions being over-reliant upon declining industries such as coal, textiles and shipbuilding. A study by Fothergill and Gudgin (1982) suggests that this *was* true until the mid-1960s, but that since then the main problem seems to be of regions, such as the North and Scotland, being dragged down by the fact that they have a disproportionate number of big cities in which unemployment is particularly high. In other parts of these regions unemployment trends are not so bad, but what is happening throughout the UK is a massive shift of jobs from the cities to the smaller towns and rural areas on a scale that swamps most other trends in industrial location. Fothergill and Gudgin suggest that the main cause of this trend is the shortage of space in urban areas, with factories becoming less profitable than their rural counterparts because so many operate in unsuitable, old-fashioned buildings, with production organized less efficiently on more than one floor.

The decline in UK unemployment since the recession of the early 1990s has been accompanied by a narrowing of the dispersion in regional unemployment rates. For example, in 2003 the region with the highest unemployment rate was London which, at 6.8%, was only 33% higher than the UK average rate of 5.1%. Similarly the North-East, Scotland and Northern Ireland had unemployment rates of 6.6%, 6.1% and 5.5% respectively, rates which were only 29%, 20% and 10% above the UK average.

Although regional unemployment disparities may have fallen and become less of a policy issue in the UK, it is worth noting that unemployment rates *within* regions still demonstrate large variations. For example in the London region, Bromley had an unemployment rate of only 3.9% whereas Tower Hamlets had an unemployment rate of 12.3% (or 2.2% and 6.4% respectively as measured by the claimant count in March 2003). In the North-East, Teesdale had a claimant count unemployment rate of 1.6% against Middlesborough's 6.0%.

Unemployment and inactivity by gender

Male unemployment rates have always been higher than female rates. The overall UK unemployment rate for the three months to March 2003 was 5.1%, with male unemployment for the same period being 5.7% compared to female unemployment of 4.4%.

Although over the longer run (since 1979) the overall unemployment and activity rates have not changed significantly, there have been other changes worth noting. The most striking has been the rise in male *inactivity rates* (neither employed nor counted as unemployed) and the fall in female inactivity rates. According to Nickell (2003), in 1977–78 male inactivity in the 25–64 age group was 4.7% but by 2002 it had risen to 14.3%. Over the same period, however, female inactivity rates (age 25–59) had fallen from 37.4% to 23.8%. This increase in female participation in the labour market arises mainly from married women whose partners are typically working, which more than compensates the fact that the participation rate of single women with children has fallen. The rise in male inactivity rates has mainly involved married men whose partners do not work (or have never worked) and single men. Nickell (2003) finds that the rise in prime-age male inactivity rates is largely accounted for by low-skilled workers claiming incapacity benefit. The weakness of the labour market for unskilled workers plus the relative ease in acquiring incapacity benefit could explain part of this rise in inactivity rates.

As a result of these changes, there has been a growing polarization between work-rich households where both partners work, and work-poor households where no one works. Nickell couples this trend together with growing UK wage dispersion (falling relative wages of unskilled workers) to explain increased poverty in the UK (see Chapter 14 for more details).

Age-related unemployment

The unemployment rate in the UK amongst young people of working age is particularly high, though the duration of these periods of unemployment tends to be relatively short for most individuals. Where young people do spend long periods out of work, evidence suggests that the damage done can have a significantly negative impact on later labour market performance. Although the rate of 'youth unemployment' (under 25 years) is lower in the UK (12.3%) than in Italy (27.7%), Spain (26%) and the EU15 (15.7%) as a whole, it is higher than in Germany (9.8%), Austria (7.0%), Denmark (8.4%) and the Netherlands (7.6%). Table 23.1 indicates that the unemployment rate tends to decline with age; for example only 3.9% of those aged 25–49 years were unemployed in

Table 23.1 UK unemployment rates (%) by age, January–March 2003.

	16–17	18–24	25–49	50 and over	16–59/64
All persons	20.5	10.8	3.9	3.3	5.1
Men	24.1	12.3	4.2	4.1	5.7
Women	16.9	9.1	3.5	2.4	4.4

Source: Office for National Statistics.

early 2003 compared to 20.5% of those aged 16–17 years.

However, those older workers who *do* become unemployed are particularly prone to long spells of unemployment. The long-term unemployed (a year or more) are disproportionately older, disproportionately male and disproportionately low skilled. Such *long-term unemployment* destroys skills and motivation and is often used by employers as an unfavourable filtering device, leading to the stark statistic that those workers who are still unemployed after two years stand only a 50% chance of leaving unemployment for a job within the following year. Table 23.2 indicates that 36.9% of the unemployed aged 50 and over had been unemployed for a year or more, compared to only 12.7% of the unemployed aged 18–24 years. The government's strategy towards both youth and long-term unemployment in the UK is discussed later in the chapter.

It is worth noting that the fall in the proportion of youths in the labour force over the last 15 years (a result of the low birth rate in the 1970s) may have contributed as much as 0.55 percentage points of the 5.65 percentage points fall in the UK unemployment rate between 1984 and 1998. It is thought unlikely, however, that shifts in the age composition of the labour force will have much effect on the unemployment rate over the first 10 years of the new millennium (Barwell 2000).

Qualifications and unemployment

The demand for low-skilled and poorly educated workers has been declining throughout the OECD since the early 1980s, whereas the demand for skilled workers has outstripped the supply. The overall result is that the employment prospects and wages of poorly educated and unskilled workers have deteriorated relative to those for better educated and skilled workers. Almost 90% of those with a degree or equivalent as their highest qualification were in employment in 2003, which compares with only 51% of people with no qualifications. People with higher qualifications are less likely to be unemployed or economically inactive. Similarly the wage gap between men aged 25–49 years with no qualifications and those with a university degree was 61% in 1979, but this gap had increased to 89% in 1998.

Ethnic unemployment

There are large differences between economic *activity rates* (employment plus unemployment) for different ethnic groups. In 2001/02 White men had an activity rate of 85% whereas Bangladeshi men had a rate of

Table 23.2 Percentage of UK unemployed who have been out of work for over a year, January–March 2003.

	16–17	18–24	25–49	50 and over	16–59/64
All persons	6.0	12.7	25.3	36.9	21.5
Men	n/a	16.0	30.8	39.5	25.7
Women	n/a	7.7	17.7	31.1	15.0

Source: Office for National Statistics.

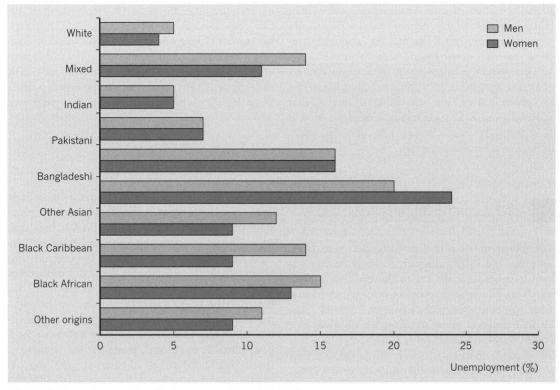

Fig. 23.3 Unemployment by ethnic group and sex, 2001/02.
Source: Office for National Statistics.

only 69%. White women and Black Caribbean women had activity rates of over 70% whereas Bangladeshi and Pakistani women had rates of only 22% and 28% respectively.

Unemployment rates also vary (see Fig. 23.3). In 2001/02 ethnic minority groups had a higher unemployment rate than was the case for White people. For example, Bangladeshi men had an unemployment rate of 20% compared to only 5% for White males. Indian men had an unemployment rate of 7% but other ethnic minorities had unemployment rates between two and three times higher than that for White males. As we have already seen, youth unemployment rates are particularly high. White males less than 25 years old have an unemployment rate of around 12% compared to 40% for young Bangladeshi men. Young Black African men, young Black Caribbean men, young Pakistanis and the young of mixed race had unemployment rates between 25% and 31%, again higher than that for young White men.

Disadvantaged groups

In 2003 a sixth of British adults (over 5 million people) did not have a job or a working partner, which is double the figure for the 1970s. A recent survey carried out by Berthoud (2003) for the Institute for Social and Economic Research highlighted six main disadvantaged groups with a high risk of unemployment: men and women without partners (particularly lone parents), disabled people, people with low educational attainment, those over 50, those living in areas of weak labour demand, and members of certain minority ethnic groups. The study found that 66% of British adults (17–59 years) had at least one of these characteristics and nearly 10% had at least three. Only 4% of the population with none of these characteristics were not in work, compared to 90% of the people with all six disadvantages. The study examines the implications for employment of various combinations of disadvantage and finds that the risk of non-employment can be explained by *adding* the effect of each disadvantage, rather than using some form of exponential model which would point to a more rapidly increasing (multiplicative) impact on non-employment from the interactions between growth in any one form of disadvantage and other disadvantages. An important implication of this for policy-makers, the authors conclude, is that addressing one kind of hindrance to employment will yield dividends without being overly concerned about its links to other disadvantages.

International comparisons

Unemployment rates in most countries have fallen since the mid-1980s, although not back to the low levels experienced in the 1960s. However, some countries have been less successful in reducing unemployment than others. As can be seen from Table 23.3, the big four countries in the eurozone, namely Germany, France, Italy and Spain, have had little success in reducing unemployment rates, whilst the Japanese unemployment rate has risen steadily since the early 1990s.

Unemployment and economic theory

The traditional way of analysing the unemployment problem has been to try and identify the various types of unemployment by cause, this being seen as the first step towards formulating appropriate policy. Economists often distinguish between frictional, structural, classical and demand-deficiency (Keynesian) unemployment. Some would argue that a further type of unemployment should be distinguished, namely technological unemployment. We now consider each 'type' in more detail.

Frictional unemployment

Frictional unemployment results from the time it takes workers to move between jobs. It is a consequence of short-run changes in the labour market that constantly occur in a dynamic economy. Workers who leave their jobs to search for better ones require time because of the imperfections in the labour market. For example, workers are never fully aware of all the possible jobs, wages and other elements in the remuneration package, so that the first job a worker is offered is unlikely to be the one for which he or she is best suited. It is rational, therefore, for workers to spend time familiarizing themselves with the job market even though there will be costs involved in this search, namely lost earnings, postage, telephone calls, etc. These 'search' costs can, however, be seen from the workers' point of view as an investment, the gain being higher future income. In principle, the economy should also gain from this search behaviour, through higher productivity as workers find jobs that are more appropriate to their skills.

Table 23.3 Comparative unemployment rates (%) (standardized).

	1960–64	1965–72	1973–79	1980–87	1988–92	1993–02	Latest (2003)
France	1.5	2.3	4.3	8.9	9.3	10.7	9.1
Germany*	0.8	0.8	2.9	6.1	5.5	8.5	8.9
Italy	3.5	4.2	4.5	6.7	9.1	10.7	9.0
Japan	1.4	1.3	1.8	2.5	2.2	3.9	5.3
Netherlands	0.9	1.7	4.7	10.0	6.1	4.6	3.6
Spain	2.4	2.7	4.9	17.6	· 17.4	18.4	11.5
Sweden	1.2	1.6	1.6	2.3	2.7	7.8	5.3
UK	2.6	3.1	4.8	10.5	8.2	7.0	5.1
USA	5.5	4.3	6.4	7.6	6.1	5.2	5.8

*West Germany up to 1992; the whole of Germany from 1993.
Source: Adapted from *OECD Economic Outlook*, various editions.

Any measures that reduce the search time will reduce the amount of frictional unemployment. Improving the transmission of job information, permitting workers to acquire knowledge of the labour market more quickly, is one such measure. A more controversial issue is how the level of unemployment benefit affects search time. It could be argued that by reducing the workers' cost of searching, increased unemployment benefit will lead to more search activity and a higher level of frictional unemployment. On the other hand, a reduction in unemployment benefit, though perhaps leading (via less search) to lower frictional unemployment, could also lead to a less efficient allocation of resources, with workers having to take the first job that comes along regardless of how appropriate it was to their skills.

Structural unemployment

Structural unemployment arises from longer-term changes in the structure of the economy, resulting in changes in the demand for, and supply of, labour in specific industries, regions and occupations. It could be caused by changes in the comparative cost position of an industry or a region, by technological progress or by changes in the pattern of final demand. Examples of structural unemployment are not difficult to find for the UK economy and might include shipbuilding, textile, steel and motor-vehicle workers, i.e. workers in manufacturing industries where the UK has largely lost its comparative advantage over other countries (e.g. newly industrialized countries). On the other hand, the emerging unemployment in the printing industry and in clerical occupations has more to do with technological progress, which enables information to be processed, stored and retrieved more quickly, so that fewer people are required per unit of output (see below). Yet again, structural unemployment may be due to a shift in demand away from an established product, as with the decline of the coal industry following the move to gas-fired power stations.

The structurally unemployed are therefore people who are available for work, but whose skills and locations do not match those of unfilled vacancies. Structural unemployment is likely to reach high levels if the rate of decline for a country's traditional products is rapid and if the labour market adjusts slowly to such changes. Indeed, adjustments are likely to be slow since they are costly to make. From the workers'

point of view it may require retraining in new skills and relocation, whilst from the firms' point of view it often means abandoning their familiar products and processes and investing in new and often untried ones. This process of adjustment is, of course, easier the more buoyant the economy.

At a broader level, one of the most important issues facing developed countries is whether they will be able to generate enough output to finance the necessary increase in service occupations required to absorb those released by the manufacturing sector. Whilst manufacturing accounted for 30.1% of employment in the EU in 1970, it accounted for only around 25% in 2002, and most forecasts see this structural trend continuing (see Chapter 1). In the UK employment in coal, steel and shipbuilding fell by 94%, 82% and 86% respectively between 1978 and 2002. The way in which the developed world manages this structural transition over the medium term will be one of the key determinants of future levels of employment.

Technological unemployment

New technologies have substantially raised output per unit of *labour input* (labour productivity) and per unit of *factor input*, both labour and capital (total factor productivity). There has been much concern that the impact of these productivity gains has been to reduce jobs, i.e. to create technological unemployment. We now consider the principles which will in fact determine whether or not jobs will be lost (or gained) as a result of technological change.

Higher output per unit of factor input reduces costs of production, provided only that wage rates and other factor price increases do not absorb the whole of the productivity gain. Computer-controlled machine tools are a case in point. Data from Renault show that the use of DNC machine tools resulted in machining costs one-third less than those of general-purpose machine tools at the same level of output. Lower costs will cause the profit-maximizing firm to lower price and raise output under most market forms, as in Fig. 23.4. A downward shift of the average cost curve, via the new technologies, lowers the marginal cost curve from MC_1 to MC_2. The profit-maximizing price/output combination ($MC = MR$) now changes from P_1/Q_1 to P_2/Q_2. Price has fallen, output has risen.

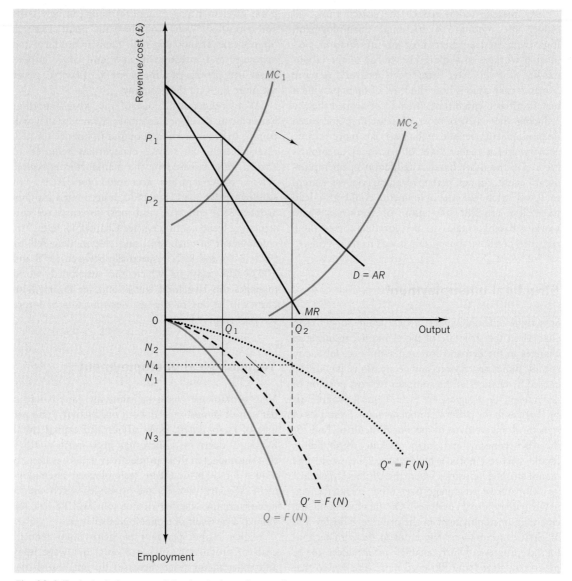

Fig. 23.4 Technical change and the level of employment.

The dual effect on employment of higher output per unit of labour (and capital) input can usefully be illustrated from Fig. 23.4. The curve $Q = F(N)$ is the familiar production function of economic theory, showing how output (Q) varies with labour input (N), with capital and other factors assumed constant. On the one hand the higher labour productivity from technical change shifts the production function outwards to the dashed line $Q' = F(N)$. The original output Q_1 can now be produced with less labour,

i.e. with only N_2 labour input instead of N_1 as previously. On the other hand, the cost and price reduction has so raised demand that more output is required. We now move along the new production function Q' until we reach Q_2 output, which requires N_3 labour input. In our example the reduction in labour required per unit output has been more than compensated for by the expansion of output, via lower price. Employment has, in fact, risen from N_1 to N_3.

This analysis highlights a number of points on which the final employment outcome for a firm adopting the new techniques will depend:

1 The relationship between new technology and labour productivity, i.e. the extent to which the production function Q shifts outwards.

2 The relationship between labour productivity and cost, i.e. the extent to which the marginal cost curve shifts downwards.

3 The relationship between cost and price, i.e. the extent to which cost reductions are passed on to consumers as lower prices.

4 The relationship between lower price and higher demand, i.e. the price elasticity of the demand curve.

Suppose, for instance, that the new process *halved* labour input per unit output. If this increase in labour productivity (1 above) reduces cost (2 above) and price (3 above), and output *doubled* (4 above), then the same total labour input would be required. If output more than doubled, then more labour would be employed. The magnitude of the four relationships above will determine whether the firm offers the same, more, or less employment after technical change in the production process.

Although a more detailed treatment must be sought elsewhere, there is in fact a fifth relationship crucial to the final employment outcome, namely, the extent to which any higher total factor productivity arising from a technological innovation can be separately attributed to capital or to labour. An innovation is said to be capital saving when the marginal product of capital rises relative to that of labour, and labour saving when the converse applies. This whole issue is surrounded by problems of concept and measurement. We can, however, use Fig. 23.4 to present the outline of the argument.

Suppose we take the dashed line $Q' = F(N)$ to represent a situation in which the new technology is capital saving (with only a small rise in labour productivity), so that the new and higher output Q_2 requires considerable extra labour to produce it (N_3 employment). If, on the other hand, the new technology were labour saving (with a substantial rise in labour productivity), then the new dotted line $Q'' = F(N)$ in Fig. 23.4 would be more appropriate. Output Q_2 would now only require employment N_4. The prospects for higher employment would therefore appear more favourable when innovations are capital saving, raising the marginal product of capital relative to that of labour.

Broadly speaking, the scenario most favourable to employment would be where a small increase in (labour) productivity significantly reduces both cost and price, leading to a substantial rise in demand.

Classical unemployment

Unemployment may be associated, in the classical view, with real wages that are 'too high'. In this case trade unions have used their power to force the *real wage* above the market clearing level or have prevented it from falling to the market clearing level after a change in the supply or demand conditions. A government minimum wage above the equilibrium wage could also generate such classical unemployment. In the 1970s there was a revival in this line of thought. The monetarist and new classical economists argued that whilst, for the most part, the economy would be at 'full employment', there might be times when firms and workers would *overestimate* the rate of inflation. If firms pay money wage increases based on such false price expectations, this will lead to (temporarily) higher real wages and reduced employment. Figure 23.5 illustrates classical unemployment using the familiar labour market diagram.

The *labour demand* curve has a negative slope to reflect the usual assumption that the demand for labour rises as the real wage falls. The *labour force* curve has a positive slope to reflect increased labour force participation as real wages rise. The *labour supply* curve represents those willing and able to take jobs at a given real wage. The market clearing real wage is $(W/P)_F$, giving employment equal to the full employment level N_F and unemployment equal to $N_1 - N_F$. This equilibrium level of unemployment is considered to be entirely *voluntary*. However, if the real wage $(W/P)_2$ is above the market clearing level $(W/P)_F$ for whatever reason, then employment falls to N_2 and unemployment increases to $N_3 - N_2$ of which the portion $N_3 - N_4$ could be regarded as 'voluntary'. In the classical view the remaining 'involuntary' unemployment $N_4 - N_2$ could not persist for long. The unemployed would exert downward pressure on money wages, and the real wage would fall back to the market clearing level.

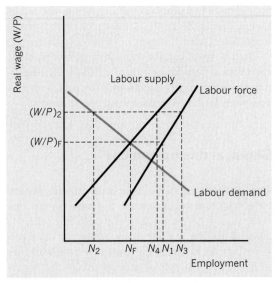

Fig. 23.5 'Voluntary' or equilibrium unemployment and the real wage.

unemployment. The downward stickiness in wages (and therefore prices) thwarts the operation of the real balance effect, whereby lower prices raise *real incomes* and thereby increase consumer spending.[1] Since no automatic tendency exists to return the economy to full employment by generating sufficient aggregate demand in the goods market, Keynesians would advocate some form of expansionary government demand-management policy. Demand-deficient (Keynesian) unemployment is illustrated in Fig. 23.6.

Aggregate demand (AD) determines the level of output Y_2 (assume Y_F is full employment output – i.e. only 'voluntary' unemployment). Given this level of output and the production function in the economy, firms will need to employ only N_2 workers to meet the demand for their product. The *effective demand* for labour is traced out by the points a-b-N_2. Note that the real wage could be anywhere between $(W/P)_2$ and $(W/P)_3$. A cut in real wages would not restore employment to its full employment level (N_F) if aggregate demand for output remains unchanged at a level consistent with output Y_2.

Demand deficient unemployment

Keynes criticized the view that unemployment is caused by too high real wages. He considered that the cause of mass unemployment in the 1930s was not to be found in the market for labour, but was rather a result of too little demand in the *market for goods*. This lack of overall demand together with an assumed downward stickiness in wages and prices leaves the economy trapped for long periods with high levels of

A framework for thinking about unemployment

One useful way of thinking about unemployment, which is especially helpful from a policy perspective, is to distinguish between 'cyclical unemployment' which results from a deficiency of aggregate demand

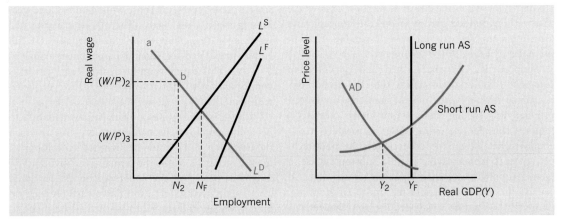

Fig. 23.6 Demand-deficient unemployment.

(e.g. during the downswing of the business cycle) and 'sustainable unemployment'. *Sustainable unemployment* is the level below which tightness in the labour market will lead to an increasing rate of wage and price inflation. The sustainable level of unemployment is variously referred to as the 'natural rate of unemployment' (NRU), the 'non-accelerating inflation rate of unemployment' (NAIRU) or, as in OECD publications, the 'structural' rate of unemployment.

At any moment in time therefore:

$$\frac{\text{Actual}}{\text{unemployment}} = \frac{\text{Sustainable}}{\text{unemployment}} + \frac{\text{Cyclical}}{\text{unemployment}}$$

Figure 23.7 illustrates these two components for 13 OECD (advanced industrialized) countries in 1998. In some countries (United States, UK, Netherlands and Ireland) the actual unemployment rate was *below* the sustainable (structural) rate. In these countries the relatively high level of aggregate demand might be expected to lead to future inflationary pressures unless corrective action is taken. In the majority of cases, however, the cyclical component was substantial so that the actual unemployment rate was well *above* the sustainable (structural) rate (e.g. Germany, France, Japan and Italy). In these countries aggregate demand might be expanded without serious

inflationary consequences. Of course the uncertainties involved in decomposing unemployment into these two components must be borne in mind.

The natural rate of unemployment (NRU) and the NAIRU

Given the central role of these concepts in discussions of unemployment, it might be useful to consider the NRU and NAIRU in rather more detail.

Natural rate of unemployment (NRU)

The NRU was introduced into economics by Milton Friedman (Friedman 1968). It can be thought of as being derived from a competitive labour market with flexible real wages, with the *natural rate* of unemployment being determined by the equilibrium of labour supply and demand. The usual labour market diagram of Fig. 23.8 can be used to illustrate this. Here labour demand, L^D, reflects the marginal revenue product of workers, i.e. the extra revenue contributed by employing the last worker. This is downward sloping in line with the assumption of a diminishing marginal physical product for workers

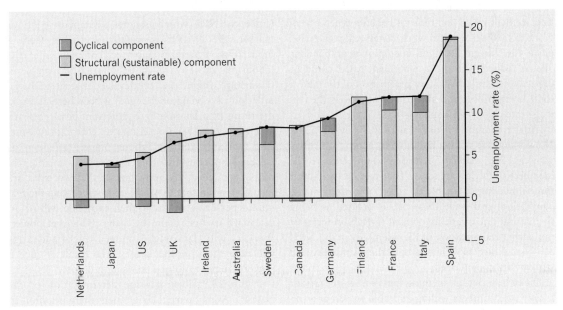

Fig. 23.7 Unemployment rates, structural (sustainable) and cyclical components for OECD countries in 1998. Source: Adapted from OECD (1999) *Economic Outlook*, June.

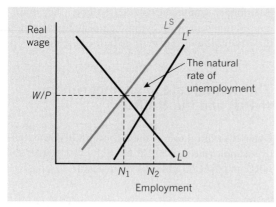

Fig. 23.8 Finding the natural rate of unemployment (NRU).

(see Chapter 15). Labour supply, L^S, represents all those workers willing and able (i.e. they have the right skills and are in the right location) to accept jobs at a given real wage. The labour force, L^F, shows the total number of workers who consider themselves to be members of the labour force at any given real wage; of course not all of these are willing or able to accept job offers, perhaps because they are still searching for a better offer or because they have not yet acquired the appropriate skills or are not in an appropriate location. Note the convergence of L^S and L^F as the real wage rises. This reflects the reduction in the 'replacement ratio' (i.e. ratio of benefits when out of work to earnings when in work) when real wages rise, given the current level of unemployment benefits. Such a reduction in the 'replacement ratio' could be expected to result in a higher proportion of the labour force being willing and able to accept jobs as the real wage rate rises (see Chapter 14).

At the equilibrium real wage (W/P) in Fig. 23.8, N_1 workers are willing and able to accept job offers whereas N_2 workers consider themselves to be members of the labour force. That part of the labour force unwilling or unable to accept job offers at the equilibrium real wage ($N_2 - N_1$) is defined as being the natural rate of unemployment (NRU). In terms of our earlier classification of the unemployed the NRU can be regarded as including both the frictionally and structurally unemployed.

It can be seen that anything that *reduces the labour supply* (the numbers willing and able to accept a job at a given real wage) will, other things being equal, cause the NRU to increase. Possible factors might

include an *increase in the level or availability of unemployment benefits*, thereby encouraging unemployed members of the labour force to engage in more prolonged search activity. An *increase in trade union power* might also reduce the numbers willing and able to accept a job at a given real wage, especially if the trade union is able to restrict the effective labour supply as part of a strategy for raising wages. A reduced labour supply might also result from *increased technological change* or increased *global competition*, both of which change the nature of the labour market skills required for employment. *Higher taxes on earned income* are also likely to reduce the labour supply at any given real wage.

Similarly anything that *reduces the labour demand* will, other things being equal, cause the NRU to increase. A fall in the marginal revenue product of labour, via a fall in marginal physical productivity or in the product price, might be expected to reduce labour demand. Many economists believe that the two sharp oil price increases in the 1970s had this effect, with the resulting fall in aggregate demand causing firms to cut back on capital spending, reducing the overall capital stock and hence the marginal physical productivity of labour.

Non-accelerating inflation rate of unemployment (NAIRU)

Unlike the NRU which assumes a competitive labour market, the NAIRU is usually developed from a model that recognizes imperfect competition in the labour market (Layard 1986). The 'sustainable' level of unemployment (i.e. the level consistent with the inflation rate being unchanged) is seen here as being the result of a bargaining equilibrium between firms and workers rather than a market clearing outcome. The two sides of the labour market are seen as engaged in a constant struggle over the available real output per head. If the claims of the two sides are inconsistent, in that they add up to more than the real output per head available, then each side will try to safeguard its own claim by using its market power. Workers will claim higher money wages and firms will raise their product prices. The result of such a power struggle will then be rising inflation.

Figure 23.9 illustrates the determination of the NAIRU. At any particular moment there is a limit to the real wage the economy can provide, given labour productivity and the mark-up that firms typically

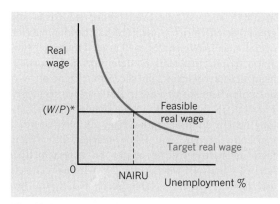

Fig. 23.9 The determination of the NAIRU.

apply to costs. This limit is the *feasible real wage* $(W/P)^*$. At the same time, the *target real wage* reflects the aspirations of workers. It seems likely that this target will be influenced by the level of demand in the economy, as reflected by the unemployment rate. When demand is high and unemployment is low, workers will feel more able to negotiate wage increases than when demand is low and unemployment high. There will be some level of unemployment where workers' aspirations are *equal* to the real wage that firms are willing to offer; this is the NAIRU. In other words NAIRU is determined by the intersection of the target and feasible real wage curves in Fig. 23.9. If unemployment were pushed *below* the NAIRU by government expansionary policy, then workers would seek a real wage above the feasible level; in an attempt to secure this they would demand higher money wages. If they were successful in securing these, firms would maintain their mark-up over costs by raising prices. If unemployment were to *remain* below the NAIRU, then a wage–price spiral would ensue. At some stage the government would have to allow unemployment to rise towards the NAIRU to end the rising inflation rate.

To sum up, then, the NAIRU is seen as being the level of unemployment necessary to keep inflation from rising. Anything which *shifts* the target or feasible real wage curves in Fig. 23.9 will affect the NAIRU.

Any factor that enables or encourages workers to *increase the target real wage* for a given level of unemployment will clearly increase the NAIRU, shifting the target real wage curve upwards and to the right. Such factors might include any or all of the following:

■ an increase in benefits and their duration;

■ an increase in trade union power or greater employment protection (both reducing the fear of unemployment);

■ increased structural unemployment (the unemployed now compete less effectively with the employed because they have the wrong skills or are in the wrong place);

■ an increase in the long-term unemployed as a proportion of total unemployment (the long-term unemployed compete less effectively with the employed for jobs);

■ an increase in taxes on earnings which reduces the post-tax real wage and leads workers to seek a higher pre-tax real wage.

Similarly any factor that *reduces the feasible real wage* will increase the NAIRU. Such factors might include any or all of the following:

■ reduced labour productivity;

■ unfavourable movements in the Terms of Trade (i.e. a fall in the ratio of export to import prices), reducing the share of output going to domestic employees and raising that going to foreign employees;

■ higher dividends reducing the share of output going to employees and raising that going to shareholders;

Table 23.4 Estimates of the UK NAIRU.

Time period	1966–73	1974–80	1981–87	1989–90	1996–99	2002
NAIRU range	1.6–5.6%	4.5–7.3%	5.2–9.9%	3.5–8.1%	6% approx.	5.25% approx.

Sources: *Bank of England Quarterly Bulletin* (1993), Vol. 33, No. 2; *Bank of England Inflation Report* (1998), August; HM Treasury, *Trend Growth: Recent Developments and Prospects*, April 2002.

- more 'leapfrogging' by which one group of workers use a pay increase by others to justify their own higher pay demands.

Although this idea of the NAIRU is a central concept in mainstream macroeconomics, its actual level is not easy to pin down. Table 23.4 shows considerable variability in the estimates of the NAIRU that have been made for the UK over selected time periods.

Unemployment in the OECD

Two important puzzles face applied economists when considering data on unemployment in the advanced industrialized countries of the OECD (Table 23.5). One puzzle involves explaining why unemployment has been much higher in almost all OECD countries during the 1980s and 1990s than it had been in the decades following the Second World War. The second puzzle involves explaining why such large variations have been recorded in unemployment rates between the OECD countries.

A study of cross-country differences in unemployment rates (Nickell 1998) attempted to assess the impact on unemployment of a variety of factors. For example, Nickell estimated that a 10% increase in the 'replacement ratio' and a one-year increase in the duration of entitlement to unemployment benefits would result in a 25% increase in unemployment, while a 10% increase in trade union density would result in a 60% increase in unemployment. On the other hand, a 5% reduction in the overall tax rate would reduce unemployment by 15% and a 2% cut in the real interest rate (a substantial cut) would reduce unemployment by around 10%. He found that policies involving an increase in labour market

'rigidity' (such as improved labour standards and greater employment protection) had little impact on overall unemployment. Nickell argued that such variables, despite problems of definition and measurement across countries, do shed some light on why unemployment varies a great deal between countries. For example, Spain, with its high replacement ratios, long benefit duration, rather high tax rates on earnings and relatively 'rigid' labour market, suffers from high unemployment, as might be expected from Nickell's analysis, whereas the US, with its relatively low replacement ratios, short benefit duration, low tax rates on earnings, flexible labour market and low union coverage, has relatively low unemployment.

Nickell goes on to argue that although his variables usefully explain cross-country comparisons, they are less useful in explaining the time series pattern of OECD unemployment (see also Bean 1994). For example, when comparing the higher unemployment of the 1990s with the much lower unemployment of the 1960s, Nickell was surprised to find that today's replacement ratios are no more generous, trade union militancy no worse, real interest rates not much higher, and labour markets not much more rigid, than all of these factors had been in the 1960s and yet unemployment is so much higher.

Concentrating on the UK alone, rather than on cross-country comparisons, Nickell (1998) estimated that the fourfold rise in the numbers unemployed since the 1960s could comfortably be explained by a model including the replacement ratio, the Terms of Trade, skills mismatch, union pressure, industrial turbulence, the tax 'wedge' and the real interest rate. The variables making the most important (percentage) contributions in explaining the overall rise in unemployment have been skills mismatch 14%, union pressure 19%, and tax 'wedge' 23%, but the real interest rate *only* 3.5%.

Table 23.5 Unemployment rates in selected OECD countries.

	UK	France	Germany (W)	Italy	Netherlands	Spain	US	Japan
1960–68	2.6	1.7	0.7	3.8	1.2	2.4	4.7	1.4
1983–97	9.5	10.5	6.2	7.9	8.1	19.7	6.4	2.7

Source: OECD, *Economic Outlook*, various.

Table 23.6 Long-term real interest rates (average of US, Germany, UK and France).

	1956–73	1974–80	1981–93
Real interest rate	1.7	0.0	5.1

Source: Adapted from Rowthorn (1995).

A rather different view was offered by Phelps and Zoega (1998) who suggested that two global forces, namely sharp rises in oil prices in the 1970s and in real world interest rates in the 1980s and early 1990s, have been the major factors responsible for the observed increases in worldwide unemployment since the 1960s.

Higher oil prices reduce labour productivity by reducing the proportion of the existing capital stock which can be regarded as 'economically efficient'; for example, oil-intensive capital equipment becomes effectively redundant. As well as diminishing the 'economically efficient' capital stock, and with it labour productivity, higher oil prices are seen by Phelps and Zoega as contributing to higher unemployment by diminishing net exports (exports minus imports) for many OECD countries. The non-oil exporting OECD countries have been particularly hard-hit by ever increasing import bills for oil and 'oil-based' products.

The Phelps and Zoega model sees hiring rates for workers as heavily dependent on both net productivity and the real interest rate. As well as the slowdown in productivity growth experienced in most countries following oil-price shocks, the steep rises in global real interest rates shown in Table 23.6 further reduce the hiring rate for labour, resulting in substantial increases in levels of unemployment. Higher real interest rates particularly discourage the hiring of workers who require a substantial investment in human capital, such as the large numbers of higher skilled and well-educated workers required by many high-technology, 'information age' industries.

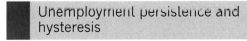

Unemployment persistence and hysteresis

In the mid-1980s oil prices fell, trade union power diminished compared to the 1970s, the replacement ratio fell, and yet unemployment kept on rising, at least in Europe. One explanation might be that demand-deficient unemployment had risen because governments were trying to control inflation by running the economy with unemployment *above* the NAIRU. However, inflation did not fall in the mid-1980s, leading some economists to the view that a period of high unemployment resulting from contractionary demand management might lead to the NAIRU itself increasing. The idea that there might be a mechanism whereby a rise in unemployment increases the equilibrium (or natural) rate of unemployment is known as *hysteresis*. There are several possible mechanisms to explain hysteresis in European unemployment.

One explanation of hysteresis involves the *insider–outsider hypothesis* (Blanchard and Summers 1986; Lindbeck and Snower 1988). *Insiders* are the unionized employed who pay little attention to the interests of the unemployed *outsiders*. For a variety of reasons (such as turnover costs, firm-specific human capital and the possibility of refusing to cooperate with newly hired outsiders), insiders do not fear that they will be replaced by outsiders. Of course in practice, if the demand for labour falls, then some insiders may lose their jobs and become outsiders. Once labour demand recovers, however, the smaller pool of insiders who remain will exploit their relative scarcity by negotiating higher wages for themselves rather than accepting wage moderation and allowing the employment of more outsiders. The economy therefore settles at a higher-wage, lower-employment equilibrium.

A second explanation of hysteresis concentrates on the role of the *long-term unemployed*; in other words this approach concentrates on the role of the *outsiders* rather than on the wage-determining role of the insiders. The long-term unemployed are seen as effectively having withdrawn from the labour force (they search less effectively, they lose their skills and employers see them as a bad risk). The result is that they do not exert much downward pressure on wage setting, so that a higher level of unemployment is required to exert the same control on inflation when the long-term unemployed increase as a proportion of the total unemployed. Empirical evidence certainly suggests that when European unemployment persists the effect is to increase the proportion of the long-term unemployed in total unemployment, so that the equilibrium (or natural) rate of unemployment rises.

A third explanation of hysteresis involves the effect of recessions on the *capital stock*. As aggregate demand falls, firms go out of business and investment plans are shelved, reducing the capital-to-labour ratio and therefore the marginal productivity of labour (shifting the labour demand curve to the left). From the point of view of the NAIRU model there has been a reduction in the 'feasible real wage'. Whichever way we look at it, the equilibrium (or natural) rate of unemployment rises.

A fourth explanation of hysteresis involves the suggestion that a more highly regulated labour market discourages recruitment, and may lead to higher equilibrium unemployment after a downturn in demand (see Bean 1994).

What can be done to reduce unemployment?

The OECD *Jobs Study* (1994) made more than 60 policy recommendations for reducing unemployment. Following on from this, the OECD *Jobs Strategy* (1998) produced a blueprint aimed at creating jobs and reducing unemployment, whilst at the same time strengthening social cohesion. The key recommendations included the following.

■ Set macroeconomic policy to encourage non-inflationary growth.

■ Enhance the creation and diffusion of technology.

■ Increase working time flexibility.

■ Encourage entrepreneurship and eliminate restrictions on the creation and expansion of enterprises.

■ Make wage and labour costs flexible and responsive to local conditions and skill levels, particularly for young workers.

■ Reform employment security provisions that inhibit recruitment.

■ Strengthen the emphasis on 'active' labour market policies.

■ Improve the education and skills of the labour force.

■ Reform 'unemployment and related' benefits and the tax system to improve the functioning of the job market, whilst not jeopardizing society's equity goals.

■ Enhance product market competition to reduce monopolistic tendencies and weaken insider–outsider mechanisms, thereby leading to a more dynamic economy.

In its latest survey of employment the OECD (2002) reinforces the view that the countries that have been most successful in reducing unemployment (e.g. Australia, Canada and some EU countries) or in holding it at a low level (e.g. the US) have, on the whole, taken the most comprehensive actions in line with the OECD *Jobs Strategy*. 'Comprehensive' in this case means reforming not only the labour market but also the goods market. Indeed the study examines the *cross-market* effects of product market policies on the labour market. It finds that anti-competitive regulation in the product market tends to lower employment, with the product market regulatory environment accounting for up to 3% points of the deviation in the non-agricultural employment rate in some OECD countries. It also found that industry wage premiums increase as product market competition decreases. Finally it argues that there is evidence to suggest that product market deregulation in one industry may reduce job security for workers in other more regulated industries. Product market policies therefore have important implications for employment.

The UK approach to reducing unemployment

The UK's strategy for reducing unemployment is in line with the OECD approach and is in the 2002 *UK Employment Action Plan*. The action plan outlines four pillars on which policy is based:

■ *Improving employability*. Included here are measures taken to prevent long-term unemployment. Key to this is the *Job Seekers' Allowance* (JSA) regime supplemented by measures such as the New Deals. Under the JSA, contracts are drawn up between the job seeker and their personal advisor which devise a route map back to employment. The agreements are reviewed fortnightly. The JSA regime is an attempt to ensure that for most people unemployment is a short-term experience.

However, for the long-term unemployed the second key element of the strategy is the *New Deal*. There are various New Deals for the long-term unemployed in different categories, e.g. 18–24, 25+, 50+ and people with disabilities, which offer opportunities such as subsidized jobs in the private sector, training and education opportunities, work in the voluntary sector or work for an Environmental Task Force. Sanctions are applied to the young or long-term unemployed who do not participate. It is claimed that the New Deal has virtually eliminated long-term youth unemployment and helped to reduce long-term unemployment by 40% amongst the 25+ age group.

Other equally important measures have also been taken to make work pay. The minimum wage and reforms in the tax and benefit system are attempts to increase the incentives to move into work (see Chapter 19). Employability will also be improved by raising UK education standards. Measures have been taken to improve both child and adult literacy and numeracy and to make life-long learning available to all.

- *Developing entrepreneurship and job creation.* The government's aim here is to make it easier to start up and run businesses, to encourage entrepreneurship and self-employment. Small firms account for over 55% of employment in the private sector so initiatives to encourage small business start-ups would help reduce unemployment. The government is particularly targeting the 20 most disadvantaged UK local authority wards and is also encouraging business support initiatives for the disadvantaged groups discussed earlier.

- *Encouraging adaptability of businesses and their employees.* The UK government initiatives here are designed to address how work is managed by employers in cooperation with trade unions. The aim is to bring flexibility to the labour market and thus raise productivity. At the same time flexibility will enable workers, especially those with small children, to better reconcile the work–life balance.

- *Strengthening equal opportunities policies for men and women.* This pillar entails a series of measures designed to ensure that women are not held back in the labour market by restricted career choice, career breaks or caring responsibilities.

Conclusion

Unemployment is determined by the level of demand in the economy. If demand is too low, then unemployment will be above the equilibrium rate (or NAIRU); if demand is too high, then unemployment will be below the NAIRU and, in the absence of other offsetting factors, the inflation rate will begin to rise. The implication for policy is that demand management should aim to keep unemployment as close to the NAIRU as possible, whilst labour and goods market initiatives should aim to reduce the NAIRU. In the spring of 2003 unemployment in the UK was at its lowest rate for over 20 years. At 5.1% it was lower than in most OECD countries, lower than the EU (15) average rate of 7.9% and lower than the US rate of 5.8%. It is clear that there has been some success in reducing the UK NAIRU since the late 1980s. Policy concerns still exist, however, not only over high European unemployment but also over getting the unemployment rates of the 'disadvantaged groups' within the UK and EU economies down to an acceptable level.

Key points

- Successive 'unemployment cycles' (peak to peak) have tended to result in higher unemployment rates.

- The ILO (survey) method of measuring the unemployed differs from the claimant (administrative record) method used in the UK.

- Unemployment in the UK can be *disaggregated* into regional, occupational, gender, age, ethnically-based and qualification-related unemployment.

- The major *types* of unemployment include frictional (temporary), structural (changing patterns of demand), technological (changing technology), classical

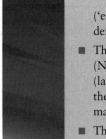

('excessive' real wages) and demand-deficient (inadequate demand) categories.

■ The *natural rate of unemployment* (NRU) is the voluntary unemployment (labour force – labour supply) existing at the real wage level which 'clears' the markets.

■ The *non-accelerating inflation rate of unemployment* (NAIRU) is that level of unemployment which equates the *feasible* real wage with the *target* real wage. It is

the unemployment rate at which inflation is constant.

■ Estimates suggest that NAIRU has risen for the UK over the past two decades or so, though falling in recent years (e.g. via more flexible labour markets). Only where the actual unemployment rate is *above* NAIRU can unemployment be reduced (to NAIRU) without stimulating inflation.

Now try the self-check questions for this chapter on the Companion Website. You will also find up-to-date facts and case materials.

Note

1. The downward stickiness in wages (wage rigidity) and therefore prices also thwarts the interest rate and foreign trade effects which might stimulate recovery. In the 'interest rate effect', lower prices mean an increase in *real money supply*, lowering the 'price' of money (interest rates) and thereby raising the invest-

ment component of aggregate demand. In the 'foreign trade effect', lower prices mean more competitive exports and more competitive (home-produced) substitutes for imports, a rise in exports and a fall in imports again stimulating (net) aggregate demand.

References and further reading

Bank of England (1998) *Inflation Report*, February, August.

Barro, R. J. (1998) *Macroeconomics*, MIT Press, Cambridge, MA.

Barwell, R. (2000) Age structure and the UK unemployment rate, *Bank of England Quarterly Bulletin*, 40(3), August.

Bean, C. (1994) European unemployment: a survey, *Journal of Economic Literature*, 32, June.

Begg, D., Fischer, S. and **Dornbusch, R.** (1994) *Economics*, McGraw-Hill, London.

Berthoud, R. (2003) Multiple Disadvantage in Employment: A quantitative analysis, Institute for

Social and Economic Research, University of Essex.

Blanchard, D. and **Summers, L.** (1986) *Hysteresis and the European Unemployment Problem*, NBER Macroeconomic Annual.

Clark, A. and **Layard, R.** (1989) *UK Unemployment*, Heinemann Educational, Oxford.

Dawson, G. (1992) *Inflation and Unemployment: causes, consequences and cures*, Edward Elgar, Aldershot.

Fothergill, S. and **Gudgin, G.** (1982) *Unequal Growth: urban and regional change in the UK*, Heinemann, London.

Friedman, M. (1968) The role of monetary policy, *American Economic Review*, **58**, March.

HM Treasury (1998) *Stability and Investment for the Long Term: Economic and Fiscal Strategy Report.*

HM Treasury (2002a) *UK Employment Action Plan.*

HM Treasury (2002b) *Trend Growth: Recent Developments and Prospects.*

Keynes, J. M. (1936) *The General Theory of Employment, Interest and Money*, Macmillan, p. 381.

Labour Market Trends (2000) July.

Layard, R. (1986) *How to Beat Unemployment*, Oxford University Press, Oxford.

Layard, R., Nickell, S. and Jackman, R. (1994) *The Unemployment Crisis*, Oxford University Press, Oxford.

Lindbeck, A. and Snower, D. (1988) *The Insider–Outsider Theory of Employment and Unemployment*, MIT Press, Cambridge, MA.

Nickell, S. (1998) Unemployment: questions and some answers, *Economic Journal*, **108**(48), May.

Nickell, S. (2003) Poverty and worthlessness in Britain, speech given at Royal Economic Society Conference at Warwick, 8 April.

OECD (1994) *Jobs Study: facts, analysis and strategies*, OECD, Paris.

OECD (1998) *Jobs Strategy: Progress Report*, OECD Working Paper, No. 196.

OECD (2002) *Employment Outlook*, OECD, Paris.

Phelps, E. and Zoega, G. (1998) Natural rate theory and OECD unemployment, *Economic Journal*, **108**(48), May.

Rowthorn, R. (1995) Capital formation and unemployment, *Oxford Review of Economic Policy*, **11**(1), Spring.

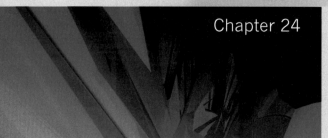

Chapter 24 — Managing the economy

In this chapter the objectives of macroeconomic policy are discussed, along with the instruments for achieving them. After a short review of the interventionist theory of macroeconomic policy, we consider the conduct of policy in the UK. Adjusting the instruments of policy to 'best' meet a set of target values for various objectives seems to fit the actual conduct of policy in the UK until 1974. The emphasis then shifted away from such 'fine-tuning' and towards the adoption of medium- and long-term rules. This change of emphasis is well illustrated by considering the policies advocated by the Cambridge Economic Policy Group (CEPG) and by the monetarists. The fortunes of the Medium Term Financial Strategy are traced from its inception in 1979 to 2003. An assessment is also made of the contribution of supply-side economics to macroeconomic policy. This chapter concludes with a study of economic policy in an international context.

The objectives of policy

The desire of most individuals is to live and work within an economic framework which gives them the prospect of steady employment, relatively stable prices and a rising standard of living. It is usually recognized that to achieve such a situation the economy must trade and 'pay its way' with other economies. Politicians realize that to attract votes and gain political power they must promise that these aspirations will be met, if only in the long run. Economic objectives at the macroeconomic level are therefore set in terms of full employment, price stability and rapid economic growth, together with long-term equilibrium in the balance of payments. All these objectives have attracted attention in the post-war period in the UK. Since they are unlikely to be achieved in their totality, they have usually been expressed in terms of target values. Whilst these target values have not always been explicitly stated, they seem to be influenced by achieved values within the recent past.

Full employment

For instance, it is recognized that full employment can never mean zero registered unemployment if only because of dynamic change within society. Following the Beveridge Report of 1944, a 3% rate of unemployment (about half a million) was used in the 1950s and 1960s as the 'acceptable' upper limit. In more recent times governments have been reluctant to commit themselves to any specific unemployment target.

Stable prices

Stable prices have always been regarded as unrealistic, but the attainment of an annual inflation rate of around 2.5% seems to have been the approximate target in the first two post-war decades. More recently the reduction of the annual inflation rate to below 4%, or to a rate equivalent to that of our industrial rivals, would appear to have been the target set during much of the 1980s and 1990s. With the advent of the new Labour government in 1997 and the establishment of an independent Monetary Policy Committee (MPC), a specific target of 2.5% for annual inflation was given to the MPC between 1997 and 2003 to guide it in setting interest rate policy.

Economic growth

Economic growth has received relatively little specific emphasis in the UK, although most governments have expressed some enthusiasm for it! We have, generally speaking, enjoyed rising living standards and have compared ourselves (favourably) with our parents and grandparents rather than with our contemporaries in Europe, the USA or Japan. A well-known statement concerning economic growth as an objective was made by the late R. A. Butler in 1954, when he suggested a doubling of living standards every 25 years as an explicit target. This was greeted as being over-ambitious, yet it entailed an annual growth rate of GDP of less than 3%. The Economic Plan of 1965 sought a growth rate of 3.8% per annum, but this was quickly seen to be unattainable and this attempt at long-term planning was soon abandoned. Between 1997 and 2003 there was a criticism that the Monetary Policy Committee had not been given a growth target to set alongside the 2.5% inflation target when deciding the level of interest rates.

The balance of payments

The balance of payments is often described as an objective of economic policy, the target being either equilibrium or a surplus over a period of time in order that accumulated international debts might be repaid. This can hardly be related to the aspirations of individuals and is thought by many to be more properly described as a constraint upon the achievement of other objectives. Nevertheless, target figures have been set in the past, e.g. the 1953 Economic Survey called for a surplus of £450m per annum as the target surplus on current account in the 1950s to finance the long-term capital outflow. It was not achieved, and since then the use of target figures has become less important. However, a relatively 'healthy' external account is still an important consideration of policy.

This list of objectives could be extended to include others, such as the redistribution of income and wealth, but target values for employment, inflation and underlying economic growth have received most attention. The recent record of achievement is displayed in Table 24.1.

Table 24.1 shows that the efforts of successive governments simultaneously to achieve the four major objectives have failed. However, this by no means indicates that it is 'worthless' for governments to intervene in the economy, as the situation could have been still worse without such intervention.

Table 24.1 Achieved values for a number of policy objectives.

Year	Unemployment as a percentage of working population (excluding school-leavers)	Annual change in RPI (%)	Annual change in GDP (at market prices) (%)	Balance of payments (current account) (£m)
1972	3.1	7.1	3.5	+142
1973	2.1	9.2	7.2	−1,100
1974	2.1	16.1	−1.6	−3,333
1975	3.3	24.9	0.0	−1,695
1976	3.5	15.1	2.7	−972
1977	4.7	12.1	2.4	−286
1978	4.6	8.4	3.3	+821
1979	4.1	17.2	2.7	−1,002
1980	5.4	15.1	−2.2	+1,740
1981	8.5	12.0	−1.3	+4,846
1982	9.8	5.4	1.8	+2,233
1983	10.4	5.3	3.8	+1,258
1984	10.7	4.6	2.3	−1,294
1985	10.9	5.7	3.8	−570
1986	11.2	4.0	3.8	−3,614
1987	10.3	4.2	4.5	−7,538
1988	8.3	4.9	5.1	−19,850
1989	6.4	7.8	2.1	−26,321
1990	5.8	9.4	0.0	−22,281
1991	8.1	5.9	−1.5	−10,659
1992	9.8	3.7	0.0	−12,974
1993	10.3	1.6	2.3	−11,919
1994	9.4	2.4	4.3	−6,768
1995	8.1	3.5	2.7	−9,015
1996	7.4	2.4	2.6	−8,709
1997	5.4	3.1	3.5	−1,720
1998	4.6	3.4	2.2	−4,814
1999	4.2	1.5	2.0	−19,729
2000	3.7	3.0	3.0	−19,208
2001	3.3	1.8	2.0	−18,038
2002	3.2	1.7	1.7	−18,965

Sources: ONS (2002) *Economic Trends: Annual Supplement*; ONS (2002), *UK Balance of Payments*; ONS (2003) *Data Releases* (various).

The instruments of policy

Governments would have no macroeconomic problems if market forces in the economy automatically led to 'full employment' equilibrium, with stable prices, and a rapid economic growth. The bulk of the evidence seems to indicate that market forces alone have failed to achieve these objectives, either in full or even at 'satisfactory' values. Such 'market failure' essentially constitutes the case for intervention by governments. If governments *are* to intervene in the economy, there still remains the problem of selecting the appropriate instruments for achieving the targets they set themselves.

In general terms the policy instruments available to the UK government are fiscal policy, monetary policy, prices and incomes policy, and policy instruments aimed at the balance of payments, such as the exchange rate or import controls. These policy instruments are sometimes called 'instrumental variables', i.e. variables over which the government has some control, and the values of which affect the behaviour of the economy itself in some reasonably systematic way.

Fiscal policy

Fiscal policy involves using both government spending and taxation to influence the composition and level of aggregate demand in the economy. Elementary circular flow analysis suggests that by raising the level of government expenditure and/or by reducing taxation, the level of aggregate demand can be raised (by a multiplied amount) with favourable consequences for economic activity and employment. Such an expansionary course of action might result in a larger budget deficit, or a reduced budget surplus, in this way affecting the Public Sector Borrowing Requirement (PSBR). This somewhat simplistic approach is the basis for fiscal interventionism as advocated by 'Keynesians', and carried out with some success in the UK for over 25 years after the Second World War. The Budget was viewed not as an accounting procedure, with expenditure and revenue to be balanced as a matter of good housekeeping, but as an instrument of policy to be manipulated as a means to an end. Deficits were financed by borrowing, short or long term, from home and abroad, with the increased National Debt seen as a means of spreading the costs of current policy over future generations.

Practical problems abound. Although tax rates can be set, the revenues they will yield are difficult to predict as income levels can vary. Also government expenditure and tax receipts are subject to time-lags, which can have destabilizing effects. For instance, the government may aim to raise spending to stimulate the economy during recession, but the effects may not be felt for several time periods, when the economy may be in a different situation. In other words, fiscal policy may move the economy away from desired values rather than towards them. There is even a problem in identifying the government's fiscal stance. A contractionary fiscal policy will, if successful, reduce incomes and tax yield, and might also have the effect of raising some government expenditures such as unemployment benefit. If we look, therefore, at the Budget *out-turn* for evidence of the government's fiscal stance, we may come to the wrong conclusion – the reduced tax yield and increased government expenditure may be the result of a contractionary fiscal policy, not evidence of an expansionary one! Problems such as these account in part for the relegation of fiscal policy in favour of monetary policy by Conservative governments during the 1980s. Even after the post-1997 Labour government brought some measure of stability into fiscal affairs by introducing its 'fiscal rules' (see Chapter 18), problems still arose in identifying accurate trends for government expenditure and revenue.

Monetary policy

Monetary policy aims to influence monetary variables such as the rate of interest and the money supply, in order to achieve the targets set for the four major objectives. Although the rate of interest and the money supply are interrelated (see Chapter 20), for convenience we examine these separately.

The rate of interest – in practice there are many – is thought to be important because it is a cost of borrowing, influencing not only long-term investment decisions by firms but also their short-term borrowing to overcome cash-flow problems. Interest rates may influence consumer spending on durable goods by affecting the cost of hire-purchase finance. Interest rates also influence household decisions as to the composition of the assets they hold. For example, low interest rates offer little reward for those acquiring financial assets, thus encouraging consumer expenditure on goods and services. The balance of payments is also affected by interest rate policy, as capital inflow and outflow depend on UK interest rates relative to those in other countries.

The money supply, as we saw in Chapter 20, 'matters' to both monetarists and Keynesians. To monetarists, money supply mainly affects prices, at least in the long run, whereas to Keynesians, the major impact is on output and employment. The measurement and control of money supply have therefore been widely regarded as an important policy instrument, and we return to this below.

Prices and incomes policy

Prices and incomes policy is used in an attempt to control inflation by directly influencing the rate at which prices, wages and salaries rise. Depending on political and economic belief, such a policy can be viewed as an irrelevance by the monetarists, or as a necessary means of influencing the institutional determinants of inflation by the Keynesians, particularly when expansionary fiscal measures are being used to overcome unemployment.

Since 1960 there have been few occasions on which this instrument of policy was not in use, either on a voluntary basis or in the form of statutory control. Prices have been directly controlled as well as wages, and wages themselves have been subject to various forms of restraint, such as 'freezes', or 'norms' for wage increases. The impact of the policy has, predictably, fallen most heavily on the public sector. Although during the operation of incomes policy the rate of wage inflation has usually been reduced below the previously prevailing figure, it has often been higher than the 'norm' set, and has always been followed, when controls have been relaxed, by a rapid and sharp increase in the rate of wage inflation. It is difficult to test the overall effects of the use of this instrument of policy, but it is generally regarded as having been less useful in the long term. Prices and incomes policy was last used formally in 1979, but an incomes policy has been used informally since then, with the introduction of cash limits for the public sector acting as a constraint on wage increases.

The exchange rate

The exchange rate is one of the instruments which can be used to influence the balance of payments. With the exception of the devaluations of 1949 (30%), and 1967 (14%), the sterling exchange rate was essentially fixed under the International Monetary Fund (IMF) system. In 1971 the convertibility of the dollar into gold at a fixed price was abandoned and the IMF fixed exchange rate system broke down. Since mid-1972 the UK exchange rate has fluctuated, in theory according to market forces (a 'clean' float), but in practice often 'managed' by the authorities (a 'dirty' float). Although the pound fell to record low levels against the dollar in early 1983, it would have fallen even lower had the Bank of England not intervened on the foreign exchange market to buy the pound with its foreign currency reserves.

A change in the exchange rate will affect the relative prices of domestic- and foreign-produced goods and services. For example, a lower exchange rate makes UK goods cheaper in the foreign markets, and foreign goods more expensive in the UK market (see Chapter 26). Given appropriate elasticities for exports and imports,[1] a lower exchange rate will improve the balance of payments.

One major difficulty in a lower exchange rate policy is that this will have an adverse effect on domestic costs, both directly and indirectly. The rise in price of imported foodstuffs and finished manufactures will have an immediate and direct effect on the price level, because these items are included in the Retail Price Index (RPI). The rise in price of imported raw materials and semi-finished manufactures will also have an indirect effect on the price level, by raising domestic costs of production. Higher prices could also stimulate higher wage demands to protect real incomes, further fuelling inflation. In these ways the competitive advantage of devaluation may well be eroded, and the objective of price stability (or reduced inflation) adversely affected. Between 1987 and 1992, the government sought to target the exchange rate at particular levels against various currencies. This was in order to prevent sterling depreciating too rapidly, thereby endangering the control of inflation. The entry of sterling into the ERM at a relatively high rate of 2.95 DM to the pound in October 1990 was also to help contain inflationary pressure in the UK. One of the concerns facing the government when the UK left the ERM in September 1992 was the fear that the 14% fall in sterling's value against the Deutsche Mark (and 20% against the US dollar) by late 1992 would rekindle inflationary pressures. As it turned out such fears proved largely unfounded. Since 1992 there has been no explicit targeting of the exchange rate, despite frequent complaints by UK manufacturers and industrialists of a 'high pound'.

Import controls

Import controls are another policy instrument for affecting the balance of payments, but have been little used in the UK since the Second World War, other than to reduce import tariffs in line with other members of the General Agreement on Tariffs and Trade (GATT). Two examples may serve to illustrate their use. Between 1964 and 1966 there was an import surcharge scheme whereby most imported manufactured goods carried a levy of 15% in an attempt to reduce imports by over £550m per annum. It was a partial success, reducing them by perhaps half the intended sum. In 1968–70 there was an import deposit scheme whereby half the value of imported manufactured goods had to be deposited with the government for six months, with no interest paid. Little effect upon the balance of payments was discerned.

Renewed interest in import tariffs emerged in the early 1980s, stimulated by the Cambridge Economic Policy Group (CEPG) who, initially at least, saw a direct and close relationship between the size of the Budget deficit and the size of the balance of payments deficit. If expansionary domestic fiscal policy is to overcome unemployment and stimulate investment, they advocate imposing tariffs to prevent the extra domestic spending from being satisfied by overseas suppliers. Their aim was not to reduce imports below the initial pre-expansion figure, but to prevent them from rising above that level.

Problems in managing the economy

Before we consider the theory of economic policy, some general points can be made concerning the objectives of policy and the instruments available to the government.

Trade-off between objectives

The most obvious difficulty is that the objectives 'trade off' against each other. For example, policy instruments that governments use to achieve the objective of lower inflation often impose a cost of higher unemployment. Curbing the money supply may reduce the value of spending,[2] and raise interest rates, resulting in the closure of many firms, with the loss of jobs. Curbing government spending as part of monetary policy can also reduce employment in the public sector. A higher exchange rate during 1981/82, from 1985 to 1988 and again from 1996 to 2001, made UK exports expensive, and imports cheaper, reducing domestic output and employment, especially in the more tradeable manufacturing sector. Lower inflation can therefore be achieved, but at the cost of higher unemployment. High interest rates and low economic activity can also discourage investment, adversely affecting another important policy objective, that of economic growth. This raises the question of 'weighting' the objectives against each other, e.g. how much extra unemployment and lower growth will be tolerated in order to reduce the inflation rate by a further x percentage points?

Interdependence of instruments

Policy instruments are not independent of each other. For example, fiscal policy has implications for the money supply and for the rate of interest. In turn, the domestic rate of interest will, by its effect upon short-term capital flows, influence the sterling exchange rate, and will also affect the money supply.

Instruments as objectives

It has to be recognized that policy instruments sometimes become objectives in their own right. This was the case with the exchange rate instrument which was used only twice in the post-war period up to the early 1970s. This was because preserving the value of the pound had itself become an objective of policy, so that it could no longer be used as a flexible instrument of policy. Again in February 1987 the UK agreed to the Louvre Accord in Paris which stated that a period of exchange rate stability was desirable. This made it more difficult to use the exchange rate as a policy *instrument* and in some respects it then becomes an *objective* of policy instead! This became even more obvious between 1990 and 1992 when maintaining sterling's parity in the ERM was seen as a major objective of policy.

Political constraints

The set of policy objectives chosen, and the instruments used, may be constrained by the fact that it is politicians who are the ultimate decision-takers. Each course of action must therefore be evaluated in its political context. The use of some policy instruments may then be inhibited, as with the Conservative government's reluctance formally to use a prices and incomes policy given its views on the efficacy of a free market system. Similarly, the decision of the government to enter the ERM in October 1990 severely limited its ability to use the exchange rate as an instrument of policy, although its subsequent withdrawal in September 1992 eased this limitation. In 1997 the decision to establish an independent body, the Monetary Policy Committee, to set interest rates effectively removed this policy instrument from government control.

The theory of economic policy

Here we look at the basic theory of economic policy, concentrating on the 'fixed targets', the 'variable targets' and the 'satisficing' approaches to policy formation.

The fixed targets approach

Perhaps the best-known approach is that of Tinbergen (1952), the so-called fixed targets approach, which establishes the condition for the simultaneous achievement of fixed target values for a number of objectives. *Tinbergen's rule* states that if these target values are to be achieved simultaneously, then there must be at least the same number of instruments as there are objectives. The values of these instruments are determined by the desired-target values of the objectives, and they

can then be assessed to see whether they are both feasible and acceptable to the decision-makers.

This rule can be illustrated in Fig. 24.1 where, for simplicity, the two-instrument/two-objective case is illustrated. Instruments I_1 (monetary policy) and I_2 (fiscal policy) are plotted on the axes of the graph. Movements along each axis and away from the origin will be used to indicate 'expansionary' policy. On the horizontal axis, for example, close to the origin we have 'tight' fiscal policy, with high taxation and low government expenditure. Movement along the horizontal axis and away from the origin indicates that fiscal policy becomes 'easier', with taxation falling and government expenditure rising. The Budget moves from surplus into deficit, with the deficit becoming greater as the movement to the right continues. On the vertical axis, points close to the origin indicate restrictive monetary policy, with high interest rates and static, or slowly growing, money supply. Movement along the vertical axis and away from the origin indicates an expansionary monetary policy, the money supply rising rapidly and interest rates falling.

The line O_1 shows the combinations of monetary and fiscal policy required to achieve the objective of *internal balance*, i.e. full employment (or something

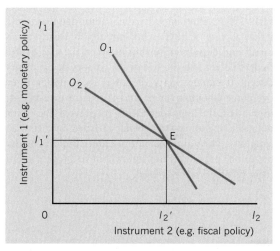

Fig. 24.1 Two-instrument/two-objective case.
Notes:
O_1 = Objective 1 (internal balance) at a particular target value.
O_2 = Objective 2 (external balance) at a particular target value.
I_1 = Instrumental variable 1, e.g. monetary policy.
I_2 = Instrumental variable 2, e.g. fiscal policy.

very close to it) with price stability (or a low and acceptable rate of inflation). O_1 will be negatively sloped, on the assumption that expansionary fiscal policy must be accompanied by contractionary monetary policy, if full employment is to be achieved without price inflation. If contractionary monetary policy did not accompany the expansionary fiscal policy then too high a level of aggregate demand would be generated, and with it price inflation.[3]

The line O_2 shows the combinations of monetary and fiscal policy required to achieve *external balance*, i.e. balance of payments equilibrium. It, too, is negatively sloped, reflecting the fact that expansionary fiscal policy raises domestic incomes, so increasing imports (and perhaps reducing exports). If balance of payments equilibrium is to be maintained, then these unfavourable effects on the current account must be offset by an improvement elsewhere in the accounts. This could be achieved by a contractionary monetary policy, which raises interest rates, attracting inflows of capital from overseas. Again, if fiscal policy is expansionary, a contractionary monetary policy will be necessary to preserve the external balance.[4]

Figure 24.1 shows that with two objectives (internal and external balance) and two instruments or instrumental variables (monetary and fiscal policy) then, by setting monetary and fiscal instruments at values I'_1 and I'_2 respectively, objectives O_1 and O_2 can be achieved simultaneously.[5] Tinbergen's rule is thereby illustrated.

Suppose now a third objective is added, perhaps a target rate of economic growth (Fig. 24.2). The line O_3 shows the combinations of monetary and fiscal policy required to achieve this target rate of economic growth. O_3 is positively sloped, on the assumption that an expansionary fiscal policy, involving extra government spending, will 'crowd out' private sector investment. Total investment can then be kept at the level required to achieve growth rate O_3 only by encouraging private sector investment through low interest rates, i.e. by expansionary monetary policy. Expansionary fiscal *and* monetary policy are in this case required to achieve the target rate of economic growth O_3.

We can now see that it would be a fortunate and unlikely coincidence if O_3 happened to pass through point E, i.e. if all three objectives could be achieved with just two policy instruments. If, as in the figure, it does not, then we can only achieve two of the three objectives with our two policy instruments. For

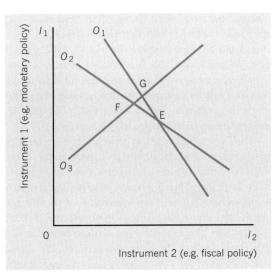

Fig. 24.2 Two-instrument/three-objective case.

instance, we could be at G (O_1 and O_3 achieved, but not O_2) or at F (O_2 and O_3 achieved, but not O_1) or at E (O_1 and O_2 achieved, but not O_3). To achieve the third objective now requires a third policy instrument, perhaps exchange rate policy![6] If we cannot find extra policy instruments, Tinbergen's rule will be violated, i.e. there will be fewer instruments (here two) than objectives (here three). Except in the fortuitous case that all three objectives intersect, at G, F or E, then an *explicit choice* will have to be made between the conflicting objectives. In our example we must choose between G, F or E.

Tinbergen's approach has the great merit of being fairly simple to understand. It has encouraged governments to be explicit about their macroeconomic objectives and has stimulated the search for new policy instruments, such as flexible exchange rates or prices and incomes policy. Its emphasis on 'fine-tuning' the economy by introducing additional policy instruments, and changing their values, reflects the spirit of 'Keynesian' interventionism.

The flexible targets approach

In Tinbergen's approach, when we were unable to achieve all three objectives simultaneously because we lacked sufficient policy instruments, the target then became the achievement of any two, i.e. at G, F or E in Fig. 24.2. A choice had to be made between these alternatives. In contrast Theil (1956) suggested that the target could be more flexible, and that any position could be chosen within the triangle GFE. In this case no single objective is achieved; instead a compromise between the three is reached, all three being 'missed', but by a narrow margin in each case. This might be preferred to achieving two objectives by missing the third by a considerable margin.

Theil's flexible targets approach therefore presupposes that since all the objectives cannot be met there must be some 'welfare loss' whatever choice of objectives is made. This approach also assumes that a social welfare function can be defined for society as a whole, the aim then being to minimize the welfare loss for any choice made. The welfare function will take into account the *deviation* between the actual value achieved for any objective and its target value, with any such deviation indicating a loss of welfare. The problem then becomes one of minimizing a welfare loss function bearing in mind that the objectives are presumably 'weighted' with respect to each other. For example, in the early 1980s a deviation between the actual and target inflation rate would appear to be weighted more heavily than a deviation between the actual and target unemployment rate. Weights W_1, W_2 and W_3 are introduced into the welfare loss function to be minimized below. The deviations between actual and target levels are conventionally squared in order to eliminate the problem of sign.

It follows that if the three objectives have *actual* values O_1, O_2 and O_3, and target values O_1^*, O_2^* and O_3^*, then the policy-makers would seek to minimize the social welfare loss function defined in terms of those three objectives, i.e.

$$\text{Minimize } U(O_1, O_2, O_3) =$$
$$W_1(O_1 - O_1^*)^2 + W_2(O_2 - O_2^*)^2 + W_3(O_3 - O_3^*)^2$$

If there had been sufficient instruments to permit the simultaneous achievement of all three objectives, then $O_1 = O_1^*$, $O_2 = O_2^*$ and $O_3 = O_3^*$; in other words, the welfare loss function would equal zero. In terms of Fig. 24.2 all three objective functions (O_1, O_2 and O_3) have coincided at a single point. More sophisticated forms of such functions recognize that it is not only the extent to which the target objectives are fulfilled that matters, but also the values of the instrumental variables themselves. For example, high tax rates or higher interest rates may themselves reduce social welfare and might therefore be included in the loss function.

No one would suggest that political decision-makers study loss minimization functions of the form indicated above, but the approach is helpful in suggesting that attempts should be made to think seriously about the relative weights given to objectives, and that if fixed target values are unattainable then flexibility might have to be accepted.

The satisficing approach

Both the Tinbergen and the Theil approaches suggest that the economy is 'fine-tuned' by the policy-makers, i.e. instruments are continuously manipulated in order to achieve target welfare-maximizing (or loss-minimizing) values. Mosley (1976) pointed out that in practice policy instruments are periodically manipulated, usually all at once, in response to a crisis. He has proposed a 'satisficing' theory of economic policy, which views the policy-maker as a 'satisficing' agent, i.e. one whose motive is not to achieve the best possible states at all times, but to achieve 'satisfactory' levels of performance. These 'satisfactory' levels are influenced, in the case of macroeconomic objectives, by recently achieved performance and are determined by compromise bargaining between such institutions as the Bank of England, the Treasury and the Cabinet. He suggests that a package of instruments will be used in order to respond to a 'crisis', which might be an unsatisfactory level of performance with respect even to one objective, with the strength of the response depending upon the amount by which the actual value differs from the 'satisfactory' level.

Testing the satisficing approach for the period 1946–71, Mosley found that *any* balance of payments deficit triggered a response – in other words only a zero or positive balance was regarded as 'satisfactory'. However, the unemployment figure considered 'satisfactory' varied over the years, following a rising trend. In 1953 it was below 1.6%, in 1965 below 2.5%, and by 1971 below 3.6%. Should a figure of below 5% be considered 'satisfactory' in the early years of the new millennium?

The fixed and flexible targets approaches to macroeconomic policy predict that policy-makers will seek to find new and effective instruments of policy in order simultaneously to achieve a growing number of economic objectives. If that search is not successful, then compromises between the target values of the objectives will be sought; more pragmatically, the policy-makers will accept quite broad ranges of values for the objectives and will intervene only when one (or more) of the target values becomes 'unsatisfactory'. In this last, 'satisficing', case the economy is 'managed by exception'.

Until the mid-1970s this reflected the interventionist 'Keynesian' approach which prevailed in the UK after the Second World War. Target values and achieved values for the objectives rarely diverged significantly, and it was generally accepted that policy-makers, armed with the predictions of increasingly sophisticated forecasting models of the economy, and using an increasing range of instrumental variables, could and should manage the economy by 'fine-tuning' it on to a desired path. However, as the 1970s progressed, the fine tuning and satisficing approaches to policy making were being replaced by theories which began stressing the inherently stable nature of the economy. These advocated the need to set 'rules' which policy-makers should follow in the medium term, instead of concentrating on short-term interventionism.

Post-war macroeconomic policy in practice

The first period – pre-1974

The major preoccupation as the Second World War ended was to put an end to the high levels of unemployment which had prevailed throughout the inter-war period when unemployment had averaged around 14%, even reaching 22% in 1932. The primacy of this objective was expressed in a famous sentence in the 1944 Government White Paper on Employment Policy: 'The Government accepts as one of their primary aims and responsibilities the maintenance of a high and stable level of employment after the War.' In the 1950s and 1960s unemployment figures of half a million led to reflationary measures, and the figure of 1 million unemployed (about 4% of the workforce) was first reached as late as 1972, when very strong measures were taken to expand demand and raise the employment level. Such expansionary measures usually took the form of fiscal activity (increased government spending and/or lower

taxation), accompanied by relaxed hire-purchase controls and some stimulus to bank lending. This was the 'Keynesian' response to unemployment.

These measures had an effect upon the level of employment but also led to periodic balance of payments crises as the stimulus to aggregate demand raised not only incomes and employment but also imports. The resulting balance of payments crises could only be tackled, given our reluctance to use tariffs, by a deflation of aggregate demand resulting in greater unemployment. This 'stop–go' cycle had adverse effects upon the rate of long-term economic growth, which was a general objective of all post-war governments. The average inflation rate was generally low (4.8% in 1946–50, 4.6% in 1951–55, 2.1% in 1956–60, 3.5% in 1961–65, 4.6% in 1966–70 and 8.5% in 1971–73), and was dealt with partly by adjusting aggregate demand but also by the use of a prices and incomes policy, itself a reflection of the Keynesian view that trade unions and other institutional features of the labour market are major factors in determining inflation.

Up to the early 1970s we can broadly say that macroeconomic policy was based upon 'Keynesian' principles, emphasizing the management of aggregate demand, mainly through fiscal policy, backed up by some form of prices and incomes policy. This kind of interventionist policy has been described as an attempt to 'fine-tune' the economy, adjusting the various policy instruments in order to achieve a set of policy objectives, and reflects the three approaches dealt with above. After 1974 the emphasis began to move away from 'fine-tuning', with its continuous exercise of government 'discretion' in varying instruments to achieve target values, and towards a more ordered path of set 'rules'.

The second period – post-1974

The subsequent period saw dramatic changes. Inflation and unemployment increased appreciably (see Table 24.1 above), and the Keynesian approach was increasingly criticized as a basis for macroeconomic policy-making. New research programmes achieved prominence with their own theoretical bases, leading to new approaches to macroeconomic policy.

Money was increasingly recognized as an important factor, that is to say 'money mattered', and less emphasis was placed on the demand side of the economy and more on supply. Even to those for whom the demand side retained its Keynesian pre-eminence, there was an interest in the influence of net financial assets on consumer expenditure in addition to the influence of income. During the period two 'new' approaches seemed to reflect these trends – that of the CEPG and that of the monetarists. These two 'schools' of economic thought might at first sight seem to have little in common, for they advocated very different policy measures and disagreed about the way the economy worked. What makes them interesting from our point of view is that they agreed that the economy was inherently stable and that the Keynesian fine-tuning interventionist approach was inappropriate. They advocated the use of 'rules' to be followed, a tax rule on the one hand and a money growth rule on the other. Short-run intervention was seen as likely to be at best irrelevant, and at worst counter-productive.

The Cambridge Economic Policy Group

The CEPG differed from traditional Keynesians in seeing fiscal policy as possibly *contributing to* the balance of payments problem rather than correcting it. They identified a strong link between the balance of payments on current account and the size of the public sector surplus/deficit.

In the conventional manner let

I = investment expenditure,
G = government expenditure,
X = exports,
S = savings,
T = taxation receipts,
M = imports.

Then, for equilibrium:

$$I + G + X = S + T + M$$

Rearranging,

$$X - M = S - I + T - G$$

i.e. the surplus on the balance of payments current account is, by definition, equal to the private sector surplus $(S - I)$ plus the public sector surplus $(T - G)$.

The private sector surplus is the sum of household and company *net* savings and this, it is claimed, is so small that it can be ignored. Household saving in the UK is normally balanced by investment in housing (channelled by building society deposits), and company saving is the major source of company investment. That being so, then:

$$S - I \simeq O$$

and

$$X - M \simeq T - G$$

i.e. the balance of payments current account surplus/deficit is approximately equal to the public sector surplus/deficit, and changes in the latter will lead to approximately equal changes in the former. The explanation is that the effect of expansionary fiscal policy will be to raise incomes and imports faster than exports.

The policy implication of the approach typified by the CEPG was that an expansion of domestic demand to alleviate unemployment must be accompanied by the use of import controls. If the expansion is not accompanied by import controls, then the balance of payments will rapidly move into a considerable deficit, with devaluation or depreciation of the exchange rate unable to correct the deficit. The favourable effects for employment of the expansionary fiscal policy will then be dissipated overseas as increased demand in the UK is met by increased purchases of foreign goods rather than domestically produced goods. Their reply to the argument that the imposition of import controls on the part of the UK would be met with retaliation from other countries, is that the aim would not be to *reduce* the level of imports into the UK but to keep the level from rising. If no other country is harmed there will be no need for retaliation! In fact, any rise in UK exports might subsequently create scope for imports to rise.

We have already seen that economists supporting the CEPG analysis believe that 'fine-tuning' the economy by pursuing an interventionist policy is actually counter-productive and destabilizing. They believe that the economy is relatively stable in the medium term and that the most appropriate policy is to apply a 'fiscal rule' within the context of a medium-term strategy. This rule takes the form of a composite tax rate – the par tax rate – set at such a level that desired targets for National Income (employment) and the balance of payments can be achieved in the medium term. This rule should be adhered to, and the par tax rate altered, *only* if the target values are themselves altered, or if there are major disturbances in the world economy, or in the trade-off between the employment and balance of payments objectives.

The monetarists

Monetarists similarly eschew the use of an armoury of policy instruments (instrumental variables) to achieve macroeconomic objectives. The monetarist economists believe that if the money stock is increased, real output is not affected in the long run, though prices are, i.e. control of the money supply is the key to the control of inflation.[7] They accept that in the short run changes in money supply will affect output as well as prices. However, there will be time-lags between the change in money supply and changes in output, making it inadvisable to use the manipulation of aggregate demand as a policy instrument for achieving target levels of output and employment. Output and employment will instead be determined at their 'natural' levels by microeconomic factors affecting aggregate supply. These are more easily influenced by measures designed to improve market efficiency or to increase the supply of factors of production.

Policy-makers are therefore encouraged to follow simple 'rules' which will influence the economy in the long run, and will not generally be subject to changes which might cause instability in the short run. The most obvious rule is to control the rate of monetary expansion, and to effect changes in it relatively gradually in order that disruption is not too great. To the monetarist the target rate for monetary expansion (given flexible exchange rates) becomes the proxy for the target rate of inflation, so that the 'target' is now set in terms of the value of the instrumental variable (money supply) rather than in terms of the objective (inflation). Short-run manipulation of the instrument to achieve the target objective was regarded as neither necessary nor even possible. Instead, the authorities are to control inflation through the long-run rate of monetary expansion. A rule for policy is therefore established.

Medium-term economic strategy

An important turning point in economic policy took place in 1979 with the election of the Conservative

government under the leadership of Margaret Thatcher. The main thrust of macroeconomic policy moved towards the evolution of a non-inflationary economic environment within which a market economy could rapidly flourish. As in many aspects of economics, a major shift in policy-making often originates from a modification of economic thinking. In this case, the theoretical basis for the anti-inflationary policy was the breakdown of the Phillips curve relationship (which seemed to have underpinned Keynesian macroeconomic policy ideas in the 1960s) and the emergence of Friedman's 'expectations augmented' version of the Phillips curve. This latter version of the Phillips relationship combined the Friedmanite inflationary expectations theory with the concept of the 'natural rate of unemployment' (see Chapter 23). As far as policy making is concerned, the intention was to achieve the goal of lower inflation by influencing aggregate demand (through the money supply) and by improving aggregate supply responsiveness, thereby creating a fall in the 'natural rate of unemployment'. The Thatcher government therefore introduced an economic strategy directed towards the medium term, which had two main components.

The first main component was *macroeconomic* in nature and was in line with monetary thinking. It involved a *Medium Term Financial Strategy* (MTFS) whose aim was to use constraints on the money supply (see below) to decrease the growth of money GDP over time, and thereby cut the rate of inflation. This obviously reflected the predominant use of monetary policy as the government's main economic policy instrument and the subordination of fiscal policy. As far as the latter was concerned, the government aimed to decrease the Public Sector Borrowing Requirement (PSBR), mainly by reducing public expenditure, since it felt that there was a close relationship between the size of the PSBR and the money supply. It was also argued that any increase in PSBR, and therefore in government borrowing, would mean that interest rates would have to rise in order to persuade the private sector to hold public debt. These high interest rates would, in turn, lead to a movement of funds from the private to the public sector, i.e. the private sector would be 'crowded out'. Therefore, the government saw the central aim of the MTFS as the control of inflation, which was to be achieved by reducing the growth of money supply and by keeping the PSBR under control.

The second main component of the medium-term economic strategy was *microeconomic* in nature, making use of the so-called *supply-side policies* in order to improve the *output responsiveness* of the economy. In terms of the economic analysis used above, these supply-side policies sought to improve the workings of markets in order to decrease the 'natural rate of unemployment'.

In the next section we will first follow the course of the MTFS before looking in more detail at the government's supply-side policies.

MTFS 1979–87: monetary targeting

The MTFS was first published in March 1980. There have been annual policy statements since 1980 which set out *targets* for monetary growth and for the PSBR over a medium-term time horizon. As noted above, the prime aim of the MTFS was to eradicate inflation, in the belief that inflation actually caused unemployment by creating inflationary wage and price expectations. Creating a stable, non-inflationary framework was therefore seen as essential, and this became the cornerstone of policy.

In the early period, $£M_3$ was chosen by the government as the most reliable indicator of spending, and targets for the growth of $£M_3$ were set in each annual MTFS statement. Unfortunately, in order to control $£M_3$, interest rates had to be raised to record levels of 17% in 1979; even then this did not seem to bring $£M_3$ within the desired bands. Interest rates remained high throughout 1980 and this pushed up the exchange rate, making UK exports uncompetitive in international markets. The continued attempts to get $£M_3$ and the PSBR under control led the government to tighten its fiscal policy in 1981 and, although interest rates fell during the early part of the year, they were back to 16% by later that year. The early monetarist experiment, plus the world recession, led to a fall in manufacturing output by 19.6% between June 1979 and June 1981 and a loss of 23% of manufacturing employment (see also Chapter 1).

Two interesting developments grew out of this early monetarist experiment. First, a difficulty arose in finding a valid measure of money which faithfully reflected movements in UK spending. Unfortunately, $£M_3$ was becoming unreliable as a measure of UK spending. For example, as the interest rate rose, depositors were induced to shift from non-interest to interest bearing accounts. Such a shift would not change the total money supply $£M_3$, but merely redistribute it from accounts where it was more likely to be spent (non-interest bearing) to accounts where it was less likely to be spent (interest bearing). As a result, although figures for $£M_3$ were not recorded as having fallen much in this period, the *actual spending* of the population decreased more significantly. Second, it was becoming clear that economic policy, whether short- or medium-term in aim, was still unable to reconcile conflicting objectives. For example, controlling money supply and the PSBR involved a policy of high interest rates; but these decreased industrial investment and also led to a fall in UK exports (as the exchange rate rose with interest rates). The early monetarist experiment was not immune to the traditional problems involved when trying to balance policy targets with policy instruments.

1982–85

In 1982 the government overhauled the MTFS and began to abandon the policy of targeting a single monetary variable, i.e. $£M_3$. For example, it had became clear as early as 1981 that *narrower* definitions of money such as M_0 and M_1 were growing much more slowly than $£M_3$ and were reflecting more accurately what was happening to the real economy. As a result, other measures of money such as M_0, M_1 and PSL_2 began to be included as target aggregates, and $£M_3$ targets were adjusted to take into consideration some of the problems noted above. The doubling of unemployment between 1979 and 1982 also weakened the government's will to continue with its severe anti-inflationary policy. By autumn 1982 interest rates had fallen to around 9% and remained reasonably steady until the middle of 1984, while at the same time the Lawson tax-cutting budgets from 1983 onwards provided some stimulus to aggregate demand. Much of the recovery of the 1982–85 period was due to a rise in consumer expenditure as earnings rose faster than inflation. This was further fuelled by a credit boom, brought about by easier access to credit and a fall in the savings ratio.

During this period the targets for the PSBR were gently eased, as money supply targets other than $£M_3$ were tried, with varying degrees of success. The government became more aware of the problems involved in using only monetary targets as the cornerstone of policy. Indeed 'squeezing' inflation out of the system by this method would not only be difficult, but might even be impossible. In a pragmatic sense, it seemed that by late 1984, both the government and the Bank of England had accepted that a 5% inflation rate might be a more realistic objective in the future. As money supply targets became less reliable, monetary policy began to shift towards targeting the exchange rate. This was to continue into the next period.

1985–87

The government's MTFS took another turn at the beginning of 1985 when economic circumstances created an exchange rate crisis. The government had shown increasing unease at the apparent rise in the underlying trend of UK inflation in 1984, together with the continued problem of unemployment. At the same time the dollar was at its peak. The ensuing loss of confidence in the UK led to a fall in the value of the pound to $1.04; this caused the UK to experience inflationary pressure as the low exchange rate increased import costs. As a result of this volatility in the exchange rate, a more 'active' policy was adopted in order to stabilize the exchange rate at a 'desirable' level which would not increase inflation. It was felt that sterling would best be pegged to a stable currency such as the Deutsche Mark, and for a while the unofficial government target for sterling was set at around DM3.0 to DM3.2 to the pound. It should be understood that the move towards stable and targeted exchange rates was not only a UK phenomenon. The major trading nations had agreed in the 'Plaza Accord' of October 1985 and in the 'Louvre Accord' of February 1987 to move towards coordinating their economic policies and to peg their currencies within agreed target zones.

What had clearly happened in 1985 was a shift in the role of monetary policy; instead of using the interest rate mechanism to control the *money supply*, it was now used to control the *exchange rate*. Inflation was now seen as being transmitted to the UK economy mainly through the exchange rate route. By November 1985, £M$_3$ was downgraded from a 'target variable' to one which was now only to be 'monitored'; and, after 1987, M$_0$ was the only targeted monetary variable in government use during the period. The 1985–87 period saw a gradual fall in interest rates and a more

relaxed approach to monetary policy in general, the interest rate weapon being used increasingly to achieve the desired exchange rate rather than any specific money supply targets. At the same time the UK experienced boom conditions, stimulated by easier credit conditions and higher post-tax incomes. Consumer expenditure on both durable and non-durable goods (such as housing) led the growth of aggregate demand. The unemployment rate fell, but many saw the rise in inflation by the end of 1987 as the inevitable 'cost' of such a policy.

This period shows that following simple monetary *rules* cannot always bring simple solutions to the economy. It also shows the conflicting nature of targets and instruments. Some members of the government (including the Prime Minister) believed that interest rates should have been higher during this period, in order to control the money supply and therefore aggregate spending and inflation. Others, such as the Chancellor, Nigel Lawson, felt that the best course was to keep interest rates rather lower in order to prevent the sterling exchange rate rising above a certain target level against currencies such as the Deutsche Mark and dollar. In this way we could still control inflation, but without squeezing the domestic money supply and credit too much.

MTFS 1987–92: exchange rate targeting

The period following the rapid expansion of the 1985–87 boom years was to prove 'costly'. As noted previously, consumer expenditure grew rapidly during these boom years as a result of lower interest rates, financial liberalization measures, and a growth of the mortgage 'leak' (i.e. the financing of spending by remortgaging and using the cash to purchase goods). The boom came to an abrupt end around the middle of 1988, with interest rates rising sharply, curbing both consumer expenditure and house prices. The UK then entered the ERM in October 1990, tying the exchange rate to European currencies within a 'band' which gave some limited room for manoeuvre. It was hoped that maintaining sterling within a relatively high exchange rate band would help keep import costs low, thus easing inflationary pressures. The tightening of monetary policy after 1988 was also complemented by a tightening of the fiscal stance, resulting in a PSBR of −£0.5bn in 1990/91. However, the rise in unemployment due to the recession was soon to result in increased government expenditure, so that the PSBR of −£0.5bn in 1990/91 soon became a deficit of £16bn by 1991/92.

The Financial Statement and the Budget Report (the 'red book') for 1992/93 reaffirmed the government's commitment to bringing inflation down to a sustainable level. However, it had very little to say about monetary policy except that it was 'primarily directed at maintaining sterling's parity in the ERM', a clear sign that the government had effectively abandoned monetary policy as an independent policy instrument for influencing domestic conditions. As far as fiscal policy was concerned, its role was to 'balance the budget over a medium term'. By 1992 it was impossible to discern any policy guidelines as being clearly derived from the monetary side of the MTFS macroeconomic 'model', while fiscal policy continued to be seen as a passive instrument. These changes left the government with one main external target, namely keeping the exchange rate within the prescribed 'band' of the ERM, and one main instrument, the interest rate. However, events in late 1992 brought fiscal policy, at least as regards public expenditure, into greater prominence. This new focus followed sterling being forced out of the ERM in September 1992. By late 1992, sterling had fallen by over 14% against the Deutsche Mark and over 20% against the dollar. Fears of renewed inflationary tendencies, via higher import prices, and alarm at a rapidly expanding PSBR, forced the government into a sharp adjustment on the public expenditure side of fiscal policy.

MTFS 1992–97: inflation targeting

After the events of late 1992, it was unlikely that even a reconstituted ERM would provide the framework for macroeconomic policy as it had done in previous years. As a result it was essential that the UK's macroeconomic policy should be based on a sustainable *domestic* strategy.

By 1993 the scene was set for a reassessment of strategy. On the fiscal side, the minimal requirement of a sound policy was seen to be 'debt sustainability'. In other words the growth in the ratio of public debt to GDP should not accelerate too rapidly. The increase in this ratio from 0% to 7.0% between 1990/91 and 1993/94 involved major problems. For example, a

high level of government borrowing left a heavy burden of debt to be financed in the future. This, in turn, led to instability in the financial markets as uncertainties about the future translated themselves into volatile interest rates. Further, a 'loose' fiscal policy placed more reliance on a 'tight' monetary policy to restrain inflation, again risking higher interest rates. The Budget Statements of 1994/95 included a programme to broaden the tax base together with measures to restrain public spending on defence, housing, social security and civil service running costs. The November 1995 and 1996 Budgets remained somewhat restrictive in nature, with the long-term aim of fiscal balance by the turn of the century.

Therefore one important medium-term objective of the goverment in the late 1990s was to achieve stable public finances, using fiscal policy as the main instrument for reducing the PSBR in the medium term. The problem about making medium-term macroeconomic forecasts for the PSBR is that they have to be based on certain assumptions about the future behaviour of indices such as economic growth and various tax elasticities. If, for example, the economic growth forecasted four years ahead actually turns out to be lower than predicted, then *actual* tax receipts will fall faster than predicted, resulting in a higher PSBR than anticipated at the begining of the four-year period.

On the monetary side, the suspension of sterling from the ERM meant that a new strategy was needed for monetary policy (Hudson and Fisher 1994). In 1993, the government introduced for the first time an explicit target for the main objective of monetary policy, namely the inflation rate. The target was to keep inflation (i.e. the retail price index excluding mortgage interest payments) within a range of 1–4% over the year. By 1995/96 the target for inflation was down to the lower end of the range, at around 2.5%. To do this, the Chancellor decided to *monitor* the variables which reflect the movement of inflation, i.e. the monetary variables M_0 and M_4. In previous years, M_0 had been assigned a *specific target*, but in 1993 this was changed to a *monitored range* of between 0% and 4% for M_0 and 3–9% for M_4. If the monetary variables moved outside these limits, there would then be some cause for concern. In addition to the monetary aggregates, indicators such as the exchange rate, asset prices and house prices were given more weight in judging the outlook for inflation.

Macroeconomic management during this period reflected two interesting aspects of the UK's fight against inflation. First, there was now a clear shift away from the 1987 to 1992 period, when the government seemed to have only one main objective to be targeted (the exchange rate) and one main instrument (the interest rate). Such a narrow focus for policy became increasingly inappropriate when an exchange rate policy designed to help the UK 'converge' with other European economies could be seen to be imposing major costs in terms of reducing both domestic output and employment. The Chancellor now began to consider a *wider range* of intermediate objectives and instruments, rather than concentrate on a narrow set of variables which had to be met precisely. In other words, a more flexible Theil-type approach was now envisaged. Although a more flexible approach was adopted towards monetary policy, we should remember that the short-term interest rate still remained the main instrument for controlling inflation. Second, a greater weight was now given to economic models in policy making. Models of the economy such as those produced by the Treasury, the National Institute of Economic and Social Research (NIESR) and the London Business School (LBS) regained their former importance as policy-makers once again looked for the optimum relationship between various objectives and instruments (Bray *et al.* 1993).

MTFS since 1997: inflation targeting and the MPC framework

Macroeconomic management took a new direction with the return of the Labour government in 1997, and in order to understand the nature of the change it might be useful to place the post-1997 policy period into its historical perspective. During the twentieth century, the macroeconomic performance of the UK economy appears to have been particularly poor during periods of transition or uncertainty, irrespective of which political party or economic ideology or regime was in vogue. This was amply illustrated by the inter-war years and by the post-1970s policy periods discussed in previous sections. In contrast, macroeconomic policy tended to work best during periods when the dominant regime was well established and was expected to continue (Britton 2002). Such periods encouraged confidence and trust which,

in turn, led to relatively stable expectations, as was arguably the case before WWI and also during the so-called 'golden age' after WWII from 1945 to the early 1970s. In other words, in macroeconomic policy-making 'nothing succeeds like success'.

In the context of the above analysis, the post-1997 Labour government's macroeconomic policy-making was geared to the establishment of stable expectations. Such policies can be viewed from a number of perspectives. First, from an *objectives* point of view, the key explicit target for monetary policy from 1997 onwards was to be the control of inflation. Although intermediate targets, such as the growth of money supply, were monitored, there were no attempts to set targets for M_0 and M_4. The erratic behaviour of the velocity of circulation of money had meant that using money supply variables for policy-making had become complicated and ineffective. Second, from an *instruments* point of view, the main monetary weapon to control inflation was to be the interest rate.

To achieve greater stability for policy-making, the Labour government made important *institutional* changes. In May 1997, the Bank of England was given operational independence to set interest rates in order to meet the government's inflation objective. The inflation target of 2.5% was to be policed by an independent Monetary Policy Committee (MPC) of the Bank of England using one main instrument – the interest rate – as its main policy weapon.[8] The MPC's work was made more transparent (minutes of its meetings published within six weeks) and accountable (MPC to report to the government and 'explain' any substantial deviations of inflation outcome from target). Because o the Bank's new independent role in policy-making, its role as supervisor of the banking sector was placed in the hands of the Financial Services Authority (FSA). The aim was to improve the quality of financial sector supervision and to protect consumer interests in an increasingly complicated financial marketplace. Finally, the Bank's responsibility for debt management was transferred to the Treasury.

In addition to the above changes, a new *fiscal policy* framework was developed under a 'Code for Fiscal Stability' approved in 1998. The code was designed to introduce more modern fiscal accounting methods, to make the reporting of fiscal matters more transparent and to ensure that the government stated its fiscal objectives explicitly (HM Treasury 2002). For example, fiscal stability was to be observed through two 'rules'. The first was the 'golden rule', whereby over the economic cycle the government would borrow only to invest and not to fund current expenditure. In other words, the government would run a current budget surplus (current receipts greater than current expenditure) over the cycle (see Table 19.2). Second, the 'public debt' or 'sustainable investment' rule was introduced, whereby net public sector debt as a proportion of GDP would be held at a stable and prudent level over the cycle (defined by the Chancellor as 40% of GDP).

The natural question to ask at this stage is whether the new arrangements, designed to introduce stability and transparency, have been successful. The record on inflation during periods covered by various monetary regimes can be seen in Figs 24.3 and 24.4. From Fig. 24.3 it can be seen that inflation continued to fall significantly in the period after inflation targeting was adopted in 1992, with a further gentle fall after 1997. Interestingly, this data suggests that it may have been the targeting of inflation after 1992, rather than the new MPC arrangements introduced in 1997, that was the key to a low inflationary environment (Allsopp 2002). However, arguably a more relevant indicator of the success of the post-1997 reforms has been the UK's ability to lower *inflationary expectations*, as seen in Fig. 24.4,

which may be the real key to controlling inflationary trends.

From a fiscal perspective, the UK's budgetary position did improve between 1996/97 and 2001/02 as can be seen in Chapter 19, Table 19.2, but forecasting future trends in current budgets and the public sector debt ratio still remains a problem despite attempts by the government to improve forecasting techniques. For example, if government expenditure turns out to be only 1% higher than forecast, and the government revenue just 1% lower, an expected current budget surplus could fall from £15bn to only £7bn (Griffiths 2001).

The independence of the Bank of England appears to have eased some of the political constraints on policy-making. However, it is the Chancellor who continues to appoint the members of the MPC, so that the political process is still not totally divorced from the management of the economy.

Supply-side strategy

As was explained previously, the Conservative government's medium-term economic strategy also revolved around improving the *output responsiveness*

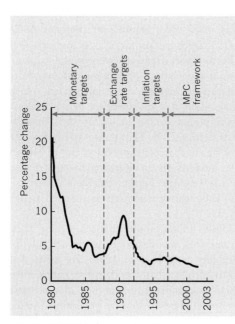

Fig. 24.3 UK inflation and policy regimes.
Sources: ONS (various); HM Treasury (2002).

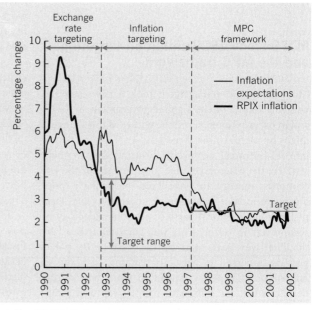

Fig. 24.4 Inflation performance and expectations.
Source: Modified from Allsopp (2002).

of the economy. Monetarists and 'New Classical' economists generally have sympathy with the view that output and employment are supply-determined, rather than with the Keynesian view that they are demand-determined.

Figure 24.5(a) represents the familiar Keynesian view, with prices and output (real national income) being determined largely by changes in aggregate demand. Our main interest here is to contrast this familiar diagram with Fig. 24.5(b), which uses the same axes to reflect the monetarist or supply-side view of economics.

In the Keynesian case, an increase in real output from Y_1 to Y_2 is most readily achieved by an increase in aggregate demand from AD_1 to AD_2. However, the supply-side view is that an increase in real output from Y_1 to Y_2 is more effectively achieved by a downward (rightward) shift of the aggregate supply curve from $SRAS_1$ to $SRAS_2$. In the former case the average price level is likely to rise as real output rises, while the supply-side approach predicts a fall in the average price level alongside a rise in real output.

In favouring the supply-side approach, Conservative governments of the 1980s argued that there were certain features of the UK economy which tended to *prevent* the supply curve shifting downwards from $SRAS_1$ to $SRAS_2$. They felt that the main task of the government was to achieve such a downward shift in SRAS through 'supply-side' policies aimed at increasing productive efficiency in the economy. However, before we look at the various policies advocated since the early 1980s in support of this approach, it is useful to consider the factors which allegedly prevent the SRAS curve from shifting downwards.

First, there is the suggestion that unemployment and social security benefits encourage people to spend more time searching for the type of employment they consider appropriate. As a result they remain on the unemployment register longer, the unemployment figures are swollen, and aggregate output is restricted from the supply side. An ancillary argument is that the difference between some low-paid jobs and the rate of unemployment benefit is so marginal that such jobs are not taken up. This problem is aggravated by the UK tax system, which may result in some workers, previously unemployed, paying marginal tax rates in excess of 100% when moving into low-paid jobs – the 'unemployment trap' (see Chapter 19). Unemployment and social security benefits may in these ways cause the short-run aggregate supply curve to remain at $SRAS_1$ in Fig. 24.5(b), thereby preventing output from rising to Y_2 and keeping the price level higher than it would otherwise be.

The second suggestion is that, quite apart from the 'unemployment trap', high taxation can affect the supply of labour (and so the level of output) through its disincentive effects. The reverse side of this is that a cut in taxes might so stimulate work effort that real output (and even total tax revenue) rises. In terms of Fig. 24.5(b) tax cuts would shift the supply curve to the right, i.e. from $SRAS_1$ to $SRAS_2$, so that output and employment would rise, and prices fall.

The third suggestion is that labour has priced itself out of the market, thereby reducing employment and

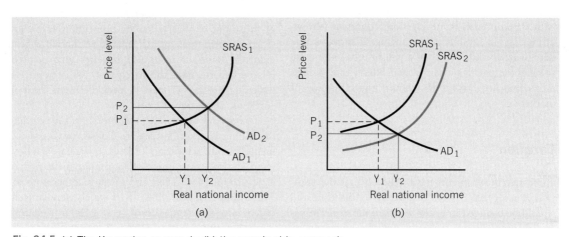

Fig. 24.5 (a) The Keynesian approach; (b) the supply-side approach.

output, because the trade unions have forced up the real wages of their members. It was estimated by Minford and Peel (1981) that unions had 'marked up' members' wages by between 12% and 25%, so raising permanent unemployment figures by between 400,000 and 800,000, although more recent research has put the average mark-up at 10% or less. Another important study (Layard and Nickell 1985) showed that the unemployment rate in the UK had risen by 11.83 percentage points between 1956 and 1983 and that union 'push' on wages accounted for 2.27 of those percentage points. The policy implication is that trade union bargaining power should be curbed. In terms of *labour market* analysis the market wage is kept above the equilibrium wage so that unemployment is higher than market conditions warrant. In terms of the *goods market* in Fig. 24.5(b), the relatively high labour costs tend to keep the aggregate supply curve artificially high at $SRAS_1$. Output and employment are lower and prices are higher than they would otherwise be.

Finally, there is the suggestion that the very high unemployment and low output figures prevailing in the UK exaggerate the true situation because there is a considerable 'hidden' or 'black' economy, encouraged by a desire to evade taxation. Some of the 'black' economy would be conducted in monetary terms (e.g. payment in cash to a local handyman), some in non-monetary terms by means of barter. The 'black' economy has always been with us, and estimates as to its size vary from 2.5% of GDP (the gap between expenditure and declared income) to 7.5% (Inland Revenue estimates of tax evasion) and even to 15%.

As explained above, successive governments have implemented a wide range of measures consistent with the approach of supply-side economics (shown in Fig. 24.5 as a shift in the aggregate supply curve downwards to the right). We will briefly summarize some of the practical changes which have to be implemented in an attempt to increase the efficiency of markets.

Taxation

Successive governments have believed that the taxation structure has become distorted over the years and should be changed in order to create more incentives and to induce more output (supply) responsiveness. For example, the decrease in tax allowances on mort-

gages in the late 1980s from £30,000 per *person* to £30,000 per *dwelling* was partly designed to curb the amount of investment in housing and to stimulate investment in company shares, i.e. to channel investment into more productive forms which would help stimulate output. Similarly, tax relief on life insurance premiums had been abolished in 1984, in an attempt to encourage people to invest in company equities. Again the rate of Capital Gains Tax had long been *less than* the basic rate of income tax, giving, for example, a better return to a person who bought and sold oil paintings than to a person buying company shares. In 1988 the CGT and the basic rate of income tax were equalized to prevent this bias. As well as bringing down personal taxation in order to stimulate incentives, successive governments have also decreased the standard rate of Corporation Tax for large companies, from 52% in 1983/84 to 30% by 2003; for small firms the rate was reduced from 35% to 19% in the same period. Those cuts in Corporation Tax were an attempt to stimulate reinvestment in capital stock.

Labour supply, efficiency and training

Successive governments have also believed in the need to improve the workings of the UK labour market, in order to make it more 'efficient' (i.e. labour should be mobile, well trained and free from institutional – e.g. union – bias). As far as *mobility* is concerned, the government felt that the UK labour market needed to be 'flexible', with workers induced to take up jobs rapidly. It was thought that this process was being inhibited by narrow differentials between the income of those out of work, thereby preventing active job search. Continuous adjustments have therefore been made in national insurance benefits and income-related benefits over the past years, with the aim of widening the gap in income levels between those in work and those out of work.

To improve the *institutional problems* surrounding the labour market, successive Conservative governments introduced a series of laws to regulate employment and the trade unions. The Employment Acts of 1980, 1982, 1988, 1989 and 1990, together with the Trade Union Act of 1984, all of which were consolidated into the Trade Union and Labour Relations (Consolidation) Act of 1992, have weakened the control of unions (see Chapter 15).

In the area of training, one of the greatest problems for the UK has been the dearth of vocational skills at the intermediate level. In 1994, for example, 64% of the UK workforce had no vocational qualifications as compared to 53% in France and 26% in Germany. At the intermediate level, only 18% of the UK workforce had intermediate craft-type qualifications as compared to 33% in France and 56% in Germany (Trade and Industry Committee 1994). A more recent report by the UK Cabinet Office pointed to the continued existence of such problems for the UK, especially in post-21 training and work skills development, as can be seen in Table 24.2. The levels of training and skill development in Fig. 24.2 are based on the International Standard Classification of Education (ISCED) and range from first and higher degree level work (Levels 5–7) to those who have passed 'A' levels, GNVQ3, NVQ3 and Trade Apprenticeships (Level 3), down to those whose maximum qualification is one GCSE (Levels 0–2).

Table 24.2 compares qualifications attained at Levels 2 and above and Levels 3 and above for certain relevant age groups in the UK, France and Germany. It shows that, in contrast to the UK, workers in France and Germany undertake significant study/training after the age of 21 in order to achieve Level 2 and above and Level 3 and above qualifications. UK statistics (for both 'all qualifications' and 'vocational qualifications') tend to show that if UK workers do *not* achieve these qualification levels by the age of 21, there is little chance of them making up the deficit in

later life. The whole problem of the UK's relative lack of intermediate-level qualifications has already been summarized in Table 1.12 of Chapter 1 where the UK's relative skills gap was discussed. The importance of raising the level of education and training is vital for the economy. Surveys have shown that raising the proportion of workers trained in an industry by 5%, say from 10% to 15%, is associated with a 4% increase in value-added per worker, and 1.6% in wages (Cabinet Office 2001).

As a result of these deficiencies, the UK government introduced a number of initiatives in the early 1990s. For example, by 1991 some 104 Training and Enterprise Councils (TECs) were in operation in Britain. These are independent business-led companies, funded by government, and charged with meeting the training, enterprise and vocational education requirements of local communities and employers. Similarly, the Technical and Vocational Educational Initiative (TVEI) was introduced in the early 1990s to influence the whole curriculum of schools and colleges to prepare pupils of 14–18 for the demands of working life. This process continued under the post-1997 Labour government. A new revised National Curriculum was introduced in September 2000 designed to make more explicit the links between education, employment and enterprise. Meanwhile, in the first few years of the new millennium, various strategies have been introduced to provide a better quality of work experience for pupils

Table 24.2 Qualification comparisons: UK, France and Germany (% of relevant age group).

	Level 2 and above			Level 3 and above		
	UK	France	Germany	UK	France	Germany
All qualifications						
19–21	70	81	65	43	43	48
25–28	61	83	85	41	54	78
Vocational qualifications						
19–21	26	25	28	14	5	26
25–28	28	43	52	17	18	48

Note:
Levels are based on International Standard Classification of Education (ISCED):
'2 and above' = e.g. achieved minimum of GCSE level pass and above;
'3 and above' = e.g. achieved minimum of 'A' Level/GNVQ3/NVQ3 and above.
Source: Modified from Cabinet Office (2001).

(Education–Business links), to encourage more entrepreneurial attitudes (National Enterprise Campaign), to improve management expertise (Council for Excellence in Management and Leadership), and to increase training initiatives (New Deal). All these policies were designed to focus on increasing the UK's stock of 'human capital'.

These types of initiatives continued with the creation of the Learning and Skills Council (LSC) in April 2001. The Council was designed to raise participation in education and training and to enhance what came to be called Work Force Development (WFD), i.e. a desire to increase the capacity of individuals in the workplace. The involvement of government departments, Regional Development Agencies and the private sector was seen as critical if the UK was to lift itself from its 'low skills equilibrium' situation.

Industrial policies

Over time, various industrial policies have played a part in improving the supply side of the economy. The process reflects government's thinking that companies in the private sector make better use of resources than those in government hands. The new Competition Act of 1998 provided enhanced powers to the office of Fair Trading to tackle anti-competitive practices and abuses of a dominant position, in an attempt to raise both productive and allocative efficiency. Urban regeneration policies such as the New Deal for Communities and the Regeneration expenditures (Chapter 11) have helped foster industrial enterprise in deprived areas. The Cruickshank report on banking, published in 2000, noted that greater efforts were needed to improve access to risk capital and to eliminate barriers to entry and anti-competitive practices in the provision of money transmission services. It concluded that the banking sector needed to be more efficient in order to increase the supply of funds for industry and improve the UK's overall supply-side competitiveness.

Many of these policies were developed further or else modified during 2000–04 as the Labour government concentrated on three main policy themes: first, to provide the UK with a properly funded science and engineering base; second, to develop an appropriately skilled workforce; and third, to encourage an enterprise culture. Although these themes have been a central concern of policy-makers from the 1960s

onwards, the government has become increasingly committed to publishing evidence of its progress. For example, *UK Competitiveness Indicators*, a regular report on UK competitiveness, provides a way of tracing the performance of its industrial policies over time (Beath 2002).

Arguably all these policies are designed to improve efficiency and help shift the supply curve downwards from S_1 to S_2 as in Fig. 24.5(b).

Policy effectiveness

As has already been noted, sound economic management from both the macroeconomic and microeconomic viewpoints is difficult to achieve at the best of times, depending as it does on so many variables which are often hard to predict. The UK has been regarded by many commentators as having had some success in changing the microeconomic environment through supply-side policies, thereby increasing the flexibility of the labour market. However, praise for UK macroeconomic policy has not been so forthcoming (Oulton 1995). Oulton compared the UK's cyclical performance with that of a number of other main industrial countries since 1970 and found that boom periods were shorter and recessions longer in the UK than in the other industrial countries. Further, countries such as the UK which have spent longer periods in recession have also experienced lower average growth rates. The point here is that more effective macroeconomic policy in the UK could provide a more balanced cyclical growth path, thereby reducing the duration of those otherwise long recessions which so damage confidence and reduce investment. This explains the Labour government's stress in its post-2000 budgets on a macroeconomic framework which sets clear long-term policy objectives using predictable and well-understood rules for monetary and fiscal policies.

Economic policy in an international context

While there has been a natural tendency in this chapter to concentrate on the macroeconomic environment of the UK, it would be instructive to place UK experience into an *international* context. Following the failure to control inflation in the late 1960s and 1970s, most industrial countries conducted macroeconomic policies in the 1980s which were designed to reduced inflation to low levels in order to achieve sustained economic growth. During the 1990s these countries often had to face the same problems resulting from the post-1988 slowdown in the world economy, namely government deficits increasing rapidly in all major countries (see Table 24.3).

It was therefore difficult for these countries to use an active Keynesian-type *fiscal policy* to help their recoveries because this would add further to budget deficits. As a result they concentrated on the longer-term aim of *fiscal consolidation*, i.e. in decreasing the burden of government deficits. The reasons for the worldwide growth of fiscal deficits apparent in Table 24.3 (at least until the mid-1990s) can be traced to five main factors.

■ First, some argue that there has been a growth across the major industrialized countries of more generous and widely available public pensions, social security benefits and other government transfers.

■ Second, higher rates of unemployment have led to increased payments of unemployment benefit while, at the same time, government tax revenues have fallen because unemployed workers have not been earning income.

■ Third, the overall productivity slowdown experienced by the major industrialized countries since the early 1970s has meant that the tax base of the government has become smaller than expected while at the same time governments have failed to adjust their spending patterns to the new reality.

■ Fourth, higher real rates of interest have added to the budget deficits.

■ Finally, greater exchange rate flexibility since 1973 together with more open capital markets have allowed governments to borrow more easily on an international basis, thereby allowing them to run up excessive deficits.

Persistent budgetary problems create serious difficulties. For example, the mounting government debts over the last 20 years have led to an increase in global real interest rates as various governments have competed for international savings to cover their deficits (Heibling and Wescott 1995). In turn, high real interest rates have led to lower global investment rates, and thus lower rates of economic growth. Large debt burdens have further meant that fiscal policy could not be used as an active policy instrument – thus overburdening the role of monetary policy. Large deficits have also influenced exchange rates, arguably contributing to a number of exchange rate misalignments.

Another likely contributor to future fiscal debt is the progressive ageing of the population. This will place increasing stress on government pensions and health budgets. The percentage of the population aged 65 and over to total population in the major industrialized countries is set to rise from 35% to 50% between 1995 and 2030. This 'invisible' (*future*)

Table 24.3 Industrial countries: general government fiscal balances including social insurance (% of GDP).

	1981–91	1994	1997	2001	2003*
Major industrial countries	−2.9	−4.3	−2.1	−1.4	−2.8
United States	−2.8	−3.8	−1.3	−0.2	−2.8
Japan	−0.4	−2.8	−3.7	−7.1	−6.1
Germany	−2.1	−2.4	−2.7	−2.8	−2.2
France	−2.2	−5.5	−3.0	−1.4	−2.1
Italy	−11.1	−9.3	−2.7	−2.2	−1.5
United Kingdom	−1.9	−6.8	−1.6	0.2	−1.1
Canada	−4.2	−6.7	0.2	1.8	1.2

* Forecast
Source: Adapted from IMF (2002) *World Economic Outlook*, 2 September, and previous issues.

debt burden is also making countries take their existing budget deficits more seriously and to aim for fiscal consolidation in the short to medium term. Studies of countries which have introduced fiscal consolidation plans, i.e. have tried to decrease public debt as a proportion of GDP, have found that the countries which have been most successful placed more emphasis on cutting spending rather than increasing taxes (IMF 1996).

As far as *monetary policy* is concerned, most industrialized economies have managed to keep their inflation rates at relatively low levels as compared with the past. In the 1980s most central banks sought to rely on the control of monetary aggregates as a means of curbing spending and inflation. However, it soon became obvious that the relationship between the various money aggregates, nominal income and interest rates was becoming increasingly imprecise. As a result, a growing number of economies moved away from targets for specific monetary aggregates during the 1990s and began focusing more directly on inflation. Although all of the major industrial countries pursued price stability as an objective of monetary policy, only a few central banks had statutory obligations to achieve price stability.

Indeed the main policy lesson of the past 25 years has been that the costs of allowing inflation to rise may be very high, with deep recessions often the only effective means of subduing inflationary pressures. This suggests that there is an *asymmetric* relationship between inflation and economic activity, i.e. excess demand has a much stronger effect in raising inflation than excess supply has in reducing inflation. This means that it is important to check inflation *before* inflationary pressures build up. This is the reason why so many countries have adopted formal targets for inflation.

However, the operation of a common macroeconomic policy within a *bloc* of different nations such as the euro area can create a different type of asymmetry problem. For example the European Central Bank (ECB) focuses on inflation trends in the euro area as a whole and often fails to take into consideration the inflationary pressures in the smaller countries of the euro area. This is because those countries have a smaller weight in the overall harmonized index of consumer prices which acts as the policy trigger, so that the overall monetary policy to control inflation might be too loose for these smaller EU countries.

As far as the *supply side* is concerned, the labour markets of most industrialized economies have experienced major changes over the last 10 years. Unemployment has risen almost universally and countries have experimented with various methods for increasing labour flexibility. First, *wage flexibility* has been encouraged by linking pay to productivity and by simplifying complicated wage structures. Second, *functional flexibility* (reorganizing methods of production to suit changing technical demands) has encouraged the growth of multi-skilling, reductions in job demarcation and more employee involvement. Finally, *numerical flexibility* has grown, i.e. the ability to adjust work levels or hours in line with changes in demand. This has involved the growth of self-employment and the greater use of part-timers and sub-contracting. To enable such labour market changes to occur with the least trauma, it has been essential for countries to introduce training schemes and more vocationally orientated courses.

The international movement towards the liberalization of industry through privatization (described in Chapter 8) was designed to introduce an efficient 'free market' discipline to previously government-owned industries. However, merely to shift more industry to the private sector may not, by itself, be a sufficient condition for a nation's economic success. This is because corporate strategy-making at the level of the firm merely reflects the ambitions of those who run the major corporations and these ambitions may not always coincide with the needs of the nation as a whole. It may be that the supply-side policies of shifting more control to the private sector should be coupled with a more positive role for government.

Conclusion

We have seen how Keynesian interventionism placed a premium on finding a variety of policy instruments to achieve a number of target objectives. Until the 1970s the Keynes/Tinbergen/Theil approach was the theoretical basis for short-term macroeconomic policy. However, evidence began to accumulate that this activity could be counter-productive, even destabilizing. The search for alternative approaches was also encouraged by the oil crisis of 1974 which destroyed old-established trade-offs and relationships between objectives. In addition, the oil-price increases deflated the non-oil-producing economies of the West and stimulated inflation. 'Stagflation' and later 'slumpflation' became new problems which the traditional 'fine-tuning', interventionist theories could not easily handle. Emphasis switched to medium- and long-term strategies which now prevail over short-term fine-tuning. In the 1980s the setting of medium-term 'rules' for the conduct of policy became central to the ideas of groups of economists as diverse as the CEPG and the monetarists. However, attempts during the 1980s to adhere to various forms of the Medium Term Financial Strategy (MTFS) failed to provide a solution to the UK's macroeconomic problems. By the early 1990s, the control of inflation remained the main long-run objective of government policy. To achieve this objective, keeping the exchange rate within its prescribed ERM 'band' became the main 'target', and using interest rate policy became the main 'instrument' of policy.

With the enforced departure of the UK from the ERM in September 1992, both the exchange rate and interest rates fell sharply. The government re-focused policy on economic growth as an objective, alongside the control of inflation. To achieve these objectives it would seek a tight fiscal policy as its key instrument, at least on the public expenditure side. The incoming Labour government in 1997 retained a tight fiscal stance, while placing still greater emphasis on achieving an inflation target of 2.5% per annum. To this end it created an independent Bank of England which, through its Monetary Policy Committee, was empowered to use its interest rate weapon to meet the inflation target laid down by government. At the same time, fiscal 'rules' were introduced to achieve fiscal balance over the economic cycle whilst providing a framework for an eventual decline in the public debt/GDP ratio. Other targets and instruments appear less clear. For example, the exchange was left to find its own level with the interest rate being used primarily as an instrument for controlling inflation rather than influencing exchange rates.

Much attention has been given in recent times to the supply side of the economy, i.e. to the efficient operation of a market economy in which the state plays a more limited economic role. Nevertheless, as noted elsewhere in this book (e.g. Chapters 5–8), examples of 'market failure' still abound, and ironically more government intervention may be needed to remedy information defects and strategic alliances within the UK economy. Managing an economy is a difficult task both nationally and internationally, and governments and their economic advisors will continue to grapple with the best ways of matching economic objects with policy instruments for some time to come.

Key points

- Macroeconomic policy seeks to achieve various *target* values as regards objectives such as employment, prices, economic growth and the balance of payments.

- To achieve such 'target values', governments use various *policy instruments*, such as fiscal and monetary policy, prices and incomes policy, exchange rate policy and import controls.

- Governments often find that there are complex linkages between policy objectives and policy instruments.

- Tinbergen's *fixed target approach* emphasizes that there must be at least as many policy instruments as policy objectives if target values for a number of objectives are to be achieved simultaneously.

- Theil's *flexible target approach* suggests that no exact target value can be achieved for any single objective or group of objectives. Instead policy instruments are geared to minimizing the (squared) deviations between the actual and target value for one or more objectives in order to minimize overall welfare loss.

- The 'satisficing' approach of Mosley moves away from the fine-tuning of Tinbergen and Theil, and suggests that 'satisfactory' rather than optimum levels of performance should be the aim of macroeconomic policy.

- Macroeconomic policy in the pre-1974 period largely followed Keynesian principles, i.e. managing demand mainly through fiscal policy, allied occasionally to prices and incomes policies.

- Macroeconomic policy in the 1974–79 period moved away from such Keynesian 'fine tuning' and towards the use of 'rules'. The CEPG and monetarists advocated such rule making.

- The Medium Term Financial Strategy (MTFS) began in 1980 and concentrated initially on controlling demand by using $£M_3$ and then the PSBR as the main *targets* for bringing inflation under control. The main *instrument* for achieving this was to be the interest rate.

- Between 1987 and 1992 the MTFS policy shifted its targets towards stabilizing the *exchange rate*, which was now seen as the main route through which inflation was transmitted to the economy. The *instrument* used to achieve this target was still to be the interest rate.

- Since the UK left the Exchange Rate Mechanism in 1992, a key target has been low inflation, seen as a prerequisite for economic growth. The main instrument for achieving this target has remained the interest rate, together with the observance of fiscal 'rules'.

- Macroeconomic policy also involved improving the responsiveness of the economy by concentrating on the *supply side* of the economy, for example by adjusting tax rates and improving labour efficiency and training.

Now try the self-check questions for this chapter on the Companion Website. You will also find up-to-date facts and case materials.

Notes

1. That is, provided the Marshall–Lerner condition is satisfied, with the sum of price elasticity of demand for UK exports and price elasticity of demand for imports into the UK greater than unity.

2. For instance, in Chapter 20 we noted that the money supply, M, times the velocity of circulation of money, V, would give the monetary value of spending.

3. If points on O_1 indicate internal balance, then points off it indicate imbalance. Check that above and to the right of the line there will be inflation, whereas below and to the left there will be unemployment.

4. Similarly, if points on O_2 indicate external balance, then points off it indicate imbalance. Check that a balance of payments surplus will occur below and to the left of the O_2 line, and a deficit above and to the right.

5. Provided that O_2 and O_1 cross! Economic objective O_2 is shown as having a shallower slope than O_1. Can you see why? Start at E, and move up the O_1, line; expansionary monetary policy reduces interest rates, so that the short-term capital inflow will diminish, and the balance of payments will deteriorate. To keep it in balance, a lower National Income would be necessary in order to reduce the import flow. This could be achieved by contractionary fiscal policy, i.e. above E, O_2 must lie to the left of O_1.

6. If the exchange rate is lowered then O_2 might shift to the right and so pass through point G (which had previously been a balance of payments deficit position). All three objectives are now achieved.

7. If $M.V \equiv P.T$, the equation of exchange where M = money supply, V = average velocity of circulation of money, P = average price level, and T = volume of transactions. Then, if both V and T are fixed (or change at a known rate), money supply M directly affects price level P. So $\Delta M = \Delta P$, and the inflation rate is determined by the growth of the money supply.

8. The inflation target changed to 2% (HICP definition) in December 2003.

References and further reading

Allsopp, C. (2002) Macroeconomic policy rules in theory and in practice, *Bank of England Quarterly Bulletin*, **42**(4), Winter.

Beath, J. (2002) UK industrial policy: old tunes on new instruments?, *Oxford Review of Economic Policy*, **18**(2).

Bray, J., Kuleshov, A., Uysal, A. and Walker, P. (1993) Balance-achieving policies: a comparative policy-optimization study on four UK models, *Oxford Review of Economic Policy*, **9**(3).

Britton, A. (2002) Macroeconomics and history, *National Institute Economic Review*, No. 179, January.

Cabinet Office (2001) In demand: adult skills in the 21st century, *Performance and Innovation Unit Report*, November, Fig. 12.

Cowling, K. and Sugden, R. (1993) Industrial strategy: a missing link in British economic policy, *Oxford Review of Economic Policy*, **9**(3).

Griffiths, A. (2001) The government's fiscal rules: origins, development and problems, *British Economy Survey*, **31**(1), Autumn.

Healey, N. (1990) Mrs Thatcher's fight against inflation: ten years without cheer, *Economics*, **26**(1), Spring.

Heibling, T. and Wescott, R. (1995) The global interest rate, *Staff Studies for the World Economic Outlook*, IMF, September.

HM Treasury (2002) *Reforming Britain's Economic and Financial Policy*, Palgrave, Macmillan.

Hudson, S. and Fisher, P. (1994) Monetary policy in the United Kingdom, *Economics and Business Education*, **II**, part 2, no. 6, Summer.

IMF (1996) World economic situation and short term propects, *World Economic Outlook*, May, Table 2.

Layard, R. L. and Nickell, S. (1985) The causes of British unemployment, *National Institute Economic Review*, **111**, February.

Minford, P. and Peel, D. (1981) Is the government's economic strategy on course?, *Lloyds Bank Review*, **40**, April.

Mosley, P. (1976) Towards a satisficing theory of economic policy, *Economic Journal*, **86**, March.

O'Mahony, M. (1998) Britain's relative productivity performance 1950–1996: estimates by sector, *National Institute of Economic and Social Research*, October.

Oulton, N. (1995) Supply side reform and UK economic growth: what happened to the miracle?, *National Institute Economic Review*, **154**, November.

Savage, D. (1982) Fiscal policy, 1974/75–1980/81: description and measurement, *National Institute Economic Review*, **99**, February.

Sentance, A. (1998) UK macroeconomic policy and economic performance, in *Britain's Economic Performance*, 2nd edn, ed. T. Buxton, P. Chapman and P. Temple, Routledge, London.

Theil, H. (1956) On the theory of economic policy, *American Economic Review*, **46**, May.

Tinbergen, J. (1952) *On the Theory of Economic Policy*, North-Holland Publishing Co., Amsterdam.

Trade and Industry Committee (1994) *Competitiveness of UK Manufacturing Industry*, Second Report, House of Commons, April.

Chapter 25   Globalization

'Globalization' is a widely used but often loosely defined term. In this chapter we take forward many of the ideas touched on in Chapter 7 (The multinational corporation). We review the major characteristics of globalization, including new markets, new actors, new rules and norms and new methods of communication.

Some indicators of these characteristics are identified and measured over recent decades to establish some of the quantitative and qualitative patterns and trends underpinning globalization. After assessing some of the strategic implications for firms operating in a global environment, attention turns to the multi-dimensional aspects of such an environment. In addition to the economic dimension, political, legal and sociocultural dimensions are briefly reviewed, including terrorism (with a review of the impacts of 9/11) and health-related issues within a globalized environment. The perspectives behind the raft of contemporary anti-globalization protests are reviewed and evaluated. The chapter concludes by reviewing the move towards global engagement by the economy most directly associated with globalization, namely the USA.

Characteristics of 'globalization'

It is widely accepted that the world has become increasingly interconnected in recent decades as the result of economic, technological, political, sociological and cultural forces. To take but one example, in 2003 BT confirmed that it would set up two call centres in India, with PowerGen and Thames Water announcing at the same time their intention to do the same. British Airways and HSBC had done the same a few months earlier, attracted by labour costs some 30% lower than in Britain. However, there is considerable debate as to whether such events merely reflect the continuation of a long-established internationalization process or a deep-seated shift in the structure and operations of the world economy. 'Globalization' is a much used but often loosely defined term, which many believe should be restricted to situations characterized by this latter perspective.

Of course globalization is by no means the preserve of economists alone. Indeed it has been approached from the perspective of at least four academic disciplines, within each of which it tends to take on different characteristics.

- *Economists* focus on the growth of international trade and the increase in international capital flows.
- *Political scientists* view globalization as a process that leads to the undermining of the nation state and the emergence of new forms of governance.
- *Sociologists* view globalization in terms of the rise of a global culture and the domination of the media by global companies.
- *International relations experts* tend to focus on the emergence of global conflicts and global institutions.

Some argue that globalization is a long-standing phenomenon and not really anything new, pointing out that world trade and investment as a proportion of world GDP is little different today from what it was a century ago and that international borders were as open at that time as they are today with proportionately just as many people migrating abroad. Nor, from this perspective, should we overestimate the power of today's global corporations. In a major study for the Economic and Social Research Council of the top 214 multinationals over the period 1995–98, Alan Rugman concluded that the vast majority were not pursuing a global strategy, were finding it difficult to make decent profits and were tending to 'de-globalize' by concentrating on tried and trusted markets at home (Elliott 2002).

However, those who believe that globalization really is a new phenomenon tend to agree that at least three key elements are commonly involved.

- *Shrinking space.* The lives of all individuals are increasingly interconnected by events worldwide. This is not only a matter of fact but one which people increasingly perceive to be the case, recognizing that their jobs, income levels, health and living environment depend on factors outside national and local boundaries.
- *Shrinking time.* With the rapid developments in communication and information technologies, events occurring in one place have almost instantaneous (real-time) impacts worldwide. A fall in share prices in Wall Street can have almost immediate consequences for share prices in London, Frankfurt or Tokyo.
- *Disappearing borders.* The nation state and its associated borders seem increasingly irrelevant as 'barriers' to international events and influences. Decisions taken by regional trading blocs (e.g. EU, NAFTA) and supra-national bodies (e.g. IMF, World Trade Organization) increasingly override national policy-making in economic and business affairs as well as in other areas such as law enforcement and human rights.

It may be useful at this point to consider some of the conceptual issues as regards 'globalization' a little further using a broadly *economic* perspective.

- *Shallow versus deep integration.* 'Shallow integration' is often used to describe an increasing volume of trade in goods and services between largely independent firms which conduct the main part of their activities within single national economies. A stereotypical version of 'shallow integration' would be the growth in international trade involving firms exchanging materials and foodstuffs with other firms mainly engaged in the manufacture and finishing of products in single national economies. 'Deep integration' is more commonly associated with the rise of the multinational enterprise and the associated *fragmentation* of production processes and their *geographical relocation* on a global scale which pays scant regard to national boundaries. The term is also used to reflect the development of communication networks, financial transactions and logistical arrangements on a global scale. In other words 'deep integration' views the linkages between national economies as being progressively influenced by the cross-border value-adding activities of multinational enterprises over a broad range of goods and services.

■ *Internationalization versus globalization processes.* Whilst the growing *quantitative* importance of multinational enterprises in global trade patterns (see Chapter 7) points inexorably towards 'deep integration', a key question is whether their

Table 25.1 Characteristics of globalization.

New markets
■ Growing global markets in services – banking, insurance, transport
■ New financial markets – deregulated, globally linked, working around the clock, with action at a distance in real time, with new instruments such as derivatives.
■ Deregulation of antitrust laws and growth of mergers and acquisitions.
■ Global consumer markets with global brands.

New actors
■ Multinational corporations integrating their production and marketing, dominating world production.
■ The World Trade Organization – the first multilateral organization with authority to force national governments to comply with trade rules.
■ A growing international network of Non-Governmental Organizations (NGOs).
■ Regional blocs proliferating and gaining importance – European Union, Association of South-East Asian Nations, Mercosur, North American Free Trade Association, Southern African Development Community, among many others.
■ More policy coordination groups – G-7, G-8, OECD, IMF, World Bank.

New rules and norms
■ Market economic policies spreading around the world, with greater privatization and liberalization than in earlier decades.
■ Widespread adoption of democracy as the choice of political regime.
■ Human rights conventions and instruments building up in both coverage and number of signatories – and growing awareness among people around the world.
■ Consensus goals and action agenda for development.
■ Conventions and agreements on the global environment – biodiversity, ozone layer, disposal of hazardous wastes, desertification, climate change.
■ Multilateral agreements in trade, taking on such new agendas as environmental and social conditions.
■ New multilateral agreements – for services, intellectual property, communications – more binding on national governments than any previous agreements.
■ The (proposed) Multilateral Agreement on Investment.

New (faster and cheaper) methods of communication
■ Internet and electronic communications linking many people simultaneously.
■ Cellular phones.
■ Fax machines.
■ Faster and cheaper transport by air, rail, sea and road.
■ Computer-aided design and manufacture.

Source: Adapted from UNCTAD (1999) *World Investment Report*.

involvement has also led to a *qualitative* change in the relationship between nation states and firms. Whereas the term 'internationalization' might be applied to the many processes resulting in more geographically extensive patterns of economic activity, 'globalization' should arguably be applied only to processes whereby geographically dispersed activities become more *functionally integrated* than hitherto. For example, a 'qualitative' change might be said to occur where the coordination and regulation functions involving the production chain become progressively 'internal' to the multinational enterprise rather than an 'external' issue whose resolution requires engagement between the multinational enterprise and national or international regulatory bodies. In such a case there has arguably been a 'qualitative' change in the relationship between nation states and the firm.

Table 25.1 attempts to capture some of the characteristics which currently underpin the use of the term 'globalization' as being something different from what has gone before.

Some would argue that the 'globalization tendencies' outlined in Table 25.1 can be at work without this resulting in the end-state of a new geo-economy in which 'market forces are rampant and uncontrollable, and the nation state merely passive and supine' (Dickens 2003, p. 5). Certainly the focus in this chapter will be on examining the impacts of these 'globalization tendencies' in today's world economy rather than on a semantic debate as to whether a deep-seated shift, involving qualitative change, has or

has not occurred in the structure and operations of the world economy.

 ## Indicators of globalization

Bearing in mind the characteristics of globalization already outlined in Table 25.1, here we review some selected quantitative indicators relevant to the debate.

New markets

Table 25.2 would certainly seem to confirm the growth of new markets within a more liberalized and deregulated global environment. We have already seen the relevance of foreign direct investment (FDI) to cross-border mergers and acquisitions by multinational enterprises (MNEs) (Chapter 7). Table 25.2 uses data from the United Nations Conference on Trade and Development (UNCTAD 2002) to indicate the progressive increase in regulatory changes affecting FDI by national governments, the overwhelming majority of which are 'more favourable' to FDI flows.

New actors

The rapid growth of MNEs themselves has already been documented in Chapter 7, as for example with employment in the overseas affiliates of MNEs rising

Table 25.2 Increasing liberalization of markets on a global scale.

	National regulatory changes in FDI regimes		
	Number of regulatory changes	Number more favourable to FDI	Number less favourable to FDI
1991	82	80	2
1993	103	100	3
1995	107	102	5
1997	158	144	14
1999	146	138	8
2001	206	194	12

Source: Adapted from UNCTAD (2002) *World Investment Report*.

from less than 18 million in 1982 to around 54 million in 2002. Table 25.3 throws further light on the increasing globalization of productive activity by showing the progressive growth in the Transnationality Index (TNI) for the world's largest 100 MNEs in their home economies between 1990 and 2000. The TNI has been defined (see p. 115) as the average of the following three ratios: foreign assets/total assets; foreign sales/total sales; and foreign employment/total employment. A rise in the TNI suggests still more international involvement of the top 100 MNEs outside their home country, which is certainly a pattern strongly supported by the data in Table 25.3.

The EU is home to almost half of the world's largest MNEs and we can see from Table 25.3 that the average transnationality index (TNI) for the EU has risen from 56.7 to 67.1 over the 1990–2000 period alone. A still more rapid growth in the TNI is indicated for MNEs with North America as their 'home' base, with Japan alone showing only modest growth. For 'all economies' the greater internationalization of production is indicated by the rise in TNI from 51.1 to 57.8 during 1990–2000. Closer scrutiny of this data reveals that the driving forces behind these observed increases in TNI have been the growth in the foreign sales/total sales and the foreign employment/total employment ratios that contribute to the TNI.

New actors within a globalized economy are also expected to include growing numbers of multilateral organizations (e.g. WTO), non-governmental organizations (NGOs) and policy coordination groups (e.g. G8/G7). These will be in greater demand in an attempt to bring some kind of order to a progressively less nationally supervised and more deregulated world trading regime. In addition, the growth of regional trading blocs is often predicted as a collective response to the progressive loss of economic power of individual nation states. Chapter 28 provides ample evidence of the growing presence of these new actors within the global economy.

New rules and norms

Not only are new international institutions and trading blocs characteristic of a more globalized economy in which nation states have progressively less influence, but so too are the 'rules and norms' by which they seek to operate. Market-oriented policies, democratic political frameworks, consensus goals involving social and environmental responsibility, and growing multilateral applications of agreed rules were all identified as characteristics of globalization in Table 25.1 above. Again Chapter 28 provides considerable empirical evidence of movements in this direction. Here we note the importance of good

Table 25.3 Transnationality Index for the world's largest 100 MNEs in their home economies, 1990 and 2000.

Economy	Average TNI (%)		Number of MNEs	
	1990	2000	1990	2000
European Union	**56.7**	**67.1**	**48**	**49**
France	50.9	63.2	14	13
Germany	44.4	45.9	9	10
UK	68.5	76.9	12	14
North America	**41.2**	**62.9**	**30**	**25**
USA	38.5	43.0	28	23
Canada	79.2	82.9	2	2
Japan	**35.5**	**35.9**	**12**	**16**
All economies	**51.1**	**57.8**	**100**	**100**

Source: Adapted from UNCTAD (2002) *World Investment Report*.

governance and transparency, an absence of corruption and appropriate property rights to the establishment of a sustainable globalized economic environment.

The World Bank (World Development Report 2001) has pointed out that good governance – including independent agencies, mechanisms for citizens to monitor public behaviour, and rules that constrain corruption – is a key ingredient for growth and prosperity. In an early study Barro (1991) had found a positive correlation between economic growth and measures of political stability for 98 countries surveyed between 1960 and 1985. More recent empirical research points in a similar direction, for example confirming that FDI inflows are inversely related to measures of corruption, as with Lipsey (1999) observing a strong negative correlation between corruption and the locational choice of US subsidiaries across Asian countries. Similarly Claugue *et al.* (1999) and

Zak (2001) found that productivity and economic growth will improve when governments impartially protect and define property rights. Underpinning these findings is the perception by firms that a non-transparent business environment increases the prevalence of information asymmetries, raises the cost of securing additional information, increases transaction costs (e.g. risk premiums) and creates an uncertain business environment which deters trade and investment. For example, Wallsten (2001) found a strong inverse relationship between investment intentions and the threat of asset expropriation, as well as a propensity for firms to charge higher prices to help pay back their initial capital outlays more rapidly when they felt less secure about the intentions of host governments, the higher prices often inhibiting the penetration and growth phase of product life cycles.

Table 25.4 Globalization: selected indicators of IT-based communication methods.

Country	IT/GDP (%)		Personal computers (per 100 people)		Telephone lines (per 100 people)	
	% change 1992–2000	2000	% change 1990–2000	2000	% change 1990–2000	2000
Developing						
Argentina	1.0	3.4	4.4	5.1	12.0	21.3
Brazil	2.3	5.8	4.1	4.4	8.4	14.9
Chile	1.1	5.7	7.5	8.6	15.5	22.1
China	3.0	4.9	1.6	1.6	8.0	8.6
India	1.8	3.5	0.5	0.5	2.6	3.2
Malaysia	2.1	5.5	9.7	10.5	12.2	21.1
Mexico	5.2	1.0	4.3	5.1	6.0	12.5
Philippines	0.9	2.7	1.6	1.9	2.9	3.9
South Africa	1.8	7.2	5.5	6.2	3.2	12.5
Advanced						
Canada	1.6	5.3	28.3	39.0	11.1	67.6
Denmark	1.0	4.5	31.6	43.1	13.8	70.5
France	0.8	3.8	23.4	30.5	8.5	58.0
Germany	0.9	4.1	23.4	33.6	16.0	60.1
United Kingdom	0.7	4.7	23.0	33.8	12.6	56.7
United States	0.9	5.2	36.8	58.5	12.8	67.3

Sources: Adapted from OECD, *World Economic Outlook* (various).

New methods of communication

Management specialist Stephen Kobrin (1994) describes globalization as driven not by foreign trade and investment but by information flows. It is this latter perspective which sees globalization as a process inextricably linked with the creation, distribution and use of knowledge and information, which is the focus here. Many contributors to the globalization debate regard the technological convergence of information, computer and telecommunications technologies in the late twentieth century as having acted as a key catalyst in the rapid growth of these information-based activities, seen here as the hallmark of the globalized economy (Held *et al.* 1999).

International communications have grown dramatically, as evidenced by indicators such as the time spent on international telephone calls rising from 33bn minutes in 1990 to over 80bn minutes in 2002, and international travellers more than doubling in 20 years, from some 260m travellers a year in 1980 to over 600m travellers a year in 2002. Contemporary discourse often seeks to express globalization in terms of the exponential growth in the creation, processing and dissemination of knowledge and information. For example, an 'index of globalization' recently compiled jointly by the Carnegie Foundation and ATKearney (a global consultant) gives considerable weight to the proportion of national populations online as well as to the number of Internet hosts and secure servers per capita. These indicators of access to information technology and associated information flows are seen here as proxy variables for 'global openness', to be used in association with the more conventional indicators of investment, capital flows, foreign income as a proportion of national income, and convergence between domestic and international prices, when compiling the overall globalization index (Walker 2001). Singapore was recorded in the 2000 index as the 'most globalized' country, helped by the fact that its recorded outgoing telephone traffic at 390 minutes per head per year was some four times as much as in the US. Sweden (ranked third) recorded some 44% of households online, whilst Finland (ranked fifth) had over 70 web-connected servers (Internet hosts) per 1,000 people. Swiss citizens (ranked fourth) spent 400% more time on international phone calls than Americans. Table 25.4 (see p. 504) presents some further selected indicators of the growth in IT-based communications methods.

Globalization and corporate strategy

It may be useful to assess the impacts of the characteristics of globalization outlined in Table 25.1 on the strategic direction of firms, where 'strategy' is defined as the guiding rules or principles which influence the direction and scope of the organization's activities over the long term. Of course, various chapters have already touched on aspects of cross-border mergers and alliances (Chapter 5), multinational involvement (Chapter 7) and price/output decision (Chapter 9). However, here we concentrate more explicitly on devising corporate strategy within a business environment exhibiting still more rapid growth in the various quantitative indicators of globalization outlined above.

Prahalad (2000) paints a vivid picture of a 'discontinuous competitive landscape' as characterizing much of the 1990s and early years of the millennium. Industries are no longer the stable entities they once were:

- Rapid technology changes and the convergence of technologies (e.g. computer and telecommunications) are constantly redefining industrial 'boundaries' so that the 'old' industrial structures become barely recognizable.

- Privatization and deregulation have become global trends within industrial and service sectors (e.g. telecommunications, power, water, health care, financial services) and even within nations themselves (e.g. Transition Economies, China).

- Internet-related technologies are beginning to have major impacts on business-to-business and business-to-customer relationships.

- Pressure groups based around environmental and ecological sensitivities are progressively well organized and influential.

- New forms of institutional arrangements and liaisons are exerting greater influences on organizational structures than hitherto (e.g. strategic alliances, franchising).

In a progressively less stable environment dominated by such discontinuities, there will arguably be a shift in perspective away from the previous strategic focus of Porter and his contemporaries, in which companies are seen as seeking to identify and exploit *competitive advantages* within stable industrial structures. The more conventional strategic models focused on securing competitive advantages by better utilizing one or more of the following five factors:

■ *architecture* (a more effective set of contractual relationships with suppliers and customers);

■ *incumbency advantages* (reputation, branding, scale economies, etc.);

■ *access to strategic assets* (raw materials, wavebands, scarce labour inputs, etc.);

■ *innovation* (product or process, protected by patents, licences, etc.);

■ *operational efficiencies* (quality circles, just-intime techniques, re-engineering, etc.).

However, the discontinuities outlined previously have changed the setting in which much of the strategic discussion must now take place. Prahalad (2000) goes on to suggest four key 'transformations' which must now be registered.

1 *Recognizing changes in strategic space.* Deregulation and privatization of previously government-controlled industries, access to new market opportunities in large developing countries (e.g. China, India, Brazil) and in the transitional economies of Central and Eastern Europe, together with the rapidly changing technological environment, are creating entirely new strategic opportunities. Take the case of the large energy utilities. They must now decide on the extent of integration (power generation, power transmission within industrial and/or consumer sectors), the geographical reach of their operations (domestic/overseas), the extent of diversification (other types of energy, non-energy fields), and so on. PowerGen in the UK is a good example of a traditional utility with its historical base in electricity generation which, in a decade or so, has transformed itself into a global provider of electricity services (generation and transmission), water and other infrastructure services. Clearly the strategic 'space' available to companies is ever expanding, creating entirely new possibilities in the modern global economy.

2 *Recognizing globalization impacts.* As we discuss in more detail below, globalization of business activity is itself opening up new strategic opportunities and threats. Arguably the distinction

between local and global business will itself become increasingly irrelevant. The local businesses must devise their own strategic response to the impact of globalized players. Nirula, the Indian fast food chain, raising standards of hygiene and restaurant ambience in response to competition from McDonald's, is one type of local response, and McDonald's providing more lamb and vegetarian produce in its Indian stores is another. Mass customization and quick response strategies require global businesses to be increasingly responsive to local consumers. Additionally globalization opens up new strategic initiatives in terms of geographical locations, modes of transnational collaboration, financial accountability and logistical provision.

3 *Recognizing the importance of timely responses.* Even annual planning cycles are arguably becoming progressively obsolete as the speed of corporate response becomes a still more critical success factor, both to seize opportunities and to repel threats.

4 *Recognizing the enhanced importance of innovation.* Although innovation has long been recognized as a critical success factor, its role is still further enhanced in an environment dominated by the 'discontinuities' previously mentioned. Successful companies must still innovate in terms of new products and processes, but now such innovation must also be directed towards providing the company with faster and more reliable information on customers as part of mass customization, quick response and personalized product business philosophies.

These factors are arguably changing the context for business strategy from positioning the company within a clear-cut industrial structure to stretching and shaping that structure by its own strategic initiatives. It may no longer be sensible or efficient to devise strategic blueprints over a protracted planning time-frame and then seek to apply the blueprints mechanically, given that events and circumstances are changing so rapidly. The *direction* of broad strategic thrust can be determined as a route map, but tactical and operational adjustments must be continually appraised and modified along the way.

Nor can the traditional strategy hierarchies continue unchallenged – i.e. top management creating strategy and middle management implementing it. Those who are closest to the product and market are becoming increasingly important as well-informed sources for identifying opportunities to exploit or threats to repel. Arguably the roles of middle and lower management in the strategic process are being considerably enhanced by the 'discontinuities' previously observed. Top managers are finding themselves progressively removed from competitive reality in an era of discontinuous change. Their role is rather to set a broad course, to ensure that effective and responsive middle and lower management are in place to exercise delegated strategic responsibilities, and to provide an appropriate infrastructure for strategic delivery. For example, a key role of top managers in various media-related activities may have been to secure access to an appropriate broadband wavelength by successfully competing in the UK or German auctions. Such access is likely to be a prerequisite for competitive involvement in a whole raft of Internet-related products for home and business consumption via mobile telephony.

Figure 25.1 provides a useful summary of the traditional and emerging views of international business strategy.

Modular strategies

Globalization has been a driving force for *modular strategies*, since these can help companies engage in large worldwide investments without a huge increase in fixed costs and with fewer of the problems typically associated with managing complex global operations. Modular strategies can embrace production, design and/or use (see Fig. 25.2).

■ *Modularity in Production (MIP)*. This provided the initial impetus to adopt modules in the car industry. Here production activities are broken down into a number of large but separate elements that can be carried out independently, with the finished vehicle then being assembled from these large sub-assemblies. Such modular production

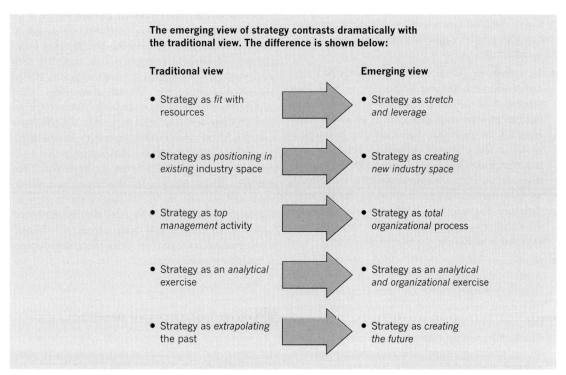

The emerging view of strategy contrasts dramatically with the traditional view. The difference is shown below:

Traditional view	Emerging view
• Strategy as *fit* with resources	• Strategy as *stretch and leverage*
• Strategy as *positioning in existing* industry space	• Strategy as *creating new industry space*
• Strategy as *top management* activity	• Strategy as *total organizational* process
• Strategy as an *analytical* exercise	• Strategy as an *analytical and organizational* exercise
• Strategy as *extrapolating* the past	• Strategy as *creating the future*

Fig. 25.1 New strategic directions in a global economy.

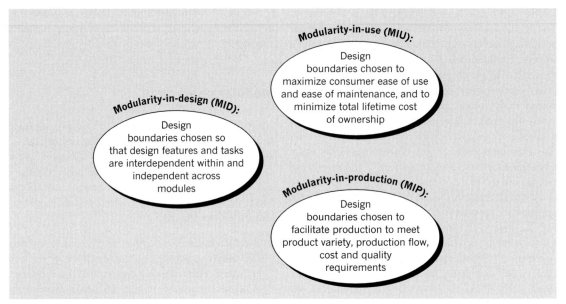

Fig. 25.2 Modular strategies.

systems can help reduce the fixed capital overhead required for production, especially where selected modules are *outsourced*. Specialization of labour and management on smaller, independent modules can also result in productivity gains and lower variable costs.

■ *Modularity in Design (MID)*. There may be more problems in establishing modularity in the design process. This will be particularly true where the finished product embodies systems as well as sub-assembly components. For example, a finished vehicle offers climate control and vehicle safety 'systems' which, to be provided effectively, require design input into a whole range of sub-assembly module operations. Modularity in design may therefore require that boundaries be carefully drawn so as to capture as many interdependencies as possible within the modular groupings.

■ *Modularity in Use (MIU)*. This was the main reason for the introduction of modularity in the computer industry. It became increasingly obvious that consumers required computer-related products that were both compatible and upgradeable. Much effort was therefore expended in standardizing interfaces between different elements of the product architecture to give these desired user attributes. The then leader, IBM, found that the

electro-mechanical system could be disaggregated without adversely affecting performance.

Of course, creating a modular product in any or all of these ways may have organizational consequences, not all of which may be foreseen. A national or international infrastructure exists which supports new firm start-ups – e.g. access to venture capital, skilled labour, etc. Further, for example, a module product architecture may result in *modular business organization*. This has certainly been the case in the computer industry. It can also stimulate certain types of organizational practice, such as outsourcing, and shift power relationships between companies. For example, IBM's decision to outsource the development and production of its operating system to Microsoft and of its chip to Intel was an important factor in shifting power away from the overall product architecture to these designers and producers of modular systems elements.

Dimensions of globalization

Of course, we should admit that a one-dimensional view of globalization, which thinks purely in terms of the economic impacts of market forces, is likely to result in only a partial picture at best. To quote Giddens (1990):

> 'Globalisation is a complex process which is not necessarily teleological in character – that is to say, it is not necessarily an inexorable historical process with an end in sight. Rather, it is characterised by a set of mutually opposing tendencies'.

McGrew (1992) has tried to identify a number of these opposing tendencies.

- *Universalization versus particularization.* While globalization may tend to make many aspects of modern social life universal (e.g. assembly line production, fast food restaurants, consumer fashions) it can also help to point out the differences between what happens in particular places and what happens elsewhere.
- *Homogenization versus differentiation.* While globalization may result in an essential homogeneity ('sameness') in product, process and institutions (e.g. city life, organizational offices and bureaucracies), it may also mean that the general must be assimilated within the local. For example, human rights are interpreted in different ways across the globe, the practice of specific religions such as Christianity or Buddhism may take on different forms in different places, and so on.
- *Integration versus fragmentation.* Globalization

creates new forms of global, regional and transnational communities which unite (integrate) people across territorial boundaries (e.g. the MNE, international trade unions, etc.). However, it also has the potential to divide and fragment communities (e.g. labour becoming divided along sectoral, local, national and ethnic lines).

Morrison (2002) usefully reviews these multi-dimensional perspectives of globalization, in particular pointing to two widely held but contrasting schools of thought (Table 25.5).

- *Hyperglobalists* envisage the global economy as being inhabited by powerless nation states at the mercy of 'footloose' multinational enterprises bestowing jobs and wealth creation opportunities on favoured national clients. National cultural differences are largely seen by these progressively powerful multinationals as merely variations in consumer preferences to be reflected in their international marketing mix.
- *Transformationalists* recognize that globalization is a powerful force impacting on economic, social and political environments, but take a much less prescriptive stance as to what the outcomes of those impacts might be. Predictions as to any end-state of a globalized economy can only be tentative and premature. Rather globalization involves a complex set of intermittent, uneven processes with unpredictable outcomes rather than a linear

Table 25.5 Globalization: two schools of thought.

	Hyperglobalists	Transformationalists
What's new	A global age	Historically unprecedented levels of global interconnectedness
Dominant features	Global capitalism; global governance; global civil society	'Thick' (intensive and extensive) globalization
Power of national governments	Declining or eroding	Reconstituted, restructured
Conceptualization of globalization	As a reordering of the framework of human action	As a reordering of interregional relations and action at a distance
Historical trajectory	Global civilization	Indeterminate; global integration and fragmentation

Source: Morrison (2002), adapted from Held *et al.* (1999).

progression to a predictable end-state. It is this more pragmatic transformationalist approach which is reflected in the rest of the chapter.

Globalization and the political environment

At the heart of governance is the notion of 'sovereignty', which implies the power to rule without constraint and which, for the last three centuries, has been associated with the nation state. We live in a world which is organized as a patchwork of nation states within which different peoples live, with their own systems of government exerting authority over the affairs within their territory. Of course groupings within those territories may arise from time to time, which seek a measure of independence from the central authorities, sometimes claiming nation statehood themselves. Many would also argue that the idea of the nation state has itself been challenged by the growth of globalization. Before turning to this issue, it may be useful to highlight some opposing and arguably contradictory tendencies in globalization.

■ *Centralization versus decentralization.* Some aspects of globalization tend to concentrate power, knowledge, information, wealth and decision-making. Many believe this to be the case with the rise of the MNE, the growth of regional trading blocs (e.g. EU), the development of world regulatory bodies such as the WTO, etc. However, such centralizing tendencies may conflict with powerful decentralizing tendencies as nations, communities and individuals attempt to take greater control over the forces which influence their lives (e.g. the growth of social movements centred on the global environment, peace and gender issues, etc.).

■ *Juxtaposition versus syncretization.* In the globalization process, time and space become compressed, so that different civilizations, ways of life and social practices become juxtaposed (placed side by side). This can create 'shared' cultural and social spaces characterized by an evolving mixture of ideas, knowledge and institutions. Unfortunately this can also stimulate the opposite tendencies, such as a heightened awareness of challenges to the established norms of previously dominant groups, which can result in determined attempts to avoid integration and instead combine against a 'common opponent' (syncretization).

Whilst there may be many theories as to the causes of globalization, most writers would agree that globalization is a discontinuous historical process. Its dynamic proceeds in fits and starts and its effects are experienced differentially across the globe. Some regions are more deeply affected by globalization than others. Even within nation states, some communities (e.g. financial) may experience the effects of globalization more sharply than others (e.g. urban office workers). Many have argued that globalization is tending to reinforce inequalities of power both within and across nation states, resulting in global hierarchies of privilege and control for some but economic and social exclusion for others.

Globalization and the nation state

It has been argued that one of the major effects of globalization is to threaten the notion of the territorial nation state, in at least four key respects: its competence, its form, its autonomy and, ultimately, its authority and legitimacy. In a global economic system, productive capital, finance and products flow across national boundaries in ever increasing volumes and values, yet the nation state seems increasingly irrelevant as a 'barrier' to international events and influences. Governments often appear powerless to prevent stock market crashes or recessions in one part of the world having adverse effects on domestic output, employment, interest rates and so on. Attempts to lessen these adverse effects seem, to many citizens, increasingly to reside in supranational bodies such as the IMF, World Bank, EU, etc. This inability of nation states to meet the demands of their citizens without international cooperation is seen by many as evidence of the declining *competence* of states, arguably leading to a 'widening and weakening' of the individual nation state.

In such a situation, the *form* and *autonomy* of the nation state are also subtly altered. The increased emphasis on international cooperation has brought with it an enormous increase in the number and influence of intergovernmental and non-governmental organizations (NGOs) to such an extent that many writers now argue that national and international policy formulation have become inseparable. For example, whereas in 1909 only 176 international NGOs could be identified, by 2003 this number exceeded 30,000 and was still growing! The formerly monolithic national state, with its own independent and broadly coherent policy, is now conceived by many to be a fragmented coalition of bureaucratic agencies each pursuing its own agenda with minimal central direction or control. State autonomy is thereby threatened in economic, financial and ecological areas.

However, as we saw earlier, globalization consists of a series of conflicting tendencies. Whilst there is some evidence that the relevance of the nation state is declining, other writers claim the alternative view. Some argue that the state retains its positive role in the world through its monopoly of military power which, though rarely used, offers its citizens relative security in a highly dangerous world. Further, it provides a focus for personal and communal identity, and finally, in pursuing national interest through cooperation and collaboration, nation states actually empower themselves. The suggestion here is that international cooperation (as opposed to unilateral action) allows states simultaneously to pursue their national interests and at the same time, by collective action, to achieve still more effective control over their national destiny. For example, the international control of exchange rates (e.g. the EU single currency) is seen by some as enhancing state *autonomy* rather than diminishing it, since the collective action implicit in a common currency affords more economic security and benefits for nationals than unilateral action.

Globalization is therefore redefining our understanding of the nation state by introducing a much more complex architecture of political power in which authority is seen as being pluralistic rather than residing solely in the nation state.

Globalization and knowledge-based economies

Most commentators agree that developments in the information and communications technologies (ICT) have played a key role in the dramatic surge in information flows associated with the globalized economies of the latter part of the twentieth century. Some have even spoken of a new economic paradigm (e.g. 'new economy') resulting in a long-term upward shift in the productivity of both labour and capital,

leading to enhanced prospects of higher long-term and non-inflationary growth. Convergence of ICT technologies and the enhanced use of the Internet and websites are often linked, in this perspective, to a new Kondratief 'long wave' cycle of the type associated with the earlier technological breakthroughs in steam power, railroads and electricity.

Recent major reports (World Economic Outlook 2001; World Employment Report 2001) have identified a number of important impacts of the expanded Internet and website usage within the global economy and associated increases in information-related activities on contemporary labour markets. A number are briefly reviewed below.

- A positive net impact on total levels of employment, with the employment-creating potential of ICT outweighing the risk of job losses. Evidence suggests that countries experiencing the greatest growth in 'total factor productivity' over the past decade have been those where ICT have been most widely adopted. These are also the countries in which employment has grown most rapidly.

- A change in the patterns of employment. ICT developments increase the demand for highly skilled workers who can push forward the technological frontier and make the new technology accessible to the rest of the workforce. Less skilled, repetitive occupations in both manufacturing and service sectors (e.g. offices) tend to be replaced by ICT, with fewer, more highly skilled workers remaining.

- A greater geographical dispersion of employment as work becomes progressively less dependent on specific locational factors (e.g. growth in work from home).

- A shift in employment towards smaller, less established firms and new entrants via 'leapfrogging', which in this context refers to the opportunities inherent in the new ICT technologies for SMEs and new entrants to bypass earlier investments by rivals in the time or cost of developments.

- A more highly skilled and better-educated workforce within economies which now depend less on physical inputs than on knowledge.

- A shift in the focus of education and training to foster generic skills, with individuals no longer seen as passive recipients of facts but as active, life-long learners. The ability at all levels of expertise to learn new approaches and transform existing knowledge into new knowledge becomes still more important in work environments that rely increasingly on rapid innovation and the interpersonal exchange and creation of knowledge.

However, some have cast doubt on the growth of knowledge-based societies as indicative of globalization. For example, it has been suggested that 'globalization' is merely a contemporary catchphrase for what in reality has been a long-established process in the growth of knowledge and information. Adams, an American historian, claimed as early as 1918 to have observed an exponential growth in various aspects of knowledge, subsequently formulated as 'Adams' Law of Acceleration of Progress' (see Rescher 1978). Similarly Rider (1944), investigating the stock of books of American universities over the period 1831–1938, found the stock to have doubled every 22 years, whilst the stock of the pure research universities had doubled every 16 years, resulting in growth rates of 3.2% and 4.4% per annum respectively. Price (1961), using similar indicators, estimated the growth rate of the stock of knowledge to be 6.5% per annum. Later writers (Machlup 1962; Bell 1973; Gershuny 1978) have identified these patterns and trends as being part of an inexorable process towards 'maturity' as developed economies pass through industrial and service-sector stages and towards 'post-industrial' societies. The acquisition and codification of theoretical knowledge, giving rise to a host of information-related activities, is seen as a key characteristic of such post-industrial societies.

Globalization and terrorism/criminality

The global growth of foreign direct investment and the increasingly 'footloose' activities of MNEs have already been documented as widely used indicators of globalization. Many commentators have also drawn attention to parallels between the rapid growth in formal, legal cross-border relationships and the rapid growth in a wide range of illegal cross-border relationships including, at one extreme, activities more commonly associated with terrorism. Some of the characteristics of globalization previously reviewed in Table 25.1 are seen as conducive to such growth, especially the weakening of power and control by nation states and the proliferation of new, less detectable methods of communication. Whilst a proper investigation of so complex an issue is beyond the scope of this chapter, we can perhaps draw attention to some of the economic impacts associated with global terrorism and criminality within more globalized economies.

September 11th 2001 (9/11)

This is perhaps the single event most closely associated with global terrorism. It may therefore be instructive to consider some of the short-term and long-term economic impacts of that event. Table 25.6 identifies what is arguably the major cost of 9/11 to the world economy over the two years following the attack on the World Trade Center, namely the difference between *projected and actual* growth of global GDP over that period. Whilst other external events may also have contributed to the cumulative discrepancy (projected – actual) of $740bn (£476bn) estimated for global GDP over the two-year period, there is little doubt that the greatest single influence has been 9/11 itself.

Of course many other more *direct* short-term costs of 9/11 can be identified, as indicated in Table 25.7. In New York alone some $95bn in costs have been estimated as directly attributable to 9/11 and some

Table 25.6 Short-run costs of 9/11 to the world economy (using $/£ exchange rates averaged over the period in question).

	09.11.01–09.11.02	09.11.02–09.11.03
Projected growth of *global GDP*	1.5%	2.5%
Actual growth of *global GDP*	0.7%	1.6%
Projected – Actual $bn (£bn)	$350bn (£225bn)	$390bn (£251bn)

Sources: Kaletsky (2002); *Economic Trends* (various).

Table 25.7 Direct cost impacts of 9/11.

$95bn cost to New York	
Wealth and capital (lost cash and lives)	$30.5bn
Replace World Trade Center	$6.7bn
Replace other offices	$4.5bn
Replace other infrastructure (roads, subways, etc.)	$4.3bn
Replace office equipment (computers, desks, telephones, etc.)	$5.2bn
Lost taxes	$3.5bn
Lost jobs	$11.0bn
Other costs	$29.0bn
$40bn cost to insurance companies	
Business interruptions	$11.0bn
World Trade Center property	$3.5bn
Other property	$6.0bn
Worker compensation	$2.0bn
Life insurance	$2.7bn
Aviation liability	$4.0bn
Event cancellation	$1.0bn
Other liability	$10.0bn

Sources: Adapted from *Comptroller of New York; Insurance Information Institute.*

$40bn in costs to an assortment of insurance companies involved with individuals and companies affected by 9/11.

Nevertheless it is the adverse impacts of global terrorism on future growth prospects that are likely to impose the greater short- and longer-run costs on the world economy. For example the cumulative loss of £476bn identified in Table 25.6 corresponds to more than half the annual output of the entire British economy.

Of course, as well as direct short-run costs there are a range of *indirect* short-run costs attributable to 9/11. Table 25.8 gives a breakdown of such 'indirect' costs estimated for three sectors, Airlines, Tourism and Luxury goods, in the 12 months following 9/11.

For example, global insurance premiums in the airline industry alone rocketed from $1.7bn in 2001 to over $6bn in 2002, whilst US airports reported extra costs and lost revenue associated with 9/11 over the following 12 months of some $4.5bn. This comprised extra security costs of $1.7bn over this time period, extra terrorism insurance and related costs of

$0.5bn and a loss in operating revenue (over projections) of $2.3bn.

When we turn to the long-run costs of 9/11 and subsequent terrorist activity, the estimates become dramatically larger, if still less capable of quantification.

Globalization and disease control

We noted earlier that increased international travel and communication featured in the 'globalization characteristics' outlined in Table 25.1. Parallel with the growth of such travel is an increasing exposure to communicable diseases.

SARS: a case study of globalized disease

The recent SARS (Severe Acute Respiratory Syndrome) outbreak provides a useful illustration of this point, with the World Health Organization believing it to be the first health episode of the twenty-first century with epidemic potential, with the

Table 25.8 Impacts of 9/11 on Airlines, Tourism and Luxury goods sectors over the subsequent 12 months.

Airlines	Tourism	Luxury goods
■ Two national flag carriers, Swissair and Belgium's Sabena, failed. ■ In America US Airways filed for Chapter XI protection from bankruptcy and United Airlines announced serious financial trouble. ■ The world's airlines made a total loss of $12bn (£7.7bn) on international flights over the 12-month period. ■ Insurance premiums have soared, costing the UK airline industry an extra $250m and the global airline industry $3bn. ■ Passenger numbers fell by 4% in 2001 and a further 3% in 2002. ■ Around 200,000 jobs were cut by airlines, 10,000 in the UK. ■ Transatlantic passenger traffic dropped by 25% over the period. ■ Hundreds of planes were mothballed in the Mojave desert, Arizona.	■ Worldwide income from tourism dropped by 2.2% to $462bn in 2001. ■ Tourists accounted for only 10% of sales in West End stores, down from 20% before September 11. ■ Between September and December 2001, tourist arrivals fell by 9.2% worldwide. ■ The hardest hit areas were the Middle East (down by 11%) and South Asia (down by 24%). ■ Tourists visiting New York spent $1bn less in 2002. ■ Delta airlines estimated a loss of $600m due to passenger delays from increased airport security discouraging 'day tripper' flights in the USA.	■ Consumer confidence in the US took the biggest plunge since the 1st Gulf war, according to the independent research group the Conference Board. ■ A substantial proportion of sales come from travellers and these have fallen as tourism and business travel has declined since 9/11. ■ US retail sales slumped by 2.4% over the period, the largest fall since 1992. ■ Exports of platinum watches from Switzerland fell by almost a quarter in the first half of 2002. ■ Luxury goods use a high proportion of skilled workers, making it harder to cope with a downturn as skilled workers are less easy to lay off. ■ Debt rating agency Fitch stated that a recovery in the retail sector following 9/11 would not take place until 2003.

Sources: Various.

ease of global travel acknowledged as playing a key role in its dissemination. Stephen Roach, chief economist of Morgan Stanley, argued that SARS would cut growth in Asia, excluding Japan, from 5% to 4.5% in 2003. Hu Angang, of Tsinghua University in Beijing, believes that without SARS, China could have achieved 9–10% growth in 2003, but expects SARS to have reduced growth by at least 1% on those projections to 8–9%. The World Bank is also pessimistic, cutting 0.5% off its pre-SARS estimate for Chinese growth in 2003.

We cannot, of course, hope to capture more than a flavour of the multi-dimensional and broad-based influence of globalization in a single chapter. What we can do is note that the economic, sociocultural and political impacts are significant and ongoing.

 Anti-globalization movements

In recent years the meetings of various international finance, trade, political and economic forums which were once routine, have become the focus of unprecedented protest and widespread media coverage. Since the Seattle meeting in November 1999, a wave of other protests has crashed around the world, including Bolivia, Ecuador, Washington, Paris, Prague, Nice, Quebec, Gothenburg and Genoa.

Seattle represented a turning point in what some now describe as the 'anti-globalization movement'. Although one account of events in Seattle maintained that people both outside and inside were confused about what they wanted, it captured the attention of the world's media and brought the issues surrounding globalization onto screens and into people's homes. International economic and political meetings now invariably focus on the major themes of trade, debt relief and globalization. Although hard to understand, this new 'movement' is now given much attention in the media.

Is the anti-capitalist movement merely the focus of today's privileged, excluded or bored OECD youth – an anarchist travelling circus? Such explanations are too simplistic. The coalitions of stakeholders taking to the streets appear to be unlikely alliances of disparate groups transcending age and economic and social classifications, including trade unionists, representatives of NGOs, shareholder activists, and students. Although the movement certainly contains anti-globalization and anti-capitalist elements, it appears to be united over the central issue of political, economic and social exclusion. All these groups have experienced the transfer of power from government to big corporations, the acceleration of inequalities within and between countries as a result of current economic policies and political ideologies, and the sense that society is itself being shaped and defined by big corporations. In rising up and dissenting against a sense of dispossession, the anti-globalization movement is in effect creating a society for those who feel excluded.

Globalization – North and South

North and *South* are terms often used to refer to the advanced industrialized and the developing economies respectively and their perspectives on globalization often differ markedly. Some Northern perspectives see globalization as liberalization, creating a climate of trust and enhancing wealth creation, whereas Southern perspectives often emphasize marginalization, exploitation, divisiveness and the exercise of power, viewing neo-liberal economic policies as destructive of livelihoods, communities, cultures and natural resources.

Many supporters of globalization are aware of its shortcomings and unintended side-effects and argue that the challenge is finding rules and institutions to preserve the advantages of globalization whilst taking account of these problems, hence the search for 'globalization with a human face', which can embrace concerns for ethics, equity, inclusion, human security, sustainability and development.

Sustainable development, open economies and trade

A key issue is whether globalization helps contribute to raising global standards of living, enhancing human and social capital in both North and South and therefore contributing to sustainable development, or whether its impacts are quite the opposite. This debate has largely crystallized around perspectives as to the role and impacts of international institutions such as the World Trade Organization, World Bank, IMF and so on. The anti-capitalist protestors regard these roles as inimical to sustainable development. But is this really so? We now address this key issue in rather more depth, with the particular emphasis on whether an 'open' world trading regime supports or hinders sustainable development.

Trade liberalization and the WTO

The World Trade Organization (WTO) is a powerful institution of international global governance whose rules and procedures are having a profound impact on global economic, social and political development (see Chapter 28). Agreeing trade rules that work for the benefit of the many and not the few is about reaching agreement on the ultimate purposes and goals of trade liberalization itself.

Trade liberalization has certainly met many of its own objectives, with various trade rounds having resulted in a tenfold reduction in border tariffs on industrial products from 50% in 1947 to around 5% in 2003. However, many believe that it is the multinational corporations and the North in general that have benefited most from these trade freedoms. Nevertheless some, even from the South, argue that the WTO is needed to protect developing countries and that it is a broadly successful institution of global governance to be reformed and improved, but not abandoned. Others stress that the WTO goes much too far, pointing out that it forces domestic laws to conform to trade law; in over 90% of the WTO cases between 1995 and 2003, national government regulation has been struck down. In essence some see the WTO as a mechanism for putting trade rules above every other kind of law, in the interests of its most powerful members. For example, Southern governments argue that the focus tends to be on Southern rather than Northern non-compliance!

Whilst any country has a chance of winning a case at the WTO, not all can impose effective sanctions. For example, a small developing country can win a WTO ruling but, even with WTO permission, would hardly benefit from imposing retaliatory sanctions on a large, advanced industrialized country. In contrast, developing countries fear the impact of trade sanctions imposed by the more powerful WTO members who have won a WTO ruling against them.

The influence of multinational companies on devising the current trade rules at the WTO arouses strong emotions. Many would like to see an end to a system in which trade rules are set after discussions between government trade representatives and the government relations representatives of multinational companies. Trade rules are widely held to have been set to the advantage of the business community, restricting the capacities of national governments to make their own trade-related decisions. Such cross-border and internally invasive intervention has been an important source of public disenchantment with the WTO and similar bodies.

The anti-capitalist protests have significantly changed the dynamic of the trade negotiations. The conventional wisdom that 'trade is good for the poor, it makes people richer – and hence improves the environment' is now being openly challenged. Whilst more trade may very well benefit higher-income groups in many countries, in some cases it would seem to have had negative effects on low-income groups in both developed and developing countries. For example, the sustained decline in commodity prices to their lowest levels in the post-war period has further eroded the incomes of the poor in many developing countries. However, many believe that the reform, not the abandonment, of institutions such as the WTO may be in the ultimate interests of the world's poor, in other words the essential maintenance of an 'open' world trading system with institutional support to prevent its worst excesses.

It is argued by those who support reform of existing multilateral institutions that market-led growth is the most effective weapon against poverty available. The only alternative to growth must be redistribution from the rich of the world. In 2002, according to the World Bank, average world income per head was US $5,140 (World Development Report 2002). The 885m inhabitants of high-income countries had average real incomes per head of $26,710, while the 3.5bn people in the low-income countries had average incomes of only $430 and in the lower-middle income countries of only $1,850. Put another way, the average income in the richest 20 countries in 2003 is now 37 times that in the poorest 20. This ratio has doubled in the past 40 years, mainly because of the lack of growth in the poorest countries. In fact around 3 billion people now live on less than $2 a day and around 1.2 billion people live on less than $1 a day.

The scale of the global redistribution of incomes needed to seriously redress these inequalities is, in the view of many, wholly impractical. With such global redistribution ruled out, only events within individual developing countries can eliminate mass poverty. Here the evidence is clear for two propositions: first, sustained growth raises the real incomes of the poor; second, intelligent exploitation of opportunities in the world economy contributes mightily to growth. On the first of these, two World Bank economists, David Dollar and Aart Kraay, provide what appears to be strong supporting evidence (Dollar and Kraay 2000). Using a sample of 80 countries over four decades, and defining the poor as those in the bottom fifth of the income distribution, they reach the following four conclusions:

1 The incomes of the poor tend to rise in the same proportion as those of the population as a whole.

2 The effect of growth on the incomes of the poor is the same as in rich countries.

3 The incomes of the poor do not fall disproportionately during economic crises.

4 The relationship between poverty reduction and growth has not changed in the era of globalization.

None of this should be controversial. We know that the bulk of the world's destitute live in the world's poorest countries: more than two-thirds of those living on less than a dollar a day live in south Asia and sub-Saharan Africa. We know, too, that the biggest reductions in mass poverty have occurred where there has been the fastest growth: in East Asia.

The paper by Dollar and Kraay also indicates that the policies economists would recommend for improving growth performance also help the poor. High inflation is bad for overall growth and particularly harmful to the poor; and an effective rule of law is good both for average incomes and for the poor. None of this should be seen as mere 'trickle-down' economics: macroeconomic stability and honest law enforcement directly benefit many of the poorest people. It would be strange to suggest otherwise.

Turn then to the second proposition: the role of increased openness to trade. The paper by Dollar and Kraay concludes that this raises average incomes. They also conclude, contrary to much of the conventional wisdom, that there is no relationship between increased openness to trade and rising inequality. Trade raises average incomes and the incomes of the poor in roughly equal proportions.

That open economies tend to grow faster than closed ones is consistent with a range of empirical studies. To take just one example, Sebastian Edwards of the University of California at Los Angeles concluded in a study of 93 countries that there is a close link between openness and rates of productivity growth (Edwards 1997). The latter is the most important determinant of long-term growth.

We conclude with a brief review of the one nation which, more than any other, is perceived as the driving force behind, and major beneficiary of, globalization, namely the United States.

The United States and globalization

Although the United States is less dependent in trade terms on the global economy than many believe, its influence is felt everywhere. The US has a population of 287,400,000, which is smaller than the EU's single market, but it has a huge land area (9,158,960 square kilometres) which is very resource rich with plentiful supplies of water, timber, coal, iron ore, oil, gas, copper, bauxite, lead, silver, zinc, mercury and phosphates, amongst others. Given the abundance of these resources, the United States was for many years self-sufficient with little need to import. However, a recurring problem has been the country's relatively low population density so that, despite its huge potential in natural resources, it has had a scarce labour supply which has made full exploitation of those resources rather difficult. For much of the nineteenth century and even in the early twentieth century, the United States was largely disengaged from the global

marketplace in terms of imports and exports. Even in the 1960s, imports and exports *combined* amounted to barely 10% of GDP. Nowadays things have changed. Today America exports around 13% of its GDP, with almost 30% of all the wealth generated in the United States (more than \$2 trillion) coming from trade.

The United States' increased role in the globalization process essentially has two strands which, while interconnected, remain distinct. The first of these strands relates to a number of happy accidents that drew a reluctant America into increased involvement in international affairs which, combined with pragmatic domestic policies, allowed it to benefit fully from that involvement. The second of these strands involves the notion of the dynamism of American culture and the endurance of the 'American dream' which in turn have given rise to the perception of US dominance in the global economy.

US international engagement

During the nineteenth century, and particularly after the American Civil War (1861–65), the American economy grew rapidly, spurred on by the advent of the railways which made development of the western territories more viable. Even more striking, however, was the growth of America's economic influence abroad. From the 1870s onward, American farmers in the midwest exported grain and meat, as improved transport links and refrigeration lowered transport costs. America began to eclipse the major European countries as a manufacturing nation, and as a producer of raw materials such as coal, iron and steel. By 1914 America was producing nearly five times as much steel as Britain and more than twice as much as the German Empire.

With a smaller population in a pre-consumer society, the United States was able to almost completely isolate itself from the rest of the world, and thanks to a highly protectionist trade policy, its imports were minimal. However, vast amounts of European, and especially British, portfolio investment had flooded into the United States to finance economic development in the late nineteenth and early twentieth centuries. By the end of World War I, with Europe an economic wreck, the allies had borrowed such large sums from American bankers that Wall Street had become the world's financial centre, and

America had become the world's largest international creditor. Under the presidency of Woodrow Wilson (1913–21) the United States took its first tentative steps towards freer international trade, but such steps were not long lasting or indeed very forthright.

The 1920s saw unprecedented growth in the American economy as the consumer age really began. Fostered by the loose regulation and pro-business framework of the classical *laissez-faire* economic policies of the government, and largely free from foreign competition due to its extensive tariff barriers, American business grew rapidly. As the population expanded so did the markets available for these firms, and developments in technology allowed for vastly increased output at lower costs.

World War II served as a kick-start for the United States to engage with the global economy, and is one of the happy accidents mentioned earlier. More activist government policies brought about by the war effort helped to start a number of virtuous circles whose effects lasted many decades. For example, the strong American presence in the world aircraft industry today came about because of the increased demand for aircraft that arose from the needs of the US military during World War II. Having thus acquired a dominant position in the aircraft industry during the war, the United States now had a large pool of workers and engineers with the skills required, and was thereby well positioned to maintain its competitive advantage. Even though the initial war trigger is long gone, the dominant position of the US aircraft industry endures. To varying degrees, the same can be said about other industries, ranging from space technology, through defence, and on to consumer goods. In summary, by the end of World War II, the United States was in an excellent position to head into the post-war period. Its industrial base was large and diverse, its technology was superior, and a number of virtuous circles had developed.

US cultural dominance

The move into the global arena was aided by the widespread perception in the 1950s and 1960s that American culture was dynamic and worthy of emulation. The fact that the United States was an English-speaking country, and English is the language of international business and commerce, also helped smooth such cultural transmission. In a time of rising prosperity and optimism about the future, the American dream seemed available to all. The growth of American firms in the consumer goods and leisure industries coincided with an increased demand for these outputs within the more affluent societies. American culture began to permeate Western Europe, driving demand further, and thus ensuring business for American firms, whether located in Europe or supplied from the US.

In the post-war period, the United States became a champion of free trade, reversing the policy plank that had been present since the early days of the union. It was a founder member of the General Agreement on Tariffs and Trade (GATT) in 1947 which sought to break down barriers to trade, especially trade in manufactures. Having developed strong and competitive industries in the US, being home to major financial centres in New York and Chicago, and finding itself drawn more into the global arena than previously, the aim was to increase its access to foreign markets. As the domestic economy developed and became ever more consumer orientated, America found itself constrained in exploiting its resources fully due to insufficient labour supply. Paradoxically for a country that, in theory, did not need to trade internationally, the ever-increasing demand from rising prosperity at home forced America to import, and the hungry ambitions of American business sought new markets outside America.

Modern American trade policy, particularly in the post-cold war period, has focused on locking the United States into each significant region of economic development. Under Presidents George H.W. Bush (1989–93), Bill Clinton (1993–2001) and George W. Bush (since 2001), the United States primarily favoured a regional and bilateral thrust to trade policy, although remaining a member of the World Trade Organization (WTO). American involvement in the APEC agreement (1993), the creation of the North American Free Trade Agreement (NAFTA) (1994), the signing of the Transatlantic Pact between the United States and the EU (1995), and the current development of the Free Trade Area of the Americas (FTAA) have all cemented the American position in the global economy. However, they mark a subtle change in what had occurred previously. The new regionalist approach to trade policy exchanges access to the American market for reciprocal access to foreign markets. It uses the power of the United

States, and the allure of its domestic economy, to force open foreign markets that otherwise may have remained closed. It also ensures that very little now goes on in the global economy without US involvement.

In the realm of international financial markets, American practices are now more widespread than in previous generations. As American financial service providers have traditionally been better financed than their British counterparts, with a work ethic less genteel and less based on historical precedents, it was much easier for them to attract the best staff and be more competitive in the European financial markets. In the 1980s, when American financial service providers arrived to do business in the City of London, they found that the London markets functioned like a gentlemen's club, with short working weeks, long lunches and a sense of tradition. The faster-paced 'greed is good' ethic of the American markets swept away much of the old city practices very rapidly, as the traditional British financial markets found that their quaint ideals, smaller capital base, and respect for tradition were no match for the flash young traders from America who worked through lunch breaks and often on into the evening in search of the lucrative bonuses. Nowadays American financial service providers are everywhere, and the culture they brought with them has displaced much indigenous financial culture.

Globalization has resulted in challenges for the United States too. In spite of the advantages it possesses, whether by virtue of natural resources, language, culture, government policy or serendipity, the move into the global market has not been without problems. Perhaps the most obvious problem has involved the trade deficits that opened up quite rapidly between 1981 and 1984. Although America had run deficits before, the deficits of the 1980s appeared year-on-year, and were much larger than any previously experienced. In part, the trade deficits were the result of the budget deficits resulting from Ronald Reagan's tax-cutting agenda. National savings fell, and capital had to be imported to finance domestic American investment. The American position as the world's largest international creditor disappeared, indeed America became the world's largest net debtor. During the 1980s, the American trade deficit was financed by the sale of American assets, including shares, bonds, real estate and eventually entire companies. There are those in America who saw this financing of the deficit as giving away the foundations of the American economy to foreigners and resulting in a loss of American economic sovereignty. The major budget and trade deficits of George Bush junior have reawakened such concerns.

Many in the United States, on both sides of the political divide, question the benefits from being involved in globalization. Some argue, for example, that the freer world trade arising from GATT/WTO and the patchwork of bilateral and regional deals negotiated by the United States has left the American worker dangerously exposed to lower wage competition from the economies of Latin America and the Asia Pacific rim. As the MNEs source labour and raw materials from whichever locations are cheapest, they now produce much of their output from outside the United States but can then sell within the American market without paying high import tariffs. They no longer employ as many American workers, or invest as much in the United States. This argument, known as the 'pauper labour argument', implies that American workers will lose out in terms of employment, pay and working conditions from the inexorable process of globalized world production.

There is also concern that in an era of global markets, where production occurs in many locations which are likely to be different from those in which the goods are sold, firms that began life as 'American' now see themselves in a different light, namely as global companies rather than national ones. It used to be said that what was good for General Motors was good for America, but if ideas such as the pauper labour argument are valid, then this is less likely to be the case now.

Again some argue that, given the size and wealth of the American market, the United States should once again be protectionist, as foreign firms would be willing to pay more in the form of tariffs for access to its huge, high-income market. They also suggest that since much of global trade is *intra-industry trade*, with parts made in a number of countries for assembly in the United States, such tariffs would make it less cost-efficient for firms to source their components outside America, and thereby encouraging productive capacity to return to America.

We might conclude that for the reluctant globalists of the United States, globalization has been remarkably successful. However, disadvantages have also been recognized, as with President Clinton's attempting to equip the American workforce to take full advantage of the opportunities resulting from intensi-fied global competition. His attempts to overhaul health care, education and job training, and bring about an improvement in skills, were aimed at raising American productivity and lowering business costs. In practice US success in promoting free trade has arguably intensified the pressure on lower-skilled Americans, whilst offering them little defence from an ever intensifying global competition in the future.

Conclusion

Globalization is more widely viewed as a process rather than an end-state, in terms of our earlier frame-work, conforming more closely to the perspective of 'transformationalists' rather than 'hyperglobalists'. That said, it is characterized by major changes occur-ring in at least four broad areas, namely new markets, new actors, new rules and norms, and new methods of communications. Quantitative and qualitative changes in these areas are arguably having major impacts in shaping corporate strategies and influenc-ing the lives of employees and individuals worldwide. Nor can we confine these impacts to the economic sphere alone, important though that undoubtedly is. The greater difficulties faced by nation states in com-bating global forces extend to the security and health-related domains, as much as the economic. At the macro level, policy responses have often involved a resort to more multilateral institutions and arrange-ments, including regional trading blocs, in an attempt to employ more effective collective influence where national influence is perceived to be lessening. At the micro level, the wide range of firm strategies (e.g. Porter's Five Forces) thought appropriate when industry structures were stable and predictable, at both national and institutional levels, are now being challenged and reshaped in the 'discontinuous com-petitive landscape' more typical of a globalized busi-ness environment.

Of course the debate as to the costs and benefits of globalization, however defined, continues apace. Supporters of the development of advanced business capitalism since the early nineteenth century point to the remarkable growth in living standards achieved. For example, in the eight centuries from 1000 to 1820 per capita incomes in Western Europe rose by 0.15% per year on average, but by 1.5% per year on average since then – 10 times as fast (Elliott 2002). On the other hand anti-globalization protesters point to the gross inequalities between rich and poor, such inequalities buttressed by the prevailing rules and norms governing the actions of an institutional super-structure (IMF, World Bank, G7/G8, WTO, etc.) which is allegedly biased against the disadvantaged.

Key points

- Shrinking space, shrinking time and dis-appearing borders are widely accepted features of globalization, however defined.

- 'Hyperglobalists' and others see global-ization as an end-state characterized by global governance, global capitalism (dominated by multinational enterprises) and rapidly eroding nation states.

- 'Transformationalists' and others see globalization as consisting of a complex set of intermittent, uneven processes linked to rapidly increasing levels of global interconnectedness. Whilst no single end-state is predictable, corporate, national and individual destinies will be reshaped by these globalization processes.

- These globalization processes are leading to new markets, new actors, new rules and norms, and new methods of commu-nication.

- In a progressively less stable environ-ment, there will arguably be a shift away from the previous strategic focus of Porter and his contemporaries in which companies seek to identify and exploit competitive advantages within stable industrial structures.

- In the new, globalized landscape the strategic focus shifts to the stretching and shaping of industrial structures by the MNEs themselves, using their own strategic initiatives.

■ Globalization is redefining our understanding of the nation state by introducing a much more complex architecture of political power in which authority is seen as being pluralistic (e.g. intergovernmental and non-governmental organizations) rather than residing solely in the nation state.

■ The growth of knowledge-based economies dominated by the creation,

processing and dissemination of information is seen by some as synonymous with globalization.

■ Globalization is a multi-dimensional process, reshaping the context of security, health control and other governmental policies just as much as their economic policies.

■ The USA, whilst seen as the major driver of, and beneficiary from, globalization, has in many respects been a reluctant participant in that process.

Now try the self-check questions for this chapter on the Companion Website. You will also find up-to-date facts and case materials.

References and further reading

Barro, R. (1991) Economic growth in a cross-section of countries, *Quarterly Journal of Economics*, 106(20): 407–43.

Bell, D. (1973) *The Coming of Post-Industrial Society*, Basic Books, New York.

Buchanan, P. (1998) *The Great Betrayal: How American sovereignty and social justice are being sacrificed to the gods of the global economy*, Little, Brown, New York.

Claugue, C., Keefer, P., Knack, S. and Olson, M. (1999) Contract-intensive money: contract enforcement, property rights and economic performances, *Journal of Economic Growth*, 4: 185–211.

Dickens, P. (2003) *Global Shift: Reshaping the global economic map in the 21st century*, 4th edn, Sage Publications.

Dollar, D. and Kraay, A. (2000) Growth is good for the poor, *World Bank unpublished paper*, March.

Duignan, P. and Gann, L. H. (1994) *The USA and the New Europe 1945–1993*, Blackwell, Cambridge, MA.

Edwards, S. (1997) Openness, productivity and growth: What do we really know?, National Bureau of Economic Research, www.nber.org

Elliott, L. (2002) Big business isn't really that big, *Guardian*, 2 September.

French, M. (1997) *US Economic History since 1945*, Manchester University Press.

Gershuny, J. (1978) *After Industrial Society? The emerging self-service economy*, Brill Academic Publishers.

Giddens, A. (1990) *The Consequences of Modernity*, Polity Press, Cambridge.

Held, D., McGrew, A., Goldblatt, D. and Perraton, J. (1999) *Global Transformations: Politics, economics and culture*, Polity Press, Cambridge.

Kaletsky, A. (2002) If leaders persist with failed economic policy they will be doing Bin Laden's work for him, *The Times*, 10 September.

Kobrin, S. J. (1994) Is there a relationship between a geocentric mind-set and multinational strategy?, *Journal of International Business Studies*, 3: 493–511.

Krugman, P. (1994) *Peddling Prosperity: Economic sense and nonsense in the age of diminished expectations*, Norton, New York.

Krugman, P. (1998) *The Age of Diminished Expectations*, MIT Press, Cambridge, MA.

Lipsey, R. E. (1999) The location and characteristics of US affiliates in Asia, *NBER Working Paper*, National Bureau of Economic Research, Cambridge, MA.

Machlup, F. (1962) *The Production and Distribution of Knowledge in the United States*, Princeton University Press, Princeton, NJ.

McGrew, A. (1992) A global society, in *Modernity and its Futures*, S. Hall, D. Held and A. McGrew (eds), Open University Press, Milton Keynes.

Morrison, J. (2002) *The International Business Environment: Diversity and the global economy*, Palgrave Macmillan, New York.

Prahalad, C. K. (2000) *Mastering Strategy*, Financial Times/Prentice Hall, London.

Price, D. de Solla (1961) *Science since Babylon*, Yale University Press, New Haven, CT.

Rescher, D. (1978) *Scientific Progress. A philosophical essay on the economics of research in natural science*, Basil Blackwell, Oxford.

Rider, M. (1944) Growth of knowledge, in *Science since Babylon*, D. de Solla Price (ed.), Yale University Press, New Haven, CT.

Spulber, N. (1995) *The American Economy: The struggle for supremacy in the 21st century*, Cambridge University Press.

UNCTAD (1999) *World Investment Report*, United Nations Conference on Trade and Development, New York and Geneva.

UNCTAD (2002) *World Investment Report*, United Nations Conference on Trade and Development, New York and Geneva.

Walker, D. (2001) Global's good side, *Guardian*, 2 May.

Wallsten, S. (2001) Ringing in the 20th century, *World Bank Research Working Paper*, World Bank, Washington, DC.

World Bank (1997) Trade development and poverty reduction, www.worldbank.org/devcom

World Bank (2003) *Global Economic Prospects*, World Bank, Washington, DC.

World Development Reports (various) World Bank, Washington, DC.

World Economic Outlook (2001) *The Information Technology Revolution*, International Monetary Fund, October.

World Employment Report (2001) *Life at Work in the Information Economy*, International Labour Office, Geneva.

World Investment Reports (various) United Nations Conference on Trade and Development, New York and Geneva.

Zak, P. (2001) Institutions, property rights and growth, *Gruter Institute Working Papers*, **2**(1): Article 2.

Chapter 26 Exchange rates

The exchange rate is the price of one currency in terms of another. The exchange rate for sterling is conventionally defined as the number of units of another currency, such as the dollar, that it takes to purchase one pound sterling on the foreign exchange market. In the market, however, it is usually quoted as the number of units of the domestic currency that it takes to purchase one unit of foreign currency. In general terms the sterling exchange rate is perhaps the most important 'price' in the UK economic system. It affects the standard of living, because it determines how many goods we can get for what we sell abroad. It influences the price of UK exports and hence their sales, thereby determining output and jobs in the export industries. It structures the extent to which imports can compete with home-produced goods, and thereby affects the viability of UK companies. Because the price of imports enters into the RPI, any variation in the exchange rate will have an effect on the rate of inflation. This chapter will consider these various issues. Chapters 20 and 29 provide additional insights into the role of exchange rate systems in general. These chapters will also consider the UK's specific experience both inside and outside the Exchange Rate Mechanism (ERM), together with the likely impacts of membership of the euro area. The chapter concludes by reviewing the operation, over time, of various exchange rate regimes, such as the gold standard, the 'adjustable-peg' exchange rate system, and freely floating exchange rates.

The foreign exchange market

The foreign exchange market is the money market on which international currencies are traded. It has no physical existence: it consists of traders, such as the dealing rooms of major banks, who are in continual communication with one another on a worldwide basis. Currencies are bought and sold on behalf of clients, who may be companies, private individuals, or banks themselves. A distinction is made between the 'spot' rate for a currency, and the forward rate. The spot rate is the domestic currency price of a unit of foreign exchange when the transaction is to be completed within three days. The forward rate is the price of that unit when delivery is to take place at some future date – usually 30, 60 or 90 days hence. Both spot and forward rates are determined in today's market; the relationship between today's spot and today's forward rate will be determined largely by how the market *expects* the spot rate to move in the near future. The more efficient the market is at anticipating future spot rates, the closer will today's forward rate be to the future spot rate.

The spot market is used by those who wish to acquire foreign exchange straightaway. Forward markets are used by three groups of people.

- Firstly, there are those who wish to cover themselves (*hedge*) against the risk of exchange rate variation. For instance, suppose an importer orders goods to be paid for in three months' time in dollars. All his calculations will be upset if the price of dollars rises between now and payment date. He can cover himself by buying dollars today for delivery in three months' time; he thus locks himself into a rate which reduces the risk element in his transaction.

- Secondly, there are *arbitrageurs* who attempt to make a profit on the difference between interest rates in one country and another, and who buy or sell currency forward to ensure that the profit which they hope to make by moving their capital is not negated by adverse exchange rate movements.

- Thirdly, there are straightforward *speculators* who use the forward markets to buy or sell in anticipation of exchange rate changes. For instance, if I think that today's forward rates do not adequately reflect the probability of the dollar increasing in value, I will buy dollars forward, hoping to sell them at a profit when they are delivered to me at some future date.

London is the world's largest centre for foreign exchange trading, with an average daily turnover of over US $900 billion. The market is growing all the time; indeed the average daily turnover in 2003 was more than double the value recorded in 1993. Some 64% of transactions are 'spot' on any one day, 24% are forward for periods not exceeding one month, and 10% are forward for longer than one month. Increasingly, however, more sophisticated types of transactions are being done. For instance, there is a growth in the following types of transactions:

1 foreign currency options, which give the right (but do not impose an obligation) to buy or sell currencies at some future date and price;

2 foreign currency futures, which are standardized contracts to buy or sell on agreed terms on specific future dates; and

3 foreign currency swaps – spot purchases against outright forward currency sales.

Foreign exchange market business in London is done in an increasingly wide variety of currencies: for example, £/$ business now accounts for only 11% of activity. However, trading transactions which do not involve the US dollar are becoming increasingly frequent.

Supply and demand for a currency

Prices of currencies are determined, as on any other market, by supply of and demand for the various currencies. Businessmen wishing to import goods will sell sterling in order to buy currency with which to pay the supplier in another country. Tourists coming to the UK will sell their own currency in order to buy sterling. Other types of transactions, too, will have exchange rate repercussions. For instance, if a German company wishes to buy a factory in the UK it will need to convert euros into sterling, as will foreign banks who wish to make sterling deposits in London, or residents abroad who wish to buy UK government bonds.

Another way of saying this is that in any given period of time the factors which determine the demand and supply for foreign exchange are those which are represented in the balance of payments account. The demand for foreign exchange arises as a result of imports of goods and services, outflows of UK capital in the form of overseas investment (short and long term), and financial transactions by banks on behalf of their clients. The supply of foreign exchange comes as a result of the export of goods and services, inflows of foreign capital and bank transactions.

It is clear from the balance of payments accounts that companies and individuals are not the only clients of foreign exchange market dealers. The Bank of England also buys and sells foreign currency, using the official reserves in the Exchange Equalization Account. In order to reflect on why this might be the case we have to remember that governments have an interest in the level of the exchange rate, and that they may on occasion wish to intervene in the workings of the foreign exchange market to affect the value of sterling. Indeed, it was estimated that on the day sterling was forced to withdraw from the Exchange Rate Mechanism (16 September 1992), the Bank of England spent an estimated £7bn, roughly a third of its foreign exchange reserves, in buying sterling. In particular it bought sterling with Deutsche Marks in an unsuccessful attempt to preserve the sterling exchange rate within its permitted ERM band.

Historically the policy stance on this has varied. As we note later in the chapter, it was only after the Second World War that foreign exchange markets began to function freely on a worldwide basis. Governments then had the option of allowing exchange rates to be market-determined, i.e. to 'float', or to establish some kind of fixed exchange rate system. The decision was taken at Bretton Woods in 1945 to adopt a fixed exchange rate regime; governments thus committed themselves to continual intervention in the market in order to offset imbalances in the demand and supply for their currencies. The Bretton Woods agreement collapsed in 1972, since when currencies have been allowed to float. However, the European Exchange Rate Mechanism (ERM) was established in 1979 to restrict the range within which member currencies could float against each other (see Chapter 29), with the ERM eventually leading to the establishment of the euro as the single currency. For a variety of reasons governments continue to 'manage' the floating exchange rate system by intervening in the foreign exchange market. In the UK the Bank of England deals in this market in order to smooth out short-term fluctuations in the value of

sterling as well as to influence the exchange rate as part of its overall economic strategy. However, intervention in the market alone is insufficient to affect the sterling exchange rate, simply because the size of speculative trading on the world's foreign exchange markets dwarfs the size of any one country's official reserves. For instance, it has been estimated that daily dealings in the foreign exchange markets totalled around $1,000bn, whereas the reserves of the six leading ERM nations in September 1992 totalled only some $250bn. Governments must therefore attempt to increase the demand for their currencies by, for instance, attracting flows of short or longer-term investment from abroad by means of high interest rates.

We have argued that in everyday terms currency prices are determined by demand and supply on the foreign exchange markets. We must now examine in more detail the forces determining any given exchange rate in the short and long term. As we shall see, all the various theoretical explanations focus on the importance of one or other of the variables contained within the balance of payments accounts. The theories vary only in the time perspective considered. The function of theory is to explain and predict; we shall consider later to what extent recent experience in the UK validates the different theoretical arguments.

Exchange rate definitions

Before we do this, however, we must consider what we mean by 'the exchange rate'. In a foreign exchange market where exchange rates are allowed to 'float', every currency has a price against every other currency. In order to allow for measurability, economists use three separate concepts:

1 *The nominal rate of exchange.* This is the rate of exchange for any one currency as quoted against any other currency. The nominal exchange rate is therefore a bilateral (two-country) exchange rate.

2 *The effective exchange rate (EER).* This is a measure which takes into account the fact that sterling varies differently against each of the other currencies. It is calculated as a weighted average of the individual or bilateral rates, and is expressed as

an index number relative to the base year. The weights are chosen to reflect the importance of other currencies in manufacturing trade with the UK. The EER is therefore a *multilateral* (many-country) exchange rate.

3 *The real exchange rate (RER)*. This concept is designed to measure the rate at which home goods exchange for goods from other countries, rather than the rate at which the currencies themselves are traded. It is thus essentially a measure of competitiveness. When we consider *multilateral* UK trade, it is defined as:

$$RER = EER \times P(UK)/P(F)$$

In other words, the real exchange rate is equal to the effective exchange rate multiplied by the price ratio of home, $P(UK)$, to foreign, $P(F)$, goods. If UK prices rise the real exchange rate will rise unless the effective exchange rate falls. We consider below the question of how one might measure this definition empirically.

Table 26.1 outlines the *nominal rate of exchange* for sterling against a variety of other currencies (columns 1 to 5) and the overall *effective exchange rate* (EER) against a 'basket' of other currencies (column 6). Of course, from 1 January 1999 onwards the French franc, German mark and Italian lira were

Table 26.1 Sterling exchange rates, 1980–2003.

	US dollar 1	French franc 2	Japanese yen 3	German mark 4	Italian lira 5	Sterling effective exchange rate (1990 = 100) 6	Euro	Consumer prices (1990 = 100) UK	US
1980	2.33	9.83	526	4.23	1992	128.1		53.0	63.1
1981	2.03	10.94	445	4.56	2287	129.8		59.3	69.7
1982	1.75	11.48	435	4.24	2364	124.4		64.4	73.9
1983	1.52	11.55	360	3.87	2302	114.1		67.3	76.3
1984	1.34	11.63	317	3.79	2339	109.8		70.7	79.6
1985	1.30	11.55	307	3.78	2463	109.4		75.0	82.4
1986	1.47	10.16	247	3.18	2186	100.2		77.5	83.9
1987	1.64	9.84	237	2.94	2123	99.2		80.7	87.1
1988	1.78	10.60	228	3.12	2315	105.3		84.7	90.5
1989	1.64	10.45	226	3.08	2247	102.3		91.3	94.9
1990	1.79	9.69	257	2.88	2133	100.0		100.0	100.0
1991	1.77	9.95	238	2.93	2187	100.7		105.9	104.2
1992	1.76	9.33	224	2.76	2163	96.9		109.8	107.4
1993	1.50	8.50	167	2.48	2310	88.9		111.5	110.6
1994	1.53	8.48	156	2.48	2467	89.2		114.3	113.4
1995	1.58	7.87	148	2.26	2571	84.8		118.2	116.6
1996	1.56	7.98	170	2.35	2408	86.3	1.21	121.1	120.0
1997	1.64	9.56	198	2.84	2789	100.6	1.45	124.9	122.9
1998	1.66	9.77	217	2.97	2925	105.3	1.49	129.1	124.4
1999	1.62	–	184	–	–	103.8	1.52	131.2	127.6
2000	1.52	–	163	–	–	107.5	1.64	133.1	131.1
2001	1.44	–	175	–	–	105.8	1.61	136.0	134.2
2002	1.50	–	188	–	–	106.0	1.59	139.0	137.3
2003*	1.62	–	189	–	–	102.4	1.40	141.1	138.4

*End 2nd quarter.
Source: *Economic Trends* (various).

replaced by the euro. It may be useful to conduct our discussion of Table 26.1 in terms of two time periods: 1980–98 and from 1 January 1999 to the present day.

1980 to end 1998

We can see that the £ sterling fell in terms of its *nominal exchange rate* against all the individual currencies over much of the period 1980–98, though rising in the latter years from 1996 onwards. A fall in these nominal exchange rates for sterling made UK exports to these countries cheaper (in the foreign currency) and imports dearer (in sterling). For example, in 1980 an American resident would have had to give up $2.33 for each pound, whereas by 1998 he or she would have needed to give up only $1.66 for each pound. British goods would therefore have cost less in dollar terms in 1998 than in 1980.

Of course our trade with America is only part of our external transactions. The sterling *effective exchange rate* (EER) was, until 1998, a weighted average of 16 major national currencies, the weights depending on the relative importance of UK trade with each country. The dollar, mark, franc and yen had the greatest weights at 21%, 20%, 12% and 9% respectively. The effective exchange rate is calculated as an index with 1990 = 100, and Table 26.1 suggests that the pound in 1998 was worth, *overall*, some four-fifths of its value in 1980.

The fall in both nominal and effective exchange rates for sterling meant that it cost less to purchase each £1 worth of UK goods abroad in 1998 than it did in 1980. Did this then mean that UK goods had become more competitive on world markets? Of course the answer depends not only on changes in the exchange rate but on relative inflation rates between the UK and the countries with which we are comparing it. In other words, we must examine the *real exchange rate*.

Returning again to the *bilateral* exchange rate between sterling and the US dollar, we can now investigate the *real exchange rate* between the two currencies from 1980 to 1998. As we can see from Table 26.1, although the nominal (bilateral) exchange rate between sterling and US dollar fell substantially over the period, consumer price inflation was higher in the UK than in the US.

Using the information in Table 26.1 on nominal exchange rates and UK/US consumer prices, we can work out the real exchange rates between pound sterling and US dollar for 1980 and 1998.

Real exchange rate =

$$\frac{\text{nominal £/\$}}{\text{exchange rate}} \times \frac{\text{price index of UK goods in £}}{\text{price index of US goods in \$}}$$

$$\text{Real exchange rate (1980)} = 2.33 \times \frac{53.0}{63.1} = 1.96$$

$$\text{Real exchange rate (1998)} = 1.66 \times \frac{129.1}{124.4}$$

$$= 1.72$$

The fall in the real exchange rate ($/£) from 1.96 in 1980 to 1.72 in 1998 clearly indicates that by 1998 fewer dollars needed to be exchanged for each £1 worth of UK goods bought in the US. Although inflation was higher in the UK than in the US over the period, the fall in the nominal sterling exchange rate against the US dollar *more than offset* the higher UK inflation. However, sterling depreciated against the dollar only by some 12.2% $\left(\frac{0.24}{1.96} \times 100\right)$ over the period using *real* exchange rates, but by 28.8% $\left(\frac{0.67}{2.33} \times 100\right)$ using *nominal* exchange rates. In other words, the loss of competitiveness because of higher UK inflation eroded *some* of the exchange rate gains between UK and US producers, though these still remained substantial.

1 January 1999 onwards

This analysis of the fall in sterling exchange rates helping to improve the UK's international competitiveness holds true over much of the period 1980–98. However, there has been a sharp upward revision since 1996 in nominal sterling exchange rates against individual countries and against the euro (i.e. resulting in a sharp upward revision in the sterling effective exchange rate). This appreciation of sterling has led to a sharp *deterioration* in the UK's international competitiveness since 1996, making UK exports dearer overseas and imports into the UK cheaper (see Chapter 1). For example, the sterling effective exchange rate rose as an index from 86.3 to 106.0 (1990 = 100) between 1996 and 2002, a rise of over 22%. A lower price inflation in the UK than in its competitors would help modify any loss of competitiveness, resulting in a smaller rise in terms of *real* sterling exchange rates. However, Table 26.1 provides no evidence of a lower price inflation for the UK against the US during this period. Euro zone countries have also experienced rates of price inflation at least as low as those recorded in the UK. In other words the appreciation of sterling since 1996 has indeed resulted in a loss of UK competitiveness against many of its trading partners.

However, in 2003 the sterling effective exchange rate has fallen sharply in value against the euro, though appreciating against the fast falling US dollar. This means that UK exports into euro area countries are becoming progressively cheaper in those markets, with imports from euro area countries becoming progressively more expensive. Given that some 60% of UK goods exports are destined for euro area countries and around 55% of UK goods imports come from euro area countries, this can only be a major boost for UK competitiveness *vis-à-vis* those countries. However the appreciating pound against the dollar will have the opposite effect for the much smaller value of UK trade with the USA (see Chapter 27). The US dollar has fallen even more substantially in recent times against the euro, helping US trade prospects with euro area countries but creating further problems for the already low growth euro area economies as their exports become more expensive in the US and imports from the US become cheaper.

Exchange rate determination

We can distinguish four theoretical approaches to exchange rate determination. It must be emphasized that these are in no sense 'competing' theories. They are simply different ways of looking at what determines the exchange rate, depending on whether we are interested in the short run or the long run, in immediate or more fundamental determinants, and on what we consider to be the most empirically relevant factors at any given time.

Exchange rates and the balance of trade

The *traditional* approach sees the exchange rate simply as the price which brings into equilibrium the supply and demand for currency arising from trade in

goods and services and from capital transactions, as explained above. This approach was formulated in the 1950s when capital flows were small in relation to trade flows, and hence its major use is to illustrate the interrelationship between current account flows and exchange rate changes. Nevertheless, it can also accommodate capital account transactions. It is essentially a perspective which concentrates on short-run influences.

Figure 26.1 shows that the demand for pounds will increase as the price falls. This is because customers abroad will perceive that the price of UK exports has fallen in their own currency as sterling depreciates, increasing their demand for UK exports and therefore for pounds with which to buy them. The supply of pounds will rise as the price of sterling rises because the price of imports in sterling falls as the pound strengthens. With cheaper imports, UK consumers now buy more imported items and firms exchange more pounds in order to buy these imports.[1]

Demand and supply curves can shift for a number of reasons. A shift (increase) in supply from S to S_1 might be due to a change in tastes in favour of foreign goods. A shift (decrease) in demand from D to D_1 might occur because UK interest rates had fallen, leading to a decrease in the demand for pounds as investors switch their funds out of the UK money markets. In either of these cases there will be a fall in the exchange rate below its original level, P. In a floating exchange rate system the rate will be allowed to fall. Should the monetary authorities wish to keep

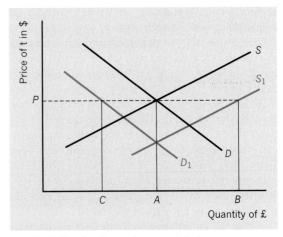

Fig. 26.1 The foreign exchange market.

the exchange rate at its original level they will be obliged to buy sterling. If the supply of sterling increases to S_1 they will buy up the excess quantity AB; if the demand for sterling has fallen to D_1 they will make up the shortfall by buying up quantity CA. In either case the price reverts to its original level.

This view of exchange rate determination predicts that the exchange rate will alter in response to macro-economic policy, because the demand for imports (and hence the supply of pounds) will depend in part on the level of income. Fiscal policy will thus affect the exchange rate. It also regards short-term capital flows (and hence both demand and supply of pounds) as being sensitive to interest rate changes. Both fiscal and monetary policy will therefore have exchange rate repercussions. Expansionary policies, whether fiscal or monetary, which raise levels of income and employment will cause the S curve to shift to S_1, as imports rise with income. Such policies will cause a balance of payments deficit and a fall in the exchange rate. The converse will be the case when policies are contractionary. In addition, in so far as fiscal and monetary policies alter interest rates in a downward direction (if, for instance, the PSBR is reduced so that fewer bonds need to be issued, bond prices rise and yields fall, or interest rates are reduced directly by the monetary authorities), capital outflows will be triggered – S will move to S_1 as people move their money out of UK financial markets; at the same time D will fall to D_1 as investment in UK money markets is no longer forthcoming.

What this model does not enable us to do is to predict the overall effect of any given policy stance. In the case of an *expansionary monetary policy* spending will increase and interest rates will fall, the supply of pounds will increase in both cases and the exchange rate will fall. But in the case of an *expansionary fiscal policy*, expansion may be associated with an increase in government borrowing, which will lead to a fall in bond prices (as the supply of bonds increases) and a rise in the interest rate. The effect on the exchange rate will then be ambiguous, depending on the marginal propensity to import from a rise in income in relation to the interest elasticity of capital flows.

Marshall–Lerner elasticity condition

We have seen how the traditional explanation of exchange rate determination is based on balance of payments flows. However, there is also a 'feedback' effect in that these flows, in particular flows of imports and exports, are themselves partly determined by the level of the exchange rate. Suppose that an exogenous disturbance, such as a change in government policy, leads to a balance of payments deficit and a consequent fall in the exchange rate. Since the demand for exports and imports is dependent on their price, will the new exchange rate level result in a further deterioration in the balance of payments and a further fall in the exchange rate, or will the balance of payments improve and the exchange rate return to its former level?

The answer to this question depends on the elasticities of demand for imports and exports. The 'elasticities' approach to balance of payments adjustment predicts that if the sum of the elasticities of demand for imports and exports is greater than one (the *Marshall–Lerner condition*) then the balance between the change in export earnings and import expenditure will be such as to improve the balance of payments, and the exchange rate will rise in consequence. In practice this principle as it stands is not empirically useful for the following reasons:

1 Trade adjustments take time. The exchange rate may adjust instantaneously, but traders take time to adjust their orders. The initial effect of a depreciation may therefore be to make the deficit larger as export demand is slow to increase at new lower prices, and importers fail to cut back their purchases. There will thus be a 'J-curve' effect as the balance of payments worsens before it improves. At the time of the UK devaluation of 1967 it was estimated that it was only in the second year after the devaluation that the gain in export volume offset the loss in revenue due to lower export prices.

2 In a floating exchange rate regime exchange rates will alter again in the time it takes for these adjustments to be made. Stability is therefore unlikely to occur.

3 The analysis takes no account of supply conditions. In a full employment situation it may not be possible to cope with the increased demand both for exports and for import-competing goods, so that the beneficial effect of a depreciation may not be realized because of supply constraints.

4 The fall in the exchange rate will increase home prices, because import prices have risen, and may therefore cause an inflation which will wipe out

the positive balance of payments effects of the devaluation. It was estimated that by 1972 the UK had lost the gain from the 1967 devaluation because of the effect of rising inflation.

5 It is assumed that only prices determine trade flows. In fact, there are several reasons why trade flows may be unresponsive to exchange rate changes. Quality and product differentiation are often more important in determining trade flows than prices (see Chapter 27).

6 The analysis takes no account of the effect of exchange rate changes on capital flows. If these latter are quantitatively unimportant this does not matter, but since they currently play a very large part in exchange rate determination the usefulness of the elasticities approach is weakened.

The 'traditional' analysis of exchange rate determination, which sees exchange rates as a function of the current balance of payments position, became less useful as historical circumstances have changed. Two major developments after the 1950s made it necessary to consider alternative theoretical approaches.

One of these was the growing importance of capital flows in the balance of payments accounts. These flows of international investment were partly caused by capital formation by multinational companies (see Chapter 7) but were also due to increasing preferences by asset holders for holding foreign assets as capital restrictions were eased. The last of these restrictions vanished in 1979 when the UK abolished exchange control. The other, later, development was the advent of worldwide inflation in the 1970s. The traditional view outlined earlier took no account of internal price changes when analysing exchange rate variations. In fact, in an inflationary situation internal and external price changes are interactive.

These two developments led to the *monetary* and *portfolio* approaches to exchange rate determination on the one hand, and to the revival of the *purchasing power parity* (PPP) theory on the other. Because the monetary and portfolio approach hinges on the validity of the PPP theory, we deal first with purchasing power parity.

Purchasing power parity

This theory originated in the nineteenth century, and was used in the 1920s to discuss the correct value of currencies in relation to gold. In general terms the proposition states that equilibrium exchange rates will be such as to enable people to buy the same amount of goods in any country for a given amount of money. For this to be the case, exchange rates must be at the correct level in relation to prices in the different countries. In order to state the proposition more rigorously we must assume that goods are homogeneous (or that there is only one good), also that there are no barriers to trade or transactions costs, and that there is internal price flexibility. The 'law of one price' will then ensure that the price of a good will be equalized in domestic and foreign currency terms. For instance, the price of a car in the UK in sterling must be equal to the price of a car in US dollars times the exchange rate (the sterling price of dollars). If the exchange rate is too high or too low, it will adjust if exchange rates are flexible. If they are fixed, internal prices will adjust as there is an excess of demand in one country and a shortfall in the other.

There are two versions of the proposition:

1 The 'absolute' version of PPP predicts that the exchange rate (E) will equalize the purchasing power of a given income in any two countries, so that

$$E = P(UK)/P(US)$$

2 The 'relative' version of the principle states that changes in exchange rates reflect differences in relative inflation rates. If internal prices rise in one country relative to another, exchange rates will adjust (downwards) to compensate.

It is easy to see how the existence of high inflation rates in the 1970s increased the attractiveness of this theory as an explanation of exchange rate determination, because the theory concentrates on showing the relationship between exchange rates and relative price movements, unlike the more traditional view which, as we have seen, had nothing to say about prices. However, what can we say about the empirical usefulness of the principle? Let us consider the problems of applying the principle first, and then look at the extent to which it was in fact successful in explaining exchange rate changes.

A number of damaging criticisms of the theory can be made:

1 The major problem relates to the choice of price index used to give empirical content to the

theory. Any overall price index includes non-traded as well as traded goods, and inflation rates may be differently reflected in these sectors, hence rendering the index unusable. Even the use of export price indices is problematic because the profitability element in export prices may vary over time. The appropriate measure would appear to be a measure of unit labour costs normalized as between countries (relative normalized unit labour costs – RNULC) which reflects differences in wage costs per unit of output and thus includes productivity measures.[2] The RNULC measures are the most accurate way of assessing the relative competitive strength of different countries in the traded goods sector (see also Chapter 1).

2   It is difficult to discuss an 'equilibrium' exchange rate without reference to some base year. The choice of representative year can pose problems in a world where inflation rates vary constantly.

3   Factors other than the prices of traded goods can affect the exchange rate. Barriers to trade such as tariffs can exist. Tastes can change, incomes can change, technology can change. The classic example of the latter is the effect on the exchange rate of North Sea oil.

4   Although in the long run the PPP theory may have some validity, exchange rates in the short run are more likely to be dominated by the effects of capital flows, particularly short-run flows. In other words, exchange rates may 'overshoot'.

Quite apart from these particular criticisms, it is doubtful whether the PPP theory provides us with an adequate explanation of changes in the sterling exchange rate. The theory would predict that if prices rise faster in the UK than in other countries the resultant trade deficit should cause a fall in the exchange rate. We can test this by examining the relationship between the effective exchange rate and RNULC. When costs rise the UK is becoming less competitive, so we might expect to see a consequent fall in the effective exchange rate if the 'relative' version of the PPP theory holds. In other words, there should be an inverse relationship between the two measures. This is clearly not the case. As Fig. 26.2 shows, relative prices (proxied by unit labour costs) and the effective exchange rate often tend to move together rather than inversely. There are various possible explanations for this:

1   Price elasticities for imports and exports may not be such as to cause the exchange rate to improve with a rise in competitiveness. In fact, with a floating exchange rate a rise in competitiveness may cause the exchange rate to fall (the J-curve effect).

2   The effective exchange rate is affected by trade in invisibles and by capital flows as well as by the relative prices of manufactured goods entering into trade.

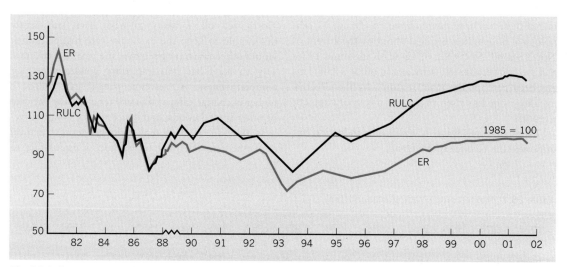

Fig. 26.2 Sterling exchange rate index (ER) and relative unit labour costs (RULC).
Source: ONS (2003) *Economic Trends*, May, and previous issues.

3 Price competitiveness is not the only factor affecting trade flows. Non-price competitiveness is also an important determinant. In other words, the crucial assumption of the 'law of one price' – that of homogeneous goods – does not hold in the real world.

We must also realize that RNULC are themselves affected by the effective exchange rate. This is because costs of production in the UK will rise faster than those in other countries if the effective exchange rate depreciates. Raw materials will become more expensive, production costs will rise, the rise in price may trigger wage demands, and RNULC will rise in consequence.

We may sum up by saying that the usefulness of the PPP theory as a theory of exchange rate determination is probably best thought of in a long-run context when changes in relative prices between countries represent the workings of inflationary forces rather than transient 'real' effects such as changes in tastes or technology. However, even in the long run it is still not possible to say whether relative price shifts determine exchange rate movements, or whether exchange rate changes influence price movements.

North Sea oil and the exchange rate

We have argued that little of the variation in the effective exchange rate can be explained by UK price competitiveness. Other factors have been more important: one of these has been the fundamental change in technological possibilities brought about by the advent of North Sea oil. North Sea oil came on stream in 1976, and the UK became self-sufficient in oil by 1980. This has been perhaps the main reason why the effective exchange rate has risen in spite of a loss of competitiveness.

There are three ways in which oil production has improved the balance of payments.

First, since 1976 the UK has been an exporter of oil and has reduced its own dependence on imported oil. As we can see from Table 26.2, the oil trading balance has been steadily improving since 1976, and moved into surplus in 1980. However, since 1985 oil production has begun to decline in volume, and this has been reflected in the reduced surplus since 1985. Nevertheless a modest recovery in world oil prices, new oil fields yielding extra output and the lower price of oil exports (after sterling depreciated on leaving the ERM) all contributed to an improvement in the oil trade balance in the 1990s. There has been a tendency for oil prices to rise in recent years, due partly to uncertainties as to future supplies of oil (e.g. Gulf War 2) and partly to more effective restrictions on the supply of oil from the OPEC oil cartel. This rise in oil prices should further improve the oil trade balance in the years ahead.

Second, the inflows of capital needed to fund investment in the oil industry helped the UK balance of payments in the 1970s. However, this effect has to some extent been offset since then by outflows of interest, profits and dividends as companies remit their gains to the country of origin.

Third, the popularity of sterling rose as an asset currency during the first and second Gulf Wars, as international asset holders speculated on the strength of sterling deriving from the favourable oil trading balance. Such problems have raised the profile of sterling as a 'petro-currency', attractive to investors at a time of potentially higher oil prices.

The net effect of the balance of payments impact of North Sea oil is likely to have been sufficiently favourable to keep the exchange rate higher than it would otherwise have been over the past few decades. This in itself has had important consequences for competitiveness. A 'resource shock' can follow a higher exchange rate, as this will tend to raise the cost of other traded goods, and hence reduce competitiveness. In addition, there may be longer-term structural adjustments as manufacturers find it impossible to

Table 26.2 Balance on oil trading account (£m).

1976	1978	1980	1982	1983	1985	1987	1989	1991	1993	1995	1997	1999	2001
−3,947	−1,984	315	4,605	6,294	8,163	4,184	1,257	1,208	2,442	4,472	4,608	4,031	5,392

Source: Adapted from ONS (2003) *UK Balance of Payments*.

maintain their position in world markets. The conventional wisdom has been to argue that this latter effect did *not* in fact happen in the UK, because the upward pressure on the real exchange rate was counterbalanced by a fall in the rate of inflation in the 1980s, as well as by a rise in domestic demand. These enabled UK firms and exporters to become more profitable and hence to compete more effectively abroad.

Of course, recession in the UK and other parts of the world economy in the early 1990s led to a renewed focus on the 'resource shock' aspect of an, allegedly, overvalued exchange rate. In more recent times, the sharp appreciation of sterling since 1996 has also brought the 'resource shock' debate to the fore, of particular concern being the negative impact of a high exchange rate on manufacturing output and employment. However, few have sought to link the rise in sterling since 1996 to North Sea oil.

The monetary approach to exchange rate determination

As we saw earlier, the growth in importance of capital account transactions led to attempts to explain the determination of the exchange rate by analysing financial flows between countries. The monetary approach to exchange rate determination, developed in the early 1970s, sees the exchange rate as the price of foreign money in terms of domestic money, determined in turn by the demand for and supply of money. If people are not willing to hold the existing stock of money there will be a shortfall in demand for it and its price will fall in relation to the currencies of other countries. What it in fact argues is that balance of payments, and hence exchange rate movements, are simply reflections of disequilibria in money markets.

Money is thought of as being an asset, the demand for which depends on income and interest rates. If the central bank in a country increases the money supply, income and interest rates remaining unchanged, people will be unwilling to hold more money and so the excess money holdings will be used to buy more goods from abroad. The result will be a balance of payments deficit and downward pressure on the exchange rate. If the authorities intervene to support the currency they will lose reserves, and so the increase in the money supply will be exactly offset by

a reduction in the external component of the money stock (see Chapter 20). On the other hand, if exchange rates are flexible, the fall in the exchange rate will simply result in internal inflation (as the price of imports rises) which will exactly cancel out the original increase in the money supply.

Suppose now that there is no increase in the money supply, but that exogenous factors cause a change in the demand for money. Suppose incomes rise: the increase in demand for money balances will then lead to an appreciation of the exchange rate as less money is available for imports. Or suppose interest rates rise: the demand for money balances will be reduced, people will spend the money on imports, the exchange rate will fall and home inflation will result. (Note that the prediction here is at variance with the usual assumption that a rise in interest rates will cause an appreciation of the exchange rate because capital flows will be attracted into the country.)

The monetary approach to exchange rate determination, incorporating as it does a whole new perspective on the role of money in the balance of payments, provides a monetarist explanation of exchange rate determination. Its strength lies in the fact that it recognizes the importance of asset market changes in determining the exchange rate, as opposed to concentrating merely on the importance of current account flows in the short or long term, as the previous approaches did. That perspective allows for the possibility of introducing the question of the effect of expectations, which is essential if we are to explain exchange rate volatility. However, in evaluating the usefulness of this approach we must first of all remember that the validity of the argument rests on very limited assumptions:

1 The demand for money is a stable function of real income and interest rates.

2 Prices are determined by the world price level and the exchange rate, i.e. the PPP theory holds.

3 There is full employment domestically.

The validity of these assumptions may be criticized on several grounds:

1 The impact of a monetary disturbance on prices and hence the exchange rate may not be predictable in the short run because of the instability of the velocity of circulation (see Chapter 20).

2 Exchange rates do not conform to the naive PPP model.

3 Changes in the money stock may produce short-run changes in output (see Chapter 20) which may make it difficult to identify ultimate effects on prices and the exchange rate.

It may help to remember the restrictiveness of these assumptions when we examine some of the implications of this monetarist view. For instance, it is clear that the theory implies that there is no need to have a balance of payments policy, since deficits are self-correcting, because increases in the money stock are reversed either by exchange market intervention or by the effects of resultant price rises. Also, under a system of fixed exchange rates it will not be possible to conduct an active monetary policy, since all changes in the money stock will be offset by changes in the reserves. But perhaps the major problem with the monetary approach to exchange rate determination, and certainly the central problem when it comes to any empirical testing of its usefulness as an explanatory device, is that it considers there to be only one asset – money – which affects exchange rate determination. This is clearly not the case in practice. We must therefore look to a wider interpretation of asset-holding behaviour if we are to account for the actual behaviour of the exchange rate.

The portfolio balance approach to exchange rate determination

The portfolio balance approach to exchange rate determination sees exchange rates as determined mainly by movements on the capital account of the balance of payments. However, it recognizes that there are a wide variety of assets represented by these transactions. Wealth holders will hold their assets in domestic and foreign securities as well as money, and their asset preferences will be determined by their assessment of the relationship between risk and return on these assets. Given the difference between domestic and foreign rates of return, the exchange rate will be determined by investors' assessment of the degree of substitutability between domestic and foreign assets. If domestic interest rates rise, the extent to which this will cause an inflow of capital and a consequent appreciation of the exchange rate will depend on investor expectations. If expectations change, so that the perceived relationship between

risk and return alters, the exchange rate will vary accordingly.

This approach, which was developed in the mid-1970s, represents the 'state of the art' in exchange rate theory. It does not discount the influence of the current account in trend movements of the exchange rate, but it does suggest a plausible explanation for the observed short-run variability in the exchange rate shown in Fig. 26.2 above. Exchange rates may vary sharply in response to asset-switching behaviour in the face of changing rates of return and expectations. Adherents of this view would argue that the major exchange rate changes of September 1992 were largely caused by asset-switching behaviour by portfolio holders. For example, once expectations moved sharply against the lira and pound sterling holding their central parities in the ERM, it became a 'low risk' one-way bet to move out of those currencies into 'harder' currencies such as D-mark and yen.

Short-term capital flows and the exchange rate

Here we consider the way in which the exchange rate is influenced by short-term capital flows. These consist mainly of borrowings from, and lending to, overseas residents by banks. Such short-term capital flows respond primarily to interest rate differentials. Asset switching between countries will take place so long as the interest rate differential is greater than any expected changes in the exchange rate. What happens is that if interest rates rise in, for instance, the US, people will buy dollars in order to invest in US money markets. This will drive the dollar rate up, but as people realize their gains by selling dollars the dollar rate will come down again. It is possible to try and hedge against potential loss by selling dollars bought today on today's forward market for delivery at some future date, but that will in turn drive today's forward rate down. In a perfect market the rise in dollar spot rate and the fall in forward rates (as investors try to make sure of their future gains today) will be just sufficient to cancel out the advantages of rising interest rates. But markets are never perfect, and some *arbitrage* is always possible.

We have no firm empirical evidence for such behaviour on the part of asset holders. There should be a positive correlation between interest rate differentials and exchange rates, as people switch funds into the UK when interest rates rise relative to US interest rates, thereby driving up the sterling exchange rate. Figure 26.3, which deals with the UK/US interest rate differential, shows as much evidence of negative as of positive correlation. There are various reasons for this. One is that the positive effect of interest rate differentials on the exchange rate may be outweighed by exchange rate *expectations*. For instance, in the period 1980–82, when interest rate differentials were very low because both the UK and the US had high interest rates, the UK exchange rate was high because people believed that a petro-currency such as sterling would remain strong.

Expectations about future exchange rates are formed by assessments about the potential demand for and supply of sterling. If asset holders see that the UK has a combined current and capital account deficit, they will *expect* the exchange rate to fall, and will move their money out of sterling, thereby exerting a further downward pressure on sterling. If the authorities do not wish this to happen, they must raise interest rates so that they are higher than those of other countries by a margin sufficient to attract funds into sterling.

Of course it is never possible to predict the effect on capital flows, and hence on the exchange rate, of any given interest rate differential. Capital flows will be more or less responsive, depending on the strength and the nature of expectations. Lacking adequate information in an imperfect market, speculators tend to be influenced by any item of information, however irrelevant. Money supply figures, political developments at home and abroad, unsuccessful summit meetings – all these tend to trigger behavioural responses in terms of flows of 'hot' money in and out

of sterling. Exogenous shocks, such as the consequences of oil price rises, or the threat of international conflict, may also lead to major flows of short-term capital. It may happen that, in spite of high interest rates, the exchange rate does depreciate. In this case there will be consequent structural changes both in competitiveness and in real rates of return on long-term investment.

Expectations would certainly seem to have outweighed interest rate differentials in September 1992, when a number of ERM currencies came under intense speculative attack. Despite sharp rises in Italian and UK interest rates, for example, the speculative pressure against the lira and pound was sustained. In the case of the UK, interest rates rose an unprecedented five percentage points (from 10% to 15%) within 24 hours. Even this, together with an estimated expenditure of £7bn by the Bank of England (roughly one-third of total UK reserves) in purchasing sterling, and further support of over £2bn by the Bundesbank, could not withstand the continued speculative pressure. Eventually the UK was forced to withdraw from the system altogether (see Chapter 29) and the Italians had to reduce the central parity of the lira within the system.

Economic policy and the exchange rate

It has become increasingly clear that there is a direct relationship between changes in the exchange rate

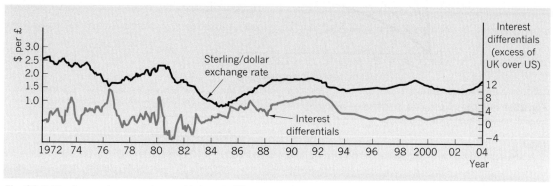

Fig. 26.3 Sterling exchange rates and interest differentials.
Sources: Derived from ONS (2003) *Financial Statistics*, May, and *Bank of England Quarterly Bulletin* (1972–87).

and the rate of inflation, because the price of imports enters into the Retail Price Index in different ways. We can illustrate this as follows. In Fig. 26.4 we consider in some detail the impact of a sterling depreciation on UK import prices. Sterling depreciation will raise the cost, expressed in sterling, of imported items. However, both the magnitude and the speed of price rise will vary with type of import. This can be illustrated for the 1980s by reference to a Bank of England short-term forecasting model. As we can see from Fig. 26.4, the full effect of the sterling depreciation on import prices will only be felt after more than two years. Imported fuel and industrial material prices will, with less elastic demands, respond most substantially and most rapidly to the depreciation. This is in part because the less elastic is demand, the easier it is to pass on cost increases to consumers.

Imported finished goods prices rise by a smaller amount, and less quickly, because some of these goods face extensive competition on home markets, i.e. face more elastic demand curves. Imported food prices will tend to be less affected, at least initially, because of the operation of the Common Agricultural Policy.

The final effect on consumer prices can be seen to be about one-quarter of the sterling depreciation, and then only after more than two years. For any depreciation, the final effect on consumer prices will depend on a number of factors:

- the import content of production;

- the extent to which cost increases can be passed on to consumers, i.e. price elasticity of demand;

- the import content of consumption; and

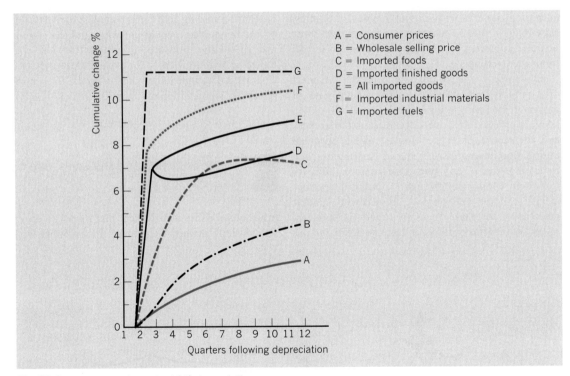

Fig. 26.4 Impact on prices of a 10% depreciation.
Source: Adapted from Bank of England.

Notes:
1 A 10% depreciation of sterling against the dollar is equivalent to an increase of 11.1% in units of sterling per dollar. As it is the latter rate which is relevant in this context, the 10% depreciation leads eventually to a rise slightly greater than 11% in some import prices.
2 The bank's short-term model assumes no wages response. The exchange rate is assumed to remain 10% below the level it would otherwise have been.

■ the sensitivity of wage demands to cost-of-living increases.

Figure 26.4 is drawn on the assumption of no wage response, i.e. that the sensitivity of wage demands to cost-of-living increases is zero. Any such response would increase wholesale and consumer prices still further.

Whereas a fall in the sterling exchange rate will increase inflation, a rise in the exchange rate will reduce it. There is, of course, another side to the picture. A high sterling exchange rate, although helping the fight against inflation, may adversely affect output and employment. United Kingdom producers may now find it more difficult to sell their goods and services, first, because competition from cheaper imports drives them out of home markets and, second, because UK exports become expensive on foreign markets. Much of the deindustrialization of the early 1980s was attributed to the high pound, which has also been blamed for lost output and employment in UK manufacturing since 1996 (see Chapter 1).

The adherence of governments to a policy of high exchange rates has often been based on a belief that high exchange rates help fight inflation by making imports cheaper, and that on the export side reliance could be placed on the 'law of one price'. In other words, British manufacturers, seeing that they could not sell on world markets unless they observed world prices for their products, would restrain the rate of growth of labour costs, thereby raising exports and further contributing to the fight against inflation.

It will be useful to conclude this chapter by reviewing the various types of *exchange rate regime* which have operated over time, before considering the system under which the UK currently operates.

The gold standard system

As the nineteenth century progressed, and as world trade expanded, the use of gold as a means of international payment broadened to take in almost all the major trading countries. Although a few, such as the US, persisted for some time with silver, by about 1873 (with the passing of the Gold Standard Act in the US) a gold standard payments system could be said to be in effect. The 'price' of each major currency was fixed in terms of a *specific weight of gold*, which meant that the price of each currency was fixed in terms of every other currency, at a rate that could not be altered. The gold standard was therefore a system of *fixed exchange rates*. Any difficulties for the balance of payments had to be resolved by expanding or contracting the domestic economy. A rather stylized account of the adjustment mechanism will highlight the main features of the gold standard system.

Suppose a country moved into balance of payments surplus. Payment would be received in gold which, because domestic money supply was directly related to the gold stock, would raise money supply. This would expand the economy, raising domestic incomes, spending and prices. Higher incomes and prices would encourage imports and discourage exports, thereby helping to eliminate the initial payments surplus. In addition, the extra money supply would lead to a fall in its price (the rate of interest), encouraging capital outflows to other countries which had higher rates of interest – a minus sign in the accounts. A payments surplus would, in these ways, tend to be eliminated. For countries with payments deficits, gold outflow would reduce the gold stock and with it the domestic money supply. This would cause the domestic economy to contract, reducing incomes, spending and prices. Lower incomes and prices would discourage imports and encourage exports. The reduction in money supply would also raise the price of money (interest rate), encouraging capital inflows – a plus sign in the accounts. Payment deficits would, therefore, also tend to be eliminated. This whole system came to be regarded as extremely sophisticated and self-regulating. Individual countries need only ensure (a) that gold could flow freely between countries, (b) that gold backed the domestic money supply, and (c) that the market was free to set interest rates. Of course, this meant that countries with payment surpluses would experience expanding domestic economies, and those with deficits contracting economies.

There seemed to be a general acceptance amongst the major trading nations that currency and payments stability took precedence over domestic production and employment. What was perhaps not realized was that the apparent 'success' of the system in the 10 years between 1873 and 1913 was largely due to the additional liquidity provided by sterling balances. The growing value of UK imports had led to an increase in the holding of sterling by overseas residents, who then used sterling to settle international debts.

If the supply of gold and other precious commodities could not keep pace with the expansion of world trade, the obvious alternative was to make use of 'paper'. In practice, of course, exporters would accept only paper and a 'paper' system could be used on a worldwide basis only when it fulfilled a number of useful criteria:

1 It had to be freely exchangeable on a global basis.
2 It had to be available in sufficient quantities.
3 It needed to be of a fixed value which did not depreciate rapidly.
4 Its value, ideally, needed to be guaranteed in terms of some other precious commodity such as gold.

The paper currency, in other words, had to be 'as good as gold'.

For a brief period in the late Victorian and early Edwardian eras sterling fulfilled the bulk of this role. Sterling continued to play a part in the funding of international debt in what was called the 'Sterling Area' well into the 1960s.

Although several attempts were made to revive the gold standard after the First World War, these largely failed. The dominance of the UK in world trade began to fade during this period, restricting the supply of sterling as a world currency. The Great Depression of the late 1920s and early 1930s also encouraged many countries to adopt protectionist measures. In such an atmosphere countries became less willing to abide by the 'rules' of the gold standard. Gold flows were restricted, and money supply and interest rates were adjusted independently of gold flow to help domestic employment rather than international payments. Wages and prices became much more rigid as labour and product markets became less 'perfect', which further impeded the adjustment mechanism. For instance, any deflation that did still occur in deficit countries led *less often* to the reductions in factor and product price needed to restore price competitiveness. Countries began therefore to resort more and more to changes in the exchange rate to regain lost competitiveness.

This breakdown of the gold standard system during the inter-war period found no ready replacement. The result was a rather chaotic period of unstable exchange rates, inadequate world liquidity and protectionism. It was to seek a more ordered system of world trade and payments that the Allies met in Bretton Woods, in the US, even before the Second World War had ended. What emerged from that meeting was an entirely new system, under the auspices of the IMF.

The IMF system

The adjustable-peg exchange rate system

Imbalances in world trading patterns, and imperfections in world money markets have at least three implications:

1 That deficits and surpluses rarely self-correct, so that foreign exchange reserves are required to fund persistent payments deficits.
2 That although surpluses and deficits are supposed to balance as an accounting identity for the world as a whole, in practice surpluses are rarely recycled to debtor countries.
3 That even though in theory the world must be in overall balance, in practice there is a substantial imbalance. As far as these missing balances are concerned, the IMF reported in 1991 a global surplus of over $100bn. A number of factors may be involved: time-lags in reporting transactions, the non-recording of arrangements conducted through tax havens, and the problem of using an appropriate 'price' to evaluate trade deals when exchange rates fluctuate several times between initiation and completion.

In order to settle deficits, theory tells us that deficit countries should be able to run down their foreign exchange reserves, or to borrow from surplus countries. Both methods have, in reality, proved next to impossible. The countries most likely to suffer deficits are those with low per capita incomes and few foreign exchange reserves. They are also in consequence those with low credit ratings on the international banking circuit, making borrowing from surplus countries difficult. It was in order to solve just these sorts of liquidity problems for deficit countries that the IMF was established. As well as providing foreign currencies in times of need, its other major objective was to promote stability in exchange rates, following the uncertainties of the inter-war period.

Exchange rate stability

Under the IMF system, each country could, on joining, assign to itself an exchange rate. It did this by indicating the number of units of its currency it would trade for an ounce of gold, valued at $35. The dollar was therefore the common unit of all exchange rates. A country had a 'right' to change its initial exchange rate (par value) by up to 10%. For changes in par value which, when cumulated, came to more than 10%, the permission of the IMF was required. The IMF would give such permission only if the member could demonstrate that its payments were in 'fundamental disequilibrium'. Since this term was never clearly defined in the Articles of the IMF, any substantial payments imbalance would usually qualify. A rise in par became known as a revaluation; a fall in par, devaluation. As well as changing par value, a member could permit its exchange rate to move in any one year ± 1% of par, but no more. Because the IMF system sought stable, but not totally fixed, exchange rates, it became known as the 'adjustable peg' exchange rate system.

The IMF also introduced – in 1961 – the idea of 'currency swaps' by which a country in need of specific foreign exchange could avoid the obvious disadvantages of having to purchase it with its own currency by simply agreeing to 'swap' a certain amount through the Bank of International Settlements. The swap contract would state a rate of exchange which would also apply to the 'repayment' at the end of the contract.

Changes in exchange rate were a means by which deficits or surpluses could be adjusted. For instance, a devaluation would lower the foreign price of exports and raise the domestic price of imports. The IMF system has, however, been criticized in its actual operation for permitting too little flexibility in exchange rates. Between 1947 and 1971 only six adjustments took place: devaluations of the French franc (1958 and 1969), sterling (1949 and 1967), and revaluations of the Deutsche Mark (1961 and 1969). It is true, of course, that adjustments of exchange rates are subject to an extremely fine balance: too many adjustments and the system loses stability and confidence; too few and the system generates internal ten-sions of unemployment and/or lower real incomes which may eventually destroy it.

By 1971, continuing US deficits (the expense of the Vietnam War was a major contributory factor), paid in part with US dollars, had led to an overabundance of dollars in the world system. Under the IMF rules all dollars could be converted into gold at $35 per ounce, and as confidence in the dollar declined, US gold stocks came under increasing strain. Although the US, even in 1971, still accounted for 30% of world gold reserves and 15% of total world reserves (gold, foreign currencies and SDRs), the enormous payments deficits of 1970 and 1971 ($11bn and $30bn respectively) imposed tremendous pressure on its gold and foreign currency reserves. President Nixon announced in August 1971 that the US dollar would no longer be convertible into gold.

The scrapping of dollar convertibility into gold at a *fixed price* caused a crisis in the IMF exchange rate system, which had been founded on that very principle.[3] This was followed by two increases in the 'official price' of gold – in 1971 to $38 per ounce, and in 1973 to $42.22 per ounce – together with revaluations of other currencies against the dollar, and increases in the width of the permitted band within which currencies were allowed to drift from ± 1% to ± 2.25%. None of these had any lasting effect, however, as first sterling (in 1972) and then the dollar (in 1973) began to float freely against other currencies. By 1976 almost all IMF members had adopted some type of floating exchange rate system. The IMF meeting of that year in Jamaica officially recognized this new situation.

The floating exchange rate system

According to basic economic theory, a system of freely floating exchange rates should be self-regulating. If the cause of a UK deficit were, say, extra imports from America, then the pound should fall (depreciate) against the dollar. This would result from UK importers *selling* extra pounds sterling on the foreign exchange markets to buy US dollars to pay for those imports. In simple demand/supply analysis, the extra supply of pounds sterling will lower their 'price', i.e. the sterling exchange rate. As we have already seen, provided the Marshall–Lerner elasticity conditions are fulfilled (price elasticity of demand for UK exports and imports together greater than one), then the lower-priced exports and higher-priced imports will contribute to an improvement in the balance of payments, perhaps after a short time-lag.

As it has developed since 1973, however, the system has not been one of 'freely floating' rates. Instead, governments have tended to intervene from time to time to support the values of their currencies (see Fig. 26.1). For instance, the UK has intervened in recent times to prevent the pound falling when cheap imports were part of its anti-inflationary strategy. The setting, for internal reasons, of particular 'targets' for the exchange rate has therefore resulted in a system of 'managed' exchange rates, picturesquely described as a 'dirty floating system'. The major advantages and disadvantages of fixed versus floating exchange rates are shown in Table 26.3.

Sterling and the ERM

In the last fifty years we have moved, as we have noted, from a fixed to a floating exchange rate regime. With the advent of world inflation in the 1970s it became impossible to maintain fixed exchange rate parities between countries because internal prices were accelerating at different rates. As world inflation subsided in the 1980s floating exchange rates became less necessary: in addition, the increased volatility of currencies led the major countries to seek some form of greater stability. The countries of the European Community had a particular problem in that it was clearly not possible to create a unified market without fixed parities.

While it has not proved possible to implement any form of fixed exchange rate regime for countries as a whole, the European economies have, since 1979, operated an Exchange Rate Mechanism (see Chapter 29). This pegged currencies to the central unit, known as the 'ecu', within a permitted band of divergence. The value of the 'ecu' was based on a weighted average of the participating currencies. The ERM of the European Monetary System can now be seen to have been an intermediate step towards the European Monetary Union (EMU) which began its transition phase on 1 January 1999 with the launch of the euro (see Chapters 20 and 29).

Table 26.3 Fixed versus floating exchange rates: pros and cons.

Fixed	Floating
Advantages	*Advantages*
1. Exchange rate stability provides a realistic basis for expectations	1. Automatic eradication of imbalances
2. Stability encourages increased trade	2. Reduced need for reserves – in theory, no need at all
3. Reduced danger from international currency speculation	3. Relative freedom for internal economic policy
4. Imposes increased discipline on internal economic policy	4. Exchange rates change in relatively smooth steps
5. Domestic price stability not endangered through import prices	5. May reduce speculation (rates move freely up *or* down)
Disadvantages	*Disadvantages*
1. Requires large reserves	1. Increased uncertainty for traders
2. Internal economic policy largely dictated by external factors	2. Domestic price stability may be endangered by rising import prices
3. No automatic adjustment – danger of large changes in rates	3. May increase speculation through coordinated buying or selling

The UK did not join the ERM when it was established in 1979, as it was feared that sterling would not be able to maintain its position within the system. After that, when sterling rose as a result of the advent of North Sea oil, it seemed inappropriate to join an exchange rate system where the dominant currency, the mark, was a non-oil currency. After 1987, when the UK signed the Single European Act designed to create the single market by 1993, the question of joining the ERM again became a live issue. In fact, before the Chancellor, Nigel Lawson, resigned in 1989 it was clear that he was attempting to target the value of sterling at DM3 = £1. However, the UK government expressed a reluctance to join until various conditions were fulfilled. Behind what were clearly political arguments and bargaining positions lay a very real apprehension about the problems which the UK might face on entry. In particular there was the fear of losing the use of a policy instrument, namely the exchange rate, which might then make it more difficult to use depreciation/devaluation to remedy any trade imbalances with individual countries or the rest of the world. A full discussion of the UK's entry into, and exit from, the ERM can be found in Chapter 29, and more detail on the operation of European Monetary Union (EMU) can be found in Chapters 20 and 29.

Key points

- The exchange rate is usually quoted as the number of units of the domestic currency that are needed to purchase one unit of a foreign currency.

- London is the world's largest centre for foreign exchange trading, with an average daily turnover of over $900 billion.

- Some 64% of transactions are 'spot' on any one day, 24% are forward for periods less than one month and a further 10% forward for periods greater than one month.

- The exchange rate is a key 'price', affecting the competitiveness of UK exporters and UK producers of import substitutes.

- A fall (depreciation) in sterling will, other things being equal, make UK exports cheaper abroad and UK imports dearer at home.

- The Marshall–Lerner elasticity conditions must be fulfilled if a fall in the exchange rate is to improve the balance of payments. Namely the *sum* of the price elasticities of demand for exports and imports must be greater than one.

- Because short-term elasticities are lower than long-term elasticities, the initial one to two years after a depreciation may *not* lead to an improvement in the balance of payments (the so-called 'J-curve' effect).

- The *effective exchange rate* (EER) for sterling is a weighted average of the 16 national currencies which are most important in terms of trade with the UK.

- The *real exchange rate* takes account of the nominal exchange rates between the various countries *and* of the relative inflation rates in those countries.

Now try the self-check questions for this chapter on the Companion Website. You will also find up-to-date facts and case materials.

Notes

1. This analysis assumes that the elasticity of demand for imports is greater than one. In the case of exports foreign buyers will demand more pounds whatever the elasticity of demand, simply because they are buying more goods as the price in their own currency falls, and the sterling price of exports has not changed.

2. The RNULC are calculated by taking indices of labour costs in the UK and dividing by the weighted geometric average of competitors' unit labour costs. 'Normalization' involves adjusting the basic indices to allow for short-run variations in productivity – so eliminating cyclical variations.

3. During the exchange rate crisis of September 1992, three countries reintroduced exchange controls aimed at reducing the capacity of international banks to borrow in their money markets and then sell the currency for speculative gain. Portugal permitted only between half and one-third of escudos in Lisbon's money markets physically to be used for currency speculation. Spain demanded that the banks deposit funds interest free for a year to match the amount they plan to sell for foreign exchange. Ireland insisted that the government now take over the management of currency swaps, with the exception of those that are trade related.

References and further reading

Buxton, T. and Lintner, V. (1998) Cost competitiveness, the ERM and UK economic policy, in *Britain's Economic Performance*, 2nd edn, T. Buxton, P. Chapman and P. Temple (eds), Routledge, London.

Goodman, S. (2002) The euro and progress on enlargement, *British Economy Survey*, **31**(2).

Jones, R. (2002) The Argentinian crisis – a case study in exchange rate inflexibility and national bankruptcy, *British Economy Survey*, **31**(2).

Kitson, M. and Michie, J. (1994) Fixed exchange rates and deflation: the ERM and the Gold Standard, *Economics and Business Education*, Spring.

ONS (2003) *Economic Trends*, May.

ONS (2003) *Financial Statistics*, May.

ONS (2003) *UK Balance of Payments*.

Sutherland, A. (1998) Why are exchange rates so important?, *Economic Review*, **16**(2).

Turner, P. (1997) Britain and the European Monetary System, *Economic Review*, **14**(3).

Chapter 27   United Kingdom trade performance

Although the UK's balance of trade in goods (previously 'visible trade') has been in deficit for most of the last 150 years, it has not presented a major problem as the surplus on trade in services, investment income and transfers (previously 'invisible trade') have usually been more than able to cover any deficit on trade in goods. However, since 1945, with the exception of oil, there has been a progressive and serious fall in the UK's export competitiveness on trade in goods and a rise in import penetration. This chapter examines such trends, particularly those for the manufactured goods sector, and investigates in detail the problem of non-price competitiveness for the UK. The chapter concludes with an attempt to assess the importance of an adverse performance on non-oil goods trade for the UK economy.

The nature of the problem

It was observed in Chapter 26 that the UK's balance of payments has two main components: a 'current account' and a 'transactions in UK assets and liabilities account'. Our main concern in this chapter will be the current account, since the items on this account are often used to measure the UK's ability to compete in world markets. In 1995, for the first time, the current account figures were shown rather differently than in previous years, and this is shown in Table 27.1.

The first item is 'balance on goods', which corresponds to the balance of visible trade found in the old accounts and, as there, is split into oil and non-oil trade in goods. The next item is 'balance on services' which provides information about the UK's net income from services such as shipping, insurance and finance. These two balances are then added together to give the 'balance on goods and services'. The current account is then completed by adding two further items, the 'total income balance' which is made up almost exclusively of the balance on investment income, i.e. net income from interest, profits and dividend (IPD), and the 'transfer balance', which relates to net transactions such as government transfers to the EU, bilateral aid, etc.

The main difference between the new format and the old current account statistics is that the services balance is now added to the goods balance instead of being included with investment and transfers to form the old 'invisible balance'. The term 'invisibles' is no longer used in the accounts. Eventually, even the 'current account' may disappear, leaving the 'balance on trade and services' as the main focus. One rationale behind the change is that the distinction between goods and services sectors is often difficult to establish in practice, so it is arguably simpler to place them both together under one heading. The changes were also designed to bring UK statistics into line with the 1995 IMF Balance of Payments format.

Apart from during the Second World War, the UK's current account has been in deficit on only 43 occasions between 1816 and 2002, giving the impression of a solid and consistent trading performance in both goods and non-goods. However, a closer look at the accounts shows that, apart from times of war, there have been only six surpluses on the goods account, and only three deficits on services and investment income throughout the whole period. It appears that the UK's weakness in her goods trade has, for the most part, been compensated for by her strength in services and investment income. Table 27.1 suggests that this is basically still the case, although the picture has become more complex in the last three decades following variations in the oil price, and the advent of UK North Sea oil.

It would seem from Table 27.1 that had it not been for the oil shock of 1973/74, the UK current account would have remained in surplus, with the earnings on services and investment more than covering any deficit on the goods balance. With the advent of North Sea oil in the late 1970s, and with the UK becoming a net exporter of oil in 1980, the future of the current account would still seem secure! However, the underlying trends would warn us against any such complacency. For example, the fall in the price of oil and therefore oil revenue between 1986 and 1991 weakened the total goods balance significantly and further exposed the difficulties which the UK has experienced on its non-oil goods account. Although the balance on services has remained positive and grown substantially since the early 1990s, as has the investment income balance (capital inflows exceeding outflows), these have not been sufficient in total to offset the negative balances for non-oil goods and transfers (net payments to EU, foreign aid, etc.), so that the current balance has been negative for the past 20 years.

Goods trade

The UK's competitive weakness on her goods trade can be viewed from three main standpoints: first, the deterioration in the non-oil goods balance; second, the change in the area and commodity composition of goods trade; and third, the adverse trends observed for trade in manufactures.

The non-oil goods balance

From Table 27.1 we see that the non-oil goods balance has experienced alternate periods of deficit and surplus. Historically these periods have to some extent followed the business cycle. Imports in particular have been sensitive to business cycles, with the growth of domestic demand during recovery periods – especially demand for investment goods (machinery

Table 27.1 Components of UK current account, 1970–2002 (£m).

| | Trade in goods and services | | | | | | | |
| Year | Balance on goods | | | Balance on services | Balance on goods and services | Total income balance[1] | Transfer balance | Current balance |
	Total	Oil	Non-oil					
1970	−18	−496	+478	+455	+437	+471	−89	+819
1971	+205	−692	+897	+590	+795	+418	−90	+1,123
1972	−736	−666	−70	+665	−71	+355	−142	+142
1973	−2,573	−941	−1,632	+803	−1,770	+1,006	−336	−1,100
1974	−5,241	−3,360	−1,881	+1,118	−4,123	+1,092	−302	−3,333
1975	−3,245	−3,062	−183	+1,447	−1,798	+416	−313	−1,695
1976	−3,930	−3,953	+23	+2,532	−1,398	+960	−534	−972
1977	−2,271	−2,774	+503	+3,306	+1,035	−432	−889	−286
1978	−1,534	−1,988	+454	+3,777	+2,243	−2	−1,420	+821
1979	−3,326	−738	−2,588	+4,076	+750	+25	−1,777	−1,002
1980	+1,329	+308	+1,021	+3,829	+5,158	−1,765	−1,653	+1,740
1981	+3,238	+3,106	+132	+3,951	+7,189	−1,124	−1,219	+4,846
1982	+1,879	+4,638	−2,759	+3,198	+5,077	−1,368	−1,476	+2,233
1983	−1,618	+6,972	−8,590	+4,076	+2,458	+191	−1,391	+1,258
1984	−5,409	+6,933	−12,342	+4,491	−918	+1,190	−1,566	−1,294
1985	−3,416	+8,101	−11,517	+6,767	+3,351	−997	−2,924	−570
1986	−9,617	+4,070	−13,687	+6,403	−3,214	+1,694	−2,094	−3,614
1987	−11,698	+4,161	−15,859	+6,813	−4,885	+917	−3,570	−7,538
1988	−21,553	+2,758	−24,311	+4,450	−17,103	+753	−3,500	−19,850
1989	−24,724	+1,263	−25,987	+3,643	−21,081	−792	−4,448	−26,321
1990	−18,707	+1,529	−20,236	+4,337	−14,370	−2,979	−4,932	−22,281
1991	−10,223	+1,274	−11,497	+4,102	−6,121	−3,307	−1,231	−10,659
1992	−13,050	+1,610	−14,660	+5,482	−7,568	+128	−5,534	−12,974
1993	−13,066	+2,612	−15,678	+6,581	−6,485	−191	−5,243	−11,919
1994	−11,126	+3,937	−15,063	+6,379	−4,747	+3,348	−5,369	−6,768
1995	−12,023	+4,323	−16,346	+8,481	−3,542	+2,101	−7,574	−9,015
1996	−13,722	+4,810	−18,532	+9,597	−4,125	+1,204	−5,788	−8,709
1997	−12,342	+4,560	−16,902	+12,528	+186	+3,906	−5,812	−1,720
1998	−21,813	+3,042	−24,855	+12,666	−9,147	+12,558	−8,225	−4,814
1999	−27,372	+4,449	−31,182	+11,794	−15,578	+2,536	−6,687	−19,729
2000	−30,326	+6,536	−36,862	+11,838	−18,488	+9,312	−10,032	−19,208
2001	−40,620	+5,577	−46,197	+13,000	−27,620	+16,188	−6,606	−18,038
2002	−46,455	+5,487	−51,942	+15,166	−31,289	+21,119	−8,795	−18,965

[1] This total includes both 'compensation to employees' and 'investment income' but in statistical terms it is nearly all investment income.
Sources: ONS (2002) UK Balance of Payments; ONS (2003) Data Releases (various).

and equipment) and inventories (material and fuel) – often leading to the rapid growth of such imports (Bank of England 2002) and resulting in a deficit on the non-oil account. Therefore, deficits have tended to be more pronounced during periods of recovery and boom, and surpluses during periods of recession. The relatively high incomes experienced during periods of expanding economic activity have tended to attract imports (see below), with an adverse effect on the non-oil goods balance, as in 1973/74 and in the short-lived 'boom' of 1978/79. Conversely, lower incomes during periods of recession have tended to curb spending on imports, improving the non-oil goods balance. However, since 1980 this pattern has been disturbed, with the non-oil goods balance moving sharply into deficit in 1982–85 despite economic recession. The further deterioration of the non-oil goods balance during the 'boom' years of 1986–88 was not unexpected. Of greater concern is the fact that the significant fall in consumer spending after 1988, with the onset of recession, should only have led to such a modest 'improvement' in the non-oil goods balance after 1989. All these factors suggest that the UK is facing even greater problems in becoming competitive in goods other than oil. The deficit on the non-oil balance grew alarmingly between the second half of the 1990s and the early years of the new millennium as the strength of the pound and relatively strong domestic growth resulted in a surge of imports.

The area and commodity composition of goods trade

Changes in the UK's pattern of goods trade, on both an area and a commodity basis, also suggest further potential problems.

An area analysis of UK trade in goods, as seen in Table 27.2, shows a clear shift since 1960 towards Western Europe generally, and the EU in particular. Both the share of UK exports to, and imports from, Western Europe nearly doubled between 1960 and 2002, with most of the shift being due to increased UK trade with EU countries. On the other hand, the share of total trade in goods with North America has fallen as regards imports, because although trade with the USA remained relatively steady, trade with Canada fell sharply. The share of UK trade with 'other OECD countries' such as Australia and New Zealand has also fallen, although trade with Japan, the remaining major country in this bloc, has increased (mainly on the import side). The oil-exporting countries (OPEC) account for a relatively steady share of UK exports and imports of goods, but since the advent of North Sea oil their share of both UK goods exports and imports has declined. The remaining significant change is the rapid fall in the importance of the 'Rest of the World' in UK trade, this category consisting mainly of Commonwealth countries and Latin American states. However, it is interesting to note the recent increase in importance of

Table 27.2 Area composition of UK goods exports (X) and imports* (M) (% of total).

		1960		1969		1979		2002	
		X	**M**	**X**	**M**	**X**	**M**	**X**	**M**
1	Western Europe	32	31	40	38	57	60	62	57
	(of which EU)	(21)	(20)	(29)	(26)	(43)	(45)	(58)	(52)
2	North America	16	21	17	20	12	13	18	15
	(of which USA)	(10)	(12)	(12)	(14)	(10)	(10)	(15)	(13)
3	Other OECD countries	13	12	12	10	6	6	6	8
	(of which Japan)	(1)	(1)	(2)	(1)	(2)	(3)	(2)	(4)
4	Oil-exporting countries	6	10	5	8	9	7	3	2
5	Rest of the World	31	23	23	20	13	11	11	18
	(of which Newly Industrial Asia)	(4)	(3)	(3)	(3)	(3)	(4)	(5)	(10)
	(E Europe and former USSR)	(2)	(3)	(3)	(4)	(3)	(3)	(2)	(2)

* Exports are measured free on board (f.o.b.), but imports include cost, insurance and freight (c.i.f.). All figures are rounded.
Sources: ONS (2003) *Monthly Digest of Statistics*, May, and previous issues.

Newly Industrial Asia (Hong Kong, Singapore, Malaysia, China, Taiwan, Thailand) in UK trade.

Table 27.3 shows the composition of UK trade in goods over the years 1960–2002. On the *export* side, the share of manufactured goods has remained at around 82% over the period 1960 to 2002, while there has been an increase in the share of oil-based products from 4% to 8%. On the *import* side, there has been a significant decline in the share of food, beverages and tobacco in total goods imports, as has also occurred for basic materials, such as textile fibres, crude rubber and metal ores. In each case the volume of imports has increased, but much more slowly than total imports, so that their *share* has fallen. The opposite is true for manufactured goods, with the volume of imports growing so fast that the share of manufactured goods in total visible imports has increased by two and a half times since 1960. In fact, the share of *finished* manufactured goods in total goods imports has increased more than fivefold.

Tables 27.2 and 27.3 show that the UK has shifted the geographical focus of her trade towards the industrialized countries of Europe, and in particular towards the EU. At the same time the UK is showing symptoms of being less able to compete with these countries in the important commodity sector of manufacturing. It may therefore be useful to look at this sector in more detail.

Trade in manufactures

The UK's problems as regards trade in manufactures manifest themselves in a variety of ways. Table 27.4 presents the share of selected countries in world *exports* of manufactures. Although not shown in detail in this table, the UK's share fell from about 17% in 1960 to 7.5% by 1984, before falling yet further to an all-time low of 6% in 2001. The significant fall in the UK share of world exports of manufactures between 1960 and 2001 was not matched by any of her main competitors.

Table 27.5 shows *export intensity* figures for the manufacturing sectors of leading economies between 1971 and 1998. The four European countries have a significantly higher *average level* of export intensity (i.e. the ratio of exports to domestic production) than countries such as the US and Japan which have much larger domestic markets to entice their producers. Between the 1970s and 1980s, the *average growth rate* of export intensity decelerated in all the countries shown in Table 27.5, with Japan and Italy actually experiencing negative growth in the 1980s. By the 1990s those two countries had improved their performance somewhat, whereas the US, Germany, France and the UK continued to experience long-term decelerations in export intensity. During the 1990s the growth of UK export intensity was about average for the group.

Table 27.5 also provides information on *import penetration* in manufacturing (figures shown in brackets). By the 1990s the *average level* of import penetration (i.e. the ratio of imports to domestic consumption) was significantly higher in the UK than in the other countries. The *average growth rate* of import penetration was positive for all countries over the 1971–98 period as they progressively specialized

Table 27.3 Commodity composition of UK goods exports (X) and goods imports (M) (% of total).

		1960		1969		1979		2002	
		X	M	X	M	X	M	X	M
(0, 1)*	Food, beverages, tobacco	5	33	6	23	7	14	5	9
(2, 4)	Basic materials	4	23	4	15	3	9	2	3
(3)	Mineral fuel and lubricants	4	10	2	11	11	12	8	4
(5–8)	Manufactured goods	84	33	85	50	76	63	84	83
	(5, 6) (i) Semi-manufactured goods	(36)	(22)	(35)	(28)	(31)	(27)	(27)	(24)
	(7, 8) (ii) Finished manufactured goods	(48)	(11)	(50)	(22)	(45)	(36)	(57)	(59)
(9)	Unclassified	3	1	3	1	3	2	1	1

* Numbers in brackets relate to the Standard International Trade Classification.
Sources: ONS (2003) *Monthly Digest of Statistics*, May, and previous issues.

Table 27.4 Share of world export of manufactures of major OECD countries (%).

	1960	1969	1979	2001
USA	22	19	16	13
Japan	7	11	14	8
France	10	8	10	6
Germany	19	19	21	12
Italy	5	7	8	5
UK	17	11	9	6
Others*	21	23	22	50

*All figures are rounded up, so that totals may not sum to 100.
Sources: WTO (2002) *International Trade Statistics 2002*; OECD (2000) *Foreign Trade by Commodities*, and previous issues.

Table 27.5 Export intensity and import penetration in manufacturing.

	Export intensity[1] (import penetration[2])			
	Average growth rate			Average level
	1971–80	1981–90	1990–98	1990–98
USA	6.9 (6.1)	1.3 (6.5)	0.6 (0.8)	13.5 (17.0)
Japan	2.8 (3.7)	−2.3 (0.8)	0.4 (0.3)	13.5 (8.0)
Germany	3.4 (4.2)	2.4 (2.6)	1.0 (1.0)	37.0 (31.0)
France	4.5 (4.0)	1.9 (3.4)	1.2 (0.9)	32.0 (31.5)
Italy	3.8 (3.0)	−1.1 (0.8)	1.1 (0.9)	26.5 (23.5)
UK	4.5 (5.1)	1.3 (3.3)	1.0 (0.9)	34.0 (37.5)

[1] Export intensity = exports/domestic production.
[2] Import penetration = imports/apparent consumption, where apparent consumption = domestic production − exports + imports.
Sources: Adapted from OECD (1994) *Assessing Structural Reforms: Lessons for the Future*, Paris, and OECD (2001) *OECD Science, Technology and Industry Scoreboard, 2001*, Paris.

in commodities for export, and imported other commodities that they required. The *growth rate* of UK import penetration, averaged over both the 1970s and 1980s, was second only to that of the US. By the 1990s, the UK rate of import penetration was about average for the group if the special case of Japan is excluded.

In conclusion, it appears from Table 27.5 that the UK's export intensity performance had stabilized by the 1990s, while on the import side the UK continued to experienced both high absolute levels of import intensity, coupled with relatively high growth rates of import intensity, for most of the period 1971–98. At the same time import penetration statistics for certain UK *sectors* have been much higher than for the equivalent sectors of other countries. For example, the UK had particularly high import penetration ratios in electrical machinery (45%), motor vehicles (53%) and computers and office machinery (116%). The main problem for the UK is that its import penetration ratios are rising relatively more rapidly than its corresponding export intensity ratios. This points to progressively more serious problems for its balance of trade in manufactures.

The problems encountered by the manufacturing sector are also revealed in Fig. 27.1, which shows the

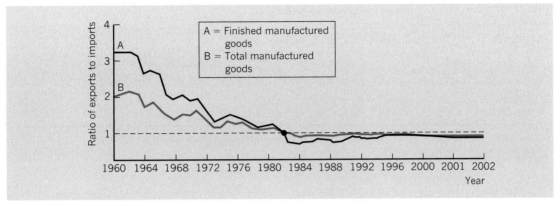

Fig. 27.1 UK balance of trade in manufactures.
Sources: ONS (2003) *Monthly Digest of Statistics,* May, and previous editions.

balance of trade (value of exports/value of imports) for both finished and total manufactured goods. The ratios have fallen progressively since the early 1960s. In fact by 1982 the UK had, on an *Overseas Trade Statistics* basis, become a net importer of *finished* manufactures and of *total* manufactures. Since the mid-1980s there has been some stabilization of this trend, but the *overall* balance of trade in both finished and total manufactures still remains in deficit.

Reasons behind UK trade performance

This deterioration in UK performance on its non-oil account, and in particular in manufactures, may be due to a number of factors: an inappropriate trade structure, a lack of price competitiveness, or an inability to compete in terms of non-price factors such as marketing, design, delivery date and product development. We examine each of these possibilities in turn.

Trade structure

It is possible to argue that the UK's relatively poor trading performance, especially in exports, has been due to its inadequate response to the changing geographical and commodity composition of world trade. The fall in the UK's share of world trade could

then be due to at least three main causes. The first is a geographical composition of exports biased towards slow-growth areas. The second is an inappropriate commodity composition of exports, with the UK sluggish in shifting her exports to commodity sectors growing rapidly in world trade. Third, it may, of course, be that irrespective of area and commodity composition, the UK has basically failed to compete *within* each geographical area and *within* each commodity group. In many analytical surveys of competitiveness, this third factor is often called the 'residual effect' since it attempts to measure the importance of factors *other* than area or commodity – such as the effects of price and non-price competition within each area and commodity group.

A major study of UK export performance was conducted by the Bank of England (Dumble 1994). Using 'shift-share' analysis, it was possible to provide information on the relative magnitudes of the 'regional' (area) and 'commodity' composition effects for UK exports. These statistics are given in Table 27.6.

From Table 27.6 it can be seen that between 1970 and 1985 the UK lost export market share valued at $8,532m. A small part of this loss ($407m) could be attributed to the UK specializing in the export of manufactured goods the demand for which was growing more slowly than the demand for manufactured goods in general (*commodity composition effect*). A larger part of this loss ($1,017m) could be attributed to the UK concentrating its exports in regional markets which were growing more slowly than the average of all world markets (*regional composition effect*). However, the main factor causing the

Table 27.6 UK export performance in manufactures ($m).

	Commodity composition effect	Regional (area) composition effect	Residual effect	Total effect*
1970–85	–407	–1,017	–7,108	–8,532
1985–90	373	6,912	3,719	11,004

*The total effect is the sum of the three effects. A positive figure represents an increase in market share.
Source: Adapted from Dumble (1994).

loss of UK export share over the period was the *residual effect*, which measures the loss of market share due to a host of factors *other than* the 'commodity' and 'regional' effects. Such residual factors included the forces of price and non-price competition which the UK faced across a range of commodities and regions over the period.

During the late 1980s the UK regained some of its export market share, to the value of $11,004m. This was due mainly to an improved performance in terms of the 'regional composition' effect. However, it is interesting to note that the 'residual' still accounted for a third of the improvement. In short, the main determinant of the UK's export competitiveness over much of the post-war period has been her competitiveness in terms of price and non-price factors *within* particular commodity groups and *within* geographical regions. This study confirms earlier work by the OECD into the loss of UK share of world manufactured exports over the period 1970–87. The OECD study also attributed the loss of market share to the effects of price and non-price factors as reflected by the size of the 'residual effect'. We now turn to an examination of UK competitiveness in terms of these price and non-price factors.

Price competitiveness

Price elasticity of demand is a traditional measure of demand responsiveness. In the trade context it can be expressed as a ratio of percentage change in quantity demanded of exports or imports, to the percentage change in price. As regards trade, however, it is not just the absolute price of UK exports or imports which is important, but UK prices *relative* to those of its main competitors. Such relative prices often reflect

differences between countries in unit costs, inflation rates or exchange rates.

International competitiveness may be assessed in a number of different ways. One is to use the UK export price divided by a weighted average of competitors' export prices. Another is to look not at prices but at costs, since even where there is no change in price, a change in costs may still affect underlying competitiveness. For instance, if price is unchanged, a rise in costs will reduce profits, perhaps reducing future investment and eventually sales. Costs, and in particular unit labour costs, are therefore often used in assessing changes in international competitiveness. Let us now examine the evidence as to whether improvements in UK price or cost competitiveness will have an important influence on trade flow.

Writers do not fully agree on the responsiveness of UK export and import volumes to changes in price. For one thing it is often difficult to identify the effect of price on quantity demanded when other factors are changing. For another, measures of price elasticity are often calculated over varying time periods, which can lead to different results. The surveys that are available suggest that the *short-run* price elasticity of demand for total UK exports varies between 0.26 and 0.46, indicating a relatively inelastic response of export demand to price change. In the *longer run*, after a time-lag of around two years, the price elasticity of demand for total visible exports rises to between 1.5 and 2.6 (Thirlwall 1980). As regards total visible imports, most studies reveal a UK price elasticity less than 1, and sometimes near to zero. Manufactured imports are rather more price-responsive, with estimates ranging from 0.9 to 1.6 (Panić 1975; Morgan and Martin 1975).

Despite the difficulties of measurement, it seems that after a time-lag of around two years, UK exports are much more responsive to price than are UK imports. This suggests that an improvement in UK price competitiveness, *vis-à-vis* other countries, would significantly raise the volume of UK exports, but have much less effect in reducing the volume of UK imports.

Of course, it is not just volumes of trade flow that matter, but also *values*. The empirical measurements of UK price elasticities are encouraging in this respect in that they fulfil the Marshall–Lerner elasticity condition. This condition must be met if a fall in export prices and a rise in import prices (e.g. via devaluation) is to raise the *value* of exports relative to the *value* of imports, thereby improving the visible balance. The condition states that the sum of the respective price elasticities of demand for exports and imports must be greater than 1. Even taking the lower bands of the elasticity estimates for total visible exports and imports, their sum is nearer 2 than 1, at least over the *longer-run* time period. In the *shorter run*, however, the sum may well be less than 1, so that observations in the UK of a J-curve effect, whereby an improvement in UK price competitiveness actually worsens the visible balance for 18 months to two years, should therefore come as no real surprise.

Another way of assessing the importance of price factors in UK trade is to look at the *share* of UK exports and imports in world trade. If, for example, UK exports became relatively cheaper, one would expect other countries to substitute UK goods for their previous purchases, thus increasing UK share of world trade in these goods. We are, in effect, measuring the ease with which UK goods are substituted for foreign goods as the former become relatively cheaper. The basic question is this: will an improvement in UK price competitiveness increase our share of the world export market, and decrease import penetration as the home market switches to relatively cheaper UK goods?

A study by J. Fagerberg looked at the factors which determined the growth of the UK's share of world export markets between 1960 and 1983. It found that labour cost (a main determinant of price competitiveness) was much less important than non-price factors (such as the capacity to deliver goods and technological competitiveness) in accounting for the UK's relatively poor ability to compete in world markets (Fagerberg 1988). Interestingly, when the UK share of world export markets improved during the period 1985–90, the relative prices and costs of UK manufacturing *vis-à-vis* her main competitors actu-

ally *deteriorated* (Dumble 1994). This tends to suggest, once again, that factors *other than price* account for much of the UK's export competitiveness.

The picture is similar for imports. One early OECD survey found little link between UK price competitiveness and import penetration. A statistical survey by the present author has substantiated these results for the period 1963–2002. The UK's ratio of imports to home demand was barely affected by observed changes in UK price competitiveness during this period, whatever the time-lags introduced. The analysis noted above should not be mistaken to mean that price factors are *not* important in the global trading environment. Indeed, price is an integral part of the 'marketing mix'. Lowering costs to enable prices to be set in a flexible manner is crucial to trading success.

Unfortunately, the UK's international cost competitiveness has deteriorated over the last few years. For example, in 2002, the US Department of Labor announced that its hourly compensation cost for workers in manufacturing was $20.32. In comparison, the hourly costs for other main economies were Italy ($13.76), France ($15.88), UK ($16.14), Germany ($23.84) and Japan ($19.59). The level of labour cost in the UK was lower than in the US, Germany and Japan, but was no longer the lowest of this group of countries, as was the case in 1995. Despite these adverse trends in the UK's price/cost competitiveness, many major studies have shown that non-price factors also have a very significant role to play in the nation's overall competitiveness.

Non-price competitiveness

Income

The level of world income is an important factor affecting demand for UK goods, and hence her trading position. As early as the 1980s, Thirlwall (1980) suggested that the income elasticity of demand for *total* UK exports (which measures the responsiveness of UK exports to changes in world income) had been relatively low over the previous 30 years, being in the main less than unity. The figure for *manufactured* exports was also generally below unity, although *individual sectors and products* often had elasticity figures which varied between 1.0 and 1.5. These values tend to be lower than those for our competitors. For Germany the income elasticity of demand for total exports is as high as 2.5, and for Japan 3.5.

However, it is well known that changes in the level of UK income have a significant effect on the UK demand for imports. In other words, the income elasticity of demand for *total* UK imports is high, ranging between 1.6 and 2. For *total manufactured* imports the value of income elasticity is even higher, between 2.6 and 3.0, and for *finished manufactured* imports higher still, around 4.6.

The UK income elasticity figure for *total imports* is not significantly different from that of other countries – USA 1.5, Germany 1.8 – but for *manufactured imports* it does seem higher in the UK than elsewhere. The study by Panić (1975) found the income elasticity of demand for manufactured products to be 3.1 in the UK, but only 2.2 in France and 2.1 in Germany. These elasticity values highlight three important points:

1   That income elasticity of demand for total UK imports is higher than for total UK exports.

2   That for manufactures, particularly finished manufactures, this gap between income elasticity of demand for UK imports and exports is even greater.

3   That other countries have similar or lower (as in manufactures) income elasticities of demand for imports, but experience higher income elasticities of demand for their exports.

The implications of these figures are clear. When income (and therefore demand) in the world economy rises, UK imports will tend to grow faster than UK exports, especially for manufactures. Other countries will not suffer to the same extent as the UK. Whilst their imports may grow steadily, their exports will grow relatively faster than UK exports, so that their visible balance comes under less strain.

Unfortunately, the effect of higher income on imports is not easily reversed. The data suggest a sort of 'ratchet effect', so that although the ratio of manufactured imports to GDP rises on the upswing of the business cycle, it does not fall to the same extent on the downswing. There is then a real danger that higher import ratios for manufactures become a permanent feature of the economy.

One reason for exports rising relatively slowly when UK and world income increases is the tendency

for firms to concentrate on the more secure home market when domestic demand is high. This shift away from the export market and towards the home market has affected our export performance, with exports progressively becoming a 'residual' market for UK producers.

Another reason for the slow growth of exports when UK income increases, and with it domestic demand, might be the failure of firms to increase their total capacity in order to satisfy *both* home and foreign markets. For instance, an increase in total capacity may require UK companies to increase their investment in plant and equipment, and this is never easy.

Unfortunately, even if UK firms *do* manage to increase total capacity by channelling more resources into increased investment, the *composition* of this investment may be biased against export growth. For example, it has been argued that during the 1980s those UK sectors which invested most in plant and equipment were the ones which were least open to foreign competition (Muellbauer 1990). In his study, Muellbauer calculates 'tradeability' and 'investment growth' ratios for 25 sectors in the UK economy. The *tradeability ratio* is defined as the ratio of exports or imports to total sales (whichever is the largest). If this ratio is high, it indicates that the sector is relatively 'open' to trade, and thus to foreign competition. If the ratio is low, then the sector is less involved in trade and is not affected so much by foreign competition. The *tradeability ratio* of each sector was compared with the *growth of investment* in that sector between 1979 and 1987 (expressed as a ratio using 1979 as the base year). The general conclusion was that the investment ratio tends to be very *high* in sectors such as Distribution, Communications and Banking which have *low* tradeability ratios, i.e. which are not so open to foreign competition. In other areas (such as manufacturing) where the investment ratio is lower, the tradeability ratio is high, i.e. they are more open to foreign competition. The argument here is that investment has not grown sufficiently in those sectors most open to foreign competition. This obviously prevents many UK industries from competing effectively abroad. Similarly, too much investment may have gone into sectors such as banking, insurance and distribution, which are not so open to foreign competition. This bias in the investment ratios may inhibit the UK's long-run ability to produce goods for the world markets. This has particular significance when placed alongside research which indicates that the growth of UK productivity is closely related to the degree of openness of the economy (Proudman and Redding 1997). This research shows that the sectors of the UK economy which are most open (i.e. have higher ratios for export/output and import/domestic sales) tend to have the highest labour and total factor productivity growth rates. Hence, low investment in these 'open' sectors will diminish the prospects for the UK closing the 'productivity gap' with countries such as the US (see Chapter 1).

Quality, service and other effects

Price and income are not the only factors influencing UK trade performance. In the home market, competition between oligopolistic firms often takes the form of non-price competition (see Chapter 6). Since much of world trade, especially in manufactures, involves competition between domestic and foreign multinationals (see Chapter 7), it is hardly surprising that it is often non-price competition that determines which nations will be successful in the export market. Indeed a major study by Hooley *et al.* (1988) of 1,380 UK companies found that only 7% of companies cited price as being a significant source of competitive advantage, with 26% citing company/brand reputation, 21% product performance, 18% product quality and 14% product design.

Two types of non-price competition seem particularly important for both domestic and overseas sales: first, competition in *product characteristics*, such as quality, design, ease of maintenance and the development of entirely new products; and second, competition in *sales characteristics*, such as delivery date, after-sales service, marketing strategies, and the use of agents and subsidiaries at home and abroad.

To quantify the relative importance of non-price factors, such as quality and service, is a difficult task, made more so by a dearth of regular statistics in this area. However, some *ad hoc* attempts have been made at statistical analysis. One prominent method for evaluating the importance of non-price factors is to compare the average value per unit weight of exports from different countries. This figure is obtained by dividing the total value of goods exported by a certain sector, e.g. mechanical engineering, by the total weight of such exports. The 'value per ton' that results from this calculation is simply the average price per ton. The rationale behind value per ton comparisons is that if goods are identi-

cal in non-price characteristics such as quality, international competition will tend to make value per ton (average price per ton) similar in whichever country those goods are produced. It follows that any discrepancy in value per ton between countries in a given export product is an indication that non-price differences exist in that product.

Research based on the years 1962–75 found that the value per ton of UK exports from the non-electrical sector (essentially mechanical engineering) was the lowest of all the major industrialized countries. Apart from Italy, the rate of growth of value per ton was also lowest in the UK between those dates. Similar results were observed in a separate study of a wide range of manufactured exports traded between the UK and Germany (Connell 1980: Chapter 3). A number of inferences can be drawn:

1   The lower value per ton of UK exports may reflect lower prices in the UK for *similar*-quality products. However, if UK exports were cheaper, and of the same quality, then the UK's share of the world market in such products should increase! Since the UK's share did *not* increase, it is unconvincing to explain lower value per ton of UK exports in terms of lower UK prices for similar-quality products.

2   It could still be argued that the lower-priced UK exports are similar in quality to those produced abroad, but that static or falling market share is due to inadequate sales back-up. United Kingdom exporters may have lowered prices (reducing value per ton) in the hope that relative cheapness would raise sales and help compensate for an inability to market the product adequately.

3   The relatively low value per ton of UK exports could be due to differences in product mix between different countries. The UK may be going progressively 'down market', exporting 'less technology-intensive' products. The price, and therefore value per ton, of UK exports would then tend to be lower than in those countries which export a higher proportion of the 'more technology-intensive' products (see Chapter 7).

Even if the precise cause of the low value per ton of UK exports is difficult to identify, it seems reasonable to assume that it must be due to factors *other than* price competition amongst export goods of similar quality, especially since in many cases the value per ton of other countries' exports was two or three times higher than that of UK exports. Non-price factors – quality, design, marketing, after-sales service, etc. – must account for much of the substantial difference in value per ton.

Other research during the late 1990s on unit values (i.e. value of exports divided by quantity of exports) have followed the approach used in the Connell survey noted above. Such surveys have indicated that about 38.8% of the UK's total manufactured exports were in the 'up market' unit value category, just below the average for the EU (39.8%) as a whole, but still behind the UK's main competitors such as the US (60.1%), Japan (55.7%) and Germany (49.5%) (OECD 2001). In other words, although there are signs that the UK's trade performance in non-price terms has improved since the 1960s and 1970s, there is still some catching up to do.

Product quality

Product quality depends on many interrelated factors, but it is clear that most high quality products are ones which tend to have a high research and development content, are technologically complex and are also skill intensive. The UK's trade performance in various technological sectors is shown in Table 27.7, which gives the export ratios and import penetration figures for 1990 and 1999. On the export side, 34% of the UK's manufactured exports were in the high-technology sector in 1999. This figure was below that of the US, but was above the EU average and similar to that of Japan. If we take both high and medium-high technology sectors together, then again the UK's export share performance was not as good as that of the US or Japan but was better than the EU average, and showed sound improvement over the decade.

When we look at the import penetration figures, we find that by 1999, some 75% of the UK's domestic demand for high-technology goods came from abroad. Although it is natural for import penetration figures in the high-technological sectors to increase over time in most developed countries as product differentiation increases, the absolute level of the UK's

Table 27.7 Export shares and import penetration in manufactures in 1990 and 1999.

	High technology		Medium-high technology		Medium-low technology		Low technology	
	1990	1999	1990	1999	1990	1999	1990	1999
France	16	24	41	41	18	14	25	21
	(39)	(56)	(38)	(48)	(22)	(23)	(21)	(25)
Germany	14	18	51	51	16	14	17	15
	(52)	(79)	(28)	(34)	(21)	(24)	(25)	(29)
Italy	10	11	38	40	19	18	33	31
	(42)	(65)	(27)	(38)	(16)	(18)	(13)	(17)
UK	26	34	38	37	16	13	18	16
	(61)	(75)	(45)	(52)	(23)	(28)	(25)	(27)
EU	15	22	41	41	19	15	25	22
	(51)	(69)	(34)	(43)	(21)	(23)	(20)	(25)
Japan	30	31	51	51	13	12	6	5
	(9)	(17)	(5)	(7)	(7)	(6)	(8)	(10)
USA	33	38	39	37	11	10	17	15
	(20)	(31)	(21)	(25)	(10)	(12)	(11)	(15)

Notes: Non-bracketed figures refer to the percentage share of the various technological sectors in total manufacturing exports. Bracketed figures refer to imports in the technological sectors concerned as a percentage of total domestic demand for that sector's goods. Figures for manufacturing exports are rounded and may not add up to 100.
(*High technology sectors* include aircraft, computing, pharmaceuticals, communications, etc.; *medium-high technology sectors* include automobiles, electrical machinery, chemicals, etc.; *medium-low technology sectors* include rubber/plastics, shipbuilding, ferrous/non-ferrous metals, etc.; *low-technology sectors* include paper/printing, wood products, textiles, food, etc.)
Source: Adapted from OECD (2001) *OECD Science, Technology and Industry Scoreboard 2001*.

import penetration ratios in this sector had reached significantly high levels by 1999. This figure was equalled by that of Germany, whose position seemed to worsen significantly in the 1990s. If we take both high and medium-high technological sectors, we again see that the UK's absolute levels of import penetration are high by the late 1990s, although other European countries such as France, Germany and Italy were also experiencing higher import penetration ratios.

In conclusion, the figures in Table 27.7 show that although the UK's export performance in the high/medium technology sectors stabilized during the 1990s, the import penetration figures were particularly high. This points to the UK's long-term inability to develop import-substitute industries on a sufficient scale in the relatively higher value added sectors of the economy. Given these tendencies, there seems a risk that the UK may revert to the down-market tendencies well documented by various case studies carried out in the 1980s and 1990s.

For example, a tendency for the UK to produce, and often export, lower quality goods can be seen in a major survey of 29 manufacturing plants producing biscuits in four European countries, i.e. the Netherlands, France, UK and Germany (Mason et al. 1994). In this sector they found that the value-added per ton of biscuits was between 15% (Netherlands/France) and 75% (Germany) higher than in the UK, and that the reason for this differential had very little to do with the type of capital equipment used. Basically, the UK industry specialized in

highly automated, mass-produced, low value-added biscuits – precisely the type of product which is prone to international competition from developing countries. Much of the reason for such a low value-added strategy was traced to the alleged lack of suitable labour skills at all company levels. Similarly, a study of the UK and German furniture industry (Steedman and Wagner 1987) showed that even though the industry was far from being in the 'high technology' class, it was still obvious that the UK furniture industry continued to use technically less advanced equipment and produced for the middle- to low-quality end of the market. German firms, on the other hand, used more advanced equipment and specialized in high-quality products, exporting some of these to the UK!

Any assessment of a country's relative strengths and weaknesses in international trade in technological goods should focus not only on exports but also on imports. Table 27.8 shows the contribution made by various industrial sectors (defined by their technological intensity) to the manufacturing trade balance of the major economies. This measure of the contribution of various sectors to a country's trade balance can help identify the structural strengths and weaknesses in each economy. A *positive value* for an industry indicates that the specific sector's trade balance performs relatively better than the total manufacturing trade balance. This means that the country concerned specializes in that particular sector to a greater extent than might be expected from the 'weighted norm' for that sector. A *negative value* indicates that the sector's trade balance performs relatively worse

Table 27.8 Revealed comparative advantage in manufacturing exports.

	High technology		Medium-high technology		Medium-low technology		Low technology	
	1990	1999	1990	1999	1990	1999	1990	1999
France	−0.4	0.4	2.0	1.6	−0.5	−0.6	−1.1	−1.6
Germany	−2.2	−2.6	9.3	7.4	−1.5	−0.5	−6.1	−4.6
Italy	−3.5	−4.2	0.2	−0.1	−0.8	0.5	4.1	3.8
UK	2.2	2.4	1.9	1.0	0.5	0.6	−4.9	−4.2
Europe (15)	−1.4	−1.2	2.3	1.8	−0.2	0.1	−0.9	−0.9
Japan	6.6	0.7	14.2	14.4	−5.7	−0.8	−15.1	−14.3
USA	5.3	5.0	1.4	0.4	−2.2	−0.9	−4.6	−4.5

Notes: The revealed comparative advantage figure is derived from the equation $(X_j - M_j) - (X - M)(X_j + M_j)/(X + M)$ where j is the type of industry (according to the technological intensity) and X and M refer to exports and imports respectively.
Source: Adapted from OECD (2001) *OECD Science, Technology and Industry Scoreboard 2001*.

than the total manufacturing trade balance, suggesting that the country concerned specializes in that particular sector to a lesser extent than might be expected from the 'weighted norm' for that sector. These figures provide the 'revealed comparative advantage' or specialization profiles of the countries involved in terms of technological intensity.

From Table 27.8 it can be seen that the UK performed relatively better between 1990 and 1999 than her main European competitors in the *high-technology sectors*, although lagging behind Japan and the US. In the *medium–high technology sectors*, the UK's revealed comparative advantage is positive but falling and is below the performance of the EU as a whole, and Japan, Germany and the US in particular. The UK's revealed comparative advantage is also positive but falling in the *medium–low technology sectors*, but this time it is above the performance of the EU as a whole. The decline in these high/medium technological intensity ratios relative to its competitors in recent years may be of some concern to UK policy-makers.

Even the UK income elasticities of demand we noted earlier could be considered symptoms of 'product inferiority'. The low income elasticity of demand for UK exports, and high income elasticity of demand for UK imports, both suggest that at higher income, goods produced by the UK export industries and by the import substitute industries are replaced by more attractive, higher-quality goods from abroad. There is some evidence to show that European exports were moving in the direction of more highly skilled, capital-intensive products in the early 1980s and that the UK needed to become more involved in these high-technology products to increase its export share and to reduce import penetration. In 1987 an important study (Patel and Pavitt 1987) attempted to assess the relationship between the UK's technological competitiveness in world markets and her trading performance. Measuring the UK's trading performance in certain sectors of the economy was relatively straightforward, since figures for exports and imports are easily available. However, it was more difficult to devise a measure which reflected the UK's technological competitiveness in relation to other countries. Patel and Pavitt overcame this problem by studying the *number of patents* which were granted in the USA between 1963 and 1984 and calculated an index which measured the share of those patents which had *originated* in the UK. For example, it was obvious that if one sector of

US industry used a large proportion of patents which had originally been invented in the UK, then this meant that the UK was technologically very competitive in this sector. Conversely, a sector with a low ratio of US patents originating from the UK indicated a relatively lower level of UK technical competence in this particular sector. By comparing these measures of UK technological competitiveness with UK trade performance, sector by sector, it was possible to see that the interrelationships between trade and technology were very close. For example, in the electrical and electronics industry, the UK's technological competitiveness was medium to low and her trade competitiveness was also low. For the chemical industry, the UK's technological competitiveness was medium to high, and so was her trade competitiveness in this sector. In other words there seemed to be a strong relationship between technological competitiveness and trading performance. Since EU exports of high technology products have grown at a faster pace than manufacturing in general, it is important for the UK to improve its technological competitiveness in such products if it is to compete successfully with its main EU rivals. This point is further reinforced by the work of Lall (1998) which indicated that even the developing countries are increasing their share of world manufactured exports in both medium and high technology products. For example, between 1980 and 1998 the developing countries' overall share of world manufactured exports had risen from 11% to 27%, and interestingly their share of medium technology exports has risen from 8% to 17% and of high technology exports from 12% to 31% over the same period (UNCTAD 2002). The pressure on the UK to progressively improve its trade performance in medium to high technology products within manufacturing seems likely to continue.

The relatively low income elasticity of demand for UK manufactured exports does tend to indicate that UK producers are unable to react promptly to world demand with good quality products. However, it has been argued that the value of income elasticity of demand for UK manufactured exports has increased since the late 1970s. This would suggest that UK manufacturing industry has become more responsive to changes in world demand since the recession of the early 1980s (Landesmann and Snell 1989). The crux of this theory is that the aggregate income elasticity of demand for UK manufactured exports rose from 0.74 in 1979 to 1.0 by 1986, and that this may be due to the shake-out of inefficient exporters during the 1979–81 slump which left a core of relatively more efficient exporters. By definition, 'poor' exporters have low income elasticities and 'good' exporters have high income elasticity figures. Improvements were found in many industries, with the income elasticity figure for electrical engineering rising from 0.78 in 1979 to 1.3 by 1986, the figure for textiles and clothing rising from 0.8 to 1.3, and for transport from 0.8 to 1.0 over the same period. These figures do tend to point to an export performance from UK industry which is more responsive to world demand since the early 1980s. Indeed, the UK has a number of companies which *export* a significant percentage of their UK turnover. For example, Lucas (vehicle/aircraft accessories), Caterpillar UK (earthmoving equipment) and SIEBE (control devices and compressed air equipment) all export more than 80% of their turnover, while Rolls-Royce and NEI plc (aero engineering), Allied Colloids (industrial chemicals), Amersham International (radioactive materials) and Polaroid (photographic and optical equipment) export over 70% of their turnover. Despite these encouraging signs, it should also be remembered that the UK manufacturing sector needs a greater *absolute number* of firms which are responsive to the market in order to increase total exports significantly. This is difficult to achieve when the manufacturing base of the economy is being eroded, as was seen in Chapter 1 of this book.

This conclusion is supported by a survey in 1994 which found that UK firms were much more likely to approve capital investment which was aimed at cutting production costs than investment to enhance new product development (Wardlow 1994). This suggests that the UK's investment growth in the early 1990s was more likely to *deepen* the industrial base rather than *widen* it across many companies. In other words, the UK's traditionally successful industries such as pharmaceuticals and aerospace have tended to strengthen their position, while the range of products offered by the UK as a whole has barely been extended.

However, even so-called successful industries should not be complacent, because research by the DTI into the office machinery and chemical industries has shown that while the UK has world-class companies in these areas, it still has a 'long tail' of relatively low productivity companies *within* each industry in comparison to Germany, France and Italy (HMSO 1996). Signs that this lower productivity and quality

record might improve in the future have come from the growth of 'benchmarking' in the UK. Benchmarking occurs when companies set out to compare themselves systematically with the best in their industry, thus helping them to establish targets for improvement. In 1996 a number of benchmarking providers, including the DTI, British Quality Foundation, the CBI PROBE initiative, and Cranfield University, agreed to work towards establishing a *National Benchmarking Network*. In October of the same year, the UK launched the United Kingdom Benchmarking Index (UKBI) which, by 2000, was providing some 60 performance measures in its benchmark system. These included profitability, return on net assets (RONA) growth, innovation, investment, cash management, customer satisfaction and operations and people management. It is through such networks that the increased quality and productivity necessary for competitive exports might be secured.

The results of a Benchmarking Index Survey in 2002 showed that the top 25% of companies achieved 10 times the profit levels, were five times as efficient and had only a third of the labour turnover as the bottom 25% of companies (Business Link 2002). This provides some evidence that the 'long tail' of UK manufacturing companies noted previously is still a problem. Interestingly, benchmarking surveys have also shed light on product quality and export potential of UK companies. For example, a benchmarking report on the UK's processing industries (chemicals, pharmaceuticals, plastics, rubber) in 2001 suggested quality problems for the UK processing industry in that its defect rate of 6.5 per 100 compared unfavourably with the world-class level in this sector of 1 per 100. The report concluded that bringing more UK companies to world-class levels could reduce costs by a fifth, increase sales by £9.5bn, and create £1.26bn worth of trade surplus for the UK (PICME 2001).

Design

Improved design of new products, as well as product quality, is also essential for UK competitiveness. Research shows that firms in both traditional and new sectors which invest significantly in design are more successful than firms which pay less attention to this feature. Further, for those companies using professional designers, around 90% of the products which reached the production stage were found to be a commercial success, with an average payback period of under 15 months (HMSO 1996). Research by the London Business School in 1998 showed that an extra 1% of sales revenue devoted to product design and development was likely to increase company sales value and profits by around 3% to 4%.

Encouraging the design aspects of product competitiveness is also important, because there is often a close relationship between the design of a product and its cost of production. For example, it is not always realized that a significant proportion of the cost of a finished product is often dictated by the specific design which is chosen at the outset. Figure 27.2 indicates two aspects of the cost structure of a typical product development cycle, from the initial 'idea' stage through to the 'design' stage and then to the final 'ongoing production' stage. The lower line indicates the percentage of total development costs *actually spent* at each stage in the cycle; the upper line indicates the percentage of total development costs *committed* at each stage in the cycle. The importance of the 'concept' and 'detailed design' stages can be clearly seen from Fig. 27.2. For example, while the absolute amount of money *actually spent* in the design stages is relatively low as compared to the pro-duction stages, it is obvious that it is in the 'concept' and 'detailed design' stages that the major share of the lifecycle development costs of the product are *committed*. From the graph, it appears that some 85% of a product's final costs have been committed by the end of the design stage.

According to executives of General Motors in the US, some 70% of the cost of producing the transmission mechanism of its trucks is determined at the design stage. Similarly, in a study of the Rolls-Royce company, John Corbett found that 80% of the final costs of some 2,000 different components were determined by the design adopted. This means that good, efficient design is an essential requirement for keeping costs at a minimum when competing in international markets (Griffiths 1989).

An important report on the relationship between design, competitiveness and manufacturing performance (Sentance and Walters 1997) provided added confirmation of the role of product development and design in UK competitiveness and UK trade performance. A survey of 800 UK companies yielded three main conclusions: first, that there was a significant and positive relationship between the amount of internally generated product development/design and the percentage of sales going to export markets; second, that there was also a significant relationship

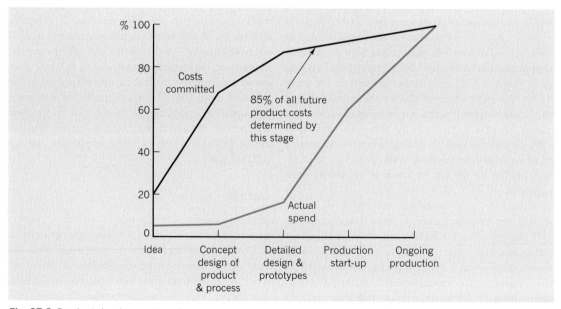

Fig. 27.2 Product development cycle.

between internally generated 'hard' design expenditure (i.e. expenditure on technical, process/system and engineering design) and export performance; and third, that the relationship between design activity and business performance varied systematically with company size, indicating that smaller firms made less effective use of design than larger companies. This work has been backed up by more recent research carried out for the Design Council which indicated that 90% of a large sample of UK businesses felt that design improvements increased the quality of their products, 84% felt that it helped increase profits and 70% believed that such improvements reduced their costs of production (Design Council 2000).

Product marketing and sales

Apart from quality, marketing and selling operations can have a substantial impact on market share. Reports in the early 1980s indicated a declining UK share in total OECD exports in the majority of the 30 industrial sectors studied – with 'inadequate marketing' the single factor most often quoted as the explanation for this poor export performance. An earlier NEDO report on the UK textile industry had concluded that most of the UK's problems in competing with its EU counterparts arose from a poor performance in packaging, delivery date and after-sales service, rather than from price.

It does appear that other countries have devoted more sales effort to the export market than has the UK. There is considerable evidence to suggest that UK competitors have larger sales forces in the export sector, and that they also employ more highly skilled marketing specialists, and pay more attention to the activities of promotion, advertising, delivery date and after-sales service.

The importance of *early delivery* in determining export success has been stressed by many writers, such as Fagerberg (1988). He found that the loss of UK market share in manufacturing exports was very closely linked to the capacity of UK companies to deliver goods efficiently. This in turn was dependent on the diffusion of technology within companies, and on the growth of UK investment in plant and equipment. It can be seen, therefore, that an efficient delivery of goods depends on many interrelated factors. However, it should be understood that even if UK companies can produce good products, there is still the problem of cutting down the time between receiv-

ing a customer's order and actual delivery. It has been calculated that between 33% and 50% of the time taken between receiving an order and final delivery is taken up by sales and distribution activities, so that any effort to cut this time period will increase competitiveness and lower costs.

The importance of marketing efficiency for a successful product launch is standard knowledge. For example, a survey of 1,000 product launches in 320 firms based in Europe and North America concluded that the failure of new product launches was closely correlated to a lack of market research and market testing, and ineffective market launches (Cooper 1994). Similarly, a survey of the Pacific Rim countries of Australia, New Zealand and Singapore found that the companies which achieved the most impressive competitive advantage were those with a clear marketing orientation (Ghosh *et al.* 1994).

To achieve marketing effectiveness, UK firms must respond actively, rather than passively, to enquiries from foreign customers. It has been calculated that UK exports could be over 10% higher if passive exporters could match the average active performer. Similarly, there is the need to increase efforts on market research. An analysis of UK-based firms aiming to invest abroad in order to penetrate foreign markets found that less than 60% had undertaken any specific consumer research or done any work on assessing market demand, distribution channels or employment regulations in the countries in which they intended to operate (HMSO 1996). The irony is that while UK market research companies have a significant (23%) share of the EU market for such services, the status accorded by UK manufacturing firms to market research was the lowest (with the exception of Italy) recorded in a major seven-country study (HMSO 1996)! The creation of the 'Marketing Council' in 1995 has helped foster a greater understanding of the importance of this form of non-price competition.

The importance of trade in goods for the UK

It could be argued that there is no reason to worry about the problems facing the UK on her non-oil goods trade, because oil and services will rectify the financial imbalance. However, the situation is not as simple as this, involving long-term competitive problems within the UK economy which other parts of the accounts may not always be able to offset.

Problems of competitiveness for goods production in general, and manufacturing in particular, are important for a number of reasons.

1 The UK's involvement in international trade is significantly higher than in large economies such as the US and Japan and tends to follow more closely the pattern of her European competitors. For example, the UK ratio of exports of goods to GDP was 20% in 2002 compared to 22% in Italy, 25% in France and 29% in Germany, but only 10% in Japan and 7% in the US. Since exports are an injection into the domestic circular flow of income, any lack of competitiveness in the international markets will have a particularly important effect on economies such as the UK's in which exports are an important component of aggregate demand.

2 The importance of manufactured goods is particularly vital to the balance of payments on current account. Around 38% of all export earnings on current account, and also about 42% of all expenditure on imports, derive from trade in manufactures. A less competitive performance in the manufacturing sector will, therefore, have a significant effect on the current account.

3 The relative performance of UK manufacturing exports *vis-à-vis* other countries can be measured by comparing the real growth of UK manufactured exports over a given period with the growth in demand for manufactures in the markets where the UK sells its goods. In other words the UK's 'relative manufacturing export' performance measures the extent to which UK manufacturing exporters maintain, expand or lose their market share. If the growth of demand for manufactures in the UK's current markets is greater than the growth of UK manufactured exports to those markets, then the UK will have lost market share, and the figure will be negative. Over the period 1991–2002, the UK lost market share in manufactured exports at the rate of −1.5% per year, twice the average figures for all the OECD countries (−0.8% per year). By 2002, the manufactured exports of China equalled those of the UK as did the combined manufactured exports of Korea and Singapore.

4 There is evidence that trade in manufactures between the developed industrialized countries is increasing at the expense of such trade with the newly industrialized countries, at a time when it is these developed countries which are the main threat to UK trade performance. For instance, in the particularly important sector of machinery and transport equipment (43% of total UK manufactured exports) the developed industrialized countries have been the source of 80% of total world exports in this category since 1965, with 60% destined for other developed industrialized countries. Complaints about competition from 'low-wage' countries, although serious, may be rather less significant to the UK than competition from these highly industrialized nations. In any case, competition from the newly industrialized countries is itself often competition from other industrialized nations through the guise of multinational company activities in those developing nations. Therefore, the fact that more and more trade is conducted between the *developed* industrial nations, and that more of that trade is in manufactures, suggests that an open economy like the UK's will encounter serious problems if it becomes progressively less competitive in non-oil goods trade.

5 The import penetration ratio in manufactures has risen in the UK from 17% to nearly 47% between 1968 and 2000. Some have argued that this loss of UK competitiveness in the production of import substitutes matters little, since the ratio of exports to total sales of manufactures (the export sales ratio) has also risen in the UK from 18% to 41% over the same period. However, it has been pointed out that the export sales ratio is often artificially high in times of recession. As demand falls, and with it total sales of manufactures, the ratio becomes artificially high since the denominator falls faster than the numerator. Although UK export performance has improved, it should be understood that a higher ratio during periods of slow growth or recession may be a misleading index of long-term UK export competitiveness. Also, it is worth noting that although the exports/sales ratio did rise up to 1985, it has not changed much since that date, while the import/home demand ratio continued to rise throughout the 1980s and 1990s.

Services, investments and the current account

Loss of competitiveness on the UK's non-oil goods balance *is* important for all these reasons. Although the UK oil surplus has alleviated many problems on current account (see Table 27.1), it would be short-sighted to see this as a cure for all our ills. The oil surplus has eased the immediate strains on the goods balance, but there is little evidence of improvement in UK price and non-price competitiveness. In fact oil has contributed to a high exchange rate for the pound (see Chapter 26), and in this sense has made UK producers less price-competitive in foreign and domestic markets.

Does the UK's deteriorating performance on non-oil goods trade in general, and manufacturing in particular, matter when we are still a major surplus country on services and investments? It is quite true that the UK has surpluses on services (in common with the US, France and Spain) and also surpluses on investment income (in common with Japan and Benelux countries), but there is no guarantee that such surpluses will *grow* fast enough to compensate for the deterioration in exports of manufactures. When we convert the UK surpluses on services and investment income into proportions of GDP (at factor cost) we find, over the last 15 years, that the ratios of surpluses on services to GDP varied between 0.7% to 2.0% and the ratios of surpluses on investment to GDP varied from 0.03% to 1.6%, but with no discernible upward trend. Essentially, the non-goods account is made up of three elements as seen in Table 27.1: first, net earnings on investments, i.e. from interest, profit and dividends (IPD); second, earnings from services such as shipping, civil aviation, general government services and financial services (such as banking and insurance); and third, transfers between the UK government and other institutions in the form of overseas aid or payments to the EU.

On average, the only element which has been in continuous deficit over the last 20 years has been the transfer element, while IPD has, in most cases, been in surplus. Earnings from services remain in surplus, with about 50% of the positive balance on services being provided by the financial services and 'other business services' sectors. It would be unwise for the UK to rely on the growth of such services to continue to compensate for the decline in manufactures and other visible items. This is particularly true when the future of London as an international banking and financial centre can depend on 'arbitrary' factors such as the decision to locate the European Central Bank in Frankfurt, and the implications of the single European Currency for European financial markets. The projected merger of the London Stock Exchange and its German equivalent in Frankfurt, though it failed to materialize, is perhaps one indication of the threat to the UK's international earnings from financial services.

Other advanced countries are also concentrating on services as a means of increasing their incomes. For example, between 1975 and 2001 the UK's share of world exports of commercial services fell from 12.5% to 7% as new countries entered the market for international commercial services. By 2001 the US share of world exports of such services was 18%, with France (5%), Germany (5%), Italy (4%) and Japan (4%) also being significant players. Despite the fact that the UK's exports of such services grew at the healthy rate of 8% per annum between 1991 and 2001, the UK imports of these services grew at 10% per annum – higher than all her major competitors (WTO 2002). Although the UK's world position in international services stabilized in the 1990s, some difficulties remain. For example, Table 27.9 shows that by 2001 the UK had an overall deficit in services with the EU of around £2.4bn. This was due in no small measure to the inability of the financial services surplus to offset the large deficit on travel/tourism.

Table 27.9 suggests that most of the UK's surpluses derive from the financial services, insurance and computing services sectors. On a country basis, the UK's surpluses in services appeared to be predominantly with the US, Germany and Japan. If these countries improve their own competitiveness in such services, as they have already done in manufacturing sectors, then it would be rash for the UK to rely on her trade in services to support progressive deterioration on the non-oil goods account.

Interestingly, if we investigate the UK's share of world trade in goods *and* services, which is the format presented in the new UK trade accounts, then the results can be seen in Table 27.10. From the table it can be seen that the UK's share of world exports of goods *and* services has dropped since the 1970s, stabilizing at around 5% of world exports. The task in the future will be to keep the UK's share at this level

Table 27.9 The UK's balance on services by sector and country, 2001 (£m).

Country	Trans-portation	Travel	Communi-cations	Construction	Insurance	Financial	Computer and information	Royalties and licence fees	Personal, cultural and recreational	Government	Other business	Total services
EU total	-3,103	-10,275	-92	16	552	5,251	1,077	872	215	-671	3,762	-2,396
Germany	-720	119	-23	3	73	1,020	350	110	143	-927	653	801
France	-676	-3,017	-47	-11	122	1,281	176	15	4	-83	33	-2,203
Italy	-368	-703	1	–	109	559	28	59	–	–	206	-142
Spain	-676	-4,273	-30	–	25	365	20	33	12	–	96	-4,482
USA	202	-1,310	-188	4	741	1,697	226	-495	27	55	3,812	4,771
Japan	3	228	-11	–	128	595	76	31	38	–	246	1,329
World	-3,556	-13,268	-348	46	3,056	9,576	1,849	1,486	464	-451	12,444	11,300

Source: ONS (2003) *UK Trade in Services 2001* (Business Monitor) UKA1.

in the face of pressures from both developed and developing countries.

A final point to observe is that the development of services is not necessarily divorced from manufacturing, in fact it is likely that some 25% of employment in the service industry depends directly on manufacturing. Service industries often need manufactured goods such as computer and data processing equipment, so that the contraction of manufacturing can have adverse repercussions on services. Indeed research in 1998 by the investment bank Paribas showed that for every 1% fall in manufacturing output there was a resulting fall of 0.4% in service sector output.

Given the strength of manufactured items, by value, in UK exports, it has been calculated that it would need more than a 2.5% rise in the exports of services to compensate for each 1% fall in manufactured exports. Members of the Cambridge-Harvard Research Group on UK Competitiveness calculated that for the period 1992–2003, even with economic growth at a modest average of 2.5% per year, the UK would continue to have a balance of payments deficit. For the accounts to balance, there would need to be a trebling in the exports of services, equivalent in value to the entire current international financial activity of New York and Tokyo put together!

Apart from these reservations, it should also be remembered that the UK export of services is only 49% of the value of manufactured exports, and only 43% of the value of total exports of goods. A given percentage change in exports of manufactures or of total exports of goods will have a larger *absolute* impact on the current account than would the same percentage change in the export of services. The same is true of imports. To concentrate on developing the invisible sector may be an inappropriate response to any loss of competitiveness experienced in non-oil visible trade.

Conclusion

This chapter has attempted to analyse the trends in the UK balance of trade on goods, with special reference to trade in manufactures. Although UK goods trade has adapted along similar lines to that of her competitors as regards both geographical area and

Table 27.10 Shares of world exports of goods and services (%).

	1970–79	1980–89	1992	1994	2002
USA	12.1	12.1	12.9	13.3	12.4
Germany	10.2	9.4	10.4	9.2	9.1
France	7.0	6.7	7.3	6.5	4.9
Japan	6.3	7.8	8.0	8.4	5.9
UK	6.0	5.6	5.2	5.0	5.1
Italy	4.5	4.6	5.6	5.3	4.0
ANIEs*	3.1	5.7	8.5	9.6	9.5

* ANIEs = Taiwan, Hong Kong, Korea and Singapore.
Source: IMF (2003) *World Economic Outlook*, April, and other sources.

commodity composition, her ability to compete *within* these areas and commodities has come under greater strain. The chapter also stressed the role of non-price factors, such as income, quality, design and marketing, in accounting for both UK export performance and import penetration. Although price considerations are important, they are often given too prominent a place in explanations of trade flow. The fact that UK manufactures have moved down-market in quality, design and marketing should perhaps be given more recognition as an important factor in restricting the growth of UK exports and in encouraging import penetration. The high income elasticity of demand for UK imports of manufactures is but one reflection of the growing importance of such non-price factors.

Ironically, the UK's problem of matching other countries in terms of non-price factors has become a still more serious cause for concern over the last 15 years with the progressive tendency for industrial countries to *specialize* in the production of traded goods. This has meant that countries have naturally increased their imports of specialized manufactured goods from each other, thereby increasing the import penetration ratio regardless of any change in other competitive factors. Although the UK has surpluses on oil, services and investment income, it would be a hazardous strategy to rely on these to 'subsidize' a progressive deterioration in trade in non-oil goods. The rapid fall in oil revenue between 1985 and 1991 vividly demonstrated this point. There were some

signs that UK industry became more supply responsive during the 1980s and that this helped to increase the income elasticity of demand for UK exports, as shown by Landesmann and Snell. The health of the manufacturing sector is highly significant in this context because most manufactured goods are potentially tradeable across international boundaries, i.e. can be sold abroad, while only around 20% of services are internationally tradeable. This means that as resources move from manufacturing to services, the balance of trade may continue to deteriorate (Thirlwall 1992). The rise in the share of UK exports of manufactures between 1984 and 1993 noted in the text appeared encouraging. However, on closer scrutiny, the conclusions of Muellbauer and Murphy (1990) that UK exports had benefited from a fall in the growth of world trade relative to world production, and the findings of Landesmann and Snell (1993) that the US and Japan's share of world trade of manufactures weakened in the same period, may have been due to the same cause – namely trade friction between the US and Japan. Since this problem eased in the second half of the 1990s, we might have to look once more at whether the UK will lose the 1% share of world manufactured exports which it recently regained. The question therefore remains as to whether UK companies in general have the flexibility to follow the ebb and flow of the international market. The evidence for this remains rather elusive and patchy.

Key points

- The UK current account was mostly in surplus until the late 1980s; problems on the non-oil goods account have subsequently resulted in the current account moving into deficit.

- The *area composition* of UK goods trade has moved strongly towards the EU and away from North America and other OECD countries since the 1960s.

- The *commodity composition* of UK goods trade shows a shift away from foodstuffs and raw materials, and towards manufactures, especially as regards imports.

- The UK's share of world exports of manufactured goods of major OECD countries fell from 17% to 6% between 1960 and 2001, whereas various measures of import penetration of manufactured goods show a sharp increase.

- The UK's poor long-term performance in manufactured goods is due to a loss of competitiveness *within* particular commodity groups and *within* particular geographic areas.

- While *price* factors are important, *non-price* factors such as income, quality, design, service, etc. also crucially affect competitiveness.

- The UK shows symptoms of going 'down-market', by exporting cheaper lower technology-based products and importing more expensive high technology-based products, although the trend has stabilized in recent years.

- Trade in goods is important for the UK, with 69% of the total value of exports of goods and services being from the goods sector.

- The UK usually achieves a balance of payments surplus from services and investment income, etc., but only 20% of all services are internationally tradeable. Manufactures and goods in general cannot therefore be neglected in trade terms.

- Some 25% of all income from services depends upon manufacturing industry itself, which also emphasizes the continued importance of manufacturing.

Now try the self-check questions for this chapter on the Companion Website. You will also find up-to-date facts and case materials.

References and further reading

Bank of England (2002) Why are UK imports so cyclical?, *Bank of England Quarterly Bulletin*, Summer.

Business Link (2002) Manufacturing – a sectoral study. The performance of manufacturing companies with Benchmark Index.

Connell, D. (1980) The UK's performance in export markets – some evidence from international trade data, NEDO, Discussion Paper No. 6.

Cooper, R. G. (1994) New products: the factors that drive success, *International Marketing Review*, **11**(1).

Design Council (2000) *Design in Britain: 2000.*

Dumble, J. (1994) UK trade – long-term trends and recent developments, *Bank of England Quarterly Bulletin*, **34**(3), August.

Fagerberg, J. (1988) International competitiveness, *Economic Journal*, **98**, June.

Ghosh, B. C., Schoch, H. P., Taylor, D. B., Kwan, W. W. and Kim, S. T. (1994) Top performing organizations of Australia, New Zealand and Singapore: a comparative study of their marketing effectiveness, *Marketing Intelligence and Planning*, **12**(7).

Griffiths, A. (1989) Manufacturing competitiveness: new sources for old, *British Economy Survey*, **18**(2), Spring.

HMSO (1996) *Competitiveness: Creating the Enterprise Centre of Europe*, HMSO.

Hooley, G. J., Lynch, J. E., Brooksbank, R. W. and Shepherd, J. (1988) Strategic market environments, *Journal of Marketing Management*, **4**(2).

Humphries, S. (1998) Geographical breakdown of export and imports of UK trade in services by component, *Economic Trends*, **530**, January.

Lall, S. (1998) Exports of manufactures by developing countries: emerging patterns of trade and location, *Oxford Review of Economic Policy*, **14**(2).

Landesmann, M. and Snell, A. (1989) The consequences of Mrs Thatcher for UK manu-facturing exports, *Economic Journal*, **99**, March.

Landesmann, M. and Snell, A. (1993) Structural shifts in the manufacturing export performance of OECD economies, *Journal of Applied Econonometrics*, **8**.

Mason, G., van Ark, B. and Wagner, K. (1994) Productivity, product quality and worker skills: food processing in four European countries, *National Institute of Economic Review*, February.

Morgan, A. D. and Martin, A. (1975) Tariff reductions and UK imports of manufactures 1955–71, *National Institute Economic Review*, May.

Muellbauer, J. (1990) A pattern biased against trade? *Financial Times*, 19 February, p. 17.

Muellbauer, J. and Murphy, A. (1990) Is the UK balance of payments sustainable?, *Economic Policy*, October.

OECD (2001) *Science, Technology and Industry Scoreboard 2001*, Paris, September.

Owen, C. and Wren-Lewis, S. (1992) *Variety, Quality and UK Manufacturing Exports*, Strathclyde University.

Panić, M. (1975) Why the UK propensity to import is high, *Lloyds Bank Review*, **115**, January.

Patel, P. and Pavitt, K. (1987) The elements of British technological competitiveness, *National Institute Economic Review*, November.

PICME (2001) Competitiveness of the UK processing industries 2001, *Process Industries Centre for Manufacturing Excellence*.

Proudman, J. and Redding, S. (1997) The relationship between openness and growth in the United Kingdom: a summary of the Bank of England Openness and Growth Project, *Bank of England Quarterly Bulletin*, **37**(4), November.

Sentance, A. and Walters, C. (1997) Design, competitiveness and UK manufacturing performance, *Design Council Report*, November.

Steedman, H. and Wagner, K. (1987) A second look at productivity, machinery and skills in Britain and Germany, *National Institute Economic Review*, November.

The Sunday Times (1990) May, p. D7.

Thirlwall, A. P. (1980) The UK's economic problems: a balance of payments constraint? *National Westminster Bank Quarterly Review*, February.

Thirlwall, A. P. (1992) The balance of payments and economic performance, *National Westminster Bank Quarterly Review*, May.

UNCTAD (2002) *World Investment Report*.

Wardlow, A. (1994) Investment appraisal criteria and the importance of low inflation, *Bank of England Quarterly Bulletin*, **34**(3), August.

WTO (2002) *International Trade Statistics 2002*, World Trade Organization.

Chapter 28   Free trade, regional
trading blocs and
protectionism

Protectionist measures are aimed at reducing the level of imports,
either because of the 'damage' they cause to particular domestic
industries, or because of their adverse effects on the balance of
payments. In this chapter we review critically the arguments in
favour of free trade, and therefore against protectionism. We
examine the international institutions which have been created to
foster trade, particularly the General Agreement on Tariffs and
Trade (GATT) and the World Trade Organization (WTO), and then
note the measures available to countries wishing to pursue a
protectionist strategy. The extent to which such measures have been
used within both the European Union (EU) and the UK is considered,
together with their alleged benefits and costs. We also consider the
shift in trading patterns towards regional blocs and assess the
implications of this development.

Free trade

Free trade was given impetus by 'The Theory of Comparative Advantage', outlined by Ricardo in the nineteenth century. Essentially, Ricardo sought to extend Adam Smith's principle of the division of labour to a global scale, with each country specializing in those goods which it could produce most efficiently. Even if one country was more efficient than another country in the production of all goods, Ricardo showed that it could still gain by specializing in those goods in which its *relative efficiency* was greatest. It was said to have a *comparative* advantage in such goods. This would raise total world output above the level it would otherwise be, with the benefits shared via trade between the two countries. The degree of benefit to any one country after specialization and trade would depend upon the terms of trade, i.e. the ratio of export to import prices.

The use of protectionist measures, such as tariffs, may distort the comparative cost ratios, by raising import prices and encouraging the domestic production of goods that could otherwise have been imported rather more cheaply. In addition to disrupting the efficient allocation of *domestic* resources, such protectionist measures are likely to reduce international specialization and to lead to a less efficient allocation of *world* resources.

Figure 28.1 shows that free trade could, in theory, bring welfare benefits to an economy previously protected. Suppose the industry is initially *completely protected*. The price P_D will then be determined by the interaction of domestic supply (S–S_H) and domestic demand (D–D_H). The government now decides to remove these barriers and to allow foreign competition. For simplicity, we assume a perfectly elastic 'world' supply curve P_W–C, giving a total supply curve (domestic and world) of SAC. Domestic price will then be forced down to the world level, P_W, with domestic demand being $0Q_3$ at this price. To meet this domestic demand, $0Q_2$ will be supplied from domestic sources, with $Q_2 Q_3$ supplied from the rest of the world (i.e. imported). The consumer surplus, which is the difference between what consumers are prepared to pay and what they have to pay, has risen from DBP_D to DCP_W. The producer surplus, which is the difference between the price the producer receives and the minimum necessary to induce production, has fallen from $P_D BS$ to $P_W AS$. The gain in consumer surplus outweighs the loss in producer surplus by the area ABC, which could then be regarded as the net gain in economic welfare as a result of free trade replacing protectionism.

Critics of free trade suggest that a number of drawbacks may outweigh the net gain shown above:

1 The theory is based on a 'full employment' model and fails to appreciate the problems raised by chronic unemployment. For instance, in Fig. 28.1 if domestic supply falls from $0Q_1$ to $0Q_2$ as a result of the removal of tariffs, then the reduced output may lead to unemployment. The welfare loss associated with this may more than offset the net welfare gain (area ABC) noted above.

2 It fails to analyse how the gains that arise from trade will be distributed. In practice, the stronger economies, through their economic power, have often been able to extract the greater benefits.

3 It assumes a purely competitive model of industry. If, in fact, industry includes both large and small firms, then area ABC may not represent net gain. For instance, a higher proportion of the remaining domestic output $0Q_2$ in Fig. 28.1 may now be in the hands of a monopoly. This growth in importance of monopoly could be construed as a welfare loss to be set against the area of net gain, ABC.

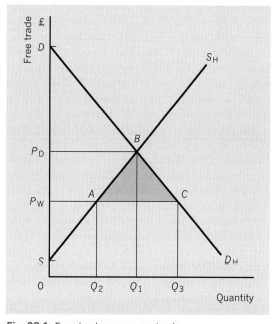

Fig. 28.1 Free trade versus no trade.

In practice a number of organizations have tried to encourage free trade in the post-war period.

General Agreement on Tariffs and Trade/World Trade Organization

The General Agreement on Tariffs and Trade (GATT) was signed in 1947 by 23 industrialized nations including the US, Canada, France and the Benelux countries. Its successor, the World Trade Organization, was established in 1995 and now has 144 members with the People's Republic of China and Chinese Taipei the latest countries to join. WTO members in total account for more than 90% of the value of world trade. The objectives of the WTO are essentially the same as GATT's: that is, to reduce tariffs and other barriers to trade and to eliminate discrimination in trade. But the WTO is much more than GATT. Although the latter still provides the principal rulebook for trade in goods, the WTO has broadened out the agreement to also include services (the General Agreement on Trade in Services) and intellectual property such as copyright, trademarks and patents (the Agreement on Trade Related Aspects of Intellectual Property, also known as TRIPS).

Since the GATT was signed there have been eight rounds of negotiations paving the way for considerable cuts in the level of tariffs being applied. In 1947 the average tariff in the industrialized world stood at some 40% but by the late 1990s the figure had dropped to around 5%. The 'Kennedy round' of negotiations in the 1960s was particularly effective, cutting tariffs by around one-third. The 'Tokyo round' in the latter part of the 1970s resulted in further reductions of a similar magnitude.

An important series of multilateral negotiations, known as the Uruguay round, was completed in December 1993. This proved to be by far the most complex and ambitious round of negotiations. It consisted of 28 accords designed to extend fair trade rules to agriculture, services, textiles, intellectual property rights and foreign investment. It was agreed to make further cuts in tariffs on industrial products, to eliminate tariffs entirely in 11 sectors and to substantially reduce the level of farm subsidies. Non-tariff barriers were to be converted into the more viable tariff barriers (Greenaway 1994). The most recent new series of negotiations, known as the Doha round, began in 2001 but has to date struggled to make very

much headway. A key reason for this has been the reluctance of the EU to countenance a wholesale transformation of the rules governing trade in agriculture. Also under consideration are the guidelines for anti-dumping and subsidies, investment and competition policy as well as government procurements and services.

GATT itself, the new accord on services and intellectual property and the codes on government procurement and anti-dumping, have now been placed under the umbrella of the WTO. Trade disputes between member states are settled in this arena by a streamlined disputes procedure with the provision for appeals and binding arbitration. Since its creation in January 1995, more than half the cases brought before the WTO have involved the US and the EU, whilst around one-quarter have involved developing countries. Trade disputes which go to arbitration still tend to be fairly lengthy affairs, as can be seen from the case of the importation of bananas into the European Union. The complaint was brought by Ecuador, Guatemala, Honduras, Mexico and the United States back in August 1998, with these countries complaining that the EU gave preferential treatment to bananas imported from former colonies of the UK, France, etc. However, it took more than three years for this matter to be satisfactorily resolved.

Although the aim of the WTO is to reduce tariff barriers, there are a number of circumstances in which a country will be allowed to maintain such barriers. Article 6 of the original GATT permits retaliatory sanctions if 'dumping' can be proven. Article 18 also provides a number of 'escape clauses' for the newly industrializing economies, allowing some protection of both infant industries and of their balance of payments. Article 19 permits any country to abstain from a general tariff cut in situations where rising imports may seriously damage domestic production. Articles 21–25 are concerned with the protection of the national interest, permitting restrictions to be placed on imported products which might affect the nation's security.

Aside from tariff cuts, the WTO/GATT has made efforts to eliminate discrimination in trade by use of the 'most-favoured nation' (MFN) principle. This means that each member country has to treat each of its fellow members equally; any trading advantage granted by one country to another must be accorded to all other member states. The MFN clause is so important that it was actually the first article of the original GATT. It has also been incorporated in the GATS (Article 2) and the TRIPS (Article 4). Some exceptions are allowed from MFN, for example when a free trade area has been established by a specific group of countries. In general, however, the MFN means that no discrimination is permitted in trade relations.

Trade and the world economy

The rapid growth of world trade during the twentieth century reflects the fact that nations have become more interrelated as they have attempted to gain the benefits of freer trade. One way of measuring this increasing integration is to compare the *relative growth* of world trade and world output, as seen in Table 28.1.

Table 28.1 shows that the growth rate of world merchandise exports (Trade) has exceeded the growth of world output (GDP) in four of the five periods, clearly suggesting an acceleration of global integration through trade. The only exception to this pattern occurred during 1913–50 when two world wars and a major world depression led to economic depression and the emergence of protectionist trade policies. The post Second World War period (1950–73) saw an unprecedented growth of world trade which far outstripped the growth of world production. This period of freer trade reflected the desire to reduce the high protective tariffs introduced during the inter-war period as a means of increasing post-war prosperity for all countries. The founding of the GATT in 1947 was a positive step in this direction. Since 1990 it is significant that developing and newly industrializing countries have achieved the fastest expansion of trade. With an average annual rise of over 8%, their share of world trade has increased from 24 to 29%,

whilst that of the industrialized countries has edged back a little to around 65%.

It may be useful to enquire at this stage whether the expanding role of world trade seen in Table 28.1 was accompanied by an increase in the share of that trade conducted on a *regional* basis. It would seem natural that nations would tend to trade more with their immediate neighbours in the first instance, thereby raising the share of world trade occurring between nations within a specific geographical region. This tendency towards *intra-regional* trade can be seen in Table 28.2.

From Table 28.2 it can be seen that the share of intra-regional trade grew most rapidly in Western Europe between 1948 and 1996. However, between 1996 and 2001, North America and Central/Eastern Europe have seen the most rapid growth in intra-regional trade. Intra-regional trade occurring in other regions has remained largely unchanged or even declined since the mid-1990s. It is also clear from Table 28.2 that intra-regional trading is not a new phenomenon and that geographically adjacent nations in many areas of the world have been trading with each other for many decades.

Regional trading arrangements (RTAs)

As we have noted above, the resumption of rapid growth in world trade after the Second World War was tied up with the desire for the resumption of *multilateral trade* under the auspices of the GATT. However, this movement towards free trade was accompanied by a parallel movement towards the formation of *regional trading blocs* centred on the EU, North and South America, and East Asia. We noted in Table 28.2 that intra-regional trading is not a new phenomenon and has been active for at least a century or more. However, what is new involves the fact that the nations of a given region have begun to create

Table 28.1 Growth in world GDP and merchandise trade, 1870–2001 (average annual % change).

	1870–1900	1900–13	1913–50	1950–73	1973–2001
GDP	2.9	2.5	2.0	5.1	2.8
Trade	3.8	4.3	0.6	8.2	4.3

Source: WTO, *International Trade: Trends and Statistics* (various) and *Annual Reports* (various).

Table 28.2 Shares of intra-regional trade in total trade, 1928–2001 (% of each region's total trade in goods occurring between nations located in that region).

	1928	1938	1948	1968	1979	1996	2001
Western Europe	50.7	48.8	41.8	63.0	66.2	68.3	67.5
Central/Eastern Europe/USSR	19.0	13.2	46.4	63.5	54.0	18.7	26.6
North America	25.0	22.4	27.1	36.8	29.9	36.0	39.5
Latin America	11.1	17.7	17.7	18.7	20.2	21.2	17.0
Asia	45.5	66.4	38.9	36.6	41.0	51.9	48.2
Africa	10.3	8.8	8.4	9.1	5.6	9.2	7.8
Middle East	5.0	3.6	20.3	8.7	6.4	7.4	7.6

Source: WTO, *Annual Reports* (various).

more *formal* and comprehensive trading and economic links with each other. By 2003 there were more than 100 RTAs in force, many of which had been established over the previous decade.

There are four types of regional trading arrangements:

■ *free trade areas*, where member countries reduce or abolish restrictions on trade between each other while maintaining their individual protectionist measures against non-members;

■ *customs unions*, where, as well as liberalizing trade amongst members, a common external tariff is established to protect the group from imports from any non-members;

■ *common markets*, where the customs union is extended to movements of factors of production as well as products;

■ *economic union*, where national economic policies are also harmonized within the common market.

Three features have characterized post-war regional integration.

1 Post-war regional integration has been primarily centred in Western Europe. More than half of all the RTAs established have involved West European countries, with many of the more recent agreements with the EU involving the Central and Eastern European countries.

2 Only a small number of post-war regional agreements have been concluded by developing countries. This is mainly due to continuing competition between these countries involving trade in similar products (e.g. primary products) together with the

difficulty of achieving the political stability in some developing countries which is so vital to trade.

3 The *type* of economic integration between the parties to agreements has varied quite significantly. Most of the notifications made to GATT have involved free trade areas, with the number of customs unions agreement being much smaller.

Table 28.3 provides examples of different types of regional trading arrangements across the globe. For example, the most advanced form of trading bloc is the EU which, before the access of 10 new members, covered 15 nations with a combined population of over 370m and accounted for some 42% of world trade. This group originated as a customs union but moved towards the common market type of arrangement in the 1990s, the majority of members effectively progressing into a type of economic union with

Table 28.3 Regional Trading Arrangements (RTAs): intra-regional export shares (%).

	1990	1995	2001
NAFTA	42.6	46.1	55.5
EU	64.9	64.0	61.9
APEC	67.5	73.1	71.8
MERCOSUR	8.9	20.5	17.3
ASEAN	20.1	25.5	23.5
ANDEAN	4.2	12.2	11.2
CEFTA		14.5	12.4

Source: WTO (2002) *International Trade Statistics*.

the advent of the euro and its related financial arrangements on 1 January 1999. In August 1993 the North American Free Trade Agreement (NAFTA) was signed between the US, Canada and Mexico, having grown out of an earlier Canadian–US Free Trade Agreement (CUFTA). NAFTA, as the name implies, is a free trade arrangement covering a population of 372m and accounting for 31% of world output and 17% of world trade.

MERCOSUR was established in South America in 1991, evolving out of the Latin American Free Trade Area, the four initial members being Argentina, Brazil, Paraguay and Uruguay. It developed into a partial customs union in 1995 when it imposed a common external tariff covering 85% of total products imported.

In Asia and the Pacific, the rather 'loose' Association of South East Asian Nations (ASEAN) with a population of 300m was formed in August 1967. In 1991 they agreed to form an ASEAN Free Trade Area (AFTA) by the year 2003. A Common External Preference Tariff (CEPT) came into force in 1994 as a formal tariff-cutting mechanism for achieving free trade in all goods except agricultural products, natural resources and services. Finally, in November 1994, the goal of an open trade and investment area was agreed in principle by members of the Asia-Pacific Economic Cooperation Forum (APEC) which includes the members of ASEAN, ANZCERTA (Australia and New Zealand) and NAFTA as well as China, Japan, Korea, Hong Kong, Taiwan, and Papua New Guinea. It is hoped that this arrangement may be realized by 2010 for developed countries and by 2020 for developing countries. This group would account for 38% of the world's population (2.1bn), and 43% of the world trade in goods.

RTAs have also featured in trade liberalization in Africa over the past decade. The Common Market for Eastern and Southern Africa (COMESA) is the largest RTA in geographic terms, with some 21 members. It has plans to establish both a free trade area and a common external tariff. In Central and Eastern Europe, a free trade bloc has been established by Poland, the Czech Republic, Slovakia, Hungary, Slovenia, Romania and Bulgaria (CEFTA).

From the above examples it is possible to see that trading blocs have adopted various types of arrangements depending on their specific circumstances.

Table 28.3 shows the share of *intra-regional exports* of each specific bloc as a percentage of the total exports of that bloc. For example, in 2001 the exports of EU members *to each other* comprised some 61.9% of total EU exports. A significant shift towards intra-regional exports took place in Europe, North and Central America, and Asia between 1960 and 1970, but since that time there has been no major growth, except in the NAFTA.

The completion of the Uruguay round in December 1993 served as a step forward in the cause of *multilateral trade*. However, frustration with the slow progress of GATT during the 1990s, and continuing friction between the US, EU and Japan, have reinforced concerns that regional trading blocs may begin to look inwards and behave more like 'regional fortresses'. Thus, the trading blocs we have been discussing above have begun to be seen as initiators of a 'new regionalism', leading to potential problems for *inter-bloc* trade. Those who favour the regional approach argue that the setting up of trading blocs can enable individual countries to purchase products at lower prices because tariff walls between the member countries have been removed; this is the *trade creation effect*. They also argue that regional trading arrangements help to harmonize tax policies and product standards, while also helping to reduce political conflicts. Others argue that where the world is already organized into trading blocs, negotiations in favour of free trade are more likely to be successful between, say, three large and influential trading blocs than between a large number of individual countries with little power to bargain successfully for tariff reductions.

On the other hand, the critics of regionalism warn that regional trading blocs have, historically, tended to be inward looking, as in the 1930s when discriminatory trade blocs were formed to impose tariffs on non-members. Some also argue that member countries may suffer from being inside a regional bloc because they then have to buy products from *within* the bloc, when cheaper sources are often available from outside, i.e. the *trade diversion effect*. Further, it is argued that regionalism threatens to erode support for multilateralism in that business groups *within* a regional bloc will find it easier to obtain protectionist (trade diversionary) deals via preferential pacts than they would in the world of non-discriminatory trade practices favoured by GATT. Finally, it is argued that regionalism will move the world away from free trade due to the increasing tendency for members of a regional group to resort to the use of *non-tariff barriers* (VERs, anti-dumping duties, etc.) when experiencing a surge of imports from other countries *inside* the group. Such devices, all part of the new protectionism, can then easily be used by individual countries against non-members from other regional groups.

Many studies have been made as to the trade and welfare effects of such regional blocs both on 'internal' participants and on countries outside the bloc.

- Analyses of the customs union formed between the original six members of the European Community (EC) have shown that trade creation exceeded trade diversion in the case of manufactures (Lloyd 1992; Srinivasan *et al.* 1993), but that the reverse was true in the case of trade in agricultural products – leaving the overall effect unclear.

- Studies of EFTA suggest that trade creation just outweighed trade diversion (Lloyd 1992).

- Studies for CUFTA suggest positive benefits for Canada but negligible benefits for the US, while trade with third countries declined (Primo Braga *et al.* 1994).

- For NAFTA, estimates indicate some net trade creation with small trade effects for third countries (Reinert *et al.* 1994).

The various studies noted above can only give a general idea of the net effects as they do not measure accurately the potential stimulus to third countries resulting from any higher rate of economic growth in the bloc being studied.

What then can be done to make sure that regionalism and multilateralism (general free trade) can coexist? First, it has been suggested that article 24 of GATT which sets the rules for regional arrangements could be modified to allow only customs unions (i.e. regions which require a common external tariff) and to prohibit free trade areas which allow countries to retain a variety of national tariffs against other countries. If this were done, the more liberal members of the region would then be able to force down the overall regional tariff level, which could then be 'locked in' under GATT rules and prevented from being subsequently raised. Second, in order to fight the 'new protectionism', GATT articles 6 (anti-dumping) and 19 (VER) could be strengthened to minimize the use of non-tariff barriers against countries outside the regional arrangement (*World Economic Outlook* 1993).

Protectionism

There are a number of methods which individual countries or regional trading blocs can use to restrict the level of imports into the home market.

Methods of protection

Tariff

A tariff is, in effect, a tax levied on imported goods, usually with the intention of raising the price of imports and thereby discouraging their purchase. Additionally, it is a source of revenue for the government. Tariffs can be of two types: lump sum, or specific, with the tariff a fixed amount per unit; and *ad valorem*, or percentage, with the tariff a variable amount per unit.

To examine the effect of a tariff, it helps to simplify Fig. 28.2 if we again assume a perfectly elastic world supply of the good S_W at the going world price P_W, which implies that any amount of the good can be imported into the UK without there being a change in the world price. In the absence of a tariff the domestic price would be set by the world price, P_W in Fig. 28.2. At this price, domestic demand D_H will be $0Q_2$ though domestic supply S_H will be only $0Q_1$. The excess demand, $Q_2 - Q_1$, will be satisfied by importing the good.

If the government now decides to restrict the level of import penetration, it could impose a tariff of, say, $P_W - P'_W$. A tariff always shifts a supply curve vertically upwards by the amount of the tariff, so that in this case the world supply curve shifts vertically upwards from S_W to S'_W. This would raise the domestic price to S'_W which is above the world price P_W. This higher price will reduce the domestic demand for the good to $0Q_4$, whilst simultaneously encouraging domestic supply to expand to $0Q_3$. Imports will be reduced to $Q_4 - Q_3$. Domestic consumer surplus will decline as a result of the tariff by the area $1 + 2 + 3 + 4$, though domestic producer surplus will rise by area 1, and the government will gain tax revenue of $(P'_W - P_W) \times (Q_4 - Q_3)$ (i.e. area 3). These gains would be inadequate to compensate consumers for their loss in welfare, yielding a net welfare loss of area $2 + 4$ as a result of imposing a tariff.

The UK was extensively protected by tariffs until the 1850s. These were progressively dismantled in an

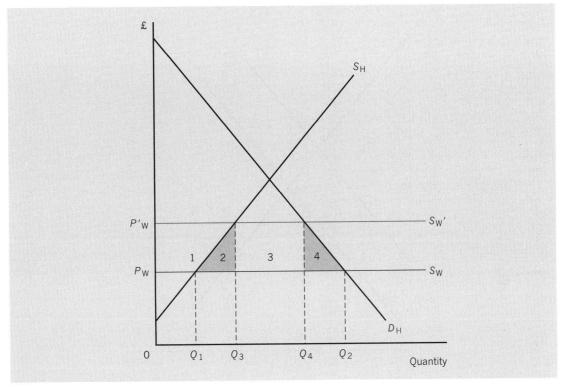

Fig. 28.2 The effect of a tariff.

era of free trade that lasted until the First World War. The first significant reintroduction of tariffs occurred in 1915 with the 'McKenna duties', a 33.3% *ad valorem* tax on luxuries such as motor cars, watches, clocks, etc. They were designed to discourage unnecessary imports in order to save foreign exchange, and thereby free shipping space for the war effort. In 1921, the Safeguarding of Industry Act extended protection to key industries. This was followed in 1932 by the Import Duties Act, which provided a comprehensive range of protection; a 20% *ad valorem* duty on manufactured goods in general, but 33.3% on articles such as bicycles and chemicals, and 15% on certain industrial raw materials and semi-manufactures.

Since the Second World War, the UK, along with others, has moved away from the protectionist doctrine of the inter-war period. We have already seen that considerable reductions in tariffs took place under the auspices of GATT. However, for the UK, entrance into the EU in 1973 has had a dual effect. Although tariffs on industrial products have been eliminated between member countries, permitting free trade, at the same time a Common External Tariff (CET) has been imposed on industrial trade with all non-member countries, with import tariffs varying by product. For example, whilst the *average* tariff on industrial imports into the EU is 4.1%, the tariff on clothing imports is as high as 9.7% but the tariff on metal imports is only 3.8%.

Non-tariff barriers

During the 1990s many quantitative restrictions on trade were gradually replaced by tariffs. Exceptions do, however, remain with significant non-tariff barriers affecting trade in textiles and clothing.

There are a number of different types of non-tariff barriers.

Quotas

A quota is a physical limit on the amount of an imported good that may be sold in a country in a given period. Its effects are examined in Fig. 28.3.

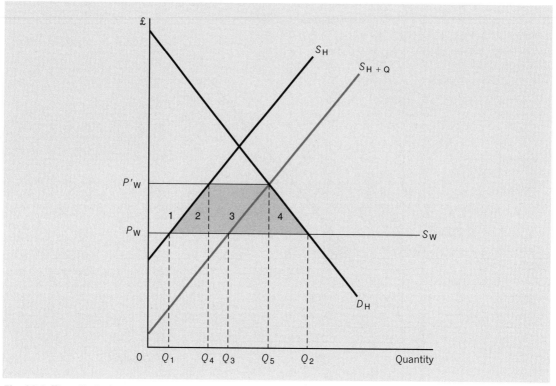

Fig. 28.3 The effect of a quota.

As in the case of a tariff, we assume for simplicity that the world supply curve is perfectly elastic at P_W. Once again, if there is free trade, the domestic price will be set by the world price, P_W. Domestic production would initially be $0Q_1$ though demand would be considerably higher at $0Q_2$. This excess would be satisfied by importing the amount $Q_2 - Q_1$ of the particular good.

If the government were now to decide that it wanted to limit the level of imports to, say, $Q_3 - Q_1$, it could impose a quota to this effect. The total supply curve to the UK market now becomes the domestic supply curve, S_H, plus the fixed quota permitted from abroad, Q. The new domestic price rises from P_W to P'_W which in turn reduces domestic demand from $0Q_2$ to $0Q_5$. Domestic supply will expand to $0Q_4$, with imports reduced to the quota level $Q_3 - Q_1$ $(= Q_5 - Q_4)$.

As in the case of the tariff, the imposition of a quota will involve a loss in consumer surplus (i.e. area $1 + 2 + 3 + 4$). However, in contrast to the tariff, the only area of welfare gain will be the producer surplus

of area 1, since the government receives no increase in tax revenue from the quota. This leaves area $2 + 3 + 4$ as the net loss of economic welfare. For *any given price rise*, the welfare loss is then greater for a quota than for a tariff.[1] Import quotas are still used on a whole range of products. They may be applied either unilaterally or as a result of negotiated agreements between the two parties. For instance, the EU has the authority to negotiate quota agreements on behalf of member states, including the UK, and does so on a whole range of products.

The import of textiles into the EU from the newly industrialized countries was controlled until recently by the Multi-Fibre Agreement (MFA), a negotiated settlement between developed and developing countries which first came into effect in 1974. A major aim has been to provide greater scope for newly industrialized countries to increase their share of world trade in textile products whilst at the same time maintaining some stability for textile production in the developed economies. The first agreement allowed for quotas to rise by approximately 6% per annum, though a subsequent agreement began to cut back on these concessions. The MFA was renewed for a third time in 1986, although there was considerable opposition from many of the textile producers who favoured a return to a more liberalized trading environment. As part of the Uruguay round, an accord was agreed which will gradually (by 2005) bring trade in clothing and textiles under normal GATT rules. The settlement provides for a phase-out period of 10 years for all existing quota restrictions. However, the deal is heavily 'back-end' loaded.

An UNCTAD study in 1986 concluded that the complete liberalization of trade barriers would bring substantial benefits for developing countries. It was suggested that their total export of clothing would rise by around 135% while textile exports could grow by some 80%. A more recent analysis carried out by the World Bank put the potential gains at an even greater level. These figures seem to indicate quite clearly that the export quotas work against the interest of the *producers* rather than the *consumers*. But there is an argument that the developing countries actually benefit through the MFA arrangement. This is because, it is asserted, they receive what may be termed *quota rents*, i.e. higher prices than would be guaranteed through a free market.

Looking back to Fig. 28.3, this benefit would amount to area 3. However research into this by Balassa and Michalopoulos (1985) estimated that the value of lost output to the US exceeds the quota rent by nine times and to the EU by a factor of seven.

Subsidies

The first two forms of protection we have described have both been designed to restrict the volume of imports directly. An alternative policy is to provide a subsidy to domestic producers so as to improve their competitiveness in both the home and world markets. The effect of this is demonstrated in Fig. 28.4.

Once again we assume that the world supply curve is perfectly elastic at P_W. Under conditions of free trade, the domestic price is set by the world price at P_W. Domestic production is initially $0Q_1$ with imports satisfying the excess level of demand which amounts to $Q_2 - Q_1$. The effect of a general subsidy to an industry would be to shift the supply curve of domestic producers to the right. The domestic price will remain unchanged but domestic production will rise to $0Q_3$ with imports reduced to Q_2Q_3. If, however, the subsidy is provided solely for *exporters*, the impact on the domestic market could be quite different. The incentive to export may encourage more domestic production to be switched from the home market to the overseas markets which in turn could result in an increased volume of imports to satisfy the unchanged level of domestic demand.

Subsidies continue to be widely employed in agriculture alongside other forms of protection. The US and the Cairns group of farm exporters, which

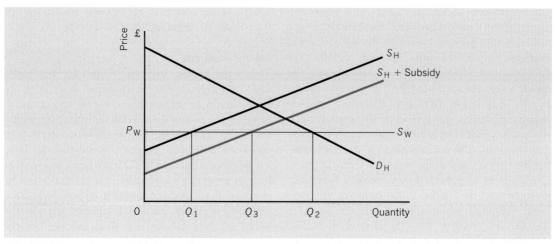

Fig. 28.4 The effect of a general subsidy.

includes Australia, Canada and Brazil, are pushing for a liberalization of trade in agricultural products. Many developing countries support this approach, though the EU, Japan and other countries are reluctant to withdraw agricultural protection. For example, producer support grant in the OECD area for agriculture still accounted for around $246bn in 2000 with the EU accounting for the largest share of this expenditure (36%) followed by Japan (24%). However, it is noteworthy that the US ranked third in the league table (20%) in terms of providing support for its farmers. Anti-subsidy cases brought before the WTO hit a peak in 1999 with 40 complaints. After moderating in the following year, they climbed back to 27 in 2001.

Exchange controls

A system of exchange controls was in force in the UK from the outbreak of the Second World War until 1979 when, in order to allow the free flow of capital, they were abolished. They enabled the government to limit the availability of foreign currencies and so curtail excessive imports; for instance, holding a foreign-currency bank account had required Bank of England permission. Exchange controls could also be employed to discourage speculation and investment abroad.

Safety, technological and environmental standards

These are often imposed in the knowledge that certain imported goods will be unable to meet the requirements. The British government used such standards to prevent imports of French turkeys and ultra-heat-treated (UHT) milk. Ostensibly the ban on French turkeys was to prevent 'Newcastle disease', a form of fowl pest found in Europe, reaching the UK. The European Court ruled, however, that the ban was merely an excuse to prevent the free flow of imports. In the mid-1990s Germany effectively blocked imports of traffic cones from a UK manufacturer while it 'upgraded' its testing requirements no fewer than 12 times. The cones passed the test each time, but the German authorities refused to issue approval certificates or to publish their standards. Eventually pressure from the UK led to the standard for cones being published which allowed sales of cones to Germany to proceed. The US, meanwhile, banned shrimp imports from countries that fish using 'Turtle Excluder Devices', a ban that included fish from India. While the policy may appear to have an envi-

ronmental motive, it was also a form of discrimination. Significantly it was applied to all Indian exports, whether farmed (as the bulk of shrimps are) or caught in the ocean. A more pertinent issue relates to genetically modified foods. The EU has effectively banned the import of GM products, much to the irritation of the US amongst others. GM crops now account for 75% of the US annual output of soya beans, 71% of its cotton and 34% of its corn. The WTO rules do allow countries to regulate imports on health and environmental grounds, but any restraints must be based on 'sufficient scientific evidence'. In the case of GM foods, this is a point of dispute.

Time-consuming formalities

In 1990, the EU alleged that 'excessive invoicing requirements' required by US importing authorities had hampered exports from member countries to the US. In Asia these problems abound. For example, Indonesian customs officials take at least a week to process imports, and this often involves considerable administrative and capital costs for many companies. A similar problem in China can lead to two or three weeks' delay.

Public sector contracts

Governments often give preference to domestic firms in the issuing of public contracts, despite EU directives requiring member governments to advertise such contracts. A number of Australian states have continued to give price preferences of up to 20% to domestic bidders for public contracts in the latter half of the 1990s. Public contracts are actually placed outside the country of origin in only 1% of cases.

Labour standards

This is not an area currently subject to WTO rules and disciplines, but some countries do believe the issue should be examined as a first step towards bringing the matter of core labour standards within the WTO framework. However, many developing and some developed nations contend that the issue has no place within the WTO framework and see it as little more than a smokescreen for protectionism by the more developed economies from low-wage competition. Areas of particular concern include the issues of child labour and slave labour, but the broader issue of setting minimum labour standards is where opinion tends to diverge. The issue is a bone of contention in the current Doha round of negotiations.

The case for protection

Protectionist measures may be applied on a selective or more widespread basis, with most of the measures currently in force falling into the first category.

Selective protection

A number of arguments have been used to justify the application of both tariff and non-tariff barriers on a selective basis:

1 to prevent dumping;

2 to protect infant industries;

3 to protect strategically important industries.

Dumping occurs where a good is sold in an overseas market at a price below the real cost of production. Under Article 6 of the GATT, the WTO allows retaliatory sanctions to be applied if it can be shown that the dumping materially affected the domestic industry. As well as using the WTO, countries within the EU can refer cases of alleged dumping for investigation by the European Commission. The Commission is then able to recommend the appropriate course of action, which may range from 'no action' where dumping is found not to have taken place, to either obtaining an 'undertaking' of no further dumping, or imposing a tariff.

Table 28.4 indicates a significant increase in antidumping cases initiated by the WTO in recent years. Indeed, according to a World Bank study, average tariffs in the US manufactured goods sector would be 23% today as compared with a nominal level of less than 6% if anti-dumping duties were included.

The US has consistently been one of the main initiators of anti-dumping investigations. Canada, India and the European Union have also initiated numerous actions. The main targets of anti-dumping probes have been the European Union, China, Chinese Taipei and India. The sectors where anti-dumping measures are most widely applied include chemical products and base metals, in particular steel. The latter is currently a battleground between the US and the EU. The US steel industry has alleged that financial support from European governments has given the EU steel industry an unfair advantage over US producers. In response the US government imposed tariffs of up to 30% on selected steel products in March 2002.

The use of protection in order to *establish new industries* is widely accepted, particularly in the case of developing countries. Article 18 of GATT explicitly allows such protection. An infant industry is likely to have a relatively high cost structure in the short run, and in the absence of protective measures may find it difficult to compete with the established overseas industries already benefiting from scale economies. The EU has used this argument to justify protection of its developing high-technology industries.

The protection of industries for *strategic reasons* is widely practised in both the UK and the EU, and is not necessarily contrary to GATT rules (Article 2). The protection of the UK steel industry has in the past been justified on this basis, and the EU has used a similar argument to protect agricultural production throughout the Community under the guise of the CAP. In the Uruguay round of GATT, the developing countries used this argument in seeking to resist calls for the liberalization of trade in the service sector. This has been one of the few sectors recording strong growth in recent years and is still a highly 'regulated' sector in most countries.

There is a small but growing body of opinion which questions the benefits to be derived from international trade and which is hostile to the drive by the WTO to liberalize trade. This movement, which is quite diverse, comprises environmentalists, trade unions, charities and Third World activists, amongst many others, and has manifested itself in WTO/IMF demonstrations in Seattle and Prague in recent years. Although not necessarily rejecting the theoretical

Table 28.4 Anti-dumping cases initiated.

1987	1988	1989	1990	1991	1992	1993	1994	1995	1996	1997	1998	1999	2000	2001
120	124	96	165	228	326	299	228	156	221	233	232	328	272	348

Source: WTO Annual Reports (various).

benefits of free trade, opponents of the WTO contend that the gains are largely expropriated by big business, leaving both workers and developing nations no better off and in many cases actually worse off. Groups such as Global Trade Watch suggest that the WTO has little regard for democracy or for environmental standards and almost always acts against the public interest.

Criticisms of protectionism

Retaliation

A major drawback to the imposition of protectionist measures is the possibility of retaliation. For example, the US has, as discussed earlier, imposed tariffs on steel products in response to European support for its industry. Meanwhile the EU was supported by the WTO in 2003 in giving the US an ultimatum in a separate dispute. This is to abolish its *Foreign Sales Corporations Act* which helps US exporters by giving them a tax rebate on sales overseas. Failure to do so will result in EU-imposed trade sanctions worth US$4bn, the largest retaliation package the WTO has ever sanctioned.

Misallocation of resources

We saw in Figs. 28.1–28.3 that protectionism can erode some of the welfare benefits of free trade. For instance, Fig. 28.2 showed that a tariff (and Fig. 28.3 a quota) raises domestic supply at the expense of imports. If the domestic producers cannot make such products as cheaply as overseas producers, then one could argue that encouraging high-cost domestic production is a misallocation of international resources.

A related criticism also suggests that protectionism leads to resource misallocation on an international scale, but this time concerns the multinational. We saw in Chapter 7 that multinationals are the fastest-growing type of business unit in Western economies, and that they are increasingly adopting strategies which locate particular stages of the production process in (to them) appropriate parts of the world. Protectionism may disrupt the flow of goods from one stage of the production process to another, and in this sense inhibit global specialization.

Work carried out by the OECD (Goldin and Van Der Mensbrugghe 1992) has attempted to quantify the costs of protection in terms of 'lost output'. The study considers two scenarios: (i) a 30% reduction in tariffs (roughly equivalent to that in the Uruguay round); and (ii) the complete elimination of tariffs. Under the first scenario, the report concludes that world output of goods and services would rise by an *additional* $195bn per annum within a decade, i.e. by around 0.75% of current annual world output. Under the second scenario, world output is expected to rise by an *additional* $477bn per annum within a decade, i.e. by around 2% of current annual world output. Although a few countries (mainly net food importers) were expected to be disadvantaged under both scenarios, the overall losses were calculated as being no more than $7bn. These anticipated losses are small in comparison to the anticipated gains from tariff reductions. Indeed the 'losses' could be fully compensated by a transfer of resources equivalent to only 3.5% of the anticipated gains under scenario (i).

On the domestic level, various studies have found that profits were higher than normal in industries which were dominated by a few large firms, reflecting their use of market power (e.g. Turner 1980). However, excess profits were smaller in the industries which experienced most foreign competition. Protectionist measures, by removing such competition, may therefore allow large firms to exert their latent market power, causing prices and profits to be raised at the expense of consumers.

Conclusion

The current Doha round of trade negotiations is struggling to make very much headway, with attempts to extend the range of goods and services covered under the auspices of the WTO proving difficult. Even the existence of multilateral, rules-based institutions such as the WTO is being questioned. Certainly the weak economic climate is encouraging countries to revert to protectionism, as indicated by increases in the number and severity of trade disputes and the unilateral decision by the US to impose significant new tariff barriers on imports of steel in 2002. Replacing the optimism of free-traders in the early 1990s, when the completion of the Uruguay round of tariff reductions was estimated as having raised world GDP by 1% per annum (Greenaway 1994), has long since vanished.

For the time being, the volume of world trade is continuing to grow. But with globalization increasingly being seen as the cause of much upheaval and insecurity in industrial countries, the risk remains of a retreat towards protectionism. Unless there is a renewed recognition of the *worldwide costs* of such a development, the protectionist lobbies in various countries may still succeed in curbing the growth of international specialization and trade.

Key points

- In a competitive, full employment framework, free trade can be shown to yield a net welfare gain *vis-à-vis* various protectionist alternatives.

- In the more realistic situation of 'market failures', the existence of monopoly power, unemployment, etc. may offset (in part or in whole) these welfare gains.

- The General Agreement on Tariffs and Trade (GATT) established in 1947, and its successor the World Trade Organization (WTO), seek to reduce tariffs and other barriers to trade, and to eliminate discrimination in trade.

- The GATT/WTO have had some success, cutting the average tariff in the industrialized world from 40% in 1947 to less than 5% in 2000.

- Since 1870, the growth of trade has *exceeded* the growth of world GDP in all but the period between the First and Second World Wars.

- *Intra-regional* trade (i.e. trade within a region) has grown substantially in recent decades. For example, 68% of all Western European trade occurs between countries in Western Europe.

- Various types of regional trading arrangement have promoted this trend. Free Trade Areas, Customs Unions (which have an external tariff barrier), Common Markets (in which factors of production can also freely move) and Economic Unions (with harmonization of member policies) have all been used to this end.

- Various types of protection have been used by countries, including tariffs, quotas, voluntary export restraints, subsidies, exchange controls, and a range of restrictions involving technological standards, safety, etc.

- Arguments often advanced in *favour* of protectionist policies include the prevention of dumping, the protection of infant industries and the protection of strategically important industries.

- Arguments *against* protectionist policies include retaliation and a misallocation of resources on both a national and international scale, leading to welfare loss.

Now try the self-check questions for this chapter on the Companion Website. You will also find up-to-date facts and case materials.

Note

1. It could, however, be argued that the welfare loss is overestimated by this analysis. Area 3, though no longer received by the government as tax revenue, may still be received by importers. Although paying only P_W to the foreign suppliers, the importers now receive P'_W when selling $Q_5 - Q_4$ on the domestic market.

References and further reading

Balassa, B. and Michalopoulos, M. (1985) Liberalizing world trade, *World Bank Discussion Paper*.

Barrell, R. E. and Pain, N. (1999) Trade restraints and Japanese direct investment flows, *European Economic Review*, **43**(1).

Bayard, T. O. and Elliot, K. A. (1994) *Reciprocity and Retaliation in US Trade Policy*, Institute for International Economics, Washington DC.

Bhagwati, J. (1992) Regionalism and multilateralism: an overview, *Columbia University Discussion Paper*, No. 603.

De Melo, J. and Panagariya, A. (1992) The new regionalism, *Finance and Development*, December.

Goldin, I. and Van Der Mensbrugghe, D. (1992) *Trade Liberalisation: What's at Stake?* OECD.

Greenaway, D. (1994) The Uruguay Round of trade negotiations, *Economic Review*, November.

Grimwade, N. (1996) Anti-dumping policy after the Uruguay Round, *National Institute Economics Review*, February.

Lloyd, P. J. (1992) Regionalisation and world trade, *OECD Economic Studies*, No. 18.

Panagariya, A. (1999) The regionalism debate: an overview, *The World Economy*, **22**(4), June.

Primo Braga, C. A., Safadi, R. and Yeats, A. (1994) NAFTA's implications for East Asian exports, *World Bank, Policy Working Paper*, No. 1351.

Reinert, K. A., Roland-Holst, D. W. and Shiells, C. R. (1994) A general equilibrium analysis of North American regional integration, in *Modelling Trade Policy: Applied General Equilibrium Analysis of a North American Free Trade Area*, J. F. Francois and C. R. Shiells (eds), Cambridge University Press.

Srinivasan, T. N., Whalley, J. and Wooton, I. (1993) Measuring the effects of regionalism on trade and welfare, in *Regional Integration*, K. Anderson and R. Blackhurst (eds), Harvester Wheatsheaf.

Turner, P. P. (1980) Import competition and the profitability of United Kingdom manufacturing industry, *Journal of Industrial Economics*, **29**, December.

Vanston, N. (1993) What price regional integration? *PECD Observer*, No. 181.

World Economic Outlook (1993) IMF.

WTO (2002) *Annual Report*.

WTO (2002) *International Trade Statistics*.

Yannopoulos, G. N. (1990) Foreign direct investment and European direct investment: the evidence from the formative years of the European Community, *Journal of Common Market Studies*, No. 23(3).

Chapter 29　The European Union

In a variety of forms the 'European Union' (EU) has been in existence
for almost 50 years. Given the almost continual controversy which
has surrounded the issue, it is easy to forget that the United Kingdom
has been a full member for over 30 years. This chapter seeks to
review the development of the Union and its impact on the UK. It
considers all major areas in which the EU now has a role and
examines the links between 'political' goals and economic structures.

From European Coal and Steel Community (ECSC 1952–57), to
European Economic Community (EEC 1958–86), to European
Community (EC 1986–92), to European Union (1993–) and a single
currency (1999), the 'European idea' has moved inexorably forward,
to such an extent that the EU 15 became the EU 25 with the
accession of a further 10 countries in 2004. Each step has taken the
idea further from its original 'pure' economic roots towards more and
more explicit declarations of political intent. The fundamental idea
behind every step of the European process has been a very simple
one: to construct a form of economic and political cooperation which
would make future wars between the nations of Europe totally
unthinkable. One forgets this 'fundamental objective' at one's peril.

Historical background

The historical background to the EU has been covered in some depth elsewhere (see, e.g., Lewis 1993). Since its foundation the EU has absorbed the two 'communities' which preceded it, i.e. the European Coal and Steel Community (ECSC) and the European Atomic Energy Community (Euratom). The ECSC had been established in 1952 to control the pooled coal and iron and steel resources of the six member countries – France, West Germany, Italy, Belgium, the Netherlands and Luxembourg. By promoting free trade in coal and steel between members and by protecting against non-members, the ECSC revitalized the two war-stricken industries. It was this success which prompted the establishment of the much more ambitious European Economic Community (EEC), subsequently known simply as the European Community (EC). The European Atomic Energy Community (Euratom) had been set up by treaty in 1957 with the same six countries, to promote growth in nuclear industries and the peaceful use of atomic energy.

The EEC was formed on 1 January 1958 after the signing of the Treaty of Rome. This sought to establish a 'common market', by eliminating all restrictions on the free movement of goods, capital and persons between member countries. By dismantling tariff barriers on industrial trade between members and by imposing a common tariff against non-members, the EEC was to become a protected free-trade area or 'customs union'. The formation of a customs union was to be the first step in the creation of an 'economic union' with national economic policies harmonized across the member countries. The original 'Six' became 'Nine' in 1973 with the accession of the UK, the Republic of Ireland and Denmark, and 'Ten' in 1981 with the entry of Greece. The accession of Spain and Portugal on 1 January 1986 increased the number of member countries to 12.

With the entry into law of the Single European Act in January 1993 the EC became the European Union (EU). In January 1995 the 12 became 15 as Austria, Finland and Sweden joined. The population of the EU now encompasses over 382 million people with a GDP exceeding €9 trillion.

The Single European Act (SEA), as it is widely known, came into force in July 1987. It constituted a major development of the Community and was based on a White Paper, 'Completing the Common Market', which had been presented by the Commission to the Milan meeting of the European Council in June 1985. It represented the first time, since 1957, that the original Treaty of Rome had been amended. The Act looked towards creating a single European economy by 1993. The objective was not simply to create an internal market by removing frontier controls but to remove all barriers to the movement of goods, people and capital. Achieving a single European market has meant, amongst other things, work on standards, procurement, qualifications, banking, capital movements and exchange regulations, tax 'approximation', communications standards and transport.

Since 1987 over 600 separate new directives have been created, ranging from common hygiene rules for meat and regulations on the wholesaling, labelling and advertising of medicines, to capital adequacy rules for investment and credit institutions and a common licensing system for road haulage. The Single Act also had political ramifications in that it formalized the use of qualified majorities for taking decisions in the Council of Ministers and gave the elected European Parliament greater legislating powers.

The European Economic Area

In the 1990s the political and economic problems of the EU itself prevented formal enlargement but did not stand in the way of intermediate arrangements for closer cooperation with certain states. In 1992 the EU signed an agreement with the seven members of the European Free Trade Association (EFTA) which led, on 1 January 1993, to the formation of the 'European Economic Area' (EEA). The EEA then consisted of 19 states which together formed a powerful and wealthy trading bloc.[1] Under the agreement, the EU extended to EFTA all of the EU's own freedoms in the movement of goods, services, people and capital while the EFTA states agreed to abide by the EU's competition rules. Under agreements existing prior to the EEA agreement, industrial tariffs between the 19 countries were already at zero. The 1992 agreement further reduced agricultural tariffs and established a new EEA fund designed to help the poorer EU regions (including Northern Ireland).

The Maastricht Treaty

The Treaty on European Union which was signed at Maastricht on 7 February 1992 represents one of the most fundamental changes to have occurred in the EU since its foundation. Although, legally speaking, merely an extension and amendment to the Treaty of Rome, Maastricht represents a major step for the member states. For the first time many of the political and social imperatives of the Community have been explicitly agreed and delineated. Maastricht takes the EU beyond a 'merely' economic institution (if it ever was such) and towards the full political, economic and social union foreseen by many of its founders. Some of its major objectives are as follows:

1 to create economic and social progress through an 'area without internal frontiers' and through economic and monetary union (EMU);

2 to develop a common foreign, security and defence policy which 'might lead to common defence';

3 to introduce a 'citizenship of the Union'.

Table 29.1 presents some of the important characteristics of the 15 member countries (the enlarged EU of 25 countries is considered further on p. 604). It shows how diverse they are in terms of population, industrial structure, standard of living, unemployment level and inflation rate. In terms of population the UK is still the third-largest member, with a smaller proportion engaged in agriculture than in other EU countries but the third largest in services. In overall wealth, however, the UK drops down the rankings. It has the second-largest GDP in absolute terms, but comes only sixth in terms of GDP per capita.

Quite apart from the political rationale behind the EU, a number of economic arguments have been advanced in its support:

1 By abolishing industrial tariff and non-tariff barriers at national frontiers, the EU has created a single 'domestic' market of around 382 million people, with opportunities for substantial economies of scale in production. By surrounding this market with a tariff wall, the Common External Tariff (CET), member countries are the beneficiaries of these scale economies.

2 By regulating agricultural production through the CAP, the EU has become self-sufficient in many agricultural products.

3 By amending and coordinating labour and capital regulations in the member countries, the EU seeks to create a free market in both, leading to a more 'efficient' use of these factors. A further factor, 'enterprise', is to be 'freed' through increased standardization of national laws on patents and licences.

4 By controlling monopoly and merger activities, competition has been encouraged both within and across frontiers.

5 By creating a substantial 'domestic' market and by coordinating trade policies, the EU hopes to exert a greater collective influence on world economic affairs than could possibly be achieved by any single nation.

These policies have been supported by a number of other arrangements, including a common form of taxation, a common currency, and policies directed towards transport, energy, education, social improvement and regional aid. Although our main concern in this chapter will be economic, we should not overlook the political objectives which lay behind the formation of the EU. As early as 1946, Winston Churchill had called for a 'United States of Europe' as a diplomatic and military counter to the Soviet Union. However, it was two Frenchmen – Robert Schuman and Jean Monnet – who were the founding fathers of the EC, with their vision of using economic involvement to tie Europe's warring countries together. Having attempted, on three occasions, to join the EU during the 1960s, the UK was finally accepted for membership in 1970, signed the Treaty of Accession in 1972, and became a full member with effect from 1 January 1973.

The UK's objectives in signing the Treaty of Accession in 1972 were a combination of the short- to medium-term economic, with the medium- to long-term political. There was an undeniable desire to share in the prosperity which the EU appeared to have stimulated for its six original members since 1958. The fact that the average growth rate of the Six had been 4.8% per annum between 1961 and 1971, compared to the UK's 2.7% per annum, seemed to show that entry into the EU might offer a solution to some of the UK's growth problems. In this chapter we examine the EU and the effect of UK membership of the EU under five broad headings:

Table 29.1 The Fifteen in 2002: some comparative statistics.

Member country	Population (millions)	Economically active population			GDP euro (bn)	GDP per capita euro (000s)	Share of EU		Index of GDP per capita	Unemployment[1] (%) 2000	Inflation[2] (%) 2000
		Agric. (%)	Industry (%)	Services (%)			GDP (%)	Population (%)			
Austria	8.2	7.2	33.2	59.6	216.4	26.4	2.4	2.1	111.2	4.3	1.9
Belgium	10.3	2.5	6.1	71.4	261.4	25.4	2.9	2.7	106.0	6.8	1.8
Denmark	5.4	4.0	27.0	69.0	186.6	34.5	2.0	1.4	145.5	4.2	2.3
Finland	5.2	7.1	27.6	65.3	139.5	26.8	1.5	1.4	112.4	9.1	2.0
France	61.2	4.6	25.9	69.5	1,504.0	24.6	16.5	16.0	103.0	8.8	1.6
Germany	82.4	3.3	37.5	59.2	2,107.0	25.6	23.2	21.6	107.2	8.1	1.3
Greece	11.0	20.4	23.2	56.4	139.9	12.7	1.5	2.9	53.5	9.9	3.1
Ireland	3.9	10.7	27.2	61.1	124.8	32.0	1.4	1.0	133.8	4.4	4.7
Italy	58.0	7.0	32.1	60.9	1,252.0	21.6	13.7	15.2	90.5	8.9	2.7
Luxembourg	0.4	2.8	30.7	66.5	21.7	54.3	0.2	0.1	203.6	2.3	1.9
Netherlands	16.2	3.9	22.4	73.7	446.3	27.5	4.9	4.2	116.0	3.1	3.4
Portugal	10.3	12.2	31.4	56.4	129.7	12.5	1.4	2.7	52.7	4.6	3.5
Spain	40.5	8.7	29.7	61.6	689.8	17.0	7.6	10.6	71.3	11.4	3.6
Sweden	8.9	2.9	26.1	71.0	246.9	27.7	2.7	2.3	116.0	4.9	2.0
UK	60.2	2.0	26.4	71.0	1,645.0	27.3	18.1	15.8	114.8	5.0	0.9
Total EU	**382.1**	**3.9[3]**	**28.2[3]**	**67.9[3]**	**9,111.0**	**23.8**	**100.0**	**100.0**	**100.0**	**7.6**	**1.9**

[1] Eurostat definition of unemployment.
[2] Private consumption deflator.
[3] Weighted averages; projections for 2002.
Source: European Commission (2002) European Economy, No. 6.

For each of these headings we discuss both EU policy in general and how it has affected the UK in particular.

Finance and the EU budget

Between 1958 and 1970 the EU was financed by contributions from member states which, although politically determined, were still broadly based on the various countries' ability to pay. However, since 1970 the EU has financed its spending using a system of 'own resources', i.e. income it regards as its own *as of right*. The composition of 'own resources' is shown in Table 29.2 and consists of three main sources of revenue. First, Traditional Own Resources (TOR) includes revenue raised from customs duties such as the Common External Tariff (CET) and agricultural duties. Second, 'VAT' is revenue from each country up to a *maximum* of 1% of its domestic VAT tax base. Third, 'GNP' is a levy of up to a *maximum* of 1.27% of the value of GNP in each member country. This levy, which was introduced in 1988, is used as a 'buffer' to equate EU revenue with its expenditure. In other words, the actual percentage of GNP required can vary according to how much revenue is required to balance the EU budget (e.g. 0.40% of GNP in 1997 but 0.56% in 2002). Finally, the table also includes 'other revenue' which consists of revenue from a variety of sources such as interest on late payments, fines, taxes on salaries of employees of EU institutions, etc.

A notable feature of Table 29.2 is the decline in the relative importance of TOR and VAT as sources of revenue and the growth in importance of the GNP element. The impact of trade liberalization on tariff levels (e.g. reductions via GATT rounds) has meant that the total yield from TOR has failed to increase in line with the expansion of world trade, so that the share of TOR in total revenue has decreased. Similarly the share of VAT in total revenue has also decreased. This is partly because of decisions made by the Commission to decrease the percentage of GNP which acts as the *tax base* for calculating the VAT paid by member states. For example, the VAT base for member states has fallen from 55% of their GNP in 1995 to 50% of GNP by 2003. Once the absolute amount of the tax base has been calculated for each country, then a VAT tax rate is applied to this amount in order to arrive at the sum which each member has

Table 29.2 Sources of revenue for the EU budget (€m and %).

	1998	(%)	2000	(%)	2002	(%)
TOR	13,743.2	(16.7)	14,564.9	(16.4)	15,892.7	(17.0)
VAT	32,752.8	(39.7)	32,554.6	(36.7)	36,603.9	(39.1)
GNP	35,985.2	(43.6)	41,593.4	(46.9)	41,147.6	(43.9)
Total 'own resources'	**82,481.1**	**(100.0)**	**88,712.9**	**(100.0)**	**93,644.2**	**(100.0)**
Other revenue	1,628.0		674.0		2,010.6	
Total revenue	**84,109.1**		**89,386.9**		**95,654.8**	

Source: Adapted from European Commission (2002) *General Budget of the European Union for the Financial Year 2002*, January, and previous issues.

to pay. The maximum rate of VAT applied to this tax base has also fallen from 1.4% in the mid-1990s to 0.75% in 2003 and to 0.5% by 2004, which has further decreased the revenue derived by the EU from the VAT source. These curbs on the VAT source of revenue reflect the view that it is a regressive tax which tends to disadvantage poorer members of the EU because a greater proportion of their national income is devoted to consumption, resulting in a greater tax burden being placed on them than on richer members. As a result of the trends noted above, the importance of the GNP element in EU revenue has increased in order to fill the revenue gap. This is regarded as a more acceptable source because the contributions of the various member countries to the EU budget are more closely related to their affluence, i.e. to their ability to pay as indicated by GNP.

A breakdown of the expenditure side of the EU budget is shown in Table 29.3.

■ During most of the 1990s and in the early years of the new millennium, around 50% of the EU's total expenditure was spent on the *Guarantee* section of

the European Agricultural Guarantee and Guidance Fund (EAGGF). This Fund is used to subsidize the farming community under the EU's Common Agricultural Policy (CAP) in various ways. The Guarantee section is responsible for a wide range of price support programmes (see p. 590).

■ The second most important expenditure group involves 'Structural Operations' which accounted for some 33% of total expenditure in 2002. Within this group, the main constituent is the 'Structural Funds' accounting for 92% of the total. Although not shown in Table 29.3, the Structural Fund is made up of four sub-funds:

(a) the European Regional Development Fund (ERDF), which aims to reduce the inequality gap between the Community's regions;

(b) the European Social Fund (ESF), which is designed to improve the labour market in member countries by increasing employment opportunities, employment flexibility and equal opportunities for the workforce;

Table 29.3 Budgetary expenditure of the European communities (€m).

Budget heading	1998	2000	2002	2006[1]
Agriculture	**40,937.0**	**40,993.9**	**45,377**	**44,209**
EAGGF guarantee	40,937.0	36,889.0	40,761	39,572
Rural Development (RDP)	–	4,104.9	4,616	4,637
Structural operations	**28,594.7**	**32,678.0**	**32,998**	**31,955**
Structural Funds	23,084.4	28,105.0	30,316	29,278
Community Initiatives	2,558.8	1,743.0	–	–
Cohesion Fund	2,648.8	2,659.0	2,682	2,677
Others	302.7	325.0	–	–
Internal policies	4,678.5	6,027.0	6,793	7,038
External policies	4,528.5	4,805.1	4,895	4,916
Administration	4,353.4	4,703.7	5,225	5,439
Other	437.0	4,072.7	3,754	3,754
Total	**83,529.2**	**93,280.4**	**99,042**	**97,311**

[1] Estimated, at 2002 prices.
Source: As for Table 29.2.

(c) the EAGGF *Guidance* Fund, which helps to adapt the structure of agriculture by encouraging small (less efficient) farmers to leave the land;

(d) the Financial Instrument for Fisheries Guidance (FIFG), which helps the restructuring of the fisheries sector.

In 2002 the average percentage shares of Structural Fund expenditure spent on these activities were ERDF 58%, ESF 31%, EAGGF 9% and FIFG 2%. These Structural Funds are spent on the EU's three priority-based objectives:

- *Objective 1* covers regions of the EU in which development is seriously lagging behind the EU average. Member countries can apply to the four funds for assistance under this objective.

- *Objective 2* covers regions undergoing economic and social conversion, involving industrial restructuring or urban problems. The ERDF and ESF provide the main funding assistance under this objective.

- *Objective 3* covers whole countries and provides support for the adoption of education, training and employment initiatives. This objective is mostly funded by the ESF.

The remaining part of the Structural Fund is 'Community Initiatives', designed to stimulate co-operation between EU member states in promoting measures of common interest, e.g. rural development (the expenditures under this heading are no longer recorded separately but are included in the overall Structural Fund).

Finally, the Cohesion Fund is a separate part of the Structural Operations and is designed to help the least prosperous member states of the EU to take part in Economic and Monetary Union. For example, it provides assistance to projects in Greece, Ireland, Portugal and Spain, such as those which contribute to improvements in the transport infrastructure and transport networks of those countries.

- 'Internal policies' refers to the funds used to help improve EU competitiveness and includes spending on Research and Development (R&D) projects.

- 'External policies' includes EU foreign aid to states such as the former Eastern bloc countries wishing to progress towards the market economy model.

In 1998 the European Commission reported on the revenue and expenditure aspects of the EU budget (European Commission 1998). On the *revenue* side it was suggested that the performance of the budget should be assessed on five criteria, namely resources adequacy, equity in gross contributions, financial autonomy, transparency and simplicity, and cost-effectiveness. To fulfil these criteria the report proposed changes which would be simpler, fairer and more cost-effective. In particular there was support for more *revenue* being derived from members' GNP contributions. On the *expenditure* side, the main proposal was to decrease spending on market support policies for agricultural products. Finally, the report suggested that those members with large budget imbalances (i.e. whose contributions are generally greater than their receipts) should be compensated by some form of correction mechanism. For example, Germany, the Netherlands, Austria and Sweden have found themselves with budgetary deficits which are arguably excessive in relation to their relative standards of living within the EU.

The nature of the imbalances problem can be seen from Table 29.4. This table shows the relative shares of member countries in total EU GNP and in relative contributions to the total revenue for the EU budget, together with figures for the imbalances, both in absolute amounts and as a percentage of the country's GNP (UK figures are net of its rebate). Some important points can be noted from this table. First, the UK had an 18% share of EU GNP but contributed only 14.3% (after rebate) to the total revenue for the EU budget. Second, the UK has often had a negative budgetary imbalance with the EU, but in 2001 it became a net beneficiary because of an unusually high amount of rebate in that year. Third, other countries such as Germany, the Netherlands, Austria and Sweden were also experiencing negative imbalances with the EU. Arguably their situations are less fair in that their negative budgetary imbalance is a much higher percentage of their respective GNPs than for other member states. Put another way, their relative contributions to the EU budget are greater than their relative prosperity within the EU. Germany's problems have been particularly difficult because, as a wealthy country with a relatively small agricultural sector, it attracts low shares of EU spending on both the Structural Funds and the CAP. Fourth, it is clear that the EU budget continues to generate major

Table 29.4 GNP and EU budgetary balances, 2001.

	Share of EU GNP (%)	Share of EU budget (%)	Imbalance (€ million)	Imbalance (% GNP)
Belgium	2.9	4.0	−629.5	−0.24
Denmark	2.1	2.0	−229.0	−0.13
Germany	23.4	24.4	−6,953.3	−0.34
Greece	1.5	1.6	4,513.2	3.50
Spain	7.4	7.7	7,738.3	1.24
France	16.5	16.7	−2,035.4	−0.14
Ireland	1.3	1.4	1,203.1	1.13
Italy	13.8	13.0	−1,977.9	−0.17
Luxembourg	0.3	0.2	−144.1	−0.66
Netherlands	4.9	6.5	−2,256.8	−0.54
Austria	2.4	2.5	−536.4	−0.26
Portugal	1.4	1.5	1,794.2	1.53
Finland	1.5	1.5	−150.4	−0.12
Sweden	2.6	2.7	−973.3	−0.44
UK	18.0	14.3	707.5	0.05
EU	**100.0**	**100.0**	**70.3**	**0.00**

Sources: European Commission (2002) *Allocation of 2001 EU operating expenditure by Member States*, September, Table 6; European Commission (2002) *Public Finance Figures of the European Union*; European Economy (2002) *European Economy*, No. 3.

financial transfers to Greece, Portugal, Spain and Ireland – the four countries that receive a substantial amount from the Cohesion Fund.

In March 1999, the Berlin European Council reached an agreement on an important communication entitled *Agenda 2000: a stronger and wider Europe*. This was directed towards stimulating economic growth, increasing living standards and preparing for the enlargement of Europe over the period 2000–06. On the expenditure side of the new financial framework, the Council agreed to ensure that the EU's budget expenditure would not rise too rapidly over the seven years to 2006 (see Table 29.3). On the revenue side, adjustment were to be introduced to ensure that the burden on the least prosperous members would be alleviated by altering the rules on VAT contributions to the EU budget. At the same time, the UK's rebate would be gradually decreased, and adjustments made to the GNP method of revenue calculation (the base) in order to reduce the contributions of Austria, Germany, the Netherlands and Sweden to the EU budget.

The UK and the EU budget

It must be stressed that the terms 'net contributor' and 'net beneficiary' relate only to the EU budget and its relatively tiny amounts of expenditure, and *not* to the members' total experience within the Community. Merely to say that Germany and the UK have usually been large net contributors to the budget has no bearing upon whether they have or have not benefited overall from membership of the EU. It is also important to understand that being a 'net contributor' does not imply a transfer of German or UK funds to the EU. The budget is 'self-financing' to the extent that contributions to it are, by treaty, never the property of the member state. It is intended (although the results in practice are very different) to be a reallocation of resources from rich to poor in much the same way as national income tax. However, it is not so much being in the position of a net contributor to the budget that has worried successive UK governments, as the relative size of that contribution.

The calculation of the UK's net contribution

involves the following procedure:

1 customs tariffs paid directly to EU; *plus*

2 agricultural levies paid directly to EU; *minus*

3 administrative costs of collecting the above returned to UK government; *plus*

4 VAT contribution (according to the rate set by Council); *plus*

5 direct UK government contribution (the GNP element)

equals gross contribution, *minus*

6 amount due to UK for agricultural support (from Intervention Board); *minus*

7 structural Fund payments

equals net contribution (or benefit for some members).

As a major importer of both manufactured goods and food (see Chapter 27), the UK collects large amounts under items (1) and (2). The VAT rate as a tax on the value added is, of course, fairly closely related to economic activity and therefore the VAT contribution is reasonably proportional across member countries. Summing items (1)–(5) gives the UK's *gross* contribution to the EU budget. However, the UK must set against this the revenue it receives for agricultural support programmes, item (6), and for regional and social projects, item (7). Subtracting items (6) and (7) from gross contribution gives the UK's *net* contribution (or benefit).

Whereas the UK's gross contribution is relatively high compared with those of other members, its receipts from the EU budget, items (6) and (7), are relatively low. The UK receives little in terms of agricultural support because the operation of the CAP largely benefits less efficient producers, and not efficient ones like the UK. The modest increase in EU support for regional and social projects in the UK has been insufficient to correct this imbalance. As a result the UK has consistently found itself a net contributor.

The UK's net contributions to the EU budget are shown in Table 29.5. The fact that the UK was a large net contributor to the EU was addressed as early as 1984 when, under the Fontainebleau agreement of that year, the UK received a 'rebate' according to a set formula which the Commission calls 'a correction mechanism in favour of the UK'. The rebate was reviewed in 1988 and 1992 and on both occasions the

Table 29.5 UK net contributions to the EU budget, 1996–2002.

	1996	1998	2000	2002[1]
Total contribution[2]	6,721	8,712	8,433	6,491
VAT and FRA[3]	−4	874	236	85
UK abatement	−2,412	−1,378	−2,085	−3,099
Total receipts	4,373	4,115	4,241	4,318
Net contribution	**2,348**	**4,597**	**4,192**	**2,173**

[1] Provisional.
[2] Net of VAT, FRA and Abatement.
[3] Fourth Resource Adjustment.
Source: Adapted from HM Treasury (2002) *European Community Finances*, July, CM 5547.

European Commission decided that it should be continued. However, as noted above, under *Agenda 2000* the UK can expect its net payments to the EU to rise over the coming years, especially in view of the substantial rebates shown in Table 29.5.

Policy areas

1. Competition policy

The theory behind European competition policy is exactly that which created the original EEC almost 50 years ago. Competition brings consumer choice, lower prices and higher quality goods and services. The Commission has a set of directives in this area which are designed to underpin 'fair and free' competition. They cover cartels (price fixing, market sharing, etc.), government subsidies (direct or indirect subsidies for inefficient enterprises – state and private), the abuse of dominant market position (differential pricing in different markets, exclusive contracts, predatory pricing, etc.), selective distribution (preventing consumers in one market from buying in another in order to maintain high margins in the first market), and mergers and takeovers. The latter powers were given to the Commission in 1990.

Two of the most active areas of competition policy have involved mergers and acquisitions (see Chapter 5) and state aid. In the former, the power of the Commission was widened in 1998 to increase the range of mergers which can be referred to it. In the latter, the Commission has attempted to restrict the aid paid by member states to their own nationals through Articles 87 and 88 (previously articles 92 and 93) of the EC Treaty and Articles 4 and 95 of the ECSC Treaty. These Articles cover various aspects of the distorting effect that subsidies can have on competition between member states. However, it is likely that the progressive implementation of Single Market arrangements will result in domestic firms increasing their attempts to obtain state aid from their own governments as a means of helping them meet greater Europe-wide competition. Overall aid given by member states to their domestic industry has been running at around 2% of their respective GNPs during the 1990s.

Between 1988 and 2002, an average of €84bn per year was spent by member countries on all forms of state aid, and an average of €29bn of that aid went to the manufacturing sector. Germany tops the league of aid recipients as it tries to help its new *Länder* in the former East Germany to restructure their industry. The main problem with state aid is that the big, industrially powerful countries – Germany, France, UK and Italy – account for some 70% of the total state aid given by EU countries to their domestic industry. This arguably gives such economies considerable advantages over the four 'cohesion' countries – Greece, Portugal, Spain and Ireland.

To counter some of these trends, the EU Commission has begun to scrutinize state aid much more closely – especially where the aid seems to be more than is needed to ensure the ultimate viability of the recipient organizations. For example, in April 1998 the Commission decided that aid paid to the German porcelain firm, Triptis Porzellan GmbH, should be recovered because it believed it to be more than was needed to restore the firm's viability, thereby distorting competition in the market.

2. The Common Agricultural Policy

When the Treaty of Rome was signed in 1957 over 20% of the working population of the 'Six' were engaged in agriculture. In the enlarged EU of 15 countries in 2002 that figure is only 3.9%, ranging from the UK with 2.0% to Greece with over 20.4% (see Table 29.1). Since one in five of the EU's workers were involved in agricultural production in 1957, it

came as no surprise that the depressed agricultural sector became the focus of the first 'common' policy, the CAP, established in 1962. The objectives of this policy were to create a single market for agricultural produce and to protect the agricultural sector from imports, the justification being to ensure dependable supplies of food for the EU and stability of income for those engaged in agriculture.

Both the demand for, and the supply of, agricultural products are, for the most part, inelastic, so that a small shift in either schedule will induce a more than proportionate change in price. Fluctuations in agricultural prices will in turn create fluctuations in agricultural incomes and therefore investment and ultimately output. The CAP seeks to stabilize agricultural prices, and therefore incomes and output in the industry, to the alleged 'benefit' of both producers and consumers.

There are, of course, a number of ways of achieving such objectives. Prior to joining the EU, the UK placed great emphasis on supplies of cheap food from the Commonwealth. The UK therefore adopted a system of 'deficiency payments' which operated by letting actual prices be set at world levels, but at the same time guaranteeing to farmers minimum 'prices' for each product. If the world price fell below the guaranteed minimum, then the 'deficiency' would be made up by government subsidy. Under this system the consumer could benefit from the low world prices whilst at the same time farm incomes were maintained. Although the UK system involved some additional features, such as marketing agencies, direct production grants, research agencies, etc., it was by no means as complex as that which has operated in the UK since 1972 under the CAP.

Method of operation

The formal title for the executive body of the CAP is the European Agricultural Guarantee and Guidance Fund (EAGGF), often known by its French translation 'Fonds Européen d'Orientation et de Garantie Agricole' (FEOGA). As its name implies, it has two essential roles: that of guaranteeing farm incomes, and of guiding farm production. We shall consider each aspect in turn.

Guarantee system
Different agricultural products are dealt with in slightly different ways, but the basis of the system is

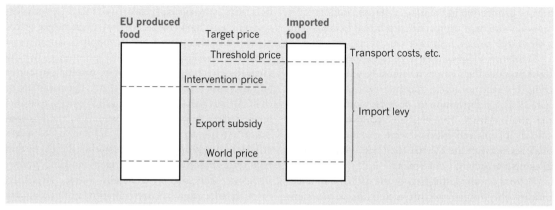

Fig. 29.1 EU agricultural pricing.

the establishment of a 'target price' for each product (Fig. 29.1). The target price is *not* set with reference to world prices, but is based upon the price which producers would need to cover costs, including a profit mark-up, in the highest-cost area of production in the EU. The EU then sets an 'Intervention' or 'guaranteed' price for the product in that area, about 7–10% below the target price. Should the price be in danger of falling below this level, the Commission intervenes to buy up production to keep the price at or above the 'guaranteed' level. The Commission then sets separate target and Intervention prices for that product in *each area* of the Community, related broadly to production costs in that area. As long as the market price in a given area (there are 11 such areas in the UK) is above the Intervention price, the producer will sell his produce at prevailing market prices. In effect the Intervention price sets a 'floor' below which market price will not be permitted to fall and is therefore the guaranteed minimum price to producers.

In Fig. 29.2, an increase in supply of agricultural products to S_1 would, if no action were taken, lower the market price from P_1 to P_2, below the 'Intervention' or 'guaranteed' price, P^*. At P^* demand is Q' but supply is Q^*. To keep the price at P^* the EAGGF will buy up the excess $Q^* - Q'$. In terms of Fig. 29.2 the demand curve is artificially increased to D_1 by the EAGGF purchase.

If this system of guaranteed minimum prices is to work, then EU farmers must be protected from low-priced imports from overseas. To this end levies or tariffs are imposed on imports of agricultural prod-

ucts. If in Fig. 29.2 the price of imported food were higher than the EU target price then, of course, there would be no need for an import tariff. If, however, the import price is below this, say at the 'world price' in Fig. 29.2, then an appropriate tariff must be calculated. This need not quite cover the difference between 'target' and 'world' price, since the importer still has to pay transport costs within the EU to get the food to market. The tariff must therefore be large enough to raise the import price at the EU frontier to the target price minus transport costs, i.e. 'threshold price'. This calculation takes place in the highest-cost

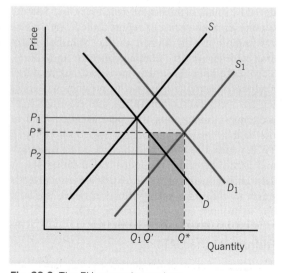

Fig. 29.2 The EU guarantee system.

area of production in the EU, so that the import tariff set will more than protect EU producers in areas with lower target prices (i.e. lower-cost areas).

Should an EU producer wish to export an agricultural product then an export subsidy will be paid to bring his receipts up to the Intervention price (see Fig. 29.2), i.e. the minimum price he would receive in the home market. Problems involving this form of subsidy of oil-seed exports were a major threat to dealings between the EU and the USA, with the latter alleging a breach of GATT rules.

Reforms in the latter part of the 1980s had a significant effect on key sectors such as dairy products. In the cereals and oil-seeds market, intervention buying now occurs only outside the harvest periods. *Maximum Guaranteed Quantities* (MGQs) are also set for most products. If the MGQ is exceeded, then the intervention price is cut by 3% in the following year.

The system outlined above does not apply to all agricultural products in the EU. About a quarter of these products are covered by different direct subsidy systems, e.g. olive oil and tobacco, and some products, such as potatoes, agricultural alcohol, and honey are not covered by EU regulation at all.

Guidance system

The CAP was, as originally established, a simple price-support system. It soon became obvious that agriculture in the 'Six' required considerable structural change because too much output was being produced by small, high-cost, farming units. In 1968 the Commission published a report called *Agriculture 1980*, more usually known as the 'Mansholt Plan' after its originator, the Commissioner for Agriculture, Sicco Mansholt. The plan envisaged taking large amounts of marginal land out of production, reducing the agricultural labour force, and creating larger economic farming units. The plan eventually led to the establishment of a Common Structural Policy in 1972, which for political reasons was to be voluntary and administered by the individual member states. The import levies of the EAGGF were to provide funds to encourage small farmers to leave the land and to promote large-scale farming units.

Reform of the CAP

The relative failure of the guidance policy has meant the continued existence of many small, high-cost pro-ducers in many agricultural areas of the EU, with correspondingly high 'target' prices. High target prices have in turn encouraged excess supply in a number of products, requiring substantial purchases by the Guarantee section of the EAGGF, resulting in butter and beef mountains, wine lakes, etc. The net effect of the CAP has therefore been, via high prices, to transfer resources from the EU consumer to the EU producer. At the same time the CAP has led to a less efficient allocation of resources within the EU in that high prices made the use of marginal land and labour-intensive processes economically viable. Arguably, resource allocation has been impaired both within the EU *and* on a world scale, in that the system of agricultural levies distorts comparative advantages by encouraging high-cost production within the EU to the detriment of low-cost production outside the EU. Finally, through its import levies and export subsidies the CAP introduces an element of discrimination against Third World producers of agricultural products, for whom such exports are a major source of foreign earnings.

The growth of agricultural spending in the early 1980s placed increasing pressure on the EU's 'own resources'. By 1983 the 1% VAT ceiling had been breached and even the steady growth in imports (providing CET revenue) was not sufficient to meet the demands on the budget. The member governments were forced to agree to special additional payments to meet deficits which arose in 1983, 1984, 1985 and 1987. With no agreement on reform during the late 1980s, the CAP began to expand rapidly and the Council was forced to agree a series of 'supplementary' budgets.

The breakthrough occurred at the Brussels Heads of Government meeting in February 1988 during which a further, new source of finance was sanctioned (up to 1.2% of GNP) in return for legislative limits on the CAP. In 1988 the CAP was limited to a fixed sum of 27.5bn ECU (€27.5bn) and from then onwards could only expand, in future years, by three-quarters of the average rate of growth in EU GNP (see Table 29.6). Other significant limits were placed on the CAP in the form of a ceiling on cereal production (160 million tonnes), a cut in producer prices of about 3%, and a new 'co-responsibility' levy of 3% on larger farmers.[2]

The reform of CAP took a further step forward in June 1992 when the so-called 'McSharry proposals' for reform were adopted. The purposes of the reforms

Table 29.6 CAP spending as a proportion of the EU budget, 1984–2002.

	% of EU budget
1984	65.4
1988	65.0
1990	59.4
1992	53.3
1996	50.4
1998	49.0
2002	41.1

Note: Figures exclude EAGGF guidance.
Sources: As for Table 29.3 and *Eurostat* (various).

were, first, to control agricultural production which had been artificially stimulated by CAP; second, to make European agriculture more competitive by reduction of support prices; and third, to discourage very intensive agricultural methods while still maintaining high employment on the land and supporting more marginal and vulnerable farmers.

To achieve these aims, support prices for cereals were to be reduced by some 30%. Also, arable land was taken out of production or 'set aside', with farmers receiving payment based on average yields for what is *not* produced. Livestock farmers were limited to a maximum head of cattle per hectare of available fodder. Other elements of the reform involved direct income-support for farmers in Less Favoured Areas (LFAs) and for those who use environmentally sound methods of farming. Finally, an early 'pre-pension' scheme was introduced to accelerate the retirement of farmers who operated unviable holdings.

In July 1997 the European Commission published *Agenda 2000* which analysed the EU's past policies and considered certain long-term future trends. As far as agriculture was concerned, it recognized the need to extend the agricultural reforms of 1992. The recommendations of 1997 were designed to continue the post-1992 trend of reducing price support to farmers (through the intervention buying system) and providing more money payments direct to producers. For example, in the cereals sector the intervention price was reduced by 15% between 2000 and 2002 to set it closer to world levels (see Fig. 29.1). In the

milk sector, the intervention price will be cut by 15% in three steps from 2005/06 onwards, although output quotas were raised by 1.5% in three steps from 2000 onwards (from 2003 in the UK) to try to alleviate the problems resulting from a lower intervention price.

Finally, a new Rural Development Policy (RDP) was introduced in January 2000 to boost a variety of restructuring schemes directed towards easing these changes in agricultural policy (see Table 29.3). This is to be the 'second pillar' of EU agricultural policy and is designed to help stimulate investment in farm business, develop forestry and forestry products, improve training for young farmers, and provide help for those older farmers wishing to retire. In the UK, expenditure on the RDP will amount to £1bn between 2000 and 2006 and it will certainly be needed to support hard-pressed farmers, given the drop in their incomes resulting from lower intervention prices. In fact since 2002 the European Commission has been involved in discussions relating to reforming the CAP by freezing agricultural spending from 2007 onwards. It has also introduced the idea of '*compulsory modulation*' which involves forcing member states to reduce direct payments to agriculture and place more funds into environmental protection and early retirement schemes for workers within the agricultural sector.

The pressure for agricultural reform has come from many sides – such as consumers who worry that CAP encourages higher prices, ministers afraid of the spiralling budget costs of agricultural subsidies, policy makers aware of the need to shift resources from an EU farming community of 7 million in order to help the 18.5 million Europeans who are unemployed, and supporters of the Single Currency who accept the need to cut member states' budget deficits in order to meet the Maastricht criteria. Agricultural reform has also been accepted as necessary by supporters of EU enlargement who recognize that if price supports are not decreased, then the enlargement of the EU in 2004 to include 10 Eastern European states will cause severe budgetary difficulties. This is because farm prices in the new entrants are already 20–40% below the EU level and would require extensive (and costly) support to be raised to the EU levels. Such increases in agricultural prices to EU levels could, of course, also cause financial hardship for the consumers in those lower-income countries, as well as giving a cost-push stimulus to inflation.

3. Structural policy

This is the term given to a combination of what used to be called the Regional and Social Policies (together with several other minor policy areas). For clarity we have separated these two central policy areas in the discussion which follows.

Regional policy

Like the UK's own regional policy, the objective of that for the EU as a whole is to attempt to ease regional economic differences (Chapter 21). Almost a quarter of the current EU budget is devoted to 'regional policy' as part of what are called the 'Structural Funds' (Social plus Regional plus other policies).

Regional policy attempts to improve the structural base of the EU's poorer regions against a background of inequality in income per head, ranging from around 30% of the EU average in some poor regions to over 200% in some rich regions. The disparities in regional income per head will clearly grow still wider should the countries of eastern Europe join. Of even greater concern were the findings of a study by Dunford (1994). This showed that, although the regions of the EU were converging up to 1976, they actually diverged in terms of incomes per head after that date, casting doubt as to the effectiveness of EU regional policy. As a part answer to this problem a *Cohesion Fund* was introduced in 1993 to help certain countries achieve the convergence criteria necessary for economic and monetary union. Four countries have already benefited from the Fund because they had GDP per head of less than 90% of the Community average in the early 1990s. They are Spain (75%), Ireland (68%), Portugal (56%) and Greece (47%). Some €24bn was spent on this Cohesion Fund over the 1993–2003 time period.

The accepted wisdom during the 1970s and 1980s was that a European *core* existed which was highly developed and very wealthy. The core consisted of the northern and western parts of Germany, Benelux, most of northern France, and south-east England. Outside the core the picture was of a less-developed *periphery*. It is now understood that the EU's pattern of economic well-being is more patchy and far more complex than the 'core and periphery' model.

To address the patchy nature of EU regional development, the EU decided in 1997 to introduce new guidelines by 2000 in order to reduce the proportion of the EU population eligible to receive regional aid, as a step towards reducing the total value of such aid to industry. Initially it will more carefully scrutinize the eligibility of regions for the *Objective 1* status which provides maximum grants, i.e. where GDP per head in the region is less than 75% of the EU average. By 2002, some 50 regions, covering 22% of the EU's population, had received money under Objective 1, accounting for 70% of the total Structural Fund budget. Meanwhile, 18% of the EU population lived in areas that received *Objective 2* money, accounting for 13% of the Structural Fund's resources. Finally, *Objective 3*, whose eligibility is not confined to any particular areas of the EU, received 12.3% of total Structural Fund resources.

In the UK, the EU has classified Cornwall and the Isles of Scilly, South Yorkshire, West Wales and the Valleys, and Merseyside as areas eligible for Objective 1 funding over the period 2000–06. These areas cover some 5m people and each has GDP per head levels of around 70% of the EU average. Northern Ireland and the Highlands and Islands will also receive transitional support until 2006 to help them consolidate on the improvements they achieved as a result of previous funding in the 1990s.

Social policy

The development of European social policy has involved both the operation of the *European Social Fund* (ESF) and developments in the 'Social Chapter' of the Maastricht Treaty.

The European Social Fund is designed to develop human resources and improve the workings of the labour market throughout the EU. Expenditure is concentrated in those regions of the EU which are suffering from high unemployment and is designed to help with retraining initiatives, improving skills and providing educational opportunities in order to make the labour force more flexible. In March 1998 the European Commission formally adopted a series of draft regulations which will form the backbone of the ESF's plans for the 2000–06 period. At the centre of these plans is the new European Employment Strategy (EES) which stipulates that each member state must submit an annual employment plan directed towards raising 'employability, entrepreneurship, labour force adaptability and equal opportunities'. A sum of €210bn has been allocated to achieving these goals by 2006.

As far as the 'Social Chapter' of the Maastricht Treaty is concerned, the UK had been opposed to many of the regulations and directives associated with the Social Chapter, with successive Conservative governments arguing that attempting to impose regulations in such areas as works councils, maternity/paternity rights, equal pay, part-time workers issues, etc. merely increased labour costs and decreased UK competitiveness. For example, German social/labour market policies have been criticized for making labour too expensive to employ! We have already noted in Chapter 1 that Germany's labour productivity in manufacturing was 29% above that of the UK in the late 1990s, yet its Relative Unit Labour Costs were 64% higher than in the UK. Part of the problem results from the fact that Germany's labour costs have been inflated by non-wage costs (e.g. social benefits) which are 32% of total wage costs in Germany as compared to only 18% in the UK. Nevertheless the Labour government in the UK has adopted many parts of the Social Chapter in order to provide basic minimum standards across Europe even if this does result in some increase in labour costs. In any case, even if the UK had remained outside the Social Chapter it would still have been subject to a great deal of EU social legislation introduced as part of other programmes from which there is no UK 'opt-out'. The UK has adopted the Working Time Directive (1998) and the Parent Leave Directive (1999) in an attempt to catch up with other EU members which had already adopted these directives (see Chapter 15).

4. Trade policy and balance of payments

The EU is the largest trading bloc in the world. It accounts for 20% of world GDP and around 40% of world trade. The EU runs a deficit on its visible trade with the rest of the world, largely due to its need for substantial imports of fuel and raw materials. As regards invisible trade the EU is roughly in balance with the rest of the world. By the early 1990s, almost 60% of both EU exports and imports involved other EU countries. The growth of this intra-European trade has been a significant factor in attracting inward investment into the EU (see Chapter 7).

The UK's trade with the EU

The UK's trade with the EU has shown important changes since the late 1960s. First, the area composition of UK visible exports and imports indicates a strong movement towards the Community. In 1969, for example, 29% of total UK visible exports were destined for the EU, whilst 26% of UK visible imports came from the EU. By 2002 the shares had increased significantly, to 58% and 52% respectively (see Table 27.2). Second, as can be seen from Table 29.7, the UK's trade with the rest of the EU has shown little improvement in trade in either goods or services. The UK had a deficit on both goods and services accounts with the EU throughout the 1990s and improvements in the current account balance after 1996 were not in fact due to any improvements as regards trade in goods and services. Rather they were arguably due to temporary financial market conditions which reduced the outflow of income earned on inward investment (e.g. losses for foreign-owned banks, etc.) which helped inflate the 'income' line. Thus there is little real evidence that the UK could earn sufficient income from the EU to cover its large trade deficit, especially in manufactures.

Any disadvantage for the UK in its trade in manufactures is particularly worrying, since exports and imports of manufactures together constitute some 66% of total trade with the EU whilst food, drink, tobacco and oil together account for only 25%. A major study (European Commission 1997) points out that the UK is still at a competitive disadvantage in high price/high quality goods compared to its European competitors.

The nature of the EU, as a bloc which allows free trade in manufactured goods, has worked to the disadvantage of the relatively less efficient British manufacturers. Similarly, the fact that the EU remains a relatively closed market with respect to both agricultural goods and invisibles (particularly the two areas of relative British strength – insurance and banking) has restricted the UK from taking advantage of the areas in which it has had a small comparative advantage.

5. Monetary policy

A single currency permitting trade at 'known prices' has been a long-standing goal of the EU. Such a currency would overcome the uncertainties created by currency fluctuations which discourage medium- and long-term contracts and therefore international trade.

Table 29.7 UK current account transactions with the EU, 1992–2001.

£mn	1994	1995	1996	1997	1998	1999	2000	2001
Balances								
Trade in goods	−5,572	−4,523	−4,870	−4,468	−6,571	−7,260	−3,271	−5,182
Trade in services	−991	−45	−397	216	244	−2,320	−2,597	−2,668
Trade in goods and services	−6,563	−4,568	−5,267	−4,252	−6,327	−9,580	−5,868	−7,850
Investment income	1,502	743	1,899	4,692	7,861	6,201	10,319	9,897
Current transfers	−3,057	−4,917	−6,606	−4,358	−6,562	−4,416	−6,790	−3,920
Current account	**−8,118**	**−8,742**	**−9,974**	**−3,918**	**−5,028**	**−7,795**	**−2,339**	**−1,873**

Source: Adapted from ONS (2002) *United Kingdom Balance of Payments.*

A common currency and common exchange reserves, together with a European Central Bank, are the major features of European monetary union (EMU). The 'Snake', and later the European Monetary System (EMS), were seen by many as steps towards European monetary union.

While now thoroughly integrated into the move towards economic and monetary union, we deal in this section with the background to EMU in the form of the EMS and its precursors and the European Currency Unit (ECU). The discussion of EMU and the euro is presented in a separate section below.

The 'Snake', 1973–79

Consultations between the 'Six' and the three applicant countries between 1970 and 1972 led in 1973 to the establishment of a currency cooperation system called variously the 'Snake', or the 'Snake in the Tunnel'. It required each central bank to maintain its currency within a band of ±2.25% against the US dollar, limiting the fluctuations that could occur between member country currencies. This had the advantage of reducing uncertainty but it did restrict the use of the exchange rate as a policy instrument for adjusting trade deficits and surpluses between members.

The oil crisis of 1973 and ensuing world recession created balance of payments problems for many member countries. Fluctuations in the balance of payments in turn led to more volatile exchange rates, making it more difficult to maintain par values within the narrow bands of the 'Snake'. As a result the UK remained a member for only a few months, with France also leaving the system in January 1974.

Although the 'Snake' itself continued, it did so in a truncated form, with three members outside (UK, the Republic of Ireland and France) and four non-members inside (Norway, Sweden, Austria and Switzerland). In effect the 'Snake' now contained only currencies with a historically close link to the Deutschmark and it was replaced in the late 1970s by the EMS.

European Monetary System (EMS) since 1979

The EMS was created in order to increase cooperation on monetary affairs within the Community, and like the 'Snake' was founded on the ultimate goal of European Monetary Union (EMU). The EMS was established in March 1979 with three main components, a European currency unit (ECU), an exchange rate mechanism, and the European Monetary Co-operation Fund (EMCF). In 1989 a fourth element was added – the Very Short Term Financing facility (VSTF). This is a means of funding deficits between member states to an unlimited amount, but for very short periods of time.

The ECU was, possibly, the most radical of the EMS innovations. Whilst superficially similar to the old unit of account in which EU dealings used to be denominated, the ECU was far more than a *numéraire*. It was valued according to a weighted basket of all the EU currencies. Being a weighted average it was more stable than the exchange rate of any single currency. In addition to its role as a unit of account, it functioned as an international reserve currency. Each member of the EMS 'bought' ECUs with 20% of their gold and dollar reserves, which were then held by a new EU institution called the European Monetary Co-operation Fund (FECOM according to its French initials). The central banks used their holdings of ECUs to buy each other's currencies and to settle debts. Of course, as of 1 January 1999, the ECU was replaced on a one-to-one basis by the euro (see Chapter 20).

The second element of the EMS involved the exchange rate mechanism which was, essentially, a development of the 'Snake'. Like its predecessor, the scheme originally set a 2.25% divergence limit, but this time not against the more volatile individual currencies but against the ECU. The new scheme also differed from the old in that it encompassed a formally recognized method of 'warning' governments that they have to take action. Each currency had a 'divergence limit'[3] computed against each of the other currencies in the scheme which, because it did not include the 'home' currency whose divergence against itself was zero, was always slightly less than the official 2.25% limit. If a currency diverged by more than 75% of this limit it had reached its 'divergence threshold' and the government was expected to intervene, either to buy its own currency for ECUs (if the exchange rate has declined) or to sell it for ECUs (if the exchange rate has risen).

The European Monetary Cooperation Fund, the third element in the EMS, consisted of all the heads of the central banks of the member states and was intended to supervise the use of the 'official ECU'. This was the currency unit originally established, and acted as a means of settling deficits between the members; it was supported by an IMF-type system of deposits of gold and foreign currency. It held the members' 20% deposits of gold and dollars, was empowered to lend up to 25bn ECUs to countries in difficulties, and was intended ultimately to become a central bank for Europe acting to support the ECU against the dollar, yen, etc.

Until mid-1987 the development of the ECU as a private currency was hampered by the refusal of the West Germans to recognize it. The ECU had been developing as a major international bond currency and, indeed, as a private European currency, but the objections of the West Germans meant that it could not be truly 'European'. In June 1987, however, the West German government removed their veto on the private holding of ECUs by their citizens and thereby opened the way for further liberalization of capital movements within the Community. Up to 1999 the ECU was used throughout the EU as a basis for travellers' cheques, and the Belgian government even issued 50 ECU gold and 5 ECU silver coins in 1987 to celebrate the thirtieth anniversary of the founding of the EC. After 1999, the ECU was superseded by the euro.

The UK and the EMS

The UK has always been a member of the EMS but, until late 1990, did not join its exchange rate system (known as the 'parity grid'). The UK government felt in 1978 that sterling would be too volatile to cope with the confines of the parity grid system. The UK anticipated a continual need to defend a weak pound within the grid, thereby putting pressure on its gold and foreign exchange reserves. The UK also held that the restricted variation in exchange rate against other member currencies would impede the use of the exchange rate as a policy instrument. Finally, by setting limits for sterling, the exchange rate could less readily be used for economic management in the UK, e.g. a high pound helping to curb inflation.

Up to 1987 there had been 11 realignments in the EMS parity grid. The West Germans felt that these readjustments were too frequent, allowing several countries to avoid the macroeconomic discipline originally intended by adopting the system. Ironically, having remained out of the parity grid due to fears of sterling's weakness, the UK government experienced for a period the exact opposite. At least until the end of 1982 the problem would have been that of having to keep sterling down within the grid rather than of establishing a 'floor' for sterling.

As indicated in Chapter 27, UK trade has become less sensitive to price factors and therefore less easily influenced by exchange rate adjustment. Further, a third of UK trade is still invoiced in the dollar or in other EMS currencies, reducing the importance of EMS currency fluctuations to the UK. For these reasons it has been suggested that the restrictions imposed on the *sterling exchange rate* by the EMS parity grid were, from the point of view of trade, less important to the UK than to other EU member countries. It would therefore seem that the restrictions imposed upon *UK demand management*, via the parity grid, proved the greater deterrent to full UK participation within the EMS. However, the arguments in favour of the UK joining the EMS parity grid became stronger as the EU became more important in

UK trade, and as dollar-invoiced oil took a smaller share in UK exports. The problem, once the UK joined in 1990, became the ability of the system to cope with three major currencies, in view of the difficulties it had experienced in coping with two, namely, the Deutschmark (DM) and French franc.

Black Wednesday

The initial phase of UK membership of the EMS lasted less than two years before the Conservative government of John Major withdrew sterling on Wednesday, 16 September 1992 – 'Black Wednesday'.

Underlying the events which led to the withdrawal of sterling and the lira from the EMS in September 1992 were two phenomena: the weakness of the US economy and the resulting low interest rates in that country, and the large amounts of capital required by Germany for economic reconstruction in the eastern part of that country and the resulting high interest rates needed in Germany to reduce inflationary pressure. Finance flowed towards the DM and out of US dollars and sterling. The UK government made it worse by refusing to realign sterling in the ERM in early September and there followed two weeks of momentous pressure on European currencies and the ERM itself.

Downward pressure on the Italian lira forced the Italian government first to increase domestic interest rates twice – first to 15% (4 September) and then to 20% (8 September). Continued speculative selling of the lira then forced the Italians to negotiate the first realignment in the EMS since 1987 – a 7% devaluation of the lira against the other EMS currencies (13 September). Finally, a small reduction in German interest rates (by 0.25% on 14 September) was not enough to prevent the lira being withdrawn from the EMS on Black Wednesday.

Sterling followed a similar path to the lira but without the intermediate rises in interest rates. On 3 September the Chancellor announced that the UK was borrowing £7.25bn in foreign currency to assist in the defence of the pound. At the same time the government made it clear that they had no intention of allowing sterling to be deflected from its rate and band in the EMS. Both German and French central banks, the Bundesbank and the Bank of France, assisted the Bank of England in trying to defend sterling's central rate in the EMS.

By Wednesday 16 September, however, the financial markets had driven sterling below its 'floor' in the EMS and the British government took drastic measures to attempt to maintain sterling's position. Unprecedented rises in British interest rates – by 2% and then by another 3% (from 10% to 15%) – were announced during Wednesday 16 September but neither was sufficient to prevent sales of sterling from reducing its rate against the DM well below the EMS 'floor' of DM2.78. Sterling was withdrawn from the EMS system – along with the lira – and allowed to 'float'. Viewed against an EMS central rate of DM2.95 and a 'floor' of DM2.78, sterling quickly fell and continued falling. By October 1992 it had reached DM2.36 – a devaluation of some 20% on its previous central rate in the EMS.

These events seemed to indicate that a fixed system of exchange rates could not stand against the sheer scale of currency movements in the new global financial markets. A number of factors might, however, have exacerbated the situation for the EMS in September 1992 which need not have been allowed to hold sway. In the absence of these factors it might have been that the system could have weathered the period in a more effective manner.

It might have been the case that the attempt – unofficially – to 'fix' the EMS currencies together as early as the late 1980s and early 1990s was just too early. No realignment had taken place since 1987 in spite of significant underlying economic changes in the economies of the member states (reunification in Germany, lower inflation and better industrial performance in France, high inflation and poor economic performance in Italy, and persistent recession and falling industrial production in the UK). Rather than relieving pressures and differentials gradually by occasional realignments, the EMS had resisted changes in parity for five years. At the same time unusually large divergencies had built up between the United States and German economies. Interest rates of 3% in the USA and 9% in Germany carried sufficient differential to create massive currency flows between the two and between Germany and other less successful economies. Large amounts of money were required by the German economy to finance reconstruction, and high interest rates were deemed to be required both to encourage this investment and to keep inflation in check. Political and financial uncertainties over the future of the Maastricht Treaty and, therefore, over the future of Economic and Monetary Union following the Danish rejection of the Treaty simply added to the problem.

The crisis in the EMS in September 1992 did not imply that such currency arrangements were impractical or irrelevant, only that the member states of the EU needed to gain more experience of their management. The key seems to lie in achieving the correct balance in the degree of 'fixity' of the rates in the system and in ensuring that 'divergence indicators' require both strong and weak currencies to take action. Concerns about the degree of 'fixity' were met in late 1992 by extending the ERM fluctuation bands to ±15%. This band continued in operation for the non-eurozone currencies after the major EMU reforms of 1999.

6. Commercial and industrial policy

The Common Customs Tariff (CCT) is common to all members of the EU and is imposed on all industrial imports from non-EU countries, though with a few exceptions. Tariff rates differ from one kind of import to another. For example, raw materials and some types of semi-manufactured goods that are not produced within the EU tend to benefit from low duty rates. Tariff rates may also be set at a low rate to stimulate competition within some sectors of the EU, e.g. for pharmaceutical and IT-related goods. Since tariffs on industrial products traded between member countries have been dismantled, the application of the CCT has created a protected free trade area or 'customs union' of some 380 million consumers.

The effect of creating a customs union is, however, double-edged. 'Trade creation' is the term used to refer to the extra trade between members of the customs union as a result of removing tariff barriers. Production of certain goods is then transferred from high-cost to low-cost producers within the customs union. It can therefore be argued that trade creation causes resources *within* the customs union to be used more efficiently. However, 'trade diversion' also occurs as a result of the CCT imposed against non-members of the customs union. This may cause some production to be transferred from low-cost producers *outside* the union to high-cost producers inside. We shall see below that the two effects are extremely difficult to quantify. However, in general terms, the higher the original tariff between member countries, and the higher the original tariff against non-members, the more likely it will be that the efficiency gains from trade creation will outweigh the efficiency

losses from trade diversion.

A major study of trade in manufactured goods in France, Germany, Italy and the UK over the period 1985 to 1995 showed a strong 'trade-creation' effect from the creation of the Single Market but found little evidence of a 'trade diversion' effect (European Commission, 1996). For example while the share of the domestic demand in these countries met from other member states (i.e. *intra-EU trade*) rose from 16.9% to 21.5% between 1985 and 1995, the share of domestic demand met from outside the EU also increased from 12.7% to 15.6%. In other words, there was a strong trade creation effect (rise in intra-EU trade) and no evidence of a trade diversion effect (fall in *extra-EU trade*).

UK industry and the EU

It is extremely difficult to evaluate the industrial effects of UK entry into the EU. Certainly the hope on entry was that the UK would secure 'dynamic gains' in this sector to offset the expected 'static costs' of the net budget contribution and higher food prices. The 'dynamic gains' were expected to include a boost to output and productivity from a large, protected market, with its potential for scale economies and greater export opportunities. However, for whatever reason, there seems little evidence in Table 29.8 of those gains in UK manufacturing output anticipated after entry into the EU in 1973. In fact, the real output of UK manufacturing has grown more slowly than that of the other EU countries.

Lord Kaldor suggested, prior to entry, that the alleged 'dynamic gains' might turn out to be 'dynamic costs', as the UK market in industrial products became more exposed to its European competitors with the dismantling of tariffs. It may be that the UK joined the wrong type of 'customs union'! If trade in agriculture and in service activities were freed between member countries, rather than trade in industrial products, then some of the alleged 'dynamic gains' might indeed have materialized. In Chapter 1 we noted that the trend towards service activities, though a feature of all advanced economies, has been most marked in the UK. It is arguable that it is in this sector that the UK's comparative advantages lie. The present industrial policy of the EU, which frees trade in industrial products whilst permitting (along with WTO/GATT) the protection of services, would seem to be to the particular disadvantage of the UK.

Table 29.8 Comparisons of manufacturing output (1970 = 100).

	1970	1975	1980	1985	1992	2002
EU (excluding UK)	100	108	133	133	154	188
Germany	100	104	122	122	138	156
France	100	108	133	133	157	188
Italy	100	107	139	132	160	176
UK	100	102	110	113	128	147

Source: Adapted from OECD (2003) *Main Economic Indicators* (and previous issues).

Monetary union

European Economic and Monetary Union (EMU)

As long ago as 1969 the Commission funded the 'Werner Report' which acknowledged what it called the 'political wish to establish economic and monetary union' and set a target of completion by 1980. Unfortunately the severe economic traumas of the 1970s intervened and it was 1979 before even the first stage – the setting up of the European Monetary System (EMS) – was accomplished.

In 1988 the Council decided to look into the matter again and set up a Committee under the then EC President, Jacques Delors. That Committee reported in June 1989 and the Council agreed to enter into Stage 1 on 1 July 1990.

The first stage of the Delors Plan – the establishment of a true Single European Market (SEM) – had, of course, already been put in train by the Single European Act of 1987. As the fundamental base of the EMU structure, the Commission felt that it was necessary to set out clearly what the economic benefits would be. They therefore commissioned a group of senior economists, financiers and business people to investigate the issues. The Committee under the chairmanship of Paulo Ceccini reported in 1988.

The Ceccini Report

Although published as a single report, the 'Ceccini Report' is simply the summary and conclusions of no fewer than 13 separate economic reports on aspects of the single market. It identifies two types of cost associated with what it calls, in shorthand, 'non-Europe', i.e. a Europe of markets separated by physical, technical and fiscal barriers:

- first are those barriers which have an immediate benefit when they are removed;
- second are those which will have benefits spread over a period of time.

It should be noted that both types include elements of both static and dynamic benefits.

The parts which made up the 'Ceccini Report' examined the single market from the point of view of microeconomic benefits (the removal of non-tariff barriers, economies of scale, X-efficiencies, etc.) and of macroeconomic benefits (the supply-side shock and its effects on GDP, inflation rates, employment, production, etc.).

Using a variety of methods, the Report came up with significant benefits which might accrue to EU members as a result of the Single Market. These included the following:

- total gains of around 216bn ECU at 1988 prices (between 4.3% and 6.4% of EU GDP);
- price deflation of an average 6.1%;
- an improvement to the EU's external trade of about 1%;
- an improvement to budget balances of about 2.2%; and
- around 1.8m new jobs (a reduction in unemployment of about 1.5%).

The Maastricht agreement set out a planned system for moving towards EMU, including the creation of a system of European central banks to precede the European Central Bank. The full schedule was delineated in three 'Stages'.

Stage 1

Theoretically this commenced on 1 January 1993 and involved the creation of an EU 'Monetary Committee' whose role included general monitoring and review of monetary matters in EU states and throughout the EU as a whole, providing advice to the Council of Ministers and contributing to the preparation for the European System of Central Banks (ESCB) and the European Central Bank (ECB) (see below).

Stage 2

In theory this Stage was to commence on 1 January 1994 with the establishment of a new 'European Monetary Institute' to strengthen cooperation between EU central banks, coordinate monetary policy, monitor the functioning of the EMS and take over the role of the European Monetary Cooperation Fund (EMCF). The EMI would seek to obtain a 'high degree of sustainable convergence' against four criteria:

1 *Price stability*. This should be close to the performance of the three best performing members. In a protocol to the treaty 'close to' was defined as not more than 1.5% above the average inflation of the three best performers.

2 *Government finance*. This should adhere to a pre-ordained 'reference value' – defined as a government deficit of no more than 3% of GDP at market prices and a government debt of no more than 60% of GDP at market prices.

3 *ERM fluctuations*. Normal margins of fluctuation should not have been breached for *two years*.

4 *Durability of convergence*. This was to be measured by long-term interest rate levels. The rate for long-term government bonds should not have exceeded by more than 2% those of the three best performing countries.

The Maastricht Treaty required that the EMI should specify – by 31 December 1996 at the latest – the regulatory, organizational and logistical framework for the ESCB (to be created in the third stage). It should also set a date for the beginning of the Third Stage. If this date was not set before the end of 1997 it would, according to the Treaty, automatically begin on 1 January 1999.

Stage 3

This stage included the establishment of the European System of Central Banks (ESCB) which would hold and manage the official reserves of all the member states. At this stage exchange rates would be fixed and the ECU would acquire full status as a currency throughout the Community. The ESCB would prepare for the establishment of the European Central Bank (ECB) which, when founded, would have the exclusive right to issue banknotes throughout the EU. It would accomplish this through the central bank of each of the member states. It would receive some 5bn ECU together with all members' reserves – excepting only member states' foreign currency, ECU holdings, IMF reserve positions and SDRs. Any reserves over 50bn ECU in value would also be left with the member country (in theory, of course, these would not be required and could be used in any way by the member state). The theoretical total reserves to be held by the ESCB would, therefore, be around 600bn ECU.

Maastricht established the shape and format of all of the institutions it envisaged. The Treaty provided for it to come into force on 1 January 1993 or on the date on which the last member country deposited an instrument of ratification with the Commission.

There were a number of protocols to the Maastricht Treaty involving most of the members. The UK had a lengthy protocol agreed which allowed it not to proceed to Stage 3 if it did not wish to and excluded it from most of the Stage 2 arrangements (in return the UK would not be allowed to have a vote in Council on arrangements to do with the ESCB or the ECB).

The path to EMU settled down into the following timetable:

1996–98	All member countries brought their economies into line to meet the Maastricht criteria (see Table 29.9).
1998	The countries which formed the first members of EMU were selected.
1999	January 1 – the EMU process began with the launch of the euro and the beginning of the transition phase (through to the end of 2001). During this phase national currencies still existed but were irrevocably fixed to each other and to the euro.
2002	January 1 – the euro was introduced in coin and note form. A period of six months was allowed for national currencies to be withdrawn from circulation. Since 1 July 2002 only the euro has been legal tender in EMU member countries.

Table 29.9 Performance of the member states in relation to convergence criteria, 2002.

	Inflation HICP (%) 2002	Deficit (% of GDP)[1] 2002	Debt (% of GDP) 2002	Change from previous year 2002	2001	2000	Exchange rates ERM participation 2002	Long-term interest rates 2002
Reference value	3.3%	3%	60%					7.0%
Belgium	1.7	−0.1	105.6	−2.8	−1.3	−3.7	yes	5.0
Denmark	2.3	2.0	44.0	−1.6	−9.3	−6.3	yes	5.0
Germany	1.4	−3.75	61.0	2.5	−1.9	−0.7	yes	4.8
Greece	3.8	−1.1	105.3	−1.6	3.2	−0.7	yes	5.1
Spain	3.3	0.0	55.0	−3.7	−8.3	−1.9	yes	5.0
France	1.8	−2.8	58.7	2.4	−1.5	−0.7	yes	4.9
Ireland	4.6	−1.0	35.3	−3.8	18.8	−13.7	yes	4.9
Italy	2.5	−2.1	109.4	−0.4	−0.8	−3.5	yes	5.1
Luxembourg	1.8	0.5	5.6	−17.3	−3.4	−6.4	yes	4.7
Netherlands	4.2	−0.8	51.0	−3.4	−10.2	−7.8	yes	4.9
Austria	1.7	−1.8	63.2	0.8	0.0	−3.5	yes	5.0
Portugal	3.7	−3.4	57.5	3.6	−2.6	0.4	yes	5.1
Finland	2.1	3.8	42.5	−2.1	1.9	−9.5	yes	4.9
Sweden	2.2	1.7	53.6	−1.3	−11.4	−6.4	no	5.3
UK	1.1	−1.1	38.5	−1.8	−7.5	−7.8	no	4.9
EU	**2.0**	**−1.9**	**63.0**	**0.0**	**−3.2**	**−4.8**		**4.9**

[1] A negative sign for the government deficit indicates a surplus.
Sources: European Commission (2002) *European News*, 18 November; European Commission (2002) *European Economy*, No. 3.

Convergence

In March 1998 the European Commission announced that 11 members had reached a sufficient degree of sustainable convergence as measured against the Maastricht Treaty criteria. The relevant criteria were (1) consumer price inflation must not exceed that of the three best-performing countries by more than $1\frac{1}{2}$ percentage points; (2) interest rates on long-term government securities must not be more than 2 percentage points higher than those in the same three member states; (3) the financial position must be sustainable. In particular, the general government deficit should be at or below the reference value of 3% of

GDP, or, if not, it should have declined substantially and continuously and reached a level close to the reference value, or the excess over the reference value should be temporary and exceptional. The gross debt of general government should be at or below 60% of GDP or, if not, the debt ratio should be sufficiently diminishing and approaching the 60% reference value at a satisfactory pace. The exchange rate criterion is that the currency must have been held within the normal fluctuation margins of the ERM for two years without a realignment at the initiative of the member state in question. Based on these figures it was agreed that 11 members of the EU had reached a sufficient degree of sustainable convergence against the criteria laid down in the Maastricht Treaty. The countries which qualified and wished to join the single currency in January 1999 were Austria, Belgium, Finland, France, Germany, Ireland, Italy, Luxembourg, the Netherlands, Portugal and Spain. Sweden and Greece did not meet the convergence criteria at that time and the UK and Denmark had already decided not to take part in Stage 3 of EMU in 1999.

The European Commission's convergence report of March 2000 concluded that Greece had met the criteria for entering the EMU and Greece was subsequently accepted as a full member from January 2001. Sweden was deemed not to have met the criteria on convergence since its legislation was not compatible with the Treaty and the ESCB Statute, and also its exchange rate had been outside the ERM II and hence fluctuated against the ERM currencies. The UK and Denmark had decided not to take part in Stage 3 of EMU in 1999 and thus remained outside 'Euroland'.

To maintain stability in Euroland, a 'Growth and Stability Pact' has been operating since January 1999 which is designed to ensure that the euro maintains its value over time by committing the participating countries to form 'convergence contracts'. These contracts are necessary to make sure that members of Euroland continue to maintain their economies under the same economic criteria as when they entered. In particular, the Pact was designed to ensure that the medium-term budgetary discipline criteria were met. At least every two years, the Commission and the European Central Bank (ECB) report to the Council on the fulfilment of the convergence criteria. If member states exceed the criteria for government budget deficit (set at 3% of GDP) or government debt (set at 60% of GDP) they would be penalized. Penalties for *excessive government deficits* can involve members having to lodge with the Commission a fixed, non-interest bearing deposit of 0.2% of the country's GDP and a variable non-interest bearing deposit of 0.1% of GDP for every 0.1% excess over the deficit criteria, up to a ceiling of 0.5% of GDP. The penalty for *excessive government debt* is a fixed amount involving a non-interest bearing deposit of 2% of a country's GDP.

The performance of EU countries *vis-à-vis* the convergence criteria in 2002, three years after the formation of the EMU, is shown in Table 29.9. As can be seen, three countries exceeded the budget deficit criterion, whilst four countries exceeded the government debt criterion. The German budgetary situation was a particular worry for the Commission during the 2002/03 period, as were those of France and Italy. Such budgetary problems are serious, especially when public age-related spending is estimated to increase by six percentage points by the middle of this century. The UK, on the other hand, was well within the criteria limits, showing relative strength and stability despite not being a member. These strict budgetary criteria are a matter of considerable debate in the EU, with some arguing that the 'Growth and Stability Pact' is unduly restrictive on EU member states, keeping unemployment high and growth low.

Single currency

The euro

The launch of the single currency, the 'euro', occurred on 1 January 1999, although it did not become a physical currency until 1 January 2002 (see also Chapter 20). However, from 1999 onwards the euro became a legal currency in its own right and the vehicle for electronic and business-to-business transactions throughout the euro-zone. As early as January 1999 some 25% of Barclays Bank customers had already been asked to invoice or pay in euros.

The long-term effects of the euro, and with it EMU, are to change the nature of the way business is carried out in Europe. For consumers, prices are more 'transparent', making it easier to see whether different prices are being charged for the same product in various EU countries. For manufacturers and other traders, the introduction of EMU means the elimination of exchange rate risks, which should benefit smaller businesses which often lack the resources for foreign exchange management.

The EMU might also produce further corporate rationalization as firms merge in an attempt to grow larger in order to derive scale economies from operating within the Single Market. The foreign exchange market is restricted in its dealings as fewer currencies are traded, with most dealings being in currencies outside the euro, together with euro-dollar or euro-yen. It is likely that a new market for government debt denominated in euros and a new pool of euro-denominated equity will be created.

For the potential benefits of the euro and EMU to

be realized in the long run, three factors will be decisive:

■ *Sustainable economic convergence.* For the smooth working of the euro, the economies of the participating countries must be in the same stage of the economic cycle and be relatively homogeneous.

■ *Strong political commitments to EMU discipline.* The European Council of Economic and Financial Ministers (ECOFIN), consisting of the finance ministers of the EU, are able to impose severe fines on member states whose budget deficits exceed the ratio of 3% of GDP. The fines could, as noted above, reach as much as 0.5% of GDP.

■ *Credible European Central Bank* (ECB). The ECB's independence is enshrined in the Maastricht treaty, as is its commitment to price stability. Short-term interest rates are set with a view to achieving such price stability. However, political pressure for reflationary policies might arise if the EU experiences slow growth and high unemployment.

The question also remains as to how the national central banks will operate under EMU. Together with the ECB, the national central banks formed the European System of Central Banks (ESCB) in June 1998. This body, through its Governing Council and Executive Board, defines and implements monetary policy and foreign exchange and reserves policies. However, the operational responsibility to carry out agreed ESCB policy is retained by the national central banks. As with the federal central banking systems of the US and Germany, the operations of the ESCB are therefore highly decentralized. There is a risk that the national central banks may try to pressurize the independent ECB to adopt policies directed towards growth and employment in situations where the ECB might be more inclined to tighten control of inflation.

Enlargement

The economic objectives of the original EEC were centred on the creation of prosperity and growth through the creation of a 'customs union' involving both reduction in tariff barriers and the establishment of common external tariffs between the union countries and the rest of the world.

During the course of its history the EU has encouraged greater liberalization in trade (particularly in industrial goods) through a series of separate – usually bilateral – agreements with third countries. These 'association' agreements usually allowed their signatories preferential – 'Most Favoured Nation' – status with respect to EU tariff requirements while encouraging them to reduce their own tariff barriers. A number of countries with association agreements with the EU are currently seeking (or have indicated their intention to seek) full membership of the Community.

In October 2002, the EU Commission approved the most ambitious expansion plans in its history when 10 countries were told that they had met the 'Copenhagen criteria' for membership. The criteria included such aspects as institutional stability, democracy, functioning market economies, and adherence to the aims of political, economic and monetary union. These 10 countries were deemed to be ready to join the EU in 2004 while a further two – Bulgaria and Romania – would be due for membership in 2007. Table 29.10 provides some economic data on these countries together with their projected dates of accession.

There have been many arguments regarding the strengths and weaknesses of enlargement. A key academic study by the Centre for Policy Research estimated that the enlargement would bring an economic gain of €10bn (£7bn) for the EU15 and €23bn (£16bn) for the new members (Baldwin *et al.* 1997). A more recent study of the period 2000–09 by the European Commission's Directorate General for Economic Affairs estimated that enlargement would result in an increase in the annual growth of GDP in the new member countries of between 1.3 and 2.1 percentage points above pre-existing growth rate levels (European Commission 2001). For the existing members, the annual increase in the level of GDP would be in the region of 0.7 percentage points on a cumulative basis. In 2002, the European Round Table of Industrialists calculated that the new enlargement should create 300,000 jobs in the EU15. In terms of budgetary consequences, the enlargement should involve only a modest (less than 10%) transfer to the Central and East European countries in the early years after entry. In UK terms, some 14,000 UK firms export to Eastern and Central Europe and the DTI has noted that each enlargement has brought a surge of exports from British companies. It estimated that

Table 29.10 EU enlargement, 2004–07: some economic indicators, 2001.

		Population (million)	GDP per capita (% of EU average)	General government budget (% of GDP)	Unemploy- ment rate (%)	Inflation (%)
Bulgaria	(2007)	7.9	28	1.7	19.9	7.4
Cyprus	(2004)	0.8	80	–3.0	4.0	2.0
Czech Rep.	(2004)	10.2	57	–5.5	8.0	4.5
Estonia	(2004)	1.4	42	–0.4	12.4	5.6
Hungary	(2004)	10.2	51	–4.1	5.7	9.1
Latvia	(2004)	2.4	33	–1.6	13.1	2.5
Lithuania	(2004)	3.5	38	–1.9	16.5	1.3
Malta	(2004)	0.4	55	–7.0	6.5	2.5
Poland	(2004)	38.6	40	–3.9	18.4	5.3
Romania	(2007)	22.4	25	–3.4	6.6	34.5
Slovakia	(2004)	5.4	48	–5.6	19.4	10.8
Slovenia	(2004)	2.0	69	–2.5	5.7	8.6

Source: European Commission (2002) *Towards the Enlarged Union*, COM (2002) 700 Final.

the new round of enlargement should increase the UK's GDP by £1.75bn.

In the meantime, establishing the EU25 will not be easy since even the optimists believe it will take a decade to fully absorb the 10 new nations, whose per capita income is less than 40% of the EU15 average. This is a much more demanding challenge than the last EU expansion which admitted three small and wealthy nations – Austria, Finland and Sweden – in 1995. Demands for larger subsidies for farming from the new entrants will become an inevitable problem; e.g. in Poland, 25% of the population gain some income from farming. Others argue that most of the gains will go to countries such as Germany, Austria and Italy which are physically closer to the new entrants. It has also been argued that accession countries add less than 5% to EU GDP and are thus more likely to help boost EU competitiveness through cost and labour benefits rather than by stimulating growth of the internal market.

Opting out?

For the UK there are both advantages and disadvantages of making use of the 'opt-outs' which it negotiated at the Maastricht conference. The advantages lie mostly in the fact that it would leave the bulk of monetary policy firmly in the hands of the UK government, thereby making it possible to use the exchange rate as a policy instrument independently of other EU countries and without 'interference' from Brussels. In most respects this translates fairly clearly into the ability to devalue in order to remain competitive (but, in so doing, probably to slip even further down the prosperity rankings).

The disadvantages stem from the opposite argument – that the UK needs external discipline over its exchange rate and monetary policy in order to ensure that difficult decisions are not fudged. Quite apart from the 'economic' arguments against opting out of EMU, there is also the possibility that other member states might 'informally' discriminate against the UK and its products. There is a strong argument that remaining outside EMU would damage our financial services trade (the one area in which we claim – probably erroneously – to have a strong competitive advantage). Non-EU companies might not regard the UK as such a good bet as far as inward investment is concerned if we did not have direct access to the single most important currency on the continent. If the effect of staying outside EMU was to create fear in financial markets (on the basis that UK policy outside EMU might result in higher inflation or continuing rounds of devaluation) then long-term interest rates may well be higher than on the continent. This would tend to deter inward investment and increase costs for UK businesses (see Chapter 20). In relation to these arguments, the Labour government's position has been to accept that entry into Euroland is broadly inevitable, although the timing of such entry must be closely linked to the government's own internal set of criteria.

Conclusion

The purely economic effects of British membership of the European Union are extremely difficult to isolate and describe. It is increasingly irrelevant to speak of economic models of what Britain's experience might have been if we had not joined the EEC in 1973.

The economic debate has centred around two different 'models':

1 Britain as a permanent and irrevocable member of the EU; and

2 Britain outside the EU – the 'non-Europe' model.

The viability of any economic argument which describes Britain outside the EU has become more and more suspect as the financial, economic and business environments have become intermeshed over the last three decades. There is little doubt that the UK has experienced a continuing budget deficit with respect to the EU, that its consumers may have suffered a slight welfare loss with respect to food and the policies of the CAP, and that there has been an observable displacement of UK-manufactured goods in our own domestic market.

Alongside these factors one must recognize the interdependence of the member states in almost every commercial and economic area. The EU represents the UK's most important trading partner by far in both visible and invisible trade. Membership of the Community has also been responsible for significant amounts of inward investment from Japan and the US into the UK. Ironically this inward investment has been so large that the UK is becoming a major exporter of motor vehicles and electronic equipment, developing trade surpluses with the EU in these categories. In a similar fashion London's place as one of the pre-eminent financial centres in the world rests strongly on its position as the financial centre in which US, EU and Japanese banks and investment houses come together. Where portfolio investment is concerned the EU has become much more important to the UK (see Chapters 7 and 21).

The UK's experience in the European Monetary System has been fraught with problems but it is clear that a number of those problems were of the UK's own devising. International freedom in financial markets meant that – even outside the EMS – the UK had to ensure that sterling 'shadowed' the DM.

However, a further question has to ask why the benefits to the UK have been less than those which have accrued to other members. The UK has not gained massive benefits from Social and Regional funds and has a relatively efficient agricultural sector. There have been few or no net real benefits from the CAP and we have suffered from having a relatively inefficient manufacturing sector which has been only modestly successful in exporting to Europe. The UK has not, therefore, gained proportional benefits from the free-trade area. Outside the EU, however, we would still have had to survive, had to manage our own agriculture, and had to find markets for our exports in a world in which the ties of the Commonwealth and EFTA would almost certainly have counted for less and less as the years went by.

Key points

- There are now 15 member states within the EU, with Austria, Sweden and Finland joining in 1995. Another 10 member countries are being added in 2004, making 25 in all.

- The 15 member EU is essentially a regional trading bloc with 380 million people within a protected free-trade area, with a high per capita income of almost €23,800 per annum.

- The EU is the largest trading bloc in the world. It accounts for 20% of world GDP and around 40% of world trade.

- Since 1992, the EU has established the European Economic Area which initially included 19 countries altogether.

- Agriculture is the most regulated sector within the EU. Around 41% of the entire EU budget is spent on various price support and intervention policies involving agricultural products.

- The Regional and Social Funds are targeted at poorer regions *within* each member state in order to relieve unemployment and poverty.

- The Social Chapter includes a number of 'directives' establishing minimum working conditions, though the UK has an 'opt-out'.

- The Maastricht Treaty in 1992 sought to widen the scope of the EU beyond a common market (see Chapter 28) to that of an economic and monetary union (EMU).

- Various 'convergence criteria' needed to be fulfilled before countries could join EMU, which began on 1 January 1999. These convergence criteria included consumer price inflation within $1\frac{1}{2}$%, and long-term interest rates within 2% of the average achieved by the 'best three' EU countries. In addition the PSBR should be no higher than 3% of GDP and total public debt no more than 60% of GDP.

- EMU has a European Central Bank, a single currency (the euro) and a 'Stability Council' acting to monitor country compliance with the various criteria. Non-compliance can result in fines for the states in question.

Now try the self-check questions for this chapter on the Companion WebSite. You will also find up-to-date facts and case materials.

Notes

1. The European Economic Area comprised the (then) 12 members of the EU plus Iceland, Norway, Sweden, Finland, Switzerland, Austria and Liechtenstein, though in 1995 Sweden, Austria and Finland joined the EU.

2. The 'co-responsibility' levy is a method by which farmers are penalized for over-production of agricultural products. Up to a certain level of production the farmer is entitled to sell his goods either on the open market, or to the EU's Intervention stocks. Above that, agreed, level of production the price allowed to the farmer reduced by a specific percentage called the 'co-responsibility' levy.

3. The divergence limit for any currency was calculated by the formula $\pm 2.25 \,(1 - w)$ where w was the percentage weight of the currency in the ECU. For Germany this resulted in a limit of $2.25 \,(1 - 0.301) = 1.57\%$.

References and further reading

Ackrill, R. (1997) *Economic and Monetary Union, Developments in Economics*, Vol. 13, Causeway Press.

Baldwin, R., Francois, J. F. and Portes, R. (1997) The costs and benefits of eastern enlargement, Centre for Economic Policy Research (CEPR), *Economic Policy*, No. 24.

Barnes, I. and Barnes, P. (1995) *The Enlarged European Union*, 2nd edn, Longman.

Barras, R. and Madhavan, S. (1996) *European Economic Integration and Sustainable Development*, McGraw-Hill.

Brittan, L. (1994) *Europe – The Europe We Need*, Hamish Hamilton.

De Grauwe, P. (2000) *The Economics of Monetary Integration*, 4th edn, Oxford University Press.

DTI (2002) *EWT: Europe and World Trade*.

Dunford, M. (1994) Winners and losers: the new map of economic inequality in the European Union, *European Urban and Regional Studies*.

European Commission (1996) Economic evaluation of the internal market, *European Economy*, 4.

European Commission (1997) Trade patterns inside the single market, *The Single Market Review*, Subseries IV, Vol. 2, Kogan Page, Earthscan.

European Commission (1998) Financing the European Union, 7 October.

European Commission (2001) The economic impact of enlargement, Director General for Economic and Financial Affairs, *Enlargement Papers*, No. 4, June.

Goodman, S. F. (1996) *The European Union*, 3rd edn, Macmillan.

Griffiths, A. (1992) *European Community Survey*, Longman.

Johnson, C. (1996) *In with the Euro, out with the Pound*, Penguin.

Kenen, P. (1995) *Economic and Monetary Union in Europe*, CUP.

Lewis, D. W. P. (1993) *The Road to Europe: History, Institutions and Prospects of European Integration 1945–1993*, Peter Lang.

McDonald, F. and Dearden, S (eds) (1998) *European Economic Integration*, 3rd edn, Addison Wesley Longman.

Rosamond, B. (2000) *Theories of European Integration*, Palgrave Macmillan.

Wistrich, E. (1994) *The United States of Europe*, Routledge.

Wolf, M. (1996) Thinking the unthinkable, *Financial Times*, 18 June.

Chapter 30 Transition economies

The process of economic transformation from central planning to a market economy in Eastern Europe has been neither smooth nor uniform. States in the vanguard of reform like Poland, the Czech Republic and Hungary quickly succeeded in creating thriving, dynamic private sectors, which are generating new jobs and contributing to economic recovery; together with Estonia, Latvia, Lithuania, the Slovak Republic and Slovenia, this group has now been accepted for entry to the European Union from 2004. In contrast, in the 12 states of the former Soviet Union that now comprise the Commonwealth of Independent States (CIS) the slump in economic activity has been much more prolonged and recovery more uneven although, as we shall see, the business environment has improved significantly for the CIS countries since 1999. This chapter assesses the progress of the former centrally planned countries in their struggle to construct modern, competitive market economies. After a brief review of the size and economic structure of the 28 'transition economies', the chapter outlines the basic operation of centrally planned economies, highlighting the scale of the structural changes entailed by 'marketization'. It then documents the early phase of the transition process, in which all the transition economies experienced a slump in output and hyperinflation following the breakdown of central planning and the liberalization of prices. The chapter then considers the main macroeconomic challenges involved in restoring stability to these economies together with the microeconomic (or 'supply-side') challenges of privatization, market liberalization and legal reform. It finally assesses the progress made over the 15 or so years since the process began in 1989 and considers the outlook for the transition economies.

Central and Eastern Europe versus the Commonwealth of Independent States

The term 'communist bloc' was formerly used in the West to describe the countries that constituted the Soviet sphere of influence, implying a high degree of homogeneity between the 28 independent states that have subsequently emerged. In reality these states vary considerably, in terms of living standards (as measured by, for example, per capita GDP), economic structure, population size, history, religion and culture.

Table 30.1 gives some idea of the differences between the transition economies.[1] It shows the contrast in size, from Russia with a population of 145 million to Estonia with 1.4 million. It highlights the vast gulf in relative living standards, from Slovenia with a per capita income (calculated in terms of purchasing power parity) of $9,509 to Tajikistan with just $165. The importance of agriculture ranges from

Table 30.1 An overview of the transition economies.

	Population, millions (2001)	Per capita GDP, $PPP (2001)	Agriculture as % GDP (2001)	Industry as % GDP (2001)	Unemployment (%) (2001)
CEE countries					
Albania	3.1	1,330	49.1	27.3	14.6
Bulgaria	8.1	1,675	12.1	25.2	19.5
Croatia	4.5	4,385	7.1	20.7	15.8
Czech Republic	10.3	5,503	3.8	37.3	8.9
Estonia	1.4	4,039	5.2	20.3	12.6
FYR Macedonia	2.0	1,753	9.2**	20.7**	30.5
Hungary	10.0	5,228	4.6*	28.0*	8.4
Latvia	2.3	3,233	4.7	18.7	13.1
Lithuania	3.5	3,450	6.3	25.6	17.0
Poland	38.7	4,649	5.0	28.6	17.3
Romania	22.3	1,743	11.4*	27.6*	8.6
Slovak Republic	5.4	3,694	4.3	26.1	19.8
Slovenia	2.0	9,509	2.7	27.4	5.9
CIS countries					
Armenia	3.1	679	25.5	20.2	9.6
Azerbaijan	8.1	706	18.1*	32.0*	1.2
Belarus	10.0	1,217	6.5	34.0	2.2
Georgia	5.4	592	28.0**	13.0**	11.1
Kazakhstan	14.8	1,505	9.7*	23.6*	11.0
Kyrgyzstan	4.8	308	42.5	25.7	5.6*
Moldova	3.6	444	22.3**	16.2**	2.1*
Russia	144.8	2,137	7.1	25.6	9.0
Tajikistan	6.9	165	22.1	18.7	2.4
Turkmenistan	5.6	525	23.0	37.0	n/a
Ukraine	49.0	767	12.5	38.2	3.7
Uzbekistan	25.4	237	27.0*	21.0*	0.6*

* 2000 figure, ** 1999 figure.
Source: Adapted from EBRD (2002).

as little as 4–7% of GDP in Slovenia, the Czech and Slovak Republics, Hungary, Estonia, Latvia and Poland, to 49% in Albania.

Table 30.1 also shows that, despite the differences between individual states, it has been possible to draw a broad distinction between the Central and Eastern European (CEE) states, here defined to include the three Baltic states of the former Soviet Union and a further 10 states in this geographical area, and the 12 states of the Commonwealth of Independent States (CIS). Taken as a group, the CEE states have a generally higher per capita GDP, less reliance on agriculture and, reflecting the labour shedding which is an inevitable consequence of enterprise restructuring, much higher rates of unemployment.

However, this broad distinction between CEE and CIS states is becoming progressively less useful. Some recent studies have broken down the Central and Eastern European (CEE) states into two separate sub-groups, namely 'Central eastern Europe and the Baltic states', comprising Croatia, Czech Republic, Estonia, Hungary, Latvia, Lithuania, Poland, Slovak Republic and Slovenia, and a less advanced grouping of 'South-eastern Europe' states comprising Albania, Bulgaria, FR Yugoslavia, FYR Macedonia and Romania. Even this newer classification of CEE states is rapidly becoming redundant with the dissolution of the Federal Republic of Yugoslavia into the separate states of Serbia and Montenegro and, of course, with the admission of Poland, the Czech Republic, the Slovak Republic, Hungary, Estonia, Latvia, Lithuania and Slovenia into the European Union from 2004 onwards. Nevertheless, for the purposes of this chapter we retain the broad classification of countries into the CEE and CIS categories, respectively.

The operation of the command economy

Despite the differences between the CEE and the CIS states, both groups started the transition process with an all-pervasive central planning system, often termed a 'command economy'. The command economy dominated every aspect of life, telling factories where to buy their inputs, how much to pay their workers, how much to produce and where to sell their output; individuals were trained in specialist schools and universities and directed to work at specific factories, which provided their wages, houses, health care – even holidays in enterprise-owned hotels and sanatoria; the national bank was told how much to lend to which factories and how much cash to print to pay wages.

As a theoretical concept, central planning was very elegant. Using 'input–output' analysis (a planning framework which calculated the inputs required for each factory in order for it to deliver its planned outputs to the next stage in the production process), the planning ministry could calculate precisely how much labour, capital and raw materials each enterprise required to achieve its production targets. The various production targets for raw materials and intermediate and final products all fitted together to ensure a perfectly balanced expansion of the economy. Input and output prices were carefully set to ensure that all firms could pay their wage bills and repay loans from the national bank, while at the same time pricing consumer goods to encourage consumption of socially desirable goods (e.g. books, ballet, theatre, public transport, etc.) and discourage consumption of politically unfavoured goods (e.g. international telephone calls, cars, luxury goods).

The overall national plan was thus internally consistent. If each of the enterprises achieved its production targets, there could not be, by definition, shortages or bottlenecks in the economy. There would be full employment, with everyone working in an enterprise for which he or she had been specifically trained at school and university. The total wage bill for the economy, which was paid in cash, would be sufficient to buy all the consumer goods produced. There would be zero inflation and all the country's citizens would have access to housing, education and health care.

While the socialist nirvana of full employment and universal social security has been tarnished by the demonstrable failure of the command economy to deliver its promises in practice, it is important not to understate its emotional appeal. Market capitalism is plagued by social injustice. Large income inequalities, poverty, homelessness and mass unemployment are all characteristics of the advanced Western economies. During the 'Great Depression' of the 1930s, for example, many Western intellectuals readily embraced the principles of socialist planning as a way to end the misery of unemployment. Indeed, for some 30 years after the Second World War, many Western and developing countries used forms of national planning to support their growth policies, the latter group with the active encouragement of the World Bank. Japan and France, for example, both had well-developed national planning systems and, for a period during the 1960s, both Conservative and Labour governments tried to copy the French system in an effort to emulate that country's economic success.

Central planning ultimately failed, both in the West and, over a much longer period, in Eastern Europe. Much has been written about the deficiencies of central planning. Clearly, there are serious practical difficulties in implementing national plans. There are also fundamental, largely inherent contradictions. The Soviet model of central planning provided little incentive for either managers or workers to work harder or to innovate. The politicization of the whole economic system, with promotion at work based on service to the Communist Party rather than on-the-job performance, encouraged passivity and strongly discouraged risk-taking and individualism – the bedrocks of innovation and technological advance.

While central planning succeeded in turning Tsarist Russia from a feudal agricultural society into an industrial power, it became increasingly unwieldy after the Second World War. Internally, as economies developed, the complexity of the coordination problem grew explosively, as consumers demanded more choice and better quality. With innovation discouraged and the central planners being encouraged to set unrealistic targets for political reasons, productivity growth slowed and official statistics for production became ever more cosmetic. Absenteeism at work and false reporting of output became commonplace. Shortages of consumer goods emerged and, with people unable to buy goods with their wages, households' deposits with the national savings bank piled up. This state of affairs was summed up in the Soviet joke, 'the factories pretend to pay us and we pretend to work'. Meanwhile, in the West, scientific progress spawned a vast array of cost-saving technologies in the areas of transport, telecommunications, manufacturing and information handling, so that, relatively, the communist countries fell behind faster and faster.

Overlaid on the declining capacity of central planning to achieve its goals and promote technological advance was the geopolitical battle between the Soviet Union and the United States known as the 'cold war'. In the 'arms race' of the 1970s and early 1980s, the Soviet Union was increasingly unable to match the United States. With only 5% of GDP devoted to military expenditure, the United States was able to field a technologically advanced military force. Sluggish economic growth and an inadequate technological base meant that the Soviet Union was forced to divert an ever greater proportion of GDP to military spending. Estimates for the share of GDP absorbed by the military–industrial complex in the 1980s range from 20% to 40%. Attempts in the late 1980s to restructure the planning system ('perestroika') and liberalize the political system ('glasnost') paradoxically had the reverse of the effect intended, causing the whole economic and political system to unravel. Suddenly released from the threat of Soviet invasion, the CEE states opted for independence and market capitalism in 1989, quickly followed by the 15 Soviet republics in 1991. By 1991, the integrated, centrally planned bloc that had comprised the Soviet Union and seven CEE countries had collapsed, splintering into 28 independent countries[2] bent on constructing functioning market economies.

The road from Marx to the market

The decades of central planning meant that the transition economies began the reform process without functioning markets for labour, goods or capital. All three had been allocated by the central planner, in accordance with an internally coherent economic plan. Because all the means of production had been in state hands, there was, moreover, no legislative framework for the enforcement of property rights, the valuation and disposal of assets or the liquidation of unprofitable enterprises. Nor in a system of directed labour was there any official unemployment and, hence, no need for a social security system. As noted above, social welfare was provided by enterprises, with the central planners setting their aggregate employment equal to the size of the labour force, with services like education, health care and housing being provided by the enterprises to their employees. Banks in the central planning system were bookkeeping operations, allocating credit according to the demands of the plan rather than on the basis of objective risk assessments, and capital markets were nonexistent. The challenge for the transition states at the end of the 1980s was to build a modern market economy on these foundations.

The early 1990s ushered in a period of economic crisis in the transition economies of CEE and the CIS. The breakdown of central plan discipline and of trade between these economies, taken together with the highly concentrated, vertically integrated nature of production (particularly in the CIS), led to an early collapse in production across the region (see Table 30.2). Recovery began first in CEE, with all countries except Bulgaria showing positive growth in 1996. Nevertheless, only in six of the 13 CEE countries, namely Poland, Slovenia, Hungary, Albania and the Czech and Slovak Republics, has recent growth been sufficient to regain the losses of the early years; in all other states, output in 2001 remains below the level in 1989. Recovery in the CIS countries started later and has been more hesitant. For the CIS countries as a group, output in 2001 remains at only 64% of its 1989 level.

Table 30.2 Recession and recovery in the transition economies (% annual change in real GDP).

	1991	1992	1993	1994	1995	1996	1997	1998	2000	2002	2001 (1989 = 100)
CEE countries											
Albania	−28.0	−7.2	9.6	8.3	13.3	9.1	−7.0	8.0	7.8	6.0	116
Bulgaria	−11.7	−7.3	−1.5	1.8	2.9	−10.1	−7.0	3.5	5.4	4.0	80
Croatia	−21.1	−11.7	−8.0	5.9	6.8	6.0	6.5	2.5	2.9	3.5	85
Czech Republic	−11.5	−3.3	0.6	2.2	5.9	4.8	−1.0	−2.2	3.3	2.5	106
Estonia	−13.6	−14.2	−9.0	−2.0	4.3	3.9	10.6	4.7	7.1	4.0	90
FYR Macedonia	−7.0	−8.0	−9.1	−1.8	−1.2	0.8	1.5	2.9	4.6	2.0	77
Hungary	−11.9	−3.1	−0.6	2.9	1.5	1.3	4.6	4.9	5.2	4.0	112
Latvia	−10.4	−34.9	−14.9	0.6	−0.8	3.3	8.6	3.9	6.8	4.0	75
Lithuania	−5.7	−21.3	−16.2	−9.8	3.3	4.7	7.3	5.1	3.8	5.2	72
Poland	−7.0	2.6	3.8	5.2	7.0	6.1	6.9	4.8	4.0	1.0	129
Romania	−12.9	−8.8	1.5	3.9	7.1	4.1	−6.6	−5.4	1.8	3.5	84
Slovak Republic	−14.6	−6.5	−3.7	4.9	6.9	6.6	6.1	4.4	2.2	3.5	110
Slovenia	−8.9	−5.5	2.8	5.3	4.1	3.5	4.6	3.9	4.6	2.7	121
All CEE*	−10.7	−3.6	0.4	3.7	5.5	4.2	3.6	2.7	4.0	2.6	108
CIS countries											
Armenia	−17.1	−52.6	−14.8	5.4	6.9	5.9	3.3	7.2	6.0	8.0	74
Azerbaijan	−0.7	−22.6	−23.1	−19.7	−11.8	1.3	5.8	10.0	11.1	8.8	62
Belarus	−1.2	−9.6	−7.6	−12.6	−10.4	2.8	11.4	8.3	5.8	3.0	91
Georgia	−20.6	−44.8	−25.4	−11.4	2.4	10.5	10.8	2.9	2.0	3.5	37
Kazakhstan	−13.0	−2.9	−9.2	−12.6	−8.2	0.5	1.7	−1.9	9.8	7.6	84
Kyrgyzstan	−5.0	−19.0	−16.0	−20.1	−5.4	7.1	9.9	2.1	5.1	2.0	71
Moldova	−17.5	−29.1	−1.2	−31.2	−1.4	−7.8	1.3	−8.6	2.1	3.5	37
Russia	−5.0	−14.5	−8.7	−12.7	−4.1	−3.5	0.8	−4.6	8.3	4.1	64
Tajikistan	−7.1	−29.0	−11.0	−18.9	−12.5	−4.4	1.7	5.3	8.3	7.0	56
Turkmenistan	−4.7	−5.3	−10.0	−17.3	−7.2	−6.7	−11.3	5.0	17.6	13.5	96
Ukraine	−11.6	−13.7	−14.2	−23.0	−12.2	−10.0	−3.0	−1.7	5.9	4.5	46
Uzbekistan	−0.5	−11.1	−2.3	−4.2	−0.9	1.6	2.5	4.4	4.0	2.5	105
All CIS*	−6.0	−14.2	−9.3	−13.8	−5.2	−3.5	0.9	−3.5	7.9	4.4	64

* (W)eighted averages.
Source: Adapted from EBRD (2002).

Unemployment and underemployment in Russia

Given the calamitous fall in output that has taken place in Russia, the relatively modest increase in unemployment shown in Table 30.1 above is, at first sight, surprising. However, as Table 30.3 shows, there are large numbers of employees working shortened hours or on compulsory leave. Between 20% and 25% of the labour force is either out of work, on unpaid leave or working reduced hours, with these numbers highest in the winter months.

With national and regional governments heavily reliant on 'profit' and 'turnover' taxes on enterprises for state revenues, the early recession led to a sharp contraction of the tax base. In the absence of developed capital markets, which in market economies offer governments the opportunity of selling securities to finance themselves in a non-inflationary way, the resulting budget deficits were financed by printing cash through the central bank. Inflationary pressures were further compounded in many transition economies by the state's attempts to avoid wholesale job losses by granting heavy subsidies to loss-making enterprises. Whether these were provided by the state directly, thereby adding to its budget deficit, or in the form of 'soft' loans from the central bank, the result in both cases was to further fuel the rate of growth of the money supply. The slump in output was thus accompanied by hyperinflation in many transition states, as price liberalization brought repressed infla-

tion out into the open. Table 30.4 shows the inflation rates suffered by countries in the region and suggests some encouraging progress in most countries in curbing inflationary tendencies in recent years.

Clearly, the challenges facing the transition economies at the start of the process were profound in both macroeconomic and microeconomic dimensions. At the *macroeconomic* level, the main priority was to construct new instruments of fiscal and monetary policy and thereby stabilize economies suffering from collapsing output and spiralling prices. Under the former system, the central planners could set both production levels and final producer prices *directly* through the national plan. In the new emerging market economies, they needed to construct the tools to achieve these goals at the macroeconomic level through *indirect* means, by changing taxes and government spending and by altering interest rates and managing the exchange rate. At the *microeconomic* level, the priority was to transform an economy of large, state-owned enterprises (SOEs) into competitive, private companies capable of trading globally.

 Macroeconomic reform

Governments in *market economies* use two main sets of policy instruments to indirectly influence economic activity: *fiscal policy* – the use of taxes and public

Table 30.3 Underemployment at large and medium-sized enterprises in Russia.

	Numbers working shortened day* (million)	As % of the labour force*	As % of employed at large and medium-sized enterprises*	Numbers on compulsory administrative leave** (million)	As % of the labour force**	As % of employed at large and medium-sized enterprises**
1996 Q1	3.0	4.1	6.1	4.4	6.0	9.1
1996 Q2	3.3	4.5	6.8	6.1	8.4	12.7
1996 Q3	3.2	4.4	6.6	6.7	9.3	14.0
1996 Q4	3.4	4.7	7.2	7.5	10.4	15.9
1997 Q1	2.4	3.3	5.2	3.3	4.5	7.3
1997 Q2	2.6	3.5	5.6	4.9	6.8	10.9
1997 Q3	2.9	4.1	6.5	4.7	6.6	10.4

*End of quarter; **during the quarter.
Source: Adapted from Goskomstat (1998).

Table 30.4 The inflationary price of transition (% annual change in retail prices, end-year).

	1991	1992	1993	1994	1995	1996	1998	2000	2002*
CEE countries									
Albania	104.1	236.6	30.9	15.8	6.0	17.4	8.7	0.1	5.3
Bulgaria	338.9	79.2	63.9	121.9	32.9	310.8	1.0	9.9	6.1
Croatia	249.8	938.2	1,149.0	−3.0	3.8	3.4	5.4	6.2	2.3
Czech Republic	56.6	12.7	18.2	9.7	7.9	8.6	6.8	3.9	2.3
Estonia	303.8	953.5	35.6	41.7	28.9	14.8	4.4	4.0	3.8
FYR Macedonia	229.7	1,935.0	241.8	55.0	9.0	−0.6	−2.4	6.5	3.6
Hungary	32.2	21.6	21.1	21.2	28.3	19.8	10.3	9.8	4.9
Latvia	262.4	958.6	34.9	26.3	23.1	13.1	2.8	2.6	2.3
Lithuania	345.0	1,161.0	188.8	45.0	35.7	13.1	2.4	1.0	0.9
Poland	60.0	44.3	37.6	29.5	21.6	18.5	8.6	10.1	2.1
Romania	222.8	199.2	295.5	61.7	27.8	56.9	40.6	45.7	22.7
Slovak Republic	58.3	9.1	25.1	11.7	7.2	5.4	5.6	12.0	3.1
Slovenia	247.1	92.9	22.8	19.5	8.9	9.0	6.5	8.9	7.4
CIS countries									
Armenia	25.0	1,341.0	10,896.0	1,885.0	31.9	5.8	−1.3	−0.8	1.4
Azerbaijan	126.0	1,395.0	1,294.0	1,788.0	84.5	6.5	−7.6	1.8	2.8
Belarus	93.0	1,559.0	1,996.0	1,960.0	244.0	39.3	181.7	168.9	41.4
Georgia	131.0	1,177.0	7,488.0	6,474.0	57.4	13.7	7.2	4.1	5.5
Kazakhstan	136.8	2,984.0	2,169.0	1,158.0	60.4	28.6	1.9	13.2	6.0
Kyrgyzstan	170.0	1,259.0	1,363.0	95.7	32.3	34.9	18.4	18.7	2.5
Moldova	151.0	2,198.0	837.0	116.0	23.8	15.1	18.2	31.3	9.0
Russia	161.0	2,506.0	840.0	204.4	128.6	21.8	84.5	20.8	16.3
Tajikistan	204.0	1,364.0	7,344.0	1.1	2,133.0	40.5	2.7	32.9	12.8
Turkmenistan	155.0	644.0	9,750.0	1,328.0	1,262.0	445.8	19.8	8.3	9.6
Ukraine	161.0	2,730.0	10,155.0	401.0	181.7	39.7	20.0	28.2	1.6
Uzbekistan	169.0	910.0	885.0	1,281.0	116.9	64.3	26.1	24.2	22.8

Source: Adapted from EBRD (2002).

spending; and *monetary policy* – the control of money supply and interest rates (and the exchange rate). Neither set of policy instruments exists in the same form in a command economy. In the central planning system, taxes were levied on SOEs, normally in the form of 'turnover taxes' (i.e. taxes on the enterprises' sales revenue or turnover), and on individuals in the form of income tax. These taxes ensured that the government could, as in a market economy, finance the army and other executive functions (e.g. law and order) that did not fund their activities by generating their own sales revenues. These taxes and associated government spending, like the configuration of input and output prices, were an integral part of the national plan and were set to ensure its internal con-

sistency. Significantly, many social services that are provided by the state in market economies like public housing, public transport, pre-school education, vocational training and health care were often provided by SOEs to their employees and families and financed out of the enterprises' own operating surpluses.

As a consequence, the tax base at the start of the process in most transition economies was small relative to that in market economies (since so many social services were financed directly by SOEs) and tax and spending decisions were part of the broader process of national planning. In contrast, in a market economy, governments need to raise taxes to finance the whole range of public goods and social services, at the same time setting the balance between taxes and public spending (i.e. the budget deficit or surplus) in order to stabilize aggregate demand and output.

In a command economy there is a unified financial system, with different branches of the national bank acting as a bookkeeper for transactions between companies in different sectors and providing deposit, but not lending, facilities (through a national savings branch) to the general population. Credit was allocated by the national bank's sectoral branches according to the requirements of the national plan. Interest rates played no part in the allocation of, or demand for, credit. Lending facilities for retail customers were unknown. Domestic currencies were not freely convertible but could (with official approval) be exchanged for foreign currencies through the national bank at artificial exchange rates depending upon the purpose (a favourable rate for exporters, a higher, penal rate for importers). There were no financial markets of the sort recognizable in market economies.

However, the creation of financial markets which can 'price' risk and allocate savings to those projects and companies with the best, risk-adjusted, returns is essential to the transition process (see below). It therefore follows that macroeconomic reform fundamentally alters the role of the national bank and of the private banks and financial institutions. Since these are now used to channel savings to private companies, the interest rate (and the exchange rate) become powerful tools for influencing saving, borrowing and spending in the economy as a whole.

Fiscal policy reform

Because the system of taxes and government spending had been constructed around the needs of central planning, the *fiscal policy* instruments at the disposal of governments in the early stages of the transition process were ill-suited to dealing with the emerging market economies. Fiscal policy was beset by two overriding problems. First, the tax base was small and not set up to deal with the tax affairs of small, private companies. As the central plan collapsed and SOEs' output and turnover slumped, the revenue from turnover taxes fell sharply. In the economic chaos that followed, many SOEs switched to bartering their outputs for inputs; other profitable SOEs took advantage of the confusion and simply stopped paying

taxes. Attempts to bolster tax revenues by introducing new tax regimes for newly established private companies often foundered, because tax rates were set so high that the companies evaded taxes. The old tax systems in many countries proved unable to deal with the changing structure of economic activity and there was a slump in tax revenues as more and more economic activity shifted into the 'informal' or 'hidden' economy.

At the same time, the pressure on government spending increased. Many SOEs quickly found themselves in genuine financial distress, unable to pay their workforces or continue to fund the social services they had traditionally provided. Many of the associated 'social assets' (public housing, schools, hospitals, public transport systems) were taken into local government control. With widespread popular resistance to attempts to levy user charges which more closely approximated the true opportunity costs of providing these services, this 'nationalization' of social services, particularly in the former Soviet Union, added to government spending. Even more significantly, there was intense political pressure on governments to 'bail out' failing SOEs, by granting state subsidies to allow them to pay wages. The fear of social unrest, prompted by periodic strikes and demonstrations by powerful groups of workers (e.g. miners, shipyard workers) encouraged many transition governments to give large subsidies to their SOEs. The impact of declining tax revenues and increasing public expenditure on the government budget balances is shown in Table 30.5 (p. 617).

By the late 1990s, however, the fiscal situation in most countries was starting to stabilize, as new, market-oriented taxes began to take effect. By 2002, budget deficits had gradually declined as compared to the early 1990s, particularly in the CEE, to levels common in advanced market economies. Extending the tax base has not been easy, however, as companies used to trading in the informal economy have sought to resist the introduction of new company taxes and systems of value-added taxes (VAT).

Tax and wage arrears in Russia

Table 30.6 (p. 618) with its data on enterprise arrears provides a useful insight into some of the problems facing the fiscal authorities of Russia. The table shows the way in which Russian enterprises have financed their growing financial deficits, which has primarily taken the form of passing the deficits on to

Table 30.5 General government budget balances (% of GDP).

	1992	1993	1994	1995	1996	1998	2000	2002*
CEE countries								
Albania	−23.1	−15.5	−12.6	−10.1	−12.1	−10.4	−9.1	−8.0
Bulgaria	−2.9	−8.7	−3.9	−6.3	−12.7	−1.5	−1.0	−0.8
Croatia	−3.9	−0.8	1.6	−0.9	−0.4	0.6	−7.1	−4.6
Czech Republic	−3.1	0.5	−1.1	−2.5	−2.3	−1.6	−4.2	−9.3
Estonia	−0.3	−0.7	1.3	−1.3	−1.9	−0.3	−0.7	−1.0
FYR Macedonia	−9.8	−13.4	−2.7	−1.0	−0.5	−1.8	2.5	−4.4
Hungary	−7.2	−6.6	−8.4	−6.7	−5.0	−5.6	−3.3	−6.0
Latvia	−0.8	0.6	−4.4	−3.9	−1.8	−0.8	−3.3	−2.5
Lithuania	0.5	−5.3	−4.8	−4.5	−4.5	−5.8	−2.8	−1.4
Poland	−6.7	−3.1	−3.1	−2.8	−3.3	−3.0	−3.2	−5.0
Romania	−4.6	−0.4	−2.2	−3.4	−6.7	−3.0	−3.7	−3.0
Slovak Republic	−11.9	−7.0	−1.3	0.2	−1.9	−5.8	−3.6	−4.5
Slovenia	0.3	0.6	−0.2	−0.3	−0.2	−1.1	−1.3	−2.9
CIS countries								
Armenia	−13.9	−54.7	−16.5	−9.0	−8.6	−3.7	−6.3	−3.2
Azerbaijan	2.7	−15.3	−12.1	−4.9	−2.8	−4.2	−0.6	−0.1
Belarus	0.0	−1.9	−2.5	−1.9	−1.6	−0.3	0.3	−0.7
Georgia	−25.4	−26.2	−7.4	−5.3	−4.9	−6.5	−4.1	−1.7
Kazakhstan	−7.3	−4.1	−7.5	−2.7	−4.7	−7.4	−1.0	−2.0
Kyrgyzstan	−17.4	−14.4	−5.7	−8.4	−8.8	−10.2	−9.6	−4.9
Moldova	−26.6	−7.6	−11.5	−8.0	−11.2	−8.9	−2.6	−2.7
Russia	−18.9	−7.3	−10.4	−6.0	−8.6	−8.0	3.0	1.5
Tajikistan	−30.5	−20.9	−5.2	−5.3	−5.8	−3.8	−0.6	−1.0
Turkmenistan	9.4	−4.1	−2.3	−2.6	−0.3	−2.7	0.4	−2.0
Ukraine	−25.4	−16.2	−7.7	−6.1	−6.1	−3.0	−1.3	−1.8
Uzbekistan	−18.3	−10.4	−6.1	−4.1	−7.3	−3.0	−1.2	−2.5

*Projected
Source: Adapted from EBRD (2002).

their suppliers (inter-enterprise arrears), workers (wage arrears) and, most significantly, the tax authorities (tax arrears). By the end of 1998, tax arrears had grown to 7.5% of GDP, a figure almost exactly equal to the federal budget deficit in 1998. Table 30.6 also illustrates the extent to which government wage arrears have increased over recent years.

Monetary policy reform

In a command economy, the national bank performs many of the functions of the central bank and the commercial banking system in a market economy, controlling the money supply, taking deposits from the general public and lending money to enterprises. The essential difference is that these activities are all part of a wider national economic plan: money emission, in the form of banknotes, is set to ensure that enterprises can pay their workers; and a separate credit plan allocates loans to enterprises to support their investment and finance stocks and work-in-progress. In the former communist countries, the *national bank* was normally structured into functional areas: the national bank which performed a coordinating role and liaised directly with the

Table 30.6 Enterprise arrears (Rbn).

| | Total enterprise arrears | | Of which: | | | |
| | | | Arrears to suppliers | Tax arrears | Wage arrears | Government wage arrears |
	4 sectors	9 sectors	4 sectors	4 sectors	4 sectors	Rbn
1994	90.4	–	56.8	19.3	4.7	–
1995	238.9	–	122.3	75.0	13.6	–
1996	514.4	–	245.9	203.4	34.7	9.3
1997	756.1	–	344.7	316.6	39.7	4.9
1998	936.3	1,082.0	417.2	391.1	56.4	10.0

Source: Adapted from *Russian Economic Trends* (1998).

planning ministry; several sectoral banks (agriculture, industry, etc.) which managed the accounts of enterprises within their designated sector; an investment bank which made loans to enterprises for capital investment; and a national savings bank, which held the deposits of the general public.

In this system, there were, in effect, *two parallel monetary systems*, one cash based, one credit based. In the *cash economy*, the national bank, as part of the planning process, set the volume of cash to be printed within a given time period (Table 30.7, p. 619). The production plan for each enterprise specified the amount of cash they could draw from their sectoral bank to pay wages; all wages and salaries were paid in cash. The general public then used their cash wages to buy goods and services and the state shops redeposited their cash takings in the national bank; household savings were deposited in the national savings bank. In the *credit economy*, the national plan set limits on the amount each enterprise could borrow from its sectoral or investment bank to finance investment and stocks. Inter-enterprise payments were all made by transfers between their accounts in the national banking system. Credits were not convertible into cash, so the two systems were separate, although integrated through the national plan.

This feature of the command economy gave rise to curious monetary problems. It was possible, for example, for the two monetary systems to become misaligned. For example, if the national bank increased the *cash* issue to allow enterprises to pay higher wages, there could be increased demand for goods by households. At the same time, there may be restrictions on *credit* availability, so that enterprises could not expand production.

The immediate priority for the post-communist countries was to integrate the cash and credit systems and create a 'two-tier' financial system, in which the national bank could assume the responsibilities of a conventional central bank, setting interest rates and ensuring the viability of the system as a whole, and a lower tier of commercial banks could take deposits and make loans on market terms. In the former Soviet republics, there was an additional decision to be taken, namely whether to remain in monetary union with Russia after independence, or to secede and establish their own currency. In the event, the political difficulties of maintaining monetary ties with Russia during the turbulence of the transition process forced the issue and even those states which might have preferred to remain within the rouble zone introduced their own national currencies.

The restructuring of the national bank system was achieved fairly quickly, with most countries choosing to privatize the sectoral, investment and savings divisions of the national bank and allowing new joint-stock banks to be created. The core of the national bank which remained in state control was normally reconstituted as a central bank and, in most countries, given a high degree of legal autonomy from the government, along with a mandate to manage monetary conditions in the pursuit of price stability. Indeed, the constitution of the Bundesbank was widely used as a model for designing the new central banks of CEE and the CIS.

Establishing monetary stability has been made

Table 30.7 Broad money growth (% change per annum).

	1991	1992	1993	1994	1995	1996	1997	1998	2001
CEE countries									
Albania	104.4	152.7	75.0	40.6	51.8	43.8	28.5	20.6	11.8
Bulgaria	110.0	53.7	47.6	78.6	39.6	124.5	359.3	9.7	49.3
Croatia*	n/a	n/a	n/a	75.7	39.3	49.1	38.3	13.0	45.2
Czech Republic	26.8	20.7	22.5	20.8	19.4	7.8	8.7	5.2	13.0
Estonia	n/a	59.0	93.0	40.1	34.5	35.6	42.3	0.1	23.0
FYR Macedonia	n/a	n/a	n/a	8.9	−59.3	−0.5	21.1	13.0	66.3
Hungary	35.7	27.6	15.7	13.0	20.1	22.5	19.4	15.2	16.8
Latvia	153.0	169.9	84.1	47.4	−23.1	19.9	38.7	5.9	29.0
Lithuania	143.0	245.9	100.2	63.0	28.9	−3.5	34.1	14.5	21.4
Poland	37.0	57.5	36.0	38.2	34.9	29.3	20.9	25.2	9.0
Romania	101.2	79.6	141.0	138.1	71.6	66.0	104.9	48.9	46.2
Slovak Republic	n/a	n/a	18.5	18.6	18.9	16.7	8.9	2.7	7.8
Slovenia	n/a	128.9	63.2	43.3	28.1	20.5	24.3	19.8	30.4
CIS countries									
Armenia	n/a	n/a	10,77.2	737.1	65.0	35.2	29.2	38.2	10.8
Azerbaijan	n/a	n/a	818.0	1,114.1	25.4	17.1	41.4	−22.6	−3.4
Belarus	n/a	n/a	n/a	1,818.0	173.7	52.4	111.4	276.0	58.9
Georgia	n/a	464.0	4,319.0	2,229.0	135.1	41.9	45.6	−1.2	18.5
Kazakhstan	211.0	391.0	692.0	576.1	109.0	16.6	28.2	−13.3	14.3
Kyrgyzstan**	84.0	428.0	180.0	125.0	80.1	21.3	25.4	17.2	3.0
Moldova	n/a	367.6	310.0	115.6	65.2	15.3	34.1	−8.2	37.8
Russia	125.9	642.6	416.1	200.0	125.8	30.6	29.8	19.8	40.1
Tajikistan	68.0	579.0	1,429.0	159.0	413.0	93.2	10.7	30.7	54.6
Turkmenistan**	n/a	n/a	n/a	983.9	448.0	411.7	81.2	83.2	17.5
Ukraine	n/a	n/a	758.0	540.0	117.4	35.1	33.9	25.3	42.0
Uzbekistan**	n/a	468.0	785.0	25.9	144.3	113.3	45.6	28.1	50.0

* = M4; ** = M3.
Source: Adapted from EBRD (2002).

more difficult for the new central banks by two main factors:

1 budget deficits;
2 the dollarization of the economies.

Budget deficits and the money supply

In a cash-based economy where the government has the monopoly over currency issue, printing cash provides a straightforward alternative to raising taxes as a means of financing government spending. In the early years of the reform process, money emission was the primary way in which governments financed the growing gap between government spending and tax revenues. There are essentially three ways of financing government spending:

1 taxation;
2 printing currency or borrowing from the banking system – which increases the money supply;
3 borrowing from the general public or abroad – which increases government debt.

Transition governments have sought to rebuild their tax bases with varying degrees of success and, by western standards, budget deficits in the CEE and the CIS are generally modest. Nevertheless, monetary financing of the residual budget deficits remains a problem. The main reason is that, in Western countries, budget deficits are normally financed by borrowing from the general public by selling bonds on the stock market. However, stock markets remain generally underdeveloped in many transition economies. The other alternative, borrowing from abroad, also has its drawbacks. While the IMF and the World Bank have been prepared to extend large loans to transition governments to assist them through the early stages, these loans are highly conditional upon the governments adhering to pre-agreed policies, restricting the

government's subsequent room for policy manoeuvre. Unlike sales of bonds to the general public, which are normally in the local currency, transition governments borrow from the international agencies in foreign currency (usually US dollars) and this must be repaid, imposing a burden in terms of interest and capital payments (Table 30.8). Clearly the transition economies have borrowed heavily from abroad, so that their external debt is a large percentage of their annual GDP and export values. 'Servicing' this debt via interest payments, etc., also takes up a substantial percentage of annual export values for many of these economies.

Table 30.8 External debt and servicing, 2001.

	External debt stock ($m)	External debt/GDP (%)	External debt/exports (%)	Debt service (% exports)
CEE countries				
Albania	1,157	28.2	137.7	4.7
Bulgaria	9,894	73.2	131.5	20.2
Croatia	11,189	57.3	116.2	18.8
Czech Republic	21,695	38.2	50.9	6.4
Estonia	3,279	59.6	65.5	7.1
FYR Macedonia	1,410	40.2	99.3	19.0
Hungary	33,871	63.6	94.6	15.4
Latvia	5,578	73.5	161.6	19.6
Lithuania	5,262	43.9	87.0	27.3
Poland	70,160	39.0	204.2	8.1
Romania	11,822	30.5	88.7	20.5
Slovak Republic	11,269	56.3	76.5	n/a
Slovenia	6,717	35.7	59.5	n/a
CIS countries				
Armenia	905	42.8	167.6	9.7
Azerbaijan	1,402	24.5	59.2	5.7
Belarus	930	11.1	7.6	2.5
Georgia	1,704	53.8	343.5	7.4
Kazakhstan	14,100	63.4	135.7	11.9
Kyrgyzstan	1,876	127.7	335.6	24.4
Moldova	1,464	91.6	200.8	30.4
Russia	134,000	53.6	145.5	n/a
Tajikistan	1,023	97.6	320.8	19.2
Turkmenistan	2,400	81.1	86.4	30.9
Ukraine	11,831	31.5	56.1	8.1
Uzbekistan	4,533	75.2	164.5	30.4

Source: Adapted from EBRD (2002).

Dollarization

In a market economy, money performs the functions of a medium of exchange, a unit of account and a store of value. The ability of a currency to perform these functions is undermined by high rates of inflation. Typically, in many transition economies, US dollars first began to circulate as an alternative store of value: individuals would switch their wages from the local currency into dollars and only switch back when they had goods to purchase, preserving the value of their wages in the interim. At higher rates of inflation, the 'menu costs' of continually altering the prices of goods and services become intolerable and dollars have been used as the unit of account. Prices in a shop, for example, are shown in dollars and, at the checkout, the till operator converts the prices into local currency at the prevailing exchange rate for payment. Finally, when there is hyperinflation, dollarization often becomes complete, with goods and services being both priced and paid for in dollars.

It is impossible to estimate accurately the volume of dollars (and other hard currencies, notably the Deutschmark) in circulation in CEE and the CIS, but the sums are huge. The Federal Reserve Bank, for example, calculates that there are more dollars being used in the region than in the United States. This phenomenon presents major problems for monetary control, since a significant proportion of the 'money supply' in transition economies is unrecorded and outside the central bank's control. Transition economies which have succeeded in stabilizing inflation have, however, been able to reverse the dollarization of their economies. The normal mechanism is that, as inflation comes under control and real interest rates for deposits in local currency become positive, it becomes more attractive to hold bank deposits in local currency than to hold dollar bills. Individuals begin to sell their dollars to the central bank and there is a virtuous circle, as stabilization leads to an increase in foreign exchange reserves.

The 'New Currency Boards': the case of Estonia

In June 1992, Estonia became the first of the former Soviet republics to leave the rouble zone and introduce its own national currency, the kroon. At the same time, Estonia set up a currency board, fixing the kroon to the Deutschmark. The government's decision was heavily influenced by the return of 11 tonnes of gold reserves from abroad, which had been deposited by the Estonian government in 1940 shortly before the Soviet occupation in that year. The early repayment of 4.8 tonnes of gold by the Bank of England in March 1992, which had a market value of DM80m, provided the capital for the initial currency issue.

Like the old colonial currency boards, the note issue was 100% backed by gold and hard currencies, and the Bank of Estonia was legally obliged to exchange notes for Deutschmarks, and vice versa, at the official rate. The advantage of the system is that, provided the government can obtain the necessary capital, it is simple to set up and operate. Latvia and Lithuania subsequently followed Estonia's example and set up currency boards of their own, also using gold reserves reclaimed from foreign central banks.

In analytical terms, a *currency board* is equivalent to using a foreign currency as the means of exchange and unit of account; that is, there is no difference in analytical terms between using dollars for domestic transactions and using local currency which is 100% backed by dollars. The obvious advantage is that a currency board provides a credible guarantee of monetary stability, thereby reducing inflationary expectations and restoring faith in the domestic currency. For transition economies which have experienced very rapid inflation rates and the resultant 'dollarization' of the economy as confidence in the domestic currency collapses, a currency board can provide a powerful mechanism for bringing about a sustainable disinflation.

There are two major risks to a currency board. One is related to the central bank's role in preserving the viability of the commercial banking system. In most countries, the central bank acts as 'lender of last resort', lending reserves to commercial banks with liquidity difficulties and thereby maintaining confidence in the banking system as a whole. Given the widespread problems of commercial banks in the transition economies, many of which have made non-performing loans to enterprises which are bankrupt, there is a danger that political and social pressure to rescue failing banks will force the central bank to issue local currency in excess of its holdings of foreign exchange reserves. The cost of avoiding a wholesale collapse of the commercial banking system may be the breakdown of the currency board.

The second risk, which applies to all forms of fixed exchange rate systems (since all involve the central bank losing control of the money supply), stems from the government's budget deficit. Introducing a currency board clearly closes off the option of financing the budget deficit through the creation of money. Indeed, it is precisely because a currency board forces the government to finance itself in non-monetary ways that this form of fixed exchange rate is so attractive to countries bedevilled by hyperinflation. However, if the government is politically incapable of reducing its budget deficit, it may be that resort to the 'inflation tax' (i.e. financing expenditure by printing money) is preferable to the social unrest that might follow from the non-payment of state workers, pensioners, etc. Unless achieving a more balanced budget is politically feasible, a currency board will fail.

The disadvantages of a currency board in economic terms are basically those of a fixed exchange system, namely the loss of monetary sovereignty. In the special case of transition economies, this can cause adjustment difficulties. Because high-inflation countries tend to be extensively dollarized, the introduction of a credible currency board will encourage residents to switch out of dollars into local currency. Under the currency board arrangements, the central bank's foreign exchange reserves and the stock of issued banknotes will grow. Because this portfolio reallocation out of dollars into local currency simply changes the form in which money is held, there need be no inflationary consequences from the subsequent rapid growth in the money supply. However, experience in the Baltic states and eastern Germany suggests that, as people switch from hoarded dollars into domestic currency, the *velocity of circulation* of money may rise. Because the exchange rate is fixed, any temporary increase in prices as a result of increased spending leads to a rise in the real exchange rate and may cause problems for exporters.

The balance of payments

Under the former centrally planned system, international trade of the transition economies was largely conducted within the framework of COMECON, the Council for Mutual Economic Assistance. Under this arrangement, trade between the economies of CEE and the former Soviet Union was organized through a central payments system (via 'trade roubles'). Exports to other COMECON members were recorded as credits, and imports as debits, in each country's 'account', with settlement for inter-country indebtedness made using trade roubles. This model of organizing and financing international trade, together with a favourable configuration of export and import prices for trade with the former Soviet Union[3] and integrated national economic plans across COMECON, meant that the trade patterns of the smaller CEE countries were heavily skewed towards Russia and the other Soviet republics. Trade with capitalist countries outside the COMECON system was heavily restricted by a range of import and export taxes and, in the case of imported goods and services, by shortages of hard currencies; as a result, a high proportion of non-COMECON trade was conducted on a barter basis, with the government negotiating goods-for-goods exchanges with western manufacturers. PepsiCo's barter deal with the Russian government of Pepsi for vodka in the late 1980s was the most famous of the barter arrangements which characterized trade between the COMECON and capitalist world before 1989.

The breakdown of the centrally planned system, the weakening of the political ties between CEE and Russia and the liberalization of prices, exchange rates and trade regimes has led to a rapid reorientation of trade patterns towards the richer economies of the EU, notably Germany, and to a lesser extent towards the United States and South East Asia. Some 45% in value of Russian external trade was conducted with the EU in 2002, with the corresponding figure over 50% for countries such as Albania, Bulgaria, Croatia and Romania. Such an outcome is consistent with the so-called 'gravity model' of international trade, which suggests that, in the absence of trade barriers, trade between countries will be a function of absolute GDP, per capita GDP and geographical distance (a proxy for transport costs).

This process of reorienting trade flows has been painful and most of the transition economies suffered a collapse in exports and trade deficits during the early and mid-1990s. The situation has since improved significantly, as Table 30.9 reveals, although some of the CIS countries still face major trading imbalances. As a major exporter of oil and other commodities, Russia stands out as one of only four transition economies with a current account surplus. However, the importance of trade within the transition economies is clear from the second column of data in the table. Table 30.9 also shows the scale of foreign direct investment (FDI) relative to current account imbalances. Historically, developing economies attracted inward FDI which allowed them to finance current account deficits as their economies industrialized. While Azerbaijan and Kazakhstan, which have extensive oil reserves, have benefited from inward FDI from oil companies, per capita inward FDI over the period 1989–2001 has been limited and concentrated in the richest CEE states (the link between inward FDI and microeconomic reform is discussed further below).

Microeconomic reform

A central planning system takes upon itself the responsibility for *resource allocation*. It therefore adopts its own procedures for the following activities which are performed in a market economy by:

1 dynamic, profit-seeking firms, which seek out profitable investment and production opportunities;

2 open competitive markets, in which domestic and

Table 30.9 Trade, the current account and foreign direct investment (FDI).

	Current account balance, 2002 (% GDP)	Share of trade 2001 (% GDP)	FDI inflows 2001 (% GDP)	Cumulative FDI inflows 1989–2001 ($m)	Per capita cumulative FDI, 1989–2001 ($m)
CEE countries					
Albania	−6.0	39.9	5.0	799	259
Bulgaria	−5.9	87.0	4.7	3,961	491
Croatia	−3.5	69.2	6.8	5,858	1,315
Czech Republic	−3.6	123.1	8.5	26,960	2,615
Estonia	−6.7	136.5	6.2	2,351	1,727
FYR Macedonia	−10.2	78.8	12.7	888	444
Hungary	−2.4	109.3	4.0	21,751	2,137
Latvia	−8.5	76.2	2.2	2,670	1,138
Lithuania	−5.8	90.8	3.7	2,826	813
Poland	−3.8	40.2	3.6	34,426	890
Romania	−5.0	66.3	3.0	7,928	356
Slovak Republic	−9.1	137.3	7.3	5,629	1,042
Slovenia	−1.2	102.6	1.8	1,847	934
CIS countries					
Armenia	−8.9	53.2	3.3	620	199
Azerbaijan	−22.4	62.0	4.0	3,973	491
Belarus	−0.4	123.3	0.7	1,315	132
Georgia	−6.2	45.8	3.2	838	157
Kazakhstan	−5.5	77.7	12.4	11,361	765
Kyrgyzstan	−2.9	62.7	1.5	405	85
Moldova	−9.2	91.3	3.8	526	146
Russia	8.0	50.7	0.0	6,762	47
Tajikistan	−4.1	135.9	0.9	155	24
Turkmenistan	0.8	159.7	4.5	1,077	191
Ukraine	4.0	90.4	2.0	4,104	84
Uzbekistan	0.6	86.8	1.2	768	30

Source: Adapted from EBRD (2002, 2003).

foreign consumers and producers come together to set prices, sales and output;

3 the financial system, which channels resources from savers to investors which can earn the highest, risk-adjusted returns.

Building a fully functioning market economy thus involves transforming state enterprises into outward-looking, profit-oriented firms opening up domestic markets to internal and external competition, and establishing a banking system and capital market in which funds are allocated on the basis of objective risk assessments and prospective returns, rather than in accordance with the demands of a central plan. Finally, transition requires the establishment of a functioning legal system to define and protect property rights, clarify ownership and, most importantly, provide a legal framework which facilitates investment.

We now consider the issues involved in each in turn.

Creating a dynamic private sector

The creation of a dynamic private sector can be achieved in one of two ways: first, by encouraging entrepreneurs to start up new businesses; and second, by transferring the ownership of existing SOEs into private hands. Experience to date has highlighted the importance of maintaining a balance between the two. The crucial difference between business start-ups and the privatization of SOEs is that the former creates jobs, while the latter inevitably leads to job-shedding, at least in the short term. In Poland, for example, approximately half the jobs created since 1989 have been in new, small-scale business ventures. When SOEs are privatized, on the other hand, the new management's first objective is often to eliminate overstaffing and thereby increase labour productivity. In the former centrally planned system, unemployment was officially non-existent, a result achieved, in part at least, by forcing SOEs to mop up all the available labour.

It is often asserted that promoting 'organic' private sector growth requires simple legal procedures for registering companies and a straightforward corporate tax structure. Strictly speaking, these conditions are essential for the growth of an 'official' private sector, rather than private sector activity *per se*. The former communist countries always had an unofficial private sector (sometimes called the 'hidden', 'informal' or 'black economy') which, despite being harshly repressed by the authorities, was active in selling smuggled goods and organizing currency trading. After 1989, state repression of the unofficial private sector was widely relaxed, while the accelerating disintegration of the command planning system created huge opportunities for entrepreneurs.

Mainstream economic theory suggests that, if markets are 'efficient' in the sense that markets are competitive and contestable and information is widely shared, then market operators cannot make abnormal profits in the long run; economic rent acts as a signal to attract new entrants, who compete down prices and eliminate the abnormal profit. In the aftermath of the democratic revolutions spreading around the CEE and CIS states, however, the fledgling markets were characterized by massive inefficiency, with the debris of the central planning structures and the absence of clear property rights preventing normal market transactions. For the new entrepreneurs, the opportunities for hugely profitable arbitrage were everywhere. Extensive price controls meant that prices bore little relation to opportunity cost and, where official prices were far below world prices, moving goods across borders offered the prospect of spectacular returns. The much publicized Russian 'mafia' is a legacy of the early years of transition, when rational speculative activity in the presence of pervasive market inefficiency created opportunities for profit undreamed of in the West. This window of opportunity closed rapidly, as prices were deregulated and markets liberalized. Nevertheless, many governments are finding it difficult to draw their new class of small entrepreneur back into the official private sector.

Small-scale privatization

In the area of privatization, it is useful to distinguish between small-scale privatization and 'mass' privatization. The former refers to the transfer to private hands of small SOEs, mainly retail shops, restaurants and other service providers (e.g. hairdressers, bars, cinemas, etc.). In the west, such companies are typically owned by their managers. Replicating this arrangement through privatization involves either transferring ownership (either free of charge or for an agreed cash price) to the present managers and/or workers, or auctioning off the enterprise to the highest bidder. Most transition economies have experimented with small-scale privatization somewhere along the continuum from a straight give-away to the incumbents to a cash auction.

Small-scale privatization plays an important role in the transition process for two reasons. First, like business start-ups, small companies offer greater scope for job creation than large, overstaffed SOEs. In the communist days, for example, state restaurants were typically dour, unattractive places characterized by poor service. Freed from state control, such restaurants can expand into new markets (e.g. fast food, ethnic food, etc.), quickly increasing turnover and jobs. Second, small-scale enterprises are 'close' to people in a way that large SOEs are not. Their transformation, with the attendant changes in shop window displays, service to customers, range and quality of goods and services sold, provides an immediate and powerful psychological symbol of the benefits of transition.

Enterprise restructuring and large-scale privatization

At the other end of the scale, the region faces the problem of privatizing the huge SOEs that made up the Soviet military–industrial complex. Many of these enterprises employed tens of thousands of workers, often producing specialist intermediate and final products for the military. The breakdown of COMECON and the Warsaw Pact and the end of the Cold War (together with the budgetary problems of many CIS governments) have radically reduced the demand for the products of many large SOEs. At the same time, the liberalization of prices and the opening up of economies to international competition have resulted in many large SOEs making heavy financial losses. In the past, the central planners arranged input and output prices so that enterprises making 'socially necessary' goods could make a profit; liberalization and foreign competition have quickly driven input and output prices to world levels, making many previously profitable activities financially unviable.

Enabling the huge SOEs to respond flexibly to the changed configuration of input and output prices requires breaking the link between the state and enterprises, so that managements are free to maximize profits rather than meet political or social objectives imposed by their sponsoring ministries. The normal approach taken in most former centrally planned economies is to 'corporatize' the enterprises, i.e. transform them into joint stock companies. The stock (i.e. shares) created is initially held by the state, but the intention of corporatization is to enable the management to pursue commercial objectives free from political interference.

One difficulty widely encountered with corporatization involves the issue of 'corporate governance', a special case of the so-called 'principal–agent' problem. In market economies, companies are owned by private shareholders (the principals) who appoint managers (the agents) to run companies on their behalf. The principals clearly have different interests from their agents, the former wanting to see profits (or growth) maximized, while the latter are better served by targeting stable, secure markets (thereby promoting job security) and increasing the wages of senior management. A combination of annual general meetings, at which shareholders can assess the performance of the incumbent management and replace it as necessary, and an active stock market in which investors scrutinize the profitability of listed companies (driving down the market price of companies with underperforming managements and opening them up to hostile takeovers) ensures that the will of the principals is, by and large, imposed on the agents.

The process of corporatization, of itself, means that corporate governance remains the preserve of the state and, quite probably, the ministry which previously managed the SOE. In such circumstances, it is difficult for corporatization, *per se*, to break the link between state and SOEs. In countries where the state has effectively abdicated its role as principal (notably Bulgaria), presumably in the belief that freed from control the SOEs would act to maximize profit, the result has been predictably disappointing. The managers, rather than concentrating on increasing sales and profit, have instead taken advantage of their freedom of action to exploit the companies for their own benefit.

One solution to the principal–agent problem, widely employed in the developing world, is to transfer SOEs to indirect state ownership, through the creation of 'state holding companies'. Unlike a ministry, the state holding company is mandated solely to control the economic performance of the companies it owns, through *ex post* monitoring of its financial accounts. This solution permits a separation of the state's ownership and management functions, allowing a decentralized management to act more independently and thereby promoting restructuring and more commercial behaviour.

However, such 'half-way house' solutions have, in general, been rare in the transition economies, with most governments regarding corporatization as merely a first step on the road to full privatization. The transfer of the shares in SOEs from the state to the private sector, taken together with measures to create a vibrant stock market, is widely regarded as the only way of satisfactorily resolving the principal–agent problem and, in the process, revitalizing large-scale industry in the CEE and CIS. The methods of privatization have varied widely and, amongst a wide array of different models, have included:

1 open-market auctions of SOEs for cash;

2 open-market auctions of SOEs for vouchers, which have previously been distributed amongst the target owners (who may be the incumbent workforce or the general public) either free or for cash at a discounted rate;

3 open-market auctions of SOEs for a mixture of cash and vouchers;

4 direct sales of SOEs to managers (so-called 'management buyouts'), workers (in the form of cooperative enterprises) or, wholly or partially, to a foreign company; and

5 direct transfer of shares (free of charge) to the incumbent management and/or workers.

A key debate is whether restructuring of SOEs should precede or follow privatization. The British government, an early pioneer of privatization in the West, adopted a strategy of overhauling nationalized industries while they were still under public ownership. This meant that the heavy costs of redundancy were borne by the state; the enterprises themselves were not sold to the private sector until they were profit-making, thereby making them attractive to private investors. This model does not transfer easily to the transition economies of CEE and the CIS, where fiscal problems preclude the heavy investment of public funds in restructuring SOEs. In cases where companies are chronically inefficient, finding a foreign investor willing to invest in new plant and equipment is often the only way to revive the fortunes of a failing SOE. The German Treuhandanstalt, the privatization agency set up to sell off SOEs in the eastern *Länder* following the reunification of Germany in 1990, agreed sales on the basis of the new owner's commitment to invest and retrain workers, as well as the actual selling price.

As noted above, whether SOEs are sold to domestic buyers, who must improve their performance with only modest initial injections of capital, or acquired by foreign companies with funds to invest, large-scale job losses are inevitable – hence the importance of a vibrant private sector which can absorb the displaced workers through organic growth. The efficiency gains in countries in the vanguard of mass privatization have been impressive. For example, output per worker in the manufacturing sector in Poland and Hungary rose by 7–18% per annum between 1992 and 1995. While part of this increase reflected greater effort on the part of workers in the privatized SOEs and increased capital investment, the European Bank for Reconstruction and Development acknowledged that the shedding of staff was the dominant factor, especially in the early years of transition.

Given the huge scale of many SOEs, particularly in the CIS, the fear of wholesale job shedding following privatization provides a powerful political obstacle to progress in this area. The mass popular unrest and demonstrations that preceded the collapse of the former communist regimes provides a reminder of the anti-government riots which might result from massive, highly concentrated job losses in particular regions and industries. As noted above, SOEs traditionally provided their workers with a raft of social benefits (housing, education, health care), which explains why many workers continue to work in the CIS even when they are not paid for months at a time. The loss of their jobs threatens not just their incomes, but the continuation of these benefits-in-kind. It is clear that, while a vibrant private sector can act as a shock absorber, governments have to begin building a basic social welfare system (to provide basic income support and social services for the poor and unemployed) if the social costs of industrial restructuring and large-scale privatization are to be politically tolerable.

Income inequality and economic transition

Economic transition has meant a sharp increase in income inequality. Table 30.10 provides an overview of income distribution in Russia. It shows that for the poorest 20% of citizens, their share of total income has fallen from 11.9% to 6.2% over the period 1991–97, while the share of the richest 20% has risen from 30.7% to 46.7%. These changes are reflected in the Gini coefficient (the standard measure of equality, with the higher figure representing greater inequality), which has increased from 0.260 to 0.374, and the ratio of the income earned by the richest 10% to the income earned by the poorest 10%, which has trebled from 4.5 to 13.2.

Market liberalization

The operation of the 'invisible hand', namely the price mechanism, lies at the heart of a market economy, with high prices/profits encouraging an influx of producers to meet demand, and vice versa. Transition thus requires an end to the practice of setting prices and profit margins centrally, in accordance with the needs of the central plan and the planners' subjective judgements of the 'social value' of different goods and services. Price control was so fundamental to the central planning system that dismantling the apparatus by which prices and costs are fixed has proved lengthy.

The abolition of controls (both maxima and minima) on the prices of final goods was achieved in most countries relatively quickly, although at great social cost. Against a backdrop of rapid monetary growth and an already large 'monetary overhang' (i.e. money balances which people had accumulated in the years when they could not find the goods on which to spend their income), price liberalization led to an explosion in retail prices, hitting vulnerable, fixed-income groups like pensioners disproportionately hard. The demonstrable social injustices occasioned by earlier price liberalization led governments in many countries to delay the ending of more subtle price controls (e.g. on 'essentials' like bread, milk, heat and light and public transport). Producers' input costs (notably energy) continue to be subsidized in some countries for fear of the inflationary consequences, while profit margins were often controlled long after final prices were liberalized for fear that consumers would be 'exploited' by the new 'capitalists'.

The opening up of foreign trade and the liberalization of the foreign exchange market are prerequisites for meaningful price liberalization. During the period of central planning, the states of CEE and the CIS traded relatively little with the outside world. The total exports of the former Soviet Union to countries outside the COMECON bloc were, in the 1980s, lower than Belgium's, for example. The isolation of

Table 30.10 Income distribution in Russia, 1991–97.

	1991	1992	1993	1994	1995	1996	1997
Income by quintile							
Poorest 20%	11.9	6.0	5.8	5.3	5.5	6.5	6.2
Next poorest 20%	15.8	11.6	11.1	10.2	10.2	10.9	10.6
Next poorest 20%	18.8	17.6	16.7	15.2	15.0	15.5	15.0
Next poorest 20%	22.8	26.5	24.8	23.0	22.4	22.4	21.3
Richest 20%	30.7	38.3	41.6	46.3	46.9	44.7	46.9
Total %	100.0	100.0	100.0	100.0	100.0	100.0	100.0
Gini coefficient	0.260	0.289	0.398	0.409	0.381	0.375	0.374
Richest 10% : poorest 10%	4.5	–	11.2	15.1	13.5	13.0	13.2

Source: Adapted from Russia–Europe Centre for Economic Policy.

domestic markets from outside competition, taken in conjunction with a regime of comprehensive import and export taxes and duties, was instrumental in ensuring that central planners could arrange internal costs and prices without reference to world prices. Artificial exchange rates, officially set and administered by national banks, achieved a similar result.

Allowing the invisible hand to operate freely implies that trade restrictions should be eased and, more importantly, that the tariff regimes should be simplified and purged of the distortions which hitherto served the purposes of the central planners. Similarly, true price liberalization needs 'current account convertibility', so that internal prices are not distorted by the government restricting access to foreign exchange. Under the former arrangements, exchange rates were administered (i.e. the rates were set by government decree), often with differential rates for importers and exporters, tourists and foreign investors. Current account convertibility does not mean that the government or the central bank cannot 'manage' the exchange rate by pegging its value to, say, the US dollar or the euro; indeed, many of the more successful transition economies in CEE have exchange rate targets of one form or another. Rather, it means that the exchange rate should be one at which importers and exporters can freely buy and sell foreign currency, so that a process of arbitrage can bring internal and world prices into line. For example if the government pegs the exchange rate of currency X at, say, X1 = \$1, then provided the government is prepared to accumulate or run down its foreign exchange reserves to maintain this parity, inflows and outflows of tradeable goods and services will bring internal prices into line with the world price of (tradeable) goods and services.

The final building block of market liberalization is, paradoxically at first sight, the creation of an effective competition or anti-monopoly policy. As noted above, central planners faced a rational incentive to try and maximize economies of scale, since, as the rulers of the economies they oversaw, they could prevent large state-owned monopoly producers exploiting their dominant market positions. At regional and local level, many similar dominant positions existed in the wholesale and retail sector. As former SOEs have been privatized, the risk that the new privately owned companies will abuse their inherited monopoly power is very real. Indeed, the fear that consumers will be exploited has deterred many governments from pressing ahead with privatization more aggressively and encouraged others to reimpose price and profit margin controls in an *ad hoc* way which threatens the viability of the newly privatized companies. The solution is a workable body of anti-monopoly legislation and, in cases where the scope for abuse is potentially extreme (e.g. in the case of a private monopoly electricity company), some form of state regulator along the lines of OFGAS and OFTEL in Britain.

Financial sector reform

In the central planning system, agencies of the national bank provided an accounting system to book the credits and debits of SOEs as intermediate and final products were transferred between one enterprise and another. These agencies of the national bank were typically organized on a sectoral basis, with an agricultural 'bank' for farms and food processors, an engineering bank for manufacturers of capital goods and so on. 'Soft' loans (i.e. loans at zero or artificially low interest rates) were available to loss-making enterprises, with decisions about credit being taken within the context of the central plan. Separate 'savings banks' provided a repository for individual citizens to save unspent income, but consumer loans were virtually unknown. Market economies, in contrast, are built upon competitive financial systems which allocate savings to their best uses – that is, to borrowers who can pay, after adjustment for credit risk, the highest rates of return.

The transition process thus implies creating a 'two tier' banking system, in which the state or national bank is split into a central bank (with responsibility for monetary policy and banking supervision) and a commercial banking system. This objective has generally been achieved by breaking up the national bank and privatizing the sectoral agencies as stand-alone commercial banks (albeit, initially, with a strong sectoral orientation). In Poland, for example, nine commercial banks were hived off from the national bank, of which four had been privatized by the end of 1996. In contrast to the industrial sector, moreover, new business start-ups in the banking sector have been very vigorous since 1989–91. In part, the rapid growth of a private sector banking system was based on market imperfections. Citizens socialized during the communist era often did not fully understand the principles of private banking, believing them to enjoy the same solid state backing as the former savings banks. The new breed of private bankers, initially loosely regulated by central banks unsure of their new role post-communism, only vaguely understood notions of capital adequacy and credit risk assessment, but quickly realized the scope for reinvesting depositors' funds at a profit in economies characterized by a lack of loanable funds and a huge demand for credit.

Recent years have seen a wave of private sector banking crashes and scandals. In Latvia, the activities of more than one-third of the country's commercial banks were suspended in 1995, after a number were found to be insolvent (i.e. to have deposit liabilities which exceeded their assets, due to loan defaults). In the same year, the Lithuanian central bank prohibited the planned merger of its two largest private banks after one was discovered to be insolvent. A number of medium-sized and local banks failed during a banking crisis in the Czech Republic in 1996. It has become clear that the challenge is not simply to promote the creation of a private sector banking system, but to properly regulate commercial banks, paying particular regard to the maintenance of minimum capital ratios – that is, the ratio of shareholders' capital to outstanding loans – and to supervise the accelerating numbers of mergers and acquisitions that will be necessary to transform the ranks of small, mainly local or regional banks that now characterize many former centrally planned economies into a much more select group of large, efficient commercial banks.

The second major area of financial sector reform concerns the development of functioning stock markets. As noted above, these are important not only as a means of mobilizing savings and channelling them to their most efficient use, but also as an integral part of the process of corporate governance. For obvious reasons, the development of active capital markets has mirrored the pace of large-scale privatization (and to a lesser extent, the needs of government to sell securities to finance their budget deficits). The stock market capitalization of the Czech Republic, for example, was 42% of GDP at the end of June 1996, reflecting the advanced nature of that country's comprehensive voucher-based privatization programme at that time. In most CIS countries, in contrast, stock markets remain underdeveloped and illiquid.

Legal reforms

In the early stages of transition, investment was strongly inhibited by the absence of clear property rights and a generally murky picture with regard to the laws concerning the ownership of land and buildings (particularly the permissible extent of foreign investments), the valuation of assets and the outlook for taxes on profits and capital, as well as the future regime for the treatment of profits made by foreign investors. While all the transition economies have attempted to set in place new legal structures and regulations, legislation in one area (e.g. foreign ownership of land) often conflicts with laws passed in another (e.g. rules relating to the repatriation of profits by foreign-owned subsidiaries), resulting in a confused patchwork of inconsistent laws and regulations. Creating a transparent, internally consistent legal structure is thus essential for the promotion of investment, particularly foreign direct investment.

Foreign direct investment could potentially play an important part in the reconstruction of CEE and the CIS. Jeffrey Sachs, a US economist and advisor to governments in Eastern Europe, famously observed in the early 1990s that Singapore attracts more foreign investment each year than all the transition economies put together. While the picture has improved slightly, Table 30.9 above suggests that CEE and the CIS attract a relatively small amount of foreign investment. Moreover, creating a receptive investment climate not only holds out the promise of drawing more foreign capital into the transition economies, but also access to the latest western technology and management methods.

Progress in transition to date

Table 30.11 sets out the performances of the transition economies in each of these key areas. The indices are ranked from 1 (little or no progress) to 4 (complete or near complete reform). The key below sets out the meaning of the indices in more detail. Table 30.11 shows that the CEE countries are far more advanced in the transition process than their CIS rivals. Strikingly, of the 12 CIS countries, Russia is in the vanguard of reform, with the private sector now accounting for 70% of GDP following a successful and extensive privatization programme. Overall, Table 30.11 and its key show that most of the transition economies have completed (or nearly completed) the comprehensive liberalization of prices, foreign trade and exchange rates; in almost all countries, small-scale enterprises have been largely privatized. The difference between the CEE and CIS countries is more stark in the field of large-scale privatization of SOEs and enterprise restructuring and financial sector reform, where the CIS countries lag markedly.

It is also worth noting that the pace of structural change is beginning to slow as compared with the early 1990s. This is because most of the 'easier'

reforms have already been achieved. It is the 'hard core' of tasks that remain, notably the restructuring and privatization of large, loss-making SOEs and the creation of an efficient financial system. These are the reforms that promise to be the most socially or politically painful. The pace of reform has slowed also, in part, because the governments that were in power in the immediate aftermath of the collapse of communism enjoyed a popular mandate to undertake radical political change, but as the social pain of the transition process has mounted, the electorate's will-

Table 30.11 The transition picture in 2001.

	Firms				Markets			Finance		Law
	Private sector % GDP	Large-scale privat.	Small-scale privat.	Ent. restruct.	Price liberal.	Trade and forex	Comp. policy	Bank reform	Capital markets	Index of legal reform
CEE countries										
Albania	75	2	4	2	3	4	2	2	2	2
Bulgaria	70	4	4	2	3	4	2	3	2	3
Croatia	60	3	4	3	3	4	2	4	3	3
Czech Republic	80	4	4	3	3	4	3	4	3	3
Estonia	80	4	4	3	3	4	3	4	3	3
FYR Macedonia	60	3	4	2	3	4	2	3	2	2
Hungary	80	4	4	3	3	4	3	4	4	4
Latvia	70	3	4	3	3	4	2	4	3	3
Lithuania	75	4	4	3	3	4	3	3	3	3
Poland	75	3	4	3	3	4	3	3	4	4
Romania	65	3	4	2	3	4	2	3	2	3
Slovak Republic	80	4	4	3	3	4	3	3	2	2
Slovenia	65	3	4	3	3	4	3	3	3	3
CIS countries										
Armenia	70	3	4	2	3	4	2	2	2	2
Azerbaijan	60	2	4	2	3	4	2	2	2	2
Belarus	20	1	2	1	2	2	2	2	2	1
Georgia	65	3	4	2	3	4	2	2	2	2
Kazakhstan	65	3	4	2	3	3	2	3	2	2
Kyrgyzstan	60	3	4	2	3	4	2	2	2	1
Moldova	50	3	3	2	3	4	2	2	2	2
Russia	70	3	4	2	3	3	2	2	2	2
Tajikistan	50	2	4	2	3	3	2	2	1	1
Turkmenistan	25	1	2	1	2	1	1	1	1	n/a
Ukraine	65	3	4	2	3	3	2	2	2	2
Uzbekistan	45	3	3	2	2	2	2	2	2	2

Source: Adapted from EBRD (2002).

Key to Table 30.11.

	4	3	2	1
Large-scale privatization	More than 50% of large enterprises privatized	More than 25% of large enterprises privatized	Privatization scheme for large enterprises about to be introduced	Little or nothing done
Small-scale privatization	All small enterprises (e.g. shops, restaurants) privatized	Most small enterprises privatized	Significant proportion of small enterprises privatized	Little or nothing done
Enterprise restructuring	Corporatization of state enterprises completed	Corporatization in progress, but incomplete	Legislative reforms passed, but not fully implemented	Few reforms passed
Price liberalization	Complete price liberalization and anti-monopoly controls	Substantial price liberalization	Price controls remain for significant number of products	Most prices still controlled
Trade and foreign exchange system	No import/export quotas or controls, convertible exchange rate	Few quotas, near full convertibility of exchange	Few quotas, but exchange controls still in force	Widespread import/export quotas and/or exchange controls
Competition policy	Signification anti-monopoly enforcement	Some enforcement to control abuse of market power	Basic competition policy rules and institutions set up	No competition policy rules or institutions
Banking reform	Well-functioning banking system	Substantial progress towards competitive banking system	Interest rates main means of allocating credit	Little or no progress
Capital markets	Functioning, liquid capital market, with legal framework approaching international standards	Substantial issues of shares by private firms on capital market	Establishment of capital market and limited trading	Little or no progress
Legal reform index: rules on pledge, bankruptcy and company law	Comprehensive legal rules, independently and consistently enforced	Legal rules exist, but enforcement patchy	Legal rules are limited or contradictory, hard to enforce	Legal rules very limited in scope, unclear and not consistently enforced

ingness to tolerate the further sacrifices necessary to maintain the rate of progress has waned. The blunting of voters' appetite for economic transformation, even in CEE where progress has been more swift and the beneficial results more tangible and evenly spread, is best illustrated by their growing propensity to elect left-wing administrations pledged to slow the pace of reform in the interest of promoting social harmony.

Conclusion

Taken together, the analysis above suggests a strong link between progress in reform and economic recovery. The CEE states have, as a group, moved furthest and fastest in transforming their economies into open, competitive market democracies and are now enjoying positive economic growth. In contrast, the CIS states have delayed reform and are still in economic decline. However, such a simplistic conclusion understates the importance of culture, history and geography. The CEE states started from a much better position, with a folk memory of capitalism and a popular antipathy towards their former Soviet colonizers and communism. With strong national identities and the massive markets of the European Union on their doorstep, transition has been economically, socially and psychologically easier than for their eastern neighbours in the CIS.

In the former Soviet Union, communist ideology pervades every aspect of the economy. The entire economic structure reflects the priorities of the plan, with mammoth, highly specialized state enterprises which have floundered outside the rigid framework of the central planning system. There is no generally shared belief that communism was fundamentally flawed and, given the large numbers of casualties of the reform process (pensioners, students, the military, employees of large state enterprises), the construction of a market system has taken place against a backdrop of growing popular hostility. Electoral resentment to the structural changes in the economy is further heightened by nostalgia for the days of the Soviet empire, which adds to a general feeling that things were better in the days of central planning.

Perhaps the most important conclusion from the transition experience to date is that transforming centrally planned economies into market democracies hurts; not only is the economy as a whole destined to undergo a painful negative output shock, with years of declining living standards, but income distribution is inevitably bound to become worse as the new entrepreneurs benefit at the expense of state employees and welfare dependants. The keys to success appear to be:

1 to rush through small-scale privatization and set in place the basic requirements for private business, so that small, dynamic start-up businesses in the private sector can begin to absorb the labour shed by state dinosaurs;

2 to establish a state welfare system which is independent of enterprises, to protect those who lose from transition in the short to medium term;

3 to 'buy off' vested interest groups such as large state enterprise managers and workers (e.g. by giving them shares when their enterprises are privatized), so that they support rather than block reform; and

4 to liberalize trade and capital movements, in order to attract foreign investment to assist the transformation process.

Finally, the challenge which lies ahead in the twenty-first century for CEE and the CIS countries alike is to maintain high rates of domestic savings in order to finance the investment needed for restructuring and economic development. The European Bank for Reconstruction and Development estimates that the region will need to invest at least 20% of GDP in order to sustain annual growth rates in the region of 4%, the absolute minimum needed to regain the losses of the last 15 years and begin to catch up with the poorer west European states. While the consolidation and extension of market reforms remains the short- to medium-term priority, the long-term objective must be to promote investment and savings and thereby accelerate development and raise living standards.

Key points

■ CEE (Central and Eastern Europe) and CIS (Commonwealth of Independent States) economies can usefully be distinguished.

■ The 16 CEE economies consist of the three Baltic States and 13 countries previously under the Soviet sphere of influence.

■ Generally the CEE economies (as compared to the CIS economies) have experienced a higher per capita GDP, less dependence on agriculture, more industrialization and higher unemployment following enterprise restructuring.

- The incorporation of eight of the former CEE economies into the EU in 2004 makes this particular classification of economies largely redundant for future analysis.

- The former *command economies* depended upon highly structured national plans, using input–output techniques.

- The transition process requires the development of labour, goods and capital markets, largely absent from the command economy era.

- Disruption of the highly concentrated and vertically integrated production system of the command economies during the early transition years has caused major losses of output and employment, together with hyperinflationary tendencies as expanding money supply 'chased' an ever smaller output of goods and services.

- Macroeconomic policies restricting public sector deficits via reform of public expenditure and tax revenue, and microeconomic policies increasing productivity via supply-side reforms, are key elements in the transition process.

- Trade patterns of the transition economies have shifted towards the advanced industrialized countries and away from trade between themselves.

- Enterprise restructuring and privatization have played significant roles in the transition process, as have market liberalization and financial sector reform. However, a basic prerequisite for 'success' is arguably an appropriate set of legal reforms concerning ownership and property rights.

Now try the self-check questions for this chapter on the Companion Website. You will also find up-to-date facts and case materials.

Notes

1. The table includes Slovenia, Croatia and Macedonia, but excludes the other states of former Yugoslavia (Bosnia, Serbia and Montenegro) where war and economic sanctions have delayed economic transformation. Some studies now split the Central and Eastern European (CEE) states into two subsections: 'Central Eastern Europe and the Baltic States' and 'South-eastern Europe'.

2. The Soviet Union's 15 republics declared independence in 1991. In 1993, Czechoslovakia split into the Czech Republic and Slovakia, and after a series of conflicts, Slovenia, Croatia, Macedonia and Bosnia Herzegovina left Yugoslavia, leaving a federal rump of Serbia and Montenegro.

3. For example, oil and natural gas from the former Soviet Union to CEE countries was exported at below world prices, while most studies now conclude that CEE countries were able to sell manufactured goods to the former Soviet Union at above world prices.

References and further reading

Aldcroft, D. and Morewood, S. (1995) *Economic Change in Eastern Europe since 1918*, Edward Elgar, Aldershot.

Aoki, M. and Kim, H. K. (1995) *Corporate Governance in Transitional Economies: insider control and the role of banks*, EDI Development Studies, The World Bank, Washington, DC.

Baldwin, R. (1994) *Towards an Integrated Europe*, Centre for Economic Policy Research, London.

Carlin, W. and Mayer, C. (1992) Restructuring enterprises in eastern Europe, *Economic Policy*, 15, 311–52.

EBRD (1995) *Transition Report 1995: Investment and enterprise development*, European Bank for Reconstruction and Development, London.

EBRD (1996) *Transition Report 1996: Infrastructure and savings*, European Bank for Reconstruction and Development, London.

EBRD (1997) *Transition Report 1997: Enterprise performance and growth*, European Bank for Reconstruction and Development, London.

EBRD (1998) *Transition Report 1998: Financial sector in transition*, European Bank for Reconstruction and Development, London.

EBRD (1999) *Transition Report 1999: Ten years of transition*, European Bank for Reconstruction and Development, London.

EBRD (2000) *Transition Report Update*, European Bank for Reconstruction and Development, London.

EBRD (2002) *Transition Report 2002: Agriculture and rural transition*, European Bank for Reconstruction and Development, London.

EBRD (2003) *Transition Report Update*, European Bank for Reconstruction and Development, London.

Estrin, S. (ed.) (1994) *Privatization in Central and Eastern Europe*, Addison Wesley Longman, London.

Gros, D. and Steinherr, A. (1995) *Winds of Change: economic transition in central and eastern Europe*, Addison Wesley Longman, London.

Healey, N. M. (1994) The transition economies of central and eastern Europe: a political, economic, social and technological analysis, *Columbia Journal of World Business*, 29, 62–71.

Johnson, S. and Loveman, G. (1995) *Starting Over in Eastern Europe: entrepreneurship and economic renewal*, Harvard Business School Press, Cambridge, MA.

Johnson, S., Kaufmann, D. and Shleifer, A. (1997) *Politics and Entrepreneurship in Transition Economies*, Working Paper Series No. 57, William Davidson Foundation, University of Michigan.

Kumar, A. (1993) *State Holding Companies and Public Enterprises in Transition*, Macmillan, London.

Lavigne, M. (1995) *The Economics of Transition: from socialist economy to market economy*, Macmillan, London.

UNECE (1995) *Economic Survey of Europe in 1994–1995*, UN Economic Commission for Europe, Geneva and New York.

A guide to sources

The following list, and associated discussion, is by no means intended to be exhaustive, but rather to highlight some of the more useful sources for statistical data and information on the UK economy. The sequence will be as follows:

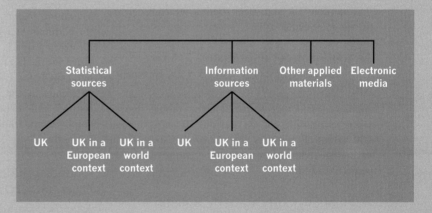

Statistical sources

The following contain important statistical series and, in some cases, articles commenting on those series or on related issues. The addresses given are those for enquiries about *orders* and *subscriptions*.

The UK economy

Guide to Official Statistics   The Stationery Office (TSO), PO Box 29, Norwich NR3 1GN

This is, perhaps, the most useful starting point in any search for statistical sources relating to the UK. It has been published at irregular intervals since 1976 and the latest enlarged edition, compiled by the Office for National Statistics (ONS), was published in 1996. The first chapter of the Guide looks at the organization of the Government Statistical Office and gives the main contact points and publishers of statistics. The remaining 15 chapters contain one subject area per chapter, e.g. population, education, labour market, environment, the economy, etc. For each subject, the main datasets are described and the sources of statistics available are provided. Information on any specific topic can be obtained by using the extensive key word index at the back of the Guide.

The other UK statistical sources we consider are presented alphabetically.

Annual Abstract of Statistics   (AAS)
The Stationery Office (TSO), PO Box 29, Norwich NR3 1GN

Annual Abstract of Statistics gives annual figures, wherever possible, for the previous 10 years, in some 400 tables. It presents the major statistics of the various government departments, grouped under 18 section headings.

Bank of England Quarterly Bulletin
(BEQB)   Publications Group, Bank of England, London EC2R 8AH

The *Bulletin* is published quarterly, providing detailed statistics on assets and liabilities of the UK monetary sector institutions, though with less detail than in *Financial Statistics* (see below). Data are also provided for money stock components, government debt, official reserves, foreign exchange rates, com-

parative interest rates, and flow of funds analyses. Each issue contains a number of articles on recent economic and financial developments and on other topics in banking and finance. The Bank of England also publishes *Inflation Report* every quarter. This contains six sections covering topics such as the outlook for inflation over the next two years, monetary aggregates, financial market data, firm's pricing behaviour, etc.

Business Monitor   (BM)   The Stationery Office (TSO), PO Box 29, Norwich NR3 1GN

Business Monitor presents summary information on the annual census of production, with a two- to three-year time-lag. The annual summary tables (PA. 1002) present data for the latest year, and previous four years, for mining and quarrying, the manufacturing industries, construction, gas, electricity and water. Detailed data are presented, by Minimum List Heading, on output, employment and costs, for both establishments and enterprises in each industry group. Separate annual (PA) reports are also available for each Minimum List Heading, together with quarterly (PQ) and monthly (PM) reports.

Economic Trends   (ET)   The Stationery Office (TSO), PO Box 29, Norwich NR3 1GN

Economic Trends is published monthly by the Office for National Statistics and contains tables and charts illustrating trends in the UK economy. Data are provided for the latest month, or quarter, as appropriate, and usually for at least the five previous years. As well as trends in the components of National Income, output and expenditure, trends in productivity, employment, trade, financial and corporate matters are outlined.

Financial Statistics   (FS)   The Stationery Office (TSO), PO Box 29, Norwich NR3 1GN

Financial Statistics is a monthly publication of the ONS. Data are provided on a wide range of financial topics, for the latest month or quarter, and for at least the previous five years. Financial accounts are presented for various sectors of the economy, central and local government, the public corporations, the monetary sector, other financial institutions, industrial and commercial companies, the personal sector and the overseas sector.

Key Data   The Stationery Office (TSO), PO Box 29, Norwich NR3 1GN

Published annually, *Key Data* is a 'student version' of the key tables and charts from a variety of official publications involving economic and social data. Over 125 tables and charts cover topics such as Finance, Population, Transport, Employment, European Union, Law and Order, Leisure and Tourism, Education, Health and Personal Social Services, and Housing and the Environment.

Labour Market Trends   The Stationery Office (TSO), PO Box 29, Norwich NR3 1GN

This is the successor to the Department of Education and Employment's *Employment Gazette* and is now published in an ONS series which includes *Economic Trends*, *Social Trends*, etc. It is published monthly and contains special feature articles which examine specific issues affecting labour markets – such as women's pay, trade unions, flexible labour markets, etc. It does not include policy developments such as training, health and safety, as these are covered by the Department of Education and Employment's *Employment News*.

Monthly Digest of Statistics   (MDS) The Stationery Office (TSO), PO Box 29, Norwich NR3 1GN

This is another monthly publication of the ONS. It gives up-to-date statistics on the output of various industries, covering a wider range of industries than *Business Monitor*. Statistics are also presented on the components of National Income and Expenditure, on demographic topics, on the labour market and on a variety of social issues.

Regional Trends   (RT) The Stationery Office (TSO), PO Box 29, Norwich NR3 1GN

Regional Trends is an annual publication of the ONS, and presents detailed data on the Standard Planning Regions of the UK. *Regional Trends* includes a wide range of economic, social and demographic indices, highlighting regional disparities in the UK.

Social Trends   (ST) The Stationery Office (TSO), PO Box 29, Norwich NR3 1GN

Much of the material in *Social Trends* is of interest to the social scientist in general rather than the economist in particular. Nevertheless, it gives a detailed breakdown of patterns of household wealth, income and expenditure, together with demographic, housing and social trends.

Transport Statistics: Great Britain
The Stationery Office (TSO), PO Box 29, Norwich NR3 1GN

Published annually by the Department of the Environment, Transport and the Regions, this is the main source of statistics on UK Transport. It is divided into nine parts covering Energy and the Environment, Vehicles and Roads, Road Traffic and Freight, Water and Air Transport and Public Transport. It also contains international transport statistics to place the UK in a world context.

UK Balance of Payments   The Stationery Office (TSO), PO Box 29, Norwich NR3 1GN

The so-called *Pink Book* is the most comprehensive single source available for balance of payments statistics. Published annually, it breaks down trade in goods and services, investment income, investment and other capital transactions, official financing, and external assets and liabilities, into their various components. Data for the previous 10 years are presented for purposes of comparison.

UK Economic Accounts   The Stationery Office (TSO), PO Box 29, Norwich NR3 1GN

Published quarterly by the ONS, this provides a useful update of some of the main components of National Income. It includes the financial accounts of industrial and commercial corporations together with those of central and local government. This publication also provides details of the Balance of Payments on goods, services and investment accounts.

United Kingdom: National Accounts
The Stationery Office (TSO), PO Box 29, Norwich NR3 1GN

Published annually by the ONS, the so-called *Blue Book* is the single most comprehensive source of data on National Income, output and expenditure, and their components. As well as data for the current calendar year, those of the previous 10 years are also provided. For some tables, data are even presented for 20 calendar years on a consistent basis and, in an annual supplement, as far back as 1946.

The UK economy in a European context

Economic Survey of Europe   The Stationery Office (TSO), PO Box 29, Norwich NR3 1GN.

Published by the UN annually. Data are presented by individual country, and by geographical groupings in Europe, including the Eastern bloc countries. Trends are identified for the various components of agriculture, industry, investment, consumer expenditure, National Income and foreign trade. The tables and charts are supplemented by written discussion.

European Economy   The Stationery Office (TSO), PO Box 29, Norwich NR3 1GN

European Economy appears three times a year, in March, July and November, and is published by the Commission of the European Union. The November issue contains an annual report on the economic situation within the Union. A statistical annex presents the main economic indicators on an annual basis, and is attached to each issue.

Europe's 15,000 Largest Companies   c/o W. Snyder Publishing Associates, 5 Mile Drive, Oxford OX2 8HT

This publication is regularly updated and contains information on the top companies of Europe. The volume contains data on the sales, profits, total assets, shareholder funds and employment of the largest companies in the Industrial, Trading and Services sectors.

Eurostat   ONS, Room 1015, Government Buildings, Cardiff Road, Newport, S. Wales NP10 8XG

Annual publications on the major indices of economic activity are provided by the Statistical Offices of the members of the European Union under the *Eurostat* heading.

Panorama of EU Industry   The Stationery Office (TSO), PO Box 29, Norwich NR3 1GN

Published annually by DGIII of the European Commission, this contains some 25 chapters covering all the main industrial and services sectors of the EU. Each chapter presents both a wealth of statistics and full commentaries. Each issue also contains special feature articles on topical subjects relating to industry and the Single Market.

The UK economy in a world context

International Monetary Fund publications   The Stationery Office (TSO), PO Box 29, Norwich NR3 1GN

World Economic Outlook Published annually since 1980. This presents and analyses short- and medium-term projections for individual countries, together with a discussion of key policy issues. The industrial countries, the oil-exporting countries, and the non-oil developing countries, are considered as separate groups.

OECD publications   The Stationery Office (TSO), PO Box 29, Norwich NR3 1GN

OECD Economic Surveys Individual country reports for the advanced industrialized economies, published annually.

OECD Economic Outlook Presents economic trends and prospects in OECD countries. Published twice a year in July and December.

United Nations publications   The Stationery Office (TSO), PO Box 29, Norwich NR3 1GN

UN Statistical Yearbook Published annually, covering a wide variety of indices of economic activity for developed and developing nations.

World Economic Survey Published every second year, examines fluctuations in the world economy, by individual countries and by groups of countries, for a variety of economic indicators. Problems and prospects are examined for the developed market economies, for centrally planned economies, and for the developing countries, together with the outlook for international trade.

Monthly Bulletin of Statistics Published monthly, this volume contains a section on special statistics compiled for that specific issue and regular information on other statistical series, including population, wages, prices, production, manpower, etc.

Information sources

The following are helpful in locating new and past articles, in newspapers and periodicals. These often provide a fund of useful contemporary data on, and analysis of, applied issues. Also included are references to sources of documents and papers produced by various official and unofficial bodies.

The UK economy

Britain: an official handbook   The Stationery Office (TSO), PO Box 29, Norwich NR3 1GN

An annual publication by the ONS which provides a compact guide to the UK. It contains information and data on Government and Administration, External Affairs, Economic Affairs, the Environment, and Social and Cultural Affairs. It is up-to-date and provides useful insights into the most recent changes in the UK economy and society.

British Humanities Index   Bowker-Saur, Windsor Court, East Grinstead House, East Grinstead, West Sussex RH19 1XA

Published quarterly, this presents titles of articles, listed by subject and by author, for over 300 current periodicals.

Clover Newspaper Index   4 The Green, Ickwell, Biggleswade, Beds SG18 9EF

Published monthly, this index covers all the main daily papers such as the *Times*, *Financial Times*, *Daily Telegraph*, *Guardian* and *Independent*, as well as the Sunday papers. It provides a single comprehensive source of all the articles written in these newspapers and is valuable for tracing most subjects of economic interest to the reader.

Monthly Index to the Financial Times
Primary Source Microfilm Ltd, PO Box 45, Reading RG1 8HF

Published monthly, this details all the articles, by subject and by author, in the final edition of the *Financial Times* during that period.

Official publications   These are particularly difficult to track down.

HMSO Government Publications The Stationery Office (TSO), PO Box 29, Norwich NR3 1GN

Published monthly (and even daily as a flysheet), this provides an index to new reports by parliamentary (e.g. House of Commons select committees) and non-parliamentary (e.g. Cabinet Office) bodies. Unfortunately a number of important reports from government departments and various official bodies are not included in the HMSO lists. A useful new publication seeks to document these.

Catalogue of British Official Publications Chadwyck-Healey Ltd, The Quorum, Barnwell Road, Cambridge CB5 8SW

Published bi-monthly, this lists British official publications *not* published by HMSO. The majority of these publications are available on microfiche from the address above.

Research Index   Broadmayne House Farm, Osmington Drove, Broadmayne, Dorset DT2 8EP

A monthly index, by subject heading and by company name, to articles and news items of financial interest in over 100 periodicals and in the national press, during the previous period.

Reviews of UK Statistical Sources
Pergamon Press, Headington Hill Hall, Oxford OX3 0BW

This is the successor to the previous series on *The Sources and Nature of the Statistics of the UK*, edited by M. Kendal. The reviews not only outline but also evaluate statistical sources for a wide and expanding range of topics.

The Times Index   Primary Source Media Ltd, PO Box 45, Reading RG1 8HF

A monthly index, by subject heading and by author, to the pages of *The Times* newspapers (excluding the *Financial Times* – see above). Available on microfilm.

The UK economy in a European context

European Access   ProQuest Information and Learning, The Quorum, Barnwell Road, Cambridge CB5 8SW

Published six times a year. This is a useful source of information on articles covering various aspects of the EU. Each issue provides a brief commentary on recent events in the EU and a list of recent articles published under 19 headings related to various EU activities, e.g. industry, business, money, environment, technology, education, etc.

European Business Intelligence Briefing

Headland Business Information, Windsor Court, East Grinstead House, East Grinstead, West Sussex RH19 IXA

Published 11 times a year. This is a newsletter which analyses the sources of European company, market and product information.

Publications of the European Community

Alan Armstrong Ltd, 2 Arkwright Road, Reading RG2 0SQ

This annual catalogue contains all the publications, including periodicals, issued during the year by the Institutions of the European Community. There is a breakdown by subject heading.

The Directory of the EU Information Sources   Euroconfidentiel, Rue de Rixensart, Genval, Belgium.

This publication is regularly updated and presents useful details of various sources of information available on the EU.

The UK economy in a world context

HMSO International Organizations Publications   The Stationery Office (TSO), PO Box 29, Norwich NR3 1GN

This annual catalogue contains all items placed on sale by HMSO in that year for the international agencies and overseas organizations for which HMSO acts as agent. These include the European Commission, the IMF, the OECD and the UN, amongst many others.

Information Sources in Official Publications   Bowker-Saur, Windsor Court, East Grinstead House, East Grinstead, West Sussex RH19 IXA

This volume provides a guide to the Government/Official Publications available in a large number of countries across the world. It discusses the main guidebooks which can help readers access the myriad of official publications produced by various government and other official bodies.

Other applied materials

The following are a number of useful sources, readily available to the reader interested in applied economic issues.

Bank Reviews   Often available free, on application.

Barclays Economic Review, published quarterly, Economics Dept, Barclays House, 1 Wimborne Road, Poole, Dorset BH15 2BB.

This publication contains statistics and brief commentary on the current economic situation in the UK and abroad. It has a regular section on forecasting inflation.

British Economy Survey   York Publishing Services, 64 Hallfield Road, Layerthorpe, York YO3 7XQ

A highly useful, twice-yearly update on the current state of the British economy. Eight main sections: Industrial Structure; Public Sector; Monetary System; Public Finance; Industrial Relations; Employment; Balance of Payments; World Economy. It also covers business topics such as human resources in business; production and operation; and marketing. Published in October and April.

Business Strategy Review   Oxford University Press, Pinkhill House, Southfield Road, Eynsham, Oxford OX8 1JJ

Produced three times a year by the London Business School's Centre for Business Strategy. This journal contains articles on practical issues which are relevant to decision making within modern business.

Business Review   Philip Allen Updates, Market Place, Deddington, Oxford OX15 0SE

Published four times a year, this journal contains a range of articles that places theory in a real life business context and addresses subjects such as marketing, finance, production operations and human resource development. It also provides guidelines on how to tackle examination questions.

Developments in Economics: An Annual Review   Ed. G. B. J. Atkinson, Causeway Press Ltd, PO Box 13, Ormskirk, Lancs L39 5HP

A yearly publication in ring binder format. Each issue includes a number of clearly written articles which update student knowledge on various micro- and macroeconomic issues.

Economics Today   Anforme Ltd, Stockfield Hall, Stockfield, Northumberland NE43 7TN

This journal is published four times a year and contains a main article section relating to economic problems in both micro and macro-economics. It also has regular features covering various topic areas, e.g. essay and multiple choice questions; making sense of economic data; views from the city; etc.

Economic Review   Philip Allan Publishers Ltd, Market Place, Deddington, Oxfordshire OX15 0SE

Four issues are published each academic year in September, November, February and April. *Economic Review* is aimed at introductory students in economics, and relates economic theory to contemporary economic problems. Each issue contains main feature articles, and a teaching section which reviews the various ways of tackling typical examination questions.

Far Eastern Economic Review   GPO Box 160, Hong Kong

A weekly publication available from main UK booksellers. It is a major source of up-to-date information about countries of the 'Pacific Rim' (such as SE Asia and Australasia) which have become an important part of the world economy. It contains sections which deal with regional issues in the Far East, and presents important articles on business and society in the different Far East countries.

Key British Enterprises   Dun & Bradstreet, Holmers Farm Way, High Wycombe, Bucks HP12 4UL

This yearly publication covers some 50,000 large and medium-sized UK companies. It provides *financial* details (profit, turnover, etc.), *operational* details (line of business, markets, brand names, etc.), and *corporate* details (registration no., parent company, etc.).

Lloyds TSB Bank Economic Bulletin

Economics and Strategy Planning, Lloyds Bank, PO Box 215, 71 Lombard St, London EC3P 3BS

Bi-monthly, on request. Each issue covers a topic of current interest, presenting economic principles in a manner understandable to non-economists. Also included is a section on changes in the main economic indicators.

National Institute Economic Review

2 Dean Trench Street, Smith Square, London SW1P 3HE

Published four times a year. Each issue of the *Review* contains comments on the economic situation in the UK and on the world economy as a whole. It also contains interesting articles on various aspects of the UK economy. This source is particularly strong in providing comparisons between the UK and her competitors in particular areas, e.g. labour costs, productivity, and education. There is a statistical appendix which offers updates on a wide range of economic variables relating to production, prices/wages, external trade, etc.

Oxford Review of Economic Policy   Oxford University Press, Great Clarendon Street, Oxford OX2 6DP

A quarterly publication which includes articles on various topics of current relevance. Some issues concentrate wholly on *one* contemporary topic, such as Exchange Rates, Education and Training, Finance, Health Economics, etc.

Regional Studies   Taylor and Francis Ltd, Customer Services Dept, Rankine Road, Basingstoke, Hants RG24 8PR

Published six times a year. This is the standard source of articles for those students who are interested in various aspects of UK and world regional and urban issues.

Teaching Business and Economics

Economics and Business Education Association, 1a Keymer Road, Hassocks, West Sussex BN6 8AD

This is the official journal of the Economics and Business Education Association and is published quarterly. As well as containing articles on various aspects of economics, business and related subjects, it also covers up-to-date teaching methods and reviews new literature.

The Economist   25 St James Street, London SW1A 1HG

This is the internationally known weekly, published by The Economist Newspapers Ltd. It includes articles on subjects such as World Politics and Current Affairs, together with Business, Finance and Science. It is an invaluable source of national and international business news and also has a useful update on basic economic statistics.

The Times 1000   Times Books, 16 Golden Square, London W1R 4BN

This is a yearly update of the basic data on the world's top companies. It covers the top 1,000 UK companies and also the main companies of many other OECD countries. It also provides information on companies in the financial sector, such as clearing banks, acceptance houses and discount houses, as well as an update on the year's main mergers and acquisitions.

United Kingdom in Figures   Central Statistical Office, Press and Information Service, Great George Street, London SW1P 3AQ

This pocket-sized abstract provides current facts and figures on population, employment, the environment, the standard of living and the National Accounts. Free from the above address.

Who Owns Who   Dun and Bradstreet, Holmers Farm Way, High Wycombe, Bucks HP12 4UL

This is a yearly publication which includes a mass of essential information about companies and their subsidiaries. It enables readers to find the main subsidiaries of UK companies, whether in the UK or abroad. It can also be used to trace the parent firm if the name of the subsidiary is known. This publication is therefore invaluable for unravelling the pattern of ownership and control in UK industry.

Electronic media

Many series of data and sources of information can now be accessed directly on-line or are available on disk or tape.

ONS Databank   ONS Sales Desk, Room 131/4, Office for National Statistics, Government Offices, Great George Street, London SW1P 3AQ

The ONS Databank contains major series such as GDP, PSBR, RPI, Balance of Payments, National Accounts, index of production, etc. Time series data for these items are available on disk or paper.

NOMIS   Unit 3P, Mountjoy Research Centre, University of Durham, Durham DH1 3SW

The National Online Manpower Information Service (NOMIS) is a database of labour statistics run on behalf of the ONS by the University of Durham. It contains a range of official statistics relating to the labour market.

ESRC Data Archive   University of Essex, Colchester, Essex CO4 3SQ

This archive provides data across the full range of the social sciences and humanities and contains information about most areas of social and economic life including Family Expenditure Surveys, Labour Force Surveys, census data, etc. The Data Archive will endeavour to locate and obtain research data for those interested.

SINES   SINES Help Line, Room 285, Ordnance Survey, Romsey Road, Southampton SO16 4GU

This source contains information about specific datasets through printouts, floppy disks or E-mail. It states the purpose, the sources, and frequency of updata, etc. of major economic, environmental and industrial, and other datasets.

CD-ROM   Many schools, colleges and public libraries now provide CD-ROM access to a range of UK and EU *databases* and *Information Sources*. The following items are indicative of what may well be available to you via this resource:

1   ABI/INFORM
    Gives 150-word abstracts and indexing to over 800 international academic business, economics and management journals.
2   ANBAR ABSTRACTS
    Abstracts and indexes articles covering business, management and IT topics from mainly UK and European journals.
3   BOOKBANK
    Gives bibliographic information on over 600,000 books from UK publishers and English language titles from overseas which are available in the UK.
4   BOOKFIND
    Includes over 2 million books, currently in print, from publishers in the UK, the US, Canada and other English-speaking countries.
5   DISCLOSURE/WORLDSCOPE EUROPE
    Contains company accounts and financial information on over 10,000 companies in 27 countries. This information enables comparisons to be made between the major companies trading in Europe.
6   EC/EU INFODISK
    Contains the official bibliographic database of the European Union (SCAD) and detailed briefings on Britain's implementation of EU legislation prepared by the DTI (Spearhead).
7   FINANCIAL TIMES
    Full text of back issues of this newspaper.
8   THE GUARDIAN
    Full text of back issues of this newspaper.
9   JUSTIS
    This is the official legal database of the European Union. It contains the full text of most of the treaties, regulations, directives, preparatory work, case law and parliamentary questions dealt with by the EU.
10 THE TIMES
    Full text of back issues of this newspaper.

Internet sources

The increasing use of the Internet as a source of information for economics and business has grown rapidly over the last few years. The usefulness of the material on the Internet largely depends on whether organizations keep their site up-to-date. The sources of information are growing daily so the list given below provides only a very brief idea of the type and range of websites available.

UK sites

Guide book

The Essential Guide to Government Websites   The Stationery Office (TSO), PO Box 29, Norwich NR3 1GN

This publication contains a very wide range of websites across all the major government departments. It therefore includes many sites relevant to economic and business issues.

Others

British Library Catalogue   (http://opac97.bl.uk)

This will provide details of books published in the UK, enabling a search to be made to identify up-to-date books on many topic areas.

CCTA government information   (http://www.open.gov.uk/)

This site will lead to most of the materials published by UK government authorities, including the Departments of State and other Agencies.

Economist   (http://www.economist.com/)

This includes the current week's issue of *The Economist*, book reviews and surveys. It also provides links to other related sites.

HM Treasury   (http://www.hm-treasury.gov.uk)

Press releases, ministers' speeches, lists of research papers, together with details of economic forecasts and budget measures are available on this site.

HMSO Online   (http://www.hmso.gov.uk)

This provides a useful guide to key UK official publications, and has a daily list of latest publications from the UK and overseas. It also has access to information on the UK's most requested Acts and has a search facility for unpublished government information.

Institute for Fiscal Studies
(http://www.ifs.com)

This is an independent research organization that does extensive microeconomic analysis on areas such as the budget, public finance, income inequality, etc.

ONS National Statistics
online   (http://www.statistics.gov.uk)

This is the premier statistical source on the UK economy. The latest updated releases of statistics are posted every day. It is possible to browse by theme, or click on the 'virtual bookshelf' to discover the range of statistics available.

TSO (Stationery Office)   (http://www.tso-online.co.uk)

This is a privately owned company which publishes for the UK Government and Parliament. It maintains a catalogue of all official publications – some 450,000 titles in all. It also distributes publications for international bodies.

Newspapers

The following list provides a guide to the main newspapers that provide search facilities, and access can be gained to up-to-date articles. Occasionally, the user is asked to register (free) before using the facility, but some of their services are not free.
Financial Times (http://www.ft.com)
Guardian Unlimited (http://www.guardian.co.uk)
Independent (http://www.independent.co.uk)
Timesonline (http://www.timesonline.co.uk)

European/international

Guide book

The Guide to EU Information Sources on the Internet   Euroconfidential S.A. Rue de Rixensart 18, B-1332, Genval, Belgium

This publication provides a guide to internet sites covering a wide range of issues relating to the EU including: agriculture; industry; banking; law; etc. The site address is given for each section and an overview of the major items covered is provided.

Others

EU Information
(Europa) (http://europa.eu.int)

This is the EU's central home page. It is the starting point for a search of the main sources of official information on the EU. It leads to an enormous range of sources, including the publications of the various Directors General (DGs) and Eurostat.

International Monetary Fund
(IMF)   (http://www.imf.org)

This site provides a guide to the material available with the IMF on a wide range of economic issues.

United Nations   (http://www.un.org)

This site provides details of the publications and activities of the United Nations, e.g. information about its yearly Trade and Development Report.

United States (US)

There are a large number of sites that give information about the US economy and business. Four useful ones are:

- *Economic Statistics* (http://www.whitehouse.gov/fsbr/esbr)
  This is a central source on current economic data from various US state agencies.
- *Statistical Abstract of the United States* (http://www.census.gov/statab/www/)
  This contains a collection of statistics on social and economic conditions in the US.
- *FirstGov* (http://www.firstgov.gov)
  This site has 51 million pages with information about all aspects of US life and business. It has a 'reference centre' which contains data and law sections.
- *Fedstats* (http://www.fedstats.gov/)
  This gateway contains statistics from over 100 US Federal Agencies.

World Trade Organization
(WTO)   (http://www.wto.org)

This site is dedicated to the publications of the WTO in the area of trade and trade policy.

G. H. Black, FCA, ILTM

Senior Lecturer in Business Finance, Harper Adams University College and previously Head of Professional Accounting Courses at Ashcroft International Business School, APU. He has held many senior examining posts and has lectured in Hong Kong, Cyprus, Malaysia and Singapore. He has written several textbooks, including *Applied Financial Accounting and Reporting*, Oxford University Press, 2004 and *Students' Guide to Accounting and Financial Reporting Standards*, Financial Times Prentice Hall, 2003. He is also (with S.D. Wall) editor of the *Modular Texts in Business and Economics* series published Financial Times Prentice Hall. Responsible for Chapter 2.

G. Burton, BSc, MSc

Principal Lecturer in European Business, Ashcroft International Business School, APU, with special reference to macroeconomics and quantitative methods. Author (with G. Carrol and S. Wall) of *Quantitative Methods for Business and Economics*, 2nd Ed. Longman, 2001. He has taught economics at various levels and has lectured in Business Schools in France, Finland and the Netherlands. Responsible for Chapters 16, 22 and 23.

P. Fenwick, BA, MA, PhD

Senior Lecturer in Human Resource Management at the East London Business School, University of East London. His research interests are strategic human resource management and the impact of technological change on employment relations. Recent publications include 'HRM and Industrial Relations' (with A. Murton) in *Organizational Behaviour: A Critical Text*, J. Barry *et al.* (eds) International Thomson Business, 2000. Previous management experience in the British car industry. Responsible (with A. Griffiths) for Chapter 15.

E. Fuller, MSc, ACMA, FRSA

Professor and Director of the Centre for Entrepreneurship and Small Business Development at Teeside Business School, University of Teeside. He has written and edited numerous publications, books, trainer manuals, expert systems and academic papers. Responsible for Chapters 3 and 9.

A. Griffiths, BA, MSc

Reader in Economics, Ashcroft International Business School, APU, and previously Tutor in Economics at the University of Wales, Aberystwyth. Fellow of the Japan Foundation, Sophia University, Tokyo 1978, and visiting Professor of Economics at Yokohama National University, Yokohama, 1987/88. Research Officer at the Research Institute for the National Economy, Tokyo 1987/88. Editor of *European Economy Survey*, Longman, 1992 and *British Economy Survey*, York Publishing. Co-author (with S. Wall) of *Intermediate Microeconomics: Theory and Applications*, Addison Wesley Longman, 2000 (2nd edn). Responsible for Chapters 1, 5, 11, 19, 24 and 27, Chapter 15 (with P. Fenwick) and Chapters 4, 6, 10, 14 and 29 (with S. Wall).

B. Harrison, BA, MA

Senior Lecturer in Economics, Department of Economics and Politics, Nottingham Trent University. Visiting Lecturer, NIMBAS Postgraduate School of Management, Utrecht. He has also held a visiting post at the National Institute for Management of the Economy in Baku, Azerbaijan. His main teaching and research interests are monetary economics and finance. Responsible for Chapter 20.

N. M. Healey, BA, MA, MBA

Professor and Head of Department of Business Studies, Manchester Metropolitan University, where he is a member of the International Business research group. His research interests are European economic and monetary integration and economic transformation in the former communist countries of eastern Europe. He has worked extensively in eastern Europe, serving as economic advisor to the prime minister of Belarus and the Russian Ministry of Economy, and has held visiting posts at universities in the United States, Poland, Bulgaria and Lithuania. He is economics editor of *Teaching Economics and Business* (the journal of the Economics and Business Education Association). Recent publications include *The Economics of the New Europe* (Routledge, 1995) and *Central Banking in Transition Economies*. Responsible for Chapters 7 and 30.

S. Ison, BA, MA, PhD, MCIT

Lecturer in Transport Studies, Loughborough University. Visiting Professor at California State University, Hayward. Author of a number of articles in the area of transport economics and specifically urban road pricing. Contributor to *British Economy Survey* and author of *Economics*, Financial Times Prentice Hall, 3rd edition, 2000. Responsible for Chapter 12.

S. Rubinsohn, BA

Chief Economist at *Gerrard Ltd.*, the investment management company and previously Lecturer in Economics at APU. Responsible for Chapters 17 and 28.

Kieron Toner, BA, MA

Is a lecturer in Business Economics at the Ashcroft International Business School, APU, Cambridge. His teaching and research interests include areas within the field of international economics, particularly global trade issues and exchange rate policy, and also in the area of modern American political economy. He is involved in teaching at undergraduate level, and regularly teaches on business courses in Germany.

S. D. Wall, BA, MSc

Subject leader in Economics and Business, Ashcroft International Business School, APU. He has returned to APU having acted as consultant to the OECD Directorate for Science, Technology and Industry and guest lecturer and examiner at the University of Cambridge. Author of a wide range of reports and articles on the economics of technical change. Author (with B. Rees) of *International Business*, Financial Times Prentice Hall, 2004 (2nd Ed.), and (with A. Griffiths) of *Intermediate Microeconomics: Theory and Applications*, Financial Times Prentice Hall, 2000 (2nd Ed.) and (with G. Carrol and G. Burton) of *Quantitative Methods*, Financial Times Prentice Hall (2nd Ed.) and with Ison, S. and Peake, S. of *Environmental Issues and Policies*, Financial Times Prentice Hall, 2002. Editor (with G. Black) of Longman Modular Texts in Business and Economics. Responsible for Chapters 8, 13, 18 and 26 and (with A. Griffiths) for Chapters 4, 6, 10, 14 and 29 and (with K. Turner) for chapter 25.

R. Webb, BA, PhD

Senior Lecturer in Banking and Finance in the Division of Risk, Caledonian Business School, Glasgow Caladonian University. He lectures on financial markets and institutions at both undergraduate and postgraduate level and is an active researcher. His main research interests are the structure, strategy and efficiency of domestic and international banks, asymmetric information in the provision of financial services, Japanese banking and data envelopment analysis. His PhD analysed the efficiency of large retail banking groups in the UK. Responsible for Chapter 21.

Index

E